> Choose your format

Print or eBook? Softcover, spiral-bound, or loose leaf? Black-and-white or color? Perforated, three-hole punched, or regular paper? No matter the format, Create has the best fit for you—and for your students.

> Customize your cover

Pick your own cover image and include your name and course information right on the cover. Students will know they're purchasing the right book—and using everything they purchase!

Introducing McGraw-Hill Create *ExpressBooks*!

ExpressBooks contain a combination of pre-selected chapters, articles, cases, or readings that serve as a starting point to help you quickly and easily build your own text through McGraw-Hill's self-service custom publishing website, Create. These helpful templates are built using content available on Create and organized in ways that match various course outlines across all disciplines. We understand that you have a unique perspective. Use McGraw-Hill Create ExpressBooks to build the book you've only imagined!

D1304133

Comparative Politics

AN INTRODUCTION

Joseph L. Klesner

KENYON COLLEGE

McGraw Hill Education

COMPARATIVE POLITICS: AN INTRODUCTION

Published by McGraw-Hill Education, 2 Penn Plaza, New York, NY 10121. Copyright © 2014 by McGraw-Hill Education. All rights reserved. Printed in the United States of America. No part of this publication may be reproduced or distributed in any form or by any means, or stored in a database or retrieval system, without the prior written consent of McGraw-Hill Education, including, but not limited to, in any network or other electronic storage or transmission, or broadcast for distance learning.

Some ancillaries, including electronic and print components, may not be available to customers outside the United States.

This book is printed on acid-free paper.

1 2 3 4 5 6 7 8 9 0 DOW/DOW 1 0 9 8 7 6 5 4 3

ISBN 978-0-07-352643-0
MHID 0-07-352643-6

Senior Vice President, Products & Markets: *Kurt L. Strand*
Vice President, General Manager, Products & Markets: *Michael J. Ryan*
Vice President, Content Production & Technology Services: *Kimberly Meriwether David*
Managing Director: *Gina Boedeker*
Director: *Matt Busbridge*
Brand Manager: *Laura Wilk*
Senior Director of Development: *Dawn Groundwater*
Marketing Manager: *April Cole*
Director, Content Production: *Terri Schiesl*
Content Project Manager: *Danielle Clement*
Buyer: *Susan Culbertson*
Design: *Laurie Janssen*
Cover Image: ©*Guy Grenier/Masterfile, Ian McKinnell/Getty Images*
Content Licensing Specialist: *Brenda Rolwes*
Typeface: *10/12 Adobe Garamond Pro*
Compositor: *Laserwords Private Limited*
Printer: *R. R. Donnelley*

All credits appearing on page or at the end of the book are considered to be an extension of the copyright page.

Library of Congress Cataloging-in-Publication Data

Klesner, Joseph L., 1958-
    Comparative politics ; an introduction / Joseph Klesner, Kenyon College.
        pages cm
    Includes bibliographical references and index.
    ISBN-13: 978-0-07-352643-0 (alk. paper)
    ISBN-10: 0-07-352643-6 (alk. paper)
    1. Comparative government. I. Title.
JF51.K54 2014
320.3—dc23

                                                                2013019257

The Internet addresses listed in the text were accurate at the time of publication. The inclusion of a website does not indicate an endorsement by the authors or McGraw-Hill Education, and McGraw-Hill Education does not guarantee the accuracy of the information presented at these sites.

A Letter from the Author

Comparative Politics: An Introduction originated with Michael J. Sodaro, professor of Political Science and International Affairs at George Washington University. A winner of George Washington's highest recognition for teaching, the Oscar and Shoshana Trachtenberg Award for Excellence in Teaching, Professor Sodaro conceptualized this book and wrote the vast majority of the text for three editions. His brilliance as a teacher came through clearly in the terrific examples he used and the features he introduced in the book. His lively prose made this challenging textbook an enjoyable read. He made this a scholarly text, demonstrating the breadth of his research and learning.

I was fortunate to be recruited by Professor Sodaro to serve as a contributing author in the first edition. From him I learned how to pitch the prose to the undergraduate reader and how to select great examples to illustrate concepts. Professor Sodaro was always generous to his contributing authors, and that generosity extended further when he decided not to write a fourth edition of the book. When I expressed my disappointment that the book would cease to be available for teachers and students of introductory comparative politics, he suggested I take up the challenge of being the lead author. He encouraged me to make the book my own, and hence I have introduced new features and modified existing ones.

Yet I must recognize that this text still has as much Michael Sodaro in it as it does me. I hope that colleagues who have used *Comparative Politics* in the past will recognize and appreciate the many good elements that Professor Sodaro introduced. I also want those who will be using this book for the first time to know that I benefited tremendously by inheriting an excellent book, well-written and crafted for the introductory student who aspires to use the study of comparative politics to prepare for a life in public service. I have sought to build on the strengths of the book, strengths that Professor Sodaro originated, and to add others that reviewers have urged the publishers to introduce. I ask that those who use this book feel free to offer me frank criticism, constructive and otherwise, so that I continue to improve it in coming editions.

I have asked two of the contributors to earlier editions, Bruce J. Dickson of George Washington University and Timothy D. Sisk of the University of Denver, to continue with me in this new version of *Comparative Politics*. I thank them for continuing to contribute excellent chapters on China and on Nigeria and South Africa, respectively. My Kenyon colleague, Pamela G. Camerra-Rowe, generously agreed to take on the Germany chapter that Professor Sodaro previously wrote, for which I am most grateful. But most of all I thank Michael Sodaro and McGraw-Hill for giving me the opportunity to take on the lead authorship of this book. I hope the result is worthy of the trust they placed in me.

Joseph L. Klesner

Brief Contents

Contents

8
Political Participation

9
Political Culture

10
Ideology

14
France

15
Germany

16
Russia

19
Nigeria and South Africa

Preface

Comparative Politics: An Introduction shows new students of world politics how the methods and concepts of comparative politics can lead them to ask critical questions to better understand the complex world around them. The majority of undergraduates in introductory comparative politics courses do not plan to pursue graduate education in political science nor embark upon careers as political scientists. Most hope to take part in public and perhaps international affairs as elected officials, civil servants, or engaged citizens. As such they will need to make countless decisions about public policy, including foreign policy, throughout their careers. In *Comparative Politics: An Introduction* we equip them to make better, more informed decisions. Central to that task are three important goals: (1) to introduce readers to the conceptual foundations of comparative politics, (2) to enhance their analytical and critical-thinking skills through an introduction to basic empirical techniques of political and social science, and (3) to promote their understanding of a wide range of countries and political leaders.

CONCEPTS AND COUNTRIES: A CRITICAL FRAMEWORK

In the study of politics and public affairs, comparative politics serves the crucial role of illuminating the many alternative political regimes, including the range of institutional options among democracies; the different forms of political participation, peaceful and violent; the way competing political ideologies have been implemented and their consequences; and the alternative economic development strategies available to policy makers and their differential results, to cite a few examples. *Comparative Politics: An Introduction* addresses these and other complex matters from a critical framework that first introduces key concepts in comparative politics (Chapters 1 to 12) and then applies them to specific countries and their respective political systems (Chapters 13 to 19).

The first part of *Comparative Politics: An Introduction* introduces many of the most essential concepts of the field and offers numerous examples of them

in the contemporary world. Extensive examples are distinguished from the main text by placement in boxes and sidebars intended to underscore for readers that we are providing illustrations of conceptual material introduced in the main text. Where possible we offer explicit comparisons of important examples such as the treatment of the Arab Spring in Chapters 1 and 7, for example.

In each of the country studies in the second part of the book we return to as many of those concepts as are relevant to each country. We show, for example, how political participation is practiced in contemporary Russia, what the key institutions of the German state are, and how Chinese leaders have sought to promote economic development but stave off democracy.

Overall, *Comparative Politics: An Introduction* provides significant coverage of nine major states: United Kingdom, France, Germany, China, Russia, Brazil, Mexico, Nigeria, and South Africa. Beyond those country chapters, however, the conceptual chapters include extensive examples of additional countries and regions. More importantly, we provide the conceptual tools that will allow well-prepared readers to learn the essentials of the politics of any other country with which they need to become familiar by knowing which questions to ask.

We illustrate the country chapters and some conceptual chapters with profiles of important political leaders and activists. The

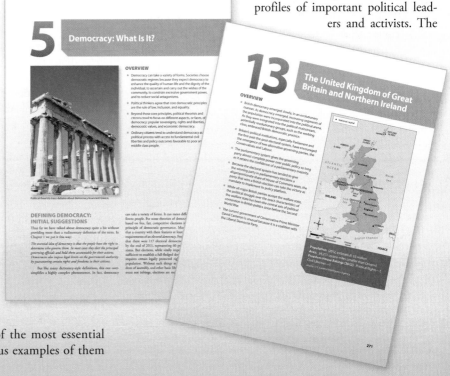

Profile features are not meant to be merely short biographies of great women and men. Rather, they illustrate typical political recruitment patterns in the countries we explore and articulate the key policy stances adopted by contemporary leaders and some key figures from the past. Each seeks to personalize conceptual points made earlier in the book. They thereby bring home in a more tangible way to college readers the ways in which a concept is expressed in a political leader's life.

CONCEPTS AND COUNTRIES: CUSTOMIZE YOUR COURSE

With McGraw-Hill Create™, instructors can combine and assign those concept and country chapters that are specific to your comparative politics course. With McGraw-Hill Create, you can easily arrange and rearrange material from a variety of sources, including your own. You can select content by discipline or collection, including 4,000 textbooks, 5,500 articles, 25,000 cases, and 11,000 readings. When you build a Create book, you receive a complimentary print review copy in three to five business days or a complimentary electronic review copy (eComp) via e-mail in about one hour. Go to www.mcgrawhillcreate.com and register today.

CRITICAL THINKING

Political science has developed many analytical techniques that can serve the decision maker every bit as well as the social scientist to think critically about our political world. We focus on *hypothesis testing,* which starts with the formation of good questions about a political phenomenon that grow out of reading the relevant literature on that topic and then moves to the statement of a hypothesis that can be rejected or accepted based on a well-designed test.

Hypothesis-Testing Exercises

The hypothesis-testing exercises in each chapter are sufficiently varied in their content and the methods we employ in

them. Readers will see how posing questions sharply enough to permit hypothesis testing can be useful in many aspects of their lives. Each hypothesis-testing exercise has a hypothesis formulated in a brief, clear "if, then" format and is set off from the text. To the extent possible, each presents empirical data (where appropriate, in a table or chart) that allows us to reject or not reject the hypothesis. Where possible, we will state where the data to test the hypothesis can be gathered by the students. One example of a Hypothesis Testing Exercise occurs in Chapter 6 (page 132). The hypothesis, relating to the topic of how democracy works, asks the question, "Do PR systems have higher turnout than plurality systems?" In it the author identifies the variables, states his expectations, provides evidence, and draws a conclusion in response to the question. This format makes the research experience come alive for students.

In some cases where we summarize another author's hypothesis testing, we provide briefly the debate in the literature between that author and his or her critics.

Most importantly, we think that decision makers must be willing to move beyond gut instincts or standard operating procedures when making choices. To do so they must both ask critical questions and have a means to put to the test the evidence they unearth as they find answers to those questions. The decision makers that comparative politics students will become—at the local, state, national, and international level, whether in their families, businesses or nonprofit organizations, or in the public sector—must learn critical-thinking skills in their college courses. We hope the approach in this book will provide new tools for our readers.

Essential Concepts and Case Study

In addition to the hypothesis-testing exercises, we offer two other features that enhance critical thinking: Essential Concepts are one- to two-page empirical applications of a concept using real-life examples, while the case studies are one- to two-page expositions that offer clear comparative analyses of actual political situations. The Essential Concepts feature in

Chapter 6 (page 119) examines the concept of "coalition formation." In this case, the author starts by asking three questions *What determines who governs? Why do political parties come together to form governing regimes? And Is there any logic to the process of how parties come together?* These questions form the basis of an exploration of the case of Irish coalition formation. Again, by providing data and analysis, students gain a strong understanding of a vital concept in comparative politics.

The Case Study in Chapter 6 addresses the concept of proportional representation by applying it to the case of the Israeli Knesset. By providing data and analysis, the author helps students deepen their understanding of a key chapter topic.

EMPHASIS ON QUANTITATIVE DATA

Both the text and the features noted above are supported by substantial survey evidence and other quantitative data to illustrate concepts and to support arguments we advance in the book. It is essential in this knowledge-based economy to know how to analyze data and use them to make informed decisions. In particular, students are exposed to public opinion data on a daily basis and should be shown how those data can be used to support arguments in political science, as well as alerting them to how they can be misused.

Along with the presentation of more empirical data, we provide that evidence in clear, brief tables, graphs, and charts that effectively illustrate the conclusions that we believe should follow from the data. These visual aids are powerful tools for summarizing evidence.

COURSESMART

This text is available as an e-textbook at **www.CourseSmart.com**. At Course-Smart your students can take advantage of significant savings off the cost of a print textbook, reduce their impact on the environment, and gain access to powerful web tools for learning. CourseSmart e-textbooks can be viewed online or downloaded to a computer. The e-textbooks allow students to do full text searches, add highlighting and notes, and share notes with classmates. CourseSmart has the largest selection of e-textbooks available anywhere.

Visit **www.CourseSmart.com** to learn more.

INSTRUCTOR RESOURCES

The password-protected Online Learning Center for *Comparative Politics: An Introduction*, contains valuable tools for instructors to use in the classroom. This site includes chapter-by-chapter instructor's manual, test bank files, and PowerPoint presentations. Contact your local McGraw-Hill publishing representative for log-in information: **www.mhhe .com/klesner1e**

Instructor's Manual

The instructor's manual provides a great starting point for instructors, with comprehensive chapter-by-chapter lecture outlines along with questions to spark discussion.

Test Bank

The test bank provides approximately 20 multiple choice questions, three essay assignments, and three hypothesis-testing assignments per chapter, with page references given alongside the answers. The Bloom's Taxonomy classified questions range in difficulty from recall questions based on the readings to thought-provoking essay prompts and hypothesis-testing assignments. All test questions are compatible with EZTest, McGraw-Hill's Computerized Test Bank program.

PowerPoint Presentations

Our PowerPoint presentations cover key points of each chapter, including graphs and charts taken from the text. These presentations are designed to be used as-is or modified to meet the individual needs of instructors.

Acknowledgments

I would like to acknowledge a number of instructors who were instrumental in the development of this text. Their input and ideas as reviewers were invaluable in the process. Thank you:

Leslie Anderson, *University of Florida, Gainesville*
Jason Arnold, *Virginia Commonwealth University*
Kathleen Barrett, *University of West Georgia*
Emily Beaulieu, *University of Kentucky*
Prosper Bernard, *College of Staten Island (CUNY – Staten Island)*
Hannah Britton, *University of Kansas, Lawrence*
Jetsabe Caceres, *University of Toledo*
Ryan Carlin, *Georgia State University*
Jeffrey Conroy-Krutz, *Michigan State University*
David Dreyer, *Lenoir-Rhyne University*
Jeffrey S. Hamill, *Bryant College*
James Kim, *Cal Poly Pomona*
Peter Koehn, *University of Montana*
Edward Kwon, *Northern Kentucky University*
Gallya Lahav, *SUNY Stony Brook*
Rebecca Larsen, *University of Utah*
Jeffrey Lewis, *Cleveland State University*
Michael F. Lofchie, *UCLA*
Mary Casey Kane Love, *Tulane University*
Michael Lusztig, *Southern Methodist University*
Christopher Muste, *University of Montana*
Saul Newman, *American University*
Jeffrey Ryan, *University of Arkansas*
Benjamin Smith, *University of Florida*
James Stone, *Mt. San Antonio College*
Katrina Swartz, *University of Florida*
Markus Thiel, *Florida International University*
Erica Townsend-Bell, *University of Iowa, Iowa City*
Anca Turcu, *University of Central Florida*
Stephen Wegren, *Southern Methodist University*
Beth Whitaker, *UNC Charlotte*
Nikolaos Zahariadis, *University of Alabama, Birmingham*
Andres Zimelis, *University of Illinois, Chicago*

I owe a deep debt of gratitude to Michael Sodaro. When he indicated that he would not be revising the previous version of this book, to which I had been a contributing author, Mike generously and graciously listened to my suggestion that I take on a major revision of *Comparative Politics: A Global Introduction* and made the necessary contacts at McGraw-Hill to get this project off the ground. Mark Georgiev, then brand manager for political science, encouraged the initial groundwork on what became this book. When Mark moved on to another role at McGraw-Hill, his successor, Meredith Grant, reinvigorated what had become a stalled project and facilitated the development of a more thorough-going redesign of this book. Laura Wilk has overseen the final stages of this project with care. I look forward to working with her on future editions.

Without the doggedness of Arthur Pomponio, my developmental editor, this book would never had seen print. I thank Dawn Groundwater, senior director of development, for assigning Art to my book. Art gave terrific suggestions about how to cut the text by 20 percent, organize it better, and make its organization more transparent. He worked with me to create and improve its features. Along the way he made many great suggestions for content and helped to make the prose more direct. My copyeditor, Nancy Dietz, likewise improved the prose immeasurably. Most importantly, Art kept me on task and adapted to the schedule of an academic administrator who took on too many other responsibilities during the project. And he did so with a wonderfully light touch—thank you, Art!

I thoroughly enjoyed working with Danielle Clement, content project manager, who responded to my many queries as we moved through the latter stages of editing, composition, and production with good humor and keen advice. To first-time authors editing, composition, and production can be very foreign places and Danielle not only helped me navigate this new terrain but made the process a terrific learning opportunity. Iris Kim prepared the first version of the glossary, an important addition to this book.

Bruce Dickson and Timothy Sisk kindly agreed to continue as contributing authors for this book, providing insightful, thorough chapters on China and on Nigeria and South Africa, respectively. Pamela Camerra-Rowe, my longtime colleague at Kenyon College, agreed to become a contributing author for our chapter on Germany. Pam and I have taught comparative politics together for close to two decades. From her I've come to appreciate an institutional approach to political science. Our work together designing our department's comparative politics curriculum made taking on this book a much easier enterprise. Nayef Samhat, Kenyon's provost, was extraordinarily patient with me, his associate provost, during the time I was completing this book. I thank him for his good humor and deeply value his friendship.

I would not have undertaken this book had I not witnessed firsthand the work that my wife, Kimberlee Klesner, does on social science textbooks for another publisher. I learned from Kimberlee the pleasures of imagining how to convey new discoveries about society and politics in creative ways to readers of undergraduate textbooks. Observing her work helped me visualize how I could take on such a major project. As I have worked through this book Kimberlee has offered frequent and excellent advice. To her I dedicate *Comparative Politics: An Introduction*.

About the Authors

JOSEPH L. KLESNER (Chapters 1–14, 16, and 18) is Professor of Political Science and Provost at Kenyon College. He received his BA at Central College and his SM and PhD at the Massachusetts Institute of Technology. He is the author of many articles appearing in journals, including *Comparative Politics, Comparative Political Studies, Latin American Politics and Society, Mexican Studies, Electoral Studies,* and the *Latin American Research Review,* in addition to many book chapters. His research has focused on politics in Mexico and on public opinion and political culture in Latin America. His research has been funded by Fulbright grants to Mexico, South America, and most recently, Ireland, and by funding from the American Political Science Association, the National Science Foundation, and the National Endowment for the Humanities. He has also written on curriculum and pedagogy in the fields of comparative politics and international studies.

PAMELA CAMERRA-ROWE (Chapter 15, "Germany") is the John B. McCoy-Banc One Distinguished Teaching Professor of Political Science at Kenyon College. She was awarded her BA by Davidson College. After working as a journalist covering the Supreme Court, she took her MA and PhD at Duke University. She has taught comparative, European, and American politics at Kenyon since 1994 and has won several teaching awards. Her research focuses on business lobbying and regulatory policy in the European Union and on political parties in Germany. She has presented papers at many conferences and published articles in *German Politics and Society* and *The Oxford Handbook of Business and Government.* During 2008–09, she worked in the U.S. Senate as an American Political Science Congressional Fellow. She has also worked in the German Economics Ministry as a Robert Bosch Foundation Fellow. She has received research fellowships from the Friedrich-Ebert Stiftung, the Social Science Research Council, and DAAD (Deutscher Akademischer Austauschdienst).

BRUCE J. DICKSON (Chapter 17, "China") is Professor of Political Science and International Affairs at the George Washington University. He obtained his BA, MA, and PhD from the University of Michigan. He is the co-author (with Jie Chen) of *Allies of the State: Democratic Support and Regime Support among China's Private Entrepreneurs* (Harvard, 2010 and the author of *Wealth into Power: The Communist Party's Embrace of China's Private Sector* (Cambridge, 2008); *China's Red Capitalists: The Party, Private Entrepreneurs, and Prospects for Political Change* (Cambridge, 2003); and *Democratization in China and Taiwan: The Adaptability of Leninist Parties* (Oxford, 1998). He is co-editor of five other books and author of articles appearing in *Asian Survey, China Quarterly, Comparative Politics,* and other leading journals. His current research examines the political consequences of economic reform in China, and in particular the Communist Party's strategies for generating new sources of popular support.

TIMOTHY D. SISK (Chapter 19, "Nigeria and South Africa") is Professor of International and Comparative Politics and Associate Dean for Research at the Korbel School of International Studies at the University of Denver, where he also serves as a faculty member in the MA program in Conflict Resolution and as Director of the Program on Fragile States at the Sié Chéou Kang Center for International Security and Diplomacy. He obtained his BA and MA from Baylor University and his PhD from the George Washington University. After experience as a journalist in South Africa and a legislative assistant in the U.S. Senate, he served as a program officer and research scholar at the federally chartered United States Institute of Peace in Washington, D.C. Sisk just completed a major new scholarly book titled *Statebuilding: Consolidating Peace after Civil War* (Polity, 2013). He is also the author of a book for policy practitioners titled *Democracy, Conflict and Human Security* (with Judith Large; International IDEA, 2006). He has written six other books and many articles, including *International Mediation in Civil War: Bargaining with Bullets* (Routledge, 2009), *Democracy at the Local Level* (IDEA, 2001), *Democratization in South Africa* (Princeton, 1995), and *Power Sharing and International Mediation in Ethnic Conflicts* (Carnegie Commission on Preventing Deadly Conflict, 1995).

1 Comparative Politics
What Is It? Why Study It? What Are Its Major Topics?

In 2011, Egyptian political activists rose against the Mubarak dictatorship, sweeping the president from power.

OVERVIEW

- Comparative politics examines in a comparative way political realities, usually by focusing on the domestic politics of countries around the world. International relations, in contrast, examines politics between and among countries.

- The Arab Spring illustrates many key themes from comparative politics, especially the forces of globalization and the pattern of democratization.

- Scientific analysis typically proceeds by comparison. Comparative politics seeks to build knowledge about politics scientifically by engaging in explicit comparison of countries, institutions, and political processes.

- A central theme in comparative politics is the difference between democracy and authoritarianism. This chapter introduces the basic differences between them.

- Differences regarding power, resources, identity, ideas, and values produce most political conflict. Comparative politics looks carefully at how these bases of conflict structure politics in countries around the world.

This book provides an introduction to comparative politics. What is comparative politics all about? **Comparative politics** examines in a comparative way the political realities in countries all over the world. It looks at the many ways governments operate and the ways people behave in political life. It considers the actions of governments and individual political behavior comparatively, drawing inferences and conclusions by comparing and contrasting. Comparative politics does not limit the study of politics to one place, one society, or one time, such as the present. It is the most comprehensive subfield in political science.

Let's begin with a brief and current example to illustrate themes of interest in comparative politics.

AN INTRODUCTION TO COMPARATIVE POLITICS

True to its subtitle, this book is introductory in nature. It assumes you have little or no background in studying the politics of different countries on a systematic basis. Our approach provides broad coverage of *countries* around the world, offers *conceptual comprehensiveness*, and promotes *critical thinking*.

CASE STUDY
The Arab Spring

Every 10 years or so in recent times, a global political event has erupted that has defined the following decade. Between the late summer of 1989 and the end of 1991, the Berlin Wall fell, oppositionists brought down the communist governments of the former Soviet bloc, and the Soviet Union itself collapsed. In the following decade newly independent states in the vast region once governed directly or otherwise effectively controlled by Moscow struggled over whether democracy would succeed the authoritarian regimes imposed by the Communist Party while simultaneously dismantling centrally planned economies. Ten years later the terrorist attacks of September 11, 2001, led to significant American and allied military interventions in Afghanistan and Iraq, a rise of tensions between Muslims and non-Muslims in Europe, increasing restrictions on personal freedoms in many democracies, and greater political instability in nations bordering the conflict regions.

In 2011, 2012, and into 2013, much to the surprise of almost all observers, a broad groundswell of opposition to the seemingly stable Arab governments of Tunisia, Egypt, Yemen, Libya, and Syria focused the world's attention. The Arab Spring, as this transnational phenomenon has been called, has led to different outcomes in these five nations, and its effects have spread across the Arab world. In Tunisia, the location of the first challenge to a long-standing autocracy, President Zine el-Abidine Ben Ali fled in January 2011 after less than a month of mass protests against his government's venality and corruption. The protests erupted after a street peddler named Mohamed Bouazizi burned himself to death to protest his dismal circumstances and the offenses to his dignity by government officials who harassed him. After Ben Ali's abdication, Tunisia held elections to an assembly in October 2011 that subsequently wrote a new constitution

Anti-Mubarak protesters celebrating his resignation as president of Egypt in Cairo on February 11, 2011.

and formed a new, democratic government headed by the moderate Islamist party Ennahda. Tunisia may be on the path to democracy.

Egypt's President Hosni Mubarak, who had governed the largest Arab country for nearly 30 years, seemingly had arranged for his son to succeed him. However, soon after the Ben Ali regime fell in Tunisia, Egyptian protesters rallied to demand that Mubarak leave power too. Within 18 days, on February 11, 2011, Mubarak resigned. Little more than six months later, Mubarak and his sons were being tried on a variety of charges of corruption and human rights violations. Egypt came under the rule of a military junta that took power when Mubarak fell. However, that junta agreed to allow elections to take place. In June 2012 Mohamed Morsi of the Freedom and Justice Party, with strong ties to the Muslim Brotherhood, won election as president. Violence between Morsi supporters and liberal opponents led the military to oust him in a coup in July 2013.

Just as Egyptians were rising against the Mubarak government in January 2011, Yemenis began to protest the rule of President Ali Abdullah Saleh. Saleh had become North Yemen's president in 1978, and took the top leadership post in united Yemen when North and South Yemen agreed to unify in 1990. Saleh responded to large Yemeni protests by first offering not to run for reelection in the scheduled 2013 presidential elections, but he otherwise struggled to stay in power until that time. In contrast to the relatively blood-free Tunisian revolution and the Egyptian power-transfer process, in which deaths were largely due to forces loyal to Mubarak shooting demonstrators, in Yemen the protests escalated to military conflict between forces loyal to Saleh and those seeking to overthrow him. Saleh was wounded in a June 2011 assassination attempt and flown to Saudi Arabia for medical treatment.

Mass protests led to the resignation of President Zine el-Abidine Ben Ali in Tunisia in January 2011.

By November the situation had advanced enough that Saleh agreed to transfer power to Vice President Abd Rabbuh Mansur Al-Hadi. Al-Hadi was subsequently elected president in February 2012.

Libya, ruled by Colonel Muammar Gaddafi since 1969, next erupted in civil war. While initial protests in mid-February 2011 took place throughout the country, the base of rebellion against the Gaddafi regime was concentrated in the eastern part of the country, and Gaddafi's regime controlled Tripoli, the capital, in the west. Gaddafi's vigorous attempt to put down the rebellion helped to convince Western nations—Britain, France, the United States, and others—to intervene in March 2011 to support the rebels militarily, particularly through air support of rebel forces and a naval blockade meant to cut off supplies to Gaddafi. After months of fighting, the rebels took Tripoli in August. Gaddafi, who fled with his family as the capital fell, was killed October 20, 2011. The rebels formed a provisional government, the Transitional National Council, after taking Tripoli in August 2011. However, the continued activity of many militias formed to oppose Gaddafi during the revolution has prevented the consolidation of central power and the formation of a new permanent government.

Protests against Syria's authoritarian government began in mid-March 2011 and were met with stiff resistance by President Bashar al-Assad's government. Assad had succeeded his father in the presidency of Syria. Hafez al-Assad had seized power and declared himself president in 1970, a position that he held until his death in 2000. Owing to Syria's strategic location bordering Israel and its long-standing conflict with that country, the nations intervening in Libya have been reluctant to repeat their intervention in Syria. Meanwhile, the Assad regime has proven willing to repress rebels with tanks and other advanced weapons systems, forcing the Syrian opposition into a military struggle, with the loss of tens of thousands of lives.

Comparative Politics Themes in the Arab Spring

The events of the Arab Spring offer an excellent jumping-off point for the study of comparative politics. To begin, the Arab Spring illustrates two central themes to which we will frequently return in this book. The first is globalization. **Globalization** refers to the growing interconnectedness of governments, non-state actors, and populations throughout the world through a variety of political, economic, technological, cultural, environmental, and other interactions. Globalization has many dimensions, and we will attempt to explore them in many later chapters. Here we highlight two—the impact of globalizing economic forces on the Arab societies subject to political protests in the past couple of years and **transnationalism**, a concept that emphasizes the increasing movement of people and ideas across borders as the result of globalization.

Globalizing economic forces affected the Arab countries briefly discussed above differently. With the exception of Libya, none is a major oil exporter, and as such, their authoritarian governments lacked that significant source of revenue to use to placate unsatisfied populations. Perhaps the most important aspect of the populations of the Arab nations is their relative youth. One in five people in the Arab region is between 15 and 24 years old, the age at which they should be entering the labor force. However, the Middle East and North Africa regions had the highest youth unemployment rates in the world in 2009, 23.4 percent and 23.7 percent, respectively.[1] In recent years, pressure from providers of foreign economic assistance has pushed some countries in the region, including Egypt and Tunisia, to adopt economic reforms that have included privatization of government-owned enterprises and reduction of subsidies to the poor. The set of reform policies they followed are sometimes known as neoliberal reforms, and they are a hallmark of economic globalization, as we'll discuss in Chapter 12. This dimension of globalization created a sizable disaffected youth population in the countries we are discussing, exactly the group that has risen to demand political change.

The aspect of globalization we call transnationalism has manifested itself in the rapid movement of ideas across national boundaries. In the Middle East this flow of ideas has been further encouraged because of a long-standing "pan-Arab" identity that has caused people in the region to view

Former Libyan dictator Muammar Gaddafi.

(Continued on next page)

(Continued from previous page)

themselves as both Arab and Tunisian or Arab and Syrian, and hence to look to happenings in neighboring countries to take their cues about politics. Media outlets such as Al Jazeera have made the transnational flow of ideas all the easier. Social media, especially Facebook and Twitter, played a large role in disseminating the messages of the protesters. The uprisings of the Arab Spring spread from country to country very rapidly. This unfolding of democratic demands is an excellent example of how transnational forces operate today.

Our second major theme illustrated by the Arab Spring is democratization. **Democratization** is the transition from nondemocratic to democratic forms of government. We are now in the midst of what political scientist Samuel Huntington called the third wave of democratization, a process that has accelerated since the second half of the 1980s. In 1987, 66 countries permitted democratic elections. By the end of 2011 there were 117, including a number of former communist countries that had been involved in nearly 50 years of Cold War confrontation with the United States and its allies. Some 87 of these 117 countries, comprising 43 percent of the world's 7 billion people, buttressed their democratic election procedures with a solid respect for human rights and the rule of law, compared with only 43 countries 30 years earlier. A majority of the world's Muslims now live under governments that have been elected democratically in countries including Indonesia, Turkey, India, and Nigeria. Although it is far too early to assess democracy's prospects in Tunisia, Egypt, Yemen, Libya, and Syria, the recent removal of blatantly authoritarian rulers in the first four holds out at least a glimmer of hope that democracy may gain a footing in those countries, however great the challenges may be.

Many proponents of democracy contend that the clash between advocates and opponents of democracy is the central political struggle of our times. It lies at the heart of such recent developments as the collapse of communism, the proliferation of civil wars and interstate conflicts, and the global confrontation with terrorism. No one can foresee the ultimate outcome of this historic confrontation or the course the latest wave of democratization will take. But the record convincingly shows that democracy, though by no means perfect, offers humanity its best chance of escaping tyranny, poverty, and relentless political violence. We will discuss democratization further in Chapter 7.

Many observers were surprised by the Arab Spring. Some political analysts thought the "moderate" tyrants in Tunisia, Egypt, and Yemen would be difficult to topple and that the Gaddafi and Assad families had firm control of Libya and Syria, respectively.[2] Students of comparative revolutions, though, have told us to expect successful revolutions when three conditions are present: an internally weak state is manifestly unjust; some elites, especially from the military, are alienated from the rulers; and a broad segment of the population is prepared to rise up to protest injustice. It helps, too, if international actors either do not intervene against the revolutionaries or actively support them.[3]

Each of the countries mentioned above had been ruled by the same person or family for decades. These regimes have been ruled by individuals who have sought to expand their personal power at the expense of formal institutions of governance, and their main claim to rule is simply their personal authority. These dictatorships typically led to gross misappropriation of public funds by the dictators and their families. The Mubarak and Ben Ali families, for example, were widely known to have built personal fortunes in the billions of dollars, and the Gaddafis appropriated to themselves and their cronies the billions earned from Libyan oil exports. Saleh and Assad similarly treated their governments as sources of personal enrichment. In light of the high levels of unemployment mentioned above and the dim prospects many young people in the Arab world face, it is not surprising that the government was very unpopular and the people were waiting to explode. They saw their rulers helping themselves to public resources while the people suffered. When significant segments of the military, which were for different reasons not happy with the rule of these dictators, sided with the protesters, the basis for a successful overthrow of the old regime was set.

A comparative analysis of the type we just did can provide clarity to situations that otherwise look chaotic. Such a study can unveil patterns in political behavior that help us to better understand the political world. But as we see even in the Arab Spring examples, the outcomes have varied. Those differing outcomes point to the unpredictable in politics. As we study the politics of many different countries, we'll find that it is difficult to predict political outcomes with much certainty. Local circumstances differ significantly across countries—the willingness of a Ben Ali or Mubarak to resign after protests lasting only two or three weeks whereas Gaddafi and Assad hung onto power tenaciously suggests such differences matter. Those differences suggest that human agency, the capacity of single human beings to make their political choices and follow them, matters a lot in politics. That's one reason we will pay attention to individual political actors through featured profiles.

The Arab Spring is an example of the kind of international event that makes front-page news almost every day and commands the attention of government officials, political activists, and average citizens in virtually every country on our planet. Such events assume life-and-death importance for millions of people caught up in the turmoil of political conflict. The world needs people of goodwill who are capable of making independent judgments on the basis of a wide knowledge of global realities and an ability to think clearly and logically. That is why the study of comparative politics is more necessary and challenging than ever.

Countries

This book is global in its coverage of a representative selection of countries spread across all the world's geographic regions. Chapters 13 through 19 are devoted to specific countries. Chapters 1 through 12 present a considerable amount of information about other states not covered in subsequent chapters—Canada, Egypt, India, Indonesia, Iran, Iraq, Israel, Japan, Pakistan, and Turkey, among others—for the purpose of illustrating various concepts in comparative politics. Though no chapter is devoted specifically to the United States, there are numerous references to it throughout the book for comparative purposes. We use material from specific countries to illustrate concepts introduced in this book. Our choice of countries for the country chapters in Part Two of the book is not accidental. All are major actors in world affairs. Young people learning about politics so as to be good citizens or policy analysts or political actors themselves will benefit tremendously by knowing more about Russian, or Chinese, or German politics

We also provide biographical *profiles* of world leaders. Portraits of leaders can tell us a great deal not only about political developments in their respective countries but also about the nature of political leadership and how political leaders are recruited to their roles. Again, as young people interested in world affairs, the readers of this book will benefit by learning more about major world leaders such as Angela Merkel or Xi Jinping.

Concepts

This book is comprehensive in its conceptual treatment of the field of comparative politics. To understand political life in the United States, Russia, or any other country, we must examine relevant facts concerning the country's history, political institutions, public opinion, and other essential features of its political system, plus we must also pay close attention to the ways general political processes and concepts apply to them. For example, to understand the way democracy works in specific countries such as Israel, France, or South Africa, we need to know something about democracy in general. What is it? How does it come about? These and other questions we raised at the start of this chapter address some critical aspects of democracy in general terms. Whether the topic is democracy or some other feature of political reality, comparative politics almost always involves the interaction of the specific and the general.

Numerous additional concepts and categories of political phenomena must also be examined if we want to get a good grasp of political reality around the world. Accordingly, chapters 3 through 12 are designed to introduce you to some main concepts in comparative politics. They include such things as *the state, nationalism, ideology, political culture,* and *political economy.* These chapters provide material drawn from a vast array of countries as well as from a broad sampling of scholarly literature produced by some of the top specialists in comparative politics. They also present some of the core ideas of prominent political thinkers whose theories have helped shape political history and the ways we think about politics. In sum, our approach is not confined to giving you just a bunch of facts about individual countries. It actively seeks to deepen your understanding of politics in general.

Critical Thinking

This book seeks to develop your capacity for critical thinking. Relevant facts and key concepts are necessary, but to appreciate the complexities of political reality more fully, we need to know *how to think* about politics and *how to analyze* it in a logical and systematic manner.

Comparative politics is a subfield of political science. Students often ask, "Is political science *really* a science?" The answer to this question obviously requires an understanding of what science is. While the term *science* may conjure up images of people in lab coats measuring chemicals or observing mice, in fact science is primarily a system of logic. **Science** is a set of rules and methods for investigating reality logically and systematically. Political science is therefore a science to the extent that it observes the cardinal rules of scientific logic. To be more specific, political science is scientific when it engages in the following operations: *definition, description, explanation, prediction,* and *prescription.*

Definition Any science must define its terms as precisely as possible, and political science is no different. Definitional clarity is especially necessary in politics because terms such as democracy, socialism, liberalism, and other commonly used political concepts often have more than one meaning and are frequently misused or misunderstood. We therefore need precise and consistent definitions of political terms as well as a subtle appreciation of their variations and shades of meaning in particular contexts.

Description Like physicists and biologists, political scientists need to describe the phenomena they are examining as accurately as possible. How does the U.S. system of checks and balances among the three branches of government actually work? How is the British parliamentary system organized? How can we categorize various types of democracy and nondemocratic regimes? These and other political phenomena need to be described carefully so that we can understand them clearly.

Explanation *Why* do things happen the way they do? Why, for example, does democracy succeed in some countries but not in others? Why did the Communist Party dictatorship collapse in the Soviet Union but not in China? The list of political phenomena begging for explanation is practically endless, and political scientists especially relish the opportunity to explain politics to others.

In an effort to explain the things they find intriguing, scientists frequently generalize about the phenomena they seek to understand. Very often these generalizations are expressed as theories or *hypotheses* that posit cause-and-effect relationships between things. Political scientists formulate generalizations that seek to address the causes of democracy, war, voter turnout, fascism, and other political realities. And like natural scientists, political scientists are frequently engaged in *testing* their generalizations against the hard facts of reality to determine whether they are true or false, or whether perhaps they are true under some conditions but not in others. *Hypothesis testing* is a central activity of political science. One of the main aims of this book is to teach you to think about politics in terms of hypotheses that can be tested against relevant evidence.

Prediction Political scientists have a spotty record when it comes to predicting the future. The Arab Spring is just the most recent major political phenomenon not predicted by political science. Today's highly sophisticated statistical models can sometimes forecast election results with impressive accuracy—but not always. The realities of human behavior and political life are so variegated that we have very little ability to foretell what will happen in any particular country over the near term, let alone the long term. The world is full of surprises. Nevertheless, we can observe trends and patterns in various aspects of political life. Sometimes we can extrapolate from these observable trends and suggest, however tentatively, what broad tendencies are possible, or even probable, assuming that certain conditions hold.

While we cannot say with certainty that democracy is bound to succeed or doomed to fail in Egypt or Russia or somewhere else, we can at least specify the factors that may make democracy's success or failure more probable. In other words, prediction in political science is *probabilistic* in nature. It can sketch out alternative possibilities and probabilities, while modestly desisting from claims to foolproof reliability.

Prescription Doctors can prescribe medicines on the basis of the findings of research biologists and pharmacologists. Can political science prescribe remedies to the political problems besetting the nations of the world?

Yes and no. In some instances we can provide recommendations that, if followed, may increase the probability that a desirable outcome will ensue at some indeterminate point in time. We can prescribe, for example, a set of actions that need to be taken to establish a democracy and enhance its prospects for success. We can urge the adoption of a body of laws ensuring fair elections, civil rights, an independent judiciary, and so forth. But no political advisor can compel any country to take her advice, and no one can guarantee that, even if all the prescribed steps are followed, democracy will inevitably succeed. The particularities of each individual country and the unforeseeability of future events may dash even the most determined efforts to make democracy work. Still, our prescriptions for democracy can at least increase the chances that democracy will succeed.

Many readers of this book may be drawn to the study of politics in order to have an impact on the real world. Whether you seek to embark on a political career, to be an activist in a political cause, or simply to become a better informed citizen, a scientific approach to politics can help you formulate your own ideas and better assess the recommendations offered by politicians, government officials, and others engaged in political action and debate. Sound government policies rest on sound analysis. A scientific approach to politics contributes to intelligent policy prescription.

Thus the analytical aspect of this book is designed to teach you how political scientists think when they study comparative politics in accordance with scientific rules and methods. In the process, this book explicitly seeks to improve your own critical-thinking skills. The value of taking a scientific approach to the study of politics extends well beyond the field of political science. The ability to think logically and coherently is a vitally necessary skill in a large number of academic disciplines and nonacademic careers. It deserves the highest priority in your education. The analytical techniques employed in this volume, while rudimentary, can be applied across a wide spectrum of intellectual and professional endeavors. In helping you understand the world of politics, this book enhances your general education by helping you think more sharply and effectively. It also seeks to help you make up your own mind about some of the world's most pressing issues. Learning *how* to think will help you figure out *what* to think.

The scientific approach to comparative politics is spelled out in Chapter 2. In addition, most subsequent chapters contain a *hypothesis-testing exercise* designed to bolster your comprehension of how scientific analysis can be applied to the study of politics.

COMPARATIVE POLITICS AND INTERNATIONAL RELATIONS

Many students take introductory comparative politics because of their interest in world affairs. World affairs or world politics is a broad subject area. Political scientists make a basic distinction between two areas of inquiry: *comparative politics* and *international relations* (see Figure 1.1). You may take a course in international relations during your college career, but the course for which you are using this book is probably in comparative politics. How are they different but related?

Historically, comparative politics has examined political activities mostly *within* individual countries. It looks at politics inside, say, the United States, Russia, Japan, Mexico, or South Africa. It then compares the domestic experiences of particular countries with the domestic experiences of others. The focus is on each country's *internal* politics, with a view to making generalizations about politics in a variety of domestic settings. For example, we can compare various democracies with one another to learn more about democracy. We can also compare various nondemocratic governments to learn more about how they work, such as communist countries or military dictatorships.

International relations, by contrast, concerns relations *between* countries. Here the focus is on the *external* relationships of individual countries. Diplomacy, international law, international economic relations, war, and peacemaking are among the chief topics studied by political scientists concerned with international affairs. Their task is to look at relationships between, say, the United States and Russia, Israel and Egypt, and so on. Sometimes the scope of international relations is understood more broadly to include the actions and interactions of international organizations such as the United Nations

Comparative Politics

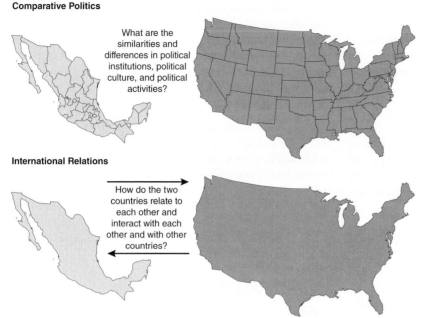

What are the similarities and differences in political institutions, political culture, and political activities?

International Relations

How do the two countries relate to each other and interact with each other and with other countries?

FIGURE 1.1 Difference between Comparative Politics and International Relations

Comparative politics examines political activities mostly within individual countries, for example the United States, Russia, Japan, Mexico, or South Africa. It then compares the domestic experiences of these countries with the domestic experiences of others. International relations concerns relations between countries. The focus is on the external relationships of individual countries that include diplomacy, international law, international economic relations, war, and peacemaking.

or the International Red Cross, or non-state actors ranging from al-Qaida to Exxon Mobil. Such investigations explain how these relationships work and provide us with a more theoretical understanding of international politics in general.

The dividing line between comparative and international politics is razor thin, however, and it's getting thinner all the time. Domestic and international politics are increasingly intertwined within virtually every country in the world today. We cannot really understand the domestic politics of most nations without some reference to their international relationships. What goes on internally is often affected by events occurring externally, beyond the country's borders. As we saw at the outset of this chapter, events in some Arab countries were strongly influenced by earlier events in other Arab countries, and in the cases of Libya and Syria, by the willingness of foreign powers to become involved in the protests against the Gaddafi and Assad regimes. Conversely, we cannot fully comprehend international affairs without a good look inside the domestic political systems of individual countries. The actions of individual governments frequently have a powerful impact on other countries or on the world as a whole. Globalization and the increase of transnational movements of people and ideas render the distinction between comparative politics and international relations less and less valuable analytically. Somewhat like biology and chemistry, comparative politics and international relations are complementary: Though they are separate fields of analysis, they are intimately interrelated.

THE PURPOSES OF COMPARISON

What exactly is "comparative" about comparative politics? What are we comparing, and for what aims?

To understand politics comprehensively, we must compare. We cannot possibly understand democracy, for example, by simply concentrating on one example of a democratic government, such as the United States or Britain. Democracies organize their executive, legislative, and judicial institutions in different ways. Some have encouraged free enterprise while others have favored greater government interference in the economy. Some democracies have succeeded while others have failed. Democracy is not a single phenomenon; it has many manifestations. The same is true of nondemocratic regimes. To fully grasp how these governmental systems work, we need to look at a variety of cases and systematically examine their similarities and differences.

Another reason for making systematic comparisons between different countries and political systems is that we can learn a great deal more about any one particular case (country X) by comparing it with other relevant cases (countries A, B, and C). If you are interested in South Africa, China, Russia, or any other country, you will acquire a deeper appreciation of its history and politics by holding it up against the experiences of other nations. This simple idea is central to the logic of comparative analysis. And it strikes very close to home: We can learn a lot more about politics in our *own* country by comparing it with other countries. Specialists in comparative politics are fond of quoting Rudyard Kipling in this regard. "And what should they know of England," the poet inquired, "who only England know?" Presumably, not much. At least, not as much as they would know if they ventured outside their homeland and savored life's possibilities in other places.

To a considerable extent, studying comparative politics is like traveling abroad. It awakens us to the varieties of human experience and shows us there are different ways of doing things than what we are used to in our own country. In the end we come home with a greater sensitivity to both the positive and negative features of our homeland as well as an enhanced appreciation of why other people do things differently.

Thus for people in the United States, a comparative analysis of Britain, Japan, Israel, or other established democracies can shed light on how the American political system actually works. Both the similarities the United States shares with these countries and the peculiarities that set America apart from them will stand out in sharp relief. For example:

- The U.S. system of government is based on a separation of powers and checks and balances. But how does this system compare with the British system? Or the German, French, or South African? In fact, these and other democracies are organized quite differently. The U.S. system is unique in many of its most essential features. What are the advantages and disadvantages of the U.S. system compared with other democratic systems of government?

- One of the most frequent criticisms Americans level at their own system of government is that it is prone to gridlock. Between Congress and the president, major decisions often do not get made effectively. Is gridlock a peculiarly American phenomenon, or do other governments have it, too? Can the United States reduce or eliminate gridlock by adopting constitutional procedures used in other democracies?

- Some of the most controversial political issues in the United States center on such topics as voting procedures, health care, and opportunities for women. How do other democracies handle these problems? Can the United States learn anything from these countries, or vice versa?

The principal purposes of studying comparative politics may therefore be summarized as follows:

- To widen our understanding of politics in other countries.
- To increase our appreciation of the advantages and disadvantages of our own political system and to enable us to learn from other countries.
- To develop a more sophisticated understanding of politics in general, including the nature of democracy and non-democratic regimes, the relationships between governments and people, and other concepts and processes.
- To help us understand the linkages between domestic affairs and international affairs.
- To help us see the relationship between politics and such fields as science, technology, the environment, public health, law, business, religion, ethnicity, culture, and others.
- To enable us to become more informed citizens, so that we can more effectively develop our own political opinions, participate in political life, evaluate the actions and proposals of political leaders, and make our own political decisions and electoral choices.
- To sharpen our critical-thinking skills by applying scientific logic and coherent argumentation to our understanding of political phenomena.

As a method of analysis, comparison is thus essential to developing a broader, better-rounded understanding of how politics and government function both at home and abroad. Throughout this book we strive to present comparative analyses

of political institutions, political behavior, and public policy. But what are the main topics of comparative politics? To what themes do we tend to gravitate in comparative politics?

THE MAIN THEMES OF COMPARATIVE POLITICS

Let's begin our study of comparative politics by defining critical terms and introducing some of the most important themes addressed by scholars in the field, themes we will spend the rest of this book examining in greater depth. We begin by defining what we mean by *politics*, thereby establishing the domain of our study. We then compare and contrast the characteristics of democratic and authoritarian regimes. Finally, we consider the main sources of political conflict across the countries we will explore in this book.

What Is Politics?

Politics, wrote the American political scientist David Easton, concerns "the authoritative allocation of values."[4] Another influential political scientist, Harold Lasswell, said politics is about "who gets what, when, and how."[5] What exactly do Easton and Lasswell mean by these definitions? And what do they have to do with the ordinary day-to-day struggles in places like Washington that we usually think about when we say "politics"?

Authoritative, in Easton's definition, means that people feel they must obey a decision because those who make that decision have the right to make it. What is being decided authoritatively? The *allocation* or distribution of those things *valued* in a society. Here we mean both material things, such as the allocation of government funding for building new roads or schools or buying a new aircraft carrier, as well as nonmaterial values, which can include many important symbolic acts, such as declaring a national holiday to honor Abraham Lincoln or the Rev. Dr. Martin Luther King, Jr. When Lasswell says politics is about *who* gets *what* and *when*, he is referring to the distribution of society's goods, its valued things, to particular individuals and groups in society. *How* that distribution occurs points us to two features of politics as we usually understand it. First, as Easton said, the distribution is authoritative. The person or persons who decided who was to get what and when are regarded as having the right to make that choice. Within a family the authoritative decision makers are typically the parents. Within a business firm, it is typically the chief executive—probably the owner in a small firm or, in a large firm, someone appointed as the chief executive officer by the firm's board of directors. So we can, and we often do, talk about politics taking place outside of government organizations because values are being authoritatively allocated in contexts other than national or local government.

However, that *how* does point us to a second feature of politics as we usually use the term. As Max Weber, the German sociologist whose work inspired many twentieth-century political scientists, wrote, "'politics' for us means striving to share power or striving to influence the distribution of power, either among states or among groups within a state."[6] Power is what determines who gets what, when, and how. Like Weber, in ordinary conversation we tend to discuss the exercise of power in the state as the defining characteristic of politics. When we talk about *politicians* we are usually referring to our elected representatives or top-level executive branch officials in Washington, or perhaps those who serve in our state capitals. Thus, most of the time when we are discussing politics we are concerned about how the government is distributing or redistributing public goods and services, and who is paying for it.

Weber's writing on politics identifies a tension in our understanding of what is at the root of the authoritative allocation of society's valued things. On the one hand, Weber pointed out that underlying political order is the threat or the actual exercise of violence. Weber defined the **state**—which we will discuss at greater length in Chapter 3—as "a human community that (successfully) claims the monopoly of the legitimate use of physical force within a given territory." That is to say, a state is the organization that monopolizes the use of violence within a territory in order to command the obedience of those living there through the laws and policies it has issued. In the end, the authoritative allocation of values that has been chosen by the officials leading a state rests on the threat that those who don't abide by the allocation decision may be subject to the state's use of force. If, for example, you decide not to pay the taxes that the government has decided you owe, the Internal Revenue Service may force you to do so anyway by seizing your bank account or other assets. Occasionally armed conflicts take place between government agents and tax resisters, underscoring that the state considers itself to have the monopoly of the use of force within the territory it rules. Tax resisters may disagree with who gets what from government and who pays for it, but the state insists that they pay their taxes anyway. On the other hand, most of us pay our taxes. That most of us do pay our taxes with little resistance other than some grumbling each April when we file our tax returns suggests that we believe in the authority of the government to decide on the particular allocation of values that leads us to owe a certain amount of taxes. In Chapter 3 we will discuss at greater length why we might grant to the state the authority to engage in major decisions for society.

It is the state that makes authoritative decisions on the people's goals, whatever those goals may be. And it is to governments—those individuals at the highest levels of authority in the state—that people turn for authoritative decisions in dealing with their conflicts. Even those who want the government to stay out of a particular matter and leave the citizens free to deal with it on their own, or those who attack a government to harm or destroy it, are still engaged in a political process insofar as they seek to define the scope and direction of government authority. Whatever their nature, conflicts are "political" to the extent that governments are somehow involved, whether directly or indirectly, immediately or potentially, extensively or minimally.

How states are organized, how they work, how people interact with them, and, in some cases, how they break down are topics of critical significance in comparative politics. So let's take a look at the two main forms of government in the modern world: democracy and authoritarianism.

Democracy and Authoritarianism

There is a fundamental distinction between two broad types of political system: democracies and authoritarian regimes. The term **regime** means, among other things, a form of government. More precisely, a regime is the set of rules and procedures, both formal and informal, that guides the operation of state institutions. The essential idea of **democracy** is that the people have the right to determine who governs them. In most cases they elect the principal governing officials and hold them accountable for their actions. Democracies also impose legal limits on the government's authority by guaranteeing certain rights and freedoms to their citizens. Whereas democracy places the people above the government, **authoritarianism** (or dictatorship) places the governing authorities above the people. The people have little, if any, say in who governs them or how they are governed. In contrast to officials elected in democracies, authoritarian rulers do not usually allow themselves to be limited by legally defined procedures. Thus they tend to be the principal violators of fundamental human rights.

There are several different types of authoritarian regime. Perhaps the oldest is the traditional **monarchy**, in which a king, queen, emperor, or prince, often flanked by blood-related aristocrats, wields effective power. Contemporary variants of monarchal government include Saudi Arabia and several other countries in the Middle East. Another form of authoritarianism is a dictatorship run by a single political party headed by an all-powerful leader or a small committee of leaders. The most extreme variant of such a regime is **totalitarianism**, a political system in which the state's domination of the individual and society as a whole is virtually total, permeating almost every aspect of political and social life. Historically, Hitler's Nazi regime in Germany, Joseph Stalin's brutal rule over the Soviet Union, and China under Mao Zedong in the 1950s and 1960s were prime examples of totalitarian regimes. North Korea is still totalitarian today. Military governments run directly by the military high command constitute yet another form of authoritarianism. Egypt after the fall of the Mubarak government was ruled by military authoritarianism until Mohamed Morsi, a civilian leader from the Muslim Brotherhood, was elected president in June 2012; the military later overthrew Morsi in a coup d'état. Some authoritarian governments are headed by civilians whose power is heavily protected by the military leadership; others are based on a combination of a dominant party and the military (this was true in Egypt during Mubarak's long rule and in Iraq under Saddam Hussein). A state run by religious authorities is called a **theocracy**. Contemporary Iran, whose Islamic government is strongly authoritarian, is a prominent example.

Although democracy and authoritarianism in their purest forms are antithetical, both forms of government come in shades of gray. There are varying degrees of democracy and authoritarianism. Quite a few countries in today's world are *mixed regimes*. Mixed regimes combine elements of democracy and authoritarianism.

The experts who produce *Freedom in the World*, an annual publication that evaluates democracies and nondemocracies around the globe, provide useful criteria for making distinctions among governments that are predominantly democratic, those that are predominantly authoritarian, and those that fall in between. Every year they investigate how nearly 200 countries measure up against a political rights checklist and a civil liberties checklist. (Table 1.1 presents the main questions on the checklists used in 2011.) Every country is given a score for its performance in meeting the requirements of each checklist. The most democratic performance merits a grade of 1; the most authoritarian gets a grade of 7. (These numbers are not based on rigorous statistical calculations, but reflect the experts' judgments of how

each country should be graded.) A country's scores on each list are then averaged to produce a combined score. Countries are considered "free" if they have an average combined score of 1 to 2.5. Those whose scores range from 3 to 5 are considered "partly free." And those whose scores run from 5.5 to 7 are categorized as "not free."[7] Map 1.1 shows how freedom is distributed across the world in accordance with this three-part categorization.

Obviously, countries with a combined score of 1 are the most democratic, and those bottoming out with a grade of 7 are the most authoritarian. *Freedom in the World* reported that by the end of 2012 there were 47 countries that topped the list with an overall score of 1, and 9 countries brought up the rear with a score of 7. But 138 countries had scores ranging from 1.5 to 6.5, and 58 of these countries were rated "partly free." How should we apply the terms *democratic* and *authoritarian* to these intermediate regimes?

Table 1.1 Checklists from *Freedom in the World*

Political Rights Checklist*

- Is the head of government or other chief national authority elected through free and fair elections?
- Are the national legislative representatives elected through free and fair elections?
- Are the electoral laws and framework fair?
- Do people have the right to organize in different political parties or other competitive political groupings of their choice, and is the system open to the rise and fall of these competing parties and groupings?
- Is there a significant opposition vote and a realistic possibility for the opposition to increase its support or gain power through elections?
- Are the people's political choices free from domination by the military, foreign powers, totalitarian parties, religious hierarchies, economic oligarchies, or any other powerful group?
- Do cultural, ethnic, religious, and other minorities have full political rights and electoral opportunities?
- Do the freely elected head of government and national legislative representatives determine the policies of the government?
- Is the government free from pervasive corruption?
- Is the government accountable to the electorate between elections, and does it operate with openness and transparency?
- For traditional monarchies that have no parties or electoral process, does the system provide genuine, meaningful consultation with the people, encourage public discussion of policy choices, and allow the right to petition the ruler?
- Is the government or occupying power deliberately changing the ethnic composition of a country or territory so as to destroy a culture or tip the political balance in favor of another group?

Civil Liberties Checklist*

- Are there free and independent media and other forms of cultural expression?
- Are religious institutions and communities free to practice their faith and express themselves in public and private?
- Is there academic freedom, and is the educational system free of extensive political indoctrination?
- Is there open and free private discussion?
- Is there freedom of assembly, demonstration, and open public discussion?
- Is there freedom for nongovernmental organizations (including civic organizations, interest groups, foundations, etc.)?
- Are there free trade unions and peasant organizations or equivalents, and is there effective collective bargaining? Are there free professional and other private organizations?
- Is there an independent judiciary?
- Does the rule of law prevail in civil and criminal matters? Are police under direct civilian control?
- Is there protection from political terror, unjustified imprisonment, exile, or torture, whether by groups that support or oppose the system? Is there freedom from war and insurgencies?
- Do laws, policies, and practices guarantee equal treatment of various segments of the population?
- Does the state control travel or choice of residence, employment, or institution of higher education?
- Do citizens have the right to own property and establish private businesses? Is private business activity unduly influenced by government officials, the security forces, political parties/organizations, or organized crime?
- Are there personal social freedoms, including gender equality, choice of marriage partners, and size of family?
- Is there quality of opportunity and the absence of economic exploitation?

*The full checklist includes subquestions under the questions listed here.

Source: Arch Puddington, *Freedom in the World 2013: Democratic Breakthroughs in the Balance* (New York: Freedom House, 2013), pp. 33–34.

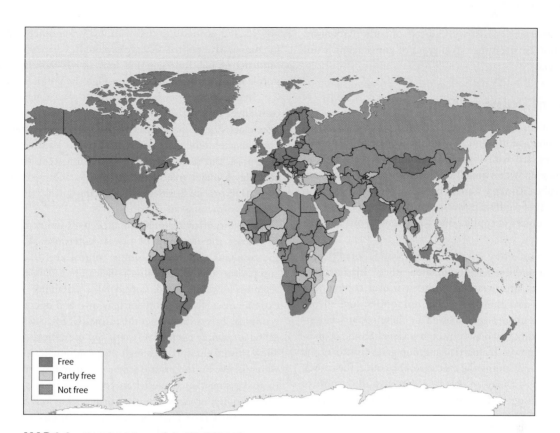

MAP 1.1 Freedom Around the World 2012
"Does the map reveal any patterns? Where are the 'free' countries concentrated? Where are most of the 'not free' countries located?"

To keep it simple, we label the countries classified as "free" in *Freedom in the World* as "democratic," and the countries classified "not free" as "authoritarian." This categorization acknowledges that some democracies are more democratic than others. Countries with a composite score of 2 or 2.5 have problems meeting all the criteria fulfilled by countries with a "perfect" score of 1. (As we'll see in later chapters, even countries with the highest score—such as Britain and France—are less than perfect when it comes to providing equal democratic rights to all their citizens.) It also acknowledges that authoritarian countries with a score of 6.5 or 6 may not be quite as tyrannical as those with a score of 7. We categorize countries labeled "partly free" in *Freedom in the World* as *mixed regimes*. They can be considered either semi-democratic or semi-authoritarian, depending on whether one regards the proverbial glass as mostly full or mostly empty (i.e., as mostly democratic or mostly authoritarian). Viewed in these terms, the relationship between democracy and authoritarianism should be seen as a continuum, with intermediate gradations between the extremes (see Figure 1.2).

The numbers represent a country's combined score of political rights and civil liberties, as reported in *Freedom in the World 2012*.

What do these labels mean in practice? According to the *Freedom in the World* checklists, a country with an overall rating of 3 or 3.5 might have such democratic procedures as free and fair elections and an independent judiciary, but is penalized for having rampant corruption, pervasive discrimination against women or ethnic minorities, limitations on press freedom, the use of torture, or other nondemocratic practices. Countries with grades ranging from 4 to 5.5 may or may not have democratic elections; in either case, political power tends to be heavily concentrated in the hands of a small elite that evades legal controls and real accountability to the populace. Countries with a grade of 6 or 6.5 may be fundamentally authoritarian in political terms, with an unelected hierarchy that wields power without much accountability to the citizenry, but there may be some redeeming democratic features such as elections to a legislature (though it is controlled by the authorities), a quasi-independent judiciary, or private enterprise. In each case,

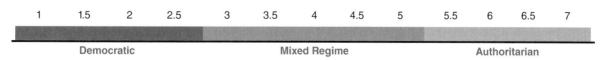

FIGURE 1.2 Democracy–Authoritarianism Continuum
The numbers represent a country's combined score of political and civil liberties, as reported in *Freedom in the World*, 2013.

aspects of democracy coexist with aspects of authoritarianism. The distinction between these two types of government is not always clear-cut.[8]

Sources of Political Conflict

What kinds of conflicts do people and their governments typically face in political life, and how do democracies and authoritarian regimes deal with them? If we think about it, we can probably come up with a long list of real or potential issues that spark political controversy. In this book, we focus on five main sources of political conflict: power, resources, identity, ideas, and values. These sources of conflict often overlap with one another.

Power In almost every country in the world, some people at one time or another have dominated others. Masters have subjugated slaves, aristocrats have lorded it over commoners, majorities have discriminated against minorities, and so on. Whenever governments get involved in these social relationships, the question of who has power in society becomes a question of political power. If a particular group gains control of the state apparatus—including the executive, the police, the courts, and the military—it may be able to get its way all or most of the time, exercising real dominance over the entire population. By contrast, if no group is able to impose its dominance on everyone else, a certain balance of power may exist. In that case, the government may play a mediating role as the various groups that compose society (businesspeople, employees, religious groups, ethnic minorities, and so forth) seek to influence the governing authorities to help them out or favor them in one way or another. In politics, the state is the prize: whoever controls the government and its institutions—whether in a dictatorship or a democracy—plays the central role in dominating or influencing political realities.

Dominance and *influence* are both forms of political power. Democracy is based on power sharing, and the main mode of exercising political power in most democracies tends to be the exercise of influence. In authoritarian regimes, dominance tends to prevail. But there can be elements of both dominance and influence in democracies and nondemocracies alike. Regardless of the nature of the regime, politics invariably involves a conflict over who controls or influences the state. At its very core, politics is thus a conflict over power itself.

Resources *Resources* are another source of political contention. Natural resources such as land, oil, and water have ignited conflicts ranging in severity from legislative wrangling to mortal combat. Money is also a resource that sparks political controversy. How much will the government spend on the military, the elderly, students, big business, the sick, the poor, the middle class? Which policies will the government adopt to stimulate economic growth, reduce prices, or alleviate poverty? Such bread-and-butter issues are the raw stuff of political controversy in virtually every country in the world.

Conflicts of these kinds are typically economic conflicts. **Political economy** refers broadly to the relationship between politics and economics. It constitutes yet another major topic in comparative politics that we explore in Chapters 11 and 12. Students of political economy look at the various ways economic resources are dealt with through the political process.

In some countries the government plays a relatively small or indirect role in the economy, leaving the better part of economic activity in the hands of private businesses and workers. Democracies tend to grant considerable latitude to private enterprise. But most democratic governments in today's world also play a major role in the national economy, raising taxes, regulating private businesses, enhancing social welfare, and in some cases owning corporations.

Authoritarian regimes, for their part, are generally prone to restrict the freedoms of private enterprises. Control over the country's population requires control over its economy. A comparison of the economic policies of various authoritarian regimes, however, reveals considerable variability. In the most extreme cases, the government may own and operate the entire economy, as was the case in the former USSR. Such a system is called a *centrally planned economy*. But even dictatorships often allow private enterprise, though the government usually keeps a watchful eye on the private sector and may impose regulations to make sure that its activities conform to the government's general policy objectives. Hitler's dictatorship in Nazi Germany, communist China since the 1980s, and various military dictatorships around the world have permitted private enterprise but have usually taken measures to ensure that the business sector complies with the government's economic and political goals.

One of the most important questions in comparative politics centers on the relationship between states and markets. How much economic activity should be controlled or regulated by the state, and how much should be left to the free play of market forces? This question is controversial in democracies as well as in nondemocracies.

Identity *Identity* constitutes a third source of political conflict. Identity refers to the ways in which individuals and groups are defined in society. (Here we define society in simple terms as a country's population.) Every individual has a multiplicity of identities. Everyone has a gender, racial or ethnic, and generational identity. Many people also identify themselves with some form of religion, whether it is an organized religion or a set of religious beliefs. (A nonreligious or antireligious attitude may also define one's religious identity.) Most people acquire an occupational identity: as a student, for example, or a factory worker, a lawyer, or an unemployed person. Educational attainments establish a person's educational identity as poorly educated, highly educated, or some intermediate category. Many people also belong to a particular socioeconomic class, such as the upper class, the middle class, or the poor. Some people may strongly identify themselves with the area or region in which they live. Southerners, rural folk, suburbanites, and city dwellers exemplify various types of regional identity. Some people may identify themselves with a particular language group (or ethno-linguistic group) such as English-speaking Canadians and French-speaking Canadians. Some may have strong attachments to a tribe, a clan, or an extended family. And most people share a national identity with their compatriots (Americans, Japanese, Swiss, and so on).

The branch of comparative politics that focuses on how the groups associated with these various social identities behave in the political process is known as political sociology. **Political sociology** is the study of the relationship between social identity and political behavior, and of how political power is distributed among social groups.

Too often, conflict is the central behavior that arises from these different group identities. Conflicts over opportunities for women and gay men and lesbians, racial or ethnic antagonisms, the clash of generations, religious strife or intolerance, class struggles, or regional rivalries can be found in almost every country. Whenever governments get involved in taking sides or mediating among conflicting identity groups, these conflicts become political conflicts over who has power or how the economy operates.

At a deeper and more personal level, however, identity conflicts can be far more intense than issues that involve just power or resources. They can be a matter of fundamental dignity and respect, qualities to which all human beings feel rightfully entitled. When our basic human worth is at stake, when the essence of who we are and how we live is bound up with profound emotional attachments to our ethnic group, our religion, or some other identity group, we can become fiercely determined to defend ourselves whenever our group is discriminated against or threatened by antagonistic forces. For this reason, identity conflicts are often extremely difficult to resolve. Unlike conflicts over money, we cannot always "split the difference" in conflicts over identity.

Democracies and authoritarian regimes tend to deal with identity conflicts, as with most other matters, in different ways. Democracies approach social conflicts through the ground rules of the democratic process: electoral competition,

political bargaining, and the right to organize interest groups. In the most successful cases, democratic governments manage to reduce social antagonisms by helping the contending parties compromise their differences and cooperate on the basis of tolerance and nondiscrimination. If cooperation proves impossible, governments may at least manage to keep the opposing groups from harming each other. Unfortunately, these ground rules are not always observed with scrupulous fairness. Democracies are not immune to social discrimination. Electoral majorities can find ways to subjugate minorities by supporting discriminatory laws. For much of its history, the United States has wrestled with the question of how—and at times even whether—to integrate African-Americans into the democratic process on an equal basis with whites. Until multiracial elections were held in 1994, South Africa's government represented the white minority, which comprised only 18 percent of the population, against the country's massive nonwhite majority. Other democracies have had their own difficulties implementing the ideals of democratic nondiscrimination with respect to various social groups.

Still, for all their problems, democracies are usually better disposed than authoritarian regimes to dealing with social conflicts with relative fairness. Fairness is a democratic ideal that many authoritarian regimes cynically spurn. Quite a few dictatorships have rested on privileged social groups such as the upper class or a dominant ethnic or religious group. Most communist governments paid lip service to social equality but were actually ruled by a privileged Communist Party elite. At times the ruling elites have oppressed subjugated groups with cold-blooded ruthlessness, taking full advantage of the government's coercive powers. Under more chaotic conditions, civil tranquillity may break down if the government cannot prevent rival social groups from assailing one another. In recent decades such violent turmoil has plagued both democracies and authoritarian regimes alike, especially in countries torn apart by intractable ethnic or religious divisions.

To get a better understanding of how comparative politics addresses identity, let's take a brief look at some issues connected with class, ethnicity, religion, gender, tribal or clan, and generational identities. We'll be looking at these and other forms of identity conflict in greater detail at various points in this volume.

The concept of **class** usually refers to the economic position of an individual or group in society. Class thus refers to a person's *socioeconomic identity*. The division of a country's population into socioeconomic classes is called *social stratification*.

There are two main ways of determining socioeconomic class. One way is the objective approach, which employs various quantitative measures. For example, we can calculate what percentage of a country's annual income goes to the richest 20 percent of the population and what percentage goes to the poorest 20 percent, as indicated in Table 1.2. (Of course, we can also divide the population into tenths or some other fraction.) The ratio of the income shares of the richest quintile and the poorest quintile is a way to compare countries with a single statistic. Another objective measure is the **Gini coefficient**

Tammy Smith is the first openly lesbian general in the US military. Until 2011 gay military personnel could not serve openly in the US armed forces, let alone be promoted to such a high rank. With Congressional authorization, the military can no longer consider sexual identity in determining membership or opportunity among its members.

Table 1.2 Social Class Identity: Objective and Subjective Measures

| Country | OBJECTIVE MEASURES | | | | SUBJECTIVE MEASURE | | | | |
| | Share of National Income | | Ratio of Richest to Poorest Quintiles | Gini Index | Which social class would you say you belong to?* | | | | |
	Poorest 20%	Richest 20%			Lower class	Working class	Lower middle class	Middle class	Upper middle class
Argentina	4%	49%	11.3	44.5	7%	24%	20%	47%	3%
Chile	4	58	13.5	52.1	20	34	18	24	3
China	5	48	9.6	42.5	25	22	21	30	2
Denmark	8	36	4.3	24.7	2	18	14	52	14
Germany	9	37	4.3	28.3	3	28	na	57	11
Poland	8	42	5.5	34.1	9	30	17	35	6
Russia	6	47	7.3	40.1	7	30	16	43	3
South Africa	3	68	25.3	63.1	7	50	14	21	8
South Korea	8	38	4.7	31.6	12	7	27	43	10
Spain	7	42	6.0	34.7	4	40	19	35	2
Sweden	9	37	4.0	25.0	1	24	12	49	13
Turkey	6	45	7.9	39.0	23	16	19	39	2
United Kingdom	6	44	7.2	36.0	3	40	18	35	4
United States	5	46	8.4	40.8	4	36	13	39	7

* The response for "upper class" equaled less than 1 percent for all countries and has been suppressed to make the table more readable.

Sources: For subjective social class, ISSP Research Group, International Social Survey Programme (ISSP): Social Inequality IV, 2009. Distributor: GESIS (Cologne, Germany), ZA5400, Data Version 2.0.0 (2012-01-6), accessed from http://zacat.gesis.org/, March 13, 2012. For Gini index and income quintiles: World Bank, World Bank Data Catalog, http://data.worldbank.org, accessed April 11, 2012.

(or **Gini index**), also shown in Table 1.2. This index is a measure of the relative degree of socioeconomic inequality within a particular country. Perfect equality equals zero—all individuals (or households) receive the same annual income; there is zero inequality. Maximum inequality equals 100: only one individual (or household) monopolizes all (100 percent) of society's income while everybody else gets nothing. Any number between 0 and 100 represents the degree to which a society's income distribution pattern deviates from perfect equality.

The significance of the Gini index figures is largely relative: They show that some countries have a more equal sharing of wealth than others do. The lower the Gini index, the greater the degree of socioeconomic equality; the higher the number, the greater the degree of inequality. As Table 1.2 shows, no country comes even close to perfect equality (zero); but among the countries selected here, real differences are evident. In Denmark and Sweden, Scandinavian welfare states that are the most equal societies shown in Table 1.2, the ratios of the income share of the richest 20 percent to the poorest quintile's share are about 4-to-1 and their Gini coefficients are about 25. In Argentina and Chile, two relatively prosperous but unequal South American countries, the richest-to-poorest quintile ratio is more than 10-to-1, while for South Africa it was an astounding 25-to-1. These countries' Gini coefficients range from 44.5 for Argentina to 52.1 for Chile and 63.1 for South Africa.

Another way to determine class is the subjective approach: Simply ask people which class they think they belong to. As a

general rule, people act on their *perceptions* of reality. If they perceive themselves as middle class or working class, they are likely to behave accordingly, such as by voting for candidates who represent their perceived class interests. Table 1.2 also shows responses to a question on the International Social Survey Program's 2009 survey on social inequality. Looking closely at the table we can see that those countries that have more equal income distributions tend to have higher percentages of their citizens self-identifying as middle class. However, as Table 1.2 also suggests, the propensity of groups of people to claim particular class identities seems to vary across countries in ways we would not predict based on the objective measures alone. Argentines, for example, don't seem to want to claim lower-class and working-class status nearly as much as other nationalities shown here, and they see themselves as a middle-class country. However, income distribution in Argentina is much more unequal than in Spain, where a large share of the people are willing to embrace a working-class identity. There is a link between the actual distribution of income in a society and how people see their class statuses, but class identity is clearly formed from other factors too.

The figures displayed in Table 1.2 suggest that all countries are socially stratified. In democracies and nondemocracies alike, class distinctions are often a powerful influence on political behavior and government policies. In democracies, class is one of the main factors affecting the way people vote. The game of politics in most democracies revolves to a considerable degree around conflicts between the rich, the poor, and the middle classes over the budget and the government's economic policies. Dictatorships of various kinds must also pay heed to class distinctions, and they often base their rule on alliances with one or more favored socioeconomic groups. Conflicts over class identity thus frequently overlap with conflicts over power and resources.

Social class often goes a long way to explaining how democracy itself comes about and endures over the long run. As many observers have pointed out, democracies tend to flourish when there is a vibrant middle class. Countries that are sharply polarized between a small number of extremely rich people and masses of impoverished laborers and peasants, with few middle-class professionals or private businesspeople in between, are more likely to succumb to authoritarianism.[9]

Ethnicity is a form of group identification or distinctiveness often based on a common biological ancestry in the distant past. More accurately, it is typically based on the belief in such a common biological ancestry, because the fact itself cannot normally be proven with scientific accuracy.

The terms *ethnicity* and *ethnic group* sometimes refer to race. Traditionally, anthropologists and other scientists have applied the term *race* to only a few large groupings of human beings who are assumed to have various biological commonalities. Caucasians (whites), Negroids (blacks), Mongoloids (East Asians), and three or four other such groupings have often been characterized as the main racial categories. Despite certain noticeable physical differences, there is no such thing as a completely distinct race that is biologically separate from all other races. Each of these groups contains a mixture of biological characteristics, including blood types and DNA.

The same can be said for the many subgroups that fall within these larger racial categories. Caucasians, for example, include Indo-Europeans, a category that is further subdivided into such groupings as Scandinavians, Anglo-Saxons, Slavs, and others. These latter groups in turn can be further divided into smaller groupings. Slavs, for example, would include Russians, Poles, Czechs, Slovaks, Ukrainians, Serbs, Croats, and still others. Although each of these groups is typically defined as an ethnic group, none is biologically distinct. Any racial or ethnic group that is defined in biological terms is bound to consist of a mixture of biological influences—the result of mass migrations, invasions, and other forms of intergroup contact—stretching far back into unrecorded time. The notion that individual races or other biologically defined groupings are fundamentally distinct is symptomatic of *racism*, which falsely exalts some ethnic groups as genetically superior while demeaning others as fundamentally inferior.

To say that no ethnic group is biologically homogeneous, however, is not to deny the reality of kinship patterns within identifiable groups. Centuries of living together within relatively circumscribed geographical boundaries and intramarriage among members of the same group can create real biological bonds among its members. These bonds explain why so many ethnic groups define themselves on the basis of blood ties. Japanese, Germans, Koreans, Russians, and hundreds of other collectivities regard themselves as distinctive ethnic groups largely on the basis of kinship ties, forged in the course of a long history of living together. In some cases these ties foster a people's sense of constituting a distinctive "nation," as we'll see in Chapter 4. It is therefore perfectly acceptable to acknowledge that ethnicity often has a genuine biological basis, at least to some extent, as long as we also recognize that no ethnic group can certify an unbroken lineage from a unique set of identifiable common ancestors. As Donald Horowitz, a noted scholar of ethno-politics, puts it, ethnicity is frequently based on the "myth of collective ancestry." Myths can be powerful integrative forces in ethnic identity, however.[10]

Despite the complexities of defining ethnicity, most people in today's world identify themselves with an ethnic group. It also happens that some people are defined by others as belonging to a particular ethnic group. In some countries, persons of mixed race, for example black and white, may be considered black (or, in some countries, "colored") by others in society, irrespective of how such individuals might prefer to define themselves. Social scientists therefore say that ethnic identity is *socially constructed;* it is created or defined by people in the course of their social interactions rather than being determined by objective criteria such as biology. Ethnic self-definitions, along with the definitions imposed on people by others, can have a profound effect on political behavior. Tragically, they can also lead to intractable political conflicts, at times with violent results.

Religion is another social identity that can have a demonstrable impact on the way people behave in politics. In the most tranquil of circumstances, societies divided along religious lines find a way to permit adherents of different religions to live peacefully side by side. The United States, for example, was established on the basis of the separation of church and state, and its traditions of religious tolerance have made a vital contribution to its success as a democracy. Many people came to America to escape religious persecution at home. Most of them practiced religious tolerance to ensure their own religious freedom.[11]

But religious identity often gives rise to sharp political conflict. (Religious conflict is sometimes called *sectarian* conflict, from *sect*.) The separation of church and state does not necessarily mean the separation of religion and politics. In the United States, for example, controversies abound over the interpretation of the clauses of the First Amendment of the Constitution, which state that "Congress shall make no law respecting the establishment of religion, or prohibiting the free exercise thereof." In accordance with the most literal meaning of these clauses, the United States does not have an official (or "established") state religion or church, and Americans are generally free to practice any religion they want, subject to laws against bigamy, drug use, and the like. Beyond a general agreement on these basic principles, however, there has been considerable disagreement among American citizens, politicians, and jurists on the extent to which the U.S. government, or state and local governments, may permit religious beliefs, practices, and symbols to cross the boundary separating church and state. Quite often the courts determine where that boundary lies, though court rulings rarely end debate on these matters. More broadly, religious doctrines and values are central to the deep disagreements dividing Americans over such issues as abortion, gay marriage, euthanasia, creationism, school prayer, and related issues. Inevitably such conflicts spill over into the political process, directly affecting the votes people cast, the laws passed by legislatures, and the cases brought before the courts.

The relationship between religion and the state has been a source of controversy in other countries as well, resulting in a wide variety of constitutional arrangements. Some countries have an *established church*—that is, an official state religion or church. The United Kingdom has two established churches—the Church of England, which is the Anglican church (its organization in the United States is called the Episcopal Church) that was founded by King Henry VIII in the sixteenth century and is still headed by the reigning monarch; and the Church of Scotland, which is Presbyterian. British citizens enjoy freedom of religion, however, and may worship as they wish; more Roman Catholics attend Sunday services in England than do Anglicans. Moreover, British citizens enjoy political and legal equality regardless of their religious faith.

Iran takes the concept of an established religion more literally. The Islamic Republic's theocratic regime is run by hardline clerics; more moderate clerics have been harassed. The Iranian legal system is based on Islamic law (*Sharia*). Christians and Jews may worship freely but they are denied political and legal equality, encountering systematic discrimination in both government and nongovernment employment, property rights, and education. In stark contrast, other countries go even further than the United States in proclaiming the separation of church and state. France, for example, passed a law on secularity (*laïcité*) in 1905 mandating the government's complete neutrality in religious matters. This law was fiercely opposed by many French Catholics at the time, in part because it limited public funding for Catholic schools. More recently the tradition of French secularism has created animosity in the country's growing Muslim community, following the government's 2004 ban on the wearing of head scarves and other religious attire in public schools. Turkey has its own concept of secularity, despite the fact that its population is 99 percent Muslim.

In addition to sparking constitutional conflicts over church–state relations, religion is frequently the source of conflict between different elements of a country's population. In some cases these conflicts involve adherents of different religions. Anti-Semitism, for example, has a particularly long history in Christian Europe and Russia, producing the Holocaust during World War II. Nigeria experiences intense strife between its Muslims and Christians. India has seen periodic outbreaks of violence between Muslims and Hindus. Other countries have witnessed sharp interreligious contention as well. In still other instances there has been antagonism between different denominations of the same religion. Sectarian violence in Northern Ireland between Protestants and Catholics has claimed more than 3,200 lives since 1969. Contemporary Iraq is seething with religious tensions between *Sunni* and *Shiite* (or Shia) Muslims, a dispute that goes back nearly 1,400 years to the formative decades of Islam. (Sunnis reject the Shiites' claim that the Prophet Muhammad's son-in-law Ali was the legitimately chosen fourth successor to Muhammad as the leader of the Muslim faith.) There are internecine feuds between various doctrinal orientations within the Sunni and Shia traditions as well.

Another source of political identity is *gender*. It took a long time for women to win the most elementary political rights in the world's democracies. Women first won a general right to vote in New Zealand in 1893. Despite their long histories as electoral democracies, Britain did not grant women the vote until 1918, the United States did not adopt a constitutional amendment according all its female citizens the right to vote until 1920, France did not extend the franchise to women until 1944, and Switzerland not until 1971. Ever since the 1960s and 1970s, feminist movements around the world have vigorously promoted public awareness of the subordinate status of women in various spheres of social and political life. Gender issues overlap with conflicts over political power and economic resources, and—in many countries—religion.

In some cases, governments have responded. Legislation has been passed to address such issues as job discrimination and sexual harassment. In other cases, governmental action has not been as effective as many women would wish, even in democracies. In most nondemocracies, women have few or no opportunities to speak up for a more equitable status in society. In India, Bangladesh, and other countries, killings and suicides over dowries are common. The deliberate abortion and infanticide of girls is practiced in India, Pakistan, China, and other countries, resulting in abnormally high male-to-female sex ratios.[12] Various African groups engage in the ritual genital mutilation of women. Rape and domestic violence are common around the world, and in many countries such acts routinely go unpunished.

In most of the developing world, especially in authoritarian regimes, women generally have less schooling and lower literacy rates than men. In the developing world and even in the most economically developed democracies of North America, Europe, and elsewhere, women have lower levels of economic activity and lower levels of political participation than men, at times substantially so.[13] Women are still underrepresented in the governmental structures of most democracies today; that is, their share of governmental positions is less than their share of the population, which is usually about 50 percent. As Table 1.3 illustrates, they do better in some national parliaments than in others.[14]

Women are especially disadvantaged in the Muslim world. A recent Freedom House survey of 16 states in the Middle East and North Africa (including the Palestinian Authority)—states with large Muslim majorities and with little or no real democracy—found that women were routinely discriminated against in every category of political, economic, and social rights. Using a rigorous scientific methodology, the team of regional experts who conducted the study found that, on a scale of 1 to 5 (with 1 constituting the lowest level of women's rights and 5 the highest), not one of these countries scored a 4 or 5 in any of five separate categories of rights. Most of these countries fell below a score of 3 in all five categories, reflecting major restrictions by the government and non-state actors on

Table 1.3 Percentage of Female Members of Lower House or Unicameral Legislature in Selected Countries (2011)

Country	%	Country	%
Rwanda	50.9	Bangladesh	18.6
Sweden	45.0	Indonesia	18.0
Iceland	42.9	Honduras	18.0
South Africa	42.7	Poland	17.9
Finland	42.5	Tajikistan	17.5
Norway	39.6	Greece	17.3
Mozambique	39.2	Venezuela	17.0
Costa Rica	38.6	United States	16.8
Belgium	38.5	Jamaica	16.0
Denmark	38.0	Azerbaijan	16.0
Argentina	37.8	Bosnia and Herzegovina	15.8
Netherlands	37.8	Burkina Faso	15.3
Uganda	37.2	South Korea	14.7
Tanzania	36.0	Uruguay	14.6
Spain	34.7	Zambia	14.0
New Zealand	33.6	Malaysia	14.0
Nepal	33.2	Thailand	14.0
Ecuador	32.3	Chile	13.9
Germany	31.7	Liberia	13.8
Bolivia	30.1	Colombia	13.8
Senegal	29.6	Kazakhstan	13.6
Australia	28.3	Paraguay	13.6
Austria	28.3	Japan	13.6
Switzerland	27.6	Niger	13.1
Peru	27.5	Syria	12.4
Portugal	27.4	Jordan	12.2
Ethiopia	25.5	Guatemala	12.0
Mexico	25.5	Russia	11.5
Iraq	25.2	Ireland	11.1
Canada	24.9	India	10.7
Croatia	23.5	Mali	10.2
Tunisia	23.3	Kenya	9.8
United Arab Emirates	22.5	Romania	9.8
Serbia	21.6	Brazil	9.6
Philippines	21.5	Armenia	9.2
China	21.3	Turkey	9.1
Pakistan	21.0	Côte d'Ivoire	8.9
Czech Republic	21.0	Ghana	8.3
United Kingdom	21.0	Ukraine	8.0
Bulgaria	20.8	Botswana	7.9
Malawi	20.8	Kuwait	7.7
Nicaragua	20.7	Nigeria	7.3
Italy	20.3	Algeria	7.0
France	20.0	Morocco	6.7
Estonia	19.8	Georgia	6.5
Uzbekistan	19.2	Sri Lanka	5.3
Israel	19.2	Haiti	4.2
Lithuania	19.1	Lebanon	3.1
Dominican Republic	19.1	Iran	2.8
El Salvador	19.0	Qatar	0.0
Cambodia	19.0	Saudi Arabia	0.0

Source: United Nations Development Program, *Human Development Report 2011: Sustainability and Equity: A Better Future for All*, http://hdr.undp.org/en/reports/global/hdr2011/, Table 4.

women's rights to equal justice and nondiscrimination, to personal freedom and security, to economic freedom and opportunity, to political participation, and to social and cultural opportunities.[15]

Even though politics is a male-dominated enterprise in every country in the world, the number of women who have succeeded in gaining positions in the executive, legislative, or judicial branches of government has nevertheless risen appreciably since the 1970s in most economically advanced democracies. In a few cases women have risen to the apex of the political pyramid, even in predominantly Muslim countries such as Bangladesh, Indonesia, Pakistan, and Turkey. When political scientists look at the role that gender plays in shaping political behavior, one of the essential questions they ask is, to what extent is the political activity of women determined mainly by their identity as women? Are the political opinions and attitudes of women shaped fundamentally by their gender, or do women behave essentially the same as men? In most democracies the answers are mixed. Some women place gender above all other considerations in their political activity, but many other women agree with men on the same topics and vote accordingly. Nevertheless, in virtually every country in the world, gender is a social identity that has important political implications, even in those countries where women's voices are largely silenced. We'll look at women's issues further in the countries to be examined in Part Two of this book, as well as in a number of countries treated later in Part One.

Close *kinship ties* are perhaps the most tightly knit forms of identity. In some countries they play important political roles, providing a strong basis of group self-interest, social and political organization, and even political power. The distinction between *tribes*, *clans*, and *families* is not always precise. All three involve kinship relationships, and their differences are based mainly on size. Tribes are typically the largest of the three groups, often consisting of interrelated families or communities that speak the same dialect and share various cultural characteristics. Native American Indian tribes are obvious examples, but roughly similar groups can be found in such diverse places as Africa and Afghanistan. Tribes tend to be smaller than ethnic groups but bigger than clans. Clans tend to be built around closer family ties than tribes. (In some cases they are subgroups of tribes.) Scotland, Ireland, China, and Japan are historically known for their clan-based societies, though the clan warfare that once characterized the struggle for power in these countries is now a thing of the past. Clan rivalries can still be highly volatile, however. Somalia, for example, has been seized by intermittent clan violence since 1991, rendering the country ungovernable. Clans also play an important political role in contemporary Iraq and other countries. Families are the smallest of the three kinship groups. Some modern political leaders have based their rule at least in part on their family connections, assigning important positions of power either to a close circle of immediate family members (like the Assad family in Syria) or to a more extended family (like Saddam Hussein, who drew on a large family centered in his home town of Tikrit). Among other things, the recent struggles in the Arab Spring have involved the patriarchs of political families striving to be able to pass power on to their heirs, as we saw above.

Yet another source of political identity is one's *age*. "Never trust anyone over 30!" was the battle cry echoed by millions of young Americans who came of political age in the 1960s, the decade in which the term *generation gap* captured the clash of attitudes between the young and their elders on a spectrum of issues ranging from the Vietnam War to sex. Although this tumultuous period has receded into history, generational factors have always played a prominent role in the political life of most countries. According to one hypothesis, every generation tends to be stamped by the political and social events of its youth. The attitudes that most people take through life, in this

Brutal fighting in Syria continues through 2012 as the Assad family seeks to maintain its decades-long hold on power.

view, are substantially molded by the political experiences they encountered in their teens and twenties.

As a general rule, different generations are likely to have different political outlooks. Throughout history, young people—especially students—have frequently been in the forefront of movements for political transformation in numerous countries around the world, waving the banners of such contradictory causes as democracy and fascism, global harmony and national assertiveness, peaceful reform and violent revolution. In recent years courageous young activists, boldly risking incarceration or death, have pressed their demands for democracy against entrenched dictatorships in Indonesia, Iran, and Nigeria. In the Arab Spring young people have played a prominent role.

On a somewhat more mundane economic level, demographic trends in recent years have set the stage for what may turn out to be significant generational conflicts in a number of countries. As the elderly come to constitute a rising percentage of the population, younger people may have to pay higher taxes and make other sacrifices to satisfy the needs of older generations for adequate pensions, health care, and other necessities. Table 1.4 shows some of these trends.

As we examine these and other identity conflicts in the ensuing chapters, we should keep in mind the distinction between cross-cutting cleavages and polarizing cleavages. **Cleavages** are social divisions that are meaningful enough to shape political preferences. *Cross-cutting cleavages* occur when the various factors that make up an individual's social identity tend to pull that person in different political directions. Take, for example, a 20-year-old African-American female student in New York City who is a devout Catholic opposed to abortion, whose parents together earn $100,000 a year, and who hopes to pursue a career in the military. Public opinion polls and voting studies demonstrate that most African-Americans, most females, most college students, and most New Yorkers in the 2010s tended to vote for Democrats in presidential and congressional elections, whereas most opponents of abortion, most upper-income families, and most military officers tended to vote Republican. This individual's ethnic, gender, generational, and regional identities are said to *cut across* her class, religious, and career identities, leading her to support Democrats on some issues and Republicans on others.

Polarizing cleavages occur when the factors composing one's social identity tend to pull in the same political direction. Consider a 45-year-old white male corporate executive who earns $250,000 a year and who is a born-again evangelical Protestant residing in Charleston, South Carolina. Every one of his separate social identities reinforces the others in a cumulative fashion to pull him toward the Republicans and away from Democratic candidates. By contrast, a 25-year-old Hispanic female agnostic earning $30,000 a year as a temp in New York City has all the attributes of a typical Democratic voter. In terms of their various social identities, these two people are polar opposites. Of course, they are both free individuals and may vote any way they please. There is nothing to prevent the former from voting for Democrats or the latter from voting solely for Republicans. All we can do as political scientists is hypothesize how these

Table 1.4 Generational Trends in Selected Countries

	POPULATION OVER 65 (%)			
	2000	**2010**	**2020**	**2050**
United States	12.4	13.1	16.1	20.2
United Kingdom	15.8	16.0	19.0	24.1
Sweden	17.3	18.3	21.1	23.6
Japan	17.4	23.1	29.2	29.6
China	7.0	8.2	12.0	29.6

Source: Organisation for Economic Cooperation and Development, *OECD Factbook 2011–12,* http://www.oecd-ilibrary.org/economics/oecd-factbook-2011-2012/dependent-population_factbook-2011-10-en.

individuals *may* vote, given the general voting patterns of the population. Once people have voted, however, and all the votes are counted, real voting patterns invariably emerge.

Now let's move from individual cases to entire countries. Suppose country X has a highly complex society with a diversity of ethnic groups (white, black, Asian, etc.). Each one of these ethnic groups has members at different socioeconomic levels (low income, middle class, rich), and each one has members who profess different religions (Catholic, Muslim, Buddhist, Protestant, etc.). This society as a whole is characterized by cross-cutting cleavages; ethnicity cuts across class and religion in a multiplicity of ways (see Figure 1.3).

Country Z, by contrast, consists of three unique groups, each with a distinctive combination of social identities. For example, all the whites are impoverished Catholics, all the blacks are middle-class Muslims, and all the Asians are rich Buddhists. There are no other combinations of ethnicity, class, and religion. Within each group, the key factors of social identity combine in such a way as to create three polarized groups with virtually nothing in common.

Most political scientists would hypothesize that the society of country X, characterized by cross-cutting cleavages, is better suited for democracy and cooperative interaction than deeply polarized societies. In view of its extreme polarization, country Z is a prime candidate for prolonged social confrontation, political stalemate, and, in the worst of scenarios, a civil war that might only be terminated by the dictatorial domination of one group over the other two. As a general rule, whenever two or more identities reinforce each other, social conflicts are likely to be all the more intense.[16]

Ideas Some of the oldest and most contentious conflicts in world history have centered on political ideas. In some cases these conflicts have revolved around what may be called the grand questions of politics: What is the best form of government? What should the community's most important goals be? Freedom? Equality? Social welfare? Military strength?

Not surprisingly, such grand questions have provoked a variety of grand answers. The most far-reaching and intellectually ambitious of these political grand designs are called ideologies. An **ideology** is a coherent set of ideas and guidelines that defines what the nature and role of government should be

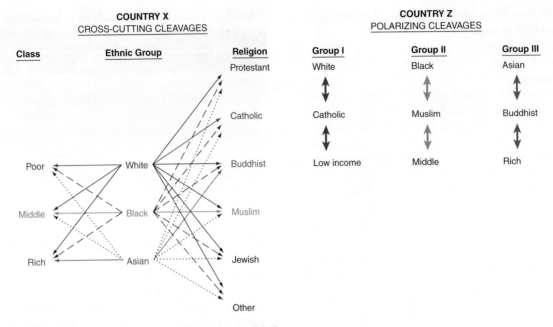

FIGURE 1.3 **Cross-Cutting and Polarizing Social Cleavages**

and prescribes the main goals the people should pursue through political action.

Liberalism, *socialism*, and *fascism* are among the most influential political ideologies that have emerged over the course of humankind's political development. Other political ideologies have derived from various religions, such as *Christian Democracy*, *Zionism* (which derives from Judaism), and various ideological orientations that stem from Islam. Each of these ideologies spells out certain ideas about the proper role of government and the relationship between the ruling authorities and the population. Whereas some ideologies and their variants favor democracy, others espouse authoritarianism. Each one of these broad ideologies, moreover, has important variations.

In the United States, the term liberalism often means, simply, the politics of the Democratic Party, or more particularly, of its most progressive wing. But in the history of ideas, liberalism has had another meaning, one that it still retains in most of the rest of the world, especially in Europe. Liberalism's most significant thinkers include John Locke, Adam Smith, and the American founders, especially Thomas Jefferson and James Madison.

In its oldest and broadest definition, **liberalism** refers to a system of government that guarantees liberty. This was the original meaning of the term as it emerged in the late seventeenth and early eighteenth centuries in Great Britain and as it developed over the course of the eighteenth, nineteenth, and early twentieth centuries, particularly in Britain, America, and France. In its earliest manifestation, liberalism posed a direct challenge to government by absolute monarchs and aristocracies, expressing the basic idea that the power of the state should be limited and that certain freedoms should be granted to the people by law. From the outset, the essence of liberalism was its opposition to tyrannical state power.

For many liberals, the concept of liberalism has both political and economic components. Whereas *political liberalism* emphasizes the concept of government by consent of the governed, *economic liberalism* stresses the notion that the state should strictly limit its role in the economy, leaving the bulk of the nation's economic activities in the hands of private individuals and companies. Early economic liberalism championed a free enterprise economy. It sought to dismantle the vast edifice of taxes, state monopolies, feudal estates, and other forms of governmental or aristocratic domination of economic life that were common under most monarchal regimes. In their place it favored the free operation of businesses and commercial farming. Liberalism generally advocates limited government, rule of law, property rights, and the advantages of free operation of market forces. As time has gone on, many liberals have begun to question the merits of the most pure form of liberalism in favor of government intervention in social and economic affairs to protect the most vulnerable members of society, but today's *libertarians* continue to sound the virtues of limited government and market capitalism.

Socialism is an ideology whose central premise is that an economy based on private enterprise (also known as *capitalism*), which economic liberals advocate, places excessive economic and political power in the hands of a small band of private entrepreneurs. Socialists contend that this capitalist elite, driven exclusively by greed for profits, uses its powers to exploit the working masses who constitute the vast majority of the population. Socialist ideology maintains that humanity would be better off if the free enterprise system were abolished. In its place, a socialist economy would put control over factories, farms, banks, stores, and other economic enterprises in the hands of the people as a whole.

While generally agreeing on these basic axioms, socialists have historically disagreed over *how* the ideals of socialism should be put into practice. Karl Marx (1818–83), the most influential theorist of socialist ideology, believed that a socialist society would not require any government. Marx did not view socialism in authoritarian terms; he saw it as a liberating force that would free the masses from economic exploitation.

Soviet-style communists, by contrast, believed in an all-powerful government operated by a well-organized Communist Party claiming to represent the workers. Under such leaders as V. I. Lenin (1870–1924) and Joseph Stalin (1879–1953) in the Soviet Union, and Mao Zedong (1893–1976) in China, communists of this type set up oppressive authoritarian regimes that placed exclusive political and economic power in the hands of a small party elite that administered a huge bureaucracy.

Additional variants of socialist ideology have been advanced by other theoreticians and political activists, as we will see in Chapter 10.

Fascism is an ideology that emerged in various parts of Europe in the 1920s and 1930s. Its most malignant manifestations were Adolf Hitler and his Nazi movement, which ruled Germany from 1933 to 1945, and the Italian fascist party under Benito Mussolini, who held power from 1922 to 1943. Fascism's essential features include an aggressive nationalism that glorifies one's own people above all others; intense racism; and devotion to an all-powerful, heavily militarized state. Efforts to whip up popular support through mass propaganda campaigns accompanied these orientations.

Although ideologies may constitute the grand ideas of politics, they are not the only examples of how ideas can stir up political conflict. On a more routine level, ideas are constantly at the heart of political debates and controversies in both democracies and authoritarian regimes. In democracies, people are constantly debating such issues as what the proper role of government should be and which policies the government should adopt in addressing the community's problems. Even authoritarian regimes must decide from a menu of alternative ways of pursuing the ruling elite's chosen goals.

Political ideologies can be placed along a left–right spectrum (see Figure 1.4). The terms *left* and *right* in politics derive from the French Revolution. When the French legislature known as the Convention convened in 1792, revolutionaries who favored replacing the monarchy with a fundamentally different political system took their seats to the left of the presiding officer, and conservatives who wished to preserve the monarchy were seated to his right. Moderates who sought some kind of compromise gathered in the center. These seating arrangements endured and so did the political alignments associated with them. Accordingly, proponents of political change became known as *leftists* (or the *left wing*), conservative advocates of the status quo

became known as *rightists* (or *right-wingers*), and those in the middle became identified, quite appropriately, as *centrists*. The most extreme right-wingers are often called *reactionaries* because they want to turn the clock back to some previously existing (or idealized) governmental system or concept of government.

We'll examine these and other ideological issues further in Chapter 10.

Values Spiritual or moral principles, ideals, or qualities of life that people favor for their own sake may be defined as **values**. Among the most important values to be found in political life are freedom, justice, equality, security, order, and community. People often cherish these principles and ideals because of their intrinsic merit in promoting human dignity and civilized relationships, not simply because they may confer wealth or power. In addition, people may attach a special value to certain qualities of life. A healthy environment, for example, or "family values" may be prized for their own sake as conditions of civilized existence. Religion is also a major source of values, and value conflicts often overlap with religious conflicts. On the whole, values make a major contribution to a country's political culture, the complex of attitudes and beliefs that shape political mentalities and behavior. As we'll see in Chapter 9, the World Values Survey and other studies clarify value orientations around the world.

Some political values tend to promote democracy; others are often invoked to justify authoritarian rule. Freedom is one of the most hallowed democratic values, one that is seldom, if ever, embraced by dictators. People who support authoritarian regimes attach a higher value to order than to freedom and justify the use of dictatorial rule and unrestrained force as necessary to ensure domestic tranquillity. Indeed, democracy ultimately rests on certain core values that include not only freedom but also the notion that human dignity and equality are impossible under dictatorial oppression and require the state's full accountability to the people. The clash between democracy and dictatorship is thus in large measure a clash over values, not simply a conflict over power or resources.

Political conflicts may arise over values for a variety of reasons. Sometimes the multiple values that a society favors may clash with one another, making it difficult or impossible to fulfill one value without limiting another. Freedom and equality are frequently in conflict, for example. The freedom to operate a business without any governmental interference may clash with employees' demands for a just wage and social welfare benefits or for the nondiscriminatory treatment of females or ethnic minorities in the workplace. To ensure a measure of social fairness, governments may infringe on the freedoms of the private entrepreneur.

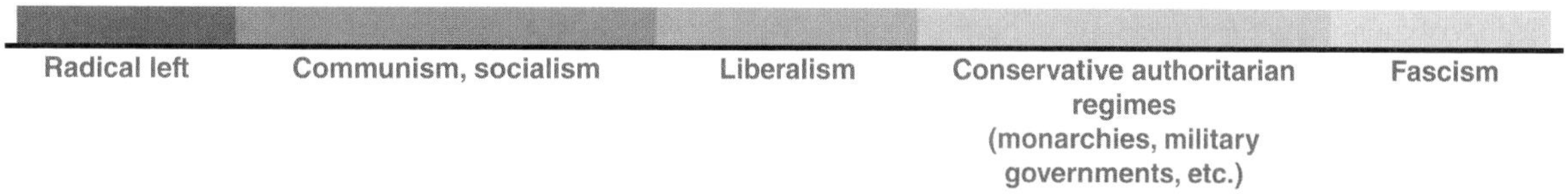

Radical left	Communism, socialism	Liberalism	Conservative authoritarian regimes (monarchies, military governments, etc.)	Fascism

FIGURE 1.4   The Left–Right Spectrum

The Chinese government regularly censors the information its population can access online. One way of understanding these restrictions is to compare the Western value of the relatively free exchange of ideas with the Chinese values of social order that such exchanges may challenge.

On a global scale, some of the most contentious issues in today's world center around values. Whereas proponents of democracy and private enterprise cherish freedom and individualism, some people reject these ideals as "Western values" that they regard as incompatible with the cultural norms and value systems of their own societies. They tend to view the West's exaltation of individual freedom as dangerously excessive and argue that it leads to decadent egoism and social breakdown. In its place they stress the individual's responsibilities to the community and the need for deference to established political or religious authorities. Variants of these arguments have been put forward by certain East Asian authoritarian leaders who assert the superiority of "Asian values," highly conservative Muslims who want Islamic law to replace civil law in Islamic countries, and various others.[17] Advocates of democracy insist that its basic values and procedures are universally applicable and can be adapted to local cultures and value systems.

In asserting our support for democracy, we argue that when people are denied the possibility to elect their government or speak freely, many of them will know that they are being politically oppressed, regardless of their culture. When people are subjected to systematic discrimination, arbitrary arrest, or brutal torture because of their political views, religious beliefs, ethnic identity, gender, or for some similar reason, they know that they are being deprived of fundamental human rights, regardless of their culture. The forms that human societies take are incredibly diverse; cultural differences abound. Nevertheless, we believe that the values that distinguish democratic rights and liberties from authoritarian repression are everywhere the same, and that they are universally recognized by those who seek a genuine alternative to exclusion, persecution, and the suppression of human dignity.

Conclusion

This chapter has shown that comparative politics covers a wide array of topics. Not surprisingly, comparativists have come up with a wide array of approaches to understanding these phenomena. Some comparativists focus on how governmental institutions work and how they affect political outcomes. Those who give greater emphasis to political culture look at the attitudes and values of various populations. Other approaches have their own perspectives. Each approach has its strengths and limitations; when it comes to the complexities of politics, no single theory or school of thought can explain everything. That is why this book does not confine itself to just one approach to comparative politics. It seeks to be eclectic, exposing you to several different ways of examining political realities. Our premise is that any theory or analytical orientation must ultimately answer two basic questions: What does it tell us about politics in general? How well can it explain specific phenomena? To figure out how to address these questions, we need to know something about how scientific methods can be applied to politics. We turn to that subject in Chapter 2.

Key Terms

Comparative politics
Globalization
Transnationalism
Democratization
Science
International relations
Politics
State
Regime
Democracy
Authoritarianism (dictatorship)
Monarchy
Totalitarianism
Theocracy
Political economy
Political sociology
Class
Gini coefficient/index
Ethnicity
Cleavages
Ideology
Liberalism
Socialism
Fascism
Values

Notes

1. International Labour Organisation, *Global Employment Trends for Youth: August 2010: Special Issue on the Impact of the Global Economic Crisis on Youth* (Geneva: ILO, 2010), available at http://www.ilo.org/wcmsp5/groups/public/---ed_emp/---emp_elm/---trends/documents/publication/wcms_143349.pdf, p. 66.

2. F. Gregory Game III, "Why Middle East Studies Missed the Arab Spring," *Foreign Affairs* 90, no. 4 (July/August 2011), pp. 81–90.

3. Theda Skocpol, *States and Social Revolutions: A Comparative Analysis of France, Russia, and China* (New York: Cambridge University Press, 1979); Jack A. Goldstone, "Understanding the Revolutions of 2011," *Foreign Affairs* 90, no. 3 (May/June 2011), pp. 8–16.

4. David Easton, *A Systems Analysis of Political Life* (New York: Wiley, 1965).

5. Harold D. Lasswell, *Politics: Who Gets What, When, How* (New York: McGraw-Hill, 1936).

6. Weber's discussion of the state is found in "Politics as a Vocation," which appears in *From Max Weber: Essays in Sociology*, translated and edited by H. H. Gerth and C. Wright Mills (New York: Oxford University Press, 1946).

7. Arch Puddington, *Freedom in the World 2013: Democratic Breakthroughs in the Balance* (New York: Freedom House, 2013). A large set of data on political regimes since 1800, known as Polity IV, is available online at http://www.systemicpeace.org/polity/polity4.htm.

8. See Marina Ottoway, *Democracy Challenged: The Rise of Semi-Authoritarianism* (Washington, DC: Carnegie Endowment for International Peace, 2003).

9. For an overview, see Patrick Joyce, ed., *Class* (Oxford: Oxford University Press, 1995).

10. Donald L. Horowitz, *Ethnic Groups in Conflict* (Berkeley: University of California Press, 1985), p. 52.

11. See Jon Meacham, *American Gospel: God, the Founding Fathers, and the Making of a Nation* (New York: Random House, 2006); David L. Holmes, *The Faiths of the Founding Fathers* (New York: Oxford University Press, 2006); and Gordon S. Wood, "American Religion: The Great Retreat," *New York Review of Books*, June 8, 2006, pp. 60–63.

12. Valerie M. Hudson and Andrea M. den Boer, *Bare Branches: The Security Implications of Asia's Surplus Male Population* (Cambridge: MIT Press, 2004); Mara Hvistendahl, *Unnatural Selection: Choosing Boys Over Girls, and the Consequences of a World Full of Men* (New York: PublicAffairs, 2011).

13. See the data in United Nations Development Program, *Human Development Report 2005* (New York: UNDP, 2005), pp. 299–302, 307–19.

14. See Monique Leijenaar, *The Political Empowerment of Women: The Netherlands and Other Countries* (Leiden and Boston: Martinus Nijhoff, 2004); Michael A. Genovese, *Women as National Leaders: The Political Performance of Women as Heads of Government* (Newbury Park, CA: Sage, 1993); and Barbara J. Nelson and Najma Chowdhury, *Women and Politics Worldwide* (New Haven: Yale University Press, 1994). See also the annual Global Gender Gap Report published by the World Economic Forum, www.weforum.org.

15. Sameena Nazir and Leigh Tomppert, eds., *Women's Rights in the Middle East and North Africa: Citizenship and Justice* (Lanham, MD: Rowman and Littlefield, 2005). See also World Bank, *Gender and Development in the Middle East and North Africa: Women in the Public Sphere* (Washington, DC: World Bank, 2004).

16. See Amy Gutmann, *Identity in Democracy* (Princeton: Princeton University Press, 2003).

17. On Asian values as conceived in Singapore, see Kishore Mahbubani, "The United States: 'Go East, Young Man,'" *Washington Quarterly* 17, no. 2 (Spring 1994), pp. 5–23. On the views of Malaysia's leader Mohamad Mahathir, see Khoo Boo Teik, *Paradoxes of Mahathirism* (Oxford: Oxford University Press, 1995).

2

Critical Thinking about Politics
Analytical Techniques of Political Science—
The Logic of Hypothesis Testing

OVERVIEW

- While students of comparative politics are often motivated by questions of justice (*ought* questions), their research methods emphasize empirical analysis to answer questions about political reality (*is* questions).

- Empirical analysis seeks to discover, describe, and explain factual relationships. In empirical analysis political scientists define expected relationships between explanatory factors (independent variables) and outcomes (dependent variables) and then seek to determine whether correlations can be found between them.

- Expected relationships can be formulated as hypotheses that can be rigorously tested to show whether there is empirical evidence to support or reject a hypothesis.

- This chapter provides an extended example of a hypothesis testing exercise that explores the relationship between economic well-being and democracy.

Comparative political analysis relies heavily on the information gathered by national census bureaus and polling organizations.

As Chapter 1 pointed out, comparative politics is a subfield of political science. Political science, in turn, is a science to the extent that its practitioners engage in the tasks of definition, description, explanation, probabilistic prediction, and prescription. This chapter explains how to apply these scientific operations to the study of politics. The first part defines important terms and provides examples of how they are used. The second part walks you through a hypothesis-testing exercise, using a step-by-step procedure that is utilized in the chapters that follow. Both parts demonstrate how the logic of scientific analysis can help you understand reality, enhancing critical-thinking skills that you can apply in a variety of academic and professional contexts.

ANALYTICAL TECHNIQUES OF POLITICAL SCIENCE

Political science asks two broad types of questions: *is* questions (What *is* political reality?) and *ought* questions (What *ought* to be done about political reality?). The two sets of questions are intimately related: we cannot adequately determine what we ought to do through practical political activity without a thorough comprehension of the realities we are facing. Good policy prescription requires good analysis! We must always keep in mind, however, that *is* questions and *ought* questions are basically different. *Is* questions concentrate on *facts* and *explanations* of facts, whereas *ought* questions mostly deal with *personal preferences* and *values*. The systematic analysis of facts is called *empirical analysis*. This chapter is mainly concerned with the logic of empirical analysis.

Within the academic traditions of political science, *ought* questions are the special province of two fields of the discipline: political philosophy and public policy analysis.

Political philosophy, which is also called *political thought*, is perhaps the oldest form of systematic thinking about politics. For most political philosophers, the central question of political philosophy has traditionally been, What is the best form of government? This broad question has inspired a chorus of related ones: What ought to be the main goals of political action: freedom? order? equality? justice? How do we define these goals in practical circumstances? These and similar questions are characterized above all by their concern with political values and with optimal standards of political organization and behavior. Such values are called *norms*. Consequently, the field of political philosophy is also called *normative political theory*.[1] While this book is not a work of political philosophy, we do turn to the work of political philosophers regularly, for example, when we discuss democracy (Chapter 5), ideology (Chapter 10), and political economy (Chapter 11), because the great works of political philosophy have determined the goals of many political activists and the founders of constitutions.

Public policy analysis is the other subfield of political science that is primarily concerned with *ought* questions, but it also employs a lot of empirical analysis to assess the impact of policy decisions. Public policy essentially means governmental policy. *Public policy analysis* concerns the decisions that governments make (or should make) to reach certain goals. Public policy analysts who pursue their careers in government agencies or in nongovernmental organizations, such as public watchdog groups, take a hard look at specific issues such as health care, homeland security, or defense policy and propose specific governmental programs or decisions. Once policies are adopted through the political process, these analysts monitor the results and recommend pertinent adjustments and corrections. These tasks require strong analytical skills as well as a personal dedication to improving government performance.[2]

This textbook concentrates on comparative politics, not on political philosophy or public policy analysis per se. But comparative politics cannot be properly understood in isolation from some of the leading traditions of political thought and the work of comparative public policy analysts.

"WHAT IS . . . ?": A GUIDE TO EMPIRICAL POLITICAL ANALYSIS

In addition to being interested in what people ought to do in the realm of politics, political science is concerned with describing and explaining political realities. To this end it takes a close look at the facts of political life and searches for patterns or relationships that help explain the facts. What is democracy and how does it work? What is a military dictatorship? Why does it tend to occur in some countries but not in others? Questions such as these probe the *what*, the *how*, and the *why* of political reality, which are all examined through empirical analysis.

Empirical analysis seeks to discover, describe, and explain facts and factual relationships, to the extent that the facts are knowable. The term *empirical* derives from the ancient Greek word for *experience*. Empirical analysis is based strictly on what we can experience or perceive through our senses—namely, *facts*. Empirical analysis is not concerned with our values, ideals, or preferences. It does not make value judgments.

At least in principle, when we study politics empirically we are supposed to put aside our personal preferences and religious faith and stick to the observable facts. As a consequence, empirical political science is sometimes called *value-free* political science. It requires us to keep our investigations of political reality free from our own particular values and biases, no matter how well intentioned our convictions may be. If we favor democracy, for example, we must not allow this preference to intrude into our efforts to understand how democracies work in actual fact. Otherwise, we may blind ourselves to certain realities about democracies that we may find unpalatable. The same admonition applies to adherents of all political persuasions. In practice, however, it can be quite difficult to keep our subjective inclinations separate from our fact-centered analyses. Personal values and preferences sometimes creep into the way we select the topics we are interested in and the way we look at them. But the canons of science require us to acknowledge our biases and make sure they do not get in the way of our quest for objective truth when conducting empirical investigations.

The principal approach of this book is empirical. Its main purposes are to present and explain facts about politics and to teach you various ways of analyzing political reality from an empirical perspective. At the same time, the authors freely acknowledge that we are not unbiased. To put our cards on the table, we unabashedly proclaim that we favor democracy over any known form of authoritarianism. Though we may differ among ourselves about how to promote democracy in the world or how democracies should be run in actual practice, we favor democracy as a general principle because it provides far more opportunities to achieve human dignity and to practice self-expression than authoritarian regimes.

All sciences must strive for definitional clarity. Unless we are clear about the terms we use, we may end up in a conceptual muddle. The same terms may mean different things to different people, or they may have several different meanings depending on the context in which they are used.

As political scientists, we must define our concepts and refine our definitions so that they apply to reality as accurately as possible. A *concept* is a word, a term, or a label that applies to a whole class or category of phenomena or ideas. In political science, such terms as freedom, power, democracy, liberalism, conservatism, socialism, and globalization are concepts whose meanings need to be spelled out carefully so that we can talk about them intelligibly and consistently. Like many political concepts, each of them can be defined in more than one way. For James Madison and the framers of the U.S. Constitution, for example, freedom meant above all freedom from the tyranny of an excessively powerful state and freedom to engage in private economic activity. For Karl Marx, however, it meant freedom from economic exploitation by private industrialists. In early twentieth-century Germany, a conservative was a staunch opponent of democracy who favored a militarily powerful authoritarian state. Conservatives in contemporary Germany, by contrast, favor both democracy and civilian control over the military. Conceptual clarity is imperative whether we are discussing political values (e.g., freedom) or describing political facts (e.g., German conservatism). Achieving such clarity is one of the main tasks of political science.

Description: Observing, Collecting, Comparing

Natural scientists must look very closely at natural phenomena, record their observations, and gather them in some systematic fashion. One of the oldest ways of studying the natural world has involved the *comparative method*. Biologists, for example, compare various forms of animal and plant life and group them into categories such as kingdom, genus, and species. In a roughly similar manner, political scientists examine systems of government, describe their similarities and differences, and classify them in various categories. Starting with democracy and authoritarianism as the two broadest categories, we can group different types of democracy under the first rubric and different forms of authoritarian government under the second. Gabriel Almond, a pioneering figure in the study of comparative politics, once suggested that it is especially useful to look for *dissimilarities* between *similar* forms of government (such as democracies) and *similarities* between *dissimilar* forms of government (such as

democracies and nondemocracies). By employing these descriptive and comparative techniques, we can get a better understanding of how governments work—and ought to work.

The precise methods used to carry out our observations and comparisons will vary from case to case. If we are interested in the way people vote, we will want to gather election returns as well as relevant information about the voters, such as their social class, religion, ethnicity, and the like. If we want to understand how political elites view politics, it may be helpful to conduct interviews with relevant officials, such as parliamentarians or bureaucrats, to see how they perceive politics and their own role in political affairs. To increase the breadth and depth of these observations, we may want to examine voting patterns or elite attitudes in a variety of countries over extended periods. The more information we observe, the more likely patterns will emerge that will permit us to go beyond merely describing reality. It will then be possible to make generalizations about reality with the aim of explaining it.

Explanation and Generalization

Are Americans increasingly fed up with their political parties? Are similar tendencies occurring in other democracies? If so, then why? Do political leaders in democratizing countries share similar conceptions of human rights or do they differ? What accounts for these similarities or differences? Are these attitudes conducive to stabilizing democracy or might they tend to undermine it?

Questions like these take us beyond merely isolated facts about politics in this or that country, however intriguing the facts may be. They prompt us to generalize from those facts to gain a broader perspective on political reality. By themselves, facts are not especially meaningful. (As one wag put it, "History is just one damned thing after another!") The facts of political life assume meaning only when we visualize them as general patterns, tendencies, or relationships.

Political scientist Gabriel Almond suggested that it is useful to look for *dissimilarities* between *similar* forms of government (such as democracies) and *similarities* between *dissimilar* forms of government (such as democracies and nondemocracies). Can you think of any similarities between Kim Jong-un, the supreme leader of nondemocratic North Korea, and the leaders of Western democracies?

Therefore, if we want to understand the significance of discrete facts or events in political life, we must integrate them into larger analytical frameworks. Today's headlines, for example, may announce that the prime minister of a major democratic country has resigned, that the government's central bank in a leading trading nation has just raised interest rates, and that the military in a country struggling to establish democracy has seized power in a coup d'état. Governments, private businesses, journalists, and other interested parties around the world must pay instant attention to these occurrences and assess their implications for decision makers or average citizens. As political scientists, we too may be interested in the immediate practical effects of these events. But we will also be interested in what they tell us about politics more generally.

What does the prime minister's resignation tell us about how democracies work? What do the central bank's actions tell us about the relationship between politics and economics? What does the latest coup tell us about military intervention in politics? Our aim here is to deepen our understanding of democracy in general, political economy in general, and military authoritarianism in general. *Generalization* is a central purpose of science. At the same time, we can apply our understanding of these general processes and tendencies to sharpen our understanding of the specific events at hand.

To construct meaningful generalizations from a wealth of political information and to determine how accurate these generalizations are, we must use scientific methods of analyzing facts and testing general propositions. Many students of science maintain that the essence of science lies in its methods of analysis.[3]

Analysis is simply the quest for understanding through close observation and broad generalization. In pursuit of this objective, scientific analysis has a toolbox of concepts and procedural operations. Variables, correlations, laws, theories, hypotheses, and models are some of the most important ones, and they are particularly important in political science. Following is a brief explanation of each of these terms, coupled with elementary examples of how they can be employed in political science.

Variables

A **variable** is an element or feature that can vary or change. That is, a variable can take different forms or be a changeable characteristic of a phenomenon. Sometimes we use the word *factor* instead of variable. The idea is the same: We want to explain something that changes—a variable or a factor—and something we think has caused the change—another variable or factor—whose causal role we want to investigate.

Suppose we want to understand democracy. Democracy has many characteristics that can vary or come in different forms. For example, there are stable democracies that endure over long periods with few major alterations (such as the United States); there are unstable democracies that experience frequent changes of government (like Italy, which has had more than 60 governments since World War II) or that alternate with nondemocratic modes of government (such as Brazil, which has alternated between democracy and dictatorship). Stability

is thus a characteristic of democracy that can vary. We can focus on stability as one among several variables about democracy that can be analyzed systematically. We can define exactly what we mean by stability and instability, we can collect information on stable and unstable democracies, compare different cases of each variant, and look for possible explanations of why some democracies are stable and others are not. The factors that account for stability or instability are also variables. For example, we may find that, of all the possible characteristics of a given country, national wealth is the variable that best explains democratic stability: Rich democracies may turn out to be the most stable, poor ones the most unstable.

Almost any general topic in political science has characteristics that can vary, such as types of government (e.g., democracy, authoritarianism), governmental institutions (e.g., unicameral and bicameral legislatures), or political behavior of people (e.g., mass voting behavior, such as whether people choose to vote or to abstain on election day). When we engage in the scientific study of politics, variables such as these occupy our direct attention. In some cases we may wish simply to observe these phenomena, collecting information about them and perhaps classifying them in some way. Things get especially interesting, however, when we find relationships between two or more observed variables.

Dependent and Independent Variables Whenever we are looking for patterns or connections between two variables, one variable is the dependent variable and the other is the independent variable. The **dependent variable** is the variable we are most interested in examining or explaining; it is the main object of our study. It is the effect or outcome that is influenced or caused by another variable or variables. It is the variable whose value changes in response to changes in the value of other variables (viz., independent variables).

Let's say that we are interested in understanding voting behavior in the United States and other democracies. One variable characteristic of voting behavior is *turnout*, the number of people who vote. Some voters go to the polls but others stay home. Electoral statistics over the past 50 years show that Americans tend to vote at consistently lower rates than West Europeans. What explains these differences? Are there any patterns we can find that might be associated with the level of voter turnout? Put another way, on what factors is turnout *dependent*? Turnout is thus our *dependent* variable. It is the variable we seek to explain; we want to see what it *depends* on. The **independent variable** is the factor or characteristic that influences or causes the dependent variable. In cause-and-effect relationships, it is the causal or explanatory variable. Changes in the value of the independent variable may produce changes in the value of the dependent variable.

In our hypothetical study of voter turnout, the independent variables are various characteristics of the electorate that may help account for variations in voter turnout. These characteristics would include income level, age, education level, ideological proclivities, and other pertinent factors. For example, low-income voters may be less inclined to vote than

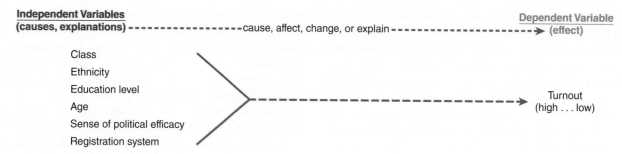

FIGURE 2.1 **Independent and Dependent Variables**

upper-income voters; younger voters may be less inclined to turn out than older ones; and so on. Independent variables could also include different attitudes about politics, as evidenced in public opinion surveys. Some people may not vote because they believe their vote doesn't really matter and that voters can't change anything for the better; they therefore have a low sense of political efficacy and feel alienated from the political system. By contrast, others may have a high sense of political efficacy: They believe that "every vote counts" and that voters can influence politicians to make desirable decisions while in office. Turnout might also hinge on registration procedures: It may be higher in countries where registering to vote is easy and lower where it is more inconvenient (as in the United States). Almost anything that might affect turnout can be an independent variable in our investigation. Figure 2.1 illustrates these variables.

In short, in the statement "A causes B," A is the *independent variable* and B is the *dependent variable*. B is dependent on A.

We can test our independent variables individually to see to what extent each one is associated with our dependent variable, or we can try different combinations of independent variables. For example, we can focus first on the relationship between ethnicity and turnout in the United States, examining turnout levels for whites, blacks, Asians, Hispanics, and so on.

We can do the same for the income-level variable, the religious variable, and so on. In these instances we are engaging in *bivariate analysis*, or analysis of the relationship between two variables, one independent and one dependent. We can also examine two or more independent variables in combination against the dependent variable (e.g., rich whites, poor blacks; Protestants who attend church regularly and Protestants who do not attend church regularly, and so on). Such analyses are *multivariate analyses*.

Our aim in this study is to determine whether, or to what extent, there are any connections between the independent variables and our dependent variable, voter turnout. Such connections between variables are called correlations, or associations.

Correlations

A **correlation** (or **association**) is a relationship in which two or more variables change together. *Correlates* are variables that are associated with each other in some way. For example, such things as a high level of national wealth, a large middle class, and a well-educated populace are often correlates of democracy: As a general tendency they go together with democratic forms of government.

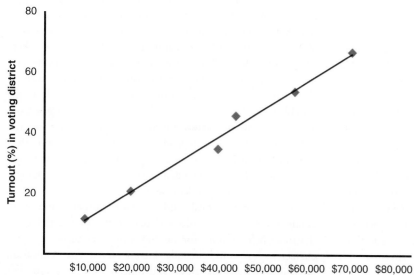

FIGURE 2.2 **Positive Correlation between Income Levels and Voter Turnout**

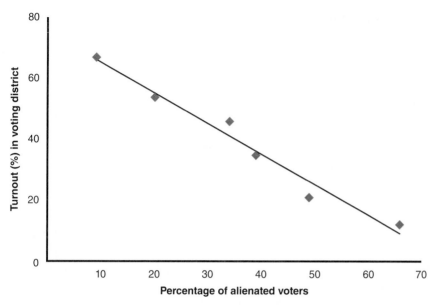

FIGURE 2.3 **Inverse (Negative) Correlation between Alienation and Turnout**

Variables are *positively* correlated when they vary in the same direction. Two variables are positively correlated when they go up or down together (i.e., they increase together or decrease together).

If our variables are quantifiable, we can plot them on a graph. Usually we plot the dependent variable along the y-axis (vertical axis), and the independent variable along the x-axis (horizontal axis). Let's measure the relationship between turn-out and the electorate's income levels in a hypothetical country. Figure 2.2 illustrates a *positive correlation* between the voters' income levels (the independent variable) and the percentage of people who turn out to vote (the dependent variable). The higher the income level, the higher the turnout; the lower the income level, the lower the turnout. Eighty percent of people in the highest income bracket turn out to vote, but only 5 percent of the people in the lowest income level show up at the polls.

Note that when the correlation is positive, the plotted line goes from bottom left to top right.

Variables are inversely correlated when they vary in opposite or reverse directions. In quantitative terms, an inverse correlation occurs when one variable increases and the other variable decreases, or vice versa. We can grasp an inverse correlation rather easily by looking at the relationship between turnout (the dependent variable) and the voters' sense of *alienation* from the political system (the independent variable). (Alienation means a low sense of political efficacy and a basic distrust of politicians and government officials.) Figure 2.3 illustrates a theoretical relationship in which voting districts in which few voters are alienated have the highest turnout rates; districts in which many voters are alienated have the lowest turnout rates. If this relationship holds up under empirical investigation there would be an *inverse correlation* between alienation and turnout. Inverse correlations are

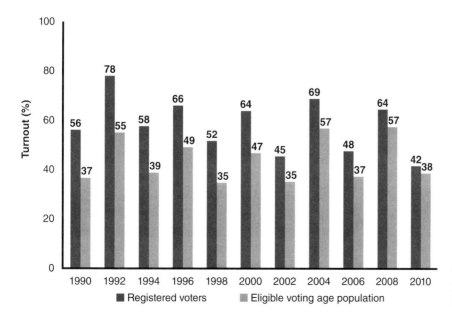

FIGURE 2.4 **Bar Chart Comparing Turnout Rates of Registered and All Potential U.S. Voters (Elections to House of Representatives, 1990–2010)**

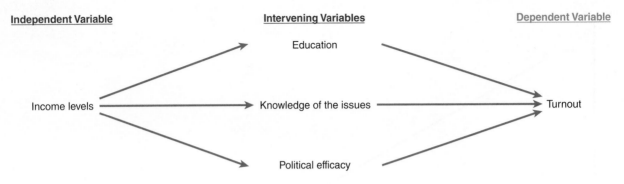

FIGURE 2.5   Intervening Variables

also called *negative correlations*. Note that when the correlation is negative, the plotted line goes from top left to bottom right.

In some cases we cannot chart quantifiable degrees of variation on a graph, but we can display different examples of the variable on a bar chart. Figure 2.4 shows the relationship between turnout and voter registration in the United States. Because we cannot distinguish among different magnitudes of "registered-ness," we cannot plot variations in turnout rates *within* these two groups. The bar chart compares the percentage of registered voters who have turned out to vote in elections to the House of Representatives with the percentage of all potential voters—registered and unregistered—who have turned out.

Keep in mind that correlations are *not* explanations. Even though our data may show a clear correlation, positive or negative, between the dependent and independent variables, they do not explain *why* the variables are related. Let's take another look at Figure 2.2, which shows a positive correlation between voter turnout and income levels. *Why* do higher-income people vote at higher rates than less well-off citizens? We cannot get answers to this question just by looking at the graph depicting the correlation.

To find out why higher-income voters come out on election day at higher rates than the less well-to-do voters do, we will have to extend our investigations by conducting surveys of voter attributes and attitudes. These surveys may reveal that wealthier citizens tend to be better educated than poorer ones and thus more knowledgeable about political issues. They may also have a higher sense of their own political efficacy, that is, their ability to have a real impact on government policies. The surveys may further reveal that poor citizens tend to be poorly educated, display less knowledge of the issues of the day, and have a markedly lower sense of political efficacy. These results suggest that income levels (the independent variable) affect turnout (the dependent variable) by working through such intermediary factors as education, knowledge of the issues, and a citizen's sense

of political efficacy. These intermediary factors are called **intervening variables**. As Figure 2.5 shows, intervening variables are located between the independent and dependent variables.

As a rule, correlations do not prove that one variable (i.e., income level) actually causes the other variable (i.e., voter turnout). All a correlation does is suggest or imply that there *may* be a cause-and-effect relationship between the variables under observation. Correlations are necessary to demonstrate causality, but by themselves they are not sufficient to do so.

Sometimes variables may be positively or negatively correlated but it turns out on further investigation that there is no direct cause-and-effect relationship between them. We then have a *spurious correlation*.

One type of spurious correlation occurs when there appears to be a correlation between the variables but in fact no real relationship of any kind exists. One of the most famous examples concerns the fairy tale that babies are delivered by storks. The story comes from actual statistical data from northern Europe that showed an increase in human births whenever stork births increased. When stork births declined, so did human births. No one ever came up with any verifiable explanations as to why human and stork birthrates were positively correlated. Obviously, the one event could not have caused the other, but neither was there any evidence that some other variable (climactic patterns? lunar cycles?) caused the two birthrates to rise and fall together. Until someone brings forward convincing evidence of a causative variable, we can assume that the correlation between human births and stork births is entirely fortuitous. Thus a spurious correlation can at times be a matter of pure coincidence, with *no* causal factors at work.

In sum, a spurious correlation occurs when two variables appear to be directly linked in a cause-and-effect relationship but in fact (a) there is no causal linkage whatever, or (b) they are linked indirectly by some other causative variable or variables. Figure 2.6 depicts the logic of spurious correlations.

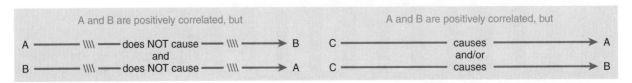

FIGURE 2.6   Spurious Correlations

As political scientists we must constantly be on guard against spurious correlations when conducting or examining scientific research. We should be similarly vigilant as citizens. In the rough-and-tumble world of politics, it is common for politicians seeking to oust their opponents from office in the next election to blame the incumbents for virtually everything that has gone wrong in the country during the government's term in office. In some cases, the elected officials may indeed be responsible for the problems they are accused of creating. But not always. It could happen, for example, that a downturn in the national economy that occurs when the Freedom Party is in power actually had its causative roots in policies pursued several years earlier when the Independence Party was in office. The correlation between the Freedom Party's incumbency and the deterioration of the economy is spurious because a third variable, the Independence Party, actually caused the economic tailspin.

Alternatively, it could happen that the actions of neither party were responsible for the economic decline. Other factors over which the two rival parties had little or no control while in office may have been at fault, such as unfavorable international economic conditions or the effects of disastrous weather on the national economy. Examples of spurious correlations in the real world of politics are rarely in short supply.

Laws

In science, a **law** is a regularly occurring association (or correlation) between two or more variables. A *deterministic* law means that whenever X occurs, Y *always* occurs. The laws of gravity are an example.

A less stringent type of scientific law is a *probabilistic* law. In this case, whenever A occurs, B *sometimes* occurs. Occasionally we can calculate the degree of probability with which B is likely to occur. In the natural world, weather predictions are frequently based on probabilistic laws. Given certain temperatures, humidity levels, and other atmospheric conditions, we can predict when snow will probably fall. Nevertheless, so many variables are at work that we cannot be absolutely certain when it will snow, or if it does, we cannot be completely sure how much will fall on which spots.

Human behavior is not as law-bound as inanimate nature. Human beings are capable of conscious volitional behavior and completely erratic irrational behavior. We can make decisions about how we wish to behave by choosing from a menu of alternative courses of action. We can change our minds. We can act singly or in all sorts of groups. We can act cooperatively or at cross-purposes. Sometimes we miscalculate, acting on the basis of false assumptions, inadequate information, or faulty logic. As a consequence, human behavior is extremely variable and unpredictable. Hence the social sciences, which focus on human behavior (especially in large social groups), cannot predict the future with unfailing accuracy.

Although there are no deterministic laws in political science or in other social sciences (such as sociology, economics, and social psychology), researchers can frequently discern real patterns and tendencies in human social activity. Thus, social

scientists can sometimes suggest which future developments are more probable or less probable, at least in the near term.

Prediction of the future in the social sciences is thus suggestive or probabilistic in nature. If we can identify regularities in a population's voting patterns, for example, we can *suggest* how people *may* vote in the next elections. The closer we get to election day, the greater the confidence we may have in our estimation of *probable* outcomes. One of the best known laws in political science is Duverger's law, named after a French political scientist who observed that electoral systems based on proportional representation were more likely to produce multiparty systems than did single-member district, winner-take-all electoral rules.[4] We will explore this law in Chapter 6.

Laws—like correlations—are not *explanations*. They simply point out that two or more variables generally go together, but they do not explain why. To find out why these patterns exist, social scientists must conduct other exploratory investigations. The principal ways of explaining political realities scientifically are by formulating *theories* and *hypotheses*.

Theories

The term **theory** can have several different meanings in political science.

1. In its broadest sense, theory simply refers to thinking about politics as opposed to practicing it. As such, it is an abstract intellectual exercise. Theorizing can mean nothing more than making generalizations about politics ("Majorities always discriminate against minorities!"), whether in accordance with strict scientific rules ("And I can prove it!") or far more informally, as in late-night political discussions with friends ("Now don't try to reason with me!").

   In this elementary definition of the term, theory also refers to general principles or abstract ideas that may not necessarily be true. For example, when we say, "In theory, democracy is government by the people," we are referring to some general principle or idea of democracy; we are not explaining how democracy actually works in practice.
2. More restrictively, theory can mean *normative theory*: that is, value-centered political philosophy (or political thought), as we defined these terms earlier in this chapter.
3. In the natural and social sciences, theory most frequently means a generalization, or set of generalizations, that seeks to explain, and perhaps predict, relationships among variables. This is explanatory theory. Explanation is the main aim of theory in empirical political science. The word *because* is stated or implied in almost every explanatory theory.

Generally, explanations that merit the term *theory* have usually gained wide acceptance over long periods because their ability to explain the facts has been confirmed in repeated scientific investigations. Theories thus tend to be more solidly grounded in empirical reality than hypotheses, which are typically assumptions that have yet to be sufficiently tested. Nevertheless, even the most widely respected theories are not unchallengeable truths. They are meant to be constantly challenged against the hard facts of reality. In political science as in the natural sciences, explanatory theories are not abstractions that are divorced from reality; on the contrary, they seek to explain reality. Theories are valid only as long as they are consistent with the facts they endeavor to explain. If new evidence comes to light that contradicts the theory, then the theory is probably either partially or entirely wrong. It must then be modified or discarded and replaced by a better theory that fits the facts. All explanatory theories need to be repeatedly subjected to verification against the hard data of reality. The main way of accomplishing this task is by breaking theories down into hypotheses and testing them against the available evidence.

Hypotheses

A **hypothesis** is an assumption or supposition that needs to be tested against relevant evidence. In some cases, hypotheses can be purely descriptive in nature. For example, we can hypothesize that democracy has broad popular support in Russia. We can then test this hypothesis by surveying a large number of Russians and asking them whether they support democracy, and if so, how strongly. After we've collected and analyzed our research data we will end up with a description, a picture, of mass attitudes toward Russian democracy. The data will permit us to describe the Russian electorate as mostly supportive of democracy or mostly unsupportive of it by providing statistical readings of the proportion of the voters who support it strongly, the percentage of those who support it with less conviction, and the percentage of those who don't support it very much or not at all.

This descriptive hypothesis simply proposes certain facts about the Russian electorate, and the hypothesis-testing survey seeks to determine whether and to what extent those facts are really occurring. The descriptive hypothesis does not suggest an explanation as to why the proposed phenomena might be occurring, however. It is not an explanatory hypothesis that explains why Russians feel as they do about democracy. But in political science as in the physical sciences, explanation is the ultimate goal.

Explanatory hypotheses posit a cause-and-effect relationship between dependent and independent variables that can be tested empirically (i.e., against factual evidence). By formulating explanatory hypotheses about politics, we force ourselves to specify our dependent and independent variables and to be clear about the sharp difference between cause and effect. By testing hypotheses empirically, we submit them to a reality check:

We look closely at all the available facts to see if they substantiate or contradict the relationships we propose in our hypotheses. For example, we might find that, contrary to our hypothesis, popular support for democracy in Russia is in fact much weaker than we had originally surmised. We must then formulate explanatory hypotheses that might suggest possible reasons for this phenomenon. We could hypothesize that public dissatisfaction with the economy is causing people to turn against democracy; or we could hypothesize that disgust at political corruption may be the main explanatory variable accounting for Russian attitudes; or we could assume that public ignorance about democracy may be the explanation; or we could develop a host of other possible explanations, whether singly or in combination.

We could then test these various explanatory hypotheses by going back to Russia and resurveying the electorate, asking them more specific questions about their attitudes on the economy, corruption, and so forth. After analyzing our survey data, we can then come to some conclusions about which of these explanatory variables explain why many Russians are suspicious of democracy. We may find, for example, that *all* of them play a role, albeit to varying degrees, among the voters. In these explanatory hypotheses, "negative attitudes toward democracy" is the dependent variable. The possible explanations to be tested are the independent variables. (See Figure 2.7.)

The second part of this chapter is devoted to an extended exercise in testing the proposition that *national wealth promotes democracy*. Is this hypothesis correct? Is it only partially correct? Or is it perhaps just plain wrong? Reading the section on the logic of hypothesis testing and the extended example in it attentively will give you a more comprehensive idea of how the logic of hypothesis testing applies to the study of politics.

Scientific Generalization and Practical Politics

Explanatory theories and hypotheses in political science greatly enhance our understanding of the real world of politics. They can also help us work out our own positions on the political problems of our times. Indeed, many of the practical policy choices facing government decision makers and average citizens are rooted in some overarching theory. Debates over the decision to invade Iraq in 2003 are connected with theories about U.S. foreign policy, with some favoring "regime change" to create a democracy as an immediate goal and others placing national security ahead of democratization as the country's

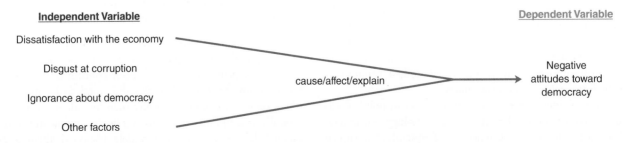

FIGURE 2.7   Independent Variables Affecting Negative Attitudes toward Democracy

number-one foreign policy priority, even when it means putting up with a vile dictator. Debates on tax policy are connected with theories about how or whether governments can stimulate economic growth while cutting budget deficits and keeping inflation low. The list of theory-related policy issues could be extended indefinitely.

Although some people dismiss theory as completely detached from the real world, in fact most individuals act in political life on the basis of certain assumptions and understandings about politics that are the equivalent of theoretical generalizations, even if they do not always realize it. As the British economist John Maynard Keynes once observed, "Practical men, who believe themselves to be exempt from any intellectual influences, are usually the slaves of some defunct economist." By the same token, politicians and the people they govern can be the slaves of political ideas they accept uncritically. An intelligent approach to politics requires a keen understanding of the relevance of explanatory theory and hypothesis testing to the real world of political action. To put it succinctly, the scientific approach to politics requires us to support our political generalizations with relevant evidence and systematic logic.

Models

In political science, a **model** is a simplified representation of reality in descriptive or abstract form. A scale model of a Stealth bomber can neither fly nor drop bombs. Its sleek proportions, however, provide some understanding of how the real aircraft is able to avoid radar detection. An auto designer's computer model of next year's dream car indicates how all its components will mesh in perfect harmony once the vehicle hits the road. Environmental scientists have built a large model of the Chesapeake Bay designed to replicate the bay's complex ecological system. Economists construct graphical and mathematical models of various dynamic economic processes, such as a perfectly competitive market economy or a global free trade system.

Though the composition of these models is different, they all serve the same function: They enable us to understand some aspect of reality, whether aerodynamics or the economy, by *representing* some of its essential features in a simplified or idealized form. Obviously, these scaled-down physical or mathematical models cannot be perfect copies of the realities they represent. The car designer does not plan for the car to malfunction, but at some point it probably will. Economists know that purely free market systems, which are devoid of any governmental interference or monopolies, exist nowhere in today's world.

The purpose of a model is not to represent reality perfectly but to enable us to understand reality by allowing us to compare it against some standard or pattern. If the car has stalling problems, the computer design can help us find the source. If world trade is declining, the mathematical model of how a free trade system works in theory may help us understand how to deal with existing trade barriers in the global economy. When viewed against the model, the complexities of the real world stand out all the more prominently by comparison with the simplified version. As one economist put it, "Models are to be used, not believed." As learning devices, models serve a *heuristic* purpose, a term that derives from the Greek word meaning "to find out."

In roughly similar fashion, political scientists use models of various kinds to help understand political realities. Sometimes these models are purely descriptive. For example, we can construct a model of democracy just by listing its characteristic features: a competitive electoral system, legal guarantees of certain freedoms and rights, and so forth. Although many democracies in today's world may actually diverge from this model of an "ideal" democracy in one way or another, these divergences will tend to stand out when compared with the model, prompting us to investigate how and why they occur.

A descriptive model of this sort is known as an *ideal type*, or one that is a model of a political or social phenomenon that describes its main characteristic features. The term was coined by Max Weber who was among the first students of modern bureaucracy. Based on his observations of European bureaucracies in the early twentieth century, Weber devised an ideal type of a modern bureaucracy that specified the features most commonly found in them. He described this standard (or ideal-typical) bureaucracy as a highly impersonal organization run in accordance with strict rules and legal procedures.

In addition to ideal types, political science uses several other types of models. *Static models* simply define the fundamental attributes of a phenomenon (like ideal types), but they do not describe how those attributes change or develop over time. By contrast, *dynamic models* describe processes of change. For example, the *modernization model* describes how so-called traditional societies develop into modern societies through the process of industrialization. As a nation's economy becomes more industrialized, people tend to move from the countryside into the cities, communications networks expand, educational opportunities improve, and traditional religious practices and superstitions give way to more secularized lifestyles and beliefs. Modernization theorists base this model on the historical development of Europe and the United States, and they believe that most countries of the world sooner or later will move in much the same directions. We shall return to this model in Chapter 12.

Dynamic models describe processes of change, such as how long it might take a traditional society to develop into a modern one.

Some models are *analogies*. In these cases, political scientists clarify political phenomena by comparing them to something else. For example, one scholar likens democracy to a market economy, with voters choosing candidates in the political "marketplace" on the basis of considerations very similar to those motivating consumers shopping for a good buy.[5] Another political scientist compares the ways governments work to cybernetic processes, complete with feedback mechanisms, communications loops, and other features of computer technology.[6]

Strictly speaking, a model is not an explanatory theory. Whereas explanatory theory *explains* reality, models *represent* and *describe* reality. However simplified or sophisticated its form may be, a model is just a picture, not an explanation. Very frequently, however, we use the term *theoretical model* (or *conceptual model*). This term can have two meanings.

In one meaning, a model is said to be theoretical if it is an intellectual abstraction as opposed to a physical representation of something. Computer models, mathematical models, diagrams, and even ideal types are theoretical models in this sense of the term. They are *intellectual* or *abstract* representations of reality, not physical objects.

In the second meaning of the term, a theoretical model *represents* explanatory theories. A theory that states, for example, that national wealth *causes* democracies to come about by promoting education and communication can be depicted in a diagram. Figure 2.8 is a *causal model* that graphically represents this theory. Causal models can be a useful way of specifying causal relationships and clarifying our thinking about how different variables interact.

Moreover, models can stimulate explanatory theory. Just as environmental scientists use their model of the Chesapeake Bay to develop theories about how marine life develops or why so much of it is dying prematurely, political scientists can use their models to come up with explanatory theories about how and why various political phenomena occur as they do. Models, in short, are yet another useful method for generalizing systematically about politics.

QUANTITATIVE AND QUALITATIVE POLITICAL SCIENCE

Political science offers two basic approaches to investigating relationships among variables: quantitative approaches and qualitative approaches.

Quantitative political science is "by the numbers." It looks mainly at phenomena that can vary in measurable degrees or quantities, such as the number of votes cast in an election or in legislative balloting, or the percentages of people who express various opinions in a public opinion survey. Statisticians have developed a variety of sophisticated techniques and software programs for performing different types of measurements involving quantifiable dependent and independent variables, and many of these tools can be adapted to research on politics.[7]

We will not use any of these sophisticated statistical techniques in this book, but they can be quite useful in the study of political science at more advanced levels, depending on the nature of the problem being investigated.

Statistical rigor is not always possible in the study of politics, however. Sometimes we would like to have relevant statistical information but it is not available, or if available, it is unreliable. Authoritarian regimes, for example, rarely permit contested elections or release public opinion poll information, and the statistics they do publish (such as economic data) may be untrustworthy. At least in these cases, Mark Twain was right when he quipped, "There are lies, damned lies, and statistics." At other times we may have statistical information available that can be quite useful in helping us understand a situation, but all we need do is report this information in tables or graphs without getting into highly sophisticated calculations. Economic statistics, election returns, and other relevant quantitative data are often used in this uncomplicated but vitally important way in political science, and we shall employ such raw data quite extensively in subsequent chapters. Finally, in some cases statistical analysis is only partially helpful in enabling us to understand political reality and must be combined with other factual information that is not readily quantifiable, such as historical accounts or other descriptions of political events, processes, or ideas.

Research and analysis in political science that is not primarily quantitative in nature is called *qualitative* political science. Political scientists who are engaged in qualitative research rely largely on descriptive accounts of the political realities they study. In seeking to explain political processes and interactions, analysts frequently use qualitative research to provide detailed (or "thick") descriptions of such things as how governmental institutions work, or how parties and interest groups are organized, or how political ideas and ideologies define the issues facing the country. These and similar political phenomena cannot be fully understood if we confine ourselves strictly to statistical analysis; descriptive detail may also be necessary.

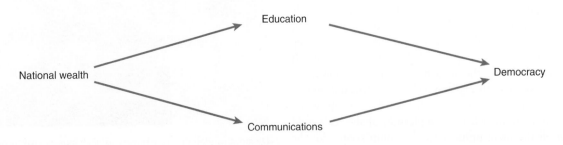

FIGURE 2.8 **Model Depicting Causes of Democracy**

Many qualitatively oriented analysts are especially sensitive to the broader historical and contemporary contexts within which political life takes place in any given country. Qualitative analysts often remind us that the specific details of politics—such as a recent leadership change or the latest elections—do not occur in a vacuum. These events have historical roots, and they may also be related to complex social, cultural, economic, or other conditions in ways that cannot be adequately explained just by referring to numerical data or by performing statistical operations. Statistics, such analysts would argue, can't explain everything. We need to immerse ourselves in the history, culture, and languages of individual countries if we want to understand their political systems.

A substantial number of political scientists today would admit that quantitative and qualitative approaches are complementary and that the approach an analyst chooses depends on the nature of the problem being studied. Most important, both quantitative and qualitative approaches must observe the same ground rules of scientific logic that we cover in this chapter.[8]

THE LOGIC OF HYPOTHESIS TESTING

Hypothesis testing is a central activity of political science. It is one of the things that makes it a science in the formal meaning of the word. By learning how to formulate and test hypotheses we can learn a lot about both political science and, not incidentally, political reality itself.

By learning some of the main rules of hypothesis testing, we can also learn a great deal about how to think logically and coherently. One of our most important tasks in this regard is to learn some of the cardinal rules of causation. Just what do we really know about politics for sure, and what are we less sure about? To what extent can we really "prove" that one thing actually causes another? How valid are our generalizations? Questions like these lie at the heart of *epistemology*, the field of inquiry that seeks to clarify the scope and limits of our ability to know. Epistemological issues are of fundamental importance in all the sciences, including political science, and they are vital to the development of critical-reasoning skills more generally.

SOURCES OF HYPOTHESES

Hypotheses about politics can spring from a variety of sources. In some instances they may derive from questions that pop into our minds from our observations of reality. Just from reading the newspaper, for example, we may notice the rather obvious fact that some countries have democratic systems of government and others do not. Why? From a superficial survey of these news accounts, a few possible answers may come to mind. One possible explanation centers on economics: The world's most successful and enduring democracies, we observe, are among the richest countries of the world. We notice, in particular, that such well-to-do countries as the United States, Canada, Britain, France, Germany, and Japan are successful democracies. Countries that lack democracy and countries that are currently engaged in the process of building democracy following the collapse of an authoritarian regime appear for the most part to be less economically developed.

A cursory glance at these facts prompts us to formulate the following hypothesis: "National wealth promotes democracy." This hypothesis implies a cause-and-effect relationship: National wealth somehow causes democracy to come about and endure, whereas national poverty precludes or undermines democracy.

The technique we have just used to formulate our hypothesis is called induction. **Induction** is a reasoning process that goes from the specific to the general. We begin with some specific facts or observations, and on the basis of these specifics we devise an overarching generalization that applies to the phenomena we have observed as well as to related phenomena that we have not as yet observed, as depicted in Figure 2.9. Thus our observation of a few specific wealthy democracies and a few specific poor nondemocracies leads us to suspect that national wealth is perhaps associated with *all* democracies and national poverty is perhaps associated with *all* nondemocracies. We say perhaps because at this point these broad generalizations are only suspicions or guesses that we have made on the basis of a small number of observations. That is precisely what hypotheses frequently are: suspicions, educated guesses, or hunches. We don't know yet if our hunch is true or false in reality. Only when we have tested our hypothesis by looking at a far wider number of democracies and nondemocracies will we have a better idea of whether, or to what extent, our proposed generalization is valid.

Another source of hypotheses consists of generalizations that have already been formulated. For example, we may read a newspaper editorialist justifying foreign assistance to poor countries on the basis of a broad generalization: "National wealth," she writes, "promotes democracy."

She sets forth a number of reasons explaining why national wealth promotes democracy: that wealthy countries have more educated citizenries, better systems of communications, and a larger middle class, all factors that are associated with democratic participation.

Generalization: "National wealth promotes democracy"

Specific facts or observations:
Countries like the United States, Canada, Britain, and Germany are wealthy and democratic;
Countries like Vietnam, Egypt, the Congo, and Cuba are poor and are not democracies

FIGURE 2.9 **Diagram of Inductive Reasoning**

In this particular case, the editorialist did not look at specific democratic and nondemocratic countries, as we did in our perusal of newspaper articles. Rather, she derived her hypothesis from *generalizations* about what causes democracies to come about. Thus generalizations themselves, not just specific facts, can also be a source of hypotheses.

STEPS OF HYPOTHESIS TESTING

Are the editorialist's sweeping generalizations correct? To find out, we need to break them into testable propositions and test them against hard evidence. Let's concentrate on her central hypothesis, "National wealth promotes democracy." How do we test this proposition?

We can choose from a variety of methods, depending on whether we are relying mainly on quantitative or qualitative analysis (or some combination of the two) and on whether we want to examine a large number of countries or confine ourselves to a few particularly illustrative ones. In most cases, however, the logic of hypothesis testing will involve the following five steps:

1. Defining key terms.
2. Identifying the variables.
3. Specifying the expectations of the hypothesis.
4. Collecting and examining the evidence.
5. Drawing conclusions from the evidence.

Defining Key Terms

Because our hypothesis is about democracy, we must define the term. *Democracy* is a multifaceted concept that includes regular elections, civil liberties, and a host of other elements. The Freedom House lists of political and civil rights that we presented in Chapter 1 encompass almost all of democracy's essential components. Moreover, the numerical rating system that Freedom House employs, with the most democratic countries meriting a grade of 1 and the most authoritarian states getting a 7, provides a useful estimate of the extent to which the countries of the world fulfill these numerous criteria, despite the system's lack of statistical precision. We shall therefore use the Freedom House criteria here as our operative definition of democracy, and we'll use the Freedom House composite political and civil rights index as a measure of each country's relative degree of democracy. In addition, we'll follow the practice of Freedom House and group the world's countries into three categories based on their composite index. Accordingly, *democracies* (labeled *free* countries by Freedom House) are countries with a composite political/civil rights index from 1 to 2.5; *partly free* countries or *mixed regimes*, 3 to 5; and *not free* countries, or *authoritarian regimes*, from 5.5 to 7.[9]

Because we are looking for a relationship between democracy and national wealth, we must also specify what we mean by *wealth* and *poverty*. Economists usually distinguish between *wealth*, a stock of assets such as investments, real estate, and bank accounts, on the one hand, and *income*, the flow of money one receives in a given time, typically a year, on the other. The understanding of material well-being we have been using to

discuss the bases of democracy is really closer to income than wealth, so we will be looking more specifically at the relationship between national income and democracy. There are several different ways of measuring a country's annual income, but we need not go into those details here. We'll simply rely on the gross domestic product per capita statistics reported by the World Bank at its website.[10]

Finally, what do we mean when we hypothesize that national wealth, or more accurately, national income, promotes democracy? Here we need to specify that national income somehow causes democracy. More specifically, we mean that (a) higher income causes democracy to come into existence, replacing authoritarian modes of government, and (b) it causes democracies already in existence to succeed over protracted periods.

Identifying Variables

The next step we must take is to identify our dependent and independent variables. Because the existence of democracy is the effect we wish to explain, it is our dependent variable.

Our independent variable is the level of national income. We want to see how varying levels of national income relate to democratic and nondemocratic systems of government. This independent variable is our presumed explanatory variable. We can manipulate it by observing how different gradations of national income are related to democracy.

Specifying the Expectations of the Hypothesis

Hypotheses are usually stated as declarative propositions. Thus far we have stated our hypothesis as a declarative sentence: National wealth promotes democracy. To test a hypothesis systematically, we must restate it in terms that will indicate what we should look for as we hunt for evidence that might confirm or contradict its validity: *If* the hypothesis is valid, *then* what would we expect to find as we sift through the available facts? In other words, what expectations does the hypothesis generate? To guide our research, therefore, it is helpful to restate our hypothesis in "if . . . then" form: If national wealth promotes democracy, then we would expect to find that (a) relatively wealthy states (those with higher annual national incomes) are democracies and (b) relatively poor states are not. Logically, we would also expect to find that (c) democracies will be relatively wealthy (have higher per capita incomes), and (d) authoritarian regimes will be relatively poor.

The process of translating our hypothesis into "if . . . then" form is an example of deduction. **Deduction** is a reasoning process that proceeds from the general to the specific. It begins with a generalization that covers a wide range or class of phenomena and then applies that generalization to specific cases (see Figure 2.10). In our example, we start with our hypothesis, which proposes that national wealth promotes democracy in general, and we apply that generalization to specific countries. In deductive logic, the applications of the generalization to specific cases must follow with logical necessity. In other words,

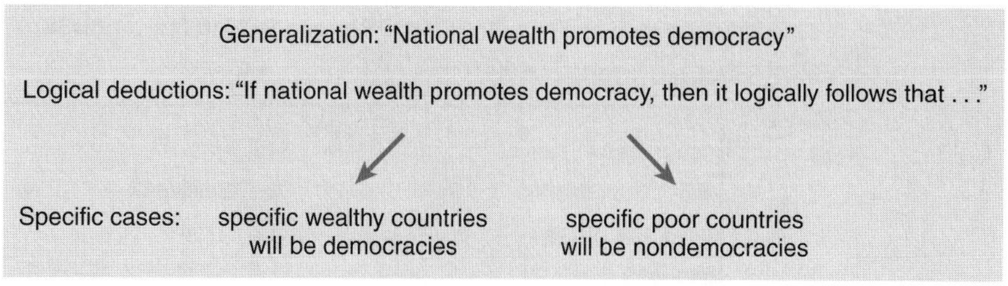

Generalization: "National wealth promotes democracy"

Logical deductions: "If national wealth promotes democracy, then it logically follows that . . ."

| Specific cases: | specific wealthy countries will be democracies | specific poor countries will be nondemocracies |

FIGURE 2.10   Diagram of Deductive Reasoning

if A is true, *then* B *must* be true; if B is true, it follows that C is true; and so on. As we've already suggested, if national wealth promotes democracy, then it is only logical that specific countries that are relatively wealthy should be democracies, while specific countries that are relatively poor should be nondemocracies. When phrased in "if . . . then" terms, a hypothesis predicts a certain research result as a logical outcome.

Collecting and Examining the Evidence

Empirical analysis is based on facts. Unless there is a sufficient body of factual evidence bearing on our hypothesis, we cannot properly test it. Suppose, for example, there is only one democracy in the world, and it happens to be quite rich. All the other governments of the world are nondemocracies, and all are economically undeveloped. On the basis of this evidence, we can conclude that the available evidence is consistent with our hypothesis linking democracy with a relatively high level of national wealth. But one case is scarcely enough to warrant high confidence in the generality of this conclusion. It does not convince us that national wealth is really necessary to promote democracies elsewhere. Other factors may be more important (such as the degree of social harmony, the nature of religious beliefs, and so on). The fact that our lone democracy is wealthy may be purely coincidental and have nothing whatsoever to do with causing or promoting democracy. Our confidence in the validity of a generalization tends to rise with the number of cases we have in its support.

Because Freedom House has rated virtually all of the countries in the world on its seven-point scale and since we have GDP per capita data for most countries, we can consider our hypothesis with evidence from 188 contemporary democracies, partly democratic regimes, and nondemocracies. A relatively simple way of examining our hypothesis is to consider the average income in our three categories of political regime. Table 2.1 shows the average (mean) income as well as the incomes of the poorest and richest countries in each category. To support

our hypothesis, the average income of free countries should be higher than that of partly free countries, which in turn should have a higher average income than the not free countries.

While Table 2.1 demonstrates that free countries (democracies) are on average the richest countries, with an average annual GDP per capita above $23,000, it also shows that the partly free countries are on average poorer than the not free or authoritarian regimes. This finding would seem to suggest that we must question our hypothesis that national wealth leads to democracy. Note too the range of incomes in each category. There are free countries with an annual GDP per capita below $1,000 (the lowest was Mali's $602—Mali was ranked a free country when this analysis was completed in 2012, before a military coup unleashed political instability) while there are partly free and not free countries with an annual GDP per capita many multiples of that figure. The relationship between income and democracy is certainly not a very tight one. Indeed, examine Figure 2.11, which plots all of the countries in our data set, with our hypothesized independent variable, national income, on the horizontal (or x) axis, and our dependent variable, democracy, measured by the Freedom House composite index, on the vertical (or y) axis. If our hypothesis held strongly, we would expect the countries to cluster closely around the diagonal trend line drawn on the chart—as countries become more wealthy, we expected them to move closer to the most democratic score (1) on the Freedom House index. Instead, we see a considerable spread across the plot space.

So, must we reject our hypothesis about the relationship of national wealth and democracy? Before doing so, let's dig a little deeper. How is it that some authoritarian regimes are extremely wealthy? Look at Table 2.2. Here the nondemocracies are listed, ordered from most to least wealthy. Do the countries at the top of the list have anything in common? Of the top 20, 15 derive a large share of their national income from the export of hydrocarbons—petroleum and natural gas. (Those countries with an asterisk are among the top 25 countries in the world in terms of hydrocarbon export revenues per capita.) Hydrocarbon exports may yield high incomes to

Table 2.1 National Income and Democracy

Freedom House Group	Average (mean) GDP/Capita	Lowest GDP/Capita Country	Highest GDP/Capita Country	Number of Countries in Group
Free	$23,248	$602	$172,676	86
Partly Free	4,068	192	41,365	58
Not Free	7,153	199	61,532	44

Sources: Freedom House, "Freedom in the World Comparative and Historical Data," at http://www.freedomhouse.org/images/File/fiw/historical/FIWAllScores Countries1973-2011.xls; World Bank, "GDP per Capita (current US$)," at http://data.worldbank.org/indicator/NY.GDP.PCAP.CD, accessed February 5, 2012.

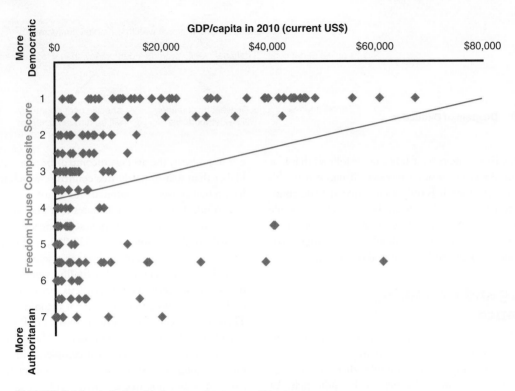

FIGURE 2.11 **Relationship between Income and Democracy**

Sources: Freedom House, "Freedom in the World Comparative and Historical Data," at http://www.freedomhouse.org/images/File/fiw/historical/FIWAllScoresCountries1973-2011.xls; World Bank, "GDP per Capita (current US$)," at http://data.worldbank.org/indicator/ny.gdp.pcap.cd, accessed February 5, 2012.

countries that produce oil and gas, but those export revenues (and hence GDP/capita) are very volatile because they depend on the world market price of oil and gas. In 2010, the year from which we have drawn our data, those prices were very high. Moreover, hydrocarbon exports do not much depend on the intervening variables that our editorialist described—education, a system of mass communications, and a middle class—because the labor force required to produce and transport oil is typically small and often composed of expatriates. Is it possible that our data are skewed by the presence of the oil exporters in our data set?

Table 2.3 excludes the major hydrocarbon exporters from all three Freedom House groups—18 from the not-free category, and 3 each from the free and partly free groups. Suddenly the relationship our hypothesis had proposed seems to emerge. What does this mean?

As it happens, quite a few democracies (with a combined political and civil rights index of 1 to 2.5) are relatively poor: 17 of the 87 in our data set have annual incomes of $5,000 per person or less. This finding provides incontrovertible evidence that *poverty does not constitute an insurmountable barrier to democracy*. Whereas a relatively low-income economy may make it more difficult for a country to build and sustain democratic institutions and practices, by no means does it doom its chances irreparably.

At the same time, even excluding the hydrocarbon exporters, several middle-income countries—Mexico, Colombia, Malaysia, and Turkey are major examples—are ranked as partly

free. Similarly, there remain some non-oil-exporting countries among the authoritarian regimes with annual per capita incomes about $5,000. Belarus, Cuba, and China are among them. The obvious lesson to be gleaned from this evidence is that *national wealth provides no guarantee of democracy*. It doesn't even provide a guarantee against highly repressive authoritarianism and flagrant abuses of fundamental political and civil rights. We now have conflicting evidence bearing on our hypothesis.

On one hand Democracies are on average the higher-income countries of the world. Moreover, a large number of the authoritarian countries are among the poorest countries, especially once we remove the hydrocarbon exporters from our consideration. These facts are *consistent* with our hypothesis.

But on the other hand some higher-income countries are not democracies or even semi-democracies. In addition, a substantial list of lower-income and even very poor countries *are* democracies or semi-democracies. These data are *inconsistent* with our hypothesis: They contradict our expectations. Our next step is to determine what conclusions we can draw from this conflicting evidence.

Drawing Conclusions from the Evidence

The first question we are tempted to ask when drawing conclusions from the available evidence is whether we have "proved" that our hypothesis is correct. The term *proof* implies absolute certitude, however, and most scientists doubt that we can ever

Table 2.2 Not-Free Countries, by National Income and Freedom House Score

Country	GDP/Capita 2010 (current US$)	Freedom House Score 2010
Qatar*	$61,532	5.5
United Arab Emirates*	39,625	5.5
Brunei*	27,390	5.5
Equatorial Guinea*	19,998	7
Bahrain*	17,609	5.5
Oman*	17,280	5.5
Saudi Arabia*	15,836	6.5
Russia*	10,440	5.5
Libya*	9,957	7
Kazakhstan*	9,136	5.5
Gabon*	8,643	5.5
Belarus	5,765	6.5
Azerbaijan*	5,722	5.5
Cuba	5,565	6.5
Jordan	4,560	5.5
Iran*	4,526	6
Algeria*	4,495	5.5
China	4,428	6.5
Angola*	4,423	5.5
Tunisia	4,199	6
Turkmenistan*	3,967	7
Swaziland	3,073	6
Congo	2,943	5.5
Syrian Arab Republic	2,893	6.5
Egypt	2,698	5.5
Iraq*	2,565	5.5
Sudan	1,425	7
Uzbekistan*	1,384	7
Vietnam	1,224	6
Djibouti	1,203	5.5
Laos	1,177	6.5
Cote d'Ivoire	1,154	6.5
Cameroon	1,143	6
Yemen	1,130	5.5
Mauritania	1,051	5.5
Cambodia	795	5.5
Chad	676	6.5
Zimbabwe	595	6
Rwanda	530	5.5
Tanzania	527	5.5
Afghanistan	501	6
Eritrea	403	7
Ethiopia	358	6
Congo (Kishasha)	199	6

*Major hydrocarbons exporting country.

Sources: Freedom House, "Freedom in the World Comparative and Historical Data," at http://www.freedomhouse.org/images/File/fiw/historical/FIWAllScores Countries1973-2011.xls; World Bank, "GDP per Capita (current US$)," at http://data.worldbank.org/indicator/NY.GDP.PCAP.CD, accessed February 5, 2012.

prove anything with complete certainty. For one thing, the evidence we collect, no matter how exhaustive our search, may not be enough to permit a final verdict on the *universal* validity of our conclusions. Instead of boasting that the evidence conclusively "proves" that a hypothesis is correct, therefore, we'll have to settle for the more modest conclusion that the evidence is *consistent* with the hypothesis. Any conclusion that a hypothesized relationship is true can only be tentative.

It is easier to *disprove* the universal validity of a hypothesis than to prove it. If we can find any evidence at all that is contrary to the results predicted by the hypothesis, we can demonstrate that the hypothesized relationship is not universally valid.

Table 2.3 National Income and Democracy, excluding Hydrocarbon Exporters

Freedom House Group	Average (mean) GDP/Capita	Lowest GDP/Capita Country	Highest GDP/Capita Country	Number of Countries in Group
Free	$22,703	$602	$172,676	84
Partly Free	$3,217	$192	$41,122	55
Not Free	$1,931	$199	$5,675	26

Sources: Freedom House, "Freedom in the World Comparative and Historical Data," at http://www.freedomhouse.org/images/File/fiw/historical/FIWAllScores Countries1973-2011.xls; World Bank, "GDP per Capita (current US$)," at http://data.worldbank.org/indicator/NY.GDP.PCAP.CD, accessed February 5, 2012.

The relationship may be valid sometimes, but not always. In some instances we can show that the hypothesis is never valid. Evidence that is contrary to the results predicted by the hypothesis is designated simply as *inconsistent* with the hypothesis. When drawing conclusions from our evidence, we have to distinguish between evidence that is consistent with our hypothesis and evidence that is inconsistent with it.

In some cases our evidence will be entirely one or the other. But in many cases it will cut both ways: Some of it will be consistent with the hypothesis, some inconsistent. In these cases the results of our research are mixed and lead us to conclude that the hypothesis appears to be partly true and partly false. In yet another set of cases, the evidence may be so evenly mixed, confusing, or simply inadequate as to be inconclusive: We cannot really be sure whether our hypothesis is true or false, or to what extent it is the one or the other. In these cases, our final conclusion must be "we don't know." Frustrating though it may be, "we don't know" is sometimes the right answer in science. *Science is characterized not by the certitude of its results but by the logic of its methods.* Taking these general observations into account, let's now draw conclusions from the evidence we've garnered on democracies and national wealth. We have evidence that is both consistent and inconsistent with the hypothesized relationship between democracy and national wealth. There are relatively wealthy democracies as well as nondemocracies; there are relatively poor democracies as well as nondemocracies. Taken in its entirety, therefore, the evidence we have examined is mixed: Some of it supports the hypothesis, some contradicts it. The evidence we have seen does not consistently and exclusively link relative wealth with democracy, nor does it conclusively rule out a relationship between these two variables.

Nevertheless, we can still discern some broad patterns. The overwhelming majority of the highest-scoring democracies have relatively high incomes. Very authoritarian regimes (with a rating of 6 or 7), excepting those that happen to have hydrocarbon resources, tend to be clustered among the countries with the lowest incomes. These data tell us that, *as a general tendency*, national wealth is a correlate of democracy (but not always).

Induction As we noted earlier, induction proceeds from the specific to the general. It is the process of drawing conclusions or generalizations from specific information or evidence. The inductive process is also characterized by the fact that, unlike deduction, the evidence does not lead to logically determined conclusions. Rather, the facts may be consistent with two or more possible conclusions, some perhaps closer to the actual

truth than others. Our specific information on democracy and national wealth, for example, does not logically compel us to conclude that national wealth always promotes democracy. It merely suggests that wealth *may* promote democracy, but only in certain cases, if then. For example, as we showed, if the source of national wealth is hydrocarbons, in most cases it has not promoted democracy. Drawing conclusions from empirical tests of hypotheses in political science is often an inductive process. In these cases, whatever conclusions we draw from our evidence can only be tentative and uncertain; the laws of logic provide no ironclad guarantee of their validity.

Indirect Hypothesis Testing Notice that we did not test our hypothesis, "National wealth promotes democracy," directly. We did not directly observe a single case in which national wealth clearly caused a democracy to come about when none existed before or caused an existing democracy to remain in existence over a protracted period. All we did was to rank the countries of the contemporary world by national income and type of government to see if any patterns emerged. We did not undertake in-depth investigations of these countries individually to see if wealth really does account for the presence or absence of democracy in each case, and if it does, how it does so. We never directly looked for evidence demonstrating the editorialist's contention that wealth promotes democracy by promoting education, mass communications, a middle class, or a government responsive to its citizens' demands.

Although the data we presented on nearly 200 countries displays a general pattern linking wealth and democracy, they do not permit us to conclude that wealth *always* promotes democracy. Indeed, we showed that in some cases it did not. These data don't even permit us to conclude that wealth is definitely responsible for creating or sustaining democracy in any of the wealthiest democracies in the world. The data simply tell us that wealth is *associated* (or *correlated*) with political and civil liberties as a general rule. Although this correlation is consistent with the hypothesis that national wealth promotes democracy, the evidence does not *definitively* demonstrate that the hypothesis is true. That conclusion would be a *false inference*.

Multicausality Sometimes a phenomenon has only one cause. Heat alone, for example, causes ice to melt. But far more often, even in the natural world, events occur because of a multiplicity of causes. These multiple causes can work simultaneously or in different sequences; they can work in a variety of combinations and quantities. Political and social phenomena, in particular, rarely have only one cause; in human affairs, *multicausality* is far more likely than monocausality. Whether we are trying to explain democracy, dictatorship, voter turnout, economic growth, or why nations go to war, two or more independent variables typically account for the dependent variable we are trying to explain. Thus the level of national wealth *by itself* may not account for democracy or its absence in any of the countries listed in our tables.

Conceivably, national wealth may promote democracy by working through other variables that may play a more direct role in stimulating the birth of a democracy or in undergirding a successful democracy over time. In a major work on this topic, Seymour Martin Lipset suggested that such variables as an educated public, mass communications, and a politically active middle class may ultimately depend on the size of a nation's wealth, but it is these intervening variables, not wealth per se, that may have a more immediate impact on the fate of democracy. These variables intervene between national wealth and democracy, enabling the one to exert a causative effect on the other, as illustrated in Figure 2.12.[11]

The recipe for a successful democracy has so many ingredients that it is virtually impossible to specify which ones are more important than others. In addition to national wealth and the intervening variables it can buy, democracies may need such things as a general respect for the law, a tradition of cooperation and compromise among social groups, a political elite that respects the rights and liberties of the population, and a host of additional factors as well. The precise mixture of these ingredients may vary from democracy to democracy. Rarely, if ever, is democracy simply the product of one sole causal variable. Although the analysis we have just conducted shows a strong association between national wealth and democracy, it by no means rules out the possibility that additional independent variables (other than those connected with wealth) may also be of crucial significance in accounting for the existence or long-term success of democracies. In trying to understand political reality, we must always be sensitive to the possibility (indeed the likelihood) of multicausality. A scientific approach to politics requires us to be on the lookout at all times for multiple sources of explanation and causation in political life and to pay close attention to the ways they interact.

THE PRACTICAL IMPORTANCE OF HYPOTHESIS TESTING

Despite the difficulties of causative logic, hypothesis testing is still a powerful analytical mechanism for understanding politics. It compels us to be explicit in our use of political terminology. It makes us check our generalizations against available evidence. It forces us to consider evidence against our prevailing assumptions and biases, not just evidence supporting them. It requires us to be systematic and logical in analyzing the evidence and drawing conclusions from it. It clarifies what we know, and what we don't know, about political life.

The logic of hypothesis testing is therefore essential to political science. But the benefits of hypothesis testing are by no means confined to the ivory-tower world of academic abstractions. They have an immense practical value as well. In the real world of political action and debate, politicians, pundits, and ordinary people hold all sorts of opinions on all sorts of political issues. Often people cling to their most cherished political beliefs with unshakable obstinacy, regarding their certainty as beyond question. In actuality, however, a great deal of what people know (or think they know) about politics really amounts to *hypotheses:* assumptions, impressions, or hunches that in many instances are only vaguely articulated or insufficiently examined. Many of us, for example, have heard such platitudes as "The longer politicians stay in office, the more they are out of touch with public opinion," or "Governments just waste money," or "Foreign aid does not work," or countless other generalizations about politics that animate everyday political discussion. Political scientists are not the only ones who like to generalize about politics; politicians and average citizens do, too. Such generalizations frequently provide the underlying rationale for important decisions political leaders make and for the way people behave within their respective political systems. But are those generalizations true? Only a systematic analysis of the evidence can tell us.

Consider as an example the editorialist's recommendation that wealthy democracies should provide economic assistance to newly democratizing countries. How do our findings about the relationship between national wealth and democracy help us formulate our own opinion on this practical policy issue?

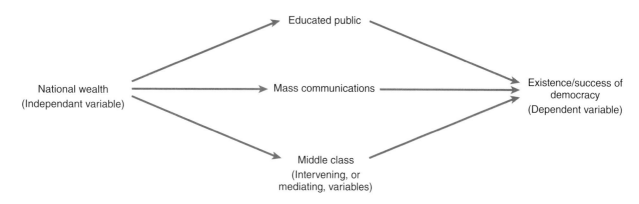

FIGURE 2.12   **Intervening Variables between National Wealth and Democracy**

As we saw, national wealth is strongly—but not perfectly—correlated with democracy. But we also saw that national wealth per se does not necessarily promote democracy; only when it is funneled into such intervening variables as education, an open communications system, or a middle class is wealth more likely to strengthen the conditions for democratic rule. And we also concluded that factors other than wealth may also be necessary to build and maintain democratic modes of government.

Thus our empirical analysis compels the conclusion that economic assistance aimed at raising the national wealth of democratizing countries may indeed be very helpful in supporting democracy, but it provides no guarantee that democracy will actually succeed. A great deal depends on how the money is spent. Will it be used to expand education or encourage the growth of a prodemocracy middle class? Or will it be spent on things that do not necessarily increase the chances for democracy, such as higher salaries for bureaucrats or graft for corrupt politicians? If key elites or broad segments of the population simply do not want democracy or do not try to make it work, wealth alone may not save the democratic cause.

Unfortunately, not everybody subjects their generalizations to a systematic reality check as we've just done. As a consequence, the generalizations people commonly make about politics often tend to oversimplify matters. But testing our political assumptions against reality is precisely what a scientific approach to politics demands. Applying scientific logic to the study of politics helps us avoid oversimplification and enables us to appreciate the complexities of the real world.

Accordingly, one of the most important scientific questions we can ask about any political generalization is, "What is the evidence to support it?" Another is, "What is the evidence against it?" We must then be very cautious and scrupulously logical in interpreting the results of these inquiries.

Scientific hypothesis testing is also important for another practical reason: It can help you examine your own political assumptions in a rational and coherent manner. One of the main objectives of your political science education should be to learn how to spell out your own political ideas in terms of propositions that can be put to a systematic test against the facts. Critical-thinking skills of this kind are invaluable in dealing not only with empirical questions about politics but with normative issues as well. As we noted earlier in this chapter, our political values and ideals need to be addressed with reference to the realities of political life. The rules of hypothesis testing provide a method for determining what those realities are and for clarifying how well we know them.

Conclusion

Now that you have examined some key scientific terminology in political science and walked through a hypothesis-testing exercise, you should have a better idea of what political science is. Of course, you won't get a deeper feel for it until you've studied it more thoroughly, but you should at least be in a position to appreciate some generalizations about what political science tries to do.

Let's emphasize what political science is *not*. First, it is not "just opinion." Although the study of politics usually provides ample opportunities to formulate and express one's personal political views, political science as an empirical science insists on the observance of strict rules of collecting, analyzing, and interpreting the facts. It requires us to support our opinions with relevant evidence and to modify our opinions (or perhaps discard them entirely) in the light of contrary information. Thus political science does not regard all political opinions as equally valid. Those opinions that can meet the acid test of empirical reality checks based on the rigors of scientific logic are generally more valid than are those based on insufficient evidence or faulty logic.

Of course, sometimes we just do not have the evidence we need to draw a reasoned, "scientific" conclusion. At times the information we need does not exist; at times it may not be readily available. In these cases, it is incumbent on us to acknowledge that the evidence we need to substantiate our case is lacking.

Even though the canons of empirical science are demanding, there is still plenty of room for rational debate and disagreement over controversial political issues. Subjective value judgments and preferences invariably play—indeed *must* play—a major role in political thinking. Just as important, the rules of scientific logic open a vast realm of empirical uncertainty with respect to many political questions. By itself, empirical political science cannot compel you to be a liberal or a conservative, a moderate or a radical. It simply tells you that, whatever your personal political predilections, you must take the rules of scientific logic into account when shaping and defending your political views.

Second, political science is not "just current events," nor is it "just facts" or "just stories." As we indicated in Chapter 1, political science is an effort to understand current events as well as the past (and, to some extent, the future) by generalizing about humanity's political experience. Political science uses facts to formulate and test these generalizations. Political scientists are just as fascinated or amused as anyone else by stories and anecdotes about politics, but as social scientists we are mainly concerned with connecting particular incidents to broader trends and processes. In telling stories about politics, we are especially interested in what the stories tell us about politics. Moreover, random facts or anecdotal evidence may not be enough to sustain a political generalization. We may need to analyze a vast array of available evidence before we can come to any reliable conclusions. And if the evidence available is incomplete or merely anecdotal, we must say so.

More than anything else, political science is a *mode of thinking* about politics. It is an academic discipline in that it disciplines our minds to think in certain ways, in accordance with a specified logic and systematic methods of analysis.

Depending on the career path you take, you may need more advanced analytical skills than we can provide in this book. This volume is purely introductory. In the pages that follow, we do not engage in formal statistical hypothesis testing, nor do we teach you how to design a research project of your own. Rather, we present numerous examples of hypotheses that have been advanced by political scientists who have written on the topics and countries covered in this volume. Along the way we introduce you to key concepts in political science, and to prominent theories and models as they apply to comparative politics. We also expose you to some of the most influential scholarship in the field. Throughout this enterprise, we are guided by one overriding aim: to help you *think for yourself* about politics in terms of the scientific terminology and logic presented in this chapter.

Accordingly, this book provides numerous synopses of scholarly arguments that use the five-step hypothesis-testing logic presented here:

1. Definition of key terms.
2. Identification of the variables.
3. Expectations of the hypothesis in "if . . . then" form.
4. Collection and examination of the evidence.
5. Conclusions (*consistent* with the hypothesis, *inconsistent*, *mixed*, or *inconclusive*).

Most chapters that follow contain a hypothesis-testing exercise that employs this format. We hope that by learning how these logical steps are used in comparative politics, you will learn not only how to think like a political scientist but also how to apply these steps yourself to analytical tasks in other areas of inquiry.

Key Terms

Empirical analysis
Variable
Dependent variable
Independent variable
Correlation (association)
Intervening variables
Law
Theory
Hypothesis
Model
Induction
Deduction

Notes

1. For an introduction to some of the timeless themes of political philosophy, see Glenn Tinder, *Political Thinking: The Perennial Questions*, 6th ed. (New York: Longman, 2003).
2. For an overview of the field, see Michael E. Kraft and Scott R. Furlong, *Public Policy: Politics, Analysis, and Alternatives*, 2nd ed. (Washington, DC: CQ Press, 2006).
3. In *The Grammar of Science*, written in 1892, the scientist and philosopher Karl Pearson wrote, "The unity of all science consists alone in its method, not its material."
4. Maurice Duverger, *Political Parties*, 2nd English ed., rev., trans. Barbara and Robert North (London: Methuen, 1959), p. 217. See also Maurice Duverger, *Party Politics and Pressure Groups*, trans. David Wagoner (New York: Crowell, 1972), and *Introduction à la Politique* (Paris: Gallimard, 1964).
5. Anthony Downs, *An Economic Theory of Democracy* (New York: Harper & Row, 1957).
6. Karl W. Deutsch, *The Nerves of Government* (New York: Free Press, 1966).
7. For example, there exist rigorous tests for determining the *statistical significance* of particular statistical results. In addition, the relative *strength* of a correlation between dependent and independent variables can be calculated and specified in numerical terms. The resulting *correlation coefficient* is a very useful tool in political analysis. Another statistical technique that is widely used in political science is *regression analysis*, which permits analysts to measure the probable effect of a change (or *variance*) in one or more independent variables on a dependent variable. It is very useful in analyzing voting patterns and other quantifiable relationships.
8. For a concise outline of the scientific approach, see Stephen Van Evera, *Guide to Methods for Students of Political Science* (Ithaca, NY: Cornell University Press, 1997). A more advanced text is Gary King, Robert O. Keohane, and Sidney Verba, *Designing Social Inquiry* (Princeton, NJ: Princeton University Press, 1994).
9. Freedom House, "Freedom in the World Comparative and Historical Data," at http://www.freedomhouse.org/images/File/fiw/historical/FIWAllScoresCountries1973-2011.xls. These figures are 2010 Freedom House indexes.
10. World Bank, "GDP per Capita (current US$)," at http://data.worldbank.org/indicator/NY.GDP.PCAP.CD, accessed February 5, 2012. The GDP per capita figures are for 2010 or, in a few cases, 2009.
11. Seymour Martin Lipset, "Economic Development and Democracy," in *Political Man* (New York: Doubleday, 1960), chap. 2.

3

The State and Its Institutions

OVERVIEW

- The state, the totality of a country's governmental institutions and officials, claims the monopoly of legal authority in a given territory.

- State structures vary significantly from country to country, but we can identify executive, legislative, and judicial structures in each.

- Major components of any state include the bureaucracy (or civil service) and the military. Understanding how the bureaucracy functions and the role of the military in politics are essential themes in comparative politics.

- While the state can seem all-powerful in some countries, many societies are threatened by state failure.

The police, such as these French officers, serve as the most frequent daily reminder that the state claims the monopoly on the legitimate use of force in the territory it rules.

DEFINING THE STATE

Often, in ordinary day-to-day conversation, we use the term *government* as a synonym for the state. However, when discussing politics and government in general, political scientists prefer the *state* as a generic term encompassing all the governmental institutions within an individual country (see Figure 3.1). As we shall see, defining the state can be complicated, and scholars offer a variety of definitional approaches. In its simplest, most commonly understood definition, the **state** is the totality of a

country's governmental institutions and officials, guided by the laws and procedures that structure their activities.

The state's *institutions* are governmental organizations and agencies that typically perform specified functions on the basis of laws, rules, directives, and other authoritative procedures and practices. Cabinets, legislatures, courts, the bureaucracy, the military, the police, public schools and colleges, your local trash removal department—these and similar bodies are all parts of the state and act as its agents. In modern states extensive regulations and operating principles guide the operations of state institutions and agencies. These include such things as the country's constitution and laws, the rules and customary practices that specify how the legislature and courts work, the procedures governing how bureaucrats are recruited and what they do, military command procedures, and so on.

Political scientists refer to these rules and procedures that guide the operation of state institutions as the **regime**. Regime principles guide the actions of state institutions. Democratic regimes limit the actions of state institutions in ways that authoritarian regimes do not. Throughout this book we will discuss democratic and nondemocratic regimes. As we do you should remember that democratic regimes set the regulations about how state institutions can operate.

While people often use state and government synonymously, for political scientists **government** means the group of individuals in the very highest levels of decision-making authority in the state. For example, in Germany, a democracy, the Merkel government is Chancellor Angela Merkel and members of her cabinet, composed of high-level leaders of her party, the Christian Democrats, and those of her coalition partner, the Free Democrats. In the People's Republic of China, a nondemocracy, the government is headed by President Xi Jinping, who is also general secretary of the Communist Party. His closest subordinates, organized into the State Council, head the various state ministries—defense, foreign relations, education, and so forth. They, too, are almost all high-level officials in the Communist Party. In the United States, we tend to use the term *administration* in the way that government is used in other democracies. Thus we say "Obama administration," meaning President Obama, his cabinet officers, and close presidential aides and advisors, whereas the British would say "Cameron government."

The most important feature of the state that distinguishes it from other entities—such as social groups or private firms—is that the state *monopolizes* legal authority. In other words, only the state possesses the legal authority to make and coercively enforce laws that are binding on the population. This legal authority makes the state's decisions "authoritative." By "coercively enforce," we mean that the state has the legal authority to use physical force, if it has to, to compel the population to obey the law. To this end it seeks to monopolize the main means of coercive power—the police, the courts, the penal system, and the military. If the state loses its monopoly of coercive power and is seriously challenged by domestic groups or individuals who routinely ignore its laws, then it is a **failed state**.

Although governmental institutions form the core of our basic definition of the state, some political scientists argue for a more expansive conception that would include certain nongovernmental organizations or groups that are very closely connected to governmental authorities and have a major impact on what they do. In Saddam Hussein's Iraq, for example, the Baath Party was not, strictly speaking, a governmental institution, yet it was so tightly integrated into Saddam's regime that it was for all practical purposes a part of his state apparatus. In contemporary China, the Chinese Communist Party is tightly intertwined with the country's governmental institutions and activities and exercises superior authority over them.

State	A country's authoritative institutions and officials, guided by the laws and procedures that structure their activities.
Institutions	Governmental organizations and agencies that typically perform specified functions on the basis of laws, rules, directives, and other authoritative procedures and practices.
Regime	The rules and procedures that guide the operation of the state.
Government	The group of individuals in the very highest levels of decision-making authority in the state.

FIGURE 3.1 **Distinguishing the Meanings of State, Institutions, Regime, and Government**

Marxists traditionally contend that, in capitalist countries, the big-business elite so completely dominates government decision makers that the state is essentially "the guardian and protector" of this economically powerful social class. At least some Marxists contend that the capitalist "ruling class" is part of the "state system."[1] Many non-Marxists would dispute this co-identification of the state and the capitalist class. Nevertheless, as all the preceding cases demonstrate, the dividing line between "state" and "non-state" may sometimes be blurry.

The definition of the state as the totality of a country's governmental institutions and officials represents only one way in which the term *state* is used in political science. As we pointed out in Chapter 1, state is also used as a synonym for an entire country. Strictly speaking, a state in international relations is a government that has authority over a national population living in a specified territory. In this sense, the United States, Japan, Mexico, and South Africa are all states; relations between their respective governments are "inter-state relations." In a third usage, state is sometimes used to designate an administrative subdivision within certain countries. The United States of America has 50 states. Germany has 16 *Länder,* a term translated into English as "states."

SOVEREIGNTY, LEGITIMACY, AUTONOMY, AND PURPOSES OF THE STATE

One of the key attributes of a state is **sovereignty**, meaning, in its classic definition, the exclusive legal authority of a government over its population and territory, independent of external authorities.

In other words, a state is sovereign to the extent that it monopolizes the exercise of governmental authority at home, rejecting the right of foreign states or other external actors to impose their own laws from the outside or interfere in its domestic political order. Traditionally, one of the most common ways for a state to bolster its sovereignty is by entering into formal diplomatic relations with other states on the basis of the mutual recognition of each other's sovereign rights. International recognition of a state's exclusive control of a given territory serves to reinforce its claim to that control because then at least it is less likely to have to struggle with foreign rivals about who can rule in that territory.

This conception of sovereignty, which has its roots in the emergence of the modern state system in seventeenth- and eighteenth-century Europe, is accepted by most governments in today's world as a fundamental principle of international law. The officials of most national governments will vigorously defend their state's sovereignty when they feel it is being undermined. But like the European state system from which it sprang, sovereignty is not what it used to be. Sovereignty is not a timeless concept that never changes. On the contrary, sovereignty is socially constructed: It is shaped and defined by the specific mixture of domestic and international factors that affect individual countries, or groups of countries, at different periods of history. Europe itself provides a vivid illustration of how sovereignty has changed in today's lattice-like, interdependent world. Since the 1950s, a growing number of European states have voluntarily relinquished some of their sovereign rights to determine their own economic policy and other policies that were formerly reserved to the exclusive competence of domestic authorities. In an effort to promote economic growth, environmental cooperation, and other mutual benefits, European states have established integrated Europe-wide institutions and engaged in joint decision-making procedures, establishing what has been described as a system of "pooled sovereignty." These efforts culminated in the formation of the European Union (EU), which by 2013 included 28 countries. (We will describe the EU in greater detail in Chapter 4). Other states around the world have not gone quite as far as the EU in the direction of shared sovereignty. Nevertheless most states find it increasingly difficult to keep out unwanted foreign influences like information on the Internet or pressures from foreign states. For many states it is also difficult to avoid the intrusion of international organizations (such as the International Monetary Fund) or rules (such as World Trade Organization rulings). Though sovereignty is still highly valued around the world—even in EU countries, which still retain sovereign rights in sensitive areas such as foreign policy—the forces of globalization are constantly chipping away at its walls.[2]

Legitimacy

Another important aspect of states is **legitimacy**, or the right to rule. For Max Weber, legitimacy is central to the very definition of the state. In his famous formulation that we saw in Chapter 1, the state "is a human community that (successfully) claims the monopoly of the legitimate use of physical force within a given territory."[3] Weber's use of the term *legitimate* implies that only the state has the *right* to employ force or to authorize others to use it. Thus the state may outlaw private militias and regulate private security companies. But what if the state is regarded as illegitimate in the eyes of its people? Weber's definition suggests that the people may have a right to use force against a government that they cannot remove in any other way. His notion that the state "claims" a monopoly on the legitimate use of force further

Max Weber

suggests that it may not be successful in getting the people (or perhaps some component of the population) to accept its claim.

What causes people to regard the state's rule as legitimate? Weber defined **authority** as occurring when there is a probability that people will obey a specific command. He defined legitimate authority as occurring when people obey the authority because they regard it as obligatory or exemplary. In his view there have been essentially three ways in which political leaders throughout history have convinced their populations to accept their authority as legitimate (see Figure 3.2).

The first way is *traditional authority*. This type of legitimacy rests on "an established belief in the sanctity of immemorial traditions." Over vast stretches of time, people come to accept the existing political realities simply because they have been there for prolonged periods. Centuries-old monarchies, such as those that once held sway in Britain, China, Japan, and elsewhere, are examples of tradition-based legitimacy. Few states rest on traditional authority today.

The second type of legitimacy is *legal-rational authority*. This type is rooted in "the belief in the legality of rules and in the right of those who occupy positions by virtue of those rules to issue commands." This type of legitimacy is most prominent in democracies, which establish very rigorous rules for determining who has the right to issue governmental commands. Conceivably, some nondemocracies may also be based on at least an element of legal-rational authority. Over the centuries, Britain's monarchs gradually came to accept the notion that they too were subject to certain laws. Today legal-rational authority undergirds most states. Even nondemocracies attempt to give the appearance of abiding by legal-rational norms. Many nondemocracies, for example, hold sham elections so that they can say their leaders were elected by their subjects. Saddam Hussein won 100 percent of the vote in his final "election" in 2002.

The third type of legitimate authority was what Weber called *charismatic authority*. This type of legitimacy attaches

Traditional	Legal-Rational	Charismatic
Political realities established over very long periods of time. Examples: Traditional monarchies of Saudi Arabia, England or Japan	Belief in the legality of rules and the right of people under these rules to issue commands. Examples: Today's democracies	Political realities established by the force of an individual's personality. Examples: Mao Zedong and Fidel Castro

FIGURE 3.2 **Weber's Categories of Legitimate Authority**

itself to a certain uniquely magnetic or inspiring leader and "rests upon the devotion" of his followers to his "extraordinary sanctity, heroism, or exemplary character" as well as to the "patterns of order revealed or ordained by him." In these rare cases, the charismatic leader is perceived by others as "set apart from ordinary men" and as "endowed with supernatural, superhuman, or at least specifically exceptional powers or qualities." Religious figures such as Moses, Jesus, Muhammad, and Buddha clearly fit this description. So, too, do certain political figures. For good or ill, such riveting personalities as Napoleon, Hitler, Stalin, Franklin D. Roosevelt, and a few other notable leaders were able to exert a charismatic effect on their followers.

Charismatic authority, in Weber's view, is the most unstable form of legitimacy. Once charismatic leaders die, their ideas and support can die with them. To prevent this from happening, the charismatic leader and successive generations of followers must institutionalize (or "routinize") the leader's charisma by building institutions that will survive, such as an organized religion, a political party, or a state. The public veneration of past leaders, such as Mao Zedong in China or Fidel Castro in Cuba, offers examples of efforts to routinize charisma in the state. These efforts are not always successful, however.

Ultimately Weber argued that political legitimacy is grounded in the beliefs of those who are governed. If the masses believe that their rulers are legitimate, for whatever reason, then the rulers are legitimate. If they believe that the state possesses legitimate authority within the territory on which they live, it possesses that authority. And if the masses believe in their leaders' legitimacy, they are more likely to comply with the laws of the land voluntarily rather than because they are forced to do so. They will accept the state's decisions about who gets what and when because they agree with how the decision was made. Governance based on legitimacy is therefore likely to be more stable and enduring than one based on sheer coercion.

Autonomy

The concept of the **autonomy of the state** refers to the relative independence of state authorities from the population. If the state enjoys a high degree of autonomy, then state officials are quite free to do what they please when it comes to governing the populace. By contrast, a low degree of state autonomy means that state officials have very little room to create laws or make decisions independently of the population as a whole or—as is more likely—independently of its politically most powerful groups. Both extremes have dangers. Maximum state autonomy means dictatorship: The people have little or no say in what their rulers do. Minimum state autonomy implies that state officials have few opportunities to use their expertise and concern for the country's common good to formulate and implement the policies they think best. Instead, they may have to cater to the wishes of society's dominant or most influential individuals and groups. A truly representative democracy, by contrast, would seek to avoid the pitfalls of too much or not enough state autonomy, giving state decision makers enough latitude to govern effectively while holding them accountable to the population for their actions.

The Purposes of the State

Why have a state? What should it do? The question of the state's ultimate purposes has provoked considerable debate through the centuries. Some theorists have argued that the state's primary function should be to guarantee order and security. To this end Thomas Hobbes (1588–1679) proposed that

In *Leviathan,* Thomas Hobbes argues that people should form a social contract with each other to obey an all-powerful state.

the people should form a kind of social contract ("covenant") with each other to obey the leaders of an all-powerful state, which he called "Leviathan." The state's main purpose would be to leave humanity free to pursue science, art, exploration, and other aspects of civilization without the pressures of "continual fear, and danger of violent death."[4]

John Locke (1632–1704)—like Hobbes, an Oxford graduate—also favored the idea of a social contract, in his view between the people and state authorities, but for aims that were very different from those laid out by Hobbes. Locke argued in his *Second Treatise of Government* (1689) that human beings are born free. Individuals enjoy a natural right to life, liberty, and "estate" (their possessions)—assets that together constitute, in Locke's formulation, one's "property." "The great and *chief end,* therefore, of men's putting themselves under government," Locke declared, "is the preservation of their property." Any state that failed to safeguard these natural rights was illegitimate. Accordingly, Locke favored a representative democracy established "by common consent," with an elected legislature constituting the highest political authority. Locke placed special emphasis on the state's responsibility to safeguard the rights and freedoms of the individual. His ideas had an enormous impact on the Founding Fathers of the American Revolution.[5]

Swiss philosopher Jean-Jacques Rousseau (1712–78), a third great "social contract" theorist, advanced yet another set of ideas about the ultimate aims of government. In contrast to Locke's emphasis on individual rights and freedoms, Rousseau stressed the *collective* rights and freedoms of the community. In his view, the people—not the state—are "the sovereign"; together they form an organic "body politic" on the basis of a

"general will," which is the common good. For each individual to be free from tyranny, the community as a whole must be free. The liberty of each depends on the liberty of all, a notion that requires each individual to conform to the general will. Rousseau recommended that "whoever refuses to obey the general will shall be constrained to do so by the whole body; which means nothing else than that he shall be forced to be free." Even the individual's right to private property "is always subordinate to the right which the community has over all." In Rousseau's vision, the chief purpose of the state is to enable the sovereign people to express and carry out their general will. In practical terms, he believed that this goal could be accomplished by a small elite making day-to-day decisions, as long as the citizens (which in his day meant property-owning males) exercised their supervisory authority by meeting periodically in popular assemblies.[6]

In contrast to the prescriptions of the social contract theorists, most modern states were fashioned out of brute force rather than the consent of the governed. Countries such as China, Japan, Russia, France, and England developed into powerful, centralized states over the course of centuries of internal turmoil, with rival clans, dynasties, warlords, or other combatants clashing over the ultimate prize—the government of the realm. Violent contention for control of the state did not die down until the eighteenth century in Britain, the nineteenth century in Japan and France, and the twentieth century in China and Russia. Once the winning faction was entrenched in power, its chief purpose was to use the state to expand its control over the domestic population and, in many cases, to make war on foreign adversaries. The early modern state was in large measure an authoritarian warfare state.

Indeed, political sociologist Charles Tilly has characterized the early modern state as a kind of protection racket. Drawing insights from Hobbes, Tilly suggested that states, which at their apex were rulers supported by heavily armed bands of soldiers, gained legitimacy by offering protection to the inhabitants of territories they sought to control. By picking fights with rival states these rulers created the need for resources to conduct war, resources that they then extracted in the form of taxes and forced loans from the people they ruled who of course feared the rival state and its armies. Early state formation thus involved war making and could be considered comparable to organized crime. Mobsters (early modern states) demand protection money (taxes) from business owners (the people, especially economic elites) to defend them against rival mobsters (other states aspiring to control the territory).[7]

Over time, states acquired purposes that were more attuned to the wishes of the population, or at least to the wishes of its most politically influential parts. Adam Smith (1723–90), the Scottish philosopher who is considered the father of modern free-market economics, argued in *The Wealth of Nations* (1776) that the state's chief purpose should be to promote private enterprise and allow the forces of the market economy to work without excessive political interference. In Smith's view, the state should limit itself to providing a legal system designed to enable commerce to flow smoothly and to undertaking large projects that are too unprofitable for private entrepreneurs to take on themselves, such as building bridges and canals and funding public education and cultural activities. Over the course of the following century, Britain and the United States adopted political philosophies that conformed quite closely to Smith's proposals. But as democracy expanded in these countries, and the vote was extended to larger segments of the populace, the state was increasingly pressured by mass publics to enhance their economic and social welfare. During the twentieth century, the state in large democracies took on a growing number of welfare functions, from expanding public education to providing pensions, unemployment compensation, health care, housing, and the like. Countries that had once been governed as warfare states evolved into welfare states. Authoritarian regimes like Nazi Germany and the Soviet Union also cultivated mass support through a cornucopia of welfare programs. Even welfare states, however, must regard their domestic and international security as a top priority.

The main goals pursued by states in today's world run a wide gamut; everything depends on who gets to define these goals. Democracies, military regimes, states based on Islamic law—these and other states will define their main goals differently. Perhaps the one universal reality is that **anarchism**, which is the notion that the people are better off without an organized government, has not been adopted as a viable option. *Anarchy* comes from the ancient Greek word meaning "without a ruler." Although fairly large anarchist movements were active in Europe and Russia in the nineteenth century and in Spain the first half of the twentieth century, anarchism has never triumphed anywhere long enough to undergo a trial run. The political world as we know it is a world built on states.[8]

ESSENTIAL CONCEPTS

Failed and Failing States

A failed state is a state that has little or no ability to govern its entire territory. In most cases, failed states do not provide basic security or services for large parts of the population. They are often confronted by organized groups that possess their own means of violence. Civil war or random chaos rages as central authority breaks down. A sizable element of the population may reject the legitimacy of the government in power or the political regime in its entirety. States attempting to govern multi-ethnic societies may be much more likely to face rejection by some ethnic groups in those societies. In some instances, what remains of the state may be captured by gangster-like elements that plunder its resources and use deadly force to impose their rule over the population. Local warlords, drug cartels, rogue militias, or bandits may carve up the countryside and assert their control over local territories.

Some analysts prefer to distinguish between a "failed state" and a "failing state." The former have become nothing more than hollow shells and have no effective control over the territory they claim, while the latter are simply in danger of losing control of critical state functions. Whether we consider failed states only or include failing states in our analysis, the fact that so many states in today's world are highly vulnerable to some form of breakdown is strikingly evident.[9]

Somalia is the quintessential failed state. A country of 10 million people on the horn of Africa, Somalia lacks any real central authority. In 1991 a coalition of clan-based armed opposition groups overthrew the military regime that had governed Somalia since 1969. Since then Somalia has been in a state of civil war. The United Nations sent peacekeepers, led by U.S. troops, to Somalia in the early 1990s. That UN involvement largely failed and led to the events chronicled in the film *Black Hawk Down* in which 18 U.S. troops and two other UN peacekeepers were killed in Mogadishu, the capital, attempting to apprehend a Somali faction leader. The UN peacekeeping force eventually left Somalia without establishing the basis of effective central governance. In its place Somalia has had the rule of local warlords. What passes for law depends on who holds power locally at a particular time. In some places power holders apply *sharia* law, in other places not. Two regional governments, Somaliland and Puntland, rule their regions autonomously but consider themselves part of the larger Somali republic. More than 1 million Somalis have fled the country and another million are internally displaced. World news often reports about another aspect of Somalia's relatively stateless condition: Pirates operate freely out of Somalia's ports, preying on everything from private yachts to oil tankers that sail by, kidnapping the occupants and holding them for ransom. The world's great powers can do little to inhibit such piracy because no Somali authorities can effectively control them. In sum, no authority successfully maintains the monopoly on the legitimate use of force in Somalia.

Pakistan is another country often in the news that is considered a failing state. What makes Pakistan a country vulnerable to state collapse?

Born in the partition of the British colony of India in 1947, Pakistan was formed to be a distinctly Islamic nation, in contrast to India, which is majority Hindu but formally secular. Although there have been tensions between Hindus and other religious groups in India, that country has managed to maintain democratic institutions and practices for all but a couple of years since 1947. (Chapter 12 discusses India in greater detail.) Pakistan has been less successful.

The country's first leader, Muhammad Ali Jinnah, paid lip service to democratic principles but gathered the reins of power in his own hands. After his death in 1948, Pakistan drifted toward chaos. There were seven prime ministers during the next 10 years, all of them ineffective. All relied heavily on the bureaucracy and the military to deal with the country's problems, which included widespread poverty, deep ethnic divisions, and doctrinal disputes between rival Muslim groups. In ethnic terms, the new country was divided among Mohajirs (immigrants from India), Punjabis, Sindhis, Bengalis, Pathans (Pashtuns), and Baluchis, along with several smaller groups. Most Pakistanis were Sunni Muslims, but Shiites constituted a sizable minority. The Sunnis themselves were divided into diverse camps, including moderates willing to support a secular state as well as radicals who favored an Islamic theocracy. The Shiites were also divided into various subsects. Intense rivalries for political power and economic benefits involving these disparate ethnic and religious groups plagued Pakistan from its very foundation as an independent state. At one time or another virtually all the country's main ethnic groups demanded greater autonomy or outright secession. But though the creation of a unified Pakistani national identity proved difficult internally, most Pakistanis were able to agree on a policy of nationalism that was directed externally against India.

Since those early days Pakistan has shifted back and forth between a parliamentary democracy and military dictatorship several times. In 1977, General Zia-ul-Haq seized power in a coup d'état and had his democratically elected predecessor, Zulfikar Ali Bhutto, executed. Zia was both a staunch anti-communist ally of the United States during the long Soviet war in Afghanistan and a devout Sunni Muslim who sought to Islamize Pakistani society. During his rule the formerly secularist army, especially its military intelligence services (ISI), became increasingly Islamist. After Zia died in a plane crash in 1988, democracy returned to Pakistan as Benazir Bhutto, daughter of the former prime minister, ascended to power. Bhutto and her husband, Asif Ali Zardari, became the subjects of allegations of corruption. She lost power to Nawaz Sharif in elections in 1990, regained the prime ministry in 1993, and lost the 1997 elections again to Sharif. Bhutto and Zardari

were then brought to trial for corruption, but their conviction was overturned when it was revealed that the Sharif government had fixed the case with the presiding judge. General Pervez Musharraf brought this sorry phase of Pakistani democracy to an end with a coup in 1999. After several years during which he was Washington's principal ally in the war on terror, Musharraf, who had appointed himself president in 2001, had the parliament indirectly reelect him as president in 2007. He then suspended the constitution, imposed a state of emergency, and removed the chief justice of the Supreme Court. Protests arose across the country in response, which forced Musharraf to hold the scheduled 2008 parliamentary elections even though he had sought to delay them. During the election campaign, Bhutto was assassinated. Facing the prospect of impeachment, Musharraf resigned the presidency in 2008, to be replaced by Zardari.

As this brief review suggests, Pakistan has been riven by deep rivalries among political elites. Its leaders have been subject to charges of corruption and worse, put on trial, and jailed (Zardari spent eight years in prison). Governments have been brought to an end in ways not prescribed by the constitution. In addition, Pakistan's long-standing conflict with India, against which it has waged two losing wars and other minor skirmishes, and the presence of conflict in Afghanistan for over 30 years have granted the military and the ISI substantial power in Pakistani politics. Yet the military is not able to control effectively all of the national territory as the Taliban, both those who have fled Afghanistan and a homegrown Pakistani Taliban, and tribal groups have prevented the central government from monopolizing the legitimate use of force in many parts of the country, especially in tribal regions. Indeed, the ISI, a segment of the military, is often accused of supporting the Taliban.

This weak state faces mounting challenges. The Fund for Peace does an annual survey to produce the Failed State Index (described in the Hypothesis-Testing Exercise). Among the indicators it tracks are social, economic, and political challenges that might make states vulnerable to collapse. We have considered several political shortcomings of the Pakistani state already, but its social and economic challenges are formidable. Already a country with a huge and growing population, in 2010 and 2011 Pakistan suffered terrible floods that displaced hundreds of thousands of people, submerged millions of acres of cropland, and set the economy back considerably. As the Fund for Peace characterizes Pakistan, it is a country facing high pressures but its state has low capacities—just the combination that can lead to widespread protest and further political conflict.[10] Pakistan may not be a failed state, but it often appears to be failing at meeting the basic criteria for being a state—maintaining the *monopoly* on the *legitimate* use of force within its territory. Rivals such as the Taliban and tribal groups exercise violence politically. They do so because they do not recognize the legitimacy of the existing state. ■

Chaos erupts in Pakistan with the assassination of Benazir Bhutto late in 2007.

■ HYPOTHESIS-TESTING EXERCISE
Ethnic Conflict and State Failure

Hypothesis In what situations might we expect to encounter failing states? One line of argument posits that state failure is more likely to occur in societies with high levels of ethnic conflict. This might occur in two situations: (1) In an ethnically divided society in which one ethnic group controls the state and discriminates against other groups, policy mismanagement (for example, poor economic performance) causes the discriminated-against groups to rebel. (2) Even if it has been inclusive and nondiscriminatory, a weak state might respond to policy difficulties by beginning to favor one ethnic group over others, leading discriminated-against groups to revolt. Either situation can lead to acute conflict, causing the state to be unable to fulfill its fundamental roles—providing legitimate law and order.[11]

Allowing that other factors might influence state failure, we can nonetheless hypothesize that *state failure is more likely to occur in ethnically divided societies.* Conversely, *state failure is less likely to occur in ethnically homogeneous societies.*

Variables In this hypothesis, the *dependent variable* is state failure. The *independent variable* is ethnic fragmentation, a measure of ethnic division.

Expectations If our hypothesis is correct, we would expect that societies with higher levels of ethnic fragmentation are more likely to experience state failure. Societies with lower levels of ethnic fragmentation (that is, those that are more homogeneous) are less likely to have failing states.

Evidence *Foreign Policy* magazine and a nonprofit organization, The Fund for Peace, produce an annual Failed States Index (FSI), a way to measure the extent to which states fail to meet the expectations of a state.[12] The FSI incorporates the following factors: demographic pressures, large movements of refugees/internally displaced persons (IDPs), a history of group grievances, large-scale human flight from the country, uneven economic development across social groups, economic decline, criminalization or delegitimization of the

Table 3.1 Ethnic Fractionalization and Failing States

HIGHEST FAILED STATE INDEX SCORES			LOWEST FAILED STATE INDEX SCORES		
Country	FSI	Ethnic Fractionalization	Country	FSI	Ethnic Fractionalization
Somalia	113.4	0.81	United States	34.8	0.49
Chad	110.3	0.86	Belgium	34.1	0.56
Sudan	108.7	0.71	United Kingdom	34.1	0.12
Congo (Democratic Rep.)	108.2	0.87	France	34.0	0.10
Haiti	108.0	0.10	Germany	33.9	0.17
Zimbabwe	107.9	0.39	Portugal	32.3	0.05
Afghanistan	107.5	0.77	Japan	31.0	0.01
Central African Republic	105.0	0.83	Iceland	30.1	0.08
Iraq	104.8	0.37	Netherlands	28.3	0.11
Cote d'Ivoire	102.8	0.82	Australia	28.1	0.09
Guinea	102.5	0.74	Canada	27.7	0.71
Pakistan	102.3	0.71	Austria	27.3	0.11
Nigeria	99.9	0.85	Luxembourg	26.1	0.53
Niger	99.1	0.65	Ireland	25.3	0.12
Kenya	98.7	0.86	New Zealand	24.8	0.40
Burundi	98.6	0.30	Denmark	23.8	0.08
Guinea Bissau	98.3	0.81	Switzerland	23.2	0.53
Myanmar (Burma)	98.3	0.63	Sweden	22.8	0.06
Ethiopia	98.2	0.72	Norway	20.4	0.06
Uganda	96.3	0.93	Finland	19.7	0.13
Mean Ethnic Fractionalization Score		**0.69**			**0.23**

Sources: Fund for Peace, "The Failed States Index 2011 Interactive Grid," at www.fundforpeace.org/global/?q=fsi-grid2011; Alberto Alesina, Arnaud Devleeschauwer, William Easterly, Sergio Kurlat, and Romain Wacziarg, "Fractionalization," *Journal of Economic Growth* 8 (June 2003), pp. 155–94.

(Continued on next page)

(Continued from previous page)

state, sharp decline of public services, widespread violation of human rights, the security apparatus (police and military) acting with impunity, increasingly factionalized elites, and external intervention in the country's affairs. These indicators are intended to capture the extent to which a state does or does not fulfill the social, economic, and political roles of an effective state, which means that it has failed or is in danger of failing as a state. Table 3.1 (on page 51) lists the 20 countries with the highest FSI scores—those least able to meet the expectations of a state—and the 20 with the lowest FSI scores in 2011.

The degree of ethnic division in societies is not easily measured because not all countries use the same census questions to establish ethnic identity. However, a group of economists led by Alberto Alesina composed an ethnic fractionalization index about a decade ago. Because the ethnic composition of societies does not change rapidly, that index remains a good indicator of how ethnically divided a society might be. It ranges from 0 for a completely homogeneous society to 1.

Table 3.1 also shows the ethnic fractionalization index for the 20 most fragile states and the 20 states with the lowest scores on the FSI (those least likely to fail in the view of the FSI's creators). As the table indicates, weak states have high ethnic fractionalization scores while strong states have relatively low fractionalization scores. There are some

exceptions—Haiti's extremely weak state attempts to govern a relatively homogeneous population while Canada's and Switzerland's strong states govern ethnically plural societies. This evidence suggests, however, that we can accept our hypothesis: Ethnic fragmentation seems to promote state failure.

Figure 3.3 plots the scores of all countries for which there are scores for both indexes. The line in the plot shows the best fit for an estimate of the relationship between ethnic fractionalization and the FSI. The actual plotted figures do not all line up on that line, indicating that ethnic fractionalization is far from a perfect predictor of a country's FSI score; indeed, knowing the countries' ethnic fractionalization scores helps us to predict about 25 percent of the variance in the FSI scores, meaning that three-quarters of the variance is due to other factors.

Conclusions What we've learned from Table 3.1 and Figure 3.3 should lead us to be modest in our acceptance of our hypothesis. Yes, ethnic fragmentation seems to contribute to state failure, but other variables also affect state failure. Based on this test of our hypothesis, we can expect that societies that are ethnically divided will be vulnerable to state failure, but we should continue to look to find other factors that undermine states.

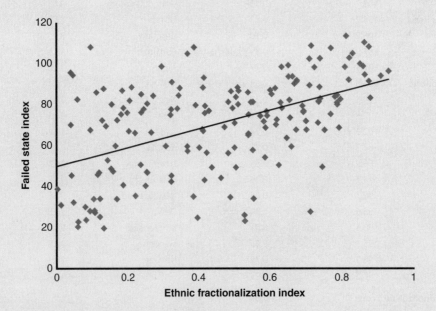

FIGURE 3.3 **Ethnic Fractionalization and State Failure**

STATE INSTITUTIONS

Ultimately the topic of the state centers on governmental institutions. **Institutionalism** (or *neo-institutionalism,* in its recent variants) is the branch of comparative politics that looks at how state institutions are set up and how they shape the political decision-making process. Its central hypothesis is that political outcomes—such as governmental decisions that determine "who gets what"—are often decisively affected by a country's institutional framework, and not simply by the direct impact of influential social groups or nongovernmental organizations. As we shall see in this and subsequent chapters, different outcomes may result depending on how a country organizes its executive branch, its legislature, its judiciary, and other institutions, and on how these organs function in practice.[13]

In most countries the legal competence of governmental institutions is spelled out in a national constitution, which is usually a single written document. The United States was the first country to establish itself from scratch on the basis of a written constitution; in this sense, it was "the first new nation."[14] The U.S. Constitution, which has been amended 27 times, is the oldest constitution in the world in the form of a single document. The constitutions of most other states are much more recent. Germany, Italy, and Japan, for instance, adopted new constitutional arrangements after World War II. France's present constitution dates from 1958. Most of the countries that abandoned communism after 1989 have written new constitutions, and some are still in the process of revising them. South Africa, Brazil, and a host of other states are also engaged in inaugurating relatively new constitutional orders.

Not all constitutions are single documents. Britain has one of the oldest continuous constitutional traditions in the world, but its constitution consists of thousands of laws and practices that have been developed over the course of centuries of parliamentary interactions with the crown and courts. Israel, established in 1948, also has no formal constitution but a set of Basic Laws and other legislation that substitute for one. The same is true of Germany.

In addition to looking at the constitutionally determined ground rules of governmental authority, political scientists also like to investigate the ways state institutions operate in real life. Often a constitution provides only the skeletal structure of a governmental system. It does not necessarily indicate how the system's institutional parts really work or how effectively the laws of the land are implemented. Constitutions can also be vague or silent on certain aspects of governmental authority or can be subject to conflicting interpretations. Authoritarian rulers sometimes ignore their country's constitution and rule by fiat. Many Latin American constitutions in past decades were modeled on the U.S. system of separation of powers. In practice, however, those provisions were largely ignored, and state authority tilted heavily in the direction of highly personalized presidential power.[15]

We need to look at several important governmental institutions to understand political realities in a variety of settings.

The Executive

The **executive branch** is of primary importance in all political systems. Presidents, prime ministers, dictators, governing monarchs, and other officials at the apex of the governmental pyramid are typically the individuals who decide government policy and who hold ultimate responsibility for the state's successes and failures. They are the individuals we typically mean when we refer to the "government."

As we look at the role of political executives in the chapters that follow, it is important to keep in mind a basic distinction between two distinct executive functions: *head of state* and *head of government.* In most countries, these are two separate offices occupied by two different people who are selected in separate procedures. Although there are some notable exceptions, usually the **head of state** is a ceremonial position that carries little or no real decision-making power. In these cases the head of state is often an individual who stands above the country's ongoing political battles and personifies the nation's unity or the continuity of its history. In some instances the person occupying this symbolically prestigious but politically neutral post is an unelected figure such as a hereditary monarch in a democracy. A **constitutional monarchy** (or **limited** monarchy) is a regime in which the monarch is head of state, but real decision-making power is in the hands of other institutional authorities such as legislators, the prime minister, and other officials who answer to them. A number of countries that once had powerful monarchs but subsequently became democracies have retained the monarchy in order to preserve their historical traditions, while radically diminishing the crown's actual power. Belgium, Britain, Denmark, Japan, the Netherlands, Norway, and Sweden are a few examples. Spain's King Juan Carlos I has played a more active political role, personally shepherding the transition from Francisco Franco's decades-long dictatorship to a successful democracy starting in the late 1970s. In 2006, Thailand's popular monarch made a rare political intervention when he called on the country's courts to invalidate recent parliamentary elections that were boycotted by opponents of the controversial prime minister, Thaksin Shinawatra. The constitutional court complied and ordered new elections. In other cases, the head of state may be an elected civilian who enjoys the respect of the country's population and political elites, including those from opposing parties. The head of state's main duties in such cases are generally limited to making speeches on ceremonial occasions, representing the state at nonpolitical functions, and greeting foreign dignitaries. In some countries the head of state has limited powers of intervention in the political process, in other countries none.

By contrast, the **head of government** is usually the country's chief political officer and is responsible for presenting and conducting its principle policies. Unlike a ceremonial head of state, the head of government has real decision-making authority. He or she normally supervises the entire executive branch of the state, including its senior ministers (who together comprise the cabinet) and their respective ministries, as well as a host

In Britain, the monarch is the head of state and the prime minister is the head of government. In 2012, these were Elizabeth II and David Cameron, respectively.

of executive-level agencies designed to propose and execute government policies. In most countries, the term *government,* in addition to being used in ordinary parlance as a synonym for the state as we defined it earlier, refers more specifically to just the head of government and the cabinet ministries. As we mentioned above, in this context it is used much the way the term *administration* is used in the United States to refer to a particular president and his executive-level colleagues: "David Cameron's government" in Britain and "the Obama administration" are analogous designations.

In Britain, the head of state is the monarch; the head of government is the prime minister. In Japan, the head of state is the emperor; the head of government is the prime minister. In Germany, the head of state is the president; the head of government is the chancellor. Many countries make roughly similar distinctions.

But as we noted, there are exceptions. In the United States, the president is both head of state *and* head of government. Another exception is France, which has an unusual "dual executive." In the French system, the president, who is the head of state, often has even greater decision-making authority than the prime minister, who is the head of government. Post-communist Russia and other countries also combine a politically powerful head of state (the president) with an active head of government (the prime minister). Not all heads of state, in other words, are purely ceremonial; some have real power. These and other variants are common, and we will look at some of them in later chapters.

The Legislature

Legislatures (or *parliaments* with a small *p*) are also important state institutions. Their chief functions, especially in democracies, are to make laws (sometimes in conjunction with the executive branch) and to represent the people in the lawmaking

process. In some cases, legislatures also keep a check on the executive branch and its bureaucratic departments by holding inquiries and investigations into their activities. This latter function is known as *legislative oversight.*

Some democracies have a *parliamentary system* of government. In these countries the national legislature actually elects (or approves) the head of government and holds that person, along with the entire cabinet, continuously accountable for their actions. Canada, Britain, Germany, Italy, Japan, Israel, India—these and a host of other countries all have one form or another of parliamentary government. We will look at this system more closely in Chapter 6.

The United States has a different system entirely, one in which the constitutional powers of Congress and the president are balanced more or less evenly. Even authoritarian regimes often have legislative bodies that play a certain role in the political system, though their real lawmaking powers may be negligible or nonexistent. In Iran, for example, the laws passed by the Majles (the parliament) can be overturned as unconstitutional by the Guardian Council, a 12-member judicial body, 6 of whose members are clerics selected by the unelected supreme leader (currently, Ayatollah Ali Khamenei). Conceivably, an elected legislature in a predominantly authoritarian political system could serve as an incubator of democracy, providing an opportunity for popularly chosen representatives to demand wider decision-making powers. We will explore this possibility further in Chapter 7.

Like the executive branch of government, legislatures around the world display considerable variation. Some countries (such as Israel and Denmark) have a **unicameral legislature**, consisting of only one house (or chamber) of parliament. Most others have a **bicameral legislature**, consisting of two houses. Typically one of these chambers is considered the *lower house* (e.g., the U.S. House of Representatives) and the second is regarded as the *upper house* (e.g., the U.S. Senate). The advantage of a unicameral legislature is that it does not have to share authority with a second legislative chamber in making laws. At least in principle, this arrangement is supposed to reduce the possibility of excessive legislative wrangling, delay, and gridlock. The main advantages of a bicameral legislature, again in principle, are that it provides greater representation for the population and requires greater deliberation in the lawmaking process. In actual practice, however, bicameral legislatures vary in terms of their representative function and their actual role.

Legislatures around the world differ in a variety of ways, including the voting systems used to elect them, their relative power, their lawmaking procedures, and so on. Subsequent chapters will discuss national legislatures in various countries around the world.[16]

The Judiciary

The **judiciary** represents a third institution whose significance, while usually considerable, varies from place to place. All states have some form of legal structure, and the role of the judiciary is rarely limited to such routine tasks as adjudicating civil and criminal cases. Inevitably the system of justice is intimately bound up with the state's political essence. Justice is not always blind; it is often keenly political. The political importance of the judiciary was especially evident when the U.S. Supreme Court decided the outcome of the 2000 presidential election. When a dispute arose over whether George W. Bush or Al Gore should be awarded Florida's Electoral College votes, the court sided with Bush by a 5–4 vote.

In some states, including the United States, Germany, and Japan, the judiciary is relatively *independent* of the political authorities in the executive and legislative branches. It may even possess the legal competence to impose restrictions on what these political leaders may do. In others (especially authoritarian ones), the legal system is often highly politicized and remains tightly controlled by the ruling clique, which manipulates the courts in an effort to keep the population in line. In Venezuela, for example, former President Hugo Chávez packed the supreme court with his followers. In some countries the legal system is based on secular law. The United States and France are prominent examples. In others such as Saudi Arabia and Iran, the legal system is based on religious law like *sharia* (Islamic law), which is itself subject to various interpretations. In yet another category of cases, the judiciary may play a critical role in defining and even widening the scope of civil rights and liberties for the population when these rights are limited or violated by other branches of government. The courts have played this quasi-independent role (or have at least attempted to play it) in such countries as Egypt, where the central executives have used heavy-handed methods of repression against political opponents, and in various countries in transition to democracy, where the formal definition of the executive's authority and the population's rights are still being worked out.[17]

Some countries, such as the United States, have constitutional courts with fairly wide latitude to interpret the highest laws of the land. In some cases these high courts have the power of **judicial review**, which is the right to invalidate laws made by the legislature and executive bodies as unconstitutional. Other countries have different patterns. In Britain, for instance, the House of Lords—the upper house of the legislature—functioned as the country's highest constitutional court until 2010.[18]

The Bureaucracy

The **bureaucracy**, or *civil service,* is an indispensable part of governance in virtually every country in the world. Without a well-developed network of state organs charged with advising political decision makers about different policy options and implementing policies once they have been decided upon, governments could not govern. The modern state invariably includes a vast array of ministries, departments, agencies, bureaus, and other officiously titled institutions whose purview may range from the domestic economy to education, health, the environment, international trade, foreign relations, and so on. The growth of bureaucracies has been a long-term political phenomenon in most countries, as have more recent efforts in some countries (including the United States) to trim their size to less costly proportions.

Although almost all large states are endowed with imposing bureaucratic structures, they differ significantly with respect to the roles their bureaucracies play. In some cases the ability of civil servants to issue regulations on their own authority is kept within fairly narrow limits. Legislative bodies, and in some cases the courts, exercise oversight functions in an effort to rein in the decision-making independence of these fairly restricted bureaucracies. The United States is an example. In other instances, bureaucrats enjoy wider discretionary powers when it comes to specifying how the government's policy aims, which may be sketched out in broad guidelines, are to be interpreted and implemented. Such broad rule-making authority can be found in democracies such as Japan and France, as well as in nondemocracies like the former Soviet Union. Measures to ensure democratic controls over the bureaucracy are among the most important tasks of newly democratizing countries that have inherited authoritarian bureaucratic structures from the old regime.[19]

Some bureaucracies consist of a fairly stable core of career civil servants who take pride in their technical professionalism and political neutrality. These *technocrats* provide government decision makers with indispensable information and policy analysis in their respective areas of expertise, such as economics, defense, technology, social welfare, and the like. Although the federal bureaucracy in the United States is populated with well-trained and dedicated careerists, the U.S. government has reserved a growing number of bureaucratic positions for political appointees, more so than in most other democracies. One of the chief spoils of political power in Washington is the opportunity given each new presidential administration to appoint faithful supporters to choice government jobs. As Barack Obama's incoming administration prepared to assume office following the 2008 presidential election, it was authorized to fill 8,000 positions, most of which were advertised in the government's aptly named "plum book."

Bureaucracies can also differ in terms of their operating procedures, the class and educational backgrounds of their personnel, their propensity to corruption, and so on. In subsequent chapters we will glance at the shape of bureaucratic structures in several countries.[20]

The Military

Military establishments can have a formidable impact of their own on the organization of institutional authority. Of course, if we consider Weber's conception of the state again, it is easy to see how essential the military is to the state. What allows the state to monopolize the legitimate use of force on the territory it claims? The military, first by denying control of the territory to outsiders—rival neighboring states—and then by taking on serious domestic challengers to the state, such as revolutionaries or secessionists if they should emerge.

Quite a few contemporary political systems have been run directly by elements of the military command. (The Spanish term *junta* refers to the leaders of a military government.) Others may be influenced indirectly by military officials who lurk in the background, keeping civilian governments dependent on their approval. A considerable number of states that made transitions to democracy in recent decades were ruled by military officials, either directly or indirectly, just before embarking on the democratic path. These include such disparate countries as Spain, Portugal, Greece, South Korea, and a host of countries in Latin America and Africa. Some countries have undergone so many cyclical oscillations between military rule and democracy that one can say with only slight exaggeration that the alternation between these two regime types in effect *is* their system of government.[21] Between 1825 and 1982, for example, Bolivia experienced periods of civilian rule interspersed with more than 180 military seizures of power. Costa Rica abolished its army in 1949 precisely to prevent military intervention in politics; it has been a successful democracy ever since. One of the main tasks that formerly military-ruled countries face as they seek to stabilize democracy is to ensure civilian control of the military.

When is a **coup d'état**—a forceful takeover of state power by the military—most likely to occur? How is it that some countries are more prone to military coups than others? Political scientists who have studied *praetorianism*—the

phenomenon of military intervention in a country's domestic politics—have identified a multiplicity of variables that answer these and related questions. Studies have shown that the likelihood and frequency of coups can be explained by such independent variables as economic stagnation, poorly developed political institutions and poor governmental performance, low levels of popular support for civilian politicians, a breakdown in law and order, and other identifiable factors. The precise mixture of these explanatory variables will vary from country to country and from one period of time to another, but certain patterns are discernible.[22]

In the following section we explore an example of the military in politics, using Turkey as our case study. Case studies provide intensive analyses of single examples. Political scientists, especially those in comparative politics, frequently employ case studies to elucidate the dynamics of politics in context. Although case studies can serve several methodological purposes, we will employ them in many coming chapters to examine in detail examples that illustrate a concept especially well—that is, examples that are particularly representative of

CASE STUDY
The Military in Politics: Turkey

As the Bush administration geared up to invade Iraq in the spring of 2003, the Turkish parliament did something unexpected: It rebuffed intense pressures from the United States, its NATO ally, to station more than 60,000 American troops on Turkish soil for use in the impending combat. With public opinion in Turkey running overwhelmingly against the war, and with U.S. offers of financial assistance falling below the Turkish government's proposed figures, a critical mass of Turkish legislators turned down the American request. The parliament's action was a turning point in the development of Turkish democracy: The Islamic party that had won two-thirds of the seats in the recently elected legislature had survived a controversial vote without serious interference from the Turkish military. In an equally momentous event, the military lifted its ban on the party's leader, Tayyip Erdogan, allowing the parliamentary majority to elect him prime minister. Only three years earlier the military had sentenced Erdogan to prison for "Islamic sedition" and banned him permanently from holding political office.

These developments were the latest in a series of uneasy encounters between the three most powerful forces in Turkish politics—Islam, democracy, and the military. Turkey's population of 70 million is 99.8 percent Muslim (mostly Sunni). For all but a few years, Turkey has been a multiparty democracy since the end of World War II. But the Turkish military command has intervened in the country's democratic processes on several occasions, removing prime ministers, outlawing parties, and even suspending democracy itself by imposing

direct military rule on the population. In justifying these interventions, Turkey's military leaders have claimed a special responsibility for maintaining a secular state and preventing it from being taken over by proponents of an overtly Islamic political orientation. They have also regarded their interventions as attempts to defend democracy rather than subvert it (or allow others to subvert it). The military's special role as the guardian of Turkey's secular and democratic principles is not a recent phenomenon. It is rooted in the very foundations of the country's post-Ottoman regime and in the ideology of its charismatic founding father, Mustafa Kemal Atatürk (1880/1–1938).

Mustafa Kemal was himself a military man. Although he defended the Ottoman Empire as a heroic commander in World War I, he also believed that the time had come for the 600-year-old dynasty to end. As Britain, France, Greece, and Armenia moved to carve up what remained of Turkey and its possessions after the First World War, in which it had allied with the defeated powers, Germany and Austria-Hungary, Mustafa Kemal took charge of a revolt against the sultanate in 1919. By the following year he headed a rival government in Ankara, backed by rising national sentiment against the weak Ottoman regime in Constantinople (Istanbul). In 1921 he was named commander-in-chief of the army by Turkey's Grand National Assembly, which formally abolished the sultanate in 1922. In 1923, after Turkey's troops had reclaimed some of its lost territory, Mustafa Kemal's ascent to power was completed as the Assembly proclaimed a republic and elected him president.

From the outset, Mustafa Kemal was determined to modernize Turkey's political, social, and cultural foundations. The principal ideas of what became known as *Kemalism* included a secular state and a commitment to raising Turkey to the ranks of the European powers. A constitution adopted in 1924 incorporated the main principles of Kemalist doctrine. In the same year, his government abolished the Caliphate, the spiritual center of Islam that the Ottoman sultans had claimed as their patrimony. In accordance with the concept of *laïcité* (secularity) inscribed in the constitution, Kemalism demanded a strict separation of mosque and state. Over the next decade Islam was deprived of its constitutional status as the country's official religion, religious courts were closed, and women's head scarves and men's clerical dress were banned outside mosques. To this day, the state's Directorate of Religious Affairs regulates many religious activities, at times even dictating the content of sermons. Women saw their civil and political rights gradually enlarged; in 1934 they won the right to vote in parliamentary elections and run for the national legislature. In 1928 the government replaced the Arabic script with the Roman alphabet for written Turkish. Mustafa Kemal moved Turkey closer to the West in other ways as well, joining the League of Nations in 1932 and signing various border agreements affirming Turkey's role as a European state. In 1934 he adopted the surname Atatürk ("Father Turk").[23]

Atatürk expected the military to be the guardian of his political legacy, but he clearly preferred civilian government to military rule. He did not want the military to play a direct role in politics. Nevertheless, events after his death induced the military to intervene several times in the political fray. During Atatürk's lifetime, Turkey was essentially a one-party state. The ruling party was the Republican People's Party (CHP), founded by Atatürk himself. After World War II, Turkey evolved into a multiparty democracy. Until 1961 there were two main parties: the Kemalist CHP and a right-wing party, the Democrat Party (DP), led by Adnan Menderes, who became

Mustafa Kemal Atatürk, the first president of Turkey.

prime minister. When violent unrest developed in 1960 after the government limited press freedoms and displayed other authoritarian tendencies, Menderes imposed martial law. (*Martial law* substitutes various military rules of justice for civil law. It typically suspends the presumption of innocence, the right to protection against arbitrary search and arrest, and other civil rights.) The military responded in May 1960 by taking power. Charging that the government was violating Kemalist precepts and that its policies were bringing the country to the brink of disintegration, the chief of the army general staff ordered troops to seize official buildings. The prime minister, the president, and numerous members of parliament were arrested. Menderes, who was accused of trying to establish a dictatorship, was later hanged. In 1961 the military leadership formed a constituent assembly to write a new constitution, which was approved in a referendum. Following parliamentary elections later in the year in which 14 parties participated, the military relinquished power.

In 1971 the military stepped into the political arena again. When rising frustration over the government's failure to adopt the economic, social, and land reforms promised in the new constitution provoked violent protests, the military leadership sent a memo to the president calling for a "strong and credible government" capable of implementing the reforms. The memo warned of military intervention if no action was taken. The prime minister promptly resigned and a new government was formed in response to what was called the "coup by memo."

The Turkish military intervened in domestic politics once again in 1980. Discontent was growing over the failure of a succession of weak center-right and center-left governments to deal with the economic problems generated by the rise in world oil prices in the 1970s. In addition, a growing number of Turkish Muslims, represented by the National Salvation Party led by Necmettin Erbakan, were demanding an end to the restrictions on religious dress and were calling for the adoption of Islamic law. There was also mounting violence in Turkey's Kurdish areas, where an independence movement was gathering strength. Strikes were occurring with increasing frequency, often with the support of the small Turkish Communist Party. And an extreme right-wing party was resorting to street violence and terrorism against its opponents, provoking the government to impose martial law. Sensing that Turkey was heading toward chaos and that the government was violating Kemalist principles, the military seized power. The Islamic party leader Erbakan was sentenced to two years in prison.

The military-appointed government stabilized the economy somewhat, and in 1982 a new constitution was approved by 91 percent of the voters in a referendum. A 10-year ban on political activity was placed on all politicians who were active before the 1980 military intervention. The military did not give up power until 1983, when elections were held for a new parliament. Only three parties were permitted to run in those elections (though more parties were permitted the following year). Martial law was finally lifted in 1984.

(Continued on next page)

(Continued from previous page)

Elections held in 1995 produced a parliamentary plurality for the Welfare Party (Refah), an ideologically Islamic party led by Erbakan, the veteran political leader who became prime minister. His efforts to ease restrictions on Islamic dress and steer Turkey's foreign policy away from its close attachment to the United States and from its long-standing cooperation with Israel provoked the military leadership into action. In 1997 the military-dominated National Security Council pressured Erbakan to resign. It subsequently banned the Welfare Party, accusing it of "conspiring against the secular order." The constitutional court barred Erbakan and five other party officials from political life for five years. Although the military's intervention was technically not a coup, it forcefully demonstrated that the military hierarchy was still the guardian of Kemalist ideals and remained the final arbiter of Turkish politics, exercising ultimate authority.

In parliamentary elections held in 2002, Tayyip Erdogan's Justice and Development Party (AKP) won a resounding victory, capturing 363 (66 percent) of the Grand National Assembly's 550 seats. The only other party to win seats in the new parliament was the Kemalist Republican People's Party. Erdogan was on record as favoring the adoption of Islamic law in place of Turkey's civil law and had been banned from holding political office for life. However, to gain power, Erdogan adopted an unmistakably moderate message during the election campaign, asserting that the AKP was a "conservative democratic party" that regarded "secularism as the guarantee of all religious faiths." He also vowed to maintain Turkey's ties with the United States, its "natural ally," and to press for Turkey's admission into the European Union. Because Erdogan was not permitted to become prime minister, his

party's deputy leader assumed that office after the elections. But in March 2003, as American pressures on Turkey mounted during the buildup to war in Iraq, Turkish military authorities lifted the ban on Erdogan's right to hold office. Shortly after he assumed his parliamentary seat, his party's large majority in the legislature elected Erdogan prime minister.

Erdogan's prodemocracy Islamic party was viewed by many in Washington and other world capitals as a role model for the Islamic world. Although Erdogan hewed to the moderate course he had promised during the election campaign, Turkey's military high command made it known that it was watching from the wings. It still retained five votes on the nine-member National Security Council, the secretive body that had a powerful behind-the-scenes influence on government decisions. But in the summer of 2003, Erdogan's government got the parliament to pass an unprecedented law declaring that the National Security Council was purely an advisory body with no decision-making authority. The legislation further stipulated that the NSC's secretary-general, typically a four-star general, could be a civilian in the future, and it opened up the military budget to parliamentary oversight.

Erdogan's government took these actions at the behest of the European Union, which had been pressuring the Turkish government to curb the military's power. Turkey has had an "association agreement" with the European community since 1963, and it applied for full membership in 1987. In 2002 the EU laid down guidelines requiring major civil rights and other reforms as prerequisites for Turkey's admission. Since then, Erdogan's government has reformed Turkey's penal code, outlawed torture and the death penalty, and extended women's rights. It has also sought to improve the government's relations with Turkey's 15 million Kurds.

More recently, the military sought unsuccessfully in 2007 to deny the largely ceremonial role of president to the AKP's Abdullah Gul, who was then foreign minister and deputy prime minister. In 2010 the AKP successfully put several constitutional amendments to a referendum, including one that removed any immunity from prosecution for former military leaders. Since then the elderly leaders of the 1980 coup have been put on trial and hundreds of other currently serving and retired Turkish military officers have been arrested on allegations of plotting to overthrow the government. In the current struggle between secularism, as represented by the military, and Islam, by the AKP, democracy seems to be the real winner. The Turkish people have not proven sympathetic to military claims to special status, which they have shown by returning the AKP to power at elections in 2007 and 2011 and by passing the AKP's proposed constitutional amendments in the 2010 referendum. Those constitutional amendments have moved Turkey closer to meeting the EU's democratic requirements for accession.

Tayyip Erdogan, Turkey's prime minister since 2003.

a concept. Case studies allow scholars to trace political processes in a single example closely, yielding insights about the calculations of political actors in ways that comparing several examples cannot provide. Here we consider Turkey, where the military has acted as a modernizing force with greater success than in any other country—indeed, it is an archetypical case, because the Turkish military's modernizing efforts were regarded by some proponents as worthy of emulation by militaries in other countries.

HOW STATES ARE ORGANIZED

Thus far our survey of state institutions has focused exclusively on the national state—that is, on the central organs (usually located in the capital city) that have responsibility for the country as a whole. But local authorities can also be of fundamental importance in determining how the political system works in a country. Just how important these subnational governmental bodies are can vary considerably from one place to the next.

Some countries provide relatively little room for subnational authorities to govern independently of the national government. In a **unitary state**, decision-making authority and disposition over revenues are concentrated in the central institutions. France and Japan are examples.

By contrast, a **federation** seeks to combine a relatively strong central government with real authority for various administrative units below the national level. These subunits may be regions, provinces or states (e.g., California), counties, municipalities, and the like. In these federal systems the subnational units usually have their own locally selected officials and, in some cases, the right to raise their own revenue through local taxes of various kinds. At the same time, they are usually dependent on the national government for some of their budgetary funding, and they must conform to certain national laws. Examples of federalism include the United States, Germany, the Russian Federation, and India. Until 1999, the United Kingdom of Great Britain and Northern Ireland used to be a classic example of a unitary state, but the establishment of local legislatures in Scotland, Wales, and Northern Ireland signified a historic shift toward a federal system.

A **confederation** is an even looser arrangement characterized by a weak central state and a group of constituent subnational elements that enjoy significant autonomy or even independence as sovereign states. In confederal systems the central government's functions are mainly confined to such basic tasks as providing for the national defense, issuing the currency, and delivering the mail. In many issues the central government cannot act without the consent of the subnational governments. Switzerland is an example. The Swiss Confederation's central government possesses only those powers—foreign affairs, national defense, the federal railways, and minting the currency—explicitly ceded to it by the 20 cantons and six half-cantons that make up the country.[24] The United Arab Emirates, consisting of seven monarchies, is another contemporary confederation. Before adoption of the U.S. Constitution in 1789, the 13 states were organized under the Articles of Confederation of 1777. That system proved to be too decentralized for many Americans, and at the urging of "federalists" such as James Madison and Alexander Hamilton, a federal system was established in its place.

Large countries—both in terms of population and geographical size—are the most apt to use federalist or confederal state structures, as Table 3.2 indicates. Geographically large countries have been more able to govern their vast regions by giving decision-making autonomy to their regional, provincial, or state governments than by trying to rule from a great distance. This challenge was obviously greater when communications and transportation were more difficult than would be the case now, but the federal structures were put into place long ago in most federalist countries. Geographically vast and highly populated countries are also likely to be ethnically diverse; federal regimes allow for the possibility of giving ethnic groups greater autonomy in decision making too. India provides a classic example. Most of the small states that are federalist—those at the bottom of Table 3.2—came together when two or more separate political entities merged or else they are island federations spread across large stretches of ocean. Switzerland is an early example, having adopted its confederal constitution in 1848. The United Arab Emirates formed in 1971, and the tiny Caribbean Federation of St. Kitts and Nevis became independent from Britain in 1983. These small exceptions aside, 40 percent of the world's population lives in the 25 federalist states listed in Table 3.2 (on page 60).

HYPOTHESES ON THE STATE

"Why can't the government get it right?" Anyone who has ever asked this question has probably experienced the frustration of watching government officials or agencies fail to respond adequately to some problem affecting the population. Sometimes the state takes too long to legislate or make authoritative decisions on pressing issues. At other times government officials make bad decisions that fail to resolve the problem or only make matters worse.

Sometimes laws or regulations are not implemented in accordance with their intended purposes. In some cases, local governments may not have the resources needed to carry out decisions imposed on them by the national government ("unfunded mandates"). In others, enforcement officials deliberately refuse to carry out laws they do not like, a phenomenon that has occurred in the United States over such issues as civil rights and gun control. Sometimes laws and regulations work at cross-purposes. (The U.S. government has routinely subsidized tobacco growers while simultaneously conducting antismoking campaigns.) And sometimes governmental institutions are unable to make *any* kind of decision in response to well-known problems, especially when the alternative solutions are politically controversial. Bureaucratic red tape, wasteful government spending, inefficient managerial practices—the catalog of complaints is a long one, and the complaints themselves are strikingly common throughout the world.[25]

Table 3.2 Federalist Countries Listed by World Population Rank

Country	WORLD RANK	
	Population	Area
India	2	7
United States	3	3
Brazil	4	5
Pakistan	5	36
Nigeria	6	32
Russia	9	1
Mexico	11	14
Ethiopia	13	27
Germany	16	63
South Africa	26	25
Spain	27	52
Argentina	32	8
Canada	36	2
Nepal	41	94
Malaysia	43	67
Venezuela	45	33
Australia	54	6
Belgium	82	141
Austria	94	114
Switzerland	96	136
United Arab Emirates	115	27
Bosnia and Herzegovina	122	129
Comoros	164	180
Micronesia	191	191
St. Kitts and Nevis	207	211

Sources: Forum of Federations, at www.forumfed.org; Central Intelligence Agency, *World Fact Book,* at https://www.cia.gov/library/publications/the-world-factbook/rankorder/rankorderguide.html, accessed May 12, 2012.

To be sure, sometimes states do get things right; people often take for granted the positive things that governmental actions actually accomplish. Nevertheless, states seldom operate at optimal levels of efficiency or effectiveness. *Efficiency* is the process of making decisions in a smooth and timely fashion, and *effectiveness* means resolving problems successfully.

Though we cannot possibly look into all the reasons for these inadequacies here, we can at least briefly examine a few hypotheses concerning the ways governments formulate and implement their policies.

Divided Government

A **divided government** exists when the executive branch is controlled by one political party and the legislature is controlled by the opposite party or parties. The United States is frequently singled out in this regard. When the president is a Republican and the congressional majority is in the hands of the Democrats, or vice versa, gridlock—the inability to agree

on legislation—may result. In a comprehensive study, Sarah Binder found that gridlock is likely to occur at statistically significant levels under conditions of divided government in the United States.[26] Nevertheless, there is no guarantee that laws will be passed quickly when the president and the congressional majority represent the same party. Democratic presidents Jimmy Carter and Bill Clinton, to name just two, did not always get what they wanted out of Democrat-controlled Congresses. France and Brazil have their own variants of divided government, as we shall see in Part Two. So do other countries.

In contrast to the American or French-style political system, in which the chief executive and the national legislature are elected separately, some people extol the British-style parliamentary system as more efficient and less prone to gridlock. In a parliamentary system, the party or parties that have the majority of seats in the legislature decide who the head of government will be. As a consequence, the executive branch and the legislative majority represent the same party or parties. Divided government occurs only in rare exceptions to this general rule. For example, Britain's Labour Party won 63 percent of the seats in the House of Commons in the 1997 elections. Labour's leader, Tony Blair, was promptly installed as the country's new prime minister as a result. Blair's government consequently managed to get virtually all its legislation passed by the Labour majority in the Commons with considerable efficiency.

As we will see in subsequent chapters, however, the parliamentary system does not always produce this happy outcome. In some countries the parliamentary majority consists of two or more parties, resulting in a coalition government that represents these multiple parties. It often happens that, the more parties there are in the cabinet, the harder it is for them to agree on government policies. Gridlock frequently results. We will discuss the parliamentary system and coalition governments in greater detail in Chapter 6. Even Britain's one-party governments can be so internally divided that they find it difficult to legislate, as we will see in Chapter 13. The evidence is quite mixed when it comes to determining whether parliamentary government is decisively better than divided government in the lawmaking process.

Rational Decision Making versus "Satisficing"

The process of transforming ideas into laws through executive–legislative interaction is invariably a complicated one, especially in democracies. Government decision makers must consider a diversity of competing demands and interests and measure what needs to be done against the resources available to do it. It should hardly be surprising that the lawmaking process does not always result in the "best" laws, if by "best" we mean the most rational solutions to specific problems or the most effective ways of improving the general well-being of the population. In a great number of cases, the laws that emerge from the executive–legislative process reflect such things as the priorities of legislative majorities, the pressures of highly influential lobbies or social groups, and the outcomes of bargaining and compromises among elected officials, most of whom are motivated largely by the desire to get reelected. Instead of "the best" or the most rational laws, the lawmaking process in democracies frequently produces laws that are *the most politically acceptable* to a majority of legislators and to relevant executive branch decision makers.

The term that most often describes this process is *satisficing*. It comes from the old English word *satisfice*, which meant "to satisfy." In contemporary political science, *satisficing* means making decisions that are satisfactory, or "good enough" rather than the best of all available options. In large organizations like states, satisficing reflects the central reality that decisions must often be reached through a bargaining process involving negotiation and compromise. Decisions reached through a process of satisficing are not necessarily the "best" decisions because those who make them cannot agree on what the best decision is, or because the best decision for the community at large may damage the interests of some specific segment of it.

What is best for the national economy? Economists may tell us that we need to reduce or eliminate budget deficits, and they may supply all sorts of statistical analyses charting the widespread benefits to be gained from such measures. Analytical studies may also provide convincing evidence that the most efficient and rational way to cut the deficit is to raise taxes *and* curtail state spending simultaneously. But if some people do not want to pay higher taxes and others do not want to give up their public jobs or welfare benefits, how can the elected officials who represent them manage to take the "best" and most appropriate action? All too often, they cannot. Rather than raising taxes and reducing expenditures in the most economically efficient manner, cabinets and legislatures may decide to raise taxes only slightly (or not at all) and to curtail state spending only slightly (or not at all).

Elected legislatures are especially prone to satisficing. Legislators are often divided among themselves for the simple reason that the people who elected them are divided. But what about the executive branch and its bureaucracies? Should we not expect the cabinet, which generally consists of a small number of relatively like-minded individuals chosen by the president or prime minister, to make policy decisions far more efficiently than a fractious legislature?

One model suggests that the executive branch of government does in fact operate in a relatively efficient and unified manner. As already noted, Max Weber was one of the first students of modern bureaucracy. Drawing his information largely from Germany's bureaucracy at the start of the twentieth century, Weber developed a hypothetical *ideal type* of bureaucratic structure and behavior emphasizing the following characteristics:

- *Hierarchy.* Bureaucracies, in Weber's model, are structured in a hierarchical fashion from the top down, with a clear chain of command enabling them to respond efficiently to directives.
- *Specialization.* There is a clearly demarcated, stable division of labor among the bureaucracy's organizational

components, and the bureaucrats themselves are chosen solely on the basis of their professional competence.

- *Impersonal rules.* Bureaucracies are run in accordance with carefully spelled out rules and regulations, another factor that makes for efficient and predictable operations. The modern bureaucracy applies these rules impersonally, without granting special favors to privileged individuals or groups.
- *Rationality.* "Bureaucracy," Weber wrote, "has a 'rational' character: rules, means, ends, and matter-of-factness dominate its bearing." The whole bureaucratic process is highly organized to achieve the state's objectives efficiently and effectively. "Precision, speed, unambiguity, knowledge of the files, continuity, discretion, unity, strict subordination, reduction of friction and of material and personal costs—these are raised to the optimum point in the strictly bureaucratic administration."[27]

Weber's model is known as the **unitary actor model** of decision making, a process in which all the elements of a state's bureaucracy work together as though they were a single actor. But do modern states actually function this way?

A far different picture of executive-level policy making emerges from more recent studies of organizational behavior. The pioneering work of economists James March and Herbert Simon demonstrated that large organizations, whether private corporations or state bureaucracies, rarely operate as rationally and efficiently as Weber maintained. Hierarchical chains of command are frequently ignored. Critical information may not be available. The "best" alternative solutions are not always carefully considered, let alone chosen. On the contrary, bureaucracies, like legislatures, often indulge in satisficing, with executives and staff personnel engaging in negotiations and compromises that lead to decisions that are good enough to win a large consensus, but are not necessarily the most effective ways to resolve the problem under consideration. Moreover, bureaucrats tend to stick to familiar "standard operating procedures": They do not like to take bold initiatives whose results are unpredictable or ambiguous. New approaches to dealing with society's problems therefore tend to differ very little from past approaches, even if they have not worked very well.

The result is *incrementalism:* Change, if it comes at all, is marginal rather than radical. Experimentation is discouraged. If asked by the head of government or cabinet chiefs to come up with innovative solutions to problems or if ordered to implement unfamiliar directives or rules, bureaucracies may misunderstand, ignore, or even sabotage the new commands.[28]

President Harry Truman probably would have recognized this model of bureaucratic unresponsiveness. Sympathizing with the problems Dwight D. Eisenhower would inherit on assuming the presidency, Truman predicted, "He'll sit here, and he'll say, 'Do this! Do that!' And nothing will happen. Poor Ike—it won't be a bit like the Army. He'll find it very frustrating."[29]

A gripping account of how bureaucratic behavior and executive-level decision making can go awry is Graham Allison's analysis of the Cuban missile crisis of 1962.

HYPOTHESIS-TESTING EXERCISE
The Cuban Missile Crisis

In October 1962, American spy planes flying over Cuba identified Soviet construction crews building missile sites. The discovery came several weeks after the missile construction program had begun. It did not occur earlier because the U.S. State Department had temporarily suspended aerial surveillance of Cuba after China shot down a U.S. spy plane. The delay was further protracted when the U.S. Air Force and the Central Intelligence Agency became snarled in a bureaucratic

battle over whose pilots would fly a new U-2 reconnaissance aircraft. This delay was one of many bureaucratic bungles and misunderstandings that complicated President Kennedy's attempts to get the Soviets to remove the missiles while at the same time avoiding nuclear war.

Hypothesis and Variables In a classic analysis, Graham Allison tested the hypothesis that bureaucratic rationality, as characterized by the unitary actor model of decision making, explained state behavior in the Cuban missile crisis. In this hypothesis, the *dependent variable* is state behavior, and the *independent variable* is bureaucratic rationality.

Expectations If the unitary actor model is an accurate representation of how the state operated during the Cuban missile crisis, then we would expect to find that the president, his key advisors, and the various agencies of the federal government involved in making policy decisions possessed all the information they needed to make well-considered, rational decisions; that they were essentially unified in their analysis of the situation and on the measures they needed to take; and that they implemented these measures smoothly and effectively, following established lines of command.

Evidence Whereas rational decision making requires relatively complete information about a problem, Allison showed that Kennedy and his advisors did not have *any* information about Soviet activities in Cuba until it was almost too late. Moreover, they had no clear information about Soviet

Photographic evidence from a U2 spy plane led President Kennedy and his staff to confront the Soviet leadership about the placement of missiles in Cuba in October 1962.

Conclusion

The state is the central reality of modern political life. How states are organized, how they operate, and how people interact with them are issues that we will examine in most of the chapters that follow. As we do, it bears remembering that the state is where authoritative decisions are made for the people living in the territory that the state claims. But who are those people the state governs? In the modern world, the group of people governed by a state is often regarded as a nation. In the next chapter, we will examine the concept of the nation and explore the extent to which national identity provides unity among the people governed by a state and eases the state's challenge of establishing the legitimacy of its rule.

Key Terms

State
Regime
Government
Failed state

Sovereignty
Legitimacy
Authority
Autonomy of the state
Anarchism
Institutionalism
Executive branch
Head of state
Constitutional (limited) monarchy
Head of government
Legislature
Unicameral legislature
Bicameral legislature
Judiciary
Judicial review
Bureaucracy
Coup d'état
Unitary state
Federation
Confederation
Divided government
Unitary actor model

motives. Were the Soviets putting missiles in Cuba in order to bomb or threaten the United States? Were they trying to set up a bargaining situation in hopes of inducing the United States to remove its missiles from Turkey, a NATO ally located on the USSR's borders, in exchange for withdrawing the Cuban missiles? Were they trying to defend Castro's regime against a potential U.S. attack? The administration similarly knew little about Soviet resolve. Would Kremlin leaders back down if the United States used military force to compel Moscow to remove the missiles, or would they risk mutual nuclear annihilation rather than give in?

The evidence also showed that the key state agencies involved in the crisis did not act in a unified fashion. Beyond the tug-of-war over the U-2 flights, the military chiefs of the Air Force and the Navy had different ideas about how to implement a possible "surgical" air strike of the missile sites and a naval blockade of Cuba, which differed considerably from the ways the president, the secretary of defense, and other top decision makers understood those policy options.

In addition, Allison saw no evidence of unity among the 14 key individuals involved in the decision-making process. Each had his own perceptions of what the Soviets were up to and how best to deal with them. Some were influenced by the nature of their professional roles. In accordance with the adage "Where you stand depends on where you sit," the chief military advisors favored military solutions, including bombardment of the missile sites and an invasion of Cuba.

Others, including the president, feared that this approach might lead to nuclear war. They favored a political solution. Over the course of the two-week-long crisis, this team of decision makers engaged in a continuing process of negotiating, bargaining, and coalition building. Some changed their minds in the process.

Ultimately the president decided on a naval blockade of the island to prevent more missile shipments from coming in. The world breathed a sigh of relief when the Soviet leadership decided to remove the missiles from Cuba.

Conclusions The evidence Allison uncovered was largely *inconsistent* with the hypothesis of rational decision making as predicted by the unitary actor model. Allison concluded that two other models offered more accurate depictions of decision making in the Cuban missile crisis. One of them, the *organizational process* model, describes decision making as a more disjointed process involving miscommunication, insufficient information, poor coordination, and other "irrational" phenomena described by analysts like March and Simon. The other one, which Allison called the *bureaucratic politics* (or *governmental politics*) model, emphasizes the different viewpoints that divided President Kennedy and the 13 other key individuals involved in finding a solution to the crisis.[30]

Far from being a smooth, "rational" undertaking, the policy process in most countries is often a disjointed affair. One political scientist famously referred to governing as "the science of muddling through."[31]

Notes

1. Ralph Miliband, *The State in Capitalist Society* (New York: Basic Books, 1969); and David Wells, *Marxism and the Modern State* (Brighton, UK: Harvester, 1981). For discussions of different conceptions of the state, see James A. Caporaso, ed., *The Elusive State: International and Comparative Perspectives* (Newbury Park, Calif.: Sage, 1989).

2. Thomas J. Biersteker and Cynthia Weber, eds., *State Sovereignty as Social Construct* (Cambridge: Cambridge University Press, 1996); Stephen D. Krasner, *Sovereignty: Organized Hypocrisy* (Princeton, NJ: Princeton University Press, 1999).

3. "Politics as a Vocation," in *From Max Weber: Essays in Sociology,* trans. and ed. H. Gerth and C. Wright Mills (New York: Oxford University Press, 1946), p. 78.

4. Thomas Hobbes, *Leviathan* (New York: Cambridge University Press, 1991); Deborah Baumgold, *Hobbes's Political Theory* (New York: Cambridge University Press, 1988); Arnold A. Rogow, *Thomas Hobbes: Radical in the Service of Reaction* (New York: W. W. Norton, 1986).

5. John Locke, *Two Treatises of Government* (New York: Cambridge University Press, 1988); Ruth Grant, *John Locke's Liberalism* (Chicago: University of Chicago Press, 1987); Maurice Cranston, *John Locke: A Biography* (New York: Macmillan, 1967).

6. Jean-Jacques Rousseau, *The Collected Works of Jean-Jacques Rousseau* (Hanover, NH: University Press of New England, 1990); Leo Damrosch, *Jean-Jacques Rousseau: Restless Genius* (Boston: Houghton Mifflin, 2005); Maurice Cranston, *Jean-Jacques: The Early Life and Work of Jean-Jacques Rousseau* (Chicago: University of Chicago Press, 1983); Maurice Cranston, *The Noble Savage: Jean-Jacques Rousseau, 1754–1762* (Chicago:

University of Chicago Press, 1991); Hilail Gildin, *Rousseau's "Social Contract": The Design of the Argument* (Chicago: University of Chicago Press, 1983); Richard Fralin, *Rousseau and Representation* (New York: Columbia University Press, 1978); Judith N. Shklar, *Men and Citizens: A Study of Rousseau's Social Theory* (Cambridge: Cambridge University Press, 1969).

7. See Charles Tilly, "War Making and State Making as Organized Crime," in *Bringing the State Back In,* ed. Peter B. Evans, Dietrich Rueschemeyer, and Theda Skocpol (Cambridge: Cambridge University Press, 1985), pp. 169–91; Mancur Olson, "Dictatorship, Democracy, and Development," *American Political Science Review* 87, no. 3 (September 1993), pp. 567–76. Also Charles Tilly, ed., *The Formation of National States in Western Europe* (Princeton: Princeton University Press, 1975), and Martin van Creveld, *The Rise and Decline of the State* (Cambridge: Cambridge University Press, 1999).

8. Robert Nozick, *Anarchy, the State, and Utopia* (New York: Basic Books, 1974); April Carter, *The Political Theory of Anarchism* (New York: Harper & Row, 1971); Emma Goldman, *Anarchism, and Other Essays* (New York: Dover, 1969); Emma Goldman, *Living My Life* (New York: AMS Press, 1970); Marian J. Morton, *Emma Goldman and the American Left: "Nowhere At Home"* (New York: Twayne, 1992); Robert Paul Wolff, *In Defense of Anarchism* (New York: Harper & Row, 1970).

9. See Robert I. Rotberg, *When States Fail: Causes and Consequences* (Princeton: Princeton University Press, 2004). The World Bank has its own quality-of-governance indicators; see Chapter 12.

10. *Country Profile: Pakistan* (Washington: Fund for Peace, 2011), available at http://www.fundforpeace.org/global/states/ccppr11pk-countryprofile-pakistan-11t.pdf.

11. Jack A. Goldstone, "Pathways to State Failure," *Conflict Management and Peace Science* 25 (2008), pp. 285–96.

12. http://www.foreignpolicy.com/failedstates and http://www.fundforpeace .org/global/?q=fsi.

13. For a good overview, see R. Kent Weaver and Bert A. Rockman, *Do Institutions Matter?* (Washington, DC: Brookings Institution, 1993).

14. See Seymour Martin Lipset, *The First New Nation: The United States in Historical and Comparative Perspective* (New York: Basic Books, 1963).

15. See Giovanni Sartori, *Comparative Constitutional Engineering: An Inquiry into Structures, Incentives, and Outcomes* (New York: New York University Press, 1997).

16. For a sophisticated game-theoretic analysis of legislative voting, see George Tsebelis, *Veto Players: How Political Institutions Work* (New York: Russell Sage Foundation, 2002). See also Gerhard Loewenberg, Peverill Squire, and D. Roderick Kiewiet, eds., *Legislatures: Comparative Perspectives on Representative Assemblies* (Ann Arbor: University of Michigan Press, 2002); Jean Blondel, *Comparative Legislatures* (Englewood Cliffs, NJ: Prentice Hall, 1973); Gerhard Loewenberg and Samuel C. Patterson, *Comparing Legislatures* (Boston: Little, Brown, 1979); Michael L. Mezey, *Comparative Legislatures* (Durham, NC: Duke University Press, 1979); Hannah F. Pitkin, *The Concept of Representation* (Berkeley: University of California Press, 1972).

17. Nathan J. Brown, *The Rule of Law in the Arab World* (Cambridge: Cambridge University Press, 1997).

18. For some comparative approaches to the judiciary, see Mauro Cappelletti, *The Judicial Process in a Comparative Perspective* (New York: Oxford University Press, 1989); Alan M. Katz, ed., *Legal Traditions and Systems: An International Handbook* (Westport, CT: Greenwood Press, 1986); Jerold L. Waltman and Kenneth M. Holland, eds., *The Political Role of the Law Courts in Modern Democracies* (New York: St. Martin's Press, 1988).

19. Randall Baker, ed., *Transitions from Authoritarianism: The Role of the Bureaucracy* (Westport, CT: Praeger, 2002).

20. On the U.S. bureaucracy, see James Q. Wilson, *Bureaucracy: What Government Agencies Do and Why They Do It* (New York: Basic Books, 1989); William T. Gormley, Jr., *Taming the Bureaucracy* (Princeton, NJ: Princeton University Press, 1989). For comparative studies, see B. Guy Peters, *The Politics of Bureaucracy: A Comparative Perspective,* 3rd ed. (White Plains, NY: Longman, 1989); Frank Fischer, *Technocracy and the Politics of Expertise* (Newbury Park, CA: Sage, 1990); Jon Pierre, *Bureaucracy in the Modern State: An Introduction to Comparative Public Administration* (Aldershot, England: E. Elgar, 1995); Joel D. Auerbach, Robert A. Putnam, and Bert A. Rockman, *Bureaucrats and Politicians in Western Democracies* (Cambridge, MA: Harvard University Press, 1981).

21. Samuel P. Huntington, *The Third Wave: Democratization in the Late Twentieth Century* (Norman: University of Oklahoma Press, 1991), p. 42.

22. Three classic studies are Morris Janowitz, *The Professional Soldier: A Social and Political Portrait* (Glencoe, IL: Free Press, 1960); Samuel P. Huntington, *The Soldier and the State: The Theory and Politics of Civil-Military Relations* (New York: Vintage, 1964); Samuel E. Finer, *The Man on Horseback* (Oxford: Pall Mall Press, 1962). For a sweeping comparative analysis, see Eric A. Nordlinger, *Soldiers in Politics: Military Coups and Governments* (Englewood Cliffs, NJ: Prentice Hall, 1977). For an advanced statistical study, see Robert W. Jackman, "The Predictability of Coups d'État: A Model with African Data," *American Political Science Review* 72, no. 4 (December 1978), pp. 1262–75.

23. Andrew Mango, *Atatürk* (Woodstock, NY: Overlook, 1999).

24. Wolf Linder, *Swiss Democracy: Possible Solutions to Conflict in Multicultural Societies* (New York: St. Martin's Press, 1994).

25. On policy implementation in the United States, see Jeffrey Pressman and Aaron Wildavsky, *Implementation: How Great Expectations in Washington Are Dashed in Oakland,* 3rd ed. (Berkeley: University of California Press, 1984).

26. Sarah Binder, *Stalemate: Causes and Consequences of Legislative Gridlock* (Washington, DC: Brookings Institution, 2003). See also Robert Elgie, ed., *Divided Government in Comparative Perspective* (Oxford: Oxford University Press, 2001).

27. *From Max Weber,* ed. Gerth and Mills, pp. 196–244.

28. James G. March and Herbert A. Simon, *Organizations* (New York: Wiley, 1958); Herbert A. Simon, *Administrative Behavior,* 3rd ed. (New York: Free Press, 1975); Herbert A. Simon, *Models of Man: Social and Rational* (New York: Wiley, 1957); James G. March, *Decisions and Organizations* (Oxford: Blackwell, 1989).

29. Cited in Richard Neustadt, *Presidential Power* (New York: Wiley, 1960), p. 9.

30. Graham T. Allison, *Essence of Decision* (Boston: Little, Brown, 1971). The notion that "where you stand depends upon where you sit" is attributed to Rufus Miles, a former U.S. assistant secretary of Health, Education and Welfare, and is known as Miles's law.

31. Charles E. Lindblom, "The Science of 'Muddling Through,'" *Public Administration Review* 19 (1959), pp. 79–88; Charles E. Lindblom, "Still Muddling, Not Yet Through," *Public Administration Review* 39 (1979), pp. 517–26. See also Brian Hogwood, *From Crisis to Complacency: Shaping Public Policy* (Oxford: Oxford University Press, 1987); Charles E. Lindblom and Edward J. Woodhouse, *The Policy-Making Process,* 3rd ed. (Englewood Cliffs, NJ: Prentice Hall, 1993).

States and Nations
Nationalism, Nation Building, Supranationalism

A nationalist in the new state of South Sudan expresses his commitment to his nation.

OVERVIEW

- The strongest bond that holds together the people governed by a state is national identity. National identities arise from various sources, most often a common ethnic identity, but each nation sees itself as unique.

- Nationalist movements seek to achieve national independence if that does not yet exist and then to build their own state.

- Although the norm or ideal in today's world may be the nation-state, or one state for each nation, in many of the most conflicted parts of the world congruence between nation and state does not exist.

- In some cases, as in the Palestinian–Israeli conflict, two nations contend for the same territory.

- In others, such as Sudan or the former Yugoslavia, a single state governs several peoples with nationalist aspirations.

- The European Union exemplifies supranationalism, the political integration of several nation-states.

WHAT IS A NATION?

In Chapter 3 we looked at states as governing organizations. We identified their main institutions and examined some of the ways they work. Of course, states do not hang loosely in the air; they must be connected with the people under their jurisdiction if they are to serve a meaningful purpose and endure over time. We've already noted the importance of legitimacy as a central element in the relationship between governments and populations. This chapter explores another feature of state–society relationships: the concept of *nation*.

When we speak of "national interests" in reference to a state's vital concerns in world affairs, or of "nation building" with regard to the tasks of reconstructing post-Taliban Afghanistan or post-Saddam Iraq, we imply that the "nation" has something to do with governments. In everyday discourse, the terms *nation* and *state* are frequently used interchangeably as synonyms for a country. The members of the United Nations, for example, are governments of countries; the term *national government* refers to a country's central government. But political scientists also use narrower definitions that highlight the distinction between states and nations. Strictly speaking, states and nations are different.

State usually refers to a country's governmental framework, as detailed in Chapter 3. In contrast a **nation** is a group of people whose members share a common identity on the basis of distinguishing characteristics and a claim to a territorial homeland.

A key distinction between nation and state is that a nation may not necessarily have a state of its own, with its own self-governing institutions. To take just one example, the Igbos (or Ibos) of Nigeria have demonstrated that they conceive of themselves as a nation, based on tribal bonds, language patterns, religious affiliations, a territorial base in Nigeria's southeastern region, and other factors. But their alienation from the Nigerian state, which has been largely controlled by groups with different tribal, linguistic, regional, and religious affiliations, prompted the Igbos to rise up in revolt in the 1960s and fight for their own independent state (country), which they planned to call Biafra. The revolt was crushed by Nigeria's military government, and the Igbos were compelled to remain part of Nigeria. But as far as a great many of them were concerned, they remained a nation nevertheless.

For its part, **national identity** is an important component of the very definition of a nation. By itself, it refers to a people's conscious belief that they collectively constitute a nation. It is a shared understanding that they belong together on the basis of certain characteristics that, in their own minds, transcend their differences and set them apart from other national groups. In other words, national identity reflects a people's sense of nationhood. Nations with a strong sense of national identity are bound together by widely diffused, and often deeply felt, attachments and loyalties on the part of the vast majority of their members. Citizens of countries with lower levels of national identity may have stronger identity attachments to smaller groups *within* the nation, such as a clan, an ethnic group, or a religious sect. Severe identity conflicts often

Many ethnic Catalans living in Catalonia, Spain, experience a more powerful regional identity than a national identity. This poster—in Catalan—urges voters in a local referendum to choose independence. While overwhelming majorities have favored independence in nonbinding local referendums in recent years, the Spanish parliament has vetoed efforts by the government of Catalonia to hold a legal referendum on independence across the whole province.

result. The Igbos have a strong sense of their own identity as a nation. Nigerians, by contrast, have a weak sense of national identity *as Nigerians:* Many of them identify more directly with their own respective tribal, linguistic, regional, or religious group, or some combination of these identity markers. The weakness of the Nigerian identity stems from the fact that the state of Nigeria and its boundaries were created by the British, not by the local people (see Chapter 19).

What are the distinguishing characteristics of a people that define their identity as a nation?

One source of national identity can be *ethnicity.* As indicated in Chapter 1, ethnicity is a form of group identification that is usually rooted in a common biological ancestry—or, more precisely, in a people's *belief* in such a common ancestry. Most ethnic groups trace their roots to a historic homeland. Most remain attached to that ancestral territory over the centuries, either physically or—in the case of émigrés or exiles—sentimentally. Ethnicity frequently includes one or more additional marks of group distinctiveness, such as language, religion, social customs, or artistic expression. Even so, it is mainly a family affair: The ethnic group sees itself as an extended family that has survived through the ages. Ethnic attachments can be reinforced by political factors such as common governmental institutions (a monarch, a legal code, a tribal council) as well as by patterns of economic interaction. Nevertheless, ethnicity is separate from government and the economy. Using these defining criteria for ethnicity, James Fearon counted 822 ethnic groups that each made up at least 1 percent of the population in 160 countries in the 1990s.[1]

Although ethnicity can provide a basis for nationhood, "nation" is not simply another term for "ethnic group." What distinguishes the two is that the members of a nation lay claim to a more or less clearly defined territory. They see this territory as belonging to them in some way, whether or not they actually govern it independently of some other governing authority. African-Americans in the United States, Hispanic whites in Mexico, and East Indians in Malaysia are all ethnic groups, but they do not claim a specific territory within their country of residence. Nations that have defined their national identity in ethnic and territorial terms include the Japanese, Chinese, and Germans, as well as smaller groups such as Basques and Catalans in Spain, Pashtuns in Pakistan and Afghanistan, Scots in Scotland, and dozens of others around the world.[2]

Another source of national identity can be a shared *civic community.* In this pattern, people feel that they constitute a nation on the basis of certain shared principles or ideals or community goals, however broadly they may be defined. The United States provides a good example. More than 300 million people representing a wide diversity of ethnic groups and backgrounds identify themselves as Americans largely because of their shared involvement in an American way of life that includes democratic rights and freedoms, private enterprise, and various cultural attitudes and behaviors. Korean-Americans, Italian-Americans, and other "hyphenated" Americans tend to see themselves as part of a larger American nation, while at the same time feeling connected to their respective ethnic groups. The country's history as a land of immigrants and imported slaves helps account for these identity patterns. Switzerland is another example. Its inhabitants speak four languages but nevertheless identify themselves as "Swiss," a national identity that was forged in medieval times and solidified in the nineteenth century. As in the case of ethnically based nationalism, civic forms of national identity include a territorial dimension: The American and Swiss nations both reside within demarcated boundaries.

In some cases a people's identity can be split between an identification with their territorial ethnic group (e.g., Tatars in Russia) and their *citizenship* as members of a state (such as the Russian Federation). If asked to identify their nation (or nationality), such people would most likely respond that they are Tatar. When asked to identify their state or country, they would probably say Russia. (When the USSR existed, they would have said "the Soviet Union" and called themselves Soviet citizens.) Only ethnic Russians would likely identify their nationality as Russian. The Russian Federation is a *multinational state:* It consists of a variety of peoples who have their own separate national identities but are also citizens of the Russian state. Most of the non-Russians were incorporated into the Russian empire in earlier centuries as it expanded across the vast Eurasian landmass, and they became citizens of the Soviet Union (or "Soviets") under communist rule. Multinational states can have serious problems staying together because some of their citizens may be more loyal to their own nationality group than to the central state. Yugoslavia provides a glaring example, and we'll look at it in depth later in this chapter.

One scholar has argued that national identity results from shared patterns of social communication. According to Karl Deutsch, membership in a people "essentially consists in the ability to communicate more effectively, and over a wider range of subjects, with members of one large group than with outsiders." The bonds that tie people together as a nation typically include group myths, historical memories, and emotive symbols such as flags, anthems, and hallowed battlefields. Another scholar has suggested that nations are *imagined* political communities. The nation is imagined, writes Benedict Anderson, "because the members of even the smallest nation will never know most of their fellow-members, meet them, or even hear of them, yet in the minds of each lives the image of their communion."[3]

Students of identity such as Anderson, David Laitin, and Russell Hardin have pointed out that national identity is not fixed forever in some primordial state; to a significant degree it is socially constructed. Individuals cannot change their DNA or their blood relations, but they can change their national identity, making choices that vary with the social and political circumstances in which they find themselves. A Russian-speaking Tatar who lived in the Ukrainian Soviet Republic in the days of the Soviet Union, and who now finds herself living in independent Ukraine, can no longer identify herself ambivalently as Soviet. She must now decide whether to identify herself as Tatar, Russian, Ukrainian, or some composite of these national identities. For their part, some Ukrainians may "construct" this person's identity as Russian or Tatar (or both), but not necessarily Ukrainian ("She's not one of us!"). The intensity of national identity can also vary with circumstances. If our group

is threatened by another, we can choose negotiation or violence, depending on the situation. But our response is not predetermined by our ethnicity or by past history: We have choices. When we think about national identity, we should be wary of fixed categories and open to the possibilities of choice, change, and ambiguity in the ways identities are formed.[4]

As our discussion suggests, while the concept of nation is broadly understood around the contemporary world, what exactly constitutes any particular nation can vary enormously. Therefore, we believe that the best way to understand nations and national identity is to observe them in practice. For that reason we offer two extended examples of the problems associated with national identity later in this chapter. In Chapters 13, 14, and 15 we discuss national identity in the United Kingdom, France, and Germany.

IMMIGRATION, CITIZENSHIP, AND NATIONAL IDENTITY

That nations imagine themselves becomes clear if we consider citizenship requirements across countries. **Citizenship** is about the relationship of a person to a state. A citizen has rights within a state's territory, such as those outlined in the United States Constitution and Bill of Rights, and reciprocally has certain duties in relation to the society and the state. In democracies the rights of citizenship include, besides the usual civil liberties, the right to vote and to stand for elective office. The obligations of democratic citizenship can include the duty to serve on juries or in the nation's armed forces. In social democracies rights may extent to an expected minimum standard of living, as we will discuss in Chapter 11.

But who should be able to claim such rights? And who owes the society and the state that governs it those obligations? That is, who should be a citizen? To be a citizen implies belonging to the community, which we often translate as belonging to the nation. We accord other people certain rights, including social rights such as access to welfare payments paid for with our tax dollars, because we believe that as fellow members of the community, that is, fellow nationals, we owe them those rights in a way that we don't owe people who live in another nation-state.

Who belongs can be a contentious question, however. For example, how do we treat those who have newly moved to our country—that is, immigrants? Do they deserve the same treatment as others who have lived here since birth and whose parents lived here before their birth? How do we treat those who were born abroad to people who have citizenship in our nation? Do they deserve the same access to public services and the same treatment before the law as we do?

If we look across several of the countries we have explored or will study in this book, we see a wide range of responses to these questions. Students of citizenship and nationality law distinguish between two principles for citizenship: **jus soli**, which means "right of the soil," and **jus sanguinis**, which translates as "right of blood." States that accord citizenship on *jus soli* principles—e.g., Australia, France, the United Kingdom, and most of the countries in the Americas, including the United States—give citizenship to anyone or nearly everyone born in the country, regardless of the citizenship of their parents, so long as the parents are legally resident (in the United States even the children of parents without legal residency are granted citizenship). In contrast, countries whose nationality law is based on *jus sanguinis* give citizenship only to those born to parents who have citizenship in that nation-state. States that have used *jus sanguinis* include Germany, the Scandinavian countries, Russia, Japan, and China.[5] Typically, *jus soli* states make naturalization (i.e., becoming a citizen if you are an immigrant) relatively easy whereas it may be impossible to naturalize to citizenship if you are an immigrant in a *jus sanguinis* country.

Comparing citizenship law in France and Germany is instructive, for it not only shows the differences in how *jus soli* and *jus sanguinis* work in practice, but it also illustrates how these two nations have come to imagine themselves.[6] Since the Revolution, France has used *jus soli* principles to define citizenship. French citizenship is about the relationship of an individual to the French state and the republican political principles upon which that state is based. Persons born in France to parents who are not French citizens nevertheless can become citizens when they reach the age of majority (18) if they have lived in France for the previous five years or at age 16 if they have lived in France continuously since birth. France will naturalize foreign-born persons after five years continuous residency and employment in much the same way the United States does. In a sense, France has decided that to be French one has to want to be French and to live there, or to be born to parents one of whom is a French citizen. Those who gain the initial residency permit and their children are on track to become French if they choose.

In contrast, Germany has followed *jus sanguinis* as its main principle for defining citizenship. Until a new law was enacted in 2000, practically the only way one became German was to be born to a German parent, although before 1975 the child of a German mother and a non-German father did not automatically qualify for German citizenship. Germany even has a "law of return" codified in Article 116 of its Basic Law (or constitution) that allows someone of German ethnic origin "who has been admitted to the territory of the German Reich within the boundaries of December 31, 1937, as a refugee or expellee of German ethnic origin or as the spouse or descendant of such person" to apply for citizenship. By this provision some 3 million ethnic Germans moved to Germany and took on German citizenship from places farther east—the former Soviet Union and East European countries—after the end of the Cold War.[7] Many of them and their parents had never lived in Germany.

As you can see, being a German does not necessarily involve birth in Germany. Rather, Germany imagines itself as a "community of descent," of people who are seen as having German blood. Meanwhile, as of 2000 about 2 million Turks were living in Germany, many of them born in Germany but ineligible to become German citizens. Only in 2000, when Germany passed a new citizenship law that adopted *jus soli* principles, were those Turks born in Germany able to become German citizens, but

In 2000 Germany adopted *jus soli* principles of citizenship, a revolutionary step in that nation's history of political participation. Here a Turkish-German casts her ballot.

then only after living in Germany for at least eight years and, at age 23, renouncing Turkish citizenship (which they acquired at birth according to Turkey's *jus sanguinis* citizenship rules).

As this summary suggests, Germany recently responded to pressures to relax its laws that restricted citizenship to those who because of their ancestry could claim German blood. Before that reform of nationality law in 2000, however, Germans tended to imagine their nation as based solely on descent. The French, in contrast, and like most people living in the Americas, tended to imagine belonging to the nation as a matter of choice—most French or Canadians or Americans or Brazilians are born into their nations, but others are free to join if they show sufficient commitment to the community. Of course, there are pressures in France, as in the United States and other high immigration nations, to be more restrictive about who can become a citizen and hence claim to belong to the nation. You will read about the rise of the National Front, a strong antiimmigrant party, in Chapter 14. National identity is about imagining the community, but the content of that imagination can vary considerably. Communities of descent based on bloodlines are quite different from communities based on choice and commitment.

NATIONALISM

The concepts of nation and national identity are usually steeped in emotional, psychological, and cultural attachments to one's people and their historic homeland. By contrast, the concept of *nationalism* is essentially political and is more explicitly articulated. Scholars have defined nationalism in a variety of ways.[8] Moreover, nationalism can have different connotations, depending on the context. In some instances nationalism connotes a *people's* resolve to take political action on behalf of their group, whether by getting an existing government to respect their rights or by insisting on some form of self-government. In other instances nationalism connotes a state's resolve in international affairs to affirm or defend the country's "national interests" (meaning state interests) in its diplomatic, military, and economic dealings with the outside world. The definition we offer here combines both of these dimensions, as follows: **nationalism** is a consciously formulated set of political ideas emphasizing the distinctiveness and unity of one's nation, specifying common interests, and prescribing goals for action.

Whereas national identity proclaims, "We are a people and we belong together in this territory," the idea of nationalism adds, "We must therefore act together to achieve our common political aims." Whereas national identity is largely a social and cultural construct (with a territorial component), nationalism is assertively political in nature: it is a call to action that invariably involves government in some way or another. And whereas national identity evokes sentiments and emotions, nationalism combines these affective inclinations—such as feelings of pride or resentment—with a more or less clearly elaborated political program. National identity answers the question "Who am I?" Nationalism addresses the question "What should we do?" and it responds with a project.

In its benign variant, nationalism calls for *patriotism,* which typically means love of one's country and a general loyalty to its laws and institutions. But in some cases the assertion of national distinctiveness can take the more extreme forms of xenophobia and chauvinism. *Xenophobia* means distrust and hatred of foreigners. *Chauvinism* is wildly exaggerated, fanatical patriotism. These attitudes often involve claims that one's own nation is superior to other groups, and they may lead to regarding outside groups as enemies. Adolf Hitler's ideology of fascism, for instance, proclaimed the superiority of the "Aryan race" (a bogus racial category), and it relegated Jews, Slavs, and others to the level of "subhumans." Hitler's Nazi government pursued a policy of *hypernationalism,* an extreme form of nationalism that unleashed Germany's military aggression and the subjugation of its defeated victims in World War II.

Like most ideologies, nationalism is propagated by political elites—professional political activists and intellectuals, for the most part—who take it upon themselves to promote a national culture and design programs for political action. Some nationalist elites may wish to secure the nation's aims through peaceful means; others do not shrink from violent confrontation. Some may favor democracy while others combine nationalism with fascism, communism, or some other authoritarian ideology. Some are exclusively concerned with the good of the nation, while others exploit a people's hopes and grievances in a cynical play for power, whipping up national passions in the process. Many a national cause has been hijacked by dictators—from Napoleon and Hitler to Mao Zedong and Saddam Hussein—who imposed their own will on the nation they claimed to represent. To be truly "national," nationalism as a political process must be democratically open to the masses who compose the nation and to their chosen representatives. The United States, for example, has managed to build a fairly high level of national unity around its Constitution (with the exception of the Civil War) while expanding democracy among its citizens. In quite a few other countries, by contrast, the process of defining the nation's goals and mobilizing the means to achieve them has been directed from above by an authoritarian elite. That elite often holds power dictatorially after self-government has been achieved.[9]

Constituting the Nation as a Political Actor

What kinds of goals do groups that consider themselves nations typically seek? What do we mean by "nationalist projects"?

Let's start with a minority group that occupies a fairly well-defined region within a country. If this group is subjected to discrimination at the hands of the majority, it will want the central government to do something about it—especially if the government is perpetrating discriminatory practices itself or permitting others to get away with it. The members of the minority nationality may also want the central government to guarantee their people's rights to economic assistance and other benefits (schools, hospitals, and so on) that other citizens of the country receive. In addition, they may want the right to use their own language in local schools, public offices, and media. In these and similar instances, the group's main aim is to get certain rights legally protected by higher state authorities within its recognized geographical area. Examples include the Hungarian minority in the Transylvanian region of Romania, historically discriminated against by Romanian governments; the indigenous peoples of the Chiapas region in Mexico; and the Baluchis in Pakistan, who have recently resorted to violence to gain a bigger share of the country's oil revenues and other benefits.[10]

Some nationalists may want more than just an end to discrimination, however; they may want some form of self-determination. **Self-determination** usually means self-government. It can take different forms. In some cases a regionally based movement may want **territorial autonomy**, which means self-government over its own territory within the structure of a larger state. Autonomy in this sense amounts to local self-administration, encompassing the group's right to elect its own local officials and administer its own laws with limited interference from the central government. Spain, for example, grants special rights of autonomy to regions whose inhabitants have a strong sense of their own national identity, such as the Basques and the Catalans. In 2006, Catalonia adopted a new autonomy statute that defined the region as a "nation." The post-Saddam Iraqi state allows Kurds significant governmental autonomy in Iraqi Kurdistan. In a process known as "devolution," the United Kingdom in recent years has granted new powers of self-administration to three of its four regional components—Scotland, Wales, and Northern Ireland. The population of each of these regions has its own ethnically rooted national identity. (England, the United Kingdom's historic heart, does not have similar autonomous powers.) The central governments of both Spain and the United Kingdom have been careful, however, to maintain higher authority over these autonomous units on certain issues, such as foreign policy and the country's economy. How much autonomy Kurds will have in Iraq, for example, over the exploitation of petroleum resources, remains a contested issue.

More assertively, a nationalist movement may want outright *independence.* In this case the nation wants its own state (country), fully sovereign over its population and territory and formal recognition by other states around the globe. Achieving this goal may require a revolt against the central government and secession from the existing state, a cause known as *separatism.* In 2011, after two civil wars that stretched back to 1955, inhabitants of South Sudan voted to secede from Sudan to form their own independent state (see the case study about Sudan later in this chapter). Similarly, in 2002, following decades of conflict that cost more than 200,000 lives, the East Timorese seceded from Indonesia and created the new state of East Timor under the auspices of the United Nations. In Russia, Chechen separatists have waged a bloody war for an independent Chechnya since the 1990s, as yet without success. In other cases the drive for independence may require a confrontation with an external power, such as an imperial state such as the British, Habsburg, or Ottoman empires. Frequently the struggle turns violent, as in the North American colonies' battle for liberation from England or Algeria's fight for independence from France in the 1950s and 1960s. But India and Pakistan gained their freedom from Britain mostly peacefully, thanks to the pacifist ideology of the independence movement's principal leader, Mohandas Gandhi.

At a countrywide level (as opposed to a regional level), a common national identity can be an important unifying force, establishing a measure of homogeneity among a people who may be otherwise divided into different religions, social classes, linguistic groups, or other identity formations. If the group's members can at least agree that they share an overarching identity as a nation (as Americans, as Pakistanis, as Iraqis, and the like), they may be able to overcome the internal differences that provoke dissension in their ranks, at least on the issues that concern their common welfare. Nationalism can thus play a *constitutive* role: It can help constitute the nation as an effective political actor, galvanizing its members' common interests and empowering them to realize their common aims.

But if people do not share a common national identity, the chances that they will be able to act in concert on the basis of a common program, such as an independence movement or a democratization process, are slim. If the inhabitants of a particular country devote their primary loyalties to their respective tribe, linguistic group, religion, or some other parochial identity group as opposed to the larger "nation," they may not be able to govern themselves effectively at all or achieve other "national" goals. In the absence of any national homogeneity, a divisive—and perhaps highly conflictual—social heterogeneity takes over. Chronic disunity can result in paralytic gridlock or civil war. Under these circumstances it is not likely that the population will agree on a central government that all can regard as legitimate. It is even less likely that they will be able to put together a stable, successful democracy. The lack of a strong, unifying national identity, in short, has a ripple effect on nationalism, the state, legitimacy, and democracy. All of these things come together under the concept of *nation building.*

NATION BUILDING

The term *nation building,* like many other entries in the lexicon of politics, means different things to different people. As Francis Fukuyama has observed, "What Americans mean by

nation-building is usually state-building coupled with economic development."[11] **State building** essentially means the effort to develop an effective government at the political decision-making level, along with supportive bureaucratic agencies that can implement government policies and programs. In a world of failed states and weak states, the task of creating and sustaining states with sufficient "institutional capacity" to maintain order and deliver human services is an urgent one. Promoting "good governance" has thus become a central goal of international development agencies. But states and nations, as we've indicated, are not the same. Accordingly, this book provides an expansive definition of nation building that combines the three tasks of forging a national identity, building an effective state, and developing democratic legitimacy. Within this context, **nation building** can be seen as the process of developing a widely shared identity among a country's population and an effective, legitimate state.

In some countries the population may already have a broadly shared national identity but lack an effective state that is accepted as legitimate by the key elements of the citizenry. In these cases, the task of "nation building" is essentially confined to state building: It centers on creating a functioning state machinery and on shoring up the state's legitimacy in the eyes of the people through democratic mechanisms and economic progress. But when a dysfunctional government with dubious legitimacy rests on a shaky foundation of national identity, as it does in a large number of countries around the world, the nation-building process becomes all the more challenging. In these cases, programs designed to construct a viable state and democracy will almost certainly require simultaneous efforts to build a common national identity capable of bridging the population's volatile divisions. If these divisions cannot be overcome, then the only way to achieve either state effectiveness or democracy may be to loosen the country into a federation or confederation (like Switzerland) that grants wide autonomy to its constituent units, or to permit the outright independence of one or more of its parts (like Yugoslavia, as we'll see later in this chapter).

Civil War

When internally divided countries fail at the multiple tasks of forging a broad-based national identity, solidifying an effective government, and building democratic institutions and practices, the results can be devastating. Civil war can ravage a society for years. Between 1945 and 1999, approximately 127 civil wars took place inside 73 countries around the globe. At least a thousand people died in each conflict, with the total loss of life amounting to more than 16 million fatalities. The average war lasted about six years.

What has been the primary cause of these conflicts? In a systematic study, James Fearon and David Laitin found that ethnic, religious, and other forms of cultural diversity are *not* the principal cause of civil wars. Many countries are culturally divided, but not all of them succumb to internal warfare. Fearon and Laitin identify civil wars as insurgencies that are conducted by fairly small, lightly armed guerrilla bands based in relatively well-protected rural areas, often in remote mountain ranges. Although the grievances expressed by these rebel groups may at times have an ethnic or religious basis, the wars themselves tend to occur when the central government is too weak, both financially and institutionally, to crush the armed uprising quickly. Corruption and brutal counterinsurgency tactics only prolong civil strife and raise new grievances. Even democratically elected governments can exhibit these tendencies, allowing civil insurgencies to develop. Fearon and Laitin call on the international community to provide financial assistance to beleaguered governments with the aim of enhancing their competence and holding them accountable for their actions. "Good governance" thus appears essential to stopping civil wars.[12]

Fortunately, the number of civil wars and other violent internal conflicts has been declining since the early 1990s. Scholars at the University of Maryland's Center for International Development and Crisis Management, using their Minorities at Risk database and other sources, report that the number of newly initiated armed conflicts for self-determination (that is, self-governance) fell from 28 cases in the 1990–94 period just after the Cold War ended to 8 in the 2000–04 period and none in 2005–08.[13] Since the end of the Cold War, most of these conflicts have been settled by granting the rebellious groups more autonomy and greater opportunities to secure their collective rights through bargaining with the central government. In addition, by 2008 more than 90 territorially concentrated groups around the world were seeking greater self-government *without* recourse to armed violence, relying instead on peaceful procedures. Significant reductions in discrimination against minorities have also occurred in the past several decades, especially in the world's democracies.

Africa has seen more than its share of protracted civil wars. Two of the most horrific examples occurred in the neighboring countries of Burundi and Rwanda, where more than 800,000 people lost their lives in ethnic warfare between the Hutus and Tutsis that began in 1993 in Burundi and then broke out in Rwanda more horrifically in 1994. Some 3 million have perished in the Democratic Republic of Congo (DRC) since 1998. Uganda was wracked by a civil rebellion from the early 1980s until 2006. Joseph Kony's Lord's Resistance Army (LRA), the strongest rebel force, failed to reach a peace agreement in negotiations with the Ugandan government in 2007 and was pushed out of the country. The LRA continues to pose threats to peace in East Africa, having operated in South Sudan, the DRC, and the Central African Republic. These and other armed conflicts in Africa have shown signs of winding down in recent years, but it is hard to say if peace will endure. Meanwhile, a new round of civil strife broke out in Sudan in 2003.

CASE STUDY
Ethno-National Conflict in Sudan

Sudan's experience illustrates vividly many of the concepts we have discussed in this chapter. Weak national identity has led to secessionist movements. Prolonged ethno-national conflict has undermined the central state's capacity to provide law and order and the services that citizens have come to expect from the state. These factors have led to major human rights violations, frequently on the part of the state's security forces. In policy terms, how to respond to these civil wars proves difficult for foreign policy makers seeking to preserve international political stability while also promoting human rights.

In January 2011 the people of South Sudan voted to secede from Sudan (Map 4.1). Their decision, in which over 98 percent of the 3.8 million voters favored independence, came after decades of conflict with the central Sudanese state. People from South Sudan are overwhelmingly black and practice animist religions and Christianity. Indeed, blacks form the majority (about 52 percent) of the 45 million people of what was before 2011 the united country of Sudan. But ever since Sudan gained independence from Britain in 1956, the central government in Khartoum has been dominated by a political and military elite drawn from the country's Arab minority, which constitutes 39 percent of the population. Sudanese Arabs are mostly Sunni Muslims, and they tend to reside in the northern part of the country.

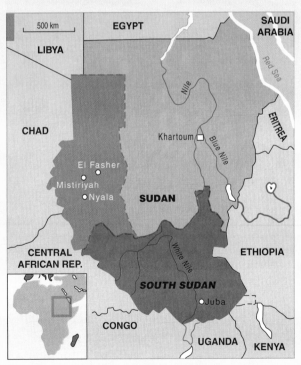

MAP 4.1 **Sudan. Darfur is the orange-colored area in the west.**

(Continued on next page)

(Continued from previous page)

Between 1956 and 1972, the central government and southerners were locked in the "Anyanya war," named after a poison used by black fighters. That conflict ended in an agreement that granted the south considerable autonomy plus representation in the central government. But fighting flared up anew in 1984 after Sudan's Muslim-dominated government imposed Islamic law on the non-Muslim south. The revived civil war lasted 21 years, leaving 2 million dead and 4 million homeless. In January 2005 a peace agreement was signed that promised to end the conflict. The deal removed the application of Islamic law from the south and gave the region a six-year period of autonomous government. The leader of the main black rebel group became Sudan's vice president. In 2011 the secession referendum led to establishment of South Sudan as an independent state.

Meanwhile, in the past decade Sudan has become notorious for the catastrophe in its Darfur region, a desert area the size of France located in the western part of the country. From 2003 to 2011 a brutal civil war in Darfur claimed an estimated 300,000 lives and displaced 2.5 million or more people, in addition to victimizing countless women, children, and other noncombatants. The hostilities began when two rebel groups from Darfur's mostly black African population attacked military and police units stationed in the region by Sudan's central government. For years Darfur's African villagers

From 2003 to 2011 a brutal civil war in Darfur claimed an estimated 300,000 lives and displaced 2.5 million or more people, in addition to victimizing countless women, children, and other noncombatants.

and farmers—who are themselves also Muslims—experienced systematic discrimination at the hands of the Arab-led central government, together with a lack of economic opportunity and property rights. They were also subjected to periodic raids by Arab militias in Darfur known as the Janjaweed.

In early 2004, government forces and the Janjaweed, armed partisans from Arab tribes, stepped up a series of coordinated attacks on Darfur's blacks, concentrating on three African tribal groups. Air strikes were followed by militia onslaughts that were accompanied by gang rapes, mass murders, and the burning of villages. Turmoil ensued as hundreds of thousands of terrorized people fled their homes, many of them ending up in refugee camps established by international organizations in Darfur and in neighboring Chad. In 2004 the U.S. government condemned the attacks as genocide. A contingent of 7,000 troops was sent to Darfur by the African Union (which represents the continent's 53 countries). The administration of George W. Bush called for a NATO force to be dispatched to the region, and the United Nations Security Council approved the deployment of a peacekeeping force of 22,500 troops to replace the African Union forces. But Sudan's president, Omar al-Bashir, who came to power in a military coup, resisted the introduction of the UN peacekeepers. In 2009 al-Bashir became the first head of state indicted by the International Criminal Court, on charges of crimes against humanity and war crimes for the actions his government has taken in Darfur. As of the printing of this book, he has not been brought to trial. In 2011 his government reached a peace agreement with the Liberation and Justice Movement, an umbrella organization for 10 Darfuri rebel groups that created a Transitional Darfur Regional Authority and envisions a referendum in the Darfur region to determine the permanent political status of the region. Sudan is near the top of the list of countries in critical condition shown in Chapter 3 in Table 3.1. By virtually every measure, it is a failed state. Clearly, the absence of a common Sudanese national identity capable of overarching the country's festering divisions has been a major source of Sudan's troubles.[14] Where the population sharing the common territory controlled by a state do not see themselves as one people, demands for regional autonomy and outright secession can be expected. Whether the group dominating the central state can retain control of the whole territory often comes down to the use of force and a test of wills, as we'll see later in this chapter.

WHEN THE NATION AND THE STATE DON'T FIT TOGETHER

Historically, the development of nationalism followed the creation of states in some cases, but preceded or accompanied the creation of new states in others. In England and France, powerful monarchal states existed for several centuries before the creation of a distinct English or French nationalism. When it came, nationalism in these countries tended to be defined in highly political terms, reflecting the development of English parliamentary processes in the one case and the French Revolution in the other.[15] In later centuries, nationalist programs were purposely elaborated to establish new states. Germans formed a central German state in the nineteenth century. At approximately the same time, Italian nationalists created a new state of Italy, putting an end to the peninsula's centuries-long fragmentation into a mosaic of different regimes and foreign occupiers. ("We have made Italy; now we must make Italians," the nationalist leader Massimo d'Azeglio proclaimed, anticipating the need for nation building.) Across the high seas, new independent states were born in Latin America as liberation movements freed their respective territories from Spain or Portugal. As the century wore on, nationalist movements within the Austro-Hungarian (Habsburg), Ottoman, and Russian empires militated for independent states of their own, processes that accelerated as these imperial regimes collapsed during or after World War I.

In most of these cases of new state creation, the overriding aim of nationalist movements was to create a **nation-state**: a sovereign state consisting of one "nation" within internationally recognized boundaries. And in most instances, the nation was characterized largely in ethnic terms. Germans, Italians, Serbs, Romanians, Poles, and a variety of other ethnically defined groups ultimately succeeded in forming new states whose populations consisted overwhelmingly of their own ethnic group. Over time, the term *nation-state* came to be used as a common synonym for state or country.[16]

In fact, however, the perfect symmetry of one state and one nation is rare. States are social constructs: They do not exist in nature. The process of state formation is invariably a complicated affair, involving internal clashes, wars, imperialism, foreign occupations, revolutions, liberation struggles, peace treaties, and other domestic and international determinants. As a consequence, the term *nation-state,* in its most literal meaning, is usually a misnomer. A 1971 investigation showed that out of 132 countries, only 12 (9.1 percent) met the strict criterion of one nation and one state.[17] The situation is not much different today. Our survey of 172 countries with populations of at least 200,000 in 2001 revealed that 53 countries (30.8 percent) had a dominant ethnic group that comprised at least 90 percent of the population. (Granted, an ethnic group is not always the same as a nation, but it often forms the basis of one.) Of these 53 states, quite a few have nationhood problems even though one ethnic group constitutes the overwhelming majority of the population. West European countries including Denmark, Germany, France, and the Netherlands have witnessed a rise in immigration from North Africa, the Middle East, and elsewhere in recent decades, resulting in the growth of antiimmigrant sentiment and political parties. These West European countries have historically defined their nationhood in ethnic terms, and the growing number of immigrants and their descendants who seek permanent residence in them has prompted a reexamination of traditional concepts of nation and citizenship. China, whose population is 92 percent Han Chinese, has continuing problems over Tibet, which was forcibly annexed in the 1950s by the Communist Chinese government, and additional problems with its large Uighur minority, which is mostly Muslim. Romania has tensions with Hungarian and Roma minorities.

Similar difficulties can be found in other countries with a large dominant ethnic group. On a more positive note, a Freedom House survey in 2001 found that countries with a dominant ethnic group comprising at least two-thirds of the population were more likely to observe political and civil rights than countries that were more ethnically divided. Political allegiances in the latter countries tended to cluster around ethnic identities, often resulting in discriminatory political practices.[18]

Today's world consists of states with more than one nation, and nations without their own states. Canada is a good example of the first category. Discord between elements of the country's English and French communities has persisted since the earliest stages of Canadian history. The predominantly French-speaking province of Quebec, originally settled in 1608, has almost 8 million people, roughly one-fourth of Canada's total population. In the 1960s a separatist movement became increasingly vocal, its leaders calling for an independent Quebec. Not all Quebecers were willing to secede from Canada, however. In 1980, 60 percent of Quebec voters (many of whom were primarily English speakers) rejected a proposal that would have given their leaders the right to negotiate an agreement establishing Quebec's sovereignty. Another referendum conducted in 1995 offered Quebec's voters the possibility of secession in the event that a new autonomy agreement could not be worked out. This time the result was much closer than before: 50.25 percent voted no, barely enough to defeat the proposal. In 2003 the pro-independence Parti Québécois lost its bid for a third consecutive term in charge of Quebec's provincial government. In 2006 the Canadian House of Commons passed a resolution that stated, "The Québécois form a nation within a united Canada," a symbolic recognition that French-speaking residents of Quebec form a separate community sociologically if not legally.

Like Canada, Sri Lanka is also a state with more than one nation. But unlike Canada, which has dealt with the Quebec issue peacefully and democratically, Sri Lanka (formerly known

In 2006 the Canadian House of Commons resolved that "the Québécois form a nation within a united Canada," a symbolic recognition that French-speaking residents of Quebec form a separate community sociologically if not legally.

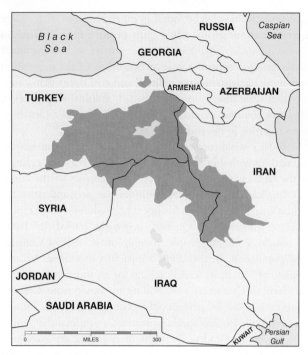

MAP 4.2   Kurdish Areas

as Ceylon) was ravaged by civil war from 1983 to 2009. The conflict raged between the majority group, the Sinhalese, who are mostly Buddhists, and their main rivals, the Tamils, who are mostly Hindus. Tamil speakers constitute about 18 percent of the country's population of 21 million. In addition to practicing different religions, the two groups are ethnically distinct and speak different languages. The Tamils reside mainly in the island's northern and eastern provinces. They claimed they have been systematically oppressed since the 1950s, when Sinhalese-led governments initiated the first in a series of discriminatory laws suppressing Tamil language rights and other basic political and civil rights. The Tamils' fight against the central government was led by the Liberation Tigers of Tamil Elam, a guerrilla group that demanded full independence for the Tamil region. Between 80,000 and 100,000 people were killed during the

conflict, which ended in 2009 with a brutal assault by the Sri Lankan army on the last vestiges of the Tigers and led to many civilian casualties.[19] Not all secessionist movements prove successful, as the American Civil War also demonstrated.

Just as there are states with more than one nation, there are also nations without a state. The Kurds, for example, are a nation of over 25 million people occupying more than 70,000 square miles of territory that spills across several countries (see Map 4.2), the largest nation without a state in the world. Though they were promised a state of their own after World War I, there is still no independent Kurdistan. Today most Kurds live in Turkey (as many as 14 million), Iran (about 8 million), and Iraq (about 4.5 million), with smaller communities in Syria, Armenia, and Azerbaijan. Kurdish fighters have been engaged in virtually continuous conflict for decades, mostly with the governments of Turkey and Iraq. Persistent attacks by Saddam Hussein's government prompted the United States, Britain, and France to provide aerial protection for Kurds in Iraq. Iraq's Kurds celebrated Saddam's fall in 2003, and struggled to achieve autonomy in post-Saddam Iraq in the form of a regional government within a federal Iraq. Turkey has been repeatedly condemned by Western governments for violating the Kurds' rights. After a five-year cease-fire from 1991 to 2004, the conflict between the Turkish state and Kurdish rebels heated up again. No resolution is in sight. For their part, Iran's Kurds complain of continuing discrimination at the hands of the country's theocratic government. Some Iranian Kurds have crossed the border into Iraq to work with the Party for Free Life in Kurdistan, which is outlawed in Iran. Despite the intense interest of Kurds in acquiring a state of their own, the states in which they live have little desire to allow them that result.

To better understand the dilemmas posed when the nation and the state do not fit together, we provide two extended case studies in the following pages. The first, the Israeli–Palestinian conflict, explores what happens when two peoples who define themselves as nations seek to control the same territory. The second examines the breakdown of a multinational state and the formation of new nation-states in its aftermath by looking at the dissolution of Yugoslavia.

CASE STUDY
Israel and the Palestinians

Perhaps the most tortured conflict over competing visions of nation and state in the modern world is the dispute between Israel, a state with territorial problems, and the Palestinians, a nation without a state. When two peoples who define themselves as nations seek to inhabit the same territory, and one or both have strong objections to sharing control of the state that governs that territory, one of those national groups will be disappointed. Conflict is bound to ensue.

Following the collapse of the Ottoman Empire's dominions in the Middle East during World War I and its

aftermath, the British assumed responsibility for the territory of Palestine. Britain's task under a League of Nations mandate was to prepare Palestine for independence, but the population—consisting of a half million Arabs and roughly 70,000 Jews—was divided on how the new state was to be constituted. The Arab majority wanted their own Palestinian state. But proponents of *Zionism,* a Jewish nationalist movement originating in Europe, demanded a state for the Jewish people, whose roots in Palestine reached back 2,000 years. In 1917, Foreign

Secretary Arthur Balfour committed the British government to the creation of a "national home for the Jewish people" in Palestine, but without prejudice to the rights of local Arabs. The Balfour Declaration's twin goals—statehood for Jews as well as for Arabs—were to prove incompatible.

Jewish emigration to Palestine grew steadily: By the time Adolf Hitler took power in Germany in 1933, Jews constituted about 20 percent of the Palestinian population. In 1939 there were about a half million Jews in Palestine (about a third of the total populace), and their well-organized businesses, farms, trade unions, and social organizations provoked an Arab backlash that occasionally turned violent. The British quelled an Arab revolt against Jewish immigration in 1936–39, but a broad-based Palestinian national movement emerged in the process, led by prominent Arab families opposed to the creation of a Jewish state. To appease the Arabs, the British clamped restrictions on the influx of Jews from abroad. But the tragedy of the Holocaust, in which 6 million European Jews perished under the Nazis' genocidal onslaught, reawakened Jewish nationalism and convinced Jews the world over that it was time for a state of their own in Palestine. Britain in 1947 asked the United Nations to propose a solution to Palestine's status, leading to a UN General Assembly resolution calling for the partition of Palestine into separate Jewish and Arab states. Palestinians initiated hostilities the next day and their attacks intensified during the next several months, but the better-organized Jewish fighters retaliated. Zionist leaders had already assumed for decades that the creation of a state with a Jewish majority would require the peaceful "transfer" of Arabs out of Jewish territory. A number of them were displeased that the UN partition plan would have left the new Jewish state with a population of a half million Jews and 400,000 Arabs, a large minority likely to reject the Jewish state. After the fighting began, many Palestinians fled their homes on their own. By the end of March 1948, about 100,000 Arabs had taken flight. But as Jewish troops took the offensive, they expelled large numbers of Palestinians by force. By the middle of May, Jewish fighters had captured nearly 200 Arab villages and towns; more than 300,000 Arab Palestinians were now dispersed. At this point, the British pulled out of Palestine, ending their mandate over the disputed territory. On May 14, 1948, Palestine's Jewish community—now numbering 650,000—proclaimed the state of Israel.

The new Jewish state was immediately attacked by its Arab neighbors. But by early 1949 it had achieved a decisive military victory, ending up with more territory than it had been awarded under the UN partition plan. A substantial number of Arabs, estimated at approximately 700,000, had fled the area or were forcibly evicted during the fighting, a mass exodus that Palestinians call "the Disaster." In all, about 150,000 Arabs stayed in Israel.[20] In 1949, the neighboring Arab kingdom of Transjordan (later known as Jordan) annexed the Arab parts of Palestine, consisting of the West Bank of the Jordan River and the eastern part of Jerusalem. Between 1948 and 1950, about 510,000 new Jewish immigrants moved into the freshly created Israeli state. In 1950, Israel enacted the "Law of the Return," which invited Jews from all over the world to settle there. An additional 600,000 arrived between 1950 and 1953. In 1955, the UN refugee organization estimated that 940,000 Arab refugees from Palestine were living in neighboring Arab countries, many of them confined to squalid refugee camps.

The hostilities surrounding Israel's emergence set the stage for the bitter Arab–Israeli conflict that persists to this day. Following Colonel Gamal Abdel Nasser's military takeover of Egypt in 1952, cross-border skirmishes between Egyptian and Israeli forces became increasingly common. In 1956, Israel attacked Egypt in conjunction with British and French landings at the Suez Canal, which Nasser had recently taken over. The United States induced the belligerents to withdraw and peace was restored, but clashes along Israel's borders with Egypt and Syria erupted periodically over the ensuing years. In June 1967, as Nasser made visible preparations for war, Israel launched a preemptive strike against Egypt, Syria, and Jordan. Following its rapid victory in the *Six-Day War,* Israel captured the Sinai Peninsula and the Gaza Strip from Egypt, the West Bank and East Jerusalem from Jordan, and the Golan Heights from Syria (see Map 4.3).

After Nasser's death in 1970, Anwar Sadat became Egypt's president. Seeking to recover their lost territories, Egypt and Syria attacked Israel in October 1973. The armies fought to a standstill, and the United States brokered a cease-fire. Israel came away from the *Yom Kippur War* with additional territory, but Egypt recovered the Sinai Peninsula by negotiation. Sadat then made a bold gesture for peace, traveling to Jerusalem in 1977 for talks with Israel's hard-line prime minister, Menachem Begin. Two years later President Jimmy Carter invited Sadat and Begin to Camp David, where the Egyptian and Israeli leaders came to terms on a peace treaty. Egypt became the first Arab state to establish diplomatic relations with Israel. Diplomatic recognition is a key component of any state's claim to legitimacy, which made Sadat's gesture so bold. Sadat paid for his reconciliation policy with his life: In 1981 he was assassinated by Islamic radicals. In later years, some of the assassination plotters would make common cause with Osama bin Laden and al-Qaeda.

As these events unfolded, Israeli governments encouraged Jewish settlers to establish communities in the West Bank, which was home to more than a million Palestinians. Though some Israeli politicians cautioned against the settlement policy, warning that it would obstruct an eventual resolution of the Arab–Israeli conflict, others favored the settlements, especially very conservative religious Jews and nationalists who regarded the West Bank as the ancient lands of Samaria and Judea, granted by God to the Jewish people. In their view, the West Bank and East Jerusalem needed to be formally incorporated into Israel, but Israeli governments refrained from taking this irrevocable step.[21]

(Continued on next page)

(Continued from previous page)

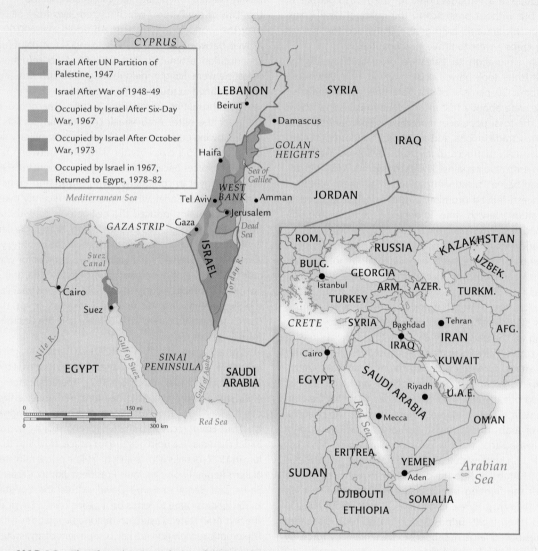

MAP 4.3 **The Changing Boundaries of the Israeli State**

These controversies reflected a broader issue of national identity: Who, exactly, was an Israeli? The answer depended in part on how various Jews defined what it meant to be a Jew. Orthodox Jews and other religious conservatives have conceived of Jewish identity primarily in religious terms. They have interpreted that identity as requiring the implementation of religious laws and traditions governing the Sabbath, marriage, dietary practices, and the like. Secular Jews, by contrast, have defined Jewishness in cultural rather than religious terms and have viewed the Jewish state in secular and national terms rather than in conformity with Biblical precepts. Initially, the Zionist movement was largely secularist. But the early Zionists

were split ideologically between socialists, many of whom took part in the creation of farm cooperatives (*kibbutzim*), and revisionists, who opposed socialist doctrines and advocated a more militant brand of Jewish nationalism. All these groups favored democracy. Nevertheless, unresolvable disagreements over identity issues prevented the elaboration of an Israeli constitution. In its place, Israel adopted "Basic Laws" establishing its secular state institutions and governing principles.

These ideological divisions in Israeli society were accompanied by a changing ethnic mix. After the 1967 war, Jews from the Middle East increasingly outnumbered Jews of European origin. The former group tended to resent the latter's continuing grip on political power. Then in the 1970s and 1980s, successive waves of Jews from the Soviet Union emigrated to Israel. About a quarter of Israel's citizenry has consisted of non-Jews—mostly Arabs (Palestinians) who remained in Israel after the 1948 war and their descendants. Today about 1.6 million Israeli citizens are Arabs. The vast majority are Muslim, but some are Christian. Throughout Israel's history, the country's sizable Arab minority has complained of discrimination at the hands of the Jewish majority, and they have had a difficult time reconciling their Israeli citizenship with their Arab ethnicity and religious affiliations.[22]

These myriad ideological orientations and geographic or ethnic backgrounds have found their political expression in a vibrant multiparty system. Socialist-oriented Zionists gravitated toward the Labor Party, while revisionists formed the basis of the Likud bloc. Other groupings formed their own parties. The existence of so many parties made for a rich and variegated democracy, but it also complicated the process of forming coherent, stable governments. We'll look at Israel's party system in greater detail in Chapter 6.

The Palestinians, for their part, have remained a stateless people. After 1948, a Palestinian diaspora fanned across the Middle East and spread into Europe and North America as well. In 2012 there were nearly 4.8 million registered Palestinian refugees living in Jordan, Lebanon, Syria, the Gaza Strip and the West Bank. The largest concentrations of Palestinians were in the West Bank, where over 2.5 million resided in 2012, and in the Gaza Strip (approximately 1.6 million). Of these, most were Sunni Muslims.

The absence of states in most of the Arab world during the centuries of Ottoman rule delayed the growth of a distinct Palestinian national identity. Until the birth of Israel, most Palestinians regarded themselves simply as Arabs, and Palestinian nationalism was articulated mainly by the leaders of prominent Arab families, both Muslim and Christian, in the context of a traditional agricultural society. In the wake of the 1948 Disaster and the mass dispersal of Palestinian Arabs to refugee camps and foreign countries, Palestinian nationalism waned, but it revived in the years just before and after the 1967 Six-Day War. A new generation of Palestinians who grew up in the poverty-stricken camps or abroad formed the social base of a more assertive national identity, led by a growing core of educated young people. This nationalist reawakening was fueled by antagonism toward Israel and by a sense that the collective experiences of the Palestinians marked them as a distinct people in the Arab world.[23]

Meanwhile, the Palestinians remained in political limbo, with no territory under their juridical authority. To provide Palestinian nationalism with an institutional foundation, Palestinian leaders formed the *Palestine Liberation Organization (PLO)* in 1964. The PLO's National Charter affirmed that the establishment of the state of Israel was illegal, that Jews did not "constitute a single nation with an identity of its own," and that the liberation of Palestine in its 1947 borders was

a "national duty" that could be achieved only through armed struggle. At the end of the decade the PLO chose Yasser Arafat as its chief. Arafat was the leader of Fatah, one of the PLO's most militant factions. Arafat steered the organization in the direction of terrorism against Israelis and got drawn into a bloody—and unsuccessful—attempt to topple the Jordanian monarchy in 1970. The PLO next moved to Lebanon, but it was evicted by the Israeli invasion of 1982.

Although the PLO in these years was militantly anti-Zionist, its platform was basically secular, not Islamic. It favored the creation of a Palestinian state on the basis of civil law, not Muslim sharia. The same was largely true of several splinter groups that broke off from Arafat's Fatah movement in the 1960s, asserting an even more militant approach to international terrorism that included airline hijackings and other spectacular operations. Since the 1980s, Palestinian nationalist organizations with a more Islamic cast have become increasingly vocal. The most prominent of these groups is *Hamas* (the Islamic Resistance Movement, whose acronym means "zeal"). Hamas rejected Fatah's vision of a secular Palestinian state with religious pluralism, calling instead for an Islamic state based on sharia. It is also militantly opposed to Israel, advocating violence as well as a patient confidence that the day will ultimately come when Israel will cease to exist as a Jewish state.

In 1987, mounting frustration at Israel's refusal to come to terms on a Palestinian state exploded into a violent uprising (*intifada*) conducted mainly by young stone-throwing Palestinians. The continuing stalemate, aggravated by casualties on both sides, led to a modest breakthrough. Starting in 1993, a series of agreements brokered in part by the government of Norway, and known as the *Oslo Accords,* provided for Palestinian self-government over the Gaza Strip and parts of the West Bank for five years. A new entity, the *Palestinian Authority (PA),* was created to exercise jurisdiction over the designated areas. Israeli Prime Minister Yitzhak Rabin and Foreign Minister Shimon Peres shared the Nobel Peace Prize with Arafat for their efforts, but Rabin was murdered in 1994 by an Israeli nationalist opposed to the Oslo peace process. As a sign of its commitment to peace, the PLO abrogated the clauses in its National Charter calling for Israel's destruction. (The Israelis, however, insisted on new clauses in the charter explicitly affirming the PLO's acceptance of Israel's right to exist.) Arafat moved quickly to assert his prominence in the new Palestinian government. In the Palestinians' first free elections, held in January 1996, Arafat handily defeated his opponent in the race for president of the PA, and his Fatah faction won 49 out of 88 seats in the newly created Palestinian Legislative Council.[24]

Although the Palestinian Authority gradually gained jurisdiction over 40 percent of the West Bank and two-thirds of Gaza, the PA was a government unconnected to a real state. Meanwhile, Israelis continued to build new settlements in the West Bank and Gaza and to encourage new housing for Jews in East Jerusalem, historically the Arab part of the city. At the

(Continued on next page)

(Continued from previous page)

end of the 1990s there were about 180,000 Jewish settlers in communities scattered across the West Bank, an area the size of Delaware. Another 5,000 Jews had settled in Gaza, and roughly 175,000 Jews were living in East Jerusalem.

There are two distinct options for resolving the struggle of these two nations over the territory comprised of Israel and the Occupied Territories. On the one hand Israel might continue the status quo, in which one state (Israel) governs two nations in the combined territories. That one state might offer equal citizenship to all inhabitants (Jews and Palestinians alike) or it might allow one group to have greater rights than the other. Currently, the latter situation reigns, with Jewish citizens of Israel having full citizenship rights in a democracy while Palestinians living in the West Bank and Gaza are occupied subjects, although with some representation through the PA. On the other hand, many advocate a two-state solution in which Israel, the Jewish nation-state, would continue to control its pre-1967 territory while the Palestinians would acquire full statehood in the Occupied Territories.

Politics in Israel in the past two decades have revolved around whether the one-state or two-state solution will prevail. In 2000, at a Camp David summit hosted by President Bill Clinton, the two sides inched toward agreement on several outstanding issues, with Israel's prime minister, Ehud Barak, offering to cede Gaza and 95 percent of the West Bank to the Palestinians and to accept a limited form of Palestinian sovereignty over East Jerusalem. But in the end neither Barak nor Arafat was ready to make difficult compromises on such sticking points as the Palestinians' demand for full sovereignty over the West Bank, Gaza, and East Jerusalem; Israel's concern for

Jewish settlers in these areas; and the fate of Palestinian refugees longing to return to their lost property in Israel. In fact, both Barak and Arafat were under intense pressure from within their own ranks to walk away from a final agreement. Barak's fragile coalition government was falling apart while he was away at Camp David. And Arafat was pressured by hardliners in the PLO as well as by terrorist groups such as Hamas, which continued to oppose Israel's right to exist.

Subsequently, a second *intifada* erupted. During three years of turmoil, nearly 900 Israelis and 2,500 Palestinians were killed. The Palestinian Authority lost control over areas it had acquired under the Oslo Accords. Arafat himself was confined by Israeli troops to his shelled-out headquarters. In 2003, the government of Ariel Sharon began constructing a protective barrier—a wall and other fortifications designed to seal off Israel proper and most Jewish settlers in the West Bank and East Jerusalem from terrorists. Prime Minister Sharon's decision in 2004 to withdraw Jewish settlers from the Gaza Strip ended up splitting his Likud Party. Sharon bolted from Likud and formed a new party called Kadima (Forward), dedicated to seeking a settlement with the Palestinians. Veteran Labor Party leader Shimon Peres and like-minded politicians from Likud and other parties soon joined him. However, other Israeli leaders, notably Benjamin Netanyahu, the Likud leader now serving as prime minister, have opposed such a settlement.

With the death of Arafat in 2004, his Fatah was challenged by Hamas, which had already proved its militancy by organizing or supporting a number of suicide bombings in Israel. Hamas entered the electoral lists for the first time in 2005, winning local council seats in Gaza and the West Bank. Hamas scored an even more stunning victory in January 2006 when it unexpectedly won a clear majority of seats in elections to the PA's legislature (74 out of 132). Conflict between Arafat's successor in Fatah, Mahmoud Abbas, and Hamas eventually led to the violent ouster of Fatah from the Gaza Strip, where Hamas has exercised de facto rule since 2006. The more moderate Abbas holds sway as president of the Palestinian National Authority in the West Bank.

With two different visions of the appropriate state for the Palestinian people, the secular nationalist version advocated by Fatah and the militant Islamist view promoted by Hamas, divisions among Palestinian leaders forestalled resolution of the conflict with Israel. Since 2011 the two factions have engaged in reconciliation talks. Without a unified national leadership with a clear nationalist vision, Palestinians will not find achieving their goals of a separate state easy.[25]

Israeli Prime Minister Yitzhak Rabin was assassinated by an Israeli nationalist in 1994.

Having considered the conflict-laden situation produced when two peoples that define themselves as nations seek to control the same territory, let's turn to another tenuous scenario: the multinational state.

CASE STUDY
The Disintegration of Yugoslavia

Though we may be tempted to think of states as enduring entities, they are by no means always so. Like geological formations, states may undergo all sorts of seismic convulsions. They can grow, disintegrate, become reconstituted, or get absorbed into larger states. One of the most volcanic examples of the disintegration of a multinational state is the former Yugoslavia. Its explosive self-destruction caused by competing nationalisms in the 1990s was accompanied by the killing of over 250,000 people and the forcible expulsion of more than 2 million from their homes and villages.

Origins

The roots of this region's intense conflicts extend more than a thousand years into the past. Starting in the late sixth century, successive waves of Slavic peoples from the eastern steppes, located in what is now Russia and Central Asia, gradually moved into the peninsula whose spine is formed by the Balkan Mountains. Their subsequent histories took very divergent paths.

Slovenes occupied the northernmost part of the area. In the eighth century the majority of Slovenes were converted to Roman Catholicism. Most of what is now Slovenia was part of the Austrian-led Habsburg Empire from 1335 to 1918. *Croats* became Roman Catholics in the tenth century and are still mostly Catholic today. Most of what is now Croatia gradually came under the control of Austria and Hungary and remained part of the Habsburg Empire until the end of World War I. *Serbs* initially occupied the valleys where Bosnia, Montenegro, and Kosovo meet. In the ninth century they were converted to the eastern rite of Orthodox Christianity—the basis of the Russian Orthodox church—by Saints Cyril and Methodius. Cyril was the founder of what evolved into the Russian (Cyrillic) alphabet. These religious and linguistic developments established a close connection between Serbs and Russians that still endures. The Turks held much of this region from the fourteenth century to the late nineteenth century. Under Russia's patronage, the kingdom of Serbia was established in 1882. Russia's support for Serbia against Austria-Hungary in 1914 was one of the key events that led to World War I.

Montenegrins were originally Serbs. They broke off from the rest of the Serbs in the early fifteenth century to escape the advancing Turks, establishing their own monarchy in an inaccessible mountainous region. Montenegro (the Black Mountain) remained an independent state until 1918. *Bosnians* were also originally Serbs. They fled Serbia proper in the fourteenth century in advance of the Turks and established their own kingdom in what eventually became known as Bosnia. In 1463 the Turks overran all of Bosnia except a small area around Mostar that was ruled by the duke (*herzeg*) of St. Sava. This area, known as Herzegovina, fell to the Turks 20 years later. Over the course of the next several centuries under Ottoman rule, most Bosnians became Muslims and became known as *Bosniaks*. But others retained their Serbian identity as

Orthodox Christians; they became known as *Bosnian Serbs*. The Austro-Hungarian Empire took over Bosnia from the Turks in 1878. It was a Bosnian Serb who assassinated Austria's Archduke Franz Ferdinand in Sarajevo in 1914, igniting World War I.

Serbs, Croats, Bosnians, and Montenegrins all speak dialects of a common language usually called Serbo-Croatian, although Croats and many Bosnians write in a Latin alphabet while Serbs are more likely to write in Cyrillic. Moreover, Croats and Bosnians prefer to say they speak Croatian and Bosnian, respectively, while Serbs prefer the notion of a single Serbo-Croatian language.

Macedonians probably stemmed from Slavic tribes but they also had close ancestral ties with the non-Slavic Bulgars. In the ninth century a Macedo-Bulgarian empire was formed, but the Ottomans took over most of its territory in the following century, ruling it almost uninterruptedly until 1913. Parts of Macedonia were taken by Serbia, Greece, and Bulgaria in the course of two Balkan wars fought in 1912 and 1913. *Albanians* are a non-Slavic people who were ruled by the Ottomans for 450 years until 1912, when Albania became an independent country. Most Albanians became Muslims. Though the majority of them live in Albania, many Albanians have lived for centuries in the region of Kosovo, which was part of Serbia.

Spread across two receding empires—Austria-Hungary and the Ottoman Empire—and several weak, newly independent kingdoms, South Slav intellectuals began to foment the idea of an independent Slav state in the Balkans in the nineteenth century. Following World War I these diverse peoples gradually formed a new country, which took the name Yugoslavia, "the land of the southern Slavs." (Albania retained its independence.) Intense rivalries virtually doomed the new Yugoslav state from the start. Efforts to establish a stable nation-state foundered on the uncompromising attitudes of the various nationality groups and their leaders. In 1934 Yugoslavia's constitutional monarch, who was a Serb, was murdered by Croatian assassins.

Internal turmoil was exacerbated by external intervention. In 1941 Nazi Germany invaded Yugoslavia, established a satellite fascist regime in Croatia, and occupied other parts of the country until 1944. While thousands of Yugoslavs took up arms against the Germans in resistance movements, the conflicts among the various Yugoslav nationalities erupted into civil war. Fighting between Serbs and those Croats allied with Germany was especially intense. Approximately 1.75 million Yugoslavs lost their lives during World War II. About half were killed by the Germans; the other half died at the hands of other Yugoslavs.

The most successful anti-German resistance movement during the war years was organized by Yugoslav communists. Their leader was Josip Broz, known by his pseudonym, Tito. Tito's

(Continued on next page)

(Continued from previous page)

communists swiftly took control of Yugoslavia following the Germans' withdrawal. Initially, the Yugoslav communists attempted to reorganize the country along the lines of Stalin's harsh Soviet dictatorship. But in 1948 Tito and Stalin got into a feud when the Yugoslav communists expressed their resentment at Soviet interference in their internal affairs. "We are good communists," Tito said, "but we are good Yugoslavs first." Yugoslavia and the Soviet Union broke off their alliance and Tito steered a more neutral course, pursuing economic ties with the West.

As long as Tito remained the country's supreme leader, the ethnic antagonisms simmering just below the surface of Yugoslavia's authoritarian regime did not explode into violence. But they did not disappear entirely. Tito, who was part Croat and part Slovene, occasionally had to take personal action to prevent excessive displays of ethnic nationalism by Serbs, Croats, and other groups. It was Tito's towering presence that held the country together. His death in 1980 at the age of 88 compelled Yugoslavia's nationalities to confront their rivalries anew.

Shortly before his death, Tito bequeathed Yugoslavia a new constitution that required the communist leaders of the country's main nationality groups to share power after his departure. (Power sharing is often attempted in multiethnic democracies where it is called consociationalism, discussed in Chapter 5.) This shaky arrangement lasted little more than 10 years. As the winds of freedom fanned across the Soviet Union and Eastern Europe in the late 1980s and early 1990s, Yugoslavs of every nationality demanded similar liberties. For most Yugoslavs, democratic self-expression meant ethnic self-assertion.

Following referendums that showed vast majorities in favor of independence, Slovenia and Croatia seceded from Yugoslavia and declared their sovereignty in June 1991. Macedonia followed suit in September, and the Muslim leaders of Bosnia-Herzegovina declared independence in

December. Serbia and Montenegro did not declare their independence but together formed what remained of Yugoslavia (see Map 4.4.). Serbia dominated this partnership under the leadership of Slobodan Milosevic, a former communist functionary who advocated the goal of uniting all the region's Serbs into a "Greater Serbia."

Though he appeared to be a typical Communist Party bureaucrat with no charismatic flair, Milosevic had a keen eye for power. Significantly, he sought to solidify his own power base by deliberately stirring up Serbian national passions. Political liberalization can be associated with the rise of ethnic conflict when politicians use ethnic or national appeals in their attempts to gain followers. In 1989 Milosevic became president of Serbia, the most populous republic of Yugoslavia. Shortly after taking office, he addressed a throng of Serbs on the site of Kosovo Pole, the "Field of Blackbirds," where the Serbian army had been defeated by the Turks exactly 600 earlier. Milosevic's fiery speech promised that Serbia would never again relinquish its control over Kosovo, the province revered as the historic birthplace of the Serbian nation. Hundreds of years of Turkish occupation had left Kosovo with a large ethnic Albanian majority, virtually all of them Muslims. Of the province's 2.2 million residents, more than 80 percent were Albanians. Tito had granted the Albanian Kosovars a number of rights and privileges, and between the 1960s and mid-1980s as many as 300,000 Serbs left Kosovo because of local Albanian domination. Milosevic was determined to reverse this process. In 1989 he began terminating the rights of the Albanian Kosovars, removing them from their jobs by the hundreds of thousands. In their place came Serbs determined to reclaim control of the province. The antagonisms set off by these actions ultimately culminated in a wholesale Serbian onslaught in Kosovo, but Milosevic first had to deal with the secession movements in Slovenia, Croatia, and Bosnia.

The Balkan Wars of the 1990s

Fighting broke out in Slovenia, Croatia, and Bosnia in 1991 shortly after the initial declarations of independence. Milosevic deployed the Yugoslav army, led predominantly by Serb officers, in an effort to halt Yugoslavia's disintegration. Slovenia quickly repulsed these forces and retained its independence. Croatia and Bosnia-Herzegovina, however, became mired in lengthy conflicts. Not only were they attacked by the Serb-controlled Yugoslav army, but they also were assaulted by local Serbs, many of whom were armed by Milosevic's Serbian government. Croatian Serbs seized control of the Krajina, a portion of Croatia where Serbs had lived since the eighteenth century.

By early 1995 Bosnian Serbs, backed by the Yugoslav government, were in control of 70 percent of Bosnia-Herzegovina. Mass murders, gang rapes, and house burnings became routine occurrences as the Bosnian Serbs carried out a policy they called "ethnic cleansing": the removal of Bosnian Muslims

Josip Broz, also known as Marshal Tito, led Yugoslavia in various offices from 1943 to 1980.

from areas claimed exclusively by Serbs. Between 1992 and 1995 the Bosnian capital of Sarajevo, once a model of multiethnic harmony, was besieged by Serb artillery.

Efforts by the United Nations and the NATO alliance to promote a settlement of these disputes proved ineffective until the summer of 1995. In August the Croatian government launched a massive assault on Krajina, evicting more than 150,000 Serbs. Prodded into action by a new wave of Bosnian Serb atrocities, including the murder of thousands of men and boys and their burial in mass graves, the U.S. government and its NATO allies launched a series of air attacks on Serb positions throughout Bosniak-Herzegovina. Bosniak forces took the offensive and regained control of several areas from the Bosnian Serbs. At the same time, fresh diplomatic initiatives succeeded in convincing Serbia's Milosevic to curtail his support for the Bosnian Serbs and come to the peace table.

Peace talks involving the leaders of Croatia, Bosnia-Herzegovina, and Serbia took place under U.S. auspices at the Wright-Patterson Air Force Base outside Dayton, Ohio. After three weeks of intense bargaining, the main parties initialed a comprehensive peace agreement on November 21, 1995. The Dayton Accords divided Bosnia-Herzegovina into the Muslim-Croat Federation and a Serbian zone known as the Serb Republic. This agreement was initially policed by a NATO force of some 60,000 troops, of whom 20,000 were Americans.

After the Dayton Accords, attention turned once more to Kosovo. Starting in 1997, a force of ethnic Albanians known as the Kosovo Liberation Army (KLA) took up arms against Serbian forces in an effort to gain the province's complete independence. Serbian reprisals were intense, and by the summer of 1998 some 700,000 refugees had fled the province. As Serb forces pressed their campaign against the KLA and civilian noncombatants, the NATO alliance began an intensive bombing campaign in April 1999. Swarms of refugees streamed out of Kosovo into neighboring Albania and Macedonia, many bearing tales of murders, rapes, extortion, and other atrocities committed by Serbian military and special police forces. The ethnic cleansing of Kosovo by some 40,000 Serbian troops

MAP 4.4   The Balkans Today

and paramilitary fighters was in full swing. After 11 weeks of bombing, which destroyed power plants, bridges, and other facilities in Belgrade and other parts of Serbia and Montenegro, Milosevic suddenly gave up and accepted NATO peace terms. All Yugoslav troops were compelled to leave Kosovo, and a 50,000 strong international peacekeeping force led by NATO took their place. By the end of 1999 most of the Kosovar Albanian refugees had returned to Kosovo, often to find their loved ones killed and their property destroyed. About 100,000 Serbs left the province, about half the number who lived there before the bombing campaign.

After giving in to NATO, Milosevic remained in office until a spontaneous revolution forced his resignation. In September 2000 it appeared he had lost the presidential election to Vojislav Kostunica, a constitutional lawyer. When Milosevic

(Continued on next page)

(Continued from previous page)

tried to suppress the election results, hundreds of thousands of protesters stormed Belgrade, seizing official buildings and media outlets on October 5. Milosevic resigned the next day. He was later handed over to the International Criminal Tribunal for the Former Yugoslavia in The Hague. Milosevic died in jail in 2006 while his trial was still in progress.[26]

Since the end of the Balkan wars, the independent states that once composed Yugoslavia have taken divergent paths. (See Table 4.1 for a comparative summary on the states that have emerged from the former Yugoslavia.) Slovenia has developed a stable democratic system, and it joined the European Union and NATO in 2004. Croatia has made substantial progress in stabilizing its democracy. In 2004 it was invited to begin talks on joining the European Union, which was scheduled to take place in 2013. Bosnia-Herzegovina has been making only slow progress toward democracy and reconciliation among the Muslims, Serbs, and Croatians who live in the two parts of the country's federated system. With the party system fragmented along ethnic lines, nationalistic antagonisms dominated the elections of 2002, 2006, and 2010, while international peacekeepers and advisors oversee a power-sharing arrangement among the three ethnic groups in which the presidency rotates among three different presidents every eight months. The ethnic groups also share cabinet posts.

In 2001, Macedonia was wracked by violent conflict between its Macedonian majority and ethnic Albanians, who compose 23 percent of the population. The Albanians demanded wider language rights, civil service jobs, and constitutional changes in their favor. As Albanian guerrillas and Macedonian armed forces squared off, NATO interposed a peacekeeping force. A settlement was reached in the same year, permitting elections to take place in 2002. In 2005 Macedonia was invited to begin negotiations on entering the European Union.

What remained of Yugoslavia formally changed its name to the State Union of Serbia and Montenegro in 2002. The newly named state was making slow advances toward democracy. But in a 2006 referendum, 55 percent of Montenegrin voters approved independence, setting the stage for the creation of a new state of Montenegro. In 2008, Kosovo declared its independence. Over 90 states have recognized independent Kosovo, including the United States.

Yugoslavia's experience suggests that multinational states are very likely to be unstable in the contemporary world. As we will see in Chapter 16, the other major communist

Table 4.1 Successor States of the Former Yugoslavia

Country	Population (in millions)	Main Language	Major Religion(s)	Political Status	Relationship with European Union	Freedom House Status
Bosnia-Herzegovina	3.8	Serbo-Croatian*	Islam and Christianity	Independent but under international supervision	Recognized to be a potential candidate	Partly Free
Croatia	4.4	Serbo-Croatian*	Roman Catholicism	Independence declared in 1991; joined UN in 1992	Joined EU July 2013	Free
Kosovo	2.3	Albanian	Islam	Independence declared in 2008 and recognized by 93 of 190 UN members	22 of 27 members recognize Kosovo's independence	Partly Free
Macedonia	2.0	Macedonian	Orthodox Christianity and Islam	Independence through referendum in 1991; joined UN in 1993	Applied to join in 2004; candidate since 2005	Partly Free
Montenegro	0.6	Serbo-Croatian*	Orthodox Christianity and Islam	Independence through referendum in 2006; joined UN in 2006	Applied to join in 2008; candidate since 2010	Free
Serbia	7.3	Serbo-Croatian*	Orthodox Christianity	Became a separate state upon the independence of Montenegro in 2006	Applied to join in 2009; candidate since 2012	Free
Slovenia	2.0	Slovene	Roman Catholicism	Independence through referendum in 1990; joined UN in 1992	Joined EU in 2004	Free

*Also known as Bosnian/Croatian/Serbian (BCS).

Sources: BBC, Freedom House

multinational state, the Soviet Union, also succumbed to nationalist sentiments in the early 1990s, although without the intense violence that characterized Yugoslavia's dissolution. Pent-up nationalist feelings can produce political explosions, especially when roused by leaders such as Milosevic.

Such leaders can easily appeal to historical memories of when one ethnic or national group was abused by others, such as the Nazi-allied Croat persecution of Serbs in World War II. Whether the injustices of the 1990s will yield nationalist conflicts in future decades remains a concern.

While the twentieth century saw enormous and bloody conflicts associated with nationalism—none more devastating than World War II—and nationalist movements have continued to provoke difficult-to-resolve conflicts such as those we have just reviewed, other experiences with national identity have proven more encouraging for those who seek a more peaceful world. Economic and political integration of sovereign states holds the promise to reduce some of the international conflict that emerges from nationalist feeling. Let's look at supranationalism, perhaps the successor to nationalism.

SUPRANATIONALISM

The state remains the central form of political organization in today's world. To be sure, the forces of globalization—

economic interactions, communications links, environmental spillovers, and the like—are driving sovereign governments to cooperate with one another more than at any other time in history, placing the very concept of national sovereignty in doubt. The realities of international relationships have in some cases led to highly structured attempts to promote cooperation across state boundaries. The most far-reaching of these efforts thus far has been the *European Union.*

The European Union (EU) is a prime example of supranationalism at work. **Supranationalism** refers to efforts on the part of two or more countries to limit their sovereignty by establishing decision-making structures over and above their national governments. In the case of the EU, these supranational bodies have the authority to make laws that are binding on the member states. We will examine the EU in detail to show how supranationalism has emerged

CASE STUDY
The European Union

In 1957, six West European countries—France, West Germany, Italy, and the three Benelux countries (Belgium, the Netherlands, and Luxembourg)—signed a historic agreement designed to expand their economic cooperation. The terms of their agreement, known as the Treaty of Rome, took effect at the start of 1958 and the European Economic Community (EEC) became a reality. Its principal aim was to promote economic growth among the member states by eliminating tariffs and other trade barriers and by jointly concluding trade agreements with nonmember states. In the early 1960s the EEC members set up a *Common Agricultural Policy (CAP)* to protect their farmers from adverse world trading patterns.

Over time, the EEC was enlarged to include new members. Britain, Ireland, and Denmark joined in 1973; Greece joined in 1981; Spain and Portugal became members in 1986. As it took on both new members and new tasks, the organization changed its name to the European Union in 1993 when the Maastricht Treaty came into force. Two years later, Austria, Sweden, and Finland brought the total number of EU members to 15. Membership rose to 25 in 2004, with the addition of 10 more new members: the Czech Republic, Estonia, Hungary, Latvia, Lithuania, Poland, Slovakia, and Slovenia—all

once ruled by communist governments—along with Cyprus and Malta. Bulgaria and Romania, two more former communist states, became EU members in 2007. Croatia became the 28th EU member in July 2013. The EU began accession negotiations with Turkey and Macedonia in 2005, Montenegro in 2008, and Iceland and Serbia in 2009 (see Map 4.5).

From the outset, Europeans have been divided between those who have wanted to accelerate the process of economic and political integration and those who have wished to keep integration within stricter limits to preserve greater freedom of action for their own national governments. Proponents of greater supranationalism have continuously sparred with advocates of state sovereignty. These debates still take place, but there has always been a general consensus that varying degrees of both tendencies should coexist. As a consequence, the organization's institutions were set up to permit significant levels of supranational activity while simultaneously preserving the member governments' rights to make important EU decisions and even to opt out of EU activities that they do not like. Following deliberations by a special convention and protracted negotiations, in 2004 the EU completed the drafting

(Continued on next page)

(Continued from previous page)

MAP 4.5   The European Union

of a constitution designed to reform its institutions and clarify their powers. That document was put on hold after French and Dutch voters rejected it in referendums held in 2006. In 2007 European heads of state returned to the negotiation table and reached agreement on the Treaty of Lisbon, which redefined the roles of key EU institutions, described below. The Treaty of Lisbon was ratified by all member states by 2009. After the Lisbon treaty, the European Union retained essentially the same organizational structure created in the Treaty of Rome, with the following key institutions:

■ The *European Commission* is one of the EU's most supra-national bodies. As such it is authorized to propose and

enforce common EU laws and policies. It may also negotiate certain international treaties. However, the commission is not empowered to make final decisions in creating new EU law, a prerogative that remains in the hands of the EU governments. At present there are 28 commission members (one from each member state), including the *President of the Commission*. After 2014 there will be one commission member for two-thirds of the member states. Although the president and the commissioners are appointed by the EU states (and must be approved by the European Parliament), they are expected to act independently of national governments, taking a pledge to place "the general interest of the Community" ahead of the interests of any member country.

■ The *Council of the European Union* is the EU's main decision-making body. It consists of regular meetings of cabinet ministers of the member states, broken down into nine functional committees. If general topics or foreign affairs are being discussed, the foreign affairs ministers meet as the General Affairs and External Relations Council. If agricultural matters are being discussed, the council consists of the agriculture ministers, and so on. The main purpose of the council is to protect the sovereign rights of the member states through a decision-making process of *intergovernmentalism,* which gives each national government a say in the making of common EU laws and policies. Some council decisions are taken under a system of weighted majority voting, in which the larger states get more votes than the smaller ones. Other decisions require unanimity, giving each country veto power. The 28 member governments take turns holding the presidency of the Council of the European Union for a period of six months. In that capacity, that member government's key cabinet ministers chair council meetings and set their agendas.

■ The *European Council* consists of the heads of government of the member countries (plus the heads of state of three of them), along with the president of the European

Commission. These powerful individuals meet as a group several times a year to make final decisions on important EU matters and chart the EU's future path. The chief executives of the member countries take special responsibility for the EU's Common Foreign and Security Policy. Although they sometimes agree to act unanimously, each member country carefully guards its sovereign independence when serious disputes arise. As a consequence, gaining agreement on issues that divide the members is difficult. For example, in 2003, as the EU states were being pressured by the United States to support its impending invasion of Iraq, the European Council was split between supporters of the U.S. action, led by British Prime Minister Tony Blair, and its chief opponents, France and Germany. Lacking a consensus, the European Council took no common action.

- The *European Parliament (EP)* has been directly elected by the people of the member countries since 1979. By the Treaty of Lisbon its size is limited to 750 delegates. The EP's approval is required in a number of specified areas before a measure can become EU law, but it still has very limited authority in foreign affairs and agricultural policy, and it has no right to raise revenue.

- The *European Court of Justice (ECJ)* consists of judges appointed by the member states. It is empowered to issue rulings and legal interpretations in cases involving other EU institutions, member governments, private businesses, associations (such as labor unions), and individuals in matters concerning European community law. In many instances, the laws of the European Union take precedence over the national laws of the member states. As a result, the ECJ plays an important role in the supranational aspects of EU activities.

In addition to these core institutions, the EU has numerous additional organs that serve as advisory bodies, policy implementation agencies, and the like. One of the most important of these institutions is the *European Central Bank*, which coordinates the monetary policies of the 17 EU states that have adopted the euro as their common currency. (Britain, Bulgaria, the Czech Republic, Denmark, Hungary, Latvia, Lithuania, Poland, Romania, and Sweden use their own national currency instead of the euro.) All the member states are included in the EU's single market, which promotes the free movement of goods, services, money, and people throughout the region (though newer members are being phased into the single market gradually). On average, about 85 percent of the member countries' business laws are now determined by the EU. In addition, the EU is engaged in coordinating immigration policies, anticrime and antiterrorism activities, environmental standards, and a plethora of other matters, with supranational laws often superseding domestic laws and policies. The EU has also played a vital role in promoting

democracy in its recently admitted states, most of which were under communist rule less than 20 years ago.

As Europe faces the challenges of a 28-member union, with a population topping 500 million, controversies continue to swirl over the central issue of supranationalism versus state sovereignty. Almost everyone wants a measure of both, but they disagree on the right mix. Supranationalists contend that individual EU member states can gain more political influence by cooperating in Europe-wide institutions than by acting alone. They also point to the economic rewards of a highly integrated European economy that had a combined gross domestic product of approximately $17.6 trillion in 2011 among its then 27 EU members (as compared with $15.1 trillion for the United States). The EU was collectively the number-one trading partner of the United States, China, and Russia. Proponents of sovereignty warn that a "democratic deficit" is developing as national governments in Paris, London, and other European capitals lose control over their own domestic and foreign policy choices to communitywide decision-making bodies. They object to ceding vast regulatory authority to some 25,000 EU bureaucrats based mostly in Brussels, the EU's headquarters.[27]

While many fear the consequence of giving over national sovereignty to an EU bureaucracy distant from national territory and disconnected to national concerns, events since 2009 have shown that the monetary interdependence forged by the use of the euro can cause the actions of small nations to have extraordinary consequences for hundreds of millions of Europeans. Because the 17 nations of the euro zone chose to use a single currency, they simultaneously made commitments to try to avoid government spending decisions that would affect the value of the currency. The most important commitment is to avoid large government spending deficits. Public policy choices made by past Greek governments—and other governments, including those of Ireland, Italy, and Spain—as well as Greece's inability to raise the necessary tax revenue to meet the spending requirements of those choices led to extensive borrowing by the Greek government, loans that it now cannot repay. If Greece were not in the euro zone, it would probably devalue its currency. Being in the euro zone, it cannot do that, and the leaders of larger European countries, especially Germany, are pressing the Greeks to drastically cut spending and increase taxes to meet their obligations. The Greek citizens on whom these decisions would have dramatic impacts have shown their rejection of that option by huge public demonstrations that have brought down governments. But while the Greeks are suffering a loss of their sovereignty to the EU, other EU countries are simultaneously at risk of a general economic setback if this crisis causes international investors to doubt that the euro zone will survive this crisis. A small nation in this supranational community could wreck the major monetary project of 16 of its partners—the common currency, the euro.

Other regions of the world have also embarked on closer attempts at economic cooperation, though none have gone as far in the direction of supranational institutions as the European Union. Meanwhile, even the EU countries have not entirely dispensed with their own national identities, as the following hypothesis-testing exercise shows.

HYPOTHESIS-TESTING EXERCISE
Are Europeans Developing a Common Supranational Identity?

Hypothesis Many early observers of the economic and political integration project in Europe thought that increasing trade, international investment, and labor migration within Europe would break down the nationalist feelings that had promoted the terrible wars of the twentieth century. In their place they expected the emergence of a European identity over and above divisive nationalism. Let's hypothesize that supranational political and economic institutions and practices are creating a common European identity that is replacing national and regional identities among the people of the member states.

Variables In this hypothesis, the *dependent variable* is a common European identity. The *independent variable* is the European Union's supranational institutions and practices.

Expectations If our hypothesis is correct, then we'd expect the evidence to show that, over time, the citizens of the EU countries have exhibited on average (1) a noticeable decline in their national and regional attachments; and (2) a correspondingly greater inclination to identify themselves as "European" rather than as French, Italian, Polish, and so on.

Evidence The evidence bearing on our hypothesis comes mainly from public opinion surveys conducted by the EU over the years and released as a Eurobarometer. It does not corroborate our expectations. Instead of diminishing their national or local attachments, people living in most EU countries have continued to affirm these loyalties. A survey in 1990 revealed that, on average, 88 percent felt attached to their country, 87 percent to their region, 85 percent to their town or village, and only 47 percent to 48 percent to the European Community or to Europe as a whole. In 2002, regional and local attachments remained much the same, but attachment to country rose to an EU-average of 90 percent and attachment to the EU dropped to 45 percent.

Similarly, the evidence contradicts our second expectation, that a common European identity is replacing separate national identities. A series of Eurobarometer surveys has asked people in the EU countries if they saw themselves in the near future as their "nationality only"; their "nationality and European"; "European and their nationality"; or "European only." The results were precisely the opposite of what our hypothesis would predict. Table 4.2 shows responses to this question for Eurobarometers conducted in spring 1992, spring 1998, and spring 2010. Remember that the EU integration project had received two big boosts with the Maastricht Treaty in 1993 (between the first two of these surveys) and the Lisbon Treaty in 2007–09 (between the last two surveys). The percentage of people who defined themselves in terms of their "nationality only" actually rose between 1992 and 1998 from about 40 percent to close to 48 percent and stayed there in 2010. Those who combined national and European identities and placed Europe first ("European and nationality") stayed quite low, at 6 percent or less. Most telling of all, the percentage of people who saw themselves as "European only" was small to begin with in 1992 (3 percent), and remains at around 3 percent in 2010.

Conclusions Evidence indicating growing levels of national identity and declining levels of European identity contradicts our expected outcome. Although the percentage of people who expressed at least some degree of European identity, either exclusively or in combination with their nationality, stood at 56 percent in 1992, their ranks fell to 48 percent by 1998 and remained about there (49 percent) in 2010. We must therefore conclude that the evidence is *inconsistent* with our hypothesis that European integration is replacing national identities with a broader European identity. Most people in the EU countries profess multiple identities, with national and local identities coexisting with attachment to Europe.[28]

Table 4.2 European and National Identities

In the near future, do you see yourself as . . . ?	Spring 1992	Spring 1998	Spring 2010
National	40.4	47.8	47.8
National and European	47.1	39.3	40.5
European and National	6.0	4.8	6.1
European	3.0	4.3	2.7
Don't Know/No Answer/None	3.5	3.6	2.9

Cells report the percentage of respondents who chose each answer.

Sources: Eurobarometers 37.0 (Spring 1992), 49 (Spring 1998), 73.4 (May 2010), available from the European Commission at ec.europa.eu/public_opinion/.

Conclusion

States and nations retain their importance in today's global system. While the norm might be that each nation should have its own state that governs the territory that it inhabits, the reality is that nations often live mixed alongside each other in territories over which they struggle, as in the case of the Israelis and Palestinians. Other states are not nation-states at all, but multinational states that are, in the contemporary world, subject to the demands of the nations within them for autonomy or secession, as we've seen in the cases of Sudan and Yugoslavia. Although political theorists may look forward to an age of cosmopolitan citizens of the world, the national idea remains powerful today and most people remain attached to their nations.

In Chapter 5 we'll begin examining what has lately become the most widely used method for the governance of states: *democracy.*

Key Terms

Nation
National identity
Citizenship
Jus soli
Jus sanguinis
Nationalism
Self-determination
Territorial autonomy
State building
Nation building
Nation-state
Supranationalism

Notes

1. James D. Fearon, "Ethnic and Cultural Diversity by Country," *Journal of Economic Growth* 8 (2003): 195–222.
2. Lowell W. Barrington, "'Nation' and 'Nationalism': The Misuse of Key Concepts in Political Science," *PS: Political Science and Politics,* vol. 30, no. 4 (December 1997), 712–16.
3. Karl Deutsch, *Nationalism and Social Communication,* 2nd ed. (Cambridge, MA: MIT Press, 1966), pp. 96–98; Benedict Anderson, *Imagined Communities,* rev. ed. (London: Verso, 1991), pp. 6, 7.
4. David D. Laitin, *Identity in Formation: The Russian-Speaking Populations in the Near Abroad* (Ithaca, NY: Cornell University Press, 1998); David D. Laitin, *Language Repertoires and State Construction in Africa* (New York: Cambridge University Press, 1992); Russell Hardin, *One for All: The Logic of Group Conflict* (Princeton, NJ: Princeton University Press, 1995).
5. T. Alexander Aleinikoff and Douglas Klusmeyer, "Plural Nationality: Facing the Future in a Migratory World," in *Citizenship Today: Global Perspectives and Practices,* ed. Aleinikoff and Klusmeyer (Washington, DC: Carnegie Endowment for International Peace, 2001), pp. 63–88.
6. See Rogers Brubaker, *Citizenship and Nationhood in France and Germany* (Cambridge, MA: Harvard University Press, 1992).
7. Veysel Oezcan, "Germany: Immigration in Transition," *Migration Immigration Source,* July 2004, available at http://www.migrationinformation.org.
8. For scholarly views on nationalism, see John Hutchinson and Anthony D. Smith, eds., *Nationalism* (Oxford: Oxford University Press, 1994). Also, Anthony D. Smith, *National Identity* (Reno: University of Nevada Press, 1991); Eric Hobsbawm, *Nations and Nationalism Since 1870* (New York: Cambridge University Press, 1970); Adrian Hastings, *The Construction of Nationhood* (New York: Cambridge University Press, 1997); Ernest Gellner, *Nationalism* (New York: New York University Press, 1997).
9. For a comparison of German and American nationalism, see Liah Greenfield, *Nationalism: Five Roads to Modernity* (Cambridge, MA: Harvard University Press, 1992), ch. 4 and 5.
10. On recent efforts to deal with "linguistic territoriality" in East Central Europe, see Zsuzsa Csergo, *Language, Division, and Integration: Lessons from Post-Communist Romania and Slovakia* (Ithaca, NY: Cornell University Press, 2007).
11. Francis Fukuyama, ed., *Nation-Building: Beyond Afghanistan and Iraq* (Baltimore: Johns Hopkins University Press, 2006), p. 3.
12. James D. Fearon and David D. Laitin, "Ethnicity, Insurgency, and Civil War," *American Political Science Review* 97, no. 1 (February 2003), pp. 75–90.
13. Monica Duffy Toft and Stephen M. Saideman, "Self-Determination Movements and Their Outcomes," in *Peace and Conflict 2010,* ed. J. Joseph Hewitt, Jonathan Wilkenfeld, and Ted Robert Gurr (Boulder: Paradigm Publishers, 2010), p. 46.
14. Julie Flint and Alex de Waal, *Darfur: A Short History of a Long War* (London: Zed, 2005); Gérard Prunier, *Darfur: The Ambiguous Genocide* (Ithaca, NY: Cornell University Press, 2005).
15. Greenfield, *Nationalism,* ch. 1 and 2.
16. Nationalism has also been defined accordingly. Ernest Gellner defined it as the political principle "which holds that the political and national unit should be congruent." See his *Nations and Nationalism* (Ithaca, NY: Cornell University Press, 1983), p. 1. Elie Kedourie wrote, "Nationalism holds that the only legitimate type of government is national self-determination." See his *Nationalism,* 4th ed. (Oxford: Blackwell, 1993), p. 1.
17. Cited by Walker Connor in Hutchinson and Smith, *Nationalism,* p. 39.
18. *Freedom in the World 2001–2002* (New York: Freedom House, 2002), p. 15.
19. Sumantra Bose, "The Implications of Ethno-National Conflict," in *Freedom in the World 2003* (New York: Freedom House, 2003), pp. 21–23. See also Partha S. Ghosh, *Ethnicity versus Nationalism: The Devolution Discourse in Sri Lanka* (Thousand Oaks, CA: Sage, 2003).
20. Benny Morris, *The Birth of the Palestinian Refugee Problem Revisited* (Cambridge: Cambridge University Press, 2004); Peter Rodgers, *Herzl's Nightmare: One Land, Two Peoples* (New York: Nation, 2005).
21. Gershom Gorenberg, *The Accidental Empire: Israel and the Birth of the Settlements, 1967–1977* (New York: Henry Holt, 2006).
22. See Nissim Rejwan, *Israel in Search of Identity: Reading the Formative Years* (Gainesville, FL: University Press of Florida, 1999); Howard M. Sachar, *A History of Israel: From the Rise of Zionism to Our Times* (New York: Alfred A. Knopf, 1976); Howard M. Sachar, *A History of Israel II: From the Aftermath of the Yom Kippur War* (Oxford: Oxford University Press, 1987); Howard M. Sachar, *Dreamland:European Jews in the Aftermath of the Great War* (New York: Alfred A. Knopf, 2002).
23. Baruch Kimmerling and Joel S. Migdal, *The Palestinian People: A History* (Cambridge, MA: Harvard University Press, 2003). See also Rashid Khalidi, *Palestinian National Identity: The Construction of Modern National Consciousness* (New York: Columbia University Press, 1997); Christina E. Zacharia, *Palestine and the Palestinians* (Boulder, CO: Westview, 1997); Glenn E. Robinson, *Building a Palestinian State: The Incomplete Revolution* (Bloomington, IN: Indiana University Press, 1997); Yezid Sayigh, *Armed Struggle and the Search for a State: The Palestinian National Movement 1949–1993* (Oxford: Clarendon Press, 1997); Joel S. Migdal, *Palestinians: The Making of a People* (Cambridge, MA: Harvard University Press, 1994).
24. Nathan Brown, *Palestinian Politics After the Accords: Resuming Arab Palestine* (Berkeley, CA: University of California Press, 2003).
25. See Shlomo Ben-Ami, *Scars of War, Wounds of Peace: The Israeli-Arab Tragedy* (New York: Oxford University Press, 2006); Bernard Wasserstein, *Israelis and Palestinians: Why Do They Fight? Can They Stop?* 2nd ed. (New Haven, CN: Yale University Press, 2003); Bernard Wasserstein, *Divided Jerusalem: The Struggle for the Holy City,* 2nd ed. (New Haven, CN: Yale University Press, 2002); Amira Hass, *Reporting from Ramallah: An Israeli Journalist in an Occupied Land,* ed. and trans. Rachel Leah Jones (Los Angeles: Semiotext(e), 2003); Daphna Golan-Agnon, *Next Year in Jerusalem: Everyday Life in a Divided Land,* trans. Janine Woolfson (New York: New Press, 2005); and Matthew Levitt, *Hamas: Politics, Charity, and Terrorism in the Service of Jihad* (New Haven, CN: Yale University Press, 2006).

26. On Milosevic, see Dusko Doder and Louise Branson, *Milosevic: Portrait of a Tyrant* (New York: Simon & Schuster, 1999); Lenard J. Cohen, *Serpent in the Bosom: The Rise and Fall of Slobodan Milosevic* (Boulder, CO: Westview, 2000); Louis Sell, *Slobodan Milosevic and the Destruction of Yugoslavia* (Durham, NC: Duke University Press, 2000); Slavoljub Djukic, *Milosevic and Markovic: A Lust for Power,* trans. by Alex Dubinsky (Montreal: McGill-Queen's University Press, 2001).

27. For an overview of the history and structure of the EU, see Desmond Dinan, *Ever Closer Union,* 3rd ed. (Boulder, CO: Lynne Rienner, 2005); also Neill Nugent, *The Government and Politics of the European Union,* 6th ed. (Durham, NC: Duke University Press, 2006); John Van Oudenaren, *Uniting Europe,* 2nd ed. (Lanham, MD: Rowman & Littlefield, 2004).

28. Eurobarometer is released periodically by the European Commission and can be accessed through the EU's website, ec.europa.eu. See, in particular, numbers 37 (1992), 49 (1998), and 73 (2010).

5 Democracy: What Is It?

OVERVIEW

■ Democracy can take a variety of forms. Societies choose democratic regimes because they expect democracy to enhance the quality of human life and the dignity of the individual, to ascertain and carry out the wishes of the community, to constrain excessive government power, and to reduce social antagonisms.

■ Political thinkers agree that core democratic principles are the rule of law, inclusion, and equality.

■ Beyond those core principles, political theorists and citizens tend to focus on different aspects, or faces, of democracy: popular sovereignty, rights and liberties, democratic values, and economic democracy.

■ Ordinary citizens tend to understand democracy as a political process with access to fundamental civil liberties and policy outcomes favorable to poor and middle class people.

Political theorists trace debates about democracy to ancient Greece.

DEFINING DEMOCRACY: INITIAL SUGGESTIONS

Thus far we have talked about democracy quite a bit without providing more than a rudimentary definition of the term. In Chapter 1 we put it this way:

The essential idea of democracy is that the people have the right to determine who governs them. In most cases they elect the principal governing officials and hold them accountable for their actions. Democracies also impose legal limits on the government's authority by guaranteeing certain rights and freedoms to their citizens.

But like many dictionary-style definitions, this one oversimplifies a highly complex phenomenon. In fact, democracy

can take a variety of forms. It can mean different things to different people. For some theorists of democracy, representation based on free, fair, competitive elections is the main defining principle of democratic governance. Many theorists contend that a country with these features at least meets the minimum requirements of an *electoral democracy*. Freedom House estimates that there were 118 electoral democracies around the world by the end of 2012, representing 61 percent of 195 sovereign states. But elections, while vitally important, are by no means sufficient to establish a full-fledged democracy. Democracy also requires certain legally protected rights and liberties for the population. Without such things as freedom of speech, freedom of assembly, and other basic liberties that the government must not infringe, elections are meaningless. Freedom House

Table 5.1 Understanding Democracy

Four purposes of democracy
1. To enhance the quality of human life and the dignity of the individual
2. To ascertain and carry out the wishes of the community
3. To constrain power
4. To reduce social antagonisms

Three principles of democracy (on which there is agreement):
1. Rule of law
2. Inclusion
3. Equality

Four faces of democracy (about which there may be disagreement or differences of emphasis):
1. Popular sovereignty
2. Rights and liberties
3. Democratic values
4. Economic democracy

ranked 90 countries as "free" in 2012, reflecting their success in combining electoral democracy with a wide range of rights and liberties. Countries that guarantee these basic liberties are often called *liberal democracies*. As Fareed Zakaria has suggested, governments that hold elections but withhold fundamental rights and liberties can be considered "illiberal democracies."[1] Illiberal democracies are not true democracies. Most illiberal democracies fall into Freedom House's partly free category, meaning they are mixed regimes having some aspects of democracy and some of authoritarianism. Later in this chapter we will discuss illiberal democracy and other hybrid regimes.

What, then, is democracy? Let's start by considering democracy's purposes. Why would a society choose to be governed by a democratic regime? Why would individuals prefer democracy to authoritarian rule? Then we will turn to a consideration of principles that all democracies must strive to achieve to merit the democracy label. Democratic thinkers agree on basic principles that must be present in any democracy. After considering what people agree are the fundamental principles of democracy, we will look at four different understandings of democracy's main emphasis, or four faces of democracy. Table 5.1 summarizes these purposes, principles, and faces of democracy that will be the main themes of this chapter. We will close the chapter by exploring what ordinary citizens say they understand democracy to be.

PURPOSES AND PARADOXES OF DEMOCRACY

Why have democracy? Why should anyone consider it preferable to a dictatorship? Democracy's four most widely acknowledged purposes answer these questions. These purposes are the goals that political thinkers and ordinary citizens alike may envision for democratic regimes. One purpose is to enhance the quality of

human life and the dignity of the individual. Democracy empowers ordinary people to participate meaningfully in the affairs of their community, to express their opinions, and to have a say in the decisions of their government. It also provides ample space for individual freedom and promotes political equality on the basis of "one person, one vote." Democracy thus has a profoundly moral dimension that dictatorships, with their tendency to ignore, suppress, and violently abuse their populations, generally lack.

Another purpose is to ascertain and carry out the wishes of the community. In an attempt to determine what Swiss philosopher Jean-Jacques Rousseau called the "general will," democracies foster open discussion of alternative programs and policies, conduct public opinion polls, and permit their citizens to choose among candidates representing competing views at election time. Democracies also allow the citizenry to be well informed about the activities of their government and to hold state officials accountable for their actions.

A third purpose of democracy is to constrain power. By imposing legal limitations on the authority of state officials, democracies hold in check the enormous coercive capabilities of the state. And, by permitting virtually the entire adult population to participate in political life, democracy promotes pluralism and counterbalances the influence of exceptionally well-advantaged social groups and organizations.

Finally, democracy seeks to reduce social antagonisms. When the various groups that compose society have a chance to be heard and to share power through their votes, democracy gives each one a chance to gain something. Recognizing that they stand to win more by playing the democratic game than by refusing to cooperate, rival social groups negotiate and compromise. Democracy thus provides incentives to replace confrontation with cooperation. But what if the aims and ideals of democracy are not realized in practice? The quality of democracy, after all, is only as good as the people who are its

Jean-Jacques Rousseau, who originated the concept of the "general will."

lifeblood. The central paradox of democracy is that its institutions and practices can be neglected, subverted, or manipulated in ways that contradict its basic purposes, even when its rules and procedures are being followed. In some cases democracy can backfire, producing results that are the very opposite of its objectives. For each of the purposes of democracy just enumerated, there can be corresponding countertendencies.

Political participation, for example, can fall well short of its potential, as we'll explore in Chapter 8. Most people do not take part in political life, except perhaps to vote every few years. Some people may feel that their voice or votes don't count for very much, and therefore retreat into apathy or cynicism. They may feel that important issues are ignored by politicians who prefer sound bites and slogans to real debate, or that there are inadequate opportunities for citizens to discuss policies intelligently in open forums. Manipulation of the issues by elites often substitutes for deliberation by citizens. Moreover, nonvoting by some confers greater political influence on those who do vote, undermining democratic equality.[2]

In addition, it may be difficult to ascertain or implement the "general will" of the people. Modern democracies are often seriously divided on important questions. In many cases there are fundamental divisions over the proper role of the state. Some segments of the population may want the state to maximize their freedom. In this so-called liberal (or neoliberal) view of government, an intrusive state with broad powers of intervention in economic and social matters is undemocratic because it limits the population's ability to control its own destiny (and its own money, if taxes are high). It is ironic that in the United States those holding neoliberal views are generally designated as "conservatives." But others may believe that democracy necessitates certain fundamental economic and social rights for the whole population, such as the right to education, medical care, and housing. Any society built on glaring social inequalities is inherently undemocratic, according to this "social democratic" perspective. Its proponents would therefore favor an interventionist state with the authority—and tax revenue—to ensure a decent standard of living for all. But if a society is sharply divided on the proper role of government, what is the "general will"?[3]

At times a population may be so divided on a controversial issue that *no* decision can be reached even by simple majority rule. People frequently criticize elected officials for failing to get things done, but politicians are often divided because the people who elected them are divided. Institutional complications can magnify these problems. The U.S. Constitution, with its governmental checks and balances, was intentionally crafted to make it difficult to enact laws. Other democracies have their own problems making decisions. The "deadlock of democracy" is a frequent phenomenon.

Under these circumstances, either no effective decision can be taken, or a decision may have to be imposed on the population dictatorially (by the courts, perhaps, or by executive decree).[4] In other instances, the "general will" may be all too clear: It may reflect the desire of the majority to discriminate against minorities. The democratic principle of majority rule thus risks producing the tyranny of the majority.

Constraining power may also prove difficult. Once elected, governing elites and their appointees often enjoy considerable discretionary power to make unpopular or blatantly discriminatory decisions before facing the voters in the next election. Indeed, the very nature of electoral democracy practically dictates that victorious politicians will favor the constituencies who voted for them and will pay less attention to the rest of the electorate. Institutions such as the bureaucracy or the courts may possess virtually unchecked authority. The political influence of privileged social groups or giant corporations may also be hard to contain, whether or not they constitute a dominant power elite. The financing of political parties and candidates by wealthy donors inflates the power of money in the political process and enhances the chances of corruption. Keeping supporters on board and reaching out to potential new voters may prompt officeholders to spend money from state coffers on pork-barrel projects that favor their own political "clients." Lying and other forms of deception on the part of public officials can go unpunished or even undetected. In sum, the abuse of power may be less flagrant in a democracy than in a dictatorship, but it does not disappear entirely.

Finally, democracy may intensify and perpetuate social conflicts rather than attenuate them. Freedom of speech gives social groups the opportunity not only to articulate their grievances openly but also to criticize one another, fanning the flames of conflict. The right to associate for political purposes may result in the formation of political parties and other organizations that are each based exclusively on the needs or desires of one ethnic or religious group or another, thereby entrenching society's divisions and making compromise all the harder.

If any of these problems should arise, it is difficult to avoid the question: If this is democracy, how democratic is it? If we want to have a realistic conception of what the term signifies, we must begin by acknowledging that no single definition of democracy suffices. As we have just seen, people have different views about what democracy is supposed to achieve. And people also differ about what kinds of behavior by public officials or social groups may be considered truly "democratic." Democracy is not a fixed thing that comes in only one size and shape; there can be different forms and different degrees of democracy.

Several different definitions of democracy are therefore possible. Consequently, this chapter will not confine itself to just one concept of democracy or insist upon some notion of the "right" definition of the term. Instead we'll expose you to a variety of understandings and let you make up your own mind about what democracy really means. Chapter 6 will examine various institutional forms of democracy, and Chapter 7 will present a number of hypotheses about what it takes to build and sustain a democracy.

THREE PRINCIPLES OF DEMOCRACY

Before we consider four multiple—and often conflicting—conceptualizations of democracy, let's consider what political theorists and politicians alike agree are fundamental to democracy. The three basic principles that most theorists and political activists in today's world would probably agree are absolutely essential for a system of government to be considered democratic are (1) the rule of law, (2) inclusion, and (3) equality.

The **rule of law** is the principle that the power of the state must be limited by law and that no one is above the law. Stated simply, the rule of law means that those who govern, including the most powerful figures in the government, shall be under the law rather than above the law. It also means that the powers of government to make and enforce laws shall be limited by legal restraints as opposed to being unlimited. These notions are captured in the famous description of the American system as "a government of laws, not of men." The rule of law is the fundamental bedrock upon which democratic government rests. It requires the state to spell out the limitations to its authority in official documents, such as a written constitution, or in some other explicit form, such as legislation, court rulings, or publicly acknowledged understandings of what the law is. Without the rule of law, power can be wielded indiscriminately by governing officials, unchecked by any limits.

For all its conceptual simplicity, the rule of law has been a scarce commodity in humankind's political history. It emerged gradually in Britain over the course of several centuries, slowly enmeshing successive monarchs in legal limitations imposed by parliament and ultimately eventuating in a mass electoral democracy in the twentieth century (see Chapter 13). The rule of law was the foundation stone of the U.S. constitutional system from the earliest days of the republic. Aside from Britain and the United States, however, until the second half of the twentieth century the rule of law in most countries was conspicuous mainly by its absence. Although all states had laws, few had laws that significantly limited the power of the state.

Before World War II only a handful of countries, mainly in Western Europe, managed to establish governments based on the rule of law. Most of them failed to last very long, succumbing to the authoritarian forces of unconstrained state power. Fascism destroyed democracy in Italy and Germany, and Nazi aggression destroyed it in France. Only after the war did these countries succeed in stabilizing democratic governance based on the rule of law. Japan established its first real democratic government based on the rule of law at the end of World War II and under the guidance of the American Occupation authorities from 1945 to 1952. Even today, a number of countries struggling to establish democratic regimes for the first time in their history (such as Mexico) are simultaneously discovering the principle of the rule of law.

Unfortunately, political leaders who publicly commit themselves to the rule of law cannot always be counted on to observe the limitations it imposes. Violations of the civil rights of the population and all sorts of corrupt practices are perpetrated by elected officials or their appointees with alarming frequency, even in countries where the rule of law has been long established. Unless the rule of law is enshrined as the first principle of government, democracy cannot exist. But unless it is routinely observed by governing officials, democracy may not survive.

Inclusion means that the democratic rights and freedoms must be for everyone. They must not be denied to specifically targeted elements of the populations, such as women or minority groups. In other words, if a country has such democratic procedures as the right to vote, the right to free speech, and other explicitly defined political rights, these rights must not be denied or limited on a discriminatory basis to particular segments of the population. All must be included; otherwise, the political system can be considered only partially democratic at best. Even then, some people may regard a partial democracy as no democracy at all.

Inclusion also means that all the main social groups that comprise the population—ethnic groups, religious groups,

Alberto Fujimori, former president of Peru, was tried in that country for human rights abuses and thus for violating the rule of law in that country.

CASE STUDY
Who Is a Citizen? Voting Rights and Inclusion in the Baltic States

Three countries bordering the Baltic Sea—Estonia, Latvia, and Lithuania—were independent states between 1918 and 1940. On August 23, 1939, slightly more than a week before the start of the Second World War in Europe, Nazi Germany concluded a secret pact with the Soviet Union pledging to hand over all three countries to the Soviet regime. Shortly after the German army overran Eastern Europe, the USSR in accordance with the agreement annexed the Baltic states in 1940, immediately imposing harsh communist rule on their populations.

Hitler's willingness to permit Soviet domination over the area was purely tactical, however. He needed Moscow's temporary forbearance while he consolidated Nazi control over the rest of continental Europe. By the early summer of 1941 the Nazis were ready to double-cross Soviet leader Joseph Stalin and invade the Soviet Union. As German troops surged eastward they quickly wrested the Baltic region from the Soviets. For the next several years the three Baltic nations were exposed to the successive horrors of the Nazi occupation and Soviet efforts to retake them. In 1944 the Soviets finally succeeded in pushing the German army out of the USSR. In the process they reasserted sovereignty over their recent Baltic acquisitions. In August 1991, with communist authority in disarray at the highest levels of the Soviet government, Estonia, Latvia, and Lithuania formally declared their independence from the USSR. In all three states the rebirth of national sovereignty was accompanied by democracy. With widespread public support, democratic constitutions were adopted and a multiparty system quickly supplanted communism's one-party rule. But the installation of democratic rights and freedoms coincided, especially in Estonia and Latvia, with blatant attempts by the ethnic majority to exclude minorities from the democratic process.

When the USSR annexed the Baltic states in 1940, ethnic Estonians comprised 88 percent of Estonia's population and ethnic Latvians constituted 77 percent of the population of Latvia. Over the subsequent decades of Soviet rule, large numbers of ethnic Russians moved into these republics. By 1991, only 61 percent of Estonia's population of 1.6 million consisted of ethnic Estonians. The rest were ethnic minorities, with Russians comprising 30 percent of the total population. Latvia's population of about 2.5 million became even more diverse, with ethnic Latvians constituting a mere 52 percent of the total and Russians comprising 34 percent. In fact, Latvians today constitute a minority in the country's largest cities. Lithuania's population of 3.7 million in the early 1990s was less heterogeneous but still ethnically mixed, with ethnic Lithuanians representing 80 percent of the total, ethnic Russians 9 percent, and other ethnic groups such as Ukrainians and Belorussians constituting the remainder. In all three of these countries, most Russians could not speak the language of the ethnic majority. Their presence was sharply resented by large segments of the native ethnic majority because it provided a constant reminder of their domination at the hands of the leadership of the Soviet Union.

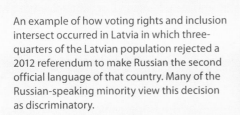

An example of how voting rights and inclusion intersect occurred in Latvia in which three-quarters of the Latvian population rejected a 2012 referendum to make Russian the second official language of that country. Many of the Russian-speaking minority view this decision as discriminatory.

(Continued on next page)

(Continued from previous page)

In 1992 Estonia instituted a new citizenship law that denied full citizenship to nearly all the country's 600,000 ethnic Russians, effectively denying them the right to vote and other democratic privileges. In 1993 the Estonian parliament passed a law that classified people who had assumed residency in Estonia after 1940 and their descendants as "aliens" rather than as citizens. Persons so designated were required to apply for special status as "permanent residents," but very few of them were allowed under the legislation to apply for citizenship.

Latvia followed a similar path. Regulations instituted by the Latvian parliament in 1991 granted full citizenship only to those who were citizens of Latvia before 1940 and their descendants. No others, including the sizable Russian minority, were allowed to apply for citizenship unless they had lived in Latvia at least 16 years, could demonstrate conversational ability in the Latvian language, and could meet various additional conditions. These guidelines disenfranchised some 700,000 people, nearly one-third of the country's voting-age population. Another law enacted in 1994 set a strict limit on the number of nonethnic Latvians who could qualify for citizenship by 2000.

These efforts to deny voting rights and other perquisites of democratic citizenship to ethnic minorities met with sharp criticism by the governments of the United States and the members of the European Union. When confronted with the disapproval of the community of democratic nations, the governing authorities in Estonia and Latvia relaxed their initial restrictions on minority rights somewhat. By 2003, there were about 170,000 noncitizens in Estonia. They had gained the right to vote (but not run for office) in local elections, but were still barred from voting in national elections. Speaking Estonian was no longer required for electoral candidates, but proficiency was required for certain private-sector jobs. In Latvia about one-fifth of the population were still noncitizens. Although the parliament in 2002 abolished a law requiring fluency in Latvian for candidates in national and local elections, the change had little meaning for noncitizens, who were forbidden to vote in state and local elections. In the same year, moreover, Latvian was adopted as the only official language in the national parliament and local councils. Noncitizens were also barred from some civil service jobs. In 2012 three-quarters of Latvian voters rejected a referendum issue that would have made Russian the second official language. Lithuania in 1992 extended citizenship to all people born there, including about 90 percent of all non-Lithuanian ethnic minorities. Nevertheless, ethnic minority groups living there have repeatedly complained of discrimination on the part of the Lithuanian majority.

social classes, and so on—should have reason to feel that they are better off under a democracy than under some nondemocratic form of government. Every group should have a realistic chance to gain something from abiding by democratic rules and procedures.[5] None should be systematically excluded from ever acquiring any advantages through the democratic process. If the "rules of the game" in a democracy are rigged against specific social groups or consistently work to some group's disadvantage, it is questionable whether such a system may legitimately be considered a democracy. Such an outcome might occur if democratic election procedures result in the permanent tyranny of the majority over minorities, for example.

Actually, almost every country that has ever been considered a democracy has either significantly reduced or denied certain political rights to targeted elements of the population. In some cases overt political discrimination against singled-out social groups may be so intentionally repressive as to place the country's democratic credentials in doubt. The denial of voting rights or other political rights to women, to nonproperty-owning classes, or to racial and religious minorities inevitably raises serious questions about how democratic such a political system really is. The definition of citizenship itself may be deliberately manipulated so as to disenfranchise certain segments of the population unfairly, as experiences in the Baltic states after the collapse of the Soviet Union demonstrate.

Equality means that democratic rights and freedoms must be accorded to everyone on an equal basis. No group in society should have fewer democratic privileges than other groups. Whereas the principle of inclusiveness asserts that democratic rights and freedoms must be for everyone, the principle of equality asserts that these same rights and freedoms must be distributed to everyone equally. No group or segment of the population should get more rights or freedoms than others. This principle is especially applicable with respect to basic civil rights, such as the right to vote, the right to free speech, and other rights that are directly related to the political relationship between the citizenry and the state. If the rules and practices of democracy are skewed in such a way as to deny the enjoyment of these civil rights to some segments of society on an equal basis with everyone else, democracy itself is diminished accordingly.

Thus if some members of society must meet higher voting qualifications than others, the distribution of civil rights is fundamentally unequal. (Until federal legislation was passed in the 1960s, for example, African-Americans in several states were required to pass much stiffer examinations than whites to qualify to vote.) Similarly, if the laws of the land are applied on a discriminatory basis, with some groups getting better treatment than others, the government violates the principle of "equal treatment under the law," a basic civil right in any true democracy.

For many decades before the Voting Rights Act of 1965, those who wanted to vote in many Southern states had to pay poll taxes. Such poll taxes fell more heavily on poor African-Americans, effectively creating inequalities in access to the franchise. Here we see a poll tax receipt paid by a white woman in Texas in the 1930s; non-whites would have found it difficult to pay $1.50 to vote at that time.

The concept of equality is a complex one, however. It can take on different meanings in different contexts. To begin with, there is an important distinction to be made between the principles of equality and equity. **Equity** means *fairness*. It requires only that we accord people a reasonably fair chance to realize their ambitions and improve their well-being under the same laws that apply to everyone else. It does not require us to make sure that everyone starts out or ends up on the same social or economic plane or enjoys the same degree of political influence. The rich usually have greater social and political advantages than the poor, but the principle of equity does not demand that we equalize wealth so that nobody is rich or poor; it simply insists that the poor be given a fair opportunity to improve their economic, social, or political welfare. Society can promote these goals by providing quality public education, medical care, legal assistance, and similar benefits to everyone at little or no cost, for example.

Equality, by contrast, is a more rigorous concept. It implies that everyone should ultimately be exactly or approximately equal whether in terms of their political rights (e.g., the right to vote) or their economic and social conditions. If everyone were truly equal in socioeconomic terms, everyone would have approximately the same amount of wealth and there would be no class distinctions. Very often when people use the term *equality* they really mean *equity*, and we should remain aware of the distinction.

While there is general agreement that democracies must grant their citizens political equality, there is continuing controversy over the question of economic equality. Some would argue that democracies should grant their citizens maximum freedom to pursue their economic fortunes with minimum government interference. If economic disparities result, creating different levels of wealth in society, so be it. Against this view, others would maintain that the equality of political rights must be accompanied by some form of equal social and economic rights. We'll examine some of these controversies later in this chapter.

As we shall see, all four faces of democracy are predicated on the notions of the rule of law, inclusion, and equality.

FOUR FACES OF DEMOCRACY

Our discussion of democratic principles focused on what people —political theorists and citizens of democracies alike—agree is fundamental to democracy. We turn now to contending perspectives or *faces* of democracy. These four faces are different understandings of the key elements of democracy. These faces of democracy are not necessarily incompatible, but different thinkers put greater or lesser emphasis on these understandings of what democracy is all about and a particular theorist may be disinclined to call a regime democratic if it doesn't measure up on the face of democracy he or she most favors.

- **Face I** is the concept of *popular sovereignty*. This is the notion that the people have the right to govern themselves. In implementing this right they either exercise control of governmental authority directly, or they establish effective mechanisms for holding their government formally accountable to them, such as periodic elections.
- **Face II** centers on *rights and liberties*. It consists of certain basic rights and freedoms that must be guaranteed by law to the citizenry. They may not be taken away either by the state acting on its own or even by the people exercising their sovereign rights of majority rule.

- **Face III** consists of core *democratic values*. Tolerance, fairness, and compromise are among the most important of these values.
- **Face IV** is the concept of *economic democracy* that establishes various criteria of fairness or equality as social and economic components of democracy.

Each of these four faces can take a variety of forms. Popular sovereignty can be exercised either directly, through the active exercise of governmental authority by the people themselves, or indirectly, through the people's elected representatives. The list of guaranteed civil rights and liberties can be a short one or a long one. Democratic values can be "moral norms" that are informally shared by the population or they can be legally binding social obligations. Economic democracy can range from a vague commitment to equity of opportunity to the systematic distribution of a country's wealth among the population on a relatively equal basis. As we might expect, people will differ not only over how to define the four faces of democracy, but also over the practical question of how to put these various aspects of democracy into practice most effectively.

Minimum and Maximum Forms of Democracy

As we have pointed out, all four faces of democracy come in different forms and degrees. To grasp these various possibilities, we should think of each face as containing a *minimum* as well as a *maximum* variant. The minimum conception prescribes certain rudimentary criteria for defining and implementing each face of democracy. It can be argued that, in order to have a democracy, a country must meet certain minimum levels or standards of popular sovereignty, civil rights and liberties, democratic values, and economic democracy. Not everyone will agree with this proposition, to be sure, and there is ample room for debate about which criteria are necessary for democracy to exist. Our discussion of minimal forms of democracy is intended mainly to spark your own thinking about democracy and provide you with a framework for organizing your ideas.

Our discussion of maximum conceptions of democracy is similarly aimed at stimulating your own understanding of what democracy is all about. Maximum conceptions widen the degree or extent of democracy in each face to the greatest feasible extent. In general, maximum forms of democracy may be viewed as desirable but not *absolutely necessary* for democracy to exist. But as our discussion points out, what some people may regard as maximum forms of democracy may be regarded by others as minimal forms of democracy and thus as essential to the very existence of democracy itself.

FACE I Democracy as Popular Sovereignty

Popular sovereignty reflects the idea that the people determine how they are governed. The people themselves, in other words, are the source of the state's legitimacy; they are sovereign over their governing institutions and officials. They have the

right to determine the type of governmental institutions and actions they want, along with other aspects of their political system. The concept of popular sovereignty is conveyed in such phrases as "government by consent of the governed" and Abraham Lincoln's famous characterization of democracy as "government of the people, by the people, and for the people."

Popular sovereignty is an essential aspect of democracy. Without it, democracy would be impossible. The very word *democracy* derives from the Greek words *demos*, which means "the people," and *kratia*, which means "authority" or "rule." Taken literally, democracy means "rule by the people."

Popular sovereignty has two key aspects: *participation* and *accountability*. If the people are sovereign, they have the right to participate in politics themselves. They also possess the right to hold those who govern them accountable for their actions. Popular sovereignty applies the rule of law by asserting the government's accountability to the people, thereby imposing constraints on the power of the state and its officials. Democracies must make sure that participation and accountability are guaranteed by the laws of the land. But how do the people participate in political life? How do they exercise accountability? Over more than 2,000 years the experiences of numerous democratic political systems and the ideas of democratic theorists have produced a number of different responses to these questions. We'll concentrate on two of them here: *representative democracy* and *direct democracy*.

Representative Democracy In a **representative democracy**, the people elect state officials to represent them and make decisions on their behalf. Representative democracy may be regarded as the *minimum* form of popular sovereignty. The main form of participation in this type of democracy is voting, in accordance with the principle of "one person, one vote." The single most important form of accountability in a representative democracy also centers on voting: The people can approve or remove state officials—executives, legislators, and at least some judicial figures—on election day. These electoral rights must be guaranteed by law on an equal basis. Representative democracy is thus based on the rule of law, inclusion, and equality. Elections are typically conducted on the basis of *majority rule*. (As we'll see in Chapter 6, however, there are different ways of counting the votes.) Legislatures generally operate on the same principle. Majority rule is thus a key feature of popular sovereignty.

To fulfill their task of ensuring citizen participation and accountability effectively, electoral procedures must meet certain basic criteria. They must be:

- *Meaningful:* The positions to be filled through the electoral process must be positions of serious governmental authority, including responsibility for making laws and for appointing senior-level state authorities.
- *Competitive:* There must be genuine competition for positions of elective office. At a minimum, there must be no laws or practices that might preclude competition or guarantee that candidates run unopposed.

- *Free:* Voters must have the freedom to vote as they see fit. They must not be subjected to any forms of coercion or intimidation by state authorities or by individuals or organizations outside the state.
- *Secret:* To protect the confidentiality of the voters' choices, elections must be held by secret ballot. The secret ballot is known as the *Australian ballot.*[6]
- *Fair:* The processes used for selecting candidates, conducting elections, and counting the votes must be untainted by favoritism, discrimination, fraud, or any other form of unfairness to the participants or to the population as a whole.
- *Frequent:* Elections must be held at regular intervals, at least every four to five years, so that voters can exercise their rights of accountability and losers can have a chance to run again.
- *Inclusive:* All adults above a certain age (say, 18) must have the right to vote, with exceptions kept to a reasonable minimum, while protecting democracy against its enemies.
- *Equal:* Voting rights should be distributed equally to individuals in accordance with the principle of "one person, one vote."

Over the centuries, dictators have dipped into a large bag of tricks intended to create the appearance of electoral accountability while subverting its true substance. They run unopposed in stage-managed elections, depriving the voters of real choice. They hold referendums asking the people to approve or disapprove their rule, then proclaim they won close to 100 percent approval. They handpick the candidates who are allowed to run, excluding the government's opponents. They intimidate voters, report false vote counts, and engage in all sorts of additional forms of electoral deceit. These fraudulent practices violate the most rudimentary notions of popular sovereignty. Elections without popular sovereignty are inherently undemocratic.

In addition to voting in elections, people can take part in electoral politics by taking an active role in a political party or by working for a candidate at election time. They can also take part in the political process by publicly expressing their opinions on issues facing their community to public officials and by joining or supporting policy advocacy organizations. People can also respond to public opinion polls and attitude surveys conducted by polling organizations. These and other mechanisms of public expression serve, however indirectly, the important function of *agenda setting*. They give the population a chance to participate in formulating the agenda of issues and priorities that government officials will be expected to address when drafting legislation or making decisions. In the process, they permit the citizenry to have an input into the political decision-making process.

Popular sovereignty thus requires *political openness* and *transparency*. To the greatest possible extent, state officials must share information with the general population regarding the decisions they make. The sphere of government secretiveness, although at times necessary for reasons of national security, should be kept as narrow as possible while the sphere of open,

To protect the confidentiality of the voters' choices, elections must be held by secret ballot. The secret ballot is known as the Australian ballot because it was introduced in Australia in the 1850s.

transparent government should be spread as wide as possible. Officials who violate this vitally important requirement by engaging in illegal or unethical acts of secret or deceitful conduct strike a harsh blow against democracy itself. Democracies must therefore keep a watchful eye on all elements of the government and probe allegations of wrongdoing. Parliaments should have *legislative oversight* capacity over the executive branch, such as the right to question officials or investigate government practices.

By the same token, openness requires the free flow of information. Freedom of the press and freedom of access to multiple sources of information bearing on governmental decisions are fundamental elements of popular sovereignty. Censorship and the deliberate spread of misinformation are typical governing techniques of authoritarian regimes; they have no place in a democracy.

How Democratic Is Representative Democracy? The essence of representative democracy lies in the delegation of governmental power and responsibility to a small number of people by the citizenry as a whole. In every democracy in the contemporary world, the actual work of government is carried on by an extremely small portion of the country's population. Representative democracies, in other words, are governed by political elites. As a practical necessity these governing elites enjoy a considerable amount of discretion when it comes to managing the community's affairs. Modern democracy operates on the principle of *democratic elitism*. Rather than being based on the concept of "government *by* the people," democracy as we know it today is government by elites who are accountable to the people. It involves a complicated mixture of popular sovereignty and elite decision making.

Robert Dahl, one of the foremost theorists of modern democracy, devised the term *polyarchy* to capture these realities. Whereas democracy means "rule by the people," **polyarchy** means "rule by the many." Dahl uses the term as a synonym for the actual practice of representative government as it emerged in the nineteenth century and developed in the twentieth century.

He uses the term *democracy* as an ideal type, a regime in which competition and participation yield a pattern of public policy that the people, weighted as equals, would prefer. In practice, what Dahl calls polyarchies are large-scale democracies, governing entire countries. They combine elite decision making with mass participation, meaningful competition for power, and the accountability of the governing elites to the governed.[7]

Direct Democracy In contrast to representative democracy, **direct democracy** is characterized by the direct exercise of governmental power by the people themselves. It is "government *by* the people" in the most literal sense. Real-world examples of direct democracies are exceedingly rare. In the ancient world a few Greek city-states, most notably Athens, had their own variants of this form of government. During the peak years of Athenian democracy, from roughly 500 to 300 BCE, citizens had the right to participate in public debates on the issues facing the city and to vote on alternative proposals for dealing with them. In effect, the citizens were the legislature. The political executive was largely an administrative body charged with implementing the citizenry's wishes; it had little authority to undertake major policy initiatives on its own, and its officials were usually chosen from among the qualified citizenry by lot for a one-year term. The city-state of Geneva in the eighteenth century provided another version of direct democracy.

Neither of these examples of classical direct democracy met very high standards of inclusion or equality, however. Both ancient Athens and eighteenth-century Geneva denied citizenship rights to women, for example. Certain categories of males were also excluded. Slaves, foreign-born "aliens," and men who did not meet property-owning qualifications were not included in the self-governing procedures of Athens. It is estimated that only about two in five adult Athenian males enjoyed the rights of citizenship. Geneva similarly imposed property requirements for citizenship. Moreover, Geneva's democracy conferred considerable decision-making powers on the elites who operated the political executive on a day-to-day basis.[8] The right to participate in direct democratic procedures was only slightly more open in town meetings in the United States, a form of direct democracy prevalent in nineteenth-century New England.[9] Even with such limited participatory rights, these direct democracies of the past could not have functioned except on a very small scale.

Though direct democracies do not exist in today's world, there still exist several possibilities for expanding the immediacy of citizen participation in decision making in between the extremes of representative democracy and direct democracy. One is **plebiscitary democracy**, a concept that has been in use for about a century. The other is a much newer possibility, one that is evolving before our very eyes thanks to the latest developments in communications technology, which some observers and proponents are calling *e-democracy*.

Plebiscitary Democracy The term *plebiscitary* derives from the Latin word *plebs*, which referred to the common people of ancient Rome as opposed to the patrician elite. Over the course of the twentieth century, a number of representative democracies have provided their citizens the opportunity to vote on specific policy questions in a *referendum* (or *plebiscite*). In the United States, referendums are quite common at state and local levels of government, but they have not been employed at the national level. In Canada, referendums have been held in Quebec on secession. Several Western European countries have held referendums on the European Union and other issues. A number of other democracies have also held nationwide referendums on various questions.

In some cases the results of a referendum are binding on government officials; in others the results are merely a popular recommendation with no binding force on official decision makers. In either case, referendums and plebiscites constitute an electoral mechanism located between representative democracy and full-scale direct democracy.

e-Democracy Political scientists and others apply the term **e-democracy** to the use of advanced information and communications technologies to allow citizens a more direct involvement in political decisions. The Internet and the profusion of social networking providers and smartphones permits ordinary citizens to follow political decision making in legislatures and the government ministries much more closely than they formerly could. Cable network news channels and their Internet sites help to promote an informed citizenry, or at least that portion of the citizenry that wants to be closely informed about political matters. These informed citizens are also much more able to register their demands and complaints with their elected representatives than they once were given the speed with which e-mail distribution lists and social media are able to spread the word to such attentive citizens that they should contact their members of congress or parliament about an issue.

In this well-known painting, *Freedom of Speech*, Norman Rockwell depicts a form of direct democracy called the town meeting, typical of some parts of New England.

Some proponents of direct democracy have advocated the use of these new communications technologies to move us closer to the active and direct involvement of each citizen in making authoritative decisions. While not yet implemented anywhere in the world, the advocates of electronic direct democracy foresee a day when each voter would be able to vote on each bill being considered in the national legislature and to author new legislation for consideration by the citizenry. Electronic balloting could make this vision a reality. Of course, whether many of a state's citizens will want to pay attention to public affairs so closely that they can participate in most public decisions is doubtful, and if they did, national productivity in most other parts of the economy would likely decline significantly as citizens spent all of their time debating national issues and voting.

In the meantime, however, some advocates of electronic direct democracy are trying to at least make representatives more responsive to those who elect them. An Australian political party called Senator On-Line (SOL) contested seats in the 2007 and 2010 parliamentary elections. SOL pledged that if its candidates were elected they would put every pending parliamentary vote to an Internet poll to determine how the citizenry wanted them to vote. SOL is far from winning seats, however, having taken only 17,441 votes (out of over 12 million total) nationally in 2010. Another party promoting electronic direct democracy is Britain's People's Administration Direct Democracy Party. It pledges that if it wins a majority of the House of Commons it would create a new political regime in which a national online voting system would allow the people to make all of the laws directly.[10] Electronic direct democracy may be a long way from implementation, but many political activists as well as political theorists have imagined how electronic communication might allow us to overcome the imperfections of representative democracy. In the meantime, many political organizations such as MoveOn.org urge us to use the Internet and our mobile communications devices daily to contact our representatives, which certainly increases the volume of information those representatives have about our policy preferences when they have to make decisions on our behalf.

The notion that legislators should faithfully carry out the wishes of their constituents is known as the *instructed delegate* model of representation. In effect, the people instruct their delegates how to vote on legislation. Edmund Burke (1729–97), an influential British political theorist as well as an elected member of parliament, rejected this concept. In a famous speech, Burke informed his constituents that he would represent their *interests*

In a 2009 referendum Irish voters approved the Lisbon Treaty, which paved the way for even closer integration of the countries of the European Union. Here, Ireland's European affairs minister, Dick Roche, celebrates with other supporters of the treaty.

as he saw fit, not necessarily their *will* on every issue. Burke saw himself as the "trustee" of the people he represented: He expected the voters to trust him to use his "mature judgment" in serving them. This *trustee model* of representation accords legislators considerable autonomy from their constituents. In practice, most legislators in today's democracies probably try to combine the delegate and trustee models of representation. They need to be very attentive to public opinion on key issues in order to get reelected. But they also want a measure of latitude to vote as they think best on specific pieces of legislation.[11] Figure 5.1 displays the continuum of popular sovereignty, showing that representative democracy reflects a minimum variant and direct democracy a maximum variant.

FACE II Democracy as Rights and Liberties

We hold these truths to be self-evident, that all men are created equal, that they are endowed by their Creator with certain unalienable rights, that among these are life, liberty, and the pursuit of happiness.

—Declaration of Independence July 4, 1776

For the founding leaders of the United States, the single most important purpose of government was to guarantee certain

Representative democracy	Plebiscitary democracy	E-democracy	Direct democracy

Minimum   Maximum

FIGURE 5.1   **Continuum of Popular Sovereignty**

individual rights and liberties through the rule of law, safe-guarding the citizenry against potential tyranny. They favored a limited suffrage, reserving the "consent of the governed" to property-owning males. (Initially, about one in 30 adults had the right to vote.) In the founders' view, a mass democracy based on universal suffrage actually threatened the survival of political liberty because the uneducated majority might mis-use their voting rights by electing a tyrant. Consequently, the word *democracy* does not appear in the U.S. Constitution. The best form of government that the founders could imagine was a republic.

Historically, a *republic* was often regarded as a form of government that did not have a monarch. Over time, the term increasingly became understood as a political system under some form of control by the people. (The word derives from the Latin *res publica*—"the people's thing.") The founders of the United States regarded their newly constituted republic as a government of strictly limited powers, with elected representa-tives and appointed officials held accountable to citizens very much like themselves: enlightened, socially respectable, and utterly devoted to civic virtue and the prevention of despotic rule. Their conception of republican government was an elitist version of popular sovereignty. Of course, the founders could not have foreseen that the term *republic* would be adopted in subsequent centuries by a wide variety of governmental sys-tems, including manifestly authoritarian regimes such as the People's Republic of China, the Democratic People's Republic of (North) Korea, and the Islamic Republic of Iran.[12]

It was not until 1791 that the founders codified into law the specific rights and liberties they regarded as sacrosanct. Known as the *Bill of Rights*, these legal guarantees against exces-sive governmental power were ratified by the end of that year as the first 10 amendments of the new U.S. Constitution, which had taken effect only two years earlier. These rights include such things as the freedoms of religion, speech, press, and assembly (First Amendment); the right to bear arms, considered neces-sary for "a well regulated Militia" (Second Amendment); the right of security against unreasonable searches and seizures (Fourth Amendment); the right to protection against dou-ble jeopardy and self-incrimination and the right not to be "deprived of life, liberty, or property without due process of law" (Fifth Amendment); and freedom from "cruel and unusual punishments" (Eighth Amendment). Nowhere in the original U.S. Constitution or its first 10 amendments is there an explicit right to vote.

As America's elitist republic evolved over the course of the next two centuries into a mass-based democracy, Ameri-can conceptions of basic rights and liberties evolved with it. Today the United States—and most other democracies around the world—are committed to providing a broad range of rights and freedoms to their citizens on the basis of the rule of law, the inclusion of virtually the entire populace, and legal equality. Although many of these rights are much the same in most democratic countries, there are some differences from one democracy to the next in the specific rights that are guaranteed and in the ways they are codified into law. We'll look at some of these differences in the countries we examine in Part Two.

One of the most important aspects of basic **rights and liberties** is that they must not be removed or infringed by the state or by the people. Although governments and the people have the right to determine how these rights and freedoms are interpreted and applied to particular cases or situations (as we'll discuss below), they may not eliminate them. A political system that has little or no press freedom, religious freedom, or any of the other rights and liberties that may be consid-ered fundamental to democracy cannot be regarded as truly democratic. Thus there is an inherent tension between popu-lar sovereignty (Face I), with its procedures of majority rule, and the basic rights and liberties of Face II, which the popu-lar majority must neither eradicate nor evade. There is ample evidence that large segments of the general public may not be willing to accept the full range of rights and liberties that are guaranteed by their own laws. When majorities discriminate against minorities and their governments let them get away with it, the dominant groups are often denying legally guaran-teed rights and liberties to the minorities. For example, public attitude surveys conducted in the United States in the 1970s revealed resistance to legally accepted applications of freedom of speech, the right of peaceful assembly, and other provisions of the Bill of Rights on the part of average citizens, at times numbering in the majority. More recent surveys have revealed similar attitudes. In 2002, 49 percent of Americans surveyed agreed that the "First Amendment goes too far in the rights it guarantees."[13]

What are the rights and liberties that, at a minimum, *must* be guaranteed to the population for the political system to be considered a democracy? The minimal list presented in Table 5.2 is not intended to be the final word on the subject. In heuristic fashion, its main purpose is to provoke you to think for yourself about the rights and liberties you regard as *abso-lutely essential* for democracy. Our list includes political, juridi-cal, and social rights. You may wish to add one or more items, such as the right to bear arms or the economic and social rights spelled out in the Universal Declaration of Human Rights. And you may want to delete an item or two from the list pro-vided here.

Whatever one's list of minimal democratic rights and lib-erties may contain, most democracies provide an expanding number of rights as demanded by their populations. These include such things as the right to privacy, the right to enjoy public accommodations such as restaurants and hotels with-out discrimination, various forms of gay rights, the right to a smoke-free environment, and so on. Some people may regard these or other rights as essential for the very existence of democracy; others may regard them as desirable but not essential. And some may not even regard certain of these rights as desirable.

Table 5.2 Democratic Rights and Liberties: A Minimal List

1. The right to life and the security of one's person and property against government interference without probable cause of illegal activity
2. Freedom of conscience, thought, and expression (including freedom of the press)
3. Freedom of religion
4. The right to vote in meaningful, fair, competitive elections and to hold governing officials accountable
5. The right to assemble and organize peacefully for political purposes
6. Freedom of movement, that is, the right to travel freely within and outside the country's borders and to live where one chooses
7. The right to equal treatment under the law and to the due process of law, including the right to a fair trial and humane forms of punishment
8. The right to own and alienate (i.e., buy and sell) private property and to engage in private business activity
9. The right to publicly funded education

As you draft your own charter of minimal rights and liberties, keep in mind that the items in Table 5.2 are stated in very general terms. Each item is subject to interpretation—very often by the courts—when it comes to their actual application. The same can be said of the U.S. Bill of Rights and similar charters around the world. What does "the right to life" mean in item 1 of our list? Does it apply in the first trimester of pregnancy, as opponents of abortion would contend? The wording in Table 5.2 does not answer that question. It simply says there is a "right to life," as opposed to *no* right to life. If there were no right to life, then presumably the state could take our lives arbitrarily. It is up to the sovereign people and their governments to determine what "life" means according to the law. Similarly, the guarantee of freedom of expression and a free press in item 2 of our minimal list does not tell us whether child pornography or incitement to riot should be allowed. In 2006, Muslims around the world rose up in indignation after a Danish newspaper published a political cartoonist's derogatory caricatures of Muhammad and other European publications reprinted them. (Islamic law forbids pictorial portrayals of the prophet.) Should democracy protect the cartoonist's right to offend people? If a freely elected government in a Muslim country banned such images, with the approval of a majority of its people and its independent judiciary, would it be a democracy?

If democracies must ensure basic rights, shouldn't they also mandate certain obligations? Should democracies require military service, or some other form of national or community service, as an obligation of citizenship? If such a duty were required by law, how should it be applied inclusively and equally? Advocates of *communitarianism* like sociologist Amitai Etzioni argue that democracy requires the acceptance of mutual obligations and responsibilities on the part of its members, including community service.[14]

ESSENTIAL CONCEPTS

Illiberal Democracy

One of the most influential popular books in international affairs in the past 15 years has been Fareed Zakaria's *The Future of Freedom*, which distinguishes illiberal democracy from liberal democracy and cautions foreign policy makers not to confuse elections with democracy. Zakaria argues that liberal democracies, of which the United States and Western European countries are exemplars, combine elections with what he terms "constitutional liberalism," essentially the rights and liberties we have just discussed plus the rule of law.[15] **Illiberal democracies**, in contrast, hold elections but do not effectively guarantee rights and liberties. Moreover, they often fail to provide the rule of law universally throughout the country.

In addition to its categories of free, partly free, and not free, Freedom House also identifies countries as electoral democracies. All of the free countries are electoral democracies, but some partly free countries are designated as electoral democracies and some are not, depending on whether their elections are for the most part free and fair. Table 5.3 lists the partly free electoral democracies as of 2012 and their Freedom House scores on political rights and civil liberties.[16] These countries, whose scores put them in the middle range of the Freedom House index, may be regarded as illiberal democracies. A brief description of politics in three of them, as summarized in Freedom House country reports, will illustrate why they may be considered as "illiberal."

- **Colombia** holds regular elections for the presidency, congress, and local government, with the most recent presidential election occurring in 2010. A long-standing two-party system has recently given way to multiparty elections. However, while Colombia has a constitution guaranteeing civil liberties such as freedom of speech and assembly, widespread violence against journalists acts as a form of censorship and many political groups find it hard to assemble in the climate of violence. For example, 51 labor leaders were killed in 2010. Judges and prosecutors are often so intimidated by violent criminals that the rule

Table 5.3 Partly Free Electoral Democracies 2012

Country	Political Rights Score	Civil Liberties Score
Albania	3	3
Bangladesh	3	4
Bhutan	4	5
Bolivia	3	3
Bosnia and Herzegovina	3	3
Colombia	3	4
Comoros	3	4
East Timor	3	4
Ecuador	3	3
Georgia	3	3
Guatemala	3	4
Liberia	3	4
Libya	4	5
Macedonia	3	3
Malawi	3	4
Mexico	3	3
Moldova	3	3
Niger	3	4
Papua New Guinea	4	3
Paraguay	3	3
Philippines	3	3
Seychelles	3	3
Tanzania	3	3
Thailand	4	4
Tunisia	3	4
Turkey	3	4
Ukraine	4	3
Zambia	3	4

Arch Puddington, *Freedom in the World 2013: Democratic Breakthroughs in the Balance* (New York: Freedom House, 2013), pp. 13–17.

of law is compromised. Armed groups—both leftist insurgents and right-wing paramilitaries—also undermine the rule of law and abuse human rights in large portions of the countryside. In sum, Colombia has a record of over a half-century of competitive elections for its most important offices but fails to protect rights and liberties and to sustain the rule of law.

- **The Philippines** also held presidential and congressional elections in 2010 that were widely viewed as legitimate and much fairer than in recent years, with fewer reports of electoral violence and more efforts to upgrade the transparency of the voting process. Filipinos generally enjoy freedom of speech and of the press, but journalists face many dangers in their work, and as Freedom House reports, "Impunity for crimes against them is the norm."[17] Rule of law is compromised by a culture of impunity for acts of corruption in government, and although legal accusations are filed against corrupt officials, their cases take an average of six to seven years to work their way through the anticorruption court. Poorly paid judges are also accused of corruption. Finally, the Philippine government has fought against a Muslim insurgency in the southern island of Mindanao for 40 years. While fighting this insurgency, the military has allegedly engaged in extra-judicial killings, disappearances, arbitrary arrest, mistreatment of suspects, and kidnappings, but prosecution of soldiers for such acts is rare.

- In **Ukraine** Viktor Yanukovych won a very close presidential election race in 2010 over Yulia Tymoshenko that was regarded as fair. His election came after six years of highly contested politics following the 2004 "Orange Revolution," in which reformist former Prime Minister Viktor Yushchenko led peaceful protests against a fraudulent electoral victory by Yanukovych and subsequently came to power as president, only to suffer a falling out with his chief ally and prime minister, Tymoshenko. After Yanukovych, an ally of Russian President Vladimir Putin, assumed the presidency in February 2010, political rights and liberties suffered, leading Freedom House to downgrade Ukraine to the partly free classification because of "deteriorating media freedom, secret service pressure on universities to keep students from participating in protests, government hostility toward opposition gatherings and foreign nongovernmental organizations, and an increase in presidential influence over the judiciary."[18]

As these brief descriptions suggest, free and fair elections do not guarantee that rights and liberties or the rule of law will be respected by those who are elected. In illiberal democracies strong leaders frequently emerge and act as limited-term despots: They can be turned out of office at election time, but until they are, they often rule arbitrarily. The citizenry in illiberal democracies often supports such leaders. When asked by the World Values Survey (WVS) whether having a strong leader who was not constrained by elections or the parliament was a good state of affairs, only about one-third of the respondents in the full 57-country sample said it was very good or fairly good. However, in five of the seven illiberal democracies surveyed (Guatemala, Mexico, Moldova, Turkey, and Ukraine), over half of the WVS respondents said having such an unfettered leader was fairly good or very good. (Colombia and Zambia, the other illiberal democracies surveyed in the 2005 wave of the WVS, mirrored the overall results.)[19]

Regimes that have committed to holding elections do not thereby become full-fledged liberal democracies. Moreover, countries that have once enjoyed both elections and constitutional liberalism can slip back into an illiberal status. Foreign policy makers must be careful not to confuse the holding of elections with liberal democracy, for a politician who wins a competitive election may well turn around and abuse the journalists who criticize him and the political groups who opposed him, hardly hallmarks of democratic practice.[20]

In addition, many regimes hold elections that are not free and fair but are meant to bolster their legitimacy at home and abroad. Elections in which hand-selected opponents are allowed to compete against ruling elites, in which other opponents are intimidated, in which the incumbents' resource advantage over their opponents is huge, in which vote counting may be rigged, and in which the incumbents have no intention of leaving office if they lose take place around the world. As we will see in Chapter 18, Mexican politics in most of the twentieth century was a form of *electoral authoritarianism*.[21] ∎

FACE III Democracy as a Value System

As we said in Chapter 1, values are spiritual or moral principles, ideals, or qualities of life that people favor for their own sake. Democracy is rooted in several key values, or *norms*. These values supply democracy's moral content and give its institutions and procedures their normative purpose.

Many people would argue that the electoral procedures associated with Face I and the rights and liberties listed under Face II are necessary but not sufficient to establish a real democracy. Democracy, in this view, also requires the observance of certain core values. The most important of these values, or norms, are:

- *Fairness*, which means that all groups in society should be treated equivalently and equitably, and none should have opportunities denied to others on a systematically discriminatory basis.
- *Tolerance*, which means respect for those who are different from ourselves and willingness to live in harmony with them.
- *Compromise*, which is the effort to reconcile our differences on the basis of cooperation, fair bargaining, and mutual willingness to make concessions.
- *Trustworthiness*, which requires the members of society, and particularly politicians and government officials, to behave in ways that inspire confidence in their dependability, integrity, and honesty.
- A *commitment to the peaceful resolution of international disputes* in the country's dealings with the outside world, with force to be used only as a last resort.

These core values may be said to exemplify the "spirit of democracy." In any democracy worthy of the name, not only must these values be publicly embraced by political leaders and others involved in setting the tone of the country's political and social life, but they must also be effectively implemented, if necessary with the full force of state authority. In other words, they must be rooted in the rule of law. To the extent that they are widely cherished and rigorously applied, these norms help democracies realize the principles of inclusion and equality. They promote inclusion by insisting that everyone is entitled to be treated on a fair and nondiscriminatory basis, regardless of religion, race, gender, or some other social characteristic. They promote equality by insisting on the equal dignity and intrinsic worth of every human being, regardless of wealth, talent, or other marks of individual distinction. Internationally,

democratic values also promote peace by ruling out naked aggression and reserving the use of force to self-defense or the defense of one's allies.[22]

Some political theorists relegate democratic values to a secondary importance. They maintain that democracy exists as long as there are fair elections and basic civil rights. Values, in their view, "are better thought of as a *product* and not a producer of democracy."[23] But a contrary view asserts that democratic values are vital to the fundamental concept of democracy. One such argument was advanced more than a century and a half ago by French political commentator Alexis de Tocqueville, who attributed the success of America's young republic in the early 1830s primarily to values that derived from such sources as religion, higher education, and the experience of interpersonal cooperation in local governments and nongovernmental associations. These values, which included the love of liberty and the spirit of cooperation, constituted what Tocqueville called the "mores" of society, "the sum of ideas that shape mental habits." Mores, in his opinion, are even more important than laws in establishing a viable democracy. "Laws are always unsteady when unsupported by mores," he wrote. "Mores are the only tough and durable power in a nation." Tocqueville contended that democratic values, far from being the end product of long experience with elections and other institutional aspects of democracy, are part of the very essence of democracy. As a Frenchman, Tocqueville exalted the values proclaimed in the credo of the French Revolution: "Liberty! Equality! Fraternity!"[24]

A more recent variant of this argument has been advanced by Robert Putnam. In a study that sought to explain why some regions in Italy were more successful than others at maintaining stable regional governments and delivering basic services to the population, Putnam and his associates found that the principal variable accounting for these differences was the extent to which civic values such as high levels of interpersonal trust and cooperativeness were shared by the local citizenry. In some regions these diverging patterns can be traced back hundreds of years. "Effective and responsive institutions depend," Putnam asserts, "on republican virtues and practices."[25]

Like the first two faces of democracy, Face III can have both minimal and maximal variants. At a minimum, some people would maintain that democracies must reject systematic discrimination aimed at selected social groups. At the very least democracies must refrain from using the law to perpetrate such forms of social discrimination. When governments make unfair laws that suppress or exclude certain target groups, they institutionalize discrimination and violate the spirit of democracy.

Moving toward a more expanded notion of democratic values, some political observers would argue that democracies must also use the law to prevent unfair discrimination or acts of bigotry in private exchanges. If private bankers or restaurant owners refuse to give service to non-green-eyed customers, for example, the government must step in and prohibit such discriminatory practices. Obviously, legal restrictions against such private discrimination would limit the right to dispose of one's property and engage in private business transactions, rights we included in our list of fundamental democratic rights in Table 5.2. Advocates of governmental action against private discrimination would reply that the right to engage in private property transactions should not be an absolute one; it must be limited by law in an effort to prevent the violation of other essential elements of democracy, such as the right to fair and nondiscriminatory treatment. The conflict between private property rights and the right to fair and equal treatment still poses thorny problems today in the United States and other democracies.

An even more expansive understanding of democratic norms asserts that governments should go beyond simply outlawing unfair discrimination: They should take special efforts to assist groups that are, or have been, the targets of discriminatory abuse. Preferential hiring laws and educational admissions policies, in this view, should be mandated by law to enable ill-treated minorities to make up for past discrimination and overcome current unfair barriers to employment or education. In the United States, affirmative action laws have been instituted in an effort to help African-Americans, Hispanics, and Native Americans achieve such goals. At times these laws have sparked resistance from white Americans who

argue that legally mandated preferences for minorities amount to reverse discrimination, resulting in unfair treatment for the white majority. Realistically, no government can force people to love one another. The most a democratic government can do is require its citizens to deal with their various conflicts peacefully and in accordance with certain broadly agreed-upon rules and procedures. But what happens when the conflicts that divide a society are so deep and contentious that the normal procedures of democracy—competitive elections, free speech, and the like—keep the main competing groups in a state of constant turmoil and uncompromising hostility? Far from being a panacea for society's ills, the normal institutions of democracy can at times actually aggravate them, just by giving everyone the right to express their hostility to other groups openly and organize for political action against them. In exceptionally divided societies, special institutions and procedures may sometimes be necessary to prevent the country from plunging into violence or its government from being mired in eternal gridlock. To save democracy itself, deeply divided societies may need the special arrangements of a consociational democracy.

HYPOTHESIS-TESTING EXERCISE
Democracy and Values

Hypotheses Do those who live in democracies actually hold values different from those who live in nondemocratic regimes? We have suggested in this chapter that citizens of democracies are more likely to trust others and to be tolerant toward those who are different from each other. In addition, we might expect that democratic citizens are much less inclined to embrace nondemocratic forms of rule. We pose three hypotheses for testing here:

H₁: Those living in democracies will express higher levels of interpersonal trust than those living in nondemocratic regimes or semi-democracies.

H₂: Those living in democracies will be more tolerant of social groups regarded as different than will be those living in nondemocratic regimes or semi-democracies.

H₃: Those living in democracies will be less likely to accept arbitrary forms of rule than will those living in nondemocratic regimes or semi-democracies.

Variables The *independent variable* is the degree of democracy of a country, which can be measured by the Freedom House rating. The *dependent variables* are (1) interpersonal trust, (2) tolerance of those who belong to groups that are usually marginalized in society, and (3) the preference for a strong, unconstrained national leader.

Expectations Residents of democracies (free societies) will express higher levels of interpersonal trust, less intolerance of marginalized groups, and less enthusiasm for strong, unconstrained national leadership.

Evidence Table 5.4 shows the responses to four sets of questions posed on the 2005 wave of the World Values Survey (WVS), which was conducted in 57 countries between 2004 and 2009. The average country responses are aggregated by Freedom House rating group (for the year corresponding to the one in which the WVS was conducted in any particular country) as free, partly free, or not free as well as a column for the countries that scored perfect 1's on both the political rights and civil liberties indexes. Most countries scoring 1's are long-established democracies.

The evidence about interpersonal trust (H₁) is mixed, as responses to the first two questions in Table 5.4 show. While respondents from the societies labeled as most free are more trusting than those from the partly free, there are relatively high percentages of trusting individuals in not free (authoritarian) countries. In contrast, the findings about tolerance (the third set of questions in the table) tend to support H₂: Those living in democracies tend to have more tolerance for those whose lifestyles or other personal attributes are perceived to be out of the mainstream. Finally, those living in free countries are more likely to reject the notion that having a strong leader who doesn't have to pay attention to parliament or electoral results is a good thing than is true for inhabitants of partly free and not free nations.

Conclusions Citizens of democracies may be somewhat more likely to hold some fundamental values about interpersonal trust and tolerance than the inhabitants of less free societies, but these fundamental values are held in surprisingly high levels even among those living in the least free countries.

This conclusion suggests that the personal values of democratic citizens are not the only factor that sustains democratic life. Indeed, some would argue that it is the experience of living in a stable democracy that encourages people to become trusting and tolerant. Of course, once those values are spread widely in the populace, they tend to reinforce democratic behavior and thus to strengthen the support for democracy as the preferred political regime. A virtuous circle results, with the experience of living in a democracy promoting values that further reinforce democracy, and so on.

Table 5.4 Democratic Values by Political Regime: Evidence from the 2005 World Values Survey

	Total WVS Sample	FREEDOM HOUSE CATEGORY			
		Countries Scoring 1 (most free)	Free Countries (1–2.5)	Partly Free (3–5)	Not Free (5.5–7)
Generally speaking, would you say that most people can be trusted or that you need to be very careful in dealing with people?					
Most people can be trusted	26%	36%	29%	18%	31%
Can't be too careful	74%	64%	71%	82%	69%
Do you think most people would try to take advantage of you if they got a chance, or would they try to be fair? (10 point scale, where 1 = would take advantage and 10 = try to be fair)					
Mean score	5.7	6.0	5.7	5.4	6.3
On this list are various groups of people. Could you please mention any that you would not like to have as neighbors?					
People of a different race	18%	9%	13%	27%	29%
Immigrants/foreign workers	23%	13%	16%	34%	40%
Homosexuals	49%	25%	38%	72%	60%
People of a different religion	18%	8%	12%	27%	29%
Unmarried couples living together	22%	6%	13%	40%	37%
I'm going to describe various types of political systems and ask what you think about each as a way of governing this country. For each one, would you say it is a very good, fairly good, fairly bad, or very bad way of governing this country?					
% responding "very good" to the option: "Having a strong leader who does not have to bother with parliament and elections"	12.1%	6%	11%	14%	12%

Selected countries and year surveyed: Andorra (2005), Argentina (2006), Australia (2005), Brazil (2006), Bulgaria (2006), Burkina Faso (2007), Canada (2006), Colombia (2005), Cyprus (2006), Chile (2006), China (2007), Egypt (2008), Ethiopia (2007), Finland (2005), France (2006), Georgia (2008), Germany (2006), Ghana (2007), Great Britain (2006), Guatemala (2004), Hong Kong, China (2005), India (2006), Indonesia (2006), Iran (2005), Iraq (2006), Italy (2005), Japan (2005), Jordan (2007), Malaysia (2006), Mali (2007), Mexico (2005), Moldova (2006), Morocco (2007), Netherlands (2006), New Zealand (2004), Norway (2007), Peru (2006), Poland (2005), Romania (2005), Russian Federation (2006), Rwanda (2007), Serbia (2006), Slovenia (2005), South Africa (2007), South Korea (2005), Spain (2007), Sweden (2006), Switzerland (2007), Taiwan (2006), Thailand (2007), Trinidad and Tobago (2006), Turkey (2007), Ukraine (2006), United States (2006), Uruguay (2006), Vietnam (2006), Zambia (2007).

Sources: World Values Survey 2005 Official Data File v.20090901, 2009. World Values Survey Association (www.worldvaluessurvey.org). Freedom House scores correspond to the WVS survey year and can be found at http://www.freedomhouse.org.

CASE STUDY
Consociational Democracy in the Netherlands

Some theorists hypothesize that a stable, effective democracy requires a relatively homogeneous population. They assume that a society whose people share a common ethnic background, a common religion, compatible economic interests, and fairly similar political outlooks is more likely to sustain democratic institutions and make governmental decisions effectively than heterogeneous societies, which are characterized by a plurality of ethnic groups, religious affiliations, economic interests, or political ideologies. Social diversity, in this view, can be expected to produce permanent political animosity rather than a viable democracy. The political history of the Netherlands provides insight into a political means to overcome the consequences of such animosity.

Political scientist Arend Lijphart pointed out that, for much of its modern history, the Netherlands has exhibited some of the distinctive hallmarks of a highly fragmented society. The Dutch share a common national identity, but they have been divided along religious lines into Roman Catholics and Protestants (mostly Calvinists) since the sixteenth century. In addition, starting in the nineteenth century the population became divided along economic and ideological lines. Middle- and upper-class liberals who favored wide freedoms to pursue their private business activities vied with working-class socialists who preferred restrictions on private enterprise along with policies designed to enhance the bargaining power of labor unions and to provide social welfare benefits to workers and their families. By the twentieth century, four well-organized "camps" had formed in Dutch society: Catholics, Protestants, liberals, and socialists. Each camp had its own political party, interest groups, newspapers, and other forms of association. Moreover, the four camps were relatively isolated from one another: their respective members did not cross over into the organizations of the other camps or interact with one another very much. Even intermarriage between camps was rare.

And yet, defying the odds, the Netherlands emerged in the twentieth century as one of the most stable democracies in the world. Competitive elections have taken place on a regular basis; political liberties flourish; the rule of law is not in doubt. Most Dutch governments have proven quite effective in making decisions that address the country's principal problems.

Lijphart concluded that the evidence of modern Dutch history indicated that instead of disintegrating into instability and ineffectiveness, as we might have expected, Dutch democracy was a stellar success. What accounted for this seemingly paradoxical combination of social fragmentation and healthy democracy? According to Lijphart's explanation, success in the Netherlands was attributable above all to the value its elites attached to *tolerance* and *compromise*. Recognizing that democratic institutions and political liberties might well founder if their respective groups did not get along, the leaders of the four camps made special efforts to tolerate their differences and accommodate their conflicting interests and demands on the basis of inclusion and equity. Through patient negotiation they worked out compromises aimed at providing each group with a fair chance at political power and a relatively equitable distribution of state revenues. Such things as educational funding and civil service jobs were divided up in approximate proportion to each group's share of the population. At the same time, the leaders of all four groups maintained an outspoken commitment to democracy and a determination to implement their agreements effectively.

For their part, most Dutch citizens deferred to their leaders, granting them considerable latitude to strike bargains with the leaders of the competing camps without pressuring them into adopting rigidly uncompromising positions. What Lijphart calls "the politics of accommodation" in the Netherlands was thus a highly elitist form of democracy. It ultimately depended on the ability of the leading personalities representing the four camps to overcome their differences and reach effective bargains, sometimes in secret, for the good of the general population. In other words, Dutch elites saved democracy by observing basic democratic *values*.[26]

Consociational democracy is the term Lijphart applied to this system of elite accommodation in a socially heterogeneous society. In the Netherlands it emerged around 1917 and reached its peak in the 1950s and early 1960s. After the mid-1960s, Dutch society no longer needed the special accommodationist practices of previous years. Democracy remains secure in the Netherlands, perhaps in large part because of the firm foundation it acquired during the long decades of consociationalism. Lijphart argues that consociational democracy, either in its pure form as it once existed in the Netherlands or in some modified variant, constitutes a distinct model of democracy that may be highly applicable in deeply divided societies. It demonstrates that "deep, mutually reinforcing social cleavages do not form an insuperable barrier to viable democracy." Variants of consociational democracy have been used in Belgium and Switzerland[27] and are being tried in contemporary Bosnia and Iraq. But its critics warn that its procedures can become so routine that they may harden a society's divisions instead of reducing them. Other critics point to failed attempts to practice consociationalism in Lebanon, where power-sharing arrangements have broken down into bloody civil war at different times in the recent past.

Today the Netherlands is facing new challenges to its democratic order. Recently arrived immigrants include many Muslims who do not fit easily into the country's freewheeling lifestyles. The Dutch initially turned to the accommodationist approach that had been so successful in their earlier history, allowing the new immigrants much autonomy within their own communities. Contacts between government officials and leaders of the Muslim community raise interesting

This Islamic school in the Netherlands is an example of the Dutch turn toward an accommodationist approach to the Islamic segment of their population.

parallels with consociational democracy. However, the unwillingness of some immigrants to abide by the Netherlands' liberal social policies led to a backlash by a significant segment of Dutch voters. In response, the government has tightened restrictions on further immigration and required immigrants to take classes in the Dutch language and culture.

FACE IV Democracy as Economic Well-Being

One of the most controversial issues surrounding the definition of democracy centers on the relationship between the citizenry and the economy. Some people may legitimately wonder whether the concept of economic well-being properly belongs in the definition of a political concept like democracy. In fact, however, welfare is a democratic value, and the economy has long been a top priority of practically every government in the world. The preamble of the U.S. Constitution states that one of the principal purposes of the American republic is to "promote the general welfare." As the 2012 presidential election demonstrated, millions of Americans expect their government to stimulate economic growth, widen economic opportunity, alleviate poverty, and provide generous welfare benefits ranging from educational assistance and unemployment relief to medical care and Social Security. Most Americans regard these benefits as basic *political* rights to which they feel entitled as citizens of a democracy. Americans may differ about *how* the state can promote economic well-being. In the 2012 election both Republicans and Democrats, however, thought their own presidential candidate was the most likely to stimulate economic growth and that it was appropriate to hold the government accountable for doing so. Similar views are shared by vast majorities in other democracies as well. Many people also believe that the

maldistribution of wealth, with wide gaps between rich and poor, is inherently undemocratic, especially when the poor have little or no chance of improving their lot in life.

Convincing evidence of the importance of economic well-being as a central aspect of democracy comes from public attitude surveys conducted in Eastern Europe in the 1990s. This was the crucial decade when the construction of democracy in that region was still in its initial phases following the collapse of communism. When asked to select "the most important elements of a democracy" from a list of political and economic categories, large numbers of Eastern Europeans—usually a substantial majority—tended to view democracy primarily in economic terms. They regarded such things as an improved economy, greater economic equality, and guarantees that their basic needs would be met as more important than political liberties like freedom of speech and an impartial judiciary. Most Western Europeans surveyed attached a higher priority to political factors, but large minorities placed economic issues first.[28]

Economic well-being is thus a widely recognized component of democracy in the minds of average citizens, as we will explore later in this chapter. Political leaders who seek their votes and who govern in their behalf are keenly aware that the voters will surely hold them accountable for the economy's performance. How, then, do democracies deal with the challenges of economic well-being?

Almost every democracy in today's world features a mixture of private enterprise and various forms of governmental intervention in the economy. These economic systems are therefore called *mixed economies*. Although private companies tend to be the primary engines of economic production and employment, the state plays a major economic role. Governments collect taxes, purchase equipment, employ bureaucrats, and transfer huge sums of money to schools, hospitals, the military, pensioners, and other beneficiaries of the treasury's largesse. The private sector, moreover, is usually subject to the rule of law. Without laws regulating contracts, stock markets, corporate finances, and the like, modern private enterprise could not function. And without laws to safeguard the rights of employees and consumers and to protect the public's health and the environment, private enterprise would have few legal responsibilities to the citizenry. The rule of law and the policies of elected governments thus act as democratic constraints on private enterprise. Whether these constraints should be reduced or increased is a matter of continuing debate in many democracies.

How do democracies observe the values of inclusion and equality (or equity) when dealing with the economy? How can they distribute society's resources—money, food, jobs, housing, medical care, education, and so on—in a fair and inclusive fashion, while at the same time preserving the value of freedom for business and property owners to dispose of their possessions as they wish? Is there a trade-off between equality and liberty in a democratic political economy?

Like the first two faces of democracy, Face IV can be viewed in terms of a continuum (see Figure 5.2). Some people would argue that, at a minimum, a democracy must strive to implement the principle of *equitable opportunity* for all. As noted earlier in this chapter, equitable means fair. Under this principle, political leaders as well as others actively involved in a country's political or economic life would work toward ensuring everyone in society a relatively fair chance at achieving economic security and advancement. Even the very poor, by this standard, should at least have a fair chance at climbing out of poverty, working their way into the middle class, and perhaps even getting rich. To be sure, different societies and individuals will measure fairness differently. Some people will say it is fair enough if the government provides free education through high school to all its citizens; others will insist that the state has an obligation to provide tuition-free education all the way to the top of the academic ladder.

The concept of fair opportunity allows ample room for economic liberty. It would permit individuals and private corporations to run their own businesses and dispose of their private possessions with considerable freedom. The government would have to impose some limitations on these private activities, but the economy could function largely in accordance with rules of the private marketplace and still meet the basic criteria for equitable opportunity.

Another possibility along our continuum is *equality of opportunity*. Equality is a more exacting standard than fairness. Fairness implies that inequalities will still exist as people start out in life and pursue their careers. Equality of opportunity, by contrast, requires efforts by the state and the private sector to make sure that everyone in society is relatively or truly equal when it comes to sharing opportunities for economic advancement. In this highly inclusive approach, no one would have a significant social advantage over anyone else in enjoying access to education or employment.

One way of moving toward greater equality of opportunity is to prohibit, or severely restrict, the right of inheritance, thereby preventing vast concentrations of wealth in the hands of particularly successful families. In an effort to provide greater equality of opportunity in the job market, the government might require businesses to set aside certain jobs on a quota basis for particular segments of the population, such as women and various minority groups. Whether such measures can actually succeed in achieving real equality of opportunity is another question; some people may still enjoy more opportunities than others. One thing, however, is certain: The scope of government intrusion in the private economy would have to be much larger in the quest for greater *equality* of opportunity than would be the case when the goal is simply *equity* of opportunity. As a general rule, the range of economic liberty for individuals and businesses declines as the pursuit of equality intensifies.

At the maximum end of our continuum is the goal of *equality of condition*. Whereas the concept of opportunity suggests that, at the end of the day, some individuals will come out ahead of others in their pursuit of economic well-being, equality of condition means that everyone will ultimately enjoy roughly the same amount of wealth. Obviously the pursuit of such an outcome would require the state to undertake major efforts to redistribute wealth throughout society and perhaps to control incomes as well. Tax policies and other modes of government intervention in the economy would be explicitly aimed at preventing the stratification of society into upper, middle, and lower classes to ensure that all citizens belong to the same socioeconomic class. Under these conditions the freedom of individuals and private businesses to conduct their economic affairs as they wish would be severely constricted. Once again, as the scope of economic equality widens, the scope of economic liberty narrows.

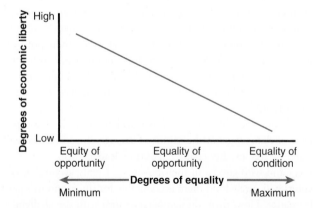

FIGURE 5.2   Trade-offs between Liberty and Equality

Thus we are faced with a real dilemma in our efforts to establish a "democratic" distribution of resources and opportunities. Democracy requires both equality and liberty, but the more equality we want, the less liberty we are likely to get (Figure 5.2 shows the inverse correlation between them). One of the most highly charged controversies in virtually every modern democracy is the clash between two conceptions of how to achieve economic well-being. Some people tend to define **economic democracy** primarily in terms of *equality*. Others prefer to define economic democracy primarily in terms of the *liberties* of the marketplace. Most democracies strive to resolve this conflict by striking a balance between equality and liberty. They may, for example, emphasize the concept of equity rather than full equality. (When people in the United States speak of "equality of opportunity," they generally mean "equity of opportunity.") At the same time, they may seek to harmonize state intervention in the economy with ample freedom for private enterprise. The modern *democratic welfare state* is the product of this balancing act; it is the most widely adopted form of political economy among the world's economically advanced democracies. Variations in the application of the welfare state model abound, however. Some countries (like the United States) place greater accents on economic liberty; others (like the Scandinavian countries) stress egalitarian and welfarist ideals. We'll take up these issues again in Chapter 11.

PEOPLE'S UNDERSTANDINGS OF DEMOCRACY

Because people differ in the purposes they ascribe to democracy, their understandings of the main characteristics of democracy differ too. Across societies, the extent to which people tend to see democracy as being about freedom and liberty or about policy outcomes such as economic prosperity or economic equality or about particular political processes varies considerably. The World Values Survey queries respondents about 10 different characteristics that people sometimes associate with democracies, asking them whether they see each of them as being an essential characteristic of democracy, not an essential characteristic of democracy, or somewhere between those two poles. Table 5.5 shows the percentage of the survey respondents in several of the countries we explore in this book who answered that each of the 10 characteristics were essential. We rank the countries in the table by their Freedom House score to see whether the citizenry in the freer countries have understandings of democracy that differ from those living in the less free countries.

The first two columns of characteristics have to do with rights and liberties: Is liberty an essential characteristic of democracy? Do women have the same rights as men? Large portions of the population the world over view the protection of civil liberties as an essential component of democracy, although it is interesting to observe that a larger share of Russians, Swedes, and Germans tend to see protecting civil rights as essential than do people in Great Britain, Japan, Mexico, Brazil, and Iran.

The importance of gender equality differs across countries too, with Japanese, Egyptian, and Iranian respondents being much less likely to see women's equality as essential than do Swedes, Germans, and Russians.

The next four columns of Table 5.5 have to do with political processes, including the roles played by particular political actors (the military and religious authorities). That significant shares of the people living in countries with little or no experience with democracy see a large role for religious leaders or the military to interpret laws or to overturn the actions of elected officials stands out. In long-standing democracies, in contrast, almost no one can conceive of a role for religious leaders to interpret laws or for military officers to step in when elected officials cannot govern effectively. The final four columns of Table 5.5 deal with policy outcomes as characteristics of democracy. Here it is notable that majorities of the citizens of countries with little experience of democracy tend to see favorable policy outcomes—economic prosperity, a safety net for the unemployed, redistribution of income via the tax system, and punishment of crime—as essential characteristics of democracy while those who have a long experience with democracy do not.

One consequence of people viewing democracy as meaning favorable policy outcomes is that if those favorable policy outcomes do not come about, disillusion with democracy as a political regime follows. Often citizens in new democracies reconsider their enthusiasm for democracy if the experiment in democratic practices coincides with hard times or a rise in the crime rate. Russia provides an important recent example in which initial enthusiasm for democracy after the collapse of the Soviet Union was followed by doubts about democracy associated with a rise in crime and economic challenges in the 1990s. Many Russian citizens even yearned for the days of Stalin, and Vladimir Putin's popular success as president of Russia owes much to the sense that he has dealt with criminality and economic problems. We will explore this situation at greater length in Chapter 16.

Conclusion

Table 5.6 summarizes our discussion of the four faces of democracy, indicating the minimum and maximum variants of democracy on each face. We can summarize our overview of democracy very simply by providing this more precise definition: **Democracy** is a political regime that offers regular opportunities for peaceful competition for political power, thereby allowing the people, no segment of which is forcibly excluded from participation, to hold their political leaders accountable. Democracy guarantees basic rights and liberties, rests on certain core values and the rule of law, and promotes the economic well being of the populace.

This chapter has presented a multifaceted concept of democracy that conforms to the views of most theorists and democracy activists in the world today. Chapter 6 looks at various ways democracies are organized.

Table 5.5 Essential Characteristics of Democracy as Seen by the Citizenry: Comparative Perspectives

Country	FH score at time of WVS 2005	RIGHTS		PROCESSES				OUTCOMES			
		Civil rights protect people's liberty against oppression	Women have the same rights as men	People choose their leaders in free elections	People can change the laws in referendums	Religious authorities interpret the laws	The army takes over when government is incompetent	Governments tax the rich and subsidize the poor	People receive state aid for unemployment	The economy is prospering	Criminals are severely punished
France	1	30%	50%	40%	25%	1%	3%	16%	15%	15%	30%
Great Britain	1	27	62	46	18	3	5	10	14	15	32
United States	1	44	57	56	27	2	5	7	12	18	17
Canada	1	33	66	50	21	1	5	7	20	17	23
Germany	1	59	74	73	53	1	3	28	37	27	38
Japan	1.5	32	43	35	34	2	2	13	18	29	40
Mexico	2	30	57	43	22	11	20	18	22	27	24
Brazil	2	31	56	48	46	6	15	9	39	21	20
Turkey	3	44	57	48	48	11	16	30	43	49	40
Russia	5.5	68	74	63	56	7	20	45	63	80	63
Egypt	5.5	57	51	79	68	48	30	58	34	68	58
Iran	6	31	35	41	29	10	8	20	32	37	37
China	6.5	49	61	46	39	6	22	30	39	49	55
Total WVS 2005		42	56	54	41	11	13	25	32	39	41

Source: World Values Survey 2005 Official Data File v.20090901, 2009. World Values Survey Association (www.worldvaluessurvey.org). Freedom House scores correspond to the WVS survey year and can be found at http://www.freedomhouse.org.

Table 5.6 The Four Faces of Democracy

ALL FOUR FACES REST ON THE PRINCIPLES OF THE RULE OF LAW, INCLUSION, AND EQUALITY				
	Key Features	**Minimum Variant**	**Intermediary Variants**	**Maximum Variant**
Face I: Popular sovereignty	Participation, accountability	Representative democracy	Plebiscitary democracy; e-democracy	Direct democracy
Face II: Civil rights and liberties	Enumerated inalienable rights (may not be abridged by majority)	Basic civil rights	Additional rights, as determined through democratic procedures	
Face III: Democratic values	Values and attitudes concerning relations between majority and minorities	Non-discrimination	Tolerance, compromise	Affirmative action
Face IV: Economic democracy	Distribution of wealth and economic decision-making power	Equity of opportunity; laissez-faire	Equality of opportunity; electoral democracy plus welfare state	Equality of condition; council or participatory democracy

Key Terms

Rule of law

Inclusion

Equality

Equity

Popular sovereignty

Representative democracy

Polyarchy

Direct democracy

Plebiscitary democracy

e-Democracy

Rights and liberties

Illiberal democracy

Consociational democracy

Economic democracy

Democracy

Notes

1. Arch Puddington, *Freedom in the World 2013: Democratic Breakthroughs in the Balance* (New York: Freedom House, 2013), p. 3. These figures compare with 66 electoral democracies recorded in the 1987–88 survey and 91 recorded in 1991–92. In 1972 there were 150 sovereign states, of which 43 were ranked "free." There were 54 free states in 1983 and 75 in 1993. Fareed Zakaria, *The Future of Freedom: Illiberal Democracy at Home and Abroad* (New York: Norton, 2003).

2. For arguments in behalf of greater citizen participation in the decision-making process, see Benjamin R. Barber, *Strong Democracy* (Berkeley, CA: University of California Press, 1984); Benjamin R. Barber, *A Place for Us* (New York: Hill & Wang, 1998); James S. Fishkin, *Democracy and Deliberation: New Directions for Democratic Reform* (New Haven, CN: Yale University Press, 1991).

3. Rousseau himself believed that on important issues, the general will should approach the unanimous opinion of the community; on less important matters a simple majority would suffice. But he also believed that reaching a wide consensus was possible only in small communities, and that large states were therefore unsuited to democracy.

4. In his famous "paradox of voting," the French philosopher Condorcet reasoned that if three individuals (I, II, and III) are faced with three different choices (A, B, and C), it is possible that no majority can be found for any of the available choices. This result would occur if I prefers A to B and B to C (and thus A to C); II prefers B to C and C to A (and thus B to A); and III prefers C to A and A to B (and thus C to B). Two out of the three people prefer A to B and B to C. However, two out of three prefer C to A! With no majority for any of the three alternatives, gridlock ensues. Nobel Prize–winning economist Kenneth Arrow showed that, when Condorcet's paradox applies to a community trying to choose from among at least three proposals for enhancing its economic welfare, and no majority can be found for any of them, it may be impossible to make a decision, or the policy choice must be imposed on the community dictatorially by state authorities. See Kenneth J. Arrow, *Social Change and Individual Values*, 2nd ed. (New Haven, CN: Yale University Press, 1951).

5. Adam Przeworski suggests that democracy works "when all the relevant political forces have some specific minimum probability of doing well," and that those who lose elections or fail to have their demands fulfilled "may stay with the democratic game if they believe that even losing repeatedly under democracy is better for them than a future under an alternative system." *Democracy and the Market* (Cambridge: Cambridge University Press, 1991), pp. 30, 31.

6. Secret voting was first employed in South Australia in 1858. It was adopted for general use in Britain in 1872 and in U.S. presidential elections only after the fraud-tainted contest of 1884. Before these dates, various forms of nonsecret balloting were the rule, such as a voice vote or show of hands at a public election meeting.

7. Among Robert Dahl's voluminous writings, see *Polyarchy: Participation and Opposition* (New Haven, CN: Yale University Press, 1971), *Dilemmas of Pluralist Democracy* (New Haven, CN: Yale University Press, 1982), *Democracy and Its Critics* (New Haven, CN: Yale University Press, 1989), *On Democracy* (New Haven, CN: Yale University Press, 1999), and *How Democratic Is the American Constitution?* (New Haven, CN: Yale University Press, 2002).

8. The population of Athens probably included 25,000 to 40,000 adult males who were classified as citizens during the fifth century BCE. Perhaps a few thousand actually took part in the deliberative assemblies that decided the city-state's laws and policies. Geneva in 1760 had a population of approximately 25,000; only about 1,500 males were qualified to take part in the town's general assembly. On Athenian democracy, see David Stockton, *The Classical Athenian Democracy* (Oxford: Oxford University Press, 1990); M. I. Finley, *Politics in the Ancient World* (Cambridge: Cambridge University Press, 1983); A. H. M. Jones, *Athenian Democracy* (Oxford: Basil Blackwell, 1969). On Geneva, see R. R. Palmer, *The Age of the Democratic Revolution*, vol. 1 (Princeton, NJ: Princeton University Press, 1959), pp. 111, 127–28.

9. Joseph F. Zimmerman, *The Massachusetts Town Meeting: A Tenacious Institution* (Albany, NY: State University of New York Press, Graduate School

of Public Affairs, 1967); Joseph F. Zimmerman, *Participatory Democracy* (New York: Praeger, 1986).

10. See http://www.senatoronline.org.au/ and http://www.paparty.co.uk/.

11. On the role of new communications technology in democracy, see Lawrence K. Grossman, *The Electronic Republic: Reshaping Democracy in the Information Age* (New York: Viking, 1995); Cass Sunstein, *Republic .com* (Princeton: Princeton University Press, 2002); Steve Davis, Larry Elin, and Grant Reeher, *Click on Democracy* (Boulder, CO: Westview Press, 2002). See Burke's speech to the electors of Bristol in 1774 in *The Portable Edmund Burke*, ed. Isaac Kramnick (New York: Penguin, 1999), pp. 155–57.

12. Martin van Gelderen and Quentin Skinner, eds., *Republicanism: A Shared European Heritage*, 2 vols. (New York: Cambridge University Press, 2002); Philip Pettit, *Republicanism: A Theory of Freedom and Government* (New York: Oxford University Press, 1997).

13. Herbert McCloskey and Alida Brill, *Dimensions of Tolerance: What Americans Believe About Civil Liberties* (New York: Russell Sage Foundation, 1983). The survey figure fell to 30 percent in agreement in 2004 and 23 percent in 2005. See the annual "State of the First Amendment Survey" conducted by the First Amendment Center, affiliated with Vanderbilt University, at firstamendmentcenter.org.

14. Amitai Etzioni, *The Common Good* (Cambridge, UK: Polity, 2004); Amitai Etzioni, *Spirit of Community: Rights, Responsibilities, and the Communitarian Agenda* (New York: Crown, 1993); Amitai Etzioni, ed., *The Essential Communitarian Reader* (Lanham, MD: Rowman and Littlefield, 1998); Amitai Etzioni, Andrew Volmert, and Elanit Rothschild, eds., *The Communitarian Reader: Beyond the Essentials* (Lanham, MD: Rowman and Littlefield, 2004).

15. Zakaria, *Future of Freedom;* Fareed Zakaria, "The Rise of Illiberal Democracy," *Foreign Affairs*, 76 (November/December 1997), pp. 23–43.

16. Puddington, *Freedom in the World 2013*, pp. 13–17.

17. Freedom House, "Freedom in the World 2011: The Philippines," http://www.freedomhouse.org/report/freedom-world/2011/philippines, accessed February 21, 2012.

18. Freedom House, "Freedom in the World 2011: Ukraine," http://freedom -house.org/report/freedom-world/2011/ukraine, accessed February 21, 2012.

19. These data are available from the online analysis function at http://www .worldvaluessurvey.org/index_html.

20. Terry Lynn Karl, "Electoralism," in Richard Rose et al., *The International Encyclopedia of Elections* (Washington, DC: Congressional Quarterly Press, 2000).

21. Andreas Schedler, *Electoral Authoritarianism: The Dynamics of Unfree Competition* (Boulder, CO: Lynne Rienner Publishers, 2006).

22. On trust, see Francis Fukuyama, *Trust: The Social Virtues and the Creation of Prosperity* (New York: Free Press, 1995); for a rational-choice perspective, see Russell Hardin, *Trust and Trustworthiness* (New York: Russell Sage Foundation, 2002).

23. Philippe C. Schmitter and Terry Lynn Karl, "What Democracy Is . . . and Is Not," in *The Global Resurgence of Democracy*, 2nd ed., ed. Larry Diamond and Marc F. Plattner (Baltimore, MD: Johns Hopkins University Press, 1996), p. 57.

24. Alexis de Tocqueville, *Democracy in America*, ed. J. P. Mayer, trans. George Lawrence (New York: Harper & Row, 1966).

25. Robert D. Putnam, with Robert Leonardi and Raffaella Y. Nanetti, *Making Democracy Work* (Princeton, NJ: Princeton University Press, 1993), p. 182.

26. Arend Lijphart, *The Politics of Accommodation*, 2nd ed. (Berkeley, CA: University of California Press, 1975).

27. Arend Lijphart, *Democracy in Plural Societies: A Comparative Exploration* (New Haven, NJ: Yale University Press, 1977).

28. *The People Have Spoken: Global Views of Democracy*, no. 2 (Washington, DC: U.S. Information Agency, 1999), pp. 32–35.

6

Democracy: How Does It Work?

Constitutional Frameworks of Democracy and Electoral Systems

The Palace of Westminster, meeting place of the British parliament.

OVERVIEW

- Democracies vary significantly in the actual institutions by which political leaders come to power.

- Two key aspects of democratic government are the relationship of executive power to the legislature and electoral systems.

- This chapter contrasts the U.S.-style presidential regime to the parliamentary governments used in much of Europe.

- This chapter shows how proportional representation differs from the single-member district plurality system the United States uses to elect its House of Representatives.

- The electoral system has a major impact on the number of parties that emerge in democracies.

- Duverger's law establishes the expected relationship between the form of the electoral system and the party system.

How do modern democratic governments work? This is a huge question with as many answers as there are democracies. In this chapter we address it by focusing on two key aspects of democratic government: *constitutional frameworks of democracy*, which establish the relationships among the executive, legislative, and judicial powers in the state, and *electoral systems*. Other important institutional dimensions of democratic government are (1) the degree of centralization of power—is a regime highly centralized or is it federalist?—a topic that we explored in Chapter 3 and (2) interest representation, which we will take up in Chapter 8. Electoral systems and the relationship of the executive to the legislative power are the two features of democratic regimes that are most easily changed, hence they warrant our close attention in this chapter.

CONSTITUTIONAL FRAMEWORKS OF DEMOCRACY

In the course of history three leading models have emerged by which representative democracies arrange the relationship between the legislature and the executive power: (1) the *presidential* system, a variant of which is used in the United States; (2) the *parliamentary system* that initially evolved in Britain, and (3) the mixed *presidential–parliamentary system*, which is currently utilized in France, Russia, and elsewhere. Each model prescribes a set of methods for selecting the three main branches of national government—the *executive*, the *legislative*, and *judicial*—and stipulates how legal authority is to be distributed among these three branches. All three models have experienced important evolutionary transformations in the countries where they first emerged. In addition, variants of all three have appeared in other countries as political leaders have sought to copy their essential features while adjusting them to the contours of their own national history and specific political conditions. Our first aim in this chapter is to help you understand these three institutional forms of democracy by comparing their main characteristics side by side. We'll concentrate here on the essential features of these systems, leaving the details of how they work in specific countries to subsequent chapters.

Some democracies have institutional arrangements that differ from the three models we are about to describe. The governmental structures of these divergent democratic systems tend to vary from one country to another, following no common patterns. Consequently, they all tend to get lumped together under the general rubric *hybrid democratic regimes*. South Africa is one example that we will examine in this book (see Chapter 19).

Presidentialism

In the presidential system of democracy—also known as **presidentialism**—the president is the sole effective head of government, constitutionally armed with real decision-making powers. Presidents in this type of system are not limited to purely ceremonial duties, and they do not share real executive power with a second executive, such as a prime minister. In most cases the president in this type of regime is not only the formal head of government but also head of state. In many countries with this type of system, the president is elected directly by the people, but in the United States the people elect the president indirectly through the electoral college.

In presidential democracies the president must share power with a separately elected national legislature (whether unicameral or bicameral) and must typically respect the authority of the highest courts in the judicial branch of

Table 6.1 Selected Presidential Regimes

Argentina	Costa Rica	Honduras	Nigeria	Philippines
Brazil	Ecuador	Indonesia	Panama	United States
Chile	El Salvador	Mexico	Paraguay	Uruguay
Colombia	Ghana	Nicaragua		

government. The legislature's role can vary across presidential regimes: Some legislatures are fairly strong, as in the United States; others are weaker and concede more power to the executive branch. Table 6.1 lists some presidential regimes in today's world. Several have been identified as illiberal democracies (see Chapter 5).

The United States has a particular form of presidentialism. Its basic features are worth summarizing here for the sake of permitting explicit comparisons with other democracies. The U.S. system was instituted with the Constitution, ratified in 1789. The United States has a federal system, with legal authority shared between the national government and the 50 states. At the national level, which is our principal focus here, the three main institutions are the *presidency*, the centerpiece of the executive branch of government; the *Congress*, which is the national legislature; and the *Supreme Court*, which is the highest judicial authority in the land.

The main architects of this system did not want any of these three branches to dominate the other two. They therefore endowed each branch with certain powers designed to check, or counterbalance, the legal authority of the others. In constructing this system of *separation of powers* and *checks and balances*, James Madison and other founders were profoundly influenced by the writings of the French philosopher Charles-Louis de Secondat Montesquieu (1689–1755). In *The Spirit of Laws* (1748), Montesquieu argued in favor of a carefully constructed separation of powers between the executive, the legislative, and

Many U.S. founders were deeply influenced by French philosopher Montesquieu's notion of the separation of powers as they drafted the U.S. Constitution.

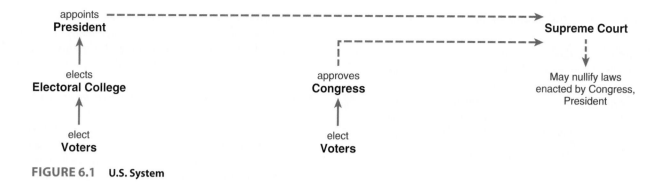

FIGURE 6.1 **U.S. System**

the judicial branches of government so that the same individuals would not be able to dominate two or more of these branches. He hypothesized that such a system would reduce opportunities for the abuse of power.[1] For Madison and other framers of the Constitution, preventing the abuse of state power was the most important priority of the U.S. system of government.

Although certain aspects of American government have evolved since the Constitution took effect in 1789, it is based today on these core principles, centering on the following features (see Figure 6.1):

- *The president and the Congress are elected separately.* The president is elected by the electoral college, which in practice is elected by the voters in each state. The two houses of Congress—the Senate and the House of Representatives—are elected by the voters. Congress does not elect the president. Members of Congress may vote to remove the president from office only for "high crimes and misdemeanors," not because they do not like his policies.
- *Lawmaking depends on a balance of congressional and presidential powers.* Strictly speaking, only members of Congress have the right to propose bills for adoption as law. The president's own legislative proposals are submitted to the Congress by members acting in his behalf. Laws are enacted when both houses of Congress pass bills by majority vote and the president signs the legislation. The president may veto congressional legislation. Congress may override the president's veto by a two-thirds majority.
- *The Supreme Court may strike down laws as unconstitutional.* Although this right of *judicial review* is not explicitly contained in the Constitution, ever since the case of *Marbury vs. Madison* in 1803 the Supreme Court has asserted the right to nullify laws on the grounds that they violate the Constitution.
- *The president, the Congress, and the states can together override decisions of the Supreme Court.* The justices of the Supreme Court are selected by the president, with the "advice and consent" of the Senate. If the court strikes down a law as unconstitutional, the constitution can be amended. Constitutional amendments require a vote of two-thirds of the members of each house of Congress and the approval of three-fourths of the state legislatures.

In keeping with the intentions of the Founding Fathers, the primary advantage of this system is that neither the president, the Congress, nor the Supreme Court can dominate American government. The primary disadvantage of the checks-and-balances system, however, is its potential for gridlock. Separate elections for the president and Congress make it possible for the president to be a Democrat and the congressional majority to be Republican (or vice versa), or even for one house of Congress to have a Republican majority while the other is controlled by the Democrats, a condition known as *divided government*. If the two sides disagree, it can be very difficult to enact legislation or concur on appointments to the Supreme Court. A more positive view of this situation, however, stresses its potential for compromise. Those who regard compromise as a good thing argue that the possibility of gridlock exerts pressure on both the president and Congress to work out mutually acceptable legislation. Madison himself shared this perspective, arguing that a slow and deliberate process of making laws was preferable to one in which laws are enacted too swiftly and without sufficient scrutiny.

Parliamentary Government

The parliamentary system of democracy, also known as **parliamentary government**, is the most widely used form of democracy in the world today. (For a partial listing of countries using the parliamentary system, see Table 6.2.)

In most parliamentary systems of democracy, the term *government* is used in its narrow sense: It refers to the head of government (usually called the *prime minister* or *premier*) and the various ministers of the executive branch (foreign minister, finance minister, etc.), plus the bureaucracies directed by respective cabinet ministers (the foreign ministry, the finance ministry, etc.). The head of government is the chief executive decision maker in the country. Most parliamentary regimes also have a ceremonial head of state: a constitutional monarch or president who possesses few, if any, real decision-making powers and whose main job is to symbolize the country's unity or the continuity of its history.

There are numerous versions of parliamentary government, and virtually every country that has this form of democracy has one or more unique features that are not found in other

Table 6.2 Selected Countries Using the Parliamentary System

Australia	Germany	Jamaica	Norway
Bangladesh	Greece	Japan	Slovenia
Belgium	Hungary	Latvia	Spain
Botswana	India	Luxembourg	Sweden
Canada	Ireland	Netherlands	Thailand
Denmark	Israel	New Zealand	United Kingdom
Estonia	Italy		

parliamentary systems in quite the same way. Nevertheless, the basic institutions of parliamentarism tend to be widely shared. Simply put, the defining principle of parliamentary government is that the government is selected in a two-step process:

1. The people elect the national legislature.
2. The national legislature (usually the lower house in bicameral legislatures) elects or approves the government.

In this system, there is no separation of powers between the legislative and executive branches as in the United States; rather, there is a fusion of powers between the legislature and the executive. To put it another way, the government in a parliamentary system stems from the legislature and is formally accountable to it. This fusion of powers and accountability are achieved in the following ways (see Figure 6.2):

- As just indicated, *the legislature elects (or approves) the government.* In most examples of the parliamentary system, the people do not directly vote for the prime minister; they vote for candidates running for the national legislature, who in turn have the opportunity to vote for (or approve) the prime minister and cabinet. Some countries provide for a formal vote of the legislature, called an *investiture* vote, to formally approve ("elect") a new government.

- *The prime minister and other government ministers serve simultaneously as members of the legislature.* This dual responsibility, observed in most parliamentary systems, tightens the connection between the executive and the legislature.

- *The government must present and defend its policies before the legislature.* Typically the prime minister and other cabinet ministers must regularly appear before the legislature to present their policies and defend them in open debate. They may also have to answer questions posed by members of the legislature in open session. In the United States, by contrast, the president is not required to answer questions in Congress but is required only to deliver an annual "state of the union" message explaining his policies.

- *The legislature can vote the government out of office.* Just as the legislature "makes" the government by voting it into office, it can also "unmake" the government by voting it out of office. Typically it exercises this prerogative through a vote of confidence.

A **vote of confidence** is a showdown vote in the legislature to determine if the government still has the support (confidence) of a voting majority of legislators. If the government loses this vote, it must usually resign and the legislature must vote a new government into office. If it cannot, the people must vote for a new legislature.

The essential features of parliamentarism provide for a system of governmental dependence on the legislature that differs fundamentally from the U.S. system of separation of powers.

Let's clarify how typical parliamentary systems of government work by providing a few examples of how the legislature elects or approves the government. Several outcomes are possible, and we'll focus here on three of them, drawing all of our examples from one country, Ireland. They are (1) single-party majoritarian government, (2) majority coalition government, and (3) minority government.

Single-Party Majoritarian Government In a **single-party majoritarian government**, one party wins a majority of seats in the national legislature and forms the government. (A majority means 50 percent plus one.)

An illustration is the 1969 Irish general election to fill seats in Dáil Éireann, the lower house of parliament (see Table 6.3). In these elections Fianna Fáil, the party that had held the majority in the Dáil since 1957 and for most of the period since 1932, won 75 of the 144 seats in the Dáil, or 52.1 percent of the total. After the Dáil assembled following the popular elections, the Fianna Fáil members of parliament used their majority to establish a government consisting entirely of Fianna Fáil ministers, led by Jack Lynch, the party leader, who served as *taoiseach* (the Gaelic word for prime minister). The other parties in the Dáil assumed the role of *opposition parties.*

With Fianna Fáil possessing six more seats than the combined total of the opposition parties, Lynch's majoritarian government was now in the position of being able to pass its legislative proposals into law with relative ease. However, this

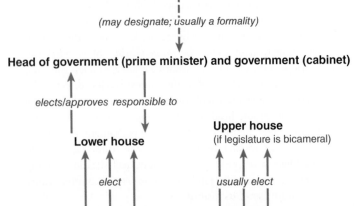

FIGURE 6.2 **Parliamentary Government**

Table 6.3 Irish Dáil Elections, 1969

Party	No. of Seats (144 total)	% of Seats
Fianna Fáil	75	52.1%
Fine Gael	50	34.7
Labour Party	18	12.5
Independent	1	0.7

enviable position required the willingness of Fianna Fáil parliamentary members to maintain party discipline. **Party discipline** is maintained when the parliamentary deputies of a particular party vote together unanimously as a bloc. Party discipline is more likely to occur in parliamentary systems than in the United States, where a tradition of greater independence on the part of individual members of Congress flourishes. This result is in no small part due to the fact that if a governing party in a parliamentary system does not maintain discipline, the government may fall, or lose a confidence vote, forcing it to give up the control of the executive power. In contrast, in a presidential system, the president remains in control of the executive branch until his or her term runs out.

As long as the governing party manages to "whip" its legislative delegation into concerted action, a single-party majoritarian government can exhibit remarkable efficiency: It can get its legislative proposals passed quickly and smoothly. The opposition parties, lacking the votes against a highly disciplined governing party, simply cannot muster a majority to defeat the government's bills. In the case of Britain, where single-party majoritarian governments have been the norm, those governments typically manage to win passage of 97 percent of the bills they propose in the House of Commons, an extraordinarily high degree of governmental efficiency.

If no party succeeds in winning an absolute majority of legislative seats, we then have a **hung parliament**. The alternatives are a majority coalition government or, failing that, a minority government.

Majority Coalition Government A **coalition government** consists of two or more parties that agree to share cabinet posts, usually to form a voting majority in the legislature. An example derives from the results of the most recent Irish elections in 2011.

As we can see in Table 6.4, no party won a majority of the Dáil's now 166 seats (i.e., 83 seats). How, then, can a government be formed? In this case Fine Gael, another political party

Table 6.4 Irish Dáil Elections, 2011

Party	No. of Seats (166 total)	% of Seats
Fine Gael	76	45.9%
Labour Party	37	22.3
Fianna Fáil	20	12.0
Sinn Féin	14	8.4
Others and Independents	19	11.4

with a long record in Irish politics, cut a deal with the Labour Party to form a coalition government. Fine Gael, being the larger of the two coalition partners, took the most important cabinet position, that of taoiseach, or prime minister. Of the remaining 14 cabinet slots, 9 went to Fine Gael, including the key ministries of finance, justice, and health. For its part, Labour got five cabinet posts. The Labour Party leader became deputy prime minister and foreign minister, while one of his colleagues took the ministry of education. By joining forces to govern the country, Fine Gael and Labour together had 113 seats (68.1 percent) in the Dáil, a commanding majority. As long as their respective Dáil delegations maintained party discipline, the bills the coalition partners proposed to the legislature would safely win passage.

Quite clearly, Labour had good reason to feel satisfied with this arrangement. With a quarter of the seats in the Dáil they managed to capture a considerable share of power—a third of the cabinet positions—in the national government. This example illustrates one of the most characteristic features of coalition government: It provides small parties with an opportunity to participate in the executive branch of government. Rather than being relegated to the status of a weak opposition party in the Dáil with little influence on the course of government policy, the Labour Party negotiated its way into the pinnacle of policy-making power, the cabinet. Their presence in the government meant they would be able to exert direct influence on practically every major political issue facing the country. Labour has, in fact, been able to share power in many Irish governments since 1948, usually in coalition with Fine Gael, but once for two years in 1993–94 with Fianna Fáil.

By its very nature, coalition government invariably involves ongoing negotiations among the parties that take part in it. The policies pursued by the cabinet are usually the product of agreements and bargains that are struck between the coalition partners. In the example shown here, Fine Gael and Labour had to agree on the bills they proposed to the legislature as well as on other decisions their government made in the day-to-day task of running the national government. Coalition government is government by bargaining par excellence.

What are the chief advantages and disadvantages of coalition government?

One advantage is that coalitions expand representation in the executive branch of government. As our example illustrates, coalition governments can permit a small party like the Irish Labour Party to participate directly in the executive branch of state decision making, giving the people who voted for that party a far greater influence on what their government could do than if Labour had been simply a small opposition party in the national legislature.

Another advantage of coalition governments is that they increase the level of bargaining and compromise in the executive branch of government. By compelling the coalition partners to constantly work together on the policies they pursue, coalitions promote the democratic ideals of negotiation and accommodation. Unlike single-party majoritarian governments, which allow one party to monopolize the executive branch as well as the legislative agenda, coalitions force the largest party to take account of the concerns and preferences of other parties. In the process they provide a mechanism for bridging the divergences and conflicts that separate the diverse elements of the electorate that these parties represent. At least in principle, coalition governments may increase the likelihood that politics will follow the path of moderation and compromise rather than the dominance of a single party's point of view.

A third advantage of coalition government is its *flexibility and adaptability*. As we've seen, the parliamentary form of democracy permits the legislature to unmake governments as well as make them. If the parties that form a governing coalition have a falling out and cannot patch up their political disagreements, it may be possible to form a new coalition government without having to wait for the next scheduled elections. The leaders of the various parties have a chance to cobble together a new majority coalition. This happened in Ireland in 1994, for example, when the existing coalition government we mentioned above of Fianna Fáil and Labour fell apart when Labour wanted to distance itself from the Fianna Fáil attorney general's mishandling of a case of clerical child abuse. A new coalition government was soon formed by Fine Gael, Labour, and another small party. This coalition governed until the next general elections in 1997.

As it happens, the disadvantages of coalition government are closely related to its advantages. Whereas the inclusion of more than one party in a coalition cabinet expands the level of representation in the executive branch, the involvement of too many parties may prove unwieldy. Generally, the greater the number of parties represented in a coalition government, the more difficult it is to reach common accord on policies and decisions. The Irish examples we have just examined are fairly simple ones involving two-party coalition governments. But some democracies have multiparty coalitions involving three or more parties. Throughout much of the 1970s, 1980s, and 1990s, for example, Italy was governed by a succession of coalition governments consisting of four to nine parties. While prolonged negotiations were often the result, Italian coalition governments, most of them dominated by the Christian Democratic Party, produced a pattern of public policy that included significant economic growth and the development of an advanced welfare state during the period. Between 1996 and 2004, India had coalition governments consisting of 19 to 24 parties. Multiparty coalitions can sometimes produce considerable governmental *inefficiency*. It is simply harder for two or more parties to formulate policies and implement decisions as efficiently and effectively as a single party that commands a majority of the legislature's seats. They can also produce governmental *ineffectiveness*: Because the coalition partners must usually agree on major policies, their decisions may reflect the lowest common denominator of interparty consensus rather than the most effective ways of addressing the country's goals and problems.[2]

Another potential disadvantage is that small parties may gain a level of influence in the government that far outweighs their share of electoral support. As we saw in the Irish case,

the Labour Party in 2011 acquired key cabinet positions even though it garnered only 22 percent of Dáil seats. While some people may applaud a political system that allows a minority party to make its way into the highest reaches of decision-making power, others may regard such a prospect as unfair because it confers excessive influence on parties with small, sometimes very small, constituencies. In 1981–82, Italy's prime minister—nominally the most powerful political figure in the country—came from a party that had captured only 1.9 percent of the vote!

A third disadvantage derives from the very flexibility and adaptability of coalition government that we highlighted earlier as one of its advantages. Whereas the institutions of parliamentary democracy and coalition government can be valuable tools enabling party leaders and legislators to remove ineffective governments, there often exists the potential for abusing these opportunities. In some democracies, governing coalitions fall apart and must be replaced fairly frequently. This phenomenon is known as **governmental instability**. Once again, Italy provides a cautionary example of what can happen in a parliamentary democracy. Between 1945 and 2012, Italy had 63 governments! A large number of them were coalitions involving three or more parties, but usually headed by the Christian Democrats. Some of these multiparty cabinets lasted no more than a few months or even weeks. Many of these instances of change in government occur when the coalition agreed that a reorganization of the government—ministers changing their portfolios—was in order. Other countries have also had periods of turbulent governmental instability.[3]

Minority Government What if no party has an absolute majority of seats in the legislature, and the leaders of the various parties cannot come to terms on forming a coalition government that enjoys the backing of the majority of legislators? Under these difficult circumstances a minority government may have to be formed. As its name implies, a **minority government** consists of one or more parties whose delegates do not constitute a majority of the legislative house. Because it takes a voting majority to pass bills into law, how can such a government legislate? There are several possibilities.

One possibility is a *parliamentary alliance*. In this case, two or more parties agree that they will not share cabinet posts, but their legislators will vote together to support the government and pass legislation. Ireland again provides an example (see Table 6.5). In the 1987 general election Fianna Fáil just missed winning a majority in the Dáil, taking 81 of 166 seats (48.8 percent). However, the remaining parties in the Dáil could not easily form a majority either, especially considering that three members of the Dáil were independents. Consequently, Fianna Fáil formed a minority government—its leader, Charles Haughey, a former taoiseach, returned to that prime ministerial role, and other party members formed the cabinet. How could a minority government govern? In this case, Fianna Fáil had an agreement with Fine Gael by which the latter would not oppose government bills that were "in the

Table 6.5 Irish Dáil Elections, 1987

Party	No. of Seats (166 total)	% of Seats
Fianna Fáil	81	48.8%
Fine Gael	51	30.7
Progressive Democrats	14	8.4
Labour Party	12	7.2
Others and Independents	8	4.8

national interest." Essentially, Fine Gael members of parliament would abstain on government-initiated legislation and it would pass with a majority of the parliamentary votes cast so long as Fianna Fáil members supported it. In most democracies, all that is needed to confirm a government in power or pass a bill into law is a majority of those *present and voting*. If some legislators abstain on a given vote or are not present in the chamber when the vote takes place, their "nonvotes" are not counted as votes against the government or against a particular piece of legislation. Minority governments of this type are usually highly unstable: The abstaining parties may not be willing to tolerate for very long a government in which they do not participate or from which they derive few, if any, benefits. The Haughey government proved remarkably stable, though, serving nearly five years. However they retain power, minority governments constitute a fragile basis for stable rule over the long run. Nevertheless, they are a relatively common occurrence in today's parliamentary systems.

Obviously, a minority government's dependence on other parties in the legislature—whether in a parliamentary alliance or on a vote-by-vote basis—can give the cooperating parties a considerable amount of negotiating power. These parties are then in a position to extract benefits from the government that they might not otherwise receive if the governing party possessed its own voting majority. If this ongoing negotiating process bogs down, the result can be gridlock. The U.S. system of government is therefore not the only type of democracy that is gridlock-prone.

But what if the parties in the legislature are unable to form *any* government, whether a majoritarian or a minority government? In that case their only recourse is to go to the voters and ask them to elect a new legislature.

ESSENTIAL CONCEPTS

Coalition Formation

Political scientists have long been fascinated by coalition formation in parliamentary democracies. What determines who governs? Why do particular parties come together to form a government in multiparty regimes? Is there any logic to coalition formation?

Political scientist William H. Riker proposed a theory that potential prime ministers seeking to form governments in parliamentary democracies will try to join together a **minimal winning coalition**, that is, the coalition that has just the bare minimum number of members to win votes on the legislation it brings before parliament.[4] Given that governing coalitions have limited numbers of cabinet and subcabinet seats to allocate and that there will be a limit on the patronage or public goods that can be distributed from government by the governing coalition, it is in the interest of all involved to have only as many participants in the coalition as absolutely necessary. By this logic, if a coalition has to be formed (i.e., if no single party has a majority), it is likely to be a coalition with just more than half of the seats. With more than half of the parliamentary seats, it can win legislative votes and govern so long as the coalition holds together.

A variation on the minimal winning coalition concept suggests that a coalition should be formed by the minimum number of parties that it takes to form a majority. Consider these possibilities: In a 100-seat legislature, four small parties could have 51 seats among them or two parties could have 55 seats. While the 51-seat group might be a minimal winning coalition in terms of seats, four parties will be more difficult to coordinate than two. Probably the two-party coalition is more likely to find the points of agreement necessary to form a government and it is more likely to stay together over time than a four-party coalition.

In another variation on this theme, what if the two parties that meet the minimal-winning-coalition criterion in a legislature (whether number of seats or number of parties) are a religiously based party and a rabidly anticlerical party? Perhaps the ideological differences between two parties that could otherwise form a minimal winning coalition are so great that the strategic logic of coalition formation just described simply cannot be followed. Such situations suggest that coalitions that approximate the minimal standard are most likely when the parties forming the coalition are close to each other on the ideological spectrum.

Let's look at an example. We will continue to use Irish elections to illustrate coalition formation. Table 6.6 shows the results of the 2007 Irish general election. Fianna Fáil had been governing in coalition with the Progressive Democrats

Table 6.6 Irish Dáil Elections, 2007

Party	Seats	Seat %
Fianna Fáil (FF)	77	46.4%
Fine Gael (FG)	51	30.7
Labour Party	20	12.0
Green Party	6	3.6
Sinn Féin (SF)	4	2.4
Progressive Democrats (PDs)	2	1.2
Independent	5	3.0
Speaker	1	0.6

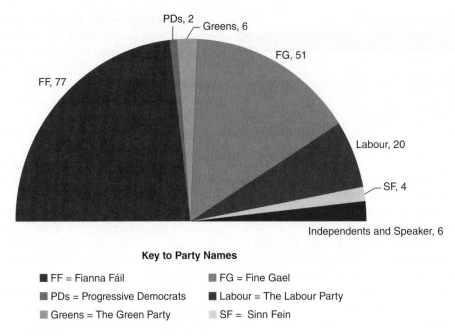

FIGURE 6.3 **Seats in the Irish Dáil, 2007**

(PDs) in the Dáil elected in 2002. The legislature's five-year term ran out, so a new election had to be called. Fianna Fáil did quite well in 2007 (the Celtic Tiger was still roaring), but the PDs did not, shrinking to two seats (from eight in the previous Dáil). The chart in Figure 6.3 shows that Fianna Fáil did not have enough seats to form a majority government on its own, nor in coalition with the PDs. So what were the options?

Table 6.7 lists a range of coalition options. Fianna Fáil and Fine Gael have never formed a government together because of long-standing animosities (their founders, in many cases the fathers and grandfathers of current party leaders, were on different sides in the Irish Civil War in the 1920s, a struggle portrayed in the film *Michael Collins*). To simplify the table, therefore, we do not list coalition options that include both of those parties. The five independent members of parliament complicate the story too. The problem with including independents in a governing coalition is that they have tremendous leverage: Because the loss of a single vote might sink the government, such independents can blackmail the coalition at every turn, seeking to extract patronage or policy concessions that the other governing partners cannot abide. And in effect, each independent must be treated like a political party—of one! Thus we are excluding them from potential coalitions, although they might vote with the government on occasion.

We see many possible coalitions in Table 6.7, but quite a few of them are too small to form a majority coalition. One of those too-small possibilities is the previous government of Fianna Fáil and the PDs, which came up four seats short of the 83 needed to have a working majority (of the 166 Dáil seats, one becomes the speaker or chairperson and does not vote except in the case of a tie). Fine Gael, if it joined with all four of the smaller parties, could form a government that just met the

83 goal. However, a five-party coalition would be unstable, and more importantly, neither Fine Gael nor Fianna Fáil was willing to govern with Sinn Fein, the radically nationalist republican party that seeks to reunify Ireland. That also ruled out the Fianna Fáil–Sinn Fein–PD coalition. Several other coalition possibilities would be *oversized*, in that they would have more seats than necessary to meet the minimal-winning-coalition criterion (see the surplus seats column). Fianna Fáil and the Green Party could govern together if they could count on the votes of some independents, as could Fianna Fáil and the PDs, but as we suggested above, independents can be unreliable or very costly to include in a coalition, hence threatening to make for cabinet instability.

In the end, Fianna Fáil's Bertie Ahern formed a government with his old partners, the PDs, and the Green Party. For the Greens, this was a difficult choice that challenged some of their most deeply held beliefs. Their party leader, Trevor Sargent, had said that if the party ever went into government with Fianna Fáil, which he saw as irresponsibly pro-development and a major threat to the environment, he would resign his post. However, Ahern courted the Greens, and after more than two weeks of talks, the Greens won the concessions they felt they needed to join the government. Keeping his word, Sargent resigned as Green Party leader while his successor became the minister of the environment in the new government.

Despite their ideological differences, the pro-development Fianna Fáil and PDs formed a minimal winning coalition with the Green Party. As you can see in Table 6.7, theirs was the coalition just able to exceed the minimum necessary to have a stable majority. (Ahern talked three independents into voting with the government just to be sure he had a margin for error.

Table 6.7 Possible Coalitions in the Irish Dáil, 2007

Potential Coalition Partners	Seats	Surplus Seats	Surplus with Independents
FF + Labour + Greens + SF + PDs	109	26	27 to 31
FF + Labour + Greens + SF	107	24	25 to 29
FF + Labour + Greens + PDs	105	22	23 to 27
FF + Labour + Greens	103	20	21 to 25
FF + Labour + SF	101	18	19 to 23
FF + Labour + PDs	99	16	17 to 21
FF + Labour	97	14	15 to 19
FF + Greens + SF	87	4	5 to 9
FF + Greens + PDs	85	2	3 to 7
FG + Labour + Greens + SF + PDs	83	0	1 to 5
FF + SF + PDs	83	0	1 to 5
FF + Greens	83	0	1 to 5
FG + Labour + Greens + SF	81	−2	−1 to 3
FF + SF	81	−2	−1 to 3
FG + Labour + Greens + PDs	79	−4	−3 to 1
FF + PDs	79	−4	−3 to 1
Fianna Fáil (FF)	77	−6	−5 to −1
FG + Labour + Greens	77	−6	−5 to −1
FG + Labour + SF	75	−8	−7 to −3
FG + Labour + PDs	73	−10	−9 to −5
FG + Labour	71	−12	−11 to −7
FG + Greens	57	−26	−25 to −21
FG + SF	55	−28	−27 to −23
FG + PDs	53	−30	−29 to −25
Fine Gael (FG)	51	−32	−31 to −27
Labour + Greens + SF + PDs	32	−51	−50 to −46

Given that he did not need their votes most of the time, he did not have to concede much to those independents either.) The other majority coalition options either included the unacceptable Sinn Fein or were oversized by a significant margin. To persuade the PDs and the Greens to join the coalition, Fianna Fáil had to give the Greens 2 cabinet posts and the PDs 1 while retaining 12. However, other coalition possibilities would have likely cost Fianna Fáil more in terms of government posts or policy concessions, making this coalition sensible for the party that led it as well as its junior partners. ■

Anticipated Elections Every democracy requires elections to the national legislature at regular intervals. In the United States, elections are held every two years for the entire House of Representatives and one-third of the Senate. In Britain, elections to the House of Commons must take place every five years. The German Bundestag has a four-year statutory term, and so on. In contrast to the United States, however, most parliamentary forms of democracy permit the possibility of holding parliamentary elections *prior to* the expiration of the legislature's full term in office. For example, until a recent law was passed setting House of Commons terms at five years, the British did not have to wait five years before holding elections to the House of Commons; elections to the Commons could take place before the expiration of this statutory term. And once these elections occurred, a new full five-year term for the newly elected House of Commons began. From 2010 forward, the possibilities for ending a parliamentary term in Britain are more onerous than in the past, when the prime minister could virtually call a new election at will. Similar possibilities prevail in other parliamentary democracies.

Parliamentary elections that take place before the expiration of the legislature's full term are called **anticipated elections**. (They are also informally known as **snap elections**.) Anticipated elections play an important role in realizing the potential of representative democracy. They provide the voters with a valuable mechanism for registering their opinions and influencing political decision makers more often than would be the case if no such mechanism existed. And because snap elections can be called at especially critical junctures in the nation's political life, during a national crisis or in the midst of severe political gridlock, they permit the citizens to have a say in the resolution of the problem in a timely fashion.

Under what circumstances, then, are anticipated elections most likely to occur? The most frequent occasions are the following:

- *No government can be formed in the national legislature.* As explained earlier, it is possible that no single party possesses a majority of seats in the legislature, and it may prove impossible to form a majority coalition government or a minority government. In some instances the government loses a vote of confidence, and the legislators are unable to form a new one. Faced with gridlock, the nation's political leaders now have no choice but to call the voters to the polls to elect a new parliament.

- *Public pressure demands immediate elections.* Suppose there is a major crisis and the existing government is in trouble. Polls show that public confidence is waning considerably. Even key leaders of the governing party or parties begin calling for change. Under these circumstances the government may feel pressured by public opinion to resign and call new elections, allowing the people an opportunity to vote for a new legislature. Even though the government is *not obliged by law* to call new elections just because the public demands them, it may do so if it feels it can no longer govern effectively. For example, in the early 1990s the Italian government was jolted by such shocking revelations of corruption that it responded to the public's disgust by calling anticipated elections in 1994.

- *The government wants snap elections so as to solidify a parliamentary majority.* Sometimes an existing government will want to call anticipated elections because public opinion polls show that, if elections are held right away instead of a year or more later, the governing party (or parties) would win. Every politician knows that the public is fickle and political fortunes cannot be predicted. A government that enjoys popular favor today may lose it next month or next year. Consequently it may be in the government's interest to call snap elections while it still enjoys enough public support to be reelected.

British Prime Minister Margaret Thatcher, for example, called snap elections in 1983, one year ahead of schedule, to capitalize on her rising popularity following Britain's victory over Argentina in the Falklands War. Her party, the Conservatives, increased its House of Commons majority from 53 percent to 61 percent. Tony Blair called snap elections in 2001 and 2005, retaining the Labour Party's majority in Parliament each time.

Most politicians understand that they risk alienating the voters if they abuse their right to call anticipated elections. Voters may react angrily if they feel they are being called out to vote too frequently or if they believe that their leaders are not trying hard enough to form a workable government. A number of democracies have rules that limit the number of times snap elections may be held within a given period. With or without such rules, political leaders tend to call them fairly rarely, with a keen eye to the public mood.

Presidential–Parliamentary Democracies

The third type of modern democracy to be sketched out is the mixed **presidential–parliamentary system**. This system is also known as *semi-presidentialism*. It features a president and a prime minister who each have significant decision-making powers. The president typically is elected by the voters. The prime minister usually must be approved by the parliament (the lower house in bicameral legislatures). In other words, this is a *dual-executive system*. Figure 6.4 provides a general model of the presidential–parliamentary system. Table 6.8 lists some of the countries that use it in one form or another.

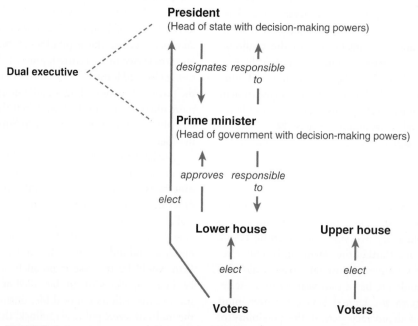

FIGURE 6.4 **Presidential–Parliamentary System**

Table 6.8 Selected Countries Using the Presidential–Parliamentary Form of Democracy

Croatia	Mongolia	Russia
France	Niger	Senegal
Lithuania	Poland	South Korea
Macedonia	Portugal	Sri Lanka
Madagascar	Romania	Ukraine

In some cases, as in France and Russia, the president has even greater constitutional powers than the president of the United States, while the legislature has fewer powers than the U.S. Congress. The French or Russian president, for example, may issue decrees or other executive decisions without parliamentary approval. The president may even possess the authority to declare a state of national emergency and govern with little or no parliamentary check on his or her authority. The parliament, for its part, can be constitutionally forbidden to propose or pass laws in certain areas that are the exclusive preserve of presidential or cabinet authority.

The main purpose of this type of regime is to expedite the process of making governmental decisions. By conferring a significant measure of legal authority on the president, it may be possible to avoid the protracted wrangling that often ensues when lawmaking is dominated by legislators. Presidential–parliamentary democracies are thus intended above all to maximize the *efficiency* of the decision-making process and the *stability* of executive authority. France adopted this system in 1958 precisely to avoid the persistent instability and gridlock that had plagued its parliamentary system of government from 1946 to 1958. Russia adopted its own variant of this system in 1993–94 with a view to managing the difficult transition from communism to democracy through strong executive power. President Boris Yeltsin, who was committed to democracy, wanted a free hand to make fundamental political and economic reforms that were opposed by the legislature's majority of Communists and other opponents of change.

The danger arises, however, that a president with too much power may abuse it, perhaps threatening the very principles of negotiation, accommodation, and compromise on which democracy ultimately rests. Russian presidents Yeltsin and Vladimir Putin have been accused of wielding quasi-dictatorial powers, and French President Charles de Gaulle occasionally exceeded his constitutional authority. Some countries not listed in Table 6.8 have a presidential–parliamentary system that is authoritarian or semi-authoritarian. They include former parts of the Soviet Union—Armenia, Azerbaijan, Belarus, Kazakhstan, Kyrgyzstan, and Uzbekistan—along with Haiti and Togo. Presidential–parliamentary regimes tend to walk a fine line between stable, efficient rule on the one hand and the abuse of executive power on the other.

Meanwhile, an efficient decision-making process firmly concentrated in the president's hands may not always come about in practice. In addition to electing the president, the voters elect the legislature. If the president represents one political party and the majority of legislators represent rival parties, divided government and gridlock may ensue. It can even happen that the president and the prime minister represent opposing parties, a prospect that can severely complicate the process of decision making at the highest executive levels of national government. In this system, the president may usually name the prime minister, but the legislature has the right to reject the president's choice. As a consequence, the president may be forced to name a prime minister of an opposing party so as to satisfy the legislative majority.

France has experienced this situation several times since the 1980s and most recently between 1997 and 2002 (see Chapter 14). Ironically, while the mixed presidential–parliamentary system is designed to streamline executive decision making, it can sometimes severely complicate it.[5]

Comparisons

Of the three types of democracy we have just examined, which one is "the best"? Seeking an unequivocal answer to this question is futile. All three systems have advantages and disadvantages. Presidentialism can be an efficient, effective, and stable form of government, provided that the executive and legislative branches work in harmony. But it risks the potential abuse of presidential power, which can reach dictatorial proportions if left unchecked by legislative and judicial authority. (Until 1997 Mexico had this problem, as described in Chapter 18.) Another potential problem is gridlock—the paralysis of the lawmaking process—in the event of a standoff between the president and the legislature, as happened in the United States between 2010 and 2012. Parliamentary government can at times function more efficiently and flexibly than the presidential system, but these advantages are most likely to occur when one party enjoys an absolute majority of seats. When this condition does not prevail, majority coalition governments and minority governments can sometimes cause just as much gridlock as in presidential systems, if not more. Finally, presidential–parliamentary systems may at times ensure stable and effective government, but they can enable the executive branch to run roughshod over the legislature, and they risk crossing the thin line that separates presidential democracy from the abuse of executive power. Far from being *semi-presidential* systems, they can turn out to be *super-presidential* systems. At other times, the decision-making powers of the presidency in this system can shrink considerably if opposing parties control the legislature and the president's chief opponent becomes prime minister.

Every system of government exists in the real-world context of an individual country's unique blend of historical, economic, social, and other characteristics. No two countries are ever exactly alike, and their political institutions are bound to emerge and develop in accordance with their own distinctive features. The U.S. system of separation of powers has evolved over more than 200 years in a country whose experiences have been very different from those of Europe, Latin America, and other parts of the world. The factors that account for the durability of this system in the United States may not be present in other countries, where other types of democracy may be more suitable or desirable.

Similarly, the factors that account for the way parliamentary government works in Britain are quite different from those that affect its operation in Japan, Israel, India, or elsewhere. The attributes of the mixed presidential–parliamentary system may be appropriate in some countries at particular stages in their history, but not at other times or in other countries. These national particularities will stand out more clearly when we examine the ways parliamentarism and the presidential–parliamentary system work in specific countries in later chapters.[6]

ELECTORAL SYSTEMS

Regular elections constitute one of the most indispensable components of modern democracy. Not all democracies have the same electoral systems, however. There are different ways of counting the votes. As a consequence, there are different ways of making the votes count in terms of who wins governing power and who does not. Vote counting is an aspect of political science that has attracted close attention for centuries. It poses some tantalizing theoretical puzzles while at the same time exerting a profound effect on the way political power is distributed in the real world of politics.

First we'll look at two methods for electing a president: the *direct election* system used in France, Russia, and some other countries, and the *electoral college* system used in the United States. Next we'll look at two methods for electing a chamber of the national legislature: the *single-member district/plurality* system and *proportional representation*. These respective electoral systems by no means exhaust the range of vote-counting methods that are in use in the world today or that have been used in the past. With all their variants, however, the systems we describe here are the most widely used electoral systems in today's democracies.

Electing a President

In some democracies, the process of electing a president is straightforward: The people vote directly for individual candidates. In France, Russia, and many other countries, the presidential electoral process can be decided in a single election, or it may require two rounds of voting. This is the *runoff* system. In the first round of balloting, virtually any number of candidates may run, subject to certain requirements for candidacy. If one candidate gets a majority of popular votes (50 percent plus one vote) in the first round, that person is declared the winner. If no one gets more than half of the votes, a second round of balloting is held a week or two later between the top two finishers of the first round. The winner of this runoff election is elected president.

This direct election system tends to give voters a wide assortment of choices in the first round. In effect, it amounts to a national primary election in which all the eligible candidates run on the same day. This system also compels the voters

to choose between two individuals in the event that a second round is necessary. If one's favorite candidate does not survive into the second round, the voter must decide whether to vote at all, and if so, for which one of the two remaining candidates to vote. The results of recent presidential elections in Indonesia and Peru, which both use runoff elections for the highest office, show that this system encourages a fairly large turnout in round one and a similar turnout in round two (see Table 6.9). It also guarantees that the person elected president is the choice of an absolute majority of those who turn out to vote. In the 2004 Indonesian election, the victor, Susilo Bambang Yudhoyono, beat the incumbent, Megawati Sukarnoputri, by pulling more votes to his side in the runoff than she did; he garnered 29,428,166 additional votes in the second round while she only gained 13,421,600. Millions of Indonesians had to cast their second ballot for a candidate less desirable than their first-round pick. Now, look closely at Table 6.9 for the Peruvian election results in the second round. Note that the eventual victor, Alan García, did not come in first in the first round. In 2006 the majority of Peruvian voters were not yet willing to have Ollanta Humala as their president. While a plurality favored him on the first ballot, when the second round was held, he gained many fewer additional votes than García. (In 2011 Peruvians did elect Humala to the top office.)

Some countries do not use the runoff model for direct election of the president. Mexico and the Philippines are two large electoral democracies that elect their presidents by plurality. Benigno Aquino III, elected president of the Philippines in 2010, won with 42.1 percent of the popular vote. One of his predecessors, Fidel Ramos, came to office in 1992 with only 23.6 percent of the votes cast. Felipe Calderón's narrow margin—35.9 to 35.3 percent—over Andrés Manuel López Obrador in Mexico's 2006 presidential election ignited a five-month political standoff between the supporters of the two candidates, casting a shadow over the legitimacy of Calderón's presidency. In 2012 Enrique Peña Nieto won the Mexican presidency with 39.2 percent of the vote. A similarly close election in Chile in 1970 brought Salvador Allende to the presidency with 36.6 percent of the vote and laid the basis for the breakdown of democracy there. When democracy returned to Chile in 1989 it came with a runoff system for electing the president. Simple plurality rules for winning direct presidential elections do not mean that all presidents will be chosen by a minority of voters; frequently one candidate in a several-candidate field does gain more than half of the votes. However, runoff elections do guarantee that presidents come into office with the support of the majority that chose to turn out to exercise their right to vote.

The U.S. system is considerably more complicated. Many of the framers of the Constitution did not want the direct election of the president by the voters because they were skeptical about the political wisdom of the population. They preferred a system that gave the final say in choosing the chief executive to a politically sophisticated elite. They therefore introduced a procedure in which voters in each state choose presidential *electors*, who in turn elect the president. The number of electors assigned to each state varies with the size of its population and

Table 6.9 Direct Election System in Indonesia and Peru

Candidate	Party	First Round	Second Round
Indonesia 2004			
Susilo Bambang Yudhoyono	Democratic Party	33.6%	60.6%
Megawati Sukarnoputri	Indonesian Democratic Party	26.6	39.4
Wiranto	Party of the Functional Groups	22.2	
Amien Rais	National Mandate Party	14.7	
Hamzah Haz	United Development Party	3.0	
Total		100.1*	100.0
Turnout		*79.6*	*77.5*
Peru 2006			
Ollanta Humala Tasso	Union for Peru	30.6%	47.4%
Alan García Pérez	Peruvian Aprista Party	24.3	52.6
Lourdes Flores Nano	National Unity	23.8	
Martha Chávez Cossio	Alliance for the Future	7.4	
Valentín Paniagua Corazao	Center Front	5.8	
Humberto Lay Sun	National Restoration	4.4	
14 others receiving less than 1% each		3.7	
Total		100.0	100.0
Turnout		*88.7*	*87.7*

* Due to rounding.

Source: Adam Carr's Election Archive, http://psephos.adam-carr.net.

equals the number of delegates it sends to the House of Representatives plus two for its U.S. senators. Several weeks after the popular elections, the chosen electors assemble separately within each state as the *electoral college* and vote for the president. To be elected, the winning candidate must win a majority of the total number of votes in the electoral college. In 2012 there were 538 electoral college votes; the winning majority had to be more than 270 electoral college votes. President Barack Obama was reelected with 332 electoral college votes to 206 for his principal opponent, Republican Mitt Romney.

One peculiarity of this system is that, in most states, whoever wins the highest popular vote total automatically wins *all* that state's electoral votes. The U.S. presidential election system thus consists of *winner-take-all* elections in almost all the 50 states plus the District of Columbia. As the controversial 2000 election showed, it is possible for a candidate to win the popular vote but lose the presidency in the electoral college. Al Gore won 48.38 percent of the popular vote and George W. Bush won 47.87 percent, but Bush won 271 electoral college votes to Gore's 266 electoral college votes. Similar anomalies have occurred in the past.[7]

Legislative Elections

As pointed out in Chapter 3, a country's national legislature is either *unicameral*, consisting of only one house, or *bicameral*, consisting of two. There are several different methods for electing these legislative chambers. The two methods we'll examine here—the *single-member district/plurality* method and *proportional representation*—each has several different variants. In this chapter we'll simply describe the main principles of these two electoral systems using a few examples, but we'll defer a more detailed explanation of how they work in specific countries to later chapters.

The Single-Member District/Plurality Method In the **single-member district/plurality electoral system**, the country is divided into electoral districts for elections to a particular legislative chamber. The United States, for example, is divided into 435 electoral districts for the House of Representatives. The United Kingdom in 2010 was divided into 650 districts for elections to the House of Commons. One person is elected to represent each district; hence the term single-member district (SMD). Because the individual who is elected is said to have a direct mandate from the voters, the SMD system is sometimes called the *mandate* system. In each district, the candidate who wins a plurality of votes—that is, the most votes—wins the legislative seat. (A *plurality* is the highest number of a set.)

One advantage of this system is that, with only one representative per district, the voters should have an easier time identifying their legislative deputy than would be the case if their district were a *multimember district*. A multimember district sends two or more representatives to the national legislature. Single-member districts are supposed to be more personalized than multimember districts. With only one representative per district, citizens should be able to know the name of the person who represents them in the legislature. This system is designed to promote greater public awareness of politics and greater accountability on the part of the elected representative to his or her constituency. In fact, however, most Americans do *not* know the name of their representative in the House of Representatives.

If there are only two candidates running in each district, the winner automatically wins by a majority. (A *majority* is more than 50 percent. In the case of only two candidates, a plurality becomes a majority.) This result frequently occurs in the United States, where most congressional races are traditionally limited to a Democrat competing against a Republican. In Britain and several other countries that have the SMD voting system, however, three or more candidates routinely compete in each district. In some of these races the winning candidate will win a majority of the votes cast, but it is not necessary to win a majority to be elected the district's representative. A plurality—the highest number of votes among the competing candidates—is sufficient to win. As a consequence, plurality election systems are also called *majoritarian* electoral systems. The candidate who wins the highest number of votes in this system is often said to be "first past the post." Table 6.10 shows the results of an actual contest in the 2008 Canadian parliamentary elections. In this riding (the Canadian term for district), Keith Martin, the Liberal candidate, is the winner with 34.1 percent of the vote. The other candidates simply lose. The SMD/plurality electoral system is a winner-take-all system. With just more than one-third of the vote, Martin wins the whole seat. Another way of thinking of this is that in the Esquimalt-Juan de Fuca riding, 20,042 voters have sent the representative they prefer to parliament; the preferred candidates of 38,692 voters (almost twice as many) are not going to take a seat in Ottawa.

France has a two-round variant of this system that like the runoff system for presidential contests is more likely to mean that a majority of voters has elected the legislator who actually takes a district's seat. In France, many candidates stand in each electoral district in the first round of voting for the National Assembly. If no candidate wins a majority (at least 50 percent plus one) on the first round, a second round occurs in which any candidate winning 12.5 percent of the first-round vote is eligible to stand again. Typically only two candidates do so, with the others being disqualified by virtue of failing to reach the 12.5 percent threshold or because they step down in favor of another candidate, attempting to throw their votes to that other candidate.

Table 6.10 Results in the 2008 Canadian Parliamentary Election Riding: Esquimalt-Juan de Fuca (British Columbia)

Party	Candidate	Votes	Vote Share (%)
Liberal	Keith Martin	20,042	34.1%
Conservative	Troy DeSouza	19,974	34.0
New Democratic Party	Jennifer Burgis	13,322	22.7
Green	Brian Gordon	4,957	8.4
Independent	Philip Ney	309	0.5
Canadian Action Party	Brad Rhodes	130	0.2
Total		**58,734**	**99.9***

*Due to rounding.

Source: http://www.cbc.ca/news/canadavotes/riding/277/.

Table 6.11 Hypothetical Election to the U.S. House of Representatives

Party	% of Total Vote Nationwide	% of Seats Won
Republicans	51%	100%
Democrats	49	0

Table 6.12 Elections to U.S. House of Representatives, 1992

Party	% of Popular Vote Nationwide	% of Seats Won
Democrats	50.8%	59.3%
Republicans	45.6	40.5
Others	3.6	(1 seat)

Source: Office of the Clerk, U.S. House of Representatives, clerk.house.gov/member_info/electionInfo/1992election.pdf.

The SMD/plurality electoral system's main advantages lie in its relative simplicity and the chances it offers to promote name recognition on the part of incumbent representatives and their challengers. But it has some potential problems. For one thing, the SMD/plurality system can lead to a disparity between a party's share of the vote on a nationwide basis and its share of the seats in the legislature. To understand this possibility, simply consider the outcome of a hypothetical race for one seat in the U.S. House of Representatives. In our example, the Republican candidate gets 51 percent of the votes cast and the Democrat gets 49 percent. There are no other candidates running in this district. The Republican is elected to Congress; the Democrat will have to wait two more years for another opportunity to campaign for the seat.

Now suppose this result, by odd coincidence, occurs in all 435 House districts. If we add up all the votes cast throughout the country for the House of Representatives, it is evident that the Republican candidates together captured 51 percent of the vote nationwide while the Democratic candidates together garnered 49 percent. Because the Republican candidate won each separate House contest, however, the Republicans end up with *all* 435 House seats; the Democrats get none. The bottom line is that the Republicans have won slightly more than half the national vote but 100 percent of the seats. The Democrats have won slightly less than half the vote but come away with no representation in the House at all. Table 6.11 displays this result.

Obviously this is an extreme example that is not likely to occur any time soon. But it illustrates a general point: Under the SMD system, a significant difference between a party's share of the national vote and its share of legislative seats *can* occur. Table 6.12 provides a real example from U.S. House of Representatives elections. Even more glaring examples of this phenomenon occur when there are three or more national parties. Tables 6.13 and 6.14 provide examples from Canadian parliamentary elections in 1993 and 2011. In 1993 Canada's Liberal Party took a commanding 60 percent of federal parliamentary seats with only 41.2 percent of the popular vote.

The Progressive Conservative Party won but two seats with 16 percent of the vote! How could this result have happened? The simple answer is that the Progressive Conservative candidates came in second or third in every Canadian riding except the two they won. While the Progressive Conservatives had been very successful in 1988, in 1993 the Bloc Québécois (a Quebec nationalist party) won many of the seats Progressive Conservatives had held in Quebec, and the Reform Party did the same in many ridings in the western provinces (taking most of the seats in British Columbia and Alberta). After a couple more poor election showings, the Progressive Conservatives united with the Reform Party to form the current Conservative Party. The Reform Party's strength in the west and the Progressive Conservatives' draw in other parts of the country combined to return them to power. Table 6.14 indicates that in the 2011 election, the Conservatives took a firm majority in parliament with less than 40 percent of the popular vote.

Another characteristic problem of the SMD/plurality electoral system is that *it tends to punish small parties*. To win a significant share of seats in the U.S. House of Representatives or the British House of Commons, a party must be able to field viable candidates throughout the country, in virtually all districts. Parties that are not large enough to mount such extensive campaigns are not likely to win many legislative seats. The SMD system, in other words, is a major reason the United States has a two-party system. Other parties are too weak within the individual districts, as well as nationally, to elect their candidates.

Table 6.13 1993 Canadian Parliamentary Elections

Party	Seats	Seats %	Vote %
Liberal	177	60.0%	41.3%
Bloc Québécois	54	18.3	13.5
Reform	52	17.6	18.7
New Democratic Party	9	3.1	6.9
Progressive Conservative	2	0.7	16.0
Independent	1	0.3	3.6
Total	295	100.0	100.0

Source: Political Database of the Americas, Georgetown University, pdba. georgetown.edu/Elecdata/Canada/parl93.html.

Table 6.14 2011 Canadian Parliamentary Elections

Party	Seats	Seats %	Vote %
Conservative	167	54.2%	39.6%
New Democratic Party	102	33.1	30.6
Liberal	34	11.0	18.9
Bloc Québécois	4	1.3	6.0
Green Party	1	0.3	3.9
Others	0	0.0	0.9
Total	308	99.9*	99.9*

*Due to rounding.

Source: Elections Canada, www.elections.ca.

Elections to the British House of Commons provide a vivid illustration of how difficult it is for small parties to win a share of parliamentary seats commensurate with their share of the popular vote. In 1992 and 1997, the Liberal Democrats, Britain's third-largest party, won nearly 20 percent of the vote nationwide but a mere 3.1 percent of the seats in the House of Commons in 1992 and 7 percent in 1997. Their voter support was spread out widely across the country, but it was sufficiently concentrated to win a plurality in only a few districts. Other parties fared even more poorly. Roughly similar results occurred in 2001 and 2005. Even in 2010, after which the Liberal Democrats were invited into a coalition government with the Conservatives, they took only 9 percent of the House of Commons seats with 23 percent of the popular vote, as noted in Chapter 13.

One of the chief problems of the SMD/plurality system, then, is that a result that is fair at the local level may seem to be unfair at the national level. "Winner take all" may be a fair way to elect someone to represent your district in the national legislature. But when all the votes are counted nationwide, there may be a significant gap between the parties' respective share of legislative seats and their share of the national vote. Statistical measures of these disparities show that they can remain quite significant over many years.

The *proportional representation* system is designed to overcome some of the defects of the single-member-district/plurality electoral system.

Proportional Representation Under **proportional representation (PR)**, a party's share (percentage) of its seats in the legislature exactly or approximately equals its share of the popular vote nationwide. To put it very simply, if a party gets 25 percent of the popular vote in legislative elections, it will get 25 percent (exactly or approximately) of the seats in the legislature. Various mathematical formulas are employed to ensure these results. There are numerous variants of the PR principle. Most of those in use today are approximate PR systems. In the *party list* variant, parties draw up lists of candidates, rank-ordering their names in accordance with their political prominence. Typically, if a party is entitled to 200 legislative seats, the first 200 people on its list will get the seats.

If a party so chooses, it can promote the election of women or minority candidates in this type of electoral system by putting the names of those candidates at or near the top of its list, so that they will be among the candidates most likely to win seats. Figure 6.5 illustrates how a party-list PR system works in principle. There are quite a few real-world variants of the PR system. Many of them deviate from our illustrative model in particular ways while adhering to PR's essential principles.[8]

Variants of PR Despite the Israeli complications detailed in the case study on page 129—problems that occur in other democracies also—supporters of proportional representation insist that it is far more representative of a country's political divisions than the single-member district/plurality system. The latter may produce more coherent and stable governments, but it may fail to represent fairly the various political

MODEL OF A PARTY-LIST PROPORTIONAL REPRESENTATION SYSTEM
(100 seats in the legislature)

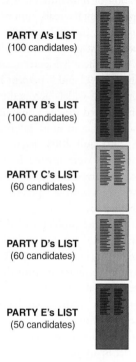

PARTY A's LIST
(100 candidates)

PARTY B's LIST
(100 candidates)

PARTY C's LIST
(60 candidates)

PARTY D's LIST
(60 candidates)

PARTY E's LIST
(50 candidates)

BALLOT

INSTRUCTIONS:
Mark an X next
to ONE Party

PARTY A

PARTY B

PARTY C

PARTY D

PARTY E

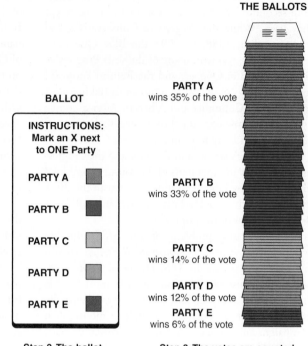

THE BALLOTS

PARTY A
wins 35% of the vote

PARTY B
wins 33% of the vote

PARTY C
wins 14% of the vote

PARTY D
wins 12% of the vote

PARTY E
wins 6% of the vote

Step 1. Party lists.

Each party draws up a list of its candidates, ranked in order of importance. Half the candidates in Parties A and B are women. The largest parties decide to run as many candidates as there are seats; the smaller parties list fewer candidates.

Step 2. The ballot.

Each voter votes for 1 party.

Step 3. The votes are counted.

Each party wins a percentage of the nationwide popular vote.

LEGISLATURE
(100 seats)

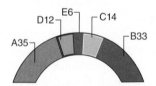

E6
D12   C14
A35   B33

Step 4. The seats are apportioned according to the popular vote.

Party A wins 35% of the seats; the top 35 candidates on its list get the seats. Party B wins 33% of the seats; the top 33 candidates on its list get the seats, and so on for C, D and E. It's a hung parliament: no party has a majority. Party A has a plurality.

(IN A PARLIAMENTARY REGIME)
COALITION GOVERNMENT
(20 cabinet ministers)

PARTY A (PM + 11 ministers) + **PARTY D** (6) + **PARTY E** (2)

Step 5. Forming a coalition government.

The country's head of state (president or monarch) asks the head of Party A to form a government. Party A cannot agree on a governing program with B or C, but comes to terms with D and E. Together Parties A, D, and E have 53 seats, a majority. They agree on how to share 20 cabinet posts. The head of Party A is prime minister, the head of D foreign minister, the head of E finance minister. All ministers are also members of the legislature. If Party A fails to form a government, the head of state asks the head of Party B to try.

FIGURE 6.5   **Model of a Party-List Proportional Representation System**

CASE STUDY
Proportional Representation in Israel

Israel provides a specific example of how a PR system can work. The country as a whole constitutes one large electoral district for the Knesset, its 120-member unicameral legislature. Voters vote for a party, not for individual candidates. Table 6.15 reports the results for the 2003, 2006, and 2009 elections.

The results show the close approximation between each party's share of the national vote and its share of the seats in the Knesset. Each party won a share of legislative seats *in rough proportion* to its share of the national vote. We do not see the wide disparities in these two figures that are possible—and that sometimes actually occur—in the SMD/plurality system.[9]

Note the large number of parties elected to the Knesset. Indeed, PR can lead to a fairly wide proliferation of political parties represented in the legislature. Under these conditions, it is not likely that a single party will win an absolute majority of legislative seats. As a consequence, PR often results in a multiparty coalition government or a minority government. If the parties that participate in these arrangements get along, such a system can work smoothly in establishing stable and effective governments. But multiparty governments can also be highly unstable and inefficient. One of the drawbacks of PR, therefore, is that it increases the chances of instability and inefficiency.

Israel is an example. The 120-member Knesset elected in 2003 included 13 party groupings; the Knesset elected in 2006 had 12; and the Knesset elected in 2009 also had 12 party groupings.

These diverse parties reflected the wide range of ethnic, religious, class, and ideological distinctions to be found in Israeli society, as noted in Chapter 4.

The center-left Labor Party is one of Israel's oldest surviving parties. It has produced a number of prime ministers, including Golda Meir (1969–74), Yitzhak Rabin (1974–77 and 1992–95), Shimon Peres (1984–86 and 1995–96), and Ehud Barak (1999–2000). Likud (Consolidation), the country's largest right-leaning party, has produced Prime Ministers Menachem Begin (1977–83), Yitzhak Shamir (1983–84 and 1986–92), Binyamin Netanyahu (1996–99 and 2009 to the time of this writing), and Ariel Sharon (2000–06). Kadima (or "Forward") resulted from a split within Likud about making peace with the Palestinians, and several Labor leaders, including Peres, joined Kadima. Its founder, Sharon (2005–06), and Ehud Olmert (2006–09) have served as prime ministers. Meretz-Yachad ("Vigor-Together") is a secular center-left party favoring compromise with the Palestinians. Its name reflects the merger of two previously separate parties. Shinui (Change) and the Center Party were also secular center-left parties, but they suffered internal leadership splits and did not win Knesset seats in 2006. Shas (the Sephardi Religious Party) is a religious right-wing party that mostly represents Jews from Morocco and other parts of North Africa and the Middle East. It is reluctant to give up Jewish settlements in the occupied territories. The National Religious Party and National Union

Table 6.15 Elections to Israel's Knesset, 2003, 2006, and 2009

Party	2003			2006			2009		
	% Vote	% Seats	No. Seats	% Vote	% Seats	No. Seats	% Vote	% Seats	No. Seats
Labor*	14.5%	15.8%	19	15.1%	15.8%	19	9.9%	10.8%	13
Likud	29.4	31.7	38	9.0	10.0	12	21.6	22.5	27
Kadima	—	—	—	22.0	24.2	29	22.5	23.3	28
Meretz-Yachad	5.2	5.0	6	3.8	4.2	5	3.0	2.5	3
Shinui	12.3	12.5	15	—	—	—	—	—	—
Shas	8.2	9.2	11	9.5	10.0	12	8.5	9.2	11
National Religious Party/The Jewish Home*	4.2	5.0	6	—	—	—	2.9	2.5	3
National Union	5.5	5.8	7	7.1	7.5	9	3.3	3.3	4
United Torah Judaism	4.3	4.2	5	4.7	5.0	6	4.4	4.2	5
Yisrael Beitenu	—	—	—	8.9	9.2	11	11.7	12.5	15
Yisrael Ba'Aliya	2.2	1.7	2	—	—	—	—	—	—
United Arab List	2.1	1.7	2	3.0	3.3	4	3.4	3.3	4
Hadash	3.0	2.5	3	2.7	2.5	3	3.3	3.3	4
Balad	2.3	2.5	3	2.3	2.5	3	2.5	2.5	3
One Nation	2.8	2.5	3	—	—	—	—	—	—
Gil (Pensioners)†	—	—	—	5.9	5.8	7	—	—	—

*In 1997, Labor ran with two smaller parties under the joint label "One Israel." In 2003, Labor joined with another small party to form Labor-Meimad. In 2006, Meretz joined with another group to form Meretz-Yachad; the National Religious Party (NRP) ran together with National Union; and the United Arab List ran together with the Arab Renewal Movement. In 2009, much of the NRP became the Jewish Home.

†Gil merged with Kadima.

Source: Adam Carr's Election Archive, http://psephos.adam-carr.net/.

(Continued on next page)

(Continued from previous page)

are hard-line right-wing religious parties that strongly support Jewish settlements in the West Bank and East Jerusalem, opposing any agreement to give up the occupied territories. The two parties ran together in 2006. United Torah Judaism (also called Torah and Sabbath Judaism) is an Orthodox religious party that appeals largely to Ashkenazi Jews, but it is opposed to Zionism as a nationalist ideology, and it is fairly flexible in its approach to the occupied territories. As a general rule, Israel's religious parties favor public funding for religious schools and strongly support Israel's use of religious law in such things as marriage and family law. (Despite these and other religious influences, Israel is a secular state based on English civil law, not Talmudic law.) Secular parties tend to oppose public funding for religious schools.

Yisrael Beitenu ("Our Home Is Israel") and Yisrael Ba'Aliya have represented Jews from the former Soviet Union, mostly from Russia and Ukraine. ("Aliya" refers to emigration to Israel.) From the start, both were hard-line right-wing parties that favored holding on to the settlements in the occupied territories. Yisrael Ba'Aliya, which was founded by the former Soviet dissident Natan Sharansky, fell apart after Sharansky and other party leaders merged into the Likud Party. The United Arab List, which ran jointly with the Arab Renewal Movement in 2006, appeals to Israel's large Arab minority, a group of Palestinian Muslims and Christians that compose about 20 percent of the population of Israel proper (i.e., not counting the occupied territories). The two Arab parties include Islamists as well as secular Palestinian nationalists. They favor an end to discrimination against Arabs inside Israel as well as a peace settlement with the Palestinian Authority. Balad appeals to secular Arab nationalists. Hadash is a left-wing party that appeals to secular Jewish and Arab voters. One Nation was also a secular leftist party that did not run in 2006.

Two parties were elected to the Knesset for the first time in 2006. As indicated in Chapter 4, Kadima (Forward) was the new center-left party created by Prime Minister Ariel Sharon after the Likud Party resisted Sharon's decision to pull Jewish settlers out of Gaza. Ehud Olmert succeeded Sharon as the party's chief after Sharon suffered a debilitating stroke in early 2006, and Olmert became prime minister after the March 2006 elections. Gil (Age) is also known as the Pensioners Party of Israel. As its name implies, it is primarily concerned with Israel's elderly population.

Israel's proportional representation does not *create* political divisions within society; like a mirror, it *reflects* them. In fact, it is a highly democratic method for representing in Israel's national legislature the numerous identities, interests, and attitudes to be found in the country's multifaceted society. At the same time, however, PR actively encourages very small Israeli parties to field their own candidates instead of coalescing into "big-tent" parties like the Democrats and Republicans in the United States. And by making it practically impossible to establish a single-party government with a coherent policy design, PR virtually guarantees that any Israeli cabinet will consist of disparate parties that are bound to disagree on this or that policy decision—including, at times, the most vital questions affecting Israel's security and the Middle East's deadly conflicts.

In effect, very small parties in Israel's government often have a veto over policy initiatives that are favored by the prime minister and the largest party in the government. The new government formed under Ehud Olmert after the 2006 elections, for example, consisted of Kadima, the Labor Party, Shas, and the Pensioners Party. Together these four parties held 67 seats, a slim 7-seat majority. Shas immediately announced that it would not support Prime Minister Olmert's plan to eventually evacuate some 80,000 Jewish settlers who had established unauthorized settlements in the West Bank. The governing parties pulled together in the summer of 2006 during the fighting with Hezbollah in Lebanon. But as his approval ratings plummeted, Olmert later invited the head of the hard-line Yisrael Beitenu Party (which had 11 Knesset seats) to join the cabinet. This government survived until January 2008. Olmert's successor's inability to form a new majority government led to new elections in February 2009. After the 2009 elections the Knesset supported a government formed by Likud's Netanyahu despite the fact the Kadima had taken the largest number of Knesset seats, showing that coming in first in a parliamentary election does not guarantee that a party will be able to form the government. Proportional representation in Israel may not be a catalyst of the Middle East crisis; but it certainly hampers the decision-making process in the Israeli government, adding one more burden to an already overburdened region.

Israel uses a system of proportional representation to elect its parties. Binyamin Netanyahu has become prime minister despite his Likud Party having won fewer seats in the Knesset than the Kadima Party.

orientations to be found in the electorate. PR systems are rarely two-party systems; they are highly inclusive of a wide spectrum of political opinion. Their advocates assert that by squeezing the voters into two or perhaps three main parties, majoritarian voting systems like SMD unduly limit voter choice and create false legislative majorities (like the British Labour Party's 63 percent majority in the House of Commons, achieved in 1997 with only 40 percent of the popular vote). Americans who complain that their own views are not adequately addressed by their two-party system might ponder the fact that the adoption of a proportional representation voting system would quite probably increase the number of parties capable of winning seats in Congress.

Critics of PR contend that it can lead to such a large number of parties in the national legislature that governing becomes next to impossible. But some democracies with PR systems have found a way to cut back on the number of parties elected to the legislature. A *hurdle* (or *threshold*) can be used to require a party to win a certain percentage of the national vote to acquire legislative seats. Parties falling below this hurdle usually do not get any seats. Sweden has a 4 percent threshold, for example, and Germany has a 5 percent threshold. Israel employed a 1.5 percent threshold in 1999 and 2003, then raised it to 2 percent in the 2006 elections. These hurdles were low enough to allow several small parties to jump over them and enter the Knesset, but they were still high enough to keep out a number of even smaller parties. (In 2003, 15 parties fell below the 1.5 percent hurdle; in 2006, 19 fell below the 2 percent hurdle; in 2009, it was 21.) Poland imposed a hurdle after the PR system that was used in 1991, in the earliest stages of the country's transition from communism to democracy, returned 30 parties to the legislature. Following the imposition of a 5 percent hurdle for single parties and 8 percent for parties running jointly, the number of elected parties fell to seven in 1993 and five in 1997. (The model displayed in Figure 6.5 has no threshold.)

Another criticism that is often leveled at PR is that it tends to be more impersonal than the SMD system. Voters in an SMD system have a chance to identify the competing candidates by name, but in most PR systems the voters vote for a party, not an individual candidate. Each party provides a list of the candidates it puts up for election, but the names on these lists are not likely to be highly publicized in the media. Except for the most prominent leaders in each party, candidates for the legislature in most PR systems do not have a high degree of name recognition among the voters. In addition, some countries with PR systems have multimember districts, with as many as 10 legislators elected to serve each district. Although some voters may like having a multiplicity of representatives catering to their district's needs, others may find it difficult to recall the name of any of them. It may therefore be more difficult to hold individual legislators accountable to their local constituents in such circumstances.

Germany tries to get around these problems by combining PR with the SMD system. Half of the Bundestag's seats are elected by PR, the other half by SMD (see Chapter 15 for more details). A statistical formula ensures that the final distribution of seats in that chamber approximates PR. Japan, Russia, and some other countries have also used a combination of PR and SMD in electing a legislative house. The combination of PR and SMD is called a **mixed-member electoral system**.[10] The choice of electoral system has weighty political implications. Russia scrapped its mixed-member system because the single-member districts produced many independent legislators with little or no party affiliation. To bring the legislature under greater presidential control, President Vladimir Putin and his allies changed the system to proportional representation in time for the 2007 elections. In the early 1990s, Italy replaced its complicated variant of proportional representation with a mixed-member system to break the power of corrupt political parties that had used the PR system to dominate Italian governments for more than 40 years. But Prime Minister Silvio Berlusconi, hoping to win reelection in 2006, had the system switched back to a new variant of proportional representation. His coalition lost nevertheless.

In sum, the main advantages of PR are (1) its *fairness* in translating popular support for political parties into equivalent shares of legislative seats; (2) its ability to *help small parties*—and perhaps women and minorities—to win a share of legislative seats (and maybe cabinet posts); and (3) its tendency to *enhance voter choice* by providing the electorate with a wide array of parties from which to choose. PR's disadvantages include (1) its tendency to promote the *proliferation of a large number of parties;* (2) its tendency thereby to increase the likelihood of *hung parliaments*, *governmental instability*, *inefficiency*, and *ineffectiveness;* and (3) its *impersonal character*.

Just as we cannot identify "the best" institutional form of representative democracy, it is equally difficult to pick either the SMD/plurality system or PR as the better legislative electoral system. Both systems have advantages and disadvantages. Most important, how these systems work in actual practice tends to differ from country to country.

One question is immensely relevant to average citizens in all democracies: Do voters turn out at the polls at consistently higher rates under one of these systems as opposed to the other? Theoretically, one would think that the PR system would attract more voters than plurality systems on the grounds that PR gives the voters a greater chance to elect representatives of their favorite party into the legislature. Under plurality systems, as in the United States or Britain, the two largest parties are likely to win the overwhelming majority of the seats. Hypothetically, PR systems thus tend to entice a greater number of parties to run candidates, giving the voters a wider array of choice on election day than they are likely to get under a plurality system.

Constitutional Design of Democracies and Electoral Rules

Usually when we think of proportional representation, we think of its operation in parliamentary systems because PR has been used in several European parliamentary systems. PR can also be used in presidential and semi-presidential systems, but

HYPOTHESIS-TESTING EXERCISE
Do PR Systems Have Higher Turnout Than Plurality Systems?

Hypothesis Proportional representation produces higher voter turnouts than plurality systems in legislative elections.

Variables The *dependent variable* is voter turnout. The *independent variables* are PR and plurality voting systems.

Expectations If our hypothesis is correct, we would expect to find that democracies with PR will have consistently higher turnout rates than those with plurality systems.

Evidence Table 6.16 lists 20 countries that held democratic elections between 1945 and 1997. Most of them retained the same parliamentary electoral system throughout the decades, the chief exception being France. Though the various PR systems differed in specific details, in principle they were sufficiently similar to justify grouping them for comparative purposes. The same was true of the plurality systems.

Table 6.16 Turnout in PR and Plurality Electoral Systems

PR Systems		Plurality Systems	
Country	Average Turnout, 1945–1997 (%)	Country	Average Turnout, 1945–1997 (%)
Iceland	89.5%	New Zealand	86.2%
Austria	85.1	Australia	84.4
Belgium	84.9	United Kingdom	74.9
Netherlands	84.8	Canada	68.4
Denmark	83.6	France, 5th Republic	65.3
Sweden	83.4	India	60.6
Germany	80.6	United States	48.3
Israel	80.0		
Norway	79.8		
Finland	79.0		
Ireland	74.9		
France, 4th Republic	72.2		
Japan	69.2		
Luxembourg	64.1		
Switzerland	49.3		

Source: International Institute for Democracy and Electoral Assistance, *Voter Turnout from 1945 to 1997: A Global Report.*

It is immediately apparent that a large number of countries with PR systems had average turnout rates of 79 percent or higher; only two of the states with plurality systems attracted more voters. Turnout in the PR countries from 1945 to 1997 averaged 78 percent; in the plurality countries the average was 69.5 percent. These figures are consistent with our hypothesis.

Conclusions Higher average turnout rates for PR systems were obviously the rule. Nevertheless, we should not lose sight of some interesting details. Notice that average turnout rates were higher in New Zealand, Australia, and the United Kingdom—countries with variants of the plurality system—than in Japan, Luxembourg, and Switzerland, which have variants of PR. Plurality systems thus do not *always* have lower turnout rates than PR systems. Our overall evidence is therefore *mixed*.

If we dig into some data not shown here, we can occasionally find significant variations in voter turnout within the same country, despite the fact that no change has occurred in its electoral system. In Switzerland, for example, turnout plunged from 63 percent in 1951 to 35.7 percent in 1995.[11] In the United States, turnout for House of Representatives elections is typically higher in years when a presidential election takes place than in off years.[12] Germany's electoral system combines PR *and* SMD/plurality: Though the final result is always approximate proportional representation, voters may be lured to the polls at least in part to vote for a single member to represent their voting district.

These and other departures from the general validity of our hypothesis serve as reminders that virtually every generalization in political science has its exceptions. Also, a correlation between two variables does not by itself explain *why* it occurs. People vote—or stay at home—for all sorts of reasons. Although people show a general tendency to vote in PR systems at higher rates than in countries with plurality systems, it would be a mistake to assume that electoral systems alone account for voter turnout. Voters can decide to troop to the polls or stay home for a variety of reasons, even though the electoral system is the same. Voter turnout in Israel, for example, fell from 78.7 percent in 1999 to 68.9 percent in 2003 and to 63.2 percent in 2006, although it recovered to 65.2 percent in 2009. Perhaps we should remind ourselves of another generalization: More often than not, multicausality is more likely to explain the complex phenomena of political reality than is reductivist monocausality.

often that combination yields significant problems. PR produces more parties than does a single-member district plurality system, but in a parliamentary system, coalition governments of multiple parties can be formed in ways that they cannot in presidential systems. In presidential systems the government does not fall if it loses a legislative vote. The president stays in office until her or his fixed-length term ends. Hence legislators or party delegations within legislatures do not have as much to risk by defying the president on some bill of importance to the president. Yet, if there is not a majority supporting the president in the congress, gridlock can result. This often happens with presidential systems that use PR to elect the congress.

Most of the examples of this combination come from Central and South America. Presidents who are stymied by legislatures that have many parties and that don't have a majority behind presidential initiatives may be tempted to use their decree powers (if they have them) to govern. A good example was Salvador Allende, president of Chile (1970–73), who lacked a majority in the Chilean congress and attempted to bring many significant changes to Chile by the use of his presidential powers. His opponents in congress, elected through a PR system, attempted to block his reform efforts. A constitutional deadlock ensued. That standoff ended when the Chilean military deposed Allende in a bloody coup.

ELECTORAL RULES AND PARTY SYSTEMS

One of the few generalizations accorded the label "law" in political science is **Duverger's law**. Maurice Duverger, a French political scientist, argued that the form of electoral system adopted in a country played a powerful role in shaping the number of parties operating there. Duverger argued, "The simple-majority single-ballot system favors the two-party system." By this he means single-member district, winner-take-all systems favor two-party systems. Conversely, he claimed, proportional representation favored multi-partism, and the majority system with a runoff vote for legislative races (such as held in France for most of the periods 1870–1940 and 1958 to the present) also favors the formation of a multiparty system.[13] How does this work in practice? Let's focus on the effects of PR and SMD rules here; we will return to the majority system with a runoff vote in Chapter 14 on France in Part Two of this book.

To explain how electoral rules shape **party systems**, by which we mean the number of parties competing in a country and their character—whether they are catch-all or ideological parties, flexible in their approach to policies or rigid—Duverger distinguished between what he called mechanical

CASE STUDY
Choosing an Electoral System in Iraq

After overthrowing the regime of Saddam Hussein in Iraq in 2003, the United States promised to bring democracy to that nation. Many Iraqis advocated democracy too and wanted to see a government of Iraqis in place as soon as possible after the war. Indeed, Ayatollah Ali al-Sistani, the premier religious figure in the country, wished to see elections little more than a year after Baghdad fell to U.S. forces in April 2003. The first elections for a transitional national assembly were held in January 2005, eight months later than Sistani would have preferred, but still less than two years after the U.S.-led invasion.

The transitional national assembly may be likened to a parliament, and from it was formed the transitional government. That national assembly also served as a constitutional convention; a committee of the national assembly drafted the constitution of Iraq. How was it elected?

In choosing an electoral system, the American-led Coalition Provisional Authority and the Independent High Electoral Commission (IHEC), which drew on the advice of a United Nations team, adopted a proportional representation system with a single national constituency and closed lists—essentially the same electoral system that Israel uses. Closed lists means that the parties propose ranked lists of candidates and that the voters cannot indicate a preference for

any particular candidate on the closed list. (An open-list system allows voters to change the order of selection from the list by indicating a preference for individuals on the list.) A feature of this closed-list system was that at least every third name had to be that of a woman. In this way, a high degree of female representation in the new assembly was guaranteed.

Why did the IHEC choose this form of PR? Two issues stand out as most critical. First, Iraqi society is highly fractured, and was even more so in the aftermath of the Hussein regime and the American invasion. Three large groups dominate Iraqi society: an Arab Shiite majority, an Arab Sunni minority, and a Kurdish minority concentrated in the north of the country. The Kurds had welcomed the American-led intervention, certain Sunni tribes had benefitted significantly during Hussein's rule, and Shiites had felt discrimination under the former regime. In addition, some Iraqis favored a stronger role for religion in politics while others preferred a more secular regime. In such a fragmented society, PR allows for each group to be represented in the national legislature in a way roughly equivalent to its weight in the population. Second, because the occupation authorities lacked an accurate census of the country, they could not draw single-member districts or even

(Continued on next page)

(Continued from previous page)

multiple-member districts to meet the one-person, one-vote norm. Also, by using a closed list (the names of which were not posted broadly), the electoral authorities allowed individuals on the party lists to "hide": They could not be easily identified by insurgents who wanted to attack those Iraqis cooperating with the invaders by participating as candidates. Moreover, with a national constituency, the candidates could avoid campaigning in parts of the country that they regarded as too dangerous.

As astute observers predicted, with a single national constituency and closed-list PR, the January 2005 election resembled an ethnic census as Kurdish voters cast their ballots for the Kurdish parties, Shiites chose parties clearly identified as Shiite, and Sunni voters unfortunately abstained in high numbers. In a sense, this election reinforced the ethnic cleavage in Iraq as the parties sought votes from specific ethnic groups that they promised to represent. In addition, with the exception of the party leaders, voters could not easily attach responsibility to individuals within the parliamentary parties because the size of the single national constituency meant they simply did not know them.

To address these shortcomings of the electoral system used in January 2005, the IHEC adopted a modified PR system when elections were held for the first permanent parliament in December 2005. That December election used the country's 18 governorates (provinces) as multimember electoral districts. The number of seats per governorate was intended to be proportional to the population (although the apportionment was based on voter registration figures rather than a census). While some complained that the Sunni governorates were underrepresented, most observers agreed that the allocation of seats was relatively fair. Because the lists were provincial-level lists, voters could more easily identify with the representatives chosen in that election, and parties were encouraged to campaign at the provincial level. This time, Sunni parties urged Sunni voters to participate, and overall participation proved to be high: Turnout was estimated to be close to 80 percent in December, whereas it had been under 60 percent in January 2005.[14] Besides the 230 seats selected in provincial multimember districts, the electoral system used to choose the parliament in the December 2005 elections also included 45 "compensatory" seats—seats that were allocated to parties to compensate for any lack of proportionality between vote shares and seat shares at the national level.

To make one more improvement on this electoral system, as the 2010 parliamentary elections approached, the electoral authorities opted for an open-list PR system, again with multimember districts whose boundaries coincided with the governorates. Open-list PR encourages voters to identify with individual representatives because they can cast a vote for an individual on a party's PR list and thereby move that person up or down the list, making them more or less likely to be elected to parliament. This change was expected to strengthen parties at the provincial level by encouraging them to put local notables on their provincial party lists.

As each of these modifications of Iraq's PR system has proceeded, the rule placing women in at least every third position on each party list has remained in place. The result has been that about one-quarter of the members of the lower house are women. The 25.2 percent of the lower house that is female compares very favorably with the Arab states' average of 11.3 percent and is above the world average, which was 20.8 percent at the beginning of 2013.[15]

The framers of the new Iraqi government selected a system of proportional representation in part to address the competing needs of three major constituents who are traditional rivals: an Arab Shiite majority, an Arab Sunni minority, and a Kurdish minority. President Jalal Talabani, center, a Kurd, sits with vice presidents, Shiite Adel Abdul-Mahdi, left and Ghazi al-Yawer, a Sunni Arab, right, during the National Assembly meeting in Baghdad, in 2005.

After an abrupt regime change, promoting democracy inevitably involves selecting an electoral system. The circumstances—how socially and politically fragmented the country might be, how much information is available about the way the population is distributed geographically, even whether the whole country is safe for the conduct of campaigns—as well as the goals of those in a position to shape the new regime affect the choices made. While the regime in place in Baghdad certainly has shortcomings—its Freedom House score of 5.5 in 2011 placed it in the not free group—it has held elections that have been judged free and fair by international and domestic observers. And its electoral system has improved with each national legislative election. Of course, a highly representative parliament in a divided society can be a blueprint for political deadlock, which has characterized Iraqi politics in the post-Saddam era.

and psychological reasons. Mechanically, the SMD, winner-take-all system tends to suppress the emergence of small parties for reasons we outlined above. Unless a small party's support is very concentrated geographically—within a single electoral district or a small number of districts where it can win outright—the votes to a party yield no seats in the legislature. Third parties in the United States are a good example—when you enter the voting booth to cast your ballot for the U.S. House of Representatives, chances are several candidates are on the ballot from parties other than Republicans and Democrats. But the Libertarian Party, which tallied more than 1 million votes in 2012, wins no seats in Congress. If the United States used proportional representation and a single, nationwide electoral district, like Israel, the Libertarians would have won at least three seats (of the 435 in the House) with 1 million votes out of a total of about 120 million. The fact that a candidate has to win the plurality of seats in a single-member district means that small parties rarely win any seats in legislative races.

Psychologically, Duverger argues, this fact means that voters will be reluctant to vote for third parties in SMD systems because they see such votes as wasted. Why vote Libertarian if your candidate is sure to lose? Perhaps you would like to influence the outcome between the Republicans and Democrats. Strategic voting leads citizens to cast ballots for two larger parties in a SMD system in order to have more direct impact on the final outcome. This voter behavior, though, dooms third parties to also-ran status.

Empirically, we tend to see proportional representation using large districts (with many seats per district) and no thresholds for representation (unlike Germany's rule that says parties have to receive 5 percent of the vote to win PR seats) yielding multiparty systems. Single-member district systems with plurality rules (first-past-the-post) tend to produce party systems with fewer effective parties.

Duverger's law is an example of how a constitutional engineer might use electoral rules to shape the party system. If you want fewer parties, SMD may be the way to go. On the other hand, if you worry that minority voices might be tamped down in a two-party system, PR offers a way to encourage small parties to emerge to represent those minority voices.

Conclusion

Chapter 5 identified democracy's defining elements. This chapter has shown how democratic governments can be organized and how various election systems work. Devising the rules that shape the relationship of the executive power to the legislative power strongly influences how power can be exercised in a country. Similarly, because electoral rules can shape how party systems develop, representation in a democracy depends greatly on those electoral rules. Both electoral rules and the constitutional design of democracies are places where human agency can have enormous impact on the way politics is played in any given society. Constitutional framers can be political engineers, if they think carefully about the electoral rules and the procedures through which legislators make laws and convey those laws to the executive to implement.

The next chapter looks at some of the main factors that account for how democracies come about and succeed in the long run.

Key Terms

Presidentialism

Parliamentary government

Vote of confidence

Single-party majoritarian government

Party discipline

Hung parliament

Coalition government

Governmental instability

Minority government

Minimal winning coalition

Anticipated (snap) elections

Presidential–parliamentary system

Single-member-district/plurality electoral system

Proportional representation (PR)

Mixed-member electoral system

Duverger's law

Party system

Notes

1. Charles Louis de Secondat, Baron de Montesquieu, *The Spirit of Laws*, 2 vols., trans. Thomas Nugent (New York: Colonial Press, 1900), especially pt. 2, bk. 11. On his influence, see Paul Merrill Spurlin, *Montesquieu in America 1760–1801* (New York: Octagon, 1969).

2. William H. Riker suggests that coalition partners often find that it is in their own best interest to share the spoils of a coalition government with as few parties as possible. They therefore tend to favor a minimum winning coalition as opposed to one that maximizes parliamentary support. See *The Theory of Political Coalitions* (New Haven, CT: Yale University Press, 1962).

3. See Wolfgang C. Müller and Kaare Strødom, eds., *Coalition Governments in Western Europe* (Oxford: Oxford University Press, 2000); Michael Laver and Norman Schofield, *Multiparty Government: The Politics of Coalition in Europe* (Oxford: Oxford University Press, 1991).

4. Riker, *Theory of Political Coalitions*.

5. See Robert Elgie, ed., *Semi-Presidentialism in Europe* (Oxford: Oxford University Press, 1999); Robert Elgie, *Semi-Presidentialism: Sub-Types and Democratic Performance* (Oxford: Oxford University Press, 2011).

6. For debates on these issues, see Juan J. Linz, "The Perils of Presidentialism," and "The Virtues of Parliamentarism," in *The Global Resurgence of Democracy*, 2nd ed., ed. Larry Diamond and Marc F. Plattner (Baltimore, MD: Johns Hopkins University Press, 1996), pp. 108–26, 138–45; Donald L. Horowitz, "Comparing Democratic Systems," in *The Global Resurgence of Democracy*, 2nd ed., ed. Larry Diamond and Marc F. Plattner (Baltimore, MD: Johns Hopkins University Press, 1996), pp. 127–33; Seymour Martin Lipset, "The Centrality of Political Culture," *The Global Resurgence of Democracy*, 2nd ed., ed. Larry Diamond and Marc F. Plattner (Baltimore, MD: Johns Hopkins University Press, 1996), pp. 134–37; and the essays in Arendt Lijphart, ed., *Parliamentary Versus Presidential Government* (Oxford: Oxford University Press, 1992). See also Lijphart's study *Patterns of Democracy: Government Forms and Performance in Thirty-Six Countries* (New Haven, CN: Yale University Press, 1999); Juan J. Linz and Arturo Valenzuela, eds., *The Failure of Presidential Democracy* (Baltimore, MD: Johns Hopkins University Press, 1994). On recent trends toward the "presidentialization" of the prime minister's office in parliamentary democracies, see Thomas Poguntke and Paul Webb, eds., *The Presidentialization of Politics: A Comparative Study of Modern Democracies* (New York: Oxford University Press, 2005).

7. Gore's plurality over Bush was 537,179 votes. Other candidates won the remaining share of the popular vote. In 1876, Rutherford B. Hayes (Republican) won 48 percent of the popular vote and 285 electoral college votes, beating Samuel J. Tilden (Democrat), who won 51 percent of the popular vote but only 184 electoral college votes. In 1888, Benjamin Harrison (Republican) won 47.8 percent of the popular vote and 233 votes in the electoral college, defeating Grover Cleveland (Democrat), who got 48.6 percent of the popular vote but 168 electoral votes. In 1824, no candidate won a majority of electoral college votes. The election was thrown into the U.S. House of Representatives, with each state's delegation receiving one vote. John Quincy Adams won the election in the House, even though he had won only 30.9 percent of the popular vote to Andrew Jackson's 41.3 percent.

8. For an explanation of various statistical methods for distributing seats in proportional representation systems, see *Electoral Systems: A Worldwide Comparative Study* (Geneva: Inter-Parliamentary Union, 1993), pp. 7–11. The same publication explains variants of other electoral systems as well.

9. "Disproportionality" in voting systems—the difference between a party's share of seats in the legislature and its share of the popular vote—is consistently higher in plurality systems than under proportional representation. Statistical calculations in which 1.0 equals the lowest level of disproportionality show that Italy's system scored an average of 1.1 over a period of three decades, while Britain's plurality system averaged 19.5 and those of Canada, Australia, and New Zealand together averaged 10.7. See Arend Lijphart et al., *Electoral Systems and Party Systems* (Oxford: Oxford University Press, 1994).

10. See Matthew Soberg Shugart and Martin P. Wattenberg, eds., *Mixed-Member Electoral Systems: The Best of Both Worlds?* (Oxford: Oxford University Press, 2001).

11. For a debate on legislative electoral systems, see the essays by Arend Lijphart, Guy Lardeyret, and Quentin L. Quade in *The Global Resurgence of Democracy*, 2nd ed., ed. Larry Diamond and Marc F. Plattner (Baltimore, MD: Johns Hopkins University Press, 1996), pp. 146–77. See also Rein Taagepera and Matthew Soberg Shugart, *Seats and Votes* (New Haven, CN: Yale University Press, 1989); G. Bingham Powell, Jr., *Elections as Instruments of Democracy: Majoritarian and Proportional Visions* (New Haven, CN: Yale University Press, 2000).

12. *Voter Turnout from 1945 to 1997: A Global Report on Political Participation* (Stockholm: International Institute for Democracy and Electoral Assistance, 1997).

13. Maurice Duverger, *Political Parties: Their Organization and Activity in the Modern State*, 2nd English rev. ed. (London: Methuen, 1959), pp. 217–39.

14. See figures at Adam Carr's Electoral Archive, http://psephos.adam-carr.net/countries/i/iraq/.

15. These data come from the Inter-Parliamentary Union, http://www.ipu.org/wmn-e/world.htm.

7

Democracy: What Does It Take?
10 Conditions

OVERVIEW

- In this chapter we develop an analytical framework for assessing the prospects for the emergence of democracy in nondemocratic settings and the consolidation of democracy in newly democratic regimes.

- We identify 10 key factors that political theorists and social scientists have considered to be associated with democratic transitions and consolidation around the world and review the evidence that indicates whether those factors have indeed been important to democratization. The absence of these positive conditions for democracy can explain why some countries remain mired in dictatorships or stuck between authoritarianism and democracy.

- Egypt serves as an example for each of the 10 conditions we discuss here. The evidence about Egypt indicates that the conditions for democracy there are not strong.

- We explore some common patterns of democratization, especially during the most recent wave of democratization over the past three decades.

King Juan Carlos played a pivotal role in Spain's 1975 transition to democracy, ushering in the third wave of democratization.

DEMOCRATIZATION

Why do some countries succeed in establishing democracies and sustaining them over long periods, whereas others cannot even build a functioning democracy or keep one for long? What must countries do to make a successful transition from a nondemocratic regime to an enduring democracy? In this chapter we'll look at a number of factors that have helped account for the success of some of the oldest democracies in the world, such as the United States and Britain. These same factors provide guidelines for countries that are now engaged in the difficult but crucially important process of democratization. To gain some insight on the utility of this list of conditions, we will consider the case of Egypt as we discuss 10 factors that influence the prospect of democratization. As we noted in Chapter 1, *democratization* is the transition from nondemocratic to democratic forms of government.

Of course, the hope of democracy's advocates is that the democratization processes now going on around the world will succeed and that countries on the verge of democracy will find a way to overcome authoritarian rule. The ultimate aim of all these efforts is the **consolidation** of democracy, by which we mean the building of a strong and lasting democracy that withstands the tests of time. States cross the dividing line between democratization and consolidation when their institutions are so widely accepted and their democratic practices are so ingrained that their populations and elites—including the military and former dictatorial parties—cannot imagine replacing democracy with an authoritarian government. Democracy becomes "the only game in town." It may be difficult, however, to pinpoint when this threshold is reached. Some democracies have appeared to be consolidated, only to collapse and give way to dictatorship.[1] The factors we enumerate in this chapter can help countries proceed from authoritarianism to democratization, and from democratization to the consolidation of a lasting democracy. Success, however, is by no means a sure thing. As we will see much later in the chapter, many countries moving away from authoritarian rule do not reach the status of consolidated democracy quickly or perhaps ever. And we must always remember that even long-standing democracies can succumb to authoritarian actors, as the countries of Chile and Uruguay tragically learned in the early 1970s. Those societies had been governed democratically for most of the twentieth century but then fell to military coups in 1973.

In the remainder of this book we will use the 10 conditions for democracy enumerated below to help us analyze the reasons democracy has emerged in formerly nondemocratic countries, to explore the prospects for democratization in currently nondemocratic settings, and to understand the persistence of nondemocratic rule in societies that have yet to experience democracy.

10 CONDITIONS FOR DEMOCRACY

The 10 factors that follow are not a magic formula. They cannot guarantee that a democracy will come about or, if it does, that it will survive over the long run. Every country must find its own path to a democratic system based on its own idiosyncrasies. Very few successful democracies or democratizing countries will possess all the factors on the list. Some may even display characteristics that are precisely the opposite of some of these factors, yet they may nevertheless succeed in building and

sustaining other democratic structures and processes. Hence we regard these factors as "conditions" for democracy in a fairly loose, rather than a deterministic, sense: It is not necessary for a country to have all 10 factors to be a democracy, and having most of the factors does not ensure a democracy's success.

Rather than constituting a foolproof recipe for how to build a democracy, what follows is simply a list of independent variables, or *explanatory factors*, in hypotheses that we can formulate about how democracies emerge and why they endure. Of course, these are two distinct processes: Creating a democracy where none exists is one thing, and consolidating a democracy that is getting off the ground is another. Nevertheless, the two processes are close enough that the same 10 factors apply to both of them in one way or another. In each case our *dependent variables*, or outcomes we are explaining, are democratization and the consolidation of democracy. And in each case our chief *expectation* is that the independent variables promote processes that are conducive to the emergence and long-term survival of democracy. This chapter is therefore an extended exploration of the hypotheses about the conditions that favor democracy. Our basic assumption is that each of the 10 independent factors on our list *increases the chances* for successful democratization and democratic consolidation. Table 7.1 provides a road map of the 10 main explanatory factors we will examine in this chapter and the hypotheses that social scientists have posed about how those independent variables affect democracy.

As we begin this analysis, we need to emphasize that how these variables work will tend to differ from one country to the next. Not all countries follow the same path from authoritarianism to democracy, and not all successful democracies manage their consolidation processes in the same ways or the same amount of time. In other words, our 10 factors do not cause democracy to come about, or to become consolidated, by interacting in some universally applicable pattern.

The factors on our list *condition* democracy, but they do not actually *cause* a democratization process to occur. No combination of the 10 conditions, not even all 10 of them acting together, can actually make a nondemocratic regime collapse or make a democracy emerge and survive. The transformation of a country's governmental system from nondemocracy

Table 7.1 10 Hypotheses on the Conditions that Support Democracy

Explanatory Factor	Favors Democracy when. . . .
1. **Elite attitudes**	Political and economic elites are committed to democratic procedures.
2. **State institutions**	The state controls national territory and is able to perform essential state functions—providing national security and law and order.
3. **National unity**	Social heterogeneity is less and national identity is strong.
4. **National wealth**	The country is prosperous.
5. **Private enterprise**	The economy is organized according to capitalist principles.
6. **Middle class**	The middle class is large and committed to democracy.
7. **Attitudes of disadvantaged**	The majority of the poor and otherwise disadvantaged favor democratic procedures.
8. **Civil society**	Civil society groups are vigorous and promote a democratic political culture.
9. **Education and access to information**	The population is well educated and has free access to information about politics and public issues.
10. **International conditions**	Foreign powers promote introduction and consolidation of democracy, the international economy is prospering, and/or transnational social movements pressure for democracy.

to democracy results from a specific set of events—political actions, economic developments, social transformations, and the like. The sequence in which these events occur will vary from country to country. In some cases they will unfold in a slow evolutionary process (as in England). In others the accretion of events over time may culminate in a sudden revolutionary eruption, with the old regime collapsing before everyone's eyes and a new form of government marching into power (as in the French Revolution). In other countries there may be a protracted struggle between a nondemocratic regime and its opponents. In these cases, democratization usually begins when the ruling elites give up power and their prodemocracy opposition takes over (as in Mexico, Nigeria, South Africa, and other countries). Such a transfer of power may result from a negotiated agreement, elections, mass demonstrations, the death of a charismatic dictator, a civil war, foreign intervention, or some other event or combination of events.

Rather than constituting the immediate causes of democratization and consolidation, our 10 conditions of democracy are general factors that can support the emergence of democratic ideas and movements under nondemocratic regimes; they can sustain a democratization process once it has already begun; they can help a new democracy become consolidated in its first decade or two of life; and they can help democracy survive and flourish in the decades that follow. We say that these factors *can* do these things because we cannot say for sure whether a democratization process will actually occur in any specific country, nor can we say when or how it will take place. Democracy does not automatically kick in when some combination of these 10 conditions exists. The victory and consolidation of democracy require specific actions in specific historical contexts, and these things inevitably vary across countries. Political actors must take action for democratization to take place, which is to say that *human agency* is involved in any particular democratization process. That said, there are some general patterns of democratization, as we'll see toward the end of this chapter.

Strictly speaking, the conditions of democracy that we are about to examine as our independent variables are really correlates of democracy. That is, their presence tends to be associated with democracy. The more of these conditions that are present, the more likely it is that a democratization process will succeed once it has been initiated, and the more likely it is that a long-term consolidation process will prove enduring. To give you a better idea about how we might use these conditions to assess the prospects for democracy in a particular context, we will briefly consider how each of these 10 conditions may be operating in Egypt today. As the largest and most complex society undergoing the changes associated with the Arab Spring, Egypt should provide us insight into how we can apply these conditions to a country in transition.

1. Elites Committed to Democracy

For democracy to succeed, people must want it. What that means in practice is that people must want to adopt the defining features of modern democracy as described in Chapter 5.

They must accept democracy's core values, above all freedom, inclusion, equality, equity, tolerance, and compromise. They must want to be governed under the rule of law. And they must want to erect the main functional pillars of democracy—popular sovereignty, guaranteed rights and liberties, and economic well-being—in accordance with these underlying values and a law-bound government.

Democracy is most likely to arise and succeed when its main tenets are embraced by the whole population. Mass support for democratic values and institutions makes for a powerful, well-grounded democracy. And prodemocracy forces are more likely to topple a nondemocratic regime when large numbers of people openly proclaim their desire for democratization—by forming democracy movements and parties (perhaps illegally), or by coming out into the streets spontaneously to demonstrate their defiance of the ruling authorities. Realistically, however, it is not "the people" who do the nitty-gritty work creating a democratic political order. As we've noted before, modern democracy is not "government *by* the people," but government *by elites* who are accountable to the people. The role of elites in building and sustaining democracy is crucial.

The actions of elites are especially important in the earliest stages of democratization, when a nondemocratic regime is weakening and a chance for democracy opens up. It is the task of a country's political, economic, and social elites to take advantage of this opening by joining and pressing for democracy. Even when there is a mass movement clamoring for democracy outside the door, it is the country's key elites who must sit at the table and hammer out the details of a new democratic system. Recently, for example, in the aftermath of the dictatorship's fall in Tunisia, newly elected elites seem to have committed themselves to designing a democratic constitution. In some countries this process can take a very long time. In England it took centuries to move from an all-powerful monarchy to a system in which the monarch shared a certain amount of power with parliament. It took even more centuries before parliament was truly supreme and the monarch was reduced to a purely symbolic role. And it took many more decades from that point to develop a mass-based democracy that gives all adult men and women the vote. Throughout this long evolution, England's political elites managed the process of building each successive expansion of democracy, though they tended to move too slowly for many British citizens. In France, the revolution that exploded in the late eighteenth century was propelled by a popular uprising for democracy, but it was organized by political leaders. Ironically, it was some of these same revolutionary elites who asphyxiated French democracy in its infancy, imposing a harsh dictatorship on the population. Democracy in France had tumultuous ups and downs for more than 150 years before finally taking hold in the decades after World War II. As we'll see in Chapter 14, France's political elites—led by a few charismatic individuals—played central roles in the country's long political drama.

In other countries, the creation of democracy has been faster. But even in most of these cases, elites have spearheaded the democratization process. In the United States, the founders, representing the cream of American society, led a popular revolution against

F. W. de Klerk and Nelson Mandela appear together in the weeks before the historic election that brought majority rule to South Africa.

British rule and then drafted the country's governing charters, first the Articles of Confederation and then the U.S. Constitution. As we saw in Chapter 5, Dutch elites stabilized democracy in the Netherlands on the basis of a consociational democracy. More recently it was two South African leaders—President F. W. de Klerk, the leader of the predominantly white National Party, and Nelson Mandela, the incarcerated leader of the largely black African National Congress—who made the critical agreement to cooperate in establishing a multiracial democracy, producing South Africa's first truly democratic elections on the basis of "one person, one vote" in 1994. And it was reform-minded Communist Party leaders in Russia, Lithuania, Hungary, and other parts of communist Europe who were instrumental in moving their governments from communism to democracy in the 1980s and early 1990s.

In some cases of democratization, society's elites may have to negotiate a democratic bargain on which to establish the foundations of democracy. At times their efforts will be supported by the vast majority of the people. In other instances the elites may be hampered by serious divisions in the population, with the values of inclusion and tolerance having weak moorings in society. Many people may approach democracy by bluntly asking, "What's in it for me and my group?" Whatever the attitudes of the masses may be, democracy may not come about in the first place, or survive in the longer run, unless the country's key elites agree to govern by agreement. This "agreement to agree" does not necessarily put an end to society's conflicts. It simply means that conflicts will henceforth be dealt with peacefully through the give-and-take of democratic procedures.

Inevitably, the true test of the elites' leadership skills comes when the leaders must convince their followers to accept whatever compromises may be necessary to establish democracy for all. In the most fortunate cases, their followers won't need to be convinced. They may be so weary of arbitrary rule, economic hardship, and civil strife that they recognize that striking a democratic bargain with their opponents is the only way out of widely shared misery. Even the supporters of a decaying nondemocratic regime, recognizing the futility of their policies,

may come to the same conclusions and agree to give up power rather than face unending civil unrest, as they did in Argentina, Brazil, and Chile in the 1980s. But when large segments of the population reject the deals their leaders have cut, democracy's chances are likely to diminish appreciably.

Political leaders—government officials, party chiefs, high-profile dissidents, and the like—are not the only ones who must accept whatever democratic bargains are struck. The leaders of a country's principal social groups—such as ethnic groups, religions, labor, farmers, and the business community—must also be on board, as must the leaders of important state institutions like the military, the judiciary, and the administrative bureaucracy. Many of these people may have worked for the outgoing authoritarian regime. It is vitally important to win their loyalty to democracy. Otherwise, they may constitute what Juan Linz has called a semi-loyal opposition, waiting in the wings for an opportunity to scuttle a fledgling democratic regime. Intellectuals and journalists need to support democracy by insisting on freedom of thought and expression, and they must be devoted to speaking and writing the truth.

In the aftermath of the toppling of Egyptian President Hosni Mubarak in February 2011, many who opposed that dictatorship advocated the holding of free and fair elections and the establishment of democracy. Two Egyptian elite groups have played the most significant roles supporting or opposing a democratic transition: military commanders and leaders of the Muslim Brotherhood. Less powerful elite actors include political and economic elites associated with the Mubarak regime, liberal intellectuals and professionals, and *salafists*—Islamic fundamentalist intellectuals and clerics.

The military high command was the force behind Mubarak's rule, but in the end the military toppled him in part because they feared he was seeking to establish a Mubarak family dictatorship. The military has not demonstrated a commitment to democracy in any of the understandings developed in Chapter 5, however, and seems most concerned about its institutional prerogatives and autonomy from civilian rule. Among the political elite groups associated with the Mubarak regime is the Egyptian judiciary, which has also played a large role in the transition. This ruling, thought by many to be intended to counter the power of the Muslim Brotherhood, left Egypt without a legislative body. The judiciary may be committed to rule of law, but whether that is meant to be the rule of law made by a democratically elected parliament seems doubtful. In July 2013 the military deposed the elected president, Mohamed Morsi, and imposed the chief justice of the Supreme Constitutional Court in his place.

Egyptian liberals include intellectuals and professionals who played a significant role in encouraging the popular uprising that brought about Mubarak's fall. They have advocated for a secular democratic regime that protects political rights and liberties, Face II of democracy (Chapter 5), including equality for women. Mass protests by liberals helped to unseat President Morsi. On the other side of the elite spectrum are salafists—Islamic clerics and intellectuals who seek a society centered on adherence to a traditional, "purified" reading of the Islamic holy

Egyptian liberals—students, intellectuals, and professionals—used social media to communicate and to turn out protesters against the Mubarak regime during the Egyptian revolution in 2011.

texts (see Chapter 10 on political Islam). Salafists reject Western notions of political rights and liberties and have sought, in the writing of a new constitution for Egypt, to reduce women's rights vis-à-vis men and to decriminalize female genital mutilation.

A critical elite actor in Egypt today is the leadership of the Muslim Brotherhood, an Muslim religious organization founded in 1928 to instill the Koran into all aspects of personal and social life. Publicly committed to nonviolence, the Muslim Brotherhood was often suppressed and forbidden to engage in open politics by the authoritarian regimes of Mubarak and his predecessors, Gamal Abdel Nasser (1956–70) and Anwar Sadat (1970–81). However, the organization developed many cultural and social organizations—welfare agencies, hospitals, and the like—that have provided for those material needs of ordinary Egyptians that the state has failed to meet. Not surprisingly, the Muslim Brotherhood emerged as the most powerful force electorally after Mubarak's fall. The Muslim Brotherhood founded the Freedom and Justice Party in 2011, nominating Mohamed Morsi as its presidential candidate. Morsi won a closely contested race in 2012.

The Muslim Brotherhood's view of democracy remains somewhat unclear. On the one hand, the organization seems to embrace democracy in the sense of Face I, popular sovereignty. As the actor that has most effectively formulated an alternative vision of society to that promoted under Mubarak, the Muslim Brotherhood is most able to win at the voting booths, as it demonstrated in parliamentary elections in 2011 and presidential elections in 2012. How the Muslim Brotherhood views democracy in the sense of individual rights and liberties (Face II) is less clear: Some Muslim Brotherhood leaders have indicated that they view non-Muslims and women as unequal to Muslim men. And while the Muslim Brotherhood has engaged in extensive charitable works, economic democracy in the sense of empowerment of the poor (Face IV) is not at the center of its program.[2] Liberals engaged in the protests that preceded Morsi's ouster out of a sense that the Brotherhood was unwilling to respect the rights of secularists and Coptic Christians.

These comments suggest that most Egyptian elite groups are ambivalent about democracy if not hostile to it. In the

conflicts leading up to the 2013 coup, all elite actors put their group interests ahead of their commitment to democracy, thereby promoting democracy's failure.

Elite support for democracy is a vitally important condition both for the democratization process right from its earliest stages and for democracy's long-term consolidation. We regard it as a *sine qua non:* Without broad elite support for democracy's core ideals and procedures, there is little likelihood that democracy will arise from the debris of a discredited nondemocratic regime. And if it does, it probably won't last very long without elite support. The evidence presented in various parts of this book, and in other countries as well, is largely consistent with this hypothesis. But even though elite support is a *necessary* condition for democracy, it is by no means sufficient.[3]

2. State Institutions

A successful democracy requires a state that has sovereignty over a defined territory and whose boundaries are accepted by the population. Its governing elites and basic institutions must also be viewed as legitimate. As Juan Linz and Alfred Stepan have pointed out, this phenomenon of "stateness" is a prerequisite of democratic development. "Without a state," they note, "there can be no citizenship; without citizenship, there can be no democracy."

Why is this so? People demand many things of their government, but first and foremost they seek security. Security means protection against foreign governments or political movements seeking to seize control of the territory on which a people lives. Security also means law and order, so that life in society does not mirror Thomas Hobbes's state of nature, where life is "solitary, poor, nasty, brutish, and short." In circumstances where the state has failed, as discussed in Chapter 3, the prospects of democracy are very dim. Anarchic conditions encourage people to see the police and the army as their friends and politicians as opportunists or ineffectual. None of the states with the highest failed states indexes listed in the left-hand column of Table 3.1 are democracies.

The legitimacy of the state is crucial. Countries where major elements of the population do not accept the state's boundaries but instead demand independence—like Yugoslavia on the eve of its dissolution in the 1990s, as discussed in Chapter 4—are bound to have serious problems. Problems are also likely to occur in countries where a significant portion of the population categorically rejects the new democratic authorities or established state institutions. If large segments of the populace believe that their leaders have assumed power improperly (through unwelcome outside intervention, for example) or maintain it through phony elections, corruption, or other manipulative stratagems, democracy will be in trouble because the state itself rests on shaky foundations.

Having state institutions that provide national security and law and order is one thing. Beyond that, successful democracies require democratic institutions. However a country's democratization process may unfold, one of the first tasks—quite often *the* first task—facing the creators of a new democracy is to construct democratic state institutions. For the long haul, thoroughly democratized state institutions are essential for democracy's consolidation.

To complete the democratization and consolidation processes successfully, democracy needs governmental institutions that will ensure popular sovereignty and basic civil rights and liberties, much as we characterized them in Chapter 5. From the start, the state must be organized on the basis of the rule of law. Those who govern must be *accountable* to the population, with fair, competitive elections permitting the removability of key officials on a regular basis. The *transparency* of the governing process must permit the citizenry to keep a watchful eye on state officials so as to detect corruption and punish those who perpetrate it. Corruption can strangle a democracy at any stage of its development, but especially in its formative period, when the population is eager to see if their new leaders are any better than their former dictators. One of the most important acts that Vicente Fox took when assuming the Mexican presidency in 2000 in its first truly democratic election was to initiate a transparency law that requires the executive branch to make information about its activities available on request. Legislatures must have real lawmaking powers as well as the right to hold the executive up to scrutiny. In Russia today the Duma, the federal congress, constitutionally a separate branch of government, is a rubber stamp for the executive, led by President Vladimir Putin (see Chapter 16). The judiciary must be independent of political manipulation by the executive and legislative branches. In much of Latin America the current struggle to consolidate democracy revolves around efforts to strengthen the judiciary. The bureaucracy must be bound by legal procedures, while at the same time possessing sufficient resources to assist elected officials in policy making and policy implementation. The military must abide by the rules of democratic governance and accept civilian controls. Only recently has the Turkish government been able to establish its control of the military, as we saw in Chapter 3. The lawmaking process must be reasonably efficient (timely) and effective, successfully addressing the country's problems. Governments need to be *stable* rather than constantly breaking down from petty squabbling among coalition partners.

Democracies must also have sufficient state power to protect themselves against their opponents. Hence there must be a single national military whose officers and troops are loyal to the democratic state. Militias or paramilitary forces that are not answerable to the central government constitute an intolerable danger. The state must also keep a watchful eye on the political foes of democracy. Antidemocratic forces may utilize elections, parliaments, and other democratic institutions for the ulterior purpose of taking power for themselves and then terminating democracy. History is replete with such forces, from Nazis and communists to generals and demagogues. Democratic states may therefore be justified in limiting the rights and freedoms of democracy's adversaries in order to safeguard democracy for those who truly want it. For example, they might ban particularly threatening antidemocratic parties and organizations.

Countries that are building democracy on the ruins of authoritarian regimes must also deal with former dictators and the remnants of their regimes, including once-powerful officials, secret police agents, judges, and torturers. A number of high-level figures from the communist era were put on trial and imprisoned after communism disintegrated in East Germany, Poland, and other parts of Central and Eastern Europe, but the extent of these efforts varied from one country to another. South Africa's first multiracial government following all-white rule set up "truth and reconciliation commissions" to investigate past abuses and hold the perpetrators accountable. In Argentina today, three decades after the most recent military regime fell, the democratic government continues to try to bring human-rights-abusing military officers to justice. The desire for retribution may be understandable when it comes to the most reprehensible figures of the old regime, and even necessary to effect a clean break with the past, but newly democratizing countries may also feel a need to put the past behind them and get on with the task of building the future. They might therefore offer a measure of forgiveness and a chance for rehabilitation to lower-level officials who are willing to abide by the rules of democracy.[4]

Egypt has a state that effectively controls its physical territory. Under Mubarak, that state suppressed its opponents openly, bringing its legitimacy into question. Moreover, the Egyptian state did not meet many of the welfare needs of the people, while its opponent, the Muslim Brotherhood, did so through its charitable agencies. The challenge as Egypt transitions away from Mubarak's rule is that elements of the Egyptian state—the military and the judiciary—that remain from the old regime may not accept the direction that a popularly elected president wants to take the nation, as Mohamed Morsi learned. Moreover, the Muslim Brotherhood and other political actors may incorporate elements into the new constitution that threaten individual rights and liberties, as Morsi's critics charged.

Evidence that can be gleaned from around the world over long stretches of history appears to be amply consistent with the hypothesis that democracy cannot emerge without an effective state in place. Beyond that, thoroughly democratized state institutions, rather than partially or inconsistently democratized ones, are vitally necessary for the stability and long-term success of democratic principles and processes—that is, democracy's consolidation. Democratic state building is thus a primary task of newly democratizing countries, and the strengthening of democratically controlled state institutions is vital to the consolidation process over the long run.

3. National Unity

Some theorists contend that democracy is most likely to succeed when it rests on a socially homogeneous society. In this view, fragmented societies that are torn by deep ethnic, religious, class, or other divisions are too unstable for steady democratic governance.

The contemporary world is not lacking in deeply polarized societies that have found it difficult or impossible to establish democratic institutions or maintain them for very long. Information gathered by Freedom House analysts shows that

In Argentina today, three decades after the most recent military regime fell, the democratic government continues to try to bring human-rights-abusing military officers to justice. While demand for retribution is understandable, many newly democratizing countries might prefer to put the past behind them and move on. Second from the left is Gen. Jorge Videla, president 1976–81, who was convicted in 2010 of human rights violations leading to 31 deaths during his time in power. In 2012 he was convicted of participating in a plan to steal babies from parents kidnapped by the regime. He died in prison in 2013.

countries in which a dominant ethnic group constitutes at least two-thirds of the population are twice as likely to be rated as "free" as multiethnic ones.[5] But some countries have found ways to make democracy succeed despite serious social cleavages. The United States, Switzerland, and the Netherlands are prominent examples. Few successful democracies in today's world, in fact, are without social cleavages of one kind or another, at times quite severe. Indeed, social heterogeneity may at times *increase* the likelihood of democracy, because democracy provides the most acceptable method for a highly divided people to reconcile their differences and live peacefully together. Conversely, in Japan and Germany, where there was historically a relatively high degree of ethnic homogeneity, democracy did not succeed until after it was imposed by victorious occupation powers after World War II.

Social homogeneity is thus no guarantor of democracy. And though social polarization can make it more difficult for democracy to flower and mature, it does not by any means make it impossible. For one thing, some societies find ways to bridge their social divisions by maintaining an overarching national unity. As pointed out in Chapter 4, a common national identity can sometimes provide a country's population with a sufficient level of homogeneity to hold its people together as a nation despite deep-seated divisions based on ethnicity, language, religion, class, and other sources of differentiation. Thanks in part to the unifying web of a shared national identity, the Swiss put together their artfully constructed confederation and the Dutch contrived their consociational democracy. National unity in the United States was founded on a desire for independence from British rule and, simultaneously, on an agreement to construct a limited government dedicated to preserving individual liberties. That unity was shattered in the events that culminated in the Civil War. But after the war was over, and a more widely shared sense of national identity gradually solidified, democracy in the United States was progressively enlarged to incorporate former

slaves, women, and successive waves of immigrants from the world over.

National unity thus played a major contributing role in helping to create and sustain viable democratic systems in these otherwise highly heterogeneous countries. Where a common national identity is lacking—as in countries like Nigeria, Sri Lanka, Iraq, and Afghanistan—the forces of social heterogeneity are less restrained. Without a common nationhood to fall back on, socially polarized societies have a difficult time making the compromises necessary to build or sustain democracy.

Dankwart Rustow has argued that national unity is the sole "background condition" of democracy, "in the sense that it must precede all other phases of democratization."[6] To be sure, any rule has its exceptions. The United Kingdom of Great Britain and Northern Ireland, for example, became a thriving democracy even though it has lacked a strong, unifying "British" national identity. English, Irish, Scottish, and Welsh national identities remain robust to this day, but the rules of democracy are accepted throughout the realm (except perhaps by violence-prone Catholic and Protestant extremists in Northern Ireland). They are also accepted in Canada, despite wide support for independence in Quebec. Of course, the United Kingdom and Canada have been democracies for a long time. Younger democracies tend to be more fragile, and more susceptible to the damaging effects of national disunity. For them, national unity is very important, especially if the population is divided into contending social groups.

Egypt is mostly a homogeneous society, with one major exception. Overwhelmingly a Sunni Muslim, Arabic-speaking people with a clear national identity as Egyptian, the society has a minority of Coptic Christians that total about 10 percent of the population. Copts have good reason to favor a secular political regime, but many of the most popular political actors in Egypt, including the Muslim Brotherhood, lean toward a legal order based on *sharia*. Copts often find themselves scapegoats

As the new Egyptian democracy takes shape, many ask whether there will be room for Christian Copts and secularists in a country where many favor law based on *sharia*. Significant intolerance to these groups has already been demonstrated.

when popular angers erupt. Many Copts were slain in religious-based conflict during Muslim Brotherhood's rule, leading Coptic Pope Tawadros II to speak out publicly against the Morsi regime. He supported the July 2013 military coup.

The evidence for the homogeneity hypothesis is mixed. Having a population that is socially homogeneous (in terms of ethnicity, religion, and class) is not an absolute requirement for democracy, but it certainly helps. But evidence from around the world appears to be mainly consistent with the national unity hypothesis, despite some exceptions. When national unity bridges over social and political differences, the chances for democracy are higher. National unity can be especially important in the early years of a democracy, when democratic institutions and practices are at their most vulnerable. But it can also help sustain a democracy that faces problems even after the consolidation process is completed.

4. National Wealth

We examined the correlation between national wealth and democracy at considerable length in Chapter 2, and thus will not repeat that analysis here. That evidence is mixed. Though national prosperity strongly correlates with established democracies, and most poor countries have not had much success in building or sustaining democracy, there are some striking exceptions. A number of relatively well off countries have failed at democracy; some poor countries have at least embarked on democratization and—in cases like India and Botswana—have registered long-term successes. Studies have shown that economic development can enhance the chances for democracy in some (though not all) countries, but it does not by itself cause democracy to come about. Democracy does not inevitably arrive when a country reaches a certain level of per capita income; political elites and elements of the mass public must take action for democracy to arise and survive. However, as Adam Przeworski and his colleagues have demonstrated, once

a democracy is already established, its prospects for survival are greater in richer countries.[7]

The World Bank ranks Egypt as a lower-middle-income country while the United Nations Development Program places it in the medium human development category. While its $5,200 gross national income per capita (PPP) is thus relatively low by world standards, Egyptians enjoy relatively equal incomes. Egypt's Gini coefficient is 32, comparable to some European welfare states, owing to decades in which the state intervened heavily in the economy. Before the 2011 revolution, Egypt had enjoyed two decades of economic growth, averaging 4.5 percent per year. However, rapid population growth limited the impact of the economic growth, causing the share of the population in poverty to rise to about a quarter of Egypt's people. Increasing poverty and the country's incapacity to provide good jobs to educated young people were among the reasons for the protests that emerged in January 2011 and brought down Mubarak. Political uncertainty since the 2011 revolution, unfortunately, has fostered dramatic declines in investment and tourism, raising unemployment rates. Many of the demonstrators whose protests provoked the military coup in 2013 were motivated by dismay about rising unemployment and difficulty feeding themselves. Egypt thus faces some barriers to democratization owing to its relative poverty and current economic difficulties. While the protestors who ignited change in Egypt joined demands for democracy and alleviation of poverty, what remains to be seen is whether the poor and unemployed will give their political support to committed democrats or to leaders who promise bread but not so much freedom.[8]

5. Private Enterprise

The connection between private enterprise and democracy reflects the idea that economic freedom promotes political freedom. People who own their own businesses or who work in privately owned companies, according to this hypothesis, will want to have a say in how the government treats them. They will especially want a say in how the government deals with property rights, taxes, business regulations, and so on. "Having a say" in what the government does and holding it accountable is what popular sovereignty is all about. In this conception, democracy emerges as a mechanism for protecting property rights. The reverse side of this hypothesis contends that the absence of economic liberty promotes authoritarianism. When the government controls the economy, it reduces the opportunities for citizens to organize themselves and take care of their economic needs independently of the state, effectively snuffing out citizen controls on state power.

One of the most influential studies of these tendencies is Barrington Moore's *Social Origins of Dictatorship and Democracy*.[9] Moore argued that democracy emerged in Britain and the United States largely because of the early appearance in those countries of a successful capitalist elite, the bourgeoisie, who made private industry and agriculture the dominant elements of the economy. They also demanded a say in the governance of their respective countries to ensure the state's protection of their property rights. By contrast, countries that failed to develop a strong entrepreneurial class did not produce successful democracies until the second half of the twentieth century, if at all. Historically, countries such as Germany, China, and Russia had a comparatively weak private business class and an undeveloped commercial agricultural class in the nineteenth and early twentieth centuries. Instead, they had a land-poor peasantry and powerful state intervention in most facets of economic life. Japan also had a landless peasantry, while its powerful business elite was closely tied to the imperial state.

As a consequence, Moore observed, Russia and China fell to the communists, Germany got a fascist dictatorship, and Japan came under an aggressive military elite before World War II. Moore concluded that a thriving capitalist class is essential to the emergence of democratic institutions. He summed up this point in the pithy phrase "No bourgeois, no democracy." Stated another way, Moore's thesis is that private enterprise stimulates the growth of a middle class that does not depend directly on the state for its livelihood. As we'll see in the next section, the middle class itself can provide essential backing for a democratic regime.

While there is ample evidence consistent with these hypotheses, there is also a considerable amount of evidence indicating that private enterprise does not necessarily promote democracy. Quite a few countries have had a thriving private sector in tandem with repressive political institutions. In some cases the owners of large corporations have actively supported nondemocratic political authority, as exemplified at various times in Latin American countries like Mexico, Argentina, Brazil, and Chile and in Asian states like Singapore and the Philippines. Communist China today combines a vibrant private sector with unrelenting one-party dictatorship. It is still not entirely evident that the expansion of private enterprise in that country is stimulating pressures for democracy; to some extent it may actually be buttressing communist rule.[10] In postcommunist Russia the rapid introduction of private enterprise has been accompanied

by the emergence of a small clique of politically influential multimillionaires and, simultaneously, by a drastic decline in living standards for large segments of the population. Some of the most disadvantaged people have responded to their plight by rejecting democracy itself, as have some entrepreneurs. As one Russian businessman put it, "If people tell me that for the sake of symbolic democracy I must give up my property—well, democracy is not worth that much to me."[11]

The Egyptian private sector includes relatively few large companies and countless small enterprises, many of the latter not included in the formal sector of the economy (the part that is licensed, regulated, and taxed). Many of Egypt's wealthiest business leaders became rich by benefiting from the privatization of the economy in recent years, often due to favors extended by Mubarak. Some of the 2011 Tahrir Square protesters' outcries against corruption were pointed at the close relationship between rich businessmen and the Mubarak regime. The perspective of these leaders of large-scale firms on democratization was at best ambivalent as a result. Egyptian business leaders seem most inclined to work with whoever promises to benefit their interests whether they are proponents of democracy or not.[12]

The evidence is therefore mixed. Though capitalism has acted to promote democratic tendencies in some countries, it has retarded, undermined, or suppressed them in others.

6. A Middle Class

A related hypothesis suggests that countries that are sharply divided into a small class of rich people and a large mass of poor, with no substantial middle class between them, are not likely to establish democracy. The rich will use their control of the economy to dominate the poor, while the poor will be mainly interested in expropriating the rich. Presumably, each of these opposing classes would be willing to use authoritarianism to impose its will on the other. A middle class, according to this hypothesis, is more favorable to democracy because its members seek to establish their own economic security on the basis of private enterprise, the rule of law, and an accountable government. These ideas are as old as Aristotle and as timely as the still-new millennium.

There is substantial historical and contemporary evidence linking the middle class with attitudes favorable to democracy. The democratic tendencies that blossomed in Britain, the United States, and France in the eighteenth and nineteenth centuries were largely the product of middle-class pressures against decaying monarchies and economically stagnant aristocracies. The middle class is still the backbone of democracy in all three countries as well as in other democracies that have emerged and flourished in the twentieth century. In recent years key elements of the middle class have played a leading role in militating for civil rights and democratic procedures in Latin America and in South Korea and Taiwan, where military or one-party regimes held sway for decades. In former communist countries such as Russia, where the middle class still consists largely of state employees, a new middle class tied to

The Philippine middle class was the base of Corazon Aquino's rise to power and the fall of the Ferdinand Marcos regime.

the emerging private sector is just beginning to make its appearance. Thus far it appears to favor democracy.

But does the middle class always support democracy? There is evidence that large elements of the middle class can turn their backs on democratic institutions and throw their support to dictators if they feel that democracy is jeopardizing their well-being. Such was the attitude of millions of middle-class Germans who were devastated by a succession of economic crises in the 1920s and early 1930s, when Germany had a democratic system of government. Having concluded that democracy itself was the source of their woes, major segments of the middle class voted for Hitler and the Nazis. "No prosperity, no democracy" may be a widespread middle-class attitude in other democracies as well. Even if a sizable middle class supports democracy in a given country, there is no guarantee that its support alone can bring democracy about where it does not already exist or sustain it where it does exist. In many cases democracy may require the backing of other classes as well, both rich and poor.

On balance, then, the evidence for this hypothesis is largely consistent with the notion that middle-class support for democracy can be very important in promoting a democratization process right from its earliest stages and in helping sustain democracy as it matures. Middle-class support definitely enhances democracy's chances. But there are mixed results in answer to the question, Does the middle class support democracy? Sometimes members of the middle class do support democracy, sometimes they don't. Much depends on their economic circumstances. If they see an opportunity to prosper under democracy, they will tend to support it, but if their fortunes diminish under a democratic government, they might turn to an authoritarian regime if they feel it can deliver prosperity. Meanwhile, keep in mind that the middle class consists of numerous individuals who do not all behave the same way.

Egypt's middle class played a big part in the revolution that ended Mubarak's regime. Some of the most prominent protesters were young people—students and young professionals—from the urban middle class. They had adopted middle-class lifestyles that included heavy use of the Internet and social media. They chafed under Mubarak's dictatorial rule that had subjected them to censorship and corruption. Egypt's liberals, who advocate for a secular regime that respects individual rights and liberties, are middle class. However, those liberals also led the protests that contributed to the popularly-elected president's downfall in 2013 and many supported the military coup. Egypt's middle class also includes conservative Muslims who support the Muslim Brotherhood and tend to be less interested in rights and liberties and more concerned about majority rule, which in the Egyptian case may mean the imposition of a political and legal order based on *sharia*.

7. Support of the Disadvantaged for Democracy

According to this hypothesis, the commitment of society's elites and the middle class may greatly enhance prospects for democracy, but if society's most disadvantaged elements feel they are left out of the democratic process or have nothing to gain from it, they could pose a serious threat to the country's democratic institutions and processes. Typically, the "disadvantaged" consist of the poorest members of the population, a group that in some countries comprises millions of people clinging desperately to survival. But other groups can also be counted among society's economically or socially disadvantaged, such as women and minorities. If democracy offers no real hope of overcoming poverty or discrimination, how can it claim to represent all the people inclusively? One result may be mass indifference on the part of the destitute and the oppressed. More ominously, seething mass discontent could provide a base of support for antidemocratic political movements and might even erupt into politically motivated violence.

Evidence relating to this hypothesis comes from a variety of countries at various stages of their historical development.

Britain, for example, managed to solidify democracy while significantly expanding mass political participation in the late nineteenth and early twentieth centuries by gradually giving the working class the right to vote. As a consequence the workers, who constituted the largest and poorest segment of British society, accepted democracy as the only legitimate method for seeking redress of their grievances, rejecting violent revolution and dictatorship. In France and Germany, by contrast, the development of democracy was slower and more turbulent than in Britain. The vast majority of workers in these countries had reason to feel shut out of the political process. The result was a greater sense of disillusionment with democracy on the part of large elements of the working masses, a sense of alienation that in the twentieth century found expression in significant working-class support for communist or fascist parties.

The support of underprivileged groups for democracy is by no means automatic, even when they are given opportunities to take part in the democratic process. Large elements of the impoverished masses, for example, may actually support an existing dictatorship if they believe the government will address their needs. Millions of poor Iranians voted for the Islamic hard-liner Mahmoud Ahmadinejad for president in 2005 in hopes that he would make good on his campaign promise to spend substantial amounts of Iran's oil revenues on social welfare and economic development projects for the country's underprivileged. For similar reasons, the poorer classes of oil-rich Venezuela provided a strong source of support for President Hugo Chávez, despite his authoritarian tendencies. Before his recent death, Chávez vigorously reached out to the poor with generous spending programs. The leaders of other authoritarian or semiauthoritarian regimes around the world have also managed to prolong their stay in power by providing economic benefits to the underprivileged, practicing a form of *populist authoritarianism*. In countries where a nondemocratic regime cannot afford to subsidize its economically deprived populations, or where it chooses not to, the ruling elites risk alienating a potentially threatening source of opposition.

Much depends on how well an elected government deals with the problems of disadvantaged groups, especially those spawned by the private marketplace. Private enterprise may stimulate extraordinary economic growth and thereby foster democratic tendencies on the part of those who profit by it. But the market economy can also produce prolonged slowdowns and deep depressions, persistent unemployment, inflation, acute poverty, and long-term financial insecurity. Those most affected by these hardships will usually look to their government for relief. To maintain mass support for democracy, therefore, elected governments must provide a panoply of social welfare measures designed to help the disadvantaged cope with economic distress.

Even in some democracies or partly free states, disadvantaged groups may turn to nondemocratic parties or engage in antigovernment violence if they feel that their basic needs are not being met. For example, in the Palestinian Authority, large numbers of Palestinians in 2006 voted for Hamas, which favors Islamic law, mainly because the Fatah-dominated PA government had failed to improve their economic conditions. Hamas won support in part because of the social services it provides to Palestinians in need. As another example, since 2006 members of the Movement for the Emancipation of the Niger Delta (MEND) have engaged in continuing violence against Nigeria's elected governments, as well as against foreign oil companies, in hopes of getting a greater share of Nigeria's oil wealth for their destitute region (see Chapter 19).

In the world's poorer countries, where the disadvantaged are often inhabitants of impoverished rural areas or overcrowded shantytowns, mass support for democracy tends to be weak or nonexistent where the masses of the population are either unable to organize broad-based democratic movements or unwilling to support democratic parties that do not adequately address their problems. It tends to be stronger where democratic parties and interest groups go out of their way to appeal to the underprivileged and make determined efforts to deal with their problems when in government.

Poor Egyptians were among those who protested against the Mubarak regime at the beginning of the revolution in 2011, joining a broad movement. A quarter of Egyptians live below the government's poverty line. Many of those poor Egyptians avoided politics under the old regime because they saw protest as futile and they needed to focus on earning what income they could. To Egypt's poor, the Muslim Brotherhood's social service networks have been a lifeline. Not surprisingly, they make up a significant electoral support base for the Muslim Brotherhood. Poor Egyptians will support a regime that improves social service delivery rather than one that emphasizes rights and liberties, as appears to have been true under Morsi.[13]

While admittedly sketchy, the evidence presented here appears to be generally consistent with the notion that the support of the disadvantaged is critical for democracy. Unless these segments of the population believe they can improve their lot by supporting democratic movements and parties, democracy will probably rest on shaky foundations. If democracy is not open to all, it may not succeed for anyone.

8. Citizen Participation, Civil Society, and a Democratic Political Culture

To give democracy life, people must participate. Political *parties* play a critical role in the participatory process, providing the main organizational link between politicians who run for office and the mass public. In most democracies, this link may be indirect at best. Typically the public has very little connection with parties except on election day; internal party affairs tend to be controlled by professional politicians and their staffs. However, some parties in the democratic world allow their members to take part in meetings to discuss policy issues and perhaps vote for the party's top leader or its candidates for office. Such parties provide a space for political participation by ordinary citizens at the grassroots level. To be sure, only small segments of the electorate may avail themselves of these opportunities. Partisanship—the extent to which voters actively identify themselves with a particular party—is in decline in most established democracies. Nevertheless, parties remain indispensable to democracy. At the very least, they provide voters with real election-day choices, and they permit legislatures and governments to function on the basis of coherent organizations. Newly democratizing countries therefore need strong parties that can be readily identified by the voters and that accurately represent the diversity of mass opinion on political issues. Unfortunately, strong parties often take decades to develop.

To maximize citizen participation, democracy also requires a strong civil society. **Civil society** refers to the population organized into associations independent of the state. Civil society includes traditional *interest groups* that are concerned primarily with issues arising out of the market economy, such as trade unions and business associations. It includes nongovernmental organizations (NGOs), which in recent decades have played an increasingly important role in democracies and even in some nondemocracies where they are able to function more or less openly. And it includes *social movements* of various kinds, such as the feminist movement or peasant movements, which may attract adherents outside the frameworks of formal organizations (see Chapter 8).

The key point is that civil society is *marked off from the state:* It consists of organizations that citizens create and join on their own, without any prompting or interference by government. Some of these associations may have overtly political purposes, such as interest groups that try to influence politicians and government officials to help their cause. In addition to unions and business associations, such groups would include ethnic and religious organizations, as well as single-issue organizations such as those advocating or opposing abortion, gun control, and the like. Other associations may be less explicitly political but may still take an interest in relevant public policy issues; examples include organizations concerned with education or health matters. And there are civic associations that have no political agenda, such as various charitable organizations, social clubs, or bowling leagues.[14]

The more the citizenry is involved in such voluntary associations, according to a widely held hypothesis, the more likely they will succeed in building and maintaining democracy. By freely entering into groups and associations, individuals learn habits of organization, cooperation, and trust that are vital to the sustenance of democratic institutions and procedures, creating patterns of interaction that link society at the grassroots level. In the process, they learn how to deal with many of the community's problems on their own, independently of government. Civil society thus can be a primary source of a democratic political culture—a pattern of widely shared attitudes and values supportive of democratic institutions and procedures. It is the social web that underlies democratic government, making it possible to limit the state's power and keeping it accountable to a self-organized citizenry. At its best, civil society promotes tolerance of other ethnic groups and religions, compromise, and a willingness to trust others and cooperate with them. Of course, citizens can also form organizations that categorically reject democratic principles, such as terrorist organizations, hate groups, or criminal gangs.

In his famous treatise on democracy in America in the 1830s, Alexis de Tocqueville placed special emphasis on the broad range of private associations that knitted Americans together in the early decades of their republic. This burgeoning network of business groups, religious societies, temperance leagues, and other forums for citizen-to-citizen contact outside the formal boundaries of government was, in his view, of fundamental importance in accounting for the success of the new nation's bold democratic experiment, providing a social bulwark against a tyrannical or domineering state. "The morals and intelligence of a democratic people would be in danger," Tocqueville warned, "if ever a government wholly usurped the place of private associations."[15]

In the 1990s another political scientist painted a more unsettling portrait of the state of American civil society. In *Bowling Alone*, Robert Putnam provides statistical evidence of a steady decline in membership in all sorts of associations in the United States, from PTAs to bowling leagues, from charitable groups to bridge clubs, starting in the late 1960s. The result has been a serious depletion of America's **social capital**, which Putnam defines as "social networks and the norms of reciprocity and trustworthiness that arise from them." Societies that have networks of people capable of working together will have large amounts of social capital that they can draw on—somewhat like a bank account—to accomplish their goals efficiently.[16]

While Putnam's hypothesis has stimulated considerable debate, few observers would question that a vibrant civil society has played a major role in building and sustaining democracy in America and other successful democracies. Striking confirmation of this reality comes from Central and Eastern Europe, where a number of countries have been consolidating democracy in the wake of communism's collapse. Poland and the Czech Republic have made rapid strides in their transition processes, while Romania and Bulgaria have moved more haltingly. These differences can be explained at least in part by the presence of a real civil society in the first two countries during the years of communist rule. In Poland, more than 10 million people joined Solidarity, an anticommunist trade union movement that openly challenged communist authoritarianism. In Czechoslovakia, a smaller but highly active group of political dissidents militated for democratic change starting in the 1960s. Romania and Bulgaria lacked such organizations, and they have taken a more circuitous route to democracy as a result.[17]

In Egypt the main axis of social organization outside of state institutions has been the Muslim Brotherhood. A formidable organization, the Muslim Brotherhood has created links to poor and middle class Egyptians through its social service networks that provide health care and hospitals, schools, job training, and support for widows and orphans. While the Muslim Brotherhood thus provides a dense social network outside of the state, the question is whether it intends to use its social linkages to create openness, tolerance, and a respect of the rights of others or rather to promote its vision of a pious, Islamic society based on *sharia* as its critics asserted happened under Morsi.

Considerable corroborative evidence links civil society with democracy. There is also strong evidence correlating a

In a widely held view, the more the citizenry is involved in voluntary political association, the more they will succeed in building and maintaining democracy. Such was the case when Lech Walesa and the Solidarity Movement helped launch Poland in its transition from a communist to democratic state.

democratic political culture with successful democracy. On the whole, the evidence is consistent with the hypothesis.

9. Education and Freedom of Information

According to this hypothesis, the prospects for democracy rise with society's education levels: The more educated the populace, the greater the support there will be for democratic values and procedures. Conversely, societies with high levels of illiteracy and a poorly educated populace are less likely to create or sustain democracy. Democracy requires the free flow of information and freedom of expression. Without the ability to discuss politics openly and debate contending points of view, it will be difficult for proponents of democracy to get organized under a dictatorship, a factor that may stall or prevent a democracy from emerging. Even after democratic institutions are set in place, the level of citizen participation in political life will depend to a considerable degree on the ready availability of relevant facts about the community's affairs and on opportunities for public discussion and citizen education about complicated political and economic issues.

There is considerable evidence in support of this hypothesis. When democracy emerged in Britain and the United States, for example, it was pushed forward primarily by society's most highly educated elites. British and American universities in the eighteenth and nineteenth centuries permitted the study of political philosophy and encouraged rigorous debate. In addition, the British monarchy permitted a certain amount of press freedom and open political discussion, a factor that was critical to the expansion of parliament's role in Britain and to the spread of democratic ideas in the American colonies. Conversely, democratic tendencies in these centuries were stultified in Russia, Japan, and China, where the study of political

philosophy was not encouraged and where oppressive state censorship smothered the open exchange of information and ideas. Meanwhile, in today's world, the most successful democracies tend to have higher literacy and secondary school graduation rates than nondemocracies.

Even when educational opportunities are widened and increasing numbers of people finish high school or enter universities, much depends on the content of what is taught and discussed. The Soviet Union, for example, greatly expanded educational opportunities for the masses, but the free discussion of political ideas was strictly forbidden. Many other dictatorships have exhibited similar patterns of restricted discussion and official censorship. Whether they can endure in the new millennium, with political information and open discussion accessible across national boundaries via the Internet, e-mail, and satellite television, is a fascinating question. A related development, in countries such as India, Pakistan, and Saudi Arabia, is the spread of Hindu or Islamic religious schools where the concept of religious tolerance is rejected, all-out opposition to other religions is inculcated in young minds, and students are given little or no instruction in other subjects. Religious intolerance can strike a death blow to democracy, regardless of who preaches it.

Egyptian oppositionists exploited the regime's inability to control information flows via mobile phones, the Internet, and social media—especially Facebook and Twitter—to mobilize a broad uprising against Mubarak's continued rule in January and February 2011. Liberal Egyptians have continued to demand press and information freedom under Morsi. They have had some success, although the armed forces continued to harass journalists and media outlets. In its review of press freedom, Freedom House moved Egypt from not free to partly free in its 2012 ratings. Censorship of film artists and writers critical of Islam remained in Muhamed Morsi's Egypt, however.[18]

As a general rule, there is a close correlation between democracy, on the one hand, and high educational levels and multiple sources of information on the other. This positive correlation is consistent with our hypothesis that education and free information can help promote democracy.

10. A Favorable International Environment

The conditions for democracy we have examined thus far are located within individual countries. But at times the external environment can have a significant impact on the prospects for democracy's emergence and subsequent development. War and its consequences can have either negative or positive effects on democracy. On the negative side, war generally requires firm centralized leadership and an influential role for the military command in the highest political councils. Under these circumstances there may be little room for interparty squabbling, an intrusive free press, or the open expression of public opinion. Not all countries involved in dangerous international conflicts have succumbed to the temptation of militaristic authoritarianism, however. The United States and its West European allies, for example, maintained their democratic institutions throughout the Cold War despite the hair-trigger nuclear standoff with the Soviet Union. On a more positive note, World War II produced democracy in West Germany and Japan, thanks to the direct influence of Western occupation authorities. Whether countries such as Afghanistan and Iraq will have similar outcomes remains an open question, however.

Global economic conditions can at times exert an equally profound impact on the prospects for democracy in particular countries. The Great Depression of the early 1930s was a major contributing factor in the collapse of Germany's democracy and the rising popularity of the Nazis. The chances for a successful transition to democracy in countries that have lately cast off dictatorship in Latin America, Africa, or Asia may depend in considerable measure on the willingness of the economically advanced democracies to provide timely economic assistance or to open their markets to mutually beneficial trade. The European Union has played a crucial role in Central and Eastern Europe by holding out EU membership to the region's former communist states. And the EU, the World Bank, and other sources of outside assistance are increasingly insisting on good governance. Good-governance projects tend to focus initially on getting governments to eliminate corruption and effectively deliver basic goods and services—such as food and medical care—to the population. At least in its early phases, good-governance projects may fall short of requiring full-scale democracy in countries where it does not yet exist, but helping to build sustainable democracies is the ultimate goal of many of these programs.

Transnational networks of nongovernmental organizations provide a growing source of outside influences on the prospects for democracy in nondemocratic or newly democratizing countries. NGOs espousing peace, voting rights, women's rights, press freedom, economic development, environmentalism, anticorruption measures, the elimination of torture, the struggle against racism, and similar causes are organized on a global scale, forming a worldwide civil society. They are using the powers of the web to publicize information, promote dialogue, and organize international letter-writing campaigns and other projects aimed at pressuring nondemocratic governments to comply with human rights standards. As Sidney Tarrow has observed, since the early 1990s a growing number of transnational activists have emerged who may be labeled "rooted cosmopolitans": They pursue their political causes both in the countries where they are rooted and in the wider world of global political activism. In the process, the number of *transnational social movements* has increased tenfold in the past 50 years, from only about a hundred in the 1950s to more than a thousand today.[19] At the same time, antidemocratic forces are also organized on a global scale, using their own financial resources and websites to influence the course of political development in a host of target countries. Terrorist networks, Islamic extremist movements, international criminal organizations, and similar antagonists of democratic principles compose an international "uncivil society" that has a long reach into states and societies around the world.

In the Egyptian case, as indicated in Chapter 1, transnational forces helped to spread the initial spark of the Arab Spring from Tunisia to Cairo's Tahrir Square. In addition, the clamor for democracy in Egypt received further support from Egyptians returning to their native country from years living abroad. Mubarak was encouraged to step aside by President Barack Obama when it appeared that Mubarak intended to try to retain his grip on power. President Mohamed Morsi's opponents used their linkages to international actors to bring pressure on his regime too, with the U.S. embassy mediating among contending forces during the 2013 protests and anti-Morsi coup.

A broader question is whether globalization will help or hinder democracy in the developing world. The forces of global economic and technological connectedness have both positive and negative consequences for developing economies, and the coming years should reveal their political effects more clearly.

The evidence is thus consistent with the hypothesis. But experience shows that, while external influences may be important, ultimately no foreign government or combination of governments is likely to prove capable of creating or propping up democratic institutions and habits in countries where the domestic conditions for democracy are unfavorable. Ultimately, the sources and nutrients of democracy must be homegrown if democracy is to germinate and blossom to its full potential.

Table 7.2 summarizes the evidence reviewed in the previous pages. As we consider prospects for democratic transition, democratic consolidation, and even democratic failure in coming chapters, we will return to this list of conditions to see what the prospects for democracy are in particular countries.

Our review of how Egypt lines up on each of these 10 conditions ought to make us cautious about seeing democracy in that nation's near future. Powerful Egyptian elites are ambivalent or even hostile to democracy, especially the military, which ended the Morsi regime in 2013. The most well-organized non-state actor in contemporary Egypt is the Muslim Brotherhood, which seems to value the promotion of a society with Islam at the center of all social organizations more than it does

Table 7.2 Evidence about the Conditions that Support Democracy

Explanatory Factor	Favors Democracy when . . .	Evidence is Mainly . . .
1. Elite attitudes	Political and economic elites are committed to democratic procedures.	Consistent
2. State institutions	The state controls national territory and is able to perform essential state functions—providing national security and law and order.	Consistent
3. National unity	Social heterogeneity is less and national identity is strong.	Consistent
4. National wealth	The country is prosperous.	Mixed; generally consistent but with major exceptions
5. Private enterprise	The economy is organized according to capitalist principles.	Mixed; evidence for and against
6. Middle class	The middle class is large and committed to democracy.	Consistent
7. Attitudes of disadvantaged	The majority of the poor and otherwise disadvantaged favor democratic procedures.	Consistent
8. Civil society	Civil society groups are vigorous and promote a democratic political culture.	Consistent
9. Education and access to information	The population is well educated and has free access to information about politics and public issues.	Consistent
10. International conditions	Foreign powers promote introduction and consolidation of democracy, international economy is prospering, and/or transnational social movements pressure for democracy.	Consistent

democracy. The Muslim Brotherhood has shaped large parts of civil society to achieve its goals. Elements of the middle class and owners of private enterprise have shown support for democracy, but other parts of those sectors have not. State institutions are powerful compared to the society they govern, and within the state the most powerful actor is the military, which brought the first elected post-Mubarak presidency to an end barely a year after it began. Egypt is not among the world's most impoverished countries, which could give us some optimism about the future of democracy there, but nearly a quarter of its people live in poverty and may find the struggle for democracy to be a luxury they cannot afford. Egyptian actors claim they seek democracy, but what they mean by it varies from one group to the next. Two differing visions animate those who collaborated to bring down Mubarak. The liberals—middle-class students, professionals, and intellectuals—tend to advocate for a view of democracy that favors individual rights and liberties. The Muslim Brotherhood tends to see democracy in terms of popular sovereignty—the rule of the people, meaning especially the majority of the people, which the brotherhood is well situated to win. That means that members of the Muslim Brotherhood believe their view of the good society—one that sees a large role for Islam in politics—should become the blueprint for the new order, whether that leads to the abridgment of the rights of some social and political groups—Copts, liberals, secularists, and women who do not embrace male patriarchy—or not. Conflict between these views provoked the 2013 coup.

PATTERNS OF DEMOCRATIZATION

As we pointed out at the start of this chapter, our 10 conditions of democracy do not by themselves *cause* a nondemocratic regime to collapse and a democracy to take its place. For such a major transformation to happen, a particular sequence of events must occur. The precise nature and timing of these events will invariably differ from one country to another. No two countries are ever exactly alike, and no two democratization processes are ever exactly alike. Still, there are general patterns of how democratization actually occurs. But even the most widely shared patterns are bound to have exceptions, and every country will have its own idiosyncrasies that deviate from the general model.

Political scientist Samuel Huntington argued that we can identify three waves of democracy over time. In the first wave, up to the 1920s, early democratizers such as Britain, the United States, France, and other European countries gradually expanded the franchise to all adults and institutionalized their democratic practices. That first wave was followed in the 1930s and 1940s by a reverse wave, as several democracies that emerged after the First World War succumbed to dictatorship before and during the Great Depression. (We will explore the example of Germany's interwar democratic failure in Chapter 15.) After the Second World War, a second wave of democratization appeared, resulting partly from military occupation (Austria, Germany, Italy, and Japan), but including several countries in Europe, Latin America, and among former colonies (such as India, as we'll see in Chapter 12). The second wave was followed in the 1960s and 1970s by a second reverse wave, with several Southern European and Latin American democracies falling to military dictatorships. Since 1974 we have seen a third wave of democratization, which has spread across the globe and includes many countries that had briefly democratized in the second wave, only to revert to authoritarianism, and many other new democracies in societies that had never known democratic rule.[20] In advancing the ideas of waves of democratization, Huntington was emphasizing the ways in which similar international conditions (condition 10 above) encouraged democratization to take place (e.g., the postwar democratization forced on Axis powers by the victorious allies). He was also drawing attention to the way democracy's advocates learn through "demonstration effects." The Arab Spring is the most recent example of how demonstration effects—seeing regime change in Tunisia and then Egypt—lead to a contagion of political change.

While Huntington provides a useful chronological typology of democratization, we can also look at democratization in another way: From what former regime types have democracies emerged? Let's start with some of the oldest democracies in today's world, all of them in Western Europe. These are democracies that have been in existence since at least the end of World War II. Most of these "elderly" democracies, listed in Table 7.3, democratized during the first wave of democratization. Their common feature is that democracy emerged from some form of monarchy. Each country on the list took its own particular path from monarchy to democracy, and we won't go into these particularities here. (We looked at the Netherlands in Chapter 5, and we'll look at the United Kingdom and France in Part Two.) The commonality of the general pattern is what we want to highlight here. Another common feature of these democracies is that, in the nineteenth and early twentieth centuries, most of them experienced pressures for democracy from an increasingly assertive middle class (the bourgeoisie). These pressures were usually augmented by an industrial working class pushing for inclusion in the political system. The result in most cases was the gradual development of a broad democratic coalition backed by conservative (bourgeois) and social-democratic (working-class) parties.

Another category includes countries that "inherited" democracy from Britain (Table 7.4). All these countries were British colonies, possessions, or dependencies at some point.

Table 7.3 European Democracies That Emerged from Monarchies

Belgium	Luxembourg	Norway
Denmark	Monaco	Sweden
France	Netherlands	United Kingdom
Liechtenstein		

Table 7.4 Contemporary Democracies Derived from British Rule

Antigua and Barbuda	Dominica	New Zealand
Australia	India	St. Kitts and Nevis
Bahamas	Ireland	St. Lucia
Barbados	Jamaica	St. Vincent and Grenadines
Belize	Kiribati	Tuvalu
Botswana	Malta	United States
Canada	Mauritius	Vanuatu*
Cyprus (Greek)		

*Governed as a joint British-French condominium.

Since achieving their independence from Britain, they have all maintained democratic government in a relatively unbroken pattern to the present day. (All the countries in Table 7.4 had a Freedom House rating of 1 to 2.5 at the end of 2011, qualifying them as "democracies" in this book.) This list includes old democracies such as the United States and Canada, along with more recent ones that emerged after World War II. Once again, these countries display plenty of individual idiosyncrasies. To state the obvious, democracy in the United States evolved very differently from the paths taken by Canada and New Zealand, not to mention Kiribati and St. Lucia. Nevertheless, the United States is one of Britain's babies, just like all the other countries on the list. (Israel was a democracy from its inception as a new state in 1948; its territory was formerly part of Palestine under the British mandate.) Several of these democracies appeared in Huntington's first wave, and others during the second wave when many British colonies separated from British rule.

Not all of Britain's former charges were equally successful in sustaining democratic institutions. The list of former British colonies that failed to sustain democracy after independence is a long one. Some of them are still not democracies, such as Bangladesh, Pakistan, Sudan, and Zimbabwe. Ghana and South Africa were authoritarian regimes for decades before becoming democracies more recently. Nigeria has been governed mostly by military dictatorships since the mid-1960s. Its elected government under President Goodluck Jonathan was considered a partly free regime by Freedom House in 2012. Sierra Leone is just coming out of a brutal civil war; it too was partly free in 2012.

Another category consists of countries that developed—or redeveloped—democracy as the result of war and foreign invasion or intervention. Major examples are France, Germany, and Japan; the stories of the first two we tell in Part Two. Italy became a democracy upon its creation as an independent state in 1859. Mussolini's fascist dictatorship put an end to that democratic system in the 1920s, but democracy returned to Italy following the defeat of fascism in World War II. Austria first became a democracy after the defeat of the Austro-Hungarian Empire in World War I. Its current democracy was established in large part as a result of World War II. In the postwar period, several of today's democracies resulted from direct U.S. military intervention against dictators (the Dominican Republic in 1965, Grenada in 1983, and Panama in 1989) or from more indirect forms of U.S. intervention (Nicaragua and El Salvador, which experienced bloody civil wars between left-wing and right-wing political groups in the 1980s).

Now let's focus on countries that have undergone transitions to democracy from either military rule, one-party rule, or rule by a regime centered around a dominant leader (a so-called "strongman") since 1986—all of these countries fall squarely in Huntington's third wave. Table 7.5 lists the main countries in this category. Most of these countries are still considered *transition countries:* They are still in the process of consolidating democratic institutions and practices. It's possible that democracy may falter in some of them and give way to authoritarianism in some old or new form. Some of the countries on the list were democracies at the end of 2012, while others were partly

Table 7.5 Transition Countries Since 1986 (Former Military, One-Party, and/or One-Leader Regimes)

Country	Regime Type	Existence of Prodemocracy Movement, Party, and/or Demonstrations/Unrest	Did Regime Allow Fair Elections?	Year Opposition Won	Freedom House Rating, 2012*
Benin	One-party	Yes	Yes	1991	2
Cape Verde	One-party	Yes	Yes	1991	1
Chile	Military	Yes	Yes	1991	1
Ghana	One-party/leader	Yes	Yes	2000	1.5
Guyana	One-party	Yes	Yes	1992	2.5
Indonesia	Military/one-leader	Yes	Yes	1999	2.5
Kenya	One-party/leader	Yes	Yes	2002	3.5
Lebanon	External influence	Yes	Yes	2005	4
Liberia	One-leader	Yes	Yes	2005	3.5
Malawi	One-party/one-leader	Yes	Yes	1994	3.5
Mexico	One-party	Yes	Yes	2000	3
Niger	Military	Yes	Yes	1993; 1999	3.5
Nigeria	Military	Yes	Yes	1999	4
Paraguay	Military	Yes	Yes	2003	3
Peru	One-leader	Yes	Yes	2001	2.5
Philippines	Military/one-leader	Yes	Yes	1986	3
Sao Tome and Principe	One-party	Yes	Yes	1991	2
Senegal	One-party	Yes	Yes	2000	2.5
South Africa	One-party	Yes	Yes	1994	2
South Korea	Military	Yes	Yes	1997	1.5
Suriname	Military	Yes	Yes	1991	2
Taiwan	One-party	Yes	Yes	1988	1.5
Tanzania	One-party/one-leader	Yes	Yes	2003	3
Thailand	Military	Yes	Yes	1992	4
Tunisia	One-party/one-leader	Yes	No	2011	3.5
Zambia	One-party	Yes	Yes	1991	3.5

Note: "One-party" regimes are run by a single ruling party. "One-leader" regimes are typically headed by an exceptionally well-entrenched individual who exercises personal power over a number of years, at times in conjunction with a ruling party, the military, or both.

* From Arch Puddington, *Freedom in the World 2013: Democratic Breakthroughs in the Balance* (New York: Freedom House, 2013), pp. 13–17.

free (with a 2012 Freedom House rating of 3 to 5). Many of these countries endured nondemocratic governments of one kind or another for two or more decades before a democratically elected, prodemocracy government took power.

Thomas Carothers argues that many countries end up in "the gray zone," of which he writes,

They have some attributes of democratic political life, including at least limited political space for opposition parties and independent civil society, as well as regular elections and democratic constitutions. Yet they suffer from serious democratic deficits, often including poor representation of citizens' interests, low levels of political participation beyond voting, frequent abuse of the law by government officials, elections of uncertain legitimacy, very low levels of public confidence in state institutions, and persistently poor institutional performance by the state.[21]

Is the gray zone a transitory state, on the way to full democratization? Or a position of semi-freedom (as the Freedom House scores in Table 7.5 imply), illiberal democracy, electoral authoritarianism? Could a society stay in the gray zone indefinitely? Our review of the conditions propelling Egypt away from Mubarak's rule suggested it could easily fall into this gray zone, with the president and a parliament elected popularly but with the regime abridging freedoms in the name of *sharia* and nondemocratic actors like the military at times bringing an end to the experiment by staging a seizure of power.

Having allowed for the possibility that countries may spend some time in this gray zone, can we nevertheless determine a pattern that successful democratization tends to follow? At the risk of making a few broad generalizations that gloss over numerous deviations and variations, we can characterize the dominant ideal type of democratization pattern in this category as follows:

1. Over time, the authoritarian regime is confronted by opponents who demand a new government based on key elements of democracy. The opposition's main demands tend to be (a) inclusion in political decision making and (b) economic improvements. In some cases a "crisis of inclusion" results from severe discrimination or persecution by the regime against its opponents.

2. The opposition forms organizations (political parties, NGOs); its adherents engage in anti-regime activities (manifestos, demonstrations, political violence, etc.); and international pressures for change mount.

3. The regime tries to co-opt the opposition with minor concessions or rigged elections, or elections to institutions that lack real decision-making authority.

4. Regime leaders realize they can no longer govern or control the situation. In some cases a *catalytic crisis* occurs, involving one or more of the following: the death or retirement of a strong leader; an economic downturn; defeat or stalemate in a war or civil war; mass anti-regime demonstrations or riots; an increase in politically motivated violence; intense international pressure or intervention; the breakup of the regime's ruling coalition (including the defection of military leaders).

5. A "democratic bargain" is struck with the opposition that permits free and fair elections. Elections are held and the opposition wins. The regime either (a) steps aside and allows the opposition to take power or (b) falsely reports that the opposition has lost, triggering a major crisis that compels the ruling elite to give up power.

In every country listed in Table 7.5 there was a serious prodemocracy movement or party, demonstrations, unrest, or some combination of these developments. In most countries, democratization got going with the victory of oppositionists at the polls. In several countries a "democratic bargain" was negotiated at a national conference aimed at facilitating fair elections and a transfer of power (Benin and Niger are examples). In some of these countries the democratization process proceeded incrementally as the ruling authorities relinquished power gradually, and often grudgingly, over a period of years or even decades (as in Mexico, South Africa, and elsewhere). In others there was a catalytic crisis that brought accumulating tensions to a head: fraudulent election results in the Philippines in 1986; a referendum against Chile's president, Gen. Augusto Pinochet, in 1988; the decision of Thailand's king to pressure the military to relinquish power in 1992; the death of Nigeria's military ruler, General Sani Abacha, in 1998; an economic crisis and mass demonstrations in Indonesia in 1998; the assassination of former Prime Minister Rafiq Hariri in Lebanon in 2005; the mass demonstrations that ignited the Arab Spring in Tunisia in 2011; and similarly crucial events elsewhere.

Several military or one-party regimes that lost power to democratization processes *before* 1986 displayed similar patterns. Several of these countries experienced catalytic crises that pushed pent-up opposition to the regime to a tipping point. Greece's military regime collapsed after its attempt to annex Cyprus by force triggered a Turkish invasion of the island in 1974. Political change gathered steam in Portugal in the early 1970s, a few years after the retirement of strongman Antonio Salazar. A highly contentious power struggle between military elements and prodemocracy civilians culminated in the stabilization of democracy in 1982. Democratization got rolling in Spain soon after the death of dictator Francisco Franco in 1975. (Salazar had come to power in 1928 and Franco in 1939.) Argentina's repressive military regime gave up power in 1982 following its defeat in a war with Britain over the Falkland (Malvinas) Islands. Brazil's military unexpectedly lost an election to an opposition candidate in 1985.

Another group of transition countries consists of former communist regimes. Table 7.6 lists countries undergoing transitions to democracy that were once part of the Soviet Union, which ceased to exist at the stroke of midnight December 31, 1991. Table 7.7 lists former communist countries outside the Soviet Union. Like the countries we've already listed, these former communist states have each taken their own idiosyncratic path of democratization, but some of them also fall into one or more of the patterns we've just observed. We've already referred to the Baltic states in Chapter 5, and we'll take a close look at the breakup of the USSR and Russia's troubled democratization process in Chapter 16.

After the USSR's collapse, power in Ukraine and Georgia was initially captured by elected governments that proved to be more authoritarian than democratic. A fraudulent parliamentary election result in Georgia in 2003 precipitated mass protests, forcing the country's strongman president, Eduard Shevardnadze, to resign. A snap presidential election that took place in 2004 was won by Mikhail Saakashvili, leader of the democratic Rose Revolution. Similar electoral crises ushered in the Orange Revolution in Ukraine in 2004 and the Tulip Revolution in Kyrgyzstan in 2005. Unfortunately, in all three cases the hopes raised by those "color" revolutions have been disappointed as more authoritarian practices have come to prevail, turning the rose, the orange, and the tulip into the grayness of the gray zone.

As communism was falling apart inside the USSR in the late 1980s and early 1990s, powerful forces for change

Table 7.6 Transition Countries (Former USSR)

Country	2012 Freedom House Rating*	Country	2012 Freedom House Rating
Armenia	4.5	Lithuania	1
Estonia	1	Moldova	3
Georgia	3	Russia	5.5
Kyrgyzstan	5	Ukraine	3.5
Latvia	2		

Note: The following former Soviet republics are not undertaking serious transitions to democracy: Azerbaijan, Belarus, Kazakhstan, Tajikistan, Turkmenistan, and Uzbekistan.

*From Arch Puddington, *Freedom in the World 2013: Democratic Breakthroughs in the Balance* (New York: Freedom House, 2013), pp. 13–17.

Table 7.7 Former Communist Transition Countries (Non-USSR)

Country	2012 Freedom House Rating*	Country	2012 Freedom House Rating
Albania	3	Mongolia	1.5
Bosnia-Herzegovina	3	Montenegro	2.5
Bulgaria	2	Poland	1
Croatia	1.5	Romania	2
Czech Republic	1	Serbia	2
Hungary	1.5	Slovakia	1
Kosovo	4.5	Slovenia	1
Macedonia	3		

* From Arch Puddington, *Freedom in the World 2013: Democratic Breakthroughs in the Balance* (New York: Freedom House, 2013), pp. 13–17.

promoted democratization in Central and Eastern Europe. In six states, communist rule effectively collapsed in 1989. In Poland, Czechoslovakia, and East Germany, mass demonstrations forced the ruling elites to permit free elections. Czechoslovakia's nonviolent transition was called the Velvet Revolution. (In 1993 the country was split into the Czech Republic and Slovakia, the so-called Velvet Divorce.) East Germany merged with democratic West Germany in 1990. In Hungary, leaders of the ruling Communist Party announced that there would be free, multiparty elections the following year. A dissident faction inside Romania's ruling elite staged a coup against strongman Nicolae Ceausescu and eventually supported democratization. The Soviet leadership replaced Bulgaria's communist strongman, setting off a democratization process there. In 1990 and 1991, noncommunist parties emerged in these states, the communists transformed themselves into prodemocracy parties, and elections were held that confirmed the transitions of power.

The events in Yugoslavia as its communist system collapsed were described in Chapter 4. It is worth reiterating that Bosnia-Herzegovina underwent a painful civil war that required international mediation. And Serbia's postcommunist strongman Slobodan Milosevic was forced to resign after fraudulent election results sparked mass demonstrations against his rule. Meanwhile, Albania's isolated regime under communist strongman Enver Hoxha dissolved in 1990; elections were held in 1992. And in far-off Mongolia, mass protests against the communist regime in 1990 pressured the government to hold free elections.

A comparative examination of transitions to democracy around the world in recent decades reveals still more general patterns. In some cases there was a *pacted transition:* State power was transferred on the basis of a negotiated agreement, or pact, between a weakened nondemocratic government and the leaders of the prodemocracy movement. Another pattern involved a genuine *revolution from below:* A broad-based movement for change shook the foundations of authoritarian rule, confronting the regime with mass protests and, in some instances, violent unrest. Yet another pattern was *democratization from above.* In that pattern, elements of the country's nondemocratic regime became convinced that reforms were necessary, and they either initiated democratization themselves or introduced reforms that ultimately produced democracy (perhaps unintentionally, as in

the USSR under Mikhail Gorbachev). Scholars have argued that the way state power is transferred from nondemocratic rulers to prodemocracy leaders has a major impact on the success and quality of the democratization process. But there has been considerable debate about how these patterns work, given the extraordinary diversity of countries that have undergone democratic transitions.[22]

A parsimonious explanation of democratization that seeks to explain a wide range of historical and recent cases has been advanced by Daron Acemoglu and James Robinson. In *Economic Origins of Dictatorship and Democracy*, they argue from a rational-choice perspective that democracy tends to come about when a nondemocratic ruling elite, consisting of a small segment of the population, is faced with a potential revolution and can no longer buy off its opponents with dubious promises of economic rewards. Rather than risk a violent struggle it cannot win, the elite chooses to hold competitive elections. The prodemocracy forces also wish to avoid a costly revolution, and democratization ensues as they are elected to power. Democracy becomes consolidated when the country's elites have no incentive to topple it. The scholars reinforce their argument with evidence of the importance of state institutions, the middle class, civil society, globalization, and other variables that support successful democratization and consolidation processes.[23]

Conclusion

Democracy's extraordinary advances in the past few decades, and the struggles for democracy that are still taking shape, have amounted to a truly global revolutionary process. They have given analysts much to think about and activists much to do. While analysts have turned transitology (the study of democratic transitions) into an academic industry, activists have joined forces around the world to support democratic movements and governments. The two groups can learn from each other, gaining a better appreciation of how democracy comes about and how best to promote it. Government decision makers concerned with democratization in their home countries and abroad can also benefit from the insights of analysts and the experiences of activists.

The 10 conditions for democracy presented in this chapter constitute a *framework for comparative analysis* that can be applied to virtually every country in the world. They provide a broad basis for understanding why some countries have succeeded at democracy and others have not. While no one of the 10 conditions is either necessary or sufficient to propel democratization, as we consider actual cases of democratic transition or consolidation in Chapter 12 and in the country studies in Part Two, we will find that this framework provides a valuable rubric.

Key Terms

Consolidation
Civil society
Social capital

Notes

1. On these points, see Adam Przeworski, *Politics and the Market: Political and Economic Reforms in Eastern Europe and Latin America* (Cambridge: Cambridge University Press, 1991), p. 26; Samuel P. Huntington, *The Third Wave: Democratization in the Late Twentieth Century* (Norman, OK: University of Oklahoma Press, 1991), pp. 266–67. Huntington suggests that democracy is consolidated when power changes hands in two successive elections. For a critique, see Guillermo O'Donnell, "Illusions about Consolidation," *Journal of Democracy* 7, no. 2 (January 1996), pp. 34–51.
2. Eric Trager, "The Unbreakable Muslim Brotherhood," *Foreign Affairs* 90, no. 5 (September 2011), pp. 114–26.
3. On the importance of elites for democracy, see Robert A. Dahl, *Polyarchy: Participation and Opposition* (New Haven, CN: Yale University Press, 1971), ch. 8; Juan J. Linz, *The Breakdown of Democratic Regimes: Crisis, Breakdown and Reequilibration* (Baltimore, MD: Johns Hopkins University Press, 1978).
4. See Donald W. Shriver, *An Ethic for Enemies: Forgiveness in Politics* (New York: Oxford University Press, 1995). For a discussion of truth and reconciliation commissions, see Priscilla B. Hayner, *Unspeakable Truths: Transitional Justice and the Challenge of Truth Commissions*, 2nd ed. (New York: Routledge, 2011).
5. *Freedom in the World 1998–1999* (New York: Freedom House, 1999), p. 9.
6. Rustow wrote that national unity "simply means that the vast majority of citizens in a democracy-to-be must have no doubt or mental reservations as to which political community they belong to." It precludes secession or amalgamation with a larger community. See D. A. Rustow, "Transitions to Democracy: Toward a Dynamic Model," *Comparative Politics* 3 (1970), pp. 337–63. Reprinted in Geoffrey Pridham, ed., *Transitions to Democracy: Comparative Perspectives from Southern Europe, Latin America and Eastern Europe* (Aldershot, UK: Dartmouth, 1995), pp. 59–86.
7. Adam Przeworski and Fernando Limongi, "Modernization: Theories and Facts," *World Politics* 49, no. 2 (January 1997), pp. 155–83; Adam Przeworski, Michael E. Alvarez, Jose Antonio Cheibub, and Fernando Limongi, *Democracy and Development: Political Institutions and Well-Being in the World, 1950–1990* (Cambridge: Cambridge University Press, 2000); Ross E. Burkhart and Michael S. Lewis-Beck, "Comparative

Democracy: The Economic Development Thesis," *American Political Science Review* 88, no. 4 (December 1994), pp. 903–10.
8. Egyptian economic data are available from the World Bank at http://databank.worldbank.org and the UNDP at http://hdr.undp.org/en/reports/global/hdr2011/. Jane Kinninmont, "'Bread, Dignity and Social Justice': The Political Economy of Egypt's Transition," *Chatham House Briefing Paper*, MENAP BP 2012/01, April 2012.
9. Barrington Moore, *Social Origins of Dictatorship and Democracy* (Boston: Beacon Press, 1966).
10. Bruce J. Dickson, *Red Capitalists in China: The Party, Private Entrepreneurs, and Prospects for Political Change* (Cambridge: Cambridge University Press, 2003); Margaret M. Pearson, *China's New Business Elite: The Political Consequences of Economic Reform* (Berkeley, CA: University of California Press, 1997).
11. *Financial Times*, November 7, 1995.
12. Kinninmont, "Bread, Dignity and Social Justice."
13. Said Sadek, "Put Women and Minorities at Ease," in "Room for Debate: Can the Muslim Brotherhood Unite Egypt?" *The New York Times*, June 25, 2012, at http://www.nytimes.com/roomfordebate; Jeffrey Fleishman, "Egypt's Poor Cannot Afford a Revolution," *Los Angeles Times*, August 2, 2011.
14. Michael Edwards, *Civil Society* (Cambridge, UK: Polity, 2004); Jean L. Cohen and Andrew Arato, *Civil Society and Political Theory* (Cambridge, MA: MIT Press, 1994); Chris Hann and Elizabeth Dunn, *Civil Society: Challenging Western Models* (London: Routledge, 1996); John Keane, *Civil Society: Old Images, New Visions* (Stanford, CA: Stanford University Press, 1998); Thomas Janoski, *Citizenship and Civil Society* (Cambridge: Cambridge University Press, 1998); Avishai Margalit, *The Decent Society*, trans. Naomi Goldblum (Cambridge, MA: Harvard University Press, 1996); John Ehrenberg, *Civil Society: The Critical History of an Idea* (New York: New York University Press, 1999); Robert K. Fullinwider, ed., *Civil Society, Democracy, and Civic Renewal* (Lanham, MD: Rowman & Littlefield, 1999).
15. Alexis de Tocqueville, *Democracy in America*, ed. J. P. Mayer, trans. George Lawrence (New York: Harper & Row, 1966), pt. 2, pp. 513–17.
16. Robert D. Putnam, *Bowling Alone: The Collapse and Revival of American Community* (New York: Simon & Schuster, 2000); Robert D. Putnam, ed., *Democracies in Flux: The Evolution of Social Capital in Contemporary Society* (New York: Oxford University Press, 2002).
17. Sarah E. Mendelson and John K. Glenn, *The Power and Limits of NGOs* (New York: Columbia University Press, 2002). Also Nancy Bermeo, *Ordinary People in Extraordinary Times: The Citizenry and the Breakdown of Democracy* (Princeton, NJ: Princeton University Press, 2003).
18. http://www.freedomhouse.org/report/freedom-press/2012/egypt; Abeer Allam, "Director Keeps Focus on Egypt Censorship," *Financial Times*, November 12, 2012.
19. Sidney Tarrow, *The New Transnational Activism* (New York: Cambridge University Press, 2005), pp. 43–45. See also William E. DeMars, *NGOs and Transnational Networks: Wild Cards in World Politics* (Ann Arbor, MI: Pluto, 2005).
20. Huntington, *The Third Wave*.
21. Thomas Carothers, "The End of the Transition Paradigm," *Journal of Democracy* 13, no. 1 (January 2002), p. 9.
22. Michael McFaul, "The Fourth Wave of Democracy and Dictatorship: Noncooperative Transitions in the Postcommunist World," *World Politics* 54, no. 2 (January 2002), pp. 212–44. See also Valerie Bunce, "Rethinking Recent Democratization: Lessons from the Postcommunist Experience," *World Politics* 55, no. 2 (January 2003), pp. 167–92; Valerie Bunce, *Subversive Institutions: The Design and the Destruction of Socialism and the State* (New York: Cambridge University Press, 1999); Richard D. Anderson Jr., M. Steven Fish, Stephen E. Hanson, and Philip G. Roeder, *Postcommunism and the Theory of Democracy* (Princeton, NJ: Princeton University Press, 2001).
23. Daron Acemoglu and James A. Robinson, *Economic Origins of Dictatorship and Democracy* (New York: Cambridge University Press, 2006).

8

Political Participation
People and Politics in Democracies and Nondemocracies

Protest is an increasingly common form of political participation even in long-established, stable democracies.

OVERVIEW

- Political participation serves as the critical linkage by which individuals and groups in society communicate their policy preferences to decision makers in the state.

- In democracies, conventional forms of participation—voting, activity within political parties, and lobbying—are supplemented by communal activity such as membership in neighborhood associations and local advocacy groups as well as by petitioning elected and appointed officials.

- In nondemocracies, individuals' interactions with the state often take the form of patronage relationships between powerful persons and their clients.

- Without formal opportunities to provide input to policy makers, individuals in authoritarian settings are often forced into confrontational forms of participation, like mass demonstrations, illegal strikes, and even armed rebellion.

- In both democracies and nondemocracies, contentious forms of political participation have become increasingly common.

POLITICAL PARTICIPATION

One of the central premises of democratic theory is that citizens will take full advantage of their opportunities to participate actively in political life. They will make their views known to the governing authorities and hold those authorities fully accountable for their actions. Political participation, hence, is the mechanism by which members of society ensure that governing authorities represent them. Contrary to these expectations, however, most people who live in democracies choose not to participate very much. One study of political participation in the United States conducted in the 1960s labeled 30 percent of the adult population "apathetics" because they knew virtually nothing about politics. Another 60 percent were labeled "spectators" on the grounds that they paid some attention to politics, though they varied in degree. Many spectators paid only minimal attention to political goings-on. Only about 5 percent to 7 percent could be termed "gladiators" who actively participated in political campaigns in presidential election years; in other years this group of political activists would typically fall to 1 percent to 2 percent of the population. Counting the gladiators and the most politically active spectators, only about 20 percent of the population regularly engaged in discussions about political issues; they were labeled "opinion leaders." These figures have remained substantially the same up to the present day. When asked in 2004, fewer than 10 percent of Americans campaigned for candidates and about 6 percent had taken part in a political demonstration or protest activity.[1] In other democracies, too, most people do not get actively involved in political life.

Nevertheless, generally a large number of citizens, quite often the majority, will turn out to vote in periodic elections. Voting is the main form of mass participation in virtually all democratic countries. Voter turnout rates differ from country to country, however, and the United States, on average, ranks close to the bottom of 22 major democracies.

Why don't people who have the privilege of democratic participation take advantage of it? Mancur Olson's acclaimed book, *The Logic of Collective Action,*[2] offers a clear explanation for nonparticipation from the perspective of rational choice.

Although Olson's rational choice logic explains why many people do not take part in political activity, it does not explain why people *do* participate. In fact, tens of millions of people around the world will at least vote every few years, and millions of others will get more actively involved in politics in one way or another. And though they may constitute a small minority in their own country, significant numbers of ordinary citizens at times feel sufficiently seized by a political issue to get up and demonstrate, sign a petition, or take part in much riskier behavior by challenging the ruling authorities in the streets. Politics is not just a matter of costs and risks;

it also offers serious opportunities and benefits. As you read through this chapter, we urge you to ask yourself, In light of Olson's conclusion that nonparticipation and free riding are the rational choices for potential participants, why are individuals choosing to act politically? We will return to this question at the end of the chapter.

Although the degree of political participation in democracies can vary considerably, the forms or modes of mass participation are generally the same. Even in nondemocracies there are often ways for ordinary people to participate in politics. The particular forms of political action an individual might choose to emphasize depend much on the opportunities available and the skills and knowledge the person brings to politics. A highly educated Canadian seeking to influence energy policy would probably opt for a very different mode of political participation than a poor Guatemalan woman hoping to convince the government to increase subsidies for food staples.

Students of political participation usually distinguish four main modes of participation:

- **Conventional political participation** includes voting, working through political parties to support campaigns and candidates, and lobbying through interest groups.
- **Communal activity** is focused on collective action at the neighborhood or village level whereby fellow citizens collaborate to achieve local needs, such as building a

ESSENTIAL CONCEPTS

The Logic of Collective Action

According to a traditional assumption about democracy, people who are free to engage in open political activity will take advantage of this opportunity by organizing or joining groups that seek to exert pressure on state decision makers on behalf of some common group interest or demand. But do they? In *The Logic of Collective Action,* Mancur Olson suggested that people in large groups usually do not behave this way. Rather than join in collective action with like-minded citizens, even people with serious grievances usually do nothing. Personal inaction is often preferred to collective action.

Olson argues that such inaction is a *rational choice* for the individual. Most social scientists define *rationality* as behavior aimed at maximizing (or at least increasing) one's expected gains and minimizing (or reducing) one's expected costs or risks. As applied to the logic of collective action, Olson hypothesizes that the average person will reason as follows when deciding whether to get involved in a group political activity:

- The costs and risks of such action may be too high (one will have to sacrifice time, comfort, or perhaps money, and one may even run the risk of being jailed, beaten, or killed if the activity is illegal).
- If a group has already been formed to militate in behalf of the individual's interests, one's own contribution may not

be all that necessary anyway ("If 10,000 are demonstrating in the streets or signing petitions, what difference will one more make?").
- If the group fails to change government policy favorably, those engaged in the collective action gain exactly what those who did not engage in it get: nothing. But if the group succeeds, the nonparticipant shares in the collective gains equally with the hardy activists who bore the costs and risks of action (lower taxes, extra social security benefits, a more responsive government, and so on).

This logic is particularly applicable in the case of **collective goods**: material or nonmaterial goods that are shared by large segments of the community rather than being divisible among individuals. Social security increases, national security, and an improved environment are examples.

Given these considerations, Olson maintains that most people will opt to be nonparticipating free riders who let others do the dirty work of political activity for them. "The paradox," Olson concludes, "is that . . . large groups, at least if they are composed of rational individuals, will *not* act in their group interest." This conclusion is strikingly counterintuitive, because it contradicts the commonsense assumption that rational people will take action in their own self-interest, or in the interest of some group to which they belong, if given the opportunity to do so. ■

Table 8.1 Forms of Political Participation

Conventional Participation	Communal Activity	Direct Contacting	Unconventional Participation
▪ Voting ▪ Campaign activity ▪ Party membership ▪ Interest group membership and lobbying	▪ Political meeting attendance ▪ NGO membership and activity	▪ Petitioning ▪ Patron–client relationships	▪ Social movements ▪ Protest ▪ Dissidence ▪ Revolution

ballpark, creating and operating a neighborhood watch organization, or launching a fund drive to finance additions to a local school or clinic.

▪ **Direct contacting** means directly petitioning elective or appointed officials or political party leaders to ask that the government address the petitioner's specific, often very individual needs.

▪ **Nonconventional** or **confrontational political participation** includes such contentious acts as creating broad social movements to promote change, mass protest, and even armed rebellion.

Democracies tend to encourage conventional participation and communal activity, while authoritarian regimes frequently do not allow those modes of political action, often forcing people to engage in contacting or confrontational acts to gain their objectives. Yet even in democracies, protest and other forms of contentious participation are growing in prevalence. Table 8.1 summarizes the forms of political participation we will be exploring in this chapter. We will work our way through these modes of political activity from left to right in the table and top to bottom within each category. Because conventional political participation is so central to the political life in democracies and has received so much attention by political scientists, our analysis will be weighted toward voting, party politics, and interest representation.

CONVENTIONAL PARTICIPATION

Voting

The scientific study of elections is called *psephology;* this term comes from the Greek word for "pebble." (In ancient Greek city-states, people voted by depositing colored pebbles into containers.) We are particularly interested in finding patterns in electoral behavior. What types of people, for example, vote for the various parties competing for power? Many observers say people tend to vote primarily in accordance with their socioeconomic status: Wealthier people tend to vote for the more conservative parties (such as the Republicans in the United States, the Conservative Party in Britain, or the Christian Democrats in Germany), and the less well-to-do tend to vote for left-of-center parties especially concerned with social welfare (such as the Democrats in the United States, the Labour Party in Britain, or the Social Democratic Party of Germany).

The scientific study of elections is called *psephology,* a particular concern of which is finding patterns in electoral behavior. Might the voting preferences of the elderly be different from those of the young?

HYPOTHESIS-TESTING EXERCISE
Socioeconomic Bases of Voting

Hypothesis People with higher socioeconomic status will support conservative parties more than will people with lower socioeconomic status.

Variables The *independent variable* is socioeconomic status, measured by household income. The *dependent variable* is the vote choice.

Expectations If the hypothesis is correct, we expect higher percentages of higher-income persons to vote for parties identified as conservative or right-leaning. Conversely, we expect higher percentages of lower-income individuals to vote for social democratic or left-leaning parties.

Evidence To test this hypothesis, we have drawn data from the Comparative Studies of Electoral Systems database, a major study that gives the same survey questionnaire to voters in many countries around the world at each major national election.[3] For this preliminary study, we will use data from four countries chosen because their party systems are simple enough to permit us to make conclusions easily. Respondents to the survey are divided into five quintiles by income—the

poorest 20 percent are in the bottom quintile; the next poorest 20 percent are in the second quintile; and so on to the richest 20 percent in the top quintile. Table 8.2 shows how voters in these income quintiles voted in the U.S. House of Representatives election in 2004 and the British House of Commons election in 2005.

As you can see, poorer Americans disproportionately voted for the Democrats and as incomes rose, the vote share for the Republicans increased. Similarly, lower-income voters in Great Britain chose Labour candidates at higher rates than did those in the richest quintile while Conservative candidates did much better among the wealthy than they did among the poor. These findings support our hypothesis. However, what about the Liberal Democrats? Where do they fit? Support for Liberal Democrats does not seem to correlate with income in quite the same way as it does for the Labour and Conservative Parties. Let's look at our other two cases quickly. Table 8.3 shows how Germans voted in their 2002 Bundestag election.

As you'll learn in Chapter 15 the German party system is more complex than the British or American examples, but here again we see some evidence that supports our hypothesis.

Table 8.2 **Income and Vote Choice in the United States and the United Kingdom**

INCOME SEGMENT	U.S. HOUSE 2004		BRITISH COMMONS 2005		
	Republicans	Democrats	Labour	Conservatives	Liberal Democrats
Poorest quintile	35	65	50	29	14
Second quintile	45	54	48	23	24
Third quintile	50	50	50	27	20
Fourth quintile	48	52	41	36	19
Richest quintile	50	47	30	39	23

Source: Author's computations based on the Comparative Study of Electoral Systems (www.cses.org), *CSES Module 2 Full Release* dataset, June 27, 2007.

Numerous factors also affect voter *turnout*. Table 8.5 shows voter turnout in the countries explored in Part Two of this book plus some other democracies. In addition to personal attributes such as one's educational level, interest in the campaign, and sense of political efficacy (Does my vote really matter?), patterns of voter turnout are also affected by such things as voter registration requirements, whether voting is compulsory, the tightness of the race, the effectiveness of political parties in getting out the vote, and even the day of the week on which elections are held (Americans vote on Tuesdays, most Europeans vote on Sundays). The generally lower turnouts in the United States compared with other countries listed in Table 8.5 are also due in part to the fact that Americans are asked to vote more often, and for more political offices, than their European counterparts are. Elections to the U.S. Congress take place every two

years, compared with every four to five years for comparable offices in most other democracies, and in the United States there are more elections for local and regional offices than there are in most other democracies.[4] Table 8.5 indicates that in the presidential and presidential–parlimentary democracies listed that have midterm or other nonsimultaneous elections for the legislature (in addition to the United States, France, Mexico, the Philippines, Poland, Russia, and South Korea), midterm elections tend to draw a significantly lower turnout than the presidential race, suggesting that voters participate more frequently in what they perceive to be high stakes elections.

Do Voters Know What They're Doing? It is a standing premise of democratic theory that voters need to be aware of what they are doing when they vote. Without a minimum level

Table 8.3 Income and Vote Choice in Germany

INCOME SEGMENT	GERMAN BUNDESTAG 2002				
	SPD	CDU/ CSU	Greens/ Alliance 90	FDP	Republicans
Poorest quintile	42	30	12	8	5
Second quintile	43	29	9	7	6
Third quintile	36	39	12	7	4
Fourth quintile	44	27	13	8	3
Richest quintile	35	38	12	10	1

Source: See Table 8.2.

Table 8.4 Income and Vote Choice in Chile

INCOME SEGMENT	CHILEAN 2005 CHAMBER OF DEPUTIES ELECTION		
	Concertación	Right	Left
Poorest quintile	47	24	3
Second quintile	49	26	3
Third quintile	49	28	5
Fourth quintile	43	33	7
Richest quintile	40	31	11

Source: See Table 8.2.

Those in the poorest quintiles tend to support the Social Democrats (SPD) at higher rates than those in the richest quintile, and Christian Democrats (CDU/CSU) tend to draw more heavily from the wealthiest Germans. But the pattern is not as clear as it was with the United States, and again, some parties don't fit into the pattern suggested by the hypothesis; for example, the Greens, who draw about equally from all income segments. Germany's radical right, the neo-Nazi Republicans, draw more heavily from lower-income sectors.

Finally, let's look at one more country in which class-based voting has a long history: Chile, shown in Table 8.4. Since Chile regained democracy in 1989, its center and left parties have aligned in a coalition called the Concertación, which controlled the government from 1990 until 2010. Its two conservative parties have usually also aligned in a right-leaning coalition. And there are two small parties of communists and ex-communists, which we have grouped here under one heading as the Left. Again the expected pattern emerges: Poorer voters disproportionately choose the center-left

Concertación parties and wealthier ones opt disproportionately for the parties of the right. But the Left parties gain higher vote shares from the wealthy than from the poor!

Conclusions Wealthier people do tend to support conservative parties disproportionately and poorer persons opt for social-democratic or labor-oriented parties of the left. However, the income variable doesn't explain all voting—almost 30 percent of the poorest quintile of German and British voters chooses conservative candidates and the figure is even higher in the United States—and many parties don't draw their support based mainly on economic issues. Knowing whether voters are richer or poorer can tell us that they may be more or less willing to support candidates of a party with a well-defined stance on economic policy, but we need to know much, much more to have a full picture of vote choice. Voting patterns in most democracies are affected by a multiplicity of factors. While income levels frequently play a major role in influencing how people vote, so do variables such as party identification, ethnicity, religion, gender, age, and ideology.

of political knowledge on the part of the electorate, the act of voting may be meaningless and the very notion of popular sovereignty illusory. Democracy thus rests on the assumption that voters are rational. Are they?

According to the standard variant of rational-choice theory, individual voters are rational to the extent that they:

1. Know what their own preferences and priorities are (lower taxes, less crime, a cleaner environment, and the like).
2. Gather as much information as they can about the various candidates and understand their positions on the issues, and they also understand what the likely consequences will be if this or that candidate gets elected.
3. Vote for those candidates who are most likely to satisfy those priorities once in office.

Some rational-choice theorists have maintained that voters are truly rational only when they seek to promote their own material self-interests. This rather narrow definition stresses personal selfishness as an essential ingredient of rationality. Voters with this type of orientation are rational if they vote for candidates who would lower their taxes or increase their social security payments, for example; they are less interested in the general welfare of the community. In a famous study published in 1957, Anthony Downs argued that voters in democracies think and act pretty much like consumers in a market economy: They know what type of product they want, they shop around and gather information about alternative models, they look at how the available products will affect their wallet, and they make a rational selection based on what is best for them. Thus each citizen, Downs hypothesized, "casts his vote

Table 8.5 Voter Turnout in Recent National Elections

Country	Date and Type of Election	Turnout (VAP)*	Good Citizens Always Vote
Brazil	2010 General	81%	69%
Canada	2011 General	54	77
France	2012 Presidential	71	80
	2012 National Assembly	51	
Germany	2009 General	65	58[†]
Hungary	2010 General	14	57
Japan	2009 General	69	67
Mexico	2009 Congressional	42	75
	2012 Presidential	65	
Nigeria	2011 Presidential	48	NA
	2011 National Assembly	26	
Philippines	2010 Presidential	65	88
	2007 Congressional	55	
Poland	2010 Presidential	49	62
	2011 Parliamentary	54	
Russia	2011 Duma	58	62
	2012 Presidential	63	
South Africa	2009 General	57	77
South Korea	2007 Presidential	64	71
	2012 National Assembly	56	
Spain	2011 General	63	68
United Kingdom	2010 General	61	56
United States	2010 Congressional	38	78
	2012 Presidential	57	

*VAP = voting age population

[†]West Germany only

Sources: International Institute for Democracy and Electoral Assistance (IDEA) voter turnout database (http://www.idea.int/vt/); U.S. Presidential Turnout: Bipartisan Policy Center (http://bipartisanpolicy.org/library/report/2012-voter-turnout); International Social Survey Programme 2004: Citizenship.

for the party he believes will provide him with more benefits than any other." Politicians, for their part, behave like sellers, rationally adjusting their "product lines" (their policies and campaign promises) so as to attract the most "buyers" (voters). Democratically elected governments and opposition parties, Downs wrote, will always act in their own self-interest: They will espouse only those policies that maximize votes, whether or not such policies are good for society in some ideal sense.[5] Do voters really behave this way?

A landmark empirical study based on election returns and interviews with voters provided considerable evidence that most Americans were anything but rational in their actual voting activity. *The American Voter,* a comprehensive analysis of elections in the late 1940s and 1950s undertaken by a team of political scientists at the University of Michigan, showed that most Americans did not vote on the issues at all. The single most important variable accounting for how the majority of Americans voted in this period was *party identification.* Those who identified themselves as Democrats tended generally to vote for Democratic Party candidates, and those who identified themselves as Republican tended to vote accordingly. Only about 20 percent of the electorate changed their long-term loyalties from one party to another. This "expressive"

explanation of voting behavior stressed the voters' psychological attachments to parties: The choices people made in the voting booth were an expression of their identification with the general long-term orientation of a particular political party (e.g., as "pro-business" or "pro-social welfare"). Voters might also identify with the party's general stance on the issues of the day and with the broad images—positive or negative—they had of the competing candidates. Thus people did not necessarily vote on the basis of a detailed knowledge of the issues or a strategic comparison of the candidates' positions, as the most stringent rational-choice criteria would assume. More recent studies have updated the concept of expressive voting.[6]

Another political scientist suggested that only about 20 percent of the U.S. citizenry is reasonably well informed about political issues, a group known as the *attentive public.* By contrast, the *mass public* has considerably less political knowledge. Additional studies have portrayed most British and French voters in a similar light.[7]

Students of U.S. voting behavior in more recent decades have somewhat altered this unflattering portrait of the average American citizen. While acknowledging that very few voters meet the strict criteria for rationality defined earlier, some scholars argue that high levels of political knowledge and analytical

Studies have shown that many people vote in terms of the party with which they identify whether or not that party stands for the individual voter's best interests.

sophistication may not be necessary for voters to make up their minds in a reasonable fashion. Most voters, they contend, have a "gut" understanding of the candidates and issues, derived in part from campaign slogans and other cues they get from politicians and the media. These simple understandings, based on information shortcuts rather than on extensive reading and analysis, are good enough for them to make electoral choices that are logically consistent with their own political preferences, however vaguely they may be articulated. Without being perfectly rational, most voters, according to this view, are not entirely irrational, either. They act in accordance with a kind of *limited rationality* (also called *low-information rationality* or *bounded rationality*).[8]

Some analysts have disputed the notion that Americans and voters in other democracies are as ignorant about politics today as voters may have been 30 or 40 years ago. Russell Dalton points out that the time costs of obtaining information about political issues are much lower nowadays than they used to be, thanks in large part to the expansion of television as an easily accessible source of news for most people. In addition, there is now a larger pool of well-educated people who have the political sophistication to process political information intelligently. Many of them no longer need to take their cues from political parties about how to vote; they can make up their own minds. The "cognitive mobilization" of ever-increasing segments of the electorate, according to Dalton, thus accounts for the rise in independent voters and for the corresponding decline in party loyalties that has been observed in the United States and Western Europe in recent decades. Other scholars have confirmed the rise of independent-minded "critical citizens" in today's democracies.[9]

One of the greatest challenges to the rational-choice perspective about voting pertains to turnout. If voters engage in a cost–benefit analysis about the act of voting, they might likely conclude that casting a ballot is not worth the effort. Why?

Each citizen's vote is one of thousands or millions of votes cast in a particular election. For example, in the 2008 California Senate election, 10,000,160 votes were registered. What is the probability that one person's vote is going to be decisive in such a contest? As you can imagine, it is near nil. Casting a vote, however, requires taking time out of your workday (because in the United States we vote on Tuesdays), perhaps standing in line for an hour or more, and, if you are not usually attentive to politics, figuring out who you plan to vote for and why. Is the expected benefit (the probability of making a decisive difference in the contest) worth the expected cost? It is hard to see how it could be if we think about voting in a narrow, cost–benefit way.

In response to this perceived paradox, an influential early analysis of the rationality of voting suggested that the benefit of voting to the individual voter included not only the voter's perceived impact on the outcome, but also a feeling of satisfaction related to having performed one's civic duty. As Table 8.5 shows, the majority of individuals in democracies believe that good citizens always vote, although that feeling is more broadly felt in some democracies than others. Political scientists have shown that there is a strong relationship between a person's sense that voting is a civic responsibility and the frequency with which one votes.[10]

Finally, a number of theorists have taken a broader view of rationality than we have been using thus far. They maintain that voters can still be considered rational even if their election-day priorities place community goals rather than personal ones at the top of the list. If a voter wants to promote environmental protection or national security, that person may still be considered a rational voter as long as she votes for candidates who openly espouse such goals. Such community-minded individuals would still gain some personal benefit if their general-welfare goals are achieved (such as clean air or a stronger national defense). Even Anthony Downs came around to this broader view of rationality, amending his original position.[11]

Campaign Activity and Political Party Membership

Political parties are organizations that seek to place their designated representatives in governmental positions. In democracies, parties are the main mechanism for providing voters with a menu of candidates and programs from which to make their electoral choices. Parties in democratic countries permit the periodic *alternation in power* between competing sets of political leaders and policy orientations. As a consequence, parties are indispensable to the functioning of contemporary democracies. But parties can also exist in nondemocratic countries. Hitler's Nazi Party, the Communist Party of the Soviet Union, the Chinese Communist Party, Saddam Hussein's Baath Party, Mexico's Institutional Revolutionary Party, and a host of others are examples of *ruling parties*. A ruling party (or power-monopolizing party) typically monopolizes state power and bans (or effectively controls) other parties. Two or more competing parties may also exist in semi-authoritarian or authoritarian states, as in contemporary Malaysia and Iran, but the government finds ways to circumscribe their influence. Any understanding of political parties must take account of the variety of roles parties can play under different political conditions and systems. For example:

- *Democratic political parties* accept democratic principles and compete for governmental positions through the electoral process in democracies.
- *Anti-democracy* or *anti-system parties* do not accept the rules and principles of democracy. Sometimes anti-system parties compete in elections, but their goal is not to promote democracy but to gain power, with the ultimate intention of destroying democracy.
- *Ruling parties* monopolize governmental power in authoritarian regimes; they are also called *power-monopolizing parties*.[12]

One thing all three party types have in common is that they seek governmental power. Whether in the legislature, the executive branch, local government, or some other state institution, or through democratic electoral procedures or force and intimidation, parties exist mainly to obtain the power to make authoritative decisions.

Particularistic and Catch-all Parties Another distinction that is commonly made when categorizing political parties is that between *particularistic* and *catch-all* parties. **Particularistic parties** are parties that confine their appeal to a particular segment of the population. When modern political parties emerged in nineteenth-century Europe and America, they often had a rather narrow appeal. Conservative parties tended to reflect the attitudes of the aristocratic upper classes and the wealthier members of the business class, while working-class parties sought their votes almost exclusively from the laboring masses in urban industrial centers. Agrarian

parties promoted the interests of farmers. These parties were defined essentially by their *social class* base. Other particularistic parties had a predominantly religious outlook. These so-called *confessional* parties usually sought the votes of Protestants or Catholics in countries with deep religious divisions. A number of them still exist. Contemporary Europe has quite a few Christian Democratic parties, but their orientation is now defined primarily by socioeconomic appeals and non-religious political issues rather than by religious considerations. Religion-centered parties are very active in a number of countries, however. Northern Ireland has Catholic and Protestant parties; Hindu and Muslim parties have large followings in India.

Islamic parties exist in a number of countries with large Muslim populations. A few of them have multiple functions in addition to trying to win governmental positions through competitive elections. In Lebanon, Hezbollah (the Party of God) has a political wing that won 14 legislative seats in the 2005 elections and placed two of its leaders in the government. It also has a well-armed militia that attacked Israel in 2006, precipitating a 33-day war; an international terrorist network that has attacked Jewish organizations around the world; a social welfare system that provides clinics, schools, cash, and other social welfare benefits to Lebanon's large Shia population; and a media operation that propagates its official positions. Hezbollah receives its weapons and hundreds of millions of dollars a year from the government of Iran. In the Palestinian Authority, Hamas (Zeal) won a majority of seats in the legislature in 2006. It has also engaged in militia and terrorist activity against Israel, and runs a network of social services for Palestinians in the West Bank and Gaza. In Pakistan, the 2008 elections saw Muslim parties on opposite sides. The Pakistan Muslim League (Q), founded by former President Pervez Musharraf, along with smaller allied Muslim parties, was opposed by the Pakistan Muslim League (N), led by former Prime Minister Nawaz Sharif. The PML(N), allied with the Pakistan People's Party (PPP), a party whose leader, Benazir Bhutto, was assassinated by a suicide bomber during an election rally, outdistanced the PML(Q) and formed a coalition government. In Chapter 7 we discussed the Muslim Brotherhood, which founded Egypt's Freedom and Justice Party to contest elections in 2011. Mohamed Morsi, ousted from the presidency in the July 2013 coup, from the Freedom and Justice Party. These and other Islamic parties around the world may participate in elections and legislatures, but their support for democratic values and procedures is ambivalent at best. Some of them openly espouse theocratic government based on Islamic law.[13]

Other particularistic parties around the world are organized to promote the interests of national or regional minorities (such as the Scottish National Party in the United Kingdom and Kurdish parties in Turkey). Still others focus on a specific issue, such as the environment, women's rights, opposition to the European Union, or the priorities of beer lovers. Ultimately, what matters is whether a particularistic

In the United States Hezbollah is known as a terrorist organization, but it is also a political party that wins legislative seats in Lebanon and provides extensive social services to its mostly Shiite Muslim followers. Here Hezbollah social workers assist residents of Beirut's southern suburbs to register the damage caused by an Israeli bombing campaign in 2006.

party accepts the rules of democracy—including compromise and cooperation with other parties when necessary to prevent gridlock or the breakdown of democracy. The particularistic religious or ethnic parties that are emerging in Iraq and Afghanistan may spell trouble for democracy if they flout these rules.

By contrast, **catch-all parties** are parties that seek to widen their base of popular support as much as possible. Their primary aim is to win elections and take control of the government. Accordingly, they try to catch all the votes they can, drawing them from a diversity of social classes, religions, ethnic groups, and other segments of the population. In the process they usually loosen their commitment to specific groups or principles and adopt more flexible positions capable of broadening their mass appeal. Sometimes catch-all parties are criticized for being so vague about the issues that the voters can't tell where they stand at all. But it is only by diluting their political consistency and opening their arms to all comers that they can amass the vote tallies they need to outpoll the other parties. Catch-all parties thus tend to be middle-of-the-road, moderate parties. They steer clear of the left and right political extremes, preferring instead to cast a wide net on either side of the political center. Over time, most of the class-based particularistic parties of Western Europe—conservative parties on the right and social-democratic parties on the left—evolved into catch-all parties. Although they may still attract their core voters from a particular tier of the socioeconomic pyramid, most of these parties today appeal to the large middle class and win votes from multiple social sectors, including the rich, the poor, women, and ethnic minorities.

According to one widely held hypothesis, catch-all parties are more supportive of stable democracy than are particularistic parties.[14] Catch-all parties, it is argued, promote moderation and compromise across social classes and other groups in society because they are so inclusive. Particularistic parties stick to their own narrow interests in a conflictual and uncompromising posture. Evidence from democracies in North America and Western Europe provides considerable support for this proposition. Virtually every generalization has its exceptions, however, and so does this one. One of the most viscerally antidemocratic parties in history, the German Nazi party, increasingly became a catch-all party as it fought its way to power through the electoral process in the late 1920s and early 1930s. With stunning rapidity the Nazis increased their share of the national vote from just 2.6 percent in 1928 to more than 37 percent by the summer of 1932, capturing votes from the upper, middle, and working classes, from urban voters and rural voters, from women as well as men, from Protestants and Catholics, and from every age group eligible to vote.[15]

In Western Europe there are party families consisting of roughly similar parties that are organized in different countries. Some of them are particularistic parties, such as the environment-friendly green parties that are organized in most countries in the region. Others are more broadly based catch-all parties like the Christian Democrats and their conservative counterparts in various countries, or the social-democratic parties that exist in virtually all Western European countries. The member parties of each family consult with one another and form voting blocs in the European Parliament, the European Union's legislature.

ESSENTIAL CONCEPTS

Responsible Party Government

For electoral democracy to work effectively, according to some theorists, three essential things must happen. First, the competing parties need to clarify as explicitly as possible what they would do if they are elected to positions of governmental responsibility. Thus each party must formulate a coherent program and spell it out to the voters in advance of election day, specifying where it stands on economic policy, social welfare policy, foreign policy, and so on. Candidates running for office need to reinforce these messages in their campaign appearances. Second, the voters need to compare the competing programs carefully and vote for the candidates most representative of their own views. And third, on taking office the victorious party must translate its campaign programs and promises into governmental action. This three-step model of responsible party government is depicted in Figure 8.1. But do things really work this way? In fact, several obstacles obstruct the smooth realization of responsible party government.

One problem arises when a political party is internally divided. Such internal fragmentation can result from disputes over party policy on domestic issues or foreign affairs; from the multiple class, ethnic, religious, or other constituencies that gravitate to the party; from leadership rivalries; or from other factors. Internal divisions of these kinds often complicate the process of what political scientists call interest aggregation.[16]

Interest aggregation is the process by which political parties gather (aggregate) the various interests, priorities, and opinions of their leaders and constituents and shape them into common goals and policy proposals. The interest-aggregation process represents step 1 in the responsible party government model shown in Figure 8.1. Some parties perform it more effectively than others. In almost all political parties in today's democracies, however, it is a complicated task that usually involves a considerable amount of negotiation and bargaining among the political elites who guide the party's fortunes. The more complex the process of internal interest aggregation, the more difficult it will be for the party to speak with a clear, unified voice to the voters.

As a consequence, the programs that parties present to the voters may be so vague or internally inconsistent that it's hard to tell exactly what the party will actually do if elected to office. Large catch-all parties are especially prone to these problems. It is quite common in the United States, for example, for candidates nominated for the presidency to casually ignore, or openly repudiate, the platform of general principles and specific proposals that is officially adopted at the party's nominating convention.

A second problem is *voter ignorance* and *shifting party alignments.* Step 2 of the responsible party government model assumes that voters have a sufficient comprehension of political affairs to make intelligent decisions in the voting booth. As we've seen, however, voters in most democracies may not be very well informed on the issues. In a recent survey, three out of four Americans could name the Three Stooges, but less than half could identify the three branches of government.[17] (Churchill remarked that "the best argument against democracy is a five-minute conversation with the average voter.") To complicate matters, in most established democracies political parties are having an increasingly difficult time holding on to a stable core of voters. *Party loyalty* is in decline in many democracies. In the United States, voter identification with the Democrats and Republicans, so prominent in the 1950s and 1960s, has diminished considerably.[18] In Western Europe, party loyalties in the 1960s were very close to what they were in the 1920s. Since then, partisan attachments have become looser in a number of European countries, and new parties have come into the picture. Party loyalties have also weakened in Japan, India, and other democracies.[19]

Voters who consistently identify themselves with one political party and vote for its candidates from one election to the next are called *partisan voters.* Sometimes certain identifiable groups in society, such as various socioeconomic classes, religious groups, or ethnic groups, tend to support a favorite party over long periods. This phenomenon is called *stable partisan alignment:* The same social groups vote for the same party time after time. But when large numbers of voters disengage their established loyalties to their favorite party and become less partisan and more independent, *partisan dealignment* is said to occur. Partisan dealignment means that once-solid supporters of a particular party no longer vote for that party's candidates automatically. They may vote for certain of its candidates depending on the stance they take on various issues, or they may gravitate to another party, or they may switch back and forth between parties from one election to the next. Voters who move back and forth in this way are called *swing voters.*

Under conditions of partisan dealignment, it becomes more difficult for parties to produce long-term programs that will attract a long-term following. By having to make frequent shifts and revisions in their programs to attract increasingly fickle and unpredictable voters, parties find it harder to represent their constituents' views in a stable fashion and support policy initiatives that may take many years to translate into effective governmental action. In short, party dealignment further complicates the task of establishing responsible party government.

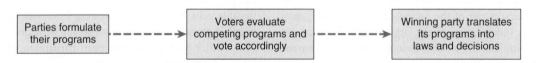

FIGURE 8.1 **Responsible Party Government Model**

Sometimes the voters may change their habits even more radically. When a large bloc of voters that traditionally votes for one party massively shifts its support to a rival party and sticks with that party over prolonged periods, *party realignment* takes place. In the United States, Southern white Protestant males were once solid Democrats. Since the 1970s, however, they have moved in large numbers to the Republicans. Whereas partisan dealignment means simply a loosening of traditional party loyalties on the part of individuals, realignment means an enduring shift from one party to another on the part of large social groups. Realignments represent major changes in a society's electoral patterns, in some cases placing new obstacles in the path of responsible party government.

A third set of obstacles is *divided* or *coalition government*. After the election, it's up to the elected officials to translate their programs and promises into authoritative actions (step 3 of the responsible party government model). This process can be strewn with hazards, however. In some presidential democracies, such as the United States, Brazil, and Mexico, the voters may elect a president of one party and a legislative majority of a rival party or parties. As such cases of divided government frequently demonstrate, it is usually more difficult to convert the competing proposals of rival parties into government actions than it is to convert the proposals of just one governing party. In democracies that have a parliamentary system of government, as explained in Chapter 6, two or more parties may be forced to form a coalition government or a parliamentary alliance to attain a working majority in the legislature. Once again, the more parties that are involved in the decision-making process, the more difficult it is for any individual party to give the voters what it promised.

A fourth obstacle blocking implementation of the responsible party government model is a *lack of party discipline*. Party discipline means the party's entire legislative delegation votes together unanimously on bills that come up for a vote. Party discipline is traditionally somewhat low in the United States, although it has increased in recent years. Members of Congress have usually financed their own election campaigns and are not financially dependent on their party. In addition, the American system of separation of powers gives members of Congress an institutional independence from the presidency. As a result, presidents may not be able to convince legislators in their own party to go along with their policies.

Party discipline is relatively higher in parliamentary democracies such as Britain and Germany. Even in these countries, however, the unity of the party's legislative delegation may occasionally break down as individual legislators diverge from their party leadership on roll call votes.

The ideal of responsible party government can be very difficult to achieve in well-established democracies; it can be even more elusive in newly democratizing countries. In countries that are making the transition from authoritarianism to democracy in Eastern Europe, Latin America, East Asia, Africa, and elsewhere, new parties must be formed from the ground up or, in some cases, re-formed on the remains of parties that once existed under earlier democratic regimes. As Chapter 18 shows in the case of Brazil it can take quite a few years before these parties solidify into stable organizations with fairly coherent political orientations, widespread voter recognition, and a core of loyal voters. Some will probably fall by the wayside. If these fledgling democracies are to take root, however, parties will have to play a major role in forging vital links between the population and the state. ■

Party Systems The term **party system** refers to the number of parties within a country, their ideological orientations, and various other general patterns. We'll consider just one variable feature of party systems here: the *number* of parties to be found within a given system.

Some democracies are dominated over prolonged periods by one party. These are called *predominant-party systems*. Japan, for example, was governed uninterruptedly by the Liberal Democratic Party (LDP) from 1955 to 1993. Although other parties ran against the LDP in freely contested elections, they were not able to win a parliamentary majority until the LDP suffered severe losses in voter support in the 1990s because of corruption scandals. A more extreme example is Mexico, which was governed by the Institutional Revolutionary Party (PRI) from 1929 until 2000, when Vicente Fox, a challenger from a rival party, won the presidential election. Although several parties had increased their share of the vote from the 1970s onward, the PRI remained Mexico's predominant party until it lost the all-important presidency to Fox.

Very few countries have a predominantly *two-party system*. The United States, of course, is one of them. While third parties have cropped up now and then on the national scene, they have not fared very well in getting their candidates elected to Congress or the presidency. Some people regard Britain as having a two-party system. To be sure, the Conservative and Labour Parties have taken turns running the government since World War II without having to take on other parties as coalition partners until the 2010 general election, after which the Conservatives and the Liberal Democrats had to form a coalition government. Britain might more appropriately be characterized as having moderate pluralism or a *moderate multiparty system*. Moderate multiparty systems typically have about three to five important parties. Contemporary France, Germany, Japan, and Canada also fall into this category.

Still other countries have *extreme multiparty systems*. Extreme multiparty systems typically have six or more parties that play a significant political role, electing their candidates to the national legislature, participating in coalition governments or parliamentary alliances, providing critical support in key legislative votes, or obstructing government actions they don't like. The Scandinavian countries, Poland, Israel, and Italy provide examples of extreme multiparty systems.

Some theorists contend that a moderate multiparty system is optimal because it gives voters more choice than a two-party system. It also creates more stable party attachments than an extreme multiparty system, which provides too many incentives to desert one party for another. In *Exit, Voice, and Loyalty,* Albert Hirschman argued that voters essentially have two choices when they no longer agree with the policies pursued by their favorite party. Either they can raise their *voice* within the party in an attempt to persuade its leaders to change course, or they can *exit* the party and shift their votes to a rival one. The choice they make will depend largely on their degree of party loyalty. Hirschman concludes that the ideal party system will have enough competing parties to give voters acceptable alternatives should they choose to exit, but it will not have so many parties that people will have no incentive to use their voice within their initial party of preference. Hirschman does not specify how many parties would meet these requirements, but he implies that a moderate multiparty system with three to five parties would be ideal.[20]

Interest Group Membership and Lobbying

Interest groups are organizations that speak up for the interests and demands of particular groups of people, often with the aim of influencing the state to do something in their behalf. They provide another means of participation in democratic political systems. They promote the aims of specific segments of the mass public by exerting pressure on political parties, candidates, and government officials. In the terminology developed by Almond and Powell, interest groups perform the function of **interest articulation** when they articulate the interests, demands, and desires of various groups in society. Political parties and interest groups are called intermediate organizations: They are located between the population and the state. At least

in democracies, one of their aims is to enable citizens to influence state actions.

The term *interest* covers a wide range of concerns. Often when we speak of people's interests we mean their material interests—matters related to their income, cost of living, quality of housing, and so forth. But many interest groups strive to promote public policies that do not directly affect members' material interests. Anti-abortion and pro-choice organizations in the United States or Britain's League Against Cruel Sports and its rival, the Countryside Alliance, which lobby Parliament about fox hunting, are examples of groups lobbying political authorities over moral concerns.

Not all interest groups are interested exclusively in political activities. In many cases they try to promote their group interests without recourse to government involvement. Trade unions, for example, may work out their problems over pay and working conditions through direct interactions with company executives, employing negotiations, strikes, and other bargaining techniques. In political science we are mainly concerned with the *political* activities of interest groups. When trade unions or business associations ask the state to take their side in a labor dispute or in support of specific governmental economic policies, their actions become decidedly political. In the United States and some other democracies, many interest groups have *lobbies,* which work directly to influence government policy, usually by establishing contacts with government decision makers. In 2005 there were about 11,500 active lobbyists in Washington, D.C., while a 2007 British study reported that many members of Parliament are approached by more than 100 lobbyists per week.[21]

Associational interest groups are organizations that speak up for specific segments of a country's population who share common problems and goals. They are more likely to be found in democracies, which permit freedom of association, than in authoritarian states, which usually do not allow such groups

Political participation includes the activities of interest groups such as Britain's League Against Cruel Sports that lobbies against the practice of fox hunting, which many view as inhumane.

to be established independently of state control. Associational interest groups display considerable variety. Some articulate the economic interests of their supporters, such as trade unions and business associations. Others may represent ethnic groups (such as the National Association for the Advancement of Colored People), gender and sexual preference groups (the National Organization for Women; the Gay Alliance), generational groups (the American Association of Retired Persons), religious groups (the Christian Coalition), and specific-issue groups (the National Rifle Association or Britain's League Against Cruel Sports).

Private institutional groups are organizations that are organized primarily for some purpose other than political action. Private corporations, such as Royal Dutch Shell or Microsoft, and established religious institutions, such as the Roman Catholic Church or the Anglican Church, are examples. Like associational groups, these private groups may also have lobbying offices to represent their interests in contacts with public officials.

No consideration of interest groups can be complete without a reference to groups in society that do *not* clearly articulate their common interests. Even in flourishing democracies, there may be segments of society with identifiable political interests that, for one reason or another, do not succeed in building interest groups or call attention to their grievances through anomic behavior. An example is people who are not covered by any kind of medical insurance in the United States. In 2006, this segment of the population amounted to an estimated 46 million people. Their problems were acknowledged by political leaders in both major parties, but they had no formal organization or other mechanism for collectively articulating their concerns. Countries all over the globe have their own examples of unorganized social groups that are not able to articulate their political needs effectively. Dayworkers, child laborers, abused or oppressed women—these and other politically voiceless people, numbering in the millions, confirm the enormous importance of interest groups precisely because they do not have them.

If you reflect on Olson's logic of collective action that we discussed at the beginning of this chapter, you begin to appreciate the challenge of pulling together the efforts of many ordinary people sharing an interest—like not having health insurance. While each may want to do something politically to address the problem, there is a powerful temptation to wait for someone else to take the lead and then to be a free rider once leaders emerge. Why should I contribute from my meager, hard-earned income to the financial resources of an organization lobbying to extend health insurance when there are 46 million others who could do it?

In recent years, political activists have sought to overcome the collective-action problem by using the Internet to organize people who otherwise find it difficult to coordinate their political efforts. By 2009 MoveOn.org claimed to have 5.2 million members who receive several e-mails weekly urging them to contribute money to an interest group lobbying the administration or the Congress on a matter of current concern, to donate to a political campaign, or to contact elected officials directly. More focused associational interest groups have also used Internet links to their advantage in encouraging their members to contact public officials or support their lobbying efforts financially.

ESSENTIAL CONCEPTS

Pluralism and Corporatism

Precisely how interest groups function can differ markedly from one country to another. There is a basic distinction, for example, between *pluralism* and *corporatism*.

Pluralism is a concept of democracy that asserts that political power is dispersed among a plurality of groups and interests. It is not monopolized by one particular social group or by a unified power elite. Interest-group pluralism emphasizes the following:

- *Freedom of association,* which means that people are free to organize their own interest groups.
- *Competition for influence,* which means that interest groups on different sides of an issue freely compete for the attention of legislators and other authoritative decision makers and seek to influence their actions.

This model of interest-group pluralism is best exemplified by the United States. Typically, as Congress considers legislation on a particular issue, interest groups concerned with how the outcome will affect their constituents' bank accounts or quality of life will seek to influence the way individual legislators vote. In the wide-open U.S. system, groups are free to use a variety of persuasive techniques to state their case: television and newspaper advertisements, e-mails and blogs, analytical reports, expert testimony, organized demonstrations, letter-writing campaigns, and so on. Those with direct access to members of Congress (an access purchased, perhaps, with generous campaign contributions) can buttonhole legislators in face-to-face meetings, at times in the comfortable settings of country clubs, conference resorts, or trendy restaurants. The line between what is legally permitted in these attempts to exercise political clout and what is illegal can be a thin one: Influence is at times barely distinguishable from bribery. Instances of corruption, whether blatant or subtle, have not been uncommon.

In some cases the American system of interest-group pluralism can delay legislation for months or even years. It can even prevent Congress from taking any action. For example, the Clinton administration attempted to win congressional approval of a new national health care system in 1993–94. Organizations on either side of the issue besieged senators and representatives, spending tens of millions of dollars to either defeat the Clinton proposal or get it passed. After a year, no congressional majority could be found for the Clinton plan, nor for any alternative. More than 40 million Americans were left uninsured. Only in 2010 did the Congress enact health care reform of the scale envisioned by the Clinton administration, and since then interest groups opposed to the Patient Protection and Affordable Care Act have sought to use the courts and electoral politics to overturn aspects of that law.

Despite these and other problems, however, Congress passes thousands of bills every session. In the process, a large number of interest groups have ample opportunity to influence the results. Other democracies have their own variants of interest-group pluralism.

Corporatism represents a different approach to involving interest groups in the policy process. Defined in very broad terms, **corporatism** is a system of formal interest-group participation in the state's decision-making processes. Different versions of corporatism have existed at different periods of time and in different political systems. Corporatism has been variously conceptualized and embraced by the Roman Catholic Church, fascist dictatorships under Mussolini and Hitler, military dictatorships in Latin America, authoritarian regimes in Portugal and Mexico, and modern democracies including Austria, Germany, and Sweden. These and other proponents of corporatist methods share some ideas but diverge, at times considerably, in their application of those ideas.

One of the most widely shared commonalities of corporatist thinking is the notion that leading representatives of the key groups in society—especially business and labor—should negotiate directly with government officials to work out the country's principal economic and social welfare policies. We'll confine ourselves in this chapter to sketching out a very generalized model (an ideal type) of modern corporatism as it works in several democracies today. Along the way we'll highlight some salient differences between corporatism and U.S.-style pluralism. We also want to note that corporatism can be applied in very nondemocratic, coercive ways, as fascists sought to do in interwar Europe and as authoritarian regimes did in Brazil and Mexico (see Chapter 18).

Corporatism in contemporary democracies (sometimes called *neo-corporatism*) typically consists of the following institutions and procedures:

1. The main groups in society involved in economic production—notably industry, labor, and agriculture—form large interest groups that represent a large proportion, sometimes the majority, of the people in their respective sector. These large interest groups are called *peak associations*. A peak association for labor will thus represent a high percentage of the country's factory workers. For example, over 80 percent of unionized workers belong to Germany's Federation of Trade Unions. The peak associations tend to be hierarchically organized; that is, their national leaders exercise considerable influence over the rank and file at local levels. (In the United States, such peak associations are rare; each industry tends to have its own labor unions that bargain with employers. The AFL-CIO, American labor's large umbrella organization, does not engage in corporatist-style bargaining.) Figure 8.2 shows the organizational chart of a peak association, the Swedish Trade Union Confederation (known as the *LO*). Note how it has a pyramidal structure: one peak association (the LO), 15 national unions, hundreds of local, regional, and enterprise-level affiliates, and about 1.5 million individual members. The LO leadership seeks to speak for all 1.5 million members.

2. Leaders of the main peak associations, especially those representing the business sector and labor, meet on a regular basis with representatives of the state, who are usually from the executive branch rather than the legislature. The executive branch representatives may include the prime minister, other cabinet ministers, their deputies, or key bureaucrats in relevant ministries. Under corporatism, the executive branch plays a more important role in dealing with business and labor groups than the legislature does. (In the United States, by contrast, Congress tends to play a more active role than the president in dealing with interest groups.)

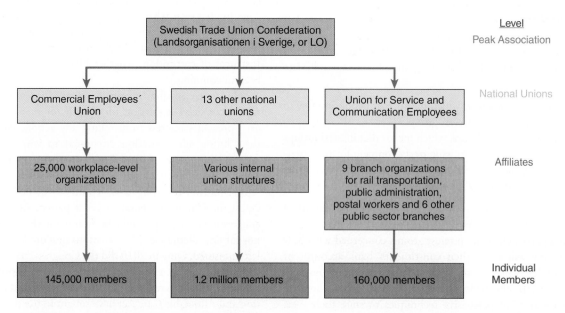

FIGURE 8.2   A Peak Association: The Swedish *LO*

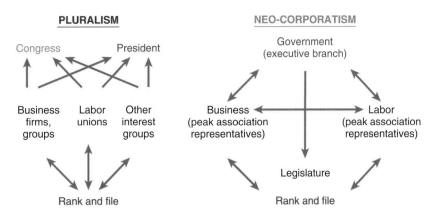

FIGURE 8.3   Models of Interest-Group Pluralism and Neo-Corporatism

3. Together these representatives of the main peak associations and the state work out deals on such economic issues as taxes, wages, working conditions, social welfare benefits, and the like. (In the United States, the government usually does not get involved in brokering agreements between unions and employers on wages or working conditions.)

4. Once agreements are worked out, the business and labor negotiators go back to their respective groups and solicit the reactions of their members. If the rank and file does not accept the agreements, they may have to be renegotiated. But the leaders of the peak associations frequently exert pressure on the membership to go along with the deals they have worked out in the tripartite negotiations on the grounds that they are the best possible under present circumstances.

5. If appropriate, the national legislature ratifies the agreed-upon arrangements by passing them into law. In parliamentary systems, the government can usually count on commanding the parliamentary majority to facilitate this procedure. Often the parliament's role is limited to voting on a done deal.

6. The peak association leaders then urge their respective members to carry out the agreements. If they fail, the agreements may have to be renegotiated.

Compared with the freewheeling style of American pluralism, neo-corporatism is typically a more orderly and regularized process. Bilateral and tripartite negotiations among business, labor, and government are often an ongoing process. However, corporatism can also be a more closed process than pluralism is. The negotiations tend to occur behind closed doors, centered in the executive branch of government. It is not always as open a process as those fought out in the legislature.[22]

Proponents of corporatist procedures argue that they provide the government with an effective way of keeping the economy running smoothly, based on constant negotiations with business and labor leaders who are armed with broad negotiating powers. (For a description of neo-corporatism in Germany, see Chapter 15.) In the United States, however, the government has less direct influence over business or labor. Critics of the American system charge that the U.S. economy is less coordinated and less efficient as a result. Critics of corporatism note that the negotiations among the key parties are often closed to outsiders, plus interests not represented in the corporatist structure have few avenues to express their demands and grievances. In Germany, for example, those who questioned the industry-centered economic development model because of its environmental consequences found that the corporatist system did not afford them a channel in which to express their concerns. Consequently they had to participate in unconventional ways, through protest movements and other forms of direct action, and these environmentally oriented Germans ended up founding a new party, the Green Party. Figure 8.3 compares pluralism and neo-corporatism. ■

COMMUNAL ACTIVITY

Although we often think of actions by which citizens attempt to shape the composition of government (voting or campaigning) or public policy (lobbying) as the principal means of participating politically, doing so overlooks many activities by which ordinary people cooperate in nonpartisan ways to deal with social problems. Most Americans are familiar with the work of Neighborhood Watch, where people living in a neighborhood agree collectively to watch their area and report any suspicious activities to the police. Similar organizations have emerged in other countries, including Britain (Neighbourhood Watch), New Zealand (Neighbourhood Support), and Canada (Block Parents Program). Many civic associations mobilize people to achieve collective objectives without primarily involving government action.

Another form of communal participation comes through the many meetings of government bodies that citizens are invited to attend. Local school boards usually open their meetings to the public and thereby hear the advice and criticism that citizens give them about the local schools. Planning agencies invite local residents to hearings when new roads or infrastructure projects are being considered. Throughout the advanced democracies, increasing citizen involvement in public debate about community issues has emerged as the result of "sunshine laws" and class-action suits by which groups of citizens seek to shape their local and regional authorities' decisions. These forms of "new politics," as they are sometimes called, are not restricted to advanced democracies, however.[23] In Porto Alegre, Brazil, a complex process of participatory budgeting has emerged by which ordinary citizens have opportunities to attend meetings throughout a yearlong budgeting cycle at which the spending priorities of the municipal government are determined.[24]

To gauge whether a person has been involved in communal activity, survey researchers often ask respondents whether they have worked together with others to solve a common problem. Figure 8.4 shows the percentage of respondents in several countries who reported doing so in the past five years. As you can see, while about a third of Americans, Canadians, and Filipinos report that they have engaged in such communal activity, much smaller shares of the populations of two former communist countries—Russia and Poland—and two East Asian democracies—Japan and South Korea—indicate that they have done so.

In many places, communal activity involves working together to achieve what the government cannot or will not do. For example, when many Latin American governments cut back on social support services in the 1980s as part of their efforts to reorient their economic development strategies, including reducing or eliminating subsidies on staple foods, citizens in poor neighborhoods often organized soup kitchens where residents took turns preparing meals that helped to share the costs of preparing food while also allowing some women to take jobs to supplement their family incomes. These groups, usually mostly women, sometimes also shared child care responsibilities, engaged in neighborhood crime watch efforts, and tried to influence public policy by contacting government officials (who were not responsive most of the time). Such groups are one example of *nongovernmental organizations* (NGOs).

NGOs

The term *nongovernmental organization* can cover a myriad of associations. NGO usually refers to a nonprofit, voluntary citizens organization. An NGO's members might be ordinary people as well as experts on the organization's special issue. NGOs perform many tasks, including humanitarian and service roles such as those described above; informing the public about social problems; and seeking to influence governments, international institutions, private corporations and other relevant bodies to take action on particular issues. NGOs' efforts can be focused locally, nationally, or internationally. While NGOs share features with interest groups and social movements, their key characteristics are that they are voluntary, independent of government, not seeking to make a profit or to benefit their members materially (unlike interest groups), and typically organized by some type of internal statutes (unlike social movements).

NGOs that focus on community improvement at the local or regional level are good examples of communal activity. India, a country with a long history of voluntarism, claims more than

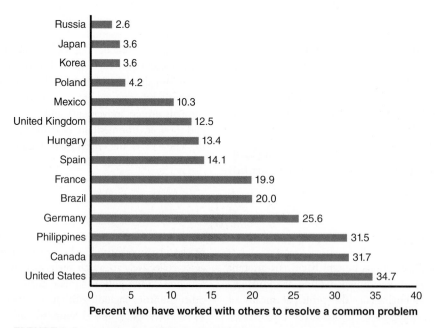

FIGURE 8.4   Communal Activity in 14 Countries
Source: Comparative Study of Electoral Systems (CSES), Module 2 (June 2007).

a million NGOs. Many of these NGOs promote the collaboration of local residents with state-level or national government development projects or with international funding agencies such as the World Bank. Often these NGOs are formed by middle-class professionals to promote the interests of the poor in a locality. As an example of how NGOs facilitate communal activity, in Baroda, a city in the Indian state of Gujarat, a local NGO, the Baroda Citizens' Council (BCC), worked with the Baroda municipal government on housing projects over many years. The local authorities provided land and some of the building materials while the BCC provided the labor to build over 10,000 homes for poor residents.[25]

Frequently, locally based NGOs become aligned with national and international NGOs in networks that seek to influence public policy. Another example from India illustrates how these networks facilitate political participation. As part of its national development policy, the government of India has promoted the erection of many large dams to provide hydroelectric power and irrigation water. One very large dam was planned for the Narmada River in the state of Gujarat; it included a 455-foot-high dam whose reservoir would have displaced as many as 320,000 people. The World Bank, the state government of Gujarat, and the national government proposed to fund the building of the dam, its electrical distribution grid, and irrigation tributaries. As the expected impact of building the dam and flooding hundreds of villages became clear in advanced planning phases, local NGOs such as Gujarat's Action Research in Community Health and Development (ARCH-Vahini) stepped forward to protest. They found allies in international NGOs, notably Oxfam, the transnational development organization that originated in Britain, and Survival International, a transnational NGO that supports tribal peoples (a large number of the affected people were from indigenous groups). While local NGOs organized demonstrations by thousands of people from affected communities to draw national attention to their cause, the transnational NGOs and ARCH-Vahini successfully pressured the World Bank to abandon its funding of the dam. The government of Gujarat was not to be stopped, however. It found alternative financing and built the dam despite an Indian Supreme Court judgment that ordered the construction to halt. In this case, a widespread mobilization of citizen participation through an alliance of many local NGOs with national and international NGOs influenced one major international actor (the World Bank) and one major national institution (the Supreme Court) to change a major policy decision, but it could not overcome the determination of another (the government of Gujarat) to complete its project.[26]

Most NGOs are based in democracies, but a growing number of them are mushrooming in nondemocratic states, boosted by Internet linkages at home and abroad. By enabling their often far-flung constituents to take part in their activities—through exchanges of information, fund-raising drives, and e-mail letter-writing campaigns addressed to governments—NGOs are playing an increasingly important role in expanding political participation on a global scale.[27]

Social Capital

Healthy communal participation of the types we described above depends on the presence of high levels of social capital. As political scientist Robert Putnam writes, *social capital* means "features of social life—networks, norms, and trust—that enable participants to act together more effectively to pursue shared objectives."[28] Putnam's definition points to two dimensions in this concept. First, social capital emerges from associational involvement—belonging to organizations such as the PTA, the Rotary Club, even sports clubs like bowling leagues. Through memberships in civic and other associations and through volunteer activities on behalf of these organizations we develop social networks of individuals we can call on to work in other endeavors, including political activities such as campaigning to pass a school levy or to support a candidate for office. Associational activities also build the second dimension of social capital, the development of attitudes such as trust in neighbors and fellow citizens, confidence in public institutions, and commitment to civic voluntarism.

Social scientists have shown that the degree to which the residents of different countries have a vigorous involvement in civic association varies dramatically. One study showed that more than twice as many Americans and Canadians are involved in organizations as French, Japanese, or Spanish citizens, and that rates of providing active, unpaid work to those organizations are about twice as high in the United States and Canada as in France, Japan, or Spain.[29] Levels of interpersonal trust vary significantly across countries too, with advanced democracies exhibiting the highest levels of social trust. Social capital, particularly in the dimension of belonging to associations, proves to be strongly associated with political participation. Those who volunteer for hospital auxiliary associations, attend weekly Kiwanis meetings, or belong to an environmental club that works to improve local parks are also more likely to vote or to engage in a campaign.[30]

DIRECT CONTACTING

Have you ever written to your member of Congress? Constituent service occupies many hours of staff time in the offices of U.S. House and Senate members, as many political science majors who intern on Capitol Hill or in the district offices of their representative learn very quickly. Writing, e-mailing, or calling your senator or U.S. House member is one example of individual contacting, a common but often underemphasized form of political participation.

Many organizations across the American political spectrum have learned how to urge their members or followers to contact elected and appointed officials to express their views on public policies currently under consideration in Congress or at a particular government agency. Much individual contacting, however, does not concern matters of general public interest. Instead, it relates to an individual's particular needs. Legislators and other elected officials in the United States and many other countries are often asked to help a constituent fix a problem—the lighting

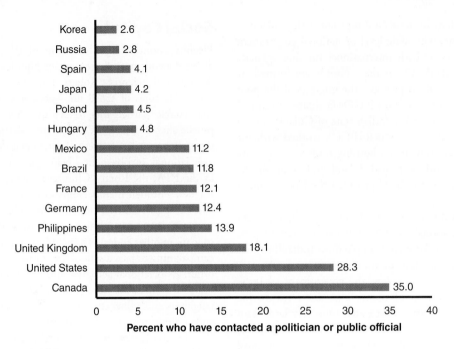

FIGURE 8.5   Direct Contacting in 14 Countries

on the street in front of one's home is inadequate or the street needs to be repaved; a family member has applied for a job with the municipal government; one's contracting company has put in a bid on a repaving project. Constituents often contact public officials to ask for special consideration on matters like these and in most democracies and many nondemocracies they expect those officials to lend an ear. In contrast to the public goods that we think most political participation is intended to influence, direct contacting is usually intended to have impact on *private goods*, government policies that have influence on individuals or small groups rather than large groups. Figure 8.5 shows that the likelihood that someone has contacted a politician or public official varies considerably across societies, with respondents in some formerly communist countries reporting almost no direct contacting, whereas in some long-established Western democracies direct contacting is fairly common. Direct contacting on matters pertaining to one's individual interest is particularly common in societies where clientelism shapes people's interactions with public authorities. Brazil, Mexico, and the Philippines are relatively new democracies in which patron–client relationships have a long history.

Patron–Client Relationships

Clientelism typically involves a political organization (such as a party) that dispenses benefits or favors to people in exchange for their votes or other forms of support. In contrast to mass electoral politics and large-scale interest-group activity, patron–client relationships generally operate on a smaller, more personalized scale. Their origins are rooted in the personal ties that developed in preindustrial societies between local authorities and ordinary villagers or peasants in need of advice, favors, or perhaps a job from authoritative figures. The patrons in these

relationships could be the village mayor, a respected landowner, or other local notables who did not necessarily hold official governmental positions. Their clients were those who came forward, hat in hand, with a favor to ask. Patrons who did favors for a large number of clients could accumulate considerable personal power and prestige in the local community.

With the advent of urban industrialism in the nineteenth century and the expansion of electoral democracy that accompanied it in the United States and certain parts of Europe, patron–client relationships moved into the big cities and became politicized. Now it was political figures, particularly those connected with vote-generating urban political machines, who became patrons for all sorts of clients struggling to make a life for themselves in the intimidating maze of mass society: local residents trying to climb out of poverty, recent arrivals from rural hinterlands, immigrants from near and far. With their hands on the apparatus of city, regional, and occasionally national government, politicians and their well-connected associates dispensed jobs, contracts, and other favors to a widening clientele. In exchange for these considerations, the clients provided their patrons with a highly cherished reward: votes. This style of political activity, as illustrated in Figure 8.6, became especially prevalent in the United States and Italy.[31]

Patron–client networks of various types continue to exist today in a number of countries. Often it is a powerful political party, one with access to government funds and jobs, that is the principal patron in these relationships. In quite a few cases these relationships are marked by bribery, favoritism, and other forms of corruption. The Congress Party of India, the Institutional Revolutionary Party of Mexico, the Liberal Democratic Party of Japan, and various parties in Greece, Italy, the Philippines, and elsewhere have been characterized by "clientelistic" relationships of one sort or another.

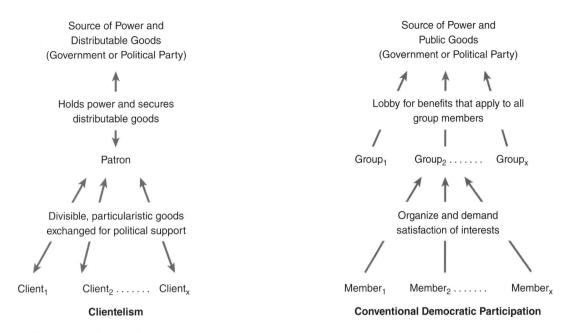

FIGURE 8.6   Clientelism Compared to Conventional Democratic Participation

CONTENTIOUS POLITICS AND PROTEST

Most of the citizen participation we have described so far in this chapter has either taken place through recognized institutional channels (e.g., voting, campaigning, or lobbying) or has involved largely cooperative activity among citizens to accomplish collective goals (much of communal activity). However, politics can be highly conflictual. Indeed, when we read in our newspapers about politics in other countries it is often because political conflict has become violent. Recent headlines have highlighted ongoing protests about who will hold power in

Egypt; demonstrations by hundreds of thousands of Greeks who opposed cuts in the public-sector budget; and public clashes between Venezuelan police and citizens protesting former President Hugo Chávez's decision to shut down a cable television channel.

In **contentious politics** one or more actors engage in disruptive activities to express a political perspective, including making demands on the government in an attempt to shape public policy. Democratic regimes are designed so as to direct political participation in peaceful ways within institutional channels like the electoral arena and the legislative process. They do not always succeed, however. While contentious

Public demonstrations such as this one of the Ecuadoran indigenous rights group CONAIE are examples of contentious politics, in which people publicly, sometimes violently contest public policy.

politics can take place within existing democratic political institutions, some of the more potent examples of the challenging types of political activity that we associate with contentious politics occur outside of the institutional framework of an existing regime. Prominent examples include social movements, protests, and revolution.

Social Movements

Social movements consist of segments of the population who engage in significant collective action because they believe that neither the state nor the established political parties or interest groups have adequately addressed their concerns. Women, gays, environmentalists, peace advocates, indigenous rights proponents, and others have formed social movements in many of the world's democracies, especially since the 1960s and 1970s. Because they view the existing modes of expressing grievances and getting the state's attention as ineffective, social movements often engage in highly contentious forms of political activity: demonstrations, strikes, disruptive behavior, and even revolutionary violence.

Why do people decide to take time-consuming and potentially risky political action instead of behaving like the inactive free riders hypothesized by Olson? Students of contentious politics like Sidney Tarrow have argued that, in democracies and nondemocracies alike, social movements tend to form when people who are dissatisfied with the status quo suddenly perceive new opportunities to pressure those in authority. Such opportunities may arise because a potentially more responsive government has come to power, or because economic conditions are conducive to change. People are also prone to act when the costs and constraints of action decline—because the ruling elites are divided or vulnerable, or because their acts of repression are no longer intimidating. And when people are able to make common cause with other aggrieved groups in society, they can build alliances and strong networks of cooperation that permit sustained political activity. National protest movements in eighteenth-century Europe and more recent struggles such as the American civil rights movement, labor unrest in Western Europe, the quest for democracy in former communist countries, and peasant protests in contemporary China have many features in common. Social movements are but one facet of the broader phenomenon of contentious politics, which has common causal mechanisms and other distinguishing features.[32]

Protest

We have typically understood political protest as an extreme expression of political dissatisfaction and frustration that cannot be handled through more institutionalized channels of participation. Who rushes to the barricades? Those who have no other options, is our standard understanding. Hence we often expect to find protest activity—whether it be organized, peaceful mass demonstrations; blocking roads and bridges; occupying buildings; even riots and the vandalism often associated with them—to be more likely in nonresponsive regimes like dictatorships. "People Power," for instance, brought down the regime of the Philippine dictator Ferdinand Marcos in February 1986 through a series of mass demonstrations in Manila that followed Marcos's blatant use of electoral fraud to defeat his rival, Corazon Aquino, in the presidential race that year. Because Filipinos did not find the expression of their democratic will respected by the Marcos regime, the argument goes, they turned to protest to demand the dictator's resignation. And they succeeded when Marcos abdicated after several days of mass protest.

A commonsense understanding of protest goes like this: Political frustration leads to small acts of protest; small acts of protest, if they receive no satisfactory response from authorities, may escalate to mass demonstrations; when mass demonstrations are met with resistance by a recalcitrant government, violent rebellion threatens to break out. While that understanding of protest describes what often occurs in nondemocratic settings, it does not explain why protest has become common in advanced democracies. Figure 8.7 shows that protest, as measured by attendance at a meeting or demonstration, is a fairly common form of participation in Spanish and French democracy. Meanwhile, in the former communist countries shown in the chart as well as East Asian democracies, protest activity is relatively rare. Those nations also had relatively low rates of involvement in other modes of participation. Filipinos, who are fairly active in communal activity (see Figure 8.4) and direct contacting (see Figure 8.5), are less likely to protest, the famous marches that brought down Marcos notwithstanding.

As Figure 8.7 shows, a considerable share of the citizens of some European and North American democracies have engaged in challenging acts, over a quarter in France and Spain. Moreover, those most likely to protest turn out to be those we expect to be most able to use the normal institutional channels—participating in election campaigns, lobbying, and communicating directly with their elected representatives. That is, protesters are more likely to be well educated, members of civic associations, and attached to political parties than are nonprotesters.[33]

These findings force us to reconsider our understanding of protest. In terms of the frequency of its use, protest rivals campaign activity as a form of participation in the advanced democracies. Indeed, in many countries it is as routine as campaigning for a candidate. One German researcher reports that in Berlin between 2,000 and 2,500 protests occur each year. In the 1990s Mexico City recorded an average of 375 protest marches annually, while in Brazil, Brasília (the capital) and São Paulo (the largest city) together averaged almost 375 demonstrations each year.[34] Why is protest becoming so common? As Dalton argues, "Protesters are people who have the ability to organize and participate in political activities of all forms, including protest."[35] The only distinct characteristic of protesters is that they tend to be young. As education and access to political information has advanced, more and more people choose to implement multiple forms of political participation. Protest has become yet one more element in the repertoire of the politically active in advanced democracies. A prominent example of the use of protest in advanced democracies is the Occupy movement to

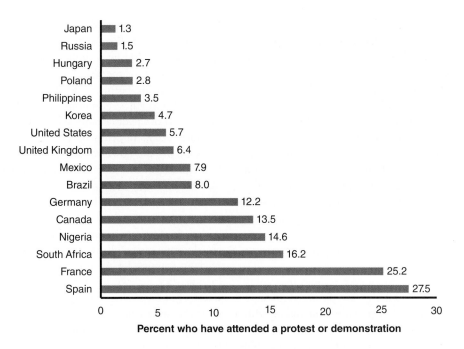

FIGURE 8.7 **Attendance at a Protest or Demonstration in 16 Countries**
Sources: Comparative Study of Electoral Systems (CSES), Module 2 (June 2007); Afrobarometer, 4th Wave (2008).

promote reform of the financial sector. The most flagrant instance took place in New York, as a broad coalition of individuals and groups sought to occupy Wall Street.

Meanwhile, protest forms one of the most effective modes of participation for those living in nondemocracies. Demonstrations led by a multi-class alliance of anti-regime protesters led to the fall of the strongman governments of Tunisia, Egypt, and Yemen in 2011. In those cases, protest was the only effective nonviolent means of pressuring those Arab governments.

In Yemen, the regime's resistance to protests led to more violent actions by anti-regime forces. In Syria, the Assad regime's use of military force against demonstrators has caused the Syrian opposition to turn to open military rebellion against Assad. The reaction of the government to an opposition movement that has opted to use nonviolent protests as its primary means of presenting its demands can play a major role in leading that opposition into even more unconventional forms of political activity, such as guerrilla war or other forms of violent protest.

ESSENTIAL CONCEPTS

Mass Participation in Nondemocratic Regimes

Authoritarian regimes usually do not allow much free political participation by the people, if any. Some of them may have the trappings of democracy, such as elections, parties, interest groups, and news media, but the population's ability to use these mechanisms is rarely free; it is typically controlled by the ruling authorities. Mass participation in nondemocratic political systems is usually *coerced participation*. The people, having no parties or interest groups of their own to represent or articulate their desires, are often reduced to an atomized "mass society": an amorphous crowd with no effective organizations to express or aggregate their interests and thus no direct way to influence the actions of the state.[36]

Nevertheless, various authoritarian governments, in the past as well as today, have seen to it that the masses do participate in political activities under the state's direction. Such participation is generally meant to provide support to the regime and its rulers. Some of these nondemocratic regimes

have staged *uncontested elections*. The population may be asked (and in some cases compelled) to approve the existing top leader in an orchestrated "election" or referendum in which the leader is unopposed. Napoleon, Saddam Hussein, and Egypt's Hosni Mubarak are among those who employed this technique. Alternatively, the people may be asked to vote for handpicked candidates for a national legislature. For each legislative seat there is typically only one candidate, someone chosen by the ruling authorities; the voters have no real choice. In most of these cases, the legislature so elected is of little importance, since the main political decisions are made by the higher-ups in the state's executive machinery. Both the electoral process and the elected organs are purely *symbolic* in nature: The symbols of democracy are present but not the reality. The ruling authorities use these procedures mainly to manipulate and control the public, giving the masses they rule a false sense of participating in the affairs of state. Before 1989, the Soviet Union and the former communist states of East Central Europe all had uncontested (or mostly uncontested) elections and powerless legislatures based on this model. Contemporary states using similar procedures include the People's Republic of China and Cuba. Sometimes uncontested elections are staged to tell the world that an authoritarian ruler commands the regime he or she rules. In October 2002, Iraqi officials declared that Saddam Hussein had been reelected to another seven-year term as president by 100 percent of the 11,445,638 Iraqis eligible to vote.

Another form of mass participation utilized in at least some authoritarian states is *mass mobilization.* In addition to being called out to vote in phony elections, the people may also be compelled to take part in mass demonstrations and parades organized by the government, listen to propaganda speeches at their school or place of work, or lend a hand in special barnstorming work projects in the factory, on the farm, or on construction sites. Cuban leader Fidel Castro many times spoke for up to seven hours to mass audiences.

It may also happen that authoritarian regimes may enjoy a measure of mass support. Quite a few dictatorships have openly cultivated popular appeal by providing the masses with improvements in their economic welfare, by enhancing their national pride through military conquests or nationalistic propaganda, or by various other means. In some cases these regimes may actually succeed in building a broad base of popularity. Such overtures to the mass population by political elites is known as *populism.* Actually, **populism** has two meanings. When it springs from the people themselves, populism means

mass anti-elitism. It expresses the people's hostility to the overweening power of elites. Sometimes these sentiments can spark significant political activity, like the Populist Party organized in the 1890s by American farmers and workers opposed to the power of big business. When the source of populist ideas is the political elites, populism means elite efforts to cultivate the support of the disadvantaged masses. Elite-driven populism routinely occurs in democracies as politicians seek to drum up votes among the downtrodden by promising to alleviate their poverty. Argentina's Juan and Eva Perón were populists as was Venezuela's Hugo Chávez until his recent death. But populism can also occur in authoritarian regimes as dictators try to win mass support, or at least acceptance, by providing the masses with various welfare benefits to alleviate their plight.

In some cases, this strategy of *populist authoritarianism* succeeds in winning broad support for nondemocratic leaders, as long as they manage to improve the lot of the impoverished masses. But the strategy does not always work. Communist leaders in the Soviet Union and in Central and Eastern Europe sought to keep their populations quiet through an unwritten "social compact" stipulating, in effect, that the people would refrain from challenging the regime politically while the regime would provide economic and social amenities in return. Communism failed at least in part because the ruling authorities, saddled with stagnating economies, did not keep their end of the bargain. ∎

Dissidence

Dissidence is anti-regime behavior that falls short of actually toppling the government. It can take many forms, from the distribution of leaflets and other peaceful activities to overt acts of terrorism. While dissidents may nourish the hope that their small sparks of personal opposition will ignite a general conflagration, they are often willing to take extraordinary risks even if they realize that a mass uprising is not an immediate likelihood. Surveillance, incarceration, and torture are often their grim rewards.

Political dissidence is by no means confined to advocates of democracy. Some may wish to replace one form of dictatorship with another. It is possible that one could be a dissident against the rule of a government elected democratically, but the usual application of the term *dissident* is to a person protesting against dictatorial rule. A number of the most prominent political dissidents in recent decades have been outspoken proponents of democratic liberty, courageously taking up the cause of human freedom and dignity against incalculable odds. Mohandas Gandhi, the leader of the movement for India's liberation from Britain, stands out as one of democracy's most inspiring heroes, as detailed in Chapter 12. See the Profiles box for recent examples of well-known dissidents.

The contributions of these and other courageous dissidents to the cause of human rights and democratic freedom dramatize the importance of leadership in the struggle against oppression. Democratization projects that lack such dynamic

and widely recognized leaders tend to have a difficult time energizing mass action in support of change.

Revolution

Revolution is a term often used for political purposes by both proponents and opponents of political change. When using the word *revolution,* social scientists usually mean the overthrow of one system of the government and its replacement by a different regime, accomplished by a violent, mass uprising. At issue in defining any particular mass uprising as a revolution is the extent of social change that follows the change in political regime. Some scholars are willing to call a violent overthrow of a regime that only changes the rules of the political game a revolution. To us, such an uprising should be called a *political revolution.* To date, the changes wrought by the Arab Spring in Tunisia and Egypt are only political revolutions. *Social revolutions,* in contrast, bring lasting results for social groups. For example, in the French Revolution, not only was the monarchy replaced by a republic, but members of the nobility also lost their legal privileges (and thousands lost their heads on the guillotine). When fundamental changes in a nation's political regime are accompanied by profound changes in the political attitudes of the masses and elites, we might refer to such change as a *cultural revolution.* Change of this scale that occurred in France after 1789 thus included political change (the replacement of a monarchy by a republic), social change (formerly privileged classes lost their legal and social privileges),

PROFILES | Prominent Dissidents

- *Aung San Suu Kyi*, winner of the 1991 Nobel Peace Prize for her efforts to bring democracy to Myanmar (Burma), was placed under house arrest by the military regime in 1989. Under intense international pressure the regime formally released her in 1995, but she was arrested again in 2003 and accused of plotting an armed uprising. After an incident in which an American swam to her home and violated the terms of her house arrest in 2009, she was sentenced to three years' imprisonment with hard labor. That sentence was reduced to continued house arrest, where she remained until released in November 2010. In 2012 she was elected to the Myanmar parliament in what may be an important step in the liberalization of the Myanmar regime.

- *Shirin Ebadi*, the Nobel Peace Prize-winning human rights lawyer, is president of the Defender of Human Rights Center in Iran, a group declared illegal in 2006. She has been in exile since 2009.

- *Akbar Ganji*, an Iranian writer, spent six years in prison for "defaming" Iran's theocratic regime. His book *Dungeon of Ghosts* and other writings have exposed the regime's repression and corruption. He left Iran in 2006 after his release from prison.

- *Chen Guangcheng*, a blind human rights lawyer in rural China, was sentenced to more than four years in prison in 2006 after organizing a lawsuit to stop the government's population-control policy of forced sterilizations and abortions. After his release from prison in 2010 he was under house arrest until he escaped and took refuge at the U.S. embassy in Beijing in 2012. After diplomatic negotiations he was allowed to move to the United States.

- *Saad Eddin Ibrahim*, an Egyptian scholar and founder of the Arab Organization for Human Rights, was arrested on false charges in 2000 after criticizing Egypt's authoritarian regime; in 2003 he was acquitted and released. Later, in 2008, another Egyptian court sentenced him to two years in prison for "defaming Egypt," forcing him to remain in exile until the Mubarak regime fell in 2011.

- *Nelson Mandela*, the South African champion of racial equality, was jailed for 27 years before reaching a historic agreement with white leaders that gave nonwhites the vote in 1994. A Nobel Peace Prize winner, he served as South Africa's first black president.

- *Kim Dae-jung*, a fearless advocate of democracy in South Korea during three decades of authoritarian rule, spent 16 years in prison, in exile, or under house arrest before being elected president in 1997. A Nobel Peace Prize winner, he served as president until 2003. He died in 2009.

- *Lech Walesa*, an electrician who led illegal strikes against Poland's communist government in 1980, spearheaded the creation of Solidarity, the communist bloc's only noncommunist trade union. Though Solidarity was temporarily banned and Walesa was arrested, in 1989 they pressured the communist regime to hold elections and subsequently give up power. Walesa served as postcommunist Poland's first president from 1990 to 1995.

- *Vaclav Havel*, an acclaimed Czechoslovak playwright, was repeatedly jailed by the communist authorities in the 1970s and 1980s before becoming the first president of postcommunist Czechoslovakia. Havel died in 2011.

- *Wang Dan* was at the top of the Chinese regime's most-wanted list at the age of 20 for his leadership role in the 1989 student demonstrations for democracy in Beijing's Tiananmen Square. Following his arrest he spent four years in prison. Upon his release in 1993 he continued his prodemocracy activities, only to be arrested again. The communist authorities released him to the United States in 1998.

- *Andrei Sakharov*, the father of the Soviet H-bomb, was exiled to the isolated city of Gorky in the 1970s for his prodemocracy views. After being freed by Soviet reformer Mikhail Gorbachev, he was an outspoken champion of democracy during the Soviet Union's final years. He died in 1989.

and cultural change (the notion that some categories of people deserved different treatment than others was replaced with an idea that all people should be treated the same before the law).

Revolution and armed rebellion are the most violent and contentious forms of political participation. They share with more conventional modes of participation the activists' desire to bring political change through collective activity. They are on the violent and unconventional end of a continuum of political participation that has elections and voting at the most conventional end and armed actions—assassinations, hijackings,

guerrilla warfare, and revolutions—at the most unconventional end. Figure 8.8 illustrates a continuum of participation, with the more conventional forms of political involvement that we discussed at the beginning of this chapter on the left-hand side of the chart and the more unconventional, contentious forms of participation on the right.

Successful revolutions are rare. The American Revolution of the 1770s and 1780s, the French Revolution unleashed in 1789, the Russian Revolution of 1917, the Chinese revolution that started in 1911 with the collapse of the Manchu

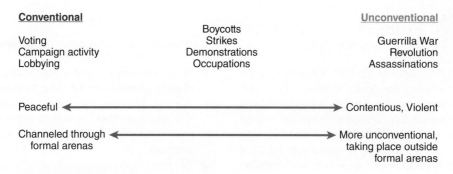

FIGURE 8.8 **Continuum of Political Participation**

dynasty and culminated in the communist takeover of 1949, and the Iranian Revolution that toppled the shah in 1979 are major examples of successful revolutions in modern history. More recently, the collapse of communism in the Soviet Union and Central and Eastern Europe and the swing toward democracy in these countries qualify as true revolutions because the social and cultural dimensions of life in the former Soviet bloc changed dramatically, not just the political regimes. Whether the new regimes resulting from the Arab Spring will be regarded as part of true revolutions depends on how much social and cultural change they introduce to the Arab world.

When do revolutions take place? The enormous scholarly literature on revolutions provides several explanations. All of them stress the importance of mass opposition to the existing government and a widespread yearning for something better as a critical element. Though political activists—*revolutionary elites*—invariably lead revolutions, they cannot succeed without establishing some kind of rapport with the masses.[37]

One set of explanations looks at the psychological sources of revolutionary violence. The other set concentrates on the social and political conditions of revolutionary situations. Any comprehensive understanding of the causes and outcomes of revolutionary tumult requires us to combine both types of analysis.

One psychological approach regards revolutionary activity as a rational choice, arguing that the logic of collective action, which views most people as politically passive, may not always apply. The people's discontent may be so great that they are willing to shake off their passivity and actively participate in anti-regime activity, even if they run the risk of being arrested or shot. Such behavior may be quite rational if there appears to be a once-in-a-lifetime chance to get rid of a despised government, the risks are tolerable, and the chances of success look good. Calculations like these may account for the popular uprisings in East-Central Europe that destroyed communism.[38]

Some of the most compelling psychological studies of revolution are rooted in *frustration-aggression theory*, which argues that people turn to violence when they are repeatedly or consistently frustrated in their attempts to achieve their goals. James C. Davies, for example, hypothesized that revolutions are not likely to occur simply because people are poor or oppressed, as common sense might lead us to expect. He

made the counterintuitive argument that revolutions are most likely when large numbers of people have experienced recent improvements in their living conditions but are suddenly confronted with a sharp reversal of fortunes as the economy takes a downward turn. In these circumstances, the "rising expectations" that people experienced under favorable economic conditions are rudely frustrated and replaced with fears of reverting back to the deplorable conditions that prevailed before the improvements. The result is a rapid increase in violent behavior, which eventually targets the political regime itself.[39]

One of the most influential students of mass violence and revolutionary psychology is Ted Robert Gurr. His widely read book *Why Men Rebel* centers on *relative deprivation* as the main source of frustration that, at least in some cases, sparks mass violence and can lead to a real revolution. Relative deprivation occurs when people perceive a gap between what they feel rightfully entitled to and what they feel they are actually capable of getting and keeping under existing circumstances. If they are continually frustrated in their efforts to satisfy their basic political, economic, or social goals and if there are no alternative ways of satisfying them, the likelihood rises that they will engage in some form of collective violence against others. Ultimately these frustrations can lead to exceptionally high magnitudes of political violence aimed directly at the governing authorities.[40] Other psychological studies have focused on "revolutionary personalities" and individual revolutionaries.[41]

The other category of research on revolutions focuses on the social, economic, and political realities (or "structures") that exist when revolutionary activity explodes. Karl Marx theorized that when a country has achieved an advanced stage of capitalism, society becomes split between a small but wealthy and politically dominant business class (the bourgeoisie) and a large mass of workers and unemployed. Once they fully understand their predicament and achieve "class consciousness," the workers will stage a revolution and wrest control of the economy from the bourgeoisie. Marx's theory of inevitable revolution was not confirmed by subsequent historical events, however.

A more recent "structural" approach by Theda Skocpol explores the causes of the French, Russian, and Chinese Revolutions and finds striking political and social similarities among all three cases. At the political level, the prerevolutionary state in France, Russia, and China consisted of a decaying absolutist monarchy that could no longer cope with the pressures posed by stronger foreign rivals. At the socioeconomic level, all three countries experienced violent rebellions by peasants who had become fed up with their inferior economic and social status. Finally, in each of the three cases the revolutionaries mobilized the masses and, upon taking power, set up a powerful centralized state with an intrusive bureaucracy. Authoritarian rule, not democracy, was the immediate result.[42]

Revolutionary activity has not subsided. During the 1980s and early 1990s, for example, a fanatical guerrilla movement known as the Shining Path conducted a systematic terror campaign in Peru in an effort to take over state power. As many as 25,000 people were killed during the prolonged insurrection, many of them as a result of the counterinsurgency efforts of the Peruvian armed forces. The Shining Path attracted most of its adherents from the urban and rural poor during a period of extreme hardship for the Peruvian economy. The movement suffered a severe blow in 1992 when its leader was captured and sentenced to prison.[43] Colombia has witnessed a decades-long attempt by revolutionaries to topple its central government. By 1999 the rebels controlled as much as half the country. They started as Marxists bent on social revolution, but their aims appear to have degenerated into the simple pursuit of power and economic control over the territory they occupy, plus access to the lucrative drug trade. In recent years the Colombian government has effectively beat back the rebel advance. A variety of rebel groups have sought to gain power in Congo, Ivory Coast, Liberia, Sierra Leone, and other African countries, though their ultimate political goals beyond taking power are unclear. For better or worse, history's great revolutions have been guided by major ideologies: nationalism, democracy, communism, fascism, Islamic fundamentalism. Rebels without a cause other than their own lust for power and plunder are scarcely revolutionaries. Most of them are little more than political thugs.

Conclusion

As we have seen, political participation can take many forms. While we may first think of voting when someone mentions political participation, turning out on election day is only one mode of political activity, and usually not the one with the greatest impact. In democracies and nondemocracies, individual and group resources combine with opportunities—what is legal or not, where in the state the decision making on an issue is located, what might gain the attention of the mass media or the outside world—to shape participation choices.

We began this chapter by pointing to what many would regard as the paradox of political participation. In strict cost–benefit terms, why do individuals cooperate with one another in promoting particular candidates for office or public policies? We can explain individual contacting behavior in narrow rational choice terms—if I ask an official to do something to specifically benefit me or my family, the cost of my doing so is probably little more than my political loyalty, or maybe a specific campaign contribution. I ask that an official grants a government contract to my firm, and that official expects me to make a campaign contribution and to vote for him or her. But most forms of participation beyond direct contacting could be subjected to the calculus about collective action that Olson posed, and we would normally conclude that it's not worth our effort to participate. Our rational decision would be to abstain or free ride.

Yet people involve themselves politically in a wide range of activities. Why? While some people may make inaccurate assessments of their costs and benefits, most do so because their rewards are not just the material rewards they expect in terms of public policies or government benefits to them as individuals. Some political scientists have posited that there is a psychic benefit from voting; casting our ballot makes us feel as though we have completed a civic duty. By that logic, many other political activities, almost all of which are more costly in time and effort than voting, must also cause activists to feel good about what they are doing collectively. One of the strong notions coming out of the literature on civil society and social capital is that for many people, involvement in group activities is inherently rewarding emotionally and intellectually. Those people are the most participative individuals in society. Scholars such as Robert Putnam argue that we need highly participative persons to make our democracy work well. Other scholars would go so far as to argue that high levels of political involvement make us more completely human. For such theorists, devising the democratic structure that creates the greatest opportunity for all citizens to participate politically is an imperative because it will further the evolution of the human race.[44]

Individuals' participation decisions are influenced by the political structures in which they operate. Those who live in authoritarian regimes have fewer opportunities to participate politically than those in democracies. Political involvement is also shaped by people's values and their knowledge about politics. In the next chapter we will explore the attitudinal components of political behavior, sometimes also called political culture.

Key Terms

Collective goods
Conventional political participation
Communal activity
Direct contacting
Nonconventional (confrontational) political participation
Particularistic parties
Catch-all parties
Interest aggregation
Party system
Interest group
Interest articulation
Pluralism
Corporatism
Clientelism

Contentious politics
Social movements
Populism
Dissidence
Revolution

Notes

1. Lester W. Milbraith, *Political Participation* (Chicago: Rand McNally, 1965). See also the second edition, coauthored with M. L. Goel (Chicago: Rand McNally, 1977). Also Sidney Verba and Norman H. Nie, *Participation in American Politics* (New York: Harper & Row, 1972); Michael M. Gant and Norman R. Luttbeg, *American Electoral Behavior: 1952–1988* (Itasca, IL: F. E. Peacock, 1991); Sidney Verba, Kay Lehman Schlozman, and Henry E. Brady, *Voice and Equality: Civic Volunteerism in American Politics* (Cambridge, MA: Harvard University Press, 1995); Russell J. Dalton, *Citizen Politics: Public Opinion and Political Parties in Advanced Industrial Democracies,* 5th ed. (Washington, DC: Congressional Quarterly Press, 2008).

2. Mancur Olson, *The Logic of Collective Action* (Cambridge, MA: Harvard University Press, 1965).

3. The Comparative Study of Electoral Systems (www.cses.org), *CSES Module 2 Full Release* dataset, June 27, 2007.

4. One scholar showed that U.S. registration requirements reduced voter turnout by at least 10 percent compared with other democratic countries; see G. Bingham Powell, "American Voter Turnout in Comparative Perspective," *American Political Science Review* 80, no. 1 (March 1986), pp. 17–43. For a discussion of turnout in the United States, see Gant and Luttbeg, *American Electoral Behavior.* For a comparative study, see Sidney Verba, Norman H. Nie, and Jae-on Kim, *Participation and Political Equality: A Seven-Nation Comparison* (London: Cambridge University Press, 1978), pp. 190–91, 234–68. When asked to agree or disagree with the statement "People like me don't have any say about what the government does," 29 percent agreed in 1964, 39 percent in 1980, and 45 percent in 1988; 69 percent disagreed in 1964, 59 percent in 1980, and 54 percent in 1988. The rest did not know or had no opinion. Reported in Gant and Luttbeg, *American Electoral Behavior,* p. 128. See also Michael Schudson, *The Good Citizen: A History of American Civic Life* (New York: Free Press, 1998); Kay Lehman Schlozman, "Citizen Participation in America: What Do We Know? Why Do We Care?" in *Political Science: The State of the Discipline,* ed. Ira Katznelson and Helen V. Miller (New York: W. W. Norton, 2002), pp. 433–61.

5. Anthony Downs, *An Economic Theory of Democracy* (New York: Harper & Row, 1957).

6. Angus Campbell, Philip E. Converse, Warren E. Miller, and Donald E. Stokes, *The American Voter* (Chicago: University of Chicago Press, 1960). The researchers also found that only an extremely small proportion of the electorate (2.5 to 3.5 percent) thought about politics in terms of a coherent ideology, such as "liberal" or "conservative" orientations. Subsequent studies by members of the Michigan group tended to corroborate this depiction of the American voter as essentially uninformed, with little appreciation of the policy implications of the candidates' positions. In a study of the political belief systems of Americans, for example, Philip E. Converse found that they consisted mainly of what he called *nonattitudes*—political opinions that are inconsistent, contradictory, and subject to unpredictable fluctuations. Angus Campbell et al., *Elections and the Political Order* (New York: Wiley, 1966); Philip E. Converse, "The Nature of Belief Systems in Mass Public," in *Ideology and Discontent,* ed. David E. Apter (Glencoe, IL: Free Press, 1964). For a summary of more recent treatments of expressive voting, see Randall Calvert, "Identity, Expression, and Rational-Choice Theory," in Katznelson and Miller, *Political Science,* pp. 568–96. See the American National Election Study data at www.electionstudies.org.

7. David Butler and Donald Stokes, *Political Change in Britain,* 2nd ed. (New York: St. Martin's Press, 1974); Philip E. Converse and Georges Dupeux, "Politicization and the Electorate in France and the United States," *Public Opinion Quarterly,* no. 26 (1963), pp. 1–23.

8. See, for example, Samuel L. Popkin, *The Reasoning Voter* (Chicago: University of Chicago Press, 1991).

9. Dalton, *Citizen Politics,* pp. 18ff, 187–09. See also Russell J. Dalton, Scott Flanagan, and Paul Allen Beck, eds., *Electoral Change in Advanced Industrial Democracies: Realignment or Dealignment?* (Princeton, NJ: Princeton University Press, 1984). Pippa Norris, ed., *Critical Citizens: Global Support for Democratic Governance* (Oxford: Oxford University Press, 1999); Pippa Norris, *Democratic Phoenix: Political Activism Worldwide* (New York: Cambridge University Press, 2003).

10. William H. Riker and Peter C. Ordeshook, "A Theory of the Calculus of Voting," *American Political Science Review,* 62 (1968), pp. 25–43; André Blais, *To Vote or Not to Vote: The Merits and Limits of Rational Choice* (Pittsburgh: University of Pittsburgh Press, 2000).

11. Anthony Downs, "Social Values and Democracy," in *The Economic Approach to Politics: A Critical Assessment of the Theory of Rational Action,* ed. Kristin R. Monroe (New York: HarperCollins, 1991), pp. 143–70. See also Donald P. Green and Ian Shapiro, *Pathologies of Rational Choice Theory* (New Haven, CN: Yale University Press, 1994); Jeffrey Friedman, ed., *The Rational Choice Controversy* (New Haven, CN: Yale University Press, 1996).

12. For a different categorization, see Kenneth Janda, *Political Parties: A Cross-National Survey* (New York: Free Press, 1980), p. 5; Kenneth Janda, "Comparative Political Parties: Research and Theory," in *Political Science: The State of the Discipline II,* ed. Ada W. Finifter (Washington, DC: American Political Science Association, 1993), pp. 163–91. A classic is Giovanni Sartori, *Parties and Party Systems: A Framework for Analysis* (Cambridge: Cambridge University Press, 1976). For information on parties around the world, visit www.electionworld.org.

13. On Hezbollah, see Judith P. Harik, *Hezbollah: The Changing Face of Terrorism* (New York: Palgrave Macmillan, 2004); Ahmad Nizar Hamzeh, *In the Path of Hizbullah* (Syracuse, NY: Syracuse University Press, 2004). On Hamas, see Matthew Levitt, *Hamas: Politics, Charity, and Terrorism in the Service of Jihad* (New Haven, CN: Yale University Press, 2006). On Pakistani parties, see Farooq Tanwir, "Religious Parties and Politics in Pakistan," *International Journal of Comparative Sociology* 43, no. 3–5 (2002), pp. 250–68.

14. On catch-all parties, see Otto Kirchheimer, "The Transformation of the West European Party Systems," in *Political Parties and Political Development,* ed. Joseph LaPalombara and Myron Weiner (Princeton, NJ: Princeton University Press, 1966), pp. 177–200.

15. Thomas Childers, *The Nazi Voter* (Chapel Hill, NC: University of North Carolina Press, 1983); Richard F. Hamilton, *Who Voted for Hitler?* (Princeton, NJ: Princeton University Press, 1982).

16. Gabriel A. Almond and G. Bingham Powell Jr., *Comparative Politics: A Developmental Approach* (Boston: Little, Brown, 1966); Gabriel A. Almond and G. Bingham Powell Jr., *Comparative Politics: System, Process, Policy* (Boston: Little, Brown, 1978).

17. The poll, conducted by Zogby International, was released in 2006. Consult www.zogby.com.

18. Paul Allen Beck, "The Dealignment Era in America," in Dalton, Flanagan, and Beck, *Electoral Change in Advanced Industrial Democracies,* p. 243. See also Gant and Luttbeg, *American Electoral Behavior,* pp. 63–74.

19. Seymour M. Lipset and Stein Rokkan, eds., *Party Systems and Voter Alignments: Cross-National Perspectives* (New York: Free Press, 1967), p. 50. See also Dalton, *Citizen Politics,* pp. 180–89.

20. The terms *moderate* and *extreme* for party systems come from Sartori, *Parties and Party Systems,* pp. 125–09. Albert O. Hirschman, *Exit, Voice, and Loyalty* (Cambridge, MA: Harvard University Press, 1970).

21. *Washington Post,* January 29, 2006. See also John R. Wright, *Interest Groups and Congress* (Boston: Allyn & Bacon, 1996); p. 23; Philip Parvin, "Friend or Foe? Lobbying in British Democracy," Hansard Society discussion paper, 2007.

22. For introductions to corporatism in theory and practice, see Peter J. Williamson, *Varieties of Corporatism* (Cambridge: Cambridge University Press, 1985); Peter J. Williamson, *Corporatism in Perspective* (London: Sage, 1989); Alan Cawson, *Corporatism and Political Theory* (Oxford: Basil Blackwell, 1986). See also Philippe C. Schmitter, "Still the Century of Corporatism?" *Review of Politics* 36 (1974), pp. 85–131; Philippe C. Schmitter and Gerhard Lehmbruch, *Trends Towards Corporatist Intermediation* (Beverly Hills, CA: Sage, 1979); Gerhard Lehmbruch and Philippe C. Schmitter, *Patterns of Corporatist Policy-Making* (Beverly Hills, CA: Sage, 1982); Peter J. Katzenstein, *Corporatism and Change: Austria, Switzerland, and the Politics of Industry* (Ithaca, NY: Cornell University Press, 1984).

23. Russell J. Dalton, Susan E. Scarrow, and Bruce E. Cain, "Advanced Democracies and the New Politics," *Journal of Democracy* 15, no. 1 (January 2004), pp. 124–38.

24. Boaventura de Sousa Santos, "Participatory Budgeting in Porto Alegre: Toward a Redistributive Democracy," *Politics and Society* 26, no. 4 (December 1998), pp. 461–510; Gianpaola Baiocchi, *Militants and Citizens: The Politics of Participatory Democracy in Porto Alegre* (Stanford, CA: Stanford University Press, 2005).

25. Siddhartha Sen, "Some Aspects of State-NGO Relationships in India in the Post-Independence Era," *Development and Change* 30, no. 2 (1999), pp. 327–55.

26. Sanjeev Khagram, *Dams and Development: Transnational Struggles for Water and Power* (Ithaca, NY: Cornell University Press, 2004).

27. Sidney Tarrow, *The New Transnational Activism* (New York: Cambridge University Press, 2005); William E. DeMars, *NGOs and Transnational Networks: Wild Cards in World Politics* (Ann Arbor, MI: Pluto, 2005).

28. Robert Putnam, "Tuning In, Tuning Out: The Strange Disappearance of Social Capital in America," *PS: Political Science and Politics* 28, no. 4 (December 1995), pp. 664–83.

29. James E. Curtis, Edward G. Grabb, and Douglas E. Baer, "Voluntary Association Membership in Fifteen Countries: A Comparative Analysis," *American Sociological Review* 57, no. 2 (April 1992), pp. 139–52.

30. Joseph L. Klesner, "Social Capital and Political Participation in Latin America: Evidence from Argentina, Chile, Mexico and Peru," *Latin American Research Review* 42, no. 2 (June 2007), pp. 1–32.

31. Theodore J. Lowi, *At the Pleasure of the Mayor: Patronage and Power in New York City, 1898–1958* (London: Macmillan, 1964); P. A. Allum, *Politics and Society in Post-War Naples* (Cambridge: Cambridge University Press, 1973).

32. Charles Tilly, *Contention and Democracy in Europe, 1650–2000* (New York: Cambridge University Press, 2004); Mario Diani and Doug McAdam, eds., *Social Movements and Networks: Rational Approaches to Collective Action* (Oxford: Oxford University Press, 2003); Jack A. Goldstone, ed., *States, Parties, and Social Movements* (Cambridge: Cambridge University Press, 2003); Doug McAdam, Sidney Tarrow, and Charles Tilly, *Dynamics of Contention* (Cambridge: Cambridge University Press, 2001); Marco G. Giungi, Doug McAdam, and Charles Tilly, eds., *From Contention to Democracy* (Lanham, MD: Rowman and Littlefield, 1998); Sidney Tarrow, *Power in Movement: Social Movements and Contentious Politics,* 2nd ed. (Cambridge: Cambridge University Press, 1998).

33. Dalton, *Citizen Politics,* p. 68.

34. Dieter Rucht, "The Spread of Protest Politics," in *The Oxford Handbook of Political Behavior,* ed. Russell J. Dalton and Hans-Dieter Klingemann (Oxford: Oxford University Press, 2007), p. 715; Kathleen Bruhn, *Urban Protest in Mexico and Brazil* (New York: Cambridge University Press, 2008), p. 36.

35. Dalton, *Citizen Politics,* p. 69.

36. A classic work on this subject is William Kornhauser, *The Politics of Mass Society* (Glencoe, IL: Free Press, 1959).

37. For introductory overviews, see Peter C. Sederberg, *Fires Within: Political Violence and Revolutionary Change* (New York: Harper-Collins, 1994); A. S. Cohen, *Theories of Revolution: An Introduction* (London: Thomas Nelson, 1975).

38. On revolution and collective action, see Michael Taylor, ed., *Rationality and Revolution* (New York: Cambridge University Press, 1988).

39. James Chowning Davies, "The J-curve of Rising and Declining Satisfactions as a Cause of Revolution and Rebellion," in *Violence in America,* rev. ed., ed. Hugh Davis Graham and Ted Robert Gurr (Beverly Hills, CA: Sage, 1976), pp. 415–36.

40. Ted Robert Gurr, *Why Men Rebel* (Princeton, NJ: Princeton University Press, 1970). See also Ivo K. Feierabend et al., eds., *Anger, Violence, and Politics* (Englewood Cliffs, NJ: Prentice Hall, 1972); Fred R. von der Mehden, *Comparative Political Violence* (Englewood Cliffs, NJ: Prentice Hall, 1973).

41. E. Victor Wolfenstein, *The Revolutionary Personality: Lenin, Trotsky, Gandhi* (Princeton, NJ: Princeton University Press, 1971); Bruce Mazlish, *The Revolutionary Ascetic: Evolution of a Political Type* (New York: Basic Books, 1976); Erik H. Erikson, *Gandhi's Truth: On the Origins of Militant Nonviolence* (New York: W. W. Norton, 1969).

42. Theda Skocpol, *States and Social Revolutions* (Cambridge: Cambridge University Press, 1979).

43. Cynthia L. McClintock, "Why Peasants Rebel: The Case of Peru's Sendero Luminoso," *World Politics* 37, no. 1 (October 1984), pp. 48–84; David Scott Palmer, ed., *Shining Path of Peru* (New York: St. Martin's Press, 1992).

44. See Carole Pateman, *Participation and Democratic Theory* (Cambridge: Cambridge University Press, 1970); Benjamin Barber, *Strong Democracy: Participatory Politics for a New Age* (Berkeley, CA: University of California Press, 1984).

9 Political Culture

OVERVIEW

- Political culture is the pattern of shared values, moral norms, beliefs, expectations, and attitudes that relate to politics and its social context.

- Fundamental attitudes about authority and the relationship of the individual to society and to the state impact people's political behavior and the political regimes that emerge in different countries.

- Four influential theories about political culture are: *The Civic Culture*, post-materialism, human development theory, and the clash of civilizations.

- The political culture of the United States differs from and is similar to that of other democracies.

Aspects of traditional society and modernity are in evidence in rural China.

POLITICAL CULTURE IN THE UNITED STATES

It is generally recognized that in the United States, certain basic attitudes about political life are widely shared. Americans tend to be rather proud of their political system, for example: They revere the Constitution, prizing it as one of the greatest political documents ever devised. At the same time, their attitudes toward politicians are rather ambivalent. Though Americans generally treat their political leaders with civility, they can be highly critical of politicians and even quite cynical about them.

Americans are also ambivalent about government in general. There is a prevailing aversion to "big government" and excessive governmental intrusion in people's lives. In fact, many Americans do not have a particularly high regard for government. Though only a few Americans are intensely angry about their government, trust in government officials has declined appreciably since the 1960s.[1] Many people regard the government as inefficient and wasteful and hold the private business sector in higher esteem as more effective than politicians or bureaucrats. Most Americans value individual responsibility and personal initiative over excessive reliance on the state. Most favor equality (or equity) of opportunity rather than a state-enforced equality of condition.

In fact, most Americans don't care much about politics. In a World Values Survey administered in the United States in 2006, only 11 percent of Americans said that politics was very important in their lives, ranking it at the bottom of their priorities, far below family, friends, religion, work, and leisure.[2] As we noted in the previous chapter, voter turnout in the United States is lower than in most other Western democracies. Still, most Americans perceive themselves as law abiding and have a high respect for law and order. They decisively reject violence as a legitimate form of political action.

Americans value hard work, believing that people are entitled to earn as much money as they can. Private enterprise, while not without problems, is viewed positively by most Americans as basically successful, even though many of them regard large corporations as excessively powerful and impersonal. Socialism is taboo, which is why labeling President Barack Obama a socialist has such power among conservatives and even nonconservatives. Americans tend to be distrustful of excessive power in any form, whether it is the power of government, of large corporations, or of special interests representing particular groups in society.

Nevertheless, most Americans believe that it is proper for the government to help take care of people who cannot help themselves. Large majorities believe that such large government programs as Social Security, Medicare, and welfare for those unable to work are necessary.[3] Some observers maintain that Americans in recent decades have become so accustomed to expecting various government benefits that an "entitlement" mentality has set in. While they may object to big government in principle, they favor it in practice as long as they can derive some gain from it.

Most Americans favor compromise. They like to get things done, and a refusal to compromise is regarded as a barrier to effective action. Quite a few Americans have become dissatisfied with the two main political parties in recent years because they believe that Democratic and Republican politicians are more interested in opposing each other than in reaching effective agreements that can help the country. This willingness to compromise helps make for moderation in American political life. Even those who regard themselves as liberals or conservatives tend to shun the more extreme tendencies of these competing orientations—only about 10 percent of Americans regard themselves as very conservative and 6 percent are very liberal.[4] Political radicalism of any kind is generally frowned upon, although the ideological spectrum has grown somewhat more polarized in the past decade in response to growing economic and foreign policy challenges.

Of all the political values Americans hold, freedom usually tops the list. Typically this means freedom from excessive governmental interference, but it is more than that. To most Americans, freedom means that they can come and go as they please and express themselves as they wish, that there are practically no barriers to what they can accomplish, and that the future is full of possibilities. Most Americans are relatively optimistic about the future; there is a continuing belief that all are entitled to fulfill "the American dream": to own one's own house, earn a

rising income, and enjoy the pleasures of life, a value extolled in the Declaration of Independence as "the pursuit of happiness." Most Americans are content and optimistic. The Pew Global Attitudes Project regularly asks people around the world where they believe they stand on a 10-rung "ladder of life." In 2010, 64 percent of Americans placed themselves on rungs 7 through 10, compared to 53 percent of French people, 52 percent of Britons and Germans, 31 percent of Russians and Chinese, 32 percent of Nigerians, and a mere 10 percent of Egyptians. Only Brazilians and Mexicans, of the societies we'll study in Part Two, regarded themselves as more satisfied with their lives, as 65 and 72 percent, respectively, put themselves on the top rung. Most Americans see their position as having improved on the ladder of life in the previous five years, too.[5] We should note, though, that although Americans are more optimistic than people in many other societies, social mobility is now greater in Europe than in the United States.

Americans are also generally tolerant of the freedoms of fellow Americans, and they have a general commitment to fair play and equity. Their tolerance has limits, however. Although there has been substantial progress in the area of racial and ethnic tolerance over the past three decades, racial divisions persist, and many heterosexuals are intolerant of homosexuals. Most Americans favor immigration, boasting that the United States is a land of immigrants, but there is unease about the influx of illegal immigrants, who are perceived as enjoying the benefits of American society unfairly.

On the whole, Americans can work together to achieve common goals. A high degree of interpersonal cooperation undergirds American society, giving rise to all sorts of civic, business, cultural, philanthropic, and other associations and volunteer organizations. But many Americans also experience a tension between their desire for freedom and individualism, on the one hand, and close community bonds on the other. Interpersonal trust is declining, especially among younger Americans, as is participation in voluntary associations.

Most Americans are religious. To a greater extent than people in most other economically advanced democracies, they believe in God, attend church regularly, and are profoundly influenced by religious beliefs and moral teachings (see Tables 9.1 and 9.2).

To be sure, not all Americans subscribe to all these notions. Public opinion survey data, however, show that large numbers of them do, often a majority. In most respects, these surveys have displayed considerable consistency over the past several decades.[6]

DEFINING POLITICAL CULTURE

The attitudes toward politics that were just described are representative of what political scientists would call the prevailing *political culture* of the United States. **Political culture** is a pattern of shared values, moral norms, beliefs, expectations, and attitudes that relate to politics and its social context.

Political culture reflects the ways people think and feel about political life. It consists of clusters of attitudes about

Table 9.1 Belief in God, 1947–2001

Country	PERCENTAGE OF THE PUBLIC WHO SAID YES WHEN ASKED IF THEY BELIEVED IN GOD.							
	1947	1968	1975	1981	1990	1995	2001	Change
Sweden	80%	60%		52%	38%	48%	46%	−33.6
Netherlands	80	79		64	61		58	−22.0
Australia	95		80	79		75	75	−19.9
Norway	84	73		68	58	65		−18.9
Denmark	80			53	59		62	−17.9
Britain		77	76	73	72		61	−16.5
Greece		96					84	−12.3
West Germany		81	72	68	63	71	69	−12.0
Belgium			78	76	65		67	−11.2
Finland	83	83			61	73	72	−10.8
France	66	73	72	59	57		56	−10.1
Canada	95		89	91	85		88	−7.2
Switzerland		84			77	77		−7.2
India			98		93	94		−4.0
Japan			38	39	37	44	35	−3.0
Austria		85			78		83	−1.9
United States	94	98	94	96	93	94	94	0.4
Brazil	96				98	99		3.0

Source: Reprinted from Pippa Norris and Ronald Inglehart, *Sacred and Secular: Religion and Politics Worldwide*, 2nd ed. (Cambridge: Cambridge University Press, 2011), p. 90.

Table 9.2 Must Political Leaders Believe in God?

Country	PERCENTAGE OF THE PUBLIC WHO AGREE THAT "POLITICIANS WHO DO NOT BELIEVE IN GOD ARE UNFIT FOR PUBLIC OFFICE" IN THE 2004–08 WAVE OF THE WORLD VALUES SURVEY.					
Country	Percentage Agreeing		Percentage Agreeing		Percentage Agreeing	
Indonesia	88%	Zambia	55% Peru	39%	Uruguay	13%
Iraq	87	Morocco	53 Cyprus	38	Italy	13
Georgia	83	Ethiopia	50 Argentina	33	Spain	11
Iran	75	India	49 United States	32	Germany	11
Ghana	73	Romania	49 Chile	30	Slovenia	11
Jordan	69	Burkina Faso	49 Bulgaria	28	Taiwan	10
Trinidad and Tobago	68	Brazil	49 Mexico	26	Finland	9
Thailand	64	South Africa	48 Viet Nam	18	N. Zealand	9
Malaysia	64	Ukraine	45 Poland	18	Japan	7
Mali	59	Rwanda	44 Canada	17	Norway	4
Guatemala	59	Moldova	43 South Korea	15	Sweden	4
Turkey	55	Serbia	41 Australia	13	Andorra	3

Source: World Values Survey 2004–08 wave, available at www.worldvaluessurvey.org.

authority, government, and society that are accepted by large portions of a country's population, quite often the majority. It includes broadly diffused core values, especially those that relate to political ideals and social relations. In some cases, the ideas of liberal and social democracy—such as individual freedom, equality, tolerance, and social welfare—are the main sources of political values. In other cases *religion* is a source of values. Many political and social values in the United States, such as

individual dignity and social equality, have been shaped by the Judeo-Christian heritage. Much like patriotism, religion itself is a *political* value in America, as reflected in the mottos "In God We Trust" and "One nation, under God." Despite the formal separation of church and state, U.S. political leaders routinely invoke the deity in political speeches and call on the citizenry to pray in times of national crisis. Christian denominations such as Roman Catholicism, Protestantism, and Eastern Orthodoxy have each made contributions of their own to political and social values in various countries, in some cases by supporting democracy, in others by propping up authoritarian regimes.

Similarly, Confucianism, a moral-philosophical tradition that functions like a religion, has exerted a profound influence on prevailing values in countries including China, Taiwan, and Singapore. It is the principal source of what some East Asians extol as Asian values, which emphasize respect for authority and the individual's responsibilities to the community, while disparaging Western notions of individualism and freedom of expression as dangerous threats to social harmony and political order. Perhaps not surprisingly, apologists of authoritarian regimes in this part of the world have argued that Asian values are incompatible with democracy. Islam has had an equally powerful impact on the political culture of numerous countries in the Middle East, Africa, and various parts of Asia, with important political and social implications for the role of women and for the state's responsibility for the enforcement of Islamic law and customs. Hinduism in India and Shinto in Japan have also had profound effects on the way people view politics in those countries. But religious beliefs and practices are in decline in many countries, reflecting long-term trends toward *secularization*, especially in economically advanced democracies (see Table 9.1). We'll discuss some reasons for these trends later in this chapter.

Nationalism (see Chapter 4) may also be a source of political values, involving a range of affective attachments to one's country or people that run from quiet patriotism to militant hypernationalism.

Closely related to political and social values are *norms* that define right and wrong in the attitudes and behavior of public officials, in the substance of government policy, and in the enforcement of legal codes. To continue our example about religion and politics, many people the world over believe that politicians must believe in God if they are to hold public office. However, from country to country the share of the population that insists its leaders be believers differs from fewer than 1 in 10 in Scandinavian countries to almost 9 in 10 in the predominantly Muslim countries of Indonesia and Iraq (see Table 9.2).

In some countries, providing gifts to officials in exchange for favors is acceptable, but in others it is condemned as corruption. Public policy relating to abortion and homosexuality largely reflects prevailing (or conflicting) moral tenets within a given country. Some countries, like the United States, have the death penalty; others, like the 28 members of the European Union, have banned it. Governments based on Islamic law—such as the regimes in Iran, Saudi Arabia, Afghanistan under the Taliban, and certain parts of Nigeria—sanction decapitation, stoning, amputation, and flogging as just punishments. Singapore practices caning. And some societies tolerate revenge killings and other customary forms of tribal or village justice.

General beliefs about the nature of politics are also components of political culture. People in one culture, for example, may view their political system as essentially transparent and accessible, with state officials sharing information with the public and making decisions in accordance with the public's wishes.

The game of politics in this perception is one in which everybody has a chance to win something, and today's losers can be tomorrow's winners. This view is how we tend to see politics in democracies like the United States, Canada, and the United Kingdom. By contrast, people in another political culture may perceive politics in darkly conspiratorial terms as the preserve of distant elites who demand obedience and play favorites. In this view, politics is rigged as a zero-sum game in which the winners take all at the losers' expense. Often in the past Latin Americans have held the latter view. Trust in government is also a critical element of a country's political belief system. Can the people who run the country's political institutions be trusted to be ethical, truthful, and fair, and to act in the best interests of the people rather than in their own self-interest? As we'll see later in this chapter, trust is declining in most of the world's established democracies. Beliefs about politics color the *expectations* people have about how their political system works. In most well-established democracies, people expect elections to take place regularly and they do not expect the military to seize power. In other countries the public's expectations may be quite different. In some political cultures there is a general expectation that political figures and other elites (such as business executives) will abide by the law or suffer serious consequences if they do not. In others, people learn to expect powerful figures to do what they want and get away with it.

Political culture thus involves a combination of things that together shape mass *attitudes* toward politics and the implications of political life. Though some regard political culture as a nebulous concept, because it refers to so many disparate perceptions and feelings, many political scientists believe that it is a real phenomenon of social psychology that can be empirically verified in studies of public opinion.[7]

Most countries have a dominant political culture, a collection of attitudes that are broadly shared by the political elites and a large proportion of the population. These dominant or prevailing attitudes frequently cut across social classes, ethnic groups, and other social strata. The attitudes we have just described as elements of the dominant political culture in the United States are broadly representative of "middle America"—the white middle class.[8] To be sure, not everyone in the United States shares all of them. A majority of African-Americans have different attitudes than most whites on a host of racial questions, for example. Nevertheless, they share quite a few basic attitudes with whites, including support for the Constitution, individual freedom, private enterprise, equality of opportunity, the importance of education and hard work, and belief in God.

Many, if not most, countries also have one or more political subcultures. A **political subculture** is a political culture that deviates from the dominant culture in key respects. In the United States, many poor and uneducated people, for example, feel more or less permanently alienated from the American political and economic systems. They may feel a fundamental dissatisfaction with life in general and a sense of being trapped in their circumstances. In some instances these orientations are combined with a hostile attitude toward authority, intolerance of different ethnic groups, and a sense that one has nothing to compromise. In the most extreme cases these attitudes may lead to violations of the law and perhaps a tendency to violence. Another example of a subculture is indigenous minorities in Latin American countries. Often indigenous Latin Americans—especially those who have lived in indigenous communities isolated from the mainstream of the countries in which they are located—evidence more communitarian values than their more individualistic countrymen who are white or mestizo. They are more likely to prefer traditional forms of governance than their mainstream countrymen who advocate democratic rules.

As we talk about political cultures and subcultures, we must at the same time avoid concluding that all individuals in a society or in a group within a society share the attitudinal features of the majority. To assume that some individual who lives in Russia, for instance, shares the political values that the majority of Russians report to a social scientific survey would be to commit the *ecological fallacy*, the error of inferring individual characteristics from the characteristics of the group to which one belongs. Any individual Russian can have values quite at variance with the values of society as a whole.

Political Socialization and Psychology

The defining attitudes of a political culture are essentially learned and transmitted in what is called the political socialization process. **Political socialization** is the process in which individuals learn about politics and the political culture of their society. One's family is the primary agent of socialization. Dinner table conversation about public affairs, observing your parents' or siblings' engagement in civic affairs, and your parents' exhortations about appropriate behavior toward others play key roles in defining how you will view politics. Secondary agents of socialization include peer groups, schools, churches, places of employment, the military, and other elements of the larger society. Americans and people in other societies send their children to public schools or parochial schools in no small part because of the particular socialization they expect to occur in one or the other. You might want to discuss with your peers who attended a different kind of school than you did the particular social and political messages conveyed during their primary and secondary education.

Mass attitudes reflect the attitudes and perceptions of individuals. At the same time, the attitudes of individuals are profoundly influenced by the cultural orientations of the larger society in which they live. Individuals interact with their political cultures in complex ways that are difficult to capture in a single parsimonious theory. While rational-choice theorists focus on the incentives and costs that structure individual decisions, some "culturalists" highlight the impact of political culture as an independent variable that shapes behavior.[9] And psychologists have provided insight into cognitive processes that are anything but rational. The perceptions and attitudes of individuals and masses alike can take irrational turns, at times with disturbing political consequences. In *The Authoritarian Personality*, a group of psychologists and political analysts concerned with how Nazism could have arisen in Germany probed the personality

Children are sent to schools in no small part to have their society's values imparted to them. The state often attempts to subtly or not so subtly influence the values of young people, as in this German school in the 1930s.

factors that inclined certain types of people to be particularly receptive to fascist or racist propaganda. A rigid adherence to conventional values, a low tolerance for ambiguity, a reliance on superstition as opposed to scientific logic, and gullibility as opposed to independent critical judgment emerged as the leading characteristics of the "antidemocratic personality."[10]

In the book about another famous study, *A Theory of Cognitive Dissonance*, Leon Festinger reported on experiments showing that many people, when faced with information that contradicts one of their deeply held opinions, preferences, or biases, find ways to ignore or explain away the undesirable messages rather than alter their views in a rational fashion to take account of the facts before their eyes. They also go out of their way to avoid information that they suspect will be dissonant with what they are accustomed to believing. Decision makers and the mass public are likewise prone to these misperceptions.[11] Critics of people's reliance on blogs and cable television for political information point out how the proliferation of political information and commentary available through blogs and cable TV has only tended to lead us to read the blogs that contain the political messages we want to hear—liberal or conservative, pro- or anti-gay, pro- or anti-environmentalist, and so forth. We seek to avoid dissonant information about political positions we hold dear.

STUDIES OF POLITICAL CULTURE

The concept of political culture has a venerable tradition. Plato and Aristotle both attached considerable importance to the basic attitudes people have about authority, about how social relationships should be conducted, and about the roles government should play in people's lives. Some of these cultural attitudes, they maintained, favor democracy, while others are incompatible with democratic self-government.

Alexis de Tocqueville placed cultural values and attitudes at the forefront of his famous analysis of democracy in America. In place of our contemporary term *political culture*, he used *mores*, a generic term meaning the broadly shared customs and values of a society. Tocqueville defined mores as "the whole moral and intellectual state of a people," and he was particularly interested in political mores, those "habits of the heart" and "mental habits" that helped shape the political behavior of Americans. In his view, American political mores were characterized above all by the love of liberty, an attitude he believed was propagated by both the Protestant and Catholic religions in America, by the educational system, and by the family, with women playing an especially important role. In addition, Tocqueville believed that Americans had a basic good sense about political life that came from generations of experience with social cooperation and local self-government at the village level. He also noted their general "restraint," "moderation," and "self-command."

In fact, Tocqueville regarded these attitudinal factors as even more important in accounting for the success of American democracy than the Constitution and other legal props of the U.S. governmental system. "Laws are always unsteady when unsupported by mores," he wrote. "Mores are the only tough and durable power in a nation." Without the proper attitudes, values, and habits on the part of the population, Tocqueville clearly implied, even the most brilliantly conceived democratic institutions would inevitably rest on shaky foundations. Other students of early American history have also underscored the impact of cultural factors on political developments. Gordon S. Wood, for example, has pointed out that Colonial-era concepts of equal dignity were a powerful component of the American Revolution against Britain. "Ordinary Americans came to believe that no one . . . was really better than anyone else," a notion that has made the United States "the most egalitarian nation in the history of the world," despite its history of slavery and great disparities of wealth.[12]

German sociologist Max Weber was also a keen student of political culture. He believed that political and economic institutions could not be understood solely on their own terms. Cultural attitudes deriving from such nonpolitical sources as religion, the family, and rules of logic can also have a profound impact on political and economic reality. In *The Protestant Ethic and the Spirit of Capitalism*, Weber wondered why Protestants tended to dominate the German economy at the turn of the twentieth century, occupying the most important corporate executive positions to a far greater extent than Catholics. His answer was that Protestantism and Catholicism had traditionally taken divergent approaches to religious asceticism (austere living). Whereas Martin Luther had placed a high value on personal engagement in worldly activities and on modestly saving one's wealth, medieval Catholic doctrine preached withdrawal from the worlds of commerce and politics in favor of worshiping God in monasteries. Although these ascetic ideals faded over time, they generated mass attitudes toward economic behavior

that endured. In the process, Weber concluded, Protestantism proved more conducive than Catholicism to encouraging entrepreneurial activity and the accumulation of wealth.[13]

A groundbreaking study of political culture was published in 1963 by Gabriel Almond and Sidney Verba. *The Civic Culture* examined political culture in five countries (the United States, Britain, West Germany, Italy, and Mexico). Based on responses to a host of questions about politics, the authors concluded that the populations of each of these countries could be divided into three groups:

1. *Participants*, who generally are knowledgeable about politics and have positive feelings about their governmental system, regarding it as legitimate and worthy of support. They vote regularly and may also get involved in other forms of political activity.

2. *Subjects*, who are less knowledgeable about what is going on in politics. Subjects evince relatively little pride in their political institutions, vote rarely, and have little confidence in their ability to get results out of government, but they are law abiding and can be quite deferential in their attitudes toward governmental authority.

3. *Parochials*, who know practically nothing about politics, especially at the national level. Their world is usually confined to their local community or village. They are basically alienated from their government and apathetic, with very low confidence in their ability to get government officials to help them or to effect political change.

Almond and Verba concluded that all the countries they studied consisted of a mixture of participants, subjects, and parochials. The countries differed, however, with respect to the relative size of the three categories in proportion to the population. At the time the studies were conducted, in the late 1950s, the United States had a high proportion of participants and subjects. Mexico and Italy had high proportions of subjects and parochials, while Britain and Germany fell in between.

Almond and Verba hypothesized that democracy would be most stable in countries possessing what they called a **civic culture**, that is, a combination of fairly large numbers of participants and subjects together with a smaller number of parochials. In their view, democracy did not require a population consisting entirely of politically active participants. Too many activists, they argued, might destabilize the political system. Democracy would be most stable if, in addition to political activists, the population also included subjects and parochials who did not make too many political demands and who quietly accepted the existing political arrangements. They believed that the United States and Britain most closely approximated this ideal mixture.

Like Tocqueville, Almond and Verba affirmed that a successful democracy requires more than just democratic governmental institutions and laws; it also requires a compatible political culture. "Unless the political culture is able to support a democratic system," they wrote, "the chances for the success of that system are slim." By contrast, the authors hypothesized that authoritarian governments of various kinds (such as communist countries and military dictatorships) would rest on a cultural foundation of subject and parochial attitudes. Politically active participants would be a small minority in such countries, confined mainly to the ruling elite and their most determined opponents. Advocates of the importance of political culture thus contend that authoritarian governments do not rule on the basis of force alone. They stay in power at least in part because large segments of the population share certain attitudes and beliefs supportive of authoritarian rule.

Though some scholars have questioned the assumptions and conclusions of *The Civic Culture*, others have supported their basic contention that attitudes and feelings do play a major role in explaining why some countries have stable democracies and others do not.[14] So, does political culture matter? In several major books and other works devoted to testing the hypothesis that cultural factors exercise an impact on the probability that countries will be democratic, Ronald Inglehart has found considerable evidence that high levels of interpersonal trust and voluntary participation in cooperative associations are strongly correlated with stable democracies. Countries that lack these cultural attributes tend to be less successful at building or maintaining stable democratic institutions. While admitting that the cultural factors associated with democracy are often correlated with high levels of national economic development, Inglehart notes, "Wealth alone does not automatically bring democracy." By the same token, he writes, "Democracy is not attained simply by making institutional changes or by clever elite-level maneuvering." Rather, cultural factors play a role of their own in affecting democracy's prospects.[15]

In an innovative study, Robert Putnam and his associates examined various explanations of why some regions of Italy have very effective governments while other regions do not. They found that economic factors were not the principal explanatory variables. The critical difference rested on a key aspect of political culture, namely, the extent to which people trusted one another enough to cooperate in forming associations. Regions with a history of social trust and cooperation—mostly in the northern part of Italy—were more successful at making democracy work than were those characterized by high levels of suspicion and noncooperation—the regions in the south and Sicily. The combination of social capital, civil society, and a civic culture forms *civicness*, an essential cultural ingredient of democracy.[16]

CONCEPTUALIZING POLITICAL CULTURE

To make the concept of political culture clearer, let's consider some patterns of attitudes and values about political and social life that can exist in different countries. We considered some features of democratic political culture when we discussed democratic values in Chapter 5, but these are central attitudes that matter politically. We'll divide these attitudinal patterns into three clusters: (1) attitudes toward authority; (2) attitudes toward society; and (3) attitudes toward politics, especially the state. Within each of these clusters, we'll look at specific dichotomies (i.e., paired opposites) that form the outer extremes of possible attitudes people may have. However, many people, perhaps the majority, are located at various points between these extreme attitudes. Hence we should conceptualize the various attitudes people have toward a given object (such as the government) in terms of a *continuum*, a line of gradations between one polar extreme and the opposite. Let's clarify these notions with specific examples.

Attitudes toward Authority

One possible dichotomy that describes attitudes toward authority is the *submissive-rebellious* dichotomy (see Figure 9.1). At one extreme, people can be highly submissive toward authority (whether in the family or in the political community). Often this attitude is tinged with fatalism and resignation (e.g., "Nothing can be changed; it is God's will."). At the other extreme are those who reject authority and seek to rebel against it. But there are various stations between. Without being humbly submissive, people can be *deferential* toward authority, like the "subjects" in Almond and Verba's analysis. These people willingly respect authority but do not seek to deal with it directly. Think of that family member you know—uncle, aunt, cousin—who would never dream of breaking the law but wants nothing to do with local authorities—couldn't imagine questioning the city council's decisions or a court's judgment—and just wants to avoid causing a ruckus. Moving along the continuum, people can be *interactive* with authority: They can share in making the decisions that affect their lives. This interactive attitude is characteristic of what Almond and Verba would call "participants." Participants attend public meetings, they sign petitions, and they campaign for candidates.

Next along the continuum we find *alienated* attitudes toward authority. Alienated people are too discontented to be obligingly submissive or quietly deferential, and they are generally quite cynical about the authority patterns under which they live. But if they do anything at all to express their alienation, the actions they take will usually be sporadic, halfhearted, and ultimately ineffective (such as persistently refusing to vote). You've probably met the alienated at some family gathering too—the relative who gripes about politicians and bureaucrats but gives no impression he will do anything to address what he is griping about. At the opposite extreme on this continuum, people with *rebellious* attitudes toward authority are so hostile to the ruling powers that they try to take action against them. In political life, rebels may undertake such dissident behavior as publicly denouncing the

| Submissive | Deferential | Interactive | Alienated | Rebellious |

FIGURE 9.1   Continuum of Attitudes toward Authority

Table 9.3 Fundamental Political Attitudes

	PEOPLE SHOULD . . .		"THERE ARE ONLY FEW PEOPLE TO TRUST."			GOVERNMENT SHOULD OR PROBABLY SHOULD . . .		
	Obey the law without exception	Follow their conscience on occasions	Agree or strongly agree	Neither agree nor disagree	Disagree or strongly disagree	Provide jobs for everyone	Provide a decent living standard for the unemployed	Reduce income differences between the rich & poor
Canada	40%	60%	71%	13%	16%	35%	63%	68%
Chile	71	29	82	10	8	72	91	91
France	23	77	71	14	15	62	70	78
West Germany	37	64	69	12	19	63	67	67
East Germany	44	56	69	12	19	80	80	83
Ireland	55	45	75	5	20	65	82	80
Israel—Jews	60	40	68	15	17	76	65	83
Israel—Arabs	64	36	87	7	6	94	60	94
Japan	24	76	63	17	20	52	57	66
Netherlands	34	66	60	12	29	56	69	72
Philippines	46	54	72	15	13	92	79	73
Poland	72	28	86	9	5	89	82	88
Russia	49	51	82	10	8	93	68	86
South Africa	77	24	85	7	8	90	83	83
South Korea	41	59	70	13	17	70	70	81
Sweden	30	71	64	16	21	59	84	68
Taiwan	59	41	56	16	28	88	72	89
United Kingdom	44	56	74	11	15	56	57	69
United States	53	47	72	8	20	40	52	52
All Countries	**51**	**49**	**73**	**11**	**16**	**73**	**74**	**76**

Source: International Social Survey Programme, "Role of Government IV," (ISSP 2006), available at http://www.gesis.org/issp/.

government, or they may actively seek to overthrow it, whether violently or through nonviolent resistance. Highly traditional political cultures, such as Middle Eastern sheikdoms, tend to have a large number of submissive and deferential citizens. Democracies thrive on an interactive citizenry, though some people may feel alienated. Any country with a large number of rebels is probably experiencing violent discontent or civil war.

Table 9.3 shows the responses to the International Social Survey Programme's 2006 survey on the role of government. The respondents live in several of the countries we explore in depth in Part Two of this book or that we use as examples in Part One. The first panel of Table 9.3 provides the responses to a question about whether people should always obey the law or follow their consciences on occasion, an item that offers insight into people's views of their relationship with authority. The cells of the table in red indicate societies in which the respondents to the survey are more likely to follow their consciences, that is, not obey the law indiscriminately. As you can see, more

Americans are willing to always obey the law than are willing to follow their own consciences on occasion. In many other democracies occasional civil disobedience is preferred over strict obedience to the law.

Attitudes toward Society

One continuum of this type is delineated by the *consensual–conflictual* dichotomy (see Figure 9.2). At one end of the line we find people with highly cooperative attitudes toward other individuals and social groups. They exhibit high levels of tolerance, interpersonal trust, and willingness to compromise. At the other end we find highly conflictual attitudes toward other individuals and social groups, defined by correspondingly low levels of tolerance, interpersonal trust, and propensity to compromise. The continuum shows various gradations between. Yugoslavia, wracked by ethnic cleansing in the 1990s (see Chapter 4), and Lebanon, with a plethora of religious groups embroiled in civil

| Highly consensual | Mixture of conflict and compromise | Somewhat conflictual | Highly conflicted |

FIGURE 9.2 **Continuum of Attitudes toward Society: Consensual–Conflictual Dimension**

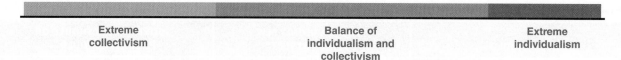

Extreme
collectivism

Balance of
individualism and
collectivism

Extreme
individualism

FIGURE 9.3   Continuum of Attitudes toward Society: Collectivist–Individualist Dimension

strife down to the present day, are examples of highly conflictual political cultures in which sectarian divisions (Roman Catholic, Eastern Orthodox, and Muslim in Yugoslavia; Maronite Christian, Sunni Muslim, and Shiite Muslim in Lebanon) have been the basis of political conflict. Japan exemplifies a highly consensual society: Political decisions typically have to meet with a broad social consensus before they can be finalized. The United States, Canada, the West European democracies, and other successful democratic states generally display a mixture of conflict and compromise, with the conflicts typically dealt with through the democratic process rather than through violence.

To examine just one of the attitudes mentioned, interpersonal trust, consider the middle panel of Table 9.3. The cells in red indicate countries in which the population is more trusting of each other than is the norm worldwide. Note, though, that most people around the world think there are few people who can really be trusted. Even in the highlighted countries in Table 9.3 more respondents are suspicious of others than are trusting of them. In any political system those seeking to form organizations and to foster collaboration have to confront people's natural propensity to be suspicious of others, although that distrust is more broadly felt in some countries (Chile, Poland, and South Africa, in the table) than in others (Taiwan, the Netherlands, and Sweden).

Another dichotomy we can expect to find in people's attitudes toward other people is the *collectivist–individualist* dichotomy (see Figure 9.3). At the far right end, the most extreme individualists have an "everyone-for-himself" mentality. Proponents of *economic individualism* reject government assistance and seek to take care of themselves and their immediate families entirely on their own. If they fail in these efforts, they proudly reject handouts or charity. Such extreme types expect everyone else in society to behave the same way. Proponents of what may be called *expressive individualism* believe that all individuals should have the right to say what they want and live as they please, with scant regard for the larger society. Whether stressing economic or expressive individualism, extreme individualists place the individual at the center of society.

At the left end of this continuum are extreme collectivists who discount individual rights and freedoms in favor of group rights and group activities. Just as extreme individualists may be willing to tolerate a high level of social inequality, at least some extreme collectivists seek to achieve as much egalitarianism as they can in all facets of social life: equality of opportunity, wealth, education, power, and so forth. But collectivism also risks producing the very opposite of political and social equality if authoritarian leaders and parties, acting in the name of the common good, establish a dictatorial regime commandeered by a narrow elite and its privileged supporters. That is what happened in Russia when the communists took power. In the

middle are those who seek a balance between the freedom of the individual and the welfare of the larger community.

Historically, the United States has gravitated somewhat toward the individualist side of this dichotomy, an attitude reflected in the old nostrum, "The government that governs least, governs best." As we pointed out at the start of this chapter, however, most Americans also expect their government to provide various social welfare benefits. This balance of individualist and collectivist values places the United States close to the middle of the continuum, though it still leans toward the pole of individualism. Most European countries are also close to the center, but they gravitate more toward the collectivist side because of public support for their well-funded welfare states. Russia has generally gravitated toward the collectivist side. Hypothetically, individualist cultures are more likely to favor market economies than are collectivist cultures, which would tend to favor strong state intervention in the economy to promote social equality.

Attitudes toward the State

The main dichotomy in this cluster of attitudes is the *permissive state–interventionist state* dichotomy (see Figure 9.4). At one end are those who favor a weak government that permits people the widest possible freedom to do what they want. The most extreme permissivists want no governmental interference of any kind in the economy (no taxes!), a minimal government role in maintaining law and order, no national obligation to defend the country; indeed, very few government intrusions of any kind. The most extreme permissivist is basically an anarchist. As one moves along the continuum, one finds increasing levels of support for various governmental tasks, starting with such elemental ones as the maintenance of law and order, regulation of transportation facilities, delivery of the mail, and control over the national defense.

At the other end of the continuum are those who favor maximum governmental intervention in all facets of life, including control over the economy and the regulation of social conflicts. Political elites who favor such an interventionist state may do so in some cases to maximize their own power over the population or over the economy. But ordinary citizens may also prefer an interventionist state, usually because they want the state to protect them against economic fluctuations, ill health, destitution in old age, or other possible hardships, whether natural or human-made. Proponents of the interventionist state may be willing to give up some of their personal freedoms in exchange for the state's assistance. Of course, there are less extreme variants of this protectivist attitude as one moves back toward the center of the continuum. In the 2012 U.S. presidential campaign, the camps of the Republican challenger Mitt Romney and Democratic incumbent Barack Obama made the degree of state intervention

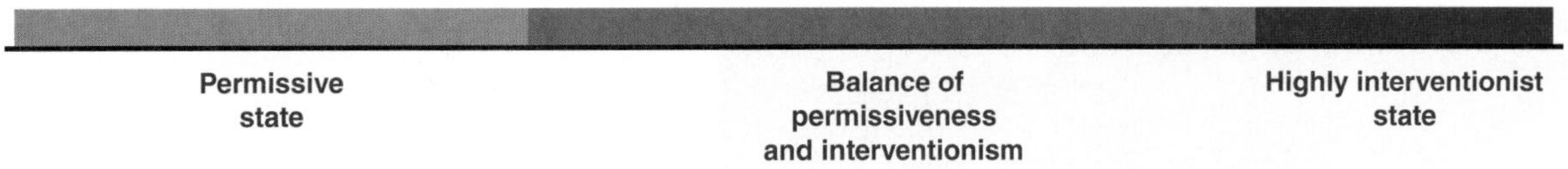

| Permissive state | Balance of permissiveness and interventionism | Highly interventionist state |

FIGURE 9.4   Continuum of Attitudes toward the State: Permissive–Interventionist Dimension

in the economy—whether the state would be more interventionist or more permissivist—the central issue of the race.

The 2006 ISSP survey on the role of government asked several questions about what the government should be expected to do. The third panel of Table 9.3 shows responses to three of those questions. The cells in red show where a society has low expectations of the government or where people do not want the government to take a significant role in economic affairs. You can see a wide range of views about the responsibilities of government. Whereas nearly everyone in the formerly communist countries (Russia, Poland, and East Germany in Table 9.3) tends to regard it as a government duty to provide jobs, to support the unemployed with a decent standard of living, and to reduce income disparities, Americans, the British, the Dutch, Japanese, and Canadians are not so enthused about significant government intervention in economic affairs. Individual responsibility for one's economic well-being and a notion that one deserves what one earns tend to characterize the more economically individualistic political cultures of the latter countries. They also tend to prefer private ownership of industry, whereas public ownership of industry is much more popular in former communist countries. As you will see in Chapter 11, many of these preferences for greater state involvement in economic and social affairs are reflected in policy choices about state expenditures and taxation.

The spectrums of attitudes shown in Figures 9.1 through 9.4 make ample room for political subcultures within a given country. Whereas the majority of the population may cluster around the middle of the spectrum along the authority continuum, favoring interactive relations with the decision makers, some people in the same country may be alienated from the dominant elites or political majority, or may even be actively rebellious. Similarly, whereas a few people may favor "rugged individualism," most segments of society may not. The point is, almost every country will have people whose attitudes can be located at different points along the attitudinal spectrums. At the same time, many countries will show majorities huddled around the midpoint. In short, we should conceive of each country's political culture as consisting of a combination of attitudes on a variety of dimensions. In most cases it would be an oversimplification to suggest that we can locate an entire country at a precise point along any of the continuums shown in this chapter.

We can hypothesize that some combinations of attitudes will be more supportive of stable democracy than others are, while alternative combinations can be expected to yield different results. For example, at least hypothetically we can assume:

- Societies with (1) high levels of interactive attitudes toward authority, (2) a high level of consensual attitudes toward society, (3) intermediate levels of individualism and collectivism, and (4) roughly balanced support for permissiveness and intervention on the part of the state will be more likely to sustain a stable democracy than will societies whose majorities deviate from these standards.

- Societies with (1) a high level of alienated or rebellious attitudes toward authority, (2) high levels of conflictual social attitudes and individualism, and (3) high levels of support for a permissive, weak state are likely to be embroiled in continuing civil conflict.

- Societies with (1) high levels of submissiveness or deference to authority, (2) high levels of social consensus and collectivism, and (3) wide support for an interventionist state are likely to be fairly stable authoritarian states of one kind or another.

Of course, these alternative combinations of attitude mixtures by no means exhaust all the possibilities. We may find other mixtures as we look directly at specific countries.

DO POLITICAL CULTURES CHANGE?

Although most systematic studies of political culture have revealed considerable continuity in the way particular populations think about politics, political culture is rarely static. Attitudinal change is real; all political cultures evolve. In some cases such changes occur slowly, shifting only every two generations or more. But in other cases they occur a bit more rapidly. As noted in Chapter 1, members of every generation tend to be influenced by the political events of their youth. When succeeding generations basically adopt the political attitudes of their parents with little or no change, shifts in political culture will be slight. But when key segments of a particular generation adopt political attitudes at variance with those of the preceding generation, a country's political culture can shift accordingly.

A good example of such generational change occurred in West Germany after World War II. In 1953, some eight years after the defeat of Nazi Germany, only about half the population said that democracy was the best form of government. With the passing of the older generation and the emergence of younger people who grew up after the war, support for democracy rose appreciably. In 1972, 90 percent of West Germans favored democracy.[17] Similar changes are occurring right now in the formerly communist countries of Russia, Poland, the Czech Republic, and others. Attitudes toward authority, society, and the state are in flux, sometimes wildly so. Some people in these countries cling to old habits of mind and behavior and long for a restoration of strong political authority and a state-controlled economy; others (especially younger people) are ready to experiment with democracy and private enterprise.[18]

Following the ouster in 2011 of Egyptian President Hosni Mubarak, the newly elected president, Mohamed Morsi, faced challenges from the competing interests of secularist and Islamist groups. In 2012, a newly drafted constitution evoked serious conflict as different elements of Egyptian society struggled to influence the direction of a new political culture. Here Morsi receives a copy of the final draft of Egyptian new constitution from the head of the Islamist-dominated constituent assembly. In July 2013 the Morsi government was overthrown in a military coup d'etat after widespread protests led by liberal and leftist political organizations. Among his opponents' complaints were that Morsi had railroaded a flawed constitution through the Constituent Assembly and that he and the Muslim Brotherhood governed in an authoritarian manner.

ESSENTIAL CONCEPTS

Post-Materialism

Another shift in attitudes has occurred since the 1960s in many Western democracies. As Ronald Inglehart has shown, an increasing percentage of citizens in the United States and Western Europe in the 1960s and 1970s shared what he calls **post-materialist values**. Instead of being motivated primarily by the need for financial security, as was the case with previous generations, a large number of citizens who came of voting age in these years, particularly those who had a secure economic background and higher education, tended to vote or engage in other forms of political behavior on the basis of broader concerns about the welfare of the community. The goals of urban renovation, environmental protection, and other communitywide considerations increasingly took precedence over personal wealth as a source of political behavior. Subsequent decades showed slight variations in these attitudes in particular countries.[19]

In a subsequent work, Inglehart undertook a sweeping investigation of the hypothesis that "economic, political, and cultural change go together in coherent patterns that are changing the world in predictable ways." With an insightful look at the historical record and an analysis of survey data from 43 countries, collected in the World Values Survey, Inglehart found substantial evidence consistent with **modernization** theory and what he calls **postmodernization**.[20]

As societies modernize from traditional, largely agricultural economies to industrialization, the attitudes and values of the population shift as well. A preoccupation with survival under conditions of acute scarcity gives way to a quest for personal economic advancement. Maximizing one's material security and wealth becomes a top priority.

As people pursue these economic goals, they seek greater political influence. Whereas premodern societies tend to have authoritarian regimes, the rising prosperity and education levels that accompany industrial modernization promote greater mass political participation. Industrialism and the value changes accompanying it thus promote democracy.

In the most economically advanced societies of the late twentieth century, industrial economies developed into *post-industrial economies*. The service sector—consisting of government, education, banking and finance, retail stores, and all sorts of consumer services—replaced manufacturing as the main source of economic growth and employment. Personal and national incomes rose appreciably. A well-funded welfare state guaranteed minimal living standards for the less fortunate as well as various other benefits for all (medical insurance, social security pensions, and the like).

Under these postmodern conditions of rising prosperity, the main priorities of a growing portion of the population shift from maximizing material wealth to maximizing nonmaterial forms of personal well-being: a satisfying job, a clean environment, more leisure time, and other postmaterialist values. Politically, these values entail less reliance on the state and declining deference to authority. People want less government intervention in their lives. Voters show greater independence at election time, loosening their traditional ties to the major political parties. Ironically, though their living standards are high, people with postmaterialist values have higher expectations and tend to display fairly high levels of dissatisfaction with their governments.

Gender roles change significantly in postmodern societies. Women are less confined to the home and more inclined to pursue higher education, careers, and political activism. People who embrace postmodern values are also more accepting of gender equality, divorce, homosexuality, abortion, and sexual liberalization than are the members of more traditional countries or less economically advanced segments of society.[21]

People who embrace postmodern values are also more accepting of gender equality, divorce, homosexuality, abortion, and sexual liberalization than are the members of more traditional countries or less economically advanced segments of society. In 2001 Klaus Wowereit became mayor of Berlin and Bertrand Delanoë the mayor of Paris. Both are openly gay men with immense power in their respective countries.

Attitudes toward religion also change with post-materialism. Pippa Norris and Inglehart have shown that the populations of all economically advanced countries have manifested a general tendency toward secularization over the past 50 years, albeit at varying rates of change (see Table 9.1). Belief in God, church attendance, the frequency of prayer, and other indicators of religious commitment have declined steadily in most of these countries as national wealth and educational levels have risen. Differences are also observable between affluent and less affluent citizens inside these countries: On average, the poor are nearly twice as religious as the rich. Even in the United States, an outlier country that has consistently remained more religious than most other wealthy democracies, two-thirds of the poor tend to regard religion as "very important" and pray every day, as compared with 47 percent of the highest income group. These and other data suggest that as lives become more secure and immune to daily risks, the importance of religion gradually fades. At the same time, however, the number of people around the globe who profess strong religious beliefs has never been higher. A major reason appears to be that countries whose populations have traditional religious attitudes are producing children at significantly higher rates than wealthier countries.[22]

In advanced industrial democracies, Green parties have most consistently promoted post-materialist values in the political system. The German Green Party is the classic example of a party that emerged among the generation that came of age in the 1970s after West Germany had achieved a high degree of material prosperity. As we'll see in Chapter 15, the German Greens (and similar parties in other Western European democracies) have protested environmental degradation, advocated direct democracy and transparency in government, and promoted the inclusion of women and marginalized groups in politics. ■

Human Development Theory

In a pathbreaking study, Inglehart and his collaborators, Christian Welzel and Hans-Dieter Klingemann, go beyond modernization–postmodernization theory and present what they call **human development theory**. Drawing on the work of other scholars, the Freedom House rankings, and the World Values Surveys conducted between 1981 and 2001, the study demonstrates causal linkages between economic development, the value of freedom, and democratic institutions. The authors begin with the well-established observation that scarce economic resources in poor countries compel people to adopt a cluster of attitudes necessary for survival. These *conformity values* include tight group discipline, distrust and intolerance of others, moral rigidity, and the acceptance of strong hierarchical authority patterns. But as the economy develops and individuals have more resources at their disposal, people become better educated and demand more liberty. Socioeconomic prosperity engenders such *emancipative values* as individual freedom and self-expression, along with greater tolerance for the freedoms and rights of others. As emancipative values spread across the population, popular demands for democracy rise.

When these trends occur in nondemocratic countries, they spark opposition to authoritarian elites and promote democratization. When they occur in countries that already have democratic institutions (including partly free states), people become less willing to put up with limitations on their political influence or with corrupt leaders. In other words, they become less satisfied with the veneer of "formal democracy" and insist on a truly "effective democracy": a democracy that requires the integrity of the elite and ensures the government's accountability to the governed. At the end of this chain of causation (depicted

HYPOTHESIS-TESTING EXERCISE
Economic Development and Post-Materialism

Hypothesis Is Inglehart's hypothesis about post-materialism supported by the evidence? Inglehart essentially argues that where economic conditions are less precarious we should find that the society includes a greater share of the population with post-materialist values. Put another way, economically more prosperous or developed societies should have more citizens who are post-materialists.

Variables The *independent variable* is a country's level of economic development. The *dependent variable* is the share of the population with post-materialist values.

Evidence One way of measuring economic development is the gross domestic product (GDP) per capita, the measure we used in our initial hypothesis-testing exercise in Chapter 2. Economists working for the United Nations Development Programme (UNDP) have created another measure of development known as the Human Development Index (HDI), which we will use here. The HDI incorporates not only income as measured by GDP per capita but also two other measures of economic well-being, one that incorporates literacy and the share of the population attending school while the other is life expectancy, a measure of the population's physical health. The HDI ranges from 0 to 1.

To measure post-materialism, Inglehart designed the following question that has been asked regularly by the World Values Survey (WVS).

> People sometimes talk about what the aims of this country should be for the next 10 years. Below are listed some of the goals which different people would give top priority. Would you please say which one of these you, yourself, consider the most important? And which is the next most important?

1. A high level of economic growth.
2. Making sure this country has strong defense forces.
3. Seeing that people have more say about how things are done at their jobs and in their communities.
4. Trying to make our cities and countryside more beautiful.

Options 1 and 2 are materialist responses while 3 and 4 are post-materialist answers. Respondents to the survey who select 1 and 2 as their top and second most important priorities are considered materialists, while those who select 3 and 4 are post-materialists. Those who select one materialist and one post-materialist option as their top two priorities are considered mixed. (Answer the question yourself. Are you materialist, post-materialist, or mixed? Does your response surprise you?)

Fifty-five countries participated in the 2004–08 wave of the WVS. Figure 9.5 plots the relationship between the HDI (the explanatory factor) and the share of the population that is post-materialist (what we're trying to explain) for those 55 countries. The line in the chart shows the best fit for a linear relationship between the two variables. As it suggests, as the HDI rises, so does the share of the population that is post-materialist. This plot does not show a tight fit of the line to the data, but there is a clear, positive relationship between economic development and post-materialism.

Conclusions Based on our evidence from a recent WVS, Inglehart's hypothesis is supported. Countries with higher levels of economic development will tend to have more post-materialists in their society. Since post-materialists tend to favor policies that are sensitive to environmental degradation and to the aesthetic quality of the spaces in which we live and

in Figure 9.6) come rising levels of *human choice:* People are increasingly free to choose the lives they want to lead. Freedom of choice is a globally shared value. Surveys conducted in 148 countries display a highly significant correlation between the perceptions of how much choice people believe they have, on the one hand, and their overall satisfaction with life, on the other hand.

All of this is good news for democracy advocates. Human development theory tells us that socioeconomic development sets in motion a train of processes that ultimately leads to democracy. But even though the causal connections laid out in the theory are valid across different countries and cultures, they cannot predict exactly when a democratization process, or a move toward "effective democracy," will occur in any specific country. As we saw in Chapter 7, transitions to democracy and democratic consolidation depend on a variety of factors, some of which cannot be foreseen. Inglehart and his co-authors acknowledge that their theory is probabilistic in nature: It

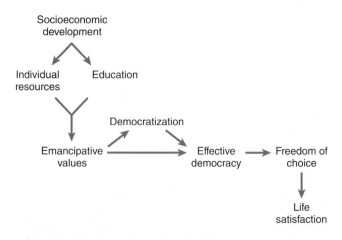

FIGURE 9.6   The Logic of Human Development Theory

Source: Based on Christian Welzel, Ronald Inglehart, and Hans-Dieter Klingemann, "The Theory of Human Development: A Cross-Cultural Analysis, *European Journal of Political Research* 42 (2003), pp. 341–79.

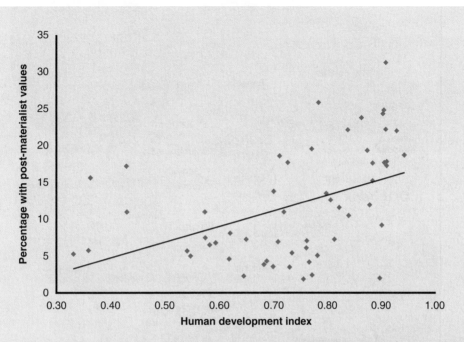

FIGURE 9.5   **Relationship between HDI and Share of Population Viewed as Post-Materialist**

work and since they advocate for equality between men and women in the household and for greater opportunities for participation for everyone in the nation's political life, we should expect the richer countries to have political systems that are more inclusive, social policies that favor women's equality in the home and the workplace, more extensive environmental regulation, and more severe zoning rules to shape the quality of the infrastructure of roads, buildings, and parks. In contrast, poorer countries will have the converse—more exclusionary politics, social policies that favor men, more pollution, and a more haphazard attention to the quality of the built environment.

highlights general tendencies that make democracy *probable* but not inevitable or predictable by a certain point. Every country moves along the path to democracy at its own pace, in accordance with its own specific economic, social, and political characteristics. Nevertheless, from human development theory and its supporting evidence come findings of global applicability: Democracy rests on both socioeconomic development *and* the value of freedom. Economic progress *promotes* support for the value of freedom. And as a key attribute of a country's political culture, freedom has a *causative* effect on democratic institutions; it is not simply a product of democratic institutions, as some scholars maintain.[23] Reinforcing these conclusions, Christian Welzel finds that when mass attitudes are shaped by aspirations of liberty, democratization tends to progress. Arguing against democratization theories that downplay mass attitudes, Welzel observes that no other independent variable, including per capita income or social capital, explains democratization processes better than emancipative values and aspirations when

they are adopted by large elements of the populace. These findings, Welzel notes, are fully consistent with human development theory.[24]

The division of the world into different countries, regions, and cultures reflects different value orientations. Some countries and regions have societies that tend on average to favor *traditional* values: strong religious beliefs, deference to authority, close family ties, intolerance of diversity, nationalism, and a few others. By contrast, other countries have populations that tend to favor *secular-rational* values, such as weaker ties to religion and family, tolerance, democratic attitudes toward authority, and a cosmopolitan outlook. A second cultural dichotomy centers on the division between societies that emphasize *survival* values, reflecting the constraints of poverty, and those that tend to favor the *self-expressive* values associated with postmodernism. These differences are portrayed in the Inglehart-Welzel Values Map (see Map 9.1). As you can see, the countries tend to cluster on these two attitudinal axes within the larger cultural

The World Value Survey Cultural Map 2005–2008

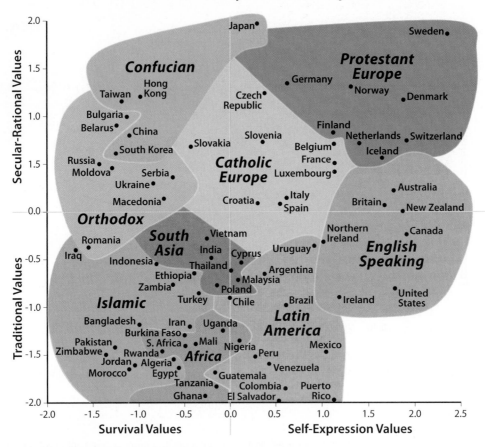

MAP 9.1   The Inglehart-Welzel Values Map

Source: Ronald Inglehart and Christian Welzel, "Changing Mass Priorities: The Link Between Modernization and Democracy," *Perspectives on Politics*, 8, no. 2 (June 2010), p. 554.

Note: The numbers represent the scores of countries on the traditional/rational-secular values dimension and the survival/self-expression values dimension.

groups from which they descended (e.g., Protestant Europe, Latin America, Islamic countries). This result leads Inglehart and Welzel to conclude that political cultures persist and matter.

A Clash of Civilizations?

In view of the striking cultural differences identified by Inglehart and Welzel, is the world facing a clash of civilizations? Some policy makers have wondered aloud whether the major axis of conflict in international politics in the post-Cold-War world is such a civilizational struggle. These views were given a powerful expression in an article and book on the "clash of civilizations" by the influential political scientist Samuel Huntington.

Huntington advanced the hypothesis that the main source of struggle in the contemporary world is neither ideological nor economic but cultural, centered in a civilizational conflict. Defining a civilization as the broadest level of a person's identity, Huntington divides the world into seven (perhaps eight) major civilizations: Sinic, Japanese, Hindu, Islamic, Orthodox, Western, and Latin American. A cohesive African civilization may also be emerging. Each one is rooted in a distinct

blend of history and culture. You can see some of Huntington's civilizations reflected in the Inglehart-Welzel Values Map. For several of them, religion is the key defining feature. With the disappearance of the ideological rivalries of the Cold War, in Huntington's view, the principal fault lines in world politics are drawn at the borders of these cultural communities. Numerous fault-line conflicts between representatives of different civilizations have recently occurred in Bosnia, Sri Lanka, Russia, Kashmir, and other parts of the globe. In addition, the presence of powerful core states such as China, Japan, India, Russia, and the United States at the head of their respective civilizations makes the prospect of a global civilization war, while highly unlikely, at least possible, with potentially devastating results. Meanwhile, the West is now at the zenith of its economic and military power, but it is simultaneously entering a period of relative decline, losing ground to Asia in economic terms and to several other civilizations in demographic terms. The Western countries are also meeting stiff resistance from almost all the other civilizations—above all from the "Confucian-Islamic connection"—in their attempts to promote democratization and human rights around the world.

Under these circumstances, Huntington argues, the West must stick to its core democratic values but repudiate the idea that the defining features of Western civilization—Christianity, the rule of law, pluralistic democracy, individualism, and the separation of church and state—are universally applicable. The West's belief in the universality of Western culture, he writes, is false, immoral, and dangerous. Instead of arrogantly foisting these values on the world, or expecting economic and technological progress to create a single, Western-oriented global culture, Huntington argues, the United States and its European allies should concentrate on solidifying their own unity while encouraging international acceptance of cultural diversity and promoting commonalities among the world's great civilizations. It is "most important to recognize," he concludes, "that Western intervention in the affairs of other civilizations is probably the single most dangerous source of instability and potential global conflict in a multicivilizational world."[25]

Huntington's views touched off a lively debate. Critics including Norris and Inglehart point out that global opinion surveys conducted up to 2001 revealed markedly little evidence of a clash of political values between Western and predominantly Muslim countries. Majorities in both cultures approved of democratic ideals in principle and the way democracy works in practice. The greatest gap between Muslim and Western societies centers on gender equality and sexual liberalization. Even young Muslims retain deeply traditional values on these issues, in contrast to young Westerners. "The central values separating Islam and the West revolve far more centrally around Eros than Demos," the authors conclude. The survey data revealed less support for democratic values and greater support for strong governments in Central and Eastern Europe, the former USSR, Latin America, and East Asia. Thus the survey evidence bearing on Huntington's thesis is mixed.[26]

Another criticism focuses on the fact that states, not civilizations, are the primary elements of organized political activity around the world. Civilizations cannot account very well for the specific forms of government and political life countries have, or for their foreign policy orientations. In fact, every civilization Huntington identifies is characterized by a variety of political regimes, ideologies, parties, and government policies, both domestic and international. For example, Orthodox civilization—Russia, Greece, Romania, and Serbia, among others—has seen kaleidoscopic changes in political regimes in the past 50 years. Russia, Romania, and Serbia have gone from different forms of communism to different degrees of democracy. Greece has had a military dictatorship as well as democratic governments of both the center-right and the center-left, plus two Communist Parties. Greece and Romania are in the European Union and NATO; Serbia appears to be heading into those organizations, whereas Russia nurtures its independence. The variety of regime types, domestic political developments, and international orientations in these states is even greater if we go back a hundred years. Much the same can be said for the other civilizations Huntington singles out.

Finally, you should reflect on the consequences of economic modernization for the emergence of the civilizational conflict Huntington predicts. To Inglehart and Welzel, further economic development is likely to lead to a convergence in values and political cultures in the way Figure 9.6 suggests. To Huntington, the more likely consequence of non-Western cultures' exposure to the consumerist, individualistic values depicted in the Western media, Hollywood films, popular music, and advertising is a rejection of such values by people in some civilizations, especially Islamic civilization. Which do you think it will be?

Conclusion

This chapter has shown that political culture—understood as shared political attitudes by whole societies or large segments of them—has a broad, long-term impact on political life around the world. Different societies have varied views about how deferential toward authority or how participative people should be in politics. They differ about the degree to which others in their society can be trusted and hence might form the basis of collective action. They have a wide range of views about the responsibility of the state toward the individuals in society, especially about how much the state should promote individuals' economic interests. Political culture is not static, however. We have also seen that economic development can spur cultural change, although it typically takes a long time to happen. Having considered how these broad social and political attitudes may shape people's political behavior in this chapter, in Chapter 10 we examine a more immediate influence on politics and policy: ideology.

Key Terms

Political culture
Political subculture
Political socialization
Civic culture
Post-material values
Modernization
Postmodernization
Human development theory

Notes

1. In 1964, 22 percent of Americans said they distrusted the federal government. This figure climbed to 62 percent in 1976 and 73 percent in 1980 before dropping to 58 percent in 1988. Cited in Michael M. Gant and Norman R. Luttbeg, *American Electoral Behavior* (Itasca, IL: F. E. Peacock, 1991), p. 144. A poll taken in 1995 revealed that 45 percent of Americans were "satisfied but not enthusiastic" about the way their federal government works, and 41 percent were "dissatisfied but not angry." Only 3 percent were "enthusiastic" and 9 percent were "angry." See the *The Washington Post*, May 18, 1995. In the 2006 World Values Survey, 38 percent expressed a great deal or quite a lot of confidence in government, while 62 percent had not very much confidence or none at all. Data retrieved from the online analysis program at worldvaluessurvey.org.

2. worldvaluessurvey.org.

3. See, for example, Jon Cohen and Dan Balz, "Poll Shows Americans Oppose Entitlement Cuts to Deal with Debt Problem," *The Washington Post*, April 20, 2011.

4. Lydia Saad, "Conservatives Remain the Largest Ideological Group in U.S.," January 12, 2012, at http://www.gallup.com/poll/152021/Conservatives-Remain-Largest-Ideological-Group.aspx.

5. "Pew Global Attitudes Spring 2010 Trends Topline," available at http://www.pewglobal.org/2010/05/08/spring-2010-survey-data/.

6. Donald J. Devine, *The Political Culture of the United States* (Boston: Little, Brown, 1972); Herbert McClosky and John Zaller, *The American Ethos: Public Attitudes Toward Capitalism and Democracy* (Cambridge: Cambridge University Press, 1985); Robert N. Bellah et al., *Habits of the Heart: Individualism and Commitment in American Life* (Berkeley, CA: University of California Press, 1985); Gary Wills, *A Necessary Evil: A History of American Distrust of Government* (New York: Simon & Schuster, 1999). See also the attitudinal orientations of various clusters of Americans in the survey conducted by the Kaiser Family Foundation, *The Washington Post*, and Harvard University titled *Why Don't Americans Trust the Government?* (Menlo Park, CA: Henry J. Kaiser Family Fund, 1996). On the intellectual history of contending political cultures in the United States, see Richard J. Ellis, *American Political Cultures* (Oxford: Oxford University Press, 1993).

7. For surveys of concepts of political culture, see Richard W. Wilson, "The Many Voices of Political Culture: Assessing Different Approaches," *World Politics* 52, no. 2 (January 2000), pp. 246–73; John R. Gibbons, "Contemporary Political Culture: An Introduction," in *Contemporary Political Culture*, ed. J. R. Gibbins (London: Sage, 1989), pp. 1–30.

8. Herbert J. Gans, *Middle American Individualism* (New York: Free Press, 1988).

9. Harry Eckstein, "A Culturalist Theory of Political Change," *American Political Science Review* 82, no. 3 (September 1988), pp. 789–804.

10. T. W. Adorno et al., *The Authoritarian Personality* (New York: Harper, 1950).

11. Leon Festinger, *A Theory of Cognitive Dissonance* (Stanford: Stanford University Press, 1957). See also Robert Jervis, *Perception and Misperception in International Politics* (Princeton, NJ: Princeton University Press, 1976); Richard Hofstadter, *The Paranoid Style in American Politics* (New York: Knopf, 1965); Robert S. Robins and Jerrold M. Post, *Political Paranoia* (New Haven, CN: Yale University Press, 1997). An early classic is Charles Mackay, *Extraordinary Popular Delusions and the Madness of Crowds* (Boston: L. C. Page, 1932).

12. Alexis de Tocqueville, *Democracy in America*, ed. J. P. Mayer, trans. George Lawrence (New York: Harper and Row, 1966), pp. 165, 274, 287–89, 291, 297–301, 309. John Adams remarked that "the source of the revolution" against England was the "systematical dissolution of the true family authority." See Gordon S. Wood, *The Radicalism of the American Revolution* (New York: Knopf, 1991), pp. 145–68, 235–36.

13. Max Weber, *The Protestant Ethic and the Spirit of Capitalism*, trans. Talcott Parsons (London: Routledge, 1992). This work was first published in 1904 and 1905. See also H. H. Gerth and C. Wright Mills, eds., *From Max Weber: Essays in Sociology* (New York: Oxford: 1946).

14. Gabriel Almond and Sidney Verba, *The Civic Culture* (Boston: Little, Brown, 1963). See also Gabriel Almond and Sidney Verba, eds., *The Civic Culture Revisited* (Boston: Little, Brown, 1980); David Laitin, "The Civic Culture at 30," *American Political Science Review* 89, no. 1 (March 1995), pp. 168–73.

15. Ronald Inglehart, *Culture Shift in Advanced Industrial Society* (Princeton, NJ: Princeton University Press, 1990); Ronald Inglehart, *Modernization*

and Postmodernization (Princeton, NJ: Princeton University Press, 1997). The quotes are on page 215 in the latter work.

16. Robert D. Putnam, *Making Democracy Work: Civic Traditions in Modern Italy* (Princeton, NJ: Princeton University Press, 1993). Putnam's findings corroborated the results of an earlier work on Italian political culture by Edward C. Banfield, who found that high levels of distrust among families undermined the effectiveness of local government. See Edward C. Banfield, *The Moral Basis of a Backward Society* (New York: Free Press, 1967). See also Christian Welzel, Ronald Inglehart, and Franziska Deutsch, "Social Capital, Voluntary Associations and Collective Action: Which Aspects of Social Capital Have the Greatest 'Civic' Payoff?" *Journal of Civil Society* 1, no. 2 (September 2005), pp. 121–46.

17. Kendall L. Baker, Russell J. Dalton, and Kai Hildebrandt, *Germany Transformed: Political Culture and the New Politics* (Cambridge, MA: Harvard University Press, 1981), p. 24; David Conradt, "Changing German Political Culture," in Almond and Verba, *The Civic Culture Revisited*, pp. 212–72.

18. The question of cultural change is also addressed in Cynthia McClintock, *Peasant Cooperatives and Political Change in Peru* (Princeton, NJ: Princeton University Press, 1991).

19. Ronald Inglehart, *The Silent Revolution: Changing Values and Political Styles Among Western Publics* (Princeton, NJ: Princeton University Press, 1977).

20. Inglehart, *Modernization and Postmodernization*. The World Values Survey is a cross-national survey of public values on a host of issues. The first wave surveyed 22 countries in 1981–83, the second one covered 41 countries in 1990–93, the third surveyed 43 countries in 1995–98, the fourth covered 59 countries in 1999–2001; subsequent surveys have been under way. Consult www.worldvaluessurvey.org and the Inter-university Consortium for Political and Social Research at icpsr.umich.edu.

21. Ronald Inglehart and Pippa Norris, *Rising Tide: Gender Equality and Cultural Change Around the World* (Cambridge: Cambridge University Press, 2003).

22. Pippa Norris and Ronald Inglehart, *Sacred and Secular: Religion and Politics Worldwide* (Cambridge: Cambridge University Press, 2004).

23. Christian Welzel, Ronald Inglehart, and Hans-Dieter Klingemann, "The Theory of Human Development: A Cross-Cultural Analyis," *European Journal of Political Research* 42 (2003), pp. 341–79. See also Christian Welzel and Ronald Inglehart, "Liberalism, Postmodernism, and the Growth of Freedom," *International Review of Sociology* 15, no. 1 (March 2006), pp. 81–108; Ronald Inglehart and Christian Welzel, "Political Culture and Democracy: Analyzing Cross-Level Linkages," *Comparative Politics* 36, no. 1 (October 2003), pp. 61–79; Ronald Inglehart and Christian Welzel, "Changing Mass Priorities: The Link Between Modernization and Democracy," *Perspectives on Politics* 8, no. 2 (June 2010), pp. 551–67.

24. Christian Welzel, "Democratization as an Emancipative Process: The Neglected Role of Mass Motivations," *European Journal of Political Research* 45, no. 6 (October 2006), pp. 871–96. This article, along with Welzel's "A Human Development View on Value Change" and a collection of graphs by Ronald Inglehart, can be accessed at www.worldvaluessurvey.org.

25. Samuel P. Huntington, *The Clash of Civilizations and the Remaking of the World Order* (New York: Simon & Schuster, 1996).

26. Norris and Inglehart, *Sacred and Secular*. The authors attribute the relatively high degree of religiosity in the United States to fairly high levels of economic insecurity and the growing number of Hispanic-Americans. For more critiques of Huntington, see *The Clash of Civilizations? The Debate* (New York: W. W. Norton, 1993).

10 Ideology

OVERVIEW

- Ideology is a coherent and elaborate set of political doctrines that serve to shape the political choices of individuals, political parties, and governments.

- Four main political ideologies have dominated the world in the past century: liberalism, socialism, fascism, and Islamist ideology. We explore each in depth, detailing their intellectual roots, examining different variants within them, and discussing the main political movements that they have inspired.

- While classical and contemporary liberalism have the same intellectual roots, they differ in fundamental ways. The terms *liberal* and *conservative* as used in the United States both fit into the liberal tradition.

- Marxism inspired two major twentieth-century ideologies, social democracy and Soviet-style communism.

- Fascism is the most important radical right ideology of the modern period. We consider its key elements and whether it is mainly a historical phenomenon or could reappear in the contemporary period.

- The religious teachings of Islam shape the views of Islamic fundamentalists about the ideal social order and the use of violence in politics. We also explore how they influence the prospects for democracy in Muslim countries.

- Observers typically array political ideologies on the left–right spectrum, but ideologies can also be placed in multi-dimensions space, as we will show.

Iranian president Mahmoud Ahmadinejad speaking before an image of Ayatollah Ruhollah Khomeini.

WHAT IS IDEOLOGY?

In virtually every country, political ideas have played a vital role in shaping the kinds of government that have evolved as well as the ways people behave in political life. Because of their presence in such a wide variety of settings, political ideas and the terminology used to express them can be a source of considerable confusion. As we've pointed out before, terms such as *liberalism*, *conservatism*, and *socialism* can have different meanings in different historical or country-specific contexts. One of the purposes of this chapter is to clear up some of this conceptual ambiguity.

To begin with, the term *ideology* itself is used in different ways. In its most informal, everyday usage, ideology frequently means little more than a person's general political orientation. When people say, "Ideologically, I'm a Republican" or "Environmentalism is my ideology," they often mean simply that they identify with the Republican Party or environmental causes in a general way, without necessarily subscribing to a carefully elaborated theory of politics or a particular form of government. But politicians, activists, political scientists, and others who take a more avid interest in politics usually have a more formal understanding of ideology. In its formal definition **ideology** is a coherent set of ideas that typically includes: (1) a theory about political relationships and the role of the state; (2) a notion of what constitutes political legitimacy and the highest political values; and (3) an action program indicating the goals, ideals, policies, and tactics to be pursued by the state, political elites, and the masses.

This second, formal definition involves a more systematically thought-out ideological orientation than the first definition does. You will note that ideologies are much more elaborate—they are usually written down and worked out in great detail—than are the more diffuse attitudes about politics that we associate with political culture, as discussed in Chapter 9. The dissemination of a political ideology to a whole society or large elements of it may cause a political culture to emerge that shares features of the ideology. Indeed, many historians and political scientists have argued that the United States has a liberal political culture because, from the time of our founding, liberal thinkers—John Locke and Adam Smith, Thomas Jefferson and James Madison—formulated the liberal ideology that is at the base of our political institutions.[1]

Although ideologies are created by sophisticated thinkers and are grasped in their entirety by very few people, they can exert a profound impact on mass political behavior. Political elites are often quite successful at attracting large followings by getting a few key points of their ideologies across to the masses. Most people living in established democracies have not read the works of Locke or Madison, but they have learned in the course of their political socialization that democracy entails the right to vote and various other rights and freedoms. Average Muslims are not scholars of the Koran and may have little or no understanding of the complicated ideological and religious values that have marked their religion's history. Still, they may be swayed by Islamic clerics to adopt any of a variety of political attitudes, ranging from extreme hostility toward the non-Islamic world to more tolerant positions.

Throughout history relatively few political orientations have been sufficiently coherent to be regarded as ideologies. Most flourished in the twentieth century, which is often called "the century of ideologies." In this chapter we'll focus on four of them: *liberalism*, *socialism*, *fascism*, and *political Islam*. The sharp differences among these ideological orientations have fueled some of the bitterest conflicts in human history. People have fought and died over ideological beliefs by the tens of millions.

All four ideologies we consider in this chapter have variants. Sometimes these variations are very similar to one another. Liberals and conservatives in the contemporary United States, for example, are in basic agreement on the Constitution and on the nature of the economy as a mixture of private enterprise and state intervention. But in other cases the diverse tendencies within an ideology can be so disparate as to constitute distinctive ideologies in their own right. At times these internal variants have sparked intense conflict between their adherents, resulting in prolonged debates and in some cases bloody feuds over the ideology's "correct" interpretation. The socialist tradition, for example, produced two fundamentally different strains: Soviet-style communism and Western-oriented social democracy. Islam has produced several competing doctrinal and political orientations.

Any attempt to understand comparative politics in the contemporary world must explore the ideological sources of political life. We must also consider the implications of ideology for the immediate future. Some scholars assert that the intense ideological conflicts of the twentieth century are dying. Have we reached the "end of ideology"? We'll examine this hypothesis at the end of the chapter.

LIBERALISM

In today's world, **liberalism** essentially means liberal democracy and its economic counterpart, free-market capitalism. Because this book devotes three full chapters to democracy, and because the next chapter will cover capitalism extensively, we do not need to devote many pages here to a detailed discussion of liberal ideology. It is nevertheless useful at this point to clarify the diverse shadings of meaning that the term *liberalism* has acquired over the course of its historical evolution.

In its oldest and broadest definition, liberalism refers to a system of government that guarantees liberty. This was the original meaning of the term as it emerged in the late seventeenth and early eighteenth centuries in Great Britain and as it developed over the course of the eighteenth, nineteenth, and early twentieth centuries, particularly in Britain, America, and France. In its earliest manifestation, liberalism posed a direct challenge to government by absolute monarchs and aristocracies, expressing the basic idea that the power of the state should be limited and that certain freedoms should be granted to the people by law. From the outset, the essence of liberalism was its opposition to tyrannical state power. It regarded the citizenry, not God, as the source of legitimacy. For its earliest advocates, such as Locke, Madison, and Thomas Jefferson, liberalism did not imply mass democracy based on universal suffrage. They espoused a highly elitist concept of liberalism, with the right to vote confined primarily to men of property.

For many early liberals, moreover, the concept of liberalism had both political and economic components. Whereas political liberalism emphasized the concept of government by consent of the governed, economic liberalism stressed the notion that the state should strictly limit its role in the economy, leaving the bulk of the nation's economic activities in the hands of private individuals and companies. Early economic liberalism championed a free-enterprise economy. It sought to dismantle the vast edifice of taxes, state monopolies, feudal estates, and other forms of governmental or aristocratic domination of economic life that were common under most monarchal regimes. In their place it favored the free operation of businesses and commercial farming.

As liberal ideas evolved over the course of the nineteenth and twentieth centuries, the notion that a liberal political order requires mass democratic participation gradually asserted itself. Universal adult suffrage finally became a reality during and after World War I as women gained the right to vote in Britain (1918), Germany (1919), and the United States (1920). A host of countries adopted universal voting rights after World War II.

The concept of economic liberalism also changed over time, especially during the second half of the twentieth century. Whereas early conceptualizers of economic liberalism advocated only the barest minimum of government involvement in the economy, since World War II most proponents of private enterprise have accepted the view that governments should play a significant role in national economic life. Instead of advocating a completely free-enterprise economic system, they accept a partially free-enterprise system. Today's economic liberals acknowledge that governments must collect taxes, regulate banks and stock markets, promote economic growth, and provide various social welfare measures for the population such as education, unemployment insurance, and pensions. Hence we can make a general distinction among economic liberals between *classical liberals*, who favored virtually no governmental intervention in the economy, and *social liberals*, who favor a *mixed economy* that combines private enterprise and a large economic role for the state. Today those who advocate a classically liberal approach to the role of the state in the economy and also prefer a maximum of freedom in their social lives call themselves *libertarians*. Libertarianism still has a significant presence in the United States where the presidential campaigns of Representative Ron Paul drew a small but intense body of supporters in 2008 and 2012.

Liberalism and Conservatism in the United States

The interacting concepts of political and economic liberalism resulted in several different strands of liberalism in the contemporary world. In the United States, for example, the term *liberalism* as used in everyday parlance has a narrower, more specific meaning than the generic ones just described. Liberalism in the United States is a variant of the liberal tradition that can be called social liberalism. **Social liberalism** means active government intervention in the economy and society for the purpose of promoting economic growth, community welfare, and social justice. With its stress on government activism, this conception of liberalism took shape in Franklin D. Roosevelt's New Deal. Assuming office in 1933 at a time when American political

traditions precluded massive governmental interference in the private sector, Roosevelt boldly broke precedent and launched sweeping measures to combat the Great Depression. In the process, proponents of federal government activism in the United States became known as liberals. They favored a liberal (i.e., permissive) interpretation of the Constitution's injunction to "promote the general welfare."

The assertions of their adversaries to the contrary, American social liberals are not socialists, because they do not favor abolishing private enterprise or drastically limiting its scope in favor of a predominantly state-controlled economic system. Historically, American liberals have tended to side with the labor movement in labor–management disputes. They have generally made their home in the Democratic Party.

Conservatism in the United States is the heir to the classical liberal tradition of minimal government interference in the economy. During the New Deal decades, many confirmed and uncompromising conservatives viewed Roosevelt's interventions in the economy as heresy. As many New Deal programs such as Social Security and the regulation of the private banking system proved their popularity, most conservatives came to accept the notion that the government must play an expanded role in the modern American economy. Contemporary conservatives do not reject government interventionism in principle but tend toward skepticism about its effectiveness in dealing with poverty or ameliorating other social conditions. They usually prefer more limited government activism, less government spending, and greater freedom for the private sector, and they tend to side with the business sector in labor–management relations. In recent decades, modern liberals and conservatives have differed more sharply on such value issues as abortion and school prayer, with "cultural conservatives," often connected with the Christian right, more inclined to take antiabortion and pro-prayer positions than liberals are. Conservatives have generally gravitated to the Republican Party.

Presidents Franklin D. Roosevelt (left) and Ronald Reagan (right) are considered by many to be the champions of modern American liberalism and conservatism, respectively.

American conservatives today are divided between those who favor a "realist" conception of foreign policy that would confine the use of military force to protecting vital U.S. national security interests, and *neoconservatives* who would use force in certain cases to promote "regime change" and democracy—an "idealist" approach previously advocated by Woodrow Wilson and other American liberals.

Liberalism and Conservatism Around the World

In many countries outside the United States, the term *liberalism* also has two meanings, roughly similar to those employed in the American context. Throughout much of the world, the first meaning of liberalism is its traditional one: As a generic political orientation, liberalism favors political and economic freedom as opposed to authoritarianism and socialism.

Its second connotation roughly approximates the more specific meaning that the term has acquired in twentieth-century U.S. politics. Like social liberals in the United States, many politicians and political parties that label themselves "liberal" in Canada, Western Europe, and elsewhere combine staunch support for private enterprise with attitudes favoring a certain amount of state intervention to improve general living conditions. European liberals, for example, constitute a centrist movement positioned between the more conservative parties on their right and the working-class-oriented social-democratic parties on their immediate left.

Conservatism also assumes different meanings in different contexts. In its most literal meaning, conservatism means resistance to any kind of change unless absolutely necessary. In the famous words of Sir Edward Grey, "When it is not necessary to change, it is necessary not to change." If change must come to save the country or preserve certain essential values, then it should be gradual rather than abrupt or revolutionary. For Edmund Burke, considered the founding father of British conservative thought, the constitutional order of monarchy, Parliament, and church had proven its legitimacy in Britain over the course of centuries. The accumulated wisdom of tradition, in his view, should not be thrown over in a headlong rush to revolution.[2]

In the United States and other democracies, today's conservatives favor democracy and the market economy. As a general rule, they attach a high priority to promoting private enterprise. European and Japanese conservatives, however, tend to favor a more interventionist state than is typically the case with American conservatives, as we'll see in Part Two.

SOCIALISM

The origins of twentieth-century socialist movements are to be found in nineteenth-century Europe. Socialism emerged as a reaction to the excesses of the industrial revolution and the free enterprise system that classical liberals championed. Over the course of the nineteenth century, the spread of manufacturing in Britain, France, Germany, and other countries rapidly blighted the cities and countryside with grimy factories and squalid slums. For much of the century, governments did virtually nothing to regulate working hours, safety standards, or child labor. Business owners were free to deal with their work force as they wished. Health care and unemployment insurance either did not exist at all or were grossly inadequate. The vast majority of the working class, lacking basic educational opportunities, faced a desperate future with scant hope of improving their lot. Peasants who owned little or no land of their own labored under similarly arduous circumstances for their landlords.

These conditions spawned several variants of socialist ideology. In the first half of the nineteenth century a number of socialist thinkers devised elaborate plans for replacing the free enterprise system (capitalism) with an entirely different economic system in which the workers, or the people as a whole, would collectively own the factories, farms, mines, and other productive enterprises. Common ownership of productive enterprises (or "communism") would thus replace private ownership. While the schemes proposed by these imaginative thinkers differed in detail, they agreed on one essential point: Capitalism was an exploitative and unstable economic system that had to be replaced by a more humane society based on the values of equality and community. These thinkers came to be known as *utopian socialists*, a term that derived from Sir Thomas More's design for an ideal society in his book, *Utopia*, published in 1516. Efforts to establish ideal socialist communities largely failed in Europe, however, and in some cases their adherents journeyed to the United States, creating utopian societies in Texas, Indiana, New Jersey, and other states. Most of these experiments also proved short-lived.[3]

A more enduring approach to socialism was elaborated by Karl Marx. Marx was significantly influenced by the utopian socialists, but in the course of his long career as an ideological theorist he developed a far more complicated system of thought that incorporated elements of philosophy, history, economics, sociology, and political theory. Marx turned out to be the principal intellectual source of twentieth-century socialism. But his complex ideas were interpreted in different ways by his contemporaries and subsequent generations.

In its original nineteenth-century conception, therefore, **socialism** was understood as a political and economic system in which private enterprise (capitalism) is abolished and replaced by some form of common ownership of factories, farms, and other productive enterprises.

Marxism

Summarizing Marx's thought is no easy task. The following brief sections convey some of the essential points of **Marxism** without underestimating its complexity, ambiguity, and internal inconsistencies.

History Has Direction Marx was born in Germany in 1818. After spending a year studying law at Bonn University in 1835–36, he moved to Berlin and became attracted to the ideas of one of the most influential figures in modern philosophy, Georg Wilhelm Friedrich Hegel (1770–1831). Marx was particularly intrigued by Hegel's philosophy of history.

Hegel maintained that human history has an identifiable direction and purpose. He argued that the long-term progression of history moves in accordance with a process he called the *dialectic*. For Hegel, the dialectic meant that history advances through recurring clashes between opposing forces. Conflicting religious beliefs, philosophical ideas, forms of government and society, modes of artistic expression: Over thousands of years, these and other elements of the human drama were always and everywhere in contention. The progress of humanity from one historical epoch to the next thus always involved conflict. Hegel termed these ongoing conflicts "contradictions."

Marx was captivated by Hegel's vision of the dialectical process of history. But as an atheist, Marx could not accept Hegel's assumption that God presided over the dialectical process. Hegel was a philosophical *idealist* in the sense that he believed in spiritual, or "ideal," forces like the deity. But Marx was a philosophical *materialist* who rejected spiritual essences. For materialists, human beings and the ideas they create are purely material substances.

Economics and Class Conflict as the Motive Forces of History

Marx moved to Paris and began his first major treatise on political economy in 1844.[4] In these early manuscripts Marx concluded that *economic* factors constitute the primary material sources of human action. Private property, in particular, stood out as a principal cause of *alienation*, which Marx described as "the self-estrangement of man from himself." He reasoned that as long as there is private ownership of productive enterprises, the workers are engaged in producing objects that do not belong to them. Their employers sell these commodities and pocket the profits, remunerating the workers with wages barely sufficient to keep them alive. The workers are therefore "alienated" from the very products of their labor. The only

way out of this inhuman predicament, Marx announced, was communism, the common ownership of productive enterprises.

Over the next several years Marx was to refine his central notion that *the principal motive forces in society and politics are economic in nature*. He was joined in this endeavor by Friedrich Engels (1820–1895), the son of a wealthy German industrialist, who had become a socialist in his youth. The two became lifelong collaborators: Marx was the creative thinker while Engels contented himself with popularizing his friend's more abstruse ideas. One of their most famous tracts was the *Communist Manifesto*, written in 1847 at the request of a group of German communists and published the following year. In this and subsequent works, Marx developed two critical ideas that defined what dialectical materialism meant in practice.[5]

The first of these ideas was the notion that *economic relations condition everything else that happens in human affairs*, including the type of government a country has as well as its prevailing beliefs and social conventions. For Marx, economics determines, or at least significantly influences, politics. In essence, whoever controls a nation's economy also controls its political system. Thus the state is always manipulated by those who possess economic power.[6]

The second idea that was critical to Marx's concept of dialectical materialism was *class conflict*. Marx maintained that whenever there is private ownership of the "means of production" (factories, the land, technology, and the human labor force), social classes come into being. The relationships between the main social classes under conditions of private property, in Marx's view, are invariably antagonistic. "The history of all hitherto existing society," he and Engels wrote in the *Manifesto*, "is the history of class struggles." Thus in the ancient world, the slave-master class and the slave class were locked in hostile confrontation. In nineteenth-century Europe, wherever capitalism was the dominant mode of production, the capitalist class confronted the working class.

Laissez-faire capitalism in Britain and the United States emerged with the industrial revolution. Entrepreneurs could earn fortunes with successful investments in mines, mills, and early factories. The fate of workers in those workplaces inspired Karl Marx to write his critiques of capitalism.

When referring to the capitalist class in the industrializing countries, Marx used the term *bourgeoisie*. The term derived from *bourg*, the old German and French word for "town" or "city." (Industrial capitalism in Marx's time was largely an urban phenomenon.) The bourgeoisie consisted of entrepreneurs who owned factories and other productive enterprises, together with other private businesspeople who stood to profit from providing their services in a free enterprise economy: bankers, lawyers, accountants, and the like. Marx used the term *proletariat* when referring to the industrial working class, which consisted mainly of factory laborers. This term came from the Latin *proletarius*, referring to a member of the non-property-owning lower class of ancient Rome. In Marx's conceptualization, these two classes were destined to clash, much like the "contradictions" in Hegelian philosophy. True to the laws of the dialectic, the bourgeoisie creates the very class that will destroy it. By building factories, the capitalists in effect create the working class. "What the bourgeoisie therefore produces, above all," Marx colorfully wrote, "is its own gravediggers."

As industrial capitalism matures, he believed, the contradictions inherent in the relationship between bourgeoisie and proletariat inevitably intensify. The rich grow richer while the poor get poorer. The most successful capitalists drive their competitors out of business, a process Marx called *monopolization*. As a consequence, the bourgeoisie shrinks in size, concentrating society's wealth in very few hands. The middle class, consisting of small, independent property owners—shop owners, artisans, small farmers, and the like—are also victimized by the relentless pursuit of capitalist competition. Crushed by aggressive large-scale businesses, the middle class literally disappears, sinking into the working class. As the ranks of the proletariat swell beyond the capitalist system's ability to employ them, the unemployed grow into a vast "reserve army of the proletariat" that Marx called the *lumpenproletariat*, the "proletariat in rags."

Meanwhile, the capitalist elite uses its control over the state to reinforce its subjugation of the proletariat. For Marx, the state is always an instrument of class domination. "Political power," says the *Manifesto*, "is merely the organized power of one class for oppressing another." In capitalist societies, "The executive of the modern state is but a committee for managing the common affairs of the bourgeoisie." In Marx's view, electoral democracy in capitalist societies is a sham that holds out no hope for the working class; it is nothing more than a "bourgeois democracy," thoroughly manipulated by the capitalist class for its own benefit. Legislatures, political parties, politicians—all do the bidding of the captains of industry. Britain, where Marx lived from 1849 until his death in 1883, impressed him as a prime example of such a capitalist-dominated parliamentary system.

Eventually, the proletariat comes to comprise the vast majority of the population wherever advanced capitalism has developed to its full potential. Only about 10 percent of the population ends up owning private businesses. Under these circumstances, the capitalists are outnumbered. Time is then ripe for revolution and socialism.

The Socialist Revolution In the *Manifesto*, Marx and Engels declared that the capitalist bourgeoisie is destined to be overthrown in a working-class revolution. Reduced to a small minority of the population, the bourgeois class is incapable of holding back the mounting tide of proletarian resentment. The proletariat, imbued with growing "class consciousness," undertakes "the forcible overthrow of all existing social conditions" in a spontaneous revolutionary outburst. Through the dialectical clash of bourgeoisie and proletariat, humanity is then "lifted up" to the higher historical plane of communism.

Once installed in power, Marx and Engels predicted, the working class dismantles the entire capitalist system. Private ownership of the means of production is forever abolished, the capitalist "expropriators" are expropriated. The workers themselves take possession of factories, farms, and other productive enterprises, reorganizing economic life for the benefit of the people as a whole. With the dissolution of private property and its transformation into "the property of all members of society," all class distinctions then cease to exist. The economic exploitation of one class by another is no longer possible. The proletariat scrupulously refrains from setting itself up as a new dominant class. Communism, in Marx's grand vision, is a truly classless society.

Most important, Marx and Engels affirmed that the abolition of private property is accompanied by the abolition of the "bourgeois" state. Indeed, the seizure of state power will be the first task of the revolutionaries. Having captured the main institutions of government, the proletariat then uses its command of the state to wrest all economic power from the bourgeoisie. In pursuing this task, the workers might have to establish a temporary "dictatorship of the proletariat," but its term would be brief, probably no more than a year.

In fact, once the capitalists have been deprived of their economic power, government itself ceases to exist as a political institution. The state, as Engels put it, simply dies out. While there may still be an "administration" in communist society to take care of basic services, the state is no longer an instrument of class domination. It has no real political power. By abolishing private property, the victorious working class abolishes class conflict; and by abolishing class conflict, which is the driving force of politics, it abolishes politics itself. Under communism, in other words, private property, social classes, conflict, the state, political power, and even politics itself all disappear.

While politics withers away in communist society, economic conditions vastly improve. Marx and Engels prophesied that the great mass of the population would respond to their newfound freedom with a tremendous burst of creativity and productive energy. Although everyone would be expected to work, they would work for society as a whole, not for greedy capitalists. The result would be a superabundance of socially useful goods from which everyone would ultimately benefit. Marx and Engels thus portrayed socialist society (that is, communism) as an idyllic utopia. In Hegelian terms, communism was Marx's vision of the final stage in the long dialectical march of human history. Beyond a few generalities about a classless, stateless society, however, the two founding fathers of modern socialist ideology had very little to say about how communism would actually work. They left no blueprint indicating how the socialist economy would be organized. Nor did they outline a communist "constitution," since there would be no politicized government. They assumed that, without any class conflicts to divide them, the people themselves would find ways to manage their common affairs harmoniously.

Scientific Socialism In the *Manifesto*, Marx and Engels proclaimed that the destruction of capitalism and the victory of the proletariat were inevitable. For Marx, the inevitability of socialism was ordained by the immutable laws of history, whose secrets he believed he had discovered. Just as Charles Darwin had discovered the laws of biological evolution, Marx maintained that he had uncovered the laws governing humanity's social evolution. On these grounds Marx always insisted that his theories of dialectical materialism were scientific. So conceived, history was the source of communism's legitimacy. Accordingly, Marx asserted that the entire course of humankind's historical development, from the most primitive preindustrial societies to the highest stage of communism, was governed by the laws of economic determinism. These laws, moreover, were immutable; no one could change them or get around them.

Both Marx and Engels believed that, as a general rule, industrial capitalism was a necessary precondition to the construction of a successful socialist society over the long term. They did not believe that predominantly agricultural societies were ripe for socialist development, and so they dismissed peasants as incapable of mounting a true socialist revolution. Only the industrial working class had the class consciousness necessary to create a stable and enduring socialist society. Consequently they predicted that socialist revolutions would occur only in advanced capitalist countries such as Britain, France, and Germany. In their view, nineteenth-century Russia was an unlikely candidate for revolution. Russia's population consisted overwhelmingly of impoverished peasants, not industrial workers, and its capitalist bourgeoisie had not yet formed itself as a dominant class.[7]

These "scientific" predictions would prove wrong. In actual fact, the proletarian revolutions Marx and Engels foresaw as imminent in Britain, France, and Germany in the 1840s never took place in these countries. Communist revolutions did not occur until the twentieth century. Ironically, they triumphed in precisely those countries where industrialism and capitalism were largely undeveloped and where a modern bourgeoisie was weak or absent. Countries such as Russia, China, and Cuba were predominantly agricultural societies when the communists came to power. The triumph of what came to be known as *Soviet-style communism* (or *Marxism-Leninism*) in these countries represented only one strand of Marx's legacy, however. In another irony of history, the advanced capitalist societies of Western Europe, which Marx's "laws" regarded as primed for revolution, did not experience socialist revolutions. Instead, they developed socialist movements that combined socialist economics with ballot-box democracy, a combination known as *social democracy*.

Soviet-Style Communism

Communism triumphed in Russia in 1917 under circumstances significantly different from those predicted by Marx and Engels. Russia was still an overwhelmingly agricultural society in 1917. Furthermore, Marx had depicted the revolution as a largely spontaneous upheaval carried out by the masses; he did not portray it as an organized conspiracy led by a handful of revolutionary leaders. But communism came to Russia as a well-orchestrated coup d'état engineered by a highly centralized political party, the Bolsheviks. It was this party, which soon came to be known as the Communist Party, that defined the essence of Soviet-style communism.

The party's principal creator was Vladimir Ilyich Lenin (1870–1924). An avid student of Marx's writings from his teenage years, Lenin placed his own stamp on the Marxist tradition by adapting its core ideas to Russia's specific conditions.

Lenin's single most important contribution to Marxist theory, as expostulated in the 1902 pamphlet *What Is to Be Done? Burning Questions of Our Movement*, was the notion that the industrial working class in modern Russia and Europe was not capable of launching a spontaneous mass revolution on its own; it had to be led to socialism by a party of professional revolutionaries. Experience had already shown that, instead of risking a potentially disastrous uprising, most workers were content to form trade unions and to seek negotiated compromises with their capitalist employers. But trade unionism, argued Lenin, amounted to acceptance of capitalism; only capitalism's complete destruction could liberate the workers from exploitation. If the workers would not destroy capitalism on their own, a "party of a new type" would have to be formed whose primary

Vladimir Ilyich Lenin argued that the industrial working class in modern Russia and Europe was not capable of launching a spontaneous mass revolution on its own as Marx had insisted; it had to be led to socialism by a party of professional revolutionaries.

task would be to organize and carry out a violent revolution at the first sign of weakness in the capitalist ruling class. This party would be the "vanguard of the proletariat," acting as its "organizational weapon."[8]

For Russia's rulers, that critical moment of weakness occurred amid the turmoil of World War I. With minimal resistance, Lenin's Bolsheviks, organized into a small militia, seized official buildings that had been abandoned by an unpopular government in November 1917. In a brutal civil war that extended into 1921, the Bolsheviks finally vanquished all their opponents. From that point onward, Russia's Communist Party monopolized power in what subsequently became known as the Soviet Union (or USSR, the Union of Soviet Socialist Republics).

The key idea of **Leninism** is the primacy of the Communist Party. It is the party that leads the revolution; it is the party that governs the country once the revolution has eliminated its foes. Lenin's definition of the "dictatorship of the proletariat" was distinctly different from Marx's conception of a temporary government in the hands of the masses. "The dictatorship of the proletariat," Lenin affirmed, "is the dictatorship of the party." Far from being a temporary phenomenon, the Communist Party exercised dictatorial rule over the Soviet Union until December 1991, when its power collapsed and the USSR disintegrated.

For much of its reign, the party leadership utilized all the coercive mechanisms at its disposal to enforce its will, at times resorting to mass murder. Joseph Stalin (1878–1953), who succeeded Lenin following a power struggle within the party hierarchy, brutalized Soviet society by imprisoning millions in concentration camps, killing the cream of the party elite, and intimidating workers, peasants, intellectuals, and others into submission through the unremitting use of violence. His successors were not as murderous as Stalin on a mass scale, but until the late 1980s they did not shrink from using severe coercive measures to ensure compliance with their dictates.

In another sharp departure from Marx's tenets, Soviet rulers erected a powerful state to undergird their dominance. Instead of dying out, the state swelled into a gargantuan bureaucratic arm of Communist Party rule. The Soviet state was a highly politicized state, moreover; it consisted of party and governmental institutions that joined in propagandizing the population, repressing dissent, and implementing policies over which the people had little or no influence. Its top officials constituted a privileged elite who enjoyed benefits denied to the mass public. This enormous governing apparatus also planned and operated virtually all economic activity in the USSR, presiding over a centrally planned economy. (We'll discuss central planning at greater length in Chapter 11.)

At no point in its history did the Soviet Union approach the stateless, egalitarian utopia that was Marx's conception of communism. The USSR was called "communist" only because it was governed by the Communist Party. The same can be said for other "communist" countries that came into being after the USSR. These included China, where the Chinese Communist Party took power in 1949 following a long civil war (see Chapter 17); Poland, Hungary, and other Central and East European states on which the USSR imposed Communist Party rule after World War II; Cuba, where Fidel Castro's communists won a revolutionary struggle in 1959; and others such as North Korea and Vietnam. All were the heirs, not just of Marx, but also of Lenin. Hence twentieth-century communism, defined in terms of Communist Party dictatorship, was rooted in the ideology of **Marxism-Leninism** (see Figure 10.1).

Today, the states that still claim to be communist—China, Cuba, and North Korea—are attempting to evolve to meet the demands of living in a capitalist world economy. China, as you'll learn in Chapter 17, has gone furthest in adopting capitalism, even while the Communist Party retains control of the political system. Cuba, still governed by the Castros (Fidel's brother Raul is now the leader), has become more friendly to foreign investment and trade, even though the United States refuses to deal with the country in most ways. North Korea has made the least progress in adapting to capitalism and remains a largely closed off society, a pariah in world politics.

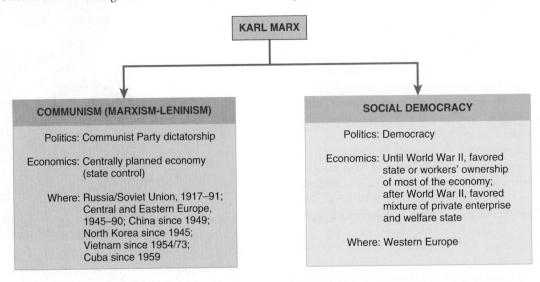

FIGURE 10.1 **Legacies of Marxism**

Social Democracy

The second main inheritor of Marx's legacy was **social democracy**, which is a combination of economic socialism and political democracy. One of the chief incubators of the social-democratic tradition was the Social Democratic Party of Germany (known by its German initials as the SPD). Founded in 1875, the SPD's backbone was the German working class, a disparate mass of mostly blue-collar workers. Deprived of economic and political power by the kaiser's authoritarian regime, Germany's workers looked mostly to the SPD to win them a share of participation in the affairs of government. The ballot box became their main political weapon. Most German workers shunned the path of revolution, sharply contradicting Marx's predictions of an inevitable proletarian uprising.

One SPD leader, Eduard Bernstein (1850–1932), drew the implications of this contradiction between Marxist theory and working-class practice with bold clarity. His book *Evolutionary Socialism*, published in 1898, was a point-by-point refutation of key tenets of Marx's thought. For Bernstein, the immediate aim of the socialist movement should not be to mount a violent revolution but to promote democracy. Bernstein defined democracy as "the absence of class government," and he advocated universal suffrage, proportional representation, equal rights for all citizens, and parliamentary control over legislation. He emphatically rejected both the kaiser's militaristic dictatorship and Marx's "dictatorship of the proletariat." And he regarded compromise and moderation as indispensable elements of democratic government. As to socialism, Bernstein conceived of it as a "cooperative society" organized for the benefit of the whole population and guided by the principle of majority rule.

Over the next several decades, the SPD's commitment to political democracy intensified. The party was a mainstay of democratic government during Germany's ill-fated Weimar Republic (1918–33), which died an early death at the hands of Adolf Hitler and the Nazis, as we'll learn in Chapter 15. After World War II a revived SPD became one of the two largest parties in West Germany, a status it still enjoys today in unified Germany. Meanwhile, starting in the 1950s the SPD began retreating from its earlier commitment to economic socialism. It accepted private enterprise and the market as the principal mechanisms of economic production. It has sought to promote the interests of the working class and other constituents by working within the capitalist system through democratic processes.

Other social-democratic parties emerged in the industrialized nations of Europe and have undergone a roughly similar historical evolution. They include Britain's Labour Party, France's Socialist Party, Scandinavian social-democratic parties, and numerous others. Like the SPD, most social-democratic parties in today's industrially advanced democracies accept private enterprise and the market economy. Today, social democracy in most democracies is practically indistinguishable from American social liberalism, though many European social democrats favor a larger welfare state than do most U.S. liberals. The United States never developed a successful social-democratic party that favored the state's takeover of factories and other productive enterprises.[9]

Socialism in the Developing World

The varieties of socialism are multiplied when we look at socialist ideas in the developing countries. In Asia, Africa, the Middle East, and Latin America, various forms of socialism have been articulated and adapted over many decades to fit social and economic conditions that are quite different from those that prevailed in nineteenth- or twentieth-century Europe. In most instances, these variants of socialism emerged in countries with little or no industrialization. A proletariat in the European sense has been either very small or nonexistent. Not surprisingly, some of the most creative socialist theorists and political activists in the less economically advanced part of the world did not base their ideas on Marxism but instead on local traditions and circumstances.

One of the most influential Third World socialists was Julius K. Nyerere (1922–99), the principal theoretician of what became known as "African socialism." A British-educated Christian from Tanzania, Nyerere rejected Marx's notions of class struggle and devised a Tanzanian variant of socialism rooted in long-standing tribal customs that emphasized the individual's responsibility to the community and the community's responsibility to care of the individual. Out of this tradition he derived the concept of *ujamaa*, or "familyhood." Under Nyerere's leadership as president of Tanzania for more than 20 years, the government abolished private ownership of land and instituted a system of communally owned rural property, touting self-reliance as the country's main economic goal.[10] Several African states embarked on roughly similar paths in the 1960s and 1970s. Over time, however, most of them, including Tanzania, were forced by economic realities to curtail or abandon their lofty goals of agricultural self-sufficiency and full economic equality. Most have reintroduced market economic mechanisms.

One of the most influential Third World socialists was Julius K. Nyerere, the principal theoretician of "African socialism."

Another source of non-Marxist concepts of socialism was the Middle East. Initially, the Muslim Brotherhood, founded in Egypt in the 1920s, had socialist leanings. A coup involving Colonel Gamal Abdel Nasser deposed the king of Egypt in 1952 and installed a new regime led mainly by military officers. Nasser elaborated a form of "Arab socialism" that placed heavy emphasis on governmental direction of the economy. These measures were accompanied by efforts to anchor the ideology of Arab socialism in the religious traditions of Islam.[11] Similar concepts of Arab socialism were elaborated in the 1960s in Syria, Iraq, and Libya. As in Nasser's Egypt, they tended to emphasize the state's responsibility for guiding the economy. They also went hand in hand with strong authoritarian governments. The popularity of socialism in the Middle East has waned in recent decades, however, in part because of pressures from the United States and international financial institutions to open these economies to market forces and in part because of the collapse of the Soviet Union, which was an occasional ally of several states in the region.

In Latin America, socialist movements have frequently tended to have a Marxist background. Some have been Soviet-oriented Communist Parties, some have espoused violent revolutions of one kind or another (at times with the support of Fidel Castro's communist regime in Cuba), and still others have been social democratic in orientation. One notable example of a radical social democrat was Salvador Allende, who was elected president of Chile in 1970. Allende's Socialist Party was committed to democracy but was equally committed to redistributing the nation's wealth from the rich to the poor and to nationalizing large privately owned corporations, including copper mines owned by U.S. companies. Although Allende was not a Soviet-style communist, Chile's Communist Party was part of his governing coalition. Irked by Allende's socialist economic policies and his friendly gestures toward the Soviet Union and Castro's Cuba, the Nixon administration conspired with Allende's domestic opponents to undermine his government. In 1973 a military coup led by Gen. Augusto Pinochet and abetted by the CIA ousted the socialist coalition. Allende was killed in the assault, and democracy itself was extinguished in Chile for the next 16 years.

Since the collapse of communism in the Soviet Union and East Central Europe, and the failure of socialist economies in the developing world, socialism seems to have receded as a major ideological force around the world. Whether economic and social conditions will lead to its revival some day is an open question.

FASCISM

Historically, fascism emerged in Europe between the two world wars. Its most successful manifestations occurred in Italy, where Benito Mussolini's National Fascist Party held power from 1922 until 1943, and in Germany, where Adolf Hitler and the Nazis ruled between 1933 and 1945. Fascist movements also existed in other European countries during the inter-war period, including France, Hungary, and Romania, but they did not acquire the extraordinary grip on power achieved by

their Italian and German counterparts.[12] Fascist-like movements and ideas have also emerged in other parts of the globe in the decades before and after World War II, particularly in Latin America. The American Nazi Party, neo-Nazi skinheads in Europe, and white-supremacist Afrikaner groups in South Africa are often singled out as examples of quasi-fascist or neofascist organizations in the contemporary era.

In most instances, fascism is a response to a specific combination of problems that face certain societies at a particular juncture in their historical development. Most fascist regimes arose in societies facing rapid economic modernization that threatened traditional groups—especially artisans, small businesspeople, and small farmers—not prepared to compete with large capitalist enterprises.[13] In addition, both Italy and Germany had emerged from defeat in World War I feeling humiliated and betrayed, and both had to confront overwhelming economic problems. In both countries, moreover, democracy failed to provide adequate remedies for the nation's misfortunes. Growing numbers of Italians and Germans concluded that democracy was the principal problem. In most instances, neofascist movements in today's world also represent extreme responses to social or economic problems for which democratic solutions are either inadequate or completely unacceptable to certain segments of society. Ethnic diversity and long-term unemployment are typical of the problems that spark neofascist resentments, particularly among poorly educated white males.

Fascism has proven to be a difficult term to define. Reduced to its basic elements, fascism consists of the following four features: hypernationalism, racism, totalitarianism, and mass mobilization through propaganda and coercion. Not all fascist movements have shared all these defining characteristics. The features enumerated here form a composite "ideal

Italian leader Benito Mussolini first applied the term fascism to his political movement.

type" of fascism extracted mainly from the experiences of inter-war Italy and Germany. To define the term, we may say that **fascism** is an authoritarian and nationalistic right-wing system of governance.

Hypernationalism

Fascism is rooted in an extreme version of nationalism called *hypernationalism*. As we discussed in Chapter 4, nationalism is the notion that the members of one's nation (or "people") must act together to achieve certain collective goals. In its fascist variant, the nation is exalted as the supreme political value. This conception of nationalism is far more intense than patriotism, which means love of one's country. For many fascists, love of one's own country requires hatred of others, particularly those marked as implacable enemies.

National glory and self-assertion therefore assume the highest priority on the political agenda of most fascist movements. Mussolini was determined to establish an Italian empire through the conquest of Ethiopia in 1936 and other territorial acquisitions during World War II. Hitler sought to subdue all of Europe and the Soviet Union by force of arms, with the express intention of creating a fascist "New Order." Chauvinism is a typical component of the fascist worldview.

Whereas militant nationalism characterizes fascist attitudes toward the outside world, national unity is often the chief priority at home. Both Italy and Germany had achieved statehood only in the second half of the nineteenth century, hundreds of years after Britain and France. Italian and German fascist leaders felt an acute need to solidify bonds of national unity among their people, many of whom still felt more attached to their local region than to the country as a whole. These efforts assumed manic proportions. The fascists sought to forge a common national identity by drumming up hatred of presumed enemies such as communists, Jews, and British imperialists. They also demanded

unquestioning loyalty to a powerful central state. For Mussolini, Hitler, and other fascists, internal divisiveness breeds external weakness; hence democracy is intolerable precisely because it promotes national discord. Democratic debate and free competition for power inevitably mean that the nation is constantly at war with itself, its domestic fissures deepened by open conflict among social classes, religions, regions, and other segments of the country. Democracy, in this view, is a prescription for national powerlessness, a condition no fascist could possibly accept.

Racism

At least some fascist and neo-fascist movements have defined the nation primarily in terms of race. Concepts of racial purity and superiority were especially characteristic of German fascism under Hitler. The notion that the Germans were members of a pure-blooded "Aryan race," a completely fabricated idea, was a central tenet of Nazi doctrine. Nazi ideology exalted the Germans as a race of "supermen" and denigrated most other racial categories as "subhumans."

Anti-Semitism assumed ferocious proportions in Nazi doctrine. After World War I, Nazi propagandists used the Jews as scapegoats for Germany's political and economic ills even though Jews comprised less than 1 percent of Germany's population. By the late 1930s the Nazi state had instituted a number of racial laws aimed at publicly humiliating German Jews and depriving them of their means of livelihood. During World War II the determination of Hitler and his principal henchmen to proceed with "the final solution of the Jewish problem" throughout Europe resulted in the Holocaust, the annihilation of some 6 million Jews throughout Europe and the Soviet Union and the infliction of untold suffering on millions of survivors. Anti-Semitism has been a characteristic feature of most other fascist or neofascist movements as well, though not all these movements have been as fanatically or blatantly anti-Semitic as the Nazis.[14]

National glory and self-assertion assumed the highest priority on the political agenda of most fascist movements. Fascists also embraced militarism. Here Mussolini and Hitler are seen leaving a meeting with their chief lieutenants.

Anti-Semitism is by no means the only form of racism to be found in fascist or quasi-fascist movements. The Nazis denounced almost all racial or ethnic groups not explicitly identified as "Aryan." Depending on local circumstances, racism has also been a defining characteristic of fascist-like movements in other countries as well, spawning hatred and even violence against immigrants and indigenous members of target ethnic groups. Hatred of homosexuals and the physically and mentally handicapped was also part of the Nazi worldview.

Totalitarianism

Fascist ideology demands a powerful state. The very word *fascism* derives originally from the Latin *fasces*, which in ancient Rome was a staff consisting of a bundle of rods bound together around an axe. The *fasces* would be held aloft on ceremonial occasions as a symbol of national unity and the state's authority.

Once ensconced in office, Mussolini and Hitler established totalitarian states. **Totalitarianism** is an exceptionally intrusive form of authoritarianism in which the state monopolizes control not only over all institutions of government but also over the educational system, the media, science, and the arts, leaving little room for private liberty. Youth groups and even organized religions also come under the watchful eye of the state. Mussolini bluntly asserted that "for the Fascist, all is in the State and nothing human or spiritual exists, much less has value, outside the State. In this sense, Fascism is totalitarian."[15] The ideal in totalitarianism is to control even the thought of the citizenry, hence the importance of controlling education and cultural institutions.

The fascists of Italy and Germany also used state mechanisms to secure their control over the economy. Unlike communists and social democrats of that era, who favored abolishing private enterprise, the fascists were willing to permit private firms to do business and make profits. These businesses were subject to all sorts of state regulations, however. To ensure that privately owned companies, especially the large industrial concerns, conducted their operations in accordance with the government's priorities, Italian and German authorities created special state institutions, which they called "corporations," in which leading representatives of the business community would meet on a regular basis with state officials to coordinate economic goals and operations. The government established similar corporations to represent the labor force, and all trade unions and other labor organizations were abolished except for those operated by the state or the fascist party. Corporations representing agriculture and other sectors of the economy were similarly organized. This system of *state corporatism* (see Chapter 8) served the central purposes of facilitating the state's supervision of the economy and, not incidentally, of organizing the economy for war.[16]

The fascist concept of totalitarianism, at least in its Italian and German variants, was also characterized by the concept of a *party-state.* The state and the fascist party were fused. The Italian fascists' motto, "Everything inside the state, nothing outside the state, nothing against the state," above all meant that the state and the National Fascist Party were one. Hitler's dictatorial state and the Nazi Party were similarly intertwined, with the Nazis monopolizing all official state institutions. As you will learn in Chapters 16 and 17, communist regimes have also imposed totalitarian regimes on their populations, with Stalin's Soviet Union and Mao's China being primary examples.

Mass Mobilization Through Propaganda and Coercion

Traditional authoritarian regimes, like the old monarchies of Europe, China, and Japan, made little effort to court popularity. Military regimes, too, typically care little about public opinion. The Italian and German fascist parties, by contrast, were authoritarian movements that made decisive efforts to cultivate mass support. Although they rejected democracy as a goal, before assuming power they took full advantage of electoral democracy to build a wide constituency. Mussolini and Hitler were charismatic orators whose speeches transfixed millions. Their parties proved highly effective at organizing parades, rallies, and other events to galvanize a mass following. The breadth of their appeal, moreover, was multi-class in nature. Though the Italian and German fascist movements started in the 1920s with a pronounced working-class orientation, over time they drew support from farmers, the large middle class, and even the wealthiest strata of society. The Nazis, for example, raised their share of the electorate from 3 percent in 1928 to more than 37 percent by the summer of 1932, becoming the largest party in Germany.

In addition to using democratic mechanisms to achieve power, Italian and German fascists freely engaged in coercive techniques in their rush to build and consolidate mass support. The *glorification of violence* against political opponents was another core element of fascist ideology. Mussolini's fascist party explicitly defined itself as a militia. From its earliest years it included "squads" *(fasci)* of black-shirted toughs whose task

Adolf Hitler was a powerfully charismatic orator, able to move crowds of thousands.

was to beat up political rivals and fight their way into local city halls, seizing power by force. In October 1922, tens of thousands of armed fascists were massed on the outskirts of Rome, poised for a final assault on the Italian government itself. To avoid a massacre, the king of Italy, acting under his constitutional authority to designate the head of government, named Mussolini as the country's new prime minister. The next day the fascist militia staged a victory parade in the streets of the capital city, an event known as the "march on Rome." The Nazis also employed force in their march to power. Hitler set up a militia in brown shirts, which developed into the notorious Storm Troopers. By 1932, on the eve of the Nazi takeover of power, there were more than 400,000 Storm Troopers. In January 1933, German President Paul von Hindenburg appointed Hitler the country's new chancellor.

Efforts to mobilize the population, both peaceful and violent, became all the more extensive after the conquest of power. Fascist Italy and Germany were *mass mobilization regimes*, resolved to enlist maximum popular support and stifle all opposition. Both regimes organized continuous propaganda campaigns designed to stir up popularity, appealing not only to national pride but also to the darkest anxieties, prejudices, and yearnings for vengeance on the part of the Italian and German populations. They also engineered massive employment programs and other efforts to improve the economic welfare of large elements of the population. And they did not hesitate to use violence against real or imagined political opponents, with secret police, concentration camps, and torture employed with intimidating effect.

Some scholars contend that fascism was an epochal phenomenon unique to inter-war Europe.[17] Nevertheless, it is far too early to consign fascism to the graveyard of history. At least hypothetically, fascist ideas may find a popular resonance wherever other forms of government, including democracy, fail to address the basic needs of the population for economic security, national pride, and social order.[18] After 1945, Germany and Italy played key roles in forming the European institutions that eventually became the European Union. Leaders of those postwar states sought explicitly to redefine their national identities in a much more positive relationship to Europe in the hope to avoid a return to the hypernationalism that led to World War II.[19]

RELIGION AS A BASE FOR POLITICAL IDEOLOGY: ISLAMISM

At one time or another, all the world's great religions have functioned as political ideologies, articulating explicit political messages and, in some cases, exercising political power. Islam has emerged as the most politically active religious force in the contemporary world. Its centrality in the convulsive politics of the Middle East, in the crucible of international terrorism, and in the global struggle between democracy and authoritarianism raises important questions about some of the most pressing political issues of our time. **Islamism**, sometimes referred to

as *Islamicism*, is "the belief that Islam should guide social and political as well as personal life."[20] Some scholars prefer to use the terms "activist Islam" or "political Islam" to refer to the same phenomenon.

Specifically, does Islam require theocratic government? Is it particularly prone to violence? And is it compatible with democracy?

Origins

Although Islam has evolved considerably over the centuries, many of its most widely held beliefs derive from its founder, the Prophet Muhammad (ca. 570–632). Proclaiming himself a prophet and messenger of God in the grand lineage of Abraham, Moses, David, and Jesus, Muhammad called for the individual's complete surrender to God's will. The word *Islam* is Arabic for "surrender"; it is etymologically related to *salam*, which means "peace." A Muslim is someone who submits fully to God. In his preaching, Muhammad extolled the virtues of moral probity, simplicity, compassion, charity, economic justice for the poor, and peace among all Muslims.

Muhammad's message represented a radical departure from the polytheistic beliefs that were still widely held in the Arabian peninsula. In 622 Muhammad fled from Mecca and emigrated to nearby Yathrib, which became known as Medina. Muhammad's "migration," known as the *Hijrah* (or *Hegira*), formally inaugurated the Islamic era. With about a hundred "companions," Muhammad established the first Muslim community, or *ummah*. A series of battles ensued against the defenders of the old order in Mecca, culminating in the Muslims' victory over the Meccan army in 627. In 630 Muhammad returned to Mecca in triumph and established his political and religious authority there. By the time of his death in 632, Muhammad was the most powerful man in Arabia, simultaneously the leader of a popular new religion and the political head of the Muslim community.

For 21 years Muhammad affirmed that he received divine revelations, which he would recite to assembled followers. After his death, his words were gathered from written fragments and oral renditions and compiled in written form as the Koran (or *Quran*, or "recitations"). Like holy books in other religions, the Koran was composed from a diversity of sources dating from different times, and its verses are sometimes ambiguous or contradictory, giving rise to different interpretations of their meaning. Another source of Muslim beliefs was the *hadith*, which are anecdotes about Muhammad and his companions. Islam has no equivalent of the pope, who is the ultimate authority for Roman Catholic doctrine. Hence there is no "official" Islamic doctrine or interpretation of its core beliefs. The interpretation of Islamic religious tenets and Islamic law increasingly fell into the hands of Islamic scholars and legal experts, known collectively as the *ulama*, "the learned men of God." The result has been considerable diversity in the interpretation of Muhammad's legacy and Islamic tradition over the centuries and across the Muslim world. In fact, conflicts within the Muslim community arose shortly after Muhammad's death.

It was not clear who should succeed the Messenger as the next head of the Muslim community, the *ummah*. In the succession struggle, Muhammad's close friend Abu Bakr and Muhammad's cousin and son-in-law Ali contended to be his first "successor" or "representative" (*khalifa*, or caliph). Initially it was agreed that the caliph would be the temporal head of the *ummah*, but there would be no religious authority. The schism split the Islamic movement into warring camps. Ali was murdered in 661 at which time Shiites proclaimed Ali's second son Hussain as the next legitimate caliph. Hussain was subsequently killed in a battle in Karbala (now located in Iraq) by rival Muslims in 680. The internecine conflict over Muhammad's succession persists: There is still no single spiritual or temporal head of Islam. Those who regard Abu Bakr and his immediate successors as the first three legitimate caliphs are mostly Sunnis. **Sunnis**, a term meaning Muslims who follow the words and deeds of Muhammad, compose about 87 to 90 percent of the world's 1.6 billion Muslims.[21] The **Shiites** continue to regard only Muhammad's blood descendants as the Prophet's true successors, or imams. Most of the about 170 million Shiites in the contemporary world belong to the "Twelver" school of Shiism. This school holds that after the death of the Eleventh Imam in 874, the Twelfth Imam was spirited away ("occulted") by God and hidden to spare his life from his Sunni enemies. The mystical doctrine of the "Occultation of the Hidden Imam" asserts that the Twelfth Imam, known as the Mahdi, will one day return to the world to usher in an era of justice. Until then, it is the task of the erudite Shiite clergy to discern his will and lead the faithful on his behalf. Shiites today are heavily concentrated in Iran, where they are 93 percent of the population; in Iraq (67 percent); and in Lebanon (40 to 50 percent).[22]

Expansion and Decline

Ironically, as these and other feuds unraveled Islam's inner core, the religion itself expanded. Once Muhammad brought peace to the unruly Arabian peninsula, Arab warriors under their new Muslim leadership charged into neighboring areas in search of plunder and territory. By the end of the eighth century the Mediterranean was a Muslim lake. Baghdad (founded in 762 in Iraq), Cairo (Egypt), Damascus (Syria), Cordoba (Spain), and Palermo (on Sicily) became flourishing centers of classical scholarship, science, and theology.

In the first half of the fourteenth century a Turkish tribe, the Osmanlis, established the first Ottoman government, forming the cornerstone of the most dynamic and expansionist of all Muslim states. After taking Constantinople in 1453 and converting it into their new capital, Istanbul, they extended their sway over most of the Arab world as well as the Balkans and Hungary.

The Islamic world reached its political apogee in the late seventeenth century. After the Ottoman Turks were defeated in their second attempt to take Vienna in 1683, their empire entered into a long process of external retreat and internal decay. Britain and Russia pressed on its flanks, slicing away at the Ottomans' territorial appendages until the end of World

War I and placing large Muslim populations under European or Russian control in the nineteenth century. In 1916, Britain and France agreed to carve up the Middle East, imposing new states on Arab populations in the region.

These political defeats were accompanied by a vast cultural divide that widened the gap between Christian Europe and the Islamic world. Although Arab, Turkish, and other Islamic intellectuals outshone European scientists until the end of the Middle Ages, Europe in the sixteenth century embarked on a path that led from the Renaissance and the age of discoveries to the scientific revolution. Because of religious dogmatism and shortsighted political leadership, the Muslim world failed to keep pace with European inventiveness, falling disastrously behind the West in scientific theory, experimentation, and technology—including military technology. (By the late thirteenth century, a "rationalist" school of Islam, stressing human reason and free will, lost out to the "traditionalist" school, which stresses divine revelation and the authority of Islamic law.) In addition, the Enlightenment and the democratic revolutions of the eighteenth and nineteenth centuries in Europe and America had no serious equivalents in the Islamic world. As the West moved in fits and starts toward the rule of law, democratic participation, the separation of church and state, and the emancipation of women, Muslim religious authorities and political elites largely ignored these ideas. The result was a gap not only in the balance of political and military power between Islam and the West, but in political culture as well. In many respects, these cultural gaps endure to the present day. Although modern Islamic states have accepted scientific-technical modernization, many of them have resisted cultural and political Westernization.[23]

Religion and Politics

Islam was intended to be an all-encompassing way of life. Consequently, Islamic doctrine recognizes no distinction between religion and politics: The *ummah* is both a religious and a political community in which Islamic law (*sharia*) prevails. Allah, not the people, is the source of legitimacy. Muhammad did not conceive of Islam as a "church" that is organized separately from the state, and he personally disapproved of monarchy, a secular form of government. In its original doctrinal form, Islam thus requires a theocratic government. But with its vast territorial expansion, the Islamic world became fragmented into a variety of states and empires under Muslim rulers who were not religious authorities. The caliphate shifted from one city to another as rivalries intensified and military and political power shifted within the Islamic world. In the process, the caliph's original role as the temporal (political) head of Islam was at times augmented by religious functions, as various caliphs proclaimed their authority as Islam's principal religious leader. Ultimately the caliphate arrived in Istanbul, reflecting the predominance of Ottoman power. In a marked departure from Islamic orthodoxy, the Ottoman Turks established a monarchy under the sultan. Over time the ties between religion and the state grew looser as the Ottoman regime implemented a limited modernization program and the sultans increasingly adopted opulent lifestyles. The leaders of other predominantly Muslim countries took steps of their own to distinguish religion from the state.

Meanwhile, the power of the *ulama*—the learned Muslim clerics—expanded throughout the Islamic world in matters of religious doctrine and interpretation. Because the Koran did not lay out a body of rules to regulate the daily life of Muslims, it was left to succeeding generations of Islamic thinkers and jurists to formulate and refine Islamic law. And because Islam did not develop an authoritative religious chief (despite the claims of certain caliphs), competing and overlapping schools of religious belief and jurisprudence have proliferated throughout the Muslim world through the centuries. As a general rule, the Shiite clergy has tended to have a tiered hierarchy, with "grand ayatollahs" outranking ayatollahs, and so on down the ranks. The Sunni clergy is less structured, permitting greater flexibility in religious and political doctrine.

"Traditionalist" Sunni Islam has stressed the Prophet's commitment to peace (except for defensive wars) and to coexistence with Christians and Jews; it generally rejects terrorism and the killing of women, children, and the elderly for any reason. Traditionalists also view Islamic law as binding on all Muslims, even though the Islamic scholars and jurists who interpret and define the law often disagree with one another. As Reza Aslan has pointed out, "It is practically impossible to reconcile the Traditionalist view of the Shariah with modern conceptions of democracy and human rights." Sunni Islam has also produced a "modernist" (or "reformist") orientation that calls for a separation of religion and the state, with Islamic law separated from the sphere of civil and political life. Some modernists have regarded Muhammad's community in Mecca as an example of such a separation. Modernists have sought to reconcile Islam with Western rationalism and democracy, without necessarily embracing a fully secular state.[24]

In addition to traditionalism and modernism, Sunni Islam has also produced more radical and extreme strains, which are often labeled "fundamentalist" or "Islamist" in the West. Despite some variations, the fundamentalist schools favor a state based on a rigid and puritanical interpretation of Islamic law, including the application of severe restrictions on women and of "eye-for-an-eye" punishments that Muhammad himself did not explicitly condone (such as amputation of a thief's hand). Some fundamentalists favor a theocratic Islamic state; others would permit civil authority, but only if it adheres to a strict code of *sharia*. Many Sunni fundamentalists also call for the creation of a worldwide Islamic political community. Sunni fundamentalists are deeply opposed to Shiism and most other strains of Islam, regarding their adherents as heretics. Most also oppose the West and Western democratic traditions. A few have advocated terrorism.

The most prominent general school of Sunni fundamentalism today is the Salafi school. In Arabic, *salaf* means "the ancient ones" or "the predecessors," a reference to Muhammad's companions. Salafis believe that they are practicing the pure form of Islam developed by the first three generations of Muslims. Salafism has several variants. In Saudi Arabia it is identified with *Wahhabism*, an orientation developed by Muhammad

ibn 'Abd al-Wahhab (1703–92), who formed an alliance with the al-Saud family, a minor desert clan, and together they founded a new state in the Arabian peninsula. Al-Wahhab accepted the temporal authority of the head of the al-Saud family, and the latter agreed to enforce a puritanical interpretation of the Koran and Islamic law. In 1932 the Saudis proclaimed the Kingdom of Saudi Arabia, basing their state on Wahhabist principles. Although the government is controlled by the royal house of al-Saud, the legal system is based on *sharia*. The Saudi state encourages Islamic religious schools (madrassas) to inculcate Wahhabism's traditional doctrines and values, but the anti-Western messages that are conveyed in many of the madrassas are diametrically opposed to the Saudi government's policy of cooperation with the United States. Fifteen of the nineteen hijackers who participated in the events of September 11, 2001, came from Saudi Arabia, a fact that some observers attribute to the doctrinal influences of Wahhabism.[25]

Another version of Salafist tradition is the Deobandi school, founded in 1867 in the north Indian town of Deoband. Deobandis are active today in Pakistan, where they comprise about 15 percent of the country's Sunni majority, and they formed the backbone of the Taliban movement, another Salafist movement, in Afghanistan. Some of the leaders of Egypt's Muslim Brotherhood have been Salafis. One of them, Sayyid Qutb, is considered the father of modern Islamic radicalism. Qutb came away from a research trip in the United States in 1948 with an intense hatred of Western political and social freedoms. (He denounced sock hops and jazz as immoral.) The Muslim Brotherhood's current leaders, who include

Ayatollah Khomeini was an ardent Iranian theocrat, who ruled the country from 1979 to 1989. He took the unprecedented step of claiming that he was the infallible representative of the Mahdi (the Hidden Imam) and was therefore entitled to the same power as the Messenger Muhammad in demanding absolute obedience from the people.

Muhamed Morsi, removed from the presidency by the military, tend to be more moderate in their views. Osama bin Laden and his closest associate, Ayman al-Zawahiri, also subscribed to Salafism, and al-Qaeda is a Salafist-inspired movement.

Like Sunni Islam, Shiism also has several different strains. Shiites have advanced three different interpretations of the relationship between religion and politics. Historically, most Shiite clerics have favored a complete withdrawal from politics, preferring instead to concentrate on the purely religious aspects of Islamic law and doctrine. This attitude comes closest to the Western concept of the separation of church and state. A second view permits cooperation between the clergy and the state for the purpose of enforcing Shiite Islamic law through the government of a just ruler. A third approach is even more politically engaged: It actively encourages Shiite clerics to get involved in politics, either by taking over the state themselves and setting up a theocracy, or by openly opposing an unjust, un-Islamic government. Iran's Ayatollah Khomeini was one of the most ardent advocates of this activist stance. Khomeini took the unprecedented step of claiming that he was the infallible representative of the Mahdi (the Hidden Imam) and was therefore entitled to the same power as the Messenger Muhammad in demanding absolute obedience from the people. The question of which of these three Shiite orientations to politics will prevail in the future is of vital importance not only in post-Khomeini Iran but also in post-Saddam Iraq.[26]

Khomeini's 1979 Iranian revolution inaugurated a Shiite revival that is still reverberating in the greater Middle East. The rise of Hezbollah in Lebanon and the growth of Shiite militias in Iraq are symptomatic of this great awakening. Both movements are actively promoted by Iran's leaders, who have not concealed their intention of playing an assertive role in the region in opposition to U.S. interests.[27]

Islam and Violence

Violence is no stranger to religion. The history of Christianity, for example, is marked by the Spanish Inquisition, Europe's wars of religion, and more recently, sectarian violence between Protestants and Catholics in Northern Ireland. In 1095, Pope Urban II preached the First Crusade against Muslims in the Holy Land.[28]

The connection between Islam and political violence has doctrinal roots in the Koran's concept of *jihad*. Muhammad understood jihad (which means "struggle") in several different senses. It can refer to the efforts of individual Muslims or the broader Islamic community to overcome sinful habits ("jihad of the heart") or to speak out against evil and in favor of the good ("jihad of the tongue"). The Prophet also understood jihad in martial terms, as reflected in the so-called "sword verses" and other passages of the Koran that call on Muslims to "kill the idolaters" (pagans) until they embrace the Muslim religion, or to fight Christian and Jews until they accept the hegemony of Islam by paying a tax to the Islamic authorities ruling over them. (Muhammad did not require Christians and

Jews to be converted to Islam.) These verses espouse "jihad of the sword."[29] But the Koran prohibits the killing of non-combatants. It also prohibits offensive wars. ("Do not begin hostilities; God does not like the aggressor.") According to a widely accepted interpretation, it permits only defensive wars undertaken by "the oppressed." Centuries later, crusaders from Catholic Europe coined the term *holy war* to justify their invasions of the Muslim-controlled Holy Land. It was during this period that Islamic scholars developed a more assertive doctrine of jihad authorizing the House of Islam to take the offensive against non-Muslims (including Christians), who were collectively consigned to the House of War. This "classical" doctrine of jihad was repudiated by subsequent Islamic jurists, but it has been resuscitated more recently by militant fundamentalists such as bin Laden, Khomeini, and the leaders of Hezbollah and Hamas. Islamic militants who favor violence against non-Muslims (including Christians and Jews) are consequently called *jihadists*.

In 1998 Osama bin Laden and his key associates issued a theological decree *(fatwa)* calling on "every Muslim who believes in God . . . to kill the Americans and plunder their money wherever and whenever they find it" in order to expel U.S. military forces from "the lands of Islam." For most Muslims, bin Laden's appeal represented an extreme concept of jihad that exceeds traditional interpretations of the term. His authority to issue such an order, moreover, has been questioned. Islamic traditions hold that only a qualified Muslim jurist has the authority to issue a fatwa. Whatever its original connotations, jihad is not viewed by most Islamic religious authorities as justifying indiscriminate terrorism against non-Muslims.

A substantial number of the violent conflicts involving Muslim states or terrorists in recent years have occurred for reasons other than the assertion of religious doctrine. As we saw in Chapter 4, Palestinians are struggling against Israel to establish their own sovereign state; most of them do not want an Islamic theocracy. Chechens fighting the Russian government want national independence. Saddam Hussein invaded the Islamic Republic of Iran to capture territory and assert his power in the Persian Gulf region. Bosnian Muslims fought mainly to defend themselves against attacks launched by Bosnian Serbs, the Serbian government, and Croats, while Kosovo's Albanian population fought Slobodan Milosevic's Yugoslav government to regain autonomy rights in Kosovo (or to win Kosovo's independence), not to create an Islamic theocracy, as we also learned in Chapter 4. Though the Muslim world today may indeed be heavily engaged in violent conflicts around the globe, few of these conflicts are driven by theological injunctions to engage in all-out holy war against non-Muslims or to create theocratic governments.

Islam and Democracy

Islamic countries have not readily taken to democracy. The authors of *Freedom in the World* point out that countries with a Muslim majority (or a large Muslim plurality) have generally bucked the historic trend toward political liberalization and democracy that has been evident in much of the non-Islamic world over the past 35 years or so. Out of nearly 50 countries around the world with a Muslim majority, 2 were classified as "free" in 1972. By the end of 2012 there were still only 2: Indonesia and Senegal. Among the Muslim-majority countries of the Middle East and North Africa, not one was "free" in late 2011; 4 were rated "partly free" and 13 were "not free." In striking contrast, much of the rest of the globe has witnessed more rapid increases in "free" and "partly free" countries since the 1970s.[30]

These realities are partly accounted for by several factors unrelated to Islamic doctrine: the proliferation of military regimes, especially in Africa; the entrenchment of dictators wielding personal power in countries such as Iraq (Saddam Hussein), Syria (led by Hafaz al-Assad from 1970 to 2000, and since then by his son Bashar), and Egypt (led by Gamal Abdel Nasser from 1954 to 1970, Anwar Sadat from 1970 to 1981, and Hosni Mubarak from 1981 to 2011); the persistence of monarchies in Saudi Arabia, Jordan, Morocco, and Persian Gulf sheikdoms; and the influence of authoritarian parties such as the Baath Party in Iraq. Of 47 predominantly or traditionally Muslim countries in 2006, only one—Iran—was an Islamic theocracy.

Nevertheless, Islamic doctrine and traditional practices have fortified resistance to democracy in the Muslim world. Religious intolerance is part of the problem. Most of the world's great religions and religious sects have shown strains of intolerance, directing animosity either at the adherents of other faiths (e.g., Christians versus Muslims) or at coreligionists (Catholics versus Protestants, Anglicans versus Puritans, and so on). Islam is by no means unique in its hostility to other religions or in its internal disputes. However, religious toleration gradually emerged as an important value in the European Enlightenment. Most importantly, religious tolerance was one of the founding principles of American democracy. Many of the immigrants who came to America precisely to escape religious persecution at home shared a basic understanding that mutual tolerance and the separation of church and state under a secular government were imperative if they were to avoid a repetition of Europe's bloody religious conflicts. Ultimately, religious tolerance became a cardinal principle of Western democracy.

Although Muhammad did not demand the conversion of Jews and Christians, and he allowed them to live freely in his Muslim community in Medina, he did not regard them as the spiritual or political equals of Muslims. As Islam extended its conquests to areas with substantial Jewish and Christian populations, like Spain and the Ottoman Empire, the "Peoples of the Book" were treated harshly by some rulers and favorably by others, but they were always second-class citizens.[31] The treatment of Christians and Jews in Muslim-dominated countries in recent decades has been mixed. In Lebanon, Nigeria, and Sudan there has been considerable sectarian violence between Muslims and Christians, but Jordan and the Palestinian areas have witnessed somewhat greater tolerance of their Christian minorities. Since the intensification of the Arab–Israeli dispute, most Jews have left predominantly Muslim countries such as Morocco and Iraq. If democracy is to take hold in the Muslim world, there will have to be genuine tolerance on the basis of political and social *equality* not only for non-Muslims but also for the various currents within the house of Islam.

The treatment of women is another major stumbling block on Islam's road to democracy. Traditional Islamic practice has been more stringent than Muhammad's teachings when it comes to the role of women in social life. After the death of his beloved first wife, Muhammad required only that his subsequent nine wives, but not other women, wear the veil (the *hijab*). And he granted women unprecedented rights of property ownership and inheritance. It was subsequent Muslim caliphs and scholars who adopted demeaning and misogynist attitudes and laws. As a general rule women in traditionally Muslim countries do not enjoy social and political equality with men. In many Islamic societies they are subject to significant restrictions with regard to dress, education, marital rights, property ownership, legal standing, and political activity. Steven Fish argues that the status of women in traditionally Muslim countries is *the* single most significant variable associated with authoritarianism in the Muslim world.[32]

Another barrier to democracy in Muslim countries, particularly in those that practice Islamic law, is the legal system. Modern democracies have a civil legal code that is independent of religious authority. Contemporary democracies have also adopted prohibitions against what the Universal Declaration of Human Rights calls cruel, inhuman, degrading punishment. European democracies have abolished the death penalty (while the United States has not), and no established democracies permit decapitation, stoning, amputation, or flogging as legitimate punishments for criminal offenses. Such punishments are condoned in Islamic law, and several of them have been routinely carried out in countries practicing *sharia*— Iran, Saudi Arabia, and Afghanistan under the Taliban. One notorious case occurred in Nigeria. In 2002 Amina Lawal was convicted of adultery by an Islamic court in a Muslim-majority Nigerian state after giving birth to a daughter two years after divorcing her husband. The court sentenced her to death by stoning. The case provoked an international outcry before an Islamic appeals court overturned the single mother's conviction in 2003.

The generalizations we have made in this book about democracy apply to traditionally Muslim countries no less than to non-Muslim countries. Definitionally, democracy must meet at least the minimal criteria discussed in Chapter 5. Appeals by reformers for "Islamic democracy" and "Islamic pluralism" must consider the full implications of these terms. If a privileged religious group does not accord *everyone*—including the adherents of other religions and women—the same political, legal, and social rights on the basis of inclusion, equality, and

Amina Lawal was convicted of adultery by an Islamic court in a Muslim-majority Nigerian state after giving birth to a daughter two years after divorcing her husband. The court sentenced her to death by stoning. The case provoked an international outcry before an Islamic appeals court overturned the single mother's conviction in 2003.

nondiscrimination, the political system is not a democracy. If a religious group monopolizes political power and refuses to allow others to vote them out in free and fair elections, and to change the country's laws through fair legislative processes, it's not a democracy. If excessively cruel punishments are imposed for victimless "crimes" or even for real transgressions, it's not a democracy. And if religious laws and practices (other than holidays, perhaps) are imposed on nonadherents against their will, it's not a democracy. Muslims who seek to combine Islam with democracy must confront some difficult questions: Does democracy require a secular state? If it does, then what is "Islamic" about it? And if it does not, then how can an "Islamic" state be reconciled with the democratic principles of equality and inclusion for all?

Ultimately, democracy is most likely to emerge and survive in Muslim countries when a critical mass of elites and elements of the population *want* it and are willing to take risks to get it, whether their purpose is to eliminate tyranny, avert civil war, or share the national wealth more equitably. Any Islamic country will have to chart its own path to democracy, based on its history and culture, and creative hybrids of democracy and Islam may very well emerge. Meanwhile, debates about Islamic "exceptionalism," which assumes that Islamic countries cannot build democracies, will likely continue.[33]

CASE STUDY
Islam and Democracy in Indonesia

Indonesia, the country with the world's largest Muslim population, provides a contemporary example of the relationship between Islam and democracy.

On a warm Saturday evening in October 2002, bombs went off outside two crowded nightclubs on the Indonesian island of Bali, killing more than 200 people, including many foreign nationals. The police quickly rounded up the main perpetrators of the attack. All were thought to be associated with Jemaah Islamiah (Islamic Community), a secretive terrorist network that seeks to create Islamic states in Southeast Asia.

In August 2003 a suicide bomber set off a car bomb that rocked the Marriott Hotel in Jakarta, killing 12 people (mostly Indonesians). Once again, suspects connected with Jemaah Islamiah were arrested; two of them quickly confessed. In addition, violence between Muslims and Christians has flared up periodically in recent years in several Indonesian provinces. Nevertheless, violence associated with Islamic militants has actually declined substantially since 1999 and 2000, when more than 2,000 people were killed in sectarian strife each year. Moreover, there seems to be little support in Indonesia for an Islamic government based on the strict observance of *sharia*. On the contrary, the country's population and political elites continue to support Indonesia's traditional tolerance of its main religious denominations.

With a population of 250 million people, 86 percent of whom are Muslim, Indonesia is the world's largest Muslim country. Since 1999 it has become the world's third-largest democracy (after India and the United States). Though problems

persist—including endemic corruption and sputtering economic growth—the process of consolidating democracy has made visible strides. The Indonesian experience suggests that democracy can emerge in an overwhelmingly Islamic society.

From Islam's first appearance in Indonesia, Islamic beliefs and practices in the Indonesian archipelago assumed a hybrid character. Traditional Sunni doctrines from the Arabian peninsula blended with Sufism, a mystical variant of Islam. As Islam spread across the thousands of islands that make up Indonesia, it fused with preexisting beliefs in each locality, including Hinduism, Buddhism, and traditional animism (paganism). During Dutch colonial rule (Indonesia was then known as the Dutch East Indies), support for Islam hardened into a source of resistance to foreign occupation. Opposition to Dutch rule was particularly fierce in the province of Aceh, located on the northwestern tip of the archipelago. Islam became well entrenched in Aceh, and it remains so to this day.

After World War II, pressured by the United States, the Dutch pulled out and Indonesia gained its formal independence in 1949. Indonesia's religious diversity, rooted above all in the variety of religious practices of the country's overwhelmingly Muslim population, convinced the new state's nationalist leader, Sukarno, to establish a legal code based on civil law rather than on *sharia*. Sukarno formed an alliance with the powerful Indonesian Communist Party. When the communists attempted to seize power in 1965, the military leadership, backed by anticommunist civilian groups, deposed Sukarno. Muslims were among those intensely opposed to the communists, and Muslim organizations took an active part in the violent anticommunist backlash.[34]

General Suharto, a top military leader, soon asserted himself as the country's new military ruler. Like many other dictators, Suharto built alliances by providing benefits to favored groups and organizations in return for their political support, or at least their quiescence. At first, Suharto kept Muslim groups at arm's length. Members of the military command and the civilian leadership (some of whom were Christian or Hindu) feared that Islamic organizations, with their large mass base, were a potential threat to the regime.

By the late 1980s, support for Suharto's long dictatorship was waning significantly. To shore up his base, Suharto reached out to the Muslim community, granting Muslims new concessions in order to co-opt Muslim leaders and their mass followings. A number of prominent conservative Muslims went along with Suharto, and some were rewarded with important posts in the government or the military. But a "modernist" group of Muslim leaders kept their distance from the regime; over time, they increasingly favored a more democratic state based on pluralism, tolerance, and civil society. One of the most independent Muslim leaders was Abdurrahman Wahid, a moderate cleric who became committed to a peaceful transformation of Indonesian politics based on these principles. During the 1990s, Wahid edged closer to an alliance with the anti-Suharto Indonesian Democratic Party, which was led by Megawati Sukarnoputri, the daughter of Sukarno.[35]

Suharto moved even closer to Muslim leaders as pressure for him to leave power increased, a situation favoring traditionalist Muslims over more reform-minded modernist Muslims. In late 1997 and early 1998, when Indonesia's economy was suddenly shaken by an Asian financial crisis, a wave of strikes, student demonstrations, and urban riots destroyed the remaining shreds of Suharto's legitimacy. More importantly, moderate Muslim leaders such as Wahid turned away from Suharto, joining forces with oppositionist forces in support of democratization, forcing his resignation.[36]

Legislative elections held in 1999 returned a plurality to a prodemocracy coalition led by Megawati Sukarnoputri. The legislature thereupon elected Wahid, her Muslim ally, as president. Megawati, a modern Muslim who did not wear a head scarf or veil, became vice president. Hopes for a stable transition to democracy rose as Megawati and Wahid pledged their support for reform. But rivalries between the two camps frayed their coalition. The ineffective Wahid was impeached in 2001, and Megawati took over the presidency.

In addition to confronting the country's continuing economic slide, Megawati had to deal with one of Indonesia's oldest problems: regional secessionism. On the eastern side of the 3,200-mile-wide archipelago, East Timor's largely Roman Catholic population renewed its demands for sovereignty. In a process mediated by the United Nations, East Timor became an independent state in 2002. On the western island of Sumatra, Aceh province had also been a hotbed of secessionist sentiment for decades. President Megawati responded to the

latest armed revolt by declaring martial law and dispatching more troops. As the country's most devoutly Islamic province, Aceh enforces a strict regimen of *sharia* over its population of more than 4 million Muslims. Couples have been flogged for engaging in "immoral behavior" in public; flogging is also meted out for the consumption of alcohol.[37] (Aceh was the site of the worst devastation of the December 2004 tsunami.)

In 2004 Indonesia held its first free, direct presidential elections. President Megawati's bid for a strong popular mandate was spoiled when a political outsider of humble origins, Susilo Bambang Yudhoyono, known as SBY, forced the president into a second-round runoff in which he handily defeated Megawati. He was reelected in 2009. Since assuming office, President Yudhoyono has sought to reach an accommodation with the Aceh rebels. But his small Democrat Party won only 10 percent of the seats in the 550-seat lower house elected in 2004; in 2009 it took 26 percent. In search of allies in 2004, SBY has found support from two moderate Islam-influenced parties: the Prosperous Justice Party, which won 45 seats, and the Crescent Star Party, with 11 seats. Neither party officially espouses an Islamic state based on *sharia*. The Prosperous Justice Party increased its share of votes after its leaders moderated the party's religious rhetoric and focused instead on the need to eliminate government corruption, running on the slogan "Clean and Concerned." The party also scored points with voters by providing tsunami relief more rapidly and effectively than the government was able to manage, at least initially. The Prosperous Justice Party continued in SBY's government after the 2009 election.

Despite the Bali bombings of 2002, Indonesia today is not on the verge of chaos or civil war. The overwhelming majority of the country's Muslims reject terrorism and support Indonesia's tradition of religious tolerance. Indonesia remains a secular state that officially recognizes five religions: Islam, Hinduism, Buddhism, Catholicism, and Protestantism. The vote for Islam-inspired parties has declined from 45 percent in the 1950s to 38 percent in 2004 and 24 percent in 2009.[38] Support for radical and terrorist groups is minimal. At the same time, support for Islamic beliefs is growing in Indonesia, stimulated by the global rise of Islamic proselytizing and political activism, and there are growing complaints of intolerance by Islamists. There is an ongoing debate between traditional and modernist Muslims, in tandem with a debate about how Islam should relate to democracy.

The chief conclusion of this section is that Islam has been quite compatible with democracy in Indonesia. Key Muslim leaders actively promoted the democratization process in the 1990s, and most of the country's overwhelmingly Muslim population supported it. They have also supported the democratic process that has developed since then, for all its flaws. Many Muslims regard tolerance, pluralism, and civility as defining features of Indonesia's Islamic tradition, and they want neither an Islamic theocracy nor an all-powerful state. The fate of democracy in Indonesia in all likelihood depends more on how Muslims view the government's efforts to eliminate corruption and improve the economy than on the political status of Islam.[39]

Many Islams

A survey of political currents in the Muslim world reveals a wide variety of political orientations and governmental structures.

- *Fundamentalists* (or *Islamists*) advocate the creation of Islamic theocracies, to be governed by clerics in accordance with a strict interpretation of Islamic law. They are vehemently anti-Western. Their ranks include the like-minded successors to Iran's Ayatollah Khomeini, the Taliban, and Osama bin Laden's followers. Some may advocate terrorism.

- *Conservatives* are devout Muslims who favor the implementation of Islamic law, whether in a very austere form or a more moderate version. As a general rule, conservatives tend to be less extreme than fundamentalists in their interpretation of Islam, and they may have a favorable attitude toward the West. Most would oppose terrorism. Some may favor a clerical theocracy (like Iran's former president, Grand Ayatollah Khamanei), while others prefer a secular government (like the royal family of Saudi Arabia or Zia ul-Haq, Pakistan's former president).

- *Authoritarian secularists* favor a dictatorial state run by secular authorities. As a rule they do not practice *sharia*. Within these broad parameters there is room for a variety of different religious, governmental, and foreign policy orientations. Some may be devout Muslims; others may only pay lip service to Islamic ideals, manipulating Muslim sentiment to their own ends. Some may be hostile to the West (like Saddam Hussein, Syria's Bashar al-Assad, and Libya's Muammar Gaddafi), while others may get along with the West (like Egypt's Hosni Mubarak and Pakistan's Pervez Musharraf). Kemal Atatürk deliberately led Turkey on the path of Westernization. The leaders of the former Central Asian republics of the Soviet Union fall into this category, as do the military or autocratic leaders and former leaders of various African states and the Mahgreb countries of Algeria, Morocco, and Tunisia.

- *Democratizing secularists* are leaders and political forces in predominantly or traditionally Muslim countries that have embarked on creating or consolidating a secular democracy. Examples can be found in Bangladesh, Egypt, Indonesia, Mali, Nigeria, Senegal, Tunisia, and Turkey—and perhaps in Bahrain and Qatar, whose monarchs appear to be moving in the direction of constitutional monarchy.

In sum there are many Islams, with a diversity of political directions. Whether the world's leading Muslim countries can find ways to blend Islam's rich religious and cultural heritage with the requirements of democracy in the years ahead will have a decisive impact on freedom and security throughout the world.[40]

ESSENTIAL CONCEPTS

The Left–Right Spectrum

Now that we've surveyed a number of ideologies, we can present a more detailed left–right political spectrum than the one in Chapter 1. In view of the complexities of political reality, however, the traditional left–right political spectrum as presented in Figure 10.2 should be taken with a grain of salt. Though anarchism is placed on the extreme left, some extreme right-wing groups in the United States are so antigovernment that they come close to advocating anarchism. Soviet-style communism (as in the former USSR or contemporary China) is placed on the left because of its historical associations with revolutionary socialism. It is virtually indistinguishable from fascism in several key respects, however. Both communist and fascist regimes have been one-party totalitarian regimes with a highly nationalistic foreign policy. Military regimes, for their part, come in left-wing socialist variants (in which the military leaders take up the cause of the working class or the poor) and right-wing variants (in which the military is aligned with a conservative ruling elite). Religiously oriented states, such as fundamentalist or traditionalist Islamic states, are placed on the right because of their reactionary tendency to implement religious and political doctrines as they were propounded more than a thousand years ago, but to the extent that they implement social welfare programs for the masses, they resemble the welfarist tendencies of the socialist left. The use of the term *Islamic fascism* to describe Islamic terrorists is inappropriate, however. Although both fascism and Islamic extremism reject democracy and embrace violence, their differences are substantial. Fascism espouses hypernationalism, military conquest, and racism; it scorns religious morality. Islamic fundamentalists want theocratic states. Their nationalism is directed mainly at getting American troops out of the Middle East, not at taking over Western countries. And their animosity toward Jews primarily reflects their opposition to the existence of Israel as a Zionist state in a predominantly Muslim region. It also reflects competing Islamic and Judaic claims of religious superiority. These anti-Jewish attitudes, however vengeful, generally do not stem from anti-Semitic racism. Arabs are themselves Semites.

As we suggested, depicting the differences among ideologies that we have discussed above in one-dimensional space along a single line greatly simplifies the richness of the views of politics that they offer. An alternative is to pose a two-dimensional chart such as that shown in Figure 10.3. Here the major ideologies discussed in this chapter are arrayed left to right according to their views about the role of the state in the economy and vertically according to their views about moral issues in politics. Here we see classical liberals and contemporary libertarians in the upper-right corner because they prefer little or no state involvement in both the economy and people's private lives. Social democrats tend to be progressive on cultural and moral issues but advocate

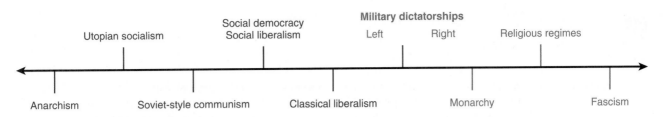

FIGURE 10.2   The Left–Right Spectrum

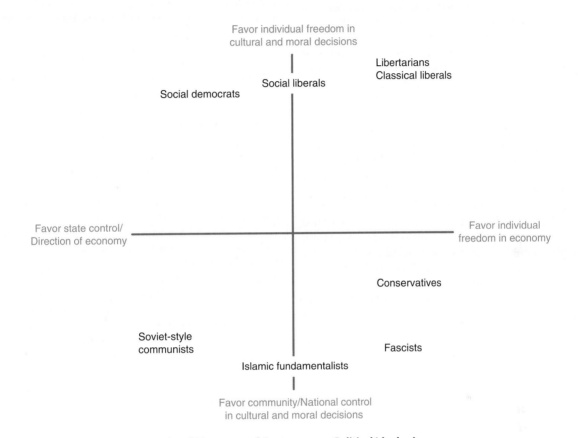

FIGURE 10.3   Two-Dimensional Placement of Contemporary Political Ideologies

a significant state role in the economy, hence they belong in the upper-left corner. Today's social liberals, who are also progressive on social issues, do not insist on the same degree of state involvement in managing the economy and redistributing income as social democrats, so they take a place between the latter and classical liberals on the upper part of the chart. Fascists allowed private property and a market economy in their societies (although regulating them to achieve their nationalist goals) but insisted on conformity to the hypernationalist and racist cultural and moral policies that they imposed, putting them in the lower-right corner. Soviet-style communists (e.g., Stalin and his successors, as we'll learn in Chapter 16, or China's Mao Zedong, discussed in Chapter 17), in contrast, insisted on the state's complete control of the economy but also allowed little nonconformity

with the cultural direction they took, so they belong in the lower left of this figure. We place Islamic fundamentalists in the middle of the lower part of the chart because, while they are dogmatic on cultural and moral matters, they have proven more pragmatic about the degree of state involvement in the economy.

The two dimensions of ideology graphed in Figure 10.3 do not exhaust the possibilities, of course. While the state–economy dimension usually appears on charts like this one, one might consider graphing the positions of these ideologies about their preference for democratic or authoritarian rule as the second dimension. As an exercise, you might attempt to place the ideologies discussed in this chapter on those two dimensions. ■

HYPOTHESIS-TESTING EXERCISE
The End of Ideology?

Hypothesis A number of scholars have hypothesized that the era of fierce ideological conflict is over. Daniel Bell, for example, argued in the 1960s and 1970s that fundamental changes occurring in the economies of most advanced capitalist countries since World War II were undercutting the basis of the historic ideological clash between capitalism and socialism. Instead of being dominated by industrialism, with its emphasis on manufacturing and manual labor, the post-industrial economies of the United States, Japan, and most West European countries were now driven by the service sector, consisting of financial services (banks, stock markets); consumer services (stores, restaurants, and the like); health and legal services; and so on. Education and technology were becoming the driving forces of economic advancement. As a consequence, Bell argued, the classic confrontation between the capitalist bourgeoisie and the industrial proletariat was essentially dying out. The evidence of recent decades largely confirms Bell's insight.[41]

A more recent "end-of-ideology" hypothesis maintains that the forces of technological advancement and economic globalization since the 1970s have undermined the traditional dichotomy between capitalism and socialism on a global scale. Most of the extraordinary technological innovations of the past several decades, especially in the computer and telecommunications industries, were pioneered by private companies. One of the principal reasons the Soviet Union collapsed, according to this hypothesis, was that its centrally planned socialist economy proved incapable of keeping up with the accelerated pace of high-technology advancement in countries with private enterprise. Meanwhile, the private-enterprise economies long ago ceased being "capitalist" in the sense in which Karl Marx understood the term. The economies of the United States, Japan, and Western Europe today are mixed economies in which the state plays a major role, at times assisting private firms and at times regulating their activities. These countries, moreover, are all welfare states in which the workers have collective bargaining rights and the government provides a host of welfare benefits to the general population. They are also mass democracies.

Our hypothesis asserts that a growing global consensus on the desirability of the democratic mixed-economy model is reducing the scope of ideological conflict both within and between countries around the world.

Variables The *dependent variable* is the end of ideological conflict, both within countries and among the nations of the world. The *independent variable* is mixed-economy democracies.

Expectations If the hypothesis is true, we would expect to find a global increase in the number of countries becoming mixed-economy democracies and a decline in competing ideological orientations such as communism, fascism, religious ideologies, and others.

Evidence The evidence required to put the hypothesis to a systematic test is vast. The most we can do for now is mention a few facts that touch on the hypothesis and the expectations that flow from it.

The hypothesis finds support in the fact that the centrally planned economies of the former Soviet Union and the communist-ruled states of East Central Europe fell far behind the mixed-economy democracies in developing advanced technologies and maintaining economic growth. As the hypothesis would lead us to expect, Soviet-style communist planning is now being replaced in these countries by private enterprise and other features of the modern mixed economy. Even China, which continues to be governed by a powerful Communist Party, abandoned central planning in the 1980s and now has a considerable amount of private enterprise. A growing number of developing countries in Asia, Latin America, Africa, as well, have made substantial changes in their economic systems since the 1980s, reducing the degree of state domination of the economy and expanding opportunities for private enterprise. In quite a few cases these economic changes have been accompanied by efforts to establish democracy.[42]

On the other side of the ledger, it is also true that ideological opposition to the prevailing Western model of the mixed-economy democracy continues to exist in various parts of the world. In Russia, for example, the triumph of private enterprise and democracy is still by no means assured. China openly advertises its own model, combining private enterprise with stern authoritarian rule. The desirability of combining private enterprise with some form of authoritarian rule has a wide following in other East Asian countries as well. In addition, as we have seen, Muslims around the world have advanced their own ideological alternatives to Western political and economic models. Finally, it cannot be casually assumed that no new ideological orientations will arise. A large proportion of the world's population lives in abject poverty; the blessings of the modern mixed-economy welfare state have eluded them. As Kenneth Jowett has observed, new political ideas and "movements of rage" may yet emerge from these desperate conditions or from other political landscapes where Western ideas are deemed inappropriate or downright unacceptable.[43]

Conclusions The sketchy evidence we have just summarized is quite *mixed*. There seems to be a wave of democracy and private enterprise billowing around the world, but the long-term success of these efforts is by no means a certainty. Islamic ideology and other orientations still pose a challenge to Western political and economic ideas.

Table 10.1 Key Characteristics of Contemporary Ideologies

Ideology	View on Government	Ideal Relationship between State and Economy	Views on Freedom and Equality	Social Values
Classical liberalism/ libertarianism	Negative: government should be limited to protect individual freedom	State allows the free market to regulate economic exchange	Individual freedom is highest goal; equality of opportunity leads to income inequality	Advocates the separation of religion and politics
Social liberalism	Positive: government can level the playing field and serve people's needs	State should regulate the economy to overcome market failures	Freedom and equality are both good; government helps to keep them in balance	Seeks the separation of religion and politics and promotion of a secular society tolerant of difference
Social democracy	Positive: government intervenes to protect the vulnerable and promote equality of life outcomes	State must regulate the economy and redistribute income to protect working people	Promoting equality of life chances will lead to freedom to do the most with one's life	Seeks the separation of religion and politics and promotion of a secular society
Communism	The state is the instrument of the dominant class for the exercise of its power	State owns means of production and plans all economic activity	Equality of economic condition is valued over individual liberty	Religion is the "opiate of the masses"
Fascism	An inspired leader should unify the core elements of the nation to confront internal and external adversaries	State should promote national economic interests through protectionism and strategic economic relationships	Individuals must be loyal to the nation; within the nation equality may prevail	Promotes traditional features of national culture; severe discrimination against "impure races"; glorifies violence
Islamic fundamentalism	Secular government is rejected; a theocracy where the state or religious authorities can enforce *sharia* law is sought	State will protect trade, prohibit charging of interest, and require charitable giving	Equality is maximized in a traditional society with limits on personal liberties	*Sharia* defines moral values; male honor, strict sexual mores, and submission to Allah emphasized

Conclusion

Table 10.1 summarizes the positions of the ideologies on several important characteristics discussed in this chapter. The table includes the perspectives of both classical and social liberals and of both major inheritors of Marx's legacy, social democrats and Soviet-style communists. While we suggested that there are different thrusts within Islamic ideology, for simplicity we provide only the views of Islamic fundamentalists. Use Table 10.1 to compare these ideologies. Which come closest to the views you hold?

Key Terms

Ideology
Liberalism
Social liberalism
Conservatism
Socialism
Marxism
Leninism
Marxism-Leninism
Social democracy
Fascism
Totalitarianism
Islamism
Sunnis
Shiites

Notes

1. See Louis Hartz, *The Liberal Tradition in America* (New York: Harcourt, Brace, & World, 1955).
2. For a biography of Burke, see Conor Cruise O'Brien, *The Great Melody* (Chicago: University of Chicago Press, 1992). See also Burke's critique of the French Revolution, *Reflections on the Revolution in France* (1790).
3. On utopian socialism, see Edmund Wilson, *To the Finland Station* (Garden City, NY: Doubleday, 1940); Robert Heilbroner, *The Worldly Philosophers*, 7th ed. (New York: Simon & Schuster, 1999); Charles Nordhoff, *The Communistic Societies of the United States* (New York: Hillary House, 1960), first published in 1875.
4. *Economic and Philosophic Manuscripts of 1844*, excerpted in Robert C. Tucker, ed., *The Marx-Engels Reader* (New York: W. W. Norton, 1972), pp. 53–103.
5. *Manifesto of the Communist Party*, in Tucker, *The Marx-Engels Reader*, pp. 331–62.
6. "The mode of production of economic life conditions the social, political and intellectual process in general." From *A Contribution to the Critique of Political Economy*, in Tucker, *The Marx-Engels Reader*, p. 4. See also Melvin Rader, *Marx's Conception of History* (New York: Oxford University Press, 1979).

7. Engels, "On Social Relations in Russia" (1875), in Tucker, *The Marx-Engels Reader*, pp. 589–99; Marx and Engels, preface to the Russian edition of the *Manifesto* (1882), in Tucker, *The Marx-Engels Reader*, pp. 333–34.

8. V. I. Lenin, *What Is to Be Done?* in *The Lenin Anthology*, ed. Robert C. Tucker (New York: W. W. Norton, 1975), pp. 12–114.

9. Bernstein wrote that the United States "apparently contradicts everything that the socialistic theory has hitherto advanced." In 1906 a prominent German sociologist addressed this curiosity. See Werner Sombart, *Why Is There No Socialism in the United States?* trans. Patricia M. Hocking and C. T. Husbands (White Plains, NY: M. E. Sharpe, 1976). See also Seymour Martin Lipset and Gary Marks, *It Didn't Happen Here: Why Socialism Failed in the United States* (New York: W. W. Norton, 2000). The American Socialist Party fielded presidential candidates between 1900 and 1932 but its candidates never obtained a million votes. For a biography of the party's last major leader, see W. A. Swanberg, *Norman Thomas: The Last Idealist* (New York: Scribner, 1976).

10. Julius K. Nyerere, *Ujamaa—Essays on Socialism* (London: Oxford University Press, 1968).

11. Abdel Moghny Said, *Arab Socialism* (London: Blandford Press, 1972).

12. Stanley G. Payne, *A History of Fascism, 1914–1945* (Madison: University of Wisconsin Press, 1995).

13. See Juan J. Linz, "Some Notes Toward a Comparative Study of Fascism in Sociological Historical Perspective," in *Fascism, a Reader's Guide: Analyses, Interpretations, Bibliography*, ed. Walter Laqueur (Berkeley, CA: University of California Press, 1976).

14. Meir Michaelis, *Mussolini and the Jews* (London: Oxford University Press, 1978).

15. Benito Mussolini and Giovanni Gentile, "The Doctrine of Fascism," in *Italian Fascisms from Pareto to Gentile*, ed. Adrian Lyttelton, trans. Douglas Parmee (New York: Harper and Row, 1973), p. 42. See also Herman Finer, *Mussolini's Italy* (New York: Grosset & Dunlap, 1965), pp. 198, 201. This classic work was first published in 1935.

16. On Mussolini's progression from socialism to fascism, see A. James Gregor, *Young Mussolini and the Intellectual Origins of Fascism* (Berkeley, CA: University of California Press, 1979).

17. Ernst Nolte, *Three Faces of Fascism*, trans. Leila Vennewitz (New York: Mentor, 1969), p. 282.

18. One leading scholar of fascism, A. James Gregor, has argued that fascist ideas may be found even in political movements that are not openly identified as fascist, including communist parties in Asia and Latin America and radical groups in the United States. Fascism and twentieth-century communism, he argues, are not mutually exclusive but share certain things, especially nationalism, totalitarianism, and mass mobilization. See *The Fascist Persuasion in Radical Politics* (Princeton, NJ: Princeton University Press, 1974).

19. Peter J. Katzenstein, ed., *Tamed Power: Germany in Europe* (Ithaca, NY: Cornell University Press, 1997).

20. Sheri Berman, "Islamism, Revolution, and Civil Society," *Perspectives on Politics* 1, no. 2 (June 2003), p. 257.

21. Pew Research Center Forum on Religion and Public Life, "The Future Global Muslim Population: Projections for 2010–2030," available at http://www.pewforum.org.

22. For overviews of the history of Islam, see Reza Aslan, *No God but God: The Origins, Evolution, and Future of Islam* (New York: Random House, 2005); Karen Armstrong, *Islam: A Short History* (New York: Modern Library, 2002).

23. Bernard Lewis, *What Went Wrong? Western Impact and Middle Eastern Response* (Oxford: Oxford University Press, 2002).

24. Aslan, *No God but God*, p. 170. See also Mansoor Moaddel and Kamran Talatoff, *Modern and Fundamentalist Debates in Islam* (New York: Palgrave, 2002).

25. Vincenzo Oliveti, *Terror's Source: The Ideology of Wahhabi-Salafism and Its Consequences* (Birmingham, UK: Amadeus, 2002); Natana J. DeLong-Bas, *Wahhabi Islam: From Revival and Reform to Global Jihad* (Oxford: Oxford University Press, 2004); David Cummins, *The Wahhabi Mission and Saudi Arabia* (London: Tauris, 2006).

26. Moojan Momen, *An Introduction to Shi'i Islam: The History and Doctrines of Twelver Shi'ism* (New Haven, CN: Yale University Press, 1985), pp. 191–96. See also Yitzhak Nakash, *The Shi'is of Iraq* (Princeton, NJ: Princeton University Press, 1994); Fouad Ajami, *The Vanished Imam: Musa al Sadr and the Shia of Lebanon* (Ithaca, NY: Cornell University Press, 1986).

27. Vali Nasr, *The Shia Revival: How Conflicts Within Islam Will Shape the Future* (New York: W. W. Norton, 2006).

28. Jonathan Riley-Smith, ed., *The Oxford History of the Crusades* (Oxford: Oxford University Press, 2002); Karen Armstrong, *Holy War: The Crusades and Their Impact in Today's World*, 2nd ed. (New York: Anchor, 2001).

29. Reuven Firestone, *Jihad: The Origins of Holy War in Islam* (New York: Oxford University Press, 1999).

30. Arch Puddington, *Freedom in the World 2013: Democratic Breakthroughs in the Balance* (New York: Freedom House, 2013), pp. 13–17.

31. See, for example, Maria Rosa Menocal, *The Ornament of the World: How Muslims, Jews, and Christians Created a Culture of Tolerance in Medieval Spain* (Boston: Little, Brown, 2002).

32. M. Steven Fish, "Islam and Authoritarianism," *World Politics* 55, no. 1 (October 2002), pp. 4–37.

33. On democracy and Islam, see Leonard Binder, *Islamic Liberalism* (Chicago: University of Chicago Press, 1988); Charles Kurzman, ed., *Liberal Islam: A Sourcebook* (Oxford: Oxford University Press, 1998); John L. Esposito and John O. Voll, *Islam and Democracy* (New York: Oxford University Press, 1996); Joel Beinin and Joe Stork, eds., *Political Islam* (Berkeley, CA: University of California Press, 1997). See also the articles in the *Journal of Democracy* 13, no. 4 (October 2002), pp. 5–68; *Journal of Democracy* 14, no. 2 (April 2003), pp. 18–49. On "exceptionalism," see *Journal of Democracy* 15, no. 4 (October 2004), pp. 126–46.

34. Steven Drakeley, *The History of Indonesia* (Westport, CN: Greenwood, 2005); J. D. Legge, *Sukarno: A Political Biography* (New York: Praeger, 1972); Rex Mortimer, *Indonesian Communism under Sukarno: Ideology and Politics, 1959–1965* (Ithaca, NY: Cornell University Press, 1974). The events of 1965 provide the background of the film *The Year of Living Dangerously*, based on the novel by Christopher J. Koch.

35. Robert W. Hefner, *Civil Islam: Muslims and Democratization in Indonesia* (Princeton, NJ: Princeton University Press, 2000); Donald J. Porter, *Managing Politics and Islam in Indonesia* (London: Routledge Curzon, 2002).

36. Edward Aspinall, *Opposing Suharto: Compromise, Resistance, and Regime Change in Indonesia* (Stanford, CA: Stanford University Press, 2005); Richard Lloyd Parry, *In the Time of Madness: Indonesia on the Edge of Chaos* (New York: Grove, 2005); Stefan Eklöf, *Indonesian Politics in Crisis: The Long Fall of Suharto 1996–98* (Copenhagen: Nordic Institute of Asian Studies, 1999).

37. "Tolerating Intolerance: Islam in Indonesia," *The Economist*, June 9, 2012; Human Rights Watch, "Policing Morality: Abuses in the Application of Sharia in Aceh, Indonesia," December 2010.

38. Norimitsu Onishi, "Indonesia's Voters Retreat From Radical Islam," *The New York Times*, April 24, 2009.

39. "Time to Deliver: A Survey of Indonesia," *The Economist*, December 11, 2004. On the tsunami, see *The Washington Post*, January 14, 19, 27, and 28 and February 27, 2005. See also Giora Eliraz, *Islam in Indonesia: Modernism, Radicalism, and the Middle East Dimension* (Brighton, England: Sussex Academic Press, 2004); Bahtiar Effendi, *Islam and the State in Indonesia* (Athens, OH: Ohio University Press, 2003); and the discussion at the conference titled "Islam in Modern Indonesia" organized by the United States–Indonesia Society (February 7, 2002), accessible at www.usindo.org. The website of the Liberal Islam Network is www.islamlib.com.

40. Mir Zohair Husain, *Global Islamic Politics* (New York: HarperCollins, 1996). See also Olivier Roy, *Globalized Islam: The Search for a New Ummah* (New York: Columbia University Press, 2004); Gilles Kepel, *The War for Muslim Minds: Islam and the West*, trans. Pascale Ghazaleh (Cambridge, MA: Harvard University Press, 2004).

41. Daniel Bell, *The End of Ideology*, rev. ed. (New York: Free Press, 1961); Daniel Bell, *The Coming of Post-Industrial Society* (New York: Basic Books, 1973 and 1999); Daniel Bell, *The Cultural Contradictions of Capitalism* (New York: Basic Books, 1976). See also Chaim I. Waxman, ed., *The End of Ideology Debate* (New York: Simon & Schuster, 1969).

42. Daniel Yergin and Joseph Stanislaw, *The Commanding Heights* (New York: Simon & Schuster, 1998).

43. Kenneth Jowett, *New World Disorder* (Berkeley, CA: University of California Press, 1992), pp. 275–77.

11

Political Economy
Laissez-Faire, Central Planning, Mixed Economies, and Welfare States

The leaders of the world's most powerful economies regularly meet at the G8 summit.

OVERVIEW

- Political economy considers the relationship between politics and economics in order to learn how governments contribute to the direction of the economy and how economic relationships shape political behavior.

- This chapter introduces key economic concepts that have political implications, such as monetary and fiscal policy, central banks and their role in regulating investment and inflation, and the problem of government budget deficits.

- Three alternative models of political economy have prevailed in the modern era: laissez-faire capitalism, centrally planned socialism, and mixed economies.

- The writings of classical political economists (classical liberals) such as Adam Smith, David Ricardo, Thomas Malthus, Herbert Spencer, and John Stuart Mill shaped the government policies that allowed free-market capitalism to dominate Britain and the United States in the nineteenth century.

- Centrally planned state socialism, a legacy of Marxist-inspired communism in which the state and the economy were essentially fused, prevailed in the Soviet Union and mainland China in the twentieth century.

- Reactions to the shortcomings of laissez-faire capitalism and state socialism led to the emergence of the mixed economy (informed by social liberalism and social democracy) in the twentieth century, especially in the United States and Europe.

- Mixed economies in high-income democracies tend to follow welfare state policies. We consider the rise of the welfare state and the barriers to its survival in the current period.

WHAT IS POLITICAL ECONOMY?

Politics and economics are intimately interrelated. Whether it is a matter of taxes, budget deficits, health care programs, or foreign trade, economic issues are invariably the stuff of intense political controversy and governmental decision making. Because of this intimate linkage of politics and economics, many political scientists and economists choose to focus on an interdisciplinary subfield of both disciplines: political economy.

Political economy is the study of how people pursue collective economic goals and deal with conflicts over resources and other economic factors in an authoritative way by means of government.

Especially in today's tightly woven global economy, a sound understanding of economics is more than just useful; it's a survival skill. Consider the following example of how international relationships affect the value of our money.

A Tourist's Guide to International Economics

Most countries have their own currency: the U.S. dollar, the Japanese yen, and the Swiss franc are among the most widely used currencies in the world. Most members of the European Union share a common currency, the euro. Just like stocks and bonds, currencies are bought and sold on world markets by banks and other currency traders. Currencies worth more than $4 trillion change hands around the globe on a typical business day.[1] And just like stocks and bonds, currencies change their relative value as a result of these global transactions.

A currency's value—its price relative to other currencies—can often be affected by political as well as economic considerations. If currency traders believe that country X may experience political instability or turmoil such as an unpredictable new government or a civil war, they may sell their holdings of that country's currency, buying the currencies of more politically stable countries instead. They may do the same thing if they believe that country X is about to experience major economic difficulties. When a country's currency is being sold in large quantities in world currency exchanges, its value relative to stronger, more desirable currencies drops, or *depreciates*, significantly.

The result of currency depreciation (or currency devaluations) can be felt instantly by tourists visiting the country whose currency is declining in value. Suppose you are an American tourist visiting Mexico. When you arrive, the Mexican peso is valued at 3.5 to the dollar. At this rate, you buy 350 pesos for $100. After a few days of dining and shopping, you need more pesos. But in the meantime, Mexico experiences a currency crisis as international traders begin a massive sell-off of pesos. The next time you go to a bank to exchange your dollars, you find to your delight that the peso is now valued at 5 to the dollar. For $100 you can now get 500 pesos in exchange. If the peso continues to slide in value, you may be able to extend your stay or buy more items, because each dollar exchanged buys more Mexican goods and services than it did upon your arrival. Mexicans involved in the tourist trade eagerly welcome your additional expenditures. Like you, they stand to benefit from the peso's devaluation.

For many Mexicans, however, the peso's depreciation brings unwelcome consequences. Mexicans who buy imported goods from the United States such as computers or autos must now pay out more pesos per dollar's worth of purchase. A $1,000 American-made computer cost 3,500 pesos before the currency crisis; it now costs 5,000 pesos following the Mexican currency's devaluation. At the new rate of exchange, a Mexican consumer or businessperson may decide that it's too expensive to buy the computer at the higher peso price. In that case, the U.S. computer exporter loses a sale. For a U.S.-based company that sells a lot of goods south of the border, the peso's decline can result in a severe loss of customers. The business may be forced to lay off workers or may even go bankrupt.

Imagine the impact of the peso's decline on billions of dollars' worth of economic transactions between the two countries. (In 2011, U.S. exports of goods to Mexico exceeded $198 billion and Mexican exports to the United States exceeded $262 billion.) Large numbers of tourists, consumers,

Table 11.1 Winners and Losers in a Currency Devaluation

AS THE MEXICAN PESO DEPRECIATES RELATIVE TO THE U.S. DOLLAR...	
Winners	**Losers**
U.S. purchasers and importers of Mexican goods and services	Mexican purchasers and importers of U.S. goods and services
Mexican sellers and exporters to U.S. buyers	U.S. sellers and exporters to Mexican buyers

and businesses on both sides of the border are directly affected by the shift: some positively, others negatively. In virtually every case of currency depreciation, there are winners and losers (see Table 11.1). Those who are economically disadvantaged will exert pressure on the Mexican and U.S. governments to do something about the peso's decline. The economic issue now becomes a political issue: People want governments to take action.

What can governments do in this situation? The most immediate option is for governments to intervene in world currency markets by buying pesos. Like stocks, the value of a currency rises the more it is purchased. If the U.S. and Mexican governments spend millions of dollars from their treasuries to buy pesos, the value of the peso will likely rise. It may not go all the way back to 3.5 to the dollar, but at least it will move closer. Most important, the object of the governments' intervention is to stabilize the peso so it will not fall or rise wildly, but will retain a fairly stable and predictable value against the dollar and other world currencies.

The case just outlined is not fictitious. At the end of 1994, the Mexican peso began falling in value against the U.S. dollar exactly as described. Within a few months the peso plunged from 3.45 to 8 to the dollar, as you can see in Figures 11.1 and 11.2. To halt the peso's slide, the Mexican government spent millions of U.S. dollars in its possession (its dollar *reserves*) to buy pesos on world markets. The U.S. government joined other governments in providing the Mexican government with a $38 billion rescue package to strengthen its economy, in hopes of making the peso more attractive to currency buyers. Though the peso's value rose in response to this assistance, it fell once again in the fall of 1995. The peso is now valued at about 13 to the dollar.

The peso's sudden deterioration had profound political consequences for both Mexico and the United States. In Mexico it triggered a severe economic crisis. The prices of imported goods rose dramatically, hurting businesses and consumers. Prices in 1995 were more than 40 percent higher than the previous year. As many as a million people were thrown out of work in 1995 alone because their employers could no longer afford to pay them. The country's domestic economy declined by about 10 percent, as Figure 11.1 shows. Inflation rates skyrocketed to as much as 100 percent, as seen in Figure 11.2. A significant increase in violent crime in Mexico City and other parts of the country was attributed to rising economic frustration. Predictably, Mexicans from all walks of life looked to their government to help them. In the United States, the Clinton administration and the Republican-controlled Congress worked out a response

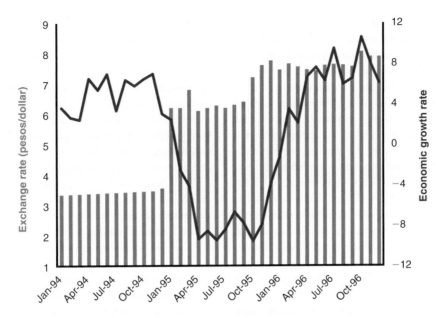

FIGURE 11.1   Impact of Exchange Rate Devaluation on Mexican Economic Growth, 1994–1996

Source: Mexico, National Institute of Statistics and Geography, http://www.inegi.org.mx/sistemas/bie/.

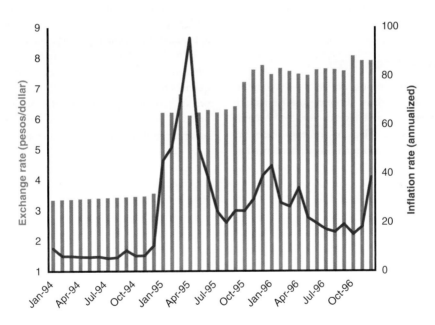

FIGURE 11.2   Impact of Exchange Rate Devaluation on Mexican Inflation, 1994–1996

Source: Mexico, National Institute of Statistics and Geography, http://www.inegi.org.mx/sistemas/bie/.

to the Mexican situation because American businesses and consumers have an interest in a stable, fairly valued peso. Approximately 700,000 jobs in the United States depended on trade with Mexico. The United States also had an interest in helping Mexico avoid potentially violent internal unrest as well as a rise in illegal immigrants coming across the U.S. border.

But as the peso fell, Mexico's exports rose more than 30 percent over the next few years. Sales to the United States, which buys 80 percent of the country's export goods, got an additional boost from the North American Free Trade Agreement (NAFTA), which reduces trade barriers between the United States, Mexico, and Canada. The steep rise in Mexico's export industry helped stabilize the economy and boosted growth rates considerably starting in 1996 (see Figure 11.1). While wages for industrial workers and other aspects of Mexico's economy deteriorated as a result of the currency devaluation, exports and other sectors improved. Winners as well as losers were still in evidence in Mexico several years after the peso's dramatic fall.

Arguably, though, being able to devalue its currency allowed Mexico to find a way out of its economic difficulties in 1994–95, but it is not coincidental that Mexico's long-ruling party, the Institutional Revolutionary Party, lost elections in 1997 and 2000 as voters punished the party in power.

Beginning in 2009 the countries sharing the euro as their currency have struggled to address what is known as the sovereign-debt crisis, in which several euro zone governments owe large debts to foreign creditors. Greece, the most prominent example, has been wracked by political conflict about how to meet its debt obligations. If Greece's circumstances today paralleled those of Mexico in 1994, Greece would have devalued its currency as early as 2010 so it could sell more goods abroad (because they would be cheaper after devaluations), earn more foreign exchange (such as dollars, yen, or Swiss francs), and pay creditors. However, as a member of the euro zone, Greece cannot unilaterally devalue the euro. The countries with large foreign debts in Europe—e.g., Ireland, Italy, Spain, and Portugal in addition to Greece—would likely benefit from devaluing the euro. Germany, whose citizens and banks have lent much money abroad, including to the Greeks, does not want a euro devaluation. Difficulties in resolving this tension between debtors and creditors within the euro zone have drawn out the euro crisis.

Defining Political Economy

Economics is the study of how people and societies choose to allocate the scarce resources at their disposal, such as natural resources, human-made goods, and human services. Accordingly, economists examine such things as the way prices are determined, the impact of taxes, and such other phenomena as production, inflation, unemployment, and the causes of economic growth and decline.

Like political science, economics is a behavioral science: One of its main ambitions is to examine the ways individuals and organizations behave when making economic choices and decisions. And like at least some political scientists, many economists employ *rational-choice theory*, the notion that people generally act on the basis of calculated self-interest to increase their anticipated gains and reduce their anticipated costs or risks. Thus *homo economicus*—economic human—is a rational actor who is able to figure out how to increase wealth and minimize losses. Viewed from the larger perspective of an entire society, however, a collection of individual and corporate rational actors may not necessarily produce economic results that maximize everyone's welfare. What is rational for you may be bad for me. If you decide to raise prices for the goods you sell me, you are increasing my costs. Sometimes decisions that are rational for an individual or a particular company may prove harmful for the larger community. If a factory keeps its costs down by refusing to use expensive pollution control devices, the pollutants its chimneys belch into the air not only damage the public's health but also raise the community's health care costs. Conversely, economic decisions that are rational for the community as a whole may be deleterious for particular individuals or groups. If the government, for example, decides to trim its budget deficit by raising your taxes, you may not personally appreciate the rationality of its choice.

In short, the economic activities of individuals, private enterprises, and governments often produce negative consequences for others. Of course, there are times when public and private economic policies benefit almost everyone to a greater or lesser degree. A growing economy can afford better roads, more medical research, and cleaner air. These cases are positive-sum games, with many winners. But all too often there are losers as well as winners. This outcome is especially likely when the resources people want—money, land, jobs, and so on—are

As a sovereign country within the euro zone struggling with a failing economy, Greece cannot make unilateral decisions to address its economic situation. The Greek government must negotiate with other, more economically powerful nations with different economic needs, such as Germany, to affect meaningful change. Austerity measures forced on Greece by the European Union prompted many large demonstrations.

limited in quantity, a common occurrence. As a consequence, the allocation of scarce resources in society can sometimes be a zero-sum game. That is, it may be impossible to improve one person's welfare without reducing the welfare of someone else.[2] In other commonly occurring cases, a decision that may improve your welfare in the long run (balanced budgets, for example) may worsen it in the short run (higher taxes).

In these and other social relationships that arise out of economic interactions, conflicts over "who gets what" often result. Whenever conflict occurs over economic issues and the state is expected to deal with them, economics is joined with politics. Every economic system, moreover, is "political" in the sense that it is embedded in laws and procedures that are sanctioned by the state. Whether it is a private-enterprise system, socialism, or some other mode of economic organization, the state invariably makes laws that determine how the economy works in practice. Economics is inseparable from politics. Political economy is about the relationship between the economy and the state and about the various ways people try to use the state to improve their economic welfare.

Viewed in the most general terms, political economy is interested in two broad sets of questions: (1) How does economics affect politics? and (2) How does politics affect economics? In the first question, economics is the independent variable (the cause or influencing factor) and politics is the dependent variable (the effect).

1. *Economics affects politics.* It frequently happens in democracies that many voters, sometimes a majority, "vote their pocketbooks": They vote for candidates who appear most likely to improve their economic well-being. Empirical evidence in the United States shows that, since World War II, incumbent presidents usually win reelection if the economy grows by about 4 percent or more in the four quarters preceding the election.[3] Another example is the tendency for growth in the U.S. economy to stimulate progressive political developments such as the expansion of civil rights, racial tolerance, immigration, and educational opportunities. By contrast, economic downturns have tended to produce cutbacks in social spending and immigration along with outbursts of racism.[4]

   In the second question the variables are reversed: Politics is the independent variable and economics is the dependent variable.

2. *Politics affects economics.* In 1996 and 1997, President Bill Clinton signed bills passed by the Republican-dominated majority in Congress designed to balance the annual federal government budget by 2002. This legislation, hammered out in long negotiations that required the Democrats and Republicans to compromise their differences, is credited with promoting one of the longest periods of sustained economic growth and high employment in decades. Other examples of this connection focus on how government institutions such as central banks can affect the inflation rate or stock markets, or how the partisan composition of the government can affect the ways the state spends its money and

thereby influences the economy. Some comparative studies show, for example, that left-leaning governments tend to spend slightly more than right-leaning governments.

Because economic transactions and political activity go on all the time, the relationship between politics and economics is frequently interactive. That is, economic variables affect political variables, which in turn affect economic variables, which then affect political variables, and so on. A central purpose of political economy is to clarify these interacting relationships.

One of the most important of these relationships is the relationship between states and markets. Such terms as *markets, the market economy,* and *market forces* refer mainly to the private sector. They apply broadly to the production, buying, and selling of goods and services by private companies and individuals, with prices and salaries determined largely by the forces of supply and demand rather than by government fiat. Political economy examines such questions as, How do government policies affect market forces, and vice versa? Should governments control or regulate the economy, or should markets have fairly free rein? Can there be an acceptable balance between states and markets? The answers to these questions, whether of an empirical or prescriptive nature, will vary from country to country and are often grist for the mill of lively debate within individual countries.[5]

Because political economy encompasses a wide range of specific issues, we'll spread our conceptual treatment of this topic over two chapters. This chapter looks first at basic terminology in economics. It then examines three systems of political economy: *laissez-faire capitalism, central planning,* and *mixed economies.* Each one entails a different theory of the relationship between the state and the economy. A prime example of a mixed economy is the modern *welfare state,* which is discussed in the last section of this chapter. The next chapter focuses on countries engaged in early stages of economic development.

ESSENTIAL CONCEPTS

Basic Economic Concepts

Grasping the main issues of political economy requires an understanding of a few central concepts in economics. The following definitions are not a substitute for a course in economics; rather they provide rudimentary information about basic economic phenomena and analytical terminology with a view to enhancing your understanding of politics. Most of these concepts come from *macroeconomics,* the part of the discipline that deals with whole economies and aggregate behavior; *microeconomics,* in contrast, examines individual behavior by firms, households, and individuals.

The **gross domestic product (GDP)** represents the market value of all goods and services produced by a country's economy in a specified time period. It includes the consumption and investment of individuals and private companies as well as government expenditures. It also includes the value of goods and services produced within the country for export abroad, minus the value of imports from abroad. The GDP does not include the income that the country's citizens earn abroad, nor does it take into account the income foreigners earn from investments within the country's borders. Because the GDP excludes the latter two figures, it measures what a country is actually producing *at home*. **Per capita GDP** is the country's GDP divided by its population. Whereas GDP refers to gross production, per capita GDP provides an *average* of the country's domestic product per person. Of course, some individuals and companies produce more than others.

The **gross national income (GNI)** equals the total market value of goods and services a country produces at home (the GDP), plus the *net* income received from foreign countries. Net income from foreign countries includes interest payments and dividends paid by other countries, plus the profits earned by the home country's citizens and companies abroad that are sent back (repatriated) to their home country. Similar payments made to other countries are subtracted from these sums. Thus, if the domestic economy of country X generated $10 trillion worth of income at home last year, and residents of X earned $2 trillion abroad and sent it back home, while foreigners earned $1 trillion from their investments in X and repatriated it back to their home countries, then X's GNI last year was $11 trillion. The GNI is essentially the same as the *gross national product (GNP)*, a term that is now rarely used. **Per capita GNI** is a country's gross national income divided by its population. It provides a picture of how much income the country's individuals earn *on average*—but it does not take account of the distribution of national income among the very rich, the very poor, and all those in between.

Economic growth refers to the increases in a country's GNI or GDP over a specified period. If a country's national or domestic income falls below the previous period's figure, it experiences negative growth.

Inflation means steadily rising prices. The *inflation rate* measures the extent to which the average price for goods in one time period exceeds average prices in some previous period. If the average price for a typical market basket of a society's goods and services in 2012 was 10 percent higher than the average price for those same goods in 2011, then the annual inflation rate for 2012 was 10 percent.

Inflation has several different causes. One is an excess in a country's supply of money in circulation. As a result, the money's value declines (or *depreciates*)—a single dollar buys less and less. The expression, "Too many dollars chasing too few goods," captures this problem. To remedy it, the government must stop printing more money or significantly reduce the amount it is printing. Governmental decisions affecting the money supply are the main concern of *monetary policy*. *Monetarism* is an economic theory that emphasizes the links between a country's money supply and such phenomena as inflation and economic growth. One of its most influential exponents was Milton Friedman (1912–2006), a Nobel Prize winner.

Prolonged inflation can be ruinous. When the inflation rate tops 10 to 15 percent per year, governments are usually expected to step in to solve the problem. Their efforts are not always successful. Between 1987 and 1991, the annual inflation rate averaged more than 1,000 percent in Argentina and Brazil and more than 2,000 percent in Peru. In 1993 Ukraine had an inflation rate of 8,000 percent. In 1923, Germany's inflation rate topped 1 billion percent! Inflation of this magnitude is called *hyperinflation*, which is usually defined as an inflation rate that exceeds 50 percent per month. Failure to reduce runaway inflation can jeopardize a government's ability to stay in power because the consequence of high inflation is that the value of people's savings is wiped out. Inflation can therefore be just as much a political problem as an economic one.

The central bank is the national government's official bank. In the United States it is the Federal Reserve System. Central banks determine how much money to print and provide loans to private (commercial) banks. They may also engage in open market transactions such as buying and selling government bonds. These various actions often raise or lower the nation's inflation rate.

The **central bank** is the national government's official bank. In the United States it is the Federal Reserve System. In most countries the central bank's main tasks are to determine how much money to print and to provide loans to private (commercial) banks. Central banks may also engage in open market transactions such as buying and selling government bonds. These various actions often have the effect of raising or lowering the nation's inflation rate.

For instance, when private banks borrow cash from the central bank for their own lending and investment operations, the central bank charges them interest. If inflation is undesirably high, the central bank may raise the interest rate it charges to commercial banks. The central bank's interest rate is called the *discount rate* or the *bank rate*. Through this action the central bank can indirectly raise commercial interest rates throughout the economy. If the commercial banks must pay higher interest to the central bank, they cover this added expense by charging their own customers higher interest rates for personal or business loans. Higher commercial interest rates discourage prospective borrowers. As interest rates go up, fewer people are willing to take out personal loans for college tuition, auto purchases, home mortgages, or other big expenditures, and fewer businesses are willing to borrow heavily to expand their operations. Less money gets circulated in the economy, the demand for goods declines, and inflation falls. But as a result of this "tight money" policy, business in general may also fall off and unemployment may rise.

Conversely, the economy could be in a recession or a depression. The difference is mainly a matter of degree. A **recession** is a period of zero growth or negative growth, resulting in declining business activity, rising unemployment, and perhaps some bankruptcies. In the United States and the United Kingdom, a recession is usually understood to mean two successive quarters (a half year) of negative growth. A **depression** is much more severe, with prolonged negative growth, massive unemployment, and widespread bankruptcies. In these situations inflation is typically low or nonexistent; prices tend to fall. To stimulate the economy, the central bank may reduce the discount rate or take other action to make money more available to businesses and consumers. If successful, this "easy money" policy revives business activity and reduces unemployment, though prices may rise in the process.

A trade-off exists between inflation and employment: Governmental policies aimed at keeping inflation low may at times increase unemployment, while policies aimed at stimulating business and increasing employment opportunities may sometimes increase the inflation rate. The aim of most governments is to sustain both high employment and low inflation simultaneously, but this dual objective is sometimes hard to achieve. Governments therefore frequently have to make difficult policy choices that may adversely affect certain segments of the population for at least the short term, if not longer. Because central banks can have such a powerful influence on the economy, their policies often trigger political conflict.

The question of who controls the central bank is therefore crucial and profoundly political. Some central banks are fairly independent of the executive and legislative branches of government and enjoy ample latitude to make tough decisions that may be good for the economy but unpopular, such as raising interest rates. (The U.S. Federal Reserve bank is an example.) Other central banks are less independent of political decision makers and may have less freedom to make politically unpopular decisions.

A **budget deficit** occurs when a government spends more than it takes in. When expenditures equal revenues, the government has a *balanced budget*. The U.S. government ran consecutive annual budget deficits from 1969 through 1998. Thanks to a booming economy, the United States finally realized a budget surplus in 1999. But a declining economy and a tax cut sent the deficit soaring above $100 billion in 2002. The costs incurred in bolstering homeland security after September 11, 2001, and the money spent on military and reconstruction operations in Afghanistan and Iraq, drove deficits still higher: The deficit surpassed $426 billion in 2005. Then the financial crisis triggered by the subprime mortgage bubble hit, and the government's effort to support the economy sent the deficit still higher, to $1.3 billion in 2011. Some economists maintain that no government should allow its annual deficit to exceed a certain limit. For advanced economies such as the United States and the European Union countries, the recommended limit is usually 3 percent of GDP. In 2011 the U.S. figure was about 8.7 percent of GDP (the figures were worse in 2010).[6]

The public **national debt** is the amount of money the national government owes its creditors at home and abroad. When governments do not earn enough revenue from taxes, import duties, or other typical sources, and thereby run up budget deficits, they may have to borrow money from private banks, foreign governments, international lending agencies, or other sources of funds to pay their bills. As budget deficits mount from year to year, the amount of money the government must borrow rises accordingly. One way governments borrow money is by issuing bonds (like U.S. savings bonds) or Treasury bills (T-bills). The government pledges to reimburse the purchasers of these securities, with interest, after a specified time ranging from 30 days to 30 years or more. The accumulated principal and interest owed to the holders of these "debt instruments" are part of the public national debt, along with any other money the government owes to lenders such as the International Monetary Fund (IMF) or the World Bank.

The U.S. public national debt reached $10.1 trillion at the end of 2011. The U.S. government owes an increasing share of this money to the central banks of foreign governments and to foreign commercial banks. Foreigners held 47 percent of the U.S. debt in 2011. (In 2005, foreigners held 43 percent, while in 2000, foreigners held 34 percent, and in 1995 the figure was 25 percent.) About two-thirds of these foreign holders of U.S. securities were governments. In other words, foreigners—especially foreign governments—have been playing a growing role in financing U.S. government expenditures. China currently has the largest amount of U.S. public securities held by one country, just ahead of Japan. In 2011, China and Japan (both the governments and private citizens) held 9.8 and 9.6 percent of the U.S. debt, respectively. Is reliance on foreign creditors dangerous? On the positive side, foreign governments, banks, and other investors buy U.S. Treasury securities because they have confidence in the U.S. economy: They can be quite sure that the U.S. government will repay them, with interest, by the promised date. The American economy is so big and its political institutions so stable that there is little likelihood the U.S. government will default on its loans or go bankrupt like individuals or private companies that get over their heads in debt. For the U.S. government, selling bonds and Treasury bills is a quick way to get cash to meet budgetary obligations. For the rest of the world, purchasing U.S. government securities is a safe investment. On the negative side, the U.S. government runs the risk that foreign governments and banks will suddenly stop or reduce their purchases of U.S. securities. Alternatively, they might sell their U.S. holdings to buy securities offered by other governments in hopes of reaping a higher return on their investment than the United States might be offering. Such decisions would deprive the U.S. government of vast amounts of money. In stark contrast to the prodigious U.S. economy, middle-income and poor countries that cannot repay the money they have borrowed abroad may have to be rescued by international agencies such as the IMF. In these circumstances they may be compelled to make difficult economic adjustments, such as drastically slashing government spending, as a condition of receiving international assistance.

Another negative consequence of national debt is that it requires indebted governments to pay interest to their creditors. These interest payments are supposed to be made on time to all creditors, whether domestic or foreign, private or governmental. Paying interest in periodic installments is called *debt servicing*. In 2011 the U.S. government paid out $251 billion in interest, about 6.5 percent of total federal government expenditures for that year. In addition, by borrowing huge amounts of cash from bond purchasers, the government is soaking up money that would otherwise remain in people's hands, to be spent by consumers or invested by businesspeople. Persistent government borrowing, in other words, deprives the national economy of funds that could be more productively utilized, through consumer spending and business investment, to boost economic growth.

Ultimately, there are only two ways to reduce budget deficits and the national debt: slash government spending or raise revenue such as taxes. For especially large debts, both may have to be done simultaneously. Obviously, these choices can be quite painful for large segments of the population.

Fiscal policy refers to government revenue and expenditure policy. The term derives from the old term "the fisc" for the state treasury. Taxation is the most widely used form of raising revenue. One of the most common political controversies surrounding tax questions centers on the fairness of the tax burden. *Progressive income taxes* are generally considered to be fair because they take a rising proportion of income as income rises. The rich must pay at higher rates than lower-income households pay. Critics of this system charge, however, that a "soak the rich" tax policy hinders overall economic growth and employment opportunities because it deprives the most well-endowed consumers and investors in the economy of money they could use to buy goods and services or invest in productive businesses.

Regressive taxes take a decreasing percentage of income as income rises. There are several types. Sales taxes, for example, are generally regressive in nature. If everyone in a certain jurisdiction (such as Maryland or France) is subject to the same sales tax rate (say, 10 percent) for certain categories of goods, lower-income people will pay out a higher portion of their income for these taxes than will wealthier people, especially if such necessities as food and clothing are taxed. Low-income people have to spend most of their earnings, whereas the rich can afford to save or invest a portion of their income, and what they do not spend is not subject to sales taxes.

In the United States the federal government has at times imposed national sales taxes on such things as gasoline, alcoholic beverages, and cigarettes. In addition, the 50 states have the right to impose statewide sales taxes. Local communities in the United States, such as cities and counties, also have certain tax powers, as in the case of real estate taxes.

Many countries in Western Europe and elsewhere have a national **value-added tax (VAT)** on certain types of goods and services. The VAT is a national sales tax imposed at every point in the production and marketing process of specified goods. Ultimately it is the final consumer who pays the entire tax. By the mid-1990s the average VAT rate was about 20 percent in most countries belonging to the European Union, though the actual rate varied with the item.

Finally, a *flat tax* taxes everyone's income at the same rate (say, 20 percent), regardless of their wealth. In the United States, a national flat tax has been proposed in recent years by both liberal and conservative candidates for president, but never adopted.

The expenditure side of fiscal policy revolves largely around the budget. The process of putting the budget together is typically highly politicized, involving bargaining among multiple actors both inside and outside the state's institutions. ∎

Let's now look at different forms of political economy, considering the differences between a model in which the state tries to play a relatively small role in economic interactions—laissez-faire capitalism—and central planning, where the state has an all-encompassing role in the economy. We will then turn to mixed economies, which characterize most of the advanced democracies in today's world.

LAISSEZ-FAIRE CAPITALISM

The form of political economy with the least amount of governmental involvement is known as **laissez-faire capitalism**. *Laissez-faire* (less-ay fair) means "let do" or "leave alone" in French. In effect, the state leaves private individuals alone in their economic activity and lets them do whatever they want. *Capitalism* involves private ownership of businesses: in other words, *private enterprise*. Classical economic liberals, as described in Chapter 10, advocate laissez-faire capitalism, as do their current intellectual heirs, libertarians.

In a completely pure laissez-faire economy, private enterprise is really *free* enterprise: The government plays little or no role in restricting private economic activity. People are free to make as much money as they can by whatever means, subject perhaps to a few laws regulating contracts and penalizing criminal behavior. In such a system there are no taxes to be paid; no health or safety regulations to be concerned about; and no laws requiring employers to pay their employees minimum wages, limit their working hours, or provide them with paid vacations. There are no laws regulating child or female labor. In its most extreme variant, laissez-faire capitalism can be quite beneficial to entrepreneurs, allowing them to concentrate on the rigors of economic competition and the laws of the marketplace. But it can be extremely detrimental to workers and other employees,

leaving them unprotected against the demands of their employers. Laissez-faire capitalism prevailed in the United States, Britain, and a few other countries during Karl Marx's lifetime.

Laissez-faire capitalism in its purest form is the most unregulated variant of a market economy. A **market economy** is an economic system in which prices are determined mainly by supply and demand. The government, in other words, does not control the price system. The prices of goods and services are established by "what the market will bear": by the independent decisions of sellers and buyers, each seeking to get the most for their money in a market characterized by open competition between businesses. One of the first exponents of this type of economic system was Scottish economist Adam Smith, the first major theoretician of laissez-faire capitalism.

PROFILES   Adam Smith (1723–1790)

In his groundbreaking book, *An Inquiry into the Nature and Causes of The Wealth of Nations*, Adam Smith argued forcefully for the removal of virtually all governmental restrictions on private enterprise, a position with which many in today's so-called Tea Party feel sympathy.

Smith's groundbreaking work, *An Inquiry into the Nature and Causes of The Wealth of Nations* (or *The Wealth of Nations*, for short), was a passionate plea for the removal of virtually all governmental restrictions on private enterprise.

The idea for which Smith is perhaps most renowned is that the pursuit of every individual's economic self-interest ultimately increases the wealth of society as a whole. Personal gain enhances the common good. Smith believed that individuals are motivated basically by the quest for social status and material wealth in their economic undertakings. Without intentionally striving to do so, however, acquisitive private entrepreneurs end up promoting the general welfare. "It is not from the benevolence of the butcher, the brewer, or the baker that we expect our dinner," he wrote, "but from their regard to their own interest." In a famous image, Smith said that the self-interested economic decisions of individuals would lead to the enlargement of society's welfare as if guided to that end by an "invisible hand." The enterprising individual, he wrote,

neither intends to promote the public interest, nor knows how much he is promoting it. (He) intends only his own gain; and he is in this, as in many other cases, led by an invisible hand to promote an end which was no part of his intention. . . . By pursuing his interest, he frequently promotes that of the society more effectually than when he really intends to promote it.

Smith therefore recommended that private self-interest be given free rein and that all governmental impediments to "perfect liberty" in economic life be removed.

The freely operating market economy, in Smith's view, would not lead to chaos. On the contrary, it would be a self-sustaining mechanism that would regulate production, prices, wages, and even population through a spontaneous combination of incentives and restraints. While he was too much of a realist to expect an earthly paradise, Smith believed that the market economy, if left unhindered, would function with clockwork regularity to maximize the welfare of all.

At the time Smith was writing, Britain's economy was a complicated mixture of private enterprise and government regulations and monopolies, many of them in place since medieval times. Like other European monarchies of the period, Britain was heavily influenced by the century-old doctrine of mercantilism. *Mercantilism* was the notion that the state should expand its direct role in the economy and control foreign trade for the purpose of maximizing national wealth and power. Smith rejected mercantilism. In his view, the government's involvement in the economy had only retarded England's economic growth. Smith denounced royal authorities as "the greatest spendthrifts" in society and praised the hard work and frugality of private individuals for having "maintained the progress of England toward opulence and improvement."

(Continued on next page)

(Continued from previous page)

The *Wealth of Nations* still stands as the veritable bible of classical economic liberalism. Nevertheless, Smith has often been misinterpreted as a proponent of unrestrained personal greed and a kind of free-market anarchy, devoid of any governmental role at all. In fact, Smith strongly maintained that the market economy presupposed a moral order characterized by human benevolence and self-restraint and by a legal system that would effectively punish wrongdoing. In an earlier work, *The Theory of Moral Sentiments* (1759), Smith said the state must rigidly enforce a strong code of justice. He also stated that the "invisible hand" would eventually produce economic equality. In Smith's view, the main beneficiaries of laissez-faire capitalism ultimately would not be a small entrepreneurial elite but the population as a whole.

Moreover, Smith argued in *The Wealth of Nations* that the state should provide public works that were too unprofitable for private capitalists to undertake (such as roads, bridges, and canals) as well as public education. Smith also expected the state to provide cultural activities to prevent the masses from being spiritually and intellectually "deformed."[7]

Within decades of Smith's dreamy vision of the wealth of nations, a new generation of British economists described the free-market economy in considerably harsher terms. David Ricardo (1772–1823) argued that private entrepreneurs had little choice but to squeeze their workers to produce everything they possibly could at the lowest possible wages. In no other way, he maintained, could productive capitalists amass the funds they needed for further investment and business expansion. Ricardo's *iron law of wages* stipulated that the development of the economy, and hence the creation of future employment opportunities, required this pitiless "capital accumulation" process at the expense of the impoverished labor force.[8]

Thomas Malthus (1766–1834) maintained that, whereas population grew in a geometric progression (2, 4, 8, 16, 32, . . .), food supplies grew in an arithmetic progression (2, 4, 6, 8, 10, . . .). Consequently, prudence dictated that the masses should not be encouraged by high wages to have lots of children. Excessive overpopulation, according to his calculations, would ultimately outstrip food supplies and provoke mass starvation. It was therefore better to keep working-class wages relatively low. Malthus's calculations turned out to be overly pessimistic, but his dire predictions prompted one observer to label economics "the dismal science."[9]

Social Darwinism represented another school of thought that drew stark conclusions from the social divisions created by the progress of capitalist economics. Stimulated by British social thinker Herbert Spencer (1820–1903) and American economist William Graham Sumner (1840–1910), the social Darwinists argued that, just as animal species had evolved by a process of natural selection, humanity also develops in accordance with the grim law of the "survival of the fittest." (It was Spencer, not Charles Darwin, who coined this phrase.) Society as a whole would advance only if it encouraged and rewarded individual economic achievement. Spencer firmly opposed all attempts by the state to assist the poor or even educate them. "The whole effort of nature," he wrote, "is to get rid of such [people], to clear the world of them, and make room for better."[10]

Social Darwinist logic made great strides not only among Britain's entrepreneurial elites but in the United States as well. The American economy reflected the principles of laissez-faire capitalism right from its origins. By the late nineteenth century, vast fortunes were accumulated as railroad magnates, steel and oil tycoons, and other infamous "robber barons" plied their trade without the burdens of labor laws or meddlesome governmental regulations. Federal income taxes barely existed until the Sixteenth Amendment to the Constitution was ratified in 1913. Only with Franklin D. Roosevelt's New Deal did laissez-faire economic theory, which had failed to halt the Great Depression, lose its grip on economists and policy makers in the United States. In Europe, meanwhile, the most vocal opponents of laissez-faire economics were socialists who favored abolishing capitalism. In Western Europe, the socialist movement became more moderate over time, as social-democratic parties came around to favoring the mixed-economy welfare state. In Russia, however, socialism took on the far more radical form of the centrally planned economy.

CENTRALLY PLANNED ECONOMIES

As we described in Chapter 10, the classical socialist doctrines of Marx have had two legacies, social democracy and communism (see Figure 10.1). Soviet communists and their followers built *centrally planned economies.*

The Russian communists seized control of the central government in the autumn of 1917. Over the next several years they consolidated their rule in a bloody civil war against their main opponents. After a brief period in which private enterprise was permitted, the Soviet government under Joseph Stalin began taking charge of the economy in the late 1920s. With rare exceptions (such as tiny family-owned plots of land), all factories, farms, stores, and services came under the all-encompassing control of government agencies. A mammoth planning bureaucracy was erected to organize the production of all manufactured goods. Agriculture was "collectivized" and subjected to bureaucratic supervision. The prices of all products and services were dictated by the planning authorities, whose decrees supplanted the market economy's laws of supply and demand. Legally binding plans were issued by the government every year requiring factories and farms to meet official production quotas, usually specified in terms of quantities of goods (pairs of shoes, tons of hay, etc.). A five-year plan set production targets over a longer term.

Beginning with Stalin and continuing under his successors right up to Mikhail Gorbachev (1931–) in the second half of the 1980s, the Soviet Union had a **centrally planned economy (CPE)**. The distinguishing feature of this type of system is the fusion of the state and the economy. The state and the economy are merged into an integrated whole. In effect, the state "owns" the economy. State authorities, not private individuals or companies, determine what should be produced and in what quantities, how these goods should be distributed, and at what price. Because the state, in effect, commands the entire economic process, the CPE is also called a **command economy**.

In Soviet theory, a fully planned economy was expected to be far more rational in the production and allocation of goods than was a capitalist economy. The market, according to the communists, was chaotic, with countless private individuals and firms making countless decisions in their own personal interest. It wasted resources on unnecessary production and led to inflation, unemployment, inequality, bankruptcies, and depressions. A planned economy, they felt, would avoid these pitfalls. In their view, growth would be higher and faster than under capitalism, and distribution would be fairer.

A planned economy would also facilitate the political elite's control over the population. One of the essential purposes of the state planning system was to stamp out all opportunities for individuals and groups to be independent of Communist Party rule. The extinction of economic freedom was deliberately intended to reinforce the extinction of political freedom.

Industrial production in the Soviet Union grew dramatically in the 1930s under the new planning system, elevating the Soviet Union from a backward agricultural country to an industrial giant in less than a decade. Agricultural production suffered, however, as the collectivization process, in which landholders were forced to hand over their fields, crops, and farm animals to the state, created havoc in the countryside. Additional setbacks occurred during World War II, as the German invasion in 1941 and three years of continuous fighting resulted in the destruction of 1,700 Soviet cities and towns and the devastation of the agricultural economy.

The Soviet economy gradually revived after the war, prompting communist officials in the early 1960s to make ambitious claims about overtaking the U.S. economy in the next 10 years.[11] Far from accomplishing that grandiose goal, the Soviet economy fell increasingly behind its mixed-economy competitors. Upon assuming the leadership of the Communist Party of the Soviet Union in 1985, Mikhail Gorbachev denounced his predecessors' years in power as an "era of stagnation." Between 1978 and 1985 the Soviet economy had experienced zero growth. As the United States, Japan, and Western Europe charted new directions in high-technology development, the cumbersome Soviet central planning bureaucracy proved no match for the rapid-production techniques of private companies competing in global markets. Over the next several years, Gorbachev tried to come up with a new formula for rescuing the central planning system, including the adoption of a modicum of private enterprise, but he never succeeded in devising a more effective economic mechanism. In late 1991,

The command economy in the Soviet Union resulted in the planning and creation of entire cities such as the industrial steel town Magnitogorsk.

Gorbachev gave up power and the Soviet Union itself ceased to exist. Starting in January 1992, Russia—now an independent country—began moving toward a mixed economy with the introduction of substantial private enterprise and market mechanisms for determining prices. Though the state continues to play a major role in the Russian economy, the centrally planned economy is a thing of the past.

Similar developments have occurred in Central and Eastern Europe since the collapse of communist rule and the installation of democracy. Most of these countries have been quite creative in developing various combinations of public and private economic activity.[12]

For its part, China began dismantling its central planning system long before Russia or East-Central Europe. The Chinese Communist Party leadership itself inaugurated privatization measures and market reforms starting in the late 1970s. Over the course of the following decade, most of China's industrial enterprises and farms came into private hands. Oddly enough, these massive economic transformations took place despite the communists retaining their grip on power, harshly repressing all demands for democracy.

One hypothesis that stands out as particularly relevant in these circumstances states that the process of economic privatization promotes democratization. Our main expectation is that a private-enterprise economy creates social groups (such as businesspeople and an upwardly mobile work force) who wish to preserve and expand their freedom in the marketplace by keeping government intervention limited and by making sure they have a say, through the electoral process and other democratic procedures, in the decisions governments make. Thus if the economic liberalization process succeeds, democracy will succeed in Russia and East-Central Europe, and it may even successfully challenge communist rule in China.

A contrary thesis suggests that the privatization process in formerly communist countries and China ultimately undermines support for democracy. If the economic transformations now under way produce unacceptable levels of inflation, unemployment, inequality, or corruption, large segments of the population and political elites may turn against economic change and, simultaneously, against political change as well. Some may long nostalgically for the "good old days" under central planning when, despite that system's disadvantages, life was more stable and predictable and prices for most basic goods, when available, were cheaper. Driven to despair by economic adversity, many people may demand a strong authoritarian government to impose order on a society they perceive as careening into chaos.

Between these extreme scenarios of triumphant success and catastrophic failure lies a third hypothetical alternative: The dual processes of marketization and democratization may inch along at a rocky pace, with alternating successes and failures, advances and retreats. Though the economic and political transformation processes present great difficulties, the populations and political elites of these countries in this scenario together manage to muddle through, achieving at least some degree of both market economics and democracy.

Whatever happens, it can be confidently anticipated that the development of stable economic mechanisms and democratic institutions and practices will be a long process, requiring perhaps decades of concerted social and political action. The hypotheses just presented, as well as others applicable to these developments, will have to be continually put to the test.

MIXED ECONOMIES

The most widely adopted economic system in the world today is neither laissez-faire capitalism nor full-scale, centrally planned socialism but something in between: the mixed economy. A **mixed economy** combines both private enterprise and state involvement in the country's economic affairs. Both social liberalism and social democracy, as described in Chapter 10, support mixed economies. However, a mixed economy can take many forms. No single model is faithfully copied by all mixed-economy countries.

For one thing, countries may differ in the relative *degree* of capitalism and state intervention. Some grant wider latitude than others to the private sector while holding governmental intervention within bounds (or at least trying to do so). Such factors as the percentage of GDP taken up by government expenditures illustrate the point (see Figure 11.3). These statistics, the latest available from the Organization for Economic Cooperation and Development (OECD), an association of the advanced industrial democracies, come from before the 2008–09 financial crisis that led the United States and European countries to increase their government spending to stimulate their economies. Note that the United States spends a considerably lower percentage of its GDP on government services compared to Sweden, France, or Denmark. South Korea, a relatively new member of the advanced industrial democracies, spends

considerably less of its GDP on government services (see the discussion of South Korea in the next chapter). Note too that several of the mixed economies reduced the size of their government sectors in the decade reported in Figure 11.3.

Mixed economies may also differ in the *forms* of state intervention they employ. In some cases the government's economic involvement is largely indirect. That is, the state allows private enterprise and market mechanisms to play the main role in the national economy but seeks to influence or adjust private behavior so as to advance certain national economic goals. The central bank, for example, may influence commercial bank interest rates to rein in inflation or stimulate growth, or the government may raise or lower taxes to advance political or economic goals. In these and other instances of indirect intervention, the state does not directly own enterprises outright but confines its role to influencing or regulating the private sector.

One of the most widely utilized forms of indirect state intervention in the economy consists of a set of policy mechanisms known collectively as Keynesianism. **Keynesianism** refers to the state's use of fiscal and monetary measures and public spending to promote growth in an economy dominated by private enterprise. Its main architect was perhaps the most influential economist of the twentieth century, John Maynard Keynes.

In addition to employing indirect forms of economic intervention, governments may engage in more direct forms of activity in mixed economies. In some countries the state may directly own certain enterprises, whether as full owner or as a

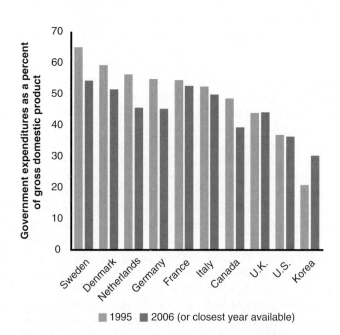

FIGURE 11.3 **Government Expenditures as a Percent of Gross Domestic Product**

Source: Organization for Economic Cooperation and Development, http://www.oecd-ilibrary.org.

PROFILES   John Maynard Keynes (1883–1946)

By providing a feasible alternative to both laissez-faire capitalism and all-out socialism, John Maynard Keynes produced a revolution in economic thinking whose tenets are widely accepted.

John Maynard Keynes (pronounced "canes") studied economics at Cambridge University at a time when economic theory had not advanced very far beyond the doctrines of Adam Smith and David Ricardo. The stimulus to Keynes's revision of classical economic theory was the Great Depression. The stock market crash of October 1929 shattered the U.S. economy and exacerbated the problems of other capitalist economies, resulting in bankruptcies, plummeting economic growth, and skyrocketing unemployment around the world. As the years ground on with little improvement, governments and the private sector appeared to be at a loss about how to resolve the crisis. The conventional wisdom of laissez-faire economics predicted that market forces would generate a recovery in the long run. As Keynes drily observed, however, "In the long run we're all dead."

He argued that the best way to stimulate economic growth during a depression was to increase total spending—that is, *aggregate demand* for goods and services—throughout the economy. When more money was spent for these things, businesspeople would amass enough profits to expand their operations and hire new workers. Unfortunately, Keynes observed, individual consumers have little money to spend in a depression. With millions unemployed, much of the population is more likely to be reduced to penury. Starved for customers, businesses stagnate or go bankrupt. Keynes thus reached a startling conclusion: A free-market economy does not possess the mechanisms needed to recover from a depression on its own.

If consumers, banks, and businesses do not have sufficient money to spend in the economy to spark a recovery, who does? Governments, Keynes replied. By spending additional funds from the national budget, governments can inject spendable money into the economy and thereby "prime the pump" of the private sector. The state can take this action by directly purchasing goods and services from private businesses (such as highway construction) or by hiring people for public works projects. By putting cash in the hands of consumers and businesses, governments would enable individuals to buy more things, thereby increasing the demand for goods, and enable businesses to increase production and hire more employees. Economic recovery would then be under way.

Keynes laid out these ideas in *The General Theory of Employment, Interest, and Money*, published in 1936. By that time, the New Deal had already begun implementing some of them, such as the mass hiring of unemployed workers through the Public Works Administration and the Civilian Conservation Corps. But in Keynes's opinion, the Roosevelt administration was not spending enough to pump the country out of the depression. Only when the U.S. government engaged in much more massive public spending during World War II did the depression in the United States end.

Keynes asserted that in certain compelling circumstances such as a depression, governments may have to engage in deficit spending to improve the overall economy. *Deficit spending* is spending by governments even though there is a budgetary deficit that cannot be balanced through ordinary revenue sources (such as taxes). To finance this excess spending, governments must borrow money from individuals or other lenders and pay them interest, thus increasing the national debt. Keynes believed that the extra money governments spent would eventually come back to the national treasury in enhanced tax revenue, collected from increasingly profitable businesses and a rising number of well-paid employees as the recovery widens and the economy grows.

After World War II, Keynes's principles of government intervention won growing acceptance. By the 1960s the United States, Western Europe, and other countries were routinely using Keynesian mechanisms to fine-tune their economies and regulate the business cycle. More recently, however, the experiences of many advanced capitalist economies have prompted debate about the pertinence of Keynes's theories. Many economists argue that national debts have reached such astronomical heights that additional deficit spending may only hamper future economic growth. A number of economists and public officials also believe that capitalist economies are better off with less government intervention rather than more. They cite the warnings of another major theorist, Friedrich von Hayek (1899–1992), that excessive government involvement in the economy is "the road to serfdom."[13]

Whatever one thinks about Keynes's theories, one thing is certain: The central question today is not *whether* governments should intervene in the economy, but *how much*. By providing a feasible alternative to both laissez-faire capitalism and all-out socialism, Keynes produced a revolution in economic thinking whose tenets are widely accepted.[14] Since the advent of the financial crisis in 2008–09 governments in advanced democracies have engaged in enormous stimulus efforts, running huge budget deficits. The influence of Keynes remains powerful.

shareholder in partnership with other investors. These state-owned firms in mixed economies are usually called *public enterprises* or *parastatal enterprises*. Such internationally known firms as Air France and Rolls-Royce have been owned by the state, along with giant companies in Italy, Spain, Sweden, Brazil, Mexico, and other countries. The U.S. government became the chief owner of General Motors after the company's bankruptcy during the 2008 financial crisis and still owned more than a quarter of the firm in 2012.

The chief difference between public enterprises and private firms is that the managers and workforce of public enterprises are employed directly by the state and the earnings of state-owned companies go into the national treasury. Such enterprises may also receive loans or other forms of financing directly from the state budget. Their proponents regard them as an effective way to combat unemployment and earn revenue for the national treasury to help finance general budgetary outlays. Opponents of public enterprises, by contrast, argue that state-owned companies might be less efficient and competitive than private firms. If they do not turn a profit, they may have to be bailed out with state subsidies, thereby draining the national treasury. In some cases, public enterprises may become nests of corruption.

These and other arguments against public enterprises have convinced many of their opponents to push for their privatization. **Privatization** means the transfer of state-owned enterprises to private ownership. (It is the opposite of **nationalization**, which is the transfer of privately owned firms to state ownership.) The privatization issue has unleashed a storm of political controversy in Argentina, Britain, France, Russia, Brazil, India, and other countries in recent years.[15]

Another variant of direct state intervention in mixed economies is *bureaucratic coordination* of the economy. In bureaucratically coordinated economies, the state plays a direct and constant role in coordinating the activities of private firms (and, perhaps, the labor market as well) for broad national purposes. There are several different variants of bureaucratic coordination in mixed economies, as the following examples illustrate:

- Contemporary Japan and South Korea have aggressively supported competitive private firms that cooperate closely with state agencies to promote exports. Such agencies as the Ministry of Finance and the Ministry of International Trade and Industry wield very important bureaucratic power in the Japanese economy, as do their counterparts in South Korea.
- Germany, Austria, and other countries have corporatist systems that involve continuing discussions and coordination among business organizations, labor unions, and government.
- France has used a system of "indicative planning" through which the state and private enterprises coordinate general guidelines and expectations of economic development. Indicative planning led to the promotion of "national champions," private enterprises meant to be globally competitive in their industries.

- Various African countries have state-managed purchasing boards and other bureaucratic institutions that help coordinate agricultural development or other economic activities.

Today's mixed economies can be measured in a variety of ways. In addition to providing statistics on gross domestic product, gross national income, and other widely used measures, economists have also devised methods for calculating the relative *competitiveness* of an economy (that is, its ability to function in the global economy), the degree of freedom that private enterprises have in individual countries, and other yardsticks.[16] In most instances, government policies and political processes play a critical role in affecting the economic bottom lines reflected in these statistics.

Whether guided by indirect or direct methods of state intervention, mixed economies cannot escape politics. This is especially the case nowadays because most countries are *welfare states*. Most welfare states today are mixed economies. While some are authoritarian regimes, the most highly developed ones are in the economically advanced democracies.

WELFARE STATES

Broadly defined, the **welfare state** is a form of political economy in which the state assumes responsibility for the general welfare of its population, especially its most vulnerable elements, through spending on such items as education, housing, health care, pensions, unemployment compensation, food subsidies, family allowances, and other programs. Both social liberalism and social democracy have facilitated the growth of welfare states.

The term *welfare state* came into vogue in Britain in the 1930s and 1940s. Though it is largely a twentieth-century phenomenon, its roots reach into the previous century. As laissez-faire capitalism advanced and the working-class population expanded, a number of European political theorists and politicians began groping for ways to maintain robust economic growth while at the same time confronting the appalling poverty of the working class and the unemployed.

In Britain the path to the modern welfare state was long and circuitous. One of its early intellectual forebears was the philosopher Jeremy Bentham (1748–1832). Bentham is perhaps most famous for his statement that the principal aim of government should be to promote "the greatest happiness of the greatest number." To this end, Bentham maintained that the chief obligation of government was to provide certain services to the population, including basic physical security against crime and foreign enemies, economic subsistence, and the legal protection of property rights, personal reputation, and private contracts. Bentham strongly believed that democracy provided the most effective means for achieving these goals.[17]

Another progenitor of the welfare state was John Stuart Mill (1806–73). Mill's essays *On Liberty* (1859) and *Considerations on Representative Government* (1861) established his reputation as a democratic theorist of the first rank. His masterwork, *The Principles of Political Economy*, first appeared in 1848, the same year Marx and Engels published their *Communist Manifesto*. Mill's work pointed in a fundamentally different direction from revolutionary socialism, however. Laissez-faire, he wrote, "should be the general practice: every departure from it, unless required by some great good, is a certain evil." He also regarded restrictions on economic competition, as advocated by socialists, as "evil."

But Mill was equally outspoken in his objections to a completely unrestrained free market. He advocated such things as state-funded education, public works, restrictions on child labor, and limited governmental assistance to those unable to work. He also supported the right of workers to organize trade unions and go on strike. To remedy the social inequalities produced by capitalism, Mill favored stiff inheritance taxes aimed at preventing the concentration of wealth in a handful of families. He also favored producers' cooperatives that would compete in the marketplace under the ownership and management of the workers themselves. These ideas flew directly in the face of the British elite's laissez-faire inclinations. Over time, however, Mill's ideas sensitized Britain to the possibility of finding a middle ground between the extremes of unregulated capitalism and revolutionary socialism.[18]

Ironically, it was the highly conservative ruling elite of nineteenth-century Germany that introduced some of Europe's first major social welfare programs. In the 1880s the kaiser's authoritarian government introduced the industrialized world's first government-financed health and accident insurance for workers and its first state-managed pension program. The kaiser and his ministers were no socialists. Their chief incentives for providing social welfare benefits to Germany's working masses were to stave off a potential socialist revolution and to reduce popular support for the Social Democrats.

The Emergence of the Modern Welfare State: Germany, Sweden, and the United States

In a few countries the twentieth-century welfare state began taking shape in the decades between World War I and World War II. After the kaiser's departure following Germany's defeat in 1918, the German Weimar Republic (1919–33) took the unprecedented step of incorporating generous welfare benefits into the constitution as legally guaranteed social rights. But the entire Weimar regime collapsed as the German economy was battered by astronomical inflation in the early 1920s and by a wave of bankruptcies and rising unemployment with the onset of the Great Depression in the early 1930s. Moreover, business, labor, and agricultural leaders were never able to agree on a mutually acceptable balance of economic policies. The failure of the Weimar Republic's political economy provided a perfect opportunity for the Nazi Party under Adolf Hitler to take advantage of widespread frustrations and thereby gain power, as you will learn in Chapter 15. While establishing one of the most tyrannical dictatorships ever known, the Nazis also established their own version of the welfare state, one that placed the economy firmly in the hands of a brutal, war-driven elite.

A far more salutary development occurred in Sweden. As the Great Depression took a heavy toll on Sweden's export-oriented economy, leaders of parties and interest groups representing agriculture, labor, and big business made a concerted effort to iron out their conflicts in a grand "historic compromise." In the process, they saved Swedish democracy and established "a model for what all of Europe would do after 1945."[19] Today Sweden and other Scandinavian countries are "cradle-to-grave" social welfare systems, with the state providing a broad spectrum of benefits to workers, farmers, and the sizable middle class.

Across the ocean, Franklin D. Roosevelt's New Deal was forging a new model for the political economy of the United States, one whose basic parameters would also set a pattern for the postwar period. Before Roosevelt, the U.S. government had provided only minimal social welfare benefits, mainly to war veterans.[20] The prevailing laissez-faire orthodoxy dictated against governmental interference in the economy and especially against deficit spending. Roosevelt himself initially accepted this view, but later vowed to try anything that might work to bring the U.S. economy out of the depression. Guided by no preconceived blueprint, FDR and his brain trust launched a wide assortment of measures aimed at reducing unemployment and reinvigorating the economy. Public works programs, the Tennessee Valley Authority, the Social Security system, and the Wagner Act, which provided legal support for trade unions, were all products of New Deal interventionism. So, too, was the National Recovery Administration (NRA), a corporatist body intended to pull together representatives from business, labor, agriculture, and government in an effort to regulate wages, prices, and production.[21]

Although the NRA was declared unconstitutional by the Supreme Court, and although FDR's critics denounced the New Deal as creeping socialism, quite a few of Roosevelt's programs remained in place long after the end of his administration. Most important, the New Deal established the legitimacy of significant governmental intervention in the U.S. economy.

The Postwar Welfare State

The heyday of the welfare state in the economically advanced democracies occurred in the first three decades after World War II. In 1945, Britain's Labour Party won its first majority in the House of Commons. Under Prime Minister Clement Attlee, the Labour government enacted a series of major welfare measures and nationalized several private corporations. (The owners were compensated.) The centerpiece of Labour's legislation was the National Health Service, which guaranteed free medical and dental care to all British citizens while preserving private care for those willing to pay for it. Although the Conservative Party, which had traditionally campaigned against such measures, returned to power in 1951, it did not abolish the National Health Service, which remains a broadly popular institution to this day.

Most other industrially advanced countries also expanded their welfare programs after World War II. In most cases, the social and political underpinnings of the welfare state were the same. From its inception, the democratic welfare state has

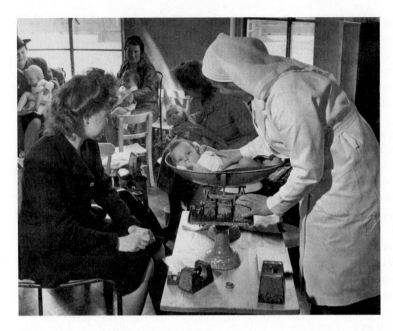

Britain's National Health Service guarantees free medical and dental care to all British citizens while preserving private care for those willing to pay for it. Inaugurated after World War II by the Labour Party, the Conservative Party, which had traditionally campaigned against such measures, did not abolish the National Health Service when it returned to power in 1951.

been based on compromises made by representatives of labor, agriculture, and the business sector as mediated and enforced by a democratically accountable state. The specific agreements reached in Western Europe soon after World War II are sometimes known as the *postwar settlements*.

Particularly rapid expansion of the welfare state occurred between 1960 and 1975. This period witnessed fairly continuous economic growth in the advanced democracies. It was during these decades that the economies of the United States, Canada, Japan, and most of Western Europe completed their transformation from industrial economies to *postindustrial economies*, characterized by the fact that more than half the workforce was now engaged in the service sector of the economy. As the economically advanced democracies blazed the trails of postindustrialism from the 1960s onward, their governments became increasingly committed to promoting not only education but also a host of other programs designed to enhance the welfare of the population and the growth of the economy. Most of these governments utilized Keynesian tax and spending policies designed to keep growth rates climbing while maintaining high levels of employment. As national wealth grew, the amount of money available for social welfare programs rose apace. Government expenditures on an array of social programs in most of these countries rose from 10 to 20 percent of GNP in the 1950s to between one-fourth and one-third of GNP in the mid-1970s.[22] The so-called *Keynesian welfare state* became the dominant mode of political economy throughout the economically advanced world of democratic states.

Not only have government welfare programs assisted the poor and the working class, but they have also benefited the middle class and even the upper class. In various welfare states, people from all income levels have taken full advantage of expanding educational opportunities, health insurance, retirement pensions, and other state-sponsored programs. In countries such as the United States, special tax breaks, such as write-offs for interest paid on home mortgages or other loans, have constituted a form of social welfare benefit for middle-and upper-class property owners.

Moreover, both left-leaning parties and mainstream conservative parties have tended to agree on the basic principle of the welfare state, though they might disagree on the extent or form of government funding for social welfare measures. Most of these parties in Western Europe, North America, and Japan have recognized that government-funded welfare measures are widely popular and that their electoral fortunes often depend on their ability to provide social benefits to key segments of the population. The main differences among these various political parties and governments have generally been a matter of degree, not principle. The gamut has extended from the extensive welfare systems of Sweden and other Scandinavian countries (commonly known as the *Swedish model*) to the less encompassing, though still significant, welfarism of the United States.[23] Table 11.2 shows that the financial commitment of the Scandinavian governments and those of France, Germany, and Italy to social expenditures is rather greater than for the United States, Canada, Japan, and the United Kingdom.

Welfare programs cost money. Some populations have been willing to shoulder higher tax burdens than others. Table 11.3 shows the top tax rates in 11 democratic welfare states. Note that the United States is a comparatively low-tax country, particularly as measured by the tax revenue as a percentage of GDP. The governments of Sweden and Denmark take in nearly double the share of national income that federal, state, and local government in the United States do.

Farewell to the Welfare State?

Starting in the mid-1970s, doubts about the sustainability of the welfare state began spreading in Western Europe and North America. In October 1973, the world's leading oil exporting

Table 11.2 Public Social Spending* as Percentage of GDP in Selected High-Income Democracies

Country	1980	1990	2000	2007
Canada	13.7%	18.1%	16.5%	16.9%
Denmark	24.8	25.1	25.7	26.1
France	20.8	24.9	27.7	28.4
Germany	22.1	21.7	26.6	25.2
Italy	18.0	20.0	23.3	24.9
Japan	10.4	11.3	16.5	18.7
Netherlands	24.8	25.6	19.8	20.1
Sweden	27.2	30.2	28.4	27.3
United Kingdom	16.5	16.8	18.6	20.5
United States	13.2	13.5	14.5	16.2

*"Public social spending" refers to central government expenditures on pensions, health care, unemployment compensation, education, family allowances, income maintenance, and the like.

Source: Organization for Economic Cooperation and Development, Social Expenditures Database, www.oecd.org/els/social/expenditure.

countries pushed for the immediate quadrupling of petroleum prices. The sudden price hike dealt a staggering blow to the energy-hungry industrialized democracies, resulting in a relatively new phenomenon dubbed *stagflation*, an unusual combination of economic stagnation and high inflation. (Classical economic theory predicted that, when the economy goes into a recession, prices should fall, not rise.)

Keynesian prescriptions for fine-tuning the national economy, which had registered some visible successes in the previous decade, no longer appeared to work. The budget deficits that many advanced industrial democracies had been running up as government welfare programs proliferated now threatened to get out of hand. Large segments of the population demanded ever-higher government-funded pensions, health benefits, and other forms of assistance to help them keep up with the rising cost of living. But government treasuries were no longer prepared to meet these demands as the decline in economic activity brought in diminishing tax revenues and necessitated rising amounts of compensation for the growing ranks of the unemployed.

Throughout the 1980s and into the 1990s, the idea gained currency in the economically advanced democracies that governments could no longer afford the high deficits and weighty tax burdens typically produced by the modern welfare state. For many people, the welfare state—and government intervention in the economy more generally—seemed to have reached its limits. In the 1980s, conservatives such as President Ronald Reagan and British Prime Minister Margaret Thatcher spoke out forcefully in favor of greater reliance on the private sector and less reliance on government. In 1991, the leaders of the 12 West European countries that then constituted the European Community (the forerunner of today's European Union) agreed to restrict their annual budget deficits to no more than 3 percent of GDP as a precondition for adopting the euro. That restriction, along with other criteria, continues to require tough budget control measures on the part of most EU countries.

Despite belt-tightening policies in a number of countries over the past two decades, the welfare state remains both viable and popular. As Table 11.4 shows, government spending on health care accounts for well over half of total health care spending in the wealthiest democracies of North America, Europe, and East Asia (with the exception of South Korea and the United States). And tax revenues still comprise a large share of gross domestic product in most of the welfare states on our list (see Table 11.3). Indeed, social welfare spending remains broadly popular in most economically advanced democracies, a fact even conservatives acknowledge. (President Reagan *raised* Social Security payments in the 1980s, and President George W. Bush pushed through the Medicare prescription drugs benefit in 2003.)[24] At times these welfarist attitudes coexist with support for cutting budget deficits and reducing taxes. Globalization poses additional problems for today's welfare states. While further constricting the resources available to governments for

Table 11.3 Highest Marginal Tax Rates in Selected Democracies and Tax Revenue as a Share of GDP, 2009

Country	Highest Personal Income Tax Rate	Income Threshold	Tax Revenue as % of GDP
Canada	46.4%	$103,785	32.0%
Denmark	54.8	47,572	48.1
France	37.6	105,114	42.4
Germany	47.5	316,732	37.3
Italy	40.2	113,446	43.4
Japan	47.3	195,812	26.9
Korea	35.4	137,865	25.5
Netherlands	50.2	63,661	38.2
Sweden	56.5	60,268	46.7
United Kingdom	40.0	68,674	34.3
United States	41.7	382,300	24.1

Notes: The highest personal income tax rate is the combined central government and subcentral government marginal personal income tax rate at the earnings threshold where the top statutory personal income tax rate first applies; the income threshold is the gross wage earnings threshold at which the top statutory rate first applies in U.S. dollars (using the purchasing power parity or PPP method of measuring GDP); tax revenue as a percentage of GDP is total tax revenue of combined central government and subcentral government.

Source: Organization for Economic Cooperation and Development, www.oecd.org.

Table 11.4 Government Spending on Health Care as Percentage of Total Health Care Spending in Selected High-Income Democracies, 2010 or most recent year

Country	Percentage	Country	Percentage
Netherlands	85.7%	France	77.0%
Denmark	85.1	Germany	76.8
United Kingdom	83.2	Spain	73.6
Sweden	81.0	Canada	71.1
Japan	80.5	South Korea	58.2
Italy	79.6	United States	48.2

Source: Organization for Economic Cooperation and Development Health Data 2012 (June 2012), www.oecd.org.

welfare spending, globalization also causes dislocations such as unemployment and poverty that raise new demands for government compensation and protection. But as citizens demand more public spending on education, job training, health care, unemployment compensation, pensions, and other items on their social welfare wish list, the governments they elect will need to figure out how to do more with less.[25]

The Politics of Welfare States

Today the most contentious issue on the political agenda of wealthy democracies is the government budget deficit. Figure 11.4 shows the budget deficits of Germany, Japan, the United States, and the combined G7 (which includes those three plus Canada, France, Italy, and the United Kingdom) in the 1990s and the first decade of the twenty-first century. As they experienced economic growth in the 1990s, the United States and Germany gradually moved from budget deficits to surpluses as the century turned. In the United States the reduction of deficits resulted from an explicit political deal between President Clinton and Republicans in Congress, as mentioned earlier in the chapter. Germany ran an unusually large deficit as it sought to integrate the former East Germany in the mid-1990s, but then grew itself out of that deficit. Meanwhile Japan, mired in a deep recession caused by the collapse of its real estate bubble in the early 1990s, moved in the opposite direction. After 9/11, the recession it caused, and the spending associated with the wars in Afghanistan and Iraq, which were not paid for by tax increases, the United States receded into large deficits again. Germany also suffered from the post-9/11 recession and its budget deficit increased to meet the needs of people dislocated in that economic downturn. Japan remained in its long recession until the middle of the last decade when it finally was able to reduce its deficit. As you can see, after the U.S. housing bubble burst in 2008 and the great recession it caused spread worldwide, all of the G7 countries began to run very large deficits as they sought to address the needs of the unemployed and to stimulate their economies.

Most democratic welfare states have difficulty coming up with the money needed to meet continuing public demands

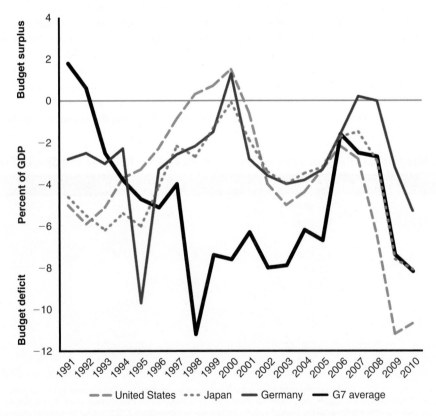

FIGURE 11.4 **Government Budget Deficits as a Percentage of GDP**

Source: Organization for Economic Cooperation and Develoment, www.oecd.org.

for welfare services. This has prompted some serious soul-searching about the nature of the state's proper role in economic affairs and, indeed, the very nature of contemporary democracy itself. One disturbing hypothesis suggests that today's mass democracies make such overwhelming demands on their governments for benefits of various kinds that the results can only be uncontrollable budget deficits, which is why most of the time the lines in Figure 11.4 are below zero. These deficits, in turn, stifle economic growth by breeding abnormally high interest rates or inflation, or both. Modern welfarist democracies are therefore by nature self-defeating: They prevent the very increases in national wealth that are needed to meet rising public demands for governmental assistance. At the same time, the argument continues, democracies place such inordinate pressures on elected officials to "deliver the goods" (better schools, more health care, higher pensions, increased poverty relief, etc.) that politicians cannot get elected unless they make promises that are inevitably unrealistic. Candidates competing in electoral contests seek to outdo one another in making fantastic promises, a process known as *overbidding*. Once elected, political leaders then find that they cannot deliver the goods as promised because of inescapable budgetary constraints or other adverse economic conditions over which they have little or no immediate control, such as sluggish growth rates, or a weak international economy.

Many elected officials find themselves locked into automatic spending commitments for programs already enacted into law. In the United States, the funds available for discretionary spending (that is, money that can be spent at the discretion of the president and Congress) typically amount only to about a third of the federal budget. The remaining two-thirds is already committed to mandatory payments for Social Security, Medicare, and other social welfare measures, plus interest payments on the national debt.

In addition to confronting demands for more benefits, political leaders must frequently confront demands for lower taxes, as the rise of the Tea Party in the United States dramatically illustrates. In the United States, though, most income taxes that are owed are actually paid to the government. In some countries, the state finds it cannot bring into the treasury the taxes that it is owed. In Greece, for example, the central government deficit that has driven its sovereign debt crisis turns out to be about the same size as the gap between what the government is owed according to tax laws and what it is actually paid by Greek taxpayers—about one-third of the total owed.[26] Other European countries, including Italy and Portugal, which also have sovereign debt concerns, have similar tax evasion problems.[27] Compounding the political challenge, it is not uncommon that demands for tax relief are raised by the very people who insist on more government assistance for themselves. Mass democracies seem to have no shortage of citizens who feel entitled to various welfare benefits but who are always ready to shift the burden of paying for them to someone else. As a consequence, democracy once again proves itself to be self-defeating: Voters make demands that their government cannot fulfill and for which they are not willing to pay. They take out their frustrations by turning against the incumbent leaders and shifting their support to challengers who make unrealistic promises of their own ("More gain, less pain"). To save themselves, the incumbents may feel compelled to outbid their opponents by providing instant rewards or grandiose pledges to their constituents at election time—tax cuts, higher pensions, and the like—even though the economy can ill afford such favors. Incumbents thus have an interest in promoting a favorable political business cycle, using the powers of their office to tilt economic policy in directions that will enhance their chances for reelection. Irrespective of whether the incumbents are victorious or the vote goes to their opponents, the cycle of broken promises and voter discontent just begins anew.

Elected officials might try to sway voters by tampering with the economy at election time, but some analysts doubt that they have sufficient short-term control over the economy to do so effectively.[28] Nevertheless, there is some evidence that many voters at election time are more likely to be swayed by economic conditions than by other factors impinging on their vote.

There are several variants of these generalizations about the corruptive nature of democratic welfare politics and the "entitlement mentality" accompanying it. One that surfaced in the mid-1970s hypothesized that the increase in mass political participation that had taken place in the United States and various West European countries over the preceding 15 years (through the enfranchisement of 18-year-olds and the increased activism of minority groups), along with the rise in welfare spending that occurred in the same period, had overloaded governments with demands they could not fulfill. The result was a crisis of governability. Frustrated by the inability of elected leaders and bureaucratic agencies to respond to their demands, growing numbers of citizens in these countries showed signs of having less trust in their governments. Paradoxically, the natural functionings of democracy—mass participation and open interest articulation—were undermining the authority of democratically elected governments in the eyes of the population.[29]

Another set of hypotheses concerning the self-destructive tendencies of modern democratic welfare states was advanced by Mancur Olson. Olson argued in *The Rise and Decline of Nations* that one of the main variables that accounts for stunted economic growth and the ungovernability of certain democracies is the existence of small special-interest groups that exert a degree of political influence that is disproportionately greater than their share of the population. These groups pressure governments into providing their members with special privileges and benefits at the expense of society as a whole. Ironically, these kinds of pressure groups are more likely to exist in countries that have had a long history of stable democracy, such as Britain and the United States. Successful democracies, in essence, breed the very political forces that undermine an elected government's ability to govern in behalf of all the people. The result, almost inevitably, is the ungovernability of democracies. Democracy, in short, is its own worst enemy.[30]

Other critics of the welfare state point out that it has failed to stamp out poverty, guarantee job security, or eliminate class conflict. Though they vary in degree, virtually all the democratic welfare states of the contemporary world continue to experience hard-core poverty, unemployment, and fairly wide disparities in personal incomes and family wealth. Because today's highly advanced postindustrial economies are particularly dependent on highly educated professionals and a technically skilled work force, income gaps between different socioeconomic classes increasingly reflect gaps in education levels.

Welfare states are also maligned for encouraging excessive dependency on government handouts, a phenomenon that may induce some people to live off welfare payments instead of holding a steady job. Efforts in the United States, Britain, and other countries in recent years to require impoverished welfare recipients to work in exchange for welfare benefits (or instead of them) reflect the frustration of many taxpayers who believe that income maintenance programs for the able-bodied poor are often abused. "Workfare" programs of this kind are sometimes hampered, however, by a paucity of well-paying jobs for poorly educated or unskilled workers.

Still, many political observers argue that the modern democratic welfare state, for all its faults, is the most stable and humane system of political economy humankind has ever developed. It has combined the freedoms and growth potential of private enterprise with the security of a social safety net that has all but eliminated the terrors of permanent impoverishment and misery. It has provided educational opportunities and community services that were undreamed of only a few generations ago. While admitting that the welfare state's detractors may have some valid points, many of its defenders would say that no superior alternative presently exists or is ever likely to exist. In this view, the democratic welfare state constitutes a model that many countries in the world are striving to emulate, especially former communist countries and others that are now in transition from authoritarianism to democracy.

HYPOTHESIS-TESTING EXERCISE
Does Globalization Force Governments to Reduce Spending?

With the advent of more rapid globalization in the 1990s and thereafter, many defenders of the welfare state have been concerned that the need to attract international investment will force governments to reduce taxes, thereby reducing the revenue they have available for social spending, the largest component of total government spending for most high-income democracies. This concern is one variant of the "race to the bottom" theme advanced by critics of globalization. They essentially argue that the need to provide the lowest possible wage rates and other similarly low costs of production will force mixed economies to reduce their regulatory efforts, to impose very low tax rates (or waive them for foreign investors), while spending their declining revenues on infrastructure and production subsidies to attract investors rather than on welfare services to help society's less fortunate. In short, the welfare state is threatened by globalization.[31] Is this true?

Hypothesis Countries that are more globalized will devote less of their GDP to government spending than countries that are less globalized.

Variables Our *independent variable* is globalization. The *dependent variable* is the percentage of GDP spent by the government.

Evidence The KOF Swiss Economic Institute produces a globalization index for 187 countries that we can use as our independent variable. Government spending as a share of GDP is available from the Penn World Tables, produced by the Center for International Comparisons at the University of Pennsylvania. Figure 11.5 is a scatterplot of these two variables for all countries with populations greater than 2 million (many very small countries are very reliant on international trade or tourism and often do not even have their own currencies, so they are hard to compare to larger countries). For our hypothesis to be supported by the evidence we should see a linear relationship characterized by a downward slope from left to right—less globalized countries would have higher government spending while more globalized would have less government spending. In fact, we see a chart in which the points that represent the 136 countries plotted here are spread across the graph, suggesting no effective relationship. (Statistically, there is a very weak negative relationship but the substantive meaning of it is practically nil.) We should reject our hypothesis. Globalization does not lead to less government spending.

Conclusions The worry that globalization leads to a race to the bottom in which states are less able to tax their people and businesses to gain the revenue needed to finance social spending appears to be balanced by a greater need for welfare state spending as the result of the impact of globalization. Globalization has led to more dislocation for workers as jobs move offshore and as rapid change in technology leaves older workers less able to compete for new jobs when they prove unable to adapt to those new technologies. Those dislocated workers need and demand social services such as job retraining and income supplements (unemployment insurance payments, food assistance) from the government. And democracies tend to respond to the needs of their citizens.

Our simple examination of the evidence by a scatterplot of the contemporary experience with globalization and public spending is supported by much more sophisticated

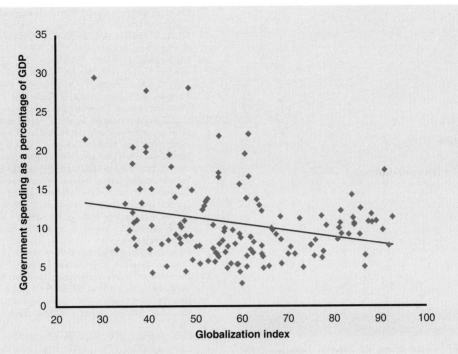

FIGURE 11.5   **Globalization and Government Spending**

Sources: Axel Dreher, "Does Globalization Affect Growth? Evidence from a New Index of Globalization,"
Applied Economics 38, no. 10 (2006), pp. 1091–1110, updated at KOF Index of Globalization, http://
globalization.kof.ethz.ch; Alan Heston, Robert Summers, and Bettina Aten, Penn World Table Version 7.0,
Center for International Comparisons of Production, Income and Prices at the University of Pennsylvania,
June 2011.

econometric analyses. In a study of 186 countries for the 1970–2004 period Stephanie Meinhard and Niklas Potrafke demonstrated that globalization actually increased government spending, especially in the countries of the OECD, suggesting that globalization does not threaten the welfare state at all. The demands of ordinary citizens for social insurance cause governments, especially democratic governments, to find ways to respond to those citizens' needs, despite the constraints allegedly imposed by globalization.[32] We need to be concerned that globalization causes serious disruptions in the lives of ordinary people and puts great strain on democratic welfare states. However, those welfare states have deep roots in their societies and hence they find the means to meet their people's needs.

Conclusion

The state and the economy have always been intertwined, although classical political economists (economic liberals) put forward a model of political economy—laissez-faire capitalism—that advocated keeping the state out of the economy, allowing market forces to determine prices, what was produced, and how income was distributed. In reaction, after the Russian Revolution the Soviets (communists in the Marxian tradition) introduced a model of political economy in which the state was completely involved in the economy, so much so that politics and economics were intertwined. In the twentieth century, democracies, inspired by social liberalism and social democracy, have tended to prefer a mixed economy that avoids the pitfalls of the earlier two approaches. Keynesian policies allowed political leaders in mixed economies to try to overcome the worst aspects of free-market capitalism: depressions or recessions in which production, employment, and incomes fall dramatically, on the one hand, and the inflation that often arises when the economy is strong, on the other. The welfare state has permitted democratic leaders to address the income maldistribution that often accompanies market capitalism. While the welfare state and Keynesian policies are often criticized by those who would prefer a return to free-market capitalism, both extensive social policies and Keynesian policies to stimulate the economy remain popular among democratic publics and politicians alike.

Key Terms

Political economy
Gross domestic product (GDP);
     Per capita GDP
Gross national income (GNI);
     Per capita GNI

Inflation
Central bank
Recession
Depression
Budget deficit
National debt
Fiscal policy
Value-added tax (VAT)
Laissez-faire capitalism
Market economy
Centrally planned (command) economy
Mixed economy
Keynesianism
Privatization
Nationalization
Welfare state

Notes

1. Morten Bech, "FX Volume during the Financial Crisis and Now," *BIS Quarterly Review*, March 2012, pp. 33–43.
2. The term *Pareto optimum* refers to a state of economic equilibrium in which no one's welfare can be improved without reducing someone else's welfare. It was named after the Italian political economist Vilfredo Pareto (1848–1923).
3. The reelection of Barack Obama is an exception to this trend. Since 1948 the only other exceptions to this rule occurred in 1956, when President Eisenhower was reelected despite 1.4 percent growth in the previous 12 months, and 1976, when President Ford was defeated despite 4 percent growth (*Economist*, May 27, 1995, pp. 25–26). In 1996, when President Clinton was reelected, the growth rate was about 3.1 percent in the previous 12 months, but 4 percent in the previous six months. George W. Bush was reelected in 2004 with a growth rate of about 3.7 percent in the four quarters before his election.
4. Benjamin Friedman, *The Moral Consequences of Economic Growth* (New York: Knopf, 2005).
5. See Herman M. Schwartz, *States Versus Markets*, 3rd ed. (New York: Palgrave Macmillan, 2009); Martin Staniland, *What Is Political Economy?* (New Haven, CT: Yale University Press, 1985). For an overview of scholarship on political economy, see James E. Alt, "Comparative Political Economy: Credibility, Accountability, and Institutions," in *Political Science: The State of the Discipline*, ed. Ira Katznelson and Helen V. Miller (New York: W. W. Norton, 2002), pp. 147–71. Barry R. Weingast and Donald A. Wittman, eds., *The Oxford Handbook of Political Economy* (New York: Oxford University Press, 2006) offers a compendium of review articles on the scope of political economy. See especially the editors' introduction.
6. Congressional Budget Office, *The Budget and Economic Outlook: Fiscal Years 2012 to 2022* (Washington, DC: January 2012), available at http://www.cbo.gov/sites/default/files/cbofiles/attachments/01-31-2012_Outlook.pdf.
7. Adam Smith, *The Wealth of Nations* (Chicago: University of Chicago Press, 1977). For biographic studies, see Jerry Z. Muller, *Adam Smith in His Time and Ours* (Princeton, NJ: Princeton University Press, 1993); Ian Simpson Ross, *The Life of Adam Smith*, 2nd ed. (Oxford: Clarendon Press, 2010); Athol Fitzgibbons, *Adam Smith's System of Liberty, Wealth, and Virtue* (Oxford: Oxford University Press, 1995).
8. David Ricardo, *The Principles of Political Economy and Taxation* (New York: E. P. Dutton, 1948). This work was first published in 1817.
9. Thomas Malthus, *An Essay on the Principle of Population* (New York: Oxford University Press, 1994). This work was first published in 1798.
10. Cited in Richard Hofstadter, *Social Darwinism in American Thought*, rev. ed. (New York: George Braziller, 1959), pp. 41, 57.
11. See the *Program of the Communist Party of the Soviet Union*, issued in 1961.
12. David Stark and Laszlo Bruszt, *Postsocialist Pathways* (Cambridge: Cambridge University Press, 1998).
13. Friedrich von Hayek, *The Road to Serfdom* (Chicago: University of Chicago Press, 1956).
14. On Keynes, see Robert Lekachman, *The Age of Keynes* (New York: Random House, 1966); Robert Skidelsky, *John Maynard Keynes: A Biography*, 2 vols. (New York: Viking/Penguin, 1994). For essays on Smith, Malthus, and Keynes, see D. D. Raphael et al., *Three Great Economists* (New York: Oxford University Press, 1997).
15. Daniel Yergin and Joseph Stanislaw, *The Commanding Heights: The Battle Between Government and the Marketplace That Is Remaking the Modern World* (New York: Simon & Schuster, 1998); Harvey Feigenbaum, Jeffrey Henig, and Chris Hamnett, *Shrinking the State: The Political Underpinnings of Privatization* (Cambridge: Cambridge University Press, 1998).
16. See the annual *Global Competitiveness Report*, released by the World Economic Forum, at www.weforum.org, and the *World Competitiveness Yearbook*, prepared annually by the IMD World Competitiveness Center, at www.imd.org. The Heritage Foundation and *The Wall Street* Journal jointly produce an annual Index of Economic Freedom, accessible at www.heritage.org.
17. For a sampling of Bentham's writings, see Bhikhu Pradesh, ed., *Bentham's Political Thought* (London: Croom Helm, 1973).
18. For a comprehensive interpretation, see Alan Ryan, *J. S. Mill* (London: Routledge & Kegan Paul, 1974). For a psychohistory that relates Mill's ideas and personality to his relationships with his father and his wife, see Bruce Mazlish, *James and John Stuart Mill* (New York: Basic Books, 1975).
19. Sheri Berman, *The Social Democratic Movement* (Cambridge, MA: Harvard University Press, 1998); Peter Gourevitch, *Politics in Hard Times* (Ithaca, NY: Cornell University Press, 1986), p. 34.
20. Theda Skocpol, *Protecting Soldiers and Mothers: The Political Origins of Social Policy in the United States* (Cambridge, MA: Harvard University Press, 1992).
21. Robert F. Himmelfarb, *Survival of Corporatism in the New Deal Era, 1933–1945* (New York: Garland, 1994).
22. Cited in Christopher Pierson, *Beyond the Welfare State? The New Political Economy of Welfare* (University Park, PA: Pennsylvania State University Press, 1991), p. 128.
23. For an analysis of different types of democratic welfare regimes, see Gøsta Esping-Andersen, *Three Worlds of Welfare Capitalism* (Princeton, NJ: Princeton University Press, 1990).
24. Pierson, *Beyond the Welfare State?* pp. 168–78. See also Paul Pierson, *Dismantling the Welfare State? Reagan, Thatcher, and the Politics of Retrenchment* (Cambridge: Cambridge University Press, 1994).
25. Christopher Pierson, *Beyond the Welfare State?* 3rd ed. (Cambridge: Polity, 2006); Miguel Glatzer and Dietrich Rueschemeyer, eds., *Globalization and the Future of the Welfare State* (Pittsburgh, PA: Pittsburgh University Press, 2005); B. Vivekanandan and Nimmi Kurian, eds., *Welfare States and the Future* (New York: Palgrave Macmillan, 2005); Gøsta Esping-Andersen et al., *Why We Need a New Welfare State* (New York: Oxford University Press, 2002); Neil Gilbert, *Transformation of the Welfare State: The Silent Surrender of Public Responsibility* (Oxford: Oxford University Press, 2002); Evelyne Huber and John D. Stephens, *Development and Crisis of the Welfare State: Parties and Policies in Global Markets* (Chicago: Chicago University Press, 2001).
26. James Surowiecki, "Dodger Mania," *The New Yorker*, July 11, 2011.
27. Edward Christie and Mario Holzner, "What Explains Tax Evasion? An Empirical Assessment based on European Data," Working Papers no. 40 (2006), Vienna Institute for International Economic Studies, wiiw.ac.at.
28. James E. Alt and K. Alec Chrystal, *Political Economics* (Berkeley, CA: University of California Press, 1983), pp. 103–25; Alt, "Comparative Political Economy," pp. 151–52, 163ff.
29. Michel Crozier, Samuel P. Huntington, and Joji Watanuki, *The Crisis of Democracy* (New York: New York University Press, 1975).
30. *The Rise and Decline of Nations* (New Haven, CT: Yale University Press, 1982).
31. An especially articulate early version of this argument made in the context of a larger study of globalization and backlash against it is Benjamin Barber, *Jihad vs. McWorld* (New York: Times Books, 1995).
32. "The Globalization–Welfare State Nexus Reconsidered," *Review of International Economics* 20, 2 (May 2012), pp. 271–87. For an early analysis of the globalization–welfare state tradeoff, see Dani Rodrik, "Sense and Nonsense in the Globalization Debate," Foreign Policy, no. 107 (Summer 1997), pp. 19–37.

12

The Politics of Development

Microfinance, as exemplified by the Grameen Bank in Bangladesh, offers poor women an opportunity for advancement.

OVERVIEW

- The *Third World* and the *Global South* are terms that mask much diversity among the more than 150 countries political scientists typically group in the developing world.

- Central on the agendas of the developing countries is promoting economic prosperity so that they may transcend the poverty that has burdened their peoples.

- While several newly industrializing countries (NICs) have made significant economic advancements in the past half century, many other countries remain mired in underdevelopment. Many countries of Asia and sub-Saharan Africa remain trapped in circumstances of dire poverty despite the pledge of the United Nations membership to meet the Millennium Development Goals by 2015.

- The causes of underdevelopment remain a point of contention among social scientists. Among proposed causes of underdevelopment are overpopulation, traditional culture, either excessive or insufficient state involvement in the market, dependency on richer countries' markets and foreign assistance, and corruption.

- India provides the textbook case of a country in development. Blessed and cursed by sociocultural pluralism, India pursued a socialist-leaning economic development strategy for decades before liberalizing its economy two decades ago. What was a slow growth economy is now experiencing rapid growth and its attendant challenges.

- India has built a democracy that demonstrates that economic prosperity is not a prerequisite for democratic governance.

DEVELOPING COUNTRIES

The *developing countries* consist of more than 150 states spread across the globe from Latin America to Africa, from the Middle East to East Asia. Together they are home to more than 80 percent of the world's population. These countries are also sometimes referred to as the "Third World," a term coined by a French economist in the 1950s. Although it had never been common previously to speak of the "First World" as a euphemism for the economically advanced democracies or to refer to the communist states as the "Second World," it was universally understood that the Third World applied to almost every other

country on the planet. Concentrated largely in the Southern Hemisphere, the Third World is also known collectively as "the South," in contrast to North America, Europe, and Japan, known collectively as "the North." "North–South relations" are relations between the more economically advanced countries and those that are less developed.

Like most blanket terms, such designations as **Third World** or the **Global South** cover a far greater variety than they imply. In fact, the nations of the developing world exhibit an extraordinary diversity of political systems, social structures, and even levels of economic development. Some are (or have been) democracies. Others are authoritarian regimes of various

Table 12.1 Colonization Patterns

Region or Country	Colonizing Powers	Period of Decolonization
Latin America	Spain, Portugal	1810–1820s
Caribbean	Britain, France, Denmark, Netherlands, United States	1950s–1970s
Africa	Portugal, Britain, France, Germany Belgium, Italy	1950s–1970s
Middle East; North Africa	Turkey, Britain, France, Spain, Italy	1920s, 1940s–1950s
India; Pakistan	Britain	1947
Southeast Asia	France, Britain, Netherlands, Japan	1945–1950s
Korea; Taiwan	Japan	1945
Philippines	United States	1946
Pacific Islands	United States, France, Japan	1945–1980s

types, such as traditional monarchies or military dictatorships. Some are fairly homogeneous when it comes to the ethnic composition or religious beliefs of the population; others consist of socially heterogeneous populations. In economic terms, a few developing countries are relatively rich, most are poor, and quite a few are in between.

Most developing states—but not all—have experienced a colonial past (see Table 12.1). Few states in these regions managed to escape long-term colonization by the imperialist powers. Even some that avoided colonial rule came under short-term domination by outside powers at one time in their history. Those colonial histories (discussed briefly in Chapters 17 to 19) often involved some degree of the extraction of the colony's resources by the imperialist power or the creation of a pattern of economic development more beneficial to the colonizer than the colonized. Creating an economic development model that proves self-sustaining and beneficial to the majority of a former colony's people has proven very difficult for many postcolonial countries.

Table 12.2 Human Development Index, 2011: Levels of Human Development in Selected Countries Based on Life Expectancy, Literacy Rates, School Enrollments, and Per Capita GDP (Total: 187)

VERY HIGH AND HIGH		MEDIUM		LOW	
Rank	Country	Rank	Country	Rank	Country
1.	Norway (0.943)	95.	Jordan (0.698)	143.	Kenya (0.509)
2.	Australia	101.	China	145.	Pakistan
3.	Netherlands	103.	Thailand	146.	Bangladesh
4.	United States	107.	Paraguay	149.	Burma
5.	New Zealand	108.	Bolivia	154.	Yemen
6.	Canada	110.	Mongolia	155.	Senegal
7.	Ireland	112.	Philippines	156.	Nigeria
9.	Germany	113.	Egypt	158.	Haiti
10.	Sweden	114.	Palestinian Authority	161.	Uganda
11.	Switzerland	115.	Uzbekistan	166.	Rwanda
12.	Japan	118.	Botswana	169.	Sudan
15.	South Korea	119.	Syria	170.	Côte d'Ivoire
17.	Israel	121.	Honduras	172.	Afghanistan
20.	France	123.	South Africa	173.	Zimbabwe
24.	Italy	124.	Indonesia	174.	Ethiopia
28.	United Kingdom	127.	Tajikistan	175.	Mali
30.	United Arab Emirates	128.	Vietnam	177.	Eritrea
39.	Poland	129.	Nicaragua	178.	Guinea
57.	Mexico	130.	Morocco	180.	Sierra Leone
66.	Russian Federation	132.	Iraq	181.	Burkina Faso
84.	Brazil	134.	India	183.	Chad
88.	Iran	135.	Ghana	186.	Niger
92.	Turkey (0.699)	139.	Cambodia (0.523)	187.	Congo (Dem. Rep.) (0.286)

Source: Human Development Report 2011 (New York: United Nations Development Program, 2011), Table 1. For the calculation of the Human Development Index Value (shown in parentheses), see http://hdr.undp.org/en/statistics/hdi/. A perfect score equals 1.000.

Another commonality that most developing states share is their relative economic inferiority to the industrially developed democracies. But here, too, there are exceptions. For example, several Middle Eastern states are rich in oil reserves or other economic assets. In 2011, eight of them—Bahrain, Libya, Iran, Kuwait, Oman, Qatar, Saudi Arabia, and the United Arab Emirates—were ranked among the world's high-income countries. An indication of the relative standing of various countries around the world in terms of their overall level of development can be gleaned from Table 12.2, which is a partial list of countries ranked in accordance with the United Nations Development Program's Human Development Index.

NEWLY INDUSTRIALIZING COUNTRIES

Yet another category of developing countries consists of a small number of relatively successful economies known as the **newly industrializing countries (NICs)**. Several of them are in East Asia: China, Indonesia, Thailand, and Malaysia would currently be called NICs. Sometimes the Philippines is mentioned as an emerging NIC. Hong Kong used to be grouped with these East Asian NICs when it was under British authority, but in 1997 it reverted to China. South Korea, Taiwan, and Singapore were the first countries considered to be NICs, but they have now moved to high-income status. The largest non-Asian countries typically categorized as NICs are Brazil, Mexico, and

Argentina in Latin America; South Africa; and Turkey. In 2011 these countries had per capita national incomes ranging from $3,051(the Philippines) to $17,674 (Argentina).

The NICs are characterized above all by the fact that, since the 1950s and 1960s, they have significantly industrialized their economies. They have also expanded the postindustrial service sector, and some have moved into high-technology production. To varying degrees they have been quite successful, but several were severely shaken by the global financial crisis that started in East Asia in 1997 and spread across the globe.

In addition to sharing certain economic features, all these countries have had problems building stable democracies. We'll examine Mexico and Brazil in Chapter 18 and South Africa in Chapter 19. The case study looks briefly at the experience of South Korea, a former NIC that has graduated to rank among the countries highest on the human development index.

LOW-INCOME COUNTRIES

Although the newly industrializing countries are considered developing countries, most countries in the developing world are considerably worse off. Quite a few middle-income countries have major pockets of poverty, especially those in the lower-middle-income range. But the most severely impoverished are the "low-income" countries. In 2011 the World Bank counted 36 countries in its low-income group, each with a per capita national income of $1,025 or less. In 2008 almost

 CASE STUDY
South Korea, Development and Democracy

Table 12.2 indicates that South Korea's Human Development Index ranks 15th globally. In 1980, it had ranked 36th. By any account, South Korea has vaulted into the ranks of the world's most developed societies. How?

Thirty-five years of imperial Japanese rule over Korea came to an end in 1945. Under Moscow's aegis, North Korea became the People's Republic of Korea, a rigid communist dictatorship led for nearly 40 years by Kim Il-Sung. Upon Kim's death in 1994, power devolved upon his son, Kim Jong-Il, and now his grandson, Kim Jong-Un, who today presides over a highly repressive, economically moribund state that has devoted its energies to developing a nuclear arsenal. In 1948, South Korea became the Republic of Korea.

Hopes for democracy in South Korea were quickly dashed as the military imposed dictatorial rule on the fledgling republic. The military's power was immediately reinforced by the Korean War, which began with North Korea's unprovoked invasion of South Korea in 1950. A United Nations force led by the United States repelled the invasion and restored the status quo ante in 1953. The ensuing military standoff, fortified

with huge armies on both sides, tightened the military's grip on South Korea. Except for a short-lived elected government in 1960–61, military strongmen governed until the 1990s, at times quite harshly repressing expressions of democratic sentiment. The regime's oppressive authoritarianism was accompanied by extraordinary economic dynamism, however. South Korea's military leadership initially attempted to achieve a certain level of economic self-sufficiency, pursuing an *import-substitution* policy aimed at substituting domestically produced goods for costly imports. When this policy failed to generate growth, the government changed course. Starting in the mid-1960s it embarked on a vigorous *export-led growth* strategy. Working closely with the country's leading private companies, organized into some 50 conglomerates known as *chaebol*, the military catapulted South Korea into the front ranks of the world's export-oriented manufacturing countries by the 1980s by adopting for its own manufacturing facilities the technologies developed earlier in the United States, Europe, and Japan. The resulting gains in economic growth were spectacular. In 1950, South Korea's per

(Continued on next page)

(Continued from previous page)

capita national income was about $100, slightly lower than that of India and Ghana; by 1990 it was $3,600. In 2011 South Korea's per capita national income was estimated at $20,870, while India's and Ghana's were both $1,410.

The South Korean experience strikingly demonstrated that political authoritarianism is not necessarily a barrier to economic growth. Under certain conditions (such as a well-planned export strategy and a robust private sector), an authoritarian regime can successfully promote a vigorous economic development policy by importing technologies and processes and by enforcing labor discipline through dictatorial practices.

But such a regime cannot always count on the support of its people, despite dramatic improvements in their standard of living. In South Korea, outbursts of democratic fervor periodically challenged the military's hegemony. Prosperity fostered the growth of a middle class that was eager to have a say in politics. The state's expansion of education produced growing numbers of students and professionals capable of articulating their political demands. In 1980 a student uprising was brutally quashed. The suppression of the labor movement, which enabled private companies to keep labor costs down, provoked strikes and galvanized support for free labor unions. The rising popularity of Christianity, with Christians eventually constituting 29 percent of the population, expanded the role of churches in associational life. Beneath the hard shell of military rule, a vibrant civil society was gathering force.

In 1992, prodemocracy opposition parties won a major victory in parliamentary elections. Later the same year, democratic reformer Kim Young Sam won the presidency. He was succeeded by Kim Dae-Jung, who won the 1997 presidential election. An internationally celebrated human rights activist and Nobel Peace Prize winner, Kim Dae-Jung had been condemned to death four times by military authorities for his outspoken support for democracy. A corruption scandal led Kim's successor as president, Roh Moo-hyun, to resign after an impeachment motion in the national legislature, but the Constitutional Court overturned the impeachment measure,

Working with the country's leading private companies, organized into some 50 conglomerates known as *chaebol*, the military catapulted South Korea into the leading ranks of the world's export-oriented manufacturing countries by the 1980s by utilizing the manufacturing technologies developed earlier in the United States, Europe, and Japan.

allowing Roh to return to the presidency. Through these presidencies the nation suffered a severe downturn associated with the 1997–98 Asian financial crisis that hit hard during Kim Dae-Jung's term. Yet, while the country's military ultimately failed to maintain authoritarian rule despite a record of economic success, Kim Dae-Jung's administration showed that democracy can survive even in periods of economic duress.

Whereas a successful rags-to-riches economic development program had sustained military rule in past decades, a more sophisticated, well-developed economy is sustaining democracy in South Korea now, despite rising fears about security.[1] In 2012, South Korea had Freedom House ratings of 1 for political rights and 2 for civil liberties. Meanwhile, North Korea remains one of the poorest and least free countries in the world, scoring 7s for both civil liberties and political rights.

1.3 billion people were clinging to the margins of subsistence on less than $1.25 a day, the threshold regarded by the United Nations as the boundary of extreme poverty. Another 1.2 billion were trying to survive on incomes between $1.25 and $2 a day. These 2.5 billion people form a global underclass with bleak prospects for climbing out of staggering poverty.[2]

The economic chasm between rich and poor around the world has been widening steadily. The income gap between the richest third of the world's countries, measured in terms of average per capita GNP, grew from about 11 to 1 in 1970 to just short of 20 to 1 by 1995. By 2005 the richest 20 percent of the world's population held 75 percent of the world's income; the poorest 20 percent held a mere 1.5 percent of the world's income. The worldwide Gini coefficient, with zero constituting perfect equality and 100 constituting the most extreme

inequality, measured 67. (For more about the Gini coefficient, see Chapter 1.) The combined income of the world's 500 wealthiest persons was greater than the combined income of the world's poorest 416 million. But income statistics tell only part of the story. Other current indicators reveal the tragic dimensions of the poorest countries' predicament with even greater harshness:

- About 7.5 million children under the age of five die every year—one every four seconds—even though almost all childhood deaths are preventable; almost all of these victims are in poor countries.
- Almost 100 people die every hour from malaria; three-quarters of them are children, and most could have been saved with bed nets and timely medication.

High death rates due to treatable illnesses such as malaria are potent indications of the impact of poverty. Simple mosquito nets such as the one protecting this mother and her baby could dramatically cut deaths due to malaria.

- Vaccine-preventable illnesses took the lives of 1.5 million children in 2008.
- More than 925 million people (one-third of whom are preschoolers) suffer from malnutrition, which can have devastating effects on the immune system and brain function.
- More than 34 million people were reported to have HIV/AIDS in 2011, 60 percent of them in sub-Saharan Africa; each year about 1.8 million die from it and 1.7 million become infected.
- Some 350,000 women die every year from pregnancy-related causes, due mostly to inadequate neonatal care.
- More than 780 million people lack access to clean water.
- About 2.5 billion lack access to modern sanitation.
- Some 67 million lack access to primary school.

On each of these indicators the world has seen improvement over the past decade, yet much severe poverty remains. Sub-Saharan Africa has been hit especially hard by the grinding effects of poverty and disease. Of the region's 47 nations, 27 are low-income countries. The region accounts for two-thirds of the annual fatalities resulting from HIV/AIDS. Life expectancy has diminished. In the mid-1980s, someone born in sub-Saharan Africa could expect to live 24 fewer years than someone born in a rich country, but the gap was shrinking. By 2005 that figure had grown to 33 years and the gap was widening.[3]

However we draw the dividing lines between middle-income and low-income nations, a large number of developing countries suffer from *underdevelopment*. **Underdeveloped economies** are somewhat different from "undeveloped" economies. Undeveloped economies are ready to grow, like the United States in the mid-nineteenth century or South Korea in the 1950s.[4] Underdeveloped economies suffer from chronic, seemingly eternal, low growth and mass poverty.

In an effort to achieve a breakthrough in combating underdevelopment, all 189 members of the United Nations signed the UN Millennium Declaration in 2000, pledging to achieve eight Millennium Development Goals by 2015. Table 12.3 lists these goals. Since the adoption of these ambitious goals, there has been some progress in reducing malnutrition and childhood mortality, advancing literacy, and providing greater access to clean water. The number of people living on less than $1.25 per day fell by about 400 million between the baseline years of 1990 and 2005, and the UN projects that the world is likely to meet its poverty reduction target by 2015. But at present rates of progress, projected outcomes will fall short of the Millennium Development Goals in many of these categories.[5]

Why haven't the chronically underdeveloped countries been able to develop their economies? This pressing question has generated a wide range of answers. The following overview presents a few independent variables that students of economic development have used in their efforts to explain the persistence of underdevelopment in different settings.[6]

Population

On October 31, 2011, the world greeted the birth of its 7 billionth resident, according to demographers' calculations. Current projections estimate that global population will be just over 8 billion in 2025 and 9.6 billion in 2050 (see Table 12.4 for projections of population growth in the world's most populous countries). Does overpopulation cause poverty? The evidence is rather mixed. On the one hand, *poverty causes overpopulation*, which in turn causes more poverty. People who live in dire conditions must confront the probability that some of their offspring will die as children. To compensate for anticipated childhood mortality, many destitute families tend to have more children than less-deprived families. The population's fertility rate (that is, the average number of children born during an average woman's fertile years) tends to be highest in poor, mainly rural countries—typically above five children. Many poor families overcompensate

Table 12.3 United Nations Millennium Development Goals

1. **Reducing poverty and hunger.** Halve the number of people living on less than $1 a day, between the baseline year of 1990 and 2015.* Halve the proportion of people who suffer from hunger in the same period.

2. **Educating all children.** Ensure that by 2015 children everywhere, boys and girls alike, will be able to complete a full course of primary schooling.

3. **Empowering women.** Eliminate gender disparity in primary and secondary education, preferably in 2005, and at all levels by 2015.

4. **Saving children.** Reduce by two-thirds, between 1990 and 2015, the under-five mortality rate.

5. **Caring for mothers.** Reduce by three-quarters, between 1990 and 2015, the maternal mortality ratio.

6. **Combating disease.** Have halted by 2015 and begun to reverse the spread of HIV/AIDS and the incidence of malaria and other major diseases.

7. **Using resources wisely.** Integrate the principles of sustainable development into country policies and programs, and reverse the loss of environmental resources. Reduce by half the proportion of people without access to safe drinking water. Achieve significant improvement in the lives of at least 100 million slum dwellers by 2020.

8. **Working together.** Develop further an open trading and financial system that is rule-based, predictable, and nondiscriminatory. Address the special needs of the least-developed countries and those of landlocked and small island developing states. Deal comprehensively with developing countries' debt problems to make debt sustainable in the long term. Develop decent and productive work for youth. Provide access to affordable essential drugs in developing countries. Make available the benefits of new technologies—especially information and communications technologies.

* The UN now uses $1.25 as its poverty threshold.

Source: The Millennium Development Goals Report 2011 (New York: United Nations, 2011).

and have more surviving children than they can afford. (Ironically, areas with high childhood mortality rates tend to have high population growth.) In these circumstances, impoverished parents may not be able to provide all their children with adequate food, health care, or education. Children who grow up in such deprivation tend to remain poor all their lives, producing more poor children in the next generation. The cycle of poverty and overpopulation thus repeats itself. In contrast, in societies that have managed to achieve a modest degree of economic development and stability, population growth rates tend to decline to something closer to replacement rate—that is, the number of children per couple necessary to maintain a stable population.

On the other hand, it cannot be said that the world has "too many" people, or that countries with a high population density are doomed to poverty. There is enough food in the world to feed *everyone* adequately. The problem is that much of this food rots or goes to waste in wealthy countries; for a variety of reasons, it does not get to the malnourished people of the world in time or in sufficient quantities. Meanwhile, high-density countries such as China, South Korea, Singapore, and India have registered extraordinary gains in economic growth. Some of the poorest rural regions of sub-Saharan Africa and Latin America, by contrast, are sparsely populated. (Of course, poverty is also extreme in densely populated urban areas in these two vast continents.) On October 17, 2006, the population of the United States reached 300 million—an increase of 100 million since 1967. Despite its size, the United States has by far the world's largest economy. Nevertheless, even the U.S. economy has attributes of poverty that by some measures are more acute than in poorer countries. The life expectancy of

Table 12.4 The World's 10 Most Populous Countries

Country	2012 Population (in millions)	Expected Population in 2025 (in millions)
China	1,350	1,402
India	1,260	1,458
United States	314	351
Indonesia	241	273
Brazil	194	210
Pakistan	180	230
Nigeria	170	234
Bangladesh	153	183
Russia	143	141
Japan	128	120

Source: Population Reference Bureau, *2012 World Population Data Sheet,* www.prb.org.

A high density population does not necessarily mean significant poverty. In many densely populated areas, such as São Paulo, Brazil, the high population may contribute to economic vitality.

African-American children, for example, is lower than that of comparably aged children in Sri Lanka, the Dominican Republic, or Costa Rica.[7]

Population can be an explosive political issue. China's communist leadership decreed in 1979 that no couple living in an urban area should be allowed to have more than one child; rural couples may have more than one child only under specific circumstances. Forced sterilization has been imposed on millions of Chinese men, a policy that has raised protests from human rights advocates both inside China and around the world. Forced abortion for women pregnant with second or third children occurs with frequency in China. In parts of China, India, and Pakistan, newborn girls are often killed or sold for adoption as birth control measures.[8] Meanwhile, India's government-sponsored birth control programs, which include sex education and encouragement for voluntary sterilization, have been regarded by many observers as inadequate or ineffective. And in countries with large Catholic or Muslim populations, birth control and abortion may be illegal or difficult to obtain.

Sociocultural Explanations

Some analysts attribute economic underdevelopment to social and institutional structures and to the cultural attitudes and modes of behavior that accompany them. One such school of thought was first conceptualized by Max Weber early in the twentieth century and later adapted by American social scientists in the 1950s and 1960s. It makes a fundamental distinction between *modern* and *traditional* societies.

Modern societies are characterized by a complex social structure consisting of differentiated, specialized professions (doctors, farmers, mechanics, etc.) and organized associations (trade unions and other interest groups), all interacting with one another over a relatively wide geographic area. They also tend to have a network of well-developed governmental institutions, including highly organized bureaucracies and a fairly sophisticated system of laws that regulate political, economic, and social interactions. Modern societies are heavily centered in urban areas and are characterized by fairly high rates of literacy and education.

Traditional societies, by contrast, tend to consist of extended families engaged in primary economic activities, such as subsistence agriculture, within a fairly small area. They display little or no professional differentiation; one person may perform multiple tasks (farmer, medicine man, priest). There are few, if any, organized associations. They also have much simpler institutional structures. Government, to the extent that it is organized, is typically built around elites who wield power arbitrarily, demanding the population's deference while freely engaging in corrupt activities. Most people in traditional societies live in rural areas. Very few are educated or even literate.

Whereas modern societies tend to be secular (though they may permit religious freedom), rationally organized, and attuned to scientific logic, traditional societies tend to attribute natural phenomena to supernatural forces over which human beings have little control. In modern societies, religion and

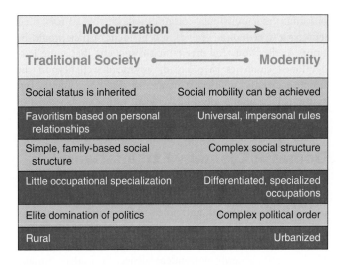

Modernization ⟶	
Traditional Society ●————————● **Modernity**	
Social status is inherited	Social mobility can be achieved
Favoritism based on personal relationships	Universal, impersonal rules
Simple, family-based social structure	Complex social structure
Little occupational specialization	Differentiated, specialized occupations
Elite domination of politics	Complex political order
Rural	Urbanized

FIGURE 12.1   Traditional Society and Modernity

science coexist. In traditional societies, religious belief or superstition substitutes for scientific rationality. As a consequence, modern societies are able to apply science to the production of sophisticated technology, while traditional societies must make do with fairly primitive technology.

Whereas modern societies are based on impersonal rules that apply to everyone, such as legal codes and the laws of the economic marketplace, social and political relationships in traditional societies are more personalized, with a high value placed on face-to-face relations and personal favoritism. Modern societies are dynamic; change is the norm. Traditional societies are resistant to change: People know their place in the existing social hierarchy and are expected to stay there. Often a sense of resignation precludes even the possibility of change.

Scholars who stress these and related distinctions between modern and traditional societies are often exponents of **modernization theory**, which contends that economic underdevelopment cannot be overcome until the society in question abandons its traditional social and institutional structures, along with their accompanying attitudes and behavioral patterns. Figure 12.1 provides a simple schematic version of the characters of traditional and modern society; *modernization* is the movement from tradition to modernity. Countries as diverse as India, Burma, and various African and Middle Eastern states have been variously viewed as possessing distinct features of traditional society that appear to obstruct their economic development.[9]

The modern-versus-traditional-society dichotomy is not without its critics. Some maintain that the distinction is too sharp, arguing that it is possible for some countries to retain certain elements of their own traditional society while simultaneously adopting specific aspects of modern society. A number of critics accuse Western social scientists of ethnocentric bias because they equate "modern" societies with Western societies. By placing American or West European concepts of modernity on a pedestal as the preferred ideal, they argue, Western advocates of modernization theory implicitly denigrate non-Western approaches to political and economic life and overlook the possibility that individual countries will be able to find their own path to economic growth, independent of their would-be tutors in the West. Another criticism suggests that some less-developed countries have already advanced well beyond the simple social and political structures of traditional society but still remain economically undeveloped. Other explanations of economic backwardness are therefore necessary.[10]

Domestic Economy Explanations

After World War II, most of the nations of Asia and Africa that had been colonized by Britain, France, and other European powers in the eighteenth and nineteenth centuries gained their independence. The process was known as **decolonization**. (See Chapter 19 for a discussion of decolonization in Africa.) Flush with their newly won independence, the leaders of many of these decolonized states embraced one form or another of what they generally called socialism. For a number of the freshly independent states, socialism above all meant two things: (1) opposition to Western neocolonialism, and (2) a powerful role for the state in organizing the national economy.

Neocolonialism and **neo-imperialism** were the terms used by many leaders of the developing world to denounce what they regarded as attempts by Britain, France, the United States, or other Western states to try to dominate their economies and dictate their political orientations even after the formal termination of colonial rule. These anti-Western attitudes often included a rejection of the market-oriented economic approaches of the advanced capitalist states and efforts to forge homegrown models of economic development. Anticolonialism thus implied anticapitalism. In several developing countries, businesses or other property privately owned by Europeans or Americans were expropriated by the state, often without compensation.

In addition to having a distinctly anti-Western bias, socialism in many developing nations meant the state would play a galvanizing role in guiding the process of national economic development. Throughout the developing world, especially in the decades extending from the 1950s to the 1980s, a considerable number of political leaders and economists subscribed to the view that a state-centered socialist system would promote development far more rapidly and far more equitably than would free-market capitalism. Denouncing capitalism as greedy and exploitative, many of them also placed a sharp emphasis on economic self-reliance and spurned trade relations with the West.

Historically, state-dominated economic systems of one type or another today have been an attractive alternative to Western-style private enterprise for many political leaders and intellectuals throughout the developing world. But the role and effectiveness of the state in economic development has varied considerably. Atul Kohli has identified three ideal types of state organization and activity in the developing world. *Coherent-capitalist states* like South Korea are characterized by a cohesive "rational-legal" central state and a fairly clear distinction between the public (state) sector and private enterprise. Such states tend to be the most successful at promoting economic

growth because they are able to organize and carry out coherent government programs aimed at stimulating vigorous private-sector development and promoting foreign trade. At the opposite end of the spectrum are *patrimonial states*. As typified by Nigeria, this pattern features government officials who regard public resources—such as the national treasury, royalties from oil exports, and other state assets—as their own personal patrimony, to be plundered for their own benefit or for the benefit of their favored group. Patrimonial states tend to do a poor job of promoting economic development. Between these patterns are *fragmented-multiclass states* such as India and Brazil. These states are better organized than patrimonial states, but state authority tends to be highly fragmented because it rests on a very diverse society and its attendant political alliances. States like these find it difficult to pursue a coherent, narrowly focused development strategy because they must meet the demands of multiple social and political groups simultaneously. They are pressured by their supporters to scatter the state's limited resources among conflicting goals, such as promoting industrial growth, subsidizing agriculture, and redistributing wealth to the poor. Though the state has invariably played a major role in the economies of developing countries, Kohli concludes, its effects on economic growth have differed widely around the globe.[11]

Over the course of the 1980s, however, calls for enhancing private enterprise and introducing market mechanisms and more international trade made a strong resurgence. These *neoliberal* economic policies were favored especially by the Reagan administration in Washington and the Thatcher government in London, as well as by leaders of Washington-based international organizations such as the World Bank and the International Monetary Fund. (The governments of the United States, Japan, Germany, Britain, and France have dominated World Bank and IMF decision making.) The term *neoliberal* is meant to imply a close policy resemblance to what the classical economic liberals that we have discussed in Chapters 10 and 11 would propose—a commitment to laissez-faire capitalism. This widening commitment to market economics as a prescription for economic growth in developing countries became known as the *Washington consensus*. It stemmed in part from the failure of a number of heavily state-managed economies to grow. Political elites in a variety of developing countries reached the conclusion that excessive government involvement in the economy had not stimulated growth but retarded it. An effort to privatize at least some government-controlled enterprises followed, especially in the Latin American countries of Chile, Mexico, and Argentina.

Yet another source of the change in attitudes toward capitalism was the undeniable success of the East Asian NICs. (Critics of the Washington consensus have argued that the East Asian NICs' version of capitalist growth was hardly the laissez-faire variety because the state played a leading role in all cases.) Finally, the collapse of the Soviet Union and its communist empire in Central and Eastern Europe took the wind from the sails of many Third World socialist movements, particularly those that depended on financial or military support from Moscow and its allies.

Although the neoliberal Washington consensus became the new orthodoxy governing economic policies toward the developing world in the 1980s and 1990s, a number of developing countries have had a difficult time meeting its requirements for *structural adjustment*—the process of trimming budget deficits, removing protectionist trade barriers, eliminating price controls on key consumer goods, privatizing state-owned enterprises, and fulfilling other conditions for receiving IMF financial assistance. Critics have charged that structural adjustment programs worsen poverty rather than alleviate it. The failure of a number of developing countries to eradicate poverty has led to recent reevaluations of the efficacy of market mechanisms as the predominant engine of growth. A World Bank report in 2006 noted that Latin America's per capita GDP increased by roughly 1.5 percent a year in the 1990s, but with no significant change in poverty levels. The authors found that poor people cannot actively participate in a market economy because they lack access to credit and insurance. And poor regions cannot attract investment from private companies because they lack basic infrastructure, such as good roads and communications facilities. With the highest income inequality in the world, Latin American countries are also generating social tensions that further reduce incentives for private businesses to invest their money. The result is a vicious circle in which low growth produces more poverty, and more poverty produces low growth.

In addition to issues relating to how a country organizes its economic institutions, domestic, geographical, and ecological factors invariably play a major role in economic development. Many developing countries have geographical features, climactic conditions, resource scarcities, and other natural conditions that have profound causative effects on their inability to promote economic growth. Sub-Saharan Africa is especially disadvantaged in these respects. Development economist Jeffrey Sachs points out that much of this region lacks navigable rivers, reliable rainfall, and irrigation. Its tropical climate breeds malaria, dengue fever, and other diseases that take a huge toll not only on the population but also on the domestic economy. These and other natural factors, Sachs concludes, are more important than adverse political conditions (such as corruption, civil war, or the lack of democracy), cultural variables (such as "traditional" values), or economic institutions (such as the absence of free markets) in explaining Africa's endemic poverty. Other developing countries are also powerfully affected by the realities of nature.[12]

International Explanations

As we have repeatedly emphasized, what happens *within* nations is very often affected by what happens *between* nations, and vice versa. Not surprisingly, some explanations as to why certain countries experience significant economic growth while others do not are rooted in the interconnection between internal factors and external ones.

One explanation of this kind was advanced by Raul Prebisch, an Argentine economist who served for many years as the head of the United Nations Economic Commission for Latin America. Prebisch and others like him have maintained that one of the chief causes of economic underdevelopment is the prevailing structure of the international economy. Specifically, most Third World countries are at a permanent disadvantage because the *terms of trade* for their imports and exports favor the rich nations of the world. In other words, the products that most poor nations must import (such as oil, technology, autos, and other manufactured goods) cost more than the products they can sell in world markets (which often consist of raw materials or cheap manufactures). The result is lingering economic backwardness. To remedy the situation, Prebisch and like-minded economists in the 1970s called for the negotiation of a new international economic order, based on preferential concessions by the advanced states of the North to compensate the poorer countries of the South. But this radical reordering of the world trading system has not come about.[13]

Prebisch's influence on economic policy in developing countries from the 1950s through the 1970s was profound. After he became director of the Economic Commission for Latin America (ECLA), a UN agency in Santiago, Chile, in 1948, his unequal exchange theory became the basis for policy recommendations that advocated a rejection of free trade and the advocacy of **import-substituting industrialization (ISI)**. ISI promotes development by substituting domestic manufactured consumer goods for like products that had previously been imported from more industrialized economies, like the United States or Western Europe in the 1950s. ISI is a type of economic nationalism; it protects domestic manufacturers (Argentine, Brazilian, and Mexican, in the 1940s through the 1970s, for example) and discriminates against foreign sellers of goods by raising high tariff barriers and other forms of trade protectionism. In Latin America, ISI led to several decades of economic growth in the middle of the twentieth century before the domestic markets for easy-to-manufacture goods were saturated and continued protectionism led the domestic producers to become so inefficient compared to the world's leading firms that economic growth stagnated. Often, ISI was accomplished by inviting foreign manufacturers to set up factories in developing countries. In such arrangements profits often returned to the home country of the multinational enterprise, although employment was promoted in the host society.

A related international explanation for Third World poverty is **dependency theory**. Some of the main authors in the dependency tradition were based at ECLA and drew their initial inspiration from Prebisch. This theory asserts that the advanced capitalist countries of the North dominate the world economy and constitute its "core" (or "metropolis"). The poor countries are relegated to the "periphery" of the world capitalist system. They are treated as mere satellites of the rich industrialized nations and remain economically dependent on them. Dependency theory has several variants. One variant asserts that capitalists in the core countries sometimes succeed in making alliances with capitalist entrepreneurs and authoritarian political leaders in particular developing countries. The result is a "dual economy" within such countries: A relatively well-to-do capitalist elite with international connections coexists with poverty-stricken masses who are cut off from such privileged contacts.

In the 1960s Mexico invited Volkswagen to produce its iconic Beetle in a factory in Puebla so that Mexicans could buy inexpensive Mexican-made cars. For a time more than 100,000 Volkswagen Beetle taxis roamed the streets of Mexico City providing inexpensive cab rides. Here the last Beetle comes off the assembly line in 2003.

The dependency hypothesis touched off a lively debate. The neoliberal critique of dependency, for example, affirms that countries that orient their national economy toward active involvement in international trade are more likely to experience growth than countries that cut themselves off from the global economy, whether for ideological reasons (e.g., anticapitalism) or others. As one might expect, neoliberals point to the Asian NICs as prime examples of export-oriented growth. At the same time, they criticize inward-looking economies based on excessive import substitution or political hostility to trade with the capitalist world as paragons of domestic economic stagnation. One early advocate of dependency theory, Fernando Henrique Cardoso, adopted neoliberal views in the period leading up to his election as president of Brazil in 1994.[14]

Over the course of the 1990s the neoliberal approach won acceptance among a growing number of governments in the developing world. By the end of the 1990s, 110 developing countries were members of the World Trade Organization, compared with only 65 members of the WTO's predecessor, the General Agreement on Tariffs and Trade (GATT), in 1987. By 2012 the WTO's membership numbered 155.

Despite undeniable correlations between international trade and economic growth in many countries around the world, wealthy countries continue to prevent developing countries from participating equitably in the world trading system. Most of the gains from trade in the developing world have been reaped by only seven countries. China and other dynamic East and South Asian states account for about half of the world's high-technology exports. But the majority of developing countries lack this technological dynamism. Africa's exports have remained a paltry 3 percent of world trade since 1990. The initiation of a new round of international trade negotiations in Doha, Qatar, in 2001 promised major gains for the developing world. But rich countries continue to impose barriers to the importation of goods from poorer countries; they still subsidize their own farmers at the expense of farmers in the Third World; and they maintain a variety of trade rules detrimental to the less-developed countries. Clearly, the gains from globalization are not being shared by many nations around the world.[15]

Foreign aid is another problematic area. The governments of many developing countries depend on grants and loans from the wealthier countries to remain economically solvent. In 1969 a UN commission headed by Lester Pearson, Canada's former prime minister, recommended that North America, Western Europe, and Japan devote 0.7 percent of gross national income in each country to foreign assistance. Most wealthy countries never met that goal. Over the ensuing decades, the United States provided the most foreign aid in money terms, but it ranked among the lowest of the donor countries when its assistance was measured as a percentage of GNI. American aid usually remained below 0.3 percent of gross income. Much of that aid was military assistance to Israel and Egypt, and a great deal of it came back to the United States because of conditions requiring governments receiving U.S. aid to spend large amounts of it in the United States on equipment and other goods and services needed for development. By 2000 the United States was spending 0.1 percent of its GNI on foreign aid, the lowest percentage among the wealthy countries. With aid allocations falling in other donor countries as well, President George W. Bush joined other world leaders at a conference on development financing in Monterrey, Mexico, in March 2002. The assembled leaders agreed to raise their respective development assistance levels to 0.7 percent of GNI. Over the next two years the U.S. government provided $8 billion in aid (much of it going to Afghanistan and Iraq). Nevertheless, by 2010 its aid assistance had climbed to only 0.21 percent of GNI, while Luxembourg, Denmark, Norway, and Sweden contribute about 1 percent of GNI annually as official development assistance.[16]

In 2005 Jeffrey Sachs provided rough calculations to estimate how much it would cost to lift approximately 1.1 billion people who then lived on less than $1 a day to a slightly higher plane of subsistence by 2015. For these extremely poor people to meet their most basic needs in terms of nutrition, health care, schooling, and the like, the wealthy countries would have to provide about $80 billion in assistance per year to the developing countries. Half that amount would go to sub-Saharan Africa. The donor countries would also have to provide development agencies such as the World Bank with additional funds amounting to $48 billion to $54 billion each year. Sachs's bottom line thus came to $135 billion to $195 billion in assistance per year between 2005 and 2015—amounts that are *less* than the Monterrey target of 0.7 percent of GNI per year from the wealthy countries. Mustering the political will to make these commitments has proven impossible, however. In 2010 18 rich countries spent an average of 0.25 percent or more of their GNI on foreign aid; the total aid by 23 members of the OECD's Development Assistance Committee summed to $128 billion, below Sachs's proposed aid goal.[17] Polls show that most Americans believe that foreign aid consumes about 20 percent of the federal budget, when in fact it is considerably less than 1 percent of the budget.[18]

Of course, foreign assistance by itself is no panacea for poverty. And development specialists readily admit that some aid is wasted on poorly planned projects, mismanagement, corruption, and other failings that inevitably raise skepticism about the utility of the billions that are spent on foreign assistance. William Easterly, a former World Bank economist, notes that the West has spent more than $2.3 trillion on foreign aid over the past five decades, yet it has failed to provide enough 12-cent medicines and $4 bed nets to prevent malaria, just as it has failed to provide equally simple remedies for other Third World problems.[19] But the need for more foreign aid—along with better oversight—is now accepted by virtually all world leaders.

International debts place additional burdens on developing countries. Over the decades, most of these countries have borrowed heavily from international agencies, foreign governments, and private banks to pay their bills at home and purchase imports. By 2010 they had run up total debts amounting to $4 trillion. For debtor countries, the interest that comes due on accumulated debts can reach tens or hundreds of millions of dollars annually. Every dollar spent on interest payments represents a dollar that cannot be spent on health care, education, or other basic needs of the population. In recent years a campaign to provide debt relief for poor countries, spearheaded by people such as Bono and Pope John Paul II, has resulted in unprecedented agreements by the world's richest countries to cancel at least some of the developing world's debts. By the end of 2010, the World Bank, International Monetary Fund, and other creditors had provided debt relief totaling $79 billion to 39 heavily-indebted poor countries.[20]

Poverty in the developing world thus has a number of causative roots in the international economy. But domestic political factors provide additional causes.

Domestic Political Explanations

Another set of hypotheses accentuates domestic political factors as important independent variables that help explain economic performance. One study, for example, compared the development experiences of more than 40 Third World countries between 1950 and 1980. Although the study was conducted by a team of economists, it concluded that political factors such as continuity of leadership and a cohesive sense of nationhood were just as important as, and sometimes even more important than, economic factors in accounting for the success or failure of a country's efforts to develop its economy.[21]

More recent studies confirm the importance of governments in fostering—or hampering—economic growth. For example, William Easterly argues that the most crucial factor in determining whether an economy grows rich or stagnates is *incentives*. Individuals, businesses, and others involved in the economic development process will perform at their most productive levels if they can see that their efforts will bear fruit. They need incentives to save, invest, create businesses, and pay taxes. Bad governments stifle these expectations by providing disincentives to productive activity. They destroy the value of people's savings by printing excess money and driving up the

inflation rate. They destabilize the currency through black-market transactions. They undermine faith in the banking system through lax regulations. They erect barriers to potentially profitable foreign trade by insisting on protectionism. They squander resources by running high budget deficits and foreign debts. And they fail to provide the infrastructure necessary for sustained economic activity, such as roads, telecommunications, irrigation, education, health care, and other basic needs. Worst of all, government corruption casts a pall over the entire development process. When leaders and bureaucrats dispense economic rewards only to a privileged class or ethnic group, or when they steal tax revenues, demand bribes, and misuse foreign aid, potentially productive citizens wallow in poverty. Easterly concludes that bad government is a primary cause of economic stagnation.[22]

Roughly similar conclusions have been reached by studies of the Arab Middle East and North Africa conducted by the United Nations and the World Bank. The studies demonstrate how the region's dictatorships are responsible for persistent economic stagnation. They further indicate that freedom, inclusiveness, accountability, and other aspects of democracy will be essential for future growth.[23]

Economist Daron Acemoglu and political economist James Robinson have articulated another political basis for economic development. They argue that most of human history and most of the regimes under which people have lived have had extractive economic and political institutions: Elites use their power to control the labor of those weaker than them and extract what the poor and the weak produce. Slavery and serfdom have been the norm rather than the exception in human history. Even modern regimes such as those in the Soviet Union and the People's Republic of China have been extractive. Inclusive political and economic institutions, in contrast, produce self-sustaining economic growth. In pluralist political regimes, even pre-democratic ones like Britain in the eighteen century (see Chapter 13), political and economic actors have been able to resist the demands of the highest elites, they have been able to insist on private property rights, and hence they have created the incentives that have rewarded entrepreneurs and promoted the introduction of new products and new productive processes. While extractive regimes can promote growth for a while, as we'll see in the chapters on Russia and China in Part Two of this book, they are less able to encourage innovation.[24] In a complementary work, political scientist Robert Bates points out that states that provide public order and allow the taxpaying population to hold the government accountable for how their taxes are used are much more likely to promote economic prosperity. His account, which echoes the political philosopher Thomas Hobbes, thus emphasizes that states must quell the violence that characterizes human societies and they must be responsible to the people they govern.[25]

As Bates's work suggests, the need for civil peace is another political requirement for economic growth. Developing countries that are torn apart by civil wars, sporadic ethnic or religious violence, and the breakdown of law and order are typically incapable of maintaining a successful economy.

Acknowledging *good governance* as a factor that can facilitate economic development, the World Bank since the late 1990s has ranked the countries of the world in accordance with six *governance indicators*. These indicators measure the extent of the population's participation in selecting the government, along with freedom of expression, association, and other political freedoms ("voice and accountability"); the degree of political stability and the absence of violence; the effectiveness of the government in providing public services and a timely policy formulation and implementation process; the quality of the state's regulatory policies aimed at promoting private-sector development; the rule of law, including the quality of the police and courts; and control of corruption. Focusing on these criteria of governance has practical policy implications. Researchers estimate that even minor improvements in governance can raise incomes and reduce infant mortality significantly, and can bring about other beneficial effects as well. As a consequence, donor countries are increasingly requiring better governance as a condition of their aid to developing states. Table 12.5 displays the World Bank scores for a number of developing countries in 2010. For the sake of comparison, it also provides the average rankings for the mostly wealthy democracies that belong to the Organization for Economic Cooperation and Development (OECD).[26]

The relationship between economic development and politics is often a complex one, however. As Samuel Huntington pointed out in *Political Order in Changing Societies*, there is always a dynamic interaction between socioeconomic modernization and political development, but the results may vary. As a developing country embarks on the path of modernization and

independence, political participation on the part of the masses tends to increase. Literacy, higher education, and urbanization expand, promoting mass political activism. To gain popular support, political leaders seek to mobilize the masses, organizing them into supporting various political ideas and programs. At the same time, the state makes a conscious effort to promote the country's economic development. Social change, economic change, and mass political mobilization are the order of the day. These processes typify what Huntington calls *political modernization*.

How the state and other political institutions deal with these changes is problematic. The process of building effective institutions is what Huntington calls *political development*. Successful political development requires the creation of interest groups and political parties that are capable of expressing popular demands and of channeling them into concrete and realistic policy proposals that governments can act upon. It also requires governmental institutions—executives, legislatures, bureaucracies, and so on—that can make decisions efficiently and implement them effectively. Only by being responsive to the newly activated masses can these political associations and institutions hope to gain popular legitimacy. If they succeed, the result can be long-term political order and steady economic growth.

But social, economic, and political modernization may explode with such force that it rapidly outpaces the ability of political institutions to keep up with the demands being placed on them. If political development fails to keep pace with modernization, the result can be long-term political authoritarianism and economic decay. "The primary problem in politics,"

Table 12.5 Rankings of Selected Countries According to World Bank Governance Indicators, 2010 (Percentile Rank, 1–100)*

Country	Voice and Accountability	Political Stability/ No Violence	Government Effectiveness	Regulatory Quality	Rule of Law	Control of Corruption
Afghanistan	8.1	1.4	4.8	4.8	0.5	1.0
Brazil	63.5	48.1	56.9	56.0	55.5	59.8
China	5.2	24.1	59.8	45.0	44.5	32.5
Congo (Dem. Rep.)	9.0	2.8	1.4	3.3	2.4	2.9
Costa Rica	80.6	68.4	64.6	68.9	64.9	72.7
Egypt	13.3	17.9	40.2	46.9	51.7	34.4
India	59.2	10.8	55.0	39.2	54.5	35.9
Indonesia	48.3	18.9	47.8	39.7	31.3	27.3
Mexico	52.1	22.6	61.7	58.9	33.6	44.5
Nigeria	27.0	3.8	10.5	23.0	10.9	15.8
Pakistan	27.5	0.5	25.8	30.1	25.6	12.0
South Africa	65.4	44.3	65.1	62.7	57.8	60.8
Sudan	4.3	0.9	6.7	7.2	6.2	4.3
Turkey	43.1	16.0	66.0	61.2	58.3	57.9
Venezuela	22.3	10.4	14.8	4.3	1.4	7.2
Zimbabwe	7.6	13.2	3.8	2.4	0.9	2.4
OECD[†]	85.3	70.1	86.5	86.7	85.3	83.1

*100 is the best score; the higher the number, the better the performance.

[†]Average scores for 34 OECD countries, including Mexico and Turkey. For a list of members, consult www.oecd.org.

Source: worldbank.org/governance.

Huntington stated, "is the lag in the development of institutions behind social and economic changes." Huntington argued that economic growth does not take place in a political vacuum. It can best flourish in a context of political order and stability, rooted in legitimate political institutions. But one of his implications is that, for modernizing countries, political order may be more difficult to achieve in a democracy than in an authoritarian regime.[27]

Indeed, the question of whether authoritarian states or democracies are more effective at promoting rapid economic growth is still one of the most contentious political issues of modern politics. The authoritarian camp derides democracy as hopelessly inefficient. And the right to vote means nothing, in their view, to populations whose bellies are empty. Democracy's advocates reply that democratic government is more effective than authoritarianism when it comes to generating and sustaining economic growth. Mancur Olson, for example, argued that democracies are more successful than despotic governments at guaranteeing property rights, which are a verifiably important catalyst of economic growth.[28]

Adam Przeworski and his associates provide substantial evidence that, on average, the differences between democracy and dictatorship when it comes to generating economic growth are only marginal. Countries such as South Korea under the military or China under the communists have produced phenomenal rates of growth, though other dictatorships have languished. Przeworski and his colleagues conclude that "regimes make no difference for growth"—ultimately, total economic output grows at similar rates in democracies and dictatorships alike.[29] Arguing against these conclusions, other scholars insist that democracy *does* make a difference when it comes to promoting growth; it just takes longer for some democracies to produce positive economic results than Przeworski and his colleagues assume.[30]

What about the economy's effects on democracy? Aren't poor countries less likely to create or sustain democracy than rich ones? Chapter 2 provides data relating levels of wealth to varying degrees of democracy and authoritarianism. As the tables in Chapter 2 show, the lower we go down the economic pyramid, the less often we encounter democracy. Nevertheless, even countries with very low levels of per capita income—like India—are capable of building and sustaining democracy, as we shall see below.[31]

Amartya Sen underscores the relationship between economic development and democracy with particular forcefulness. In *Development as Freedom*, the Nobel Prize-winning economist redefines the very concept of development in terms of the value of freedom. Instead of focusing exclusively on such economic measures as gross domestic product or per capita income, Sen argues, development should be seen as a process for promoting various kinds of freedom, such as the freedom to live a long and healthy life, the freedom to participate in political and social activities, and the freedom to enjoy educational and cultural opportunities. Sen places human *agency*, centered on the individual as the key "agent" of action and change, at the heart of the development process. Expanding individual freedom is both the principal *means* of promoting development as well as the principal *purpose* of development. The best way to stimulate development, in Sen's view, is to remove the various "unfreedoms" that prevent individuals from realizing their full potential: dictatorship, excessive state controls over the economy, unemployment, inadequate educational facilities, the repression of women, and so on. When people are freed of these constraints, they will expand these and other freedoms all the more. "The people have to be seen as being actively involved in their own destiny," Sen insists. Sen's freedom-based approach to development has directly influenced *human development theory*, as discussed in Chapter 9, as well as the creation of the United Nations Development Program's human development index (HDI), the primary alternative measure to GNI per capita as a way to rank countries' economic progress.[32]

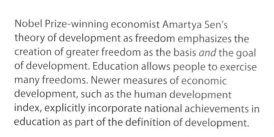

Nobel Prize-winning economist Amartya Sen's theory of development as freedom emphasizes the creation of greater freedom as the basis *and* the goal of development. Education allows people to exercise many freedoms. Newer measures of economic development, such as the human development index, explicitly incorporate national achievements in education as part of the definition of development.

Ultimately, no single variable neatly explains underdevelopment, nor is there a single "one size fits all" cure for it. Endemic poverty and economic stagnation have a multiplicity of causes, and their elimination will require concerted efforts on multiple fronts. Political, economic, social, cultural, environmental, medical, and other modes of attack must all be pressed simultaneously. These tasks are both doable and—for the rich countries of the world—affordable. A commitment on the part of citizens in both the developing world and the developed countries to support effective actions is needed, as well as bold decisions by their governments to make them work. In every country, economic development requires political choices.

To people in the rich countries of the Global North, no other country has framed the challenge of development in the way India has. China and India together form 45 percent of the developing world's population. A far more open society than China was for most of the post-World War II period, India's attempts to promote economic development while maintaining its democratic regime have been wide open to the world's scrutiny. For many decades India seemed mired in poverty and underdevelopment even while sustaining democracy. In the past two decades India has apparently broken out of its stagnation. Today it is one of the most dynamic economies in the Global South, and one of its largest. Along with Brazil, China, Russia and South Africa, India is one of the five BRICS (after the first letter of the five countries' names), the largest of the emerging economies that together have 40 percent of the world's population, 20 percent of its economic output, and 25 percent of its landmass.[33]

INDIA: POLITICS IN THE QUINTESSENTIAL DEVELOPING COUNTRY

"At the stroke of midnight, while the world sleeps, India will awake to life and freedom." With those words, Jawaharlal Nehru proclaimed India's independence on August 15, 1947, after centuries of foreign domination.

As independent India's first prime minister, Nehru (1889–1964) inherited the world's second most populous nation after China. Nearly 350 million people formed a vast mosaic of religions, languages, classes, and castes, squeezed into an area only about a third the size of the United States. Before independence, the country consisted of more than 500 states and subdivisions, most with their own distinct traditions and social patterns. Out of this tangled human web, Nehru was determined to shape the structures of an enduring democracy and lay the groundwork for steady economic development.

The challenge was daunting. India's freedom was accompanied by fierce bloodletting between its two largest religious groups, Hindus and Muslims. The confrontation was the result of the breakup of British India into two separate states, India and Pakistan.

After gaining their first foothold in India in 1614, the British gradually extended their domain on the South Asian subcontinent over the course of the seventeenth and eighteenth centuries, ousting Portuguese, French, and Dutch settlers in the process. In 1858, when it officially became a crown colony, British India extended from the borders of Iran and Afghanistan in the north to the southern tip of the subcontinent, opposite the island of Ceylon (now Sri Lanka), another British possession.

Throughout these centuries, the British were at best tolerated but never fully accepted by the population as the legitimate rulers of India. In 1885, a small group of nationalists formed the Indian National Congress, an organization intended to give Indians a greater say in their own affairs and, eventually, freedom. For the next several decades the Congress was largely ineffectual, its membership confined to the country's urbanized, educated elite and its small middle-class following. When Mohandas Gandhi (1869–1948) became the organization's leader, however, the Congress took on the character of a surging mass movement rooted in India's populous rural villages.

As a young lawyer, Gandhi had worked in South Africa, using Western legal concepts and his own doctrine of *satyagraha* (moral persuasion) in an effort to obtain civil rights and racial justice for the country's Indian minority. After returning to India in 1915, Gandhi began employing the same techniques of persuasion and nonviolent agitation to rouse India's masses against British rule. He organized several demonstrative campaigns of civil disobedience in the 1920s and 1930s, including his famous salt march, a 240-mile trek to the Indian Ocean, where he clutched a handful of salt in defiance of British regulations requiring payment of a salt tax. Gandhi was arrested, and the event became an international sensation. Over the next 17 years, Gandhi stood out as the charismatic political and spiritual leader of India's impoverished masses and an inspiration throughout the world to oppressed groups seeking to overcome domination through nonviolent means. His followers called him *Mahatma* (Great Soul).

Although a devout Hindu, Gandhi believed strongly in religious tolerance and the national unity of India's diverse peoples. He had no desire to see British India partitioned into separate

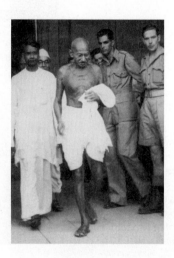

Mohandas Gandhi led India's quest for independence from Great Britain.

states after independence. Islamic leaders led by Mohammed Ali Jinnah (1876–1948), however, insisted on the formation of a separate state composed mainly of Muslims. The British authorities agreed. After intensive negotiations it was decided to partition Punjab and Bengal, two northern provinces located 900 miles apart. Each was divided roughly evenly into Muslim and Hindu populations. Portions of these provinces were split off from India to form the new state of Pakistan. A part of Punjab became West Pakistan and a part of Bengal became East Pakistan (now Bangladesh). The border regions of Kashmir and Jammu were also divided, and the boundary line is still hotly contested. The partition plan resulted in the uprooting of more than 10 million people, as Hindus moved to the Indian side of the border and Muslims moved to Pakistan. Periodic outbursts of violence between the two groups in 1947 and 1948 resulted in hundreds of thousands of casualties. Gandhi himself was assassinated by Hindu fanatics infuriated at his efforts to accommodate the Muslims.[34]

Following these unpropitious beginnings, Nehru focused his attention on the political and economic modernization of India. An ardent nationalist and a descendant of the country's select Brahmin caste, Nehru had spent seven years in Britain, where he was educated at Harrow and Cambridge University and admitted to London's prestigious Inns of Court. Although determined to win India's freedom from British rule, he was a great admirer of Western democracy and socialist conceptions of economic justice. He presided over the adoption of India's 1950 constitution, which adopted British-style parliamentary democracy.

Succeeding Gandhi as the leading figure in the Indian National Congress, Nehru helped shape the organization into a political party capable of representing not only India's elites and middle class but also its poor, uneducated masses. Under his guidance, the secular, centrist *Congress Party* quickly dominated India's emerging political system. Aided by a single-member-district/plurality electoral system, the Congress Party from 1952 to 1967 converted a popular vote ranging from 45 percent to 48 percent of the ballots into control of about 75 percent of the seats in the House of the People (Lok Sabha), the lower house of the national parliament. (It got roughly similar shares in the 1980s.) In these years the Congress Party evolved into a large grassroots movement as well as the principal party of government at the national level. Its success appeared to be just what Huntington would have ordered for a country in the throes of modernization: an effective political organization responsive to the newly mobilized masses. Nehru's charismatic leadership and the Congress Party's early dominance helped legitimize India's democratic system among a majority of its citizens. Voter turnout for national elections has averaged about 60 percent of eligible voters since the 1960s.[35]

But neither Nehru nor the party was able to resolve India's two most haunting problems: the immense scope of its economic underdevelopment and the potential explosiveness of its social and regional diversity. Either of these challenges would be enough to keep democracy at bay, or destroy it, in most any other country.

Economic Development

Two years after Nehru's death in 1964, India faced a severe food shortage that compelled the government to appeal to the outside world for immediate assistance. India remained dependent on food imports until 1978. Since then the country has been relatively self-sufficient in food supplies despite a burgeoning population. Nevertheless, the challenge of eradicating poverty has not been surmounted. The Nehru government's economic strategy of achieving self-sustained growth through a combination of private enterprise and government planning yielded some significant gains in national income, but it set India on a course of import substitution and escalating government involvement in the economy that led to waste and inefficiency.[36] For decades, India's industrial growth rates lagged behind those of other developing countries, such as China, South Korea, and Mexico. Early plans to revitalize the agricultural economy were never seriously implemented. India's rural villages, where 70 percent of the population still resides, remain much more impoverished than urban India.

Inspired by the economic growth of the inward-looking Soviet Union, India under the Congress Party pursued an economic development strategy that aspired to a local version of socialism and emphasized government planning of the economy (India used five-year plans, like the Soviet Union, explained further in Chapter 16), state-owned enterprises, and extensive regulation of business. India essentially had a mixed economy (see Chapter 11). This period of Indian economic history is sometimes called the "License Raj," a play on the name often given to the period of imperial rule, the "British Raj." The License Raj involved the imposition of many regulations on private business, especially the requirement of government licenses for those who wished to engage in particular types of manufacturing or commerce, and the red tape that went along with it. Not surprisingly, such bureaucratic oversight encouraged the emergence of corruption, for which the License Raj was famous. Economic growth during this period of inward-oriented development was very modest, averaging increases of a little more than 1 percent of GDP per capita annually.

In the mid-1960s, farmers in India began planting the high-yielding grain varieties associated with the green revolution. Whereas Indian agricultural productivity had been largely stagnant, the green revolution allowed a significant increase in the production of wheat and rice from the mid-1960s onward. India became self-sufficient in these staple grains, even exporting rice. The increased output of grain associated with the green revolution and the consolidation of Indian democracy have allowed independent India to avoid what had occurred frequently in its own history: famine. As Amartya Sen argues, no democracy has suffered famine.[37] While India struggled to achieve its modest economic growth rate in the 1950s through 1980s but managed to avoid famine, China suffered the famine associated with the "Great Leap Forward" (see Chapter 17), and famines hit Ethiopia, Sudan, and other countries of the Sahel in northern Africa. Millions had died in India itself during terrible famines in 1876–78, 1899–1900, and 1943 during British rule of the subcontinent, but independent, democratic India avoided that fate.

India's slow growth under socialism and the License Raj, along with political instability we will mention below, eventually produced a balance of payments crisis in the late 1980s that led India to accept an IMF bailout plan in 1991. That agreement, made by the minority Congress-led government of Prime Minister P. V. N. Rao and his finance minister, Manmohan Singh, who is currently prime minister, began the dismantling of the inward-looking economic development model. Economic reforms reduced government regulation, encouraged direct foreign investment, and began the privatization of government-owned enterprises. In response, the Indian economy surged, with GDP per capita nearly doubling in the 1990s. In the past decade the Indian economy has achieved economic growth rates approaching 10 percent annually.

Much foreign investment that entered India in the 1990s and after concentrated in the high-technology sector and what is sometimes called "business process outsourcing." Investors capitalized on the presence in India of many highly educated English speakers to develop the call centers that Americans have come to know well. In addition, because its time zone means that day in India corresponds to night in Europe and North America, computer programmers and systems analysts in India can continue the work of their colleagues in Europe or North America in a continuous 24-hour cycle. These developments have led to significant advancement for the highly educated in India, but less opportunity for those who are not educated. Education in India is highly unequal, and that social imbalance in education along with the economic opportunities occasioned by economic liberalization is leading to increased income inequality.[38]

Social Pluralism

Intense social divisions provide a continuing source of political conflict. Socioeconomic divisions are one source of turmoil, but cleavages along religious, ethnolinguistic, and caste lines play an important role also.

Today's India is still a predominantly Hindu country: 81 percent of the population adheres to this ancient faith. Muslims comprise about 13 percent of the populace. Even after the partition of British India in 1947–48, some 50 million Muslims remained in India; today they number about 150 million. Approximately 2 percent of Indians are Sikhs, the adherents of a Hindu sect that branched off from traditional Hinduism some 500 years ago. Christians of various denominations comprise 2.4 percent of the population, and a host of other religions have smaller groups of followers.

Ethnolinguistic distinctions are even more abundant. Though Hindi and English are the main official languages, the constitution recognizes 14 other official languages. There are 24 languages spoken by at least a million people each, and over 1,600 dialects. These divisions lead to considerable regional diversity and fragmentation. India's federal structure now consists of 28 states and seven union territories, and local

distinctions within these subdivisions abound. Separatist movements have flared up in Punjab (with its large Sikh population), Assam and Nagaland in the northeast, in the largely Muslim border areas of Kashmir and Jammu, and elsewhere. Communal violence involving Hindus, Muslims, Sikhs, ethnic and tribal groupings, and ideologically motivated guerrilla movements have shaken India's democracy from its foundations to the present.[39]

The ties of caste also exert a profoundly divisive effect on Indian society, even though Nehru's government abolished the caste system in legal terms. With deep roots in Hindu cosmology, more than a thousand castes still exist, separated by doctrines and traditions that forbid contact between members of specified castes. A prevailing hierarchy differentiates higher castes from lower ones, with millions relegated to the lowest caste, the untouchables, a group Gandhi sought to dignify by calling them *harijans* (children of God).

Thus far, India's democracy has proved sufficiently resilient to withstand the acute challenges posed by these economic and social realities. Maintaining democratic procedures and political stability has been a challenge, however.

Political Dynamics

The Congress Party dominated Indian national politics so thoroughly in the first three decades of independence that political scientists sometimes called India a predominant party system, meaning that one party dominated even though competitive elections with multiple parties took place.[40] That predominance lasted until 1977, as Figure 12.2 shows. While policy challenges associated with India's relatively stagnant economy played some role in the decline of the party's predominance, political mistakes by Congress Party leaders in India's highly pluralist society have at times proven to be the party's undoing.

In 1966 Nehru's daughter, Indira Gandhi (1917–84, who was no relation to Mohandas Gandhi), became prime minister. Three years later, deep divisions within the Congress Party over policy issues and personalities split the organization into two parties, one loyal to Mrs. Gandhi and the other opposed to her. Prime Minister Gandhi used her control over political patronage to build a new Congress Party concerned mainly with winning elections rather than serving as the country's prime force for national political integration, as it had in the past.

Meanwhile, long-standing tensions with Pakistan reached a boiling point. In 1971, as 10 million refugees streamed into India in an attempt to flee a civil war, Prime Minister Gandhi ordered the Indian army into East Pakistan to put a decisive end to Pakistani control of the area. The Pakistani army quickly surrendered, and with India's blessing, East Pakistan became an independent country, Bangladesh.

On the heels of this triumph, Prime Minister Gandhi and her Congress Party allies won a smashing victory at the polls. In 1975, however, a court invalidated the 1971 elections on the grounds that civil servants had openly aided Mrs. Gandhi's reelection campaign in violation of the constitution. Besieged with demands for her resignation, the prime minister

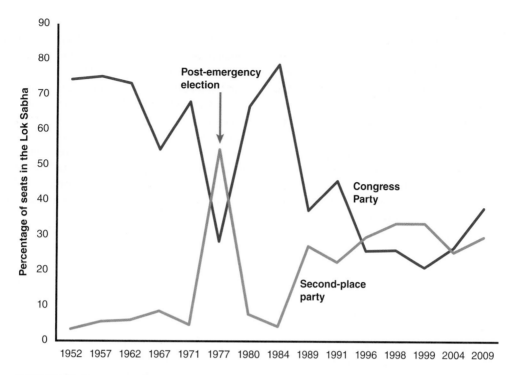

FIGURE 12.2 **Shares of the Seats in the House of the People, Indian Congress Party and Second-Place Party since 1952**

Source: Adam Carr's Election Archive, psephos.adam-carr.net.

instead declared a state of emergency and suspended normal democratic procedures. She had her chief political opponents arrested and imposed strict censorship on the press. Two years of repressive emergency rule followed. India's fragile democracy appeared finished.

Under intense pressure, Mrs. Gandhi lifted the state of emergency in 1977 and allowed parliamentary elections. Her Congress Party was soundly defeated, garnering only 34 percent of the vote and a mere 28 percent of parliamentary seats. But the new government of M. R. Desai's Janata Dal Party did not last long. With an emotional appeal to India's masses, Mrs. Gandhi led the Congress Party to a decisive comeback. In 1980, her party won two-thirds of the seats in the lower house.

Religious tensions reached new heights in 1984 when Sikh militants demanding greater autonomy for the state of Punjab ensconced themselves in the Golden Temple, a sacred Sikh shrine, and began using it as a base for terrorist operations. Mrs. Gandhi dispatched the Indian army to dislodge the terrorists; more than a thousand Sikhs lost their lives in the raid. The tragedy created an outpouring of resentment among India's 14 million Sikhs. Several months later, Prime Minister Gandhi was assassinated by two Sikh bodyguards. An organized massacre of Sikhs in New Delhi ensued.[41]

The Congress Party then named Indira's son, Rajiv, as prime minister. Rajiv led the party to an impressive electoral victory later in the year. From the outset, however, his government was plagued by mounting sectarian violence in Punjab. Rajiv Gandhi also failed to heal festering divisions within the Congress Party, which became increasingly factionalized. His

efforts to reduce the heavy hand of the government in India's economy also fizzled. By 1985, central government expenditures amounted to more than 35 percent of GNP, up from about 19 percent in 1960. Elections in 1989 swept the Congress Party from power in the aftermath of a kickback scandal, but the next two prime ministers could not establish a stable base of power in the divided parliament. Fresh elections were ordered in 1991, and during a campaign appearance, Rajiv Gandhi was assassinated by Tamils linked to Sri Lankan guerrilla movements. Tamil resentments at the Indian government stemmed from India's unsuccessful military intervention in Sri Lanka several years earlier as well as from ethnic animosities in the southern Indian province of Tamil Nadhu, where the Tamil population was a source of resistance to central government authorities.

The next prime minister, P. V. N. Rao, formed a new Congress Party-led government following the elections. As described above, one of Rao's principal ambitions was to reduce the state's role in the economy by promoting an extensive privatization program, a policy initiative that many now regard as the beginning of the Indian economy's recent economic surge. Meanwhile, however, India's smoldering religious tensions erupted once again as more than 150,000 Hindu fundamentalists demolished a sixteenth-century mosque cherished by Muslims, claiming that it occupied a holy Hindu site. The incident, occurring in the town of Ayodhya, was inspired by the rightist *India People's Party (Bharatiya Janata Party,* or *BJP),* a stridently pro-Hindu organization. Some 1,700 people were killed as sporadic confrontations between Hindus and Muslims flared up over the next two weeks. Anti-Muslim violence in Bombay and elsewhere in early 1993 produced an additional thousand casualties. Corruption scandals aggravated Rao's difficulties, along with persistent unemployment and inflation. In the 1996 parliamentary elections the Congress Party suffered a major defeat, with the BJP winning a plurality of seats in the Lok Sabha but not enough to form a government on its own.

The remaining years of the decade witnessed a succession of weak minority governments. In the 1996 elections, the Congress Party's share of seats fell from 47.5 percent to 25.7 percent, rising only to 30.1 percent in the snap elections of 1998. The BJP and its allies raised their share from 21.5 percent in 1991 to 35.4 percent in 1996 and 46.2 percent in 1998. Following the 1998 elections, a BJP-led minority government was formed under Atal Bihari Vajpayee, a moderate in a party noted for its fanatical pro-Hindu attitudes. Vajpayee backed away from the BJP's earlier pledges to build a Hindu temple on the site of the old Ayodhya mosque, but he sought to awaken national pride through a series of nuclear weapons tests several months after taking office. The underground explosions provoked Pakistan into conducting its own nuclear tests and prompted considerable international concern at the prospect of a nuclear confrontation between the two archrivals. Conflicts over Kashmir, most of which is in India, intensified these tensions, and fighting broke out in the summer of 1999 as Pakistani troops invaded the area. Despite India's internal political turmoil, its army evicted the intruders.

In 1999 Vajpayee's multiparty minority government fell apart and lost a vote of confidence. Because no new governing coalition could be stitched together, Indian voters were called to the polls for the third time in as many years. As its new leader the Congress Party chose Sonia Gandhi, Rajiv's widow and an Italian by birth. The choice was roundly criticized by numerous opponents of the Congress Party, and even some Congress members questioned the appropriateness of selecting a non-Indian female as the country's potential next prime minister. "Every drop of my blood says this is my country," Gandhi replied. The elections were spread out over four weeks and provoked sporadic outbursts of violence; more than 300 people were killed in campaign-related incidents. Only half the eligible electorate voted, an unusually low turnout. When the vote counting was over, Vajpayee and his coalition partners had managed to win a plurality of seats in India's Lok Sabha. But with only a third of the total, they fell far short of a majority. Both the BJP-led coalition and the Congress Party lost seats, while several regional parties, reflecting the enormous importance of local issues in Indian politics, increased their share of votes in parliament. The final result was an even more fractionated lower house than before the elections. Vajpayee, reelected prime minister, formed a government consisting of the BJP and 21 smaller parties.

Despite the defection of one of its coalition partners and several defeats in local elections, Vajpayee's BJP managed to hold the government together in the face of explosive Hindu–Muslim violence and another dangerous confrontation with Pakistan. In February 2002, a train carrying Hindu extremists was set ablaze in Godha, in the western Indian state of Gujarat; more than 50 people were killed. The fire, allegedly set by a Muslim mob, incited Hindu attacks on Muslim neighborhoods, businesses, and mosques. About 2,000 were killed and 100,000 were rendered homeless as local officials and the Gujarat state government, dominated by the BJP, actively cooperated with Hindu extremist groups in organizing the rampage. At the end of the year Gujarat's BJP, campaigning for reelection with a stridently anti-Muslim message, won an overwhelming majority in the state legislature. Tensions with Pakistan escalated in December 2001 when Muslim terrorists fighting for control of the Indian parts of Kashmir, where Muslims are in the majority, staged a raid on India's national parliament. India held Pakistan responsible for failing to rein in terrorist groups based on its territory, and Vajpayee's government placed its troops on high alert. A military standoff between the two nuclear-armed countries lasted for several months before diplomatic intervention and fears of an all-out war calmed the situation.

The foregoing chronicle indicates that India's pluralism has put its political stability to the test. One way in which this is manifested is the decline of national-level parties and the rise of state parties (see Figure 12.3). Only six parties are now regarded as national parties—Congress; its splinter, the Indian National Congress; the BJP; Bahujan Samaj Party (BSP), a party formed to represent Scheduled Castes, an Indian term for those castes eligible for affirmative action; and the Communist Party of India and the Communist Party of India (Marxist), two separate, although aligned, communist parties. The remaining parties—more than 200 of which postulated candidates in the 2004 general elections—operate at the state level, although some are active in two or three states.

In anticipation of gaining a third straight electoral victory, Prime Minister Vajpayee called snap elections a few months ahead of schedule in 2004. To his surprise, his BJP party lost more than 40 seats in the House of the People and his allies dropped more than 50. Despite record economic growth of about 8 percent, two-thirds of the voters in India's heavily populated villages were dissatisfied with the government's efforts to improve their conditions. The winner of the three-week electoral contest was the Congress Party, which staged a major comeback under Sonia Gandhi's leadership. Before the elections, Congress had joined with several smaller parties in forming the United Progressive Alliance (UPA). The Congress Party won 145 seats outright, and its partners won 73 seats (see Table 12.6). Vajpayee's BJP won 138 seats, and allied parties won 43. Although the United Progressive Alliance held only about 40 percent of the seats, it was able to form a minority government with the support of India's Communist Party and a collection of smaller parties that agreed to vote with the UPA on most bills.

Shortly after the final vote tallies came in, Sonia Gandhi stunned India by announcing that she would not become prime minister. Cognizant of the opposition within the country, and even within her own party, to having a foreign-born woman lead India, Gandhi stepped aside to allow Manmohan Singh, a respected Congress Party leader, to take the premiership. An economist with degrees from Cambridge and Oxford, Singh had played a critical role in Rao's Congress Party government in the 1990s, masterminding the government's economic

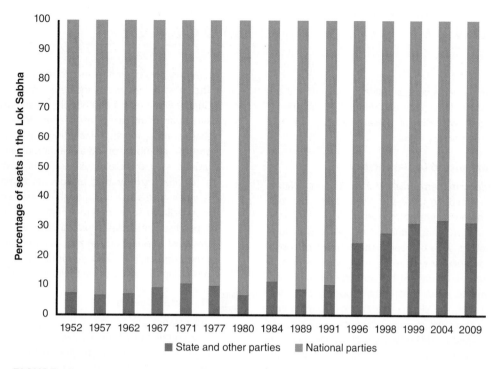

FIGURE 12.3   The Rise of State-Level Parties in India

Source: K. C. Suri, *Parties under Pressure: Political Parties in India since Independence* (New Delhi: Centre for the Study of Developing Societies, 2006).

liberalization program. Singh was also India's first Sikh to head the government. Singh put together a coalition government that counted more than 20 parties. The relatively booming Indian economy helped Singh win reelection in 2009, as the Congress Party gained seats while the BJP and its allies lost ground.

The Congress Party continues to govern, but governing India, with its complex, pluralistic society and the continuing challenges of development, is far from easy.

Table 12.6 India's House of the People (Lok Sabha), 2004 and 2009 (543 seats)

Parties	2004		2009	
	Seats	% of Seats	Seats	% of Seats
United Progressive Alliance				
Congress Party	145	28.4%	206	38.0%
Other UPA	73	13.4	56	10.3
Left Front (2004) / Third Front (2009) (Communist Party and others)	59	10.9	79	14.5
National Democratic Alliance				
BJP	138	25.4	116	21.4
Others	43	7.9	43	7.9
Other parties	85	15.7	43	7.9

Source: Adam Carr's Election Archive, psephos.adam-carr.net.

Manmohan Singh, who became prime minister in 2004, introduced economic reforms to reduce government regulation when he was finance minister in the 1990s.

10 CONDITIONS FOR DEMOCRACY

India

How do India's experiences match up against the ten conditions for democracy enumerated in Chapter 7? Let's explore how each of these conditions has had impact on democracy in India.

1 Elites Committed to Democracy

The creators of modern India—Mahatma Gandhi, Nehru, and their immediate successors—were uniformly committed to democracy, as were most of those leading the country's major ethnolinguistic and religious groups. Arend Lijphart, who pioneered the concept of consociational democracy with respect to countries torn by social strife (see Chapter 5), has argued that the consociational model, which stresses the importance of power sharing among the elites representing the main conflicting social groups, explains why democracy survived in India despite its diversity. Lijphart argues that even when India was governed under the Congress Party's large parliamentary majorities, key elements of the consociational model were present.[42]

While consociational power sharing has diminished since the 1960s, and while Indira Gandhi suspended democracy in the 1970s, the elites who have dominated India's political parties, social groups, and the military for most of the post-1947 period have not been willing to replace democracy with a nondemocratic system.

2 State Institutions

India appears to be saddled with insurmountable weaknesses in its institutional structures. Fissiparous tendencies rooted in the country's ethnolinguistic and religious heterogeneity are institutionalized in its federal system and exacerbated by separatist movements. Extensive official corruption eats away at public support for state officials and politicians, as do persistent inefficiency and ineffectiveness at all levels of government. Police and military personnel routinely abuse their authority, engaging in torture, rape, "disappearances," and murder against insurgents, Muslims, Sikhs, members of the lower castes, women detainees, and other victims.

Yet the central government has managed to hold India's explosive parts together without civil war or the outright secession of any of its states. Most important, the electoral process retains an enduring legitimacy in the eyes of most Indians. Political life is lively at the state and local levels; elite and mass support for democracy is widespread. The traditions of parliamentary government adapted from Britain remain intact.

3 National Unity

Obviously, India is the very opposite of a homogeneous society. Communal violence flares up on occasion as tensions persist among India's religious communities. The most recent major incident occurred in 2002 in Gujarat when over 1,000 people, mostly Muslims, were killed and many places of worship desecrated. Nevertheless, most Indians—including millions of Muslims and the members of India's numerous ethnolinguistic groups—still think of India as a single state, sharing a national identity that bridges its myriad divisions. A widely held sense of national unity thus coexists with extraordinary social heterogeneity, religious strife, and separatist tendencies. Most Indians see democracy as the most effective way to keep national unity intact by preventing civil war and permitting the country's various groups to have a say in their own destiny.[43]

4 National Wealth

India stands out as one of the chief exceptions to the rule correlating national poverty with nondemocratic regimes. With a per capita gross national income (GNI) of a mere $1,410 in 2011, India is one of the poorer countries in the world. In 2009, 69 percent of the country's population was living on less than $2 a day, and 32 percent were subsisting on less than $1.25 a day. At the same time, its GNI per capita grew at an average annual rate of 6.9 percent from 2003 to 2010, an impressive result.

India's annual population growth is 1.5 percent. Even if the economy expands by more than 5 percent a year through 2050, per capita GNI will still be low. Moreover, the economic gains from globalization have been highly concentrated in certain states and urban areas, particularly in the south.[44] The northern states tend to languish in extreme poverty. India's economy thus combines pockets of dynamism with massive poverty. Although poverty of this magnitude would seem to be highly inconsistent with democracy, it has not unleashed a mass outpouring of support for nondemocratic solutions to the country's economic problems.

5 Private Enterprise

Efforts to promote private enterprise intensified in the 1990s. Since then, private-sector development has been quite vibrant. A number of government-owned firms have been privatized, and investment in India's stock market has swelled. India has acquired a global reputation as a hub of software production and outsourced services, such as call-center services, but such businesses employ less than 1 percent of India's workforce. Barriers to private-sector development remain, obstructing foreign investment. Nevertheless, neither the persistence of state interventionism nor the uneven growth of private-sector development appears to have affected Indian democracy in any negative way.

6 The Middle Class

India's middle class is estimated at about 5 percent of the population. In a country with 1.26 billion people, that's a sizable number (about 60 million), and it's growing very rapidly. In conformity with our expectations, the Indian middle class has provided a large and consistent bloc of support for democracy. To be sure, many middle-class Indians are gripped by the same ethnolinguistic and religious fervor that characterizes large elements of the population, but the overwhelming majority of them appear to favor democracy over authoritarian rule.[45]

7 Support of the Disadvantaged for Democracy

If endemic poverty is to constitute a serious threat to democracy, the masses must be mobilized against it. Thus far, however, no mass political movement has managed to whip up an organized protest of the poor against democracy. On the contrary, political activism is increasingly energized in many of the all-important states in India's federal system.

Although millions of Indian women have made great strides in getting educated and pursuing careers, millions of others are severely disadvantaged, particularly in areas where local authorities turn a blind eye to flagrant abuses. Dowries are outlawed, but thousands of women every year are immolated, beaten, or driven to suicide in dowry disputes. Rapes and other violent offenses are often unreported or ignored by police and judicial officials. Male births inordinately outnumber female births in several states, no doubt because of abortion and infanticide aimed at girls. Gender inequality is thus both a source of flagrant human rights abuses and an obstacle to economic development. To remedy these problems, though, politically active Indian women have demanded more democracy, not less.[46]

In most cases, apathy and resignation, rather than revolutionary unrest, mark the political attitudes of India's destitute masses. The simple struggle to survive leaves little time to care about elections and party programs. While support for democracy may not be the consequence, there is little in the way of mass opposition to it, either.

8 Citizen Participation, Civil Society, and a Democratic Political Culture

In a country as variegated as India, torn by so many unresolved conflicts, it should not be surprising to find that a thriving civil society shares the social landscape with a notoriously uncivil, violence-prone society. India has an estimated 1 million nongovernmental organizations. Women's rights groups are proliferating, and human rights organizations have also become more active. Trade unions are organized and energetic. And civil society has played an especially important role in

An estimated 1 million nongovernmental organizations (NGOs) in India address the countless conflicts that exist within the diverse and violence-prone Indian society. NGOs address many sectors within Indian society, including education.

(Continued on next page)

(Continued from previous page)

curbing Hindu–Muslim violence. Ashutosh Varshney has shown that associational civic groups with mixed Hindu and Muslim memberships—business associations, labor unions, and the like—are often quite effective at halting communal violence in various cities before it gets out of hand.[47] India's experiences with civil society are therefore very mixed: Some non-state organizations exist mainly to exacerbate conflict, thereby undermining democracy, while others seek to reduce conflict in a democratic spirit.

9 Education and Freedom of Information

Here, too, India's record is a tangle of contradictions. The country can boast millions of college graduates and recipients of graduate and professional degrees. Advanced technology and MBA programs are proliferating. Many college grads remain unemployed for years, however. Illiteracy is a mass phenomenon, affecting one-fifth of males over age 15 and more than one-third of females.[48]

India's press freedoms are secure; national and local newspapers and magazines thrive. Journalists have been physically attacked for their political views, however. The Indian government holds a monopoly on domestic television broadcasting, but foreign-based networks have been allowed to broadcast in recent years. Radio and television stations are mostly in private hands, but All India Radio dominates the airwaves. There are no Internet restrictions.

10 A Favorable International Environment

India's external environment is also a source of both negative and positive influences on its democratic order. Its tormented relationship with Pakistan inevitably has an impact on the delicate ties between Hindus and Muslims in India itself. India has a long-standing border conflict with China, but relations between the two neighboring giants have been improving. Overall, though, India's international environment appears to pose no threat to its democracy.[49]

In 2012 India had Freedom House ratings of 2 for political rights and 3 for civil rights. What is most striking is that several of the factors that we tend to think of as potentially crippling for democratic governance—such as ubiquitous poverty, violence-prone social heterogeneity, and vast numbers of grievously disadvantaged people—have not combined to smother democracy in India. On the contrary, a commitment to democratic ideals and practices is powerful throughout the country. Amartya Sen argues that India's conflicting cultural and intellectual traditions are the very sources of its tolerance for diversity and its widely shared commitment to democracy.[50]

Conclusion

Countries in the developing world have faced their share of challenges over the past half century and more. Many have made significant progress in improving the lot of their people, none more than South Korea. The developing world is a complex place and its experiences and challenges cannot be easily summarized, however. The difficulties in generating self-sustaining growth in sub-Saharan Africa are compounded by political weaknesses; it is not coincidental that the impoverished societies of that region are governed (or frequently, not) by many of the states highest on the failed state index (see Table 3.1). Many of those same countries have found it nearly impossible to generate a sense of national identity (see Chapter 19 for a discussion of Nigeria and South Africa). The states in the NICs, in contrast, are often among the strongest and most able to promote national unity (China and South Korea are prominent

examples). Given that many societies in the developing world are governed by weak states and lack a sense of national purpose, it is not surprising that they continue to struggle to improve the lives of their people. Those same societies have not found much success introducing democracy. India is an important exception that demonstrates that democracy can survive difficult economic conditions, and the critical case that indicates that development and democracy do not always go together.

Key Terms

Third World (or the Global South)
Newly industrializing countries (NICs)
Underdeveloped economies
Modernization theory
Decolonization
Neocolonialism (neo-imperialism)
Import-substituting industrialization (ISI)
Dependency theory

Notes

1. On South Korea, see Sung-Joo Han, "South Korea: Politics in Transition," in *Politics in Developing Countries*, ed. Larry Diamond, Juan J. Linz, and Seymour Martin Lipset (Boulder, CO: Lynne Rienner, 1990), pp. 313–50; Stephan Haggard, *Pathways from the Periphery* (Ithaca, NY: Cornell University Press, 1990), pp. 51–75, 130–38; Nigel Harris, *The End of the Third World* (London: Penguin, 1986), pp. 31–45; Robert Garran, *Tigers Tamed* (Honolulu: University of Hawaii Press, 1998), pp. 119–36; Dennis L. McNamara, ed., *Corporatism and Korean Capitalism* (London: Routledge, 1999); *The Kwangju Uprising*, Henry Scott-Stokes and Jai Eui, eds. (Armonk, NY: M. E. Sharpe, 2000).

2. The poverty statistics are calculated with PovcalNet, the World Bank's online poverty analysis tool, available at http://iresearch.worldbank.org/PovcalNet/index.htm.

3. *Human Development Report 2005* (New York: United Nations Development Program, 2005), pp. 1–48, passim.

4. See W. W. Rostow, *The Stages of Economic Growth*, 3rd ed. (Cambridge: Cambridge University Press, 1990).

5. *Human Development Report 2005*, pp. 19–21, 40–45; *The Millennium Development Goals Report 2011* (New York: United Nations, 2011).

6. For an overview, see John Rapley, *Understanding Development: Theory and Practice in the Third World*, 3rd ed. (Boulder, CO: Lynne Rienner, 2007); Howard Handelman, *The Challenge of Third World Development*, 6th ed. (New York: Longman, 2010).

7. This phenomenon was originally highlighted by Amartya Sen, "The Economics of Life and Death," *Scientific American*, May 1993, pp. 40–47; Amartya Sen, "Demography and Welfare Economics," *Empirica*, no. 22 (1995), pp. 1–27. Since the early 1990s the African-American life expectancy has improved dramatically but remains below that of several developing countries.

8. Mara Hvistendahl, *Unnatural Selection: Choosing Boys Over Girls, and the Consequences of a World Full of Men* (New York: PublicAffairs, 2011).

9. Daniel Lerner, *The Passing of Traditional Society* (New York: Free Press, 1958); David E. Apter, *The Politics of Modernization* (Chicago: University of Chicago Press, 1965); Cyril E. Black, ed., *Comparative Modernization: A Reader* (New York: Free Press, 1976).

10. For a critical appraisal, see Irene L. Gendzier, *Managing Political Change: Social Scientists and the Third World* (Boulder, CO: Westview, 1985). An early study that recognized a mixture of the traditional and the modern in developing countries is Gabriel A. Almond and James S. Coleman, eds., *The Politics of the Developing Areas* (Princeton, NJ: Princeton University Press, 1960).

11. Atul Kohli, *State-Directed Development: Political Power and Industrialization in the Global Periphery* (New York: Cambridge University Press, 2004).

12. Jeffrey Sachs, *The End of Poverty. Economic Possibilities for Our Time* (New York: Penguin, 2005), pp. 57–59, 188–209, 311–28.

13. Raúl Prebisch, *The Economic Development of Latin America and Its Principal Problems* (New York: United Nations, 1950); Joseph L. Love, "Raul Prebisch and the Origins of the Doctrine of Unequal Exchange," *Latin American Research Review* 15, no. 3 (1980); Mahbub ul Haq, *The Poverty Curtain: Choices for the Third World* (New York: Columbia University Press, 1976).

14. For examples of dependency theory see Fernando Henrique Cardoso and Enzo Faletto, *Dependency and Development in Latin America*, trans. Marjory Mattingly Urquidi (Berkeley, CA: University of California Press, 1979); André Gunder Frank, *Capitalism and Underdevelopment in Latin America* (London: Penguin, 1970); André Gunder Frank, *Critique and Anti-Critique* (New York: Praeger, 1971). On the capitalist world system, see Immanuel Wallerstein, *The Capitalist World-Economy* (Cambridge: Cambridge University Press, 1979); Immanuel Wallerstein, *The Politics of the World-Economy* (Cambridge: Cambridge University Press, 1984). For review essays, see James A. Caporoso, "Dependency Theory: Continuities and Discontinuities in Development Studies," *International Organization* 34, no. 4 (autumn 1980), pp. 605–28; Tony Smith, "Requiem or New Agenda for Third World Studies?" *World Politics* 37, no. 4 (July 1985), pp. 532–61.

15. National Science Board, *Science and Engineering Indicators 2010* (Arlington, VA: National Science Foundation, 2010); United Nations Economic and Social Commission for Asia and the Pacific, *Statistical Yearbook for Asia and the Pacific 2011* (Bankok: UNESCAP, 2011); *Human Development Report 2005*, pp. 113–48.

16. OECD, "DAC Members' Net Official Development Assistance in 2010," http://www.oecd.org/dataoecd/31/22/47452398.xls.OEO

17. Ibid.

18. Sachs, *The End of Poverty*, pp. 290–308.

19. William Easterly, *The White Man's Burden. Why the West's Efforts to Aid the Rest of the World Have Done So Much Ill and So Little Good* (New York: Penguin, 2006). Easterly does not reject foreign aid out of hand, but argues that it can be distributed to needy individuals far more effectively by people who know the local conditions than it can by planners in international agencies.

20. World Bank, *Global Development Finance: External Debt of Developing Countries 2012* (Washington: World Bank, 2012); International Monetary Fund, "Debt Relief under the Heavily Indebted Poor Countries (HIPC) Initiative," June 26, 2012, at http://www.imf.org/external/np/exr/facts/pdf/hipc.pdf.

21. Lloyd G. Reynolds, *Economic Growth in the Third World* (New Haven, CT: Yale University Press, 1985).

22. William Easterly, *The Elusive Quest for Growth: Economists' Adventures and Misadventures in the Tropics* (Cambridge, MA: MIT Press, 2002).

23. *The Arab Human Development Report 2004: Towards Freedom in the Arab World* (New York: United Nations Development Program, 2005); *Better Government for Development in the Middle East and North Africa: Enhancing Inclusiveness and Accountability* (Washington, DC: World Bank, 2003).

24. Daron Acemoglu and James Robinson, *Economic Origins of Dictatorship and Democracy* (New York: Cambridge University Press, 2006); Daron Acemoglu and James Robinson, *Why Nations Fail: The Origins of Power, Prosperity, and Poverty* (New York: Crown, 2012).

25. Robert Bates, *Prosperity and Violence* (New York: Norton, 2009).

26. For definitions of the World Bank's six governance indicators and other information, see Worldwide Governance Indicators, info.worldbank.org/governance/wgi/resources.htm.

27. Samuel P. Huntington, *Political Order in Changing Societies* (New Haven, CT: Yale University Press, 1968); Samuel P. Huntington and Joan M. Nelson, *No Easy Choice: Political Participation in Developing Countries* (Cambridge, MA: Harvard University Press, 1976).

28. Mancur Olson, "Dictatorship, Democracy, and Development," *American Political Science Review* 87, no. 3 (September 1993), pp. 567–76. Elsewhere, Olson argued that narrowly based political or social groups, such as India's caste system, can impede economic development. See Mancur Olson, *The Rise and Decline of Nations* (New Haven, CT: Yale University Press, 1982). Emphasizing the rule of law, Hernando de Soto contends that the key to capitalism's success in the West and Japan is codified property laws, which many developing countries lack. See Hernando de Soto, *The Mystery of Capital: Why Capitalism Triumphs in the West and Fails Everywhere Else* (New York: Basic Books, 2000).

29. Adam Przeworski, Michael E. Alvarez, Jose Antonio Cheibub, and Fernando Limongi, *Democracy and Development: Political Institutions and Well-Being in the World, 1950–1990* (Cambridge: Cambridge University Press, 2000), pp. 103, 106, 178–79, 212–13.

30. John Gerring, Philip Bond, William T. Brandt, and Carola Moreno, "Democracy and Economic Growth: A Historical Perspective," *World Politics* 57, no. 3 (April 2005), pp. 323–64.

31. Larry Diamond, Juan J. Linz, and Seymour Martin Lipset, eds., *Democracy in Developing Countries* (Boulder, CO: Lynne Rienner, 1988); Larry Diamond, Juan J. Linz, and Seymour Martin Lipset, eds., *Politics in Developing Countries*, 2nd ed. (Boulder, CO: Lynne Rienner, 1995). See also Larry Diamond, *Developing Democracy* (Baltimore: Johns Hopkins, 1999); Stephan Haggard and Robert R. Kaufman, eds., *The Political Economy of Democratic Transitions* (Princeton, NJ: Princeton University Press, 1995).

32. Amartya Sen, *Development as Freedom* (New York: Random House, 1999).

33. Antoine Van Agtmael, "Think Again: The BRICS," *Foreign Policy*, no. 196 (November 2012).

34. On Gandhi and the origins of independent India and Pakistan, see Larry Collins and Dominique Lapierre, *Freedom at Midnight* (New York: Simon & Schuster, 1975). For a biography of Gandhi by a prominent psychologist, see Erik H. Erikson, *Gandhi's Truth* (New York: W. W. Norton, 1969). See also Richard Attenborough's epic film *Gandhi*.

35. Myron Weiner, *Party Building in a New Nation: The Indian National Congress* (Chicago: Chicago University Press, 1967); Samuel J. Eldersveld and Bashiruddin Ahmed, *Citizens and Politics: Mass Political Behavior in India* (Chicago: University of Chicago Press, 1978).

36. Shashi Tharoor, *Nehru: The Invention of India* (New York: Arcade, 2003).

37. See Sen, *Development as Freedom*, ch. 7.

38. World Bank, *Perspectives on Poverty in India: Stylized Facts from Survey Data* (Washington, DC: World Bank, 2011).

39. Amrita Basu and Atul Kohli, *Community Conflicts and the State in India* (Delhi: Oxford University Press, 1998).

40. Giovanni Sartori, *Parties and Party Systems: A Framework for Analysis* (New York: Cambridge University Press, 1976).

41. Katherine Frank, *Indira: The Life of Indira Nehru Gandhi* (London: HarperCollins, 2001).

42. Arend Lijphart, "The Puzzle of Indian Democracy: A Consociational Interpretation," *American Political Science Review* 90, no. 2 (June 1996), pp. 258–68.

43. On India's diversity, see Robert W. Stern, *Changing India: Bourgeois Revolution on the Subcontinent*, 2nd ed. (Cambridge: Cambridge University Press, 2003). See also Amartya Sen, *Identity and Violence: The Illusion of Destiny* (New York: Norton, 2006).

44. "The Tiger in Front: A Survey of India and China," *The Economist*, March 5, 2005. See also "Now for the Hard Part: A Survey of Business in India," *The Economist*, June 3, 2006; "India's Shining Hopes: A Survey of India," *The Economist*, February 21, 2004. For an analysis of this regional concentration, see Travis G. Coan and Tadeusz Kugler, "All Foreign Direct Investment Is Local: Indian Provincial Politics and the Attraction of FDI," *South Asia Economic Journal* 13, no. 2 (March 2012), pp. 27–50

45. See Shimelse Ali And Uri Dadush, "The Global Middle Class Is Bigger Than We Thought," *Foreign Policy*, May 16, 2012, at www.foreignpolicy.com.

46. *Financial Times*, February 8–9, 2003; *Sun* (Baltimore), September 30, 1999; *Freedom in the World 2006* (New York: Freedom House, 2006), pp. 323–28; Carol Lloyd, "Defending Women from 'Dowry Death': Is India Going Too Far in Its Efforts to Prevent Violence against Married Women?" Salon.com, May 10, 2007.

47. Ashutosh Varshney, *Ethnic Conflict and Civic Life: Hindus and Muslims in India*, 2nd ed. (New Haven, CT: Yale University Press, 2000).

48. On India's educational system, see Thomas Friedman, *The World Is Flat: A Brief History of the Twenty-first Century* (New York: Farrar, Straus and Giroux, 2005), pp. 104–05, 261–62, 465–68.

49. Stephen Cohen, *India: Emerging Power* (Washington, DC: Brookings Institution, 2001).

50. Amartya Sen, *The Argumentative Indian: Writings on Indian History, Culture and Identity* (New York: Farrar, Straus and Giroux, 2005).

13

The United Kingdom of Great Britain and Northern Ireland

OVERVIEW

- British democracy emerged slowly, in an evolutionary manner. As democracy emerged, increasing segments of the population were incorporated into the political arena. As they were integrated into the political mainstream, potentially revolutionary groups, such as the working class, embraced British democratic practice.

- Britain's political institutions, especially Parliament and the first-past-the-post electoral system, have encouraged the emergence of two alternative governing parties, the Conservatives and Labour.

- The parliamentary system gives the governing party almost complete power over public policy so long as it retains the confidence of a parliamentary majority.

- Because the electoral system has tended to give the winning party in parliamentary elections a disproportionate share of House of Commons seats, the party that wins a British election can take the victory as mandate to implement its policy platform.

- While all major British parties accept the welfare state, the political struggle over the exact characteristics of the welfare state has been the central axis of political contention in British politics since before the Second World War.

- The current government of Conservative Prime Minister David Cameron is unusual because it is a coalition with the Liberal Democrat Party.

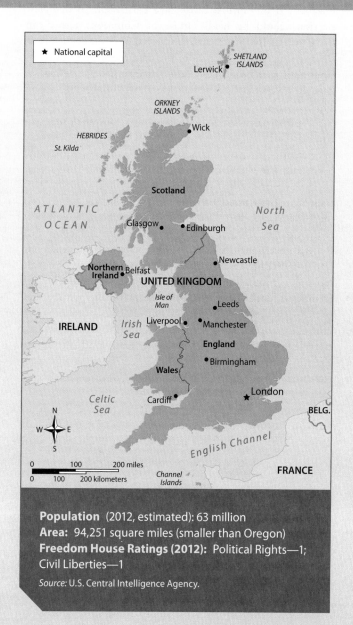

★ National capital

Population (2012, estimated): 63 million
Area: 94,251 square miles (smaller than Oregon)
Freedom House Ratings (2012): Political Rights—1; Civil Liberties—1

Source: U.S. Central Intelligence Agency.

A COALITION GOVERNMENT

On May 6, 2010, voters in England, Wales, Scotland, and Northern Ireland went to the polls to elect their representatives to the House of Commons, the United Kingdom's more powerful lower house of Parliament. The election came about when Gordon Brown, the sitting prime minister, asked Queen Elizabeth II on April 6 to dissolve Parliament so that new elections could be held. House of Commons terms can stretch up to five years, and the May 6 election day came as close to exactly five years from the date the sitting House of Commons had been voted into office on May 5, 2005, as it could given that UK general elections are always held on Thursdays.

Brown's party, the Labour Party, had controlled the government since his predecessor, Tony Blair, had led the party to a majority of Commons seats in 1997. Brown had become prime minister when Blair stepped down as Labour Party leader in 2007, so Brown had never led his party in a parliamentary campaign. Brown and Labour faced a strong challenge from the Conservative Party, led by David Cameron, himself new to the Conservative leadership. Cameron's party had controlled the UK government for the 18 years before Blair and Labour (1979–1997) but had struggled to win over voters since Blair took office. Complicating the picture, a third party, the Liberal Democrats, under the leadership of another rising political star, Nick Clegg, also vied for the votes of the UK's electorate. The Liberal Democrats had descended from the Liberal Party, which last ruled the country at the time of the First World War almost a century earlier. Clegg hoped his party could win enough parliamentary races to deny either Brown or Cameron an outright majority of seats in the Commons.

Labour or the Conservatives had almost always won an outright majority of Commons seats during the twentieth century, allowing whichever party won that majority to form a single-party government as described in Chapter 6 for parliamentary democracies (see Table 13.1 for British governments and prime ministers since World War II). As a consequence, British politics has had clear governing and opposition parties–known as Her Majesty's Government and Her Majesty's Loyal Opposition, respectively. While parliamentary systems often involve extensive coalition formation negotiations after elections, making the ultimate result of voting unclear to voters at the time they cast their ballots, the UK's tendency toward one-party governments had always made the general election vote a clear choice for the voters—choose your constituency's Labour candidate if you favor the Labour leader (e.g., Brown) as prime minister, select the Conservative candidate if you want the Conservative Party leader to form the new government. This typical result frequently caused observers to call Britain a two-party system. Once in the post-World War II years, in the February 1974 general election, neither party won a majority of seats in the Commons. As a result, neither could form a one-party majority government from that "hung parliament," a term the British use for a parliament without a majority party. The Labour Party leader then, Harold Wilson, formed a minority government but found himself unable to pass the laws he needed to govern effectively, so another election had to be held in October 1974.

The February 1974 hung parliament came as a surprise to all observers. Because the polling industry has advanced considerably over the past 35 years, the prospect of a hung parliament was widely expected before the 2010 general election. By the morning of May 7, the BBC could acknowledge that the votes had produced a hung parliament. While the Conservative Party gained 97 seats over its 2005 results, it remained 19 seats short of the 326 needed to form a majority government. Gordon Brown would face a more difficult challenge forming a government because even with the seats of the third-place Liberal Democrats, a Labour–Liberal Democrat coalition would be

Table 13.1 British Prime Ministers Since World War II

Prime Minister	Parties in Government	Duration in Power
Clement Attlee	Labour	1945–51
Winston Churchill	Conservative	1951–55
Anthony Eden	Conservative	1955–57
Harold Macmillan	Conservative	1957–63
Alec Douglas-Home	Conservative	1963–64
Harold Wilson	Labour	1964–70
Edward Heath	Conservative	1970–74
Harold Wilson	Labour	1974–76
James Callaghan	Labour	1976–79
Margaret Thatcher	Conservative	1979–90
John Major	Conservative	1990–97
Tony Blair	Labour	1997–2007
Gordon Brown	Labour	2007–10
David Cameron	Conservative–Liberal Democrat coalition	2010–

11 seats short of a majority. If Britain ever had a two-party system, it no longer did.

Table 13.2 shows the many parties that run in the constituent units of the United Kingdom. In addition to the Conservatives and Labour are national parties, including the Liberal Democrats and the Greens, and regional parties. The proper name of what we commonly call "Britain" is the United Kingdom of Great Britain and Northern Ireland (or the UK). Great Britain consists of England, Scotland, and Wales. Northern Ireland is juridically separate from the sovereign republic of Ireland, which is an independent country. These four regions of the UK all elect representatives to the House of Commons and recognize the monarch as the UK's head of state. In Northern Ireland, the main national parties don't even contest parliamentary seats, as the table suggests. In Wales and Scotland, there are long-standing national parties (Plaid Cymru and the Scottish National Party, respectively). There's a lot more going on in British politics than the typical story of a three-party contest for control of the House of Commons suggests. Indeed, the presence of these smaller parties contributed in both 1974 and 2010 to hung parliaments.

Without an outright majority, David Cameron had to negotiate to form a coalition government. He turned to Nick Clegg, the Liberal Democrat leader. Gordon Brown also tried to attract the Liberal Democrats into a coalition, but any Labour–Liberal Democrat coalition would be far more complex to operate since it would have had to rely on the support of yet other parties. After five days of negotiations, Cameron and Clegg struck a deal whereby Clegg would be Cameron's deputy prime minister and his party would have five seats in the Cameron cabinet. The Conservatives would hold 18 cabinet seats.

The coalition deal also included Conservative promises to the Liberal Democrats to consider serious political reforms. One demand of the Liberal Democrats imagined a national

Prime Minister David Cameron, left, and Deputy Prime Minister Nick Clegg outside No. 10 Downing Street, the Prime Minister's residence.

referendum on replacing the British "first past the post" electoral system, which had long produced disproportionate electoral results that disfavored the Liberal Democrats, with the alternative vote system, a form of proportional representation. A second involved replacing the House of Lords, Britain's unelected upper chamber of Parliament, with an elected body. The

Table 13.2 2010 United Kingdom General Election Results

Party	Constituencies Contested	Seats Won	Votes	Percent of Votes
Conservative Party	631	307	10,726,614	36.1%
Labour Party	631	258	8,609,527	29.0
Liberal Democrat Party	631	57	6,836,824	23.0
Democratic Unionist Party (Northern Ireland)	16	8	168,216	0.6
Scottish National Party	59	6	491,386	1.7
Sinn Fein (Northern Ireland)	17	5	171,942	0.6
Plaid Cymru (Wales)	18	3	165,394	0.6
Social Democratic and Labour Party (Northern Ireland)	18	3	110,970	0.4
Green Party	310	1	285,616	1.0
Alliance Party	18	1	42,762	0.1
Others, including independent candidates	—	1	2,082,129	6.9
Total	—	650	29,691,380	100.0

Source: BBC.

Liberal Democrats argued that both reforms would make Britain more democratic. In 2011, the British voters decisively rejected the alternative vote. The coalition continues to struggle about replacing the House of Lords because many Conservatives strongly oppose that suggestion.

At the time the coalition was formed, observers did not have high hopes for its success. Britain has little experience with coalition government outside of wartime. Its parties are accustomed to the single-party majority rule that political scientists have come to call the Westminster model, named after the Palace of Westminster, where Parliament meets. Cameron and Clegg were both young, rising politicians whose ambitions were likely to clash. Yet, at this writing more than two years after the coalition was formed, it survives. How does this coalition diverge from recent British experience? How have British institutions and parties operated to make coalition government the exception rather than the norm? How can it be that a major political party, the Liberal Democrats, would be advocating *democratic* reforms in what many regard as the world's oldest democracy? Let's start by exploring how democracy came to the United Kingdom and then look at its institutions carefully. We'll then return to contemporary politics and policy to consider the policy issues and political challenges that Cameron, Clegg, and their parties face.

HISTORICAL BACKGROUND: THE EVOLUTION OF BRITISH DEMOCRACY

In some countries, democracy came about as the result of a fairly sudden turn of events. Examples include the Allied occupations of Germany and Japan after the Second World War, the periodic swings between military rule and democracy that have occurred in various Latin American nations, and the outbursts of democracy in Eastern Europe that accompanied the collapse of communism. By contrast, democracy developed in Britain in a slow, piecemeal fashion that took centuries to unfold. Evolution, not revolution, has characterized the British democratic experience.

Following the collapse of the Roman Empire in the fifth century, England was governed by a succession of monarchs until the middle of the seventeenth century. Though most of them ruled through military force and other forms of coercive power, from the Middle Ages onward there was a growing tendency to justify the crown's legitimacy according to the **divine right of kings**, the doctrine asserting that the monarch derived his or her power from God and not from the people. The concept of divine right provided the legal basis for **sovereign monarchy**, or **absolutism**, which meant that the monarch was the supreme political authority in the land and enjoyed the right to absolute power. Rarely, however, did the crown sit easily on the English monarch's head. Challenges to individual claimants to the throne, as well as to royal authority itself, were frequent and sometimes violent. Over the span of centuries,

rivalries over the coveted English crown fueled dynastic wars with France and Spain as well as civil wars, palace intrigues, and strategic marriages involving both native and foreign-born noble families.

The first real break with the principle of monarchy occurred in the 1640s. Civil war led to the defeat of the royal army, followed by the trial and decapitation of King Charles I. In 1649, England was declared a republic. Oliver Cromwell, a commoner, ascended to power and ruled as "Lord Protector" under the country's first written constitution. Shortly after Cromwell died, the monarchy was restored in 1660. A monarch has served as Britain's official head of state ever since, though with diminishing effective power.

Other countries have also experienced extended periods of sovereign monarchy. For hundreds of years France, Spain, Germany, Russia, China, and Japan, to mention only a few, were governed by kings, queens, or emperors who asserted their royal preeminence over all other institutions and political forces within their respective realms. In stark contrast to these countries, England began moving as early as the thirteenth century toward a less autocratic form of monarchical power. When viewed in comparative perspective, England's gradual evolution to democracy under the aegis of monarchy stands out as one of very few examples of such a transition. What accounts for it?

As the discussion of conditions for democracy in Chapter 7 revealed, the forging of a successful democratic system usually requires a constellation of favorable factors, not just one or two. Britain began developing most of these conditions at exceptionally early stages in its history. They included:

- Parliament, a *state institution* of paramount importance that fostered *elites* opposed to royal absolutism and dedicated to the rule of law.
- English nationalism, which took a form that proved especially favorable for the creation of a democratic *political culture*.
- *Private enterprise*, which promoted *national wealth* and the development of a democratic *middle class*.
- Political parties that embraced democracy rather than antidemocratic ideologies, bringing *disadvantaged* groups such as the working class into the democratic fold; trade unions and other elements of *civil society* also promoted democratic practices.
- A system of *education*, centered in universities such as Oxford and Cambridge, that fostered freedom of thought, scientific inquiry, and artistic creativity.

Meanwhile, the British have found ways to deal with a number of serious challenges that at various times have threatened to place democracy in jeopardy or severely limited its scope.

- From its very inception the United Kingdom suffered from weak *national unity*: It was formed by force, as England compelled Wales, Scotland, and Ireland to join it in forming a unified state under the English monarchy. In 1922 a self-governing state was created in the south of Ireland, where Catholics had a majority, while six largely Protestant counties remained in the United Kingdom as Northern Ireland. The consequences of the UK's formation are still being addressed through the government's devolution policies.

- Britain's *elites*, though committed to Parliament, took a long time to permit popular sovereignty, granting the vote to the mass citizenry only in the twentieth century.

- Glaring socioeconomic inequalities produced fairly rigid class distinctions that still leave many Britons feeling *disadvantaged* and excluded from the full range of political and social opportunities democracy is expected to provide.

- A frequently tumultuous *international environment* has included more than two centuries of imperialism, two world wars, the Cold War and the complicated post-Cold-War order, with its challenges of globalization and terrorism.

Let's examine the development of British democracy by considering these conditions in more detail.

The Mother of Parliaments

Parliament began in England as an extension of monarchical rule. In 1212 and 1213, King John summoned various clergymen, barons, knights, and other prominent personages "to speak with us concerning the affairs of our realm." The term *parliament* derives from the French *parler*, "to speak." From the outset, however, these elites displayed a marked interest in protecting their own powers and liberties as prelates of the Catholic Church or as leaders of England's counties and villages. In 1215 they prevailed upon King John to sign the **Magna Carta** (the Great Charter), a document specifying their rights in such matters as taxation, judicial appointments, and private property. The Magna Carta affirmed the *rule of law*, plainly indicating there were limits to the king's sovereign power and that the monarchy was not above the law. A Parliament summoned in 1265 included representatives of the common elements of society—the equivalent of the middle classes—rather than just the upper ranks of the nobility and church.

These ideas and practices solidified during the fourteenth century as a succession of monarchs called Parliament into session with growing frequency and acknowledged its responsibility in providing advice and passing legislation. In the process the institution became divided into two houses. The "lords spiritual and temporal" consisted of bishops and other members of the cloth, along with earls, dukes, and various members of the country's higher nobility. The "commons" consisted of knights and other elements of the so-called lesser nobility, together with "burgesses," who were prominent citizens from local communities. Typically the crown summoned the **House of Lords** into session by invitation and appointed many of its members to lifetime noble ranks (peerages); eventually, most lords inherited their seats. The **House of Commons** was usually elected by local property-owning elites in counties and towns. By the late 1370s it was generally accepted that no statutes could be issued without parliamentary consent. The House of Lords was

developing into England's highest court, while the Commons acquired the right to approve taxes.

Over the next two centuries Parliament became a permanent fixture of England's governmental system. Even Cromwell relied on parliamentary support, and it was Parliament that restored the monarchy after his death.[1]

Despite its importance, Parliament remained constitutionally subordinate to the crown until the late seventeenth century. England's monarchs insisted that their reliance on parliamentary consent in no way compromised the principle of sovereign monarchy or the doctrine of divine right. They viewed Parliament as an instrument of monarchical rule, not as a democratic substitute for it. Most members of Parliament shared this notion until the dramatic events of 1688–89 brought about a fundamental reordering in the balance of constitutional power in England.

James II, a Catholic, assumed the throne in 1685. England was by now a predominantly Protestant country, however. Its Protestant Reformation had begun in the 1530s when King Henry VIII broke with the Roman Catholic Church and established the Church of England (or Anglican Church), with himself as its head. (To this day the British monarch is still the official head of the Anglican Church, which is the country's *established church*.) James II managed to antagonize virtually all the leading elements of English society through his efforts to restore Catholics to the political prominence they had once enjoyed before the Reformation and through his determination to assert royal powers in the face of widespread opposition to autocratic rule. Acting with extraordinary boldness, the king's opponents invited the Dutch monarch William of Orange to invade England and take power. William was married to James II's daughter Mary, and his own family had distant ties to the English aristocracy. Just as significant, he was a Protestant who proclaimed his willingness to respect the rights of Parliament and the established liberties of English society. Upon William's arrival in England at the end of 1688, King James fled into exile. A special parliamentary assembly thereupon declared that James had abdicated the throne and bestowed the monarchy jointly on King William and Queen Mary. For the first time in English history, Parliament had deposed one king and elected another. A declaration of parliamentary rights issued in early 1689 explicitly forbade the crown from suspending the laws of the land without Parliament's approval.

These events, occurring without bloodshed, are celebrated as England's *Glorious Revolution*. They established a solid precedent for *parliamentary supremacy*, which evolved over the following centuries into the foundation of modern British government. **Parliamentary supremacy** means that Parliament—not the crown, the courts, or any other institution—is the supreme authority in the British political system.

Over the course of the eighteenth and nineteenth centuries, Parliament persistently whittled away at the monarch's remaining powers. In the process, Britain's system of government became a *constitutional monarchy*, a system in which the monarch performs the largely symbolic functions

To counter efforts by James II to reestablish the political prominence of Catholics and to strengthen royal power, opponents invited William of Orange and his wife, Mary (the daughter of James II), to invade England and to assume the throne. James II fled into exile. For the first time in history, the British Parliament deposed one king and elected another.

Monarch (Ceremonial head of state; succession by inheritance)

(symbolically designates)

Government (Prime minister and other ministers)

responsible to

House of Commons

House of Lords (hereditary and life peers; lords spiritual)

elect

Voters

FIGURE 13.1 **Britain's Parliamentary Government**

of a ceremonial head of state while day-to-day decision making rests firmly in the hands of a prime minister and cabinet, backed by their supporters in Parliament. "The monarch reigns but the government rules" became the standard characterization of this system.

Meanwhile, the balance of power between Parliament and the government (the cabinet plus additional ministers) has undergone its own evolution. By the nineteenth century the Parliament's legislative powers and the cabinet's executive powers had become fused. Under the influence of increasingly assertive prime ministers and the rise of political parties, Britain in the nineteenth century possessed an institutional framework in which:

1. The qualified electorate voted for the House of Commons, whereupon
2. The Commons advised the monarch in selecting the prime minister, held the government accountable for its actions, and enacted bills into law.

The Commons also acquired the right to dismiss governments and form new ones, while the prime minister acquired the right to advise the monarch to dissolve the Commons and order new elections (see Figure 13.1).[2] Chapter 6 describes this Westminster system in general terms. We'll examine how it works in contemporary Britain later in this chapter.

Two additional developments occurring over the nineteenth and twentieth centuries strengthened the democratic aspects of this evolving system: the expansion of the franchise and the ascendancy of the Commons over the House of Lords.

Just as it took centuries for Parliament to become the institutional bedrock of democracy, it also took Britain a long time to confer the right to vote on all its adult citizens. Only in the twentieth century was the franchise extended to virtually all adult males and females.

- Before 1832, only males who met stringent property-owning requirements had the right to vote, a group constituting only 5 percent of all adults over the age of 21.
- The Great Reform Act of 1832 extended the franchise to about 7 percent of the adult population, while continuing to limit it to men of property.
- Another voting reform passed in 1867 eased these qualifications somewhat, enabling a segment of Britain's urban working-class males to vote for the first time. Still, only about 16 percent of the total adult population was allowed to vote.
- In 1884 the franchise was widened to include all males over age 21 who owned a home, a group comprising about 28 percent of people in that age group.
- Only in 1918, under the impact of the widely shared sacrifices of World War I, were most property qualifications eliminated for males over age 21. At the same time, women obtained the right to vote for the first time, a triumph due in part to the critical role women played in the workforce during the Great War. The international environment thus promoted democracy in Britain in the war years. Female suffrage also came about because of decades of militant campaigning for enfranchisement by Britain's suffragettes. Initially, however, only women over age 30 gained the right to vote; it was not until 1928 that the female voting age was lowered to 21.
- Though virtually all adults over age 21 were now able to vote, graduates of elite universities and various business owners still enjoyed the right to cast *two* votes in parliamentary elections. This plural voting privilege was not abolished until 1948, when the Representation of the People Act formally established the principle of "one person, one vote" throughout the United Kingdom.

- In 1969 the voting age was lowered to 18, and in 1985 about 4 million British citizens overseas were granted voting rights.

Some individuals, such as the royal family and other titled peers, still have no right to vote.[3] Figure 13.2 illustrates the extension of the suffrage in the UK from the time of the Great Reform Act of 1832 through the lowering of the voting age to 18. It also shows how during the twentieth century the extension of the franchise was paralleled by growing electoral participation of the voting age population.

The gradual extension of the suffrage was accompanied by the increasing authority of Parliament's elected body, the House of Commons, over the House of Lords. Until the early twentieth century the House of Lords retained the right to approve all bills passed by the Commons before they could become law. Because the House of Lords was an unelected body representing the aristocracy and the Anglican Church hierarchy, it constituted the last bastion of nondemocratic rule in a country that was increasingly opening itself to democratic influences and procedures. In 1911 the lords lost their veto privilege, retaining little more than the right to delay the enactment of legislation by up to two years. In 1949 their ability to delay legislation was reduced to one year. In 1999, Tony Blair's government effected another major reform of the upper house, to be described later in this chapter. As indicated in the introduction, the current coalition government is considering replacing the House of Lords with an elected upper house.

Nationalism and Political Culture

A contributing factor in the development of British democracy was the particular brand of nationalism that accompanied Parliament's institutional evolution. As noted in Chapter 4, *nationalism* is a set of political ideas that emphasizes the distinctiveness and unity of one's nation, specifies common interests, and prescribes goals for action, self-government being the most important. In some countries the development of nationalism had pronouncedly antidemocratic accents. Japan, Russia, and Germany stand out as prominent examples. The development of nationhood in these countries, extending from medieval times until well into the twentieth century, was orchestrated largely by aristocratic elites who had no intention of sharing power with elected parliaments. The military establishment, rather than legislative bodies, was their favored institutional partner. In England, by contrast, nationalism from its inception was understood by the country's politically active elites and broad segments of the population in terms that promoted democratic ideals.

Liah Greenfeld points out that England was the first country to develop a modern national consciousness.[4] This national self-conception emerged in the sixteenth century, spurred by both religious and political developments. One of its chief catalysts was the Protestant Reformation. By 1600, the majority of English people belonged to a church that explicitly defined itself as "Anglican." Protestantism was thus a defining element of the English nation, shaping not just the country's most prominent religious orientation but its basic national identity as well.

From its origins, English nationalism was infused with a specific political content. It arose at a time when Parliament was already well established as a vital component of English government, with widespread support among nobles and commoners, Catholics and Protestants. The English concept of national identity included the notion that, at least in principle,

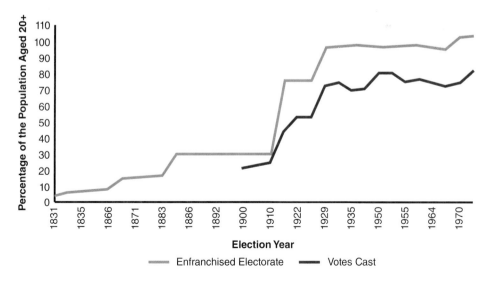

FIGURE 13.2 **Enfranchised Electorate and Votes Cast as a Percentage of the UK Population Aged 20 and Above, 1831–1974**

Note: The enfranchised electorate line exceeds 100 percent after 1969 because the ratio is based on the population aged 20 and above while the franchise was extended in 1969 to 18-year-olds.

Source: Peter Flora, *State, Economy, and Society in Western Europe, 1815–1975: Vol. 1, The Growth of Mass Democracies and Welfare States* (Frankfurt: Campus Verlag, 1983), pp. 148–50.

the English people were free and equal individuals under the law, with the right to participate in politics and government. The political values of individual freedom, equal dignity, and self-government—values that are at the heart of modern democracy—became defining characteristics of the English nation. Ultimately, what defined the English nation more than anything else was the way the English governed themselves. English nationalism, in short, was defined in part by democratic principles.

It therefore gave rise to a political culture that proved highly conducive to the expansion of democracy. As we saw in Chapter 9, *political culture* refers to a pattern of shared values, moral norms, beliefs, expectations, and attitudes that relate to politics and its social context. In their classic study of political culture, Gabriel Almond and Sidney Verba described Britain in the 1950s as having a *civic culture:* that is, a cluster of attitudes favoring the rule of law, individual liberty, equal human dignity, and political moderation. They also pointed out that the British tended to be more deferential to established authority than did people in other democracies, including the United States. Though these deferential attitudes have declined in more recent decades, the basic contours of Britain's civic culture, including a vibrant civil society, remain largely the same today.[5]

Private Enterprise and the Middle Class

Another variable that promoted the development of English democracy was the emergence of private agriculture and other business enterprises owned and operated by individuals, families, and corporations independently of the state and its chief partner, the centuries-old aristocracy. These economic processes stimulated the emergence of a property-owning middle class, centrally located in Britain's social pyramid between the wealthy aristocratic elite and the masses of poor peasants and laborers. By acquiring land or businesses of their own, these ambitious entrepreneurs acquired a personal stake in how they were governed. They wanted a say in shaping the laws of the land, especially laws regarding taxes, contracts, and other regulations affecting private property. By electing sympathetic representatives to the House of Commons, they not only advanced their own economic interests, but they also simultaneously promoted the principle of representative self-government. In their view, the defense of property rights required the assertion of political rights.

An early catalyst to private business activity was the growth of commercial agriculture in the sixteenth and seventeenth centuries. Though the process was frequently violent as peasants were thrown off the land, its main result was that—unlike Russia, China, and some other countries—Britain entered the late nineteenth century unencumbered by a large, landless peasantry whose discontent might serve as a source of revolutionary ferment. Instead, the country's rich green countryside was cultivated by wealthy estate owners and a rising middle class

of commercial farmers. These rural property owners ultimately promoted England's democratization through their support of Parliament and their insistence on voting rights for themselves, along with other legal privileges and freedoms.

The ranks of the propertied middle class swelled with the expansion of private manufacturing and other commercial activities in the sixteenth to eighteenth centuries. By 1800 the English middle class had firmly established itself as the driving force behind a dynamic market economy. As its contributions to the wealth of the country became increasingly indispensable, its influence on Parliament and government decision making grew apace. Sociologist Barrington Moore maintained that, without such a capitalist bourgeoisie, there can be no democracy. Countries that failed to develop large-scale private agriculture and industry before the twentieth century—like Japan, Russia, and China—generally failed to develop democracy until much later, if at all.[6]

The expansion of capitalism in Britain was by no means without problems, however. Large numbers of landless peasants, laborers, and others who made up the uneducated mass of British society found it difficult to climb out of the bottom of the social heap despite the new opportunities offered by the market economy. Even the middle class led a precarious existence, as the volatile dynamics of the marketplace produced bankruptcies, inflation, and recessions alongside vast personal fortunes and rising national wealth.

These conflicting tendencies intensified in the nineteenth and early twentieth centuries as Britain's industrial revolution, which had taken off in the late 1700s, well ahead of other European countries, flourished and matured. In an economy increasingly functioning according to laissez-faire principles, with minimal government involvement, industrial capitalism generated a huge working class whose fate was determined almost entirely by employers bent on raising profits at all costs. Subsistence-level wages, long working hours, and unsanitary living conditions became the unalterable lot of millions of men, women, and children, with little or no state assistance or protection.[7]

On top of all this, Britain's aristocratic elite, the descendants of blue-blooded families whose lines stretched back centuries, managed to maintain their lofty status at the apex of British society. Though they had ceded place to the business class as the principal creators of England's wealth in the eighteenth and nineteenth centuries, their hereditary titles, accumulated riches, and superior educational attainments at universities such as Oxford and Cambridge gave them a social preeminence and political influence that far exceeded their numbers.

The result of these economic and social transformations was a society that by the nineteenth century, if not earlier, was demarcated by increasingly rigid class distinctions. The "class system" became synonymous with social reality throughout Britain (especially in England, where industrialization was the most pronounced). The social class into which one was born largely determined one's life chances, including educational prospects, occupation, and income. Contrary to the predictions of Karl Marx, detailed in Chapter 10, both capitalism and democracy have flourished in the United Kingdom to the present day. They have continued to survive despite persistent social divisions in contemporary British society. What accounts for these results? One of the main reasons Marx's prognostications did not come true can be found in the ideological development of Britain's leading political parties.

The Rise of Political Parties

Since the end of World War II, British politics has been dominated by two parties, the Conservative Party and the Labour Party. A third, which now calls itself the Liberal Democrat Party, has played a less important role but still attracts a wide following. With few exceptions, postwar British governments have been *single-party majoritarian* governments, with the Conservatives and Labour alternating in power. Until 2010 there had been no coalition government since the war. Numerous other parties also exist, but their electoral support is much smaller than that of the three main parties, all of which have roots in the past.

Modern political parties emerged in Britain in the nineteenth century. The two parties that dominated the latter half of the 1800s—the Conservatives and the Liberals—could trace their origins to earlier political orientations rooted in the religious and constitutional disputes of the two previous centuries. The **Conservatives** descended primarily from the **Tories**, a moniker they informally retain today. In the seventeenth and eighteenth centuries the Tories were identified by their devotion to absolutist monarchy, aristocratic rule, the House of Lords, and the established Anglican Church. The Liberals' chief antecedents were the *Whigs*, who tended to favor a more limited monarchy, one whose power would be reined in by the House of Commons acting on the principle of government by consent of the governed. Although the terms *Tory* and *Whig* were originally insults leveled by each side's detractors, in practice the two orientations shared certain positions. A majority of both groups favored a monarchy of real stature, an authoritative role for Parliament, Protestantism as opposed to Catholicism, and government by propertied elites rather than mass democracy. Both strove to avoid a recurrence of the civil wars of the 1640s and recoiled in horror at the French Revolution. These commonalities helped set British politics on a course of moderation, consensus, and compromise that endures to this day.

Party development remained embryonic in the first half of the nineteenth century. The Tories, who began referring to themselves as Conservatives in the 1830s, were divided into competing factions, as were the Whigs. By the end of the century, party ideology and organizational structure began to solidify. The Conservatives under the leadership of Benjamin Disraeli emerged as the chief advocate of the landed aristocracy, while the Liberals under leaders such as William Gladstone stepped forward as the main party of the urbanized, business-oriented middle class, championing laissez-faire and free trade. Even these distinctions, however, reflected general

tendencies rather than strict demarcations. Most important, both parties accepted the existing constitutional framework of a limited monarchy, cabinet accountability to Parliament, and a restricted franchise confined to property-owning males. At a time when France, Germany, Russia, and Japan experienced authoritarian rule undergirded by the military, Britain's leading parties were wedded to parliamentary government and entertained no thought of military authoritarianism.[8]

At the same time, both Conservatives and Liberals feared the mounting resentments of the working class. Britain's proletariat grew steadily in the nineteenth century. Early government efforts to alleviate their plight did little more than reduce working hours for women and children to about 60 per week. The Poor Law of 1839 actually *decreased* state expenditures for the destitute. None of this legislation addressed the fundamental problem, which was the workers' lack of political power, a weakness that left them completely subservient to their employers. To redress this imbalance, a working-class group known as the Chartists was formed in 1838. Their "charter" of demands called for universal male suffrage, the secret ballot (as opposed to open elections by show of hands), and salaries for members of Parliament so that politicians other than the superfluously wealthy could afford to hold office. Two petitions to Parliament expressing these wishes were decisively rejected, as neither the Conservatives nor the Liberals in the reign of Queen Victoria were prepared to open the floodgates of democracy to the masses. Both parties were strongly committed to preserving the property rights of land and factory owners. The resulting social conflicts occasionally sparked violence, as strikes, lock-outs, and worker demonstrations led to bloody police crackdowns. Most workers, however, hewed the path of peaceful democratic change. Collaboration with sympathetic Liberals such as Gladstone yielded a few gains, such as the legalization of trade unions and the right to strike in 1871. But the predominance of business interests in Liberal ranks precluded the critical breakthrough to mass suffrage.

It was therefore incumbent on the workers' movement to establish a party of its own. Accordingly, in 1900 the leaders of several worker-oriented groups held a conference in London and formed the Labour Representation Committee. After electing 29 candidates to the House of Commons in 1906, this organization renamed itself the **Labour Party**.

From its inception the new party's main source of support came from Britain's trade unions. By 1900 some 1.2 million workers were affiliated with the Trades Union Congress, an umbrella organization formed by unions representing railway workers, factory laborers, miners, and other industrial occupations. Another early source of Labour support consisted of intellectuals, artists, and other middle- and upper-class sympathizers of the labor movement who objected on ethical grounds to laissez-faire capitalism's exploitative tendencies. Such people formed groups like the Fabian Society to give voice to these sentiments.[9]

What is perhaps most significant about the various founding elements of the Labour Party is that the overwhelming majority decisively rejected Marxism, anarchism, and other ideologies calling for violent revolution and the creation of an entirely new social and political order. Most of them believed that working-class demands for political participation and economic justice could be accommodated within the framework of parliamentary democracy and peaceful industrial development under the aegis of the British state. While many of the Labour Party's founders called themselves "socialists," most understood this term to mean a system in which national and local government agencies would play a greater role in the economy for the benefit of the working class, without necessarily eliminating private enterprise. Though many believed that the state should take over the main factories, mines, utilities, and other privately owned industries, very few advocated the wholesale government absorption of all the farms, stores, and other small- and medium-sized businesses that gave millions of British families a personal stake in private property. Only a minority of British socialists favored the gigantic state-run centrally planned economy that the Soviet Union was to set up in the 1930s. Quite a few continued to favor cooperation with the Liberal Party on certain issues, the so-called Lib-Lab orientation.

Just as significant, the early Labourites were true social democrats who believed in ballot-box democracy. They categorically rejected dictatorship. Far from opposing democracy, the Labour Party and its adherents wanted to extend its blessings to the working masses through universal male and female suffrage. Moreover, a large number of Labour leaders and voters resisted Marxism because its atheistic tenets conflicted with their strong religious convictions.[10] In short, the Labour Party helped enfold Britain's poorest classes into the democratic process. As a result, Britain did not develop a large alienated working class that felt left out of the mainstream of democratic politics. By contrast, France, Germany, and a number of other countries entered the twentieth century with many discontented workers who became radicalized and ultimately supported antidemocratic parties such as the communists and fascists.

Another comparison worth noting is that the Labour Party envisioned a much greater economic role for the state than the Democratic Party in the United States tended to favor. Though both parties had deep roots in the labor movement, Labour's call for the nationalization of private companies was not echoed by Franklin Roosevelt's New Deal, which sought instead to revive private economic activity rather than replace it with government ownership. In advocating the takeover of at least some private enterprises by the state, Labour was more socialist than the Democrats ever were.

As the Labour Party gained strength, the Conservatives and Liberals underwent their own evolution in the direction of greater democracy for all. It was a Liberal government under Prime Minister David Lloyd George that conferred voting rights on most males and females in 1918, and it was a Conservative government that expanded female suffrage in 1928. In the 1930s, as the Great Depression wracked the British economy, several Labour leaders joined with Liberals and Conservatives in forming a broad coalition government. Another three-party national unity coalition governed Britain during World War II under Prime Minister Winston Churchill. (Churchill was a Conservative who had once belonged to the Liberal Party.) These crucial developments forged an unshakable consensus among the main parties of the left (Labour), right (Conservatives), and center (Liberals) that the British system of government must consist of ballot-box democracy under a limited monarchy. The three main parties also developed a consensus on Britain's economic system, embracing the general principle that it should be a mixed economy that combines private enterprise with state intervention aimed at stimulating growth and

Table 13.3 The 10 Conditions for Democracy: The British Experience

Explanatory Factor	British Experience
1. Elite attitudes	Elites have supported democratic practices such as parliamentary sovereignty since the Glorious Revolution (1698) or before.
2. State institutions	The central state has been able to provide law and order via democratic institutions such as Parliament since the Glorious Revolution.
3. National unity	Society's whole sense of national identity has been intertwined with notions about its capacity for democratic self-governance.
4. National wealth	As the first industrializer, Britain was the world's wealthiest nation until the twentieth century.
5. Private enterprise	Commercial agriculture came to Britain from the 16th century onward; rural landholders supported parliamentary sovereignty.
6. Middle class	Small capitalists developed industry in the 18th and 19th centuries—separate from government power.
7. Attitudes of the disadvantaged	The working class was integrated into the electoral arena via gradual extensions of the ballot; a democratic Labour Party emerged to represent the working class.
8. Civil society	Independent clubs emerged in the 18th century and served as the basis of a rich associational life in the 19th and 20th centuries.
9. Education and access to information	Compulsory education was adopted in 1880; independent newspapers emerged in the 18th century.
10. International conditions	As the world's dominant power in the 19th century, Britain was the least subject to foreign domination; it led the effort to defend democracy in Europe against German hegemony in the 20th century.

providing for the welfare of the population. Fatefully, this wide consensus on democracy and the mixed economy was precisely what eluded Germany, Italy, Spain, Russia, Japan, and a host of other countries in the first half of the twentieth century, resulting in brutal dictatorships and two world wars. By contrast, Britain emerged from the First and Second World Wars with its democracy strengthened.

The preceding paragraphs have shown how several of the 10 factors identified in Chapter 7 as conditions that support the emergence and consolidation of democracy have been present in the UK from an earlier period. Table 13.3 summarizes the British experience with those factors.

BRITISH POLITICS IN THE POST-WORLD WAR II ERA

Consensus on the fundamental principles of British democracy has by no means prevented real differences from emerging among the main parties when it comes to the specifics of government policy. Since World War II, Labour and the Conservatives have sparred vigorously over how Britain's mixed-economy welfare state should be managed. The question of what role the state should play in the economy has been the single most contentious issue in postwar British politics.

Labour and the Welfare State, 1945–51

In July 1945, slightly more than two months after Germany's surrender, British voters ousted Churchill's government and swung massively to the Labour Party. With 48 percent of the popular vote and a 146-seat majority in the House of Commons, Labour formed its first majoritarian government under Clement Attlee and used its mandate to break new ground in expanding the state's role in the economy. Between 1946 and 1949 the Attlee government nationalized the Bank of England, civil aviation, and the iron and steel industries, along with the country's coal mines, railroads, gas and electricity utilities, and long-distance trucking companies. The owners of these businesses were compensated out of state revenues. In addition, the Labour government established the *National Health Service* (NHS), providing virtually free medical care for the entire population. (Private medical care and health insurance remained available for those willing to pay for it.) Other welfare measures included a vastly extended state-funded insurance program to cover unemployment and job-related accidents; maternity allowances; and pensions for widows and retirees, plus direct income assistance for the poorest families. To maintain full employment at a time when Britain's economy was still recovering from the hardships of World War II, the Labour government utilized Keynesian tax-and-spend principles (see Chapter 11). By 1950 the Labour Party had succeeded beyond all expectations in laying the foundations of Britain's large postwar welfare state, adapting to the realities of British capitalism its long-standing commitment to a social-democratic conception of economic democracy.[11]

Conservative Acceptance of the Welfare State

Despite the unprecedented scope of Labour's nationalizations and welfare measures, Conservative and Liberal politicians generally went along with most of them. Both parties had introduced their own welfare schemes before World War II, albeit on a considerably smaller scale.

Accordingly, when the Conservatives were voted back into power in 1951, they did not set out to reverse everything that Attlee's government had accomplished. Though they reprivatized the iron and steel industries and long-distance trucking, they kept the other nationalized companies firmly in state hands. Under Prime Ministers Winston Churchill (1951–55), Anthony Eden (1955–57), Harold Macmillan (1957–63), and Alec Douglas-Home (1963–64), a succession of Conservative governments significantly expanded spending on the NHS, public housing, education, and other welfare services. As one wag put it, "Labour gave us free teeth and the Tories didn't pull 'em out!" To prevent strikes, these Conservative governments acceded to a number of trade union demands for higher wages and other benefits, even though the unions were the principal financial and electoral backers of the Labour Party. And like the previous Labour government, the Conservatives used Keynesian mechanisms such as tax incentives and direct government spending to promote economic growth and reduce unemployment.

While continuing to present themselves as the party most favorable to private business and the middle class, the Conservatives in these years amply demonstrated their adherence to Britain's "postwar settlement," which combined private enterprise with a significant amount of state intervention in the economy.

Although he led a Conservative government, Winston Churchill accepted the welfare state measures put in place by Labour when he returned to power in 1951.

Conservative acceptance of this expansive state role reflected a broad popular consensus in Britain at this time on the need for "collective," that is, state-centered, solutions to national problems as opposed to private initiatives centered in the economic marketplace. The period of British politics extending from 1945 through the 1970s has been aptly described as "the collectivist age," with the value of community welfare predominating over free-market individualism in public and elite opinion to a greater extent than in the United States.[12]

Labor Unrest Challenges the Welfare State

After losing to Labour in the elections of 1964, the Conservatives were voted back into power in 1970. Prime Minister Edward (Ted) Heath (1970–74) assumed office with a pledge to preserve the essentials of the welfare state while scaling back some of its more costly programs. British economic growth was weak compared to France and Germany in the late 1960s and early 1970s, raising questions about the economic viability of the welfare state. Heath also believed that some of Britain's largest trade unions were abusing their right to strike and should be obligated to keep their agreements with private companies. In 1972, when unemployment reached 1 million, the coal miners' union declared a nationwide strike for higher wages. Several attempts to reach a settlement fell through, and violence flared up as picketers prevented coal and oil supplies from reaching electric power plants. Strikes by shipbuilders and dockworkers intensified the crisis. Brownouts and heating fuel shortages made for a dark and cold winter. In the face of these challenges, Heath abandoned his previous attempts to confront the unions and instead called on the Trade Unions Congress to join with the government and the main interest group representing the business community, the Confederation of British Industry, in negotiating a series of agreements on pay scales, prices, and production. The unions rebuffed the offer, and Heath called new elections for February 1974 in the midst of a rapidly deteriorating economic situation. "Who governs Britain?"—the unions or the government?—was a central issue of the campaign.

The result was a defeat for the Conservatives but a less than satisfactory victory for the Labour Party. Labour emerged as the largest party in the House of Commons but lacked an overall voting majority. Harold Wilson, who had been prime minister from 1964–70, thereupon formed a minority Labour government, but he called new elections in October 1974 that gave his party a slender three-vote majority.

The Labour Party itself was divided about the power of the unions. The rise of trade union militancy during Heath's government was cheered by those who believed that Britain's working class was fully justified in demanding a greater share of the nation's wealth. But Labour moderates insisted the economy could not function unless the unions accepted limits on their wage demands and strike activities. Accordingly, when Wilson reassumed office in 1974 he called for a social contract in which the unions would agree to wage restraint in return for government welfare measures. This policy calmed Britain's troubled

industrial relations for the next two years, providing Wilson with a favorable opportunity to announce his retirement.

His successor was James Callaghan (1976–79), who was quickly forced to shoulder the burdens of the British economy's continuing slide when the pound's depreciating value against other currencies required financial assistance from the International Monetary Fund. The IMF required sharp cuts in welfare expenditures that did not sit well with the Labour left. The pressures on Callaghan intensified during the winter of 1978–79—the "winter of discontent"—as a series of strikes by truck drivers, trash collectors, and other workers inconvenienced the public, prompting widespread fears that the unions were out of control.[13]

As Callaghan wrestled with these troublesome long-term trends, his own troubles were exacerbated by dwindling support in the House of Commons. Defections from Labour ranks and defeats incurred in by-elections (which take place upon the death or retirement of a Commons member) deprived the party of its majority. To save his minority government, Callaghan formed a parliamentary alliance with the Liberal Party, which had 13 seats. The "Lab-Lib" alliance lasted barely a year. The alliance did not include Liberals taking cabinet seats, and hence it was not a coalition government. In a last-ditch effort to secure a voting majority, Callaghan cut deals with the Scottish Nationalist Party and its Welsh counterpart, which together held 14 seats. But this new parliamentary alliance was shaken after government-sponsored referendums on devolution in Scotland and Wales failed. With rumors flying that Callaghan's government and its allies no longer commanded a voting majority in the House, the Conservatives supported a no-confidence motion. The tense showdown came late in the evening of March 28, 1979. By the slimmest of margins, 311–310, Callaghan's government was defeated, setting the stage for new elections to the House of Commons only six weeks later.[14]

The result was a convincing victory for the Conservatives, whose combative leader was to serve as Britain's prime minister for the next 11 years: Margaret Thatcher. Before we consider how Prime Minister Thatcher redefined the British political agenda and explore the main issues that have animated British politics since 1979, let's examine the UK's political institutions and its main mode of political participation: electoral politics and political parties.

STATE INSTITUTIONS

It is often said that the UK does not have a written constitution. In fact, the UK does have a constitution, but it is not codified in a single written document like the U.S. Constitution or the constitutions of France, Russia, or numerous other countries. The UK's constitutional laws are instead inscribed in thousands of Acts of Parliament and court rulings that have accumulated over the centuries. And they are reinforced by traditional practices and procedures that also tend to have a long history. As in other democracies, Britain's constitutional arrangements prescribe how the country's governmental institutions are organized and how they should function. They also provide the institutional framework for political competition between parties and other participants in the political process. As the pages that follow reveal, the UK's constitutional framework is marked by both enduring tradition and adaptability to changing conditions.

Parliament

The State Opening of Parliament is one of the most colorful rituals of British political life. Normally it takes place every autumn as Parliament begins a new session, but it also occurs when a new government assumes office soon after parliamentary elections. Garbed in flowing robes and bearing the Imperial State Crown, the monarch strides into the House of Lords, accompanied by peers of the realm in ornate attire. After the reigning monarch ascends the throne, the sergeant-at-arms knocks on the door of the House of Commons with a black rod and formally commands its members to join His or Her Majesty. With both houses assembled, the monarch then delivers the King's or Queen's Speech, which outlines the legislative priorities the government will pursue in the coming session. While custom prescribes the ceremonial aspects of the occasion, the speech is written entirely by the government. Over the next several days its contents are subjected to a vigorous debate as the two houses get down to business. With the first vote on legislation the government is confirmed in office.

At the opening of Parliament, Queen Elizabeth II outlines the legislative priorities her government will pursue in the coming session.

Commons: The Legislative Process To become law, a bill usually must be passed by a majority of those present and voting in both the House of Commons and the House of Lords. A bill introduced in one house may not be considered in the other until it is passed; unlike the U.S. Congress, the two British houses do not consider similar legislation simultaneously. Members of both houses have the right to debate bills proposed by the government and, within certain limits, to propose legislation and amendments of their own. The procedures for voting on legislation are also roughly the same in both houses. As the democratically elected house, however, the Commons enjoys important prerogatives not accorded the Lords. These include above all the right to hold the government directly accountable, and to vote it out of office if a majority of the Commons no longer has confidence in the prime minister and cabinet.

The government takes the initiative in drafting most legislation and shepherding it through Parliament. In Britain, as in most other parliamentary democracies, the legislative process rests on the principle of *party discipline*. That is, all the members of a party's parliamentary delegation are expected to vote together unanimously on most pieces of legislation. Should a government's support in the Commons fall below 50 percent on key bills, it could be forced to resign. Consequently, government "whips" stay in close contact with the party's parliamentary membership to ensure a bloc vote, especially on bills the government deems crucial, such as the budget or high-priority manifesto promises.[15]

The concept of party discipline applies no less to opposition parties than it does to the governing party. Members of Parliament (MPs) who vote against their leadership's clearly enunciated position can be penalized, whether by being excluded from party meetings or, in the most extreme cases, by being denied the right to run for reelection as the party's official candidate. Occasionally a party's leaders will relax party discipline and allow their colleagues to vote as they wish on matters of conscience, such as abortion, the death penalty, or gun control. And it sometimes happens that members of Parliament will defy their leadership and vote against its legislation, a reality John Major, Thatcher's successor as Conservative Party leader, frequently encountered during his time as prime minister (1990–97). Tony Blair also faced a number of rebellions by Labour Party MPs in his second term, more than a hundred in 2003 alone. As a general rule, however, British legislators maintain party unanimity about 90 percent of the time, far more often than members of the U.S. Congress have over the years.

Once the government has readied a bill, it announces its topic to the Parliament in a first reading. The bill is then debated on the floor in a second reading. Depending on the issue, debates in the House of Commons can be soporifically dull, with few members in attendance, or emotionally charged and bristling with partisan invective. The physical layout of the Commons lends itself to face-to-face exchanges between the governing party and the parties representing "Her Majesty's loyal opposition." The Speaker of the House presides from a raised chair, facing a center aisle. Since 2009 the Speaker has been John Bercow, a Conservative MP whose position requires general impartiality. (The Speaker may vote only to break a tie.) Five rows of green benches rise on either side of the aisle. The benches to the Speaker's right are occupied by the governing party, those to his left by the opposition parties. The seating arrangements are said to date from the sixteenth century, when the Commons met in St. Stephen's Chapel, seated in choir stalls located on opposite sides of the altar.

In the front rows of each side sit the parties' top leaders. The government's *front benches* are typically occupied by its ministers, at times led by the prime minister. The front benches of "parties opposite" are occupied by their respective leading personalities. Whenever the Conservative or Labour Party is in opposition, its front benches are taken up by members of the **shadow cabinet**, each of whom is assigned a portfolio corresponding to a cabinet post. The leader of the chief opposition party is the shadow prime minister, whose main task in Parliament is to challenge the governing prime minister. The shadow defense minister keeps tabs on the government's minister of defense, the shadow foreign secretary "shadows" the cabinet's foreign secretary, and so on. Should fortune bring the opposition party into power, the shadow cabinet will be ready to take office, its members having already immersed themselves in the details of their portfolios while in opposition.

Behind the front benches sit the *backbenchers*, ordinary MPs who have no spot in the government or shadow cabinet. Though they are fully cognizant of their duty to observe party discipline, they tend to be more than simply complacent followers of their party's leadership. Backbenchers have opinions of their own, and they must also consider the interests of the constituencies they represent. Government leaders frequently consult their backbench supporters to make sure bills under consideration meet with the approval of the backbench. Opposition leaders must also seek to harmonize their policy positions with their backbenchers' wishes.

After the first debate on a bill, a vote is taken. If a majority supports it, the bill then moves to a committee for detailed scrutiny. British parliamentary committees lack the authority, staff, and financial resources that U.S. congressional committees possess. Until the 1980s the House of Commons had no permanent committees such as those in Congress. Instead, it created standing committees, which are ad hoc bodies formed to consider specific bills, disbanding once their work is done. Since 1980 the Commons has also established more than a dozen departmental select committees patterned on the U.S. model, albeit with less intrusive investigatory powers.

It is in the standing committees that most bills are examined and amendments proposed. Government ministers and MPs loyal to the governing party's position generally have the upper hand in these committees. As a result, amendments to government-drafted bills are less frequent than in the U.S. Congress, where legislative proposals—even those with strong presidential endorsement—are often significantly amended before going to the floor for a final vote.

Once the bill comes out of committee in a form the government is willing to accept, it then goes before the whole House for a third reading and the decisive vote. If an initial voice vote is too close to call, a "division" takes place. Members of the House then divide into two lobbies located just outside the chamber. Those voting "aye" scurry into one lobby, those voting "no" into the other. No abstentions are recorded. The Speaker appoints "tellers" to count the votes as each MP files past them. Faithful to tradition, Parliament has resisted the use of electronic voting devices.

Throughout the legislative process, the government's priorities predominate. Well over 90 percent of all government-drafted bills are typically passed into law, often unamended. Even the most controversial measures are often passed quite rapidly. The Attlee government, for example, proposed 75 bills

The physical layout of the House of Commons lends itself to face-to-face exchanges between the governing party and the parties representing "Her Majesty's loyal opposition." Here Prime Minister David Cameron (second from left) and Deputy Prime Minister Nick Clegg (third from left) listen as Chancellor of the Exchequer George Osborne delivers a budget statement to the House of Commons in 2012.

in 1945–46. All of them passed in one year, including such sweeping measures as the creation of the National Health Service and the nationalization of several major companies. In 1997, the Blair government's bill to ban handguns was enacted by the House of Commons shortly after it was introduced. In the United States, by contrast, Congress finally passed comprehensive health care reform in 2009 after it had been proposed in 1993, and it took six years to pass the "Brady bill," a firearm regulation measure considerably less comprehensive than Britain's total ban on handguns. As a general rule, Britain's parliamentary system is more efficient at passing legislation than the U.S. separation-of-powers system. Especially when compared with periods of divided government in the United States, when the president represents one party and the congressional majority the other, British lawmaking is considerably less susceptible to gridlock.

Individual members of the Houses of Commons and Lords have the right to propose their own legislation, called "private members' bills," but only as long as the primary purpose of these bills is not to spend money or raise taxes. The government must approve virtually all spending and taxation legislation. Most private members' bills die, especially if the government is not willing to support them. British MPs thus have considerably less latitude for independent legislative initiative than do members of Congress.

Parliamentary Questions One of the most distinctive features of British politics is the practice of allowing members of the House of Commons to address questions directly to the prime minister and other government ministers. More than 50,000 queries are submitted in writing by MPs in an average year, and most receive a written response. Highly controversial inquiries, however, usually surface in open session during the periods devoted to the ministerial *question time*. By custom, the prime minister and other government ministers must appear before the House of Commons on a regular basis to answer questions posed by the members. Prime minister's question time now takes place once a week for 30 minutes. The highly charged atmosphere surrounding the prime minister's grilling guarantees a packed chamber, with many members obliged to remain standing since the benches cannot accommodate the full membership. Since 1989 the proceedings have been aired live on television.[16]

MPs who wish to ask a question must submit a written notice in advance of the session. The submissions are then drawn in lottery fashion to determine the order of questioning. Only about a dozen backbenchers will be able to raise a question in the allotted time, since the leaders of the two main opposition parties are given precedence in confronting the prime minister with several questions, often on different topics. The Speaker recognizes each questioner in turn, struggling to maintain order amid the bellowing and heckling that typically accompany a sharply worded question. After each question the prime minister rises to a lectern, the "despatch box," and delivers a response. Prime ministers do not know the content of the questions in advance, so their staff prepares them for a variety of likely queries. No amount of preparation can substitute for the cool nerves, quick wit, and debating agility required to answer—or artfully evade—a succession of hostile queries addressed by opposition leaders and backbenchers.

Members of the prime minister's own party also ask questions, usually of a friendly nature designed to elicit a glowing account of the government's achievements. On occasion, however, party disunity shows through when backbenchers raise questions indicating their dissatisfaction with their leader's policies, as occurred when Labour MPs questioned Tony Blair on Iraq.

Margaret Thatcher said no head of government in the world is as accountable as the British prime minister, largely because of the rigors of question time. No U.S. president has ever had to withstand the grueling ordeal of open questioning in Congress. The U.S. Constitution requires only that the chief executive submit to Congress an annual "state of the union" report. George Washington and the Congress discussed a questioning procedure but it was never instituted.

Other government ministers must also go before the House of Commons and answer questions, each appearing about once a month. Unlike the prime minister, who is responsible for all the government's policies, the other ministers are questioned primarily on their specific area of responsibility. Even so, the cut and thrust of the process can be unnerving. In 1983 a Conservative undersecretary collapsed while being grilled by Labour MPs and died.

Votes of Confidence Perhaps the most compelling indication of the executive's accountability to Parliament resides in the House of Commons' right to remove the government in a vote of confidence. A confidence motion may be posed either by the opposition (as in 1979) or by the government itself, as in 1994 when Prime Minister John Major sought to determine whether his government still enjoyed majority support. The procedure has been used quite sparingly, however. Since 1885 only two British governments have actually been defeated in a confidence vote. Both were Labour minority governments: Ramsay MacDonald's in 1924 and James Callaghan's in 1979. This record is remarkable when compared with the more frequent defeats that governments in other democracies have suffered in confidence votes, and it testifies to the enduring stability of British politics.

Members of the House of Commons What types of people get elected to the House of Commons? About 35 percent of the MPs elected from each of the three main parties in the 2010 election came from professional backgrounds, including lawyers (86), civil servants, and academics. Of these, 35 Labour members were college professors or schoolteachers, compared with just 4 Conservatives. Of the Labour MPs, 52 were professional politicians or party workers, and 15 were journalists or publishers while the corresponding number of Conservatives from these backgrounds were 31 and 18. Some 125 Conservative MPs came from private business, compared with 20 Labour members. Labour's parliamentary delegation also included 22 manual workers, fewer than in past decades but still 11 times as many as the Conservatives elected. Most Liberal

Democrats came from the professions (22) and business (11). About 12 percent of members of Parliament graduated from Oxford or Cambridge, a substantial number that was nevertheless smaller than in previous decades (see Figure 13.3).[17]

The representation of women has undergone slow but observable change over the years. In the seven Parliaments elected between 1964 and 1983, women held as few as 19 seats and no more than 28 (2.9 percent and 4.3 percent of the total membership, respectively). In 1987 the figure jumped to 41 members (6.3 percent) and edged a bit higher in 1992. In an effort to increase the number of women in Parliament, Labour in the 1990s adopted a candidate selection procedure aimed at electing women to half the party's seats in the House of Commons in future elections. In 1997, 121 women were elected (18.5 percent of the total), of whom 101 were in the Labour Party and 14 in the Conservative Party. In 2001, the number of female MPs fell slightly to 115 (of these, 95 were Labourites). In 2005, 128 women composed 19.8 percent of the Parliament. In 2010, 143 women were elected to Parliament (22 percent). Eighty-one were Labour members (31 percent of the Labour contingent), 49 were Conservatives, and seven were Liberal Democrats (see Figure 13.3).

The growing representation of women in Labour's parliamentary ranks coincides with rising numbers of women who voted for Labour candidates in the past two decades. From 1945 until 1979, British women tended to vote for Conservative candidates at higher rates than men—so much so that Labour probably would have formed *every* government in those decades if women had voted the same way as men. Gender differences on election day gradually disappeared in the 1980s as women increasingly abandoned the Tories, apparently out of antipathy to Margaret Thatcher's policies. With Thatcher gone, in 1992 women swung decisively

to the Conservatives again, but Labour's efforts to win them back paid off. In 1997, 49 percent of women voted Labour and only 30 percent voted for the Tories. Those figures were the same for male voters. In 2010, 31 percent of women and 28 percent of men voted Labour; 36 percent of women and 38 percent of men voted Conservative.

The House of Commons has not been very representative of the United Kingdom's nonwhite minorities. Britain's history as a colonial power resulted in the creation of the British *Commonwealth of Nations* in 1919. The organization initially sought to regulate relations between the United Kingdom and its colonies, but as Britain relinquished control over most of its dominions it evolved mainly into a forum for promoting economic cooperation. Today the commonwealth has 54 members, most of which are independent states. Until the 1960s, residents of commonwealth countries had the right to settle in the UK with full citizenship rights. But rising immigration in the 1950s and 1960s, especially from India, Pakistan, Africa, and the Caribbean, sparked resentment among large numbers of white Britons. The Wilson, Heath, and Thatcher governments imposed successive restrictions on immigration. The number of legal and illegal immigrants and asylum seekers wanting to stay in Britain has continued to grow in recent years, prompting the Blair government to work with the European Union to keep the flow within limits.

By 2011 some 6.6 million nonwhites were living in England and Wales, just over 12 percent of the population. Between 1929 and 1987 the House of Commons had no nonwhite members. Nonwhite representation in the House of Commons has risen steadily over the past three elections, to 4.2 percent of the House of Commons elected in 2010 (see Figure 13.3). Public opinion polls consistently show that a majority of blacks, Asians, and even whites regard Britain as a "fairly" or "very"

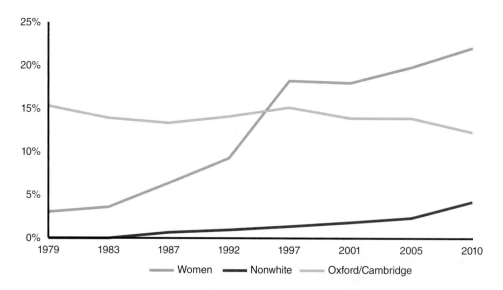

FIGURE 13.3 **Share of Parliamentary Seats Held by Women, Nonwhites, and Oxford and Cambridge Graduates, 1987–2010**

Source: Feargal McGuinness, "Social Background of MPs," House of Commons Library Research Note SN/SG/1528, December 14, 2010, www.parliament.uk/briefing-papers/SN01528.pdf.

racist society. Blair admitted before a hushed House of Commons in 1999 that "racism still exists in our society" after a report accused the London police and other British institutions of "institutional racism."

The House of Lords At the start of 1999 there were 1,294 members of the House of Lords. In accordance with centuries-old custom, the membership has traditionally included various bishops of the Church of England and so-called hereditary peers, who may bequeath their membership to an heir. In early 1999 there were 26 "Lords spiritual" and 759 hereditary peers (including 16 women). Laws were passed in 1876 and 1958 permitting the creation of "life peers," who serve in the House of Lords only for the duration of their lifetime without the right to pass their membership on to their children. Life peers are named by the monarch on the advice of the prime minister, usually as a reward for exemplary achievement in political or professional life. In the first months of 1999 there were 500 life peers (87 women), including Margaret Thatcher and the composer Andrew Lloyd Webber.

Most members of the nonclerical "Lords temporal" are affiliated with a political party. There were also more than 300 "cross-benchers" who did not align themselves with any party. Attendance at House of Lords sessions has often been spotty; traditionally, only a minority of members would show up on an average business day, while a few "backwoodsmen," usually from remote parts of Britain, rarely participated at all.

In 1999, the Blair government prevailed upon the House of Lords to accept a drastic change: The ranks of hereditary peers were reduced to 92 members. Those permitted to stay had to be elected by their colleagues in a special vote; the rest were required to relinquish their cherished parliamentary seats, abandoning a patrimony that in some cases stretched back to the fifteenth and sixteenth centuries. In 2012, the House of Lords had 765 members, including 650 life peers. A number of additional reforms have been proposed. The Conservative–Liberal Democrat coalition government agreement included a plan to reduce the size of the House of Lords to 450 members, 80 percent of whom would be elected. Many Conservative MPs, however, rejected the plan when it was raised in the House of Commons in July 2012, angering the Liberal Democrats and putting the coalition under strain.

Until the next stage of reform occurs, the House of Lords still has the right to vote on legislation passed by the House of Commons as well as to propose and pass legislation of its own. If the two houses cannot agree on a piece of legislation, a compromise is usually worked out. But if no compromise can be reached, the House of Lords under current procedures may not kill a bill already passed by the House of Commons. Laws enacted in 1911 and 1949 permit the House of Lords only to delay the passage of legislation the members do not accept, in some cases for no more than one month and in others for up to a year. If the House of Lords fails to pass the disputed bills within the allotted time, the bills automatically become law. The House of Commons has invoked this automatic enactment provision only once since 1949.

Although its legislative importance has progressively diminished, the House of Lords continues to have an impact on the legislative process. Since 2004, for example, it has managed to amend government-sponsored bills passed in the House of Commons on such controversial issues as antiterrorism, personal identity cards, acts of racial and religious hatred, and the banning of fox hunting.

Until 2009 the House of Lords stood at the apex of Britain's legal system as the supreme court of appeal for the entire country in civil cases, and for England, Wales, and Northern Ireland (not Scotland) in criminal cases. In stark contrast to the United States, Britain had no separation of powers between its legislature and its highest court. However, a government-backed constitutional reform act passed in 2005 created a new *Supreme Court* of the United Kingdom, which will take over the judicial functions of the House of Lords as well as other judicial responsibilities. Because of the concept of parliamentary sovereignty, the Supreme Court does not have the authority to overturn primary legislation, unlike the highest courts in the United States, France, and Germany. It can, however, rule on the legality of administrative and executive acts and review laws to determine their compatibility with human rights law and European Union law.

The Government

In a parliamentary system, the term *government* refers to the chief decision-making body of the executive branch. It is used in the same way people refer to a president's administration in the United States. In Britain the government consists of about a hundred individuals, all of whom must be members of Parliament. Most are members of the House of Commons, but some also come from the House of Lords.

The Cabinet The most prestigious 20 or so government ministers constitute the cabinet. Its leader is the prime minister, who also bears the titles of first lord of the treasury and minister for the civil service. Most cabinet ministers are formally known as secretaries of state, though a few have more high-sounding titles such as the chancellor of the exchequer and the lord chancellor. Each cabinet member assumes responsibility for a particular functional area, such as foreign affairs, health, or trade and industry, and most preside over a department of civil servants engaged in the bureaucratic tasks of policy planning and implementation within their respective domains. By tradition, two or three cabinet ministers are members of the House of Lords, but the prime minister and all others belong to the House of Commons.[18] Immediately after winning reelection in 2001, Prime Minister Blair increased the number of women in his cabinet to seven, an all-time high. In 2006 there were eight women in Blair's reshuffled cabinet, including the country's first female foreign secretary, Margaret Beckett, but the current Conservative–Liberal Democrat cabinet that took power in 2010 includes only five women. By the coalition agreement, 18 members (including Prime Minister Cameron) are Conservatives and five (led by Deputy Prime Minister Clegg) are Liberal Democrats.

Although it is customary—and correct—to say that Britain's political system rests on the principle of parliamentary supremacy, in actual practice the government tends to exercise more authoritative power than Parliament enjoys. The government dominates the legislative process, taking the initiative in proposing most bills and invoking party discipline when the bills come up for a vote. The Parliament may always hold the government accountable for its actions and retains the right to remove it from office in a confidence vote, but on a day-to-day basis it is the government that steers the legislature's activities rather than the other way around.

The prime minister, moreover, steers the government. The head of government possesses an impressive array of powers, all of which derive from customary practice and are not codified in legal statutes. These include the right to appoint and dismiss other cabinet members and top bureaucratic officials, or change their positions, without having to secure Parliament's approval. (The U.S. president may appoint cabinet members and many other officials only with the Senate's approval.) The government has the exclusive right to propose bills affecting revenues (such as taxes) and expenditures. The prime minister may order British military forces into action in wars, peacekeeping missions, and other operations without parliamentary approval. Some observers have suggested that the British prime minister's powers amount to an "elective dictatorship." Though there is more hyperbole than accuracy in this characterization, the fact remains that Britain's prime minister usually has more powers of initiative and greater control over the cabinet and the legislative process than do most heads of government, including the president of the United States.

Leadership styles have varied among Britain's prime ministers. Some have been dynamic leaders determined to seize the policy-making initiative and impose their preferences on their cabinet and party. Others have been more consensus oriented, seeking to balance and coordinate the diverse opinions expressed by other party leaders and the various groups and constituencies connected with their party. Thatcher and Blair are examples of dynamic initiators; Attlee and Major tended to be consensus seekers. Other prime ministers have combined aspects of both leadership styles to varying degrees.

British cabinets tend to meet far more regularly than do cabinets in the United States and to assume a greater collective role in debating and deciding government policy. In Britain the entire cabinet usually meets once a week. While its deliberations are secret, the memoirs of former ministers and occasional leaks to the press reveal that it is a lively institution whose leading members speak up on a range of issues, even those not immediately concerned with their particular functional responsibilities.[19] Budget debates can be especially intense, as the various ministers defend their own department's claims to financial appropriations. The prime minister is not formally bound to follow the cabinet's preferences on any issue, but even a strong-willed leader such as Thatcher or Blair cannot stray too far from the cabinet's wishes without risking a potential loss in leadership authority.

Once a decision is made and the prime minister enunciates it, the principle of *collective responsibility* demands that all cabinet ministers fall into line behind the policy in their public statements.

The Civil Service Visitors to Parliament and No. 10 Downing Street (the prime minister's residence) soon find themselves on an imposing boulevard called *Whitehall*. Along its wide expanse are some of the most important ministries and agencies of the British government. Just as "No. 10" is synonymous with the prime minister and "Westminster" with Parliament, "Whitehall" connotes the country's bureaucracy, or *civil service*. From the Foreign Office to departments concerned with local government, Britain's civil service is a vital part of the executive branch, playing a critical role in the formulation and execution of the government's policies.

Like many bureaucracies, the civil service is both indispensable and maligned. No cabinet official can do without the expertise of its professional cadres, many of whom have devoted their entire careers to specific policy issues. Quite often an experienced civil servant will know more about a policy matter than the cabinet minister or agency chief who supervises that office. Tensions sometimes arise when the prime minister or cabinet ministers are determined to pursue a policy initiative at variance with the preferences of the senior civil servants who advise them. Although they are expected to be politically neutral, following the government's lead in policy matters and dutifully carrying out its decisions, highly experienced civil servants may on occasion disagree with the government's policy and seek to alter its course, primarily through articulate persuasion rather than bureaucratic sabotage. Both Margaret Thatcher and Tony Blair often relied more heavily on their personal advisors than on civil service experts, especially in controversial policy areas.

The president of the United States has the right to fill some 2,000 to 3,000 plum positions at the highest levels of the American federal bureaucracy, thus ensuring compliance with presidential policy preferences throughout the executive branch. The prime minister may fill only about a hundred. Career civil servants occupy most of the remaining posts. About 700 officials comprise the Higher Civil Service, a prestigious elite heavily populated with "Oxbridge" graduates (men and women who attended Oxford or Cambridge Universities), about two-thirds of whom are male. These highly influential career civil servants owe their positions to professional accomplishment within the bureaucracy, including success in competitive midcareer examinations, rather than to political patronage. From their ranks a smaller group of about 60 to 70 are selected as "permanent secretaries," a uniquely British "elite of the elite" of career bureaucrats who work intimately with government ministers. While it is sometimes criticized as a bastion of elitism with little direct accountability to the population, Britain's civil service also wins wide praise as a model of bureaucratic professionalism and incorruptibility.[20]

The Monarchy

Although its power has been whittled down to practically nothing and its prerogatives are largely ceremonial, Britain's thousand-year-old monarchy nevertheless fulfills an important function in British politics: It provides a living symbol of the long continuity of the country's history, people, and institutions. In recent years the British royal family has suffered a number of widely publicized indignities and tragedies such as the marital troubles of the Queen's sons, Princes Charles and Andrew, and the death of the popular Princess Diana, who was killed in an auto accident in Paris not long after her divorce from Charles. And Queen Elizabeth II has been subjected to criticism for her aloofness from the general public. Nevertheless, both the queen herself and the monarchy as an institution continue to enjoy wide popularity in Britain as demonstrated by the enthusiasm at the recent diamond jubilee celebration of Queen Elizabeth's 60-year reign. Approximately 70 percent of Britons favored retaining the monarchy. However, mounting criticism of the royal family's lavish lifestyle has led to reductions in the amount of public revenue devoted to its upkeep, and in 1992 the Queen agreed to pay income taxes.

The distinction between the monarch's *formal legal* powers and her *actual decision-making* powers remains fuzzy in a number of areas. Constitutionally, the monarch is part of Parliament. She retains the formal legal authority to designate the prime minister, dissolve Parliament, and call parliamentary elections. No act of Parliament may take effect as law until the monarch signs a document of royal assent. The monarch is the nominal commander-in-chief of the armed forces and the head of the British Commonwealth. In actual practice, however, the monarch is not a voting member of Parliament like the members of the Houses of Commons and Lords. Her right to designate the prime minister is limited by the majority party's right to recommend its preferred designee. Her rights to dissolve Parliament and call elections are formalities that are superseded by the prime minister's prerogatives. She cannot refuse her royal assent without creating a grave constitutional crisis. (Not since 1707 has a British monarch refused to assent to an act of Parliament.) In actuality it is the government that directs the armed forces in war and peace and sets policy on the Commonwealth.

Devolution and Local Government

For much of its history, the United Kingdom has been a *unitary state:* Most political decisions have been taken by the central government and Parliament in London, with very little decision-making authority left to regional or local governments. In his first term as prime minister, Tony Blair secured the *devolution* of local decision-making power to newly created legislatures in Scotland and Wales. He also began the process of reviving Northern Ireland's defunct local parliament in the aftermath of the 1998 "Good Friday Accords," which were aimed at ending decades of violent conflict between Protestants and Catholics in that troubled region. In the process, Blair moved the UK closer to the model of a federal state (see Chapter 6).

Today, the Scottish Parliament and the regional government formed out of it deals with issues such as health, education, justice, rural affairs and transportation. Wales, too, has a National Assembly and a Welsh Assembly government that deals with similar policy areas. The Northern Ireland Assembly and its corresponding Northern Ireland Executive also address concerns such as culture, arts, education, agriculture and rural development, health, social services and public safety.

Many parts of England have a two-tier local government structure of county governments with district governments below them. County governments provide services such as education, social services, and public transport, while district governments look after trash collection and recycling, leisure facilities, and more local needs. In the larger cities, there is a single-tiered government structure, known as metropolitan district councils, borough councils, or city councils depending on the size of the local government unit. Most are governed by local councils, with the council leaders drawn from the council itself in a way parallel to the selection of the prime minister by the Parliament. The Cameron government had sought to replace many council leaders with directly elected mayors, like in the United States and many other democracies. However, when that plan was put as a referendum before the voters of 10 large local government units in 2012, 9 rejected it.

Even with the political reforms that recent governments have enacted, Parliament remains sovereign in the UK. Devolution and reform of local government have put more power in the hands of local officials, but Parliament remains supreme. Hence, the focus of political participation in the UK revolves around the political parties and the election of MPs because they form the government that emerges out of Parliament.

POLITICAL PARTICIPATION

Political participation can take many forms, as we learned in Chapter 8. In the UK, electoral participation and the organization of parties and campaigns for contesting elections is at the heart of citizen involvement in British politics. Hence we will focus on elections, campaigns, and parties in this section.

Parties and Elections

Political parties are vital to the electoral process in all democracies, but especially so in a parliamentary system of government. British parties are more centrally organized than are parties in the United States and play a more direct role in defining policy goals, nominating candidates for office, conducting election campaigns, and coordinating legislative and government activities. The three largest parties—Labour, the Conservatives, and the Liberal Democrats—are particularly well organized. Each has a national headquarters and a bureaucracy, representatives in Parliament (the "parliamentary party"), and local organizations in all House of Commons districts in Great Britain (the "constituency parties"). (Neither Labour nor the Liberal Democrats contest elections in Northern Ireland, while the

Conservatives have only a token following there.) Unlike the Democrats and Republicans in the United States these parties also have dues-paying members. Only those members whose dues are paid are allowed to vote at constituency meetings to nominate candidates for the House of Commons.

The Party Leader All the main parties in the United Kingdom have explicit procedures for choosing the party leader, who is the person most likely to become prime minister should the party win a majority of seats in the House of Commons. By contrast, the two main U.S. parties do not have a formal chief. While a serving president is usually regarded as the leader of his party, he does not carry this title officially. The party that does not occupy the White House may be even less certain who its leader is.

Just as important, Britain's parliamentary system requires any prospective prime minister to be a member of Parliament, preferably of the House of Commons. It is therefore unthinkable that a British politician could become leader of one of the main parties or rise to "the top o' the greasy pole" as head of government without parliamentary experience. Several have also gained executive experience serving in the cabinet before assuming party leadership. However, it is quite possible for a political figure in the United States to have no experience in national government, in either Congress or the cabinet, and still win election to the highest office of the land. Presidents Carter, Reagan, Clinton, and George W. Bush are recent examples.

British prime ministers are elected by a much smaller group of voters than are U.S. presidents. In Britain, the party leader's name appears on the ballot only in one House of Commons district (constituency). In 2010, David Cameron was the Conservative candidate for Parliament in the Oxfordshire constituency of Witney, which he has represented since 2001, and nowhere else. Voters living in other constituencies who favored Cameron for prime minister had to vote for the Conservative Party candidate running in their own constituency and hope that Conservative candidates would win a majority of these single-member constituency contests. By contrast, all American voters have a chance to choose among the competing candidates for president in the general elections.

Every year the Labour Party and the Conservatives hold a conference at which their leaders make major pronouncements and party activists debate policy alternatives. The Liberal Democrats convene twice yearly for these purposes. By contrast, American parties hold national conventions only every four years, mainly to confirm as their nominee for president the candidate who has emerged from the primary elections of the preceding months as the front-runner.

British Parties The three largest British parties share several features, though they differ in details. All three are moderate, mainstream catchall parties. Labour tends to be a left-of-center party, with its lower-middle-class and working-class base and social welfare priorities. The Conservatives are right of center, with a large upper-middle-class and upper-class following and strong ties to private enterprise. But these two large parties

garner votes from all social classes, especially the large middle class, and their leaders have calculatingly edged closer to the center since the 1990s. The Liberal Democrats position themselves squarely in the center of Britain's political spectrum. All three parties have struggled in recent years to articulate a distinctive message, a task complicated by the fact that they all favor the mixed economy's combination of private enterprise and social welfare, and all favor Britain's alliance with the United States and its membership in the European Union. At the same time, all three parties are internally divided into competing wings and policy tendencies.

The Conservatives, who have been formally known as the "Conservative and Unionist Party" since the days when they favored the union of Ireland with Great Britain, were Britain's most successful party for much of the twentieth century, producing prime ministers such as Winston Churchill, Harold Macmillan, and Margaret Thatcher.[21] From 1997 to 2005, however, the Tories suffered their three worst defeats.

One of their problems was that Tony Blair and the New Labour Party managed to occupy the center ground of British politics by embracing some traditional Conservative goals—such as low inflation, labor union restraint, and business incentives—while pursuing social welfare policies popular among voters in the middle and on the left. Blair stole the Tories' thunder by depriving them of their ability to brand Labour as a high-tax party dominated by trade union militants and pacifists. Another problem was the Conservatives' failure to find a popular, charismatic leader capable of uniting the party's various wings. After William Hague resigned following the 2001 elections, the Tories instituted new procedures for choosing the Conservative Party leader. In the past, the party chief was selected by the Conservatives' House of Commons delegation (the "parliamentary party"). Under the new rules, Tory MPs would pick two nominees for the leadership post, and then the party's dues-paying members would vote on the final choice by mail-in ballots. When this process was used for the first time in 2001, Iain Duncan Smith won the leadership in a hotly disputed contest. But Duncan Smith proved ineffectual, provoking calls for his resignation. In 2003 the Tories' "1922 Committee," consisting of all the Conservative MPs with the exception of the party leader, removed Duncan Smith and selected Michael Howard as his successor. As the parliamentary party's only nominee, Howard did not require confirmation by the party membership. After Howard resigned in 2005, the Tories chose David Cameron as their new leader.

As described in more detail in the next section, the Labour Party has undergone profound transformations of its own. Under the informal moniker "New Labour," Tony Blair and his key lieutenants guided the party to unprecedented electoral successes by pulling it away from the influences of the labor unions and the party's left wing and accepting many of the market-oriented reforms that Thatcher introduced when she was prime minister. Blair also proved more aggressive in foreign affairs than the Labour Party had been, strongly supporting President Bush in the wars in Afghanistan and Iraq. But the controversies arising from his stewardship as prime

PROFILES   David Cameron

Coming to the Conservative Party leadership at age 39, David Cameron had relatively little experience in politics. His background marked him as a traditional blue-blooded Tory. A descendant of King William IV and two Conservative MPs, Cameron was sent to boarding school as a child and rounded out his education at Eton and Oxford. The third of four children, Cameron witnessed his father, a stockbroker, struggle with adversity. Born with deformed legs, Ian Cameron eventually had to have them amputated. David Cameron said his father did not understand himself to be handicapped and said of this family that "whingeing (that is, whining) was not on the menu." His mother, Mary Cameron, served as a justice of the peace for 30 years. David Cameron married Samantha Sheffield, herself the daughter of a baronet and the step-daughter of a viscount, in 1996. They have had four children, one of whom, Ivan, required round-the-clock care for cerebral palsy and a form of epilepsy and died in 2009.

After taking his Oxford degree in philosophy, politics and economics, Cameron spent his early years as an aide to Conservative leaders, beginning with a stint in the party's research department in the late 1980s and then serving as a junior advisor to John Major's chancellor of the exchequer in the early 1990s. He was at the chancellor's side during the events of "Black Wednesday," when the pound was forced out of the European Exchange Rate Mechanism. Knowing he wanted to run for Parliament, Cameron left politics to gain corporate experience with a large communications firm from 1994 to 2001. He ran unsuccessfully for Parliament in 1997, but won his race in 2001 in the Oxfordshire constituency of Witney. In 2004 he became the Conservatives' parliamentary spokesperson for education. Although leader Michael Howard took him under his wing and made him responsible for policy coordination in the party, Cameron was a relative unknown until his three-minute speech at the 2005 party conference won a spirited response from the delegates for its rousing appeal to modernize the party. After being nominated to succeed Howard in the leadership by Tory MPs, Cameron won 68 percent of the vote among party members,

soundly defeating a more experienced right-winger favored by Thatcher.

Perhaps owing to his family's experiences with adversity, Cameron has rejected the hard-line policies associated with Margaret Thatcher. Vowing to pursue "compassionate conservatism," Cameron announced plans to steer the Conservative Party closer to the centrist mainstream, much as Tony Blair had led the Labour Party to the center in the 1990s. The main policy idea in the 2010 Conservative election manifesto was the "Big Society," which promised to take power out of the hands of politicians and give it to local communities by encouraging volunteerism, supporting co-ops and non-profit organizations, and transferring more power to local governments. These policies, Cameron hopes, will make for a more vigorous civil society.

Cameron also declared that he was "fed up with the Punch and Judy politics of name-calling, backbiting, point-scoring, and finger-pointing" in House of Commons debates. Acknowledging that the Conservatives had "a vast mountain to climb," Cameron hoped to transform a party riven by continuing differences between centrists and right-wingers on taxes, social welfare policy, Europe, and other issues. The Tories also faced declining support among young voters, women, ethnic minorities, college graduates, and even its base of "true blue" supporters from the worlds of business and the professions. By the time the Labour government's parliamentary term came to its end in 2010, David Cameron faced a far more experienced opponent, Gordon Brown. Labour, however, was deeply unpopular as the incumbent government during the economic crisis that emerged after the U.S. housing bubble burst in 2008, making Cameron and the Conservatives the odds-on favorites to sweep the election. But Cameron was blindsided by Nick Clegg, who proved to be a vigorous campaigner and who performed much better than Cameron in an early, televised public debate. Consequently, coming to power Cameron was encumbered by having to take on a coalition partner, something none of the recent Conservative Party prime ministers had to do.[22]

minister ultimately compelled Blair to step down as party chief far earlier than he probably would have liked. And the divisions within the Labour Party between Blair-oriented centrists and more left-leaning politicians and voters have by no means disappeared. Opposition to such things as the war in Iraq, college tuition payments, the privatization of traditional social services, and other Blair policies arose to a considerable extent from the party's traditional left-of-center base. Brown followed Blair into the party leadership upon the former's resignation in 2007. When Labour failed to win the 2010 election and then was unable to prevent the formation of the Conservative–Liberal Democrat alliance, Brown stepped down. Ed Miliband won

the internal party election to replace Brown. Miliband, whose father was a famous Marxist academic and whose brother was Brown's foreign minister, has been critical of Blair and Brown's policies, especially the war in Iraq, and advocated a return to Labour's more progressive tradition. Like the Conservatives, the Labour Party must redefine itself in the light of its traditional values and rapidly changing domestic and international environments.

The **Liberal Democrats** are the descendants of the old Liberal Party. The liberals originated as the Whigs and remained the country's second most important party after the Conservatives until shortly after World War I, when they were increasingly eclipsed by the Labour Party. Another antecedent of the Liberal Democrats was the Social Democratic Party (SDP). The SDP started in 1981 when a number of moderate Labour MPs, distraught at the leftist direction of the Labour leadership, bolted from the party and formed a new one. The Liberals and Social Democrats formed an alliance that won 25 percent of the vote (but only 3.5 percent of the seats) in 1983. Five years later they formally merged as the Liberal Democrats. The party has sought to forge its identity as a centrist alternative to the Conservatives on its right and Labour on its left. After the 1997 elections, the Liberal Democrats sought to make common cause with Blair's New Labour government on issues such as electoral and constitutional reform and the euro. But Labour's huge voting majority in the House of Commons enabled Blair to pursue his government's priorities independently of Liberal Democrat support. Nevertheless, the Liberal Democrats continued to support a more proportional electoral system, the replacement of the House of Lords by a democratically elected Senate, and the adoption of the euro. They also held back from supporting Blair's policies on Iraq in 2003.

With only about 70,000 paid members, the Liberal Democrats elect their leader by means of a mail-in ballot of the membership. Paddy Ashdown was elected in 1988 and was followed in 1999 by Charles Kennedy. After leading the "Lib Dems" to small but encouraging gains in the elections of 2001 and 2006, Kennedy was pressured by party leaders into resigning in January 2006 because of a drinking problem. In two rounds of postal-ballot voting, party members elected Sir Menzies "Ming" Campbell, the party's number two, as their new leader. In 2007 the elderly Campbell stepped down and Nick Clegg, only 40 at the time, took the party leadership.

All three major parties—Labour, the Conservatives, and the Liberal Democrats—have suffered from declines in their membership and core identifiers. The number of dues-paying Conservatives has tumbled from 1.2 million in the halcyon days of Thatcherism in 1982 to about 177,000 by 2011. The Labour Party's membership spiked from 280,000 in 1992 to 405,000 when Tony Blair led the party to a spectacular victory in 1997, but then slid to 190,000 in 2011. And the Liberal Democrats have fallen from 145,000 members during the time of the Liberal–SDP Alliance in 1983 to 66,000 in 2011. The problem is not money: Annual dues are £43 (less than $70) in the Labour Party while the Liberal Democrats recommend that members contribute £60 but accept members who contribute only £12, and fees are typically even less for students and workers. Even well-heeled Conservatives are asked simply to contribute only £25. Though dues-payers have the privilege of participating in the nomination process for House of Commons candidates, as explained below, a diminishing number of British citizens are willing to take part in this process by joining a particular party. In a trend observable in the United States and other long-term democracies, today's voters in Britain are increasingly independent. In 1964, 44 percent of British voters identified themselves as "very strong" adherents of a particular party (typically one of the three main parties), and 40 percent said they were "fairly strong" party identifiers. In 2005, only 8

percent were very strong party identifiers, and 37 percent were fairly strong party adherents; fully 18 percent claimed no party affiliation. In 2010, 8 percent of the voters cast their ballots for parties other than the "big three," or for the Scottish or Welsh nationalist parties.[23]

Several smaller parties have managed to win seats in the House of Commons fairly consistently. They tend to have weak organizations dominated by a few leaders, with few or no dues-paying members. The more successful of these parties are based outside of England. The *Scottish National Party* (SNP), founded in 1934, advocates independence for Scotland. In 2010 it won 20 percent of the Scottish vote and six seats in the House of Commons. Its main competitor is the Labour Party, which won 41 of Scotland's 59 House of Commons seats; the Liberal Democrats won 11, the Conservatives just one. The *Welsh Nationalist Party*, Plaid Cymru, founded in 1925, wants more autonomy for Wales (but not outright independence) and greater use of the Welsh language. It polled 11.3 percent of the Welsh vote in 2010 and won only 3 of the 40 seats reserved for Wales in the House of Commons.

Northern Ireland's parties reflect that region's tormented history of sectarian strife between Protestants and Catholics. The Protestants (or "unionists") have an intransigent party, the *Democratic Unionists*, which was founded in 1971 and led until 2008 by the Reverend Ian Paisley, and a moderate party, the *Ulster Unionists*, which supported the Protestant–Catholic peace process under David Trimble (leader, 1995–2005). The Catholics (or "nationalists") are also divided into an intransigent party and a more moderate one. *Sinn Fein* (We Ourselves) is the political wing of the Irish Republican Army (IRA), which has a tradition of terrorism. The *Social Democratic and Labour Party* has been more supportive of the peace process. After sectarian violence erupted once again in Northern Ireland in 1969, the UK government in 1972 suspended the region's local legislature and imposed direct rule from London, policed by British troops. Over the following decades, more than 3,200 people lost their lives in bombings, assassinations, and other acts of violence. With citizens on both sides of the religious divide increasingly eager for peace, Protestant and Catholic negotiators engaged in protracted negotiations mediated by the Clinton administration's envoy, former Senator George J. Mitchell. On Good Friday in 1998, accords were signed aimed at ending the stalemate. After the accords were ratified by 71 percent of Northern Ireland's voters, British rule was supposed to be lifted and the local legislature was supposed to resume its work in the historic building known as Stormont. But these measures were repeatedly rescinded or postponed as the IRA refused to disarm its militants and Protestant hard-liners refused to deal with the IRA. Only in 2006, after the IRA certified that it had disarmed, did the Stormont legislature reconvene. Tensions between Protestant and Catholic hard-liners remain, however. Northern Ireland is allotted 18 seats in the UK's House of Commons. In 2001 and again in 2005, the Protestant and Catholic intransigent parties each won seats from the moderate parties. In 2005, Trimble lost his seat to a candidate from Paisley's party. In 2010 the Ulster Unionists won no seats.

Former U.S. Senator George Mitchell brokered a peace agreement between Catholics and Protestants in Northern Ireland in 1998. David Trimble of the Protestant Ulster Unionist Party and John Hume of the Catholic Social Democratic and Labour Party won the Nobel Peace Prize for working with Mitchell to reach the peace agreement, known as the Good Friday Accords for the day on which the pact was signed. Here UK Prime Minister Tony Blair (sitting, left) and Irish Taoiseach Bertie Ahern sign the accord.

Dozens of parties and well over a hundred independent candidates participated in the UK's 2010 elections. Only 10 parties and 1 independent won seats, however (see Table 13.2). Among the smaller parties, the environmentally oriented *Green Party*, with its support centered mainly in urban constituencies with large student populations, fielded 310 candidates, up from 202 in 2005. They averaged 1 percent of the vote but won only one seat. The *UK Independence Party*, which favors a referendum on withdrawing from the European Union, ran in 572 constituencies. It won 3.1 percent of the vote but no seats. Several fringe parties on the left (like the British Communist Party) and right (like the anti-immigrant British National Party) also came up short.

Elections to the House of Commons: The Nomination Process

One of the first things most candidates for elective office must do is obtain the official nomination of a political party. Like most parliamentary democracies, the United Kingdom does not have primary elections. Rather, each party has its own procedures for choosing its nominees to compete in the general elections to the House of Commons. In the three largest parties it is the party activists and dues-paying party members in each constituency who ultimately select their party's nominee. In the smaller parties that have few, if any, dues-paying members, the nomination process tends to be controlled more tightly by professional party elites.

The Conservatives, the Labour Party, and the Liberal Democrats have roughly similar procedures for selecting their candidates. People who wish to run for Parliament are typically interviewed by a party's selection committee in the constituency they wish to represent. (As noted earlier, MPs do not have to reside in the constituency they represent.) If a constituency is considered fairly safe for one of the parties and the nomination is up for grabs, quite a few apply, sometimes between 25 and 100. But if an incumbent MP is popular or if a challenging party is not likely to win, there will usually be far fewer applicants for the nomination. The selection committee screens the applicants and draws up a short list, normally consisting of between 2 and 10 applicants. This all-important short-list decision is invariably made by a very small group of people; constituency selection committees generally consist of only about a dozen local activists in the Conservative Party and around 20 in the Labour Party.

Once prospective nominees have made the short list, they appear before an "adoption meeting" of the local constituency membership. (Conservative Party constituency associations often have a further screening of the short-list candidates, only one or two of whom may be presented to the full constituency membership for final approval.) In the Conservative, Labour, and Liberal Democrat Parties, these nomination meetings are rarely attended by more than 200 dues-paying members; in most cases only about 50 to 150 show up to vote.[24] Assuming a generous average turnout of 160 voting members in each constituency, this means that slightly more than 100,000 people in each of Britain's two largest parties participate in the nomination process for about 650 House of Commons seats. The Liberal Democrats' nominees are chosen by an even smaller number of members. Far fewer people are eligible to take part in the nomination process in the smaller parties. With about 44 million registered voters in the UK in 2010, it appears that fewer than 1 percent of British voters participated in the party nominations process for the House of Commons in that year. In the United States, fewer than 20 percent of eligible voters sometimes participate in primary elections for the House of Representatives. Yet, while many Americans regard these turnouts as lamentably low, they are considerably higher than in Britain and other democracies that do not have primaries.

Meanwhile, the central headquarters of the main parties plays its own role in the selection process. The dossiers of prospective nominees for Parliament are usually scrutinized by the party's central office, and some applicants are personally interviewed. While the national headquarters rarely forces a candidate of its own choosing on a local constituency, all candidates nominated by the constituency parties must be vetted by the party's central organs. As a consequence, candidates for Parliament—as well as serving MPs—tend to be more dependent on their national party leadership than are candidates for Congress in the United States, who compete in primary elections on their own initiative and raise most of their own campaign funding. If a party's national leadership refuses its endorsement of a prospective candidate, that person will not be able to run for Parliament as the party's official nominee. No similar process of interference by the Democratic or Republican national committees exists in the United States, giving candidates and elected members of Congress greater independence from their party leadership than their British counterparts enjoy.

Campaigns and Campaign Financing Another salient difference between British and American electoral processes is that until a new law was passed in 2011 the UK did not specify the timing of general elections very far in advance of their occurrence. American law designates the first Tuesday after the first Monday in November every two years for congressional elections and every four years for presidential elections. Before the law passed in 2011, the British prime minister could ask the monarch to call elections to the House of Commons at any time. While the old British law required parliamentary elections to take place at least every five years, prime ministers were allowed to call anticipated ("snap") elections before the expiration of Parliament's full five-year term. If public opinion polls looked favorable for the government, the motivation to call a snap election was especially high. In fact, snap elections were the rule rather than the exception in Britain. Since 1918, John Major's second government (1992–97) and the Blair–Brown Labour government (2005–10) were the only ones in peacetime to serve out their full terms. Except for the crisis years of 1935–45, all other prime ministers called snap elections. However, with the Fixed-Term Parliaments Act of 2011 British general elections will now occur on the first Thursday of May each five years starting in 2015. The law does still allow for early elections in the event that the government falls and no new one can be formed from the existing Parliament or if two-thirds of the House votes for early elections. The new law essentially denies the prime minister the right to call snap elections unilaterally.

Once the prime minister gets the monarch's symbolic approval and announces the date of the elections, an official campaign period begins that has important legal consequences. In 2010 Gordon Brown formally announced on April 6 that the elections would take place in four weeks. Parliament is formally adjourned during this period and ceases to meet; hence no new legislation can be enacted.

Once the campaign is under way, the main parties issue an election "manifesto" that outlines the policies they promise to pursue if elected to form the government. The formulation of these manifestos is taken more seriously by British parties than by the two largest parties in the United States. Presidential candidates in both large U.S. parties are notorious for ignoring their party's platform in the ensuing campaign.

Strict spending rules apply during the official campaign period in the UK. It is only during these weeks that parties and candidates may spend money for advertising and related election purposes. Most of the advertisement money is for handouts and billboards; British law forbids paid political ads on television or radio. The British Broadcasting Corporation (BBC) provides each major party with a limited amount of free airtime during the campaign period, while the national treasury picks up the tab for campaign mailings.

One of the most significant differences between British and American elections is that, since the passage of the Corrupt and Illegal Practices Act in 1883, British law limits how much may be spent on behalf of individual candidates running for the House of Commons. While the precise amount varies from one election to another and depends in part on the number of voters in each constituency, candidates in the 1990s were allowed to spend no more than about £7,500 on average—about $10,000. That amount went up only slightly in 2001 and 2005. Most candidates spent less. In the United States, individual candidates now spend about $1 million in contested primary and general elections to the House of Representatives. The cost of running for the U.S. Senate or the presidency is, of course, vastly higher.

National party organizations, however, may spend large amounts of cash on political campaigns. In recent years these costs have soared, as British parties have adopted American election techniques such as hiring ad firms and distributing literature and videos. In 2005 the Conservatives and Labour each spent about £18 million (about $34 million), and the Liberal Democrats spent £4.3 million (about $8 million). However, in 2010 the totals spent by the main parties declined. Even though each party was allowed to spend up to £19.5 million, the Conservatives spent £16.6 million, Labour £8 million, and the Liberal Democrats £4.7 million. This contrasts to the billions of dollars spent in the 2012 American election.

All candidates in parliamentary elections are required to put up a deposit of £500. If they fail to garner at least 5 percent of the vote in their constituency, they forfeit the deposit, which reverts to the national treasury.[25] Small parties and independents who just want to be on the ballot thus pay a fee for the privilege. In 2010 1,860 candidates forfeited their deposits.

Voter Registration and Turnout Unlike American voters, British citizens are not required to go to a designated location to register to vote. In Britain, voters may register by mail, and election authorities may conduct a door-to-door canvass of some residences before an upcoming election to make sure all citizens eligible to vote are on the registry. In 2011 it was estimated that about 6 million eligible voters in the UK were not registered to vote, about 15 percent of those eligible. This figure was much lower than in the United States, where 35 percent of citizens eligible to vote are not registered.[26]

Voter turnout in Britain has remained consistently higher than in the United States, even though the two countries have similar election procedures for the lower house. Between 1945 and 1997, turnout in 15 elections to the House of Commons averaged 76.8 percent of registered voters. The 2001 turnout of 59.4 percent was the lowest since World War I. It climbed slightly to 61.2 percent in 2005, and to 65.1 percent in 2010.

The Electoral System The electoral system used to elect the House of Commons is the *single-member-district (SMD)/plurality* method. There is only one round of elections: Hence it is a *single-ballot* procedure. The United States employs the same system for elections to the House of Representatives.

The United Kingdom was divided into 650 electoral districts (constituencies) for the 2010 general election. In the past there was no fixed number of constituencies, nor was there a precise limit on the size of their population. A neutral electoral commission fixed the number of constituencies and their boundaries, avoiding the political gerrymandering of districts that occurs in the United States. In 2001 there were 659 constituencies, but the number fell to 646 in 2005 as Scotland lost 13 seats in the Commons. In recent years the English constituencies have tended to represent about 68,000 voters each, with lower numbers in Scotland, Wales, and Northern Ireland. Prime Minister Cameron has ordered the electoral commission to reduce the number of constituencies to 600 for the next election, with about 76,000 eligible voters in each. In the United States, each of the 435 members of the House of Representatives represents, on average, 450,000 eligible voters, but the actual figure varies by state.

One person is elected to represent each district in a winner-take-all contest. Because at least three candidates compete in most UK districts, the victor does not have to earn an absolute majority of the votes cast (more than 50 percent) to win; a *plurality* suffices. Each candidate's name is listed on a paper ballot, followed by her or his party affiliation (see Figure 13.4). Britain does not use voting machines.

As we saw in Chapter 6, one of the chief results of the SMD/plurality system is that it sometimes produces a disparity between a party's percentage of the total vote and its percentage of the seats in the legislature. In Britain these disparities can at times be very wide, generally much wider than in the United States. One of the most glaring examples is the Parliament elected in 1997. With slightly more than 43 percent of the popular vote, the Labour Party won more than 63 percent of the seats—a 20-point disparity! The results of the 2001 elections were just as striking: Labour won 40.7 percent of the popular vote and 62.5 percent of the seats. In 2005 Labour won 55.1 percent of the seats with just 35.2 percent of the popular vote, the lowest popular percentage ever in the United Kingdom for a single-party majoritarian government. When voter turnout is considered, Labour won only 21.6 percent

VOTE FOR ONE CANDIDATE ONLY

1	**BARROW** Giles Timothy Barrow Avenue. Morden, Surrey, SM4 4 Green Party		
2	**CASALE** Roger Mark Casale Road, Ravnes Park, London, SW20 The Labour Party Candidate		
3	**COVERDALE** Christopher Joseph Coverdale Woodside, London, SW19 Independent		
4	**GEE** Stephen Mark Gee Banstead, Surrey, SM7 1 Liberal Democrats		
5	**HAMMOND** Stephen William Hammond Road, Wimbledon, London, SW19 The Conservative Party Candidate		
6	**MILLS** Andrew Thomas Mills Road, Merton Park, London, SW19 UK Independence Party		
7	**WEISS** George Weiss (known as "Rainbow") Street, Hampstead, London, NW: Vote For Yourself Rainbow Dream Ticket		
8	**WILSON** Alastair Pitcairn Wilson Close. Tooting, London, SW17 Tigers Eye The Party For Kids		

FIGURE 13.4   Sample Ballot
Source: Electoral Services Office, London Borough of Merton.

of registered voters. In 2010 the Conservatives' share of seats in the Commons was 47.2—a near majority—with just 36.1 percent of the vote (see Table 13.4).

While victorious parties have good reason to cheer the results of the British electoral system, less successful parties feel it discriminates against them. The SMD/plurality system punishes small parties. What matters in this system is not the percentage of votes a party gets nationwide, but *how many districts* its candidates win. A small party may have a substantial following spread throughout the country, but its candidates may amass enough votes to win only in a small number of constituencies. The Liberal Democrats and their predecessors, the Alliance and the Liberal Party, provide telling examples, as Table 13.4 shows. Not surprisingly, they have called for a new, more proportional system to replace the SMD/plurality system. Tony Blair once promised a referendum on changing Britain's electoral system, but he backed off the idea soon after his party's landslide win in 1997. The Liberal Democrats insisted the Cameron government present a referendum as part of the 2010 coalition agreement, which was held in 2011.

Proportional representation (PR) means that a political party is entitled to a share of legislative seats that is proportional to its share of the popular vote nationwide. There are several different variants of proportional representation. In a *pure PR system*, such as a *party list* system, a party that gets 30 percent of the

Table 13.4 House of Commons Elections, 1945–2010

| | PERCENTAGE OF POPULAR VOTE | | | | PERCENTAGE OF SEATS | | | |
| | | Liberals, Alliance, | | | | | Liberals, Alliance, | |
	Conservatives	Labour	Lib. Dems	Others	Conservatives	Labour	Lib. Dems	Others
1945	39.7%	47.7%	9.0%	3.6%	33.3%	61.4%	1.9%	3.4%
1950	43.3	46.1	9.1	1.5	47.8	50.4	1.4	0.3
1951	48.0	48.8	2.6	0.6	51.4	47.2	1.0	0.5
1955	49.6	46.4	2.7	1.3	54.6	44.0	1.0	0.3
1959	49.4	43.8	5.9	0.9	57.9	41.0	1.0	0.2
1964	43.3	44.1	11.2	1.4	48.1	50.3	1.4	—
1966	41.9	47.9	8.5	1.7	40.2	57.6	1.9	0.3
1970	46.4	43.0	7.5	3.1	52.4	45.6	1.0	1.0
1974 (Feb.)	37.8	37.2	19.3	5.7	46.8	47.4	2.2	3.6
1974 (Oct.)	35.7	39.3	18.3	6.7	43.5	50.2	2.0	4.1
1979	43.9	36.9	13.8	5.4	53.4	42.2	1.7	2.5
1983	42.4	27.6	25.4	4.6	61.1	32.2	3.5	3.5
1987	42.2	30.8	22.6	4.4	57.7	35.2	3.4	3.5
1992	41.9	34.4	17.8	5.9	51.6	41.6	3.1	3.7
1997	30.7	43.2	16.8	9.3	25.0	63.6	7.0	4.4
2001	31.7	40.7	18.3	9.3	25.2	62.5	7.9	4.3
2005	32.3	35.2	22.1	10.4	30.7	55.1	9.6	4.8
2010	36.1	29.0	23.0	11.9	47.2	39.7	8.8	4.3

Source: John Bartle and Anthony King, eds., *Britain at the Polls 2005*, (Thousand Oaks, CA: CQ Press, 2005), pp. 177, 221; BBC.

vote nationwide would automatically get about 30 percent of the seats. Another variant, which for several years was favored by the Liberal Democrat Party, is the *single transferable vote (STV)* system used in Ireland. This somewhat complicated system rests on multimember election districts and permits voters to rank the candidates in their order of preference. The 2011 referendum offered the British voters the choice of the existing single-member district system and the *alternative vote* (AV), a PR system similar to STV used since 1918 in Australia. British referendum voters decisively rejected the alternative vote.

Whichever of several different PR systems is used to distribute the seats, the final result would be somewhat closer to each party's share of the popular vote than the current plurality system (see Table 13.5). If Britain were to adopt some form of PR, it could probably count on a significant reordering of its governing processes. In all likelihood it would be more difficult for one party to win an absolute majority of seats in the House of Commons. Hung parliaments would be more common. One simulation of what the outcome of the 2010 election would have been using AV instead of first-past-the-post suggested that the Liberal Democrats would have gained 32 more seats while the Conservatives would have lost 23 and Labour 20. In that circumstance, the Liberal Democrats would have been able to form a majority coalition with either of the other parties instead of just the Conservatives.[27]

Britain's single-ballot, single-member-district/plurality electoral system is one of the main reasons British politics tends to be dominated by the two largest parties. Many observers, in fact, have described Britain as having a two-party system. But other parties are also involved in the political process, indeed considerably more than in the United States. At times these other parties can play a vital decision-making role. As we have seen, Callaghan's government relied on support from the Liberals and non-English nationalist parties. Major required

Table 13.5 Distribution of Seats under SMD and PR Systems, 1997

| | ACTUAL RESULTS UNDER SMD/PLURALITY | | | UNDER PURE PR | | UNDER STV | |
Party Seats	% of Vote	Seats	% of Seats	Seats	% of Seats	Seats	% of Seats
Labour	43.3%	419	63.6%	285	43.3%	342	51.9%
Conservative	30.7	165	25.0	202	30.7	144	21.9
Liberal Democrats	16.8	46	7.0	110	16.7	131	19.9
Others	9.3	29	4.4	64	9.7	42	6.4

Source: Bill Coxall and Lynton Robins, *Contemporary British Politics*, 3rd ed. (New York: Palgrave, 2002), p. 144.

HYPOTHESIS-TESTING EXERCISE
Social Class in British Politics

One of the oldest hypotheses about voting behavior suggests that people tend to vote in accordance with their class interests. People in the lower levels of the income pyramid can thus be expected to vote for labor- and welfare-oriented parties, while those in the upper echelons vote for conservative parties that pledge to keep taxes low and protect private business freedoms. To what extent does social class explain British voting behavior?

Hypothesis Social class best explains election outcomes in Britain.

Variables The *dependent variable* is election outcomes. On what is it dependent? The *independent variable* is social class.

Expectations If this hypothesis is correct, then we would expect the evidence to show that (1) working-class voters and others at the lower end of the socioeconomic pyramid vote consistently for the Labour Party; (2) people with higher incomes tend to vote consistently for the Conservatives; and (3) those whose incomes fall between unskilled workers and the middle class split their votes, with the less affluent strata tending toward Labour and the more affluent voting Conservative.

Evidence "Class is the basis of British party politics," a political scientist wrote in 1960. "All else is mere embellishment and detail."[28] Indeed, class-based voting patterns were especially evident before World War II and up until the 1960s. Between 1945 and 1970, for instance, the Conservatives won a solid 60 percent or more of the votes of nonmanual (white-collar) voters, while Labour won similarly large shares of the manual working-class vote. How does it look for more recent elections?

British survey researchers use a concept called "social grade" to distinguish the occupational backgrounds of chief income earners in households. This concept is not exactly the same as class but it can serve as a close proxy. There are six social grades, as shown in Table 13.6.

The British survey firm Ipsos MORI reports voting results by social class since 1974 by combining grades A, B, and C1 into the middle class, grade C2 into the skilled working class, and grades D and E into the semi- and unskilled working class.

Figures 13.5 and 13.6 show the class vote for the Conservative and Labour Parties since the October 1974 election.

As you can see in the charts, in the mid-1970s, a significant gap existed between the middle-class partisan preference and the voting tendencies of the working class, either skilled or semi- and unskilled. Only about a quarter of working-class voters chose the Conservatives, while nearly 60 percent preferred Labour. Meanwhile, nearly 60 percent of members of the middle class voted Conservative but less than 20 percent went Labour. That finding conforms with our hypothesis about class voting.

However, as the charts also show, the differences in partisan preference between the working and middle classes have narrowed considerably in the nearly 40 years since 1974. Working-class support for Labour declined during Thatcher's long tenure as prime minister. Middle-class support for the Conservative Party similarly declined during the long reign of Blair and his New Labour team. In 1974, the Conservative lead over Labour among the middle class was 37 points, and it stayed in that vicinity until Blair's first election. In 1974, the Labour lead over the Conservatives among semi- and unskilled workers was 35 points. In 2010 it was only 9 points.

Conclusions The evidence is *mixed*. British elections since 1945 demonstrate that social class indeed accounts for a substantial amount of voting behavior. The Conservatives and Liberal Democrats together have consistently managed to attract well more than half of the middle- and upper-class vote. The Labour Party has always won at least 40 percent of the least-skilled working-class vote. Nevertheless, British voters in the postwar period have not voted in strict accordance with their social class. The three main political parties, which started as *particularistic* parties representing specific class interests, developed over the course of the twentieth century into multiclass *catchall* parties. Increasingly, British voters of all classes punish incumbents in bad times (Labour in 2010), and reward them in good times (Conservatives in 1983 and 1987). In conclusion, class does matter in British elections, but class alone does not determine British election outcomes.[29]

Table 13.6 Social Grade in the United Kingdom

Grade	Description	% of Population, 2008
A	High managerial, administrative or professional	4
B	Intermediate managerial, administrative or professional	23
C1	Supervisory, clerical and junior managerial, administrative and professional	29
C2	Skilled manual workers	21
D	Semi- and unskilled manual workers	15
E	State pensioners, casual or lowest grade workers, unemployed with state benefits only	8

(Continued on next page)

(Continued from previous page)

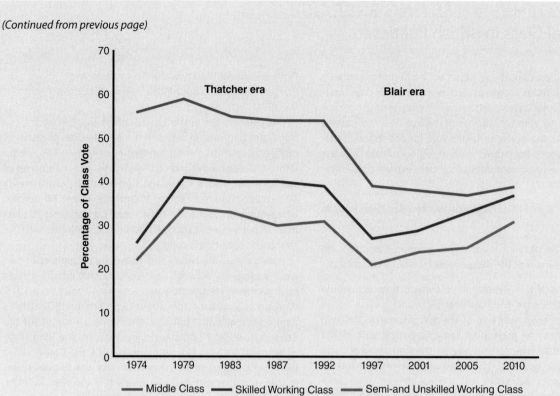

FIGURE 13.5   **Conservative Vote by Social Class, 1974–2010**
Source: Ipsos MORI.

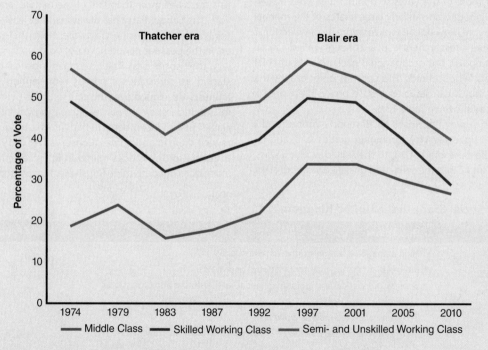

FIGURE 13.6   **Labour Vote by Social Class, 1974–2010**
Source: Ipsos MORI.

the votes of Northern Irish MPs to get his legislation on the Maastricht Treaty passed and to survive a vote of confidence. And David Cameron now relies on Liberal Democrats as part of his coalition government. Thus it would be inaccurate to describe Britain's party system as similar to the more pronouncedly two-party system that prevails in the United States. Accordingly, we describe the United Kingdom as having a *moderate multiparty* system: It has more than two parties, but fewer parties actively involved in the government than one would find in *extreme multiparty* countries such as Italy, where four or five parties have routinely joined in governing coalitions or parliamentary alliances. Had Britain adopted a form of PR, three or more parties would probably play a greater role in government than they do today.

POLICY AND POLITICS SINCE 1979

With the ascension to power of Margaret Thatcher in 1979, new approaches to major policy themes came to the fore in British politics. Most significantly these involved the nature of the British welfare state, the relationship of Britain to Europe, and the growing heterogeneity of British society.

Trimming the Welfare State

"I am a conviction politician," Margaret Thatcher affirmed as the 1979 election campaign got under way, serving notice that she did not intend to be bound by the prevailing consensus of postwar British politics. One by one, Thatcher repudiated the main tenets of British collectivism.

- Refusing to exalt the state as the mainstay of the British economy, she emphatically favored the private sector as the force of job creation. No government, she believed, could overturn the rules of the marketplace.
- She vowed to scale back the soaring costs of welfare by attacking the "culture of dependency." In her view, too many able-bodied citizens preferred government handouts to individual responsibility and hard work.
- Far from favoring the nationalization of private enterprises, Thatcher called for the privatization of nationalized enterprises. She also vowed to promote an "enterprise culture" aimed at encouraging entrepreneurism in a country that, in her view, was permeated with a socialist mentality placing excessive reliance on the state.
- Instead of placating trade unions in an attempt to avoid strikes, Thatcher declared her readiness to confront union leaders whenever their demands were economically unjustifiable or their actions illegal. She also favored greater democracy within trade unions, requiring union leaders to poll their membership before calling strikes.
- In a sharp critique of Keynesianism, Thatcher disavowed the principle of boosting government expenditures to stimulate economic activity. Instead, she embraced *monetarism*, the notion that inflation is fueled by an excess of money placed in circulation by the state's currency

authorities. For Thatcher, the battle against inflation took a higher priority over the battle against unemployment, at least in the short run.

These views constituted, in Thatcher's words, a "root-and-branch" reversal of the guiding assumptions of British politics. They also reflected a neoliberal view of economic democracy, one that stressed the liberties of the marketplace and the opportunities of a "people's capitalism" against the Labour Party's more welfarist, egalitarian approach to economic democracy. Thatcher's outspoken decisiveness and buoyant optimism about Britain's possibilities at a time of mounting pessimism captured the mood of a growing number of British voters. In May 1979 the Conservatives won a 43-seat majority in the House of Commons, and Margaret Thatcher became the first female prime minister in British history. In her more than 11 years in office, she reoriented British social and economic policy, scaling back the welfare state, weakening the unions, and setting the stage for a post-industrial society.

Thatcher changed the discourse on the British welfare state much more than the reality of public spending. Public spending remained about 40 percent of GDP from the late 1970s through the end of John Major's government, with the welfare component of that spending actually rising. Even while Thatcher privatized many state-owned firms and sold 1.7 million public housing units, most to the tenants living in them, thereby reducing public obligations, other factors prevented her from making greater headway against public spending. For one, the demand for public support increased. Her tight monetary policies and the worldwide recession that spread to Europe from the United States in the early 1980s caused unemployment to rise dramatically, increasing the need for unemployment benefits. The aging of the British population meant more pensioners began to draw on state-provided benefits too. Moreover, the British public was not as eager to abandon the welfare state as Thatcher. In 1983, 9 percent of the British population supported Thatcher's policy of cutting taxes and benefits while 32 percent preferred higher spending and taxes. By 1995, well into Major's prime ministry, 61 percent favored more spending and taxation while the share of the population supporting cutting taxes and spending had fallen to about 5 percent.

However, Thatcher reset the terms of the debate about the welfare state. When Tony Blair took leadership of the Labour Party and then won an overwhelming victory in the 1997 general elections, he brought to government a different view of the welfare state than his Labour predecessors. Blair proved more effective than other Labour leaders in convincing the party faithful that fundamental changes had to be made in Labour's ideological orientation if it ever hoped to recapture power. In the process he abandoned his own leftist positions on several issues and accommodated himself—and the party—to selected aspects of Thatcherism. Blair combined a moral commitment to social welfare and compassion for the needy with a traditionalist's attachment to God, family, and individual responsibility to the larger community. This combination of "welfarist" and conservative values defined Tony Blair's political viewpoint.

PROFILES   Margaret Thatcher

Margaret Thatcher (1925–2013), British prime minister, 1979–1990

The daughter of a small-town shopkeeper, Thatcher went to Oxford and became involved in the Conservative Party's student organization. Soon after graduation in 1947 she decided to run for Parliament. After losing her first two electoral contests in 1950 and 1951, Thatcher won the endorsement of the Conservatives of the Finchley constituency, and in the general elections to the House of Commons, Thatcher won her seat. In eight subsequent elections she never lost.

A tireless worker, Thatcher quickly ascended the party's ranks. In 1970 Prime Minister Ted Heath appointed her education secretary. But she regarded Heath's decision to change his free-market policies in 1972 as a mistake. Vowing never to make such a U-turn, Thatcher declared, "You turn if you want to; the lady's not for turning." In 1975 Thatcher was elected by Conservative members of Parliament as their party's new leader. Under her leadership the Conservatives won convincing majorities in the House of Commons in 1979, 1983, and 1987. Her overall record includes successes and disappointments.

- *Inflation.* One of Thatcher's biggest successes was her struggle against inflation. In 1980 Britain's inflation rate was 21 percent; by 1982 it was down to 5 percent and in 1986 it fell to 2.5 percent.

- *Growth.* Economic growth rates increased modestly in the 1980s to about 1.9 percent, higher than the previous decade. Business profits and real wages also rose under Thatcher's stewardship, but the gap between rich and poor widened, as did the gap between the prosperous southern parts of Britain and the declining north.[30]

- *Trade unions.* The Thatcher government faced down a yearlong strike in 1984–85 by the National Union of Mineworkers. It also secured legislation holding unions responsible for illegal actions and expanding democratic voting procedures within the unions. Many British workers supported Thatcher's policies, and the Conservatives won 37 percent of the working-class vote in the 1987 elections.

- *Privatization.* More than 25 state-owned companies were sold, in whole or in part, to private bidders. They included

Blair and political commentators have referred to it as the "third way," a centrist position located between the socialist orientations of the Labour left and the antigovernment inclinations of Margaret Thatcher's market-oriented conservatism.

With a keen eye to American politics, Blair identified Bill Clinton as a kindred spirit. Clinton's "New Democrat" approach, which stressed education and training for workers as well as tax breaks and other benefits for the middle class, struck a responsive chord in the Blair camp. Like Clinton, Blair knew that union members and nonunionized workers alike had reason to worry about job security at a time of accelerating economic globalization, but he also believed that an open global trading system ultimately creates more jobs and greater national wealth than protectionist trade barriers do. Blair further believed that the interests of all Britons, including workers, would be best served through closer ties to the European Union, an issue explored below. Given these views he and his chancellor of the exchequer, Gordon Brown, promoted education and worker training as well as programs focused on eliminating child poverty so that a culture of dependence on the state would not be established early. Yet during the Blair–Brown

years, the government share of the British economy drifted upward to reach about half of all economic activity in the crisis years after the housing bubble burst in 2008. After taking criticism during the 2001 election campaign for failing to deliver on public services, Blair and Brown injected new funds into health care, education, and other social programs. The National Health Service saw its budget rise by 7 percent a year starting in 2002. The money spent on new hospitals, clinics, and other facilities reduced the number of people on NHS waiting lists for non-life-threatening services, as well as the time spent in these queues. (In 2000, more than a quarter million Britons had to wait more than six months for an operation; by 2005 the list approached zero.) Spending on schools and other social sectors also rose. Despite these expenditures, the British economy retained a low inflation rate (2 percent or less). Interest rates also remained relatively low, stimulating a boom in real estate and consumer spending. However, those booms became bubbles just as they did in the United States by 2008.

While elements of the Conservative Party have continued to advocate Thatcherite policies to cut government spending, David Cameron came to the leadership of the party in 2007

British Petroleum, British Airways, British Telecom, and the Jaguar, Rolls-Royce, and Rover auto firms.

- *Unemployment.* The Achilles' heel of Thatcher's administration, unemployment soared from 5 percent when she assumed office to more than 10 percent from 1982 to 1987. It began edging downward in 1988, falling to 5.5 percent in 1990.

- *Spending and taxes.* Although one of Thatcher's top priorities was a reduction in government expenditures, state spending *rose* during her tenure in office due to mounting outlays for unemployment compensation, pensions, defense, public safety, and various welfare measures, including the National Health Service. Though the government kept its commitment to lower income tax rates, it raised the value-added national sales tax from 8 percent to 15 percent.

- *Social issues.* Although Thatcher favored abortion rights and the legality of homosexuality, her record on women's issues was mixed. Thatcher did not embrace feminist causes and she filled her cabinets with men. Her campaign to change British political culture by inculcating the values of the "enterprise culture" in place of collectivist values met with only modest success.

- *Foreign policy.* Thatcher achieved an international reputation as the "iron lady" for her toughness in foreign policy. In 1982 she sent the British fleet to repel Argentina's invasion of the Falkland (Malvinas) Islands, a small territory off the Argentine coast that had been governed by Britain for nearly 150 years. A staunch opponent of communism,

Thatcher had an especially close partnership with President Ronald Reagan, who shared most of her beliefs, and she played a critical diplomatic role in the West's dealings with the Soviet Union when Mikhail Gorbachev sought to end the Cold War.

Describing herself as single-minded, Thatcher pursued a take-charge leadership style, firing Conservative cabinet ministers who disagreed with her and mobilizing loyal grassroots party activists in support of her agenda. In 1990, however, the acrimony of opponents within her own party reached the boiling point after her government proposed supplementing the existing real-estate tax system with a head tax on individuals. More than 60 percent of the country opposed it, and Thatcher's approval ratings plunged to the lowest levels ever seen for a British prime minister. Taking advantage of her weakness, two Conservative leaders challenged Thatcher at the annual vote of Conservative members of the House of Commons to select the party's leader.

Thatcher fell short of the minimum votes necessary to win on the first ballot. Convinced that her position was hopeless, she withdrew from the second ballot and resigned as prime minister.

After 11 and a half years in office, Margaret Thatcher was ousted by her own party's parliamentary delegation. Nevertheless, as the dominant figure in British politics in the 1980s, she left a lasting imprint on the 1990s and beyond.[31] When Thatcher stepped down from her Commons seat in 1992, she was made Baroness Thatcher and joined the House of Lords. She died at age 87 in 2013.

with the promise to follow policies that would be more compassionate. However, facing a huge government budget deficit, he campaigned on a platform to cut government spending. After coming to 10 Downing Street he proposed to cut the budget by 25 percent with the goal of returning the government spending share of GDP to about 40 percent by the end of his term in 2015. The spending cuts led, among other things, to a tripling of tuition rates at British universities, which led to widespread and violent student protests in 2010. Cameron's coalition partner, Clegg, faced intense criticism from the Liberal Democrat faithful for supporting Cameron in the tuition hikes. The benefits the welfare state offers remain widely popular among the British people.

Britain and Europe

Another issue that has led to much debate in the UK in the post-World War II period is the country's relationship with Europe. As Europe integrated its economies, first in the European Economic Community and then in the European Union, the British have felt ambivalent about the merits of joining France

and Germany at the heart of this integration project. Britain's historical insularity as an island nation and its heritage as the center of the world's largest empire made many people resist the ties of interdependence that economic integration would bring. At the same time, though, Germany and France were enjoying much higher rates of economic growth as the leaders of the EEC and British producers could benefit from more favorable access to European markets. Britain became a member of the EEC in 1973 after its attempts to join in 1963 and 1967 were effectively vetoed by French President Charles de Gaulle. A 1975 referendum indicated the British people wanted to be part of the EEC. However, Thatcher was a "Euroskeptic" and tried to maintain a distance from the organization.

After new Prime Minister Major led the Conservatives to their fourth straight electoral victory in 1992, world currency traders began massively selling British pounds, fearing that they were overvalued in relation to other currencies such as the U.S. dollar and the German deutsche mark. Britain at this time was a member of Europe's Exchange Rate Mechanism (ERM), an agreement among Western Europe's largest economies to keep their currency exchange rates within certain limits, or "bands." As the pound's value deteriorated, Major's government announced its withdrawal from the ERM on a day that became known bitterly as "Black Wednesday." Not only did this decision represent a humiliating admission of the UK's economic weakness, but it also demonstrated that Britain could not necessarily count on Germany or its other European partners to come to its rescue in times of acute economic stress. Major spent his next five years in office gamely struggling to maintain party unity in the face of severe internal discord over European issues.

Earlier, in November 1991, leaders of the 12 countries that composed the European Community at that time held a summit in the Dutch town of Maastricht and agreed to substantially increase their economic and political integration over the decade. Their principal aim was economic and monetary union (EMU), to be anchored in the creation of a single European currency (the euro) and a European central bank to manage it. A treaty to this effect was signed in February 1992. In 1993, with a view to the eventual achievement of these and other cooperative goals, the European Community changed its name to the European Union (EU).

From the outset of these negotiations, Major let his European partners understand that his government was in no position to commit itself to abandoning the pound in favor of an all-European currency. He signed the Maastricht Treaty only after negotiating Britain's right to opt out of the clauses pertaining to European monetary union. He also refused to accept the EU's "Social Charter," which granted Europe's workers greater rights and welfare benefits than they currently enjoyed in Britain. Major also had doubts about the treaty's sections on establishing a "common foreign and security policy," something he feared would loosen Britain's close political and military ties with the United States. Despite these reservations, however, Major himself was not nearly as reluctant to join the European integration process as the more diehard anti-Europeanists within his own party. He believed that Britain's long-term economic interests required closer trade and financial ties to its EU partners over the coming years, a view strongly endorsed by the pro-European wing of his party.

The Labour Party, like the Conservatives, had long been internally divided about Europe. At different times it had supported membership in the community (in 1967 Wilson's Labour government applied unsuccessfully for membership) and opposed it, including favoring withdrawal from the EC in the early 1980s. As the Labour Party began to move in a more moderate direction under party leader Neil Kinnock in the late 1980s, it began to embrace the concept of closer ties to Europe, including openness to the EMU and the Social Charter. When he became prime minister in 1997, Tony Blair was much more openly pro-Europe than his predecessor. However, Britain has remained outside the EMU, continuing to use the pound sterling instead of the euro. Domestic political constraints impeded the Blair government and Gordon Brown, then chancellor of the exchequer, from moving into the EMU. In particular, worries about the limits on Britain's ability to

The citizens of the United Kingdom typically have the lowest sense of attachment to the European Union of any EU member state. Most Britons do not favor abandoning the pound in favor of the euro.

regulate its own economy through the central bank's interest rate policies and concerns about the potential impact of EMU membership on the huge financial industry centered in the City of London have discouraged further British integration into Europe.

The citizens of the United Kingdom typically have the lowest sense of attachment to the European Union of any EU member state. Most Britons do not want to abandon the pound in favor of the euro, and most probably breathed a sigh of relief when the proposed European Constitution was shelved by French and Dutch voters in 2006, obviating the need for a British referendum. When the EU members opted to pursue most of the features in the proposed constitution via the Treaty of Lisbon instead, Brown's Labour government approved it by parliamentary vote rather than a referendum despite the criticism of the Conservatives and many Euroskeptics. As it is, 85 percent of Britain's commercial laws are now EU laws made in Brussels.

During the sovereign-debt crisis in the euro zone the Cameron government has sought to protect Britain's financial sector. One proposed component of a Europe-wide solution to the financial difficulties of the Greek, Spanish, and other governments was a financial transaction tax on all financial dealings among EU members. Such a tax would have made the City of London a less attractive place for the world's financiers to conduct business, and so the Cameron government opted out of the comprehensive agreement the EU members made in December 2011. During the sovereign-debt crisis in the euro zone, many Britons have felt much relief that the UK retained the pound in the 1990s. Yet others have called on Cameron to hold a referendum to secede from the EU. Britain's relationship with Europe remains ambivalent.

An Increasingly Diverse Society

As mentioned above, British society includes an increasing number of immigrants and children of immigrants, many of them nonwhite. A first major wave of migration to the UK began in the 1950s when British Commonwealth residents, especially from the Caribbean, India, Pakistan, and Bangladesh, moved to the imperial metropole. In the postwar period the wave of immigrants included significant numbers of Irish, too. Much of the migration of the 1950s and 1960s was driven by a demand for labor in the UK and the search for better economic opportunities on the part of the migrants. As the British economy stagnated in the later 1960s and 1970s, labor demand declined and the government enacted restrictions on the inflow of commonwealth citizens. However, having established legal residence in Britain, the early immigrants began to bring their families to join them under family reunification policies. Much of the nonwhite immigration to Britain in the 1970s and after owes to family reunification. In the process, large communities of immigrants and their children formed. By 2010, more than 900,000 residents of England and Wales alone said they were of Caribbean ethnicity, about 1.4 million were Indian, 1 million Pakistani, more than 400,000 Bangladeshi, almost 1 million African, and more than 400,000 Chinese (many from the former British colony of Hong Kong). About 12 percent of the population was nonwhite. In addition, about 575,000 identified themselves as Irish.

As the economy boomed in the 1990s and the start of the new millennium, the British allowed EU residents to move to the UK to take jobs the new prosperity had created. This openness to EU migration led especially to an inflow of new residents from countries that had joined the EU after the fall of the Berlin Wall, such as Poland. Almost 2 million non-British, non-Irish white people lived in England and Wales in 2010.

As the result of immigration from former colonies, the United Kingdom is an increasingly diverse society, with 12 percent of the population of Britain and Wales people of color. British gold medal winners at the 2012 Summer Olympics in London included Mo Farah, who won two gold medals.

The New Labour government generally encouraged this migration. However, by the turn of the century, tensions associated with large-scale immigration had begun to appear. In the summer of 2001 race riots occurred in the declining industrial cities of Oldham, Bradford, and Leeds as nonwhites and white racists clashed, with much destruction of property.

In addition, terrorist actions by Islamic extremists from Britain's growing Muslim community have indicated that some significant element of the immigrant population has not been effectively integrated into the larger British nation. An al-Qaeda plot to set off a bomb in Birmingham was foiled in 2000. In December 2001 a British-born al-Qaeda operative, Richard Reid, was subdued on an aircraft headed for Miami while trying to set off explosives hidden in his shoe. On July 7, 2005, four British-born Muslims set off bombs in the London subways and on a bus during the morning rush hour, killing 52. In early 2006 an Islamic cleric based in London was sentenced to seven years in prison for hate crimes and incitement to murder. In the summer, British intelligence agents thwarted a plot by British Muslims to blow up as many as 10 airliners. And later in the year, the director general of MI5, Britain's security service, revealed that her agency was tracking some 200 British terrorist groups involving more than 1,600 known individuals; at least 30 terrorist plots had been discovered. Many of these potential terrorists had ties to al-Qaeda in Pakistan.

Britain has never really had a policy for integrating its immigrants and their descendants. While some observers have said that Britain under New Labour had pursued a multiculturalist strategy toward newcomers—providing state support and funding to minority groups to preserve their culture—that greatly overstates the extent to which Britain had a unified approach to immigrants. There was never a comprehensive set of policies toward immigrants, just piecemeal policies backed up by rhetorical multiculturalism. Today, as a consequence, Britain faces challenges regarding the integration of its immigrants and their descendants, both nonwhites and those who have moved from Central and Eastern Europe. Perhaps most central, what does it mean to be British? To the extent that national unity arose around the idea of the British as a democratic, freedom-seeking, self-governing people, the emergence of multiple ethnicities should not stand in the way of the regeneration of British identity. Some Britons, though, have felt threatened by immigrants. The British National Party, which has restricted membership to "indigenous British," has advocated the repeal of antidiscrimination legislation and pushed for immigrants to go home. Small matter that many "immigrants" were born in the UK, and some of their parents were too, since the communities founded by early postwar immigrants are at least third generation now.

Britain has made strides in implementing antidiscrimination legislation over the past decade and a half. Many of its communities, though, are quite segregated, with whites and Asians living in very distinct neighborhoods. The tensions associated with long-term unemployment and other manifestations of the economic downturn will surely exacerbate the potential for racial conflict. Prime Minister Cameron has argued that the culture of welfare dependency creates the need for immigrants because Britons will not accept certain low-pay or low-status jobs. At the same time he has criticized immigrant communities for failing to integrate into the larger British society. Like many postindustrial societies with large-scale recent inflows of immigration, such as the United States, France, and Germany, the integration of immigrants will remain a major challenge to the political system in coming decades.

Conclusion

Along with the United States, the United Kingdom is one of the modern world's two oldest continuously functioning democracies. Its success reflects the evolutionary development, over more than 300 years, of a democratic system as described in Chapter 5 and promoted by the 10 conditions for democracy spelled out in Chapter 7. Starting in the Middle Ages, England built the structures of modern democratic government on the foundations of the rule of law and democratic values such as freedom from tyranny and the right to private property. Over the centuries these values were supplemented by support for the values of legal equality and equity. The value of political inclusion for Britain's large working class was successfully implemented with the growth of the Labour Party. And racial and religious tolerance also gained support, though these values are always difficult to inculcate universally, as Britain's religious and ethnic conflicts continue to demonstrate today. Nevertheless, during the twentieth century Britain raised and solidified three essential aspects of democracy—popular sovereignty, based on mass suffrage; civil rights and liberties, based on the long traditions of English civil law; and economic well-being, based on private enterprise and a generous welfare state.

Despite its long lineage, British democracy is still evolving. With change on the horizon on a number of important constitutional and social issues, the United Kingdom continues to forge new directions in areas of vital importance to the functioning—and at times the very definition—of democracy.

Key Terms

Divine right of kings
Sovereign monarchy (absolutism)
Magna Carta
House of Lords
House of Commons
Parliamentary supremacy
Conservatives (Tories)
Labour Party
Shadow cabinet
Liberal Democrats

Notes

1. R. G. Davies and J. H. Denton, eds., *The English Parliament in the Middle Ages* (Manchester: Manchester University Press, 1981); Conrad Russell, *The Crisis of Parliaments* (London: Oxford University Press, 1971). King Charles I's determination to rule without Parliament in the 1630s provoked intense opposition and helped precipitate the Civil Wars of the 1640s and his own execution in 1649.

2. One historian notes that in the years between 1832 and 1867 Britain changed "from a system in which the Crown was the dominant influence in Parliament to a system in which the mass electorate began increasingly to call the tune." See Robert Blake, *Disraeli* (New York: St. Martin's Press, 1967), p. 259. Though the monarch today still formally names the prime minister, by 1834 the monarch could no longer appoint a head of government unacceptable to the House of Commons majority. For a classic description of Britain's governmental system in the latter half of the nineteenth century, with comparisons with the United States, see Walter Bagehot, *The English Constitution* (Brighton, UK: Sussex Academic Press, 1997).

3. See Dick Leonard, *Elections in Britain Today: A Guide for Voters and Students*, 3rd ed. (New York: St. Martin's Press, 1996), pp. 12–23. On the suffragettes, see George Klosko and Margaret G. Klosko, *The Struggle for Women's Rights* (Upper Saddle River, NJ: Prentice Hall, 1999); Barbara Winslow, *Sylvia Pankhurst* (New York: St. Martin's Press, 1996); Martin Pugh, *The Pankhursts* (London: Penguin, 2002).

4. Liah Greenfeld, *Nationalism: Five Roads to Modernity* (Cambridge, MA: Harvard University Press, 1992), chap. 1.

5. Gabriel Almond and Sidney Verba, *The Civic Culture* (Boston: Little, Brown, 1963). On the decline of deferential attitudes in British political culture, see Dennis Kavanaugh, "Political Culture in Great Britain: The Decline of the Civic Culture," in Gabriel A. Almond and Sidney Verba, eds., *The Civic Culture Revisited* (Boston: Little, Brown, 1980), pp. 124–76.

6. Barrington Moore, *Social Origins of Dictatorship and Democracy: Lord and Peasant in the Making of the Modern World* (Boston: Beacon Press, 1966).

7. Eric Hobsbawm, *Industry and Empire* (London: Penguin Books, 1990); E. P. Thompson, *The Making of the English Working Class* (New York: Pantheon, 1964).

8. For biographies that provide extensive accounts of the times, see Blake, *Disraeli;* Stanley Weintraub, *Disraeli: A Biography* (New York: Truman Talley/Dutton, 1993); Roy Jenkins, *Gladstone: A Biography* (New York: Random House, 1997); and Philip Magnus, *Gladstone* (New York: E. P. Dutton, 1964).

9. See Norman and Jeanne MacKenzie, *The Fabians* (New York: Simon & Schuster, 1977).

10. Henry Pelling and Alastair Reed, *A Short History of the Labour Party*, 11th ed. (New York: St. Martin's Press, 1996); Stanley Pierson, *Marxism and the Origins of British Socialism* (Ithaca, NY: Cornell University Press, 1973).

11. Kenneth O. Morgan, *Labour in Power 1945–1951* (Oxford: Oxford University Press, 1986); Jim Fyrth, ed., *Labour's High Noon: The Government and the Economy 1945–51* (London: Lawrence & Wishart, 1993).

12. Samuel Beer, *British Politics in the Collectivist Age* (New York: Vintage Books, 1969).

13. Howard R. Penniman, ed., *Britain at the Polls 1979* (Washington, DC: American Enterprise Institute, 1981); Richard Coopey and Nicholas Woodward, eds., *Britain in the 1970s: The Troubled Economy* (London: University College of London, 1996).

14. Callaghan was deserted by an erstwhile supporter from a Northern Ireland Catholic party and lost the vote of a dying Labour member who was too ill to take part. For his account, see James Callaghan, *Time and Chance* (London: Collins, 1987), pp. 558–63. See also Anthony Seldon and Kevin Hickson, eds., *New Labour, Old Labour: The Wilson and Callaghan Governments, 1974–79* (London: Routledge, 2004).

15. The term *whip* has two meanings. In addition to referring to the persons charged with keeping a party's legislative delegation in line, a whip also refers to the message sent by the party leadership to its MPs indicating the relative importance it attaches to bills coming up for a vote. Bills of relatively minor importance are underlined once; more significant bills are underlined twice or three times. MPs who vote against a "three-line whip" risk severe disciplinary action by the party leadership.

16. A taped broadcast of prime minister's question time is aired weekly in the United States by the C-SPAN network.

17. Feargal McGuinness, "Social Background of MPs," House of Commons Social and General Statistics Section, SN/SG/1528, December 14, 2010.

18. When Sir Alec Douglas-Home became prime minister in 1963 he was a member of the House of Lords. He thereupon renounced his title and subsequently won a seat in the House of Commons in a by-election.

19. For example, David Blunkett, *The Blunkett Tapes: My Life in the Bear Pit* (London: Bloomsbury, 2006).

20. David Marsh, David Richards, and Martin J. Smith, Changing Patterns of Governance in the United Kingdom: Reinventing Whitehall? (London: Palgrave Macmillan, 2002).

21. Anthony Seldon and Stuart Ball, eds., *Conservative Century: The Conservative Party since 1900* (Oxford: Oxford University Press, 1994).

22. Chris Philp, ed., *Conservative Revival: Blueprint for a Better Britain* (London: Politico's, 2006); BBC News, "David Cameron: Life and Times of New UK prime minister," May 11, 2010, http://news.bbc.co.uk; Sarah Lyall, "Cameron Faces Challenges beyond His Coalition," *The New York Times*, May 11, 2010.

23. Brian Wheeler, "Can UK Political Parties Be Saved from Extinction?" BBC News, August 18, 2011, at http://www.bbc.co.uk/news/uk-politics-12934148. The Labour Party's website is www.labour.org.uk; the Conservative Party's website is www.conservative-party.org.uk; the Liberal Democrats Party's website is www.libdems.org.uk.

24. Leonard, *Elections in Britain Today*, p. 97.

25. See www.electoralcommission.org.uk.

26. U.S. Census Bureau, "Voting and Registration in the Election of November 2010," www.census.gov.

27. David Sanders, Harold D. Clarke, Marianne C. Stewart, and Paul Whiteley, "Simulating the Effects of the Alternative Vote in the 2010 UK General Election," *Parliamentary Affairs* 64 (2011), pp. 5–23.

28. Peter G. J. Pulzer, *Political Representation and Elections in Britain*, 3rd ed. (London: Allen & Unwin, 1975), p. 102.

29. For a confirmation of this conclusion, see John Bartle, "Left-Right Position Matters, But Does Social Class? Causal Models of the 1992 British General Election," *British Journal of Political Science* 28 (1998), pp. 501–29. See also Andrew Adonis and Stephen Pollard, *A Class Act* (London: Penguin, 1998).

30. In 1979 the bottom tenth of the population shared 4.1 percent of the national income while the top tenth got 20 percent. By 1991 the bottom tenth's share was only 2.5 percent while the top tenth's share had grown to 26 percent. Income inequality grew faster in the United Kingdom in the 1980s than in any other economically advanced democracy except New Zealand.

31. Margaret Thatcher, *The Path to Power* (New York: HarperCollins, 1995); Margaret Thatcher, *The Downing Street Years* (New York: HarperCollins, 1993); Hugo Young, *The Iron Lady* (New York: Farrar, Straus, & Giroux, 1989); Dennis Kavanaugh, *Thatcherism and British Politics*, 2nd ed. (New York: Oxford University Press, 1990); Christopher Johnson, *The Economy under Mrs. Thatcher, 1979–1990* (London: Penguin, 1991); David Butler, Andrew Adonis, and Tony Travers, *Failure in British Government: The Politics of the Poll Tax* (New York: Oxford University Press, 1994); Eric Evans, *Thatcher and Thatcherism* (New York: Routledge, 1997).

14 France

OVERVIEW

- The emergence of democracy in France has been more discontinuous than the British or American experience. France experienced alternating periods of democratic and nondemocratic rule from the Revolution in 1789 until 1945.

- The centralized French state plays a strong role in society, with French democracy defined more by one's relationship to the state than in the more individualistic Anglo-Saxon democracies.

- Charles de Gaulle designed the presidential–parliamentary regime of the Fifth Republic to allow for a strong presidency. His successors learned how to cope with a circumstance, known as cohabitation, when the parliament has a majority different from the president's party.

- France's two-ballot single-member-district electoral system has gradually allowed for the emergence of two strong political tendencies, a neo-Gaullist party on the right and a socialist party on the left, while many small parties remain active.

- Like other European democracies, France struggles to retain the main features of its advanced welfare state while facing the challenges of globalization and an increasingly diverse society that has resulted from immigration.

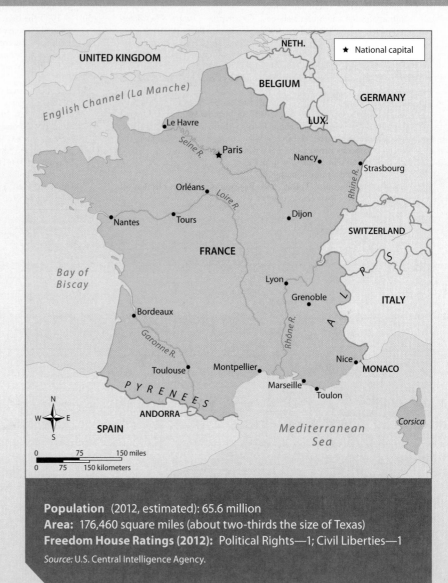

Population (2012, estimated): 65.6 million
Area: 176,460 square miles (about two-thirds the size of Texas)
Freedom House Ratings (2012): Political Rights—1; Civil Liberties—1
Source: U.S. Central Intelligence Agency.

FRENCH POLITICS ENTERS THE TWENTY-FIRST CENTURY

In the fall of 2005, President Jacques Chirac solemnly announced that France was experiencing a "deep malaise" and an "identity crisis." Voicing similar sentiments, Nicolas Sarkozy, the leader of Chirac's own political party, the Union for a Popular Movement (UMP), France's main center-right party, declared the country needed "a radical transformation." Repudiating the policies of the very president he had served, Sarkozy called for a complete rupture with a political, economic, and social system that, in his view, had produced little more than stagnation over the previous 30 years. In 2007 Sarkozy succeeded Chirac in the presidency after defeating Socialist Party (PS) candidate Ségolène Royal in a runoff election.

Sarkozy had been Chirac's interior minister. He was well known for taking tough stands on law-and-order issues, having called young people from France's housing projects, many of them immigrants or children of immigrants, "rabble," and cracking down on civil unrest based out of those housing projects in 2005. Sarkozy favored a U.S.-style quota system in restricting future immigration, with preference given to those with desirable job skills. He also favored efforts to reach out to the country's Muslim community, having previously joined in forming a new organization to represent France's Muslims, the French Council of the Muslim Religion. To this end he favored relaxing French secular traditions by permitting the use of public funds to build mosques. In economic policy he promised a pragmatic mixture of new incentives for private enterprise, including tax reductions and adjustments to the 35-hour workweek law, with continued state support for popular social welfare programs, and he pledged to reduce France's budget deficit.

In addition to his promises to modernize French politics and policy, Sarkozy came to the presidency with a background different from his predecessors. Many high-level French politicians and government officials are graduates of France's *grandes ecoles*, the country's elite graduate schools (similar to Harvard's Kennedy School of Government, only even more selective and influential in politics), and they are often from upper-middle-class Parisian families. Sarkozy, in contrast, was the son of a Hungarian immigrant father and attended law school, beginning his career as an attorney rather than a government official. He was also willing to live a flamboyant lifestyle, in contrast to predecessors who sought to protect their private lives and live discreetly. Shortly after coming to office Sarkozy divorced his second wife and then wed a fashion model, Carla Bruni, with whom he had a child while president. Sarkozy also socialized with billionaires and show business celebrities, leading one French newspaper to label him the "bling-bling president."

Sarkozy acted on his promise to lower tax rates and ease restrictions on the 35-hour workweek, but his goal of reducing the government deficit ran into the 2008–09 world economic crisis. Initially Sarkozy showed considerable pragmatism in responding to the crisis by allowing government spending to rise, but later in his term he became increasingly associated with German Chancellor Angela Merkel's policy of austerity. Sarkozy's tax breaks benefited the wealthy while the economic crisis produced more French unemployment. Between a personal image that irritated many French people and an economic program that, while relatively successful by the standards of European countries during the economic crisis, had not improved the lot of most voters, Sarkozy was vulnerable when standing for reelection in April 2012.

French presidential elections typically occur in two rounds. In the first round, virtually any number of candidates may run, subject to certain qualifications. If one of the candidates wins an absolute majority of popular votes (more than 50 percent), that person wins the presidency and there is no need for a second round. But since this electoral system was first used in France in 1965, no one has ever won a decisive first-round majority.

After a dozen years of the presidency of the rather austere Jacques Chirac, left, the French public enthusiastically greeted the more flamboyant Nicolas Sarkozy to the Élysée Palace in 2007. That enthusiasm waned quickly, however, and many analysts attribute his loss in 2012 to Sarkozy's extravagant lifestyle, including his divorce of his second wife and subsequent marriage to model Carla Bruni.

Incumbent Nicolas Sarkozy and challenger François Hollande squared off in a televised debate just before second-round voting in the 2012 French presidential election.

Round two, which takes place two weeks later, is a runoff election between the top two finishers of round one. As most observers expected, the 2012 elections ultimately came down to a second-round face-off between Sarkozy and the PS candidate, François Hollande, who ironically is the former common-law spouse of Royal, the 2007 Socialist Party nominee.

In contrast to Sarkozy, Hollande projected an image of a modest individual who abhors ostentation. Rather than driving a flashy car, he rode a motor scooter to his PS office. However, he is the graduate of a *grand école* and has been a prominent leader within the party organization for three decades. More-over, Hollande offered a clear alternative to voters: He rejected Sarkozy's calls for austerity, saying France and Europe needed an economic policy that emphasized growth, and he promised a more immigrant-friendly approach than his opponent. For his part, Sarkozy aggressively courted the supporters of the far-right National Front (FN). The FN's founder, Jean-Marie Le Pen, was renowned for his virulently antiimmigrant opin-ions. He had once advocated expelling France's immigrants, especially those of non-European descent, and sending them back to their countries of origin. His daughter and successor as FN leader, Marine Le Pen, had finished third in the first-round ballot on April 22 (see Table 14.1), but had refused to throw her support to Sarkozy who she viewed as too connected to Merkel and the European Union integration project. Hollande, who held a large lead in early polls, held on despite Sarkozy's vigorous campaigning to win the runoff vote. Sarkozy became the first incumbent to lose reelection in over 30 years but the ninth European leader to be thrown out of office after the onset of the economic crisis in the fall of 2008.

About a month later, on June 10, balloting began for the lower house of France's parliament, the **National Assembly**.

Table 14.1 2012 French Presidential Election Results

		FIRST ROUND		SECOND ROUND	
Candidate	Party	Votes	%	Votes	%
François Hollande	Socialist Party	10,272,705	28.6%	18,003,617	51.6%
Nicolas Sarkozy	Union for a Popular Movement	9,753,629	27.2	16,863,881	48.4
Marine Le Pen	National Front	6,421,426	17.9	-	-
Jean-Luc Mélenchon	Left Front	3,984,822	11.1	-	-
François Bayrou	Democratic Movement	3,275,122	9.1	-	-
Eva Joly	Europe Écologie–The Greens	828,345	2.3	-	-
Nicolas Dupont-Aignan	Arise the Republic	643,907	1.8	-	-
Philippe Poutou	New Anticapitalist Party	411,160	1.2	-	-
Nathalie Arthaud	Workers' Struggle	202,548	0.6	-	-
Jacques Cheminade	Solidarity and Progress	89,545	0.3	-	-

Source: European Election Database, Norwegian Social Science Data Services, http://www.nsd.uib.no.

Like the presidency, the 577-seat National Assembly is also elected in two rounds of voting. For these elections, metropolitan (mainland) France and several overseas territories are divided into 577 electoral districts. In accordance with the *single-member-district/plurality* electoral system, one person is elected to represent each district. The American and British variants of this system have a single round of voting on one election day. In the French variant, a candidate for the legislature who wins an absolute majority of votes in round one is declared the winner; no second round is held in such districts. But in districts where no candidate wins an outright majority in the first round, a second round of voting occurs one week later. In these districts, all candidates who won a percentage of the vote equivalent to at least 12.5 percent of the district's registered voters are eligible to compete in the second round. A plurality—the highest number of votes—is sufficient to win in round two.

The National Assembly elections of 2012 would prove just as important as the presidential elections. Not only would the president have to rely on the Assembly to pass bills into law; even more significantly, the French National Assembly has the right to approve the selection of the country's prime minister. Unlike the United States, whose chief executive is the president, and unlike the United Kingdom, whose chief executive is the prime minister, France has *two* executives. As pointed out in Chapter 6, France has a mixed *presidential–parliamentary system* of government. The chief distinguishing feature of this system is its *dual executive:* France is co-governed by its president, who has real decision-making powers, and by its prime minister, who also has real decision-making powers. The president is formally the country's head of state, while the prime minister is its head of government. To govern effectively, the two executives must try to get along and agree on a common policy agenda. If they do not agree, the result can be *immobilisme*, the French term for gridlock.

If the majority of the deputies elected to the National Assembly (at least 289 out of 577) belong to the same party as the president, the president can safely nominate a like-minded prime minister from his or her own party in the expectation that the party's parliamentary delegation will approve the choice. At least in principle, the French political system works at peak efficiency and effectiveness when the president, the prime minister, and the parliamentary majority all belong to the same party, or at least a coalition of like-minded parties. In contrast, if the president's party and its allies do not control a majority in the National Assembly, the possibilities of a standoff are much greater. The majority of the National Assembly is likely to reject a president's nominee for prime minister if the deputies do not like the president's choice. Under these circumstances, the president would be compelled by the logic of French politics to choose a prime minister who represents the opposing parliamentary majority. When the president is of one party and the prime minister represents an opposing party, the French call this situation **cohabitation**. In effect, cohabitation is the French version of *divided government*. In the United States, under a very different political system, divided government occurs when the president belongs to one party and one

or both houses of Congress are controlled by the other party. This predicament has marked the presidency of Barack Obama since the Republicans took control of the House of Representatives in 2010.

Cohabitation has occurred three times in France. The first manifestation was in 1986–88, when President François Mitterrand, a Socialist, was forced by a newly elected center-right majority in the National Assembly to select his archrival, Jacques Chirac, as prime minister. The second came in 1993–95, when Mitterrand was again compelled to pick a leader of the rival party, Édouard Balladur, as prime minister. And from 1997 to 2002, President Chirac had to select Socialist leader Lionel Jospin as prime minister after the Socialists wrested control of the National Assembly from Chirac's party in the snap elections of 1997. Although these rival leaders avoided political paralysis and even managed to cooperate, none of them regarded cohabitation as a satisfactory method of governing.

The Socialists and their allies did win a majority of National Assembly seats (see Table 14.2), allowing Hollande to name his preferred choice for prime minister, Jean-Marc Ayrault. Winning an election does not equate to success in governing, as Sarkozy learned. Hollande and Ayrault face significant challenges in France's highest offices. One set of problems centers on globalization and its regional variant, *Europeanization*. France is a rich country, with a gross national income of $2.78 trillion that ranked fifth in the world in 2011. Its per capita GNI of $42,420 made it comparable to Germany, Japan, and Canada. Nevertheless, many French people and political leaders are troubled by economic and social pressures emanating from abroad. Economic globalization features unprecedented levels of trade and foreign investment as well as relentless competition between private and state-owned companies in the global marketplace. These market forces are pushing French firms to widen their international activities and reduce operating costs. In the process, French companies are under pressure to merge with foreign-owned firms to form globally competitive corporate giants. In some cases these mergers result in layoffs of workers and staff, boosting unemployment and job insecurity. They can also diminish the executive controls previously exercised by French business owners and managers. As a consequence, anti-globalization sentiments have proliferated on both the left and right sides of the French political spectrum. When French survey respondents in their early twenties were asked in 2006, "What does globalization mean to you?" 48 percent replied, "Fear."[1]

Some of these globalization trends are being actively promoted by European Union institutions in Brussels. In the 1950s, France was a founding member of the European Economic Community, the forerunner of today's European Union (see Chapter 4). Until the 1990s, France asserted a leading role in the European integration process, acting in close concert with Germany. But the enlargement of the EU to 25 states in 2004, plus the addition of two more in 2007 and one in 2013, has diminished French influence. Hopes that France might take the lead in fashioning the EU's "common foreign and security policy" foundered when the governments of Britain, Spain, Italy, and several new East European member states backed

Table 14.2 2012 French National Assembly Election Results

Parties and Coalitions	FIRST ROUND		SECOND ROUND		TOTAL	
	Vote %	Seats	Vote %	Seats	Seats	Seat %
Presidential majority (Left)	**39.9%**	**25**	**49.9%**	**306**	**331**	**57.7%**
Socialist Party (PS)	29.4	22	40.9	258	280	48.5
Miscellaneous Left	3.4	1	3.1	21	22	3.8
Europe Ecology–The Greens (EELV)	5.5	1	3.6	16	17	3.0
Radical Party of the Left (PRG)	1.7	1	2.3	11	12	2.1
Total Parliamentary Right	**34.7%**	**11**	**44.1%**	**218**	**229**	**39.7%**
Union for a Popular Movement (UMP)	27.1	9	38.0	185	194	33.6
Miscellaneous right	3.5	1	1.8	14	15	2.6
New Centre (NC)	2.2	1	2.5	11	12	2.1
Radical Party (PRV)	1.2	0	1.4	6	6	1.0
Centrist Alliance (AC)	0.6	0	0.5	2	2	0.4
Left Front	6.9	0	1.1	10	10	1.7
National Front (FN)	13.6	0	3.7	2	2	0.4
Regionalists and separatists	0.6	0	0.6	2	2	0.4
Centre for France (MoDem)	1.8	0	0.5	2	2	0.4
Other far-right	0.2	0	0.1	1	1	0.2
Other far-left	1.0	0	–	–	0	0.0
Other ecologists	1.0	0	–	–	0	0.0
Others	0.5	0	–	–	0	0.0

Source: French Interior Ministry, http://elections.interieur.gouv.fr/LG2012/FE.html.

the U.S. invasion of Iraq in 2003, spurning efforts by France and Germany to block it. The possibility that Turkey may be admitted to the EU in the foreseeable future has raised fears of a further diminution of France's weight. In part for these reasons, a majority of French voters (55 percent), in a referendum held May 29, 2005, rejected the adoption of the EU's proposed Constitution for Europe. The vote was a stunning blow to the country's mainstream political leaders, most of whom had supported the constitution. French voters were uncomfortable with Sarkozy's support of Merkel in the German chancellor's effort to impose austerity on all of Europe, beginning with Greece, during the sovereign debt crisis (see Chapters 11 and 15), worrying that it reflected another example of EU institutions imposing economic policies on sovereign countries. France's new leaders will need to find new ways of dealing with the exigencies of globalization while redefining France's role in a new Europe.[2]

Another set of problems concerns France's ethnic and religious minorities. In 2008, more than 20 percent of adults in the country, approximately 10 million of the people aged 18 and older, were born abroad or had at least one parent who was born abroad. Roughly 45 percent of these people with foreign roots traced their origins to other EU countries, especially Southern Europe—Italy, Portugal, and Spain. About 3.5 million immigrants and second-generation French residents stemmed from one of France's former colonies in North Africa, the so-called "Mahgreb" countries of Algeria, Morocco, and Tunisia. Many others came from sub-Saharan Africa, Vietnam and neighboring parts of Southeast Asia, and the Caribbean— areas where France once had additional colonial dependencies.

French law prohibits compiling official statistics on religious affiliation, but it is believed that 5 million to 6 million Muslims reside in metropolitan France today. Many recently arrived immigrants and their families are crowded into ghetto-like suburbs (*banlieus*) of Paris and other cities. Unemployment rates, especially among youth, run as high as 40 percent of the local working-age population in some of these areas. Crime is a daily occurrence, discrimination and racism are constant realities. In an effort to integrate Muslims more fully into the country's secular education system, the government in 2004 banned the wearing of head scarves and other religious apparel or jewelry in French grade schools and high schools.

One night in October 2005, two Muslim teenagers were electrocuted to death after scaling a wall and falling on cables in an electric power substation located in Clichy-sous-Bois, about an hour's ride from Paris. Witnesses charged that the boys were being chased by police officers. The police denied this account, but accused the boys of trying to dodge a checkpoint where they would have had to show their identity documents. (One of the boys had left his identification papers at home.) Word of the deaths quickly spread, sparking anti-police disturbances. Over the course of the next three weeks, full-blown riots jolted more than 300 towns and suburbs in the Paris region and other areas with concentrations of immigrants. Even central Paris was affected. During this tumultuous period, more than 10,000 vehicles were torched and 200 public buildings set afire; 4,500 people were taken into custody. Political leaders were taken aback as events spun out of control. President Chirac was silent for 10 days before he addressed the public on the mounting

Large numbers of immigrants live in *banlieus*, or suburban ghettos, where they face crowded conditions, high crime rates, low unemployment, and ethnic and religious discrimination.

turmoil. His comments about France's "malaise" and "identity crisis" came more than a week after that. Prime Minister Dominque de Villepin and Interior Minister Sarkozy—rivals for the presidency after Chirac's expected retirement—each promised a crackdown on criminal behavior. De Villepin declared a state of emergency to permit curfews and other preventive measures. Just before the disturbances began, Sarkozy had called for a "war without mercy" against crime in the suburbs. When the riots broke out he initially called the rioters "scum" and "riff-raff" who needed to be hosed down, but he subsequently joined with Chirac and Villepin in proposing economic measures to deal with unemployment while deploring the marginalization of France's immigrant population.

Although many of the rioters were already known to French authorities as criminals, their actions reflected widespread anger in immigrant communities. Most of this discontent sprang from the frustrations of everyday life resulting from housing shortages, inadequate medical care, meager job opportunities, police harassment, and the like. Radical Islamic ideology and support for terrorism did not play much of a role in fomenting the riots. Most tellingly, the 2005 turbulence revealed the French political elite's inattentiveness to the grievances of the immigrant community, a problem that remains high on the agenda of President Hollande.

A third set of problems facing France's new leaders are socioeconomic in nature. The country's immigrants are not the only ones facing unemployment: France's overall unemployment rate has hovered around 10 percent since the 1980s. For much of that time, more than 40 percent of the unemployed have been jobless for more than a year—a figure six to nine times higher than in the United States or Canada.

As they confront these challenges, Hollande and Ayrault will operate in a political context that imposes constraints of its own, as you will learn in the coming pages. French politics has been characterized by long-established traditions of authoritarian decision making, populist demands for welfare guarantees, and intense contestation that spills out into the streets. The

nation has had a political culture that mixes support for a strong state with a passion for liberty, elite power with egalitarian ideals. The society includes those who need the state to ensure a basic safety net against poverty and those who want the state to provide the keys to the good life, including tuition-free university education, five-week paid vacations, a 35-hour workweek, subsidies for culture and entertainment, and retirement by the age of 60. Many—perhaps most—French people want a *protected society*, with the state assuming the predominant role in protecting them against the precariousness of the market economy. Many—perhaps most—of the French reject the American and British "liberal" models of political economy, which permit businesses and even the government to fire employees rather easily, and which pad employment rates with low-paying jobs (often without medical insurance, in the United States). In the "Anglo-Saxon" model, people are expected to fend for themselves to a greater extent than in France. In France, the state is expected to take care of people.

We continue the discussion of France by considering how its democracy has evolved, then turn to the major issues and political figures that dominated French politics in the second half of the twentieth century. We then pay special attention to French political institutions—above all, the presidential–parliamentary regime and the two-ballot electoral system. Following our examination of state institutions, we consider the main political parties in the country before closing this chapter by returning to the current political issues raised above.

HISTORICAL BACKGROUND: THE EVOLUTION OF FRENCH DEMOCRACY

As noted in Chapter 13, British democracy evolved in a long process that stretched from the origins of the British Parliament in the 1200s to the full flowering of universal suffrage in the twentieth century. The French democratic experience was considerably more spasmodic. Instead of a fairly steady evolution, France experienced a convulsive revolution. The French Revolution that began in 1789 was far more radical and violent than Britain's Glorious Revolution a hundred years earlier. Instead of paralleling Britain's gradual expansion of democratic rights in the nineteenth and twentieth centuries, French democracy suffered a succession of failures, giving way to authoritarian regimes of various types. And instead of developing a single concept of democratic governance like Britain's parliamentary system, France tried several democratic constitutions before settling on its current variant of the presidential–parliamentary model.

In tracing France's tortuous road to stable democracy, we can point to several factors on our list of conditions for democracy presented in Chapter 7 that distinguish the French political tradition from Britain's. They include the following:

- A long history of strong but not always democratic *state institutions*, characterized by a very effective centralized state and weak parliamentary traditions.
- The prolonged influence of authoritarian *elites*.
- A prominent role for the state in promoting *national wealth* despite substantial *private enterprise*.
- A concept of French *nationalism* that, at least until the Revolution, centered on the state and its authority rather than on the people and their liberties, retarding the emergence of a moderate and tolerant *political culture*.
- A *middle class* that did not constitute a steady source of support for democracy but divided its sympathies between democratic and various nondemocratic orientations.
- Prolonged difficulties integrating the working class, the country's main *disadvantaged class*, into democracy, resulting in the political alienation of many workers and the emergence of revolutionary socialist parties.
- A turbulent *international environment* that at various times suppressed, destroyed, or threatened to destroy democracy.

Though France has traditionally had more national unity and ethnic and religious homogeneity than the United Kingdom and developed an elite system of higher education at about the same time as England, these factors alone were not capable of overriding the other factors that made democratic stability much more difficult for the French to achieve than it was for the British. Let's look at these factors in greater detail.

The French State

"*L'Etat c'est moi*" ("I am the State"). This famous utterance is attributed to King Louis XIV, who reigned from 1651 to 1715. Though perhaps apocryphal, it plainly indicated where power resided in France. Fancying himself the Sun King (implying that he was at the center of everything and the source of all power), Louis XIV was determined to fortify royal authority through a firm application of the principle of the *divine right of kings*: the notion that God—not the people—was the source

of the government's legitimacy. The kingdom he inherited from his father, Louis XIII, was already anchored in centralized state institutions built around the monarch, his ministers, and an expanding cadre of professional bureaucrats. Louis XV, grandson of Louis XIV, allegedly expressed his own lack of faith in the ability of the French people to govern themselves by haughtily predicting, "*Après moi, le déluge*" ("After me, the deluge").

In marked contrast to England, the assertion of royal dominance in France was accompanied by the absence of an assertive national parliament.

Initial meetings in the fourteenth century of the *States General*, a nascent parliament, included representatives of the First Estate, the nobility; the Second Estate, the Roman Catholic clergy; and the Third Estate, the populations of cities, towns, and rural villages. The French crown was not ready to concede power to an elected parliament, however. King Philip IV quickly disavowed any idea of sharing power, and successive French monarchs called the States General into session with diminishing frequency. After 1439 it met once in 1614 and then not again until Louis XVI summoned it in 1789. By that time, popular demands for representation in government had been suppressed for so long that, when at last given a chance for expression, they exploded in a revolutionary frenzy.

The Revolution The **French Revolution** was such a shattering series of events that it redefined the significance of almost everything that had come before it in the country's political history. Centuries of royal absolutism, the absence of parliamentary representation, a disaffected nobility with little influence over the monarch and his ministers, financial mismanagement, an unfair tax system, festering urban and rural poverty—these and a variety of additional factors can all be viewed as antecedent causes of the Revolution.

The sorry plight of the government's finances compelled the crown in 1789 to convene the first meeting of the States General in 175 years with the hope that King Louis XVI would get the new taxes his lavish administration required. From the outset the newly assembled parliament was led by the largely middle-class deputies elected to represent the Third Estate. Shortly after convening, most of the Third Estate's 600-member delegation demanded a constitutional monarchy. The king relented, and the States General quickly reconstituted itself as a unicameral National Assembly. Also known as the Constituent Assembly, the legislature immediately set about the task of drafting France's first written constitution. Its preamble was a "Declaration of the Rights of Man," which enshrined private property along with "resistance to oppression" and citizen participation in the lawmaking process as fundamental civil rights. It formally granted citizenship to all French males over age 25 and extended voting rights to those citizens who could meet various property qualifications. Demands for "Liberty! Equality! Fraternity!"—the battle cry of the Revolution—filled the air.

At this juncture in the summer of 1789, France appeared to be moving steadily toward a moderate constitutional monarchy roughly similar to Britain's. But more radical elements known as the *Jacobins*, organized mainly in political clubs,

In the early days of the French Revolution in 1789 a crowd of demonstrators stormed the Bastille, a medieval fortress serving as a prison that was regarded as a symbol of royal despotism. Bastille Day, July 14, is now France's national holiday.

favored abolishing the monarchy and establishing a republic.[3] The Jacobins quickly took political control of the capital city, aided by the poorest classes of Paris, whose smoldering discontent erupted in mass outbursts such as the storming of the Bastille prison July 14, 1789. (The anniversary is still celebrated as France's national holiday.) Over the next three years, relations between the crown and the Assembly deteriorated. Finally in August 1792, Jacobin elements orchestrated an insurrection in Paris that drove the king from power. A new legislature was elected the following month. Known as the Convention, its members were considerably more radical than the deputies elected to the first National Assembly of 1789 or its successor, elected in 1791. One of the Convention's first acts was to declare France a *republic* in September 1792. Left-leaning delegates persuaded the Convention to put the king on trial. Out of 721 deputies, 394 voted to condemn Louis XVI to death. He died on the guillotine in January 1793.

The king's execution set in motion an orgy of bloodletting known in French history as "the Terror." Over the next year and a half, some 20,000 "enemies of the people" met their grim fate on the guillotine or in front of execution squads. They included members of the nobility as well as Catholic priests and nuns, victims of the Revolution's anticlericalism. Outbursts of antirevolutionary activity were ruthlessly suppressed in various parts of France. The Revolution also began consuming revolutionaries. Factional struggles broke out between its most zealous adherents and advocates of a more moderately ordered republic devoted to social peace and respect for property rights. Even heroes of the Revolution died on the scaffold.

As the Terror unfolded, the power of the central government intensified. The radical revolutionaries established a 12-member Committee of Public Safety that exercised harsh dictatorial rule, sending out "national agents" to impose the central government's will on local governments. The term *Jacobinism* became synonymous with a highly centralized form of government.

The trend toward greater centralization continued even after more moderate factions seized power in July 1794. The next group of revolutionary leaders, solidly middle class and committed to private property rights, abolished the Committee of Public Safety, executed its leaders, and put an end to the Terror. But they also set up a strong executive government of their own, known as the *Directory*. Five directors were selected by the Council of Five Hundred to govern the country. Voting rights were restricted and parliamentary powers withered.

Though it imposed a measure of tranquillity on an exhausted nation, the Directory could not establish an enduring government. In 1799 it gave way to yet another strong-willed authoritarian regime as General Napoleon Bonaparte grabbed power with the support of the French military. Napoleon's coup d'état effectively terminated France's decade of revolution. It had begun with lofty dreams of democracy, defined in the context of eighteenth-century Europe as constituting a limited monarchy, an elected national legislature, limited male suffrage, and private property rights. Within a few years the Revolution had degenerated into dictatorship, fanaticism, and civil strife. The elimination of royal absolutism led not to democracy but to new forms of centralized state power.[4]

After the Revolution: From Napoleon to the Fifth Republic Napoleon accentuated these centralizing tendencies. After proclaiming himself first consul of France at the start of his rule, he assumed the crown of emperor in 1804. A brilliant military commander whose armies brought most of Europe under French domination, Napoleon took an equally domineering approach to domestic affairs. He organized a secret police and pioneered the use of plebiscites to cultivate popular support for his dictatorship. In three such referendums he won the approval of 99 percent of the voters, though the voting procedures were manipulated by the authorities and the official tallies were surely suspect. Another innovation was the creation of a corps of *prefects* charged with ensuring the central government's control over more than 80 new administrative departments into which France had been divided during the Revolution. The prefecture system endured with only minor changes until the 1980s, undergirding France's long tradition as a *unitary state*. A unitary state emphasizes the central government's primacy over local governments. (It contrasts with *federalism*, which combines central government authority with significant decision-making powers for local officials.) Even today, despite reforms granting more powers to local governments, France retains the defining features of a unitary state. Prefects still exist, albeit with less power than in the past.

Napoleon's authoritarian rule lasted until his army was finally defeated by an alliance of European powers at Waterloo in 1815. With his defeat, the *restoration* of the monarchy was confirmed. The new king, Louis XVIII (a brother of Louis XVI), agreed to a constitution permitting an elected legislature, but his regal powers were substantial. After he died in 1824, his brother Charles X tried even more vigorously to reestablish a sovereign monarchy similar to the *ancien régime* (old regime) that had existed before the Revolution.

But the clock of history could not be turned back to the eighteenth century. Popular agitation resulted in his replacement in July 1830 by a constitutional monarchy under King Louis-Philippe of the house of Orleans. Reigning as the "citizen king," the new monarch was content to leave affairs of state in the hands of middle-class politicians allied with the country's rising business elite. Prime Minister François Guizot explicitly exhorted the country's businessmen, "Gentlemen, get rich!"

In kaleidoscopic fashion, one regime succeeded another. Louis-Philippe's so-called *July Monarchy* lasted only until 1848, when working-class uprisings forced his departure and swept into power a new government devoted to the Revolution's principles of liberty, equality, and fraternity. France's *Second Republic* proved to be as ill-fated as the First Republic of the 1790s. The new leaders proved unable to fulfill their promises to hire the unemployed and improve social welfare. The frustrated working class rose in rebellion once again, and the government resorted to military force to put down the upheaval. With the specter of revolution hanging over the country, the military seized power at the end of 1850 under the leadership of Napoleon's nephew, Louis-Napoleon. A new period of authoritarian rule ensued as the *Second Empire* reasserted the state's undisputed authority. Like his uncle, Louis-Napoleon (also known as Napoleon III) sought mass approval in manipulated plebiscites but could not survive military defeat. When the French army suffered disaster in the Franco-Prussian War of 1870–71 and Louis-Napoleon was captured, France found itself without a government yet again.

As in 1848, the vacuum was filled in 1870 by devotees of democracy. The *Third Republic* got off to a shaky start, marked by the bloody suppression of a revolutionary uprising in Paris, but it eventually righted itself and promulgated a new constitution in 1875. Its parliamentary system expanded male suffrage, fostered the growth of political parties, and guaranteed civil rights and freedoms, sparking a renaissance in the arts and sciences. But although the Third Republic enjoyed the longest run of any French regime since the Revolution, lasting until 1940, it was no model of governmental stability. Between the 1870s and 1940 it produced no fewer than 108 governments! In the same period Britain had fewer than 30 governments and the United States had 17 presidents. Vilified by monarchists on the right and revolutionary socialists on the left, at several junctures the Third Republic teetered on collapse.[5]

When Hitler's army invaded France in 1940 and defeated French forces in six weeks, the Third Republic perished and France fell under the grip of Nazi occupation. Initially, the Germans divided the country roughly in half, imposing direct rule in the north and organizing a puppet government under accommodating French officials in the south. The puppet regime, based in Vichy, was headed by Marshal Philippe Pétain, a World War I hero who agreed to collaborate with the occupiers in hopes of mitigating the rigors of Nazi rule. The occupation split France into antagonistic camps. *Collaborationists* assisted the Germans; the *Resistance* took extreme risks in organizing underground opposition to Nazi rule. In 1942 the Germans disbanded the Vichy government and took control of southern France for the remainder of the occupation.

Nazi rule finally ended in 1944 as American and British forces joined with the troops of "Free France" under General Charles de Gaulle (1890–1970) in driving out the Germans. De Gaulle thereupon installed himself as chief of a provisional government whose principal purpose was to preside over the elaboration of a new constitution. It took two years to accomplish this task, and de Gaulle retreated into retirement once it became clear that his own constitutional design would not win approval. The *Fourth Republic*, formally inaugurated in 1946, was a parliamentary system with a ceremonial presidency and a bicameral legislature. From the outset it was dogged by governmental instability: A parade of 22 coalition governments struggled to exercise power over the next 12 years. Like other unstable French republics before it, the Fourth Republic ultimately fell apart, the victim of its internal conflicts and external disasters.

After failing to reimpose colonial rule on Vietnam and other parts of Indochina after World War II, the Fourth Republic's leaders decided to suppress an independence movement in Algeria that began in 1954. Algeria had come under French control starting in 1830, and its European minority looked to the French government for protection against the Arab–Berber majority. The war ground on inconclusively, splitting French society as devastatingly as the Vietnam War was later to divide Americans. In May 1958 a group of French generals in Algeria, disgruntled at the government's reluctance to prosecute the war more aggressively, staged a mutiny. The Fourth Republic quickly crumbled. A majority of National Assembly deputies voted to confer power on de Gaulle, who came out of retirement with the determination to reorganize the state under a new constitution. The result was the **Fifth Republic**, whose presidential–parliamentary system was approved in a referendum at the end of 1958. With only a few alterations since then, the Fifth Republic's constitution remains in force today.

Table 14.3 French Constitutional Regimes

Until 1789	Sovereign monarchies	1848–1850	Second Republic
1789–1792	Constitutional monarchy	1851–1870	Second Empire (Napoleon III)
1792–1799	First Republic	1870/75–1940	Third Republic
1793–1794	Committee of Public Safety	1940–1944	German occupation
1794–1799	Directorate	1940–1942	Vichy regime
1799–1804	Consulate (Napoleon Bonaparte)	1944–1946	Provisional governments
1804–1814	First Empire (Napoleon I)	1946–1958	Fourth Republic
1814–1830	Quasi-sovereign monarchy	1959 to present	Fifth Republic
1830–1848	Constitutional monarchy		

The key points that emerge from the preceding historical account, summarized in Table 14.3, are the following:

- France has experienced an extraordinary multiplicity of political regimes over the past 200-plus years. Since the start of the Revolution in 1789 it has had 11 governmental regimes and 15 constitutions. This *regime instability* (or *constitutional instability*) contrasts quite starkly with the far less turbulent constitutional development of Britain and the United States.
- French regimes have tended to alternate between more or less democratically organized *republics* and *authoritarian regimes* of one kind or another.
- The first four French republics themselves proved to be highly unstable, exhibiting various forms of *governmental instability*. Here, too, the contrast with Britain and the United States is striking.
- There has been a continuing tradition of *centralized state authority* throughout French history. While the powers of the central government were especially pronounced under authoritarian regimes, even the republics have maintained the institutions of a unitary state and refrained from reconstituting France as a federation.

French Nationalism

Just as the development of French state institutions diverged sharply from Britain's, French nationalism also displayed palpable differences with British conceptions of national identity. Over the course of the sixteenth and seventeenth centuries, the term *nation* in England became associated with the people rather than the state and with the British Parliament rather than an all-powerful monarchy. As Liah Greenfeld has shown, French nationalism until shortly before the Revolution revolved overwhelmingly around the state and its crowning authority, the monarchy. Especially during the height of the monarch's absolute power in the seventeenth century, "the nation" referred mainly to the royal government rather than to the people. The people were relegated to the status of servile subjects.[6]

The Revolution made decisive changes in French national consciousness. More than anything else, the Revolution signified the French people's assertion of their right as citizens to constitute the French nation. The word *national*, as used in such terms as *National Assembly* and *national defense*, placed the people of France squarely in the center of the country's political and social life. Popular sovereignty replaced sovereign monarchy. Still, Greenfeld notes that, even during the Revolution, the French conception of popular nationalism continued to differ from Britain's. While the British conceived of their nation as consisting of individuals, the French tended to think of "the people" as a collective entity. This difference mirrored the distinction between John Locke's devotion to individual liberty and Jean-Jacques Rousseau's preference for collective liberty. It was to have long-term implications for political culture. In greater proportions than in Britain or the United States, political elites of both the right and left in France have tended to look to the state more than to private enterprise or society as the chief source of responsibility for the country's economic well-being, a concept known as *étatisme* (statism). Meanwhile, it took centuries to develop a unified French national identity out of the "hexagon" of its diverse regions. As late as the 1860s, local dialects still predominated over French in much of the country.[7]

Social Class and Democracy

Among the many factors that impeded France's advance toward stable democracy, the political roles played by elites and various social classes stand out as particularly prominent. Once again, a comparison with Britain is instructive.

The Nobility In Britain, the nobility contributed to the evolutionary unfolding of democratic institutions and practices: From the start, the nobility formed a vital component of Parliament. In the twentieth century the House of Lords, the aristocracy's parliamentary preserve, was willing to accept significant limitations on its legislative powers, ceding pride of place to the House of Commons and thus widening popular democracy.

Because they were cut in on British democracy, Britain's aristocratic elites supported it. By contrast, the French nobility tended to be cut out of political developments, shunted aside by absolutist monarchs adamantly opposed to sharing power with a national parliament. Feeling neglected and powerless under the monarchy, some nobles joined the Revolution in 1789. (The Marquis de Lafayette, who fought in the American Revolution, was typical.) Even more nobles died on the guillotine, however. From then on, what remained of the French aristocracy was politically marginalized, depriving French democracy of a potential source of elite support.

The Middle Class The various strata of the British middle class made indispensable contributions to democracy in England, promoting Parliament along with the Conservative and Liberal Parties as the main vehicles for achieving their class interests. The relationship between the middle class and democracy was more complicated in France. By 1789, centuries of exclusion from governmental power had created a split in middle-class ranks between moderates willing to settle for a constitutional monarchy and radicals determined to wipe out the detested monarchy forever. After the First Republic was established in 1792, a further split occurred among the largely middle-class Jacobins, as one faction unleashed the Terror and their more temperate rivals replaced them with the Directory. Neither group advanced the cause of stable democracy.

Over the course of the nineteenth century, the French middle class was split between those who favored a republic and more democracy (largely to protect their own property rights) and those who believed that their economic interests were best protected under authoritarian regimes. When democracy finally steadied itself in the Third Republic (1870–1940), it was dominated by middle-class politicians and their followings.

During World War II, the French middle class found itself split once again. While the majority of the population stayed aloof from political action and concentrated on coping with the daily realities of the German occupation, French fascism and the resistance movement each had middle-class support. The two republics that came after World War II have been solidly middle class in orientation.

France's middle class has thus traveled in two political directions: While providing crucial support for democratic institutions at various times, some of its members have also supported nondemocratic movements and governments.

The Working Class The industrial working class was the main disadvantaged social class in France and Britain in the nineteenth and twentieth centuries. Class conflict between workers and capitalists was sharp in both countries, but Britain managed much earlier than France to contain these conflicts within the structures of parliamentary democracy. Significantly, it was Britain's middle-class parties, the Conservatives and the Liberals, that extended the franchise to working-class voters. But it was the establishment of the Labour Party at the start of the twentieth century that most decisively incorporated Britain's working class into democracy. Britain's Communist

Party never gained much support, and the country's trade unions—even those led by radical socialists—have tended to support the Labour Party rather than more extreme parties.

A number of events in French history made for a more radicalized segment of the labor movement than in Britain, with results that are visible to this day. As industrialization intensified in the 1820s and subsequent decades, French manual laborers had to contend with the same wretched conditions as their British counterparts. Especially after the July monarchy came to power in 1830, the government firmly supported the profit-maximizing ambitions of the capitalist elite. The blatant exploitation of the French working class fueled a rage that boiled over in February 1848. As workers took up arms, King Louis-Philippe fled the country and his regime disintegrated.

The Second Republic was forged in the crucible of this workers' revolution. Its leaders immediately vowed to ameliorate working-class conditions through various welfare measures, including the creation of public-sector jobs for the unemployed. The government's promises outran its financial capacities, however. As many as 100,000 workers applied for the jobs, but the state could afford to hire only about 10,000. Short of cash, the Second Republic canceled the employment programs after several months. The workers took to the barricades once again, this time arming themselves against a democratically oriented republic that was ostensibly on their side. Fatefully, it was precisely this republic that crushed the uprising in July 1848, leading many workers to feel betrayed by democracy itself.

An even bloodier sequence of events occurred in 1871, with similar implications for French democracy. As Emperor Napoleon III's government collapsed and France capitulated to Prussia, opponents of the makeshift new regime took control of several parts of Paris and created their own government. Proclaiming themselves the "Commune" of Paris, the insurrectionists included working-class revolutionaries and their supporters who sought to establish a socialist society. But the leaders of the nascent Third Republic, determined to impose their authority on the entire country, dispatched troops to put down the insurrection. As many as 15,000 people lost their lives in a bloodbath marked by atrocities on both sides. When the smoke cleared, the Commune was liquidated, but large numbers of working-class citizens and their sympathizers once again felt subjugated by a French government that professed democratic ideals.[8]

In the wake of these events, several socialist parties were formed in France to militate for workers' rights. In 1905 various socialist organizations merged to form a single party that joined the Socialist International, a group of European socialist parties. The party called itself the French Section of the Socialist International, known by its French initials as the *SFIO*. Many of its members were social democrats: Like Britain's newly established Labour Party, they disavowed revolutionary violence and dictatorship and instead favored improving the lot of workers through ballot-box democracy and trade union activity. In 1920, proponents of a more radical approach to socialism organized the *French Communist Party (PCF)*. Its founders were a disparate group of ideological socialists and pacifists, but the Soviet government in Moscow used its influence to help a pro-Soviet faction take over the party leadership. From the mid-1920s until the late 1980s, PCF leaders generally provided faithful support for Soviet dictates and preferences. The French Communists also dominated a trade union federation, the General Confederation of Labor (CGT), and frequently used it to call strikes and demonstrations against French businesses and governments.

In 1936, as the Great Depression boosted unemployment in France, the SFIO and the PCF won an electoral victory in the lower house of the French parliament that permitted the establishment of a socialist-dominated government. Known as the *Popular Front*, the Third Republic's first left-wing government produced a spate of laws providing for unemployment compensation, state-sector jobs, trade union bargaining rights, paid vacations, and other measures benefiting the country's most disadvantaged groups. France's equivalent of President Franklin D. Roosevelt's New Deal lasted only about a year, however. By 1937, more conservative, pro-business parties used their influence in the legislature's upper chamber to block further reforms. Once again, many French workers had reason to feel let down by French democracy.

This long history of working-class radicalism and disaffection from democratic governments helps explain why France, in contrast to Britain, ended up with a comparatively large Communist Party that was allied with the Soviet Union and militantly hostile to private enterprise. Although PCF leaders increasingly expressed their adherence to democratic principles after World War II, they remained vague about what a "socialist democracy" would look like if they were given the opportunity to establish one in France. During the Fourth Republic, from 1946 to 1958, the French Communist Party was the country's largest political party, routinely capturing about 25 percent of the vote in elections to the national

legislature. Some 2 million workers were affiliated with the communist-dominated trade union organization, the CGT.

Consequences The clash between left and right has thus tended to be sharper in France than in Britain, reflecting a somewhat more antagonistic confrontation between the working class and the business community. In the 1970s this situation prompted a French sociologist to describe France as a "stalled society," incapable of resolving its economic disputes because both sides have a fear of face-to-face negotiations. As a consequence, the French government has often had to play a mediating role between business and labor.[9] Inevitably, those in power tend to side with those who elected them, the conservatives supporting business leaders (known collectively as the *patronat*) and the Socialists and their allies supporting labor.

The confrontational nature of labor–management relations in France reflects a more general tendency toward conflict and contention in French history than in British history. Charles Tilly points out in *The Contentious French* that France has experienced a multitude of politically motivated disorders over the past four centuries, largely in reaction to the expansion of the state and the growth of capitalism.[10] Whereas British political culture has generally emphasized moderation, pragmatic problem solving, and compromise in dealing with its problems, France's more conflictual political culture has placed a greater emphasis on ideological differentiation, demands for radical change, and negotiating intransigence. These attitudinal predispositions have mellowed in recent decades, but a penchant for mass protest remains a vital part of French political culture.

Table 14.4 summarizes how the 10 conditions for democracy have played out in France. You might constructively compare it to Table 13.3, in which we summarized the British experience.

Table 14.4 The 10 Conditions for Democracy: The French Experience

Explanatory Factor	French Experience
1. Elite attitudes	The nobility supported the monarchy and monarchist tendencies through the Revolution and periods of postrevolutionary political instability.
2. State institutions	A highly centralized political executive in Paris has often ignored or sought to neutralize parliament and has imposed its will on the regions of France.
3. National unity	A sense of popular-based national identity emerged from the Revolution but it emphasizes the collective or general will over the individual.
4. National wealth	France has been a relatively wealthy country for centuries. National wealth has been based on both agriculture and industry.
5. Private enterprise	The state has often sought to direct private enterprise via planning; private enterprise has often been family-based and smaller than corresponding firms in the United States, United Kingdom, or Germany.
6. Middle class	Although often the opponents of dictatorial power, such as during the Revolution, the middle class has also supported harsh rule targeted at the disadvantaged.
7. Attitudes of the disadvantaged	A strong sense of injustice has led the working class to adopt strategies of confrontation and many of the disadvantaged supported the pro-Moscow PCF.
8. Civil society	Civil society organizations have tended to be class based; strong central state has encouraged social groups to organize to demand state action.
9. Education and access to information	Education was highly politicized in the 19th and early 20th centuries, with the outcome that prosecular forces dominated public education and promoted democratic values, defeating conservative forces aligned with the church.
10. International conditions	Military remained a strong force in society owing to long-standing tensions with Germany, often exerting an antidemocratic influence in politics.

FRANCE AFTER 1945

Hoping to never again see France collapse before a foreign invasion in the way it did in 1940, de Gaulle, who headed the provisional government, favored replacing the institutions of the Third Republic with a new democratic regime that would have a strong presidency able to take vigorous action in times of national emergency. To his chagrin, the Constituent Assembly elected in October 1945 for the purpose of writing a new constitution did not share his vision, favoring instead a return to parliamentary government without the super-executive de Gaulle wanted. De Gaulle therefore resigned as president of the provisional government in January 1946. He was convinced that British-style parliamentary government was ill suited to France and doomed to certain failure.

In effect, de Gaulle sought to be a bridge linking the two warring traditions of French political history: the tradition of authority, order, and stability historically represented by the monarchy, the army, and the Catholic church; and the tradition of "liberty, equality, fraternity" associated with the Revolution and subsequent republican regimes. In the past, France had never succeeded in combining democracy with stability. De Gaulle believed that the only way to achieve a stable democracy was to anchor democratic institutions in a powerful presidency that would guarantee firm and decisive governance. A strong and stable government at home, moreover, was for de Gaulle the precondition of an active foreign policy that would place France in the front rank of the world's most powerful countries. However, the Constituent Assembly preferred a constitutional order more like the Third Republic's parliamentary regime.

The Fourth Republic

Events were to prove de Gaulle right. The Fourth Republic witnessed a steady succession of revolving-door governments. The lower house of the legislature, elected by proportional representation, was divided among five main parties and several smaller ones. The Communist Party usually had the largest delegation, but most of the other parties refused to deal with it because of its implacable pro-Soviet orientation at a time of mounting Cold War hostilities. (France was a charter member of NATO in 1949, an alliance the Communists vehemently denounced.) De Gaulle and his followers established their own party dedicated to criticizing the Fourth Republic's deficiencies. Governments tended to be shaky coalitions consisting of three or more parties. One government lasted only two days, another merely one. Gridlock reigned.

After World War II, de Gaulle and the Fourth Republic governments that followed him decided to retain control of France's imperial domains. This fateful choice resulted in a protracted struggle in Vietnam, where local communists as well as noncommunists fought to rid their country of French domination. Unable to sustain the fight, France reached a negotiated settlement with the Vietnamese in 1954 that put an end to its political presence in Indochina.

No sooner had the French withdrawn from Vietnam than a new independence movement flared up in Algeria. By virtue of its proximity to France and the presence of more than a million Europeans among its 13 million inhabitants, Algeria was France's most prized colonial dominion. In the fall of 1954 an Arab insurgency took arms against French forces. Though a majority of France favored preserving Algeria's colonial status at this time, French military leaders in Algeria believed that the floundering coalition governments in Paris were incapable of providing the support they considered necessary for a decisive military victory. In May 1958 they decided to take matters into their own hands. In a calculated act of insubordination, they engineered the military takeover of France's official government facilities in Algeria. They also proclaimed their own "Committee of Public Safety" to govern the colony. At the heart of the generals' strategy was the hope that their mutiny would precipitate the downfall of the Fourth Republic and motivate their trusted military comrade, General de Gaulle, to come out of retirement and form a "Government of Public Safety" in Paris. Though de Gaulle was informed of the generals' plans, there is no evidence that he participated in the planning of their revolt or approved

Out of the crisis in facing down the Arab insurgency in Algeria, Charles de Gaulle came out of retirement to assume the powers of the republic, first as appointed prime minister and later as the first president of the Fifth Republic.

of its execution. In any event, de Gaulle issued a statement affirming, "I am ready to assume the powers of the Republic."

The Fourth Republic's president, exercising his right to designate the prime minister, thereupon invited de Gaulle to form a new government. De Gaulle agreed, but only on condition that he be granted exceptional powers to govern France by decree for six months, during which his government would have the authority to formulate a new constitution for the voters' consideration. After an intense debate, a large majority of the Fourth Republic's lower house accepted de Gaulle's terms and voted to abolish the Fourth Republic.

The Fifth Republic

After its origins in the Fourth Republic's fatal crisis of 1958, France's Fifth Republic was profoundly influenced by two exceptional political leaders: Charles de Gaulle and François Mitterrand. As the republic's founder, de Gaulle was the source not only of its constitution but of a political movement—**Gaullism**—that still bears his name. (Contemporary Gaullists such as Jacques Chirac and Nicolas Sarkozy are known as *neo-Gaullists* because they have adapted and modernized de Gaulle's seminal ideas.) Mitterrand was the organizer of France's Socialist Party, the party of the current president, François Hollande.

Asked to take power in the midst of the Algerian crisis, de Gaulle believed that only his firm presence at the helm of the French government could prevent a chaotic civil war and preserve democracy. He immediately moved forward with the business of framing a new constitution. For this task he assembled a small group of experts led by Michel Debré, a trusted advisor and former member of the French parliament. De Gaulle himself took an active role at every stage in the elaboration of the document. The final draft reflected a combination of a powerful presidency, which was de Gaulle's highest priority, and a prime minister and government answerable to the legislature, as favored by parliamentarians such as Debré. Thus the Fifth Republic constitution was a compromise that resulted in two executives, each with significant decision-making authority.

As conceived by its framers, the new constitution's creation of a dual executive was not expected to be troublesome. The president, it was widely assumed, would lay out broad policy guidelines and ensure overall political stability, while the prime minister would take charge of day-to-day governmental activities. But early critics of the proposed constitution, including François Mitterrand, were quick to criticize de Gaulle for seeking excessive decision-making authority. Some warned that the high-powered presidency amounted to an elected dictatorship, and accused de Gaulle of **Bonapartism**—a reference to Napoleon's military autocracy. But when it was submitted to the people for their judgment in September 1958, de Gaulle's constitution was approved by 79 percent of the voters, a landslide of unprecedented proportions in French democracy. Two months later, de Gaulle's party and its conservative allies outpolled the left-wing parties in elections to the new republic's first National Assembly, ensuring an invincible parliamentary majority in favor of de Gaulle's constitution. And in December, de Gaulle won 78.5 percent of the votes cast in the electoral college established to select the president.

From the beginning it was evident that de Gaulle viewed the presidency as the central decision-making office in the Fifth Republic. At times he would announce policy initiatives without even informing his prime minister in advance. "True, there was a government which 'decides the policy of the nation,'" de Gaulle later wrote. "But everyone knew that it would proceed from my choice and act only with my blessing." Although the new presidential–parliamentary system was called "semi-presidentialism" by some French political analysts, de Gaulle was anything but a semi-president. On the contrary, he fully intended to be a super-president.

When de Gaulle ordered a referendum in 1962 asking the people to approve the direct popular election of the president, his critics charged that he ignored the constitution's provision requiring him to obtain parliamentary approval before holding a referendum. The legislature thereupon voted to censure Prime Minister Georges Pompidou's government, an act that required the prime minister's resignation. Incensed at the National Assembly's presumptuousness, de Gaulle promptly reappointed Pompidou and dissolved the Assembly, calling new elections. In 1965, when he ran for reelection, de Gaulle barely bothered to campaign. To his surprise he failed to win an absolute majority in the first round. As a result he was forced into a second round with his most serious challenger, François Mitterrand. After campaigning more vigorously, he defeated Mitterrand by 54.6 percent to 45.4 percent.

1968

The extraordinary events of 1968 began with a series of small protests by students dissatisfied with conditions in several of the country's large public universities. In March a few dozen

Daniel Cohn-Bendit, called "Danny the Red," was a charismatic leader of the 1968 student uprisings in France.

PROFILES   Charles de Gaulle

Charles de Gaulle dedicated his life to rescuing France from international humiliation and fratricidal strife. At times he spoke of embodying in his own person the legitimacy of national political authority. In his own mind, de Gaulle was France.

Born in 1890, de Gaulle entered the military academy at St. Cyr in 1910. In World War I he was wounded in three separate engagements, taken prisoner by the Germans, and tried to escape five times. After the war he distinguished himself as an original strategic thinker, criticizing French defensive strategy, unsuccessfully arguing for a mobile defensive force heavily reliant on tanks, planes, and other mechanized weapons.

The merits of de Gaulle's advice became painfully (and ironically) evident in the spring of 1940, when Hitler's quick-moving armies rapidly devastated French forces.[11] De Gaulle repaired to England in hopes of reorganizing French armed resistance to the Germans in conjunction with Winston Churchill's government.

From London, de Gaulle created a provisional government. Over the next four years he galvanized the Free French army. The anti-German resistance movement answered to him as the country's true leader. However, Churchill and U.S. President Franklin D. Roosevelt tended to dismiss de Gaulle as a minor ally and an overblown egotist. The wartime alliance left de Gaulle with a lifelong vision of collusion between the "Anglo-Saxons" (the Americans and the British) to keep France down, a humiliating affront he would never accept.

When French troops entered Paris in August 1944, de Gaulle assumed the reins of power. De Gaulle was firmly committed to democracy, but he did not want France to return to the governmental instability of the Third Republic. He deplored the "regime of the parties" that he thought had only heightened France's social and ideological divisions. He favored a constitution that would counterbalance the powers of the legislature with a strong executive, and conceived of this supreme role for himself. When the Constituent Assembly opted for a parliamentary regime like the Third Republic,

de Gaulle left the presidency rather than associate himself with it.

De Gaulle returned to power in 1958 with the advent of the Fifth Republic, the institutions of which he designed to give himself significant powers. He was 68. In two episodes de Gaulle demonstrated how he conceived the strong presidency should operate. Responding to coup attempts by French generals in Algeria, de Gaulle faced down the coup leaders and then facilitated Algerian independence. During civil unrest in 1968, de Gaulle called for new elections that returned a solid majority for his conservative forces, quelling the unrest. But in 1969, when he decided to make a constitutional referendum on senate reform a plebiscite on his continued rule, the French rejected him. He immediately resigned. He died in November 1970.

De Gaulle was a man of contradictions. Like the Bourbon monarchs, he believed that he personified the French state and that the deluge would surely follow him. And yet he reined in these authoritarian instincts with a principled commitment to democracy. Though he occasionally violated the spirit of democracy, de Gaulle more than once saved democracy in France from its challengers of both right and left. He detested the routine transactions of everyday parliamentary politics and felt a personal connection with the people of France that went over the heads of ordinary politicians. Though conservative in social matters, in 1944 he gave French women the vote for the first time. "Gaullism" became a synonym for strong presidential authority at home and foreign policy activism on the world stage. To a considerable extent, most of France today accepts the Gaullist consensus that the Fifth Republic's constitution should remain in force essentially as it is and that France needs to play a role of its own in world affairs, independent of the United States while at the same time allied with it. Although France has changed considerably since Charles de Gaulle's lifetime, its state institutions and prevailing political attitudes remain deeply affected by his powerful imprint.[12]

---

students led by Daniel Cohn-Bendit, a charismatic redheaded idealist later dubbed "Danny the Red," took over some lecture halls at the University of Paris campus in the suburb of Nanterre. As the protests continued, students at the Sorbonne in central Paris tore up paving stones and erected barricades. The government ordered the police to clear the area. From this point on, the protests escalated wildly and the brutality of the police inflamed public opinion. As de Gaulle remained stonily silent and his ministers appeared befuddled, some 300,000 students and political opponents of de Gaulle's regime staged a massive demonstration, with many shouting for the president's resignation. De Gaulle responded by casually leaving the next day on a trip to Romania.

On that very day, factory workers at a state-owned factory staged a wildcat strike, setting in motion a nationwide strike movement that soon involved industrial workers and white-collar employees throughout France. Within weeks some 10 million French people were on strike. Factories and offices closed, public services virtually ceased, and the nation's transportation system came to a standstill. Most workers had little in common with the students. Cohn-Bendit and other student leaders spoke of destroying the Fifth Republic and replacing it with a utopian society whose precise contours they admittedly could not define. "Take your dreams for reality!" was one of their slogans. Many drew their inspiration from Mao Zedong, the leader of communist China. But the striking workers were mainly interested in bread-and-butter issues, not revolution. A slowdown in the French economy over the previous year had reduced their purchasing power and boosted unemployment.

With the entire country sliding toward anarchy, de Gaulle cut his trip short and returned home. "In five days, 10 years of struggle against rottenness in the state have been lost," he thundered at his ministers. But when de Gaulle's televised address failed to quell the turmoil, and when striking workers rejected a negotiated settlement, the president announced that he was dissolving the National Assembly and setting new elections. Shortly after he spoke, a crowd that swelled to more than 500,000 people filled the boulevards of Paris in a massive display of support for de Gaulle. The atmosphere of revolutionary chaos was suddenly broken.

The results of the elections of June 23 and 30 were a triumph for de Gaulle's party and its allies on the right. They won 360 of the National Assembly's 485 seats. Mitterrand's social-democratic grouping lost half its seats and so did the Communists. As workers returned to their jobs, the student revolt quietly dissipated in the fine spring weather.[13]

Pompidou, Giscard, and Mitterrand

After de Gaulle's resignation, a special presidential election brought Georges Pompidou to the Élysée Palace. (The constitution does not provide for a vice president to fill out the term of a president who vacates the office. New presidential elections must be held within 35 days.) He had proved invaluable to de Gaulle as his second prime minister, dutifully deferring to the president in matters of the highest political importance.

However, a devastating illness prevented Pompidou from serving out his full seven-year term. Upon his death in 1974, presidential elections were held that signaled major shifts in the French political landscape after 16 years of Gaullist dominance. The victor in a close contest against Mitterrand was Valéry Giscard d'Estaing, a conservative who had served as finance minister under de Gaulle. He had his own small political party that rivaled the Gaullists for the center-right vote. Giscard's presidency was largely uneventful, at least when compared to the tumultuous 1950s and 1960s. His government secured the passage of a liberal abortion law, lowered the voting age to 18, and promoted women's rights. Giscard's governing style reflected his emphasis on technocratic competence, especially in monetary and fiscal matters. He jealously guarded the powers of the presidential office and kept the National Assembly in its subordinate position, reinforcing the concept of *etatisme*.

However, a quadrupling of oil prices in 1973–74 dealt a severe blow to the French economy and those of its trading partners, pushing France into a recession. Oil prices rose dramatically again in 1979–80, so that by the time Giscard's term ended in 1981, France was staggering under a 10 percent inflation rate and an unemployment figure of 7.2 percent, the highest in decades,[14] setting the stage for a reprise of the Giscard–Mitterrand duel for the presidency. This time, however, France's waning economic fortunes played into the hands of the challenger from the left.

Like the previous presidential elections, the 1981 contest did not produce a victor with an absolute majority in round one. In the second ballot Mitterrand narrowly defeated Giscard d'Estaing by 51.8 percent to 48.2 percent. Ten days later Mitterrand took office and quickly announced the dissolution of the conservative-dominated National Assembly. Riding a crest of popularity, Mitterrand's Socialist Party defied most predictions and won nearly 55 percent of the seats, giving it full control of the lower house.

Within their first two years in power the Socialists fully nationalized eight major conglomerates, including some of the country's leading firms in telecommunications, electronics, chemicals, steel, and airplane construction, and took over 36 banks. The nationalizations cost the state some 39 billion francs (about $8 billion). To improve the lives of French workers, the government raised the minimum wage nine times between 1981 and 1983; added a fifth week of paid vacation; reduced working hours for most categories of workers from 40 hours a week to 39; enhanced trade union bargaining rights; cut the minimum retirement age from 65 to 60; and raised pensions. To finance these and other social programs, the government in 1982 imposed a wealth tax on large fortunes and the following year it raised the average income tax rate from 42 percent to 44 percent. (The average income tax rate in the United States at the time was about 35 percent.)

Mitterrand believed that the best way to combat France's rising unemployment was to increase government spending. But this economic strategy turned out to be ill timed. France was caught in the snares of globalization. International economic conditions in the early 1980s were not conducive to the free-spending policies of Mitterrand's new government, which vastly increased budget deficits and the national debt while aggravating France's inflation rate.[15] By 1983 it was also evident that the government's Keynesian spending programs and its nationalization of private corporations were not succeeding in reducing unemployment.

And so the Mitterrand government slammed the brakes on its costly programs and reversed course. It froze wages and prices, cut subsidies to nationalized companies, laid off employees, imposed fees on various social services, and raised taxes. Mitterrand was compelled by events to pursue a conservative austerity policy for most of the next dozen years. He appointed a succession of Socialist prime ministers who shifted the government's policies toward promoting private-sector development. "Profit" and "entrepreneurism" replaced "regulation" and "nationalization" in the Socialist vocabulary.

In 1986, the neo-Gaullist party and its allies won control of the National Assembly, confronting President Mitterrand with the unpalatable necessity of appointing the conservative former prime minister (under Giscard) and mayor of Paris, Jacques Chirac, as prime minister (French elected officials may hold multiple offices simultaneously). In the Fifth Republic's first case of cohabitation, Mitterrand worked out a power-sharing arrangement with Chirac and accepted his plans to privatize more than 60 state-controlled companies. Polls showed that the vast majority of French people wanted the two ideological adversaries to get along and maintain governmental stability. But Chirac had little more success than the Socialists in stimulating the French economy.

Cohabitation came to an end in 1988 after Mitterrand defeated Chirac in the presidential elections and the Socialists led a comeback of the left-leaning parties in retaking control of the National Assembly. But Mitterrand had to endure another period of cohabitation after the right-leaning parties took back the National Assembly in 1993. The Gaullist prime minister, Édouard Balladur, launched a new round of privatizations, dealing another blow to Mitterrand's earlier visions of a socialist economy. Meanwhile, Mitterrand had essentially given up the pursuit of constitutional reform. The man who had been an incessant critic of de Gaulle's presidential authority declared after assuming office in 1981 that he would exercise the full powers of the constitution, later asserting that they "suited" him. However, during the two periods of cohabitation, Mitterrand stepped into the background and behaved somewhat like a semi-president, allowing Prime Ministers Chirac and Balladur to take the lead in formulating national policy. It appears that Mitterrand's most important legacy was his acceptance on behalf of the French left (or at least a substantial part of the left) of both capitalism and the Fifth Republic's constitution. While the left still favors state intervention to promote the welfare of the bottom sectors of the social pyramid, most of its leaders now also accept the need to promote growth in the private sector. "Socialism" in France—as in most of Europe—has become little more than a euphemism for the modern mixed-economy welfare state, at least in the eyes of all but the extreme left.

In 1996, François Mitterrand died after a long battle with prostate cancer. (It was later revealed by his physician that he had suffered from the disease throughout his presidency.) In the end, his main political contribution to French politics was his willingness to compromise some of the differences between right and left. In the process he established a precedent for the regular alternation of power between center-left and center-right parties, bringing moderation, stability, and "normalcy" to French politics. In a country wracked through much of its history by stormy conflict, this was no mean achievement.[16]

FRENCH STATE INSTITUTIONS

The *presidential–parliamentary system* of the Fifth Republic involves a mixture of presidential authority, a prime minister responsible to the parliament, and a weak but important legislature. The basic structure of the system is modeled in Figure 14.1.

The Dual Executive

The President   The Fifth Republic's constitution permits the direct election of the president by the people in a one-round or two-round procedure. Any number of candidates may run in the first round. To be eligible, each prospective candidate must be nominated by at least 500 elected officials from national or local bodies. In effect, round one is a national primary, with all the candidates for president running on the same day. (See Table 14.1 for the results of the 2012 presidential elections.) If one of the entrants gets more than 50 percent of the first-round ballots, he or she is elected president, but that has not yet happened. Round two is a runoff election between the top two finishers of the first round. Voter turnout tends to be roughly the same in both rounds. French voters whose preferred first-round candidate does not advance into the runoff usually turn out to vote for one of the remaining two candidates. (See Table 14.5 for second-round results of all presidential elections in the Fifth Republic.)

The president is France's head of state and—thanks to de Gaulle—possesses considerable decision-making powers. These powers are summarized in Table 14.6. Unlike the presidents of Germany, Italy, and some other democracies, and like the president of the United States, France's president is far more than just a ceremonial head of state.

During the presidency of François Mitterrand, France twice had cohabitation governments. In the second instance (1986–88), the Socialist Mitterrand (right) co-governed with Gaullist Prime Minister Édouard Balladur.

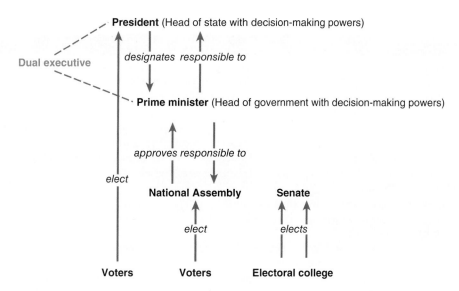

FIGURE 14.1 **France's Presidential–Parliamentary System**

The prime minister (PM) is head of government. The PM is nominated by the president, but must be approved by a voting majority in the National Assembly. When the president's party and its allies have the legislative majority, the president is usually free to pick his or her own personal favorite to serve as prime minister. But when the president's opponents dominate the National Assembly, the president is constrained by political realities to designate a prime minister from the ranks of the opposition parties. The result is cohabitation—the sharing of executive authority between the leader of the right-of-center parties and the leader of the left-of-center parties.

The constitution designates the president "the highest authority of the state" and commander in chief of the armed forces. At the same time, it gives the prime minister and the government the right to "determine and direct the policy of the nation." On paper, the constitution appears to be tantalizingly ambiguous about which of these two officers possesses ultimate decision-making authority. Indeed, the French constitution's text is not a precise guide to determining who calls the shots at the apex of the political system. All presidents of the Fifth Republic have tended to regard foreign affairs and security policy as their "reserved domain" of responsibility. But all have intruded into domestic matters as well. While they have granted their prime

ministers a certain latitude to pursue their own initiatives in economic and social policy, the extent of this ministerial freedom has varied considerably.

President de Gaulle tended to treat his prime ministers as mere executors of his will. President Giscard d'Estaing had a prickly relationship with his first prime minister, Chirac, and replaced him. President Mitterrand appointed five Socialist prime ministers. (One of them, Édith Cresson, was France's first female head of government.) Acting under the constraints of cohabitation, Mitterrand allowed his neo-Gaullist prime ministers, Chirac and Balladur, wide latitude to conduct their own economic policies, even though those policies dismantled some of the achievements of Mitterrand's early years. President Chirac similarly allowed Prime Minister Jospin, a Socialist, a great deal of leeway to elaborate the government's domestic agenda, even though it differed from Chirac's priorities. Table 14.7 lists the Fifth Republic presidents and the prime ministers who served with them.

Ironically, the relationship between president and prime minister has been more enduring under cohabitation than it has been when the two belong to the same party. The president cannot easily dismiss a prime minister of an opposing party, because the National Assembly majority would object. It is much easier for the president to fire a fellow party member

Table 14.5 French Presidential Elections (Second Round Percentages)

1965	De Gaulle	54.5%	1981	Mitterrand	51.8%	2002	Chirac	82.2%
	Mitterrand	45.5		Giscard d'Estaing	48.2		Le Pen	17.8
1969	Pompidou	57.6	1988	Mitterrand	54.0	2007	Sarkozy	53.1
	Poher	42.4		Chirac	45.9		Royal	46.0
1974	Giscard d'Estaing	50.8	1995	Chirac	52.6	2012	Hollande	51.6
	Mitterrand	49.2		Jospin	47.4		Sarkozy	48.4

Source: French Interior Ministry, www.interieur.gouv.fr/Elections/Les-resultats/Presidentielles; Manuel Álvarez-Rivera, "Election Resources on the Internet: Presidential and Legislative Elections in France," www.electionresources.org/fr.

Table 14.6 France's Dual Executive

President	
Election	■ Elected by the people. Candidates must be born or naturalized French citizens, at least 23 years old, nominated by 500 elected officials (legislators, mayors, etc.). Winning candidate must get absolute majority of voters turning out in first or second round.
	■ Until 2002, presidents served a seven-year term, with no limit on the number of terms. In 2000, the presidential term was reduced to five years, starting in 2002.
Powers	■ Head of state ("the highest authority of the state"). Likely to be de facto chief decision maker (except in periods of cohabitation).
	■ Commander of armed forces. Presides over higher councils and committees of national defense.
	■ Names the prime minister. De facto power to force prime minister to resign (except under cohabitation).
	■ With prime minister's approval, may appoint and dismiss other cabinet ministers.
	■ Chairs cabinet meetings.
	■ May veto government ordinances and decrees.
	■ May dissolve National Assembly and call new elections, which must take place within 20 to 40 days. May not dissolve Assembly again for one year.
	■ May *not* veto bills passed by parliament but may ask the deputies to reconsider legislation.
	■ May address a joint session of parliament once a year.
	■ On the proposal of the government or the two legislative chambers, may submit questions to the voters in referendums on bills dealing with "the organization of the public authorities," European Union agreements, or international treaties requiring ratification.
	■ May declare a state of national emergency under circumstances specified in Article 16 and govern by decree.
	■ Until 2007, could be impeached (indicted) only for high treason. Under reforms passed in 2007, can be impeached for "dereliction of his duties manifestly incompatible with the exercise of his mandate," but not for offenses unrelated to presidential functions. Impeachment requires a two-thirds majority of each house of parliament in an open vote. Upon impeachment, the president must relinquish office in favor of the president of the senate. The president is tried by the High Court of Justice, composed of various members of the two houses of parliament. If parliament votes to remove the president from office, new elections must be held. An ex-president may be tried as a civilian for criminal offenses, but may run for reelection.
Prime Minister	
Selection	■ Designated by the president; approved by majority of the National Assembly.
Powers	■ Head of government. "Shall direct the operation of the government," which in turn "shall determine and direct the policy of the nation." Likely to be chief decision maker in periods of cohabitation, subject to agreements with president.
	■ Responsible for national defense. The government "shall have at its disposal . . . the armed forces."
	■ Makes appointments to civil and military posts. The government is responsible for the civil service.
	■ May replace president as chair of national defense committees and, under exceptional circumstances, may chair cabinet meetings.
	■ May seek parliamentary "investiture," that is, vote of approval by National Assembly upon presenting the government and its program.
	■ May be dismissed by National Assembly, subject to provisions concerning vote of censure (see later in this chapter).

or someone from an allied party (see Table 14.7). In a number of cases the president has enjoined the same prime minister to form a new government by reassigning cabinet posts. In an effort to prevent cohabitation in the future, the leaders of the two main political parties—Chirac's neo-Gaullists and the Socialists—agreed to amend the constitution in time for the 2002 presidential elections. Until that year, France's president served a seven-year term. In addition, elections to the presidency and the National Assembly (whose members serve a five-year term) took place in different years. As a result, some voters who cast their ballots for a conservative candidate in the presidential elections tended to switch their support to the Socialists in the next National Assembly elections, and vice versa, leaving the presidency in the hands of one party and the National Assembly in the hands of its opponents. Starting in 2002 the president's term of office was reduced to five years. National Assembly elections were due to take place in the same year. It was hoped that, if the National Assembly could serve out its full five-year term without being dissolved for snap elections, presidential elections could henceforth take place in the same year as the National Assembly elections. (Presidential and legislative

elections do not take place on the same day, however, but are spaced about a month apart.) The main assumption underlying these reforms was that voters would be more likely to vote for presidential and legislative candidates *of the same party* if the two sets of elections were held close together. If the majority voted for a neo-Gaullist president, they would therefore be likely to elect a neo-Gaullist majority in the Assembly, obviating the need for cohabitation. The Socialists hoped that the same logic would apply to them.

The 2002, 2007, and 2012 elections have verified these assumptions. In May 2002, President Chirac was reelected president. In the following month his neo-Gaullist party, the UMP, won a large majority in the National Assembly. Chirac thereupon nominated Jean-Pierre Raffarin, a UMP political figure, as his new prime minister. After Sarkozy's election in 2007, parliamentary elections yielded a solid majority for the UMP, and François Fillon became prime minister for the entirety of Sarkozy's presidency. In 2012, the Socialist Party and its allies took the National Assembly majority following the Socialist Hollande's victory in the presidential election. While the Fifth Republic's dual executive creates real problems of power sharing, thus far

Table 14.7 Fifth Republic Presidents and Their Prime Ministers

Year	President	Party	Year	Prime Minister	Party
1958	Charles de Gaulle	Gaullists	1958	Michel Debré	Gaullists
			1962	Georges Pompidou	Gaullists
1965	Charles de Gaulle	Gaullists	1968	Maurice Couvre de Murville	Gaullists
1969	Georges Pompidou	Gaullists	1969	Jacques Chaban-Delmas	Gaullists
			1972	Pierre Messmer	Gaullists
1974	Valery Giscard d'Estang	PR/UDF	1974	Jacques Chirac	Gaullists
			1976	Raymond Barre	UDF
1981	François Mitterrand	PS	1981	Pierre Mauroy	PS
			1984	Laurent Fabius	PS
			1986	Jacques Chirac*	Gaullists
1988	François Mitterrand	PS	1988	Michel Rocard	PS
			1991	Édith Cresson	PS
			1992	Pierre Bérégovoy	PS
			1993	Édouard Balladur*	Gaullists
1995	Jacques Chirac	Gaullists	1995	Alain Juppé	Gaullists
			1997	Lionel Jospin*	PS
2002	Jacques Chirac	Gaullists	2002	Jean-Pierre Raffarin	Gaullists
			2005	Dominique de Villepin	Gaullists
2007	Nicolas Sarkozy	Gaullists	2007	François Fillon	Gaullists
2012	François Hollande	PS	2012	Jean-Marc Ayrault	PS

*Cohabitation

French leaders have found ways to deal with these complications without intractable disagreements or prolonged indecision.[17]

The Government

The American term *cabinet* refers to the various cabinet secretaries who run the main departments of the U.S. government or who enjoy similarly high status. In France the cabinet is called the *government* and its members are known as *ministers*. In the language of the Fifth Republic's constitution, the government is formally called the *Council of Ministers*. Normally the government consists of *full ministers*, who are the most important figures, and *junior ministers* of somewhat lesser rank.

One of the distinctive features of the Fifth Republic is that the government is responsible to two authorities, not just one. It is delicately positioned between the president and the National Assembly and is accountable to both of them. Both the president and the Assembly have explicit or implied rights to choose and dismiss the prime minister and other cabinet ministers. In Britain, by contrast, the government is responsible only to the House of Commons.

The constitution gives the president the authority to name the prime minister. It does not expressly say the president also has the right to dismiss the prime minister, stating only that the head of state "terminates the functions of the prime minister when the latter presents the resignation of the government." Presumably, therefore, the prime minister can always resign but the president has no constitutional authority to compel him or her to do so. Nevertheless, every president of the Fifth Republic has removed prime ministers he no longer wished to see in office. Sometimes a president wants a new PM in order to try new policies or give the government a fresh look. On occasion a president has sought to deflect public indignation at his own failures by sacking the prime minister as a scapegoat. Whatever the reasons, French presidents at various times have simply told the PM to resign.

As to picking the other cabinet members, the constitution grants the president the right "to appoint and dismiss" them, but only "on the proposal of the prime minister." Here again, actual practice has often diverged from the letter of the law. All six presidents up to 2012 at times took it upon themselves to appoint their own preferred choices to various cabinet positions. As might be expected, the president's ability to impose cabinet choices on the prime minister diminishes considerably under cohabitation. In these awkward circumstances the premier chooses the cabinet, though the president's primacy in foreign and defense policy tends to be respected. During the precedent-setting first cohabitation of 1986–88, President Mitterrand insisted on the right to veto Prime Minister Chirac's choices for foreign minister and defense minister. Chirac complied when Mitterrand rejected his first picks, appointing ministers more acceptable to the president.

Censure In addition to being responsible to the president, in practice the government is formally responsible to the National Assembly. Most important, the Assembly has the right to vote the prime minister and government out of office in a vote of censure, the French equivalent of a vote of no confidence. The Fifth Republic's provisions for the censure procedure are very exacting. De Gaulle and the constitution's framers were determined to avoid the experience of the Fourth Republic, whose legislature was able to depose a government relatively easily by majority vote, thereby exacerbating the regime's chronic instability. To topple a government in the Fifth Republic, the National Assembly must meet the following conditions:

1. A censure motion must be signed by at least 10 percent of the Assembly.
2. The vote may not take place until after a 48-hour "cooling off" period.

3. The motion is adopted only if it is passed by a majority of the full Assembly (289 out of 577). A majority of those voting is insufficient; abstentions do not count.

If the censure motion passes, the prime minister must submit his or her resignation to the president, along with that of the rest of the government. Presumably, the president must then select a new prime minister. In 1962 President de Gaulle flouted this provision when he reappointed Prime Minister Pompidou immediately after the Assembly passed a censure motion against Pompidou's government. To add insult to injury, de Gaulle then sent the Assembly packing and called snap elections. The 1962 incident was the only case of a successful vote of censure against a government in the Fifth Republic, though more than 30 censure motions have been filed. If a censure motion fails to obtain the necessary majority, its signers may not introduce another one in the same legislative session except under special circumstances.

If the prime minister wishes, she or he may ask the Assembly for a vote of confidence on the government's initial program or on a general declaration of its policies. Although this procedure is not mandated by law, most prime ministers have sought an early vote of support of this kind shortly after assuming office. Known as *investiture*, this practice is followed in a number of parliamentary systems (in effect, the legislature vests power in the government). Alternatively, a government that has already been in power for some time may ask the Assembly to approve its policy orientations. Prime ministers who make such a request typically want to force a divided Assembly to clear the air and decide if the majority backs the government or not. If a government fails to muster a majority in the Assembly on a vote of investiture or a policy declaration, it must resign.

Question Time As in Britain, French government ministers—including the prime minister—are required to answer questions posed by members of parliament. Question periods are held every week in both the National Assembly and the Senate. Most of the questions are in written form, as are most of the ministerial responses. Since 1989 a weekly oral interrogation of a minister or deputy minister has occurred in the Assembly. Thus far, however, the Fifth Republic has not followed the British custom of requiring the prime minister to answer questions spontaneously every week. The president is never required to appear before parliament.[18]

Cabinet Membership The size of the cabinet has varied from as few as 15 members to as many as 49. So, too, has its composition. Typically the cabinet includes political leaders from the parties forming the Assembly majority. It may also include other individuals, such as technocrats who have no significant leadership role in a political party but who bring a special expertise to their cabinet portfolio. Some cabinet members, including prime ministers, are graduates of the *grandes écoles*, France's elite graduate schools. These prestigious academies, which admit only about 4 percent of French university students, include the École Normale Superieure, the most prestigious institution for future academics; the École Polytechnique, founded by Napoleon to train engineers and technicians; and the National Academy for Administration (École nationale d'administration, or ENA), an institution established under de Gaulle after World War II to train the country's policy elite. Various efforts have been undertaken or proposed to broaden the student body's social base beyond the Parisian middle and upper classes.[19]

De Gaulle, Pompidou, and Giscard d'Estaing typically presided over governments consisting of Gaullists and members of Giscard's party. Mitterrand's first prime minister, Pierre Mauroy, had a cabinet comprised mainly of Socialists, but four Communists also held cabinet posts temporarily. Jospin's first coalition government in 1997 consisted of 18 Socialists, three Communists, and five other leftists. The government formed by Jean-Marc Ayrault after the 2012 elections included 30 members of the Socialist Party, two from the Greens, and two from the Radical Party of the Left.

Incompatibility Clause Although most cabinet ministers are chosen from the parliamentary ranks of the parties, the Fifth Republic's constitution specifically forbids members of the government from simultaneously serving as elected deputies to either the National Assembly or the Senate. The so-called *incompatibility clause*, which makes cabinet service incompatible with membership in parliament, was designed to reduce the government's dependence on the legislature and give it greater autonomy than it enjoyed under the Fourth Republic. Members of the French Parliament who are invited to join the cabinet must relinquish their legislative seats. Consequently, candidates for the National Assembly typically run together with a substitute (*suppléant*), whose role is to take over the winning candidate's seat in the legislature if the latter is tapped for a cabinet post. This practice is the exact opposite of the British procedure, which *requires* cabinet members to serve simultaneously as members of Parliament. It is nonetheless permissible, however, for a member of the French government to hold other official positions at the same time. Quite a few government ministers work simultaneously as mayors, members of town councils, regional government officials, and the like, such as Chirac, who was simultaneously prime minister and mayor of Paris. In the past there have been cabinet ministers holding as many as five posts at the same time! In 1987 a new law limited this "accumulation of positions" (*cumul des mandats*) to no more than two.[20]

Parliament

The bicameral French Parliament (*Parlement*) consists of the National Assembly, its lower house, and the Senate, the upper house.

The National Assembly The National Assembly currently has 577 deputies. Each deputy is elected in accordance with a two-round variant of the single-member district (SMD) electoral system described in the introduction. The SMD system often leads to disparities between a party's share of the popular vote and its share of legislative seats. In 2012, for example, the Socialists won 29 percent of the popular vote in the first round and then 41 percent in the second round but captured almost 49 percent of the seats in the Assembly. Seeking to work the electoral system to their own advantage, President Mitterrand's Socialists introduced proportional representation in 1986, but Chirac's center-right legislative majority changed it back to SMD two years later.[21]

The French electoral system has allowed the emergence of dozens of parties, many of which contest fewer than 100 of the 577 constituencies. Many elect only a handful of deputies, as Table 14.2 shows for the 2012 National Assembly election. Once the Assembly meets, members may form into

parliamentary groups of 15 or more members. Many such groups are essentially the deputies belonging to a single large party, particularly the UMP and the PS; others are assemblages of deputies from small parties. Groups are seated together in the Assembly chamber and allocated offices, committee assignments, and opportunities to speak and otherwise shape the Assembly's work.

When electing the National Assembly, registered voters check in with election officials at a polling place in their electoral district (*circonscription*). On a table there are paper ballots, each one bearing the name of a single candidate, along with the name of the candidate's *suppléant*, the person who will take over the Assembly seat if the winner is invited to enter the government (see Figure 14.2). There is no limit to the number of

ÉLECTION LÉGISLATIVE DU 16 JUIN 2002 - 3ᵉ CIRCONSCRIPTION DE PARIS

Marie-Claire CHAMPOUX

suppléant
Marc LAROCK
Chevalier des Arts et des Lettres

 R   CANDIDATE DE LA GAUCHE UNIE
SOUTENUE PAR LE PARTI SOCIALISTE,
LES VERTS, LE PRG ET LE PCF

imprimerie Autographe/GP • Paris, Vu les candidats

RÉPUBLIQUE FRANÇAISE
DÉPARTEMENT DE PARIS, 3E CIRCONSCRIPTION.
ÉLECTIONS LÉGISLATIVES DES 9 ET 16 JUIN 2002

MARTINE
Aurillac
DÉPUTÉ, MAIRE DU 7E ARRONDISSEMENT

CANDIDATE **Union pour la Majorité Présidentielle**

JEAN-PIERRE
SUPPLÉANT : **Lecoq**
MAIRE DU 6E ARRONDISSEMENT

FIGURE 14.2   **Sample French legislative ballots, 2002.**

candidates eligible to run in the first round of balloting. In one district in Paris, for example, there were 23 first-round candidates in 2012, the highest in the country. Twenty-three stacks of ballots were therefore lined up across the tables. A voter may choose to pick up either the one ballot bearing the name of the candidate she wishes to vote for, or as many other ballots as are available. She then goes into a voting booth, closes the curtain, and inserts a single ballot into an envelope that is provided. (If she puts two or more ballots into the envelope, they are not counted.) Upon exiting the booth, she is rechecked against the voter registry and then deposits her envelope into a ballot box on the table. At this point she may discard any other ballots she may have picked up. When the polls close, the ballots are counted by hand. In 2012, only 36 candidates won their seats by an absolute majority in the first round. The remaining 541 districts required a second round of balloting a week later. In all but 34 of these districts there were only two candidates who survived into round two; the other 34 districts each had three surviving candidates.[22] Voters in these districts thus had to go to the polls once again (the French vote on Sundays), casting their ballots by the same procedure as in round one.

Senate The **Senate** has 348 members elected to six-year terms by a special electoral college that represents local governments throughout France. One half of the Senate is elected every three years. About 150,000 mayors, city council members, and departmental officials constitute the bulk of the electoral body's membership; the 577 members of the National Assembly make up the rest. Historically, the upper house of the French legislature has usually been dominated by local notables and rural interests, a phenomenon that has not substantially changed. The Senate has traditionally represented the provincial areas Parisians call *la France profonde*—"deep France."[23] Most senators tend to be conservative and antisocialist in their political leanings.

The Senate normally works with the Assembly in drafting common language for bills their members propose. But if the Senate objects to government-drafted legislation, the government can get around these obstacles by bringing its bills directly before the Assembly for a decisive vote. Thus the French Senate may be able to delay the passage of legislation but not block it.

Parliament's Limitations The French Parliament's principal distinction is the relatively narrow scope of its importance compared with legislatures in most other democracies. One of de Gaulle's chief purposes in 1958 was to downgrade the parliament of the Fifth Republic, eliminating the principle of parliamentary supremacy that formed the basis of the Fourth Republic's unstable political system. As a consequence, the Fifth Republic's constitution specifically identifies the policy areas in which parliament has competence to legislate. All other governmental matters are reserved to the "rule-making" authority of the executive branch, which may issue decrees or ordinances without parliamentary approval. The constitution also spells out additional limits on parliament's decision-making powers.

Items that fall within parliament's legislative purview include nationality issues, criminal law, the electoral system, tax rates, and the nationalization of private enterprises. It may also pass civil rights legislation, as the constitution does not contain an enumerated bill of rights.[24] Additionally, parliament may "determine the fundamental principles" of such things as the organization of the country's national defense, local government, education, property rights, commercial law, and labor law, though the details of these matters may be subject to the government's intervention. Parliament has the exclusive right to declare war and ratify most international treaties.

Aside from possessing these and a few other specified powers, France's parliament has been severely restricted by the overriding authority of the president and the prime minister's government, although reforms passed in 2008 give it greater powers than it once had. These restrictions affect both the substance of the law and the procedures used to make it. For example:

- The government and parliament share control of the agenda of bills to be considered and their order of priority. For two weeks of the month, the government sets the agenda. One week is given over to parliamentary scrutiny of the government's work, and the last week the parliament controls. The government can also limit the time allotted for parliamentary consideration of legislation. (Until 2008 the government set the agenda almost entirely. In the United Kingdom, the government and parliament jointly work out the agenda and calendar, though the government's wishes usually prevail. The U.S. Congress controls its own agenda and calendar.)
- Although parliamentary deputies have the right to initiate bills, so does the government. Government bills take priority over private members' bills in parliamentary deliberations and have a far greater likelihood of being passed. (Much the same can be said about Britain. All legislation in the United States is proposed by members of Congress, though some of it may be at the behest of the administration.)
- Members of the French parliament have no right to introduce legislation or propose amendments to bills that entail an increase or reduction in public expenditures. Only the government may propose spending bills or amendments. (The same is essentially true in the UK, but not the United States.)
- Finance bills, including the annual budget bill, must be passed by the two houses of parliament within 70 days. Otherwise, they automatically become law by government decree. (Neither Britain nor the United States imposes a time limit on finance bills or provides for their automatic enactment by decree.)
- The government may attach the question of confidence to financial bills, those that pertain to the finance of the health service, and one other bill per legislative session. Before 2008 any bill was subject to these provisions. In these circumstances, the bill becomes law automatically,

without a parliamentary vote. The only way parliament can block such a bill is to pass a censure motion against the government in accordance with the procedures outlined earlier. In effect, the government may adopt a law on its own authority and dare the Assembly to vote it out of office! This "provocation" procedure has been utilized more than 70 times by various prime ministers since 1958, always with success. (No similar provision exists in the United States or the United Kingdom.)

- Under special circumstances, the government may ask parliament to refrain from passing legislation on matters that are normally reserved to the legislature's lawmaking competence, permitting the government to enact measures in these areas by decree. (Britain has roughly similar "statutory instruments." Though U.S. presidents may issue "executive orders" in certain areas, they cannot ask Congress to give up its legislative prerogatives.)

- The government may limit parliament's right to propose amendments to bills after they are introduced and may compel parliament to vote only on amendments proposed by the government. (This so-called "blocked vote" procedure does not exist in Britain or the United States.)

- All legislation goes through parliamentary committees, but they have minimal decision-making powers. (Parliamentary committees are also fairly weak in Britain but are more powerful in the United States. In the 1990s French parliamentary committees gained the right to query cabinet ministers about relevant legislation, as in the United States.)

In sum, the French parliament is much weaker than the legislatures of Britain, the United States, and indeed most other democracies. Its deputies exhibit rather high rates of absenteeism and comparatively low levels of independence from their respective party leaders. Nevertheless, the partisan composition of the parliament, and particularly of the National Assembly, ultimately determines which parties can form a viable government. In periods of cohabitation, this reality has conferred on France's legislature a decisive political importance.

The Constitutional Council

What happens if the executive branch and the legislature cannot agree whether a piece of legislation falls within the lawmaking competence of parliament or the decree-making privileges of the government? The Fifth Republic constitution provides for a *Constitutional Council* to adjudicate such controversies. At the request of either the government or parliament, the council must hand down a definitive ruling within eight days. In addition, the council has the authority to rule on the constitutionality of so-called "organic laws" that are under consideration in parliament. Organic laws relate to the operation and legal authority of state institutions. Parliament may not enact any measure in this sensitive area if the Constitutional Council decides it is incompatible with the constitution. In Britain, by contrast, Parliament is supreme: It has the exclusive right to enact bills into law without judicial oversight.

When the Fifth Republic was first established, de Gaulle and his associates wanted the Constitutional Council to act as yet another brake on parliamentary initiative. Rather than applying judicial checks and balances on both the executive and legislative branches as the U.S. Supreme Court does, the council was conceived by the republic's framers essentially as a check on the legislature, not on the executive. Three of its nine members are appointed by the president of France, including the head of the council, who alone is empowered to break tie votes. The other six are appointed by the presiding officers of the National Assembly and the Senate. These nine members serve one nine-year term each, but former French presidents become members of the council for life. In keeping with the framers' intentions, most council rulings have in fact supported the government and have run against the preferences of the parliamentary opposition.

Another difference between the Constitutional Council and the U.S. Supreme Court is that the council has less extensive powers of *judicial review*, which is the authority to invalidate laws as unconstitutional. The U.S. Supreme Court may review laws already in existence, for example, but the Constitutional Council must confine its rulings to draft laws that have not as yet taken effect. Moreover, only the central government or members of parliament may bring cases before the council, not local officials or private citizens as in the United States. Nevertheless, since the 1970s the council has issued a number of decisions widening the civil liberties of the population as against the authority of the state. And in 1974 the constitution was amended to allow 60 National Assembly deputies or 60 senators the right to bring cases before the council. Until then, only the president, the prime minister, and the two speakers of parliament had this privilege. The change has allowed opposition legislators to initiate proceedings, resulting in more cases as well as more rulings that have run against the government's preferences. Both the conservative parties and the Socialist Party have availed themselves of the extended opportunities to challenge government decisions. The Constitutional Council is an example of an institution that has evolved during its existence, becoming more influential than it was conceived to be.[25]

The Civil Service

Since the Middle Ages, the French state has sought to solidify its control over the country through a powerful administrative bureaucracy in Paris. The authority of the civil service not only to implement the law of the land but also to create it through bureaucratic regulations grew stronger in the nineteenth century as parliament's authority remained comparatively weak. Today the French civil service still wields significant power in virtually every aspect of the country's economic and social life. The scope of its activities extends from economic planning and financial affairs to the worlds of education, scientific research, health care, foreign policy, and a host of other areas. Its personnel, especially some 10,000 functionaries in the highest echelons, enjoy considerable prestige as highly competent policy professionals. Many of them were educated at ENA or other selective graduate schools, and quite a few are socially and politically well connected. Although the state-funded *grandes écoles* are tuition-free, and students may even be paid a stipend, a disproportionate number of those who take the stiff entrance exams tend to come from upper-class and upper-middle-class Parisian families. In every sense of the word, the top layers of the French civil service constitute a true political elite.

One of the distinguishing characteristics of the French civil service is its close interaction with private enterprise. To a far greater extent than in the United States, Britain, or many other democracies, the top managers of state agencies and the directors of major private corporations in France often share similar educational and social backgrounds and switch back and forth from the public sector to the private. This connection between the public and private sectors is reinforced by the large number of *public enterprises* in France—companies that are wholly or partially owned by the French state. Besides the usual postal service, utilities, and major transportation concerns such as the railroads and airports, the French state partly owns the automaker Renault and Air France-KLM, among other companies. A privatization process launched in the 1980s has reduced the number of these para-statal enterprises, and the French state has sold part of its shares in many firms since 2000. However, the state bureaucracy remains heavily populated with civil servants engaged in managing their affairs. The French state also cooperates with private firms in a process of *indicative planning*, which aims at forecasting future economic conditions and planning decisions accordingly.

As of 2006, some 6.7 million people are employed in the public sector throughout France (including teachers and other nonbureaucrats)—3 out of every 10 employed people. More than half of adults either work in the civil service or are closely related to someone who does—an exceptionally high percentage by European standards. Natural attrition will trim this costly public sector, as much of the civil service is now of retirement age. The French government has not released data on employment in the public sector since the onset of the economic crisis in 2008. Yet civil service jobs, which have been well paid and highly secure, remain popular: Three out of four French university students said in 2006 that they would like to work in public administration.[26]

Local Government and Decentralization

The trends underlying France's long history as a unitary state administered from Paris have not gone uncontested. From its earliest foundations as a national entity, France has always been composed of a diversity of regions, some with their own traditional languages or dialects (such as Brittany, the Basque area, and Alsace). Paris and other large cities experience many of the problems of modern urban centers, while more than 20,000 small towns still dot the French countryside. Many people living in these areas have sought greater powers for their local governments to manage their own affairs with greater freedom from the central state.

France is divided into 22 "regions" (counting Corsica), 96 mainland and 5 overseas "departments," and more than 36,700 "communes" ranging from large cities to rural villages.[27] In 1982 the Socialists enacted a decentralization scheme that increased the powers of various subnational governments without dismantling the predominance of the central state. The reform weakened the traditional powers of France's prefects, who had been since Napoleon's time the central government's agents in the various departments. No longer were they expected to impose the central government's will on the localities; instead, they were to function in a consultative capacity, facilitating communication between the center and the rest of the country. Greater authority was now devolved upon elected councils at the communal, departmental, and regional levels.

These subnational bodies now received the green light to impose various local taxes and assume wider responsibility for local matters in such areas as transportation, the environment, and various economic and welfare functions. Jospin's government permitted wider official usage of local traditional languages, such as Breton in Brittany. Despite these changes, the national government continues to control the bulk of France's tax collections and public spending. It also monopolizes the administration of the entire educational system and plays the predominant role in transportation, the environment, and social welfare. Meanwhile, France does not experience mass separatist tendencies as powerful as those present in Quebec or Scotland, though nationalist movements in Brittany and Corsica that favor greater autonomy or full independence are fairly active.[28]

POLITICAL PARTICIPATION

Much of French political activity centers on formal participation in the electoral arena, involving membership in political parties, campaigning, and voting. Hence we will focus on parties in the coming pages. However, France also has a strong tradition of protest, as mentioned above, that will be discussed briefly later in this section.

French Political Parties

Typically, a large number of political parties and groupings put up candidates for office in France, giving voters a wide array of electoral choices. (In 2002 there were more than 60 in the first round of voting in France and its overseas territories.) The two-round SMD electoral system for elections to the National Assembly keeps most of them from winning a greater share of seats than they might otherwise get under proportional representation (PR). Nevertheless, more parties are represented in the National Assembly today than in the U.S. Congress or the British House of Commons. What explains this bounty of parties and independents in an electoral system that tends to punish small parties in the United States and Britain?

Compared to countries such as the United States, Britain, and Germany, France still has a substantial number of small parties whose ideas remain tied to the past, reflecting ideological tendencies of the left and right that in most Western democracies either have receded into history or have never attracted a significant following to begin with. The 10 candidates who ran for president in round one of the 2012 elections included a Trotskyite—the intensely anticapitalist heirs of Leon Trotsky, a hero of Russia's communist Revolution of 1917 and an exponent of "permanent revolution" around the world—and two other explicitly anticapitalist parties in addition to the Socialist Party on the left. Together the three far-left parties won nearly 4.6 million votes—12.8 percent of the total. Another candidate represented the French branch of the movement headed by Lyndon LaRouche, who has run as a minor-party candidate for U.S. president eight times. To no small extent, the persistence of some of these parties and even smaller splinter groups (especially those on the left) is rooted in continuing debates over socialism versus capitalism—a discourse that is often conducted in terms reminiscent of the first half of the twentieth century, when the two competing economic systems were regarded as diametrical opposites rather than as adaptable components of the modern mixed economy. In addition, several small parties are built around a single prominent leader, typically one whose idiosyncratic views do not easily fit into the mainstream parties.

In short, the French party system is dominated by two large mainstream catchall parties, the center-right neo-Gaullists (currently the UMP, the party of Chirac and Sarkozy) and the center-left Socialists. But it is also fragmented into a multiplicity of smaller parties and their offshoots. In 2012, candidates from parties other than the Socialists and the UMP won 44 percent of the first-round vote for president and the same percentage of the first-round vote for the National Assembly. New parties are assembled, disbanded, and reconstituted under new names with bewildering frequency. For example, 14 parties that fielded candidates in the 1997 elections were not around to compete five years later. By 2002, there were nearly 50 new parties. Most of these mini parties exist because of attachments—at times quite strong—on the part of millions of French men and women to ideas and attitudes that, in their view, are not supported by the two mainstream parties. As a consequence, neither the two-round direct elections for the presidency nor the two-round single-member-district/plurality legislative electoral system has produced an American-style two-party system or a British-style moderate multiparty system. Numerous parties continue to exist in France despite the fact that the second round of both the presidential and legislative balloting tends to hurt the small parties and to favor the two largest ones. Analysts have debated whether the political space along the left–right spectrum in France since the late 1980s is characterized by bipartition into fairly stable left–right orientations, or whether the far-right movement headed by Le Pen has resulted in tripartition, with three distinct blocs of parties and voter orientations.[29] Time will tell if a distinct fourth bloc consisting of extreme-left parties and orientations will solidify.

HYPOTHESIS-TESTING EXERCISE
Duverger's Law in France

When Charles de Gaulle returned to power in 1958, he and Michel Debré advocated a return of the second ballot system, used in the Third Republic, to replace the Fourth Republic's system of proportional representation for the election of National Assembly deputies.[30] They deplored the "regime of parties" that they thought characterized the Fourth Republic and wanted an electoral system that would produce fewer parties.

In an early statement of the hypotheses that eventually became known as Duverger's law (see Chapter 6), the French political scientist stated, "The double ballot majority system and proportional representation tend to multipartism." More specifically, he stated with regard to the second ballot system, "The simple majority with a second ballot tends towards a system of many independent but flexible parties."[31] The logic is this: Ambitious politicians or individuals with distinct policy perspectives can form parties and run on the first ballot and expect voters to support them because if they are eliminated after the first ballot, they (both small party leaders and their voters) can still throw their support (or sell it for the right political price) to larger parties on the second ballot. These smaller parties need to be flexible to form political alliances on the second ballot. So, in contrast to de Gaulle and Debré, Duverger expected the second ballot system to yield many parties, just like proportional representation.

Hypothesis The reintroduction of the second ballot system in the Fifth Republic did not reduce the number of parties.

Variables The *independent variable* is the type of electoral system, proportional representation (PR) or second ballot. The *dependent variable*, what we are explaining, is the number of parties.

Evidence Political scientists have developed a measure of the number of parties in a party system, the effective number of parties, which weights larger parties more than smaller parties in an index. The effective number of parties in the United States is almost exactly 2.0 because the two parties are almost exactly the same size in terms of vote share and the share of seats in Congress. In Britain the effective number of parties in terms of votes has been about 3.5, taking into account the Liberal Democrats and the Scottish and Welsh national parties, but in terms of parliamentary seats Britain has about

(Continued on next page)

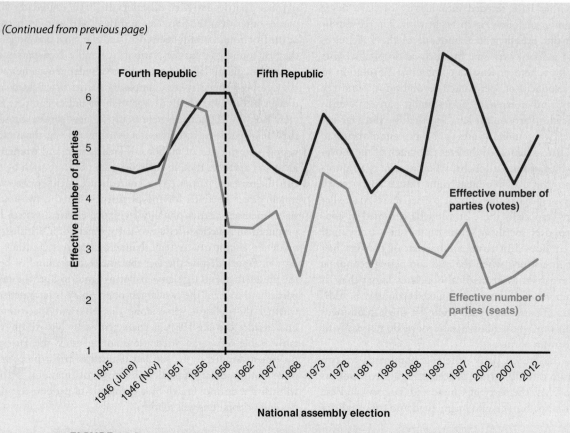

(Continued from previous page)

FIGURE 14.3   **Effective Number of French Parties in the National Assembly since 1945**

Source: "Election Indices," at Michael Gallagher's Electoral Systems website, http://www.tcd.ie/Political_Science/staff/
michael_gallagher/ElSystems/.

2.5 effective parties. Figure 14.3 shows the evolution of the effective number of French parties in terms of votes and seats in the National Assembly.

Conclusion   Here we see that both the Fifth Republic's architects and Duverger are right. De Gaulle and Debré sought to reduce the number of parties in the National Assembly so that the multiparty coalitions associated with the "regime of parties" would be transcended. Figure 14.3 shows a steady decline of the effective number of parties in terms of seats, which reflects the emergence of the PS and the UMP as the dominant catchall parties. The effective number of parties in the 2012 Assembly is 2.83, compared to 5.73 in 1956. However, the effective number of parties competing for votes remains large, as Duverger hypothesized. In the 2012 election (first ballot) the effective number was 5.27, not that different from 1956's 6.09.

One might say the second-ballot system allows the French to have it both ways: many political parties that can reflect a broad spectrum of interests and strong governing parties—often single-party majorities or close to it in the National Assembly—that can support the government.

French parties tend to be categorized as belonging to political "families" of the left and right. The main left-leaning party (the Socialists) and the main center and right-leaning parties (the neo-Gaullists and the Democratic Movement, known as MoDem, the successor to Giscard's Union for French Democracy) tend to be moderate catchall parties, avoiding the extremes of all-out socialism or all-out laissez-faire capitalism. They are also dedicated to democratic principles and the institutional framework of the Fifth Republic. These large parties, along with several moderate smaller ones, hug close to the political center, where most of the voters cluster. Hence the Socialists may be considered a center-left party, while the neo-Gaullists and UDF/MoDem parties are center-right parties. The Communists and a few small leftist parties are situated to the left of the Socialists, while the antiimmigrant National Front is an extreme right-wing party.

The Right   The *right* in French politics is a term burdened with heavy historical connotations. From the time of the Revolution to World War II, the French right was mainly associated with authoritarianism, imperialism, and in some cases, anti-Semitism. Its principal exponents were monarchists,

Bonapartists, the military, the Catholic church hierarchy, the upper classes, and others who never accepted the Revolution. After World War II the right was redefined by de Gaulle and his followers to embrace democracy and the civil liberties promised by the Revolution. Today's center-right parties are "conservative" to the extent that they oppose socialism, embrace private enterprise, and champion French nationalism (though the term *conservative* is not used as widely in France as in the United States or Britain).

But these parties also tend to advocate a strong central state. Deviating from the preferences of American and British conservatives for less government and more private initiative, most politicians of the French center-right openly embrace the principle of government intervention in the economy—through state-owned enterprises, a large civil service, relatively high taxes, and generous welfare spending. They also tend to favor a strong arm for the police and the courts in maintaining law and order. In 2003 President Chirac said, "The state does not have to decide everything," but he also reaffirmed his commitment to the "French model": a combination of private enterprise with a robustly interventionist state sector. Chirac was a very French conservative; he was no Margaret Thatcher.

The Neo-Gaullists

As the name implies, the neo-Gaullists are the political heirs of Charles de Gaulle. As such, they are devoted above all to the constitutional principles of the Fifth Republic. After de Gaulle's retirement in 1969, their most challenging task was to perpetuate their charismatic leader's legacy by maintaining an effective political organization, a process known to social scientists as the "institutionalization of charisma." To that end, over the decades the neo-Gaullists have set up several different parties bearing different names. In 1976, they reconstituted themselves as the Rally for the Republic (Rassemblement pour la République, or RPR). During the 2002 elections they formed a broader grouping called the Union for the Presidential Majority (Union pour la Majorité Presidentielle, or UMP). And several months after the elections they converted this enlarged party into the Union for a Popular Movement (Union pour un Mouvement Populaire, again UMP). While the Fifth Republic's institutional framework and a generally center-right political orientation hold them together, the neo-Gaullists display a variety of attitudes on economic policy, social issues, the European Union, and other political controversies, and there are several different currents within their broad-based organization.

The Democratic Movement (Mouvement démocrate, or MoDem)

MoDem is the successor to the Union for French Democracy (*Union pour la démocratie française*, or UDF), which was founded in 1978 at the instigation of President Giscard d'Estaing. Its initial raison d'être was to support Giscard d'Estaing's presidency. From its inception the UDF has consisted variously of about four or five parties and political clubs. The UDF's principal problem was that its main constituencies were similar to those courted by the neo-Gaullists. Still, the

UDF won a respectable 21 percent of the second-round vote as late as 1997, electing 109 National Assembly deputies.

But a succession of splits after the 1997 elections seriously reduced the UDF's appeal. The formation of Chirac's UMP in 2002 also cut deeply into its ranks, as a large number of UDF political figures joined the new center-right grouping. UDF leader François Bayrou struggled to maintain the group's independence. But he won only 6.8 percent of the vote in the first round of the 2002 presidential elections, and UDF candidates captured only 21 seats in that year's National Assembly elections. Bayrou and his followers are centrists who favor a balance of private enterprise and state-funded welfare, along with a pro-EU orientation. In 2007, Bayrou created MoDem between the first round of the presidential election, in which he finished third with 18.6 percent of the vote, and the subsequent National Assembly elections. In those legislative elections MoDem won but four seats. In 2012, Bayrou's first-round presidential vote share fell to 9.1 percent and MoDem's deputy candidates won only two seats in the National Assembly races, with Bayrou losing his own seat. Given these results, MoDem's future is highly uncertain.

The National Front

Perhaps the most controversial party in France is the *National Front* (*Front national*, or *FN*). The party was established in 1972 under Jean-Marie Le Pen. Le Pen had fought as a paratrooper in Indochina. After winning a seat in the Fourth Republic's parliament, he left the legislature to fight in Algeria. When several extreme right-wing factions consisting of Vichyites, anti-Semites, fundamentalist Catholics, die-hard proponents of French imperialism, and theorists of European racial and cultural superiority resolved to form a new party, Le Pen was their man.

In 1987 Le Pen touched off a storm of controversy with his statement that the Nazi gas chambers were just "a point of detail" in World War II, a remark that infuriated France's 600,000 Jews. (After he uttered a similar remark in Germany nine years later, a German court fined him for demeaning the Holocaust.) In 1984 Le Pen won a seat in the European Parliament. In 1988 he shocked the political mainstream again by polling 14.4 percent of the first-round vote for the presidency. In 1995 he increased his presidential support to 15 percent, winning more than 4.5 million votes. And in a succession of elections to the National Assembly, the FN saw its share of the first-round vote rise from 9.7 percent in 1986 to 15.1 percent in 1997. During the 1997 legislative election campaign Le Pen assaulted a female candidate. In 2003 the European Court of Justice stripped him of his seat in the European Parliament for this offense.

Le Pen's surprise second-place finish in the first round of presidential balloting in 2002 left the rest of the electorate stunned. Le Pen's second-round showing of 17.8 percent represented more than 5.5 million votes. But the rapid collapse of the National Front's political fortunes in the National Assembly elections that immediately followed the 2002 presidential contests suggested that Le Pen had a wider appeal than his party. The

FN won no Assembly seats in 2002. In 2007, Le Pen's vote share fell to 10.4 percent, and again the FN won no Assembly races. In 2011 Le Pen stepped down from the leadership of the FN. His daughter, Marine Le Pen, said to be more democratic and republican than her father, won an internal election to succeed him. She finished third in the 2012 presidential election, taking 17.9 percent of the first-round vote, as strong a result as her father had ever achieved. However, she could not win her own legislative election as the party's candidates took 13.6 percent of the first-round Assembly votes but only two seats.

The FN's success cannot be explained exclusively by its antiimmigrant positions. The party has also reached out to a wider constituency concerned about taxes, unemployment, crime, AIDS, globalization, and other woes afflicting French society. Its wide electoral base encompasses blue- and white-collar workers, small business owners, affluent voters, and young people. By the late 1990s, 25 to 30 percent of French voters had voted for the FN at least once. In 2002 the party and its standard-bearer made inroads into urban and suburban working-class districts once dominated by the French Communists. But their main electoral support came from France's northeast and northwest corners, where economic decay or pockets of immigrants turned more than 20 percent of the voters to the extreme right. Some 38 percent of the unemployed voted for Le Pen in the 2002 presidential race, and for the first time he scored gains in small communes where immigration was not so noticeable. In 2012, Marine Le Pen's voters were disproportionately working class with relatively less education than the general electorate. Many of the National Front's voters may be dyed-in-the-wool bigots. But an indeterminate number of them—perhaps as many as half—are mainly protest voters who are incensed at what they perceive to be the insensitivity of the other parties to their economic distress and social frustrations. Marine Le Pen's success in 2012 is attributed by some to extreme dissatisfaction with Sarkozy's presidency by those on the far right, who saw his close relationship with Chancellor Merkel as a sellout of French national independence.[32]

The Left

The Socialists The main party of the French left today is the *Socialist Party* (*Parti socialiste*, or PS). Although it is customary to identify socialism with the industrial working class and the underprivileged more generally, the PS has never been a predominantly workers' party or a party of the poor. Since its foundation in 1970, it has mainly been a center-left party, attracting those segments of the French middle class who attach a high priority to enhancing social welfare and civil rights for the population as a whole. The party's core voters as well as its dues-paying members and candidates for office include a high proportion of teachers, professors, civil servants, doctors, and other white-collar professionals. Despite the harsh anticapitalist rhetoric of the early Mitterrand years, the PS has also drawn a significant number of votes from private businesspeople and managerial personnel. Less than half its constituency is working

class, with most of it consisting of better-paid skilled workers rather than unskilled laborers.

Its main trade union support comes from the two noncommunist federations, the Workers' Force (*Force Ouvrière*, or FO) and the traditionally Catholic-oriented French Democratic Confederation of Labor (*Confédération française démocratique du travail*, or CFDT). Neither of these union organizations maintains formal institutional links with the Socialists, however.

Upon becoming prime minister in 1997 (in a cohabitation arrangement under President Chirac), Lionel Jospin pursued a middle course that combined private-sector growth with a welfare orientation that was more state-centered than that of his British contemporary, Tony Blair. "My project is not socialist," Jospin declared, while also affirming his "socialist identity" and calling himself a "democratic socialist." Acknowledging the need for more budgetary income, Prime Minister Jospin reaped more revenue by selling shares of French-owned companies such as Air France and France Telecom than all five previous prime ministers put together (including Chirac and Alain Juppé) had managed to do. He kept the state's annual budget deficits within the limits mandated by the European Union, and he explicitly rejected old leftist nostrums about the primacy of the state in the economy. But Jospin also responded to the left wing of his party by supporting a long list of social welfare measures, culminating in the Aubry law that mandated a 35-hour workweek.

Jospin's ouster from the 2002 race after falling third behind Le Pen was a devastating blow. After Jospin's immediate retirement, the party leadership fell to François Hollande, a moderate who had only a few weeks to pick up the pieces before the National Assembly elections took place. The Socialists were routed, capturing less than a fourth of the Assembly's seats. Several of their star candidates failed to win reelection.

In an effort to reinvigorate the party, Hollande brought a large number of young people, women, and immigrants into the Socialists' executive board, the 200-member National Council. During Chirac's second term he led the Socialists' vigorous opposition to the government's attempts to dilute the 35-hour workweek law and to create a new youth employment law. After shoring up his own leadership position within the Socialist camp, Hollande sought to forge a programmatic consensus in a party divided between its conservative wing, led by former cabinet ministers such as Laurent Fabius and Dominique Strauss-Kahn, and its left wing, personified by another cabinet veteran, Martine Aubry. But Fabius broke ranks with other party leaders when he called for the rejection of the European constitution in the 2005 referendum. And none of these leading "elephants" of the party emerged as the Socialists' presidential candidate for 2007. That honor went to Hollande's then common-law spouse, Ségolène Royal.

The Communists The *French Communist Party* (*Parti communiste français*, or PCF) has seen its fortunes wane appreciably in recent decades, losing votes to the Socialists and the National Front. In addition, the PCF's trade union partner, the General

PROFILES   François Hollande

François Hollande was elected president of France in 2012.

François Hollande was born in Rouen, in northern France, in 1954. His mother was a social worker, while his father, a doctor, ran for local office as a far-right candidate. His family relocated to an exclusive Paris suburb when Hollande was 13. He attended the *Institut d'études politiques de Paris* (Paris Institute of Political Studies) and the *École nationale d'administration* (ENA), the exclusive training ground of French political elites.

Hollande worked for François Mitterrand's presidential campaign in 1974 and then joined the Socialist Party in 1979. A close advisor of Mitterrand, Jacques Attali, encouraged Hollande to stand for the National Assembly election in 1981 in Corrèze, a race he lost to Jacques Chirac. However, Hollande landed a position as an economic advisor in the Mitterrand presidency, gaining critical experience and making the connections that have served him since. He ran in Corrèze again in 1988, this time winning. However, he was turned out of office at the next election in 1993, an election in which the PS lost 207 of the 261 seats it held before.

Hollande became the official PS spokesperson when Lionel Jospin became the party leader in 1995. After the 1997 Assembly elections, when Jospin became prime minister, Hollande moved into the PS first secretary role. He also retook the Assembly seat in Corrèze in that election.

For 10 years Hollande served as the Socialist first secretary. Relatively moderate by party standards, he was often opposed by more left-wing elements in the PS. After Jospin's embarrassing third-place finish in the 2002 presidential election, Hollande effectively became the national leader of the party and was considered a potential presidential candidate

for 2007. Squabbling among Jospin and rival Socialists Laurent Fabius and Dominique Strauss-Kahn created an opportunity for another candidate to take the party nomination. After Jospin stepped down, Ségolène Royal beat Hollande to the punch, putting her name into consideration before he did.

Royal and François Hollande had met as students at ENA and formed a long-term relationship. Though they never married, they have four children and for over 30 years they were partners under French laws governing civil unions—the same laws that applied to same-sex unions before Hollande's government passed its same-sex marriage law. After several debates with her chief opponents for the Socialist Party's presidential nomination, Royal in November 2006 won a convincing majority of the nearly 18,000 votes cast by party members. It later was revealed that Royal and Hollande's relationship had broken down in 2006, although they maintained the façade of domestic tranquillity during her presidential campaign. Royal lost the 2007 election to Sarkozy, and the couple split up the following year. Hollande now maintains a romantic partnership with a well-known journalist, Valérie Trierweiler, and their relationship provides much to promote French tabloid sales.

In the 2007 legislative races, the PS did poorly too. Hollande took much criticism for that result, and he stepped down from the party leadership in 2008. Despite his political setback and the breakup of his relationship with Royal, Hollande began planning for a presidential run in 2012. Strauss-Kahn, who had become the head of the International Monetary Fund, seemed poised to become the PS standard bearer, but sexual scandals, including a charge of sexual

(Continued on next page)

(Continued from previous page)

assault in New York (later dropped by prosecutors), wrecked Strauss-Kahn's prospects. Hollande defeated Martine Aubry, who had succeeded him as party first secretary, in the PS primary elections in October 2011.

From the start, Hollande was the favorite in the 2012 presidential race. He was able to project an image of normalcy in contrast to Sarkozy's seemingly hyperactive public life. A moderate Socialist, his policies were not threatening to most voters. Yet he has proposed a return to the social and economic policies that have characterized the French welfare state—higher taxes on the rich (a 75 percent tax rate passed by the PS government that would have affected the 1,500 highest French income earners was overturned by the Constitutional Council), returning the retirement age to 60 from 62 (Sarkozy had raised it), and same-sex marriage and adoption rights, among others. The most important matter on Hollande's agenda, though, is maintaining the relationship with Germany that has allowed France to be an EU leader. Given that Hollande is less enthused about austerity than Angela Merkel, this challenge may prove difficult.

Confederation of Labor, has experienced a sharp decline in membership and political clout since the 1970s. Finally, the collapse of the Soviet Union in 1991 left the PCF without a clear ideological compass.

Battered by these challenges, the Communists in 1994 picked a new chief, Robert Hue, to replace Georges Marchais, who had dominated the party since 1972. But Hue garnered scarcely more than 3 percent in the 2002 race for the presidency. And in a shocking upset, he lost his National Assembly seat to a Chirac follower who cashed in on the votes of local Le Pen supporters. The Communists came away from the debacle with only 21 seats, 16 fewer than in 1997. Under Marie-George Buffet, leader from 2002 to 2010, the party's fortunes continued to decline, with Buffet winning less than 2 percent of the vote in 2007. The PCF chose to ally with other small parties of the left in the Left Front in 2012, postulating Jean-Luc Mélenchon, a former Socialist, for president. The PCF's traditional source of support, the unskilled industrial working class, continues to shrink. Today the PCF's support still remains concentrated in industrial and mining regions, especially the factory areas outside of Paris, which are known as the "Red Belt" because of the party's decades-long control of local governments. But even these areas are increasingly slipping away.

Women in Politics

Women did not acquire the right to vote in France until 1944, following the country's liberation from German occupation. Even today, women are underrepresented in the French national legislature to a considerably greater extent than in many other democracies (Table 1.3). In 2011 20.0 percent of the National Assembly was female, up from 12.2 percent in 2003, but still well below most other democracies. In the 2012 elections, women elected to the Assembly rose to 26.9 percent. In an attempt to raise the number of women taking an active part in politics, a constitutional amendment in 1999 was enacted formalizing "the equal access of men and women to all electoral mandates and elective functions." In the following year, a nearly unanimous National Assembly passed legislation requiring an equal number of male and female candidates for most

elections—the first such law in the world. The measure had the approval of both President Chirac and Prime Minister Jospin. (Jospin's Socialists had already adopted a rule in 1996 ensuring that 30 percent of its candidates would be women.)

Although the "parity law" applies to elections to the National Assembly, the leading parties failed to follow its provisions in 2002. Chirac's Union for the Presidential Majority ran women in just 20 percent of the districts where its candidates vied for a National Assembly seat; the Socialists fielded women candidates in only 36 percent of the races it contested. Quite a few of these women candidates were assigned to run in districts where they stood little chance of winning. As a result, the number of women elected in 2002 (71) was only slightly higher than the number elected in 1997 (66), before the parity law was passed. Parties that failed to meet the parity requirement were penalized by having to forgo a portion of the state-funded subsidies that supplement private campaign contributions. The parity law does not apply to presidential elections.

The Socialists have proven more successful in posting winning female candidates, with 36.8 percent of their elected deputies in 2012 being women. The UMP, in contrast, elected only 13.6 percent women. Half of François Hollande's cabinet is female. Nicolas Sarkozy's first cabinet had seven women of the 15 total positions.

The parity law has proved quite successful in boosting the number of women running in municipal elections for city councils. In local elections held in March 2001, nearly twice as many women were elected to municipal councils as were elected before the parity law took effect. About half of the council members in cities with a population of more than 3,500 are now women. The parity law also applies to regional elections, certain Senate elections, and elections to the European Parliament.[33]

Protest and Other Forms of Participation

As suggested above, the French are known to turn to protest as a means to express political demands. No French government is immune from public demonstrations. De Gaulle experienced the 1968 student and worker movement, but recent

The French have a tradition of active political participation that often takes the form of mass protest. Here members of the General Confederation of Labor (CGT) demonstrate in 2010.

history provides many examples of the French turning to the streets to attempt to shape public policy. In 2005, for example, France was rocked by the protests of youths of North African descent described in the introduction to this chapter, but the government of Chirac and de Villepin also faced a demonstration by about 1 million labor unionists dissatisfied by government austerity plans. The following year, a new labor law that would have made new employees more vulnerable to being laid off from their jobs brought thousands of French youths into the streets several times over three months. Attempts by the Sarkozy government to introduce reforms that would make universities more independent and responsible to make decisions at the local level, including possibly charging tuition, led to student protests from 2007 through 2009. Sarkozy's bill to raise the retirement age from 60 to 62 led to violent protests in 2010. The Hollande government's need to adopt austerity measures in 2012 also produced large-scale demonstrations.

Is this level of protest unusual? While French levels of participation in conventional forms of political activity are about average for European countries, the French are more inclined to engage in more challenging political acts than others. For example, while 17 percent of Europeans responding to a European Social Survey said they had boycotted products as consumers, 27 percent of French respondents said they had done so. And although 9 percent of all Europeans had attended a legal protest (one that had a permit), 18 percent of French said they had done so. Whereas 1.3 percent of Europeans had engaged in an illegal protest, twice as many French people had done so. In comparative perspective, then, the French are more inclined to protest behavior.[34]

CONTEMPORARY POLITICAL ISSUES

In 1995, Gaullist Jacques Chirac came to the presidency after François Mitterrand had held the office for 14 years. Chirac

would hold the office for a dozen more years. As president of France, Chirac inherited the massive center-right majority that had been elected to the National Assembly in 1993, with three more years to run before the next regularly scheduled Assembly elections. But after appointing his fellow Gaullist, Alain Juppé, as prime minister, Chirac quickly ran into trouble. The president was compelled to follow the European Union's criteria for creating the euro. Under Mitterrand, France had assumed the obligation of reducing its annual budget deficit to no more than 3 percent of GDP and of cutting its substantial national debt. Chirac, like Mitterrand, was caught in the web of globalization emanating from European economic integration.

To comply with these requirements, Juppé announced new budgetary austerity measures in November 1995. Budget cuts, which were sprung on the populace with little or no explanation, sparked the most widespread outpouring of mass protest since 1968.

As economic paralysis loomed, Juppé was forced to enter negotiations with the trade unions and public-sector employees in an effort to reach a compromise. Some of his austerity plans had to be curtailed or canceled. Fearing that the center-right's popularity would sink even lower by 1998, the year of the next regularly scheduled National Assembly elections, Chirac decided in 1997 to call snap elections a year early. His hope was to retain a large enough majority for the RPR and its allies to pursue their policies of budget cutting and privatization for five more years. His calculations proved wrong, and in June 1997 the left under Jospin's Socialists retook control of the lower house. Now it was Chirac's turn as president to accept the reality of an opposing parliamentary majority. In naming Jospin prime minister, Chirac launched the Fifth Republic's third experience with cohabitation.

The experience was frustrating for the head of state. Just as President Mitterrand had stepped back and allowed Chirac to take the lead in conducting domestic policy as prime minister, President Chirac accorded Jospin a similarly wide latitude. For his part, Jospin pursued a number of policies Chirac supported, including the privatization of a record number of state-owned companies, the reduction of budget deficits and corporation taxes, and cooperation with other NATO countries during the war over Kosovo. But the prime minister also pursued policies that Chirac and his followers strongly opposed. Perhaps the most controversial of these contested initiatives was the decision to reduce the average workweek for most employees in France from 39 to 35 hours, with employers required to pay their workers for the equivalent of 40 hours. The measure, known as the Aubry law after its principal advocate, Labor Minister Martine Aubry, was intended to open jobs for France's large pool of unemployed workers. Despite a booming economy, with annual growth rates between 1998 and 2000 at 3 percent or higher for the first time in decades, France continued to suffer from chronic unemployment. The jobless rate topped 11 percent in the late 1990s, and youth unemployment was roughly double that figure. Jospin also introduced more generous minimum wage laws and other welfare measures aimed at assisting a large—and growing—population of marginalized people living at the fringes of France's fast-growing, high-tech economy. Chirac shared the views of those in the business community who objected to the Aubry law and various other policies emanating from Jospin's government. But despite the vast assortment of presidential powers at his command, he lacked the authority to veto legislation passed by parliament.

Cohabitation came to an end when Jospin failed to even make the second round in the 2002 presidential election, which Chirac won in a runoff against the National Front's Jean-Marie Le Pen. But Chirac's second term was rocked by a succession of failures. His term included the defeat of the government-backed European constitution, the explosion of rage in immigrant communities in 2005, and the withdrawal of the youth employment law in the face of demonstrative public protests in 2006 mentioned above.

Similarly, Sarkozy's term, which started with an outpouring of support for the flamboyant president, ended with widespread public disappointment. Sixty-four percent of French people disapproved of Sarkozy by the time of his run for reelection in April 2012. Sarkozy faced an even more difficult policy environment than Chirac given the worldwide economic recession that erupted in the fall of 2008 and the European sovereign-debt crisis that it aggravated.

Leading a new Socialist government after four years of global economic crisis, President Hollande and Prime Minister Ayrault will have to deal with a host of accumulating problems. Two of the major ones are the economy and the integration of recent immigrants.

The Economy

France's per capita GDP ranked 21st in the world in 2012. But in 1980 France ranked seventh in that category. Over much of that period, the country's unemployment rates either rose or

remained virtually immovable. Average net pay, with inflation taken into account, grew by only 1 percent in the first half of the past decade. French women earned about three-quarters of average male earnings and continued to come against glass ceilings at the upper-managerial levels of both the public and private sectors. Tax burdens on individual citizens and on private companies were high by OECD standards, with tax revenues at well over 40 percent of GDP. France's trade deficit has grown considerably in recent years, along with its public debt and pension deficit. The finance minister stated in 2005 that the country was living beyond its means. Government spending still takes up more than 50 percent of GDP, well above the OECD average of just over 40 percent. Because half the members of the National Assembly are former civil servants, it is unlikely that the French parliament will vote to trim the country's costly bureaucracy.

Most French employees work an annualized average of 35 hours a week and benefit from five weeks of paid vacation and an equal amount of sick leave. As a result, they put in fewer work hours than their counterparts in all but 3 out of 34 economically advanced OECD countries. American employees work 21 percent more hours. With an average retirement age of 59, only one out of five French citizens between the ages of 60 and 64 is still employed. In the United States, more half the people in that age group are working. In 2005 the French labor force was 2.7 times the size of the over-65 population, but by 2025 it will be only half as large, placing even heavier burdens on the pension system. Although tuition is free at France's 84 public colleges and universities, and admission is virtually guaranteed except in the highly selective *grandes écoles*, research and development in France has not kept pace with the highest world standards. None of these academic institutions has broken into the world's top 40 universities as measured by online faculty publications.

Globalization is transforming French businesses—including state-owned companies—to a greater extent than many people in France would like. When a large Italian energy company tried to take over a privately owned French utility group called Suez in 2006, de Villepin's government arranged Suez's merger with the state-owned energy giant Gaz de France, fending off the takeover bid in the name of "economic patriotism." Even Sarkozy, who favored a more vigorous private sector in France, applauded the French government's protection of large corporate "national champions" against foreign takeover. These interventionist practices contradict European Union policies favoring cross-border mergers that enhance Europe's competitiveness in the global marketplace. The French government has also resisted enforcing EU rules that require annual budget deficits to be kept at 3 percent of GDP or below. While all euro zone governments have struggled with those injunctions since the onset of the economic crisis, France has been less compliant than others. The EU has formally warned France to comply with these strictures or face mandatory fines.

But France also benefits from its participation in the EU. French farmers have been especially well compensated out of funds from the EU's Common Agriculture Policy, which has subsidized European agriculture and protected it against competition from the United States and other food-exporting countries. (France has also banned the import of genetically modified food from the United States.) French farm owners and vintners form powerful political lobbies that heavily influence government policies. And French firms are benefiting from globalization, reaping handsome profits from sales and investments abroad while purchasing companies around the world, including American brands. French state-owned companies often fetch hefty prices when the government sells them or offers partial ownership to outside bidders. To be sure, there are losers as well as winners in these transactions. When the French communications supplier Alcatel purchased the American firm Lucent in 2006, creating a company worth nearly $40 billion, the new management team announced it would reduce its 88,000-strong workforce by 10 percent in a cost-cutting measure. For his part, President Chirac displayed his pique at the linguistic implications of globalization. He and two French cabinet ministers walked out of an EU summit in 2006 when the president of France's largest business association, the Enterprise Movement of France (Medef), addressed the meeting in English. English "is the accepted business language of Europe today," the Medef chief said. French citizens are also taking advantage of opportunities in the global economy. Though half the population in 2006 had no faith in the market economy, the number of French men and women who have moved to Britain and other European countries or to the United States in search of better job opportunities has risen more than 40 percent since 1990.

The news is not all grim, by any means. France continues to be a prime choice for overseas investors. With a workforce that tends to have a high level of productivity, along with a quality of life that few countries can match, France remains an attractive location for foreign companies and investors. It is also the world's top tourist destination, drawing close to 80 million visitors a year, a figure higher than the domestic population. Despite the economy's doldrums, only 7 percent of France's people live with less than 50 percent of the median income, compared with 11 percent in Germany and 18 percent in the United States. Through a variety of insurance programs, the French enjoy universal health care coverage. And the French services sector has been booming, accounting for virtually all the new jobs created in recent years. When these and other pluses are added into the mix with the French economy's minuses, it is clear that the country's new leadership will face not only serious challenges but also extraordinary opportunities.[35]

Immigration

An increasingly diverse society, France has more than 5 million foreign-born residents and many more with a parent or grandparent who emigrated from abroad. As noted earlier, there are between 5 million and 6 million Muslims living in France, constituting 8 to 10 percent of the national population. In a country whose residents are accustomed to defining French identity in ethnic terms, the presence of so many people of foreign origin—especially of non-European origin—creates problems both for *les Français de souche* (people of French stock) and the immigrant community. Young Mahgrebis, who call themselves *beurs* (a play on the French word *Arabes*), have joined with other immigrants in forming groups like "SOS Racisme" that are dedicated to fighting racism. French officials, meanwhile, appear determined to integrate the country's Muslim population into the secular traditions of the French Republic. The separation of church and state was not established in France until 1905, following a long battle between secularists and the proponents of a privileged status for Roman Catholicism. Article 1 of the Fifth Republic's constitution enshrines this principle by describing the republic as *laïque*—"secular." When President Chirac called for a ban on head scarves and other religious attire in French public schools, he pointedly declared, "Secularism is not negotiable." (Ironically, however, French law permits public funding for religious schools, including Muslim schools.)

Fears of terrorism, particularly in the aftermath of September 11, 2001, have heightened the urgency of these issues. French police and prosecutors have wider authority to investigate, detain, interrogate, and expel suspected criminals and illegal aliens than their counterparts in the United States possess, and they use it. (France has no habeas corpus law or Miranda rights.) Presumed terrorists are rounded up periodically, and surveillance agents routinely stake out mosques. Allegations of police brutality aimed at immigrants have been publicized by Amnesty International, as has the rise in violence directed against France's Jewish community. The kidnapping, torture, and killing of a young Jewish man in Paris in 2006 by a gang calling itself the "barbarians" raised fears of rising anti-Semitism in the country's Muslim community.[36]

The disturbances in immigrant communities that shook France in 2005 placed the country on edge, serving notice of an incendiary discontent seething just below the surface of everyday appearances. Members of the French political elite have advocated various measures to address the immigrant minority's sense of alienation from French society. A report commissioned by de Villepin's government provided blatant evidence of discrimination in the hiring practices of French companies. Recommendations to rectify the problem accompanied the report. Conceivably, efforts to improve employment opportunities and living conditions in immigrant communities may evoke a positive response. France's Muslims, who form a large part of the country's minority population, do not seem to be as alienated as their co-religionists in Britain or other European countries. According to surveys conducted by the Pew Research Center, 42 percent of France's Muslims regarded themselves as French citizens first and as Muslims second, while 46 percent saw themselves as Muslims first. But 81 percent of British Muslims considered themselves Muslims first and only 7 percent saw themselves as British citizens first. Muslims in Spain and Germany were also considerably more inclined than French Muslims to see themselves as Muslims first. Some 72 percent of French Muslims (but only 49 percent of British Muslims) saw no conflict between being a devout Muslim and living in a modern society. These attitudes suggest that large numbers of France's Muslims want to be included in French society rather than alienated from it.[37]

Nevertheless, before the 2007 elections, people of non-European origin were practically absent from the French parliament (except for less than a dozen who represented overseas territories). In 2007 one Parisian of Guadalupean origin was elected to the National Assembly, and in 2012 six nonwhite deputies, all Socialists, took seats. Non-European origin French people were severely underrepresented in the civil service and corporate management too. In 2000, 60 percent of the French said there were too many foreigners in France, and a mere 29 percent said they were "not racist." Despite the joyous celebrations that greeted France's soccer team when it won the World Cup in 1998, the dominance of players of foreign origin like Zinedine Zidane on the championship club had little lasting effect on French racial attitudes. In the following year, 36 percent of French people surveyed believed that there were too many foreign players on the team. And as the French team battled into the World Cup final in 2006, with 17 minority players out of 23, many French citizens with similar minority backgrounds expressed doubts that the team could bring the country together politically or socially. Integrating France's large minority population into the mainstream of the country's political and economic life will surely be a major test of the country's vaunted traditions of tolerance, inclusion, and equality for many years to come.[38]

Conclusion

France took a long and winding road to stable democracy. The threat of authoritarianism hung over French politics until well into the 1960s. Starting with the Revolution, the French have sought to build a lasting democracy on the values of "liberty, equality, and fraternity." The values of tolerance, nondiscrimination, inclusion, and fairness have been harder to achieve, much as they have been in many other democracies, including the United States and Britain. Despite repeated setbacks, the rule of law has been cemented as a fundamental element of French democracy since World War II. Since then, the French have embraced all four faces of democracy described in Chapter 7: popular sovereignty, guaranteed civil rights and liberties, democratic values, and economic well-being, centered on a generous welfare state and a vibrant private sector. The wide consensus that now prevails on these basic understandings of democracy has blurred the historic distinctions between right and left in France, despite day-to-day conflict over the details of policy. (By the late 1990s, 86 percent of the French perceived no difference between Socialist and neo-Gaullist governments.)[39] Along the way, the French have also met all 10 conditions for democracy delineated in Chapter 7.

Though the years ahead may bring renewed friction and vigorous contestation, the French can be confident that they can deal with their conflicts—and enjoy their extraordinary cultural and economic blessings—on the foundations of a solid democracy.[40]

Key Terms

National Assembly
Cohabitation
French Revolution
Fifth Republic
Gaullism
Bonapartism
Senate

Notes

1. *The Washington Post*, March 25, 2006. On France's "fearful society," see Christophe Lambert, *La société de la peur* (Paris: Plon, 2005).
2. Sophie Meunier, "Globalization and Europeanization: A Challenge to French Politics," *French Politics* 2, no. 2 (August 2004), pp. 125–50; Emiliano Grossman and Sabine Saurugger, "Challenging French Interest Groups: The State, Europe and the International Political System," *French Politics* 2, no. 2 (August 2004), pp. 203–20.
3. The Jacobins (JACK-o-bins) took their name from an order of friars who were established in the church of St. Jacques (i.e., St. Jacob) in Paris. The Jacobins held meetings in the dining hall of the church convent.
4. The literature on the French Revolution is voluminous. For overviews, see Simon Schama, *Citizens* (New York: Knopf, 1989); William Doyle, *The Oxford History of the French Revolution* (Oxford: Oxford University Press, 1989); Emmet Kennedy, *A Cultural History of the French Revolution* (New Haven, CT: Yale University Press, 1989).
5. The Third Republic's first president, Marshal Patrice MacMahon, was a monarchist who tried to reestablish authoritarian rule. Electoral victories by pro-Republic forces in 1876 and 1877 prevented him from succeeding and he resigned. In the late 1880s General Georges Boulanger, "the man on horseback," almost took power in a coup. See James Harding, *The Astonishing Adventure of General Boulanger* (New York: Scribner, 1971), and William D. Irvine, *The Boulanger Affair Reconsidered* (New York: Oxford University Press, 1989). Between 1894 and 1906 the Dreyfus Affair, which took its name from a Jewish officer unjustly accused of treason, triggered an intense struggle between the republic's authoritarian opponents and "Dreyfusards" who supported democracy. Dreyfus served years of hard labor on Devil's Island, a penal colony off the coast of French Guyana, before being exonerated. See Jean-Denis Bredin, *The Affair: The Case of Alfred Dreyfus*, trans. Jeffrey Mehlman (New York: G. Braziller, 1986). Also Sanford Elwitt, *The Making of the Third Republic* (Baton Rouge, LA: Louisiana State University Press, 1975).
6. Liah Greenfeld, *Nationalism: Five Roads to Modernity* (Cambridge, MA: Harvard University Press, 1992), pp. 89–188.
7. Pierre Birnbaum, *The Idea of France*, trans. M. B. de Bevoise (New York: Hill and Wang, 2001); Sudhir Hazareesingh, *Political Traditions in Modern France* (Oxford: Oxford University Press, 1994). See also Fernand Braudel, *The Identity of France*, 2 vols., trans. Siän Reynolds (London: Collins, 1988).
8. Edward S. Mason, *The Paris Commune* (New York: Macmillan, 1930). For Karl Marx's views on the Commune, see "The Civil War in France," in *The Marx-Engels Reader*, ed. Robert C. Tucker (New York: W. W. Norton, 1972), pp. 526–76.
9. Michael Crozier, *The Stalled Society* (New York: Viking, 1974).
10. Charles Tilly, *The Contentious French* (Cambridge, MA: Belknap, 1986). See also Philip G. Cerny, *Social Movements and Protests in France* (New York: St. Martin's Press, 1982).
11. Robert O. Paxton, *Vichy France* (New York: Knopf, 1972); Michael R. Marrus and Robert O. Paxton, *Vichy France and the Jews* (New York: Basic Books, 1981). See also the film by Marcel Ophuls, *Le chagrin et la pitié (The Sorrow and the Pity)*.
12. Charles de Gaulle, *The Complete War Memoirs of Charles de Gaulle*, trans. Jonathan Griffin and Richard Howard (New York: Simon & Schuster, 1959); Charles de Gaulle, *Memoirs of Hope*, trans. Terence Kilmartin (New York: Simon & Schuster, 1971). See also Jean Lacouture, *De Gaulle: The Rebel 1890–1944*, trans. Patrick O'Brien (New York: W. W. Norton, 1993); Jean Lacouture, *De Gaulle: The Ruler 1945–1970*, trans.

Alan Sheridan (New York: W. W. Norton, 1993); Charles Williams, *The Last Great Frenchman: A Life of General de Gaulle* (New York: Wiley, 1995); Robert O. Paxton and Nicholas Wahl, *De Gaulle and the United States* (Providence, RI: Berg, 1994); Charles Cogan, *Charles de Gaulle: A Brief Biography with Documents* (Boston: Bedford, 1996).

13. Alain Touraine, *The May Movement*, trans. Leonard F. X. Mayhew (New York: Random House, 1971); Alain Schnapp and Pierre Vidal-Naquet, *The French Student Uprising, November 1967–June 1968*, trans. Maria Jolas (Boston: Beacon Press, 1971). For a fictionalized account, see the novel by James Jones, *The Merry Month of May* (New York: Delacorte, 1971). See the analysis by Richard Johnson, an American student who witnessed the 1968 events, in *The French Communist Party Versus the Students* (New Haven, CT: Yale University Press, 1972).

14. Valéry Giscard d'Estaing, *French Democracy*, trans. Vincent Cronin (Garden City, NY: Doubleday, 1977); J. R. Frears, *France in the Giscard Presidency* (London: Allen & Unwin, 1981).

15. For a comparison of Mitterrand's economic policies and Margaret Thatcher's, see Peter Hall, *Governing the Economy: The Politics of State Intervention in Britain and France* (Oxford: Oxford University Press, 1986).

16. Julius W. Friend, *The Long Presidency: France in the Mitterrand Years, 1981–1995* (Boulder, CO: Westview Press, 1998); Ronald Tiersky, *François Mitterrand: A Very French President* (Lanham, MD: Rowman & Littlefield, 2003); Mairi Maclean, ed., *The Mitterrand Years* (New York: St. Martin's, Press, 1998); Anthony Daley, ed., *The Mitterrand Era* (New York: New York University Press, 1996); Alistair Cole, *François Mitterrand* (London: Routledge, 1994); Wayne Northcott, *Mitterrand: A Political Biography* (New York: Holmes & Meier, 1992); George Ross et al., eds., *The Mitterrand Experiment* (New York: Oxford University Press, 1987); Jean Lacouture, *Mitterrand: Une histoire de Français*, 2 vols. (Paris: Seuil, 1998).

17. A thorough reference work on French institutions is Chagnollaud Quermonne, *La Ve Republic*, 4 vols., rev. ed. (Paris: Flammarion, 2000).

18. Sébastien Lazardeux, "'Une Question Ecrite, Pour Quoi Faire?' The Causes of the Production of Written Questions in the French Assemblée Nationale," *French Politics* 3, no. 3 (December 2005), pp. 258–81.

19. ENA graduates only about 80 students a year, École polytechnique about 300. By 2002, six out of nine previous prime ministers were ENA graduates, two out of the three most recent presidents, and a large number of cabinet ministers. Two out of three chairmen of the top 40 companies listed on the French stock exchange had graduated from either ENA or the École polytechnique. *The Economist*, June 5, 1999; and *The New York Times*, December 18, 2005.

20. On the *cumul des mandats*, see the articles in *French Politics* 4, no. 3 (December 2006).

21. On France's double-ballot electoral systems, see the articles in *French Politics* 3, no. 2 (August 2005).

22. "Législatives: 34 triangulaires et quelques accrocs aux consignes," *Le Monde*, June 13, 2012.

23. Out of a population of 59 million in 2001, only about 15 million lived in France's 10 largest cities (9 million in Paris). There were more than 20,000 communes having a population of fewer than 500 people. The number of rural folk fell to 627,000 in 1999, 38 percent less than in 1989 (*The Economist*, November 16, 2002). On "deep France," see Richard Bernstein, *Fragile Glory: A Portrait of France and the French* (New York: Plume, 1991).

24. The preamble affirms the "attachment" of the French people to the Declaration of the Rights of Man of 1789 and to the rights listed in the preamble to the Fourth Republic's constitution. Article 2 states that the Fifth Republic ensures "the equality of all citizens before the law, without discrimination of origin, race or religion."

25. Alec Stone Sweet, "Judicialization and the Construction of Governance," *Comparative Political Studies* 31, no. 2 (April 1999), pp. 147–84.

26. Ezra N. Suleiman, *Elites in French Society* (Princeton, NJ: Princeton University Press, 1978); Harvey Feigenbaum, *The Politics of Public Enterprise: Oil and the French State* (Princeton, NJ: Princeton University Press, 1985). See also *The Economist*, November 16, 2002; October 28, 2005; and October 27, 2012. Public-sector employment figures come from the United Nations Economic Commission on Europe, w3.unece.org/pxweb/.

27. France maintains five "overseas departments" (*départements d'outre-mer*, or DOMs): Guadeloupe, Martinique, and Guyana in the Caribbean and Réunion and Mayotte in the Indian Ocean. It also has three "overseas territories" (*territoires d'outre-mer*, or TOMs): French Polynesia, New Caledonia (near Australia), and the Pacific islands of Wallis and Futuna. In addition, it possesses two "territorial collectivities": St. Pierre-et-Miquelon, located next to Canada, and Mayotte, located near Madagascar. These overseas areas, which are not considered part of "metropolitan France," elect 22 seats in the French National Assembly. The Mediterranean island of Corsica is part of metropolitan France. It has enjoyed a special autonomous status since 1982 and elects four deputies to the National Assembly.

28. Vivien A. Schmidt, *Democratizing France: The Political and Administrative History of Decentralization* (Cambridge: Cambridge University Press, 1990). In 2003, Corsica's voters narrowly rejected the French government's proposal for slightly more local autonomy.

29. Gérard Grunberg and Étienne Schweisguth, "French Political Space: Two, Three or Four Blocs?" *French Politics* 1, no. 3 (November 2003), pp. 331–47; Robert Andersen and Jocelyn Evans, "The Stability of the French Political Space, 1988–2002," *French Politics* 3, no. 3 (December 2005), pp. 282–301. See also Andrew Knapp, *Parties and the Party System in France: A Disconnected Democracy?* (New York: Palgrave Macmillan, 2004); Michael S. Lewis-Beck, ed., *How France Votes* (New York: Chatham House, 2000).

30. Robert Elgie, "France: Stacking the Deck," in *The Politics of Electoral System*, ed. Michael Gallagher and Paul Mitchell (Oxford: Oxford University Press, 2005), pp. 119–36.

31. *Political Parties: Their Organization and Activity in the Modern State* (New York: Wiley, 1954); "The Influence of the Electoral System on Political Life," *International Social Science Bulletin* 3 (1951).

32. Peter Fysh and Jim Wolfreys, *The Politics of Racism in France* (New York: St. Martin's Press, 1998); Jonathon Marcus, *The National Front in French Politics* (Basingstroke, UK: Macmillan, 1995); Françoise Gaspard, *A Small City in France: A Socialist Mayor Confronts Neofascism* (Cambridge, MA: Harvard University Press, 1995).

33. Karen Bird, "Who Are the Women? Where Are the Women? And What Difference Can They Make? Effects of Gender Parity in French Municipal Elections," *French Politics* 1, no. 1 (March 2003), pp. 5–38; Rainbow Murray, "Why Didn't Parity Work? A Closer Examination of the 2002 Election Results," *French Politics* 2, no. 3 (December 2004), pp. 347–62; Raylene L. Ramsay, *French Women in Politics* (New York: Berghahn, 2003); *Le Monde*, October 25, 2005.

34. Kenneth Newton and Heiko Giebler, "Patterns of Participation: Political and Social Participation in 22 Nations," Discussion Paper SP IV 2008-201, Wissenschaftszentrum Berlin für Sozialforschung (WZB), 2008; Markus Steinbrecher, "Report on Non-Electoral Participation," unpublished paper, CIVICACTIVE Project, 2008, available at www.ucd.ie/civicact/workingpapers.html.

35. "France: A Divided Self," *The Economist*, November 16, 2002; "Special Report: France," *The Economist*, October 28, 2006; Marie-Béatrice Baudet, "Emploi: le CNE ne Créerait que 70 000 Postes de Plus," *Le Monde*, February 25, 2006; "Embouteillages Générationnels," *Le Monde*, February 28, 2006; "Thierry Breton: 'Tous les Indicateurs sont au Vert,'" *Le Monde*, August 12, 2006; Peter S. Goodman, "Tech Development: A French Resolution," *The Washington Post*, December 9, 2005. See also the periodic OECD reports on the French economy at www.oecd.org.

36. Molly Moore, "Killing in France Seen as 'Wake-Up Call'; Anti-Semitism Blamed in Kidnapping, Torture of 23-Year-Old Salesman," *The Washington Post*, February 25, 2006; "A Killing Horrifies France," *The New York Times*, March 5, 2006; Craig S. Smith, "Jews in France Feel Sting as Anti-Semitism Surges Among Children of Immigrants," *The New York Times*, March 26, 2006. On anti-Semitism in contemporary France, see Michael Wieviorka, ed., *La tentation antisémite: Haines des Juifs dans la France d'aujourd'hui* (Paris: Hachette, 2006).

37. See the Pew Global Attitudes Surveys, "The Great Divide: How Westerners and Muslims View Each Other" (released June 22, 2006) and "Muslims in Europe: Economic Worries Top Concerns About Religious and Cultural Identity" (released July 6, 2006), at www.pewglobal.org.

38. "Black, Blanc, Beur," *The Economist*, June 5, 1999; "France: A Divided Self," *The Economist*, November 16, 2002; Sylvia Zappi, "Appel a des Obeir a la Loi Sarkozy sur l'Immigration," *Le Monde*, June 9, 2003; Simon Kuper, "Racism Lives on in France as World Cup Win Fades," *Financial Times*, November 12, 2005; Charles Truehart, "Questions of Color; Racism in France Persists Despite Egalitarian Creed," *The Washington Post*, June 11, 2000; Michael Dobbs, "In France, Judge Fights Terrorism and

Critics, "*The Washington Post*, November 23, 2001; John Ward Anderson, "French Firm Tests Colorblind Hiring," *The Washington Post*, January 29, 2006; John Ward Anderson, "A Multi-Hued National Team Thrills Racially Uneasy France," *The Washington Post*, July 7, 2006. On alienated rappers, see *The Washington Post*, November 24, 2005. See also Paul A. Silverstein, *Algeria in France: Transpolitics, Race, and Nation* (Bloomington, IN: Indiana University Press, 2004); Fadela Amara and Sylvia Zappi, *Breaking the Silence: French Women's Voices from the Ghetto*, trans. Helen Harden Chenut (Berkeley, CA: University of California Press, 2006).

39. "Jacques Chirac, Out of Steam," *The Economist*, July 31, 1999.

40. Recent texts include Andrew Knapp and Vincent Wright, *The Government and Politics of France*, 5th ed. (New York: Routledge, 2006); Anne Sa'adah, *Contemporary France: A Democratic Education* (Lanham, MD: Rowman & Littlefield, 2003).

15

Germany

PAMELA G. CAMERRA-ROWE

Population (2013, estimated): 81.1 million
Area: 137,826 square miles (about the size of Montana)
Freedom House Ratings (2012):
Political Rights—1; Civil Liberties—1

OVERVIEW

- Despite a history of democratic failure and of authoritarianism in the early twentieth century, Germany has become one of the most stable, effective, and prosperous democratic countries in the world.

- Late state formation, late industrialization, lack of support for democracy among elites, and a weak party system delayed the emergence of a stable democracy in Germany.

- Since the end of the Second World War the major German parties, the Christian Democrats and the Social Democrats, have built a prosperous economic model known as the social market economy, which has served to create enthusiasm for democratic rule among postwar Germans.

- Postwar German political dynamics were strongly shaped by the division of the nation into two states, West and East Germany, and the West Germans' quest to achieve unification while remaining closely linked to the Western powers.

- Postwar Germany's political institutions were designed to avoid a repeat of the democratic failure that allowed Adolf Hitler to come to power. Those institutions include a parliamentary system, federalism, an electoral system that mixes proportional representation and majoritarian features, and neo-corporatism.

- Despite considerable success in building a prosperous and relatively equitable democracy, Germany faces challenges associated with globalization, its role as the leader of European economic and political integration, and the presence in Germany of millions of immigrants and their children.

GERMANY: A DEMOCRATIC SUCCESS

In the summer of 2012, Germany was awash in red, gold, and black. Giant German flags hung from apartment building windows; red, gold, and black material adorned the side-view mirrors of BMWs, Volkswagens, and Mercedes; flags waved from the backs of bicycles. The flags were in support of the German national soccer team, a multiethnic group of Germans, Turks, Poles, and Spaniards, who were playing in the European Cup soccer tournament. While the German team did not win the European Cup, German fans wrapped themselves in national colors and painted their faces to show their support.

This public display of national colors was an unusual sight in Germany. Political culture in Germany after the Second World War has been marked by an embarrassed reticence about patriotism because of the hypernationalism of the fascist period of Adolf Hitler during the 1930s and 1940s. It was not until 2006, when the Federal Republic of Germany hosted the World Cup soccer championship, that Germans began more readily to display flags in public places other than government buildings. Some Germans still express discomfort with these displays of national symbols.

These greater displays of patriotism demonstrate how far Germany has come in the past decades from an authoritarian regime under Adolf Hitler to a divided nation after World War II to a unified, stable, prosperous, democratic regime in the twenty-first century. The appearance of flags reflects a new generation of postwar Germans, who are proud of what their country has achieved. The Federal Republic of Germany has been a stable democratic regime for more than 60 years. It has the largest, and among the most successful, economy in Western Europe. In 1990, the Federal Republic successfully absorbed the 16 million citizens who lived in the former communist German Democratic Republic (East Germany). In the past decade, unified Germany has also become increasingly assertive in the European Union (EU).

This chapter explores Germany's path to democracy. It begins by examining why it took Germany until after World War II to create a successful stable democratic regime. It analyzes Germany's earlier history, especially its first failed experience with democracy in the 1920s during the Weimar Republic and its authoritarian past under Adolf Hitler, and shows how that history shaped the post–World War II democratic regime. The chapter then examines the Federal Republic's key political institutions including its parliamentary system of government, its mixed-member proportional electoral system, its constitutional court, and its strong emphasis on federalism, many of which newly democratizing countries have sought to emulate. The chapter also explores the ways in which citizens participate in politics through political parties and interest groups and the impact of that participation on the consolidation and effectiveness of democratic rule in Germany. It underscores the importance that consensus building, compromise, and representation have played in creating a stable political regime and a prosperous economy. Finally, the chapter analyzes the current political situation in Germany. It explores the results of the past four national elections and examines some of the current political challenges and issues facing Germany including globalization, immigration, and the European debt crisis.

HISTORICAL BACKGROUND: GERMANY'S DIFFICULT PATH TO DEMOCRACY

Perhaps the most striking feature about German history before World War II is that unlike Britain and France, Germany failed to develop a sustainable and successful

For many years following the Nazi era and World War II, robust displays of German national spirit were rare, considered by many to be an invitation to national shame. In recent years, the expression of German patriotic feelings has started to reemerge, as in the case of the 2012 European soccer tournament when the German team was in contention for the title.

democratic regime. Germans lived under authoritarian rule from the creation of the German state in 1871 until 1918 and again from 1933 until 1945. Although it had a short-lived parliamentary system from 1918 until 1933, democracy did not strike lasting roots on German soil until it was implanted by the United States, British, and French occupation forces in West Germany in 1949. What accounts for this failure of democratic ideas and institutions to take hold from within Germany itself?

If we consider the factors that help to account for the success of democracy, we see that the country lacked several of the conditions important in building and maintaining democratic rule.

- Germany suffered a *national unity* problem because of the late creation of a central German state in 1871, a process that was accomplished by forces opposed to democracy.
- Late industrialization in Germany led to a more *centralized economy* and to close relations between private industrialists and authoritarian leaders who sought to suppress the working-class movement.
- *State institutions* before 1919 were characterized by authoritarian governments and a weak and unstable parliamentary tradition.
- There was a profound weakness of support for democracy among German *elites* and the *middle class,* many of whom supported the right and far-right parties including the Nazis.
- Germany experienced difficulties promoting economic growth and *national wealth* because of the absence of a central German state before 1871, the high costs of World War I, and the severe economic problems during the 1920s and 1930s.
- German society before 1945 was marked by *strong class divisions* and a *fragmented civil society.*
- Germany faced a hostile *international environment* throughout much of the late nineteenth and early twentieth centuries promoted by the hypernationalism of German elites.
- A number of antidemocratic parties such as the Communists and the Nazis exploited the weaknesses of the regime.

We explore these explanatory factors briefly by examining the major historical developments in Germany from 1871 through 1945.

The Creation of the German State

Germany did not exist as a nation-state until 1871 and that state was not shaped by forces amenable to democracy. Britain and France formed states much earlier and developed democratic institutions over a long period. Britain, which became a state in 1066, established its first parliament in the 1200s and began moving toward democratic rule in the late seventeenth century with the adoption of the doctrine of parliamentary supremacy. France had been a state under a succession of monarchs since the late tenth century. In France, support for democratic ideas could be found within many of the major segments of society when the French Revolution began in 1789.

For hundreds of years, most Germans lived in the Holy Roman Empire (800–1815), sometimes referred to as the First Reich. But during that time, it was not a nation-state, but rather a collection of more than 1,790 principalities, duchies, city-states, and other governmental entities, each of which were independent from one another. After the Napoleonic wars and dissolution of the Holy Roman Empire in the early nineteenth century, there was some consolidation of German states. They created a loose confederation but remained independent. Virtually all of the states were ruled by a prince, a duke, or some other noble lord. Some were predominantly Protestant, others Catholic. The fragmentation of the German people into numerous political sovereignties promoted narrow local identities and retarded the development of an overarching German national consciousness. People tended to think of themselves as Bavarians, Prussians, Saxons, or Hanoverians rather than as Germans. In 1848, German liberals or nationalists tried unsuccessfully to establish a nation-state.

Moreover, Germany's Protestant Reformation did not have the same liberating effect on elite or mass attitudes as did England's Reformation. Martin Luther, who led the Protestant reformation, did not conceive of the German people in democratic terms, nor did he promote a common national identity. Only later did certain strands of German Protestantism promote such democratic values as individualism, equality, and capitalist entrepreneurship.[1] Thus, the German people for much of the eighteenth and nineteenth centuries did not have a single nation-state or strong feelings of nationalism.

When Germany finally came together as a single nation-state in 1871, it was not democracy that forged a German unity but military force. Germany was unified under the most powerful German state, the kingdom of Prussia, which was ruled at the time by Wilhelm I, king of Prussia. Prussia had become one of Europe's most important powers over the course of the eighteenth century. By the 1860s it possessed a nascent industrial economy and one of the largest and most disciplined armies on the continent. Kaiser Wilhelm's prime minister, Otto von Bismarck (1815–1898), was determined to create a unified German state under the Prussian monarchy. His principal aim was to make Germany into a great power, capable of competing with the British and French empires on the world stage. He declared his intention to unite the Germans by "blood and iron" rather than by ballots. Bismarck fanned the flames of German nationalism by leading Prussia into three successful wars. In 1864, Prussia attacked Denmark and came away with two provinces, Schleswig and Holstein, that remain part of Germany today. In 1866, the Prussians trounced Austria, a rival power that had its own hopes of leading the German people to national unity. And in his boldest stroke, Bismarck led Prussia to victory over France in the Franco-Prussian War of 1870–71. These wars convincingly demonstrated the effectiveness of Prussian power and won the agreement of more than 20 smaller German states to join together under the Prussian

Otto von Bismarck dominated European politics for most of the second half of the nineteenth century. Using military force, he unified many German states under Prussian leadership into a powerful empire lasting from 1871 until 1918.

monarchy to form a single Germany. Thus, the creation of a unified German state was a top-down affair, orchestrated by authoritarian political elites; the process had virtually no input from the masses below, thus precluding a democratic approach to nation building.

The new central government that Bismarck created had the outward appearances of a democracy. A national legislature, the *Reichstag*, was seated in Berlin; all German males had the right to elect its deputies. However, the Reichstag's powers were strictly limited. Under the constitution, the Reichstag had no right to unseat the government. The chancellor, as head of government, was responsible solely to the *kaiser*, not to the legislature. (In Britain and France at this time, the reverse was the case: The prime minister and the government were responsible to the legislature, which could vote them out of office.) Whenever the Reichstag showed any signs of opposing his policies, Chancellor Bismarck simply ignored or circumvented its actions. The kaiser's Germany was an authoritarian state, firmly controlled by the Prussian nobility and its main institutional arm, the military.

Late Industrialization

Not only was Germany late in forming a central state, but it also industrialized late in the nineteenth century, considerably later than Britain. For Germany to successfully compete with the British in world markets, the German state played a prominent role in the economy in supporting industrialization. This too impeded the development of democracy. Even though private enterprise was allowed to flourish, most industrialists cooperated with state authorities in supplying what the Kaiser's regime wanted most: a well-equipped army and navy, an extensive railroad network, and a modern economic infrastructure, all of which were dedicated to enhancing Germany's military prowess and diplomatic influence.

Far from favoring mass democracy, the country's leading industrialists joined with the aristocratic owners of Prussia's large rural estates in providing support for the kaiser's dictatorial regime, an alliance known as the "marriage of iron and rye." A large portion of Germany's owners of small and

medium-sized businesses—the backbone of the middle class—in principle favored democratic institutions but were neither able nor willing to organize effective opposition to the prevailing order. Many middle-class Germans, in fact, took pride in the international glory their country had achieved under the kaiser. Many of Germany's most prominent intellectuals and artists looked down on politics as unworthy of their attention and refrained from taking up the cause of democratic values.

The rapid industrialization of German society created an industrial working class. To push for more economic and political rights, the working class founded the **Social Democratic Party** of Germany (*Sozialdemokratische Partei Deutschlands*, or **SPD**) in 1875. In 1878, Bismarck banned the party and tried to placate the working class by providing health insurance and old-age pensions in what is considered the first modern social welfare state. But by 1898, the SPD was no longer banned and became the largest party in Germany, winning more than 27 percent of the vote for the Reichstag. In 1912, the party won 34.8 percent. The SPD called for greater democratization and a parliamentary democracy. It also pushed for a socialist economy based on workers' control of enterprises and state-managed welfare programs. The party's followers espoused pacifism, disarmament, and international cooperation. Despite their sizable support among Germany's voters, the SPD's efforts to alter the kaiser's regime failed.

While the economy grew during the end of the nineteenth century, Germany needed raw materials and access to world markets. But it was often checked by other colonial powers. Kaiser Wilhelm II, who assumed power after Wilhelm I's death in 1888, became increasingly aggressive toward other nations. This contributed to Germany's decision to declare war in 1914. In a dramatic turnabout, the Social Democratic leadership rallied to the kaiser's side in the feverish first days of World War I and voted to finance the war in August 1914.

The Weimar Republic: Germany's First Unsuccessful Attempt at Democracy

In November 1918, with the collapse of the German army imminent, Kaiser Wilhelm II abdicated and fled the country. On November 9, the Social Democratic Party proclaimed a republic and the chancellor, Prince Max of Baden, handed power over to Friedrich Ebert, the leader of the moderate wing of the Social Democratic Party and a member of the Reichstag. Two days later, Germany surrendered and the First World War came to an end. With the sudden disappearance of the entire governmental structure that had ruled the country since its inception in 1871, power in Germany was up for grabs. There was widespread violence in the country, as revolutionary communists fought pitched battles with right-wing militias, each hoping to take control of Germany. Despite the violence, the provisional German government led by the Social Democratic Party staged elections for a national assembly in the beginning of 1919. The assembly met in Weimar, the hometown of Goethe and the symbolic heart of German culture. After six months of intense deliberation, the assembled delegates adopted a new constitution and thereby created the **Weimar Republic**, so called because of the birthplace of its constitution.

The constitution adopted in Weimar in 1919 was in many respects the most democratic in the world at that time. It gave all men and women over age 20 the right to vote, securing a victory for women's suffrage that surpassed Britain, the United States, and most other democracies. It also guaranteed certain economic and social rights that were not to be found in the constitutions of other democratic states, including the right to a job or unemployment compensation, decent housing, comprehensive health insurance, allowances for the "protection of motherhood," and a pension. Workers earned a host of new rights, including "equal rights" with their employers in regulating wages and working conditions. In short, the Weimar constitution's framers strove to institute not just popular sovereignty and civil rights, but also a measure of economic democracy, as discussed in Chapter 5.

The structure of the national government was also novel. The constitution created a mixed *presidential–parliamentary* democracy, which today's French and Russian constitutions strikingly resemble. The president of the republic was directly elected by the people for a seven-year term and possessed real decision-making powers. In a risky departure from standard democratic practice, however, the Weimar constitution gave the president extraordinary powers to suspend basic civil rights and liberties during an emergency and to exercise virtually dictatorial authority. As things turned out, the republic's last president, Field Marshall Paul von Hindenburg, abused this authority and used it to rule the country by decree, eventually turning the government over to Hitler and the Nazis. In addition to creating a powerful president, the Weimar constitution's "dual-executive" system also featured a powerful head of government, the *Kanzler* or chancellor, who was nominated by the president and approved by the lower house of parliament and who could be dismissed by the president.

The Weimar constitution established a bicameral national legislature. The *Reichsrat* or upper house, represented the governments of the German states and had limited powers. The more important, directly elected lower house, the *Reichstag*, functioned much like the British House of Commons, holding the chancellor and the rest of the cabinet accountable. The electoral system used for popular elections to the Reichstag was proportional representation, with no minimum threshold. This system allowed a multiplicity of small parties, many of them with less than 5 percent of the vote, to win Reichstag seats. A dozen parties or more would typically win Reichstag representation. As a result, it became extremely difficult to form stable majority governments. No party ever won an absolute majority of seats, making coalition governments inevitable. The inability of the coalition partners to stick together on the basis of compromise proved one of the downfalls of the Weimar system.

Aside from some institutional weaknesses, Germany's fledgling democracy was plagued with problems from the start that undermined support for the democratic regime. Economic disasters topped the list. The republic started life under conditions of severe unemployment. Millions of soldiers, beaten and humiliated, straggled home from the front to find the civilian economy in no shape to employ them. As time went on, large numbers of these angry and demoralized troops gravitated to the Nazis' brown-shirted militias, enabling Hitler and his followers to intimidate their opponents in the streets. Many others supported the communists and other extreme left-wing groups militating for a socialist revolution.

Germany's economic woes were aggravated by a steep bill for war reparations imposed by the victorious powers. In 1921, Britain, France, and the United States demanded the payment of $33 billion in gold marks, to be paid out in installments starting immediately. The reparations only aggravated an inflation rate that was already spinning out of control because of war debts. As the German government printed money around the clock, prices rose more than 300 percent per month. The average inflation rate for 1922–23 was over 1 billion percent! Deft financial maneuvers by the government finally brought the inflationary spiral under control at the end of 1923, but millions of Germans in all social classes were financially ruined. The middle class was especially hard hit. Instead of constituting a bastion of support for democracy as in the United States and Britain, large numbers of the middle class in Germany turned away from the Weimar democratic regime and flocked to the Nazis and other antidemocratic groups.

The hyperinflation of the early 1920s was followed by the Wall Street stock market crash of 1929. The Great Depression spread even more economic misery to Germany. Banks and other businesses plunged into bankruptcy while unemployment skyrocketed, exceeding 30 percent of the workforce by 1932. People in virtually every sector of the economy were driven to despair.

These mounting economic and social crises took place in a political environment in which support for democracy remained feeble. The absence of democratic traditions in Germany deprived the Weimar Republic of a solid foundation. The republic started with a broad base of popular support. The three political parties most committed to democracy—the Social Democrats, the Center Party (a largely Catholic-oriented organization), and the middle-class German Democratic Party—together captured more than 75 percent of the vote in 1919. A fourth party, backed by business circles, soon joined their ranks and played a role in several coalition governments. Because the parties often could not agree, Weimar's coalition governments were characterized by instability, inefficiency, and ineffectiveness. Shaky coalition cabinets frequently fell apart. Between 1919 and 1933, Germany had 22 governments. Many of them were *minority governments:* That is, they did not have the support of a majority of Reichstag delegates. As a consequence, they could be easily toppled in no-confidence votes posed by their adversaries. The ineffectiveness of these governing coalitions in addressing Germany's problems progressively eroded their electoral base. By 1924 the combined popular vote for the four main prodemocracy parties fell to 48.8 percent, a minority of the electorate. In the fall of 1932, in the last elections held before Hitler came to power, it plummeted to 35 percent.

Not only were the political parties divided, but so too was the civil society, which made it easy for antidemocratic politicians to demonize other groups. Class was the major dividing line. Members of the working class, middle class, and upper class had separate social organizations. They read different newspapers; they went to different bars; they belonged to different political parties. Because there was little horizontal integration among the classes, there was little trust between citizens and the parties, which represented different classes.[2]

As the economic situation in Germany worsened in the late 1920s and early 1930s, the electoral fortunes of the antidemocratic parties rose apace. On the left, the German Communist Party increased its electoral support from only 2 percent in 1920 to nearly 17 percent in 1932. On the right, most hardline conservatives who opposed democracy initially cast their support to the Nationalists (formally known as the German National People's Party). The Nationalists doubled their vote in the first six years of the republic, peaking at 20.5 percent in late 1924. Their most revered figure, Field Marshal von Hindenburg, was elected president of Germany in 1925 and handily reelected in 1932. At first, Hindenburg endeavored out of patriotic loyalty to keep Germany's new democratic system afloat but he remained a Prussian aristocrat devoted to the army. As the Depression took its devastating toll, Hindenburg used his emergency powers to govern the country by decree, ignoring the Reichstag and relying on a coterie of archconservative cronies.

Increasingly over the course of the late 1920s and early 1930s, it was Adolf Hitler and his **National Socialist German Workers Party**, or **Nazis** for short, who picked up a growing share of the right-wing nationalist vote. Hitler was neither a Prussian (he was born in Austria), nor an aristocrat (his background was lower middle class), nor a high-ranking officer (he was a corporal in World War I). But he nourished a fiery German nationalism, fueled by fierce hatred of Britain, France, and the United States. He was also a rabid anti-Semite. Endowed with spellbinding oratorical skills, Hitler built up the Nazi party from obscurity to mass popularity. Starting with just 3 percent of the vote in 1924, the Nazis capitalized on the widespread misery generated by the Depression and captured more than 37 percent in the summer of 1932, by far the highest vote ever won by any party in the Weimar Republic (but still less than a majority).

Electoral support for the Nazis came from virtually every corner of German society. The upper crust, the sizable middle classes, and even a substantial minority of workers (about 25 percent) gave the Nazis their vote. The Nazis won about a third of the urban vote and did even better in rural areas. They were very popular among older voters and had a growing following among Germany's youth. And despite their glorification of violence, they ultimately attracted more female voters than male voters.[3] Hitler's inflammatory oratory combined with the most well-organized election campaign machine in Germany to make the Nazis the most successful catchall party in the Weimar Republic, seeking to win as many votes as it could rather than concentrating its appeal on a particular segment of the electorate. Unlike most catchall parties, however, the Nazis were not friends of democracy but its vehement opponents. They took skillful advantage of the Weimar Republic's democratic institutions and its fragmented civil society to destroy democracy. They also built up their own uniformed militia, numbering 400,000 by 1932, to beat up political rivals and threaten the republic with a potential coup d'état.

In the summer of 1932, more than half of Germany's voters (51.6 percent) voted for either the Nazis or the Communists, the two most stridently antidemocratic parties in the country. Having few options left, President Hindenburg named Hitler chancellor of Germany in January 1933. The president and his entourage thought they could keep the upstart corporal under control, but Hitler proved more than their match. By the end of the year, democracy was essentially extinguished and Germany was in the grip of a totalitarian fascist dictatorship.[4]

The Fascist Regime

When Hitler was appointed chancellor in January 1933, he worked quickly to consolidate his own power and to destroy the democratic regime. Nazi rule took the form of a *totalitarian dictatorship*. A single party, the Nazis, monopolized state power; all other parties were outlawed. Hitler exercised supreme personal authority over the party and the state. The Nazi party-state regulated almost every aspect of social life in Germany. The educational system, the arts, the media, scientific research, and other aspects of social and intellectual life all came under Nazi supervision.

The state also assumed responsibility for coordinating the economy, though private enterprise was allowed to exist. Nazi governmental authorities set up a system of *state corporatism*, in which state representatives would meet with leaders of the country's largest businesses as well as with individuals handpicked by the regime to "represent" farmers, workers, and other segments of the economy. This system enabled the Nazi party-state to impose its priorities on the country's private entrepreneurs. Hitler and his adjutants were bent on war, so their highest economic priority was to build a vast military machine, a goal they accomplished in violation of the provisions of the 1919 Treaty of Versailles, which strictly limited Germany's military capacity. State corporatism also enabled the regime to regulate the labor force. All trade unions and other organizations representing workers or farmers were abolished except for those run by the Nazis. These characteristics of fascist rule made Nazi totalitarianism considerably more repressive and intrusive than the kaiser's authoritarian regime had been.

The Nazi worldview was grounded in *hypernationalism* and *racism*. The German people (*Volk*) were conceived as the "Aryan race" and "the master race," while non-Aryans—especially Jews and Slavs—were vilified as "subhumans." Soon after the Nazis took power, German Jews, who represented only 0.9 percent of the population, were accused of ruining the country and subjected to strict limitations on their economic and educational activities. They were also compelled to suffer public harassment

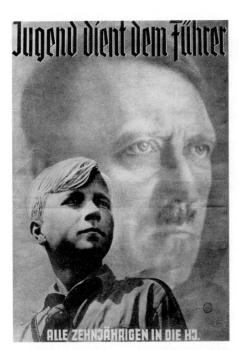

Jugend dient dem Führer

ALLE ZEHNJÄHRIGEN IN DIE HJ.

The Nazi worldview was grounded in hypernationalism and racism. It asserted that German "Aryans" consituted the master race with all other races, especially Slavs and Jews, vilified. This message was reinfocrced endlessly through Nazi propaganda, often aimed at German youth.

and indignities orchestrated by the regime. Gypsies, homosexuals, and the mentally retarded were also targeted for abuse. Members of these groups were rounded up and sent to concentration camps, where they were systematically slaughtered.

Another defining feature of German fascism was *mass mobilization*. From their earliest days as a political party in the Weimar Republic, the Nazis under Hitler's firm direction were determined to cultivate broad popularity. They devoted considerable attention to propaganda, using every means at their disposal—marches, rallies, posters, fliers, party newspapers, radio, and film—to drum up mass support. They used their control over the media and schools and a host of organizations such as the Hitler Youth organization to instill their ideas in the population.

Before the dark days of World War II, the Nazis enjoyed considerable popular support within Germany. By flouting the Versailles Treaty, Hitler restored pride to millions of Germans. In addition, the Nazi government put a decisive end to the political instability and social chaos of the Weimar Republic. While the republic's supporters were appalled at the demise of democracy, millions of other Germans were gladly ready to give up their democratic liberties in exchange for political and social tranquillity. The longing for a strong state and dutiful obedience to official authority were integral elements of German political culture at that time.[5] The Nazis appealed to these attitudes. In elections held in March 1933, shortly after Hitler was named chancellor and under conditions marked by Nazi suppression of opposing parties, the Nazis won 44 percent of the vote: not a majority, but still a substantial figure.

Perhaps most important, the Nazis achieved popularity by arresting Germany's economic slide. With tight control over the state budget, they rapidly addressed the unemployment problem by hiring people for public works projects and for service in the military or in Nazi party organizations. Orders for military weapons and other equipment reinvigorated German industry and kept factories humming, creating jobs for workers and managers. Inflation was brought under control. The Nazis also introduced a series of welfare measures to assist the most vulnerable parts of the population. The Nazi economy represented a kind of militarized Keynesian welfare state: The state stimulated growth and soaked up unemployment by spending large sums of money in the economy (see Chapter 11), and much of this money was spent for military purposes (in accordance with Nazi priorities). The years 1936–39 were perhaps the best years the German economy had ever seen up to that point.

Finally, the Nazis gained popularity by engineering a social revolution. Germany's old political elites, heavily populated with aristocrats and the scions of distinguished families, were summarily pushed aside by the Nazis to make way for less pedigreed Germans. The Nazi leaders were overwhelmingly from the middle classes, especially the lower middle class. Once ensconced in power, they opened positions in the swelling party and state bureaucracies as well as in the army, the educational system, and other institutions to people like themselves.[6]

It was World War II that ultimately destroyed Hitler's "thousand-year reich," devastating the German economy and inflicting misery on the population. Initiated with Germany's invasion of Poland on September 1, 1939, the war delivered control over virtually all of continental Europe to Hitler and Mussolini before the Nazi military was finally vanquished in 1945 by the combined efforts of the United States, the USSR, Britain, and Free France. (As Japan's ally, Germany had declared war on the United States after Pearl Harbor in 1941.) More than 50 million lives were lost in the European theater of the conflict; tens of millions more were uprooted. At the end of the war, Germany was dismembered: The Soviet Union annexed part of its territory and gave other parts to Poland and Czechoslovakia. The remaining area was then divided among the four victorious allies into occupation zones, which in 1949 were consolidated into the two separate German states.[7]

As Germans nervously entered the postwar era, uncertain of their political fate, they could look back on the first half of the twentieth century as a succession of catastrophes. Their traumatic experiences could not help but have a powerful impact on their postwar attitudes. Two world wars imprinted an instinctive pacifism on millions of Germans, along with a reluctance on the part of many of them to engage in any display of nationalist sentiment. The tribulations of the Weimar Republic, constituting a paradigm of a failed democracy, left many Germans with a lasting fear of inflation and unemployment, along with an object lesson in what happens when political leaders refuse to compromise their differences. As a consequence, political culture in postwar Germany—particularly in democratic West

Table 15.1 The 10 Conditions for Democracy: The German Experience

Explanatory Factor	German Experience
1. Elite attitudes	German elites were generally hostile to popular forces and democracy during the Second Reich and the Weimar Republic. Elites opted for Hitler during difficult days of Weimar Republic in 1930s.
2. State institutions	The German state came together late and was dominated by the kaiser and antidemocratic Prussian aristocrats during the Second Reich. Weak state institutions in the Weimar Republic discredited democracy.
3. National unity	German unity came only in the mid- to late nineteenth century and national identity became tied to aggressive, militarist nationalism.
4. National wealth	A late industrializer, Germany nevertheless adopted social welfare provisions early. Relatively wealthy, Germany was badly impacted by the Great Depression.
5. Private enterprise	Large landowners in Prussia were hostile to democracy as were large industrialists.
6. Middle class	The lower middle class provided the social basis for Nazism owing to fears of being reduced to parity with the working class.
7. Attitudes of the disadvantaged	Part of the working class formed the social base of the Social Democratic Party, a strongly prodemocracy force; another, smaller part supported the Communist Party, which sought a dictatorship of the proletariat in the interwar period.
8. Civil society	German society was highly organized into clubs and other associations but usually they were divided along class lines until after World War II.
9. Education and access to information	A highly educated society in the nineteenth and twentieth centuries, Germany had the educational foundation for democracy.
10. International conditions	Prodemocracy parties in the interwar period were identified with the harsh conditions imposed on Germany by the Allies and thereby discredited. German desires to revise the Treaty of Versailles made militarists, who were antidemocratic, popular during Weimar Republic.

Germany—was marked by antimilitarism, an embarrassed reticence about patriotism, a strong aversion to economic instability, and a prevailing inclination to political consensus and compromise. Until the 1960s most Germans wanted little to do with politics; they focused on their jobs and families, leaving political matters in the hands of their new democratic leaders. These attitudes profoundly shaped the development of the Federal Republic.

Table 15.1 summarizes the German experience up to 1945 in terms of the 10 conditions for democracy discussed in Chapter 7. As you can see, Germany faced numerous barriers to the effective introduction of stable democracy.

DEMOCRACY IN THE FEDERAL REPUBLIC OF GERMANY

In May 1945, the western Allies—Great Britain, the United States, and France—and the Soviet Union divided Germany into western and eastern occupation zones (along with the division of the capital city of Berlin, a special case). This division was supposed to be temporary with the victorious combatants speaking about reestablishing a single unified Germany. But it became increasingly apparent by 1947 that the Soviet Union and Western powers were at loggerheads over the direction of the new government. In 1948 the three Western occupation governments established a common currency for all three of their zones. The Soviets responded by blockading the land passage between West Germany and West Berlin, provoking the West to respond with the Berlin airlift of 1948–49.

As the crisis heated up, the Western powers in July 1948 ordered the German authorities under their control to convene an assembly to write a constitution for a West German government. Most Germans were reluctant to take this step, fearing that a separate constitution for West Germany would dash all hopes of reestablishing a single German state, but they bowed to Allied pressure. The elected leaders of the various regions into which West German was divided at the time selected the members of the constitutional assembly. After nine months of deliberation, the delegates produced a document they called the **Basic Law**.

On May 23, 1949, the Basic Law went into effect and the **Federal Republic of Germany** was formally proclaimed in the Western occupation zones. To this day, the Basic Law has never been submitted to the voters for their approval and it remains the constitution of modern Germany. The Basic Law was designed to be a temporary document until Germany was unified. Its framers established Bonn as the Federal Republic's capital. The choice of this small town instead of a large city such as Frankfurt or Munich reflected the hope that Germany's division would not last long and that Berlin would once again stand proudly as the capital of a large, united Germany and a new constitution could be written. In addition, the Federal Republic proclaimed the Basic Law's validity for *all* Germans, including those in communist East Germany and other parts of former German territory. West Germany's main political parties were all in agreement that the Soviet-imposed communist dictatorship in East Germany was illegitimate and that eventual reunification should be a national goal.

In the Soviet's eastern occupation zone, the USSR created a dictatorship under a single party of German communists. The **German Democratic Republic** (the **GDR**, or *East Germany*) was also formally established in 1949.[8] West Germany assumed de facto control over West Berlin and the East German authorities took control over East Berlin. Over the next 40 years, these two countries developed separate identities and followed different historical trajectories. They created two separate political cultures. The *Federal Republic of Germany*, based in the western part of the country, developed a successful and prosperous democratic regime and market economy and alliances with the United States and Western Europe. The GDR became a one-party state under the control of the communist party known as the Socialist Unity Party (*Sozialistische Einheitspartei*, or SED) and a state-directed economic system. Berlin, which was located deep inside East Germany, 110 miles from the West German border, remained a divided city. It was encircled by more than 300,000 Soviet troops based in the GDR.

The two countries were not only culturally and politically divided but also physically divided. To prevent East Germans from moving to the West, the East German authorities in August 1961 built makeshift barriers that they subsequently fortified into a massive concrete wall, known as the Berlin Wall, that blocked the two parts of Berlin from each other. Armed East German guards stood at the borders and shot anyone who tried to escape. The partition of the two countries divided some 80 million Germans into two ideologically antagonistic states and created a powder keg of confrontation in the heart of Europe that on several occasions threatened to explode into nuclear war. It would take until 1990 before the two countries were unified.

Developing Support for Democracy

The Federal Republic started in an environment marked by considerable skepticism about democracy. In a public opinion survey taken in 1951, West Germans were asked, "When in this century do you think Germany has been best off?" Perhaps unsurprisingly, only 2 percent named the current period. Barely two years after the formation of the Federal Republic, West Germany was still reeling, economically and psychologically, from the war's devastation. But only 7 percent named the Weimar Republic, Germany's previous democracy. No fewer than 45 percent of the respondents identified the kaiser's empire before the start of World War I in 1914 as Germany's best period, while 42 percent said Germans had lived best under Hitler before the start of World War II (1933–39). Another survey taken in 1953 asked whether democracy was the best form of government for Germany; only half the respondents said yes. Another survey conducted in these years revealed that more than a third of West Germans would have supported a bid by a new Nazi party to seize power or would have remained indifferent if it occurred. Another third favored restoring the Kaiser's monarchy.

Clearly, democracy had to prove itself to most West Germans. Over the course of the late 1950s and 1960s, mass attitudes swung overwhelmingly in democracy's favor. By 1970,

90 percent of West Germans said democracy was the best form of government for Germany. This shift in the country's political culture was no doubt promoted by the Federal Republic's economic successes. Germany experienced an "economic miracle" from the 1950s until well into the next decade. Part of that success was due to the Marshall Plan, officially known as the European Recovery Program. This program was an American plan intended to promote political stability by rebuilding the economies of European countries. Inspired by then Secretary of State George Marshall, the plan provided approximately $13 billion of assistance to 16 nations, including Germany between 1948 and 1951. Marshall Plan assistance, along with effective German government actions and the hard work of millions of individual Germans, led to considerable and sustained economic growth in Germany after the war. The boom benefited Germans in every social class and created a large and growing middle class. This helped to change political attitudes toward democracy across various classes. In this process, the West German government developed a so-called **social market economy**, which combines a private-enterprise system, a generous welfare state for all citizens, and social protections for workers. Germany developed a distinctive socioeconomic system known as *Modell Deutschland* that included export-oriented industries, democratic participation of workers on the job, and cross holdings of banks and industrial firms and that was widely credited for Germany's economic success.

By 1959, 42 percent of survey respondents named the contemporary period as the time when Germans lived best, while support for the Nazi era dwindled to 18 percent. Those identifying the Federal Republic as Germany's best period rose even further over the following years, reaching 62 percent in 1963 and 81 percent in 1970. Nostalgia for Hitler or the kaiser waned dramatically; by 1970 these bygone eras were fading fast in historical memory, esteemed by only 5 percent of the population each as the time when Germans lived best. As older Germans passed from the scene, their children and grandchildren acquired a much greater respect for democracy and the prosperity it had brought them in the postwar period. Some 25 years after the end of World War II, not only had West Germany undergone a profound transformation of its political and economic systems, it had also witnessed one of the most thoroughgoing transformations in political culture ever documented.[9]

As the following outline of its political evolution shows, the Federal Republic developed into a stable democratic regime, characterized by considerable political stability; a broad consensus on political and economic fundamentals among its main political parties; a record of considerable economic achievement over the long term, despite periodic downswings; and close ties with the United States and the European Union. (For a list of the Federal Republic's governments, see Table 15.2.) In the paragraphs that follow we briefly review postwar political dynamics in the Federal Republic. The leading German parties, the Christian Democrats (CDU/CSU) and the Social Democrats (SPD), as we will see, agreed on the broad outlines of economic and social policy, together promoting Germany's social market economy—a capitalist economy with broad

Table 15.2 Governments of the Federal Republic of Germany

Governing Coalition	Chancellor (Party)	Came to Power Following . . .	Opposing Chancellor Candidate (Party)
CDU/CSU, FDP, DP*	Konrad Adenauer (CDU)	Elections, 1949	Kurt Schumacher (SPD)
CDU/CSU, FDP, DP, G†	Adenauer	Elections, 1953	Erich Ollenhauer (SPD)
CDU/CSU, FDP, DP/FVP‡	Adenauer	Elections, 1957	Ollenhauer
CDU/CSU, FDP	Adenauer	Elections, 1961	Willy Brandt (SPD)
CDU/CSU, FDP	Ludwig Erhard (CDU)	Adenauer retirement, 1963	
CDU/CSU, FDP	Erhard	Elections, 1965	Brandt
CDU/CSU, SPD	Kurt Georg Kiesinger (CDU)	Coalition change, 1966	
SPD, FDP	Willy Brandt (SPD)	Elections, 1969	Kiesinger (CDU)
SPD, FDP	Brandt	Elections, 1972	Rainer Barzel (CDU)
SPD, FDP	Helmut Schmidt (SPD)	Brandt resignation, 1974	
SPD, FDP	Schmidt	Elections, 1976	Helmut Kohl (CDU)
SPD, FDP	Schmidt	Elections, 1980	Franz-Josef Strauss (CSU)
CDU/CSU, FDP	Helmut Kohl (CDU)	Coalition change, no-confidence vote, 1982	
CDU/CSU, FDP	Kohl	Elections, 1983	Hans-Jochen Vogel (SPD)
CDU/CSU, FDP	Kohl	Elections, 1987	Johannes Rau (SPD)
CDU/CSU, FDP	Kohl	Elections, 1990	Oskar Lafontaine (SPD)
CDU/CSU, FDP	Kohl	Elections, 1994	Rudolf Scharping (SPD)
SPD, Alliance '90/The Greens	Gerhard Schröder (SPD)	Elections, 1998	Kohl
SPD, Alliance '90/The Greens	Schröder	Elections, 2002	Edmund Stoiber (CSU)
CDU/CSU, SPD	Angela Merkel (CDU)	Elections, 2005	SchröderSchröder (SPD)
CDU/CSU, FDP	Merkel (CDU)	Elections, 2009	Frank-Walter Steinmeier (SPD)

*DP = Deutsche Partei (German Party)

†G = All-German bloc

‡FVP = Freie Volkspartei (Free People's Party)

participation by the organized working class in the management of large firms and with well-developed social welfare features. While prosperity came to West Germany via the social market economy, Germans' quest to reunify the country, divided into two states that were the forward lines in the contest between the capitalist West and the communist bloc, meant the foreign policy was always at the forefront of political debate in West Germany. However, that debate often produced division within the parties as much as between them.

Adenauer Era, 1949–1963

Konrad Adenauer became the first chancellor of Germany in 1949 and played a pivotal role in helping to secure the foundations for a stable democratic regime. He altered the course of Germany's domestic and foreign policy. A member of the Center Party during the Weimar regime, he served as the mayor of Cologne from 1917 until Hitler's takeover in 1933. Adenauer was one of a small number of conservative politicians untainted by cooperation with the Nazis. He spent most of the Nazi period in seclusion. He was in his early seventies when he was encouraged by the Western occupation authorities to assume the leadership of the newly formed **Christian Democratic Union (CDU)**, one of the major political parties founded after World War II. That party combined Catholics and Protestants

across Germany into a single party that subscribes in a general way to Christian principles such as fellowship and reconciliation. The CDU competed in all German states except Bavaria, where the **Christian Social Union (CSU)** competed in state elections and allied with the CDU in national elections.

Adenauer formed a succession of coalition governments with either the **Free Democratic Party (FDP)**, a new liberal party formed in 1948, or other smaller, short-lived parties. Though he favored private enterprise, like many Christian Democrats, he had a strong welfare orientation and was an avid supporter of equitable compensation for West German workers and for social welfare guarantees. He favored a role for German workers in sharing responsibility with their employers in determining wages, working hours, and other company policies, a concept known as **codetermination** or *Mitbestimmung*. Under his leadership, codetermination was introduced in the coal and steel industries.

Adenauer also made a mark in foreign policy. Although he was a strong proponent of German unification, he also wanted to integrate the Federal Republic firmly into the democratic West to rehabilitate West Germany's international reputation. The Federal Republic became one of the founding members of the European Coal and Steel Community (ECSC) in 1952. France and other Western European countries hoped that it could better control Germany's industrial production through the ECSC, while the Germans hoped that integration into the ECSC would help to alleviate the fears of other countries. West Germany also helped form the six-member European Economic Community (EEC) in 1958, the forerunner of the European Union. European integration through the EEC was viewed by the French as a means of providing political leadership in Europe and controlling Germany, while for Germany it provided a means of regaining international credibility and achieving economic recovery. Adenauer enjoyed a close personal rapport with French President Charles de Gaulle. At the same time, Adenauer worked closely with the United States, engineering the creation of a new German army and its integration into NATO in 1955. West Germany also regained some of its sovereignty. Under an agreement with the Western Allies in 1952, the occupation status was formally ended and full sovereignty in internal and external policy was conferred on West Germany. However, the Allies did continue to station large numbers of troops on German soil, and West Berlin remained under Allied control.

It was his success in piloting West Germany's economic revival that won Adenauer the most plaudits and that helped to consolidate democratic rule in Germany. Starting in the late 1950s and early 1960s, the West German economy took off on a ride of sustained economic growth. When he retired from the chancellorship in 1963 at the age of 87, Adenauer ceded his place to Ludwig Erhard, the man most responsible for designing Germany's economic miracle and creating the social market economy.

Erhard, Kiesinger, and the Grand Coalition, 1963–1969

Ludwig Erhard (CDU) served as chancellor for three years, from 1963 to 1966. He is considered the father of Germany's economic miracle during the 1950s, but by the mid-1960s, a

recession set in and West Germany's workers began to grow restive as their gains in living standards slowed. Moreover, Erhard had less success than Adenauer in maintaining smooth relations with France and President de Gaulle. Although the CDU and Free Democratic government won the 1965 election, it was split by domestic and foreign policy problems that led several Christian Democratic leaders to propose sharing power with their rivals, the Social Democratic Party (SPD), in an effort to head off an economic crisis. The result was the first **Grand Coalition** government between the Christian Democrats (CDU/CSU) and the Social Democrats that lasted from 1966 to 1969.

The SPD, with its roots in the late nineteenth century and its legacy of being the largest party during the Weimar Republic, entered the government of West Germany for the first time in 1966 after undergoing an ideological transformation. The SPD had emerged from the war with much of its socialist ideology still intact. The party was led by Kurt Schumacher, a committed Social Democrat, who advocated both economic socialism and ballot box democracy. Schumacher believed that a middle path had to be found between American-style capitalism and Soviet-style dictatorship that included state ownership of productive capacities and a paramount role for workers' councils in running factories and other places of work. He opposed German rearmament and the close U.S. alliance that Adenauer had nurtured. Schumacher helped reestablish the SPD as one of Germany's staunchest supporters of democracy after the war.

But after Schumacher died in 1952, other more moderate voices in the SPD became influential. Recognizing that the majority of West German citizens did not favor the party's socialist orientation and fearing that the party was doomed to garnering little more than a third of the vote unless it changed its tune, the Social Democratic leadership held a special conference in the town of Bad Godesberg in 1959 and made major doctrinal changes. They formally accepted private enterprise and the market as the underlying bases of the Federal Republic's

Chancellors Konrad Adenauer, right, and Ludwig Erhard led Germany's postwar economic revival. Erhard was the man most responsible for designing Germany's economic miracle and creating the social market economy.

economy. They agreed to work within the structure of the market mechanisms to improve the lot of the working class through nonconfrontational measures designed to promote cooperation between business and labor. In essence, the Social Democrats now accepted the social market economy promoted by the Christian Democrats. They also explicitly renounced their previous antireligious views and assured Germany's believers that they would be welcome in the Social Democratic Party. These changes were followed in 1960 by a decision to accept West Germany's rearmament and its membership in NATO. These changes made the Social Democrats a more mainstream, moderate party and more acceptable partners in the eyes of most Christian Democrats.

The chancellor of the Grand Coalition, Kurt-Georg Kiesinger, was a Christian Democrat, but the chief credit for the economy's rebound went to the Social Democratic finance minister, Karl Schiller. Perhaps the most prominent member of the cabinet was another Social Democrat, Foreign Minister Willy Brandt. Brandt had fled Germany during the Hitler years, adopting Norwegian citizenship. Brandt made a rapid rise up the SPD's leadership ranks after the war, serving as mayor of West Berlin in 1961 at the time the wall was built. Like many other Social Democrats, Brandt was revolted at the nation's division and longed to see Germany restored to unity in a peaceful, democratic Europe. The Social Democrats' success in government during the Grand Coalition paved the way for an electoral win in 1969 and Brandt's accession to the chancellorship.

The SPD and Willy Brandt, 1969–1974

In 1969, with a new election, the SPD managed to form a coalition with the Free Democrats, the small liberal party of the center, which had served previously in government with the CDU/CSU. Brandt became chancellor and Walter Scheel, the FDP's reform-minded leader, became foreign minister.

One of Brandt's major and most significant policy accomplishments was the opening of ties with East Germany. While keeping the Federal Republic firmly planted in NATO and the European Community, Brandt devised a new eastern policy (*Ostpolitik*) that directly approached the Soviet Union and engaged the East German leadership in face-to-face negotiations, steps regarded as heresy by previous West German governments. In the 1970s, his government concluded a renunciation of force agreement with the Soviets, pledging to resolve all disputes peacefully. Brandt also sought immediate relief for thousands of German families living in the GDR. In 1972, the two German states agreed to a sweeping set of new regulations that greatly facilitated the ability of West Berliners and other West Germans to visit East Germany. East Germans, however, did not win any new rights from their government to visit West Germany. In yet another set of negotiations, the USSR came to terms with the United States, Britain, and France in formally guaranteeing unhindered passage on the access routes between West Germany proper and West Berlin, thereby removing a source of dangerous frictions.[10]

For these efforts, Brandt won the Nobel Peace Prize in 1971. His place in history was assured the following year when his eastern treaties passed in the Bundestag, narrowly surviving the opposition of the Christian Democrats and a few defectors from the governing coalition parties. (The Federal Constitutional Court affirmed their constitutionality.) Brandt's political luster did not last long, however. In 1974 it was revealed that an East German spy was working on his staff; the spy's wife was also nabbed for espionage. Though Brandt had been unaware of their true identity, he took responsibility for the mishap and resigned.[11]

Schmidt Governments, 1974–1982

Brandt's successor was Helmut Schmidt, a Social Democrat with a razor-sharp intellect and special expertise in economics and defense policy. He assumed office at a time when his financial skills were critically needed. In 1973, the world's leading oil-producing nations quadrupled the price of oil, triggering a global economic crisis. The United States, Western Europe, and Japan sputtered into recession and suffered an unusual combination of diminishing growth and high inflation, a phenomenon called *stagflation*. As the leader of the SPD's right wing, Schmidt favored relatively austere budget-tightening policies designed to dampen inflation. He also maintained close ties with the leaders of West Germany's trade unions, traditionally the SPD's most reliable supporters, and with leading members of the business community, a connection reinforced by the business-oriented Free Democrats. These consultations paid off, as the unions kept their wage demands within limits and big business strove to maintain production, holding unemployment in check. While inflation rates in other countries spiraled into double digits, the Federal Republic held the line at about 7 percent. It also enjoyed a peaceful labor environment, with few strikes.

Schmidt's attempts to hold the line on government spending did not sit well with the SPD's left wing, which favored higher spending on social welfare. The party's youth organization, the Young Socialists, or Jusos, favored even more radical policies aimed at imposing higher taxes on corporations and wealthy individuals and redistributing the nation's wealth to ensure greater socioeconomic equality. Future chancellor Gerhard Schröder was the head of the Jusos from 1978 to 1980.

Schmidt's defense policies provoked even greater consternation within the party's left-wing ranks. In the late 1970s the Soviet Union ratcheted up the arms race by installing a new generation of guided missiles, equipped with deadly nuclear warheads, within easy striking distance of West German territory. Schmidt responded by convincing the United States and other NATO partners to develop new counter-missiles of their own in an effort to get the Soviets to reach an agreement that would restore the nuclear balance in Europe at lower levels of missile deployments. In 1979 NATO agreed to start developing its counter-weapons, some of which would be based on West Germany's densely populated territory. The NATO decision unleashed one of the most intense crises of the Cold War. It also touched off a wave of protest within West Germany, as hundreds of thousands of people took to the streets in large demonstrations against the missiles. The effects of the crisis were particularly tumultuous inside the Social Democratic Party, as left-wingers—like Schröder—and a growing number of moderates joined the opposition to Schmidt's counter-missile scheme. Schmidt himself became increasingly isolated within his own party.[12]

Conflict with his coalition partners, the Free Democrats, exacerbated Schmidt's difficulties. Although the FDP maintained its governing coalition with the Social Democrats during the 1980 elections, within a year the two parties were squabbling over economic policy. In a reversal of alliances, the FDP in the fall of 1982 announced it was withdrawing from Schmidt's government and was prepared to form a new governing coalition with the Christian Democrats. The FDP's turnabout in 1982 caused Schmidt's government to lose a constructive vote of confidence in the Bundestag. It was immediately replaced by a new coalition consisting of the Christian Democrats and the Free Democrats, and the chancellorship passed to the leader of the CDU, Helmut Kohl.

Helmut Kohl and German Unification

Immediately after assuming power by a vote of the Bundestag, Kohl arranged for snap elections to be held six months later to seek the public's approval. The Christian Democrats and their FDP allies won a solid Bundestag majority, ensuring their government's survival.

From 1982 until 1998, Kohl played a critical role in some of the most crucial events of the postwar era. One of his first decisions was to go ahead with the controversial deployment of the new NATO missiles starting in 1983, despite substantial public opposition in Germany. The Soviet Union strenuously objected to the deployments, but in 1985 a new leadership team under Mikhail Gorbachev took power in the Kremlin (see Chapter 16). Kohl and Gorbachev soon struck up a close working relationship that blossomed into a real friendship. In a startling turnabout, Gorbachev and the NATO countries agreed in 1987 to destroy all the intermediate-range missiles they had installed in the European area over the previous 10 years, removing in one bold stroke a major source of East–West frictions. The Kohl–Gorbachev connection also smoothed the way to improvements in Bonn's ties with East Germany's communist regime, which was openly resisting Gorbachev's reform program. Kohl was also a committed Europeanist and he played a leading role in boosting West European integration, putting Germany's weight behind such measures as the Treaty of Maastricht of 1992, which established the European Union and later in the decade led to the creation of the euro as the common currency and the European Central Bank. And Kohl got on well with the three American presidents whose administrations coincided with his years in office—Ronald Reagan, George H.W. Bush, and Bill Clinton.

Kohl's center-stage role in Germany's unification process was his greatest triumph. During 1989, the East German government's grip on the population, which had been tightened by the most pervasive surveillance network in the communist bloc, was weakening and the government was growing increasingly nervous. Thousands of East Germans on vacation in neighboring communist-ruled Hungary took advantage of that country's recently opened border with Austria and simply walked or rode to freedom, their possessions stuffed in a few suitcases. Many headed to West Germany, where they were considered citizens under the Basic Law. East German vacationers in Czechoslovakia, which was a more rigidly governed communist state than Hungary, swarmed into the West German embassy in Prague and pressured the West German and Czech authorities to agree to let them leave for West Germany. These actions by allied communist governments mortified East Germany's leaders, but there was little they could do about it as long as the Soviet Union did not take action to stop it.

Gorbachev was committed to reforming the Soviet system of repressive government and state-centered socialism. He wanted to fix the system with more openness, public debate, more democratization within the Communist Party and a restructuring of its political and economic institutions, while at the same time maintaining the communist system of one-party government and a socialist economy. He also wanted to maintain favorable relations with the United States and its allies. The Cold War, with its exorbitant military expenditures, had to be ended so the USSR and its allies could shift resources to rebuilding their flagging economies. Hence, the use of coercion to suppress demonstrators or stop them from emigrating to the West would dash these hopes. So the USSR stood by as 40 years of Soviet hegemony in East Central Europe slipped through it fingers over the course of 1989. Communist reformers in Hungary opened their borders to Austria. Polish Communist leaders came to an agreement with the Solidarity trade union leaders on free elections. And in East Germany, between July and October 1989, more than 120,000 people found a way to leave East Germany.

Things became more tense in the fall as anti-regime demonstrations began taking place in East German cities including Leipzig and Dresden. Once it became clear that the East German authorities were not prepared to crush the protests with overwhelming force, growing numbers of people were emboldened to take to the streets. By October demonstrations were a weekly occurrence. Clearly rattled, the Communist Party leadership decided to replace the party's aging leader, Erich Honecker, who had led the GDR for 18 years under an iron fist, with a younger leader in the hopes of convincing the population of its readiness for change. But the protest movement intensified. In early November more than a million people gathered peacefully in East Berlin in an unprecedented show of opposition to the regime's dictatorial practices.

Unexpectedly, on the evening of November 9, 1989, one of the leaders of East Germany's Communist regime declared in a televised press conference that East German citizens would henceforth receive immediate and unconditional permission to travel abroad. The statement seemed to represent a complete reversal of three decades of stringent Communist controls over

On November 9, 1989, one of the leaders of East Germany's Communist Party regime stated that East German citizens could henceforth receive immediate and unconditional permission to travel abroad. When guards opened the barriers to the west, huge crowds engaged in spontaneous celebration.

the travel rights of the East German population. News of the announcement spread rapidly throughout the country. Crowds quickly gathered on the eastern side of the Berlin wall to see if the official declaration was really true. For several hours they waited while the border crossings remained shut. Then around midnight, the guards calmly opened the barriers and thousands of East Germans flocked into West Berlin. It shocked the world. By the hundreds of thousands, people who had never seen the western part of the city stepped across the frontier. A state of almost delirious mass euphoria gripped the country. More than 5 million East Germans crossed the inter-German border in the first four days after the wall's opening.

The opening of the Berlin Wall triggered a chain of events that occurred so rapidly political leaders in all countries with a stake in Europe could barely keep up. While the leaders of the two German states talked of stability and long-term reform, most East Germans wanted radical change immediately. French President François Mitterrand and British Prime Minister Margaret Thatcher, evoking memories of World War II, warned that a unified Germany might be too powerful and would be a threat to Europe. But the East German regime quickly disintegrated, making unification almost inevitable. East Germans demanded elections in the GDR. In March 1990, free elections were held there for the first time with dozens of newly formed political parties participating. Fledgling party organizations connected with West Germany's three large parties—the Christian Democrats, the Social Democrats and the Free Democrats—handily won more than 75 percent of the East German vote. Their chief goal was the same—the dissolution of East Germany as a separate state and its incorporation into the Federal Republic. In July 1990, as the East German currency collapsed, a currency union took place, in which East German marks were exchanged for the West German currency at a 2:1 ratio.

On October 3, 1990—less than one year after the opening of the wall—the two Germanies were united into an enlarged

Federal Republic of Germany. Berlin became the capital of the united Germany and during the 1990s several federal ministries and eventually the parliament moved to Berlin. Chancellor Kohl played a key role in the negotiations on unification. His bonds with Gorbachev were critical in winning the Soviet leader's acceptance of the liquidation of East Germany's communist state. Kohl also allayed the fears of many Europeans who believed that an enlarged Germany would seek to dominate the region, assuring them his aim was "a European Germany, not a German Europe."

In December 1990, Kohl led the CDU-FDP coalition to a resounding victory in the first Bundestag elections to be held in unified Germany. But after being reinstated as chancellor, Kohl was forced to admit that reunification would cost much more money than he had led the voters to believe. His campaign promises of "blossoming landscapes" in East Germany proved embarrassingly unrealistic during the arduous post-unification decade. In his next term Kohl sought to build as large a consensus as possible on bearing the costs of modernizing eastern Germany's economy. The government of the Federal Republic invested 1 trillion deutsche marks (more than $500 billion in today's terms) in eastern Germany during the 1990s in an effort to modernize its communications and transportation infrastructure, restructure its education system, and establish new government institutions. A large chunk of the money was also used to provide jobs or unemployment compensation for eastern Germans thrown out of work by the liquidation of the GDR's enterprises, government bureaucracy, and military. To pay for these expenditures, new taxes had to be imposed on the population, with West Germans footing most of the bill. The average income tax rate rose from about 43 percent to 50 percent. Rising discontent in both parts of Germany led many political analysts to predict Kohl's defeat in the 1994 elections. Once again, however, Kohl confounded the doomsayers. In 1994 Kohl was elected chancellor for the fifth straight time, though his coalition government had a mere five-vote majority in the Bundestag (338 seats to 333).[13]

Kohl's final four-year term was marked by continuing efforts to build up the eastern German economy while contending with mounting unemployment, exploding social welfare costs, and a troubling loss of Germany's famous economic dynamism. With a mixed record of achievements and difficulties, the embattled Kohl went before the voters once again in 1998, only to lose to a new coalition consisting of the Social Democrats and the Greens, an environmental party. After 16 years at the helm of the Federal Republic, the chancellor of German unity stepped down.

POLITICAL INSTITUTIONS IN THE FEDERAL REPUBLIC OF GERMANY

Germany's stability in the postwar period can be attributed, in part, to its institutional structure. This institutional framework, set out in Germany's Basic Law, reflects many of the lessons that Germany learned from the failed Weimar democracy and the authoritarian fascist regime. Under the Basic Law, the Federal Republic is a parliamentary system, in which political power in the Federal Republic is divided horizontally and vertically. There are clear lines of accountability and checks and balances. We examine the various political institutions in turn.

A Federal System

The Basic Law establishes the Federal Republic as a federal system. *Federalism* is a political system that combines a meaningful central government with a multiplicity of regional or local governments that have specific real powers. (The United States is an example.) In Germany, policy-making power is divided between the federal government and Germany's 16 **Länder**, or **states**. After the devastating fascist experience, the Allied occupation powers and most Germans themselves had no desire to re-create a powerful central government. They therefore created states that play an important role, particularly in education and domestic security policy, and that receive representation at the national level through the upper house of the legislature, known as the Bundesrat.

The original Basic Law established 11 *Länder*. After unification, the number of *Länder* rose to 16. With the collapse of the communist government of the German Democratic Republic, East Germany was united with the rest of the Federal Republic in 1990 on the basis of a provision in the Basic Law that permitted the incorporation of new states into the FRG. After the 1990 elections in East Germany demonstrated overwhelming popular support for unification, the GDR was reorganized into five states—Brandenburg, Saxony, Saxony-Anhalt, Thuringia, and Mecklenburg-West Pomerania. These five states then entered the Federal Republic in a procedure roughly similar to the way various territories once joined the union of the United States of America. Some political forces in both eastern and western Germany objected to this procedure, arguing that Article 146 of the Basic Law mandates a new

German constitution and a national referendum on it when unification occurs. Former anticommunist East German dissidents joined with western German Greens and Social Democrats in demanding a new constitution, but their proposals were blocked by their opponents, the Christian Democrats, in the mid-1990s.

Thus, the Federal Republic now consists of 16 *Länder*. Three of these states are actually large cities (Berlin, Hamburg, and Bremen). Each *Land* (state) has its own legislature, typically known as the *Landtag* (state diet), elected every four or five years by the state's voters. The elections are usually staggered; rarely do more than two of them occur on the same day, with some occurring in different years.

All of the state legislatures are unicameral. The majority party (or parties) of each newly elected legislature elects a state government, whose chief usually bears the title *minister-president (Ministerpräsident)*. (The three city-states have different titles for their respective legislatures, governments, and heads of government. Berlin's legislature, for example, is called the House of Delegates, its government is the Senate, and its head of government is the governing mayor.) Each state's head of government is roughly analogous to an American governor, though they are elected differently and the extent of their legal powers differs. The position of head of government at the state level is an important one in German politics, at times serving as a stepping-stone to higher office. Just as several U.S. presidents, such as George W. Bush, Bill Clinton, Ronald Reagan, and Jimmy Carter, were previously governors, several German chancellors and candidates for that position once served as minister-presidents of individual German states. Helmut Kohl, for example, was minister-president of Rhineland-Palatinate before becoming chancellor. Unlike American governors, however, most state leaders in Germany serve simultaneously as members of the federal legislature, thus participating in national government. Presidents Carter, Reagan, Clinton, and G. W. Bush had never held national office before assuming the presidency.

From the very beginning, the Basic Law conferred extensive powers on each state to regulate education, the administration of justice, the police, and the mass media, including radio and television, within its territory.

In constitutional law, the legal powers accorded the regional subunits of a federal system are known as "reserved powers" (i.e., they are *reserved* to the subunits). In addition to having these considerable reserved powers, the states were given the right to supervise the administration of *federal* laws—laws enacted by the Federal Republic's national legislature and central government—within their respective jurisdictions. Because virtually every law touching on domestic affairs in Germany has an administrative component, the states have their hand in practically every aspect of government administration. Most taxes imposed by the federal government, for instance, are actually collected by the states. Though the 50 states in the United States also have extensive reserved powers, they do not have such sweeping rights to administer federal laws and regulations as their German counterparts do. As a result of reforms passed in 2006, some competencies or reserved powers were passed to the *Länder*, such as the right to regulate pay and conditions for civil servants, and university construction.

The only major policy areas where the states play little or no role concern Germany's international dealings, such as foreign and defense policy. Even in foreign affairs, however, the states are expanding the scope of their authority. In 1992 the Basic Law was amended to give the states a major role in shaping the German government's policies toward the European Union. Fearing that the process of European unification might give EU authorities in Brussels excessive powers to interfere in their internal state affairs (for example, by imposing regulations on their broadcast media), the *Länder* won the right to veto any agreement the German government might conclude with the European Union that intrudes on their local powers.

Local governments in Germany at the county and municipal levels within these states are heavily dependent on money transferred to them from the federal and state budgets.[14] In addition to their powers at the state level, the *Länder* also enjoy representation at the national level through the Bundesrat (see below).

The Federal Government

The Basic Law established a *parliamentary system* of government in the Federal Republic. Policy-making power is divided at the national level between the legislature, which is made up of two houses—the *Bundestag*, which is the popularly elected lower house, and the *Bundesrat*, which represents the states—and the executive (the *chancellor* and cabinet), who are dependent on the support of the majority of the legislature. Germany also has a strong independent judiciary, the *Federal Constitutional Court*, which has the power of judicial review. Germany has a federal president, who is indirectly elected and serves as the ceremonial head of state. The president has little independent power and is supposed to serve as the conscience and unifier of the nation.

Bundestag The **Bundestag**—or federal diet—is the lower house of the national legislature. In most respects, it functions much like Britain's House of Commons. It has approximately 598 members who are elected at four-year intervals. Its seat is the Reichstag building in Berlin. The 17th Bundestag (2009–13) had 622 members.

The Bundestag is the center of the policy-making process in Germany. Preparing and adopting legislation is its most important function. The Bundestag also elects the chancellor, scrutinizes the government, supervises the bureaucracy and military, adopts the federal budget, and selects judges to the Federal Constitutional Court.

After national elections, the Bundestag's first order of business is to elect the federal chancellor or head of government. A majority vote is needed to elect the chancellor. The Bundestag can also remove the chancellor through the constructive vote of no confidence (see below). Unlike in the Weimar period, where it was easy to remove the chancellor through a simple vote of no confidence, now the Bundestag must also have a majority in

favor of a new chancellor candidate before removing the sitting chancellor. The Bundestag also holds the government accountable by open debate and by enabling its members to pose questions directly to cabinet ministers. Unlike Britain, where the prime minister must face questions in the House of Commons every week, Germany does not require the chancellor to undergo an oral grilling in the Bundestag on a weekly basis. Still, even the chancellor must answer oral questions from time to time.

The Bundestag is organized by party caucuses known as *Fraktionen*. The leadership of these *Fraktionen* control the work of the Bundestag. Each party caucus determines the committee assignments of its members, and even office space and debating time. To be influential in parliament, deputies must have the support of the leadership. In the 17th German Bundestag (2009–13) there were five parliamentary groups. The largest was the CDU/CSU with 237 seats, the SPD follows with 146, the FDP had 93, the Left Party had 76, and Alliance '90/The Greens were the smallest group with 68.

Like the U.S. Congress, the Bundestag has a standing committee system. These committees can initiate, review, and amend legislation, similar to the U.S. House of Representatives and the U.S. Senate. The committees reflect the partisan makeup of the Bundestag. Committee chairmanships are awarded proportionately according to party strength. The committee system is more powerful than that of Britain, although less powerful than the committees in the U.S. Congress.

Bundestag Elections Bundestag elections occur at least every four years. Elections can be called before the expiration of the full four-year term, but this has rarely been the case. Unlike Britain's single-member district/plurality system, Germany uses a **mixed member proportional representation (MMP)** system or a personalized proportional system to elect members to the Bundestag. This mixed member PR system is a combination of the two main systems for electing a legislature: the single-member-district (SMD) system and proportional representation (PR). Half the members of the Bundestag (299) are elected by SMD; the other portion by PR. Once all the votes are counted, a formula is used to ensure that the final distribution of entire Bundestag seats approximately resembles proportional representation.

The German variant of the mixed members electoral system is a bit complicated, but an understanding of its main features is essential to understanding how political power is acquired in the Federal Republic.

Germany is divided into 299 single-member electoral districts (*Wahlkreisen*). These districts are distributed among the 16 states on a population basis and each district sends one representative to the Bundestag. Each of these districts averages out nationally to about 249,000 inhabitants and 170,000 voters. The other 299 seats in the Bundestag are also distributed proportionally to the states based on population.

Each voter gets two votes—on the first ballot, the voter casts a district vote, and on the second ballot, the voter casts a party vote (see Figure 15.1). Individual candidates are listed on the district ballot and a voter votes for one candidate to

Stimmzettel

für die Wahl zum Deutschen Bundestag im Wahlkreis 81 Berlin - Charlottenburg-Wilmersdorf
am 22. September 2002

Sie haben 2 Stimmen

hier 1 Stimme
für die Wahl
eines/einer Wahlkreisabgeordneten

hier 1 Stimme
für die Wahl
einer Landesliste (Partei)
- maßgebende Stimme für die Verteilung der
Sitze insgesamt auf die einzelnen Parteien -

Erststimme   **Zweitstimme**

#	Erststimme	Zweitstimme	#
1	**Merkel**, Petra-Eveline — Kaufm. Angestellte, Transvaalstr. 6, 13351 Berlin — **SPD** — Sozialdemokratische Partei Deutschlands	**SPD** — Sozialdemokratische Partei Deutschlands — Wolfgang Thierse, Dr. Christine Bergmann, Dr. Ditmar Staffelt, Petra-Eveline Merkel, Andreas Matthae	1
2	**Helias**, Siegfried — MdB, Friseurmeister, Britzer Damm 77, 12347 Berlin — **CDU** — Christlich Demokratische Union Deutschlands	**CDU** — Christlich Demokratische Union Deutschlands — Günter Nooke, Verena Butalikakis, Roland Gewalt, Peter Rzepka, Siegfried Helias	2
3	**Rottka**, Natalie — Journalistin, Krumme Str. 64, 10627 Berlin — **PDS** — Partei des Demokratischen Sozialismus	**PDS** — Partei des Demokratischen Sozialismus — Petra Pau, Dr. Bärbel Grygier, Dr. Gesine Lötzsch, Sandra Brunner, Evrim Baba	3
4	**Eichstädt-Bohlig**, Franziska — MdB, Dipl.-Ing., Architektin, Droysenstr. 6, 10629 Berlin — **GRÜNE** — BÜNDNIS 90 / DIE GRÜNEN	**GRÜNE** — BÜNDNIS 90 / DIE GRÜNEN — Renate Künast, Werner Schulz, Franziska Eichstädt-Bohlig, Michael Cramer, Anja Schillhaneck	4
5	**Dr. Rexrodt**, Günter — Dipl.-Kaufmann, Chausseestr. 99, 10115 Berlin — **FDP** — Freie Demokratische Partei	**FDP** — Freie Demokratische Partei — Dr. Günter Rexrodt, Markus Löning, Hellmut Königshaus, Gabriele Heise, Dr. Hans-Peter Schlaudt	5
		REP — DIE REPUBLIKANER — Dr. Konrad Voigt, Wolfgang Seifert, Thomas Weisbrich, Marieluise Jeschke, Reinhard Haese	6
7	**Peuker**, Dieter — Kaufmann, Galvanistr. 14, 10587 Berlin — **GRAUE** — DIE GRAUEN - Graue Panther	**GRAUE** — DIE GRAUEN - Graue Panther — Dieter Peuker, Karl-Heinz Augustin, Thorsten Hartje, Helga Nönnig, Armin Behrmann	7
		NPD — Nationaldemokratische Partei Deutschlands — Klaus Beier, Albrecht Reither, Andrea Lammok, Horst Sinning, Mike Ducherow	8
		DIE FRAUEN — Feministische Partei DIE FRAUEN — Helga Trachsel, Elke Bleich, Ilona Braune, Eva Bornemann	9
		ödp — Ökologisch-Demokratische Partei — Kerstin Heinrich, Dr. Eva Börsch-Supan, Dr. Larissa Dloczik, Andreas Schinzel, Heiner Fauteck	10
11	**Köster**, Heinrich — Geschäftsführer, Duisburger Str. 19, 10707 Berlin — **BüSo** — Bürgerrechtsbewegung Solidarität	**BüSo** — Bürgerrechtsbewegung Solidarität — Helga Zepp-LaRouche, Heiko Ziemann, Monika Hahn, Tombolo Wa Kadima Mukengechay, Ulrike Lillge	11
		HP — Humanistische Partei — Michael Steinbach, Johanna Krappmann, Benjamin-Christopher Krüger, Michael Daniel Winkler, Dirk Wanner	12
		KPD — KOMMUNISTISCHE PARTEI DEUTSCHLANDS — Werner Schleese, Günther Bandel, Alfred Fritz, Anny Wagner, Alfred Wagner	13
		PBC — Partei Bibeltreuer Christen — Klaus Lange, Matthias Gardain, Bernd Matthes, Bettina Lange, Dagmar Briegel	14
		Schill — Partei Rechtsstaatlicher Offensive — Prof. Dr. Lothar Staeck, Dr. Christian-Friedrich Eigler, Manfred Ehlert, Claas Weseloh, Valeska Jakubowski	15

FIGURE 15.1   **German Sample Ballot**

"You Have 2 Votes": The left-hand column lists candidates by name for the single-member-district vote. The right-hand column lists parties for the proportional representation vote, along with the names of prominent party leaders. *Source:* Federal Statistical Office, FRG.

represent his or her district. Whichever candidate wins the most votes in the district wins the seat in the Bundestag to represent that district. This is called the "direct mandate."

On the second ballot, the parties are listed with the names of some of the most prominent politicians in the voter's home state. Voters may vote for one of the parties. The second ballot is important in determining the overall makeup of the Bundestag. The proportion of votes the party receives on the second ballot determines the overall number of seats that party receives from a particular state. So, for example, if North Rhine-Westphalia had 100 seats (50 single member and 50 party seats) and a party were to win 40 percent of the second-ballot votes in North Rhine-Westphalia, it would receive approximately 40 percent of the Bundestag seats allocated to North Rhine-Westphalia. First, the candidates who won district mandates would take their seats, followed by members from the party's list for a total of 40 percent. If a party won no district mandates, all of the elected legislators would come off the party list.

One of the most unusual features of Germany's electoral system is the so-called "overhang mandate" (*Ueberhangmandat*). To refer to the hypothetical example above, if a party wins 40 percent on the second ballot in a state that sends 100 delegates to the Bundestag, then it is entitled in principle to 40 of those delegates, assuming the party clears the 5 percent hurdle nationwide (see below). If its candidates win more than 40 seats in the state's single-member-district (first-ballot) vote, then the size of the Bundestag is enlarged by five "overhang seats" to accommodate 105 deputies from that state. "Overhang mandates" are thus *additional Bundestag seats* that are created when a party wins a percentage of single-member-district seats in a particular state that exceeds its percentage of the popular vote for parties in that state. Overhang votes can be critical in determining who wins control of the Bundestag. In 2009, there were 24 overhang votes: 21 to the CDU and 3 to the CSU. The Bundestag was enlarged from 598 to 622 seats.

A party must receive at least 5 percent of the national vote or win three district seats to gain its proportion of seats on the second ballot. This **5 percent threshold** was introduced in the 1950s to avoid the proliferation of small parties in the legislature—a problem that plagued the Weimar Republic. Candidates who win a district seat take their seat regardless of whether their party crosses the 5 percent threshold. In 2002, for example, the Party of Democratic Socialism (PDS)—the offspring of East Germany's ruling Communist Party—failed to breach the 5 percent threshold barrier, winning only 4 percent of the national vote. However, two PDS candidates won direct-mandate victories in Berlin, giving the party two delegates in the Bundestag.[15] In 2009, six parties cleared the 5 percent hurdle—the CDU, the CSU, the SPD, the FDP, Alliance '90/ The Greens, and the Left—but 23 smaller parties did not and therefore received no representation in the Bundestag.

A growing number of German voters split their vote. They often do this to ensure that a smaller party receives enough votes on the second ballot to get over the 5 percent threshold and secure seats in the Bundestag. So, for example, in 1998, one-third of the voters who voted for the Greens as a *party* on the second ballot voted for a Social Democrat *candidate* on the first ballot. The voters who engaged in this kind of ticket splitting hoped to provide the two parties with enough seats in the Bundestag to form an SPD–Green coalition government. In 2009, vote splitting reached a new high of 26.4 percent of voters.[16] Table 15.3 shows the electoral results in the 2009 Bundestag elections.

Germany's complicated electoral system ultimately produces a distribution of Bundestag seats that amounts to approximate proportional representation for all the parties that surmount the 5 percent threshold. By capturing the advantages of candidate recognition that come with the single-member-district system, together with the fairness in party representation that accompanies proportional representation, Germany has sought to reap the benefits of both systems. Because of the proportional nature of the electoral system, every government in the Federal Republic of Germany has been a coalition government since 1949, when the FRG was founded in West Germany.

The Bundesrat The upper house of Germany's national parliament is known as the federal council or **Bundesrat**. The Bundesrat directly represents the states. The members of the Bundesrat are chosen *by the state governments*. Unlike the U.S. Senate, its members are *not* directly elected by the people of each state. Instead, the majority party (or parties) within each state legislature selects the state's representatives in the Bundesrat (because it is this legislative majority that forms the state government). Thus, if the Christian Democrats have the majority of seats in the state legislature of Hessen, they will establish Hessen's government and pick its minister-president. That government will in turn send Christian Democrats to represent Hessen in the Bundesrat. In fact, each state's head of government typically serves as a member of its Bundesrat delegation, along with other ministers in the state government. The opposition parties in these state legislatures have no role in selecting their state's Bundesrat deputies.

Table 15.3   Bundestag Elections, September 2009 (Minimum 598 Seats, Increased to 622)

Parties	% Vote Nationwide (2nd vote)	District Seats Won (1st vote)	Total Seats*
Social Democrats (SPD)	23.0%	64	146
Christian Democrats (CDU/CSU)	33.8	218	239
Alliance '90/The Greens	10.7	1	68
Free Democrats (FDP)	14.6	0	93
Left Party	11.9	16	76
Others	6.0	0	0

*Seats won in first and second votes, plus overhang mandates.

Source: Federal Returning Officer, Federal Statistical Office, FRG, www.bundeswahlleiter.de.

Though each state is represented, the Bundesrat's voting procedures are not based on "one state, one vote." Because Germany's 16 states come in different sizes, the Bundesrat uses a *weighted voting* procedure. The largest states, with a population of more than 7 million each, are each entitled to six votes in the Bundesrat. A state with between 6 million and 7 million inhabitants is entitled to five Bundesrat votes; those with between 2 million and 6 million people are entitled to four votes; all the rest are entitled to three votes each. Thus the 16 states that comprise the Bundesrat together dispose of a total of 69 votes, distributed somewhat proportionately by size. If the four largest states, with six votes each, choose to vote together, their 24 votes are enough to block the passage of any bill requiring a two-thirds majority, such as a proposed constitutional amendment. In these circumstances the four largest states can use their weighted votes to block action favored by the 12 smaller states. Even so, the Bundesrat's malapportionment favors the smaller states, which have more representation per person than the largest states have.

Each state may send as many representatives to the Bundesrat as it has votes, but each state deputation must vote together as a bloc. Thus if Bavaria sends six deputies to the Bundesrat, all six must vote in unison as instructed by the Bavarian state government. Thus, Bundesrat members have much less independence than U.S. senators. Each Bundesrat member votes on instructions from his or her state government and all members of a state delegation vote as a bloc.

These voting members of a state's Bundesrat delegation tend to be ministers in the state's government (cabinet). When Bundesrat sessions mainly involve committee work and no votes are taken, the state governments usually delegate civil servants from the state's bureaucracy to take their place on the committees. Such people tend to be technical experts on policy issues such as budgetary matters, education, the environment, and so on. Sometimes a state's Bundesrat delegation will be instructed not to vote. If the state government is a coalition between two parties (say, the Social Democrats and the Christian Democrats) and the partners cannot agree on certain pieces of legislation that come up for a vote in the Bundesrat, it may instruct its delegation in that body to abstain from voting. But abstentions count as nay votes because Bundesrat decisions require a majority of all the votes (at least 35 out of the 69 votes).

Table 15.4 lists Germany's 16 states, along with their populations and state capitals, the number of votes they are entitled to in the Bundesrat, the year of their most recent election, the parties that governed them in September 2012, and the names of their respective minister-presidents at that time.

The national government must submit its bills to the Bundesrat first and to the Bundestag subsequently. The Basic Law gave the upper house *veto power* over bills whose passage into law would require the state governments to implement or administer their provisions including tax measures, educational reforms, environmental laws, the regulation of cable television, and the like. If a bill is specifically designated as one that *requires*

Table 15.4 Germany's 16 States

State (*Land*)	Population (millions, 2011)	State Capital	Bundesrat Votes	Last Elections	Government (September 2012)	Head of Government
North Rhine–Westphalia	17.8	Düsseldorf	6	2012	SPD, Alliance '90/The Greens	Hannelore Kraft (SPD)
Bavaria	12.6	Munich	6	2008	CSU, FDP	Horst Seehofer (CSU)
Baden-Württemberg	10.8	Stuttgart	6	2011	Alliance '90/The Greens, SPD	Winfried Kretschmann (Alliance'90/Greens)
Lower Saxony	7.9	Hanover	6	2013	SPD/Alliance '90/The Greens	Stephan Weil (SPD)
Hessen	6.1	Wiesbaden	5	2009	CDU, FDP	Volker Bouffier (CDU)
Saxony*	4.1	Dresden	4	2009	CDU, FDP	Stanislaw Tillich (CDU)
Rhineland-Palatinate	4.0	Mainz	4	2011	SPD, Alliance '90/The Greens	Marie-Luise "Malu" Dreyer (SPD)
Berlin	3.5	Berlin	4	2011	SPD, CDU	Klaus Wowereit (SPD)
Schleswig-Holstein	2.8	Kiel	4	2012	SPD, Alliance '90/The Greens, SSW†	Torsten Albig (SPD)
Brandenburg*	2.5	Potsdam	4	2009	SPD, Left	Matthias Platzeck (SPD)
Saxony-Anhalt*	2.3	Magdeburg	4	2011	CDU, SPD	Reiner Haseloff (CDU)
Thuringia*	2.2	Erfurt	4	2009	CDU, SPD	Christine Lieberknecht(CDU)
Hamburg	1.8	Hamburg	3	2011	SPD	Olof Scholz (SPD)
Mecklenburg–West Pomerania*	1.6	Schwerin	3	2011	SPD, CDU	Erwin Sellering (SPD)
Saarland	1.0	Saarbrücken	3	2012	CDU, SPD	Annegret Kramp-Karrenbauer (CDU)
Bremen	0.5	Bremen	3	2011	SPD, Alliance '90/The Greens	Jens Böhrnsen (SPD)

*Formerly part of communist East Germany.

†SSW—South Schleswig Voter Federation, a regional party representing Danish and Frisian minorities.

Bundesrat approval, the Bundesrat can veto it by majority vote even if the bill has already passed the lower house, the Bundestag. If the two chambers cannot come to an agreement, a conciliation committee is convened to try to negotiate a compromise.

The Bundesrat also gets to vote on some bills that do not directly affect state governments, such as foreign or defense policy. On these issues, a negative Bundesrat vote can be overridden by a vote in the Bundestag. Thus the Bundesrat's approval is not required on all legislation, unlike the U.S. Senate. If the Bundesrat by a two-thirds majority rejects a bill that does not require its approval, the Bundestag can pass it only with a two-thirds majority of its own. If it fails to do so, the bill is dead. Thus, the Bundesrat gives Germany's 16 state governments a direct role in the national parliament that the 50 state governments in the United States do not possess. It forces the central government in Berlin to pay close attention to the wishes of each state's elected officials, injecting a considerable measure of decentralization into Germany's federal system. So important are the states in Germany's political decision-making process that one student of German affairs has called the Federal Republic's central government a "semi-sovereign state," in large measure because it must constantly share power with the *Länder*.[17]

Sometimes, however, the Bundesrat's ability to kill legislation passed by the Bundestag can produce gridlock. When one house is largely controlled by the Social Democrats and the other house is controlled by the Christian Democrats, resulting in a German version of divided government, these rival parties must compromise their differences for legislation to be enacted. At times it can be very difficult—or impossible—to find acceptable compromises. This problem became more acute after reunification. The heterogeneity among the new states, coupled with more parties competing successfully for seats in state government, has meant that the composition of state governments has become more diverse.

With politicians growing increasingly frustrated with this situation, in 2003 a committee consisting of members of both houses of the legislature was formed with the task of recommending changes in Germany's federal structure. As part of a package of reforms that passed in 2006, changes were made in the Basic Law that reduced the proportion of laws needing approval of the Bundesrat from 60 percent to about 35 percent to 40 percent. In return, some competencies were fully passed to the *Länder*.

Chancellor and Cabinet The chief executive or head of government in the Federal Republic is the **chancellor**, who serves as the head of government. The chancellor has more authority and is more difficult to remove than a prime minister in the British model. The chancellor is chosen by the majority of the Bundestag. The president of the Federal Republic, the ceremonial head of state, formally proposes someone to serve as the chancellor, but like the queen of the United Kingdom, the German president has little choice but to designate the person whose party is in the strongest position in the Bundestag to form a government. If one party holds an absolute majority of the seats, then it will be able to form a majoritarian government with no need to rely on coalition partners. Although

majoritarian governments are the norm in Britain, in the Federal Republic there has never been one: Every government since 1949 has been a coalition government.

After the coalition partners have agreed to form a government, the Bundestag holds a formal vote for chancellor. Invariably this vote falls along party lines, with the coalition partners voting to ensure a majority for the new head of government and the minority parties asserting their opposition. After this *investiture vote*, the chancellor names the cabinet ministers, usually on the basis of a previous agreement between the coalition parties. The junior partner in most coalition governments is assigned the post of foreign minister, generally considered the second most prestigious position after the chancellor, and several other cabinet ministries. Once the government is in place, the chancellor presents a formal "government declaration" (*Regierungserklärung*) to the Bundestag, a policy address indicating the government's main priorities. After the 2009 election, the CDU, CSU, and FDP together held 332 of the 622 seats in the Bundestag, and the CDU had the largest share of seats. Angela Merkel (CDU) was reelected as the chancellor.

The size of the cabinet varies from one government to the next, ranging from 16 to more than 20 members. Most cabinet members are also members of the Bundestag. The current CDU/CSU and FDP coalition has 16 members. There are eight members of the CDU, three are members of the CSU, and five are members of the FDP. There are six women in the cabinet including Chancellor Merkel.

It is more difficult to remove the chancellor during the term in office than in other parliamentary systems. The Bundestag has the right to vote the government out of office. But in the Federal Republic, the Basic Law imposes strict conditions under which a vote of confidence can be used to unseat the government. In what is called the **constructive vote of confidence**, the opposition not only must form a voting majority against the government, but it must also have the majority votes necessary to support a new chancellor and form a new government within 48 hours of the vote. The constructive vote of no confidence was implemented to avoid the rapid turnover of government prevalent in the Weimar Republic. In view of these obstacles, the confidence procedure has been used only twice in the history of the Federal Republic. In April 1972, the CDU/CSU opposition attempted unsuccessfully to bring down the government of Social Democratic Chancellor Brandt. In October 1982, the CDU/CSU successfully brought down the Schmidt government and replaced it with the Kohl government.

Government stability in the Federal Republic requires fairly strict *party discipline*: All the members of a party's Bundestag delegation are expected to vote in unison, except on special occasions when the party leadership allows its deputies to vote as they wish. Party discipline is higher in Germany than in the United States. The result is relatively smooth sailing through the Bundestag for bills drafted by the government. Roughly 85 percent of government bills pass the lower house, as opposed to about 40 percent of legislation introduced by individual members. Thanks to party discipline, Chancellor Helmut Kohl was able to maintain his coalition government with a mere five-vote majority from 1994 to 1998, and the Social Democrats and Greens were also able to govern with a 10-vote majority from 1998 to 2002 and with a 4-vote majority from 2002 to 2005.

Another factor that facilitates the legislative process in Germany centers on the unusually close relationships between the cabinet, the Bundestag, and the civil service. Most cabinet ministers and their deputy ministers are themselves members of the Bundestag; they are therefore well acquainted with the procedures and norms of parliamentary practice. The same has *not* been true of most U.S. cabinet secretaries. Moreover, a sizable number of Bundestag deputies tend to come from the civil service. U.S. law prohibits civil servants from running for office while holding down their bureaucratic positions, but Germany permits it. It even allows civil servants to get promoted within the government bureaucracy while serving in the legislature. Another large group of Bundestag deputies tends to come from trade unions, business associations, and other nongovernmental interest groups involved in the policy-making process. Upward of 70 percent of the Bundestag thus has considerable experience in government or interest groups, giving them professional expertise in their various policy specialties.

The President The federal *president* is Germany's head of state. Unlike in the Weimar period, the position of president in the Federal Republic is largely ceremonial, analogous to that of the British monarch. Germany's president in no way possesses the powers of the president of the United States, France, or Russia. The president's principal duty is to nominate a party leader to form a government after a Bundestag election, upon the chancellor's resignation, or following the government's defeat in a constructive vote of confidence. This task is usually ritualistic, as the person to be designated as the next chancellor has invariably been predetermined by the alignment of parties in the Bundestag.[18] All federal laws must be signed by the president before they can take effect.

The federal president is not elected by the people but by a special federal convention (*Bundesversammlung*). This body consists of the Bundestag and the Bundesrat, plus an equal number of delegates elected by the 16 state legislatures. The president serves a five-year term and may be reelected only once. The president is usually a former popular politician or an individual held in high esteem. He is expected to be nonpartisan after taking office. The current president is Joachim Gauck, an independent, who was elected in 2012. He is a former East German Lutheran pastor known for his anticommunist activism against the East German government.

The Federal Judiciary The Basic Law established an elaborate court system, crowned at the federal level by several superior courts. These include the Federal Supreme Court (*Bundesgerichtshof*), which is Germany's highest court of appeals in ordinary civil and criminal cases, and specialized courts concerned respectively with administrative law, labor law, financial law, and social affairs. By far the most important of these high courts is the **Federal Constitutional Court** (*Bundesverfassungsgericht*). From its inception the court was endowed with the power

of *judicial review:* the right to interpret the Basic Law and to strike down as unconstitutional laws passed by the parliament and actions taken by the government. With this considerable discretionary authority, the Federal Constitutional Court has been called the most powerful judicial body in Europe. In some respects its authority surpasses that of the U.S. Supreme Court.[19] (Britain has no comparable supreme court, while France's Constitutional Council has substantially more limited powers.)

Seated in Karlsruhe, the Federal Constitutional Court consists of 16 justices, most of them former judges or eminent constitutional scholars. Half are appointed by the Bundestag, the other half by the Bundesrat. Each house must confirm a nominee for the court by two-thirds vote, a supermajority deliberately intended to require the approval of the two largest parties, the Christian Democrats and the Social Democrats. Germany's political leaders have sought to ensure a scrupulous balance on the court between adherents of the two major parties, along with an occasional Free Democratic Party member. Even the main left and right factions *within* the main parties are often represented on the court. Once seated, however, the justices are expected to be nonpartisan, delivering their rulings on the basis of complete political independence. The court is divided into two eight-person "senates," each of which is responsible for specific categories of constitutional issues. The president of the court presides over the first senate, the vice president over the second. All justices serve a maximum 12-year term.

In assuming ample powers to interpret the Basic Law, the Federal Constitutional Court broke with a long tradition in German legal theory known as "positivism." That doctrine held that the laws were so clearly written and detailed that they did not need much interpretation by the courts. Germany's judges thus had little latitude to define the scope of the law through interpretative rulings, but were expected to rigidly apply the state's official interpretations. As a consequence, many of them blindly followed the antidemocratic legal strictures laid down by the Kaiser's imperial government and, later, by Hitler and the Nazis. The founders of the Federal Republic wanted a clean break with the past and endowed the court with broad powers to interpret the Basic Law's provisions on human rights and to protect the country against democracy's adversaries. For example, Germany's Basic Law explicitly bans all political parties whose adherents "seek to abolish or impair the free democratic order" or to endanger the FRG's existence. In the 1950s the Federal Constitutional Court upheld the government's right to ban the German Communist Party and a neo-Nazi party on these grounds. In 2003 the court narrowly rejected the government's attempt to ban another neo-Nazi party after federal and state authorities made legal errors in gathering evidence. But in the same year, the court upheld the government's decision to ban a militant Islamic organization on the grounds that it was engaged in "combative-aggressive" activities against Germany's constitutional foundations. In interpreting these constitutional rights and prohibitions, Germany's Federal Constitutional Court has a special responsibility for defending democracy.

Unlike the U.S. Supreme Court, Germany's court does not hear cases. Instead, it is asked to rule on constitutional issues upon the request of the federal government, state governments, or one-third of the members of the Bundestag. Individual citizens may also bring complaints before the court if they believe their constitutional rights have been violated. The court itself decides which of these thousands of requests it wishes to adjudicate. Not only does it possess the right to invalidate, approve, or attach conditions to laws already passed, but it may also rule on "differences of opinion and doubts" about pending legislation if so requested. Within its vast scope of authority, the court may rule on jurisdictional disputes between different branches of government and may even rule on sensitive foreign policy matters—areas the U.S. Supreme Court usually avoids on the grounds that they are "political" issues best left to the Congress and the president.

Among the plethora of landmark decisions the Federal Constitutional Court has handed down, one of its most controversial was its invalidation of Germany's 1992 post-unification abortion law, which had departed from the Federal Republic's statute outlawing abortions by adopting East Germany's practice of permitting them. Without banning abortions entirely, the court called for greater measures to protect the unborn (such as counseling for pregnant women) and abolished funding for abortions through the national health insurance system. In light of this ruling, the legislature passed a new law in 1995 permitting abortions in the first trimester but requiring counseling aimed at the "protection of unborn life."

Among its foreign policy rulings, the court affirmed the government's decisions to deploy military forces in Somalia and Bosnia. Its other most important recent ruling was in 2012, when the Federal Constitutional Court approved the European stability mechanism (ESM), which was negotiated by euro-zone governments including Germany, to lend money to struggling euro countries and possibly their banks in return for promises of economic reforms. The ESM is designed to replace temporary rescue packages for countries such as Greece and Spain that have had difficulties meeting their public obligations. The ESM will be a permanent fund with €700 billion in capital (with €190 billion pledged by Germany). The court ruled, however, that Germany's liability must be capped at €190 billion unless the Bundestag explicitly votes to increase the limit.

POLITICAL PARTICIPATION

As the earlier part of this chapter has suggested, German political participation revolves around political parties and elections. In addition, Germans advocate for their political preferences through interest groups, which have been organized in a neo-corporatist way. We explore these forms of political participation in more detail below.

Political Parties and the Party System

Political parties play an important role in providing representation and shaping state policy in Germany. Germany is known as a "party state." It has a moderate, multiparty system, with two larger parties and several smaller parties. For much of the early postwar period, Germany had two and a half parties—the Social Democratic Party (SPD), the Christian Democrats (comprised of the Christian Democratic Union and Christian Social Union of Bavaria CDU/CSU), and the Free Democratic Party (FDP). During the 1980s, a new party that promoted environmental issues and peace issues, the **Greens**, emerged. It merged with the Bundnis '90, an alliance of three East German prodemocracy groups, after reunification. The Left Party (Die Linke) was formed in the 1990s as a merger of leftist mavericks from the SPD, who were opposed to Schröder's labor reforms, and the former Party of Democratic Socialism, the communist party, in East Germany. Most recently, a party devoted to Internet freedom, the Pirate Party, has won seats in four state legislatures.

The Christian Democrats and Social Democrats are *catchall parties* that reach out to a broad base that includes working-class voters, entrepreneurs, educators, and Germany's large middle class. So wide is their appeal that they are known in Germany as the people's parties *(Volksparteien)*. The Free Democrats, the Alliance '90/The Greens, the Left Party, the Pirate Party, and Germany's far-right parties tend to have a narrower appeal. We examine each of these political parties below.

Christian Democrats (*Christlich Demokratische Union/Christlich Soziale Union*, CDU/CSU)

The CDU/CSU is one of the two largest parties in Germany. As we learned above, the Christian Democrats were led by the first postwar chancellor, Adenauer, for many of West Germany's formative years. The CDU was created immediately after World War II everywhere in West Germany except Bavaria. Bavarian politicians wanted to set up their own wing of the newly founded Christian Democratic movement, the Christian Social Union (CSU). The two parties have generally cooperated as one party and are usually referred to as the CDU/CSU. The CSU tends to be more conservative than the CDU, however, and the rivalries between their leaders occasionally produce friction.

The Christian Democratic Party is a *Volkspartei* designed to appeal to a broad array of the population. To overcome the religious divisions of the Weimar period, party leaders sought to combine Catholics and Protestants into a single party that emphasized a free-market economy, Christian values, and social welfare programs, the so-called social market economy. It tends to be conservative on social issues. It was also founded on a strong anticommunist and pro-U.S. platform. It has moved to a more conservative neoliberal economic policy since the 1980s.

Social Democratic Party (*Sozialdemokratische Partei Deutschlands*, SPD)

The SPD is the oldest party in Germany and one of the country's two largest parties. It is the major party of the left. The party was founded in 1875 as a Marxist party to represent the working class. It was outlawed from 1878 to 1890 by Chancellor Otto von Bismarck for its revolutionary and antimonarchical sentiments, but by 1912 it had become the largest party in the Reichstag. The SPD played a key role in the Weimar Republic. It was one of the parties that made up the first government of the Weimar Republic in 1919. The SPD was banned under Hitler. Several of its most prominent figures spent a large part of the Nazi period in prisons or concentration camps; others fled the country.

At the end of the war, the party was reconstituted to represent the views of the working class and labor unions. It favored state ownership of firms and was opposed to Germany's postwar rearmament and adherence to NATO. The SPD found itself in the opposition during the early years of the Federal Republic and unable to garner more than about 30 percent of the vote. To broaden its electoral appeal, the party abandoned its socialist orientation at a party congress in Bad Godesberg in 1959. Its members formally accepted private enterprise and the market as the underlying bases of the Federal Republic's economy. They accepted the social market economy and agreed to work within the free enterprise system to improve the lot of the working class through nonconfrontational measures designed to promote cooperation between business and labor and social welfare programs. They also explicitly renounced their previous antireligious biases. In 1960 they also agreed to accept West Germany's rearmament and its membership in NATO.

These changes led the Social Democratic Party to become a *Volkspartei* with broad support across an array of classes in Germany. The SPD's support comes mainly from the largest cities in the northern and western parts of Germany and in Berlin and in Protestant rural and small town areas. It was in government in a Grand Coalition with the CDU/CSU from 2005 to 2009. But in the 2009 elections, its electoral support dropped to 23 percent of the vote and 162 seats. It is now in the opposition and is led by Sigmar Gabriel. The party chose Peer Steinbrück as the SPD's chancellor candidate for the 2013 election.

The Free Democratic Party (*Freie Demokratische Partei*, FDP)

The Free Democratic Party (FDP) is a small center party in Germany formed in 1948 under the leadership of Theodor Heuss, who was the first president of the Federal Republic. Its roots are in the liberal tradition, and it is often referred to as the Liberal Party or the Free Democrats. The party is committed to individual freedom, capitalism, secularism, and democracy.

It has links with Germany's private sector and business-oriented middle class.

The FDP's size belies its influence. Although it is a small party, averaging less than 10 percent of the national vote, it has played a critical role in the Federal Republic to the present day and has served in the government longer than any other party. The FDP has been a coalition partner of either the Christian Democrats or Social Democrats in almost every government formed at the national level between 1949 and 2013. The exceptions have been the Grand Coalition of the SPD and CDU/CSU from 1966 to 1969 and from 2005 to 2009 and the SPD's coalition with the Greens from 1998 to 2005.

The FDP benefited from unification because of the work of Hans-Dietrich Genscher, its foreign minister and vice chancellor. Genscher, who was born in East Germany but came to the west in 1952, played a critical role in the negotiations with the United States, Great Britain, France, and the Soviet Union over German unification. Genscher was the longest serving foreign minister in Germany, serving from 1974 to 1992. During the 1990s, however, the FDP's electoral fortunes declined. Although it continued to be represented in the Bundestag, it failed to meet the 5 percent threshold in several state elections in the early to mid-1990s. The FDP reassessed its policies and moved from the center to the center right. Under the leadership of Guido Westerwelle, who took over as the party chair in 2001 and served until 2011, it pursued a more conservative economic policy, focusing on privatization and liberalization, and a more assertive foreign policy. The party's electoral support surged to 10 percent and 63 Bundestag seats in the 2005 election and to 14.6 percent and 93 seats in the 2009 election, which were the best election results ever for the party. It has been the junior partner in Angela Merkel's CDU-led government since 2009. The FDP is currently chaired by Philipp Rösler, who was born in Vietnam and is the first Asian-born cabinet member in Germany. He has served as the minister of economics and technology and vice chancellor since 2011.

The Free Democratic Party is currently chaired by Philipp Rösler, who was born in Vietnam, and is the first Asian-born cabinet member in Germany.

Alliance '90/The Greens This party is the merger of two distinct party groups—the Green Party and Alliance '90. The Green Party first emerged on the German political scene in the late 1970s. It began as a social movement concerned with addressing quality of life issues such as environmentalism and disarmament that were not being addressed by the major parties or interest groups. It was a heterogeneous movement made up primarily of students, farmers, environmental and peace activists, and nuclear power opponents. These social groups formed a party in Germany in 1979. The founders of the Greens were particularly concerned with preserving the environment and preventing nuclear disasters. They called for the elimination of West Germany's nuclear power plants and the removal of American nuclear weapons from German territory. They were also very active in the peace movement that arose in the late 1970s and early 1980s when NATO moved to install a new generation of nuclear-armed missiles in Germany in response to the Soviet Union's deployment of new missiles aimed at Western Europe.

In 1983, the Greens cleared the Bundestag's 5 percent threshold and sent their first delegates to the German parliament, most of them attired in sandals and jeans. From the outset, the party was split between two camps. The "fundamentalists" (known as *Fundis*) tended to oppose industrialization itself as environmentally threatening; some of them favored the dismantling of factories and a ban on personal automobiles. They were opposed to collaboration with existing parties. The "realists" (*Realos*) wanted stronger environmental protections without destroying the German industrial economy and believed it was important to enter political institutions and work with other parties. Germany's unification in 1989–90 caught the Greens by surprise. Their abhorrence of patriotic sentiment as excessively nationalistic clashed with the public mood at the time, and they were voted out of the Bundestag in the elections of December 1990. Following this defeat and the death of Petra Kelly, one of the founders of the Green Party in 1992, the realist wing took control of the party under the leadership of Joschka Fischer.

Alliance '90 at first represented a collection of East German dissidents who were eager for democracy. After the 1990 elections, the group formed a joint party with the Greens known as *Alliance '90/The Greens*. Under Fischer's leadership, the new party accepted Germany's membership in the NATO alliance and the European Union. Alliance '90/The Greens entered a national coalition government with the Social Democrats after the 1998 election. Fischer became foreign minister. The red-green coalition won reelection in 2002 and the Greens were in power with the SPD until 2005. In 2009, they won 10.9 percent of the vote and 68 out of 622 seats in the Bundestag.

Although the Alliance '90/The Greens Party is situated on the left of Germany's political spectrum, it has a largely middle class following, with a high proportion of educators, civil servants, executives and specialists in technology companies, and social activists, who share their agenda. They do not appeal as much to the working class, the unemployed, pensioners, or eastern Germans. The party is currently led by Claudia Roth and Cem Özdemir.

HYPOTHESIS-TESTING EXERCISE
Post-Materialist Values and the Green Party

Chapter 9 discussed the emergence of post-materialist values in postindustrial societies. Instead of being motivated primarily by the need for financial security, many people who came of age in the 1960s and 1970s and thereafter tended to vote or engage in other forms of political behavior on the basis of broader concerns about the welfare of the community. The goals of urban renovation, environmental protection, and other communitywide considerations increasingly took precedence over personal wealth as a source of political behavior. These broader concerns we call *post*-materialist because they come after people need to be so concerned about meeting their material needs. Post-materialist parties have emerged in Europe, often originating as environmentally focused Green parties. Germany's Green Party has been the most successful example.

Hypothesis Germans who have post-materialist values will tend disproportionately to support the Green Party.

Variables The *independent variable* is post-materialist values. The *dependent variable*, what we want to explain, is party choice.

The World Values Survey asks questions designed to tap post-materialist values. The essential question asks:

People sometimes talk about what the aims of this country should be for the next 10 years. Below are listed some of the goals which different people would give top priority. Would you please say which one of these you, yourself, consider the most important? And which is the next most important?

1. A high level of economic growth.
2. Making sure this country has strong defense forces.
3. Seeing that people have more say about how things are done at their jobs and in their communities.
4. Trying to make our cities and countryside more beautiful.

From the two answers each respondent gives to this question we can categorize people. Those answering 1 and 2 are materialists; those who answer 3 and 4 are post-materialists. Those with other combinations of answers we label mixed.

The WVS also asks respondents which party they would vote for if an election were held tomorrow.

Evidence In 2005, Germans participating in the WVS responded to the above questions as shown in Table 15.5.

The table shows that of the major German party groups, Alliance '90/The Greens have the highest proportion of their supporters that evidence a post-materialist value system. While about 17 percent of Germans are post-materialists, 32 percent of those who would have voted for Alliance '90/The Greens in 2005 are post-materialists. It is also interesting to note the supporters of the two largest parties, the Christian Democrats and the Social Democrats, the parties that build the social market economy, are the most materialist in their orientation.

Conclusions The evidence in Table 15.5 supports our hypothesis: The Greens have a disproportionate share of voters that are post-materialists. Our hypothesis is confirmed.

It is important to note, though, that the Alliance '90/The Greens share of the sample here is very small—only 6 percent of the respondents. That means that more of the post-materialists who responded to this survey said they would vote for the Christian Democrats or the Social Democrats than would vote for the Greens. The other relatively new party of the left, the PDS (now merged into the Left Party), also is disproportionately supported by post-materialists. The rise of post-materialism in Germany may have encouraged the emergence of the Green Party, but most post-materialists actually support other parties.

Table 15.5 Materialism, Post-Materialism, and Party Choice in Germany

| Party Preference | SHARE OF PARTY VOTE FROM | | | |
	Materialists	Mixed	Post-Materialists	Percent of Sample
CDU/CSU	26%	58%	13%	24%
SPD	23	57	17	22
FDP	17	59	19	4
Alliance '90/The Greens	11	53	32	6
PDS	9	65	23	9
Far Right	13	61	18	2
Don't know/no answer/refused	20	61	16	29
Total	21	59	17	100

Source: World Values Survey, www.worldvaluessurvey.org.

The Left Party The **Left Party** was founded in 2007 as a result of the merger of the Party of Democratic Sociality (PDS), which was the successor of the Socialist Unity Party of East Germany, and the Electoral Alternative for Labor and Social Justice (WASG), an offshoot of the SPD. The Left Party combines two leftist alternatives to the mainstream political parties. The PDS was hastily formed out of the remnants of the GDR's ruling Communist Party, as the East German regime was falling apart in 1990. Under the leadership of Gregor Gysi, a dissident East German lawyer who had opposed the communist regime's dictatorial practices, the PDS accepted the rules of democracy. It immediately identified itself as the party that would seek to protect East Germans from unemployment, pension cuts, and other harsh realities of the disappearance of the communist state's welfare system. In 2002 the PDS fell below the 5 percent threshold, but it managed to send two directly elected delegates to the Bundestag thanks to a provision in the electoral law permitting exceptions to the threshold rule. As in previous elections, the PDS won the overwhelming majority of its votes in the former East Germany. Lothar Bisky, a moderate, succeeded Gysi as party chief.

In 2005 Oskar Lafontaine, the outspoken leader of the Social Democratic Party's left wing, bolted from the SPD in protest of Schröder's pro-business economic reform policies and formed a new group, the Electoral Alternative for Labor and Social Justice Party. This split has been one of the reasons for the decline in votes for the SPD and the ability of the CDU/CSU to remain the largest party. As the 2005 elections approached, Lafontaine and the Left Party joined forces in an electoral alliance, agreeing not to run candidates against each other. A number of leftist independents also adhered to the new grouping. They became the fourth largest party in the Bundestag as a result of that election with 8.7 percent of the national vote and 53 seats. Party leaders then negotiated a merger agreement and held a founding congress in Berlin in June 2007. Domestically, the party called for more expansionary fiscal and monetary policy. In foreign policy, they call for international disarmament and are opposed to Bundeswehr activity outside of Germany. In the Bundestag elections of 2009, the Left Party increased its share of the national vote further to 11.9 percent and 76 seats and remains the second largest opposition party.

The Left Party reaches out to working-class voters and those displaced by unemployment and other social problems, particularly those occurring in the former communist East Germany, where the Left Party has its base. The party has been controversial because of its roots in the Socialist Unity Party (SED) of East Germany and its decidedly leftist views. At the national level, neither the SPD nor the CDU/CSU has been willing to include the Left in a coalition government. At the state level, they are currently in the government with the SPD in Brandenburg.

The Far Right—The National Democratic Party of Germany (NPD), The People's Union (DVU), and the Republican Party (*Die Republikaner*)

Germany has three major far-right parties. The oldest far-right party is the National Democratic Party of Germany, which was founded in 1964. It is an antiimmigrant, German nationalist party. It is often referred to as a neo-Nazi party. In 2003, the federal government and legislature attempted to ban the NPD but failed. The case was thrown out by the Federal Constitutional Court. The NPD has never won seats in the Bundestag, although it did receive 4.3 percent of the national vote in 1969. It has won seats in state parliaments since 2000. In 2004, it won 9.2 percent of the vote in Saxony. It lost votes in Saxony in 2009, but still has representation in the state legislature there. In 2006, it won 7.3 percent of the vote in Mecklenburg-Western Pomerania.

The second far-right party is the Deutsche Volksunion (DVU) or German People's Union, which has its origins in the 1970s. It is a nationalist party. It first won representation in state legislatures in the 1990s and fared particularly well in eastern Germany. It won 13 percent of the vote in Saxony-Anhalt's state election in 1998. It has never won seats in the national legislature. Between 2004 and 2009, the NPD and DVU reached a noncompetition agreement, in which the two parties agreed not to compete against one another. The two parties agreed to merge in January 2011, but a regional court blocked the merger.

The Republican Party (Die Republikaner) is also a far-right nationalist party, founded in 1983. Its founders were dissidents from the CSU. It has an antiimmigrant and low tax, market liberalization platform. Unlike the NPD and DVU, which draw most of their support from eastern Germany, the Republican Party was most successful in the more affluent south, particularly in Bavaria and Baden-Württemberg. The Republican Party had seats in the state parliament of Baden-Württemberg until 2001. The party has not won seats in the national legislature and received only 0.4 percent of the vote in 2009. The Republicans have refused to join an alliance with the NPD and DVU.

The Pirate Party (*Piratenpartei Deutschland*)

The *Pirate Party* is the newest party in Germany. (Pirate Parties also operate in other European democracies.) It was established in 2006. Founded primarily by young people, the Pirate Party views itself as a party of the information age and was founded to promote freedom on the Internet and prevent its regulation by the government. It also promotes greater political transparency and direct democracy via the Internet. Its members vote on all policy positions via the Internet. The party received 2 percent of the vote in the national election of 2009 and has no seats in the Bundestag since it did not pass the 5 percent threshold. Since 2011, however, the party has won representation in four state legislatures. In 2011, it received 8.9 percent of the vote in the city-state election in Berlin and won 15 out of 141 seats in the legislature. Later that year, it received 7.4 percent of the vote in Saarland and received four seats. In 2012, it won 8.2 percent of the seats in the state election in Schleswig-Holstein and six seats. It also received 7.8 percent of the vote in the state elections in North Rhine-Westphalia and 20 seats. Its success, though, has forced the Pirate Party to consider how to organize to win representation in the Bundestag, an issue that has pitted those who seek to create a professional party organization against party members who joined the Pirates to avoid bureaucracy. Internal conflict threatens to sink the Pirate Party before it wins Bundestag seats.[20]

Established in 2006 primarily by young people, the Pirate Party is the newest party in Germany. It views itself as a party of the information age and was founded to promote freedom on the Internet and prevent its regulation by the government. It also promotes greater political transparency and direct democracy via the Internet.

Interest Groups in the Federal Republic

One of the most striking differences between Germany's postwar democracy and the disastrous Weimar Republic was the determination of the country's elites after World War II to strive for consensus on major political, economic, and social issues. Over the course of the 1950s, 1960s, and 1970s, the Federal Republic created a system of decision making known as neo-corporatism. As explained in Chapter 8, corporatism is a form of formal interest group representation in the state's decision-making processes. The form of corporatism that developed in West Germany after World War II was democratic in nature and included business and labor. It featured several elements that make it distinct from earlier forms of state-mandated corporatism and is thus labeled **neo-corporatism**.

The basic idea is simple: Representatives from Germany's main business association and trade unions sit down with government officials on a regular basis and map out the main lines of the country's economic and social welfare policies. Wage parameters, working conditions, paid vacation time, welfare benefits, profit margins—these and other labor-management issues are heavily influenced and often largely determined by these tripartite negotiations. The aims of neo-corporatism in a democracy are to widen participation in economic decision making and to reinforce socioeconomic stability by giving everyone a sense of where the economy should be heading over the coming years.

The Social Democrats, the main party of the working class, were particularly supportive of neo-corporatist mechanisms and expanded their scope when they were in power in the 1970s. They have been especially sensitive to the demands of the German Federation of Labor (*Deutscher Gewerkschaftsbund*, or DGB), which is the peak association of the labor movement that consists of 16 major trade unions. Even Christian Democrats and Free Democrats were often supportive of neo-corporatist arrangements because their backers in the business community benefited from the system's virtual guarantee of a productive workforce, moderate wage demands, and few strikes. The Christian Democrats and Free Democrats have close ties with peak associations representing big business such as the Federation of German Industry (*Bundesverband der Deutschen Industrie*, or BDI) as well as those representing smaller businesses and agricultural interests.[21]

This consensus decision making is credited with much of the economic stability that Germany enjoyed in the 1970s. In contrast to the stormy business–labor relationships that rocked Britain, France, and other European countries in the 1970s, the Federal Republic was an island of labor peace and enjoyed higher rates of growth and lower unemployment. But in the 1980s, after Helmut Kohl became chancellor, the government began backing away from corporatist procedures, preferring instead to rely on market forces to work themselves out without undue state interference.

Once the Berlin Wall opened and German reunification occurred, neo-corporatism made further retreats as individual firms sought to make separate agreements with employees to give themselves greater flexibility in a global market. Membership in labor unions has declined from a high of over 35 percent in 1950 to below 20 percent of the workforce today. Similarly, membership in employer associations has declined. While union and nonunion members are covered by collective agreements, only employers who are in employer associations are formally bound by sectoral negotiations. The decline of this form of consensus decision making has been accompanied by a more pluralist interest group organization and decision making.[22]

POLITICS IN UNIFIED GERMANY (1998–2013)

German Politics in the Berlin Republic

The formation of the SPD-Green coalition following the September 1998 elections broke new ground in German politics. It marked the ascendancy of Germany's postwar generation to the highest rungs of power. Gerhard Schröder, the new SPD chancellor, was born in 1944 and belonged to a generation that grew up in a democratic country, bearing no guilt for the collapse of democracy in the Weimar period or the crimes of Nazism. Joschka Fischer, the Greens' principal leader, was born in 1948. The new coalition marked the first time the Green Party had a role in the government.

The SPD-Green Coalition, 1998–2005

The red-green coalition turned out to be far more moderate than the two parties' previous leftist convictions would have foreshadowed. Its move to the center of the political spectrum was carefully guided by Chancellor Schröder.[23]

Schröder entered office with a mixture of neoliberal views favoring private-sector expansion and traditional Social Democratic positions favoring an active role for government in fostering social justice for the less advantaged. The new chancellor was also looking for ways to tame the uncontrolled forces of globalization. His finance minister and political ally, Oskar Lafontaine, the leader of the SPD's left wing, shared most of these views but favored larger infusions of government spending as a means to boosting overall demand and eventually reducing unemployment, a classic Keynesian recipe. When Schröder opposed this approach under pressure from large German corporations, Lafontaine quit the government and launched a broadside attack on Schröder's policies.[24] He eventually formed a splinter party that has now merged into the Left Party.

Schröder managed to secure his party's approval for several economic reforms that neoliberal economists considered vital to raising Germany's sluggish economic growth rate (which had been falling to the lowest level in Europe since 1994), to reducing unemployment, and to cutting the country's huge national debt. The reforms included major tax cuts for corporations and individuals, efforts to alleviate the country's overburdened pension system, and a short-term employment program aimed at creating 100,000 new jobs immediately for young people.

In addition to pursuing a centrist economic course, Schröder took a firm position in favor of engaging German military forces in world trouble spots. Germany's reluctance to use military force in areas where the country was not overtly threatened rested on a broad national consensus that included all the major parties. After the Dayton Accords brought peace to Bosnia-Herzegovina, Schröder sent German troops to the region as part of the international peacekeeping contingent. Germany also accepted several hundred thousand refugees from the war-torn area. In 1999, Germany participated in NATO's Kosovo campaign. And in a move that created heated controversy within his own party and among his coalition partners, the Greens, Schröder took the bold step of ordering up to 3,900 troops for duty in connection with the U.S.-led war in Afghanistan in the months that followed the events of September 11, 2001, bucking opposition from anti-war Social Democrats and Greens.

Voter dissatisfaction with the government's economic record, however, led to low approval ratings for Schröder's government as the 2002 elections approached. Contrary to Schröder's promise in 1998 to cut unemployment to no more than 3.5 million, 4 million Germans were still out of work. The Christian Democrats were poised to take advantage of the government's plight under their new standard-bearer, Edmund Stoiber. Stoiber headed the Christian Social Union (CSU), the Christian Democrats' Bavarian wing. As the chief of Bavaria's government since 1993, he had won acclaim for his state's enviable economic record, especially in high-technology development. The CDU/CSU chose Stoiber as the candidate for chancellor instead of Angela Merkel, the party chief of the CDU, because he was considered a stronger candidate.[25]

The Bush administration's resolve to invade Iraq and Schröder's opposition to it was a major factor in turning Schroeder's reelection campaign around. A majority of Germans opposed the war, in part because of the deep-seated pacifism that still shaped the country's political culture more than 50 years after World War II. Schröder eked out a victory on September 23, 2002. While the SPD lost 47 seats, they won more seats than the CDU/CSU. The Social Democrats were saved by their coalition partners, the Alliance '90/The Greens, who won eight new seats, bringing their total to 55 deputies in the Bundestag. With the 251 seats won by the Social Democrats, Schröder's red-green coalition had a total of 306 seats—a slender four-vote majority.

Schröder's major accomplishments in the second term were economic reforms. The economy's growth rate in 2002 was a feeble 0.2 percent and the unemployment rate topped 9.6 percent. Hourly wages in Germany exceeded the EU average and the costs of the contributions employers had to make to their employees' nonwage benefits package was, according to Schröder himself, "too high." In March 2003 Schröder unveiled a package of reforms known as "Agenda 2010." The reforms were based in part on recommendations by a government-sponsored commission headed by Peter Hartz, a Volkswagen executive. Introduced in phases starting in early 2003, the reforms initially sought to improve the state employment agency and create new types of "mini jobs" with lower tax and insurance obligations for employers. The final phase, known as Hartz IV, reduced the amount of time unemployed workers could receive full unemployment pay and lowered the monthly stipend for most of those qualified for unemployment compensation.

These and other reforms provoked considerable opposition from the Social Democratic Party's left wing and from trade unions. In mid-2003, Schröder threatened to resign if SPD deputies blocked passage of his reform program. He also had to work out compromises with the more business-friendly Christian Democrats, who controlled the Bundesrat. Once in effect, these various reform efforts scarcely made a dent in the unemployment rate, and economic growth remained sluggish. The government's budget deficits exceeded 3 percent of GDP, the level mandated for countries using the euro. (Ironically, it was the German government and its powerful central bank, the *Bundesbank*, that had insisted on the 3 percent ceiling when the euro was being created in the 1990s.) With opposition to Schröder's reforms mounting within his own party and few tangible results to show for them, the chancellor's popularity sank to historic laws. Within less than a year of his reelection, his approval rating was only 20 percent. A succession of SPD defeats in Landtag elections in 2004 and 2005 further weakened Schröder's stature. In May 2005, when the Social Democrats lost to the Christian Democrats and Free Democrats in North Rhine-Westphalia, Germany's most populous state and an SPD stronghold for 39 years, Schröder decided it was time to clear the air. He intentionally lost a Bundestag motion of confidence vote in order to trigger new Bundestag elections in the fall, one year ahead of schedule. This time his opponent would be Angela Merkel.

The Grand Coalition— CDU/CSU/SPD 2005–2009

The 2005 election was unusual in several respects. First, the CDU/CSU nominated Angela Merkel to be the Chancellor candidate, which was the first time one of the large parties had selected a woman for the top of its ticket. Second, the CDU began the campaign with a 21 percent lead over the SPD in the polls, but this lead evaporated over the course of the campaign, and they won only 1 percent more of the vote and four more seats than the SPD in the end. Third, neither of the coalitions– the SPD and Greens or the CDU/CSU and FDP won enough seats to hold a majority in the Bundestag. Both of the major parties and the Green Party lost seats. The only party to gain significantly was The Left, which was not viewed by the other parties as a possible coalition partner at the federal level.

Both of the main parties claimed victory in the election although neither had a majority with its preferred coalition partner to rule. The inconclusive electoral results left the SPD and CDU/CSU with little choice but to begin negotiations to form a Grand Coalition. On October 10, they reached an agreement in which Angela Merkel became Chancellor and the Cabinet positions were equally divided between the two parties. The Social Democrats gained control of two of the most powerful ministries–the Foreign and Finance ministries. Merkel became the first female Chancellor of Germany after her election by the Bundestag on November 22. Many analysts believed this coalition would not last long given the differences between the two parties. However, Merkel was able to navigate and mediate the differences between the parties. While the government did not produce many wide-ranging reforms, the coalition was more harmonious than most analysts expected. Chancellor Merkel and the Social Democratic Vice Chancellor, Frank-Walter Steinmeier, worked together to pass two economic stimulus programs worth a total of €81 billion

($119.9 billion) in response to the financial crisis in 2008. Prior to that, it had introduced the biggest tax increase in post-war Germany in January 2007 by increasing sales tax three percentage points to 19 percent in order to rein in a budget deficit. It also managed to raise the pension age to 67 from 65 to help offset the rising costs of its aging population. At the same time, it was less successful at tackling the rising costs of health care and restructuring its banking system.

While many analysts thought the Grand Coalition would not last the full four-year term, Chancellor Merkel was able to find common ground with the SPD on a number of economic and foreign policy issues. Her pragmatic approach allowed the government to stay in power for the full four-year term.

PROFILES   Angela Merkel

Angela Merkel became chancellor of Germany in 2005.

"I'm an optimist," Angela Merkel declared. "Change does not frighten me." Merkel, who grew up in East Germany and became Germany's first female chancellor in 2005, has not only been a witness to much change in Germany but a catalyst for change in Germany and the EU. Her political rise was rapid and unexpected. Born in 1954 in Hamburg, she moved to East Germany as a baby after her father, a newly ordained minister in the Lutheran church, was assigned to a small parish in Templin, 50 miles north of Berlin. She studied physics at the University of Leipzig, receiving a doctorate. She worked for 12 years as a researcher.

Merkel did not take part in the anti-regime demonstrations that fanned across East Germany in 1989, nor did she join any of the early protest groups that emerged from the dissident Protestant churches and intellectual circles. But after the opening of the Berlin Wall in November 1989, she joined an East German group called *Demokratischer Aufbruch*, a small gathering of people looking for a coherent orientation and policy program, becoming the group's unofficial press secretary. As the first free East German elections approached in March 1990, *Demokratischer Aufbruch* formed an electoral

alliance with the Christian Democrats. After the election Merkel became the new government's deputy press secretary. She learned her new responsibilities on the job and won an instant reputation as one of the best informed and most approachable figures in the government.

Just before reunification in October 1990, Merkel joined the CDU and then successfully ran for Bundestag in Germany's first post-unification election held in December 1990. Her ascent up the political ladder accelerated. She became one of Chancellor Kohl's protégées. In only her first term in the Bundestag she served as Germany's minister for women and youth affairs (1991–94). She became minister for the environment, one of the most politically sensitive posts in the German government, in Kohl's next cabinet, winning international respect for her contributions to the U.N. Climate Conference in Berlin in 1995 and the Kyoto conference on greenhouse emissions in 1997.

In 1998, after the Kohl government went down to defeat, Merkel was elected the CDU's new general secretary, the number two leadership position in the party behind the party chairman. When a political scandal brought down Kohl and the CDU's leader, Wolfgang Schäuble, in 1999, Merkel was elected as the CDU's new chair in 2000. Merkel worked to restore voter confidence in the party and to stave off the party's bankruptcy in the face of more than $20 million in fines related to Kohl's financial improprieties.

Merkel became the party's chancellor candidate in 2005. After that election, neither the SPD/Green coalition nor the CDU/CDU and its preferred coalition partner, the Free Democratic Party (FDP), held enough seats to form a majority in the Bundestag. Both the SPD's Gerhard Schröder and Merkel claimed victory. After three weeks of negotiations, a grand coalition was formed with Merkel as chancellor. This grand coalition government, which lasted from 2005 to 2009, included her own party, the CDU; its Bavarian sister party,

(Continued on next page)

(Continued from previous page)

the CSU; and the Social Democratic Party. Much of the focus of that government was on the country's pressing economic problems including reducing unemployment and dealing with Germany's increasing national debt. Merkel's ability to mediate between the two major parties along with the economic recovery in Germany helped fuel her popularity. In the 2009 federal election, the CDU obtained the largest share of the votes and formed a coalition government with the CSU and the liberal FDP.

Merkel was named the most powerful woman in the world by *Forbes* in 2011 in part because of her ability to steer Germany out of a recession and her leadership within the European Union. Her style has been cautious, unflashy, and

pragmatic. She seeks to work as a consensus builder. She favors strong trans-Atlantic relations with the United States and wants a strong Europe and strong Germany. But she is also unwilling to sacrifice German interests. Germany decided not to join France and Britain in the NATO campaign against Libya's Muammar Gaddafi. Within the EU, she played a central role in negotiating the Treaty of Lisbon. More recently, during Europe's financial crisis Merkel helped to negotiate the bailouts for Greece and Spain. She does not want to see the euro fail or to walk away from European integration, which have benefited Germany, but she faces domestic pressure not to provide more public funding for bailing out other countries.

As the 2009 elections approached, both parties made clear their intention to try to form governments with other parties. The CDU/CSU entered the election saying it would prefer a coalition with the pro-business, liberal FDP, while the SPD looked to form a new government with the Greens.

The 2009 Election

The 2009 election was marked by increasing political fragmentation among the political parties and declining electoral participation. Electoral participation in Germany has traditionally been strong. During much of the 1950s, 1960s, and 1970s, it was more than 80 percent. It began to decline in the mid-1980s and reached a low of 65 percent in 2009. Traditionally, there have also not been volatile electoral swings. But in the 2009 election, the two major parties lost significant shares of the vote. Whereas the SPD and CDU together received 69 percent of the vote in 2005, in 2009 their vote share fell to 58 percent.[26] The SPD's decline was the steepest. Its vote share fell to 23 percent in 2009 from 34 percent in 2005. The smaller parties were the main beneficiaries. The FDP had 15 percent of the vote, up from just under 10 percent in 2005; the Left Party earned 12 percent of the vote, up from less than 9 percent in 2005 and Alliance '90/ the Greens vote share was almost 11 percent, up from 8 percent in 2005.[27] In part this loss stems from a belief among voters that the two parties are too similar in their approach, particularly since they were in a Grand Coalition from 2005 to 2009, and agreed on several economic and foreign policy issues. Moreover, the SPD has been on a more moderate path since the Schröder government, and it suffered vote losses from a split by its left-wing activists, who have joined the Left Party.

After the election, Merkel formed a coalition government with the FDP. The first several months of her government were marked by strife between the coalition partners, particularly over tax cuts and health care reforms. But the FDP has suffered more as a result of this strife than the CDU. An Emnid

poll in May 2012 showed that the FDP's support level had dropped to 4 percent, below the 5 percent necessary to clear the electoral threshold were elections to occur. CDU support was at 34 percent. Merkel, on the other hand, received credit for helping to guide Germany well through the financial crisis and for her leading role in seeking to save the euro. According to a public opinion poll in the summer of 2012, 70 percent of Germans felt Merkel was the best person to save the euro. Another survey showed that if Germans could vote for the head of government directly, 49 percent of Germans would choose Merkel.[28] Merkel was to face Peer Steinbrück, the SPD's former finance minister in the Grand Coalition government, in the 2013 election.

ISSUES IN CONTEMPORARY GERMAN POLITICS

As Germany moved to the end of the second Merkel government and toward the 2013 elections, the country faced a challenging array of problems. These included restructuring economic and social programs to deal with the aging population, globalization, and the debt; forging a more unified identity as a nation-state that includes both Germans living in the eastern portion of the state and the influx of non-Germans; and dealing with the continuing euro crisis in the European Union and seeking to maintain its commitment to European integration.

Restructuring the Economy and Social Welfare Programs

Germany weathered the financial crisis much better than most countries in Europe. Its unemployment rate, for example, was 5.5 percent in August 2012, lower than the 8.1 percent in the United States and the higher rates in much of Europe. Its economy also grew in 2011 and 2012, unlike many European economies. However, the German economy faces a number of challenges. Growth was expected to slow by the end of 2012 as Europe's sovereign-debt crisis slowed demand for Germany's export trade (for more on the sovereign-debt crisis, see below). Germany is also experiencing sluggish to zero job growth. Germany will have to continue to look for new markets and work to resolve financial problems in the euro zone to maintain its growth rates.

Germany also has an aging population and a below replacement birthrate, which are major challenges for the country's social welfare and family policy. The number of young people who are working is decreasing while the number of elderly people is rising and their life expectancy is increasing. In the early 1990s, there were almost three people of employable age for every person over 60. In the early 2000s, the ratio was only 2.2 persons of employable age for each German of retirement age, and it is expected to worsen.[29] As a result of these trends, the German government has already moved to raise the retirement age and change the pension scheme so that people have to contribute more on their own. It is also seeking to increase the child benefit allowance and to invest more money in kindergartens and day care facilities.

Maintaining the social welfare state and economic growth are considered vital to the stability of the German political system and hence government will have to further reform health care, pension, social welfare, and family policies to meet the changing demographics while seeking to prevent increasing social inequalities.

Immigration and Ethnic Diversity

"Germany is not a classical immigration society," Angela Merkel has said, echoing the words of a report by a government-sponsored commission. However, the German population has become increasingly heterogeneous. Approximately 7 million of Germany's 82 million inhabitants are legally considered foreigners. About 2.5 million are descendants of "guest workers" from Turkey who, along with workers from other countries, flocked to West Germany in the 1960s as the Federal Republic's long postwar economic miracle gathered steam. Others are refugees from war-torn Yugoslavia or ethnic Germans who lived for generations in the former Soviet Union and other eastern European countries, but came to Germany as communism collapsed. Still others are asylum seekers from Africa, Asia, and other corners of the globe who seek to escape persecution in their native countries. Nearly 90,000 people a year seek asylum in Germany—the highest number seeking entry to any European country. According to the United Nations Population Fund, Germany has the third highest number of international migrants worldwide behind the United States and Russian Federation.[30] Tens of thousands of immigrants have come to Germany every year to fill job vacancies.

Historically, Germans have tended to define their nationality in strictly ethnic terms: To be a German citizen, one had to have German blood. Thus, ethnic Germans from the states of the former Soviet Union and Eastern Europe were automatically granted citizenship, but many Turks and other foreigners, who had lived in Germany for many years, and their children, who were born in Germany, were not citizens. Germany has relaxed its citizenship requirements. Starting in 2000, a new law grants German citizenship at birth to children born of non-German parents, as long as one parent has resided in Germany at least eight years. (Every year about 100,000 children are born in Germany to non-German citizens.) In addition, the waiting period for acquiring German citizenship through naturalization procedures was reduced from 15 years to 8 for those who have a valid residence permit.[31] This law has made it easier for foreigners to acquire full rights as German citizens and it led to an initial increase in the number of naturalizations of foreigners in Germany in the early 2000s.

Relaxed citizenship requirements in Germany have made it possible for many children born to resident non-Germans to be recognized as German from birth. One significant group of new German citizens can trace their origins to Turkey.

The rise of international terrorism and the war in Iraq heightened public concern about immigrants. Three of the terrorists involved in the September 11 attacks had previously lived in Germany. According to government estimates, there were approximately 31,000 Islamic extremists living in Germany in 2003. In the summer of 2006, when the World Cup soccer championship was taking place in Germany, police found suitcase bombs in two German trains; the bombs were timed to detonate but failed to go off. Within a few days the authorities arrested two Arab suspects who had been living in Germany before fleeing to Lebanon immediately after setting the bombs.

In 2012 approximately 4 million Muslims were living in Germany. A survey published in 2006 revealed that 66 percent of Germany's Muslims considered themselves Muslims first and German citizens second. For their part, 59 percent of Germans regarded immigration from the Middle East and North Africa as a "bad thing"—a much higher figure than in Britain (32 percent) or France (41 percent). And 82 percent of the general public in Germany was concerned about the rise of Islamic extremism in their country (compared with 77 percent in Britain and 76 percent in France). Three out of four Germans believed that Muslims who reside in their country want to be distinct from the rest of society (as opposed to about two-thirds of the British and slightly more than half the French).[32] Germany's Federal Constitutional Court has ruled that German states have the right to enact legislation banning head scarves in public schools. A spring 2008 survey found that unfavorable opinions of Muslims, as well as Jews, have increased. The survey found that 50 percent of Germans rated Muslims unfavorably, up from 46 percent in 2004. It also shows that 25 percent of Germans expressed negative opinions of Jews, up from 20 percent in 2004. In general the survey found that anti-Muslim and anti-Jewish opinions were more common among older people and those with less education.[33]

A darker side to these ethnocentric attitudes is the violence aimed at foreigners in recent years, perpetrated by a fanatically prejudiced minority. A neo-Nazi cell has been credited with the deaths of eight Turkish and one Greek immigrant between 2000 and 2006 and the death of a German policewoman in 2007.[34] The National Democratic Party (NPD), an ultra-right antiimmigrant party, holds seats in 2 of Germany's 16 state legislatures. The DVU, another nationalist, antiimmigrant party, holds seats in one state legislature. Both parties fell well short of the 5 percent threshold in the Bundestag elections in the 2005 and 2009 elections. In the years ahead, Germany's small but growing ethnic and religious minorities will likely pose challenges not only to the broader population's security but also to its commitment to tolerance and inclusion.

European Integration and the Euro Zone Crisis

Germany has been a strong advocate for European integration since the European Union's inception in the early postwar period. Germany was one of the founding members of the European Coal and Steel Community and the European Economic Community, and it played a significant role in supporting the removal of trade barriers in Europe during the 1980s and 1990s and in creating monetary union in the 1990s.

Since 2009, several members of the euro zone (the countries in the European Union that have adopted the euro as their currency) have found themselves in a sovereign-debt crisis.[35] They are unable to finance their government debt. The crisis started in Greece in late 2009, when the Greek government revised its fiscal deficit from 6 percent for the fiscal year 2009–10 to 12.7 percent. It became clear that Greece's budget deficit and its overall debt were not sustainable. This led credit agencies to downgrade Greek debt in 2010 and made it difficult for Greece to borrow money. The country could not pay its public obligations. Greece got into this situation because it ran fiscal deficits and increased its share of government spending between 2001 and 2009. It also suffered from high tax evasion rates. The Greek government had borrowed money every year from private and foreign markets to finance deficit and roll over debt that it could not repay. Banks across Europe including in Germany continued to lend the Greek government money at rates that its economy did not merit on its own.

If Greece was not a member of the European Union's monetary union, it could have resolved this crisis by devaluing its currency. But Greece had given up its currency in 2001 to join the euro zone. In 2010, Germany and the other countries of the European Union had to decide whether to allow Greece to go bankrupt or to rescue it. In May 2010, the euro zone's countries and the International Monetary Fund, agreed to a €110 billion rescue package on the condition that Greece undertake austerity measures.

Unfortunately, this was not enough. A second bailout with another austerity package had to be worked out in late 2011. Greece was asked to make cuts of €11.5 billion or 5 percent of GDP, including pension cuts, reductions in public services, and tax increases as a condition for EU aid. This led to widespread demonstrations in Greece in 2012.

The financial crisis spread to other countries in the European Union. Ireland, Spain, Portugal, and Italy also faced difficulties financing their debt although the causes of their debt crises differed from those in Greece. The members of the European Union also negotiated financial assistance for these countries.

Chancellor Merkel played a leading role in the negotiations to negotiate financial assistance for these countries and to prevent countries from leaving the euro zone. Germany's economy is the strongest and largest in the EU and it is contributing the most to resolve Europe's financial crisis. Its export industries have benefited significantly from the euro zone since 40 percent of its exports go to other EU member states.[36] German banks lent substantial amounts of money to the Greek government. But German taxpayers are also reluctant to bail out other countries. For many Germans, the European financial crisis is due to Greece's overspending during the past decade. While Germany undertook labor market, tax, and social welfare reforms over the past two decades that led to lower wages, increased charges for health care, lower pensions, and more flexible labor markets, other countries did not. Germany therefore has grown faster in the past decade than other euro zone countries. Germans fear that they will have to bail out all of the troubled economies in Europe and that such expenditures will threaten German prosperity.

Chancellor Merkel pushed for harsh austerity measures in return for aid and has been reticent to support sharing the debt through the sale of Eurobonds. This led to resentment in other euro zone countries. In a visit to Greece in October 2012, Merkel was greeted by protesters who argued that she was seeking to ruin Greece and establish German dominance over Europe through its economic and financial clout. Protesters and Greek commentators have referred to Merkel and her finance minister, Wolfgang Schaubele, as Nazis.

Chancellor Merkel is in a difficult position. Some of the difficulties of this financial crisis are due to the single currency.[37] When it was created in 1992, there was no mechanism for bailing out countries in trouble. Germans are committed to European integration and to monetary union. It has benefited their terms of trade with other members of the European Union. German banks have also heavily invested in other EU economies including Greece. But they also fear that they will end up having to transfer much of their wealth to other countries to secure financial stability in the euro zone. Germany will have to play a key role in resolving this crisis and working to create further political and financial integration in the European Union, which has played a key role in maintaining peace on the European continent for the past 60 years. The role played by Merkel and the assessment of it by German voters will surely play a big part in determining who prevails in the 2013 German elections.

Conclusion

In the decades since World War II, the Federal Republic of Germany has achieved considerable success in adopting the core values of democracy and in solidifying the rule of law. It has also succeeded in further developing popular sovereignty, guaranteeing rights and liberties, extending social welfare, and achieving a high level of economic well-being that is widely shared across the population. Postwar Germany has also fulfilled, in varying degrees, all 10 conditions for democracy enumerated in Chapter 7. One of Germany's biggest problems today centers on the need to forge a broader sense of national unity, one that embraces the "Ossies" of the former East Germany as well as people of non-German origin who wish to be full participants in the country's increasingly heterogeneous society. Another problem is that of ensuring the well-being of the entire populace on the basis of fairness and community welfare while addressing the pressures of globalization, domestic financial challenges and the sovereign-debt crisis in the euro zone. Though they may differ on how these challenges should be addressed, Germany's mainstream political leaders appear to be fully committed to meeting them.

Germany has made extraordinary strides in the postwar era in building and sustaining a viable democratic system. When viewed against the mistakes of the past—especially the failures of the Weimar Republic and the atrocities of Nazism—Germany's success provides important lessons for peoples who seek to replace the terrors of dictatorship with the benefits of stable democracy.

Key Terms

Social Democratic Party of Germany (SPD)
Weimar Republic
National Socialist Workers' Party (Nazis)
Basic Law
Federal Republic of Germany
German Democratic Republic (GDR)
Social market economy
Christian Democratic Union (CDU)
Christian Social Union (CSU)
Free Democratic Party (FDP)
Codetermination
Grand Coalition
States (*Länder*)
Bundestag
Mixed member proportional representation (MMP)
5 percent threshold
Bundesrat
Chancellor
Constructive vote of confidence
Federal Constitutional Court
The Greens
Left Party
Neo-corporatism

Notes

1. Joshua Mitchell, "Protestant Thought and Republican Spirit: How Luther Enchanted the World," *American Political Science Review* 86, no. 3 (September 1992), pp. 688–95. On later developments, see Max Weber, *The Protestant Ethic and the Spirit of Capitalism*, trans. Talcott Parsons (London: Routledge, 1992).
2. William Sheridan Allen, *The Nazi Seizure of Power*, rev. ed. (New York: Franklin Watts, 1985); Sheri Berman, "Civil Society and the Collapse of the Weimar Republic," *World Politics* 49, no. 3 (April 1997), pp. 401–29.
3. Richard F. Hamilton, *Who Voted for Hitler?* (Princeton, NJ: Princeton University Press, 1982); Thomas Childers, *The Nazi Voter* (Chapel Hill, NC: University of North Carolina Press, 1983).
4. Sheri Berman, *The Social Democratic Movement* (Cambridge, MA: Harvard University Press, 1998); Anton Kaes, Martin Jay, and Edward Dimendberg, eds., *The Weimar Republic Sourcebook* (Berkeley, CA: University of California Press, 1994); David Abraham, *The Collapse of the Weimar Republic*, 2nd ed. (New York: Holmes & Meier, 1986).
5. Erich Fromm, *Escape from Freedom* (New York: Holt, Rinehart, and Winston, 1941); Bertram Schaffner, *Fatherland: A Study of Authoritarianism in the German Family* (New York: Columbia University Press, 1948); T. W. Adorno et al., *The Authoritarian Personality* (New York: Harper, 1950).
6. Kurt Dietrich Bracher, *The German Dictatorship* (New York: Praeger, 1970); David Schoenbaum, *Hitler's Social Revolution* (New York: W. W. Norton, 1980).

7. In addition to being divided into West Germany and East Germany after the war, Germany lost a considerable amount of territory to its eastern neighbors. The Soviet Union, whose armies occupied the region, gave some parts of Germany to Poland, including the cities of Danzig (now Gdansk) and Stettin (Szczecin) and the industrial region of Silesia. The USSR annexed the city of Koenigsberg and its surrounding region, renaming it Kaliningrad. It is still part of Russia. The Soviets also restored the Sudetenland to Czechoslovakia. In 1938 Hitler had annexed this region, with its large German population, winning British and French acceptance of his action at the Munich conference.

8. John H. Backer, *The Decision to Divide Germany* (Durham, NC: Duke University Press, 1978); Norman M. Naimark, *The Russians in Germany* (Cambridge, MA: Belknap, 1995); Henry Krisch, *German Politics Under Soviet Occupation* (New York: Columbia University Press, 1972); Ann L. Phillips, *Soviet Policy Toward East Germany Reconsidered* (Westport, CT: Greenwood, 1986).

9. David P. Conradt, "Changing German Political Culture," in *The Civic Culture Revisited*, ed. Gabriel A. Almond and Sidney Verba (Boston: Little, Brown, 1980), pp. 212–72; Kendall L. Baker, Russell J. Dalton, and Kai Hildebrandt, *Germany Transformed* (Cambridge, MA: Harvard University Press, 1981).

10. On Soviet–German relations from 1963 to unification in 1990, see Michael J. Sodaro, *Moscow, Germany, and the West from Khrushchev to Gorbachev* (Ithaca, NY: Cornell University Press, 1990).

11. Willy Brandt, *My Life in Politics* (New York: Viking, 1992); Willy Brandt, *People and Politics: The Years 1960–1975*, trans. J. Maxwell Brownjohn (Boston: Little, Brown, 1978); Barbara Marshall, *Willy Brandt: A Political Biography* (New York: St. Martin's Press, 1997).

12. Helmut Schmidt, *Men and Powers: A Memoir*, trans. Ruth Hein (New York: Random House, 1989); Jonathan Carr, *Helmut Schmidt: Helmsman of Germany* (London: Weidenfeld Nicholson, 1985).

13. Karl Hugo Pruys, *Kohl, Genius of the Present*, trans. Kathleen Bunten (Chicago: Edition q, 1996).

14. Local government in Germany is based on some 16,000 cities, towns, and villages; all have elected councils and have various responsibilities for schools, fire safety, sanitation, and other activities. All but about 100 of these communities (*Gemeinden*) fall within county (*Kreis*) administrations. Though local and county governments may raise some of their revenue locally, most of it comes in the form of grants from the federal and state governments.

15. Another provision of the electoral laws is the "three-mandate waiver" rule. If a party fails to clear the 5 percent hurdle *but wins at least three district mandates*, the hurdle clause is waived and it is entitled to a share of Bundestag seats in proportion to its share of the second vote. If the PDS had won a third district mandate in 2002, it would have been entitled to 4 percent of the seats in the Bundestag, its share of the party-list vote nationwide.

16. The Federal Returning Officer, "Representative Electoral Statistics of the 2009 Bundestag Election," February 5, 2010 at http://www .bundeswahlleiter.de/en/bundestagswahlen/BTW_BUND_09/presse/ 77_Repr_WStat.html.

17. Peter Katzenstein, *Policy and Politics in West Germany: The Growth of a Semi-Sovereign State?* (Philadelphia: Temple University Press, 1987). On federalism and other aspects of Germany's institutions, see Oscar W. Gabriel and Everhard Holtmann, eds., *Handbuch politisches System der Bundesrepublik Deutschland*, 2nd ed. (Munich: R. Oldenbourg, 1999).

18. In the event that the parties cannot agree on a chancellor, the president may have some discretion in picking someone of his or her own choice; even then, however, the Bundestag majority would have to agree. The president co-signs all bills before they become law, but has no veto power; the signature is usually automatic.

19. Donald Kommers, *The Federal Constitutional Court* (Washington, DC: American Institute for Contemporary German Studies, 1994); Donald Kommers, *The Constitutional Jurisprudence of the Federal Republic of Germany* (Durham, NC: Duke University Press, 1989).

20. "'Liquid Democrazy': Pirate Party Sinks amid Chaos and Bickering," *Der Spiegel*, February 18, 2013, http://www.spiegel.de.

21. In addition to BDI (*Bundesverband der deutschen Industrie*), the business community's peak associations include the Federation of German Employer Associations (BDA) and the German Industrial and Trade Conference (DIHT). Germany's 2.5 million farmers are represented mainly by three highly influential associations that together call themselves the "Green Front" (although they are not related to the Green Party). They are the Farmer's League, the Association of Agricultural Chambers, and a cooperative organization, the *Raiffeisenverband*.

22. For a discussion of the changes in the German political economy, see Wolfgang Streeck, *Re-Forming Capitalism* (Oxford: Oxford University Press, 2010), esp. chs. 2, 3, and 6.

23. See Volker Herres and Klaus Waller, *Gerhard Schröder: der Weg nach Berlin* (Munich: Econ and List, 1998); Reinhard Urschel, *Gerhard Schröder: eine Biographie* (Stuttgart: Deutscher Verlags-Anstalt, 2002).

24. For Lafontaine's views, see his book, *The Heart Beats on the Left*, trans. Ronald Taylor (Cambridge: Polity, 2000). On the SPD's situation during the Kohl years, see Fritz Scharpf, *Crisis and Choice in European Social Democracy* (Ithaca, NY: Cornell University Press, 1991). See also "The Parties Are Ripe for Realignment," *The Economist*, February 6, 1999.

25. Michael Stiller, *Edmund Stoiber: der Kandidat* (Munich: Econ, 2002).

26. Frank Decker and Jared Sonnicksen, "Coalitions and Camps in the German Party System After the 2009 Bundestag Election," *German Politics and Society* 28, no. 3 (Fall 2010).

27. Data from the 2009 election is from Forschungsgruppe Wahlen e.V. Mannheim available at http://www.forschungsgruppe.de/Wahlen/ Wahlanalysen/Newsl_BTW09.pdf.

28. Jochen Hung, "Why Germans Love the Enigmatic Angela Merkel," *The Guardian*, August 15, 2012, http://www.guardian.co.uk/commentisfree/ 2012/aug/15/why-germans-love-enigmatic-angela-merkel.

29. "Demographic Trends," *Facts About Germany*, http://www.tatsachen -ueber-deutschland.de/en/society/main-content-08/demographic-trends .html.

30. UN Population Division, "Trends in Total Migrant Stock: The 2005 Revision,"(POP/DB/IG/Rev.2005/DOC), p. 11, as cited in UNFPA, *State of the World Population 2006*, ch. 1, http://www.unfpa.org/ swp/2006/english/chapter_1/index.html.

31. For a discussion of the recent changes in German citizenship law, see Marc Howard, *The Politics of Citizenship in Europe* (New York: Cambridge University Press, 2009), pp. 119–47. For a discussion of Germany's earlier citizenship law see Rogers Brukbaker, *Citizenship and Nationhood In France and Germany* (Cambridge, MA: Harvard University Press, 1992).

32. "Muslims in Europe: Economic Worries Top Concerns About Religious and Cultural Identity: 13-Nation Pew Global Attitudes Survey," July 6, 2006, available at www.pewglobal.org.

33. Pew Global Attitudes Survey, "Unfavorable Views of Both Jews and Muslims Increase in Europe," September 2008, http://www.pewglobal .org/2008/09/17/unfavorable-views-of-jews-and-muslims-on-the- increase-in-europe/.

34. Katya Adler, "Germany's New Breed of Neo-Nazis Pose a Threat," BBC News, March 27, 2012, http://www.bbc.co.uk/news/world-europe-17514394.

35. For a history of the crisis and its implications, see "Staring into the Abyss," *The Economist*, November 12, 2011.

36. See, for example, Brigitte Young and Willi Semmler, "The European Sovereign Debt Crisis. Is Germany to Blame?" *German Politics and Society* 29, no. 1 (Spring 2011), pp. 1–24.

37. Andrew Moravcsik, "Europe After the Crisis," *Foreign Affairs* 91, no. 3 (May/June 2012), pp. 54–68.

16 Russia

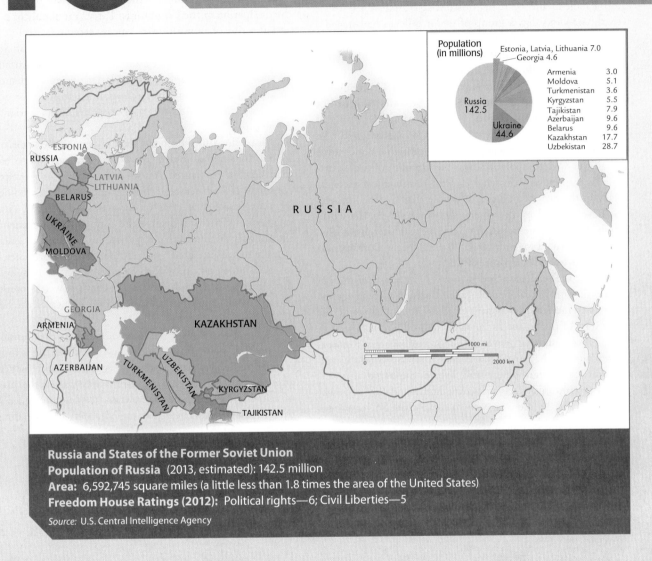

Population (in millions)

Estonia, Latvia, Lithuania	7.0
Georgia	4.6
Armenia	3.0
Moldova	5.1
Turkmenistan	3.6
Kyrgyzstan	5.5
Tajikistan	7.9
Azerbaijan	9.6
Belarus	9.6
Kazakhstan	17.7
Uzbekistan	28.7

Russia 142.5
Ukraine 44.6

Russia and States of the Former Soviet Union
Population of Russia (2013, estimated): 142.5 million
Area: 6,592,745 square miles (a little less than 1.8 times the area of the United States)
Freedom House Ratings (2012): Political rights—6; Civil Liberties—5

Source: U.S. Central Intelligence Agency

OVERVIEW

- Russia entered the twentieth century under the severely autocratic rule of the Romanov dynasty, with no experience of democracy and conditions highly unfavorable to democracy.

- Lenin and the Bolshevik Party imposed communist rule during the Russian Revolution, creating the Union of Soviet Socialist Republics from the remnants of the Russian Empire.

- Stalin mobilized Soviet society for rapid industrialization by establishing a centrally planned economy, nationalizing property, and collectivizing agriculture.

- Those who resisted Stalin's plan were imprisoned in labor camps or killed.

- Post-Stalinist rulers sought to soften the totalitarian regime but failed to reform unproductive features of the communist economy, leading to stagnation in the 1980s.

- Gorbachev's attempt to restructure Soviet society led him to sponsor liberalizing reforms, but he lost control of the processes of change, leading to the regime's collapse and the dissolution of the Soviet Union.

- Putin's Russia has seen a retreat from liberalization as Putin rules with very few constraints on power and with popular acclaim.

SCENES FROM POST-SOVIET RUSSIA

Seven scenes illustrate the dramatic transformations that have swept through Russia since the early 1990s, capping a century of revolutionary change.

In scene one, Boris Yeltsin (1931–2007)—the first person ever elected president of Russia by popular vote—stands atop a tank in the heart of Moscow. It is August 19, 1991. On the previous day, a group of senior officials had staged a coup against the government of the Soviet Union and placed its chief, President Mikhail Gorbachev (1931–), under house arrest. Under the Soviet constitution, Yeltsin was legally subordinate to Gorbachev. Russia was just one of 15 "republics" that constituted the **Union of Soviet Socialist Republics** (the **USSR**, or **Soviet Union**). Yeltsin was president only of Russia, while Gorbachev was president of the whole Soviet Union. But Russia, sprawling across 11 time zones and home to half the Soviet population, was the USSR's political heartland. As its popularly chosen president, Yeltsin enjoyed a legitimacy in the eyes of millions of people that Gorbachev, who was never elected by the voters, did not have. As the world watched in amazement, power was up for grabs in the USSR, a dictatorship ruled for more than 70 years by the **Communist Party of the Soviet Union (CPSU)**.

The coup leaders included some of the most prominent figures in Gorbachev's regime. Their decision to turn against their supreme leader was motivated by their dismay at the sorry state of the Soviet Union as a result of Gorbachev's policies. Since assuming power in 1985, Gorbachev's attempts to restructure the Soviet state, revitalize its economy, and reorient its foreign policy had led to the rapid unraveling of Communist Party power at home and Soviet power abroad. While he did not wish to replace the Soviet system with a full-blown Western democracy, he believed that he could humanize communist rule through the "restructuring" of state institutions. In place of an implacable dictatorship run by a handful of CPSU oligarchs, Gorbachev called for "democratization" and "openness" in the party's dealings with the population. The consequences of policies intended to restructure the state and the economy were plain to see: the dissipation of the Communist Party's monopoly of power and the rise of oppositionist voices; economic decline and organizational confusion; and the disintegration of Soviet hegemony in Central and Eastern Europe, where communist dictatorships were replaced by Western-oriented democracies. The coup plotters were determined to halt the Soviet system's headlong slide and restore strong authoritarian rule at the top.

But Yeltsin unexpectedly took charge of the situation as soon as the coup unfolded. An advocate of even more reform than Gorbachev wanted, Yeltsin was resolved to prevent the conspirators from reestablishing dictatorial rule. Emboldened by Yeltsin's defiance, tens of thousands of Russian citizens staged demonstrations against the coup, and key elements of the military high command refused to support it. Isolated, the plotters capitulated two days later and Gorbachev was released. This event proved to be a watershed in Russian history. It undermined not only Gorbachev's power as president of the Soviet Union but also the very existence of the Soviet Union itself.

Scene two marks a defining moment in the transfer of real political power from Gorbachev to Yeltsin. At a historic session of the Russian republic's legislature held only days after the coup plot fell apart, Gorbachev was in the process of acknowledging his mistakes when Yeltsin interrupted him to announce that he had just signed a decree suspending all

Boris Yeltsin gestures to supporters after denouncing the coup against Soviet President Mikhail Gorbachev.

activities of the Soviet Communist Party within Russia. The stunning disclosure effectively ended more than 70 years of the party's monopoly of power in Russia and the rest of the Soviet Union. Humiliated, Gorbachev resigned as chief of the Communist Party the next day.

Over the next three months the Soviet Union fell apart. Soon after the coup was thwarted, Gorbachev announced that any Soviet republic wishing to declare its independence should be allowed to go free. One by one, the 15 Soviet republics split off from the USSR and declared their independence. The first to go in September 1990 were the three states on the Baltic Sea that had been forcibly incorporated into the Soviet Union in World War II: Lithuania, Latvia, and Estonia. Ukraine, the second-largest Soviet republic after Russia, also announced plans to secede, followed over the succeeding weeks by all the remaining republics. On December 8, Russian President Yeltsin collaborated with the leaders of Ukraine and Belarus in forming a new grouping, the **Commonwealth of Independent States (CIS)**. Two weeks later they were joined by eight more Soviet republics, a development that effectively sealed the fate of the Soviet Union.

Following these events, Gorbachev resigned as president of the Soviet Union on December 25, setting the stage for scene three: Moments later, the Soviet flag was hauled down and the flag of independent Russia was hoisted in its place over the Kremlin, the historic seat of the Russian government. The USSR was passing into history. It officially ceased to exist December 31, 1991.

As the Kremlin's bells rang in the New Year on January 1, 1992, Russia formally began its new life as an independent state. The ensuing years would bring unprecedented transformations, combining fresh hopes with widespread hardships. The Russian government under President Yeltsin immediately launched economic initiatives designed to transform the still largely state-run economy into a mixed economic system with considerably more private enterprise. Although these measures produced rapid benefits for a few "new Russians" who understood the nature of the changes, most people saw their living standards deteriorate. Prices for a wide range of goods rose astronomically, far outpacing wages. Economic growth remained at a standstill. Hefty loans from the International Monetary Fund and other lenders were needed to keep the economy afloat. Organized crime reared its head as a Russian mafia pursued such illegal activities as gambling and extortion. And a small group of politically well-connected businessmen quickly became billionaires, taking over the country's largest banks, newspapers, television stations, and other major assets.

These problems could only sap popular support from Yeltsin's government and undermine the legitimacy of Russia's newborn democracy. But the difficulties of building a solid foundation for democracy in a country where it had never truly existed for very long became all the more evident in 1993, when a confrontation between President Yeltsin and the Russian legislature that had been brewing since the last years of the Soviet era came to a head. As Communist Party legislators opposed to Yeltsin's reform programs dug in their heels and barricaded themselves in the parliament building, Yeltsin called in the army to flush them out. Determined to start anew, Yeltsin scrapped the communist-era constitution and presided over the drafting of a new document that was consciously modeled on France's Fifth Republic. Like Charles de Gaulle's constitution, Yeltsin's constitutional project established a mixed *presidential–parliamentary system*, anchored in a powerful presidency. In December 1993, a majority of Russian voters approved the Yeltsin constitution in a referendum, according it a measure of popular consent.

Ukrainian President Leonid Kravchuk (left), Belarus's Supreme Soviet Chairman Stanislav Shushkevich (center), and Russian President Boris Yeltsin (right) on December 8, 1991, after signing a communiqué agreeing that "the Soviet Union as a geopolitical reality [and] a subject of international law has ceased to exist" and announcing the creation of a new entity in the post-USSR territory—the Commonwealth of Independent States.

The promise of a fresh start quickly evaporated. The long-awaited spurt in economic growth and production consistently failed to materialize. By the end of the decade, nearly 40 percent of the population lived below the official poverty line of $37 a month. Though private businesses increasingly sprouted and a new middle class was emerging, the penury of the masses glaringly clashed with the accumulating riches of the new capitalist elite. Meanwhile, postcommunist Russia was just as fractionated as the former Soviet Union in its last stages. Its most violent challenge was in Chechnya, a largely Muslim region where a separatist movement launched a guerrilla war for independence. Yeltsin sent Russian troops to the breakaway province in December 1994; the bloody confrontation ended with a truce in 1996. The conflict flared anew in 1999, and troops once again were dispatched to the troubled region.

Yeltsin himself hobbled through the decade in a state of near-permanent illness. A serious heart problem, respiratory illnesses, excessive drinking, and other infirmities required him to spend long weeks and months in sanatoriums or at home, away from the center of political life in the Kremlin. These problems culminated in scene four: On December 31, 1999, as the world prepared to greet the new millennium, Boris Yeltsin went on television and stunningly announced his immediate resignation. "Russia must enter the new millennium with new politicians, new faces," he said, asserting that he had already completed his main task, which was to ensure that "Russia will never return to the past."

With Yeltsin's unexpected departure only six months before the completion of his term, the presidency automatically passed to the prime minister, Vladimir Putin (1952–). A former officer in the KGB—the Soviet Union's notorious spy agency—Putin was practically unknown. President Yeltsin had aroused considerable puzzlement in Russia and around the world in September 1999 with his surprise appointment of 46-year-old Putin as Russia's prime minister. Putin's detachment from the secretive Kremlin inner circle, and the calm decisiveness he exuded when announcing his determination to defeat the Chechen rebels for good, won him instant public approval. Yeltsin endorsed Putin as his successor. In the fall of 1999, a new political party was organized with the principal aim of providing Putin with greater support in Russia's parliament. Known as *Unity*, the party scored an unexpected triumph in the December 1999 legislative elections, finishing behind the Russian Communist Party as the second-largest delegation in the State Duma, the legislature's lower house.

Following the terms of the 1993 constitution, new presidential elections had to be held within three months of Yeltsin's resignation. In March 2000, Putin bested 10 rival candidates, winning the presidency with an absolute majority of 52.8 percent in the first round of voting.

Scene five dramatizes some of the critical challenges facing Putin's regime. It also illustrates Putin's governing style, providing instructive clues about his conceptions of Russian democracy. On the morning of September 1, 2004, more

Boris Yeltsin endorsed the relatively unknown Prime Minister Vladimir Putin to succeed him when he retired from the presidency in 1999.

than 30 armed rebels from Chechnya stormed an elementary school in the nearby Russian town of Beslan. Ceremonies celebrating the first day of the school year had just concluded. More than a thousand children, parents, and teachers were suddenly taken hostage in the school building. Terror gripped all of Russia as the rebels threatened to kill 50 hostages for every one of their own who might be killed if Russian security forces attacked them. As a tense standoff entered its third day, with Russian troops surrounding the school, bombs went off inside the building and pandemonium broke loose. The rebels began shooting indiscriminately, killing children as they ran, while the soldiers fired away at the rebels. After the guerrillas were subdued and the smoke cleared, some 331 people lay dead, half of them children.

The Beslan tragedy had a profound effect on President Putin. Survivors of the Beslan tragedy faulted Putin for the scale of the carnage that resulted from the gun battle. Some witnesses accused Russian troops of precipitating the catastrophe by shooting first. Putin, disappointed in the performance of Russian security officials, called for a "fundamentally new approach" to law enforcement. The Putin government's attempts to withhold information and muzzle the media in the Beslan and earlier hostage incidents fit into a larger pattern of measures aimed at limiting freedom of the press. Putin has been considerably less tolerant of public criticism than Yeltsin was. Shortly after Putin assumed office, his administration closed an independent television network whose principal owner, Boris Berezovsky, was a powerful business tycoon with close ties to Yeltsin. It also wrested control of a separate network from another tycoon, Vladimir Gusinsky. Both Berezovsky and Gusinsky, whose media outlets were vocally critical of Putin, fled Russia after being charged with criminal offenses. Efforts to intimidate journalists or deny them information have proliferated since.

Scene six provides a chilling example of the dangers that journalists face in Putin's Russia. In October 2006 the lifeless body of Anna Politkovskaya, an internationally renowned critic of Putin's government, was found in the elevator of her Moscow apartment building. She had died from a bullet to her head and three to her body. The assailant left the murder weapon at the scene, signifying a contract killing. Politkovskaya was widely known for her reports of abuses by Russian security forces and their allies in what she called the "dirty war" in Chechnya. In 2000 she was arrested, beaten, and forced to undergo a mock execution by military authorities. Russian agents once poisoned her. Her editor revealed that Politkovskaya was about to file a story on the use of torture by pro-Russian Chechens on the very day she was murdered.

President Putin made no comment on the case until he assured President George W. Bush in a telephone conversation several days after the murder that the matter would be thoroughly investigated. Subsequently, Putin told reporters during a visit to Germany that the murder "was a dreadful and unforgettable crime which cannot be allowed to go unpunished." But he caustically dismissed Politkovskaya's influence in Russia as "extremely insignificant." Russian journalists have regularly faced intimidation for their willingness to print stories unfavorable to the powerful.

In scene seven, three young women, Nadezhda Tolokonnikova, Maria Alyokhina, and Yekaterina Samutsevich, members of a feminist punk-rock group calling themselves Pussy Riot, were arrested in 2012 for hooliganism motivated by religious hatred, tried in a much-followed case, and sentenced to two years in a penal colony. Pussy Riot had staged an unauthorized performance in the sanctuary of Moscow's Cathedral of Christ the Savior of a song called "Punk Prayer: Mother of God Drive Putin Away" that they released on video later that day. The song criticized the Russian Orthodox Church for its traditional views on women and its support for Putin's election campaign. While the Pussy Riot members claimed their performance was a political statement, government prosecutors argued the group was trying to "incite religious hatred" against the church. The government later successfully asked a judge to declare several of Pussy Riot's videos "extremist" and ban their distribution on the Internet. Most Russians supported the arrest and prosecution of the young women as threats to public order or offenses against the sanctity of the church, although strong advocates of freedom of expression saw the prosecution as one more example of the abridgement of civil liberties in contemporary Russia.

Because of the assaults on the press and other limitations on democratic freedoms that we will examine later in this chapter, Russia under Putin has retrogressed in the annual Freedom House evaluations of how governments around the world measure up against criteria for democracy (see Chapter 1). In the mid-1990s, Russia under President Yeltsin was doing relatively well, meriting a composite political and civil rights rating of 3.5. That score qualified Russia as "partly free" in Freedom House's rankings. By 2002 Freedom House had dropped Russia to a composite score of 5, and in 2012 Russia was ranked at 5.5 (6 for political rights and 5 for civil rights). Accordingly, we now categorize Russia as an authoritarian regime.[1]

Unquestionably, the fate of democracy in Russia stands out as one of the most vitally important issues facing today's world. The end of the Cold War, the collapse of the Soviet Union, and the replacement of a Communist Party dictatorship with a regime in transition to democracy have had

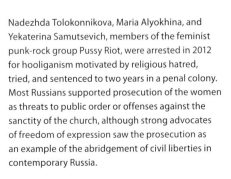

Nadezhda Tolokonnikova, Maria Alyokhina, and Yekaterina Samutsevich, members of the feminist punk-rock group Pussy Riot, were arrested in 2012 for hooliganism motivated by religious hatred, tried, and sentenced to two years in a penal colony. Most Russians supported prosecution of the women as threats to public order or offenses against the sanctity of the church, although strong advocates of freedom of expression saw the prosecution as an example of the abridgement of civil liberties in contemporary Russia.

profoundly positive consequences for Russia's relations with the United States, Western Europe, Japan, and other democracies around the world. These developments have replaced decades of global confrontation and the danger of nuclear war with unprecedented progress in arms control, diplomatic collaboration, and economic cooperation. The reversion to authoritarian rule in Russia could have a devastating impact on international comity and, conceivably, world peace.

The problems Russia faces in building a real democracy—both immediately and in the coming decades—cannot be grasped without a clear understanding of the country's thousand-year history of authoritarianism and the momentous social experiment that was Soviet communism. This chapter takes a more historical approach than earlier country chapters as we seek to understand how the ideologies surveyed in Chapter 10 and the approaches to political economy studied in Chapter 11 have been variously implemented in the Russian context. This chapter is more a study of *political development* than political institutions, for what has characterized much of Russia's history is the failure to adhere to the practices called for by formal political institutions. The timeline of the Russian past in Figure 16.1 provides the road map of the path that we will be following in coming pages. The chapter first surveys Russia's panoramic past under tsars and communists, considering the consolidation of communist control in the 1920s, Stalin's totalitarian regime, and the rule of Stalin's successors. It then explores the country's more recent efforts to move away from a centrally planned economy and toward a more liberal economy and political regime. We will give ample attention to the barriers to the establishment of a stable democracy at the end of the chapter.

RUSSIA'S HISTORICAL TRADITIONS: WHY NO DEMOCRACY?

Throughout its history, Russia was never able to sustain real democratic institutions and practices. Under the tsars (or czars) and their predecessors, Russia deviated substantially from the historical paths to democracy taken by Britain and France. Subsequently, under the communists, national wealth improved but most of the other conditions for democracy discussed in Chapter 7 remained far short of fulfillment.[2]

Tsarism

Russia's state institutions were entirely or mostly undemocratic from their earliest appearance to the final decade of the twentieth century. In 1613 an assembly of Orthodox prelates and Russian nobles elected Michael Romanov, the 16-year-old son of the patriarch of the Orthodox Church, as the new tsar. The Romanovs were destined to rule Russia for more than 300 years, up to the abdication of Tsar Nicholas II in 1917 only months before the communist revolution. Ordinary Russians would not be invited to elect their leader until Boris Yeltsin's election in 1991.

Tsarist power, autocratic and arbitrary from its origins (Grand Prince Ivan III began referring to himself as "tsar" in the fifteenth century), expanded even more pronouncedly under Peter I, better known as Peter the Great (1682–1725). Peter compelled even the most distinguished nobles to identify themselves before him as "your majesty's lowliest slave." Russia's commoners (99.7 percent of the population) remained in a state of servitude, deprived of rights and subjected to

Russian Empire	Up to 1917	Romanov Dynasty	Tsarist autocracy
Revolution	1917–21	Initially broad anti-tsarist revolutionary coalition; Bolsheviks seize power and defeat anti-Bolshevik forces in the civil war	
Soviet Union	1922–28	Lenin and Bolsheviks	CPSU consolidates power while pursuing the New Economic Policy
	1929–53	Stalin	Imposition of command economy and collectivization of agriculture; totalitarian rule by Stalin and CPSU
	1953–64	Post-Stalinist CPSU	Khrushchev's de-Stalinization
	1964–82		Brezhnev
	1982–85		Brezhnev's successors
	1985–91	Mikhail Gorbachev	Perestroika/Glasnost
Russian Federation	1992–2000	Boris Yelstin	Half-hearted attempts at democratization; severe market-based reforms
	Since 2000	Vladimir Putin	Reassertion of executive power

FIGURE 16.1 **Timeline of Modern Russia**

onerous taxes. Compulsory military service and slave labor were integral elements of Petrine Russia.

Peter clearly recognized Russia's economic inferiority to the West and he was resolved to overcome it. He extended an open hand to scientists and technicians from Germany and other countries and opened a "window on the West" by building the city of St. Petersburg on the Gulf of Finland. Peter's adaptations of Western methods stopped short of political and social reform, however. Like his predecessors on the Russian throne, Peter had no tolerance of parliamentary bodies or civil liberties.[3]

Peter's approach created an ambivalence in Russian attitudes toward the West that endured throughout the entire tsarist epoch and that persists to this very day. From Peter's time onward, the defining hallmark of Russian nationalism became its double-edged orientation to Western Europe (and, later, to the United States). On the one hand, Russian leaders and intellectuals have simultaneously recognized and resented their country's economic backwardness vis-à-vis the West. But until quite recently they resisted copying the political freedoms and social structures that underlay Western economic dynamism, preferring instead to pursue their own models (whether tsarist or communist) while asserting their country's spiritual or moral superiority to "decadent" Western norms and practices. The "Slavophile" strain in Russian culture, which crystallized as a body of thought in the nineteenth century, explicitly articulated these notions of spiritual supremacy. As Liah Greenfeld has argued, however, Slavophilism and "Westernism" were simply two sides of the same coin: Both were rooted in Russian resentment at the West's achievements and in a gnawing sense of humiliation. Neither concept of nationalism favored the development of democracy.[4]

Several of Peter's successors initiated reforms aimed at loosening some of the more extreme aspects of the country's political and social rigidity. None, however, permitted real democratization. Empress Catherine II (Catherine the Great), who ruled from 1762 to 1796, initiated administrative reforms, but she opposed sharing power with a parliament modeled on Britain's constitutional monarchy. Like her predecessors, she regarded the vast majority of the populace as mere subjects, unworthy of guaranteed rights.[5]

The revolutionary unrest and terrorism that shook Russia in the second half of the nineteenth century provoked Tsar Alexander III, who reigned from 1881 to 1894, to tighten the regime's grip on power more assertively. Over the course of the 1880s and 1890s, a series of new laws on crimes against the government gave Russia the institutional foundations of a modern police state. With no judicial system to set limits to its practices, the secret police became the principal effective authority in Russia when it came to day-to-day governance. Local government bodies were restricted in their activities, and thousands of people were exiled to Siberia.[6]

In January 1905, military units brutally dispersed a crowd of peaceful petitioners in front of the tsar's palace, an event that set off revolutionary and anarchistic outbursts throughout the country. Faced with the most severe crisis in the history of tsardom, Tsar Nicholas II, who reigned from 1894 to 1917, agreed to the creation of a parliamentary body, the Duma. The first Duma was elected in 1906 under fairly democratic conditions of universal male suffrage. But the tsar subsequently severely circumscribed the Duma's powers and reasserted his own status as "Autocrat of All the Russias." The tsar continued to rely on the old aristocratic elite to govern Russia and opposed a genuine constitutional monarchy.[7] Then in 1917, in the midst of World War I and mounting domestic unrest, Nicholas was forced to abdicate, bringing an end to more than 400 years of tsarist autocracy.

Reinforcing the tsars' success in maintaining authoritarian state institutions over the centuries was widespread indifference to democracy on the part of Russia's elites. Whereas England's parliamentary traditions had originated in the landed nobility, most Russian nobles did not own large estates. Peter the Great kept the nobility subservient, forbidding them to own private property and compelling them to change their residences so as not to develop an attachment to landholdings that might serve as a base of local power, as it had in England. He also compelled them to render lifelong service to the state. When Catherine II allowed the nobility to own land and released them from their service obligations, they gladly accepted these concessions and raised no serious demands for a parliamentary share of power, taking little interest in the consultative assemblies she established.

Russia's religious elites, consisting of the Orthodox Church hierarchy, provided consistent support for tsarism, as did the military elites. Both were props of the tsarist ruling structure and ill-disposed to democracy.

The country's intellectual elites included many people with a passion for improving social conditions. Some were genuinely interested in democracy and formed the basis of the Constitutional Democratic Party, which emerged as the largest party in the first two Dumas. Others tended toward the populists or socialists. But a sizable portion of the Russian intelligentsia, perhaps the majority, remained politically inert, exhibiting a greater interest in literature and the arts than in politics.

The absence of national unity, reflecting Russia's ethnic, linguistic, and religious heterogeneity, also worked against democracy. The state's appetite for territory brought a diversity of non-Russian peoples under tsarist rule—from Poles, Lithuanians, and Finns in the west to Georgians and Armenians in the Caucasus and an array of Turkic groups across Central Asia. These subjugated peoples had as few rights as the Russians themselves and were subjected to military reprisals for acts of insubordination. Any steps in the direction of democracy for these populations could only spell suicide for a polyglot empire. Ethnic Russians also exhibited a noticeable social heterogeneity, rooted mainly in class and status distinctions. Nineteenth- and early-twentieth-century Russian society consisted of the nobility, a mid-level gentry, a large peasantry, a small merchant class, the Orthodox clergy, a small core of professionals, and a growing industrial working class. The tsarist regime played one group against another while striving to keep them all down. Most Russians therefore developed a closer attachment to their own social class than to Russia as a whole, with few espousing a democratic conception of the common good.

A relatively low level of national wealth constituted another barrier to democracy in precommunist Russia. Until the communist era, Russia was an agricultural country, with far lower levels of industrialization than in Britain, France, Germany, or the United States. Its agricultural system was grossly inefficient. Russia was not significantly engaged in international trade, and even its domestic trade was subject to a panoply of government restrictions and disincentives. It was not until the 1860s that a private banking system developed, hundreds of years behind the commercial nations of Europe. Relatively paltry amounts of money circulated among the population, far too little to stimulate economic growth.

A major cause of both the lethargy of Russia's economy and the authoritarianism of its political institutions was the lowly status of private enterprise. Until the reign of Catherine the Great in the eighteenth century, the tsars refused to allow the private ownership of land. The tsars literally owned Russia, holding title to all its territory, natural resources, cities, and towns along with virtually all its manufacturing enterprises. In this respect Russia was vastly different from Western Europe, where private property was enshrined in ancient Roman law and respected by monarchs in legal theory and actual practice from the Middle Ages onward. It was largely to defend their property that European (and subsequently American) farmers and businesspeople demanded a say in how they were governed, advancing the cause of representative democracy and political rights through the assertion of their economic rights. In 1785, Catherine II finally permitted members of the nobility to own property. But more than 90 percent of the population, consisting mostly of peasants, did not acquire property rights until the nineteenth century. The tsars who followed her continued to regard the Russian state as their own exclusive preserve—a "patrimonial state."

On the eve of the twentieth century, Russia continued to lag far behind Britain, the United States, France, and Germany in both the level of its industrial development and the scope of its private enterprise. When private industrial capitalism finally emerged in Russia, it did so under the guiding influence of the state. Stimulated by infusions of state investment and direction from above, the economy surged forward at a rate of 8 percent a year in the 1890s.[8] However, though Russia had become the fifth-largest industrial economy in the world by World War I, one-third of its industrial investment and half of its bank capital was in foreign hands. The veritable absence of private property in Russia until late in the eighteenth century, and its narrow diffusion and weak development in subsequent phases of tsarist rule, provided slim grounds for the development of a Russian middle class that might have militated for democratic reform. With the fortunes of their businesses heavily dependent on state favors, a large number of Russia's businesspeople preferred to lend their support to tsarist authoritarianism rather than threaten it with demands for democracy.

In addition to lacking support from society's elites and middle class, democracy in Russia also failed to capture the allegiance of its disadvantaged masses. From the earliest inception of the Russian state to the ultimate demise of tsarism, the vast majority of the country's population consisted of impoverished peasants. Between 1550 and 1650, virtually the entire peasant population became serfs under the dictates of an increasingly centralized Russian autocracy.

Unlike American-style slavery, the landlords did not legally own the serfs, but they controlled them. In actual practice, the serfs were not much better off than slaves. Like slaves, Russian serfs had no rights of any kind. Tsarist law forbade them from moving without permission. Runaways, if apprehended, were to be returned to their landlords. Despite the fact that they were not legally owned by their landlords, they were nevertheless bought and sold as chattel (though Russian landlords tended to refrain from breaking up families). And yet, despite their subjugation, most serfs supported tsarism and displayed little inclination to demand a more democratic regime. Displays of mass rebellion were rare and tended to be spontaneous eruptions directed at the local landlords rather than organized political movements aimed at overthrowing the government. The notion that the tsar was a benevolent father, ordained by God to care for his people, was a common assumption in peasant lore.

In February 1861, Tsar Alexander II signed an emancipation decree abolishing serfdom in Russia. (President Lincoln's Emancipation Proclamation was issued in January 1862.) The decree freed more than 22 million peasants, roughly 38 percent of Russia's population at the time, from their obligation to serve the landlords. But just as emancipation in the United States abolished servitude in legal terms without providing the former slaves with an accompanying measure of economic self-sufficiency, so the terms of emancipation in Russia imposed new shackles of economic dependency on the former serfs. One-third of the landlords' property was made available to the liberated peasants, but they had to buy it. Unable to meet the demanding schedule of payments to the state and the landlords, many sank hopelessly into debt. Emancipation also failed to provide the full range of civil rights.

Widespread dissatisfaction with these conditions ignited a series of peasant revolts that intensified between 1905 and 1907. Though the government canceled the debts and instituted reforms promoting private land ownership, a smoldering discontent pervaded the Russian countryside. By 1917, self-employed peasants owned two-thirds of the country's farmland, but most were impoverished. Family farms tended to be small and land hunger was rampant, a predicament that induced many peasants to heed the siren call of revolution rather than seek an orderly passage to democracy.

Meanwhile, as Russia's industrial development quickened, a new class of disadvantaged people voiced their indignation. The industrial working class, toiling in the factories that proliferated in the late nineteenth and early twentieth centuries, grew from slightly more than half a million in 1860 to about 3 million by 1914. Although they still constituted only a small portion of the population (estimated at 170 million in 1914), their concentration in and around the country's main urban centers allowed them to join forces. Though trade unions and strikes were not allowed, strikes began in the 1870s and 1880s. In the revolutionary explosion of 1905, workers in the capital of St. Petersburg and in Moscow closed factories and spontaneously formed workers' councils that were poised to replace government authority until the regime suppressed them.

As World War I imposed new hardships on the working population—an increasing number of whom were women—labor agitation intensified. Strikes and mass demonstrations for "bread and peace" convulsed the cities and other areas where workers clustered, such as mines and oil fields.[9] By 1917, Russia's exploited working class was ready for radical solutions. It was the communists who spoke to their grievances more successfully than did the advocates of liberal or social democracy.

Democracy in precommunist Russia was also hampered by the absence of a civil society and a democratic political culture. One of the defining features of the tsarist era was the gaping chasm that separated the state from society. The heavy hand of tsarist rule remained so oppressive that the people had little latitude to develop viable associations of their own. Virtually all organizations independent of the state—civic associations, trade unions, political parties—were deemed seditious by the ruling authorities. A pervasive sense of resignation and alienation from the government thus settled over the bulk of the population in the nineteenth century. Predictably, the values and behaviors associated with a democratic political culture—participation, cooperation, consensus building, trust, and the like—also failed to blossom in Russia's rocky political soil.

Before the nineteenth century, education was reserved to the upper nobility and clergy. The expansion of secondary and higher educational opportunities in the second half of the nineteenth century increased the size of the intelligentsia, but the tsarist regime permitted no real outlets for mass participation in the country's political life on the part of its educated strata. The political orientations of high school and university graduates therefore got diverted into a quiescent resignation or a desperate revolutionary radicalism, with only a relative few seeking a moderate democratic constitution. The bulk of the population continued to consist of illiterate peasants, scarcely a promising basis for mass democracy.

The flow of information was seriously restricted by the regime. Official activities were tightly guarded state secrets, and the public was fed official versions of the truth as deemed appropriate by the authorities. A censorship system monitored nonofficial publications.

Finally, Russia's position within the international environment proved just as obstructive to democracy as its domestic characteristics. Russia was geographically and culturally removed from the crucial developments in European society that promoted the rule of law and the evolution of democratic attitudes and institutions, such as the traditions of Roman jurisprudence, the social obligations of feudalism, the Protestant Reformation, the Enlightenment, and the advancement of bourgeois liberalism. From the time of Peter the Great, Russians were impressed against their will into military service to fight for the emperor's personal ambitions rather than for their

"country" in any democratic or patriotic sense of the term. When World War I broke out, it only exacerbated the social and political conflicts that had been building up to a revolutionary explosion for decades. Far from promoting democracy, the First World War led Russia to communism.

With respect to all 10 conditions for democracy, then, events consistently conspired to inhibit democratic development in Russia over the course of a thousand years. The barriers to democracy would be even more imposing under communist rule.

Communism

The defining event of the twentieth century was the Russian Revolution. The Soviet experiment—implanting socialism in Russia through a centrally planned economy—challenged the visions of the good society held by both old regime autocrats such as the Romanovs and Western liberals. It created the bases of the ideological conflict that divided the world until the Soviet Union collapsed in 1991.

Marx and the Russian Revolution
If Karl Marx's predictions had been right, Russia would not have experienced a socialist revolution in 1917. As noted in Chapter 10, Marx believed that socialism had to be built on the foundations of an industrialized capitalist economy in an advanced state of development. Only a highly industrialized economy could provide a working class large enough to wrest economic and political power from the capitalist bourgeoisie in a spontaneous revolution. But 70 years after Marx and Friedrich Engels authored the *Communist Manifesto*, Russia was still a predominantly agricultural nation. Industrial workers and their families amounted to barely 5 percent of the populace in 1917, a far cry from the majority Marx required for a successful proletarian revolution.[10]

Contrary to Marx's expectations, however, a socialist revolution succeeded in Russia. But the Russian Revolution deviated from Marx's predictions in several ways. Instead of being a spontaneous working-class uprising, it was a carefully orchestrated coup d'état, skillfully managed by a revolutionary party that was in turn led by a charismatic personality, Vladimir Ilich Lenin (1870–1924). Although it was accompanied by working-class agitation in Russia's largest cities, its timing was due more to the decades-long dissolution of tsarism, the land hunger of the peasantry, and the general turbulence fostered by World War I than to a mass upheaval of the industrial working class. Political power in Russia was seized by a Communist Party elite acting in the name of the workers, not by the workers themselves.

The Russian "dictatorship of the proletariat" was not a temporary affair under the direction of the workers, as Marx had forecast; rather, it turned out to be a dictatorship of the Communist Party that endured until the final collapse of party rule in the early 1990s. Rather than withering away, in accordance with Marxist notions, the state in the Soviet Union burgeoned into one of the most oppressive totalitarian regimes ever seen, bolstered by a giant bureaucracy that imposed itself on almost every facet of the country's economic and social life. And instead of becoming a classless society, in conformity with Marx's utopian vision of communism, the USSR developed stark divisions between the mass of society (itself divided into several layers) and a select Communist Party elite (at most 2 percent of the population) who arrogated to themselves a cornucopia of privileges and material goods not available to the wider population.

Lenin and Leninism Lenin, the person most responsible for Russia's deviation from the Marxist paradigm, was not a proletarian but a product of the Russian intelligentsia.

In 1902, Lenin made his first major mark on the socialist movement with the publication of *What Is to Be Done?* The tract boldly staked out several positions that diverged from the tenets of classical Marxism. Whereas Marx regarded the industrial proletariat as the standard-bearers of revolution, Lenin insisted that the workers, if left to themselves, would never mount a revolution; at best they would form trade unions and come to terms with the captains of industry who controlled their lives. And whereas Marx foresaw spontaneous proletarian outbursts, Lenin called for the creation of a "party of a new type": not a mass party concerned with winning votes, like the German Social Democrats or the British Labour Party, but a smaller party consisting of professional revolutionaries who would act as the "vanguard of the proletariat," seizing power whenever the right opportunity presented itself. Armed with its "organizational weapon," such a conspiratorial party might be able to topple the state, along with its economic base, long before capitalism had created a sizable working-class population.

As Lenin's train arrived in Petrograd (St. Petersburg) in April 1917, almost three years into World War I, Lenin's party, the **Bolsheviks** (the name means *majority*, derived from their false claim to be the majority faction of the Social Democratic Party) could count on no more than 23,000 adherents. Between April and July, their ranks swelled to nearly a quarter million. The war's widespread unpopularity played directly into their hands, sapping the Russian government of what little support it may have possessed. In March, Tsar Nicholas II was persuaded to step down, leaving power in the hands of a provisional government consisting of politicians from the conservative right to the moderate left. (Because Russia was still using the Julian calendar, which lagged two weeks behind the more widely used Gregorian calendar, the transfer of power is known in Russian history as the "February Revolution.") Though the new government immediately conferred on Russia's citizens a wide range of democratic rights and freedoms they had never before enjoyed, its decision to prosecute the war hastened its undoing.

One-fourth of Russia's troops deserted the army over the ensuing months. Life on the home front was continuing turmoil: Shortages of food and heating fuel intensified public outrage, resulting in strikes, work stoppages, and demonstrations in the cities. In the countryside, peasants intensified their demands for more land. In Petrograd and Moscow, workers set up councils to take over the management of their factories and, in a bold challenge to the governing authorities, acted as though they constituted the only legitimate political authority. The Russian word for council is *soviet*. As the crisis deepened, soldiers and peasants formed soviets of their own, electing deputies to join with representatives of the workers' soviets to coordinate their activities.

Bolshevik propaganda deftly exploited these discontents. Lenin and his followers called for an immediate end to the war, land for the peasants, and "all power to the soviets!" By early fall the provisional government was virtually powerless. In a methodical coup d'état, Bolshevik militia units moved into the main government buildings in Petrograd, most of which had already been vacated by Russian officialdom. The tsarist regime and the short-lived provisional government had each collapsed like a house of cards. The Russian state fell into Bolshevik hands on November 7, 1917. (The date was October 25 on the Julian calendar; hence the Bolshevik takeover of power is known as the **October Revolution**.)

The Bolsheviks—also known as Communists—promptly pulled Russia out of the Great War, moved the capital to Moscow, and turned their attention to consolidating power at home. Their first moves were calculated to court popularity. During their first months at the helm, the Communists granted independence to nationality groups such as the Poles, the Finns, and the Ukrainians, who had been incorporated into the Russian Empire under the tsars. They granted power to the workers' soviets, encouraged peasants to take over land, and allowed previously scheduled elections to a constitutional assembly to go forward. The Bolsheviks won nearly 25 percent of the vote in these elections, capturing a majority in Petrograd and Moscow.[11] Then, one by one, the new rulers proceeded to take back most of their concessions: Ukraine was reincorporated into Russia, the soviets came under Communist Party control, farmland and produce were confiscated by the state, and the constituent assembly was liquidated the day after its first meeting, consigned to the dustbin of history.

Private businesses were expropriated by the government in the name of socialism. Nicholas II and his family were executed so as to preclude any return to tsarism. Over the next several years the Bolsheviks (the "reds") fought a bitter civil war against a variety of enemies, known collectively as the "whites." As fighting and famine claimed millions of lives, the Red Army, under the command of Leon Trotsky, finally vanquished its remaining foes in 1921. In 1922 the Union of Soviet Socialist Republics (USSR) was formally proclaimed, uniting under communism the remnants of the Russian empire. The country lay in ruins.

From the outset, Lenin was determined to impose Communist Party authority over all other political and social forces in the country. The primacy of the Communist Party's power was the single most characteristic feature of what came to be known as *Leninism*. By Lenin's own candid admission, the dictatorship of the proletariat in Russia effectively meant the dictatorship of the Communist Party.

A second defining aspect of Leninism was what he called *democratic centralism*. While discussion and debate among party

Leon Trotsky, a Marxist theorist, proved to be a brilliant military leader of the Red Army during the civil war (1918–20), defeating the anti-Bolshevik forces. He was later assassinated by order of Joseph Stalin.

members were supposed to be permitted until a final decision was reached, all were required to follow the policies eventually decided by the top party leaders. In actual practice, internal party democracy quickly dissipated in favor of a top-down structure of command not unlike a military hierarchy.

Violence and a highly centralized state were ruthlessly employed to secure party rule. Lenin set up a powerful secret police—the forerunner of the KGB—and presided over the creation of a large state bureaucracy dominated by Communist Party adherents. Though he recognized that bureaucratic routine threatened to smother revolutionary élan, Lenin was in practice a devotee of strong, centralized state power.

The Soviet system of government that took shape under Lenin's aegis thus revolved around two institutions: the Communist Party of the Soviet Union (CPSU) and the state. The two were so intertwined as to be virtually indistinguishable. Both the party and the state had large bureaucracies with overlapping responsibilities for governing the country. And both were topped by small, powerful committees that constituted the leading decision-making bodies in Russia. The highest party committees were the Political Bureau, or *Politburo*, and the *Secretariat*. The highest state committee eventually became known as the *Council of Ministers*, the country's formal executive branch of government. The links connecting the parallel party and state institutions were strengthened by the simultaneous presence of several key individuals in the Politburo, the Secretariat, and the Council of Ministers. In the Soviet system, the Communist Party and the state were fused. Over time, as we shall see, the *party* institutions emerged as more powerful than the state institutions when it came to making the key decisions. Until Mikhail Gorbachev began restructuring this fused

party-state institutional system in the late 1980s, its basic structure remained largely intact.

Another feature of Leninism was *tactical flexibility*. After the civil war, Lenin recognized that the Bolsheviks needed to buy time and rebuild the economy to stabilize their authority. In 1921 Lenin initiated a reform known as the *New Economic Policy (NEP)*, which reversed the state's efforts to take over the economy, putting socialism on hold. Peasants were allowed to buy and sell land; industrialists and merchants were invited to lease property from the state and run their own businesses, with strong encouragement to turn a profit. The Russian state retained control of what Lenin called "the commanding heights" of the economy: energy and steel production, the communication and transportation systems, and the like. The partial reintroduction of private enterprise was only supposed to be temporary, however. Once economic activity revived, Lenin had every intention of reimposing socialist controls over the economy under the Communist-run central government. But he set no time limit to the New Economic Policy, allowing Russia to have a respite from rigid state controls in hopes of building popularity for the communist regime over time.

The founder of Bolshevism never lived to see the reimposition of socialism in Russia. In 1922 Lenin suffered a debilitating stroke, and in January 1924 he died. He can be rightfully credited with leading the Russian Revolution and creating the bases of Communist Party rule. Although he reinterpreted a number of the central axioms of Marxism to fit Russia's peculiar conditions, Lenin always considered himself a good Marxist. Following his death, Soviet ideology officially became known as **Marxism-Leninism**, a concept that combined Marx's revolutionary anticapitalism with Lenin's reliance on the communist party-state.

One of Lenin's most enduring legacies was to haunt all the Soviet governments that followed him: his failure to establish an orderly procedure for succession to power. Lenin ruled through his charismatic hold over the Communists and unrelenting coercion against his party's opponents. He had no taste for the procedures for transferring power spelled out in written constitutions, especially those in the hated "bourgeois democracies" of the West. Moreover, he designated no successor. As a consequence, a struggle for power within the highest reaches of the Communist Party leadership commenced as soon as Lenin was incapacitated. Through a combination of manipulativeness, guile, and bureaucratic intrigue, the winner of the struggle was Joseph Stalin (1878–1953), a man who developed Lenin's legacy of centralization and coercion to unimaginable excesses.

Stalin After the Bolshevik seizure of power, Lenin entrusted Stalin with a number of sensitive party and government posts, including that of general secretary of the Communist Party. Initially, that position was nothing more than a routine bureaucratic office charged with managing the party's records. But Stalin transformed it into a sinecure of personal power, building a loyal following by promoting people to both party

Through a combination of manipulation (including extensive propaganda), guile, and bureaucratic intrigue, Joseph Stalin (right) succeeded Lenin as head of the Communist Party.

and government jobs. Through the calculated use of political patronage, Stalin created a large party bureaucracy, or "apparatus" (*apparat*), dependent on his favors. Toward the end of his life, Lenin criticized Stalin as "too rude" for the post and called for his removal, but was in no physical condition after his stroke to press his views. Stalin stayed on as general secretary until he died some 30 years later.

During the 1920s, in the years that followed Lenin's untimely illness and death, Stalin masterfully exploited rivalries and disagreements among the party's top leaders, playing off one faction against another while quietly cultivating his own coterie of loyalists. By the end of the decade he could count on a voting majority in the party Politburo. Utilizing this support, in 1928 and 1929 he engineered the wholesale reversal of the Soviet Union's economic course. The broadly popular New Economic Policy was abandoned and the first in a series of five-year plans established the bases of a **centrally planned economy (CPE)** in the Soviet Union. These measures constituted the building blocks of the Soviet model of socialism, which represented another deviation from classical Marxism. Marx, whose descriptions of socialism were inscrutably vague, had left no clear blueprint for building a socialist economy other than to imply that it would *not* be run by a powerful state. The brand of socialism that Stalin and the Communist Party now forced upon the population was a *command economy* controlled by the leadership of an all-intrusive party-state dictatorship. Stalin applied his policy with a vengeance. The first five-year plan, introduced in 1928, had set a series of ambitious growth targets to be achieved in various sectors of the economy. In 1929, Stalin suddenly raised these targets astronomically, especially in such critical industrial areas as coal, iron, steel, and electricity production. Although Stalin's plan targets were too unrealistic to be achieved, by the end of the first five-year period the Soviets had nevertheless accomplished one of the most rapid spurts of industrial development

in human history. From its inception, however, this forced-pace industrialization policy was guided by a political motivation: to impose stringent controls over the economy for the purpose of retaining the Communist Party's control over Russia's political and social life.

An even more severe policy accompanied the accelerated industrialization drive: the *collectivization* of agriculture. By 1929 there were 25 million private farm households in Russia. In an operation conducted with unparalleled brutality, the Stalinist regime liquidated all privately owned farms and corralled the rural population into newly created *collective farms*. Farm produce was confiscated by government agents, often at gunpoint, for distribution to the cities; animals were also taken from their owners and attached to the collectives. Anyone resisting these measures, or even suspected of potential resistance, might be executed on the spot or rounded up for deportation to the work camps (*gulagi*) that now proliferated in the empty vastness of Russia. Lacking the means to resist, many peasants killed their horses, cows, and other livestock rather than surrender them. Starvation stalked the countryside as food production plummeted. Stalin justified his actions with cynical distortions of Marxist ideology.[12]

By 1934, when the job was done, perhaps as many as 14.5 million Russian peasants had perished in the collectivization campaign, though estimates vary and no precise figure can be authenticated. In contrast to the relative success of Stalin's industrialization campaign, however, it took several decades for Soviet agriculture to recover from the catastrophe of the collectivization process.[13]

Having imposed his will on the population and the economy, Stalin next turned his attention to the Communist Party itself. Between 1934 and 1939, he cleansed the party's ranks from top to bottom, dismissing undesirable members and in many cases consigning them to labor camps or firing squads. Known as the *Great Purge*, the process took on the macabre pathology of a witch hunt. An atmosphere of paranoia haunted the party as accusations and denunciations, most of them fabricated, struck terror into the membership from the highest to the lowest echelons. More than 1.6 million members were expelled from the CPSU.

Stalin's terror fanned out from the Communist Party to the general population. According to one estimate, between 1936 and 1938 there were 7 million arrests and at least a million executions; in 1939 the camps contained as many as 8 million prisoners. Stalin's deadly reach even extended to the military high command, decimating about a fourth of the officer corps by the eve of World War II. A relentless assault on religion accompanied these brutalities. Clerics were murdered, churches and mosques were destroyed, and atheism was propagated as official communist doctrine. By the end of the 1930s there was little question that Stalin was the unchallenged autocrat of the USSR and that the Soviet system was a paradigm of *totalitarianism*.[14]

The sufferings of the Soviet masses did not end with the attenuation of the *Great Terror*, however. World War II exacted an even heavier price. Though Stalin managed to delay a German invasion by cutting a deal with Hitler in 1939, the Nazi regime broke the agreement and invaded the USSR with massive force in June 1941.[15] By the time the war ended in 1945, more than 22 million Soviet people had died and some 1,700 Soviet cities were destroyed.

Stalin emerged from the war with his powers intact. In fact, the war allowed him to expand his influence beyond Soviet borders. After the USSR's Red Army rolled into Eastern Europe and Germany, Soviet agents and local Communist Party leaders imposed communist dictatorships on East Germany, Poland, Czechoslovakia, Hungary, Romania, and Bulgaria between 1944 and 1948. Later these states were incorporated into a Soviet-led military alliance known as the Warsaw Pact. Yugoslavia and Albania were also taken over by local communists after the war, but they escaped Soviet domination. Victory even brought Stalin a measure of respect and popularity among a portion of the Soviet masses, though the magnitude of this support is hard to estimate. Anyone expecting a postwar diminution of autocratic rule was in for a disappointment, however. The concentration camps remained crowded and the Kremlin voiced suspicions of dark plots. The Cold War added fears of impending nuclear annihilation. Stalin was said by his successors to be planning a new party purge when he died in 1953.

Khrushchev Although the Great Purge had expelled or killed nearly 2 million party members, it also opened up new opportunities for eager young recruits as well as for more senior party members who were fortunate enough to survive the onslaught. Most of the men who were to run the Soviet Union from Stalin's death until the mid-1980s rose up the ladder of the party apparatus during the purges and World War II. Stalin's party enticed this generation to its ranks by offering careers, social status, and, for the politically ambitious, the prospect of power.

One of the most ambitious was Nikita Khrushchev (1894–1971). Khrushchev joined the party in 1925 as a full-time *apparatchik*—a member of the party apparatus—just as Stalin was gathering effective control over it.

In the early 1930s Khrushchev won swift promotions within the party's Moscow branch and supervised the construction of the city's subway system, a task accomplished by conscripted laborers forced to work in 48-hour shifts. As the Great Purge got under way, Khrushchev wholeheartedly supported Stalin.[16] His loyalty was rewarded with a seat in the powerful CPSU Politburo, where he replaced one of Stalin's purge victims, and an even more spectacular appointment as the party's top leader in Ukraine. Khrushchev's notoriety among the Soviet people escalated during World War II, when he assumed responsibility for organizing the Ukrainian war effort. One of his sons perished in the battle of Stalingrad.

When Stalin died in 1953 without leaving a designated successor, a struggle for his mantle broke out among his closest associates. Over the next two years, Khrushchev outmaneuvered his chief rivals and emerged as the Soviet Union's top leader by 1955. Khrushchev's main claim to fame in Russian history derives from his sweeping denunciation of Stalin and his effort to rid the Soviet system of Stalinism's horrors. In a speech delivered in February 1956 at the Twentieth Congress of the Communist Party of the Soviet Union, a gathering of several thousand top party bureaucrats, Khrushchev excoriated Stalin as a madman whose actions had repeatedly brought the Soviet Union to the brink of disaster. Denouncing the "cruel repression" and "mass terror" of the Great Purge as an utterly unjustified breach of legality and berating Stalin for military blunders that had cost hundreds of thousands of lives, Khrushchev denounced the former Soviet dictator's megalomaniacal "cult of personality" and his callous disregard of the people's welfare.

Shortly after Khrushchev's speech, the Soviet Communist Party embarked on a campaign of *de-Stalinization*. Everywhere throughout the USSR, anything bearing Stalin's name was renamed, from streets and schools to the city of Stalingrad (which became Volgograd). Statues and paintings of Stalin, once ubiquitous, were pulled down. Stalin's body was removed from the Red Square mausoleum it shared with Lenin's and reburied in a nondescript grave beside a Kremlin wall. Khrushchev even allowed writers such as Alexander Solzhenitsyn (1918–2008) to publish works denouncing Stalin's deeds.[17]

Throughout his life, Khrushchev remained a devout Soviet communist, committed to the authoritarian system he served. He asserted Soviet controls over Central and Eastern Europe and vigorously pursued the Cold War rivalry with the United States. While acknowledging the necessity of avoiding nuclear war, he deployed troops to crush the Hungarian uprising against communism in 1956, approved the Berlin Wall in 1961, and put missiles in Cuba in 1962. (On the Cuban missile crisis, see Chapter 3.) He was also convinced of the inherent economic superiority of communism over capitalism, vowing that the Soviet Union would overtake the U.S. economy by 1970 and would build the most productive and egalitarian welfare state in the world by 1980.

Throughout his life, Nikita Khrushchev remained committed to the authoritarian system he served. He asserted Soviet controls over Central and Eastern Europe and vigorously pursued the Cold War rivalry with the United States.

In the end, however, Khrushchev proved that he was no Stalin. Having antagonized a number of key party officials and bureaucratic agencies with his unsettling reforms, arrogant manner, and occasionally erratic behavior, Khrushchev proved far less adept than his predecessor in maintaining his authority. In October 1964, upon returning to the Kremlin from a trip, he was informed by his Politburo colleagues that he was no longer in power. Chastised by his successors for "harebrained scheming," Khrushchev became a "nonperson" and was never seen in public again. In 1971, the party newspaper *Pravda* carried a brief notice in its back pages reporting that "pensioner N. S. Khrushchev" had died.[18]

The Brezhnev Years Many of the events of the next 25 years in Soviet politics were reactions to Khrushchev's reformist impulses. His immediate successor, Leonid Brezhnev (1906–1982), was opposed to any rash tampering with the basic Stalinist model of firm party rule and central planning. Under his guidance, the Soviet leadership undertook virtually no reforms, with critical consequences by the end of his life.

Just as Nikita Khrushchev had turned on Stalin, so Leonid Brezhnev turned on the man who had been his chief benefactor during his own climb up the apparatus of the Soviet Communist Party. Thanks to Khrushchev's patronage, Brezhnev had risen from obscurity to the most powerful leadership committees in the USSR. After Stalin's death, Khrushchev entrusted Brezhnev with a succession of important positions. But gratitude is a rare virtue in politics, and its absence was especially conspicuous in the conspiratorial world of the Kremlin. Brezhnev joined the cabal that unseated his benefactor in October 1964. From then until his death in 1982, Brezhnev was the official leader of the

Communist Party of the Soviet Union, and thus the single most powerful figure in the USSR.

It was not long before the transfer of power brought noticeable changes in style and substance. Whereas Khrushchev was prone to impromptu declarations and unilateral initiatives, Brezhnev governed as part of a team. Though he shrewdly demoted his principal opponents, he presented himself as the chief spokesman of an oligarchy acting on the basis of consensus. In the policy realm, one of Brezhnev's first departures from his predecessor was his termination of public attacks on Stalin. Brezhnev even allowed positive accounts of Stalin to appear sporadically in the heavily controlled press.

A grim pall of uniformity descended on the country's cultural life. Marxist-Leninist propaganda continued to pervade the educational system, with obligatory courses on ideology imposed on Soviet students all the way through graduate school. The official censorship system became even more intrusive than it was under Khrushchev, who had allowed some freedom for anti-Stalinist writers. Political repression as a whole grew tighter. The Brezhnev regime was determined to keep the USSR's small collection of dissidents—mostly writers, artists, and academics—under close surveillance. The dreaded KGB (the Committee on State Security) had carte blanche to investigate, harass, and arrest anyone suspected of engaging in dissident activities, such as writing or disseminating of anti-communist literature. Internationally renowned figures such as physicist Andrei Sakharov and writer Alexander Solzhenitsyn were objects of continuing repression. Although the Stalin-era prison camps for the most part had been closed under Khrushchev, a few survived under Brezhnev. They were augmented by psychiatric prisons where political dissidents could be subjected to debilitating drug regimens on fabricated diagnoses of mental illness.[19]

Lest there be any uncertainty about the government's readiness to use force against challenges to its authority, the Brezhnev regime intervened vigorously on two occasions when Communist rule was threatened in its hegemonic preserve of Eastern Europe: in 1968 with an invasion to overthrow a reform movement initiated by the Communist Party of Czechoslovakia and in 1981 with an order to Polish authorities to impose martial law and outlaw the Solidarity labor movement. This dedication to projecting Soviet power abroad was another defining element of the Brezhnev regime. Brezhnev's unrelenting military buildup against the West required massive expenditures, which came to undermine the regime. He is also known for the Brezhnev Doctrine, which asserted that any move away from socialism by an existing communist regime threatened all communist societies and warranted intervention by other communist powers, especially the USSR, to put the backsliding regime back on course.

The USSR's escalating military expenditures exacerbated the Brezhnev regime's most pressing problem, the economy. Khrushchev's attempts to tinker with the central planning system were little more than cosmetic in nature; he had no taste for free enterprise. Brezhnev retreated from even these modest changes and shelved plans for future experiments proposed by members of his leadership team. Aside from small private plots that collective farmers were allowed to maintain to grow food for their own consumption, the USSR had no private property. Everything from paper clips to space rockets were planned, produced, priced, and distributed by the government under the direction of the State Planning Commission (*Gosplan*). Basic consumer goods and services were heavily subsidized so as to curry favor with the population. Prices for bread, milk, potatoes, and other staples of the Russian diet were kept artificially low; so were prices for beef and pork, which were in shorter supply and quickly sold out. Transportation fares were minimal; rents were cheap; education was free from the lowest to the highest levels. Conversely, many goods were relatively more expensive than in the West. In the 1970s, an ordinary pair of shoes could cost a third of an average monthly wage; new cars were inordinately expensive and potential owners had to wait years before taking delivery.

Although in material terms most Soviet citizens lived better in the Brezhnev years than ever before in Russian history, by the 1970s the economy was stagnating. Between 1978 and 1985, the Soviet Union experienced zero economic growth. Annual increases in military spending took a growing slice out of a diminishing budgetary pie. After Gorbachev came to power and decided to cut military expenses drastically, the Soviets disclosed that their military spending was between one-fourth and one-third of GNI, far higher than the U.S. figure of about 6 percent of GNI.

Meanwhile, the Soviets were falling far behind the West and Japan in high-technology development. The information age left the USSR trailing its adversaries by a wide margin, particularly in such sectors as computers, software, and telecommunications. Communication, after all, is not something a dictatorship likes to encourage among its citizens. The Soviet Union's cumbrous planning system moved with bureaucratic lethargy and lacked the financial incentives that lure capitalist entrepreneurs and stimulate innovation. It proved poorly equipped to make the rapid improvements that market-oriented companies must constantly make to stay competitive.

Despite these problems, Brezhnev and his colleagues were even less inclined than Khrushchev to change the system they had known all their lives. Triumphalist slogans substituted for realistic self-criticism ("We are steadfastly fulfilling the plans of the 26th Party Congress!"). Rather than institute reforms, they purchased industrial goods from the West, such as pipelines and turbines. Even here, their resistance to capitalism was barely surmountable: Soviet trade with the outside world lagged far behind the averages for most other advanced economies and was conducted mainly with the Communist-ruled states of Central and Eastern Europe.

When Brezhnev died in 1982, after nearly 18 years in office, the ruling elite that clung to power for a few last years was a veritable gerontocracy: most members of the Politburo and other key committees were in their sixties or seventies. Brezhnev's immediate successor as party general secretary was former KGB chief Yuri Andropov (1914–1984)*)*, who was 68

when he took over. He was soon overcome by a debilitating illness and died in 1984. The next party chief, Konstantin Chernenko (1911–1985), was an old Brezhnev crony who assumed power at 83. He died the following year. An entire generation of Soviet leaders was receding into history, a generation whose political careers and policy outlooks rightfully labeled them as Stalin's successors.[20]

THE COLLAPSE OF SOVIET COMMUNISM

The accession of Mikhail Gorbachev to power brought to the fore not only a new generation but a radically new political orientation as well.

"We can't go on living like this." Mikhail Gorbachev's words, spoken in March 1985 on the eve of his assumption of power in the Soviet Union, reflected his conviction that the USSR was on the brink of disaster. "By the mid-1980s," he later recalled, "our society resembled a steam boiler." Major changes were absolutely necessary; otherwise, he feared, "an explosion of colossal force would be inevitable."

The inertial forces that had led the USSR to such a catastrophic turning point were plainly visible. Growth rates had fallen by more than half since the early 1970s, leading Gorbachev to characterize the late Brezhnev years as an "era of stagnation." The country's industrial infrastructure, much of it built in the Stalinist epoch, was woefully outdated, and its high-technology lag behind the West and Japan was widening to unbridgeable lengths. Consumer goods were shoddy and scarce, environmental hazards widespread. Public health and even mortality rates were deteriorating. Military expenditures gobbled up nearly 40 percent of the national budget. And the population lived in a state of political powerlessness and cultural isolation, demoralized by the regime's routine indifference to its everyday problems.

Starting the Reform Process

Gorbachev ascended the throne of Soviet power with a sure conviction that change was imperative, but with little clear idea of what to do. During his first year in power he adopted the term *restructuring* (**perestroika**) as the masthead of the reform process. But for nearly two years he provided no clear blueprint for a comprehensive economic or political transformation. From the start, however, Gorbachev recognized that no perestroika of any kind would be possible without broad public support. Shortly after assuming office he embarked on a series of trips around the country, employing his natural charm and communicative talents in exchanging views with crowds assembled on the streets and in factories. These spontaneous dialogues with the population stood in marked contrast to Gorbachev's distant and incommunicative predecessors and stimulated a groundswell of popular support for the new leader.

Gorbachev knew that any reform process would surely meet with resistance from the party apparatchiks and state bureaucrats who had run the Soviet political and economic

PROFILES   Mikhail Gorbachev

Mikhail Gorbachev led the Soviet Union from 1985 until 1991.

At 54, Mikhail Gorbachev was the youngest of the 21 men who occupied the highest rungs of power in the Communist Party of the Soviet Union when he assumed power in 1985. Born in 1931 to a peasant family in southern Russia, Gorbachev grew up in a poverty-stricken collective farm region. Both of his grandfathers had been arrested on spurious charges during Stalin's terror. Young Mikhail also retained lifelong impressions of World War II. His village was occupied by German troops for several months, and his father fought in a number of major battles before returning home with a leg injury.

In 1950 Gorbachev was admitted to Moscow State University, the most prestigious university in the country. Following graduation in 1955, he returned to his native region of Stavropol, where he became a full-time Communist Party employee. Over the course of the next 23 years he remained in Stavropol as a CPSU functionary, rising to the top of the local political heap in 1970 with his appointment as chief of the district's party organization. Khrushchev's secret speech in 1956 was an event of profound importance in Gorbachev's life. In later years Gorbachev stated that he approved of the anti-Stalin campaign as a thoroughly justified attack on the oppressiveness of the Soviet system.

Though Stavropol is located at considerable distance from Moscow, Gorbachev took advantage of its attractiveness as a vacation resort for Soviet leaders to ingratiate himself with leading members of Brezhnev's ruling clique. These ties paid off in 1978, when he was appointed to the party's powerful Secretariat in Moscow and assigned responsibility for overseeing the Soviet agricultural system. His ability to point out shortcomings in the party's agricultural policies without calling the system itself into question won him quick promotions in Brezhnev's oligarchy. Within a year he was appointed a candidate member of the party Politburo, and the following year he became a full (voting) member.

After Brezhnev's death in 1982, his successor, Yuri Andropov, who understood the urgent need for economic reorganization, took Gorbachev under his wing and gave every indication that he was grooming the younger man as his eventual replacement. But it was the aged Konstantin Chernenko who stepped into Andropov's shoes in early 1984. As Chernenko's decrepitude proved an embarrassment to the mighty Soviet Union, Gorbachev increasingly stepped forward as the country's most dynamic spokesman. In 1984 he was chosen to lead a Soviet delegation to Italy and Britain; it was only his second trip outside the Soviet bloc. Prime Minister Margaret Thatcher was instantly impressed with Gorbachev's straightforwardness, assuring the world he was "a man I could do business with."

Gorbachev's crowning moment finally came March 11, 1985. On the day after Chernenko's death, the party hierarchy elected him general secretary. Gorbachev's conviction that the Soviet Union had to change to survive was not matched with a clear plan about how to accomplish the needed reforms. The deeper into the reform process that Gorbachev went, the more radical his proposed changes became, in no small part because of the stiff resistance he faced. In six years, Gorbachev ended the Cold War. His attempted reforms also ended the Soviet experiment, begun in 1917, when the Soviet Union imploded. At the end of 1991, Gorbachev had no job. Not surprisingly, he has since come to be regarded as one of the most reviled former leaders among the citizens of the Soviet successor states even while people in the rest of the world admire how he challenged the Soviet power structure and ended the Cold War.[21]

system for decades. These officials were collectively known as the *nomenklatura*. Since Stalin's time, the nomenklatura were the occupiers of party and state jobs who were selected from lists of people approved by the Communist Party. This vast group, numbering 18 million by Gorbachev's account, had prospered under Brezhnev, constituting the Soviet Union's power elite. Gorbachev had no illusions about the fact that any serious reorganization of the economy and political institutions would have to upset the nomenklatura's power, privileges, and arrogant disdain for the people's needs and wishes.

Not long after taking office, Gorbachev therefore began combining his call for restructuring with equally persistent appeals for "democratization" and "openness" (*glasnost*). At least during his initial years in power, Gorbachev did not intend democratization to mean the replacement of Communist Party rule by a Western-style electoral democracy with competing political parties. Rather, he meant that the people should be granted greater latitude than in the past to articulate their demands for more effective government and for better treatment at the hands of party and government bureaucrats.

Gorbachev's object was to give voice to public discontent as a means of exerting pressure on Soviet officials to support his reform plans. He fully intended to lead and guide the democratization process, channeling public frustration in the directions he desired rather than giving the population complete freedom to replace the communist system.

Gorbachev's concept of openness was similarly limited in its aims. It meant that the party and government elites who controlled the Soviet system should be more forthcoming with information about the true state of the Soviet Union's economic and social problems. Gorbachev wished to share essential information with the public with a view to stimulating open discussion of the country's problems. As with democratization, the aim of glasnost was to exert public pressure for change on the lethargic bureaucratic elite. At least in its initial stages, it was not designed to introduce full-scale freedom of speech of the kind guaranteed by the world's democracies. The explosion of a nuclear reactor in the Ukrainian town of Chernobyl in April 1986 provided Gorbachev with a powerful pretext for promoting his openness campaign. After some hesitation, his government informed the public about the gravity of the situation and opened the damaged site to foreign technicians. From the outset, Gorbachev's dilemma was how to release the forces of democratization and openness without losing control over them. "What we had in mind," Gorbachev later wrote of his first years in power, "was not a revolution but a specific improvement of the situation."

But improvements were painfully slow in coming. Gorbachev's thoughts on perestroika remained vague, as a book he published on the subject testified.[22] Halfhearted, piecemeal reshufflings of the planning bureaucracy and shifts in its accounting procedures only seemed to generate confusion and opposition among the bureaucrats charged with implementing them, at times provoking outright sabotage. The introduction of market forces, such as privately owned restaurants and other services, remained strictly limited.[23]

As industrial production fell in 1987 and 1988, Boris Yeltsin, Gorbachev's appointee as the Communist Party boss of the city of Moscow, emerged as an outspoken critic of the slow pace of the reform process. But as the radical reformers pressed their attacks on Gorbachev, so did the entrenched party elite and their supporters, now openly in revolt at the changes being forced on them.

1989

In an effort to undercut the power of the party apparatchiks and encourage their replacement by reform-minded communists more attuned to his own thinking, Gorbachev called for the creation of a new legislative body, the Congress of People's Deputies, to act as the country's supreme lawmaking organ. Daringly, he insisted that a portion of the new legislature be elected by the people rather than handpicked by the party. Once again, Gorbachev's hope was to energize his reform process through limited democratization without fully relinquishing control over it. Of the 2,250 congress deputies,

750 were to be elected; the rest (including Gorbachev himself) were to be appointed by the party hierarchy. Candidates for the electoral contests were to be nominated by organizations traditionally dominated by the Communist Party, such as the Communist Youth League and the official trade union organization. Gorbachev thus had good reason to believe that friendly Communists would thoroughly dominate the new legislature. To his surprise, the nomination process sparked considerable participation by people eager for far more radical reform than Gorbachev was offering. The country became politically energized as 170 million people were given the right to vote in the first contested elections since 1917. Gorbachev's efforts to effect change from above had awakened long-dormant demands for change from below.

The results of the 1989 elections to the congress were a shock to the Communist Party elite. Although approved party stalwarts won the majority of contests, dozens of fairly prominent officials were humiliatingly defeated. In a number of races where unpopular officials ran unopposed, the candidates lost when a majority of voters took advantage of their right to vote against them. The winners included reform-minded party candidates as well as academics and others calling for more radical reforms. The most prominent winner of all was Yeltsin, who scored a resounding triumph in Moscow after being demoted by Gorbachev for criticizing the government's feeble reform policies.

From this moment on, Gorbachev increasingly lost control over the reform process. Far more alarmingly, the winds of democratic change swirling in the Soviet Union could not help but have a devastating effect on the communist-run governments of Central and Eastern Europe. Within only a few hectic months, the emergence of democracy in the USSR would sweep away Communist Party rule from the Soviet Union's hard-won postwar empire.

Gorbachev's Foreign Policy

From its very beginnings, Gorbachev's policy of domestic reform had an important foreign policy component. One of the principal obstacles to economic growth and modernization in the Soviet economy was the stultifying effect of military spending. Gorbachev knew that if the economy was to be rescued, he had to remove the dead weight of the Soviet military-industrial complex on the budgetary process and the powerful political influence of the high command. Changes of this sort inevitably required a radical reorientation in the Kremlin's policies toward the West. In 1987, Gorbachev and President Ronald Reagan agreed to eliminate all the intermediate range missiles they had installed in the European theater in recent years, a major step toward ending the Cold War. In 1988, Gorbachev declared his intention of withdrawing all Soviet troops from Afghanistan in the following year.

It was in East Central Europe that the Gorbachev phenomenon had its most unexpected consequences. Gorbachev hoped that the ruling Communist Parties in the area would replace their repressive, Brezhnev-style regimes with more pliable reform-oriented Communists like himself. The tumultuous East European revolutions of 1989 began quietly enough. As the year got under way, Hungary's ruling Communist Party, whose reformist wing was even more radical than Gorbachev's, announced it would hold democratic, multiparty elections the following year. In April, the Polish government completed eight weeks of intensive bargaining with representatives of the once-outlawed Solidarity organization that led to parliamentary elections in June that Solidarity swept. In 1990 Lech Walesa, Solidarity's leader, was elected Poland's president.

By far the most dramatic transformation occurred in East Germany, where a hard-line Communist elite incensed at Gorbachev's reformism clung to power. In November, the East German authorities decided to open the Berlin Wall. The opening released a surge of pent-up opposition to communism and a desire on the part of most East Germans to be united with West Germany. The Communist state swiftly disintegrated, permitting the incorporation of eastern Germany into the Federal Republic of Germany in 1990 (see Chapter 15).[24]

Inspired by the East Germans and with no signs of imminent assistance from Gorbachev, the Czechoslovak authorities quietly yielded power to democratic forces led by Vaclav Havel, the playwright who epitomized the country's courageous dissident movement. In December, scarcely a month after Czechoslovakia's "velvet revolution," demonstrators in Bucharest shouted down Romania's tyrannical dictator, Nicolae Ceausescu, who was arrested by rivals within Romania's Communist elite and subsequently executed. Meanwhile, the Soviet Union engineered a behind-the-scenes transfer of power in Bulgaria, replacing an aging Communist autocrat with a more flexible party leadership.[25]

To the world's astonishment, the Soviet Union's reformist government had let East Central Europe and the Warsaw Pact military alliance slip through its fingers. In the West, Gorbachev won universal acclaim and was awarded the Nobel Peace Prize. But at home, hard-line critics of his reformist policies were mortified. At the same time, proponents of an even more radical reform course set the stage for the USSR's eventual disintegration.

The USSR Falls Apart

As resistance to Gorbachev stiffened at all levels of the CPSU, Gorbachev sought to shift the locus of decision-making power in the Soviet Union from the party organs, over which he presided as general secretary, to newly created state institutions such as the Congress of People's Deputies. In March 1990 the congress elected him to a new post as president of the Soviet Union. At no time, however, was Gorbachev ever elected to any of his positions by popular vote. His failure to obtain a mandate from the people was a significant factor in accelerating the collapse of his authority.

Time, however, was running out on Gorbachev's efforts to reform a one-party system that was proving highly resistant to change. The public's patience was also wearing thin as the economy continued to deteriorate. Lacking a clear policy vision,

Gorbachev was caught in a tug-of-war between traditionalists, who hoped to preserve the central planning system with as few alterations as possible, and an increasingly vocal group of radicals who believed that the system was incapable of being reformed and needed to be replaced by a market economy. Attempts to forge a compromise between a market economy and central planning proved futile. Gorbachev's refusal to permit the privatization of Russia's collective farms was another major disappointment for the market-oriented reformers.[26]

An equally serious problem was the growth of independence movements in key Soviet republics. Gorbachev's democratization policies had mobilized the populations of Lithuania, Latvia, and Estonia to militate for independence. After elections held in 1990 brought pro independence forces to power, Lithuania declared its independence and the other two states announced their intention to secede from the Soviet Union in the near future. Separatist movements also sprang up in Georgia, Armenia, and other Soviet republics. Far more ominously for Gorbachev, the Russian Republic, the largest and most populous part of the USSR, was also moving toward greater independence from the central government. In March 1990 Russia elected its own parliament. Two months later, Russian legislators elected Boris Yeltsin as the Russian Republic's top official despite Gorbachev's explicit opposition to the move. The Russian legislature then took the bold step of declaring that its laws superseded the laws of the Soviet Union within its territory, a flagrant repudiation of Gorbachev's central Soviet government.

Over the summer of 1990, Ukraine and several other Soviet republics declared their sovereignty within the USSR. Gorbachev's efforts to halt the Soviet Union's progressive dismemberment proved futile. The USSR was crumbling beneath his feet.

In June 1991, the first popular elections ever held for president of Russia gave Boris Yeltsin a strong popular mandate to lead the Russian Republic. It also gave him a popular legitimacy that Gorbachev, who never faced the voters, could not claim. Gorbachev worked assiduously to negotiate an agreement with most of the constituent republics of the USSR to establish a new set of ground rules for the Soviet Union. However, while on a fateful vacation in the Crimea in early August, Gorbachev became the target of a coup attempt.

The 1991 Coup and Its Aftermath

Vladimir Kryuchkov, the head of the KGB, led a plot to remove Gorbachev from power and reimpose a stern Communist Party dictatorship. A delegation sent to the Crimea by the conspirators, who held other top positions in the state apparatus, instructed Gorbachev to sign a decree declaring a state of emergency throughout the USSR and urged him to resign. According to his own account, Gorbachev refused both ultimatums. Right from the outset, the coup attempt went awry. On hearing the news, Russia's President Yeltsin rushed to the White House, the home of the Russian parliament. Mounting one of the tanks the plotters had ordered into downtown Moscow, Yeltsin denounced the coup as illegal and called on the citizens of

Russia to oppose it. Together with a group of Russian officials, he then ensconced himself in the White House while barricades went up outside its doors. Yeltsin called for a general strike of the whole population.

The coup then unraveled like a bizarre comedy. One of the plotters called a televised press conference only to be bombarded with embarrassing questions. Another plotter, the prime minister, was drunk. The next day, Yeltsin addressed 100,000 people from the White House balcony. Soviet generals and KGB leaders met to discuss how to disperse the throng, but the high command was divided: A number of commanders and other officers were clearly reluctant to attack the civilians in front of the White House. Later that evening, the plotters made the crucial decision to back away from the use of force. The coup was over. Returning from the Crimea, Gorbachev found himself in "a new country": For the first time in their history, Russian citizens had openly defied the coercive power of the state and won a victory for democracy.[27] For Gorbachev himself, the end of his extraordinary run in office was at hand. Now enormously popular, Yeltsin orchestrated the final disintegration of the Union of Soviet Socialist Republics. On December 25, Gorbachev resigned the presidency of a country that was about to expire. As the bells tolled midnight on December 31, the USSR formally ceased to exist. Looking back on his experience several years later, Gorbachev wrote, "I never for a moment thought that the transformations I had initiated, no matter how far-reaching, would result in the replacement of the rule of the 'reds' by that of the 'whites.'" With the failure of his attempt to reform Soviet communism, the fate of Russia now passed into non-communist hands for the first time since the October Revolution 74 years earlier.

Gorbachev's Legacy

Unquestionably, Gorbachev left office having granted the Russian people far more freedom than they had ever before enjoyed. Greater freedom of speech and the ability to criticize the ruling authorities without fear of violent retribution; growing freedom of political association and opportunities to vote in competitive elections; freedom of religious worship; freedom to leave the country; freedom to own private property and start a business—these and other liberties that emerged in the course of Gorbachev's tenure, however limited in scope, would have been unimaginable under previous Communist leaders. Most of the political liberties Gorbachev permitted (as opposed to the economic liberties) were unprecedented in Russian history, if one regards the few brief months of constitutional democracy under the provisional government in 1917 as but a momentary aberration.

However, while Gorbachev's policies triggered a real revolution in Russian politics, it was an unintended revolution. It was a revolution pushed forward by the forces of mass expectations for change and by elite disarray that he had unleashed but could not rein in. In his heart of hearts, Gorbachev was a reformer, not a revolutionary. Perhaps no one better understood the limitations of Gorbachev's approach more deeply than the

man who would rise as his most vocal challenger and ultimate successor: Boris Yeltsin.

YELTSIN'S RUSSIA

In 1985, Gorbachev summoned Boris Yeltsin to Moscow and put him in charge of a party Central Committee section that supervised the Soviet construction industry. At the end of the year Yeltsin gained even more prestige when he was named chief of the Communist Party's Moscow city organization. Yeltsin now had the authority to govern the Soviet Union's capital city, the hub of its highly centralized political system. Although Yeltsin's main task was to implement Gorbachev's reform program, it soon became apparent that the two men had radically different concepts of both the scope and the pace of the reform process.

Yeltsin vigorously charged into his assignment, immersing himself in the daily life of the city. Before long he was railing against the privileges of the party elite, who had their pick of special shops, hospitals, cars, and other perquisites of power that the mass of Soviet citizens could only dream about. Convinced that the local party apparatus was riddled with inefficiency and corruption, he fired half its members. In the process, Yeltsin became increasingly critical of Gorbachev himself, viewing him as indecisive and far too reticent to take on the entrenched bureaucrats who were determined to block reform. At a meeting of the Communist Party's powerful Central Committee in 1987, Yeltsin delivered a stinging critique of the party's failure to implement a concrete reform program. He accused Gorbachev of building a "personality cult"—the very same charge that Khrushchev had leveled at Stalin in his famous secret speech of 1956. For his transgressions, Yeltsin was summarily dismissed from his Moscow post and consigned to a demeaning job in the bureaucracy.

Ironically, Gorbachev's political reforms provided Yeltsin with unexpected openings to revive his political career. In the 1989 elections to Gorbachev's newly created legislature, the Congress of People's Deputies, Yeltsin captured more than 89 percent of the votes in his Moscow legislative district, soundly thrashing his Gorbachev-backed opponent.[28] In 1990, Yeltsin became a member of Russia's parliament, which soon declared that its laws would henceforward take precedence over Soviet laws throughout the Russian Republic. Yeltsin then dramatically announced his resignation from the Communist Party. Yeltsin got another boost in June 1991, when he went before the people in the first-ever popular election to Russia's presidency. Deftly playing upon mounting dissatisfaction with Gorbachev's ineffectiveness, he won a convincing 57.3 percent of the vote, besting five rivals.

Scarcely two months after this electoral triumph, the coup aimed at unseating Gorbachev from power suddenly presented Yeltsin with his greatest challenge. Yeltsin bravely resisted the plotters in Gorbachev's behalf. In the process, he became the effective leader not only of the coup's opponents but of all those who wanted a clean break with the hard-line Communists. After the coup collapsed, Yeltsin pushed Gorbachev to the sidelines. Over the next several months, Yeltsin worked frenetically to dismantle the last vestiges of the Soviet leader's power by dismantling the Soviet Union itself. In December, Russia and eight other Soviet republics formed the Commonwealth of Independent States, a loose organization in which each member state agreed to respect the sovereign independence of all the others.[29] On January 1, 1992, the Russian Federation formally entered the world as an independent country under President Boris Yeltsin.

Transforming the Economy

Yeltsin and his advisors wasted no time in their attempts to transform Russia's economy from a largely state-run operation to a mixed economy with market mechanisms. To some extent they were guided by prescriptions offered by Western economists, who called for a rapid "shock therapy" approach to restructuring the economy, arguing that it would be better to change the economic system all at once rather than in a piecemeal process stretched out over a long period. But quite a few Russian economists and political leaders feared that an excessively rapid transformation program might trigger social disruptions and political instability. Yeltsin's government therefore began with a partial approach to shock therapy, adopting bits and pieces of the shock therapists' guidelines rather than their entire program. Even so, Yeltsin's initial measures went considerably farther than Gorbachev's, and their effects were shocking enough for many Russians.[30]

On January 2, 1992, the day after Russia formally became an independent state, the government removed government price controls on a host of products and lifted wage controls on various job categories. The new administration also announced substantial cuts in military spending and other items to reduce the budget deficit. Several months later it declared the convertibility of the ruble, permitting it to be exchanged into other denominations in world currency markets. Most important, over the course of its first year in power the new Russian government unveiled an ambitious privatization timetable. Half the state's large and medium-size companies were expected to be privatized by 1995, and all state-owned small industries and consumer services and a considerable portion of the nation's housing were to be in private hands by 1994. A plan to turn Russia's population into shareholders in the newly privatized companies went awry, however. In 1992 the government handed out vouchers to more than 140 million people. The vouchers were investment securities, to be retained or sold like stocks. But many Russians failed to understand what the vouchers were all about, or they simply did not believe they were worth very much. Some sold them cheaply or gave them away, with shrewd investors and insiders acquiring a disproportionately large share.

From the outset, the Yeltsin government's economic initiatives failed to meet the expectations of the optimists in the president's entourage. Inflation soared 20 to 30 percent per month, finishing 1992 at 2,500 percent for the year. Though more food and other goods began appearing on store shelves,

prices were too high for many Russians, long habituated under the old central planning system to cheap government-subsidized prices for milk, bread, and other staples. Gross domestic product in 1992 was 14.5 percent lower than in the previous year and plummeted another 8.7 percent in 1993 and a further 12.6 percent in 1994. The Russian government's budget deficits bulged to as much as 20 percent of GDP, a figure more than double the IMF's recommended target. The government lacked the funds to pay millions of people employed in the state sector, while pensions fell far behind the galloping price increases. Unemployment grew to more than 150,000 in 1992, a far cry from the zero unemployment the old Communist regime used to boast. By 1994 some 24 million people—more than 16 percent of the population—lived below the government's official poverty line, a subsistence level of $1 to $2 a day. Meanwhile, a small minority of ambitious capitalists, some of them with exceptional political connections or ties to criminal elements, reaped overnight fortunes, resulting in a widening gap between rich and poor. The stresses of economic change and uncertainty had a visible impact on public health.[31]

Not surprisingly, support for market reforms and even for democracy itself began to dissipate during Yeltsin's first years as president of independent Russia. By 1992, only 42 percent of Muscovites identified themselves as part of the "democratic camp," down from 62 percent following the previous year's coup attempt against Gorbachev. Less than two years later, only 25 percent of Russians said they favored market reforms, compared with 40 percent in 1989; a majority described privatization as "legalized theft." Nevertheless, the Yeltsin government persevered in its reform course. By the end of 1994, half the workforce was employed by private enterprise, while 70 percent of Russian industry was privatized and over a million small businesses were in operation. It was the *political* aspect of economic reform that was to cause Yeltsin more headaches than the privatization process per se.

The Politics of Reform

On assuming control of the newly independent Russian state, Yeltsin inherited the legislature that had been elected in the Russian part of the Soviet Union in March 1990, a time when the Communist Party of the Soviet Union still dominated the Soviet political system. Of 1,046 deputies elected to Russia's Congress of People's Deputies that year, only about a hundred were strongly committed to Yeltsin's vision of radical economic transformation, with perhaps another 150 willing to support Yeltsin fairly consistently. Divided into as many as 17 factions, the Congress included more than 350 hard-liners opposed to the wholesale dismantling of the state-controlled economic system. At the end of 1992 the antireform majority in the Congress pressured Yeltsin to jettison his young prime minister, Yegor Gaidar.[32]

The clash between President Yeltsin and his antireform opponents escalated throughout 1992 and 1993. In April 1993 a referendum gave Yeltsin a boost of popular approval: Some

58 percent of those who turned out to vote expressed their confidence in him. Yeltsin dissolved the legislature in September and ordered new parliamentary elections to be held three months later. Yeltsin admitted that his action violated the existing constitution, but he insisted that the April referendum had given him the right to take extraordinary measures to break the country's political gridlock. Incensed at Yeltsin's breach of constitutional authority, hard-line politicians declared that Yeltsin was no longer the legitimate president of Russia. They barricaded themselves in the White House, the legislature's home, and named one of their leaders, Vice President Alexander Rutskoi, as Russia's new president.

The crisis threatened to crack the fragile foundations of Russian democracy. After 11 days of confrontation, Rutskoi ordered thousands of anti-Yeltsin demonstrators to storm the pro-Yeltsin, state-owned television station. Waving Communist Party flags, the crowd next marched on the Moscow mayor's office. Yeltsin responded to this provocation by ordering a military attack on the White House. Leading generals decided to support Yeltsin as the only duly elected president of the country. The operation was quick and effective: Rutskoi and others were arrested, and parts of the White House were set ablaze with more than a hundred people killed.

Yeltsin declared a state of emergency, imposed censorship, and reaffirmed his plan to set new legislative elections for December. The Russian people would also be asked to vote on a new constitution prepared under his direction. The manner in which Yeltsin used his manifestly superior power over his opponents in the fall of 1993—imposing a new constitutional order on Russia with practically no public debate—was bound to have long-term effects on the quality of Russia's democracy. It made for a prolonged transition process in which the balance of institutional power would tilt heavily in the direction of a strong presidency, leaving the legislature and the courts in considerably weaker positions.[33] In a constitutional referendum held on December 12, 1993, the voters overwhelmingly approved Yeltsin's proposed constitution, with 58.4 percent voting in its favor. The new charter created a dual executive modeled on the French constitution, with a politically active president sharing power with a prime minister. The bicameral legislature, as in France, was kept relatively weak. (We'll discuss the constitution's provisions later in this chapter.)

However, the vote for the new lower house held the same day, the State Duma, turned out considerably less satisfactory from Yeltsin's point of view. The electoral system involved a combination of proportional representation (with a 5 percent hurdle) and single-member districts: Half the Duma's 450 seats were elected under PR and the other half under the SMD/plurality system. (See Chapter 6 for a description of these electoral systems.) Thirteen parties fielded candidates, most of them fairly new.

Shockingly, the party to emerge with the largest share of the popular vote and 14.1 percent of the Duma seats was the Liberal Democratic Party (LDP), an arch-nationalist grouping under the leadership of Vladimir Zhirinovsky, a flamboyant right-winger with outrageously chauvinistic views. Another determined foe of Yeltsin's economic policies was the Communist Party of the Russian Federation (CPRF; also known as the Russian Communist Party, or RCP). Led by Gennady Zyuganov, a party apparatchik since the 1960s, the Communists opposed the rapid economic transformation process but offered no clear alternative program. Professing their acceptance of democracy, they blasted Yeltsin for abusing his authority. Together with the Agrarian Party, their ally, the Communists took 17.3 percent of the seats in the Duma.

The most outspokenly pro-reform party, Russia's Choice, garnered a disappointing 14.4 percent of the seats in the Duma. Quite a few voters gravitated instead to moderate parties that were favorable to economic reform in principle but opposed to the accelerated tempo of shock therapy. The most successful was Yabloko, a party whose name derived from Grigory Yavlinsky and two other co-founders. (Yabloko is the Russian word for "apple.") Yavlinsky, a Western-oriented economist, advocated a socially harmonious path to reform and opposed Yeltsin's constitution, with its highly centralized presidential power. The divisions in the Duma among these and other contending parties were further complicated because 30.2 percent of the elected candidates had no party affiliation.

The elections held two years later, in December 1995, were a sharp rebuke to Yeltsin. The Communists staged a comeback. With slightly more than a third of the Duma, the Communists emerged as Russia's largest party. Opponents of Yeltsin's reform policies held the majority. The Duma's checkered political composition was to create insurmountable problems for Yeltsin. The lack of a clear popular mandate for radical reform and the absence of a reliable majority of Duma deputies in Yeltsin's favor resulted in a series of policy flip-flops and political maneuvers that were to plague Yeltsin's presidency until his resignation in 1999.

The electoral rebuke for Yeltsin in 1995 should have come as no surprise. Between 20 percent and 40 percent of the population lived below the poverty line in 1995. The richest 10 percent earned 14 times the income of the poorest 10 percent—a gap that had widened appreciably since 1993. Some 40 percent of state employees had not been paid in full or on time. Out on the land, the 1995 grain harvest was the worst in 30 years.

Meanwhile, the privatization process was slowing. With some of the largest state-owned companies still in government hands, managers, banks, and political insiders worked quietly behind the scenes to acquire large stakes in their privatization. Gazprom, the largest gas company in the world, shifted more than 60 percent of its assets to politically connected insiders, with the state retaining the rest. Hopes for a "people's capitalism" based on widespread stock ownership were giving way to "crony capitalism" and "market Bolshevism." A new breed of powerful tycoons, some with ties to the old Soviet regime and all with carefully cultivated connections with the current political elite, was taking over the "commanding heights" of the Russian economy, including banks, energy firms, mines, television stations, publishing houses, holding companies, and other lucrative assets.[34] In addition, the criminal networks that made up the Russian mafia cast an ominous shadow over the entire economy, extorting protection money from businesspeople, bribing public officials, and extending their criminal operations across Russia and around the world. Crime in general was also on the rise, especially violent crime.[35]

Russians also worried about the war in Chechnya, which illustrated both the concerns of non-Russian peoples in the new Russian Federation and the approach that the government in Moscow was likely to take toward them.

Chechnya

On December 11, 1994, an invasion force of 40,000 Russian troops stormed into *Chechnya*. The operation sought to put a quick end to a secessionist movement that threatened to unravel Russia's structure as a federated state. Based largely on the territorial subdivisions of the former USSR, the Russian Federation consists of 83 administrative units (see Map 16.1). Though most had an ethnic Russian majority, 21 of these subdivisions, designated as *republics*, had a non-Russian majority. Most had been incorporated into Russia's expanding empire in the tsarist era, Chechnya in 1859. The Chechens are a distinct ethnic group practicing Islam.

From the first months of Russia's existence as an independent state in 1992, the leadership of the Chechen Republic, nestled in the Caucasus Mountains, began militating for complete independence. Chechnya had a population of about 1.2 million in that year, of whom only about 250,000 were Russians. But any attempt to break out of the freshly established Russian Federation constituted a serious provocation to the central government in Moscow, which had reason to fear that other regions might insist on independence as well if the Chechens succeeded. Open conflict between Chechen rebels and the central government began in the summer of 1994, when Yeltsin sent in troops from the Federal Counterintelligence Service, a successor to the Soviet-era KGB. The Chechens quickly repulsed the small force. On December 2, Soviet planes began bombing Grozny, Chechnya's capital city. With the invasion nine days later, the war was on. While the Russian military had expected the conflict to be over very quickly and easily, casualties mounted heavily, with estimates running between 40,000 and 60,000 civilians killed by the end of 1995.[36]

The 1996 Presidential Election

At 65 and in poor health, Yeltsin entered the 1996 presidential fray against nine other contenders with surprising vigor. But the

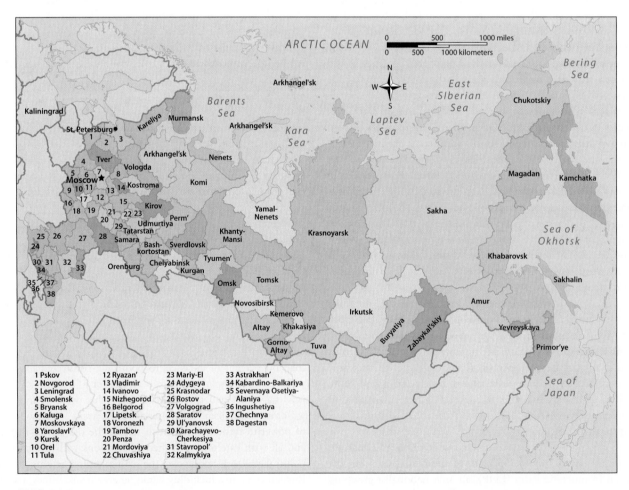

MAP 16.1   The Russian Federation

first polls showed him trailing his chief rival, Gennady Zyuganov of the Russian Communist Party. Zyuganov appealed to Russian voters nostalgic for "the good old days" of economic stability and international respect in the former USSR.[37]

Recognizing that his chances were slim as long as the bloody Chechen war dragged on, Yeltsin arranged a hasty meeting with a separatist leader and signed a cease-fire, promising Chechnya maximum autonomy within the Russian Federation. With the state-owned television station at his disposal, Yeltsin dominated the airwaves as the campaign intensified, aided by Western political advertising specialists. He dipped deeply into a lavish war chest of nearly $1 billion in campaign funds, provided largely by a group of tycoons who were determined to stop Zyuganov and the Communists.

In the first election round, held June 16, 1996, Yeltsin topped the list with 35.3 percent of the vote. Zyuganov finished second, with 32 percent. Mikhail Gorbachev was a forgotten figure, winning only 0.5 percent of the vote. Because Yeltsin had not won an absolute majority of the votes cast, he was obliged to run head-to-head against Zyuganov in a second round. But several days after his first-round triumph, Yeltsin collapsed and dropped out of sight. Panic gripped his entourage as rumors circulated about a heart attack or stroke. He finally reemerged on election day, looking haggard and expressionless as he cast his ballot. But the returns were positive: On July 3, the president edged out Zyuganov by 53.8 percent to 40.3 percent. Nearly 5 percent had voted against both contestants. Yeltsin's margin of victory was surprisingly high in some regions, the result of pressures exerted on local officials to report an exaggerated result in the president's favor.[38]

Yeltsin's 1996 electoral victory marked the high point of his presidency. From then until his resignation at the end of 1999, his declining health required him to spend long periods away from his desk at the Kremlin. Yeltsin's prolonged absences created a void at the highest levels of Russia's political system, stimulating intense rivalries for power among a handful of well-placed intimates in the executive branch—including his daughter. The absence of a legislative majority in the Duma in favor of radical market reforms and amicable relations with the West further constricted Yeltsin's ability to pursue a consistent reform course and a more cooperative pro-Western foreign policy.[39]

The Russian economy veered from one obstacle to the next. Privatization came to a near stop, tax revenues withered, and the budget shrank. Corruption festered, with possibly more than 40 percent of the Russian economy controlled by organized crime. Cronyism remained pervasive, with political and economic power concentrated in the hands of rival "clans."[40]

But Yeltsin's infirmities quickly overshadowed everything. The president had a quintuple bypass operation after his 1996 election, and entered a sanitarium in October 1998, returning briefly only to be hospitalized in January 1999 with a bleeding ulcer. His health continued to fluctuate until his retirement at the end of 1999.

Economic Woes

In the power vacuum opened by Yeltsin's afflictions, ambitious figures jockeyed for influence behind the scenes. About a dozen tycoons had amassed spectacular wealth since the collapse of the USSR by acquiring some of Russia's most lucrative businesses, including television stations, banks, and other holdings. Even the majority of shares in Russia's lucrative energy sector fell into private hands, with the state retaining minority ownership. As the so-called oligarchs grabbed control of the most important branches of Russia's private sector, they also competed with one another for political clout. With Yeltsin almost permanently incapacitated, financial barons such as Boris Berezovsky acquired powerful positions at the highest echelons of the Russian government. In effect, the financial oligarchs and a small group of insiders close to Yeltsin were running Russia in secret, with little or no accountability to the legislature or the voters.[41]

Meanwhile, Yeltsin shuffled prime ministers at a dizzying pace. Several of them got caught in the crosswinds of the global financial crisis buffeting developing economies from Asia to Latin America in 1997 and 1998. On August 18, 1998, the government announced a 34 percent devaluation of the ruble and a moratorium on Russia's payments on its international commercial debts. (At the time, Russia's total foreign debt was $200 billion.) The ruble's devaluation spelled economic ruin for millions of Russians as the value of their meager savings collapsed.

Yeltsin's popularity continued to nosedive. In the spring of 1999 the Communists launched an impeachment process against him for presiding over the Soviet Union's demise and other alleged political offenses. Like French presidents, Yeltsin let his prime ministers take the blame for the government's problems. He fired one after another before naming a relative unknown, Vladimir Putin, to that precarious position in 1999. After Yeltsin announced his resignation on New Year's Eve, tearfully acknowledging that "many of the dreams we shared did not come true," he declared his support for Putin in the presidential race set for 2000, a proposal Putin immediately accepted.

Vladimir Putin

In the years since he was brought to power by Yeltsin, Vladimir Putin has put his personal stamp on the evolution of post-Soviet Russian society. Putin has firmly held the reins of power since 1999, whether as president or prime minister. Alternative centers of power, such as regional authorities, have found their autonomy and their effective power diminished even as Putin is more and more able to rule impose his will. Despite what many regard as the reassertion of autocratic power, Putin remains widely popular in Russia and shows no indication that he will relinquish control of the Russian state until at least 2024, when he will next be barred from standing for reelection as president.

Putin Takes Over Putin had spent his early career from 1975 to 1990 in the KGB, mostly as an agent in communist East Germany. One of his law professors had been Anatoly

Sobchak, a liberal reformer who became mayor of Leningrad (later renamed St. Petersburg) and a staunch opponent of the anti-Gorbachev coup in 1991. Sobchak offered his former student a position as the city's unelected deputy mayor, a slot Putin held from 1990 to 1994, the formative years of post-communist Russia. In 1994 the government's privatization chief brought Putin to Moscow, where he initially headed the bureau responsible for Kremlin property and subsequently the office overseeing Russia's 89 regional governors. In the summer of 1998, Yeltsin named him director of the Federal Security Service (FSB), a powerful intelligence agency that succeeded the KGB, and later appointed him to the National Security Council.

Despite the votes of Communists and some radical reformers against him, Putin was confirmed on August 16, only a week after his nomination. He retained his predecessor's cabinet and announced no new policy initiatives, but his government was quickly thrown into a severe crisis. A week earlier, Chechen separatists had invaded the neighboring Russian province of Dagestan and declared their intention of creating an independent state. As soon as Putin took office, he gave the military one week to oust the rebels. Russian forces accomplished their task within the deadline, driving the rebels back into Chechnya. Within weeks a large-scale invasion force was in place, with aerial and artillery bombardments pounding Grozny and rebel strongholds. Casualties on both sides mounted rapidly. Putin received strong public endorsement from most Russians for his determination to defeat the rebels, especially after a series of random bombings of apartment buildings and other civilian centers rattled Moscow and other urban areas.

December 1999 Legislative Elections Another immediate challenge confronting the new prime minister was the upcoming parliamentary election set for December. In the months preceding the vote, Russia's fledgling party system underwent a number of changes. Five reform-oriented parties consolidated their forces in a new grouping, the Union of Right-Wing Forces. Traditionalists led by Moscow's mayor,

Yuri Luzhkov, formed a new party, Fatherland, dedicated to a "strong state" within the framework of democratic freedoms and a mixed economy. Support for the new party widened when another new grouping, a collection of regional leaders calling themselves the All Russia Movement, linked up with Fatherland. Prime Minister Putin's followers took urgent steps to create a new pro-government party called Unity. Unity was a curious mix of liberals, Christian democrats, communists, nationalists, and pure opportunists.

To the surprise of many observers, Unity did quite well, garnering 73 seats. The pro-reform parties all lost seats, with the Union of Right-Wing Forces capturing only 29. The Communists won the largest share of popular votes in the party list vote (24 percent) and remained the largest party with 113 seats. The traditionalist Fatherland-All Russia bloc came close to matching Unity's performance (68 seats). Zhirinovsky's party, the Liberal Democrats, was disqualified before the election for failing to meet election law requirements, but Zhirinovsky quickly assembled a new bloc of candidates. His supporters lost seats, falling from 51 in 1995 to 17. The real political coloration of the new Duma ultimately depended on more than 100 deputies elected as independents or as representatives of small parties (see Table 16.1).

Unexpectedly, a scant two weeks after the Duma elections, President Boris Yeltsin stepped down from the presidency. By the terms of the constitution, Prime Minister Putin immediately assumed the role of acting president while preparations began for a rescheduled presidential election to be held within three months. In the interval, Putin enlarged his own share of popular support, winning plaudits for his success in providing full financing for Russia's social welfare programs for the first time since independence while simultaneously raising pensions and paying a substantial portion of back wages. His government also achieved a measure of economic stability, aided by a global rise in prices for oil, Russia's most valuable export commodity. Despite more than a thousand Russian army casualties in Chechnya and international criticism for harsh battle tactics, Putin's prosecution of the war against the secessionists remained acceptable to many Russians.

Table 16.1 **1999 Elections to State Duma**

Party	% PR Vote	PR Seats	SMD Seats	Total Seats	% Seats
Communists	24.3%	67	46	113	25.1%
Unity	23.3	64	9	73	16.2
Fatherland-All Russia	13.3	37	31	68	15.1
Union of Right-Wing Forces	8.5	24	5	29	6.4
Yabloko	5.9	16	4	20	4.4
Zhirinovsky bloc	6.0	17	0	17	3.8
Our Home Is Russia	1.2	0	7	7	1.6
Independents	—	—	114	114	25.3
Seven small parties	(<2.0 each)	0	9	9	2.0
Against all candidates	3.5				
Turnout: 61.7%					

Source: Richard Rose and Neil Munro, *Elections Without Order: Russia's Challenge to Vladimir Putin* (Cambridge: Cambridge University Press, 2002), p. 132.

Table 16.2 Presidential Elections, 2000 to 2012

2000		2004		2008		2012	
Candidate	**Vote %**	**Candidate**	**Vote %**	**Candidate**	**Vote %**	**Candidate**	**Vote %**
Putin (Independent)	53.4%	Putin (Independent)	71.9%	Medvedev (United Russia)	70.3%	Putin (United Russia)	63.6%
Zyuganov (Communist)	29.5	Kharitonov (Communist)	13.8	Zyuganov (Communist)	17.7	Zyuganov (Communist)	17.2
Yavlinsky (Yabloko)	5.9	Glazyev (Independent)	4.1				
Tuteev (Independent)	3.0	Khakamada (Independent)	3.9	Andrei Bogdanov (Independent)	1.3	Prokhorov (Independent)	8.0
Zhirinovsky (Liberal Democrats)	2.7	Malyshkin (Liberal Democrats)	2.0	Zhirinovsky (Liberal Democrats)	9.3	Zhirinovsky (Liberal Democrats)	6.2
Six others	3.6	Mironov (Russia's Rebirth—Party of Life)	0.8			Mironov (Fair Russia)	3.9
Against all candidates	1.9	Against all candidates	3.5				

Source: www.russiavotes.org, based on Russian Federal Election Commission, www.fci.ru.

Once his most serious challenger, former Prime Minister Yevgeny Primakov, dropped out of the race, Putin was able to secure a convincing first-round victory, garnering 53.4 percent of the vote. Because of his absolute majority, a second round of voting was not necessary. More than 39.9 million citizens had voted for him. Putin was reelected on March 14, 2004, winning over 71 percent in the first round against five rivals[42] (see Table 16.2). Limited by the constitution to two terms, Putin selected his successor, Dmitry Medvedev, elected in 2008. Putin and Medvedev made a deal: While Medvedev was president, Putin would be his prime minister. In 2012, they would switch roles. Thus, in 2012, Putin won election again, and Medvedev became prime minister. After we consider the post-1991 institutional structure carefully, we'll consider the politics of Putin's Russia.

PUTIN'S RUSSIA

The years since 2000 have been dominated by Vladimir Putin, who many regard as a new tsar or dictator. Putin served as president until 2008, then as prime minister under President Medvedev until 2012, and has now returned to the presidency, which he could hold until 2024 if reelected. Having dominated the first dozen years of the twenty-first century, Putin threatens to be Russia's ruler for the second dozen.

The Institutional Structure

The constitution approved by Russia's voters in the December 1993 referendum established a mixed *presidential–parliamentary* institutional structure modeled to a considerable extent on the constitution of contemporary France (the Fifth Republic—see Chapter 14). At the national level it consists of the following:

- A dual executive with a powerful decision-making president, who is head of state, and a responsible prime minister, who is head of government.

- A bicameral legislature, the *Federal Assembly*, consisting of the *State Duma* (the lower house) and the *Federation Council* (the upper house).

- An independent judiciary, consisting at the national level of the *Constitutional Court*, empowered to rule on the constitutionality of laws and treaties and to settle disputes concerning the competence of state institutions; the *Supreme Court*, the highest court with jurisdiction over civil and criminal law and other cases arising from courts of common pleas; and the *Supreme Arbitration Court*, the highest court authorized to settle economic disputes arising from lower economic arbitration courts. Most of the constitution can be amended only with the approval of two-thirds of the citizenry in a referendum.

The President Russia's president is elected directly by the people to a six-year term (with a limit of two consecutive terms; until a constitutional amendment in 2008, the term length had been four years). A candidate who wins more than half the votes is elected president. If no one wins more than half the votes in the first round, a second round is held between the top two finishers of the first round. The president is the country's single most important decision maker. In addition to being the "guarantor" of the population's civil rights and freedoms and commander in chief of the armed forces, the president enjoys the right to "determine the guidelines of the domestic and foreign policy of the state," thus possessing considerable authority to initiate and conduct policy. Like France's president, the president of Russia has real political power, in contrast to ceremonial heads of state such as the presidents of Germany and Israel. The most important presidential prerogatives in the 1993 constitution include the authority to

- Nominate the prime minister for approval by the Duma.
- Appoint and remove deputy prime ministers and other cabinet ministers upon the prime minister's proposals (and without Duma approval).

- Preside over government (cabinet) meetings.
- Submit bills directly to the Duma.
- Veto federal laws passed by the Federal Assembly, subject to an overriding vote by two-thirds of the membership of each house.
- Dissolve the Duma in the event that it rejects three presidential nominations for prime minister or passes a vote of no-confidence in the government.
- Issue decrees and directives binding throughout the country.
- Nominate the chairman of Russia's State Bank for approval by the Duma, and nominate the justices of the three high courts for approval by the Federation Council.
- Place referendums before the voters.
- Announce a state of emergency in all or part of Russia, informing the Federal Assembly of this decision.
- Take charge of Russia's foreign and defense policies and sign international treaties.

The president may be removed from office only for high treason or some other "grave crime." The procedure requires the Duma to pass formal accusations by two-thirds majority, followed by validation of the charges by the Supreme Court and the Constitutional Court. The Federation Council may then remove the president by two-thirds vote.

In some respects the Russian president's powers are even greater than those of France's president, especially the right to issue decrees and veto bills passed by the legislature. Although the constitution stipulates that presidential decrees may not violate its provisions, it specifies no other limitations to this important prerogative, thus creating a potential for the abuse of power. As we'll see, President Putin has used his presidential powers forcefully, acting at times solely on his own authority to issue decrees and at other times with the support of his sizable majority of supporters in the legislature.

The Prime Minister and Government

The prime minister—more formally, the chairman of the government—also has significant constitutional powers, though they are less sweeping than the president's. Most important, the premier is authorized to "determine guidelines" for the government's activities and to "organize its work," a somewhat vaguely worded provision that grants the head of government a certain amount of latitude to initiate and conduct domestic and foreign policy without trespassing on the president's primacy in these domains.

The six prime ministers who served under President Yeltsin had ample latitude to conduct the government's business, but Yeltsin ultimately held them accountable for the country's deteriorating economic situation. In his first eight years as president, Putin had three prime ministers. Putin's hands-on presidential style kept those prime ministers in distinctly subordinate positions. Putin was Medvedev's only prime minister. Since Putin returned to the presidency in 2012, Medvedev has been his prime minister. The Russian prime minister and the government are responsible to both the president and the Duma. The president

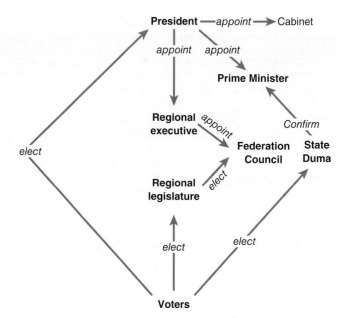

FIGURE 16.2   **Russia's Constitutional Structure**

nominates the premier, but the Duma has the right to confirm or reject the nominee by majority vote. If the president's nominee is rejected in three votes, the president must either nominate somebody else or dissolve the Duma and call snap elections. Yeltsin had trouble getting two of his nominees for prime minister confirmed. In the first case he threatened new elections, and the Duma approved his nominee on the third vote; in the second case he backed down and submitted a new nominee more acceptable to the Duma majority. The president has the right to dismiss the prime minister and other cabinet ministers. The Duma has the right to vote the government out of office in a no-confidence vote passed by the majority of its 450 members. If the president opts to reject this vote, the Duma may override his decision by passing another vote of no confidence within three months. If it succeeds, the president must then either nominate a new prime minister or dissolve the Duma and call snap elections. Snap elections called under these circumstances may not be called again for at least a year. Figure 16.2 illustrates the relationship among the major state institutions.

The Duma

The **State Duma** consists of 450 legislators elected to a five-year term (the term was four years until the 2008 constitutional amendments). As noted earlier, the 1993 constitution established a hybrid electoral system for the Duma: Half of the deputies were elected in single-member districts and the other half were elected by proportional representation on the basis of nationwide party lists. (Germany and Japan have variants of this "mixed-member" system.) This system was used in the Duma elections of 1993, 1995, 1999, and 2003. A 5 percent threshold prevented the proliferation of very small parties in the Duma. But the combination of weak, leader-driven parties, local political loyalties, and other factors resulted in the election of a large number of independent

Table 16.3 2003 Elections to State Duma

Party	% PR Vote	PR Seats	SMD Seats	Total Seats	% Seats
United Russia	37.6%	120	102	222	49.3%
Communist Party	12.6	40	12	52	11.6
Liberal Democrats	11.5	36	0	36	8.0
Motherland	9.0	29	8	37	8.2
People's Party	1.2	0	17	17	3.8
Yabloko	4.3	0	4	4	0.9
Union of Right-Wing Forces	4.0	0	3	3	0.7
Agrarian Party	3.7	0	2	2	0.4
Other parties*	11.6	0	6	6	1.3
Independents	—	—	68	68	15.1
Against all candidates	4.7	—	—	3[†]	—

* Smaller parties winning seats were Rebirth of Russia (three seats), and one each for New Course–Automobile Russia, Development of Enterprise, and Great Russia–Eurasia Union.

†Three seats went vacant because "against all candidates" took more votes than any individual candidate in three districts.

Sources: Central Election Commission, http://gd2003cikrf.ru; "Russia Votes," http://www.russiavotes.org/duma/duma_elections_93-03.php.

deputies with little or no party affiliation. Just about all of them were elected in the single-member districts. The presence of so many independents confused voters and made it difficult to form consistent parliamentary majorities without protracted negotiations between the main parties and independents whose votes were needed to pass legislation.

In his first term, Putin engineered an electoral reform aimed at reducing the number of parties by requiring all parties to have at least 10,000 members, spread out over at least half of "the subjects of the federation," the term used for Russia's constituent territorial units, or *regions*. Despite this reform, about 70 independent or small-party candidates were elected in 2003 (see Table 16.3). In 2004, shortly after the Beslan terrorist incident, Putin proposed an even more drastic electoral reform. As passed by the Federal Assembly the following year,

the new law abolishes the single-member districts and requires the entire Duma to be elected on the basis of party-list proportional representation. The threshold that a party must meet to be represented in the chamber was raised from 5 percent to 7 percent. Parties are no longer allowed to form electoral blocs or alliances to surmount the threshold jointly. Other changes to the electoral law include a ban on independent domestic election monitors (with international observers permitted by invitation only); the introduction of electronic voting in some areas; and permission for voters to vote in polling places other than the one in which they are registered without getting the prior approval of their local election officials. These changes took effect in the Duma elections scheduled for 2007. As a comparison of Tables 16.3 and 16.4 suggests, these changes in electoral rules significantly reduced the number of parties

Table 16.4 2007 and 2011 Elections to the State Duma

Party	2007			2011		
	Vote %	Seats	Seat %	Vote %	Seats	Seat %
United Russia	64.3%	315	70%	49.3%	238	52.9%
Communist Party	11.6	57	12.7	19.2	92	20.4
Fair Russia	7.7	38	8.4	13.2	64	14.2
Liberal Democrats	8.1	40	8.9	11.7	56	12.4
Agrarian Party	2.3	0	-			
Yabloko	1.6	0	-	3.4	0	-
Patriots of Russia	0.0	0	-	1.0	0	-
Civic Strength	1.0	0	-			
Union of Right-Wing Forces	1.0	0	-	0.6	0	-
Democratic Party of Russia	0.1	0	-			
Party of Social Fairness	0.2	0	-			

Civic Strength, the Union of Right Forces, and the Democratic Party of Russia became Right Cause for the 2011 election.

Source: www.russiavotes.org/duma/duma_electoral_system.php.

winning seats in the Duma to four in the past two elections, with independents now eliminated. Putin's critics charged that the electoral reforms were deliberately intended to make it more difficult for opposition parties to get elected and easier for Putin and his allies to manipulate the election process and its results. With no viable opposition to the governing party and its allies, there can be no alternation in power between competing parties. Electoral democracy is seriously diminished as a result. We look more closely at Russia's party system later in this chapter.

The Duma's chief functions are to hold the government accountable and enact legislation. As noted, it may accept or reject the president's nominee for prime minister, and it may unseat the government in a vote of confidence initiated either by the Duma or by the government. It is to the Duma that the president or the government submits bills for adoption into law. In addition, the Duma has the right to lodge accusations against the president for possible impeachment by the Federation Council. (The Duma may not be dissolved once the impeachment process begins, nor may it be dissolved during an emergency period.) And the Duma may approve or reject the president's nominee for State Bank chairman and dismiss the incumbent. In short, the Duma has ample authority to check certain presidential powers and to hold the prime minister and cabinet accountable. Nevertheless, it is a relatively weak body when compared to the U.S. House of Representatives or the British House of Commons.

Among its limitations, the Duma can be dissolved by the president under specified conditions. Moreover, its members may not propose any financial legislation, such as tax bills or proposals to increase or reduce budgetary spending, without the government's approval. The Putin administration has weakened the Duma's influence even further. For example, it terminated the Duma's previous ability to speak directly with government ministries and agencies, a practice that gave the Duma some influence over government activities in the Yeltsin years. Under Putin, the Duma has had to talk with a single representative appointed by the government.

Federation Council The **Federation Council** consists of two members from each of Russia's 83 constituent federal units. One is appointed by the local governor, the other by the local legislature. The council's principal function is to vote on legislation already adopted by the Duma. (Members of the Federation Council who wish to initiate legislative proposals must submit their bills to the Duma.) However, the council's assent is not always required for a bill to be enacted into law. If the council rejects a law passed by the Duma and the disagreement cannot be settled by a reconciliation committee of the two houses, the Duma may pass the bill on its own by two-thirds majority. Certain particularly important areas of legislation require the Federation Council's consideration, including the federal budget, tax laws, the ratification of international treaties, and declarations of war. In addition, the upper house has the sole authority to approve or reject presidential decrees declaring a state of emergency or imposing martial law in case

of war. The Federation Council also has the exclusive right to remove the president from office once the Duma passes articles of impeachment. Both houses have the right to establish investigative committees.

As part of his attempt to rein in the autonomy of the regions from the central government's authority, President Putin diluted the upper chamber's authority by getting the Duma to pass a law prohibiting the heads of Russia's 83 regional governments from serving in the Federation Council. In their place, regional governments have to appoint less powerful officials to represent them in the Russian parliament.

The Constitutional Court Of Russia's three highest courts, the Constitutional Court is empowered to interpret the constitution, settle disputes involving the competency of state institutions, and determine whether laws and the activities of state authorities are in compliance with the constitution. The court's 19 justices are nominated by Russia's president and confirmed by the Federation Council. Compared with constitutional courts in many other democracies, Russia's Constitutional Court is relatively weak. Its jurisdiction is limited to issues that are brought before it by the president, the government, the legislature, and a few other state institutions. Unlike the U.S. Supreme Court, the Constitutional Court does not hear cases that have been submitted to it by citizens involved in the appellate process. Its powers of judicial review are thus largely dependent on the issues that other state authorities wish to have adjudicated. President Putin's widening authority over the government, the Duma, and the Federation Council gives him wide personal discretion to determine which matters will be submitted to the Constitutional Court for adjudication, and which ones will not. Putin broadened his authority over the court during his second term when the legislature approved his request for more presidential influence in the selection of the Supreme Qualification Collegium, the body that approves appointments to the Supreme Court and other federal courts. These realities impose serious limitations on the court's independence from the executive and legislative branches of the Russian government.

Of course, no court system can be effective if state authorities refuse to abide by judicial decisions or if they do not conscientiously enforce court rulings. The laws that governments issue may be authoritative, but the *rule of law* prevails only when state authorities and the citizenry agree to submit themselves to the law. Unfortunately, bribery and other forms of corruption on the part of state officials is rampant. And the sorry state of Russia's finances deprives government agencies of the resources they need to enforce court rulings effectively. In addition, government prosecutors have undermined the jury system by asserting their right to appeal not-guilty verdicts. Perhaps as many as 50 percent of these verdicts are subsequently overturned. (Double jeopardy is permitted in Russia.) Authorities have used intimidation tactics against defense attorneys who represent clients involved in disputes with the state. There has been a return to the old Soviet practice of incarcerating human rights activists in mental institutions on trumped-up claims of mental illness and forcing them to take debilitating doses of psychiatric drugs. The use of torture and brutality on Chechen rebels and various criminal elements constitute yet another abuse of the state's judicial and penal powers.[43]

Regional Governments With the dismemberment of the Soviet Union at the end of 1991, the 15 "soviet socialist republics" that constituted the Soviet Union all became formally independent. The three Baltic states—Estonia, Latvia, and Lithuania—have made considerable strides toward democracy, entering the European Union and NATO in 2004. The other 12 states—grouped in the Commonwealth of Independent States (CIS), a loose organization primarily concerned with promoting economic cooperation—have moved much more slowly, or not at all, in democracy's direction. In 2008 Georgia withdrew from the CIS after the South Ossetia War. According to the Freedom House composite index for political and civil rights, and the categories used in this book to characterize countries on the basis of this index, at the end of 2012 there was no democracy among the CIS countries. Five CIS countries were semi-free: Armenia (4.5), Georgia (3.0), Kyrgyzstan (5.0), Moldova (3.0), and Ukraine (3.5). Most of these semi-free CIS states have moved in the direction of less freedom in the past five years as their earlier "color" revolutions, which brought more democratic rulers to power—e.g., the "Rose" Revolution in Georgia in 2003, the "Orange" Revolution in Ukraine in 2004–05, and the "Tulip" Revolution in Kyrgyzstan in 2005—have been reversed. Several of these countries have fairly large Russian minorities. In all, some 25 million Russians reside in former Soviet republics along Russia's periphery, areas known in Russia as "the near abroad." On numerous occasions the Russian government has asserted its responsibility to speak up for the rights of these external Russian minorities whenever a neighboring government is believed to be discriminating against them.

Russia itself incorporates a diversity of non-Russian peoples who were gathered into the Russian Empire in tsarist times. Approximately 80 percent of the country's population is ethnically Russian. Although most Russians who profess a religion are Orthodox, there are 14 million people from ethnic groups that traditionally followed Islam living in scattered parts of the country, roughly 10 percent of Russia's population. Many of the 20 percent of the population who are not Russian are concentrated in administrative subdivisions that might provide a territorial basis for wide autonomy or outright independence. The Russian Federation's structure consists of 83 regional subdivisions, based on the territorial units and nomenclature that prevailed in the Soviet Union. In addition to the cities of Moscow and Leningrad, there are 21 republics, 46 provinces (*oblasts*), nine territories *(krais)*, four autonomous areas *(okrugs)*, and one autonomous region (autonomous *oblast*, the Jewish region created in the Stalinist era). A province has an appointed governor and a locally elected legislature. Republics differ from provinces in that they are also allowed to have their own official language.

The large numbers of Russians living in neighboring states, together with the non-Russian minorities living in Russia, have saddled the Russian government with what Juan Linz and Alfred Stepan call a "stateness" problem: the problem of defining the country's territorial boundaries and the distribution of decision-making power among its constituent units.[44] Furthermore, Russia's ethnic and religious heterogeneity makes for a fragile sense of national unity. These problems came close to shattering the Russian Federation in its infancy, as regions with a strong sense of their own separate identity began to distance themselves from President Yeltsin's shaky central government. As Chechnya exploded in a violent independence movement, other regions moved more quietly to wrest greater autonomy for themselves while remaining within the Russian Federation. Regions with indigenous sources of wealth and assertive leaders insisted on greater freedom from central authorities to shape their own laws and policies and even to conduct economic relations with foreign countries. Scrambling to hold the federation together, Yeltsin's government negotiated bilateral treaties with a number of these restive regions to clarify their rights and obligations.

In stark contrast to Yeltsin, President Putin moved swiftly to reassert the central government's primacy over the provinces. Within weeks of his election in May 2000, Putin issued a decree reorganizing the country's regions under seven new super-regions known as "federal *okruga*." Putin appointed the head of each super-region, with the express purpose of enhancing the central government's controls over regional affairs. There followed other measures aimed at bringing the regions to heel, including the law barring regional chief executives from sitting in the Federation Council. Another law required the provinces to align their laws with those of the central government and gave the president the authority to replace governors who refused to implement a federal law. Governors who commit crimes can also be replaced by central authorities. Bilateral treaties between the central government and various regions were being phased out in a further effort to subordinate Russia's regional periphery to the Kremlin. And Putin backed his own favorite candidates for election to leadership posts in regional governments. Charges of fraudulent vote counts and other election irregularities have accompanied the victories of some Putin-sponsored candidates.

In his second term Putin launched an even more aggressive assault on regional governors. In September 2004, immediately after the Beslan crisis, he announced a plan to terminate the direct election of Russia's then 89 governors by giving himself the presidential authority to select them. (The president's nominee in each region would be subject to confirmation by the regional legislature, but the president may now dissolve that body and call snap elections to it if it rejects his nominee in two successive votes.) The new system significantly strengthens the president's power over Russia's regions, scoring another victory for Putin's policy of recentralizing power in the Kremlin and restricting the centrifugal tendencies of federalism. Before this change, some of the regional governors had managed to wield considerable local power, escaping the influence of the large national political parties such as Putin's United Russia and suppressing political competition in their respective regions.

Although the reassertion of central authority was fairly effective in most regions, Chechnya remained troublesome. In March 2003, the Putin administration held a referendum on a new constitution for Chechnya, promising the region considerable autonomy as a member of the Russian Federation. Russian authorities said the document was approved by 96 percent of the voters, with a turnout of 80 percent, but secessionists boycotted the vote. In 2005 regional legislative elections were stage-managed to ensure a lopsided plurality for Putin's party.[45]

In view of Russia's institutional framework and President Putin's steady accretion of power, can it be said that Russia's presidential–parliamentary system lends itself to the abuse of presidential authority and thereby places democracy itself in jeopardy?

HYPOTHESIS-TESTING EXERCISE
Is Russia's Political System Undermining Democracy?

Hypothesis A mixed presidential–parliamentary system tends to produce the worst possible outcomes: authoritarianism or gridlock. When the president and the majority in the lower house of parliament share the same political orientation, the president monopolizes power and tends to abuse it. When the president's opponents dominate the legislature, the result is gridlock, and the lawmaking process comes to a standstill. The presidential–parliamentary system is thus especially dangerous for young democracies.

Variables The *independent variable* is the presidential–parliamentary system. The *dependent variables* are the concentration and abuse of presidential power and, alternatively, gridlock.

Expectations If the hypothesis is correct, then we would expect that (1) when Russia's president enjoys the support of the majority of the National Assembly, decision making is heavily concentrated in the presidency as opposed to the government and the legislature; (2) the president tends to exceed his legal authority of the office, violating democratic principles; and (3) opposition between the president and the legislative majority produces an inefficient governmental process bordering on paralysis.

Evidence Not long after his election as president in 2000, Vladimir Putin put together a fairly stable majority of Duma members who were willing to approve his policies. As Putin's parliamentary support grew, so did his exercise of presidential power. Putin has issued more decrees than Yeltsin did. He moved swiftly against three oligarchs who challenged him—Boris Berezovsky, Vladimir Gusinsky, and Mikhail Khodorkovsky. The first two live in exile while Khodorkovsky is imprisoned. Although Putin justified these moves as legitimate attacks on the excessive power of the financial oligarchy, he did not hesitate to curry the support of more favorably inclined oligarchs. And Putin moved vigorously to retain state control over significant sectors of the Russian economy.

Putin also made it clear he would not tolerate openly critical media. The murder of the journalist Anna Politkovskaya in 2006 was only one among many examples of the threatening climate that now surrounds the Russian press. By contrast, President Yeltsin tolerated open criticism. As we have seen, President Putin has also moved boldly to restore the central government's authority over regional governments. Putin has further reinforced his personal authority by bringing trusted former KGB officials into his administration, along with representatives of the defense establishment and other "power ministries" concerned with national security.[46]

The evidence attesting to Putin's vigorous use of presidential power is consistent with our first expectation: It demonstrates an unmistakable concentration of power in the president's hands. There are also indications that Putin has on occasion exceeded his constitutional authority, in conformity with our second expectation. Nevertheless, public approval for Putin remained consistently high, above 60 percent. After more than 20 years of turmoil, most Russians appeared to favor political order and a strong state over press freedoms or the formalities of constitutional law.[47]

President Yeltsin had to contend with a considerably less pliable Duma than Putin. Communists, arch-nationalists, regional elites, and others opposed at least some of Yeltsin's policy initiatives. The Duma challenged two of Yeltsin's nominees for prime minister. Yeltsin's prime ministers could never count on the solid support of a majority in the Russian Duma. As a consequence, prolonged wrangling over the budget, economic reform, and other issues paralyzed the decision-making process.

Yeltsin's failing health further complicated the decision-making process. Executive power became lodged in a Kremlin cabal accountable neither to the Duma nor to the voters. The Yeltsin regime was an "elective monarchy," even though the "tsar" was unable to wield power for months at a time.[48]

The Yeltsin years were therefore characterized by a weak, fractionated parliament with no stable majority; a succession of weak prime ministers who could not rely on a parliamentary majority; and a president who alternated between decisiveness (when starting the economic reform process, for example) and absenteeism, allowing unelected advisors to wield significant executive power and to engage in massive corruption with virtually no accountability to the legislature or the judiciary. These realities are largely consistent with our third expectation.

Conclusions The evidence we have just presented is basically consistent with all three expectations from our hypothesis. Under varying conditions, Russia's mixed presidential–parliamentary system has permitted the concentration and even abuse of presidential authority as well as an inefficient, disjointed decision-making process. Far from being a "semi-presidential" system, as it is often called, it can sometimes function as a *super-presidential* system.[49] It therefore seems ill-suited to stabilizing a law-bound democracy in Russia. It certainly has not worked as well in Russia as in France, where democratic traditions are older, parties are stronger, and public opinion more supportive of democracy.

Socioeconomic Conditions: National Wealth, Private Enterprise, the Middle Class, and the Disadvantaged

Inevitably, economic conditions play a critical role in democracy's success. As we've seen in this chapter, the Russian economy suffered a prolonged depression from the stagnation of the late Brezhnev era to the ruble devaluation of 1998. By the late 1990s, Russia's per capita GDP hovered around $2,700, less than in Thailand, Turkey, or Mexico. President Putin inherited an economy marked by high levels of foreign indebtedness, laggard tax collections, inflation, unemployment, and a host of other problems. But rising prices for oil and natural gas exports fueled significant increases in Russia's gross domestic product. The Russian economy grew by an average of 6.9 percent between 1999 and 2008. Russia was set back by the world financial crisis of 2008–09, but in 2010 and 2011 its GDP growth exceeded 4 percent. Although these growth spurts eased pressures on the domestic economy and led to modest standard-of-living increases for millions of Russians, the country's dependence on natural resources for 80 percent of its exports left it vulnerable to unpredictable price fluctuations for these commodities in world markets. To ensure steady growth in the future, Russia still needed to diversify its economy by promoting the production of manufactured goods; it also needed to attract more foreign investment. Both tasks faced serious political obstacles.

During his first four years in office, President Putin confirmed his commitment to economic reform, including the privatization process, budgetary discipline, the sale of farmland, and related measures. He appointed dedicated reformers to key economic policy posts and sent a welter of reform proposals to the Duma. At the same time, however, Putin failed to keep the pledge he made to Russian voters in the 2000 election campaign that, following his election, "the oligarchs will cease to exist as a class." As we've noted, Putin moved against oligarchs who challenged him politically, but he left other tycoons unmolested as long as they pursued their business activities in conformity with the wider interests of the Russian state. Many of them owned shares in giant corporations that were co-owned by the state, blurring the boundaries between the public and private sectors. Between 2004 and 2008, Putin's government expanded state ownership and direct intervention in the most vital components of the Russian economy, including energy, banking, automobiles, and aviation. In 2006 the national government owned 93 percent of the natural gas industry, 41.3 percent of the electricity industry, and 5.4 percent of the oil industry. Privatization and private-sector development have slowed, while the state's stake in the country's largest enterprises has increased.[50] Under Putin's regime, eight giant conglomerates controlled 85 percent of the value of more than 60 large companies. Two oligarchic clans exercised particularly strong political influence in several of Russia's regions, pouring money into regional election campaigns to secure victory for their favored candidates.

This tight concentration of economic and political power, which started under President Yeltsin and intensified under Putin, has emerged as a primary reason for Russia's retreat from democratic consolidation and its descent toward authoritarianism. Steven Fish has argued that the Russian state's continuing—and widening—control over the economy and its overreliance on energy as its main source of wealth are two of the most important independent variables accounting for the retreat from democracy in Putin's Russia. Like Saudi Arabia, Iran, and other oil-rich authoritarian regimes, Russia has some of the key characteristics of a "petro-state." Together with the institutional framework of a super-presidency and a weak national legislature that is incapable of applying checks and balances to executive power, these economic realities are more important than cultural or historical factors in explaining Russia's latest authoritarian tendencies, Fish concludes.[51]

President Medvedev, recognizing Russia's reliance on hydrocarbon exports, initiated a "modernization" program in 2009 intended to diversify the economy into high-tech and medical and pharmaceutical fields, among others. A showpiece for Medvedev was to be the Skolkovo project on the outskirts of Moscow, where his government sought to sow the seeds of a Russian Silicon Valley. To date the modernization program has shown few results.[52]

Perhaps the biggest drains on the Russian economy have been corruption and extortion. There has been widespread bribery of public officials for permits, licenses, and other necessities of doing business, and mafia-like organizations have routinely extorted money from private businesses, depriving them of the profits they needed for investments in the future. As a consequence, Russia had one of the worst ratings in Transparency International's 2012 Corruption Perceptions Index— 133rd in the world, ranking well below any other major economy. A World Bank report released in 2002 estimated at that time 40 to 50 percent of Russia's economy was in the hands of illegal organizations, many of them with close ties to state officials.[53] Inconsistent enforcement of Russia's commercial code created additional barriers to business activity, scaring away foreign investors. Regulations made in Moscow were often ignored in the provinces. Until the rule of business law, including intellectual property rights, is universally observed throughout Russia, the climate for both domestic and foreign investment will remain uninviting. Medvedev claimed he would crack down on corruption as part of his effort to modernize the economy, but made little progress.

The Putin government's arrest and sentencing of Mikhail Khodorkovsky sent a chill through the domestic and international business community. In the 1990s Khodorkovsky learned how to take advantage of loopholes in Russia's emerging commercial laws as he embarked on new ventures. He soon established a large bank and purchased a number of newly privatized factories and plants. Khodorkovsky then parlayed his instant fortune into political influence by joining with other financial moguls in funding President Boris Yeltsin's 1996 reelection campaign. In return, he received majority ownership in an oil company called Yukos, which became Russia's leading oil producer with a market value of $35 billion. Within a few years Khodorkovsky was the richest man in the country; his net worth of $15 billion placed him among the 20 richest people in the world.

After assuming power, President Putin allowed financial oligarchs such as Khodorkovsky to keep their fortunes as long as they stayed out of politics. But Khodorkovsky openly criticized Putin at a meeting and gave large sums of money to human rights groups and to anti-Putin political parties, including Yabloko. In 2003 he was arrested on charges of fraud, embezzlement, and tax evasion. After a long trial, he and his chief partner were sentenced in 2005 to nine years in prison. Khodorkovsky was sentenced on further charges of embezzlement and money laundering while in prison, extending his term to 2017. Meanwhile, the government acquired Yukos's prime oil assets and declared the company bankrupt. Putin tried to calm nervous investors by offering assurances of his commitment to "human rights and freedoms," but his government raised new fears when it ordered several Russian companies to pay massive sums in allegedly unpaid back taxes and extended its Yukos probe to one of the firm's American executives.

As the financial elite tightened its grip on Russia's largest corporations, the development of small and medium-size enterprises continued to lag behind European standards. In Western Europe, such firms employed 50 to 70 percent of adult employees; in Russia, they accounted for only 20 percent of adult employment.[54] These figures help explain the relatively slow development of Russia's postcommunist middle class. Although the size of the Russian middle class is difficult to specify statistically, a number of investigators have concluded it constitutes one-fourth to one-third of the population. Professionally, they include such diverse groups as bureaucrats, teachers, scientists, and other state employees; independent professionals such as doctors, lawyers, and accountants; and people owning or working in private companies. Income varies widely among these groups; in effect, there are several layers of middle class, ranging from well-heeled "new Russians" to employees who scrape by from paycheck to paycheck. An indeterminate number of people

Mikhail Khodorkovsky, once the wealthiest man in Russia, was arrested in 2003 on charges of fraud, embezzlement, and tax evasion and was sentenced to nine years in prison. Many interpreted this gesture as President Vladimir Putin's response to Khodorkovsky openly criticizing Putin and for giving large sums of money to human rights groups and to anti-Putin political parties such as Yabloko.

work in Russia's "second economy"—unlicensed businesses that do not report their income to the tax authorities. A large portion of the emerging middle class was devastated by the 1998 ruble crisis, but they slowly regained their footing in the following decade. When Russians demonstrated against what they perceived to be fraud in the December 2011 Duma elections, protesters came disproportionately from the urban middle classes. The stirrings of democracy may emerge from middle-class Russians frustrated by their lack of political voice.[55]

The disposition of vast numbers of Russians left destitute by the political and economic shocks of the post-Brezhnev decades remains a major question mark. By mid-1999 nearly 38 percent of the population lived below the official poverty line of $37 a month; that figure had fallen to 25 percent in 2002 and to 13 percent by 2012. Maldistribution of wealth has remained a problem, however, with the bottom 20 percent of the population in 2009 sharing only 5.1 percent of the national income and the richest 20 percent holding 47.8 percent of it, figures that had worsened over the previous decade.[56] Though the constitution commits the state to a raft of welfare supports, such as free medical care, family allowances, unemployment compensation, disability payments, pensions, and other benefits, the money to finance them has been scarce. Russia's long economic decline since the late 1970s has taken a heavy toll on the nation's health. A rise in chronic illnesses, HIV and AIDS, alcoholism, suicides, and other life-shortening factors has combined with inadequate health care funding to reduce the life expectancy of Russian males from 70 in 1985 to 59 by 2005. The life expectancy of Russian women has fallen from 74 years in 1985 to 73 years, nine years less than Western European women. In the past half-decade, those declining life expectancy figures have reversed. As of 2010, men could expect to live to 63, women to 75, still well below world standards. The fertility rate declined from 2.22 births per woman in 1987 to 1.29 in 2005 before reviving and now standing at 1.54 (2010). Those figures are well below replacement values. Consequently, Russia's population shrank by three-quarters of a million persons per year for several years after 1991, reaching its nadir in 2008. Although the population has grown slightly since then, the Population Reference Bureau estimates Russia's population will drop from 146 million in 2000 to 127 million by 2050. President Putin has called this demographic decline "the most acute problem of contemporary Russia."[57]

Civil Society and Political Culture

Another important task confronting democratizers in Russia is the development of an active civil society. For a country with virtually no tradition of independent citizen associations, the challenge is to create grassroots organizations from scratch. Political parties can help channel citizens into the political process—but only if they are open to the participation of party members in meaningful ways. Thus far, Russia's main parties have failed to open their policy-making and candidate selection processes

to ordinary citizens. Not surprisingly, less than 20 percent of Russians expressed trust in political parties during Putin's first term. Most Russians regarded the parties as nothing more than vehicles designed to serve the personal interests of party leaders. A majority of people surveyed could not clearly distinguish one party from another.

With the exception of the Russian Communist Party, which descended from the Communist Party of the Soviet Union, all parties formed in Russia since its independence in 1992 have been brand new. Almost all these new parties have been built around prominent political personalities rather than around large groups in Russian society, such as social classes or religious denominations. A few parties are committed to human rights and other democratic ideals, while others are more concerned with asserting the power of the Russian state or other aspects of Russian nationalism, but most parties lack distinct ideological convictions. Russia's parties are elite centered and have practically no roots in civil society. The Communist Party claims to have hundreds of thousands of members, but it remains a hierarchy run by its leaders, much as in Soviet times. Until recently, most other parties have been considerably smaller, with only a few hundred, or at most a few thousand, members. Party policy and the selection of candidates for office are largely determined by professional politicians rather than by citizen-activists or membership votes.

The fragmentation of Russia's party system is due in part to the electoral system that governed Duma elections before 2007 and to Russia's structure as a federation of 83 constituent units. In 2001, there were more than 200 parties. A party (or a bloc of parties that fielded candidates jointly) had to get at least 5 percent of the nationwide vote to elect representatives to the Duma. In the four Duma elections between 1993 and 2003, only about a dozen parties or party blocs cleared that hurdle. The single-member-district vote, however, enabled smaller parties or independent candidates unaffiliated with any party to enter the Duma, sometimes in large numbers. Nearly one-fourth of the Duma members elected in 1999—123 deputies—were independents or the representatives of very small parties. Most of the independent deputies ultimately joined a party, but only after presenting themselves to the voters on election day as independents. Some 23 parties fielded candidates in the December 2003 Duma elections (compared with 26 in 1999 and 43 in 1995); only 4 won seats in the proportional-representation ballot. In the single-member-district contests, there were 15 candidates per district in 2003 (compared with 10 in 1999) and nearly 70 independents were elected.[58] The electoral system introduced in 2007 has considerably reduced representation in the State Duma (see Table 16.4) to four main national parties—Putin's United Russia, the Communists, Zhirinovsky's Liberal Democrats, and the social-democratic and nationalist A Just Russia.

Russia's federated system has exacerbated party fragmentation. More than three out of four deputies elected to serve in the country's 83 regional legislatures have not been members of any of the nationally organized parties. The governors of most regions and other executive-level regional officials are similarly detached from the national parties. Thus the parties represented in Russia's Duma do not speak for the vast majority of political elites in the provinces, another source of the Duma's weakness.

Henry Hale has described Russia's nascent party system in terms of an electoral marketplace. In the Russian political market, candidates and voters have been able to make their choices from among a variety of competing parties as well as *party substitutes*. Even though both the Yeltsin and Putin presidential administrations intervened directly in the political market to help the parties they favored and weaken the ones they opposed, dispensing or withholding the favors of political patronage from the central government, local political forces at the regional level have managed to cultivate their own political support outside the framework of the parties. Russia has thus far developed only a "partial party system," Hale observes, because candidates and their constituents have found options other than parties to meet their political needs. Examples of such party substitutes have included local political machines, politically engaged financial–industrial groups, and powerful regional officials who have often formed patron–client relationships with their followers. In many instances these party substitutes have fared better than the parties themselves.[59]

During his second term, President Putin undertook strenuous efforts to revamp the party system. In addition to changing the Duma's electoral system starting in the 2007 elections and curtailing the power of regional governors, Putin actively promoted the development of his United Russia Party. In mid-2008 this "party of power" reported having nearly 2 million members. The government also went after parties it opposed. At the end of 2005, the Motherland (*Rodina*) Party, the right-wing nationalist group that was becoming Russia's most rapidly growing party under Dmitry Rogozin, was banned from participating in the Moscow city elections after it sponsored an inflammatory advertisement implying that immigrants were "rubbish." In the following year Putin personally arranged Rogozin's replacement by a businessman and orchestrated Motherland's merger with two smaller parties to become A Just Russia whose leaders duly announced their support for Putin's policies. The government also quashed the National Bolsheviks, a small ultra-right party supported by disruptive skinheads. In addition, the changes in the electoral system have sidelined many parties who now get no representation in the Duma.

After the Duma elections in December 2011 produced a victory for United Russia candidates, many members of the Russian middle class and professionals took to the streets to protest what they perceived to be electoral irregularities. These protests, concentrated in Moscow, continued until the presidential election produced a Putin victory. Initially, they caused some observers to see an awakening of Russian civil society, but in the end the Putin win in March 2012 took the steam out of the prodemocracy movement. The regime also orchestrated large-scale demonstrations of its supporters in response to the initial protests.

Women have been significantly underrepresented in the political process. They accounted for only 7.9 percent of the Duma elected in 1999 and 9.8 percent of the one elected in 2003. The 2007 and 2011 Dumas counted 14.0 and 13.6 percent women members, respectively. The new 7 percent threshold and the ban on multiparty electoral blocs will likely keep small parties concerned with women's issues out of future Dumas.[60]

Nongovernmental organizations (NGOs)—the main base of civil society—have increased appreciably since Russia's independence. By 2003 there were 300,000 NGOs registered with the authorities, with 2.5 million participants. About one-fourth of these organizations were charitable in nature; others were concerned with the environment, health care, human rights, and other issues. Putin's administration clamped down heavily on human rights organizations and watchdog groups that were critical of his government. In 2006 Putin got the legislature to pass a new law severely restricting the rights of NGOs funded from abroad. The legislation, clearly aimed at Western human rights organizations that promote democracy, forbids them to engage in "political activity" but does not define that term. Putin himself accused foreign NGOs of funding espionage in Russia. In 2012 the Duma passed another law that requires any NGOs receiving foreign funding to include the phrase "foreign agent" in their printed materials, makes them subject to frequent audits, and requires them to issue twice-annual reports. The NGOs regard this law as intended to harass and intimidate them. Though business associations have been proliferating, membership in Russia's postcommunist trade union umbrella organization, the Federation of Independent Trade Unions of Russia, is much lower than communist-era levels, falling to under 30 million in 2005 from 60 million in 1993.[61]

Political attitudes are an important barometer of a country's political culture. Russian attitudes toward politics changed profoundly and rapidly once Gorbachev flung open the windows to greater freedom of expression in the 1980s, but interest in politics quickly subsided during the economic shocks of the early Yeltsin years. Sizable segments of the population have clung to nondemocratic attitudes well after independence. In 1995, for example, one-third (33 percent) said they thought Russians needed a ruler with an "iron hand" at all times while only 24 percent felt that it should never be possible for one person to have full power. This preference for strongman rule has only increased. In 2010, 44 percent believed Russians need an iron hand while only 19 percent felt one person should never have full power. About one-quarter of Russians say democracy is unsuitable for their country. When asked what they think democracy is, about one-third of Russians say it's economic prosperity. While in 1998 many more Russians said they wanted a political arrangement in which the local governments had extensive authority than that local authorities should be appointed by a strong central state (52 percent favored the former, 25 percent the latter), by 2010 many more respondents

(46 percent) preferred a strong central state over a regime in which local authorities had extensive powers (32 percent).[62]

Russians have consistently opted for order over freedom. In 2011, 56 percent of those polled were willing to accept violations of basic democratic values or limitations on personal freedoms to maintain the public order, whereas only 23 percent said the state should stay true to democratic principles regardless of its impact on law and order. As in previous years, Russians in 2012 overwhelmingly regarded a strong economy as more important than a good democracy. Only 19 percent placed democracy first, whereas 75 percent prioritized economic considerations.[63] Xenophobic sentiments are also visible in contemporary Russia: About 60 percent of both younger and older Russians agree with the slogan "Russia for ethnic Russians!" In 2005 approximately 40 percent favored deporting all immigrants and their children. Russians have increasingly favored a more restrictive immigration policy, including toward undocumented immigrants from CIS countries (former Soviet republics).[64]

Russians continue to hold many of the collectivist values they learned under communism. When asked to rank which human rights were most important to them, 70 percent responded "the right to have a free education, medical care, maintenance in old age and in illness," and 53 percent said "the right to have a well-paid professional job," whereas only 36 percent chose freedom of speech, 21 percent said freedom of religion, and 19 percent responded "the right to elect one's representatives to governing bodies." However, the respect for civil rights seems to be growing relative to the preference for order. In 1997 60 percent of Russians preferred order over human rights when asked, "Which is more important for Russia now: order in the country or observance of human rights?" Twenty-seven percent opted for human rights and 13 percent responded that it was hard to say. By 2011 the preference for order over human rights had narrowed to 53 percent to 42 percent, with 5 percent saying it was difficult to answer.[65]

Political culture can take a long time to change, though cataclysmic events like war or civil turmoil can sometimes hasten its transformation. For now, however, it appears that support for civil rights and democracy is fragile in Russian society.

Education and Freedom of Information

Russia's new constitution guarantees tuition-free higher education on a competitive basis. Since the fall of communism the country's educational system has freed itself from the shackles of communist ideology and the censorship of politically unacceptable ideas. Russians are now free to pursue artistic creativity and scientific research without government interference. Unfortunately, Russia's economic doldrums have left the educational system seriously underfunded. Moreover, teachers, professors, and researchers—the backbone of the Soviet intelligentsia—were hit very hard by the collapse of the economy in the 1990s. Many of Russia's best-educated people have had a difficult time

coping with the country's painful transition to democracy and private enterprise.

As we have seen, freedom of information has been a problematic issue, especially since Vladimir Putin assumed the presidency. In his first state-of-the-nation address in 2000, Putin acknowledged that "without really free mass media, Russian democracy simply will not survive." Print media are more free and abundant than in the days of Soviet censorship. Some 6,000 newspapers and 4,000 magazines are now available. But the killing of Anna Politkovskaya and 36 other journalists between 2000 and 2012 sends an unmistakable message that the Putin and Medvedev administrations, and perhaps others subjected to journalistic investigations, will not tolerate a free press. Most privately owned publications are in the hands of a few tycoons, some with close connections to state authorities. Moreover, the government has taken numerous measures to extinguish the last vestiges of editorial independence. In 2004, for example, it imposed a $10 million legal bill on *Kommersant*, a paper owned by the exiled Boris Berezovsky, after the paper won an antidefamation case against the government. In the same year some 6,000 lawsuits were filed by the government against media outlets and journalists accused of libeling state officials. In 2005 the state used its large stake in Gazprom, the energy conglomerate, to acquire the respected newspaper *Izvestiya* from its billionaire owner. This was not the first instance in which Gazprom's media arm was used to bring the print or broadcast media under government control. Later that year the country's last remaining independent television news anchor was fired. In addition, President Putin aggressively exploited the state's control of broadcast media to boost his candidacy in his three presidential elections and Medvedev's, denying opponents equal time. His administration has continuously used the state television networks to manage the news, largely by giving Putin and his allies massive positive coverage and their critics less time and more negative attention.

Although the constitution guarantees the secrecy of private communications, e-mail transmissions are monitored by the federal intelligence service, a fact that raises concerns among human rights groups and other politically oriented NGOs. Internet usage has risen dramatically: While only about 4 percent of the Russian population used the Web in 2002, by 2011 the Internet usage has risen to half of the population.[66]

The International Environment

From the inception of Russia's postcommunist regime, the international environment has had a mixture of positive and negative consequences for Russian democracy. On the positive side, Russia's democratization—especially in the Yeltsin years—was greeted warmly by the United States, Western Europe, and Japan. These former enemies of the Soviet Union joined with the International Monetary Fund and other international organizations in providing billions of dollars in loans, technical advice, food, and other forms of assistance. The end of the Cold War also brought a major diminution of the nuclear arms race between Russia and the West: Both Yeltsin and Putin signed historic arms reduction agreements with the United States that resulted in the destruction of nuclear warheads and guided missiles. In part for these reasons, the power of Russia's military establishment as a bastion of support for dictatorship has diminished appreciably. The United States also financed programs aimed at keeping Russia's nuclear material from being stolen and transferred to other countries seeking to build nuclear weapons. Nevertheless, postcommunist Russia has always had its own national interests, just like any other independent country. Not all of these interests have coincided with those of the West.

Despite generally cordial relations with the United States and its allies during the Yeltsin years, there were frictions over several issues. Yeltsin's government voiced objections to NATO's enlargement, which incorporated into the trans-Atlantic alliance the USSR's former allies in Central and Eastern Europe along with the former Soviet republics of Estonia, Latvia, and Lithuania. The Yeltsin government also had doubts about the NATO bombardment of Serbia, Russia's historic ally, during the war over Kosovo in 1999. (The Russians joined the NATO-organized postwar peacekeeping mission there, however.)[67] Disputes between Russia and the West have multiplied since Putin became president in 2000. Putin declined to support the U.S.-led invasion of Iraq in 2003, siding openly with France and Germany in opposing the war. The United States has tried to persuade the Putin government to cancel an agreement to sell nuclear reactors to Iran, fearing that the Iranian government will use them to build nuclear weapons instead of limiting their use to electricity generation. The U.S. government has tried to enlist Putin's support at the United Nations for strong sanctions against Iran. Putin made moves to accommodate U.S. concerns, some of which Russia shares (Russia has no interest in seeing Iran become a nuclear military power), but he did not cancel the reactor deal. The United States and Russia have also engaged in an ongoing rivalry for control over energy resources in the Caspian Sea region.

Putin clashed with the West more directly over Ukraine as the Orange Revolution unfolded. While the United States and the European Union strongly backed the prodemocracy candidate Viktor Yushchenko, Putin's administration supported his opponent, Viktor Yanukovich.

The leaders of the Western alliance and Russia appear to understand that neither side stands to gain anything from a return to the harsh confrontation of the Cold War. President Putin no doubt wishes to assert Russia's basic interests and independence, but he recognizes that Russia is no longer a military or economic superpower. It is therefore likely that frictions and disputes will continue to mark Russia's relationships with the West, but these discords will be contained within an overall structure of agreement on the need to keep them from getting out of hand. The big question is whether the West can influence the fate of democracy inside Russia. Thus far it appears that President Putin feels a need to assure the West of his commitment to democracy in principle, but he does not seem willing to alter his authoritarian tendencies in practice.

Table 16.5 summarizes the 10 conditions for democracy as just reviewed. As you can see, while Russia today compares well to the situation under Soviet rule, the conditions for democracy are still far from favorable.

President Vladimir Putin of Russia publicly assures the West that he remains committed to democracy in Russia while maintaining authoritarian tendencies in practice.

Table 16.5 The 10 Conditions for Democracy: Contemporary Russia

Explanatory Factor	Contemporary Russia
1. Elite attitudes	Oligarchs who emerged from privatization of the state-owned Soviet economy view democracy instrumentally and violate it whenever it benefits their purposes.
2. State institutions	Post-Soviet constitutional structure creates a super-presidency. Putin regime has scaled back the autonomy of regional governments.
3. National unity	While less nationally diverse than the USSR, the Russian Federation continues to incorporate many non-Russian peoples, some of whom suffer under the oppression of the Russian majority. Many Russians hold chauvinist values.
4. National wealth	Russians have enjoyed a sustained period of economic development after a disastrous first decade following the USSR's collapse.
5. Private enterprise	The state still holds most of the "commanding heights" while oligarchs grabbed some prizes in the privatization of the communist state enterprises. Small and medium enterprises exist but remain weak in the face of the state, oligarchs, and foreign investment.
6. Middle class	The middle class is growing but diverse, ranging from traditional state employees to new information sector workers.
7. Attitudes of the disadvantaged	The post-Soviet economic collapse created much poverty and increased inequality, leading to a politics of nostalgia for the command economy on the part of pensioners and the poor.
8. Civil society	Civil society organizations have grown but remain weak in the face of state oppression.
9. Education and access to information	Education is broad but under communism had a significant element of antidemocratic Marxist–Leninist ideology. While the press is freer and more vigorous than under the USSR, censorship, intimidation of journalists, and state and oligarch ownership of media outlets limits access to information critical of the regime.
10. International conditions	The end of the Cold War reduces the need for state control of society to harness efforts against the West. Continuing tensions with the West create excuses for the government to limit freedom.

Conclusion

The developments surveyed in this chapter make it clear that, after the Gorbachev era, Russia took a historic leap in the direction of democracy, reversing a thousand years of unyielding suppression of democratic ideals by authoritarian rulers. Although the current Russian regime can be highly repressive, Russians have the sense that expressing one's opinions, practicing one's religion, and joining a political organization are rights they should be able to exercise in post-Soviet society. During the rule of Stalin and his successors, such ideas could not even be mentioned. Nevertheless, there have been major shortcomings in Russia's democratic transition. Many of the successes of Yeltsin's first years in power have been dismantled under President Putin. Respect for such values as individual freedom, trust, and compromise is on the wane. The principle of the rule of law has been repeatedly violated by an increasingly heavy-handed national leadership. Popular sovereignty has been vitiated by attempts to manipulate the electoral process—first under President Yeltsin and his entourage, and more brazenly by President Putin. Key rights and liberties, especially freedom of the press, have been trampled. For the vast majority of Russians, economic well-being has been absent from the very beginning of postcommunist Russia; the spoils of private enterprise have been snapped up by a handful of politically favored cronies of the country's two presidents. In addition, negative tendencies have marked virtually all 10 conditions for democracy presented in this book. As a consequence, Russia's political system slipped in status from a semi-democratic regime to an authoritarian regime in just a little over 10 years.

President Putin's rhetoric has matched this retrogression. He has explicitly advocated a "dictatorship of the law," and his advisors have described his government as a "managed democracy."[68] In his second inaugural address following his landslide reelection in 2004, he did not mention the word *democracy*. After critics at home and abroad pointed out this omission, Putin referred to democracy repeatedly in a subsequent speech. But he also spoke about the need for a "mature civil society," combining this vague phrase with threats against human rights and prodemocracy organizations. Putin's blatant attempts to intimidate the press, reorganize the electoral process, and harass political opponents have raised troubling questions about what he means by a "mature civil society." The way Putin imposed his own successor, Medvedev, in 2008, and then supplanted him four years later, indicates the degree of power he exercises in twenty-first-century Russia. However, for all his faults, Putin is not a Soviet-style dictator or a new tsar. He owes his legitimacy to Russian voters, and after his return to the presidency in 2012 he enjoyed a sky-high approval rating of 72 percent. Prime Minister Medvedev had a similarly high approval rating at 67 percent. His assertion of strong state authority is viewed by millions of Russians as a welcome barrier against a return to the uncertainties and free-fall disorder of the Gorbachev and Yeltsin years. Widespread support for a "strong leader" instead of a more pluralistic democracy props up Putin's brand of *popular authoritarianism*. And though the windows of free expression, electoral honesty, and judicial fairness are closing, Russians today still enjoy more freedoms than they were ever allowed under communism. Among other things, they may join NGOs and political parties, they may worship freely (though some non-Orthodox faiths are discriminated against), they may travel abroad, they have access to information and culture from around the world, and they are free from the incessant drumbeat of Marxist–Leninist propaganda and the stultifying Communist censorship system. In addition, Putin has repeatedly reaffirmed his commitment to private property, a value now regarded by 80 percent of the Russian population as a basic right.

It would be foolhardy to predict what the coming years will bring for Russia. The unpredictability of Russia's future reminds us of Winston Churchill's famous observation more than half a century ago that Russia is "a riddle, wrapped in a mystery, inside an enigma."

Key Terms

Union of Soviet Socialist Republics/USSR/Soviet Union
Communist Party of the Soviet Union (CPSU)
Commonwealth of Independent States (CIS)
Bolsheviks
October Revolution
Marxism–Leninism
Centrally planned economy (CPE)
Perestroika
Glasnost
State Duma
Federation Council

Notes

1. Freedom House, *Freedom in the World: The Annual Survey of Political Rights and Civil Liberties 1994–1995* (New York: Freedom House, 1995), pp. 477–82; Freedom House, *Freedom in the World 2003* (New York: Freedom House, 2003), pp. 458–65; Freedom House, *Freedom in the World 2005* (New York: Freedom House, 2005), pp. 519–24; Freedom House, *Freedom in the World 2006* (New York: Freedom House, 2006), pp. 586–92. See also the annual reports on Russia published by Freedom House in *Freedom of the Press*, www.freedomhouse.org, and by Reporters Without Borders, www.rsf.org. On Politkovskaya, see the *Washington Post*, October 7, 8, 9, 11, and 13, 2006. On Pussy Riot, see the *Guardian*, August 17, 2012.
2. A classic survey is Nicholas V. Riasanovsky and Mark Steinberg, *A History of Russia*, 7th ed. (New York: Oxford University Press, 2004).
3. Robert K. Massie, *Peter the Great* (New York: Knopf, 1980).
4. Liah Greenfeld, *Nationalism: Five Roads to Modernity* (Cambridge, MA: Harvard University Press, 1992), ch. 3 (especially p. 265). She argues that whereas the Slavophiles abandoned the attempt to catch up with the West on the economic and political planes, exalting instead the pristine Russian "soul," the Westernizers favored borrowing technology from the West with the ultimate aim of demonstrating Russia's economic or military capabilities (like Peter the Great) or of eventually overtaking the West (like the communists).
5. Isabel de Madariaga, *Russia in the Age of Catherine the Great* (New Haven, CT: Yale University Press, 1981).
6. Richard Pipes, *Russia Under the Old Regime* (New York: Scribner's, 1974), pp. 281–318.
7. Dominic Lieven, *Russia's Rulers Under the Old Regime* (New Haven, CT: Yale University Press, 1989).
8. Alexander Gerschenkron, *Economic Backwardness in Historical Perspective* (Cambridge, MA: Harvard University Press, 1962).
9. Victoria E. Bonnell, *Roots of Rebellion* (Berkeley, CA: University of California Press, 1983).
10. See, for example, Engels's letter to the Russian revolutionary Peter Tkachov in Robert C. Tucker, ed., *The Marx-Engels Reader* (New York: W. W. Norton, 1972), pp. 589–99.
11. The big winners were the Socialist Revolutionaries, with 40 percent of the vote. The Socialist Revolutionaries were the heirs of the populists and had a large rural following. Though their left wing was quite radical, their large right-wing faction favored Western-style democracy. The Western-oriented liberals, the Constitutional Democrats, won 5 percent.
12. In 1930, Stalin said, "We are for the withering away of the state. But at the same time we stand for the strengthening of the proletarian dictatorship. . . . Is this 'contradictory'? Yes, it is 'contradictory.' But this contradiction is life, and it reflects completely the Marxian dialectic." In justifying the terror, Stalin said the closer one gets to socialism, the more intense the class struggle becomes. Biographies include Adam B. Ulam, *Stalin* (New York: Viking, 1973); Robert B. Tucker, *Stalin as Revolutionary, 1879–1929* (New York: W. W. Norton, 1973); Robert B. Tucker, *Stalin in Power* (New York: W. W. Norton, 1990); Isaac Deutscher, *Stalin* (New York: Vintage, 1960).
13. Robert Conquest, *The Harvest of Sorrow* (New York: Oxford University Press, 1986).
14. Robert Conquest, *The Great Terror* (Harmondsworth, UK: Penguin, 1971); J. Arch Getty, *Origins of the Great Purges* (Cambridge: Cambridge University Press, 1985).
15. On August 23, 1939, the Soviet Union and Germany signed an agreement to partition Poland. Several weeks after the German army invaded that country on September 1, 1939, Soviet forces moved into eastern Poland and annexed it. (The annexed territory today is part of Ukraine.) The Germans also handed over Lithuania, Latvia, and Estonia to the USSR.
16. Lazar Pistrak, *The Grand Tactician* (New York: Praeger, 1961).
17. Solzhenitsyn's *One Day in the Life of Ivan Denisovich*, published in a Soviet literary journal, was based on his own incarceration in a Stalinist labor camp.
18. Nikita Sergeyevich Khrushchev, *Memoirs of Nikita Khrushchev: Commissar (1818–1945)*, trans. George Shriver and Stephen Shenfield (University Park, PA: Pennsylvania State University Press, 2005); N. S. Khrushchev and Sergei Khrushchev, *Memoirs of Nikita Khrushchev: Reformer (1945–1964)* (University Park, PA: Pennsylvania State University Press, 2006); William Taubman, *Khrushchev: The Man and his Era* (New York: W. W. Norton, 2003); Sergei N. Khrushchev, *Nikita Khrushchev and the Creation of a Superpower*, trans. Shirley Benson (University Park, PA: Pennsylvania State University Press, 2000); Carl A. Linden, *Khrushchev and the Soviet Leadership, 1957–1964* (Baltimore: Johns Hopkins University Press, 1966).
19. Sidney Bloch and Peter Reddaway, *Soviet Psychiatric Abuse* (London: V. Gollancz, 1984).
20. Seweryn Bialer, *Stalin's Successors* (Cambridge: Cambridge University Press, 1980).
21. Mikhail Gorbachev, *Memoirs*, trans. Wolf Jobst Siedler (New York: Doubleday, 1995). The most substantial monographs are Archie Brown, *The Gorbachev Factor* (Oxford: Oxford University Press, 1996); and Jerry F. Hough, *Democratization and Revolution in the USSR, 1985–1991* (Washington, DC: Brookings Institution, 1997). See also Stephen Kotkin, *Armageddon Averted: The Soviet Collapse, 1970–2000* (New York: Oxford University Press, 2003); Mark R. Beissinger, *Nationalist Mobilization and the Collapse of the Soviet State* (New York: Cambridge University Press, 2002); Steven L. Solnick, *Stealing the State: Control and Collapse in Soviet Institutions* (Cambridge, MA: Harvard University Press, 1998). For an insider's account, see Yegor Ligachev, *Inside Gorbachev's Kremlin*, trans. Catherine A. Fitzpatrick, Michele A. Berdy, and Dobrochna Dyrcz-Freedman (New York: Pantheon, 1993). See also Carl Linden, "Gorbachev and the Fall of the Marxian Prince in Europe and Russia," in *Russia and China on the Eve of a New Millennium*, ed. Carl Linden and Jan A. Prybyla (New Brunswick, NJ: Transaction, 1997), pp. 59–87.
22. Mikhail Gorbachev, *Perestroika* (New York: Harper and Row, 1987 and 1988).
23. Anders Åslund, *Gorbachev's Struggle for Economic Reform* (Ithaca, NY: Cornell University Press, 1989); Marshall I. Goldman, *Gorbachev's Challenge* (New York: W. W. Norton, 1987).

24. Michael J. Sodaro, *Moscow, Germany, and the West from Khrushchev to Gorbachev* (Ithaca, NY: Cornell University Press, 1990).

25. Gale Stokes, *The Walls Came Tumbling Down* (New York: Oxford University Press, 1993); David Pryce-Jones, *The Strange Death of the Soviet Empire* (New York: Henry Holt, 1995).

26. Grigory Yavlinsky, Boris Fedorov, Stanislav Shatalin, et al., *500 Days*, trans. David Kushner (New York: St. Martin's Press, 1991). See also Marshall I. Goldman, *What Went Wrong with Perestroika?* (New York: W. W. Norton, 1991).

27. On the coup, see Victoria E. Bonnell, Ann Cooper, and Gregory Freidin, eds., *Russia at the Barricades* (Armonk, NY: M. E. Sharpe, 1994).

28. On the formation of opposition movements in this period, see Judith Devlin, *The Rise of the Russian Democrats* (Aldershot, UK: Edward Elgar, 1995); Michael Urban, Vyacheslav Igrunov, and Sergei Mitrokhin, *The Rebirth of Politics in Russia* (Cambridge: Cambridge University Press, 1997); M. Steven Fish, *Democracy from Scratch: Opposition and Regime in the New Russian Revolution* (Princeton, NJ: Princeton University Press, 1995).

29. Boris Yeltsin, *Against the Grain: An Autobiography*, trans. Michael Glenny (New York: Summit, 1990). See also Andrei S. Grachev, *Final Days*, trans. Margo Milne (Boulder, CO: Westview, 1995).

30. Martin J. Peck and Thomas J. Richardson, *What Is to Be Done? Proposals for the Soviet Transition to Market* (New Haven, CT: Yale University Press, 1991); Anders Åslund, *How Russia Became a Market Economy* (Washington, DC: Brookings Institution, 1995).

31. Olga Bridges and Jim Bridges, *Losing Hope: The Environment and Health in Russia* (Aldershot, UK: Avebury, 1996).

32. Yegor Gaidar, *Days of Defeat and Victory*, trans. Jane Ann Miller (Seattle: University of Washington Press, 1999).

33. Michael McFaul, *Russia's Unfinished Revolution: Political Change from Gorbachev to Putin* (Ithaca, NY: Cornell University Press, 2002), pp. 121–312.

34. Peter Reddaway and Dmitri Glinski, *The Tragedy of Russia's Reforms: Market Bolshevism Against Democracy* (Washington, DC: United States Institute of Peace Press, 2001); David E. Hoffman, *The Oligarchs: Wealth and Power in the New Russia* (New York: Public Affairs, 2002).

35. Phil Williams, ed., *Russian Organized Crime: The New Threat?* (London: Frank Cass, 1997); Stephen Handelman, *Comrade Criminal: Russia's New Mafiya* (New Haven, CT: Yale University Press, 1995).

36. Carlotta Gall and Thomas de Waal, *Chechnya* (New York: New York University Press, 1998); Anatol Lieven, *Chechnya* (New Haven, CT: Yale University Press, 1998).

37. Jerry F. Hough, Evelyn Davidheiser, and Susan Goodrich Lehmann, *The 1996 Russian Presidential Election* (Washington, DC: Brookings Institution, 1996), p. 40.

38. Lilia Shevtsova, *Yeltsin's Russia* (Washington, DC: Carnegie Endowment for International Peace, 1999), pp. 180–93. On Zyuganov and his party, see Joan Barth Urban and Valerii D. Solovei, *Russia's Communists at the Crossroads* (Boulder, CO: Westview, 1997).

39. See George W. Breslauer, *Gorbachev and Yeltsin as Leaders* (Cambridge: Cambridge University Press, 2002).

40. According to the Institute of International Finance, a Western organization, Russia by the spring of 1998 had borrowed $99 billion from abroad, but $103 billion had left the country (Paul Blustein and Daniel Williams, "Policymakers Fear Political Fallout of Latest Russian Financial Turmoil," *The Washington Post*, May 30, 1998). Another Western estimate reported $136 billion in capital outflows between 1993 and 1998 (John Thornhill and Charles Clover, "The Robbery of Nations: Billions of Dollars Are Flowing out of the Former Soviet Union," *Financial Times*, August 21/22, 1999). The organized crime figure was estimated by American scholar Louise Shelley, *Financial Times*, March 20, 1997. See also "Crime Without Punishment," *The Economist*, August 28, 1999, and the views of IMF Managing Director Michel Camdessus in Sharon LaFraniere, "Moscow May Get New Loans; IMF Director Says Russia Is Making Economic Strides," *The Washington Post*, June 17, 1999.

41. On the financial oligarchy and Russia's economic development, see Rose Brady, *Kapitalizm* (New Haven, CT: Yale University Press, 1999); Bertram Silverman and Murray Yanowitch, *New Rich, New Poor, New Russia* (Armonk, NY: M. E. Sharpe, 1997); Juliet Johnson, *A Fistful of Rubles: The Rise and Fall of the Russian Banking System* (Ithaca, NY: Cornell University Press, 2000); Chrystia Freeland, *Sale of the Century: Russia's Wild Ride from Communism to Capitalism* (New York: Crown Business, 2000).

42. For Putin's background and ideas upon assuming the presidency, see Vladimir Putin, with Nataliya Gevorkyan, Nataliya Timakova, and Andrei Kolesnikov, *First Person: An Astonishingly Frank Self-Portrait by Russia's President Vladimir Putin*, trans. Catherine A. Fitzpatrick (New York: Public Affairs, 2000).

43. Freedom House, *Freedom in the World 2003*, p. 464; *Freedom in the World 2006*, p. 591; *The Washington Post*, September 30, 2006; Human Rights Watch, *Country Summary: Russia*, January 2012; the U.S. State Department's annual reports on human rights practices in Russia, accessible at www.state.gov/g/drl.

44. Juan J. Linz and Alfred Stepan, *Problems of Democratic Transition and Consolidation* (Baltimore: Johns Hopkins University Press, 1996), p. 28.

45. On regionalism, see Mary McAuley, *Russia's Politics of Uncertainty* (Cambridge: Cambridge University Press, 1997); Vladimir Shlapentokh, Roman Levita, and Mikhail Loiberg, *From Submission to Rebellion: The Provinces Versus the Center in Russia* (Boulder, CO: Westview, 1997); Kathryn Stoner-Weiss, *Local Heroes: The Political Economy of Russian Regional Governance* (Princeton, NJ: Princeton University Press, 1997); Mikhail Stoliarov, *Federalism and the Dictatorship of Power* (London: Routledge, 2000). On the role of the seven federal *okrugs*, see Peter Reddaway and Robert W. Orttung, eds., *The Dynamics of Russian Politics: Putin's Reform of Federal-Regional Relations*, vol. 1 (Lanham, MD: Rowman and Littlefield, 2004). See also Gulnaz Sharafutdinova, "When Do Elites Compete? The Determinants of Political Competition in Russian Regions," *Comparative Politics* 38, no. 3 (April 2006), pp. 273–93; Grigorii V. Golosov, "What Went Wrong: Regional Electoral Politics and Impediments to State Centralization in Russia, 2003–2004," www.csis.org/ruseura/ponars/pm.

46. Arkady Ostrovsky, "Putin Oversees Big Rise in Influence of Security Apparatus," *Financial Times*, November 1–2, 2003; Brian D. Taylor, "Power Surge? Russia's Power Ministries from Yeltsin to Putin and Beyond," www.csis.org/ruseura/ponars/pm.

47. Peter Baker and Susan B. Glasner, *Kremlin Rising: Vladimir Putin's Russia and the End of Revolution* (New York: Scribner, 2005); Andrew Jack, *Inside Putin's Russia: Can There Be Reform Without Democracy?* (New York: Oxford University Press, 2004); Cameron Ross, ed., *Russian Politics Under Putin* (Manchester, UK: Manchester University Press, 2004); Timothy J. Colton and Michael McFaul, "Putin and Democratization," in *Putin's Russia: Past Imperfect, Future Uncertain*, ed. Dale R. Herspring (Lanham, MD: Rowman and Littlefield, 2003), p. 13.

48. Lilia Shevtsova, *Putin's Russia* (Washington, DC: Carnegie Endowment for International Peace, 2003), p. 59ff.

49. McFaul, *Russia's Unfinished Revolution*, pp. 310–12; Shevtsova, *Yeltsin's Russia*, p. 277ff.

50. Peter Baker, "Oligarchs' Power Unfettered under Putin; Once-Ruthless Entrepreneurs Cede Politics to Kremlin for Free Economic Rein," *The Washington Post*, December 14, 2002. See also the 2006 and 2011 OECD "Economic Survey of the Russian Federation," www.oecd.org. Carsten Sprenger, "State Ownership in the Russian Economy: Its Magnitude, Structure and Governance Problems," ICEF Working Paper, February 11, 2010.

51. M. Steven Fish, *Democracy Derailed in Russia: The Failure of Open Politics* (New York: Cambridge University Press, 2005).

52. Juliet Johnson, "Mission Impossible: Modernization in Russia after the Global Financial Crisis," PONARS Eurasia Policy Memo No. 196, George Washington University, June 2012.

53. Transparency International, *Corruption Perceptions Index 2012*, http://www.transparency.org/cpi2012/results; Freedom House, *Nations in Transit 2003* (New York: Freedom House, 2003), p. 523.

54. Center for Citizen Initiatives, http://www.ccisf.org/pep/stabilizes.htm.

55. Harley Balzer, "Russia's Middle Classes," *Post-Soviet Affairs* 14, no. 2 (1998), pp. 165–86; Harley Balzer, "Routinization of the New Russians?" *Russian Review* 62 (June 2003), pp. 15–36; Thane Gustafson, *Capitalism, Russian-Style* (Cambridge: Cambridge University Press, 1999), pp. 43–44, 176–79; Andrew E. Kramer and David M. Herszenhorn, "Boosted by Putin, Russia's Middle Class Turns on Him," *The New York Times*, December 12, 2011.

56. Irina Denisova, "Income Distribution and Poverty in Russia," OECD Social, Employment and Migration Working Papers, No. 132, 2012.

57. Population Reference Bureau, *2012 World Population Data Sheet*, www.prb.org See also Judith Ingram, "Putin Hits Back, Criticizing U.S. in Yearly Address," *The Washington Post*, May 11, 2006.

58. Richard Rose and Neil Munro, *Elections Without Order: Russia's Challenge to Vladimir Putin* (Cambridge: Cambridge University Press, 2002); Timothy Colton, *Transitional Citizens: Voters and What Influences Them in the New Russia* (Cambridge, MA: Harvard University Press, 2000);

Christopher Marsh, *Russia at the Polls: Voters, Elections, and Democratization* (Washington, DC: Congressional Quarterly Press, 2002).

59. Henry E. Hale, *Why Not Parties in Russia? Democracy, Federalism, and the State* (New York: Cambridge University Press, 2006).

60. Freedom House, *Nations in Transit 2003*, p. 504. See also Valerie Sperling, *Organizing Women in Contemporary Russia: Engendering Transition* (Cambridge: Cambridge University Press, 1999); "The Fair Sex in an Unfair System: The Gendered Effects of Putin's Political Reforms," www .csis.org/ruseura/ponars/pm.

61. Sarah Ashwin and Simon Clarke, *Russian Trade Unions and Industrial Relations in Transition* (Basingstoke and New York: Palgrave, 2002); International Labor Organization, Subregional Office for Eastern Europe and Central Asia Newsletter, September 2005.

62. For a compilation of public views about politics, see Levada Analytical Center, "Russian Public Opinion 2010–2011," 2012. See also Matthew

Wyman, *Public Opinion in Postcommunist Russia* (New York: St. Martin's Press, 1997); Vladimir Tismaneanu, ed., *Political Culture and Civil Society in Russia and the New States of Eurasia* (Armonk, NY: M. E. Sharpe, 1995).

63. "Russians Back Protests, Political Freedoms," www.pewglobal.org.

64. Mikhail A. Alexeev, "Xenophobia in Russia: Are the Young Driving It?" www.csis.org/ruseura/ponars/pm.

65. Levada Analytical Center, "Russian Public Opinion, 2010–2011."

66. The data are from the World Bank.

67. James M. Goldgeier and Michael McFaul, *Power and Purpose: U.S. Policy Toward Russia After the Cold War* (Washington, DC: Brookings Institution, 2003).

68. Timothy J. Colton and Michael McFaul, *Popular Choice and Managed Democracy: The Russian Elections of 1999 and 2000* (Washington, DC: Brookings Institution, 2003). See also Herspring, ed., *Putin's Russia: Past Imperfect, Future Uncertain.*

17 China

BRUCE J. DICKSON

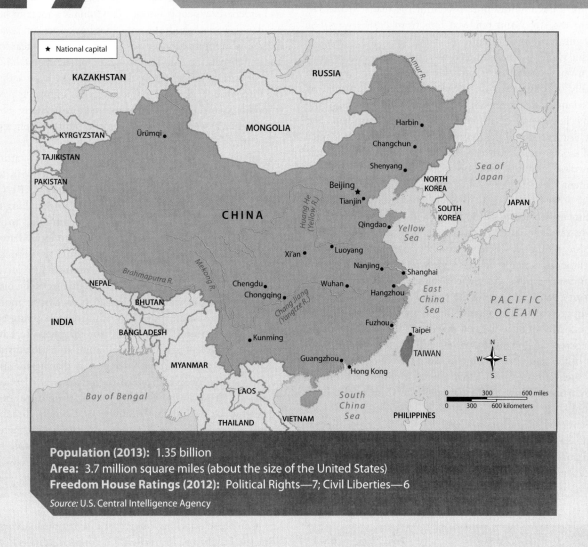

★ National capital

Population (2013): 1.35 billion
Area: 3.7 million square miles (about the size of the United States)
Freedom House Ratings (2012): Political Rights—7; Civil Liberties—6

Source: U.S. Central Intelligence Agency

OVERVIEW

■ The key to understanding politics in China is that it is governed by a Leninist party, the Chinese Communist Party (CCP), which dominates the government through personnel appointments and prevents the formation of alternative political organizations.

■ While the government structure has some superficial similarities with parliamentary systems, the CCP plays a much larger role than in any democracy and even more than many authoritarian regimes.

■ China presents a paradox: an increasingly vibrant economy combined with a strong authoritarian political system. China's economic development in recent decades owes to a liberalization of the economy, but the CCP has not permitted a similar liberalization of the political regime.

■ China faces many challenges today—how much to rely on the state and the market for economic development, how to balance growth with equity and environmental protection, how to reconcile the political system with a rapidly changing economic and social environment—that also confront most countries. However, given China's size and growing global presence, how its political leaders address those challenges will have implications not only for Chinese citizens but also for the world.

■ China presents an informative test case for many of the conventional theories of democratization, political economy, and political participation, which we examine in detail.

POLITICS IN A ONE-PARTY STATE

On the morning of June 5, 1989, a young man blocked a line of tanks moving through downtown Beijing. Holding nothing but a paper shopping bag, he faced off against the first tank in the line. As it tried to maneuver to one side or the other, he would also move to remain in its way. This bizarre little drama lasted for a few minutes until several of the man's friends ran out into the street and removed him from harm's way. The tanks continued on their path.

This vignette—as short as it was, and in the end as fruitless as it was—had a lasting impression on people in China and especially on observers overseas who had been captivated by the prodemocracy movement that gripped China in the spring of 1989. For several weeks, hundreds of Chinese students had staged unprecedented demonstrations in favor of democracy in Beijing's famed Tiananmen Square, issuing a bold challenge to China's communist dictators. Although the prodemocracy movement captured the world's attention and spread to hundreds of other Chinese cities, it was crushed overnight once the government decided to call in troops and tanks to arrest demonstrators and impose martial law. Unlike the Soviet Union and Eastern Europe, where the forces of democratization that were gathering strength at this time would ultimately topple communism, China experienced only a brief outburst of democratic sentiment before the communist authorities forcefully suppressed it. The picture of the man defying the tanks became a symbol of individual bravery in the face of tyranny, of the power of nonviolent protest against the overwhelming power of the state. But it also reminds us of the potential futility of such efforts. Since 1989, China's political institutions have remained firmly in the hands of the Communist Party leadership.

Nevertheless, it cannot be said that China has been standing still since that extraordinary year. There is little dispute that China is a rising power on the world scene. Its diplomatic activities are expanding regionally and globally. Its dramatic economic growth, driven and sustained in large part by foreign

A young man defies tanks as Chinese authorities crack down on the prodemocracy demonstrations in Tiananmen Square in 1989.

investment and trade, has boosted China's impact on the global economy. In 2011, China passed Japan to become the second largest economy in the world, surpassed only by the United States. China is also the world's second largest trading country and the second largest recipient of foreign direct investment, again second to the United States. Its military is also becoming stronger and more capable of wielding influence beyond its borders. Few people doubt that China is a force to be reckoned with in the world; the only question centers on *how* it will behave as an international actor. Will China be a threat to peace and stability in the Asia-Pacific region, or to American interests in that area or elsewhere in the world? Will it be a threat to the international economy? Or can China's growing power be smoothly incorporated into the international system? The reality of China's ascendancy is self-evident, but the implications of this reality are hotly debated.

In contrast to China's rising international stature, the country's domestic political situation is fraught with tension and turmoil. The **Chinese Communist Party (CCP)**, China's ruling party since 1949**,** shows no sign of undertaking fundamental political reforms. Instead, it is determined to remain in power by finding short-term solutions to immediate problems. But the party leadership faces mounting popular protests in the cities as well as in the countryside. Corruption seems to be endemic, and yet the party elite lacks the means or the will to crack down on corrupt officials, despite more than three decades of admitting rhetorically that stopping corruption is a matter of "life or death" for the party. In addition, China is experiencing a surge of popular nationalism: Elements of the population are increasingly placing the interests of the Chinese people ahead of the interests of the Communist Party. Criticisms of the Communist regime are spreading in cyberspace, as growing numbers of Chinese discuss their country's problems over the Internet. Faced with these challenges, the party has attempted to control the expression of critical views, but success has proven elusive. In contrast to their robust international presence, China's leaders are beset on the domestic scene with a host of problems for which they have no ready answer.

Can these opposing images of international strength and domestic fragility be reconciled? Of course, China is not alone in experiencing a mismatch between its international and domestic levels of political activity. Success in one realm does not readily transfer to the other. Moreover, the standards people use when assessing China's domestic politics vary widely. Many observers both inside and outside China evaluate the political reforms the country's leaders have initiated in recent years primarily in terms of whether they are making China more democratic. But democratization is not the only measure of political development. If we recognize that greater democracy is not the immediate goal of China's leaders, we may conclude that China's domestic environment is not so desperate or fragile after all.

The CCP has been more adaptable and more resilient than it often gets credit for being. It is pursuing a variety of political reforms that are intended to enhance the capacity of the state to govern effectively, if not democratically. It relies on a mix of measures to shore up popular support, resolve local protests, and incorporate those who have benefited from economic reform into the political system. At the same time, it forcefully represses challenges to its authority. As a result, public opinion is surprisingly complacent. Although many Chinese are unhappy with their current situation, they remain optimistic about the future. These attitudes are not a recipe for imminent revolution. The ruling elite faces serious problems, but the issues tend to be chronic rather than dangerously acute. Absent a sudden and unexpected flare-up, they do not pose an imminent threat to the Communist regime.

Despite the many economic, social, and political changes under way in China, the central fact of the Chinese political system remains the same: China is governed by a communist party. Virtually every aspect of Chinese politics—including the policy-making process, relations between state and society, and opportunities for political participation—are derived from that one fact. The top government officials, at the central level and at the local level, are party members. As in the former USSR, the party and the government are tightly integrated in communist China. Policies are normally debated, decided, and implemented by party members (often in their additional capacity as government officials) with little consultation with nonparty people or organizations. Most large organizations, including universities, factories, and government offices, have party organizations within them to monitor compliance with party policies. Whether organized to represent labor or business, to pursue sports or other hobbies, or to enhance any common interest, every organization must be authorized by the party or else it runs the risk of being disbanded and having its leaders face arrest. The goal of these organizations is not to be independent of the state, which is often the case in a pluralist democracy. Instead, the goal is to be connected to the state, to be "within the system," because everyone knows that to be outside the system means you are powerless.

These realities do not mean the CCP is monolithic or omnipotent. The history of the CCP's rule in China after coming to power in 1949 and establishing the People's Republic of China (PRC) has been marked by occasionally intense conflict over issues of power and policy. Party leaders do not always agree on the proper course of policy or even on the question of who should be in a position of power to make those decisions. The central state often cannot get lower levels of government, from the provincial level to the grass roots, to comply with its current policies. Moreover, the economic and political reforms of the past 30 years have reduced the state's control over the daily lives of most Chinese people, giving them greater independence to switch jobs, change their place of residence, travel, and have access to ideas and sources of information not controlled by the state. These changes have complicated the policy process and relaxed the state's dominance over society, but they have not challenged the CCP's

preeminent position in China's political system. In a word, China's party leaders and state officials enjoy considerable autonomy when it comes to making decisions that affect the population, but the population does not have much autonomy from the party and government authorities to act in its own behalf.

The 1989 protests in Tiananmen Square and elsewhere in China demonstrated that there are few legitimate and effective means of political participation for aggrieved individuals and groups in Chinese society. Even though the basic demands of the movement—a crackdown on corruption and inflation, enforcement of the rule of law—were consistent with the government's own policies, the state felt threatened by the spontaneous nature of the movement and the growing popular support it elicited from all walks of life. Moreover, the Communist Party-state saw the formation of autonomous (but short-lived) student groups and labor unions as a direct challenge to its authority and an unacceptable change in China's political system. Without these types of autonomous groups, there is little accountability for government officials and very limited access to decision-making arenas by people affected by policy decisions. On an everyday basis, *clientelism*—that is, one-to-one relations based on the personal exchange of favors—is very common, and collective action by interest groups and other organizations is extremely rare. (See Chapter 8 for more about clientelism.) Episodes of mass participation are rare, tend to be sporadic and unpredictable, prone to rapid escalation and extreme demands that result in a government crackdown rather than a negotiated compromise. In contrast, localized protests are increasingly common, tend to focus on the improper implementation of policy instead of the merits of the policy itself, and utilize the formal rhetoric of the state to justify their demands. The state has been more willing to compromise with these types of protests. Regardless of whether it cracks down or chooses to compromise, it is motivated by reinforcing sentiments: a deep-rooted cultural fear of instability and the self-interested desire to preserve the Communist Party's power.

In this chapter we will explore the rise of Communist Party dominance in China and consider how the CCP ruled in its early years. CCP domination meant, at times, the imposition of extreme policies such as the Great Leap Forward that led to tremendous hardship for the Chinese people. The CCP's decision to step back from a centrally planned, communist economy came after extensive discussion within the ruling elite about the merits of the market versus the continuation of state planning. Economic reform in the 1980s and since has led to rapid economic growth and the reinsertion of China into the world economy, but it has not led to a parallel liberalization of the political system. We will consider how the CCP rules China and the extent to which the Chinese people can participate politically. Whether economic liberalization may lead to political democratization remains a key topic for students of Chinese politics, and we will consider that theme toward the end of this chapter.

CHINA'S HISTORICAL LEGACIES: WHY NO DEMOCRACY?

A fascination with democracy began in China early in the twentieth century, but the Chinese have never had a democratic government on any meaningful scale for any length of time. Instead, twentieth-century China was governed by a succession of authoritarian governments of the right (mostly nationalists and military leaders) and the left (the communists). These regimes were more concerned with maintaining order and national unity and fostering economic development than with promoting liberty or government accountability.

The first major turning point in the direction of fundamental political change in China came in 1911, when a revolution put an end to the long succession of imperial dynasties that had ruled China almost continually for nearly 4,000 years. As one of the world's oldest civilizations, China is believed to have established its first dynasty sometime around 1875 BCE. With the establishment of the Qin (or Ch'in) dynasty in 221 BCE, followed by the Han dynasty (206 BCE to AD 200), the rulers of China embarked on a period of territorial expansion and laid the groundwork for the institutional structures whose basic pattern would endure for much of the ensuing millennia.

Despite long periods of disunity and the breakdown of centralized authority, until the twentieth century China would be governed for most of its history by an imperial bureaucracy emanating from the personal authority of the emperor. The emperor, in turn, typically based his legitimacy on the "mandate of heaven," a Chinese variant of what would later be known in Europe as the divine right of kings. The teachings of Confucius (K'ung-Fu-tzu, approximately 551–479 BCE) provided ethical guidance to imperial rule, emphasizing the hierarchical principles of moral leadership from above and the importance of authority in political and social relationships.

As the centuries unfolded, the most successful dynasties reinforced the system of government they inherited. They appointed scholar-bureaucrats to manage the government's affairs, and they established the central authority of the state over all of China. Nothing in the way of democracy ever emerged from dynastic rule, however: no parliaments or social movements that might pry open the closed world of imperial administration. If we measure imperial China against the 10 conditions for democracy specified in Chapter 7, it would come up short in every respect.

State institutions were authoritarian from the beginning and remained so until the collapse of the dynastic system. The governing elites were wholly committed to the imperial system, with its claims to divine legitimation and its Confucian ethos. The nation's wealth was based on an agricultural economy, with the imperial tax collection system assuring the state a large share of the national product. Commerce and private enterprise were frowned upon until late in the dynastic era, leaving little room for the emergence of a European-style entrepreneurial bourgeoisie or a middle class. China's masses, mostly destitute, illiterate peasants, were too dispersed, disorganized, and subjugated by the power of local landlords and ruling authorities to provide a groundswell of support for democracy on the part of the disadvantaged.

Civil society was dormant, and China's political culture was thoroughly imbued with Confucianism's reverence for authority and social harmony. The educational system was tightly connected to the state power structure, as the ruling dynasties created a system of rigorous examinations for entry into the prestigious state bureaucracy. Faithful adherence to the Confucian classics, rather than innovation or independence of thought, was the ultimate litmus test for a qualified Chinese official.

The quest for national unity also played a major role in strengthening the power of the imperial state. In the seventeenth century, invaders from Manchuria swooped into China and took over the government, capturing Beijing (Peking) in 1644. China's new rulers, who established the Qing (or Manchu) dynasty, were not ethnic Chinese; they constituted only about 2 percent of the country's population, whose dominant ethnic group was the Han. To impose their authority on a foreign people, they had to fortify the strong arm of the imperial state. The Manchus compelled the Chinese to wear the queue (pigtail) as a sign of submission and never integrated themselves into the population. But they also allowed about a million Han Chinese to earn prestigious degrees and to occupy the vast majority of some 40,000 administrative posts. Most importantly, they adopted the main political institutions and Confucian philosophy that had governed China in past dynasties.

The nineteenth century was a period of catastrophic decline for imperial China. A series of humiliating defeats at the hands of "barbarians" from abroad and organized challenges to imperial rule at home, coupled with the long-term consequences of several centuries of rapid population growth without any increase in the number of officials to govern the now much larger country, resulted in a spiraling process of political disintegration. By the start of the century, Britain was already in command of the tea trade in the southern coastal region of Guangdong (Canton). To finance their purchases, the British imported opium from India and sold it in China for substantial profits, spreading drug addiction among a growing segment of the Chinese population in the process. When the Chinese authorities tried to halt the drug traffic and suspended all trading, the British refused to back down. The "Opium War" began with a naval skirmish in 1839; it ended in 1842 with a British victory as the Chinese government was forced to cede Hong Kong and grant extraterritorial rights to foreigners in China. Another defeat in 1860 compelled the Chinese to open their doors even wider to foreign businesses and diplomatic representatives. These and other "unequal treaties" intensified the government's xenophobia, an attitude shared by many Chinese. It began what is popularly known in China as the "century of humiliation," when foreign countries took advantage of China's weakness to extract a series of concessions and territorial control. Meanwhile, a series of rebellions broke out in China's provinces, further sapping the central government's authority.

With China reduced to a shadow of its former glory, a debate broke out over how to rescue the country. Some blamed China itself for its predicament. The more iconoclastic thinkers argued that Confucianism was such an obstacle to China's progress that it had to be abandoned, rooted out of both government

The "Opium War" began with a naval skirmish in 1839; it ended in 1842 with a British victory as the Chinese government was forced to cede Hong Kong and grant extraterritorial rights to foreigners in China.

and society, and replaced with an alternative system of beliefs. Confucianism valued harmony over competition, stability over change, and deference to authority over individual freedoms. In the eyes of its critics, it was unsuitable to handle the challenges of the modern world. They believed there was nothing to be salvaged from China's past; the only way forward was the wholesale replacement of China's tradition with the values and technology imported from the West.

Others did not want to go that far and advocated balancing a reliance on Chinese ways as the nation's ethical foundation and Western ways for practical purposes. In the late nineteenth century, conservative writers argued that the solution to China's problems was not the adoption of Western ways, but the exact opposite: They believed that foreign pressures were the cause of China's problems, not their solution, and those pressures needed to be countered with a determined return to orthodox traditions.

Thus began an intense debate in China that has endured to the present: How should China become modern, what parts of its past are compatible with modernity, and what are the reasons for China's current backwardness? Ultimately, the debate concerns what it means to be Chinese at a time when there is little consensus on which elements of the country's traditions should be preserved and which should be abandoned.

Initially, reformers in the imperial entourage won the upper hand. Their aim was to import Western technological and administrative ideas in an effort to save the monarchy. But their ambitious reform efforts ended when conservative elements in the court, led by the empress dowager (who ruled on behalf of the last emperor of China, then still a young boy), regained control and imprisoned or exiled the erstwhile reformers, returning China to the traditions that were no match for the modern world.

In October 1911, a Chinese army garrison staged a revolt, triggering a stampede of independence movements in China's provinces. The revolutionaries named Sun Yat-sen, a reformist intellectual trained in Western schools, as China's president. Sun reached an agreement with the imperial officials ruling in the child-emperor's behalf to dissolve the monarchy. In February 1912, the Republic of China was established.

Following the collapse of the imperial system, China was governed by a succession of authoritarian governments. The new republican government was weak from the start. It never established its full authority over China's disparate provinces, some of which fell under the sway of local warlords.[1] Rival governments were established in Beijing under the influence of northern warlords, and in Guangzhou under the influence of Sun Yat-sen and his successor, Chiang Kai-shek.

Meanwhile, the debate over how far China should go in adapting Western methods gained intensity. The May 4th Movement epitomized the critique of Confucianism.[2] It began around 1915, reaching full flower in 1919 after the conclusion of World War I. During the May 4th Movement, Chinese intellectuals advocated the superiority of democracy and science over China's Confucian traditions: democracy because it entails a plurality of voices debating the common good rather than the obedience to orthodoxy required by Confucianism; science because it entails empirical investigation of nature and society in the pursuit of truth rather than the sterile application of an outmoded philosophy to rapidly changing times. Their slogan, "Let a hundred flowers bloom, let a hundred schools of thought contend" (a slogan that would be reprised in the 1950s), was itself based on Confucian traditions. China's liberal intellectuals saw the solution to China's problems in the political traditions and systems of government in the West.

That attitude abruptly changed with the end of World War I in 1918. At the Versailles conference that met at the war's end, the allies gave the German concessions in China—territories that had been granted to Germany by a weakened imperial government—to Japan instead of returning them to Chinese control. Chinese who were inspired by the enlightened beliefs that seemed to be the foundation of Western governments were disillusioned by this turn of events. Once it became known that the Beijing government's representatives at the Versailles conference had acquiesced in this action, anti-Western protests turned into antigovernment protests.

For their part, the leaders of the republican government were in no hurry to embrace Western liberal democracy. Although they abandoned Confucianism, the preference for a single orthodoxy prevailed over the uncertainties inherent in liberalism. Sun Yat-sen, the republic's leading ideologist, expounded an odd mixture of Western scientific and educational theories, Christianity, Chinese nationalism, and a residual adherence to certain Confucian traditions. His lasting contribution was the establishment of a political party, the **Chinese Nationalist Party**, or **Kuomintang (KMT)**. Sun devised the influential "three principles of the people" (nationalism, democracy, and social well-being) as the KMT's guiding political doctrine. But despite his concern for the people's welfare, Sun also believed that China was not ready for democracy and advocated a prolonged period of political tutelage to educate and prepare the Chinese people for participation in a future democratic government. Subsequently this notion was used as a rationale to maintain authoritarian controls over the country after the KMT became the ruling party of China in the late 1920s and even after it fled to Taiwan upon its defeat by the CCP in 1949.

This paternalistic belief that the Chinese people are not ready for democracy and unable to govern their own affairs remains influential in China, affecting elites and masses alike. One of the main challenges facing democratic reformers in China today is to convince not only the state but also society at large that democracy is valuable and will not generate chaos, a fundamental concern in Chinese political culture.

The Chinese Communist Party and China's Civil War

After a brief flirtation with liberalism, socialism grew in popularity in China for two reasons. First, it had the ironic appeal of being a Western theory that criticized the West. The writings of Marx and Lenin were used to criticize capitalist and Western imperialist influences in China. Second, the new Communist government of the Soviet Union, which took power in 1917, renounced the "unequal treaties" that the previous tsarist government had used, much like the Western countries, to gain trade and other concessions from China in the past. The new Soviet government returned the territories it controlled in China, a gesture that gained the Soviet Communist regime tremendous popular appeal within China, especially among urban intellectuals. These events culminated in the formation of the Chinese Communist Party (CCP) in 1921. One of its first adherents was Mao Zedong,[3] who would eventually rise to prominence as the party's supreme leader. The son of peasants from Hunan province, Mao developed the unconventional strategy of relying on the potential of the rural peasants, as opposed to urban workers, to lead the revolution in China. His ideas were a leading cause of both the Communist victory and enormous political and human tragedies after the CCP became the ruling party in 1949.[4]

The CCP and the KMT fought a prolonged civil war from the late 1920s to 1949, with a temporary halt after Japan invaded China. The CCP and KMT agreed in 1936 to a "united front" against Japan instead of fighting each other, although there was little actual cooperation. This allowed the CCP to regroup its forces in its wartime headquarters in remote Yanan. After Japan's defeat in World War II, the Chinese civil war resumed, eventually ending in the establishment of the People's Republic on October 1, 1949.

The Nationalists' defeat in the Chinese civil war led not only to a change of government in China but also to a fierce debate in the United States over "who lost China?" in the 1950s. Meanwhile, as the Nationalists retreated to Taiwan to relocate their government of the Republic of China, Chiang Kai-shek and his followers hoped one day to retake the mainland. Since 1949, Taiwan has been a source of tension in China's foreign policies, especially in its relations with the United States. The United States retained diplomatic relations and a mutual defense treaty with the Republic of China on Taiwan until 1979, when it altered its China policy by recognizing the People's Republic as the sole legitimate government of all China. Although the United States recognizes Beijing's claim that there is but one China and that Taiwan is part of it, it continues to sell defensive arms to Taiwan and has an implicit commitment to defend Taiwan against an attack from mainland China.

Following the the death of Sun Yat-Sen in 1925, Chiang Kai-shek became the leader of the Kuomintang (KMT) and the nationalist government.

PROFILES Mao Zedong

Mao Zedong led China's communist revolution.

Mao Zedong was the dominant figure in Chinese politics from the 1930s until his death in 1976. His personality and proclivities shaped the policies of the CCP and the fate of his nation. No one else enjoyed the charisma and power that let him convert his revolutionary vision into policy, and no one else brought as much tragedy and suffering to his people.

Mao was born in 1893 in Hunan province, the son of successful small farmers. He was an avid reader of Chinese history and fiction, and often drew upon this knowledge for military and political strategy.

In 1921, he attended the founding of the CCP in Shanghai, although he was not elected to the party's Central Committee or given other leadership posts then. In the 1920s, advisors from the Soviet Union counseled the CCP to refrain from revolutionary activities and to cooperate with the Kuomintang (KMT) in a "united front" until the prospects for a proletarian revolution improved. Mao favored a different approach, relying on the revolutionary potential of the peasants, the vast majority of the population. But other party leaders generally ignored his unorthodox views.

Mao returned to Hunan and organized several peasant associations and became inspired by their revolutionary potential. Although his efforts at leading peasant rebellions in Hunan failed, he never lost faith in his strategy, which seemed heretical to orthodox party leaders.

In 1927, the KMT led a surprise attack on the CCP and its supporters in Shanghai, destroying the united front. Some of the CCP leaders who managed to escape this assault joined Mao at his base camp in the mountains along the Hunan-Jiangxi border. But in 1934, they were forced again to flee the approaching KMT army. Thus began the historic Long March—a harrowing, circuitous journey of more than 6,000 miles across some of China's roughest terrain. When their journey ended more than a year later, only 8,000 of the 100,000 or so people who started the journey still remained. Those who survived formed a bond that would last for decades.[5]

During the Long March, Mao became the leader of the party, marginalizing those who favored an urban-based revolution and accepted Soviet advice. From the end of the Long March until the establishment of the PRC in 1949, the CCP under Mao was headquartered in the northwestern town of Yanan, an area so poor that many—including party leaders—lived in cavelike homes dug by hand out of the soft soil.

It was also in Yanan that the "cult of Mao" began. His writings, speeches, and poetry were studied and discussed closely. This veneration of Mao took on near-religious qualities during the Cultural Revolution of the 1960s, when his sayings were collected in the "little red book" that everyone was expected to carry and memorize, his portrait was hung in all Chinese homes and buildings, and people performed songs and dances to show their loyalty to Mao.

The triumph of Mao's CCP was based on a combination of policy moderation, nationalistic appeals, and flexible responses to changing conditions. Once in power, however, Mao became less patient about achieving his ideological goals. He grew suspicious of other leaders who were more concerned with economic development than with ideological rectitude. His charisma was so strong that even those who disagreed with him rarely challenged him directly, nor did they come to the defense of people Mao criticized, even if they shared the same views. In his later years, hobbled by old age, disease, and (according to his physician) years of drug use, Mao became increasingly erratic, throwing his support behind one faction of rivals, only to withdraw it soon after. His utterances were nearly indecipherable and open to conflicting interpretations, leading to bitter disputes between individuals and groups who hoped to gain support for their policy prescriptions. Only in the years after Mao's death was it possible to abandon his goals.

Mao was not the only communist leader to advocate a rural revolution, nor was he the party's only influential military strategist. But it is impossible to imagine the history of the post-1949 era without him. Although his policies brought widespread hardship to his people, he succeeded in unifying the country after decades of political conflict and allowing China to "stand up" against international pressure. Mao Zedong remains a symbol of power and pride for many in contemporary China.

The Communists Take Over

After the CCP became the ruling party in 1949, it promised a "new democracy" with the active involvement of non-CCP elites and organizations. Two key institutions begun during the civil war years were intended to be the basis of this new democracy. The *mass line* was a process by which concerns and suggestions would come *from the masses* and the policy decisions would be communicated by officials *to the masses*. This cycle of deliberation envisioned a close relationship between the state and society in which society would better understand policy decisions and thereby support them, and the state would better understand the concerns of society and the impact of its policies and thereby devise more effective policies.

The second political institution that was central to China's "new democracy" was the *united front*. The CCP promised to consult and cooperate with non-CCP elites, such as business-people, scholars, and even religious leaders, to promote China's modernization. The united front promised a policy process that would be consensual rather than conflictual. Today, united front policies are again being publicized to promote cooperation between the party and key groups—such as business, churches, and overseas Chinese—in China's economic modernization.

Although the mass line and united front policies had some democratic aspirations, in practice they provided at best consultation without accountability. The party-state could listen to a variety of viewpoints, but it selected which views would be heard and which would be suppressed. If the state chose to ignore the concerns of society or the suggestions of non-CCP elites, there was little these groups could do to seek redress. If state policies failed, there was no way for the public to replace the policy makers. In fact, the mass line and the united front more often than not have been means of enforcing dictatorship and state domination at the expense of democratic principles and procedures.

CHINA'S POLITICAL INSTITUTIONS

As noted at the beginning of this chapter, the most basic fact of China's political system is that it is ruled by the Communist Party. The party is organized along Leninist lines: Like Lenin's Bolshevik Party, the CCP resembles a military hierarchy, with the chain of command going from the top down. Though lower-level party officials may have a chance to have their views communicated to the party's upper echelons, once a final decision has been taken by the top leaders, all party members are obliged to fall into line. The party elite rules. Virtually every other aspect of China's politics and government, including the policy process and relations between state and society, are derived from that fundamental truth.

The Chinese Communist Party

At the top of China's political system, and integrated throughout it at all levels, is the Chinese Communist Party. Although it came to power relying on the support of peasants, workers, and soldiers, the CCP today is a broad-based party, drawing its members from all walks of life, including bureaucrats, teachers, and other people in white-collar jobs. It has more than 80 million members, a group that is roughly 6 percent of China's population but larger than the population of many countries in the world.

The most important organization within the CCP is the **Politburo**. This body consists of the top two dozen or so leaders in China. Members of the Politburo often hold other important positions in the central government and the military simultaneously. Some local governments, especially Beijing and Shanghai, are also represented on the Politburo. It approves all major policies and personnel changes. Its actual deliberations are clouded in secrecy, but it is believed to make its decisions by consensus rather than majority rule. Within the Politburo there is a subgroup of China's most powerful leaders, known as the *Standing Committee* of the Politburo, which currently has seven members (see Figure 17.1).

The Central Military Commission is the CCP's organization for overseeing the military. The Central Discipline Inspection Commission and lower-level discipline inspection commissions are responsible for monitoring the behavior of party members, especially party and government officials. They have the authority to charge and punish those guilty of corruption, malfeasance, and other violations of party policy. Primary-level party bodies are organized at workplaces, schools, neighborhoods, military companies, and small towns.

The top party official is the **general secretary**, currently Xi Jinping. Mao Zedong had the title of chairman of the party, but that post was eliminated after his death in 1976 to prevent any leader from accumulating the degree of uncontrolled power that Mao had. The general secretary is formally in charge of the *Secretariat*, a small organization connected to the Politburo that handles the daily affairs of the party leadership, such as the flow

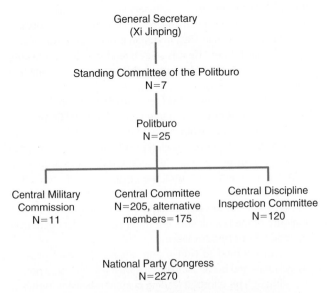

FIGURE 17.1   **Organization of the Chinese Communist Party**

of reports and memos among party leaders and the organization of important meetings.

According to party statutes, the Politburo and Secretariat are supposed to be elected in a sequential process by two larger bodies: the *National Party Congress* and the *Central Committee*. The National Party Congress has about 2,000 delegates and meets every five years, although in the past it met on an irregular basis. The Seventh Party Congress met in 1945, and the next ones did not meet until 1956 and 1969. Since then the body has met more regularly: Beginning in 1977, it has met every five years, most recently in 2012 (the Eighteenth Party Congress). Very little actual debate occurs at these weeklong sessions; the congress typically provides the party leadership with an opportunity to review past achievements and outline the main lines of policy to be pursued in the coming years. Though the congress takes a formal vote in electing the Central Committee, higher party authorities have already decided the Central Committee's membership, leaving the congress only marginal influence. For instance, the number of candidates for the Central Committee presented to the Eighteenth Party Congress in 2012 exceeded the number of those elected by just over 8 percent (205 were elected, but the CCP did not reveal the exact number of candidates).

The Central Committee is a group of about 200 people that meets once or twice a year to formally endorse important policies and leadership changes that have been approved by the Politburo beforehand. The members of the Central Committee represent a broader range of the party's top elites, mostly senior party and government officials from around the country. Some discussion takes place, but the Central Committee rarely, if ever, initiates policy or forces the senior leaders to change course. The Central Committee formally elects the Politburo and its Standing Committee, the Secretariat, and the general secretary. These votes, too, are usually pro forma, as the top leaders invariably decide among themselves how the senior decision-making positions will be distributed. These various bodies are nested: All members of the Standing Committee are on the Politburo, and all Politburo members must first be elected to the Central Committee.

Party supremacy over the government, the military, and other institutions is achieved through a combination of oversight and personnel appointments. Within all government ministries, factories, schools, and other organizations is a party committee that monitors compliance with party directives. The party also nominates or approves all key personnel, from cabinet ministers and department heads to even such relatively low-level positions as heads of university departments and bank officials.

Although far from democratic, the top of China's political system has become increasingly institutionalized. Not only do the National Party Congress and Central Committee meet on a regular basis, but the top leaders in the party and government are replaced on a regular and predictable basis. They are subject to both term limits and age limits. Leaders may serve two five-year terms in a post, and then have to either be appointed to a new post or retire. Once they turn 68, the central leaders must retire at the end of their term; they can finish their terms, but cannot be reappointed or appointed to a new position. Age limits decline at lower levels of the political system—for central ministers and provincial leaders, it is 65; for municipal leaders, it is 60; and so on. The term limits and age limits ensure a regular rotation of top leaders. In the Maoist era, leaders would serve until they died or were purged in a political struggle. China's post-Mao leaders adopted a more routine and institutionalized process to avoid the turmoil that often accompanied leadership transition.[6]

The Government

Structurally, China's government looks very much like a parliamentary system: The governing party appoints ministers and other key government officials, and it drafts most legislation. The key difference is that China's ruling party was not voted into office and does not have to stand for reelection. China's state institutions are highly centralized (see Figure 17.2). The executive branch is headed by a **prime minister** (or **premier**), currently Li Keqiang, who appoints officials to head the other ministries and commissions of the government. This group of people comprises the State Council, the equivalent of a cabinet. Almost all top officials in the government are also CCP members, with a few symbolic exceptions to show the party's continued adherence to a "united front" approach to governing. Even nonparty officials, however, are approved and appointed by the CCP. Although the CCP approves the broad principles of policy, the government has the main responsibility for actually implementing policy and monitoring results.

China's legislative branch is called the **National People's Congress**. It is the weakest of the three main political institutions (the other two being the party and government), although it has been getting more assertive and more influential in recent years. Formerly derided as a rubber-stamp legislature because it unanimously approved all motions proposed by the CCP without dissent or discussion, it now takes an active role in drafting legislation, approving annual budgets, and monitoring the results of reforms. In the past, it met irregularly to ratify party policy; it now has permanent committees with full-time staffs that work year-round. Despite these changes, the National People's Congress is not a democratic or deliberative body. Though its 3,000 members are elected by lower-level "People's Congresses," the Communist Party hierarchy carefully supervises their selection. Even those who advocate a more active role for it do not see it as a vehicle for democratization. Instead, they want to make it an institution capable of overseeing the work of the party and government, perhaps delaying or reversing policy decisions made by higher authorities when necessary. They seek to make it a stronger institution, but not necessarily a more liberal or democratic one.[7]

One of the duties of the National People's Congress is to elect the *president* of the PRC. In March 2013, Xi Jinping was elected president, replacing Hu Jintao, who had held the post for the previous 10 years. The presidency is a largely ceremonial post that gives the incumbent formal standing as China's head of state, a useful status when engaging in international

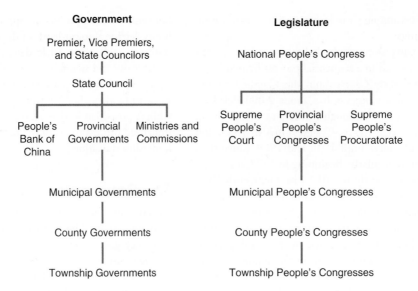

FIGURE 17.2 **Structure of China's State Institutions**

diplomacy with other heads of state. Within China, however, Xi's power is derived from his post as general secretary of the party and chairman of the party's Central Military Commission. Despite holding the top posts in the party, the state, and the military, Xi still must develop the support of other officials in the party and government—and replace those still loyal to Jiang—to wield true power.

The provincial level includes 23 provinces, five autonomous regions, and four large cities (Beijing, Shanghai, Tianjin, and Chongqing). Below the provincial level, there are almost 300 cities and almost 3,000 county-level units (including more than 800 urban districts). The basic level consists of towns and villages. The people elect basic and county-level people's congresses as well as neighborhood and village committees, but their choices are usually limited to candidates picked by the party.

These three main institutions—the party, the executive branch of government, and the legislature—are present at all levels of the political system, from the center in Beijing to the local levels around the country, including provinces, cities, counties, and townships. At each level, the party is the most important body, and the party secretary is the most important leader. Higher-level party officials appoint or approve lower-level officials to maintain some degree of oversight over local affairs. Nevertheless, making sure that local governments faithfully and efficiently carry out the policies decided by higher levels has been an ongoing challenge in China, as it is in many countries. Very few officials are directly elected by the people.

China's formal political institutions are designed to enhance the authority of central leaders. Central leaders appoint provincial-level leaders, who in turn appoint city-level officials, and so on. The power of appointment gives higher-level leaders direct control over lower level officials, whose political futures are dependent on meeting the goals set by those who appoint

them. In practice, however, the center does not have complete control over local leaders. In a country with 32 provincial-level units, 300 major cities, 3,000 counties, 80,000 townships and towns, and over 600,000 villages, leaders in Beijing are not able to directly monitor the actions of local officials and ensure compliance with central policies and procedures. The CCP is often reluctant to replace local officials except when major cases of corruption, malfeasance, or political disputes are involved, and even then only when they are publicly exposed. Moreover, the economic reforms of the post-Mao era (explained below) have made many localities quite prosperous, in turn giving local party and government officials the financial autonomy to ignore central policy. This is a point of continuity between China's imperial past and its present (and indeed common to many countries): how to make sure local officials are loyal agents of central policy, and not pursuing individual and local interests at the expense of central goals.[8]

Since the 1980s, China has been experimenting with direct village elections for the positions of village chief and villagers' representative assemblies. But even where these elections have been successful, the people elected have authority over only a small range of issues. (These elections will be described later in this chapter.) Delegates to county-level people's congresses are directly elected, but then these delegates elect delegates to the next level of people's congress, a process that is repeated up to the National People's Congress. In practice, all people's congress delegates are screened and approved by the party before assuming their posts.

POLITICS IN MAO'S CHINA

The leader of China's communist revolution, Mao Zedong, once said, "A revolution is not a dinner party, or writing an essay, or painting a picture, or doing embroidery; it cannot be so refined, so leisurely and gentle, so temperate, kind, courteous, restrained, and magnanimous. A revolution is an insurrection, an act of violence by which one class overthrows another."[9] By the time the civil war was over in 1949, China had suffered more than a century of decline, due to both internal problems and foreign encroachment. As Chairman Mao declared in Beijing in the fall of 1949, after the revolution was won, China had finally stood up for itself. But the problems faced by China after decades of war were numerous and severe. Mao and the CCP had three main goals.[10]

The first goal was *national unification*. After a period of national disunion, China needed to reintegrate its fractured society. China had long been a unified country, but after being carved into sections formerly occupied by the Japanese, the KMT, and communist armies, plus areas controlled by warlords, the first task was to create a unified country and system of government. Although the civil war was essentially over in 1949, extending the CCP's control over the entire country lasted into the early 1950s.

The second goal was *transformation*. Mao and the CCP leadership were determined to carry out a revolution of the political and social system, which they viewed as the ultimate cause of China's backwardness. In some ways, the revolution truly *began* in 1949; only the civil war had ended. During the early 1950s, the CCP implemented land reform on a nationwide basis. It overthrew the traditional hold of landlords—who comprised a class of about 15 million people—over the rest of rural society and gave their land to the peasants. It is estimated that tens of thousands—and perhaps hundreds of thousands—of landlords were killed in the process. The party also implemented a new marriage law that outlawed the traditional arranged marriages. The marriage law was designed not only to enhance the rights of women, but also to break down the traditional power of clans and heads of families. On the basis of the political and social revolution, China's new leaders believed that economic modernization would then be possible.

Their third task was *modernization*. This entailed both economic recovery (especially ending inflation and restoring agricultural and industrial production to their levels before the Japanese invasion) and economic development, using the Soviet model of rapid industrialization and a centrally planned economy. Mao wanted China to be recognized as a great power among nations. But this goal could be accomplished only if the other two goals were accomplished first.

In the early 1950s, they took a moderate approach to governing. Most officials from the old regime were retained out of necessity: The CCP simply did not have enough members with the skills necessary to take over a nationwide bureaucracy. These old officials had the requisite experience and were therefore relied on, at least in the early 1950s. This practice caused resentment among the CCP's veterans, who felt they had devoted themselves to the revolution and deserved to be given these important positions as a reward. They also resented the party's efforts to recruit better-qualified members and to upgrade the qualifications of existing members. The revolutionaries felt insulted by this emphasis on skills over experience and political reliability.[11]

These conflicts gave rise to one of the most divisive issues in Communist China, the *red versus expert debate*. During the Maoist period (1949–76), many policy debates and power struggles were linked to the issue of whether to emphasize "redness" or expertise. "Reds" were the most ideologically oriented revolutionaries, characterized by their political reliability and ability to mobilize the masses rather than by their technical, administrative, or scientific skills. "Experts," by contrast, were more interested in creating a sound, growing economy that would provide the basis for achieving the Communists' ultimate goals. They typically had better educational backgrounds than most reds and had not served in the guerrilla armies. But the reds questioned the experts' commitment to the CCP and resented their arrogance. Experts in turn resented the intrusion of poorly trained zealots into their complicated work.

The red versus expert debate was closely related to the question of the party's primary goal: whether to promote the country's economic development or to be more concerned with utopianism.[12] Party policy in the Maoist period therefore oscillated between these two goals. When economic development was the primary goal, party and government policies emphasized production goals and allowed a limited amount of private enterprise and market activity, permitting people to make a little money on the side (thereby creating incentives for more production). They emphasized technical skills in personnel matters and minimized the intrusiveness of political campaigns. In contrast, when utopian goals were paramount, party-state policies prohibited or greatly constrained markets, the "class struggle" against the party's enemies became more coercive and dangerous, and economic growth suffered.

Mao was the champion of both sets of policies, and he often shifted between the two as he felt national conditions mandated. As a result, during Mao's lifetime China lurched back and forth between these divergent goals of development and utopia. As time went on, Mao seemed to favor utopian goals above all else. Mao wanted to modernize China, but for him, the means were as important as the ends. His supporters often said it was better to be poor and communist than rich and capitalist.

Key episodes in the post-1949 history of China are impossible to understand without appreciating Mao's central role in the political system. In 1953 the Central Committee passed a resolution that authorized Mao to personally approve all decisions made by the Politburo and Central Committee or else they would be invalid. In 1987 the Central Committee passed a similar secret resolution, this time allowing Deng Xiaoping, Mao's successor as supreme leader, to approve all decisions. Both resolutions violated not only democratic procedures but also the party's traditional norms of consensual decision making. Nevertheless, they reflected the preeminent authority these two men held within China's political system.

Mao's Influence over the Policy Agenda

During the Maoist period policy shifted from development to utopianism in three main episodes. The first came with the *collectivization* of industry and agriculture in 1955–56. By the mid-1950s, the CCP had consolidated its power, eliminated its rivals, and restored the economy to prewar production levels. It then decided to eliminate all remaining private ownership of land and capital. On the land, some 110 million farm households were converted into about 300,000 communist "cooperatives" under the party's direction. In cities and towns, privately owned factories and other businesses were taken over by the Communist authorities. This turning point was of major significance in party policy: The CCP's basis for popular support had been its land reform policies, and now the land that had just recently been given to the poorest peasants was being taken away. However, there was none of the violence that accompanied the land reform of the early 1950s, which in turn had been much milder than the Soviet experience under Stalin in the 1920s.

The collectivization of agriculture and industry was followed by the **Hundred Flowers Movement** in 1957.[13] The slogan came from a saying of Confucius (and also used in the May 4th Movement), "Let a hundred flowers bloom, let a hundred schools of thought contend." It implied that the give and take of ideas was not only healthy but also beneficial to the state. Mao invited criticisms of the party's performance from experts and intellectuals, confident that his policy successes so far had created considerable enthusiasm and support for the regime. He expected mild criticism of the bureaucratic work style of some party and government officials, in line with his own view that the conservative nature of bureaucracies would inevitably slow progress toward the nation's development. What he got instead were complaints about the fundamental nature of the political system: the absence of democracy, the rule of law, free expression, and free scientific inquiry; complaints about party interference in all walks of life; and above all, complaints about the intrusion of incompetent and illiterate reds in the work of the experts. Mao seems to have been genuinely taken aback by the vehemence of the intellectuals' complaints. Rather than address their concerns, he labeled them "rightists" (akin to being a counterrevolutionary, a very serious crime). He then launched an anti-rightist campaign to persecute them, replacing many of them with his own political supporters. The anti-rightist campaign alienated most of China's intellectuals and made them wary of voicing their political views again.[14]

Following the anti-rightist campaign, the second episode of promoting utopian goals took shape. After disregarding the concerns of China's experts, Mao decided to tap into the latent energy of the masses to create economic growth. The party would encourage people to work harder, not with higher wages, but with propaganda and persuasion. This campaign became known as the **Great Leap Forward** (1958–59), the period

when the communes were created.[15] Communes were large-scale economic and administrative units, each combining 10 or more villages. At first, it seemed that the Great Leap policies were working: Most communes reported a bumper harvest, and the counties and provinces began competing with one another to claim the highest production achievements (thus proving that they were the most loyal to Mao). But in fact, the harvest was far below the forecast. Much of the grain that would normally have been stored for the winter and for spring planting was eaten in the summer and fall. By 1959, it became clear that the country was in deep trouble. Economic forecasts were drastically cut back. Reports of unrest in the countryside and general unhappiness with the mass mobilization tactics of the Great Leap Forward circulated among the party leadership. The policy excesses of the Great Leap combined with unusually bad weather to create a crisis of huge proportions. During the "three bad years" of 1960–62, close to 30 million people starved to death.

This calamity resulted in a full-scale retreat from the policies of the Great Leap Forward and a period of recovery that lasted for several years.[16] Once again, restoring order and increasing production through proper planning and the use of economic incentives became official policy. Private plots, banned with the creation of the communes, were approved again. These plots allowed farmers to grow a little extra fruit and vegetables for themselves and to sell some for cash. Mao grudgingly tolerated these recovery policies, recognizing that they were necessary to solve the severe crisis facing his country.

Mao encouraged everyone to contribute to industrialization in China during the Great Leap Forward. While he encouraged people to work harder to increase economic productivity, the policies he encouraged, such as backyard blast furnaces, led to greater poverty and famine.

But he was unwilling to accept them as long-term policies for fear that they would restore capitalism to China.

By 1965, Mao had several main grievances against his colleagues. For one, he felt their policies were leading the country in the wrong direction. The recovery policies sponsored and implemented by such party leaders as Liu Shaoqi and Deng Xiaoping were successful in creating growth and restoring order, but they were leading the country away from the communist utopia Mao envisioned.

Another grievance was that Mao was being marginalized. He was no longer consulted in the policy-making process. He complained that Deng had stopped giving him policy briefings and at meetings sat with his bad ear toward Mao. The party chairman referred to himself as a living Buddha: revered but generally ignored.

Finally, with his life running out, Mao wanted to be sure that loyal successors were in place at the top of the party. He wanted a new generation of party members filled with his revolutionary zeal and preference for redness over expertise to fill posts at all levels of the political system. By the mid-1960s, however, Mao felt betrayed by his heirs apparent, Liu and Deng, and he felt that the next generation of leaders lacked the experience necessary to instill the correct virtues.

These frustrations led him to launch the **Great Proletarian Cultural Revolution** in 1966, the third episode of utopianism.[17] Mao purged Liu, Deng, and other veteran leaders from the leadership posts in the party, government, and military, and subjected them to harsh and relentless criticism in the media and large public events. He encouraged young people, especially students, to form groups of Red Guards to attack, verbally and physically, the representatives of the party and state: local leaders, teachers, factory managers, and even high-ranking party leaders and cabinet ministers. The Red Guards attacked people who exercised or symbolized power, along with anyone else suspected of not being loyal to Mao. They fanned throughout China bearing copies of the "little red book" of Mao's choice quotations, haranguing people in lengthy propaganda sessions in factories, on farms, and in the streets. They broke into party and government offices and released information that supposedly revealed the anti-Maoist activities of the officeholders. They held public "struggle" sessions, in which selected targets were harshly criticized and assaulted. Those being attacked were subjected to beatings, imprisonment, and killings, and some committed suicide. They included many who had fought in the civil war alongside Mao and whose involvement in the CCP dated to the 1930s. Most schools and government offices closed, and most regular activities ceased; all but one of China's ambassadors was called home. Economic production ground to a halt.

This convulsive part of the Cultural Revolution came to a close in 1968 after armed clashes between Red Guard groups, each proclaiming to be the most loyal to Mao, broke out all over China. To restore order, the country came under effective martial law for several years because the military was the only nationwide organization still intact and able to carry out government responsibilities.

The Legacy of the Cultural Revolution

After being nearly destroyed during 1966–69, the party now had to be rebuilt. Many of China's best qualified and most experienced leaders were falsely accused of various crimes, removed from their posts, put in prison, or sent to remote areas of China to perform menial tasks. Eventually many of these people were brought back to their old posts, but they were forced to work alongside the very people who had accused them and caused their suffering.

Although the CCP was weakened by intense factional conflict at all levels, from society's point of view the party was stronger than ever. Virtually every aspect of life had political implications, from opinions about Mao and the party to the clothing one wore, hairstyles, and taste in books and music. It was a period of political correctness run rampant, with decisions about jobs, housing, access to food, and opportunities to travel or see a play determined by the local party committee. By the end of the Cultural Revolution, society had grown weary of the incessant political campaigns and frequent policy shifts. People had become disillusioned by a political system that seemed intrusive, arbitrary, inconsistent, and unresponsive to society's desire for higher standards of living. With Mao's death in 1976, an opportunity arose to fundamentally change the style and direction of policy.

The Cultural Revolution left several different legacies for China's leaders and members of society. The CCP's elites recognized the danger of charismatic authority, as epitomized by Mao, and acknowledged the need for regular institutions to debate and implement policies. Mao had resisted this institutionalization because he felt it would diminish revolutionary zeal, the creative spontaneity of the masses, and his own authority. But most other leaders felt the costs of Mao's preferred methods were too high. China's leaders were also aware of the CCP's failure to improve the lives of most Chinese. Party and government leaders who became victims of the Cultural Revolution and were sent to live and work in the countryside learned firsthand that the political system they had created could be completely arbitrary. They realized it had failed to bring China out of its extreme poverty and that it had thereby lost the legitimacy with which it came to power in 1949.

The Cultural Revolution left lasting marks on Chinese society. People learned that it was acceptable to challenge authority and that it was necessary to think for themselves. Mao's assault on his colleagues and the party as a whole taught Chinese society that it need not, indeed should not, accept the prevailing political orthodoxy as the truth. For the same reason, many people experienced a loss of idealism. They learned too late that the Cultural Revolution was not about revolutionary goals at all, but just a cynical struggle for power among party elites. Contrary to Mao's assumptions, many Chinese came to believe it was not necessary to assume that the leaders always knew what was best or that they had the best interests of society at heart. For a Leninist party, these ideas could only undermine the party's ability to rule. By the time Mao died in September 1976, there was a crisis of confidence, a feeling that the party and the government were no longer legitimate. Even Mao's reputation was tarnished.

The Post-Mao Transition

With Mao's death, the party was in crisis. Society had grown weary of the continual political witch hunts and had lost confidence in the party's wisdom. The party itself was divided between the reds, who believed the goals of the Cultural Revolution had to be continued, even intensified, and the experts, who believed the Cultural Revolution had done more harm than good and needed to be abandoned. The economy was shrinking, political instability was rising, and factions within the party prevented any single policy line from being agreed upon and pursued. The end result was a state so weakened by internal divisions that it was unable to adopt and implement a coherent and consistent set of policies, and a society that was unable to influence the policy-making process in any institutionalized way.

This conflict between continuing and ending the Cultural Revolution was resolved a month after Mao's death when the main reds, the so-called Gang of Four (one of whom was Mao's widow), were arrested. After a brief succession struggle, a new consensus emerged: The utopian goals of the Maoist era had to be abandoned for the sake of economic development. This decision was solidified at a historic Central Committee meeting in December 1978. Henceforth, the party would abandon class struggle as its main task (a rationale for needing a strong party), and the victims of past political campaigns would be rehabilitated. More important, the party would concentrate its energies on the economic modernization of the country and shift its policy choices and selection of personnel with this goal in mind. Throughout the post-Mao period, the party's ability to foster economic growth, rather than its ideology or the charisma of its leader, has been the basis of its legitimacy.

While several of the party's leading figures wanted these policy shifts, the man most responsible for initiating them was Deng Xiaoping. Just as Chairman Mao was unquestionably the leader of the CCP from the Long March of the 1930s until his death in 1976, Deng was the symbol of the "second generation" of leaders. Deng was never chairman or general secretary of the CCP, prime minister, or president, nor did he have indomitable power like Mao's, but he was widely seen as China's paramount leader from 1978 until his death in 1997. His preferences for policies and personnel largely set the tone for the post-Mao era.

During the Cultural Revolution, Deng was castigated as "the number two party leader taking the capitalist road" (number one was President Liu Shaoqi) and removed from all his posts in the party and government. He was placed under house arrest, and then sent to work at a tractor repair plant where he and his wife raised their own food. When Mao and Zhou Enlai became too ill to handle affairs of state, Mao called Deng

back to Beijing in 1973, appointing him vice premier of the government. Deng took over the daily work of the government, including economic and foreign policy. By 1975, he had resumed all of the party and government posts he had lost at the beginning of the Cultural Revolution. However, his leftist opponents in the Gang of Four, who included Mao's wife Jiang Qing, remained opposed to Deng and his pragmatic policies. After Zhou died in January 1976, they convinced Mao to once again purge Deng from his posts.

After Mao died and the members of the Gang of Four were arrested, in the summer of 1977, Deng was reinstated to all his former positions in the party and government. In 1981 he became chairman of the party's Central Military Commission. For nearly 20 years thereafter, Deng Xiaoping would be the principal figure in Chinese politics. His policies of "reform and opening up" were responsible for the remarkable economic growth China has enjoyed since and for the loosening of political controls over society. This legacy, however, was tarnished by his role in the 1989 popular demonstrations in Tiananmen Square, which Deng condemned as "turmoil" and "planned conspiracy." Because he believed the demonstrations were a threat to economic reform, he supported the decision to impose martial law, which led to the deaths of hundreds and perhaps thousands of peaceful demonstrators and innocent bystanders and damaged both his and China's reputation abroad. To the end of his life, Deng remained firmly committed to the belief that economic modernization required a stable domestic environment and a peaceful international environment, and his policies were designed to ensure both. Twice named *Time* magazine's "Man of the Year," Deng Xiaoping will be remembered for dramatically improving the lives of many in China, but also for disappointing those who believed that political reform should accompany economic reform.

POLITICS IN THE REFORM ERA

During the 1980s, Deng and other party leaders identified a series of problems inherited from the Maoist period and attempted reforms to remedy them, but with mixed results.[18]

Overconcentration of Power

Most Chinese leaders agreed that Mao had wielded too much power. The solution was to create a collective leadership and prevent any one individual from dominating the political system. Although Deng Xiaoping was the paramount leader from 1978 until his death in 1997, he had to build and maintain a consensus behind his policy preferences and was forced to abandon some policies when faced with opposition among his colleagues. Although he never held the top post in either the party or the government, symbolizing his commitment to collective leadership, he was nevertheless recognized as China's preeminent leader. The title of party chairman was abolished because it was so closely identified with Mao and because there were no suitable checks on the power of the office. Instead, the post of general secretary was created as the party's top leadership position.

At lower levels, efforts were made to more clearly distinguish the party from the government. The party was to limit itself to making decisions, allowing the government to implement the policies. To this end it was decided to limit the number of concurrent posts held by top party leaders. During the Maoist period, the top party leader in a province was also its governor, and the top party leader in a city was also its mayor. Beginning in the 1980s, these posts were separated and held by different people. However, all key positions were still held by party members (with rare and usually symbolic exceptions), and party committees remained more powerful than their government counterparts.

Lack of Formal Institutions

Because Mao preferred to rule by virtue of his charismatic authority, formal bodies became virtually meaningless. In the post-Mao period, reforms were implemented that emphasized collective decision making and restored the regular operations of formal bodies. The National Party Congress was convened every five years as required by the party constitution, and plenary sessions of the Central Committee were held at least once per year. The Politburo, which had fallen into disuse under Mao, again began to meet regularly (in recent years, once per month). The National People's Congress, China's nominal legislature, became rejuvenated, passing a variety of laws and overseeing government operations. In addition, the decision-making process was opened to a wider variety of people. The most important decisions are still made by a handful of people at the top, but now they consult with government officials, experts, local leaders, and others whose opinions are valued or who will be affected by the decision.[19]

However, Deng and other top leaders continued to intervene in the policy-making process. The personal attributes of individual leaders, their connections with other leaders, and their reputations as revolutionaries were still more important than their formal posts. In fact, during the 1980s and 1990s, a group of elders constituted the true center of political power in China even though they had formally retired from their party and government positions. They continued to shape policy and personnel decisions from behind the scenes and through their younger protégés. The clearest example of this was the 1987 decision giving Deng authority over all major decisions. Under the leadership of Hu Jintao (2002–12), the party even ended the informal summer meetings at the beachside resort city of Beidaihe in order to limit the influence of retired leaders over incumbent officials.

Rejuvenation of the Party

At the end of the Maoist era, the party had about 35 million members, up from fewer than 5 million in 1949. From the perspective of Deng and his allies, the composition of the party's membership had several danger signs. Many members were too old. Less than 5 percent of the members were younger than 25, compared to about 25 percent in 1949. The majority were still poorly educated: 45 percent had only a primary education, and

Deng Xiaoping is remembered on a huge billboard in Shenzhen, a modern city in southern China whose development was spurred by Deng's economic reforms.

11 percent were illiterate. More important, party members were not educated enough to handle the technical matters required by the new tasks of economic modernization. And most party members had been recruited during periods of utopianism and therefore had dubious political and professional qualifications. This state of affairs led to a change in recruitment policies. The CCP began to target the young and educated, the new elites of the reform era. By 2011, the party had grown to over 80 million members; 25 percent of them were under 35, and 39 percent had college degrees. The CCP also began to recruit more women, although they still represent less than 25 percent of party members.

These changes led to inevitable conflicts. There was strong ideological opposition to letting people formerly designated as "rightists" into the party, especially the newly emerging class of private entrepreneurs. In 1989, the party banned the recruitment of private entrepreneurs into the party, although this ban was widely ignored at the local level. The ban was not lifted until 2002, when the CCP formally adopted the "Three Represents" policy. According to this slogan, the party no longer represented just the "three revolutionary classes" (peasants, workers, and farmers) but also the advanced productive forces (a euphemism for entrepreneurs and high-tech specialists), advanced culture, and the interests of the vast majority of society. This was a very inclusive set of provisions and indicated the growing irrelevance of ideology in party policy.[20]

Weak Bureaucracy

China's officials suffered from the same problems as the party membership as a whole: They were too old, poorly skilled, and more supportive of Maoism than modernization. To address these problems, the party undertook two somewhat contradictory policies: It rehabilitated victims of the Cultural Revolution, and it recruited skilled expertise. The rehabilitation of veteran officials denounced in the Cultural Revolution was designed to build support for reform policies and to push the reds out of their posts. Once the goal of replacing the reds was accomplished, the party introduced a retirement program for veteran officials that would entice them to leave their posts and allow younger and better-educated people to be appointed.[21]

One of the most important transitions has been the recruitment of large numbers of young, highly educated officials to staff the bureaucracy. China is often described as a government of "technocrats," a term referring to bureaucrats with high levels of technical training.[22] With the period of class struggle over and the party concentrating on economic modernization, it needed new people with new skills to staff the bureaucracy. The party recruited young, better-educated and better-skilled people to replace the aged veterans, many of whom had first been appointed in the 1950s. It established minimum requirements for certain positions, such as a college degree or a specialized degree in engineering or management. In the past, no such requirements existed, and people were appointed not on the basis of their professional merit but on their political virtue. In the post-Mao period, the emphasis has been on upgrading the quality of party and government officials.

Reconciliation of Party and Society

Party leaders recognized they had lost much of their prestige and public support during the Cultural Revolution by trying to micromanage all aspects of daily life. In the post-Mao period, they have tried to limit the scope of politics. Traditional festivals and customs have reappeared, especially in the countryside. Citizens can read traditional novels or listen to Western music without accusations of being a counterrevolutionary. New social organizations are allowed to form as long as they are not politically oriented. In recent years, China has witnessed an explosion of chambers of commerce; sports leagues; hobby groups; professional associations for writers, teachers, and businesspeople; and other types of civic and professional groups. The foundations of a civil society are increasingly emerging, albeit under the ever-watchful eye of the Communist authorities.[23]

Above all, the party declared that the period of class struggle was over, replaced by a commitment to economic modernization. Those who had been falsely accused and punished during the Maoist period had their records cleared. Unfortunately, many of the victims of past class struggle campaigns had already died, but even they had their good names restored. In some cases, their families got property or personal belongings back or received cash settlements.

But not everything has changed. The party still remains the most important institution in the political system. The party makes all decisions, and there is little opportunity for nonparty people to be involved in the decision-making process. While the party now tolerates a wider assortment of nonpolitical activities, the definition of what is nonpolitical has varied considerably. The boundaries are not always clear, but the punishments can be severe for those who cross over. And anything clearly political is strictly prohibited and immediately repressed. Citizens who have tried to create new political parties and

autonomous labor unions have been severely punished, losing their jobs and housing, and in some cases, receiving long jail sentences. The CCP, like all Leninist parties, insists on protecting its monopoly on political organization. It does not allow the existence of any organization that it does not approve of or that it perceives as a threat to its power.

CHINA'S ECONOMIC DEVELOPMENT STRATEGIES

During the more than 60 years of the People's Republic, China's government has pursued three separate strategies of economic development: the Soviet model, self-reliance, and the post-Mao emphasis on markets and "openness."

The Soviet Model, 1953–1957

Following the Communist victory in 1949, China was first concerned with controlling hyperinflation and restoring industrial production to its prewar levels (in 1949, industrial production was only 56 percent of prewar levels). After restoring stability, it adopted the Soviet model of development, which emphasized heavy industry at the expense of agriculture, light industry, consumer goods, and commerce and trade. To achieve this commitment and to promote heavy industry, new central planning institutions were created.

New central ministries were needed to create and implement the plans governing the economy. All key decisions were made at the top in Beijing. Central planning, which did not rely on market mechanisms, required a bureaucracy to run the economy, and the bureaucracy needed experts to do the planning. Production targets were set for each province, which then set targets for lower administrative levels, which then set targets for individual enterprises. Prices were set by the bureaucracy, not by the market forces of supply and demand. Supplies of raw materials, energy, and other inputs to the production process were also determined by planning agencies. Manufactured goods were also distributed according to the plan.

Initially, the Soviet model was largely successful. During the period of the first five-year plan (1953–57), industrial output grew by 128 percent and agriculture by 25 percent. This success was accomplished not only with the Soviet model, but also with direct Soviet assistance. The Soviet Union sent over 10,000 advisors, blueprints for factories, the machinery and technology for running them, and plans for over 150 major projects in addition to training almost 40,000 Chinese engineers in the Soviet Union. This aid made the Soviet model successful in China.

Not all Chinese leaders were satisfied with the adoption of the Soviet model, especially its emphasis on expertise for planners in the bureaucracy and managers in factories. One reason was practical: The CCP simply did not have enough members with the necessary skills or education. The second reason some of China's leaders were unhappy with the Soviet model was political: Mao resented the way the Soviet Union treated China as a nation and himself in particular. Above all,

Mao was a revolutionary, and he was not satisfied with planned, incremental progress. He preferred struggle, transformation, turmoil, even violence as a learning experience. He also did not trust intellectuals, who were necessary for the Soviet model to work. The result was a change in economic planning strategy that had major implications for China's development and for its relationship with the Soviet Union.

Self-Reliance, 1957–1976

By the end of the first five-year plan, Mao and other CCP leaders designed a new strategy of "self-reliance," initiated by the policies of the Great Leap Forward and continuing until Mao's death in 1976. Rather than rely on markets or central planning, the Maoist strategy of self-reliance used mass mobilization to tap into China's most abundant resource: its people, not capital or technology. The CCP used propaganda and mobilization to create a spirit of teamwork, emphasizing collective well-being at the expense of personal self-interest. The careful planning and setting of feasible targets that characterized the Soviet model were replaced with political enthusiasm.

The most enduring feature of the Great Leap Forward era was the commune. There were roughly 80,000 communes, with each commune divided into brigades, and each brigade into teams. (Communes, brigades, and teams corresponded to the traditional townships, villages, and neighborhoods, respectively.) Farming was not done by individuals or families but by teams. Wages were set according to a person's work as well as his or her political attitudes, a very subjective evaluation. There was little financial incentive to work harder, and little available to buy even if money had been plentiful. The self-reliance strategy preserved the low emphasis on consumption that was a key feature of the Soviet model.

Just as China itself was to become self-reliant, each region was supposed to be self-reliant as well. Instead of producing according to its comparative advantage, concentrating on those items in which it excelled, and instead of trading with other areas of the country for other types of food, each area had to provide its own grain, meat, fruit, and vegetables even if the climate was not appropriate. Factories were built throughout the inland areas, often far from transportation lines and sources of energy and other raw materials. This effort was also part of Mao's preference for regional balance and self-reliance, but it led to wasteful duplication and inefficient farming.

Chinese leaders who promoted self-reliance wanted to cut China off from all economic ties to foreign countries, which were suspected of wanting to undermine the integrity of the communist revolution in China. But the war scenario never materialized, and the cost of preparing for it was tremendous.[24]

Self-reliance was an unmitigated disaster. Factories and communes had no incentive to operate efficiently or to turn a profit because their losses were compensated by the state. Projects were started in the wrong areas of the country, often without adequate resources, inputs, or skilled labor. These policies cut China off from the outside world, with little trade or other interactions. At a time when other Asian countries were experiencing rapid growth, industrialization, and modernization, China was out of touch with the technological advances of other countries and fell increasingly behind. Self-reliance also had a personal price for most Chinese: Wages were frozen after the early 1960s. By 1976, those with 15 years of experience were earning the same amount as those with much less seniority. However, this egalitarianism did not seem fair to most workers, who resented policies that did not recognize their seniority or personal needs.[25] A greater share of the older workers' wages went to providing housing, food, education, medical care for spouses, children, and elderly parents; many younger workers only had to support themselves, and many lived with their parents if they were not married. For all these reasons, self-reliance led to stagnant growth. The Maoist approach ignored the principles of comparative advantage and material incentives that would have provided more efficient and rapid growth.

The Reform Era, 1978 to the Present

By 1978, Deng Xiaoping and his allies were able to consolidate their position and adopt new policies that ended the political campaigns and ideologically oriented policies of the past in favor of economic modernization. In the early reform era, this goal was pursued by a variety of experiments, such as promoting private—as opposed to communal—farming, attracting foreign trade and investment through the creation of special economic zones along the eastern coast of China, and allowing small-scale enterprises and street vendors to operate. Many of these experiments later became national policy.

Although China's post-Mao leaders agreed that the Maoist policies had to be abandoned, they disagreed about the proper set of policies that should be adopted and the pace at which they should be introduced. Above all, they debated the proper balance between the state and the market for regulating the economy. Some saw the early 1950s, when China followed the Soviet model, as a golden era during which the economy achieved high growth rates without having to rely on the market. Others preferred to push ahead to a fully market-oriented economy, believing that a planned economy is too inefficient. Ultimately, this market-oriented group prevailed. These "reform and opening" policies have transformed China's economy, creating prosperity and a dynamism that were unimaginable in the Maoist era. Although rapid economic growth has created a number of problems, such as regional inequalities, corruption, environmental damage, and occasionally dangerously high inflation rates, support for economic reform remains strong.[26]

The post-Mao economic reforms have had several main goals. First, China's leaders wanted to achieve technological dynamism. They have sought access to Western technology, capital, and management practices essential for modernization.

The reformers also wanted to liberalize the state's control over the economy. A centrally planned economy needs bureaucratic controls to establish production goals, disseminate materials, monitor results, and redistribute industrial and agricultural goods to consumers and other end users. But these controls also stifle technological dynamism. Markets are needed to enliven the economy via competition and material incentives. Economic liberalization was accompanied by decentralization: the devolution of decision making to local governments and firms. Deng wanted to make local governments and individual firms responsible for their own profits and losses and reduce subsidies paid by the central government to compensate for their losses. But he also believed that, if they were to be given responsibility, they also had to be given the authority to make decisions they thought best and the right to keep a larger share of the profits. These benefits provided incentives for experimentation and new investments that created the explosive growth seen in China during the past generation.

Another goal of the reforms was to raise living standards. Mao made a virtue out of poverty, but most people want higher living standards and a more comfortable life and are not very enthusiastic about ideological purity. Self-reliance and the resulting poverty and stagnation damaged the prestige of the party and undermined the legitimacy of the government. In the post-Mao period, China's leaders have based their legitimacy on their ability to create economic growth and better living standards rather than on political correctness.

Along with the goals of creating a more vibrant and prosperous economy came a political goal: maintaining stability in general and the unquestioned leadership of the CCP in particular. Although most of China's leaders are willing to accept competition within the economy, they do not want a similar logic to seep into the political system. They believe that China must still be ruled by a unified, authoritarian political system in order to provide overall coordination and to keep the country unified. They believe that economic growth cannot be allowed to create political instability, including demands for democracy. Although some within China (and most foreign analysts) believe that the resulting imbalance between economic openness and political controls cannot be sustained indefinitely, most of China's leaders are worried that introducing more ambitious political reforms would threaten the party's hold on power. They view the collapse of the Soviet Union and of communist governments in Central and Eastern Europe as a warning of the dangers of initiating reform before achieving a stable and prosperous economy.[27]

Finally, China's reformers wanted to maintain a peaceful environment in which development could occur. Before 1989, when antigovernment demonstrations took place throughout China, Deng and other reformers thought they could enjoy prolonged peace via astute diplomacy, allowing them to divert resources away from military spending toward the civilian economy. Since 1989, military spending has risen sharply, as the party leaders seek to guarantee the support of the military. Moreover, many of China's leaders, especially conservative elites, believe that the power of the United States has risen dramatically since the collapse of the Soviet Union and the end of the Cold War, and they wonder if China should not perhaps give greater priority to security issues, even as it continues its economic modernization. One of the major questions facing the United States and other countries today is whether China still puts a priority on maintaining peace and stability or is preparing to have a more disruptive influence on its neighbors and the international

system more generally. The evidence remains ambiguous on this important question, but it has generated an ongoing debate among American policy makers and China's neighbors about the international implications of China's rapid modernization.[28]

If these have been the goals of the economic reforms, what have been the means for achieving them?

Increasing Market Forces In the early 1980s, the CCP dismantled the communes, perhaps the most prominent symbol of the Maoist approach to economic development. In their place, new policies encouraged individual and family farming and allowed farmers to sell their produce on the open market after they sold their quota to the state.[29] China gradually eliminated price controls on most industrial and consumer goods, allowing prices to better reflect supply and demand. State controls over the economy were reduced, including production targets and monopolies on the distribution of supplies and finished goods.[30] After China joined the World Trade Organization in 2001, Chinese firms began to face more foreign competition in the Chinese market. Finally, comparative advantage was made a priority, allowing regional variation and specialization.

State-owned enterprises (SOEs) were hard hit by competition from private and foreign firms. Long accustomed to support from state subsidies, possessing out-of-date technology, and providing a wide range of welfare provisions to their employees, SOEs had a difficult time surviving in the new economic environment. In the 1990s, the CCP adopted a "grasp the large, release the small" policy toward SOEs: The largest and most strategically important SOEs (such as those in telecommunications, energy, construction, and aerospace) were given renewed support, while smaller and medium-sized firms were either privatized, merged with larger firms, or forced to close. Upward of 50 million industrial workers lost not only their jobs during this restructuring, but also their housing, medical insurance, and even their pensions. As the CCP embraced market reforms, it also abandoned its commitment to social welfare.

Increasing Foreign Trade and Investment China created special economic zones along its coast and "open cities" to encourage greater foreign trade and investment. This approach was part of its comparative advantage strategy: The cities with already developed industrial bases and access to external markets were allowed to exploit their advantages. As a result, coastal areas have developed much more rapidly than inland China, creating much resentment from officials and residents in the disadvantaged areas.[31] Whereas China closed itself off during its self-reliance phase, it now encourages joint ventures and other types of foreign investment. The state no longer has a monopoly on foreign trade: Private enterprises are allowed to make deals on their own.

There has been tremendous growth in the volume of China's foreign trade and foreign direct investment (FDI) in China. Trade increased from about $40 billion in 1980 to almost $3.64 trillion in 2011; because its economic development strategy promotes exports and limits imports, China has accumulated the world's largest foreign exchange reserve,

Since the 1990s the CCP has encouraged foreign investment in export-oriented industries such as the Foxconn factory shown here.

estimated at over $3 trillion in 2012. FDI increased from a negligible amount in the early 1980s to almost $125 billion in 2010. As a result of increased trade and foreign investment, factories have been upgraded technologically, allowing them to be more innovative and better able to respond quickly to market demands. For example, most consumer electronics—computers, cell phones, and the like—are produced in China.

China's current development strategy presents a contradiction: It is the major supplier of consumer goods, such as electronics and clothing, and its foreign trade surplus creates conflicts with other countries (especially the United States), yet it has not created internationally recognizable brands. Instead, its exports are mostly sold under foreign brand names, such as Apple, Dell, and Nike. This represents the complexity of economic globalization: Although most consumer goods bought in the United States are produced in China, this is because American firms have chosen to outsource their manufacturing operations to China because of lower labor costs there.

Reliance on the Private Sector China's private sector was virtually eliminated during the 1950s. However, it began to reemerge in the 1980s with the opening of very small-scale firms, and it then exploded in the 1990s. In 1990, there were barely 10,000 privately owned firms in China; by 2010, there were

4.7 million. For more than a decade, the private sector has generated most new jobs, economic growth, and tax revenue. The state sector, in contrast, has been steadily shrinking, especially since the late 1990s when SOE restructuring began. More and more Chinese are migrating from the countryside in search of jobs in the new private and foreign-invested enterprises. Less than half of China's population now lives in the countryside, and an estimated 220 million workers have joined China's population of migrant workers.[32]

The results of reform have been both positive and negative (see Table 17.1). On the positive side, China has experienced extraordinarily rapid growth. Per capita GDP doubled between 1978 and 1988, and China averaged growth rates of almost 10 percent per year between 1978 and 2010. China is now the second largest economy in the world in aggregate terms, but still remains relatively poor in per capita terms: in 2011, it ranked 91st, between the Dominican Republic and Cuba. The fastest growing sectors have been commerce, light industry, and services, the reverse of the Maoist years. Higher incomes have created new markets for a wide variety of consumer goods, better quality and more fashionable clothing, fresh and processed foods, better entertainment, and tourism within China and abroad. In sum, the living standards for most Chinese are higher now than ever.

Table 17.1 China's Economic Growth (Various Years)

	1980	1985	1990	1995	2000	2005	2010
GDP ($ billions)	$189.4	$306.7	$356.9	$728.0	$1,198.5	$2,256.9	$5,930.5
GDP per capita ($)	193.0	291.7	314.4	604.2	949.2	1731.1	4433.0
Exports ($ billions)	20.2	28.3	57.4	147.2	279.6	836.9	1752.4
Imports ($ billions)	20.9	40.8	46.7	135.3	250.7	712.1	1520.3
Foreign direct investment ($ billions)		1.0	2.7	33.9	37.5	105.9	124.9

Note: All figures are in current U.S. dollars.
Source: World Bank, World Development Indicators database.

At the same time, a variety of negative consequences also emerged. Most important, the problem of corruption exploded as party and government officials at all levels took advantage of rapid growth, the desire of Chinese and foreign entrepreneurs to develop new projects, and weak laws and regulations to line their own pockets. China now ranks among the more corrupt countries in which to do business, according to surveys of foreign businesspeople, ranking 80th in the world in the Corruption Perceptions Index—better than Russia's rank of 133rd, but similar to India and many developing countries in Africa and Latin America.[33] Corruption was the primary cause of the 1989 student demonstrations and it continues to provoke local disturbances. The CCP tends to target cases of corruption that result in large losses of state revenue, such as embezzlement, the use of public funds for private purposes (banquets, homes, cars, etc.), and illegal privatization of state-owned enterprises' assets. In contrast, illegal confiscation of property, excessive collection of taxes and fees, and other abuses of authority by local officials are seen as mere "irregularities" and do not receive the same level of publicity or punishment.[34]

A related problem arising from rapid economic development has been rising inequality. Although incomes have generally risen, they have not risen equally. There is a growing gap between the city and the countryside and between coastal and inland areas. During the Mao era, China had one of the most equitable distributions of wealth in the world, although most people were equally poor. During the reform era, that picture changed dramatically. In 1980, the beginning of the reform era, China's Gini coefficient was 0.33; in 1995 it had grown to 0.44, and in 2012 it was officially 0.47, although other estimates put it higher than 0.50. (For more about the Gini coefficient, see Chapter 1.) As a consequence of reform and opening policies, the gap between rich and poor has grown at an alarming rate.

There is a growing perception that opportunities to succeed are also unequal. The increasingly close relationship between the party and the private sector has created the widespread perception that economic success is based on personal connections with party and government officials, not on individual initiative or quality work. This is particularly the case for the sons and daughters of high-ranking officials, who use their parents' stature and connections to become successful in business.

For the past decade and more, China's top leaders have been categorized as either "elitists" who favor increased economic liberalization and comparative advantage to achieve high growth rates or "populists" who favor greater equity in the regional and individual distribution of wealth in order to address social tensions and political instability arising from economic inequality. During the 1990s when Jiang Zemin was the CCP's general secretary, China pursued an elitist strategy, focusing on private entrepreneurs and coastal areas. Under his leadership, the liberalization, privatization, and globalization of the Chinese economy expanded greatly, but so too did levels of inequality. After Jiang Zemin retired and was replaced by Hu Jintao, China adopted more populist policies. The state shifted new investment funds from the coastal areas to inland provinces. It also boosted rural incomes through subsidies, income transfers, and tax relief. One immediate effect has been the return of migrant labor to the countryside, creating labor shortages in some cities and putting upward pressure on wages and working conditions. The government has also given renewed attention to providing health insurance, elderly care, poverty alleviation, and other social welfare policies it had largely abandoned during the 1990s. Despite the commitment to more balanced development and populist policies, inequality continued to grow under Hu's leadership.

Inflation has also been a recurring problem and was another contributor to the 1989 demonstrations. Inflation ate up most of the gains of rapid growth during the 1980s. Since then, inflation has been kept under better control.

The push for rapid growth also created tremendous environmental pollution. China is now the second largest polluter in the world (after the United States), and its CO_2 emissions more than doubled between 2000 and 2008. Of the world's 20 most polluted cities, 16 are in China. The World Bank estimates that as many as 300,000 people die every year of respiratory ailments caused by air pollution. Thirty percent of river water is so badly polluted that it is not suitable even for agriculture and industrial use, much less human consumption. China loses more than 10 million hectares of forestland each year, and its deserts are growing by 1,300 square miles each year; 25 percent of China's land is now desert. One study predicted that 30 million to 40 million farmers will lose access to adequate land and water in the coming decades and will be forced to migrate. China's pollution problems have become so severe that they have triggered riots in recent years.[35] China's water, air, and land are being damaged by companies that find it cheaper to pollute than to be energy efficient or to dispose of waste properly. A growing number of cars and trucks contribute to this increasingly serious problem. Energy prices are set by the state at below-world-market levels, giving firms and individuals little incentive to use energy more efficiently.

In addition, another unexpected consequence of economic development has been a spiritual crisis. The emphasis on making money and material interests has taken a toll on Chinese society. Many feel there has been a loss of a commitment to group welfare and collective well-being. China no longer has a shared set of values that binds the country together. First, the communists denigrated the Confucian traditions and promoted the revolutionary virtues associated with Mao; then the post-Mao leaders rejected the values promoted by Mao without offering an alternative ideology or belief system. Deng's emphasis on pragmatism, symbolized by the slogans "seek truth from facts" (as opposed to ideology) and "to get rich is glorious" may have been the basis for policy making, but it did not give people much to believe in.

This nearly exclusive interest in materialism has led to the revival of traditional religious practices and a growing interest in Christianity. Local temples have been rebuilt, usually with public funds, and individual families have rebuilt ancestor shrines. Some Protestant and Catholic churches are officially recognized by the state, but others are "underground churches" that meet in private homes without official approval. Some of these churches are persecuted by local officials, their leaders and parishioners arrested and often mistreated. But in other areas, the churches operate with the tacit approval and even the encouragement of the local leaders. Despite foreign criticisms of widespread and systematic persecution of religious practices in China, the number of religious believers has never been higher than it is today. There is no question that religious freedoms still do not enjoy full protection, but at least in some communities the growth in religious faith has come with the knowledge and often the support of local officials. More important, it reflects the search for a meaning to life that goes deeper than just rising living standards.

One of the greatest challenges facing China's leaders is to shift the economy away from infrastructure investment and exporting as engines of growth and rely more on domestic consumption. Many local governments are now burdened with massive debt from previous construction projects and cannot commit to new ones. The global financial crisis that began in 2008 led to a sudden and dramatic drop in demand for China's exports, leading to slower growth and the closing of many firms in China. But this transition will be difficult. Many local governments and firms have profited from China's export-oriented economy and have resisted changing directions. In addition, Chinese consumers have not increased their purchases enough to offset declines in exports, instead preferring to save for the future. This transition will be necessary for the long-term interests of the economy, but short-term interests interfere with its success.

To summarize, in the post-Mao era, economic growth has been the primary goal, and equity has been deemphasized. Deng in particular was a fan of rapid growth at any cost. But he was forced to compromise with those who were more concerned about order and stability and believed that the negative consequences of reform required a slower pace of reforms and even a periodic rollback. Even among China's current leaders, many feel that economic equity should not be abandoned, because rising resentment against the regions and individuals who are getting rich faster than others may also threaten political stability and ultimately the legitimacy of the CCP. Despite these negative and generally unintended consequences, the benefits of reform—a more dynamic economy, rising standards of living, a flourishing cultural life, greater access to an increasing variety of goods and services, opportunities for entrepreneurship and innovation, improvements in transportation and housing, and so on—have created tremendous popular support for further economic reform.

STATE–SOCIETY RELATIONS IN CHINA

In looking at state-society relations in China, it is important both to compare key features of its authoritarian regime with democratic regimes and to compare changes over time within its incumbent regime. Compared to democratic regimes, the Chinese party-state is extremely strong, limiting freedoms and liberties available to Chinese citizens. Compared to China's past, however, most Chinese are less encumbered by the state than ever before.

One-Party Rule Means No Organized Opposition

The CCP zealously guards its monopoly on political power. One of its primary goals has been to prevent the organization of any group outside its control. To this end the CCP operates a network of party cells throughout the government, the military, and society to monitor compliance with party policies. The government must sanction all labor unions, student organizations, professional associations, and even religious groups, and their leaders are subject to official approval. The party proscribes independent trade unions, student groups, political parties, and religious organizations like the Roman Catholic Church, which is banned in China because its priests are loyal to the pope in Rome, not to the leaders in Beijing.

The CCP justifies its political monopoly on the ideological grounds that it is a vanguard party with special insights into the laws of history. Therefore, it is uniquely qualified to decide what is best for the nation. Individuals and interest groups are not allowed into the decision-making process—except at the invitation of the party—because they only represent their narrow special interests. Only the CCP, in its own estimation, is concerned with collective well-being and the national interest. On a more basic level, the CCP recognizes that its own rise to power was based on its ability to organize society against the former government, which was unaware of what was going on. The CCP is determined not to be the victim of the same methods that brought it to power. Hence it does not allow alternative voices to be a part of the political process; it has no intention of competing with others for popular support.

There is no possibility for organized political action except by officially recognized groups. As part of the economic reform process, the state has created a variety of corporatist-style organizations, especially for businesspeople and enterprise managers, to serve as bridges between state and society. These groups tend to cooperate with the state and do not seek autonomy or an adversarial role, contrary to the ways we expect such groups to operate in a democracy. However, these groups do communicate the perspective of their members to the state and are no longer confined to simply transmitting the state's position downward to the population, as in the Maoist era. It has been difficult to organize other types of interest groups, such as those concerned with the labor or ethnic minorities. The policy-making process has gradually become more inclusive, allowing a wider range of people and perspectives to be involved, but many voices are still excluded from the process.

These organizations and the state's relationship with them follow an authoritarian variant of *corporatism* (see Chapter 8) as well as the logic of Leninism. Most organizations are created, or at least approved, by the state, and many have government officials as their leaders. For instance, local branches of the Industrial and Commercial Federation, whose members include the largest of China's manufacturing and commercial enterprises, are normally headed by the party official in charge of united front work (which handles relations between the CCP and nonparty individuals and groups), and their offices are often in the government compound. In addition, there is normally only one organization for any given profession or activity. In cases where two groups with similar interests exist in a community, local officials will often force them to merge or will disband one in favor of the other. This practice prevents competition between the associations and limits how many associations are allowed to exist, making it easier for the state to monitor and control them.

Moreover, the CCP has sponsored the creation of numerous civic and professional associations to both liberalize social life and promote economic development. As the state pulled back from micromanaging society and operating a centrally planned economy, it created new organizations to link the state with key sectors of society. China allowed some organizations even during the Maoist era for officially recognized groups, such as workers, women, and youth, but they were generally seen as "transmission belts" that monitored and enforced state policy toward these groups but had little ability to represent the interests of their nominal members or to influence policy. In the post-Mao era, the state has allowed new organizations to form and has even allowed the older organizations to be more active in representing their members, not simply conveying the official line. China now has a dense variety of associations for businesspeople, for specific professions (e.g., software writers, factory managers, lawyers, etc.), for various religions and traditional practices, and for many others. However, there are still no independent trade unions.

In addition, Chinese companies are banding together to form their own associations to lobby the government on technical standards, protection of property rights, and similar common interests.[36] Typically they do not raise broader public policy issues, but their activities may create public space for other groups. For example, homeowners, teachers, retirees, and other groups have their own organizations to promote their collective interests. They are not necessarily politically oriented, but just as all politics is local, local achievements can have broader implications. In particular, these new professional and civic organizations are not based exclusively on where people work or live, or on what community or clan they came from. Because they attract members from diverse backgrounds and experiences, and because individuals can belong to more than one group, they may create the types of social networks that create not only a more orderly society, but also one that seeks more from its government.

This growth of civic and professional organizations in China has created a great deal of excitement among outside observers. By the end of 2010, China had roughly 500,000 officially registered NGOs, and perhaps twice that many unregistered ones. Most are apolitical, providing social welfare services the state has largely abandoned (health care, poverty alleviation,

emergency relief, environment awareness, job training, legal aid for migrants, and so on).[37] Many see these organizations as forming the foundation of a *civil society*, a key component of liberal democratic government. The emergence and spread of such organizations in China may facilitate a transition from authoritarian rule to democracy. But democratization is not the only possible outcome. A key component of civil society is autonomy from the state, and that element is largely missing in China. In fact, members of these associations do not seek autonomy, because they recognize that, in China's political system, being autonomous means you are powerless and inconsequential. Instead, they want to be embedded in the state in order to increase their influence. China may be undergoing a transition from a corporatism dominated by the state to a more diverse situation that gives greater leeway to the associations and the economic and social interests they represent. Can such a shift in the balance of power between the state and society occur without a more fundamental change in China's political system? That is the question that China's leaders, its citizens, and even foreign observers cannot definitively answer.

Political Mobilization

In the United States and most democracies, political participation is primarily voluntary and spontaneous. People may join interest groups, donate time or money to a cause they support, sign petitions on various policy issues, write letters to their elected representatives or a newspaper, or take a variety of other actions to make their views known to policy makers and other influential observers. In nondemocratic countries, taking part in these kinds of political participation is often risky or even illegal. Rather than allow spontaneous participation, authoritarian states often mobilize participation to support their policies and strictly limit society's opportunities to influence policy making.

During the Maoist era, most participation was mobilized by the state. China underwent periodic mass political campaigns to both educate society on current policy and promote proper implementation. Often a campaign occurred when policy changed suddenly, as when the anti-rightist movement followed the Hundred Flowers campaign or when the Cultural Revolution got under way. People were expected to study the new policies and the propaganda that accompanied them, learn the new slogans, internalize the new party line, and change their behavior accordingly. The regime engaged in mass mobilization, requiring everyone to actively support the new policy in word and deed. However, people were *not* expected to question the new policy or its goals, to compare the results of the new policies with the past, or to criticize their leaders for changing policy. People were expected to publicly affirm their support of the new policy, even if inwardly they did not.

In the post-Mao period, the campaign style of policy implementation has generally been abandoned and the state has tried to be less intrusive in most aspects of social life. There are exceptions, of course: The state resorted to these old tactics after the violent end of the 1989 demonstrations and again beginning in the summer of 1999 against the Falun Gong spiritual movement. The general theme of the reform era has been to have the state pull back from its direct involvement in most areas, including the economy, social life, and even politics. People are no longer required to voice their approval of all policies, to denounce the old policies and the leaders who promoted them, or to refer to the ideology as the measure of correct policies.

Communication between State and Society

China developed the "mass line" concept during the revolutionary period when it was competing with landlords and the Nationalist government for popular support. The ideal of the mass line was that the state would get information from the masses to create correct policies and then communicate those policies to the masses. But after 1949, there was no competition for popular support, and the need to solicit public opinion as a guide to policy became less important. The mass line remained, but it became ritualized. Citizens learned the high price of offering contrary opinions and instead learned to recite current slogans.

Moreover, newspapers and other forms of media are owned by the state, a reality that limits their effectiveness as a form of feedback on the state's performance. During the Maoist era, the state often required participation in political study groups after work as a form of thought control. It did not provide objective information but only the party's current propaganda line, thereby imparting important clues about how to think and behave. Even today, Chinese media reports rarely break news of scandal, the abuse of power, poor governmental performance, or other exposés that people living in democracies come to expect of their media. However, in the post-Mao period the state seems to have taken a greater interest in investigating these allegations than in the past. Writing letters to national newspapers to report on local problems, such as corruption or the abuse of authority by local officials, is common.

Chinese citizens are now more able to complain about local conditions to higher levels of government. Villagers may send a team to the county government to report on excessive taxation or misuse of government funds, and if they are not satisfied with the response there, they may appeal to the provincial and even central government. What is distinctive about this trend is that the people lodging complaints are becoming better versed in official policy and are using that knowledge to further their cause. So long as people complain only about how they have been adversely affected by the improper implementation of policy, their complaints stand a better chance of being resolved. However, they may not complain about the merits of the policy itself or its general impact. For instance, they do not complain that taxes are simply too high: They complain that local officials are demanding taxes higher than what is allowed by the central government. In other words, they do not seek a change in policy, they seek to make local officials actually comply with the existing policies.[38] Once deviations from policies

are brought to the attention of higher-level officials, they are very difficult to ignore.

Although the number of complaints and petitions has skyrocketed, the number of successfully resolved cases remains minuscule. The growing use of this system, combined with frustrations created when people cannot get the relief they are entitled to, presents a potential challenge to the state. As Samuel Huntington noted, when the level of participation overwhelms the available institutions, instability is likely to rise.[39] If the state cannot reduce the demands that are percolating up or increase its responsiveness to those demands, the alternative is to have the demands raised outside official channels, as is seen in the growing number of public protests throughout the country.

These conventional forms of participation are not always effective and are often risky. In a political system with only one political party and limited citizen's rights, the state does not have to be responsive to the wants and needs of society. Those making complaints are often subjected to intimidation, arrest, the loss of their job, and occasionally beatings and even death. Nevertheless, some people are willing to appeal to higher and higher levels and even to travel to Beijing, if necessary, to seek justice. Politics can be a high-stakes game in China with tremendous costs and benefits for all involved.

State Autonomy

Because the Chinese party-state allows no organized opposition and imposes limits on the flow of information, it is largely free to decide for itself what policy should be. Decisions are made in secret, and officials are not subject to voter approval; nor are they held accountable to the population through such democratic mechanisms as citizen initiatives, referendums, and the recall of unpopular, ineffective, or corrupt officeholders. The results of policy cannot be assessed through citizen feedback because of the lack of information on public opinion and the danger of punishment for excessive criticism of Chinese officialdom. But the state does not always get what it wants: Bureaucratic inertia, lower-level resistance, or outright evasion are quite common in China and prevent new policies from being implemented in a timely and proper fashion.[40]

In addition, Deng Xiaoping's economic reforms undermined the state's control over society. This effect was largely intentional. As noted earlier, Deng Xiaoping and other leaders learned firsthand during the Cultural Revolution about the irrationality and arbitrariness of the political system they helped create. They recognized that the state was too intrusive and only inhibited development rather than fostering it. During the Maoist period, housing, education, medicine, and welfare were all tied to the workplace; if you were fired, you would no longer have access to any of these things. You would therefore have to cultivate good relations with your superiors, especially the party boss, to make sure you got your share of these scarce goods and services.[41] But the market now gives people more options: They can change jobs at will, buy their own housing, move to a new locale, and even open their own business. The state cannot threaten to withhold things it does not control, and individuals have become less dependent upon the state.

In fact, many local officials are somewhat dependent on local businesspeople. Rewards and promotions are increasingly based on local economic performance, and the fastest growing sectors are not the state-owned enterprises but private firms. Local officials now cooperate with businesspeople to help them succeed—they procure loans, find inputs and markets for goods, give tax breaks, protect local firms from outside competition, and do other similar things to promote economic growth in their communities.

China's villagers are now able to elect their own leaders. In the past, all local officials were appointed by higher levels of government, which made officials accountable to their superiors but not to the people they actually governed. This system meant, not surprisingly, that many local officials became petty tyrants in local society. Now, villagers can use the opportunity of village elections to replace unpopular or abusive officials.[42] It is still common to hear of incidents in which higher authorities refuse to let a person be a candidate, or throw out the results of elections they do not like, or even refuse to hold elections. However, national law now requires periodic elections for village chief and village councils, and the Ministry of Civil Affairs is in charge of publicizing and monitoring compliance with the law. These types of elections are limited to villages, however. City mayors, provincial governors, and party secretaries at all levels are still appointed by the CCP. Direct elections for legislative posts are similarly limited to the grass-roots level: Township- and county-level people's congresses are popularly elected, but they in turn select city-level congresses, which then select provincial-level congresses, which finally select the National People's Congress.

China has been experimenting with local political reforms to make the state more responsive to public opinion, even if it is still not fully accountable. Some local officials now have to receive majority support in a public referendum on their tenure in office to be reappointed. China has actively embraced e-government, with many national, provincial, and local government offices having their own websites to disseminate information and receive opinions and complaints. In some public policy areas, China now requires a period of public comment before projects can be approved. Township governments are expected to post annual budget plans, showing both income and expenditures. These types of reforms are still experimental and not fully institutionalized, but they indicate that important political reforms, short of full democratization, may be under way.[43]

The CCP has begun to incorporate new economic and social elites into the political system, while still excluding those with more explicitly political goals. The "Three Represents" slogan, originally coined by Jiang Zemin and enshrined in the party constitution in 2002, provides the justification for admitting "advanced productive forces" (i.e., entrepreneurs, high-tech specialists, professionals, and other new urban elites) into the CCP. Entrepreneurs increasingly run in elections for village chiefs and for local people's congresses, and they are frequently appointed to higher-level people's congresses, government posts, and even party committees. It remains to be seen whether the party manages to keep legitimate participation within the existing institutions, or whether the urban elites create pressures for broader democratization that might weaken the CCP's grip on power, thereby putting the CCP's adaptation policies at risk.

At the same time, the CCP still excludes those who pose a direct challenge to the status quo. Attempts to create an opposition party, the China Democracy Party, were blocked and the leaders of the effort sentenced to lengthy jail sentences. Those who seek true autonomy from the state, including labor unions, Christian churches, and advocates of free speech and freedom of the press, are normally punished for their efforts. Separatist movements in Tibet and the western province of Xinjiang are harshly suppressed.

Rule of Law

Democracies are based on the rule *of* law: the same laws bind both state and society (Chapter 5). Many laws are designed to restrict the ability of the state to interfere in the citizens' private lives. The courts enforce these laws, preventing the state from infringing on individual rights and civil liberties. These democratic concepts are very foreign in China, whose system is more aptly described as rule *by* law: Laws are tools of governance but they do not restrict the scope of the state's actions. A legal code was not adopted until the late 1970s, 30 years after the founding of the People's Republic of China, and many laws and regulations remain secret or are revised at the discretion of China's leaders to meet current needs. Moreover, there is no independent judiciary to mediate public and private disputes; the courts are an arm of the state, not part of a checks and balances system. For major cases, such as for student demonstrators in 1989, political dissidents, or corrupt officials, the party determines verdicts and sentences in advance.

China is trying to strengthen its legal system, in part to support the push for economic modernization (enforcement of contracts, protection of property including copyrights, etc.) and in part to create more predictability by clearly spelling out which types of conduct are appropriate and which are not. This strengthening of the legal system also gives people the power to defend their interests and protect themselves from capricious actions by their neighbors, other businesses, and even government officials. Private entrepreneurs have turned to the courts to force the government to honor its contracts or to compensate them for confiscating their property. Artists have been known to sue government-owned media for printing libelous accusations against them or for criticizing their works on political grounds. These types of suits are not always successful; China's courts are still not independent of the party-state nor are they neutral interpreters of the law. Almost 100,000 lawsuits are brought against local officials each year, but less than 25 percent of them are settled in favor of the plaintiffs. But even this low success rate is enough to encourage more and more to pursue this avenue. As businesspeople, artists, and other groups in society are becoming better educated about the state's own laws and regulations, they are increasingly using them to their advantage.[44]

Political Protest and Dissent

Political and social tensions have accompanied economic reform. Mass protests, including strikes, rallies, marches, traffic blocking, and seizure of buildings, increased from fewer than 9,000 in 1993 to an estimated 180,000 in 2010. Incidents of protest are usually provoked by unpaid wages, unsafe working conditions, confiscation of farmland and housing without fair compensation to its residents, or official corruption.[45] Local officials respond with a combination of carrots and sticks: They often grant the monetary demands of protesters, paying back wages, medical insurance, and pensions, for example, but they arrest the individuals seen as the leaders of the protest. Still, the number and size of labor protests continues to grow.

Meanwhile, modern technology is providing new opportunities for people to express their views.[46] Internet chat rooms and radio call-in shows in China are full of criticisms of official corruption and ineffective governance. The number of Internet users has grown from less than a million in the mid-1990s to over 500 million in 2011, making China the most connected country in the world. The Chinese government has repeatedly issued new regulations aimed at bringing electronic communications by individuals and private companies under tighter control. It monitors Internet chat rooms, electronic bulletin boards, e-mail, and (according to some) even instant messages to root out subversive content. It routinely limits access to the Internet and the electronic exchange of ideas to stymie dissent. In December 2008, Liu Xiaobo was arrested for drafting a pro-democratic Internet petition known as Charter 08; while serving an 11-year prison sentence, he won the 2010 Nobel Peace Prize. But most people in China had never heard of him because his works are censored within China and he was under state surveillance even when he was not in custody. Despite these efforts, the rapid growth and ingenuity of China's Internet users allow them to circumvent "the Great Firewall" almost as fast as obstacles are put up.

The Chinese government not only tries to police the Internet directly, but it also enlists others in its efforts. Microsoft monitors blogs on its servers in China and removes items that may be offensive to the Chinese government. Yahoo has turned over e-mail records that have led to the arrest and imprisonment of several political activists. Google is the only major American Internet company to end this cooperative relationship with the Chinese government. In 2010, it announced it would no longer comply with Beijing's rules censoring search results and web content, and moved its servers to Hong Kong. As cell phones have become ubiquitous in China, text messages are a quick and easy way to share information and organize protests.

These trends suggest a change in the CCP's treatment of political activity. Rather than periodic swings between liberalization and retrenchment, the CCP now has a more nuanced strategy of including supportive individuals in the political process but excluding the ideas and individuals it perceives

Mass protests, including strikes, rallies, marches, traffic blocking, and seizure of buildings, increased from fewer than 9,000 in 1993 to an estimated 180,000 in 2010.

to be threatening. The boundary between threatening and acceptable is not always clear, and those who choose to explore this border often suffer the consequences. Both inclusionary and exclusionary policies are promoted simultaneously, with frequent ebbs and flows in the extent to which each is emphasized.

While noting the changes in political participation that have occurred in the reform era, it is also important to note what has not changed. There have been no dramatic *political* changes comparable to the economic and social changes of the post-Mao period. The opportunities for political participation are still limited and the risks remain high. One reason is the legacy of the Cultural Revolution: Every episode of mass political participation, whether the goals are greater government responsiveness or more citizen representation, has been categorized by party leaders as similar to the Red Guard activities during the Cultural Revolution and is therefore quickly repressed. Unlike South Korea and Taiwan, where demands for political change were gradually accepted and the opportunities for participation within the system gradually enlarged, in China all demands from society have been met with a tightening of party controls and a retreat from political reform. Although there are supporters of political reform within the CCP, they have been on the defensive since 1989. Indeed, there is a fear (among party leaders and society as well) that the post-Mao reforms have created economic and social freedoms that will lead to political instability, and chaos is perhaps the greatest fear in China's traditional political culture. Although the party is willing to allow experimentation with economic policies, complaints about improper policy implementation, and village elections, it is not willing to

HYPOTHESIS-TESTING EXERCISE
Which Aspects of Social Media Does China Censor?

The Chinese authorities are well known for their censorship of the Internet. Even though Chinese social media providers are far more decentralized than their American counterparts—no one dominates like Facebook and Twitter, indeed there are many hundreds of social media outlets—the number of censors and their degree of sophistication is staggering, allowing the authorities to control what they want to control on the web. There are 20,000 to 50,000 Internet police and monitors, the hundreds of individual sites employ up to 1,000 censors each, and some 250,000 party members participate in censoring Internet communications. But toward what kinds of communications do the authorities direct this massive effort? There are two contending theories: (1) Censors act against criticism of local and national political leaders and their actions, and (2) the authorities seek to stamp out any online communications that threaten to facilitate horizontal linkages among Chinese citizens that could develop into independent organizations. The first is easy to understand: Local and national power holders may be thin-skinned or they may worry that Internet criticism can be used by their rivals to undermine their power. The second theory implies that Chinese authorities are most worried about the potential for autonomous political organization to emerge and threaten their monopoly on power.

Hypothesis There are two contending hypotheses:

H₁: The Chinese state censors social media messages that directly criticize individual leaders, the party, the policies they have designed, or their implementation of those policies.

H₂: The Chinese state censors social media messages that suggest the formation of independent organizations or collective action—e.g., demonstrations—whether it is directed against the CCP or not.

Variables The *dependent variable* is whether a particular social media message is censored or not. The *independent variable* is the content of the message, including whether it is

(1) directly critical or authorities or their policies or (2) suggests collective action in some way.

Evidence Gary King, Jennifer Pan, and Margaret E. Roberts directed a major study of these hypotheses by which they monitored and downloaded social media posts from 1,382 Chinese websites from January to June 2011. They then reexamined each site daily to observe which message threads were censored and when. They and their team of researchers downloaded millions of individual posts and randomly analyzed more than 125,000. They engaged in content analysis, a procedure whereby computers and human researchers code texts for the content of their messages following rigorous coding rubrics.

King et al. concluded that the first hypothesis was less strongly supported than the second. Fifteen percent of posts were censored, but message threads that were directly critical of government officials or policies were not as likely to be censored as those proposing collective action. In cases in which a post or a thread develops in a topic area in which there is a possibility of independent collective action, such posts are more likely to be censored, even if they are supportive of the authorities.

Discussion King and his collaborators have produced evidence that what Chinese censors most fear is the possibility that problems emerging from the enormous social change now going on in China will encourage the emergence of collective action independent of the state. Such collective action might involve the emergence of independent organizations that could become an alternative locus of problem solving or a possible political opposition to the ruling CCP. Criticism of the party, of particular power holders—national or local—or of specific policies is often punished, but can also be seen as a form of venting that does not challenge the CCP and is therefore tolerated. In contrast, independent collective action threatens the CCP's monopoly on politics and power, and is thus far more worrisome to the authorities. The sophistication of the CCP's efforts to maintain power can be seen in this massive censorship effort.[47]

---

allow direct challenges to its authority or demands for changes in the basic political system.

During the reform era, three episodes of demands for political reform and democracy occurred in China, always with the same result: The movements were suppressed, their leaders arrested, and their demands ignored. Let's take a quick look at the Democracy Wall Movement in the late 1970s, student demonstrations in the mid-1980s, and the Tiananmen crisis in 1989 to see how political authorities tend to respond to demands for change.

The Democracy Wall Movement, 1978–1979 In the
immediate aftermath of the Cultural Revolution, a group of

intellectuals began putting up posters in an area of downtown Beijing that became known as Democracy Wall.[48] Initially, the protesters were supportive of Deng's efforts to replace the remaining Maoists in the party and government. They wanted to hear official criticism of the Cultural Revolution, of Mao, and of those leaders pledged to remain loyal to his policies. The protesters also called for the rehabilitation of the Cultural Revolution's victims and for political reforms to loosen state controls over society. The movement led to the formation of politically oriented journals and inspired similar developments in other cities. Most of the writers of the posters and the new journals that arose at this time portrayed themselves as loyal citizens who were seeking to reform and improve the political system but not to challenge or replace it. But some advocated positions more radical than even Deng and his allies were willing to permit.

The best-known dissident to emerge in China at the time was Wei Jingsheng, who bemoaned the absence of democracy and rule of law in China.[49] He characterized Deng Xiaoping as just another authoritarian ruler who was not chosen by Chinese society and who would not be bound by the public's interest. As the demands of the Democracy Wall protesters moved in this direction, the state initiated a crackdown, arresting leading figures (including Wei) and sentencing some to long prison sentences. It also moved the authorized site of Democracy Wall from a downtown street to a remote park. In 1980, the party removed from the constitution the right to put up wall posters, eliminating one of the few avenues for public criticism of the government. China's leaders were still not willing to be accountable to public opinion.

Student Demonstrations, 1986–1987 During the early 1980s, while dramatic economic reforms were occurring, political reforms were more limited. The political system was not opened to new voices and groups; instead, political reform was primarily administrative and bureaucratic in nature. The number of government ministries, commissions, and offices was reduced (although the number of officials continued to grow); new criteria for appointing and promoting officials were put in place; and mandatory retirement rules were established for officials. Officials debated policy matters more extensively and drew upon feasibility studies and other technical considerations, rather than ideological rhetoric, in making their decisions. These measures had important implications for how well the party and government did their work, but they did not make the state more responsive to popular opinion. The state may have been more efficient, but it was not more democratic.

By the mid-1980s, many in China, especially in academic and intellectual circles, grew frustrated at the slow pace of political change. In December 1986, college students in Shanghai began public demonstrations about poor living conditions on their campuses; these demonstrations soon included calls for more extensive political reform.[50] Reports on these demonstrations spread to other campuses, and other areas of China reported similar outbreaks. Although the official media initially described the demonstrators as patriotic, the leadership soon changed its viewpoint and chose to crack down on the demonstrations without offering political concessions. Moreover, the general secretary of the CCP at that time, Hu Yaobang, was forced to resign his post and to accept responsibility for the outbreak and spread of demonstrations, which other leaders feared might lead to increased instability if not handled forcefully.

The Tiananmen Crisis, Spring 1989 Hu Yaobang's death in April 1989 sparked the largest popular demonstrations in post-1949 China. From the point of view of China's leaders, the **Tiananmen Square** demonstrations of 1989—ostensibly

about issues such as inflation and corruption—were aimed at overthrowing the government and were seen as a serious threat to their hold on power. The students, workers, professionals, and others who joined in the growing demonstrations in the following weeks were motivated by a variety of concerns. Some were concerned that double-digit inflation was undermining standards of living, wiping away the gains of a decade of reform. Others were alarmed at the rise of rampant corruption accompanying economic reforms. Both these issues in fact mirrored the government's own position. But others used the opportunity of these demonstrations to demand more fundamental changes in China's political system, calling for labor unions and student organizations free of government and party controls and even for the removal of Deng Xiaoping and Li Peng, the unpopular prime minister who was widely viewed as an opponent of reform. In the end, it was the form of these demands—popular demonstrations without government approval—more than their content that frightened China's leaders and led to the tragic outcome of June 4, when martial law was imposed with deadly force and thousands of people were killed or wounded.[51]

This outcome was not predetermined. It was the result of a long and divisive debate among China's top leaders about how to respond to the demonstrations. In fact, it was the perceived divisions among the elite that fueled the demonstrations, creating expectations that the state might actually give in. The longer the state delayed its response, the more these expectations grew. Some of China's leaders were sympathetic to the demands of the protesters and sought a compromise to bring the demonstrations to a close. Others saw the dramatic surge of protest as a repetition of Red Guard activism, from which they had suffered earlier in their careers, and wanted to nip the movement in the bud. Others were embarrassed by the swelling numbers of protesters and the diversity of people who joined, including government officials and journalists connected with the official media, people who were responsible for conveying the official line to the public.

The open display of discontent indicated a severe loss of legitimacy for the leadership in Beijing, which appeared incapable of controlling events in Tiananmen Square, the political and symbolic center of China. For more than a month, demonstrators occupied the square and began a hunger strike to dramatize their cause. The willingness of these young idealists to march in defiance of the state's orders, to remain in the square after the declaration of martial law, and to persist in their hunger strike created sympathy and support among other Chinese citizens and foreign audiences, who watched the drama unfold live on their television sets at home. Foreign television crews had arrived in China to cover the visit of Soviet leader Mikhail Gorbachev, but his visit was quickly overshadowed by the growing popular protests. The television crews stayed in China even after Gorbachev departed, providing almost continuous coverage of the protests.

The failure of these demonstrations in Beijing and elsewhere in China to bring about lasting change was due to several factors. First and most important, the party refuses to

PROFILES   Xi Jinping

Xi Jinping became China's leader in 2012.

Xi Jinping is the leader of the fifth generation of leaders in the PRC. He became general secretary of the CCP in fall 2012. Like the two CCP leaders who preceded him, he is also the president of China and chairman of the Central Military Commission. On paper, these positions make him the most powerful leader in the country. But in the Chinese political system, political power is derived from informal sources—personal experience, political connections, and family ties—as much as from formal titles. Whether Xi will accumulate the personal authority that should go with his titles will be a test of his leadership in the years to come.

Born in 1953, Xi is considered to be one of China's "princelings," children of high-ranking officials. Xi's father, Xi Zhongxun, was a revolutionary hero who was a vice premier before being purged during the Cultural Revolution. In the past-Mao era, Xi Zhongxun was rehabilitated along with many other victims of the Cultural Revolution and became a member of the Politburo. He was also a strong ally of Deng Xiaoping and helped pioneer economic reform as party secretary of Guangdong, where the special economic zones were first created. Because of his father's career, Xi Jinping was familiar with both the

relative comfort of elite families in Beijing and the hardships faced by ordinary people when his family was exiled to China's impoverished northwest region during the Cultural Revolution.

Xi spent most of his career in the prosperous coastal areas, promoting the pro-business policies of the "elitist" wing of the party. He was a leading advocate of integrating the CCP and the private sector, building party cells in private firms, lending state support to the private sector, and appointing private entrepreneurs to legislative and advisory posts. He actively sought foreign direct investment, including from Taiwan investors, giving him extensive experience in the global economy. In 2007, he became party secretary of Shanghai, replacing the former leader who was fired in a pension fund scandal. Six months later, he was elevated to the Standing Committee of the Politburo and later became vice president and vice chairman of the Central Military Commission, signifying his status as Hu Jintao's heir apparent. He was also in charge of supervising the 2008 Olympics in Beijing, by all accounts a huge success.

Xi's economic policies reflect his elitist background. He is a proponent of economic liberalization, economic integration with the global economy, and rapid growth. However, his political views are not well known. In China, leaders do not rise to the top by advocating innovative political ideas, but by publicly affirming the party line. They can be adventurous when it comes to economic reform, but not on political reform. As he rose to the top, it was not clear if he would move the CCP in a new direction or remain on the current course.

Although Xi has supported China's economic integration, he has occasionally made blunt comments about foreign pressure on China. In a widely quoted statement while in Mexico in 2009, Xi said, "Some foreigners with full bellies and nothing better to do engage in finger-pointing at us. First, China does not export revolution; second, it does not export famine and poverty; and third, it does not mess around with you. So what else is there to say?"

Unlike other post-Mao leaders, Xi was not hand-picked by Deng Xiaoping for the top post. His selection as CCP general secretary reflects a consensus among the CCP's elitists and populists. Also unlike his predecessors as general secretary, Xi has ties to the military, an essential resource for a party leader. Early in his career, he worked on the staff of the Central Military Commission and was also senior aide to Geng Biao, a prominent military and foreign policy leader. Whereas Jiang Zemin and Hu Jintao had to build personal ties with the military, primarily by promoting potential supporters to higher ranks, Xi comes to office with existing connections. Another contrast with other top leaders concerns his family: Whereas the spouses of most Chinese leaders are kept out of public view, Xi's wife is a popular singer who frequently appears on television and other public shows.

recognize the legitimacy of any group of which it does not approve and refuses to accept demands for change from outside the limited channels of communications. The political system was created to change society, not to be changed by it, and the party defends its monopoly on political organization quite vigorously. One consequence of this monopoly is that there are no organizations in China with which the state can negotiate a peaceful settlement. There is no equivalent of Poland's Solidarity or the Catholic Church, which in various ways contributed to political change in Central and Eastern Europe, Latin America, and elsewhere. As a result, the students, workers, and others who participated in the demonstrations had no durable organization to plan their protests and shape their demands. Organizations formed spontaneously during the demonstrations, but they had little interaction with each other or with the state. The protesters themselves were divided over their agenda: Some were seeking the reform of existing policies and institutions, others had more revolutionary ambitions, feeling the system was incapable of reform. Ultimately, it was the CCP's past success in preventing autonomous organizations and its refusal to negotiate even with those making demands that echoed the state's own policies that led to the tragic outcome of the demonstrations.

The Tiananmen legacy was devastating and long-lasting. Hard-liners in the party ousted many of the most prominent reformers, including Zhao Ziyang, who had been prime minister and later general secretary of the party and who was widely seen as Deng's heir apparent. Diplomatic and foreign economic relations were frozen and are still haunted by the image of tanks and soldiers firing on civilians. For those who participated in the protests, the crackdown led to months and years of anxiety. Some fled the country rather than risk arrest and jail; others were arrested and subsequently jailed for years. Some had career prospects dimmed because of their involvement. Nearly all were disillusioned by the outcome, convinced more than ever that the party was beyond hope. If it refused to accommodate even the moderate demands of the protesters, it would never sponsor more far-reaching political reforms. The party's willingness to use overwhelming force against unarmed demonstrators suggested that it was foolish to try to bring about change through popular appeals. This was a depressing revelation, but one deeply learned. Most people decided to focus on career opportunities made possible by the ongoing economic reforms and to avoid engaging in idealistic talk about democracy. This is, of course, exactly how the CCP wanted it. The new social contract in China is built on this trade-off: People who are prospering are unlikely to rebel.

In the years after, protests continued to occur, but on a smaller scale: localized, shorter in duration, and focused on the implementation of policies rather than broader political demands. With limited organizational resources and knowledge of the lengths the CCP would go to to remain in power, China has not had a sustained nationwide protest movement since 1989.

China's Leaders Today

One of the dynamics of Chinese politics is the steady decline in the power held by the top leader. Mao was able to change policies and personnel with little resistance from other top leaders. Deng was seen as the preeminent leader of the early reform era, but had to work hard to build support for his policies and occasionally had to retreat in the face of opposition. Jiang Zemin had little of the charisma of Mao and Deng, even though he eventually built up a strong network of supporters. Hu Jintao had even less personal authority and had to reach a consensus with Jiang's many protégés. China's new leader is Xi Jinping. One of the uncertainties of Xi's tenure as party leader is whether he will simply be the first among equals or will have the political skill to assert his own leadership. China's political system is increasingly governed by a collective leadership that constrains the power of the top leader. This avoids the excesses of the Maoist era, but can also prevent a more effective decision-making process.

Several other leaders of the People's Republic of China today should be singled out for their prominence.

Li Keqiang, born in 1955, is prime minister (head of government) and a member of the Standing Committee of the CCP's Politburo. He is a protégé of Hu Jintao and belongs to the populist wing of the party. His promotion to these posts represents the party elite's commitment to balancing the political power of the elitist and populist perspectives within the party.

Wang Qishan, born in 1948, is a member of the CCP's Politburo Standing Committee, former mayor of Beijing, and one of China's most influential people on banking, financial affairs, and overall economic policy. He has been China's chief negotiator with the United States on trade and other economic issues. He currently heads the Central Discipline Inspection Commission, the CCP's body for investigating and punishing corruption.

Zhang Dejiang, born in 1946, is a member of the Politburo Standing Committee and also chairman of the National People's Congress, China's legislature. A protégé of Jiang Zemin, he is a conservative on most issues, especially concerning political reforms. His appointment to these important posts reflects the more conservative nature of China's current leaders.

Although leaders such as Jiang Zemin, Hu Jintao, and former Prime Minister Wen Jiabao are now formally retired, they remain influential behind the scenes. They maneuvered to put their supporters in key jobs before they retired. Political decision making is often described as a "black box," where much is hidden from view. This is true in China more than most countries. Much of the political process is informal, allowing these and other retired officials to continue to shape policy.

10 CONDITIONS FOR DEMOCRACY

China's Prospects

What are the chances that China will undergo democratization in the future? Chapter 7 outlined 10 independent variables that influence the establishment and survival of democracies and that provide us with a framework for answering this question. As Chapter 7 indicates, we can fairly confidently expect most of these variables to promote democracy, while a few others are likely to produce mixed results, depending on local circumstances. Analyzing China's situation against these 10 conditions provides a useful exercise for examining how theories of democratization might be applied there.

1 Elites Committed to Democracy

China lacks elites committed to democracy in numbers large enough to influence decision making. China certainly does have leaders who favor political reform, even including democratization, but they are wary of being too open in their beliefs for fear of losing their jobs. Ironically, the leaders who were instrumental in promoting village elections were not supporters of democratization. Instead, they were concerned with maintaining political order over the restive countryside. Supporters of reform had a potential window of opportunity in 1989, but were outmaneuvered by hard-liners.

2 State Institutions

China has strong state institutions that exercise sovereignty over Chinese territories (with the important exception of Taiwan, as noted earlier). But these institutions are, in general, not compatible with democracy. The rule of law, as described earlier, is not protected; the courts and even the constitution are political tools of the state and are strongly influenced by the changing preferences of the leaders rather than by constraints on the state's own actions. The leaders themselves are not accountable to the people, except at the grassroots level. Obviously, the state and those who lead it are major obstacles to democratization in China.

3 National Unity

The preservation of national unity is also a factor. Roughly 92 percent of China's population belongs to the Han nationality. However, minority groups, though few in number, occupy strategically important areas of the country. The largest such areas are Tibet, the Buddhist nation that was forcibly annexed in 1949–51, and the western province of Xinjiang, where the indigenous people are predominantly Muslim. The periodic activity of independence movements in these areas has provided the Chinese government with a rationale to keep them under control. It denies them autonomy and cracks down severely on political restiveness. Thus China's ethnic and religious heterogeneity works against democratization.

4 National Wealth

Economic reform is bringing about changes that may increase pressures from below for democratic change. For more than two decades, China has experienced rapid growth in its national wealth (see Table 17.1). Its GDP exceeded $5.9 trillion by 2010, though its per capita income remained low (just under $4,500). However, this new wealth has been accompanied by other changes that may influence democratization.

5 Private Enterprise

The growth of private enterprise in China has created less state control over the economy and society, and most people are less dependent on the state than at any time since before the communist revolution. However, private entrepreneurs themselves do not seem interested in promoting democracy, at least not now. As in some other authoritarian countries, especially in East Asia, private entrepreneurs in China are partners of the state and benefit from many of its policies. They are indifferent, or even opposed, to calls for political change, a reality strikingly inconsistent with our supposition that private enterprise generally fosters democracy.[52]

6 A Middle Class

The growth of China's private sector may have indirect effects on potential democratization. It may, for example, give rise to a middle class and a civil society that will be more supportive of democracy. Here, too, the evidence thus far is limited. China's growing middle class is closely tied to the state and remains generally passive in its political behavior, another reality at variance with our expectations.[53]

7 Support of the Disadvantaged for Democracy

How China's large numbers of economically disadvantaged workers and peasants will affect the prospects for democracy is an intriguing question. The growing gap between rich and poor may prompt demands for change, but so far inequality has not become politicized. Most Chinese recognize inequality is getting worse, but do not support state actions to narrow the gap.[54]

8 Citizen Participation, Civil Society, and a Democratic Political Culture

Attitudinal issues are also important. Many people—including Chinese intellectuals—have argued that Chinese political culture, with its emphasis on hierarchy and order and its lack of emphasis on individual rights and interests, is not compatible with democracy. According to this perspective, only after an extensive period of economic growth, rising levels of education, increased freedom of information, and greater interaction with the outside world, will China's political culture be suitable for democracy.

China's civil society is still undeveloped, largely because the state makes it difficult to organize groups independent of its control. China has a large and growing number of NGOs, but they tend to cooperate with the state and steer clear of political issues. Rather than threaten the regime, these nonpolitical groups may help uphold it.[55]

However, the success of village-level elections suggests that people can participate in government even before a democratic culture is created. The gradual democratization of Taiwan—where traditional Chinese values were even more important than on the mainland—shows that democratization creates democratic values.[56] So even though democratic values may be necessary for democracy to survive, they may not be necessary to get the process started.

9   Education and Freedom of Information

Literacy levels have been rising, allowing people to absorb more information, and the state is no longer able to control the flow of information as thoroughly as in the past (especially in an age of Internet access and fax machines). Ironically, not only do the new communications technologies allow for more diverse sources of information, but the commercialization of information also allows people to avoid politics more than ever, diverting their attention to other areas of interest.

10   A Favorable International Environment

The international environment is an ambiguous factor. Clearly, many countries, including the United States, would like to encourage China's democratization. But this very willingness to promote political change makes the international environment seem threatening to China's leaders. They recognize that foreign governments would prefer that China not remain communist, a direct threat to their hold on power. They see the foreign promotion of "peaceful evolution" toward liberal democracy and a market-based economy as an attempt to undermine their political system. Direct intervention to overthrow authoritarian governments in Iraq and Afghanistan and support for regime change during the Arab Spring of 2011 further makes China's leaders suspicious of Western intentions (and makes them oppose UN efforts to intervene in Syria, Iran, and other countries).

These attitudes cannot help but create difficult dilemmas for the world's democracies in their policies toward China. Those who wish to promote democracy from outside China have few tools at their disposal. Financial and logistical support for nongovernmental organizations in China often proves counterproductive: It only raises the government's suspicions. Although the United States and other countries often criticize China's human rights record, that issue generally ranks below trade and security in the U.S.–China relationship.[57] Moreover, China frequently suspends or cancels dialogues on human rights with the United States and the United Nations when it feels the criticisms are too sharp. Some have hoped that increased foreign trade would help promote political change in China, but American businesses have successfully resisted efforts to attach political conditions to U.S.–China trade. Ironically, international efforts to promote democratization are often criticized by political activists in China. Michael Anti (the pen name of Zhao Jing, a prominent Chinese blogger whose blog was removed from Microsoft's server at the request of the Chinese government in 2005) did not welcome congressional hearings on the business practices of Google, Yahoo, Microsoft, and Cisco in China. "I don't feel that the freedom of speech of the Chinese people can be protected by the U.S. Congress," he wrote. Even the best of intentions can backfire.

International support for democratization in China is motivated not only by concerns over the human rights of China's vast population. Many advocates of democratization also believe that a democratic China will be a peaceful China. The Communist government's current efforts to strengthen its nuclear arsenal, its occasionally bellicose statements regarding Taiwan, and its expansive territorial claims in the East China Sea (also claimed by Japan) and the South China Sea (also claimed by Vietnam, the Philippines, and Malaysia) provide continuing cause for concern about its military intentions in the Pacific region. If advocates of the "democratic peace" are correct, then a democratic China would help lower tensions in the Asia-Pacific region.

For their part, the PRC's leaders are suspicious of foreign motives and critical of efforts to meddle in their internal affairs. As we've seen, mistrust of foreigners has deep historical roots in China, and any attempt by outside powers to manipulate the Chinese people or its government invariably strikes a nerve, evoking bitter memories of past exploitation. China's pride was fully evident during the celebrations in July 1997 that greeted its assumption of sovereignty over Hong Kong, which reverted to the People's Republic upon the expiration of Britain's 99-year "lease."[58] Chinese sensitivities were also on view during the Kosovo conflict in 1999 when U.S. warplanes hit the People's Republic's embassy during a bombing run over Belgrade. Washington quickly apologized for the incident, insisting it was an accident. In Beijing, thousands of angry protesters surrounded the U.S. embassy for weeks, chanting anti-NATO slogans; relations between the two

(Continued on next page)

(Continued from previous page)

governments remained chilly for months. When foreign leaders criticized Beijing's crackdown against Tibetan protesters in 2008, angry Chinese accused foreign countries and international media of being biased against China and wanting to disrupt the Olympics held in Beijing later that year.

As a general rule, China's leaders have tried as much as possible to suppress foreign pressures for political change. Thus far, efforts to promote democratization from the outside have had the opposite of their intended effect.

On the whole, some of the conditions for democracy are weak in China, while others are getting stronger.

Perhaps the most striking phenomenon is the failure thus far of economic growth and the emergence of a large private sector to stimulate more intense pressures for democratization, a development largely inconsistent with our expectations. Nevertheless, as the spontaneous student demonstrations of 1989 showed, events can take a sudden turn. Hopes for democracy may still lie just beneath the currently placid surface of Chinese society. The events of 1989 also showed, however, that if democracy is to take hold, it must have the support of key elites, both in the government and in society, who are committed to a democratic transition. So far, China lacks sufficient numbers of those kinds of elites.[59]

Conclusion

As China faces the future, many of the most important issues it faced at the beginning of the twentieth century are still unresolved. Is the West the cause of China's problems or part of their solution? Which Chinese traditions and values are appropriate for the modern world? Is democracy suitable to China, given its traditions, distinctive characteristics, and current level of economic and social development? In addition, new questions have arisen during the period of reform and opening. Should the state or the market play the leading role in shaping economic development? Must economic inequality and environmental degradation be the price for growth? These questions are fundamental ones, and no definitive answers may be possible any time soon. Nor are these questions unique to China; many developing countries face the same dilemmas. Given China's size and potential for future development, however, how China answers these questions is likely to affect not only its future, but also the future of its neighbors and perhaps even the international community of nations as a whole. For that reason, China's future is worth watching.

How China develops will also have important implications for the study of comparative politics as well. As our examination of the 10 conditions for democracy showed, China will be an important test case for many theories in comparative politics. At first glance, China often seems exotic, difficult to understand, an exception to many theories developed on the basis of the experience of Western countries. Indeed, China prefers to portray itself as exceptional and argues that conventional theories cannot capture the country's complexities. But it is only by comparing and contrasting contemporary China with its own past and with other countries that we can gain a clearer understanding of what is truly distinctive and what fits more general patterns of behavior. All countries are unique to some extent, and China no more so than many others. Its ultimate fate will surely tell us a great deal about democracy's

potential as a universally applicable system of government and about the capacity of societies to change their political order. For centuries, China has captured the imagination of scholars and policy makers, and it will continue to do so.

Key Terms

Chinese Communist Party (CCP)
Chinese Nationalist Party (Kuomintang, KMT)
Politburo
General secretary
Prime minister (premier)
National People's Congress
Hundred Flowers Movement
Great Leap Forward
Great Proletarian Cultural Revolution
Tiananmen Square

Notes

1. Edward A. McCord, *The Power of the Gun: The Emergence of Modern Chinese Warlordism* (Berkeley, CA: University of California Press, 1993).
2. Chow Tse-tsung, *The May 4th Movement* (Cambridge, MA: Harvard University Press, 1960).
3. In Pinyin, China's official system of transliteration into the Roman alphabet, *zh* is pronounced "j," *x* is "sh," and *q* is "ch." However, some names (e.g., Sun Yat-sen) are still widely transliterated in the more traditional Wade-Giles system.
4. Jonathan Spence, *Mao Zedong* (New York: Viking, 1999); Philip Short, *Mao: A Life* (New York: Holt, 1999); Jung Chang and Jon Halliday, *Mao: The Unknown Story* (New York: Knopf, 2005).
5. Edgar Snow, *Red Star over China* (New York: Grove Press, 1968); Harrison E. Salisbury, *The Long March: The Untold Story* (New York: Harper and Row, 1985).
6. Andrew Nathan, "Authoritarian Resilience," *Journal of Democracy* 14, no. 1 (January 2003), pp. 6–17.
7. Kevin J. O'Brien, *Reform Without Liberalization: China's National People's Congress and the Politics of Institutional Change* (New York: Cambridge

University Press, 1990); Randall Peerenboom, *China's Long March Toward Rule of Law* (New York: Cambridge University Press, 2002); Yong Nam Cho, *Local People's Congresses in China: Development and Transition* (New York: Cambridge University Press, 2010).

8. Pierre Landry, *Decentralized Authoritarianism in China: The Communist Party's Control of Local Elites in the Post-Mao Era* (New York: Cambridge University Press, 2008).

9. *Selected Works of Mao Tse-tung*, vol. 1 (Beijing: Foreign Languages Press, 1965), p. 28.

10. Frederick C. Teiwes, "Establishment and Consolidation of the New Regime," in *The Politics of China*, 2nd ed., ed. Roderick MacFarquhar (Cambridge: Cambridge University Press, 1997), pp. 5–86.

11. Harry Harding, *Organizing China: The Problem of Bureaucracy, 1949–1976* (Stanford, CA: Stanford University Press, 1980).

12. Richard Lowenthal, "Development Versus Utopia in Communist Policy," in *Change in Communist Systems*, ed. Chalmers Johnson (Stanford, CA: Stanford University Press, 1970).

13. Roderick MacFarquhar, *Origins of the Cultural Revolution, Volume 1, Contradictions Among the People, 1956–1957* (New York: Columbia University Press, 1974).

14. Deng Xiaoping was in charge of running the anti-rightist campaign. As far back as 1957, Deng was associated with strictly enforcing the limits on free speech and dissent. Despite his emphasis on science and technology in later years and his support for rehabilitating many of the victims of Mao's campaigns (including the anti-rightist campaign), he was also opposed to letting the experts turn their expertise into political influence.

15. Roderick MacFarquhar, *Origins of the Cultural Revolution, Volume 2, The Great Leap Forward, 1958–1962* (New York: Columbia University Press, 1983); David M. Bachman, *Bureaucracy, Economy, and Leadership in China: The Institutional Origins of the Great Leap Forward* (New York: Cambridge University Press, 1991).

16. Kenneth Lieberthal, "The Great Leap Forward and the Split in the Yanan Leadership," in MacFarquhar, *Politics of China*, pp. 87–147.

17. Harry Harding, "The Chinese State in Crisis," in MacFarquhar, *The Politics of China*, pp. 148–247.

18. Richard Baum, *Burying Mao: Chinese Politics in the Age of Deng Xiaoping* (Princeton, NJ: Princeton University Press, 1994).

19. Kenneth Lieberthal and Michel Oksenberg, *Policy Making in China: Leaders, Structures, and Processes* (Princeton, NJ: Princeton University Press, 1988).

20. Bruce Dickson, *Wealth into Power: The Communist Party's Embrace of China's Private Sector* (New York: Cambridge University Press, 2008).

21. Melanie Manion, *Retirement of Revolutionaries in China: Public Policies, Social Norms, Private Interests* (Princeton, NJ: Princeton University Press, 1993).

22. Hong Yung Lee, *From Revolutionary Cadres to Party Technocrats in Socialist China* (Berkeley, CA: University of California Press, 1991).

23. Timothy Brook and B. Michael Frolic, eds., *Civil Society in China* (Armonk, NY: M. E. Sharpe, 1997); Qiusha Ma, *Non-Governmental Organizations in Contemporary China: Paving the Way to Civil Society?* (Abingdon and New York: Routledge, 2009).

24. Barry Naughton, "The Third Front: Defence Industrialization in the Chinese Interior," *China Quarterly*, no. 115 (September 1988), pp. 351–86.

25. Martin King Whyte, "State and Society Under Mao," in *Perspectives on Modern China: Four Anniversaries*, ed. Kenneth Lieberthal et al. (Armonk, NY: M. E. Sharpe, 1991), pp. 255–74.

26. Joseph Fewsmith, *Dilemmas of Reform in China* (Armonk, NY: M. E. Sharpe, 1994).

27. David Shambaugh, *China's Communist Party: Atrophy and Adaptation* (Berkeley and Washington, DC: University of California Press and Woodrow Wilson Center Press, 2008).

28. A recent example of the "China threat" perspective is Aaron Friedberg, *A Contest for Supremacy: China, America, and the Struggle for Mastery in Asia* (New York: W.W. Norton, 2011); the alternative viewpoint is presented in Edward Steinfeld, *Playing Our Game: Why China's Rise Doesn't Threaten the West* (New York: Oxford University Press, 2010). A balanced analysis and forecast can be found in David Shambaugh, ed., *Power Shift: China and Asia's New Dynamics* (Berkeley, CA: University of California Press, 2006).

29. Jean C. Oi, *Rural China Takes Off: Institutional Foundations of Economic Reform* (Berkeley, CA: University of California Press, 1999).

30. Barry Naughton, *Growing Out of the Plan: Chinese Economic Reform, 1978–1993* (New York: Cambridge University Press, 1996).

31. Yasheng Huang, *Selling China: Foreign Direct Investment During the Reform Era* (New York: Cambridge University Press, 2005).

32. Rachel Murphy, *How Migrant Labor Is Changing Rural China* (New York: Cambridge University Press, 2002); Leslie Chang, *Factory Girls: From Village to City in a Changing China* (New York: Spiegel and Grau, 2009).

33. Transparency International, "Corruption Perceptions Index 2012," at www.transparency.org.

34. Yan Sun, *Corruption and Market in Contemporary China* (Ithaca, NY: Cornell University Press, 2004); Andrew Wedeman, *Double Paradox: Rapid Growth and Rising Corruption in China* (Ithaca, NY: Cornell University Press, 2012).

35. An excellent study of China's environmental problems and fledgling environmental movement is Elizabeth Economy, *The River Runs Black: The Environmental Challenge to China's Future*, 2nd ed. (Ithaca, NY: Cornell University Press, 2010).

36. Scott Kennedy, *The Business of Lobbying in China* (Cambridge, MA: Harvard University Press, 2005).

37. Jonathan Schwarz and Shawn Shieh, eds., *State and Society Responses to Social Welfare Needs in China: Serving the People* (Abingdon and New York: Routledge, 2009).

38. Kevin J. O'Brien and Lianjiang Li, *Rightful Resistance in Rural China* (New York: Cambridge University Press, 2005); Merle Goldman, *From Comrade to Citizen: The Struggle for Political Rights in China* (Cambridge, MA: Harvard University Press, 2005).

39. Samuel Huntington, *Political Order in Changing Societies* (New Haven, CN: Yale University Press, 1968). For a summary, see Chapter 12.

40. Kenneth Lieberthal and David Lampton, eds., *Bureaucracy, Politics, and Decision Making in Post-Mao China* (Berkeley, CA: University of California Press, 1992); Susan Shirk, *The Political Logic of Economic Reform in China* (Berkeley, CA: University of California Press, 1993).

41. Andrew Walder, *Communist Neo-Traditionalism: Work and Authority in Chinese Industry* (Berkeley, CA: University of California Press, 1986).

42. Tianjian Shi, "Village Committee Elections in China: Institutional Tactics for Democracy," *World Politics* 51, no. 3 (April 1999), pp. 385–412; Kevin J. O'Brien and Rongbin Han, "Path to Democracy? Assessing Village Elections in China," *Journal of Contemporary China* 18, no. 60 (June 2009), pp. 359–78.

43. This is a hotly debated issue among China specialists. For an optimistic view that China is undertaking important institutional reforms, see Dali L. Yang, *Remaking the Chinese Leviathan: Market Transition and the Politics of Governance in China* (Stanford, CA: Stanford University Press, 2004); for an argument that China's leaders are unwilling to engage in meaningful reform, see Minxin Pei, *China's Trapped Transition: The Limits of Developmental Autocracy* (Cambridge, MA: Harvard University Press, 2006).

44. Neil J. Diamant, Stanley B. Lubman, and Kevin J. O'Brien, eds., *Engaging the Law in China: State, Society, and Possibilities for Justice* (Stanford, CA: Stanford University Press, 2005).

45. Kevin O'Brien, ed., *Popular Protest in China* (Boston: Harvard University Press, 2008); Yongshun Cai, *Collective Resistance in China: Why Popular Protests Succeed or Fail* (Stanford, CA: Stanford University Press, 2010).

46. Guobin Yang, *The Power of the Internet in China: Citizen Activism Online* (New York: Columbia University Press, 2009).

47. Gary King, Jennifer Pan, and Margaret E. Roberts, "How Censorship in China Allows Government Criticism but Silences Collective Expression," *American Political Science Review*, forthcoming 2013.

48. Andrew J. Nathan, *Chinese Democracy* (Berkeley, CA: University of California Press, 1985).

49. Wei Jingsheng, *The Courage to Stand Alone: Letters from Prison and Other Writings* (New York: Viking, 1997).

50. Orville Schell, *Discos and Democracy: China in the Throes of Reform* (New York: Anchor Books, 1989).

51. See Michel Oksenberg, Marc Lambert, and Lawrence Sullivan, eds., *Beijing Spring 1989: Confrontation and Conflict* (Armonk, NY: M. E. Sharpe, 1990); Andrew J. Nathan and Perry Link, *The Tiananmen Papers* (New York: Public Affairs, 2002).

52. Kellee S. Tsai, *Capitalism without Democracy: The Private Sector in Contemporary China* (Ithaca, NY: Cornell University Press, 2007); Jie Chen and Bruce J. Dickson, *Allies of the State: China's Private Entrepreneurs and Democratic Change* (Boston: Harvard University Press, 2010).

53. Cheng Li, ed., *China's Emerging Middle Class: Beyond Economic Transformation* (Washington, DC: Brookings, 2010).

54. Martin King Whyte, *The Myth of the Social Volcano: Perceptions of Inequality and Distributive Injustice in Contemporary China* (Stanford, CA: Stanford University Press, 2010).

55. Michael W. Foley and Bob Edwards, "The Paradox of Civil Society," *Journal of Democracy* 7, no. 3 (July 1996), pp. 38–52.

56. Shelley Rigger, *Politics in Taiwan: Voting for Democracy* (London: Routledge, 2002).

57. James Mann, *The China Fantasy: How Our Leaders Explain Away Chinese Repression* (New York: Viking, 2007).

58. Only a portion of Hong Kong's legislature is directly elected, giving Beijing significant influence over its actions. In addition, the chief executive is handpicked by Beijing. This amount of PRC control over Hong Kong affairs has allowed Beijing to block all efforts to promote further democratic reforms.

59. A more optimistic assessment can be found in Bruce Gilley, *China's Democratic Future: How It Will Happen and Where It Will Lead* (New York: Columbia University Press, 2004).

18

Mexico and Brazil

OVERVIEW

- As large, middle-income Latin American countries, Mexico and Brazil have many similarities that allow a focused comparison of their experiences with democratization and economic development.

- Mexico was governed by a single party for most of its postrevolutionary, twentieth-century history. That party, the Institutional Revolutionary Party (PRI), brought economic development to Mexico but effectively limited the capacity of its opponents to compete for power until the 1990s.

- Mexico's democratization came about due to the country's socioeconomic modernization, the PRI's policy failures, and a long struggle by opposition parties and grassroots organizations to expand democratic participation.

- After the end of the Brazilian Empire in 1889, the country suffered from regime instability, alternating between more democratic and more authoritarian regimes during the twentieth century.

- The military government (1964–85) ruled dictatorially, but sought to retain some features of democratic politics, which eventually allowed for a peaceful transition to democracy.

- Brazil's contemporary democracy suffers challenges of governability due to its size and diversity as well as institutional shortcomings in the regime launched in the 1988 constitution.

Protesters place the shoes of people who have disappeared in Mexico's drug war before the statue of independence in Mexico City. The sign asks, "Where are they?"

Global news headlines frequently highlight gruesome incidents of violence in Mexico. Selected headlines from the *Los Angeles Times* from 2011 provide telling examples:

"Mexico's drug war disappearances leave families in anguish" (March 7).

"Body count from mass graves in Mexico rises to 145" (April 16).

"Mexican journalist, family slain" (June 21).

"At least 20 killed in Mexico bar, officials say" (July 10).

"Mexico gunmen set casino on fire, killing at least 53" (August 26).

"Mexico violence claims another member of peace movement" (December 8).

Those six stories told just a few examples of widespread violence related to drug-trafficking that in 2011 claimed more than 12,000 lives, by conservative estimates. The violence in 2011 was but one year in a six-year war on drug trafficking organizations by the Mexican federal government under President Felipe Calderón (2006–12). Estimates of the scale of the bloodletting during his term as president vary widely, but by one account it exceeded 100,000.[1] How

451

could death and mayhem take place to such an extreme in the U.S. neighbor?

The drug-related violence may be an unexpected and unintended consequence of Mexico's political liberalization, described extensively in the first half of this chapter. For more than 70 years, Mexico was ruled by the **Institutional Revolutionary Party** (**PRI**, pronounced "pree"), a party that dominated the political regime by overwhelming its challengers at the polls and then governing Mexico's states and localities at times with an iron fist and at other times with a velvet glove. The drug violence has its origins in the huge demand for illegal narcotics in the United States, an appetite that long predated Calderón's presidency. During its rule from 1929 to 2000, the PRI worked out many understandings at the regional and local levels with those who operated on the other side of the law, including narcotics traffickers. The unstated agreement was that if criminal organizations did not engage in egregious acts or challenge their authority, local officials would look the other way and perhaps accept bribes too. Police and military units, often closely linked to local PRI leaders, were complicit in the arrangement. Specific drug-trafficking organizations arose to route cocaine, heroin, marijuana, and methamphetamines to particular markets in the United States. In fairness to the politicians, police, and soldiers caught up in this racket, they were often offered the choice of *plata o plomo*, "silver or lead," accepting a bribe or taking a bullet. And the profits to be made in narco-trafficking are huge; the Mexican organizations were estimated to have made profits of almost $14 billion in 2006.[2]

Calderón and his predecessor, Vicente Fox (2000–06), did not come from the PRI, but from the **National Action Party (PAN)**, which had unseated the former ruling party and brought democracy to Mexico. Fox and Calderón came under pressure from the United States to take action against the huge flow of narcotics passing through Mexican territory. That the Mexican state could not stop narco-trafficking implied that it lacked the essential qualities of a state identified in Chapters 1 and 3. Calderón deployed the Mexican army against the drug gangs and continued Fox's efforts to clean up police and army units by removing those officers and soldiers identified as collaborating with traffickers. Unlike the long-ruling PRI, PAN elected officials did not have long-term relationships with the police and army. Thus they often found that simply wanting to clean up corruption within the forces of order did not achieve the goal.

Calderón's offensive against the criminal organizations focused on eliminating by capture or death the high-ranking members of particular gangs—so-called kingpins. To the extent that kingpins were arrested or killed, Calderón's policy tended to have a perverse and unintended consequence. When kingpins were eliminated, the struggle by their lieutenants to succeed them proved extremely violent. The removal of kingpins also tempted rival trafficking organizations to try to seize the routes controlled by the gangs losing their leaders—to take their turf. Thus, while some violence in the Mexican drug war has been between the authorities and the

traffickers, even more has taken place within and between rival drug gangs. In the process, many innocent bystanders—including friends, neighbors, and family members of people involved in these criminal organizations—have become victims of the violence. Violent deaths lead to calls for revenge against the perpetrators, and a vicious circle develops. Because the trade is so lucrative, aspiring kingpins have huge incentives to try to take some of their rivals' business. Recent estimates place the number of Mexicans working in illegal narcotics trafficking at as many as 500,000, underscoring the scale of the trade.

Calderón unleashed a struggle for power and profits that the Mexican state was not prepared to win. In the heyday of the PRI, if rivals for power took up arms, federal and state authorities would not hesitate to stamp them out. That began to change in 1994, when the federal government under President Carlos Salinas (1988–94) of the PRI hesitated after initially deciding to suppress a rebellion in the southern state of Chiapas. Fear that Mexico would be branded a ruthless, authoritarian regime by international observers at a time when it wanted to promote an image of a modernizing society ready to join the **North American Free Trade Agreement (NAFTA)** motivated the Salinas government's softer approach to the rebels. The PAN governments of Fox and Calderón, more committed to democracy and human rights than the PRI had been, were even less ready to use the full force of the military and the police against those who challenged their monopoly of the use of force. Not surprisingly, critics have begun to ask whether Mexico might be a failing state (see Chapter 3). When Mexicans went to the polls in 2012, a top issue on their minds was whether the PAN had the capacity to end the drug war. Voters elected the PRI's candidate, Enrique Peña Nieto, while the PAN's candidate, Josefina Vázquez Mota finished a distant third (see Table 18.1). Peña Nieto's greatest challenge as president will be to reestablish order in his country. However, because the PRI itself has changed since it lost power in 2012, he will not likely be able to reestablish the many informal agreements by which the PRI ruled before 2000.

Further south, the Brazilian state has at times faced similar challenges in controlling its territory. Brazil will host the 2014 World Cup and the 2016 Summer Olympics. International sports officials remain anxious that Brazil will be unable to protect international visitors from street crime and criminal organizations that have had a strong presence in Rio de Janeiro and São Paulo. At times criminal organizations have controlled large neighborhoods, called *favelas*, in Brazilian cities to the degree that the police have been reluctant to enter them. Violent crime, as evidenced by high homicide rates, plagues much of Latin America, and the states there have not been able to bring it under control. Despite economic growth over the past two decades and the establishment of more democratic regimes in the region, Brazil, Mexico, and many of their neighbors have not resolved law and order issues.

In this chapter and the next, we depart from the single-country studies provided in Chapters 13 to 17 to engage in

Table 18.1 Mexican Presidential Elections, 2000, 2006, and 2012

Candidate	Party or Coalition	% of Valid Vote
2000		
Vicente Fox	Alliance for Change*	43.4%
Francisco Labastida	Institutional Revolutionary Party (PRI)	36.9
Cuauhtémoc Cárdenas	Alliance for Mexico[†]	17.0
Others		2.7
2006		
Felipe Calderón	National Action Party (PAN)	36.7
Andrés Manuel López Obrador	Coalition for the Good of All[‡]	36.1
Roberto Madrazo	Alliance for Mexico[§]	22.7
Others		4.5
2012		
Enrique Peña Nieto	Institutional Revolutionary Party (PRI)	39.1
Andrés Manuel López Obrador	Democratic Revolutionary Party (PRD)	32.4
Josefina Vázquez Mota	National Action Party (PAN)	26.0
Others		2.5

*Alliance for Change was composed of the National Action Party (PAN) and the Mexican Green Party (PVEM).

[†]Alliance for Mexico (2000) was composed of the Democratic Revolutionary Party (PRD) and four smaller parties of the left.

[‡]Coalition for the Good of All was composed of the PRD and two smaller parties: the Labor Party (PT) and Convergence.

[§]Alliance for Mexico (2006) was composed of the PRI and the PVEM.

Sources: Instituto Federal Electoral and Tribunal Electoral del Poder Judicial de la Federación.

systematic, paired comparison. Comparative politics has a long history of contributing to area studies, and these two chapters represent our foray into area studies. Area studies scholars typically take a broad interdisciplinary look at the countries and regions they study so as to fully understand the context and then focus on themes that most interest them (for us, politics). Area studies allows us to apply a version of most-similar systems comparison. The countries in particular regions often have several contextual factors that are relatively similar. In this chapter, the pair of Latin American countries we study, Mexico and Brazil, share an Iberian cultural heritage. Mexico is now the world's largest Spanish-speaking country and Brazil the most populous Portuguese-speaking nation in the world. They were colonized at a similar time in the sixteenth century and became independent in the beginning of the nineteenth century. Large and diverse countries, they have histories in which forces favoring more centralized rule have fought others seeking more power for states and localities. Both are federalist, but how effectively the federal units have been able to exercise independent authority has varied. Brazil and Mexico have achieved somewhat similar levels of economic development. They are now middle-income industrial economies that export both agricultural and manufactured products, but for much of the twentieth century they practiced an inward-looking model of development, import-substituting industrialization. Despite these similarities, Brazil's and Mexico's political histories diverged in the twentieth century.

In this chapter we will use the tools developed in Part One of this book, especially in Chapters 6 and 7 on democratic institutions and the 10 conditions for democracy, to systematically examine how the political development of Brazil and Mexico has differed and why. We begin each case by describing the setting and identifying distinctive elements of politics in Mexico and Brazil. We then review key episodes and forces in the national history of each country to show roots of contemporary politics. Along the way we use the 10 conditions for democracy (see Chapter 7) to explain why a nondemocratic regime had a long duration in Mexico (1929–2000) and Brazil (1964–85). We then turn to the democratization process to describe how the current regimes came to be, consider the contemporary political institutions, review the societies' experience with economic development, and introduce the key issues that animate politics today.

These and related issues are especially important in Mexico and Brazil. The size and economic potential of these nations are so immense that their fate cannot help but influence future developments throughout Latin America. Nearly 200 million people live in Brazil, while the population of Mexico is 115 million. Together, their 315 million form over half of the population of Latin America and the Caribbean.[3] Further, their economies ranked eighth (Brazil) and fourteenth (Mexico) in gross national income in the world in 2011.[4] To foreign policy makers and to the leaders of banks and other transnational corporations in the United States, what happens in Mexico and Brazil can have

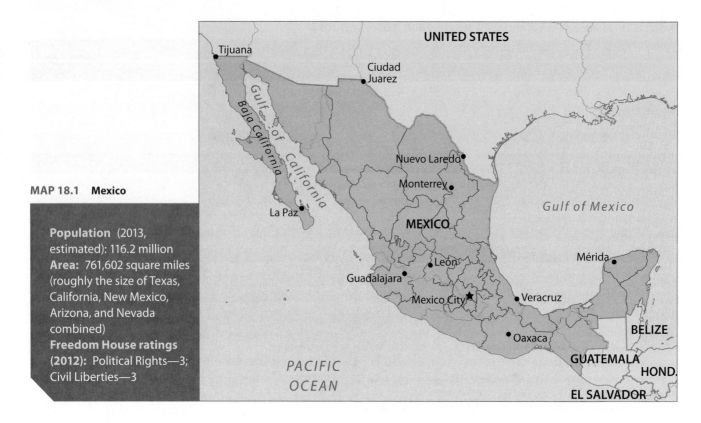

MAP 18.1 Mexico

Population (2013, estimated): 116.2 million
Area: 761,602 square miles (roughly the size of Texas, California, New Mexico, Arizona, and Nevada combined)
Freedom House ratings (2012): Political Rights—3; Civil Liberties—3

major repercussions for U.S. political and economic interests in the hemisphere, as financial crises in Mexico in 1995 and in Brazil in 1998 proved and the ongoing violence in Mexico shows.

MEXICO

For students of comparative politics, Mexico has proven to be an endlessly fascinating but difficult-to-describe country. On the one hand, in a continent beset by political crises and upheavals, twentieth-century Mexico demonstrated remarkable political stability. The constitution promulgated at the end of the Mexican revolution has been in place since 1917, amended but not changed in its fundamentals. The PRI, whose leaders sat in the president's chair for over 70 years after the party was founded in 1929, was the longest-ruling party in the world until Vicente Fox was inaugurated as Mexico's president December 1, 2000. (Current President Enrique Peña Nieto is from the PRI.) Mexicans elect a new president every six years; none has refused to hand over power to his successor. Moreover, the PRI oversaw 70 years of economic development—not without setbacks, of course—but the Mexico of the twenty-first century is profoundly different from the nation that came out of the revolution around 1920. It is now predominantly urban, not rural; it has industrialized; most of its people can read and write; and modern health facilities, sanitation, communications systems, and electricity are available almost everywhere in Mexico today. In many ways, Mexican politics since the revolution can be considered a success story in the turbulent twentieth century.

Yet, during the last three decades of the twentieth century, political observers said Mexico was in crisis. The end of Mexican stability seemed always just around the corner. The same party ruled for seven decades, making it seem as though no real alternative existed (or was allowed to exist). Formally democratic institutions hid an authoritarian political regime, but only to those who did not look closely. The PRI's challengers only as recently as 2000 defeated the ruling party in the electoral arena; previously, many opponents of the PRI considered guerrilla insurrection or other unorthodox challenges to its supremacy. Economic modernization has failed to reach many of Mexico's millions of poor peasants and urban dwellers because of severely inequitable distributions of income and wealth. Apparently often at the edge of breaking into the First World, Mexico's great economic promise has repeatedly gone unfulfilled.

The Setting

Mexico's 115 million people occupy a country that is about a quarter the size of the 48 contiguous states of the United States, meaning the population density is nearly twice that of the United States.[5] Mexico's vastness makes for considerable regional diversity, from the deserts of the north to the semitropical regions of the south. The greatest concentration of Mexicans lives in the center of the country. Mexico City is one of the world's largest cities, with over 20 million inhabitants. Its growth has been phenomenal: In 1950, Mexico City had fewer than 4 million people.[6] Also in the central region are the states of Puebla, Guanajuato, and Jalisco, and with them several large cities, including Puebla, León, and Guadalajara. While the center of the nation has experienced rapid urbanization, the cities have grown even faster in the north, where the industrial center of Monterrey has been joined by Ciudad Juárez, Tijuana, and other border cities.

With such rapid urbanization has come a wholesale uprooting of much of Mexico's population. The cities have grown because many citizens living in the countryside have seen no prospect for employment and prosperity in their families' villages. As they have moved to the cities, neighborhoods have mushroomed in rings around the old central cities, posing enormous challenges to city planners and to those local politicians and administrators charged with providing services and amenities.

At the same time, nearly 25 million Mexicans still live in rural areas, a number larger than the populations of many Latin American countries.[7] Mexico's south has been slower to urbanize than other parts of the country. For all the challenges facing country people moving to large cities such as Mexico City, rural conditions are even more rigorous: Imagine life without running water, sewage systems or even a septic tank, sometimes even electricity. Millions of Mexicans likewise send their children to rudimentary schools and get along without doctors or 24-hour emergency room personnel.

Regionalism Mexico's regions differ in their economic pursuits, too. The northern states, for example, have concentrations of export-oriented industries, such as assembly plants in border cities that have benefited from NAFTA. Central Mexico, especially the greater Mexico City area, has historically been the site of heavy industry—automobiles and steel, among others—and has not prospered so much from hemispheric economic integration. The south remains more agricultural than the rest of the country and has been especially threatened by cheap grain imports from the grain belt of the United States.

One other important regional difference is culture. Like the Western states of the United States, Mexico's north has been a frontier region since colonization. Northern Mexicans thus share some characteristics Americans associate with their own West, especially an emphasis on rugged individualism. The much greater influence of the United States on northern Mexico has probably reinforced the individualism of northerners. Northerners have preferred private enterprise to state ownership of industry. Mexico City residents, in contrast, see themselves as urbane and even cosmopolitan and sometimes view the northerners as too rough around the edges—barbarians of the north. They have been much more inclined to support a large state presence in the economy and in other aspects of social life, perhaps because so many of them work for the state. In many parts of Mexico's south, indigenous peoples remain concentrated in their traditional villages, practicing communal landholding and rejecting private ownership of the land. In the states of Oaxaca, Chiapas, and Guerrero, indigenous groups have sought to retain whatever control of their communities' political arrangements they can, arrangements that are sometimes based on long-standing community traditions.

Associated with these different regional economic and political cultures are perceptions of racial differences. Northerners, for example, are more likely to be Caucasians or people of mixed European and indigenous heritage (**mestizos**).

Southerners are more likely to be of indigenous heritage. A latent racism can often be witnessed in statements by northerners of their perceptions of the other regions of the country. For example, some years ago a newly elected governor of the northern state of Aguascalientes couldn't contain himself after his victory, describing the regional differences this way: "The north works, the center thinks, and the south rests."[8]

It is almost impossible to understate the importance of Mexico's proximity to the United States. The countries share a long, often porous border. The bulk of Mexico's trade is with the United States—as much as 80 percent annually. Millions of Mexicans have traveled to the United States to work, visit family members, shop, or just vacation. U.S. cultural influences have become very powerful in Mexico—many Mexicans look to the United States for their popular culture and for cues about their own futures.

Moreover, the border has served as Mexico's social safety valve: When Mexicans have not been able to find satisfactory employment in their country, they often have gone to the United States, legally or illegally. Many Mexicans go to the United States to work several times in their lives; many others go only once to earn money for an important purchase, like a car or improvements to their home; and still others go to the United States and don't return. Because everyone involved in the U.S.–Mexican relationship knows about this phenomenon, everyone also worries about the consequences of political instability in Mexico because that would likely increase the flow of Mexicans northward. Mexico's relatively slow economic growth in recent years has meant that more and more Mexicans now move to the United States with the intention of settling there permanently. Only with the 2008 start of the financial crisis in the United States has migration abated.

The Evolution of Mexican Politics

Prominent Features of Mexican Politics When students of comparative politics looked at Mexico in the 1970s, they noted that, although Mexicans elected their president, a congress, state governors, and state assemblies, the political regime had more in common with the military-ruled political systems of South America than it did with the democracies of North America or Europe.[9] Mexican authoritarianism had several features, the most noticeable being the long rule of the PRI. The PRI controlled Mexico's presidency and dominated the country's political system as its ruling party from the time it was founded in 1929 until Vicente Fox's victory in 2000. Until the 1980s, the PRI did not lose *any* significant elections. Democracy without alternation in power—or the serious prospect of it—could hardly be called true democracy, and no opposition party posed any real challenge to the PRI even as late as the 1970s.

Another feature of Mexican politics that everyone recognized was *presidentialism*. Mexican presidents have been in some ways akin to limited-term dictators. During his six years in office, each PRI president dominated congress, the judiciary, the military, the states and their governors, the party that elected him, and the media that reported his every move. Observers also agreed that the Mexican political system was highly centralized, despite a constitution that was formally federalist. Mexican *centralism* meant that Mexico City dominated the nation and that the federal government dictated to the states in ways that other federalist societies such as the United States or Canada would find unacceptable. Another aspect of the central role of the government in Mexican life was the heavy *state intervention* in Mexico's market economy. The Mexican government held many state-owned enterprises and the economy was highly regulated. Associated with the state's close regulation of the economy was its control of the interest groups spawned by that economy; Mexico was a clear example of *state corporatism*. The labor movement, peasant associations, state employees, small-business owners—all were captured in a system of interest representation that channeled their demands through the PRI.

Two other features of Mexican politics also caught the attention of political analysts: *clientelism* and *corruption*. The Mexican political elite was recruited through a system of patron–client relationships "in which the 'patrons'—persons having higher political status—provide benefits such as protection, support in political struggles with rivals and chances for upward political or economic mobility to their 'clients'—persons with a lower political status."[10] Clientelism (as described in Chapter 8) has extended beyond the political class, however, so that many organizations and individuals have found themselves regularly approaching powerful individuals in politics and government agencies to petition for assistance, usually with the expectation that those being helped by powerful patrons will reciprocate by supporting those politicians as they seek to climb the political ladder.[11] It is not surprising that corruption becomes bound up with clientelism; the favors asked by clients of patrons often involve gaining access to public resources for those clients' private gain. At the same time, the asymmetrical power relationships fostered by clientelism encourage the powerful to demand a great deal of their clients or would-be clients. Mexican clientelism intersects in an unpleasant way with one other feature of Mexican politics: *caciquismo*. *Caciques* are local political bosses. In rural Mexico caciques associated with the PRI are known for resorting to violence against individuals not willing to accept their subordinate position in a patron–client relationship. A cacique might be the local mayor, a union or peasant association leader, or a large landowner.

How did Mexico come to exhibit these features of political life? As the next sections explain, each feature has some antecedent in Mexican political history.

Conquest and Colonialism
The makings of the modern Mexican nation came together in the **Spanish conquest**, when Hernán Cortés led his band of 550 Spaniards against the mighty Aztec empire in 1519.[12] The conquest led to widespread miscegenation (racial interbreeding) between Europeans and indigenous people, mostly between Spanish men and indigenous women, who created a nation whose majority is now mestizo.

During the following 300 years of colonial rule, Europeans and those of European heritage held complete political control. The idea that Indians were meant to work for white people became firmly embedded in the minds of Mexico's elites. At the same time, indigenous communities were allowed to hold their lands communally and to decide how to farm them through community institutions, an arrangement known as the *ejido*.

Independence and the Creation of a Mexican Nation
Independence came to Mexico and other Spanish colonies not as a consequence of an uprising of the exploited indigenous peoples and mestizos, but rather because of a conflict between whites born in America and those who came from Spain. However, in the course of Mexico's struggle for independence, the poor and nonwhite became mobilized in a rebellion against the Spanish.

Political instability characterized the first half-century after Mexico became independent in 1822. Conservatives and liberals struggled over the definition of the new nation and its political institutions. Conservatives favored a restoration of some form of monarchy, centralized power, and a privileged political position for the Catholic church. Liberals, in contrast, sought a federal republic without an established church, as in the United States. Battles between liberals and conservatives contributed to much political instability, with coups d'état and civil wars leading to very short terms of office for Mexico's presidents. In the 32 years from 1823 until 1855, 24 men served as president of Mexico, some of them multiple times. General Antonio López de Santa Anna, whom Americans know best as the Mexican commander at the Alamo, was president 11 times.

Meanwhile, Mexico's restive neighbor to the north proclaimed the doctrine of *manifest destiny*, the notion that the United States should stretch from the Atlantic to the Pacific. Mexico's weakness—a product of its domestic political turbulence—contributed to the success of the Texas independence movement (1836) and to Mexico's defeat in the Mexican-American War (1846–48), known in Mexico as the War of North American Aggression. In addition, Mexico was invaded by French forces in 1861 while the United States was preoccupied with its own Civil War. After a six-year struggle for independence, liberal forces led by Benito Juárez defeated the French in 1867.

Mexico's unfortunate history of foreign invasion during the nineteenth century played an important role in the formation of Mexican national identity. Mexico's colonial heritage had provided little to unite its people: Colonial institutions and practices tended to divide Mexicans into rigid social categories based on race. But the struggle against foreign intervention united Mexicans of all classes by casting them as victims of foreign aggression. And while Mexico's experiences with the United States reinforced Mexican perceptions of weakness, its successful ouster of the French produced a great national hero—Juárez, who was a Zapotec Indian from the southern state of Oaxaca—and solidified the conception of Mexico as a republic.

Mexican nationalism became further defined by the nation's experiences on up to 1910. In 1876 General Porfirio Díaz led a successful military rebellion against President Sebastian Lerdo under the slogan "Effective Suffrage and No Reelection." After ousting Lerdo, Díaz was duly elected by Mexico's very restricted electorate. He served one term, then stood aside so that one of his political allies could be elected in 1880. But he returned to the presidency in 1884, not to step down until the revolution of 1910. During his long rule, he relied on a small coterie of political followers known as *cientificos*.[13] Many of them espoused social Darwinism, the notion that only the fittest would survive in social life. In the Mexican context, social Darwinists suggested that Europeans or their descendants would be most likely to survive the social struggle, while the indigenous would not. In their view, it would be better for Mexico if the indigenous population remained marginalized.

During Díaz's 35-year rule, Mexico experienced unprecedented economic growth, spurred by major investments in mining and in the railroads. These investments came disproportionately from the United States, and they gave Mexicans of all classes a feeling that they were being cheated out of the fruits of the new economic advances. Americans, in contrast, had been favored so as to attract their investment dollars. In addition, many investors from the United States became large landowners in Mexico, and U.S. banks became major lenders to Mexico's economic elites.[14] In reaction, a strong sense of economic nationalism emerged by the turn of the century.

Throughout Díaz's rule, the poor were further marginalized. The liberal constitution of 1857 had outlawed land ownership by corporate groups. By this provision, the church lost its lands to large landholders, mostly to people associated with the liberals. But this provision also barred communal property holding in *ejidos*, so individual families in rural villages were given properties previously owned by the entire village. Many such villagers subsequently lost their lands because of economic failures or were cheated out of them by rich landowners intent on consolidating large estates that increasingly produced commercial crops for the national and international markets. Thus, Mexico's peasantry became proletarianized, forced to become wage laborers on land they formerly owned or to seek employment on the railroads or in the new factories.

The Revolution Mexico's 1910 revolution brought together several social groups dissatisfied by Díaz's regime. The initiator of the revolution, Francisco Madero, came from a northern landowning family. Madero and many like him were angry that Díaz had excluded them from political power and frustrated because U.S. investors seemed to get most of the best investment opportunities. Madero remembered Díaz's slogan, "Effective Suffrage and No Reelection," and raised it as his own revolutionary battle cry. Madero's followers were political liberals and economic nationalists, but not very interested in serious social reforms.[15]

Other Mexicans sought more revolutionary changes. Emiliano Zapata, a villager from Morelos, led an army of peasants demanding land reform. They wanted to reclaim the land they had lost to investors in sugar plantations and they sought a return of the *ejido*, the system of communal land ownership.

Díaz abdicated the presidency in 1911. Madero became president, but he was overthrown and assassinated by a counterrevolutionary coup d'état in 1913 orchestrated by the U.S. ambassador, Henry Lane Wilson. After Madero's assassination, chaos reigned as revolutionaries of all stripes united to defeat the counterrevolutionary leader, General Victoriano Huerta. After ousting Huerta in 1914, however, the revolutionaries fought among themselves for direction of the new regime.

The revolution became a conflagration: As many as a million Mexicans lost their lives and much property was destroyed. Millions more were mobilized into revolutionary armies that marched or rode (on horses and the railroads) the length and breadth of Mexico, learning thereby what the rest of their country and their countrymen looked like. Although Mexicans were divided during their revolution, a sense of national identity and unity emerged from the struggle, breaking down some of the provincialism that had to that point characterized Mexican society. Those revolutionary soldiers, the majority of them peasants and workers, were now mobilized by their involvement in the revolution and became experienced in using violence against their adversaries. They would not be easily demobilized and excluded from having a political voice after the revolution.

In the end, the revolutionary faction that most closely followed Madero's political philosophy, the Constitutionalists (led by Venustiano Carranza, also a large landowner from the north), emerged as the dominant force. The Constitutionalists defeated the armies of Zapata and Pancho Villa and wrote a new constitution in 1917. Although the Constitutionalists did not favor changes as radical as those proposed by the forces of Zapata and Villa at an earlier convention in 1914, they did include clauses that reserved subsoil mineral rights to the nation, facilitated agrarian reform, permitted labor to organize and to strike, and placed heavy restrictions on the activities of the Catholic church. However, few of these progressive clauses could be implemented immediately because Mexico had to rebuild after the destruction of the revolution and reestablish political stability, a task that took up the entire decade of the 1920s.

Mexico under the PRI

In 1928, former president Alvaro Obregón (1920–24) had the 1917 constitution amended so that he could run for another presidential term.[16] Shortly after winning the presidential race, Obregón was assassinated. A political crisis immediately ensued because Mexico has no vice presidency. With Obregón dead, the most powerful politician in Mexico was the sitting president, Plutarco Elias Calles (1924–28). But Calles could hardly run for reelection, especially given that a reelected president had just been killed. To resolve the crisis, Calles proposed the creation of a national political party that would unite all "revolutionaries" in one political organization that would resolve the problems of political succession. Thus was born the National Revolutionary Party (or PNR), the predecessor to today's PRI. With all revolutionaries united in a single party and agreeing to join forces to support its candidates, a PNR nomination became tantamount to an electoral victory. This scheme proved itself when the PNR candidate, an unknown named Pascual Ortiz Rubio, defeated the well-known philosopher and former secretary of education José Vasconcelos by a margin of 1,948,848 to 110,979 in 1929.[17]

In 1934, General Lázaro Cárdenas became the party's presidential candidate. Cárdenas embarked on a program of extensive land reforms, finally fulfilling the revolutionary goals of Zapata and other agrarian leaders. When Calles objected to this and other progressive reforms, Cárdenas used his authority as president to exile the former leader. Presidentialism, a pattern of executive dominance in the political system that had been firmly established under Díaz and practiced by Obregón and Calles, was thus reestablished in Mexican politics. (For a list of Mexico's presidents, see Table 18.2.)

Cárdenas Fulfills Revolutionary Promises
Cárdenas (1934–40) did more than any other man to build the political regime we have come to describe as uniquely Mexican. In policy terms, Cárdenas engaged in an energetic program of land reform,

Table 18.2 Mexican Postrevolutionary Presidential Administrations

President	Years	Vote (%)
Venustiano Carranza	1917–20	98.1%
Alvaro Obregón	1920–24	95.8
Plutarco Elías Calles	1924–28	84.1
Emilio Portes Gil	1928–29	appointed
Pascual Ortiz Rubio	1929–32	93.6
Abelardo Rodríguez	1932–34	appointed
Lázaro Cárdenas	1934–40	98.2
Manuel Avila Camacho	1940–46	93.9
Miguel Alemán	1946–52	77.9
Adolfo Ruiz Cortines	1952–58	74.3
Adolfo López Mateos	1958–64	90.4
Gustavo Díaz Ordaz	1964–70	88.6
Luis Echeverría	1970–76	85.5
José López Portillo	1976–82	98.7
Miguel de la Madrid	1982–88	74.3
Carlos Salinas de Gortari	1988–94	50.7
Ernesto Zedillo	1994–2000	50.1
Vicente Fox	2000–06	43.4
Felipe Calderón	2006–12	36.7
Enrique Peña Nieto	2012 to present	39.2

Source: Mario Ramírez Rancaño, "Estadísticas electorales: presidenciales," *Revista Mexicana de Sociología* 39, no. 1 (1977), pp. 271–99; Instituto Federal Electoral.

redistributing more land to Mexican peasants than any other president before or since. He had governed the southern state of Michoacán and understood the desire of indigenous communities to have their land returned to them and to be able to return to a communal ownership of that land. As Cárdenas undertook land reform, he thus preferred to distribute land not to individuals, but to villages set up as *ejidos*. To represent the new beneficiaries of land reform, Cárdenas created the *National Peasant Confederation (CNC)*, a peak association of peasant groups.

He also promoted labor organization and militancy. During his presidency, the *Mexican Workers' Federation (CTM)*, a peak association of labor unions, was formed and won substantial wage increases for industrial workers. In 1938, taking advantage of a labor confrontation between petroleum workers and U.S.- and British-owned oil companies, Cárdenas nationalized the oil industry, thereby creating the giant state-owned enterprise Petroleos Mexicanos (PEMEX). The oil expropriation was the defining moment of Mexican economic nationalism, as Mexico stood up against powerful foreign firms and the countries from which they came, especially the United States. The United States, sensing the coming war in Europe, chose not to get into a confrontation with Mexico about the expropriations. Under Cárdenas, then, the PRI became known as the party that struggled for justice for workers and peasants and that protected the national interest by building state-owned enterprises in crucial economic sectors.

Political Institutions
In political terms, Cárdenas had a lasting impact. In 1938, the PNR became the Party of the Mexican Revolution (PRM). More important than the name change, however, was an organizational innovation. Cárdenas organized the PRM into four sectors, one for peasants (organized into the CNC), another for the workers (represented by the CTM), a third for state bureaucrats (organized into the *Federation of Unions of Workers in Service to the State*, or *FSTSE*), and a fourth for the military. This organizational structure made the PRM a *corporatist* institution (see Chapter 8). By incorporating these organizations of peasants, workers, bureaucrats, and the military into the PRM, Cárdenas gave them privileged access to decision makers. At the same time, the incorporation of these groups within the party, and especially of their leaders within the PRM hierarchy, made them vulnerable to co-optation and control. In particular, labor and peasant leaders were co-opted (incorporated or taken over) by the PRM's national leadership (and later by the PRI). They were offered personal political opportunities in return for exercising restraint in their demands on behalf of their constituents.

The PRM's corporatist organization also provided the party with an unparalleled capacity to turn out voters on election day. Local representatives of the CNC served as political bosses in their villages, and turned out rural voters to vote for the ruling party. Labor union leaders were similarly able to convince their membership to vote for the PRM. With so much of Mexico still rural in the 1930s and 1940s (65 percent of the labor force was involved in agriculture in 1940)[18] and millions of Mexicans incorporated into the official labor movement, the ruling party could easily overcome challengers. It demonstrated this capacity in the elections of 1940, 1946, and 1952, when mavericks from the ruling party ran for president at the head of hastily arranged parties, but lost by considerable margins.

Under Cárdenas, the powerful position of the presidency within the political regime became cemented too. He built a presidency that could dominate congress effectively, a pattern known as *presidencialismo*, or presidentialism. The president of the United States, of course, has also had great political power, especially since the time of Franklin Delano Roosevelt, and Americans mark political time by presidential administrations in much the same way as Mexicans do. But in the United States, presidents often find themselves unable to be the "chief legislators" because Congress often refuses to pass the bills sent to it by the White House, sometimes openly defying presidential wishes on important policy issues.

The Mexican congress is charged with the responsibilities of auditing the public accounts of the previous year, approving the budget of the coming fiscal year, and voting on all bills introduced to it by the president or by members of the *Chamber of Deputies* or the *Senate*, the two houses of the bicameral legislature. In the formal rules for making laws established in the Mexican constitution, a bill becomes a law in ways that are similar to the process in the United States. Bills must pass both houses of the congress; they can be approved or vetoed by the president; and if they are vetoed, the veto can be overridden by a two-thirds vote of both houses. However, until the 1990s, the Mexican congress had not rejected a presidential bill since the 1930s.

How can we explain *presidencialismo?* When we consider the incredible advantages that accrued to the PRI because of its having been the incumbent party between 1929 and 2000 (it could take credit for all the benefits of economic development that came to Mexico in those years) and the mobilizational capacity it enjoyed because of its corporatist organization of peasants, workers, and urban popular groups, we should not be surprised that a PRI nomination was equivalent to an appointment to that "elected" position. This quasi-automatic election ensured by the PRI's endorsement applied not just to presidential candidates but also to candidates for congress, governor, state assembly, mayor, or membership on municipal councils. If we then remember that postrevolutionary Mexico has forbidden reelection to the many positions just mentioned, it becomes easier for us to understand why the president has been so powerful.[19]

Politicians cannot develop support bases in constituencies that will return them to office in the way that U.S. politicians can. Each "elected" PRI politician thus had to expect to be looking for a new position, either elected or appointed, within three years (for municipal officers, state assembly members, or federal deputies) or six years (for governors or federal senators). Likewise, because each new president brought a new administration, those appointed to political positions in the bureaucracy knew that they had to plan to be appointed to some new position—probably in another area of the bureaucracy—or nominated for an elected post within six years. Who controlled these appointments and nominations? Ultimately, the president. However,

Lázaro Cárdenas established a presidency in Mexico that could dominate congress effectively, a pattern known as presidentialism.

for younger politicians to gain presidential approval, patrons in their *camarrillas*, or political groups, could provide essential support to indicate that an aspiring politician was worthy of appointment to a lesser elected or appointed position. Hence, clientelism became an essential means of ascent in a system in which political recruitment was dominated at the top by the president.

In this situation, the reasons for congressional subordination to the president become clear. Even though the PRI typically had ample majorities in the congress, which PRI deputy or senator would want to demonstrate opposition to a presidentially initiated bill? What would a vote against a bill proposed by the president accomplish? Since a member of the congress could not be reelected, why would he care about his constituents' reactions to a bill that might not be favorable to their district? Since his career required getting another position within three or six years, why would he risk antagonizing the president by voting against a presidential initiative?

This logic produced an incredible record of legislative accomplishment for Mexican presidents. As mentioned earlier, between the 1930s and the late 1990s, no presidential bill was turned down by the Mexican congress. Opposition members of the congress usually spoke against bills emanating from the presidency, but to little practical effect, especially if the national media paid little attention to their speeches, as was generally true before the 1970s.

Mexico's 1917 constitution also enshrined the concept of the "free municipality": In principle, local governments have had the autonomy to make local laws and policies. But in actual practice, municipalities (the lowest level of government in Mexico) have been subordinate to the federal government in the same way that the congress has been dominated by the president. This local political subordination to the center developed despite the strong regionalism described at the outset of this chapter.

Central government domination of the states can be attributed to three factors. First, the federal government raises by far the greatest proportion of tax revenues, which it then shares with

10 CONDITIONS FOR DEMOCRACY

Explaining Mexican Authoritarianism

Until the 1990s, Mexicans were governed by an authoritarian regime, despite living with a constitution that provided for democratic institutions. Let us briefly review some of the factors discussed in Chapter 7 that can best explain Mexican authoritarianism.

1 Elites Committed to Democracy

When Mexico was debating an electoral reform initiative in 1977, the PRI representative to the Federal Electoral Commission said his party could not support a reform that undermined the two central institutions of postrevolutionary Mexico: the presidency and the "party of the majority," meaning the PRI.[20] This assertion captured the view that the continued rule of their party was more important to the PRI than democracy. The willingness of PRI militants and PRI party leaders to engage in electoral fraud to ensure their party's victories provided further testament to their lack of commitment to democracy.

However, within the PRI political elite there were proponents of democratizing reforms and the rule of law. Many PRI members and leaders wanted to ensure that the party continued to win and thereby to rule Mexico, but they believed it essential that the party win fair and square for its continued rule to be legitimate. The relative moderation of Mexican authoritarianism owed much to this commitment on the part of liberals within the PRI elite.

2 State Institutions

Although Mexico's constitution prescribes a set of democratic institutions that would ensure popular sovereignty, the no reelection clause effectively removed the capacity of the electorate to hold elected officials accountable for their actions. Because the PRI so monopolized the electoral process until 2000 and the president so dominated the PRI, Mexico would be better described as having had *presidential sovereignty* instead of popular sovereignty. *Presidencialismo*, which was encouraged by the no reelection principle and by the PRI's control of the electoral process, explains the absence of democracy in Mexico for most of the past century better than any other factor.

3 National Unity

Revolutionary nationalism, the ideology prevailing in postrevolutionary Mexico, stressed national unity amid the nation's diversity. Much earlier than the United States, Mexico adopted a public policy that officially promoted multiculturalism. Far from being homogeneous, Mexico remains a heterogeneous society even five centuries after the conquest. Indeed, one key element of the

A trip to Mexico City's Museum of Anthropology, the largest in the world, reinforces the view that Mexico is a multicultural society and that multiculturalism is good for the nation. Each surviving indigenous group has its own celebratory exhibit. However, in reality indigenous groups face considerable discrimination.

official postrevolutionary national identity celebrates the heterogeneity of Mexican society. However, closer analysis reveals a bitter truth: Mexico's indigenous communities have been marginalized by the dominant mestizo culture. The areas of the country with high densities of people who speak indigenous languages tended to produce the highest rates of voting for the PRI. Although the Mexican state under the PRI voiced a respect for the nation's multicultural heritage, its policies encouraged the assimilation of Indians into mainstream mestizo culture. Those who chose not to be assimilated were left to the poverty and violence of rural life.

4 National Wealth

In Mexico as in other Latin American countries, the growth of national wealth did not bring democracy in the direct way that many political scientists predicted. Although Mexico has been near the top of rankings of developing countries in income per capita and other measures of wealth, that wealth has been inequitably distributed. Many of the richest Mexicans were PRI supporters over the decades and encouraged the government to control the political activities of the poor.

5 Private Enterprise

Mexico was a market economy throughout the twentieth century, but one in which the state has played a large part as "banker and entrepreneur of last resort."[21] The Mexican state played a crucial role in promoting the development of business by providing subsidized loans, building the infrastructure needed by industry, selling critical manufacturing inputs such as energy at subsidized prices, offering government contracts to preferred businesspeople, and protecting the economy from foreign competition. Important segments of Mexican private enterprise became highly dependent for their business success on good relationships with government officials and the continued rule of the PRI. Thus the business sector did not serve as a counterweight to the authoritarian tendencies of the state. As Mexican development proceeded through the postwar decades, the Mexican state came to directly control larger and larger portions of Mexican enterprise. Many Mexicans owed their very livelihood to the PRI-controlled state, not a situation likely to lead them to support opposition to the PRI.

6 A Middle Class

For many members of the middle class, advancement depended upon the success of the PRI-controlled system, especially those employed by the state. Teachers, for instance, were one of the bulwarks of the PRI's efforts to get out the vote. Others were more critical of the PRI's domination of Mexican politics and criticized the existing political arrangements because of their independence from the state. The middle class has been the support base of the longest-lived of the opposition parties, the PAN, at the head of which Vicente Fox defeated the PRI in 2000. On balance, in Mexico the standard hypothesis that the middle class has been in favor of democracy is supported.

7 Support of the Disadvantaged for Democracy

Whether the members of the Mexican working class or peasantry have been in favor of democracy or not mattered less than whether they were able to support democracy. At times large sectors of the working class sought to break free of the official labor movement. A railroad workers strike in 1958–59 and the growth of an independent union movement in the early 1970s are examples. At other times there were many efforts to create peasant associations independent of the official peasant sector of the PRI. However, the PRI's corporatist organizations for peasants and workers proved very durable. The party was able to co-opt (buy off) the leaders of independent worker and peasant associations, and the government demonstrated a willingness to repress those insurgencies within unions or peasant associations that threatened union leaders who had cozy relationships with the state.

8 Citizen Participation, Civil Society, and a Democratic Political Culture

Early psychoanalytically oriented studies by Mexican intellectuals Samuel Ramos and Octavio Paz (who was later awarded the Nobel Prize for Literature) tended to emphasize the *machismo* of Mexican men and to see a collective sense of national inferiority as a national characteristic. These traits, Ramos and Paz argued, promoted political violence and a desire to dominate others, both inhibiting democratic practices.

In the late 1950s, Mexico became a case study in Gabriel Almond and Sidney Verba's famous *Civic Culture* study (see Chapter 9). Almond and Verba categorized the respondents to their surveys into *parochials*, those who expect nothing from the political system; *subjects*, those who look to government for the outputs they can get from it; and *participants*, those more inclined to be actively involved on the input side of government.[22] Participants would be expected to form the basis of an active civil society and hence to lay the foundations of democracy. However, few participants could be found in Mexico, where about one-quarter of respondents were parochials and two-thirds were subjects. Because few independent organizations could be found in Mexican civil society, one might chalk up that absence to the lack of participant citizens to lead and to join them.

However, the situation may have been more complex than these early studies suggested. So long as people saw the government as a dispenser of individualized benefits via the clientelist networks promoted by the PRI and government agencies, they would not likely organize viable civic organizations or opposition parties to oppose the PRI and the captive organizations it had created (like the official labor and peasant movements). However, perhaps a more fruitful way of explaining Mexicans' "subject" political attitudes is to argue that the structures of government and the official party had been created precisely to encourage individuals to contact elected officials and bureaucratic agencies. The PRI understood that it was cheaper and less politically threatening to provide benefits to individuals (such as the extension of a water line to a petitioner's house or help in obtaining a government job) than to favor large groups of mobilized people who might challenge the PRI's rule. Mexicans who tended to see themselves as subjects instead of participants were simply reacting rationally to the clientelist institutions that had been created in the 1930s and 1940s.[23]

9 Education and Freedom of Information

Studies of Mexican voting behavior have consistently reported a close correlation between education levels and voting for the PRI.[24] In parts of the country where illiteracy has been high, the PRI performed much better than in areas populated by more educated people. Why? The simple answer is that less educated people can be persuaded or coerced to vote *against* their interests more easily than is true of more educated people.

(Continued on next page)

(Continued from previous page)

Perhaps more important, they have been less able to read between the lines for the truth in the esoteric prose that has characterized political reporting in the Mexican press. Thus, they can be strongly urged—or coerced—to vote for PRI candidates by local power holders. Illiterates (who made up 38 percent of the population as late as 1960, and over half the rural population then)[25] received another voting cue: Ballots have included both the name of the candidates' party and the parties' symbols in full color. The PRI's symbol—despite a legal restriction against it—has the same colors as the Mexican flag. So when voting, illiterates were reminded to do their patriotic duty by putting their X over the colors of the flag.

Even the well-educated had to struggle to obtain independent political information and analyses, however, because until the 1970s, the Mexican press censored itself. And until the mid-1990s, television and radio were strongly in the PRI's camp. For years, many articles in newspapers were simply government-written stories placed in the papers in the guise of independent reports. Newspaper reporters often took payoffs from government agencies to place these reports or to write their own favorable articles about those agencies. Newspapers depended on government-placed advertisements to meet their costs and thus they declined to threaten those advertising revenues by writing critically about the government. Broadcast media were even less critical of the government than the print media were. Like the U.S. government, the Mexican government controls broadcast licenses. This situation alone can explain why Mexican television and radio were very favorable to the PRI in their reporting and unwilling to grant much paid advertising time to the opposition parties. On top of that, Mexican television was dominated by Televisa, a broadcast conglomerate that has accounted for as much as 85 percent of the Mexican viewing audience. Over the years Televisa, in essence, exchanged a strongly pro-PRI, pro-government television news orientation for access to new broadcast licenses in Mexico's growing media market. In short, even in the absence of formal censorship, with a comparatively undereducated population and government-manipulated press and mass media, we should not be surprised that competitive democracy was hindered in its development in Mexico.

10 A Favorable International Environment

Porfirio Díaz reputedly said of Mexico's international situation, "Poor Mexico! So far from God and so close to the United States!" For much of Mexico's postrevolutionary era the Mexican government sought to keep the United States at arm's length, but the overpowering influence of the United States proved impossible to avoid. While the U.S. government has often made the promotion of democracy a key plank in its foreign policy platforms, that commitment to democracy has often been subsumed to other national interests. Particularly in view of the already large migration flows across the 2,000-mile U.S.-Mexican border, U.S. foreign policy makers have tended to define the chief U.S. national interest in terms of promoting political stability in Mexico rather than democracy, because instability—which could result from a democratic revolution—would surely lead to massive refugee flows into the United States. The United States has also benefited from the business opportunities created by a succession of Mexican presidents. In short, official U.S. foreign policy did not emphasize promoting democracy in Mexico until quite recently.

At the same time, the huge volume of migration between the two neighbors, most of which was temporary in nature, meant that millions of Mexicans were exposed directly to U.S. culture and the political system. Cultural impacts include Hollywood movies, television, and popular music. Many members of the Mexican political and economic elite have been educated in U.S. universities. In this interchange, the example of the world's oldest democracy has been conveyed to Mexicans of all social classes. Of course that message has not always been uniformly positive. Many Mexicans who come to the United States as undocumented workers learn about racial discrimination and the circumvention of the law rather than about equality before the law. Yet, on balance, the impact of social interactions between the two nations has promoted democracy in Mexico.

In sum, in the latter decades of the twentieth century some factors supported and others undermined the prospects for democracy in Mexico. Eventually, those factors that favored democracy grew stronger. Until they did, a moderate authoritarianism characterized Mexican politics.

---

states and localities. State and local governments thus have had to be careful about their relationship with the federal government, especially with the all-powerful executive, for fear of getting relatively small shares of federal revenues.[26] Second, once the PRI was formed and came to control political recruitment throughout the nation, further political advances for state governors and other aspiring politicians in a state depended on staying in the good political graces of the president. Third, like other

elected officials in Mexico, governors cannot be reelected; thus they have been constrained in the degree to which they could build local political machines that would be support bases for resisting central government demands. In effect, because most or all state governors had higher political ambitions in the PRI, the president had the *de facto* power to appoint and remove them. Thus the power of the Mexican presidency extended beyond the federal government to the states and the municipalities.

Economic Development

The political system that Lázaro Cárdenas built survived long after the policy direction he represented no longer held sway. Presidents coming to power after 1940 were much friendlier to business interests than Cárdenas was. After World War II, Mexico began to implement an economic development strategy centered on **import-substituting industrialization (ISI)**, which substituted domestically produced goods for foreign imports. The country's relatively large and growing population permitted Mexican manufacturers of formerly imported products to have privileged access to a large market of consumers, especially among the middle and working classes of the rapidly growing cities, as long as foreign suppliers were prohibited from selling their goods to Mexico. High tariffs on imported finished goods as well as import licensing and nontariff barriers to trade effectively promoted Mexico's "infant industries" in the postwar decades, and the economy and industrial employment took off. A class of Mexican industrialists with close links to the political elite grew out of the ISI policy. To promote industrial development, the state made large investments in infrastructure, especially around Mexico City, where ISI-oriented industries tended to locate. In addition, the official labor movement, which was tightly associated with the PRI, practiced wage restraint. It advocated a philosophy of economic nationalism, promoting the national interest of industrialization in lieu of Marxist-style class conflict.

The result came to be known as the "Mexican miracle." From the mid-1950s until the mid-1970s, Mexico's economy grew at rates of 6 to 7 percent per year, while inflation remained below 5 percent. Once a largely rural, agricultural nation, Mexico urbanized extremely rapidly in the 50 years between 1940 and 1990. Whereas the country was 22 percent urban in 1940, 72 percent of the population lived in cities by 1990. Government investments modernized the nation's transportation system. Illiteracy, once characteristic of half the population, was nearly eliminated.

Yet the Mexican miracle did not spread its benefits equitably across the population. Because of the emphasis on ISI and the growing urban population, Mexican governments after Cárdenas tended to grant government credit to larger, commercial farmers at the expense of the *ejidatorios* who had been granted land for the community in the agrarian reforms of the 1930s. Continuing poverty among rural villagers coexisted with the income gains of industrialists, the middle classes, and to a lesser extent, organized labor. Meanwhile, new generations of villagers fled their rural poverty, moving to the cities where they lived in the impoverished neighborhoods that mushroomed around Mexico City, Monterrey, Puebla, and other cities.[27] Few of these new urban poor were able to land the jobs protected by the labor movement, so their wages remained low. Many others were unable to land wage-paying jobs at all, becoming itinerant salespeople or domestic workers. Mexico's distribution of income has been among the most inequitable in the world, rivaling that of Brazil, with the richest 20 percent of the population sharing nearly 60 percent of national income, while the poorest half of the society has had to make do with less than 12 percent of the nation's income. The Mexican Gini index is 51.7 (compare to Table 1.2). For the poorer half of Mexican society, the years since 1940 have hardly been miraculous.

Another outlet for the rural poor has been emigration to the United States. Emigration has often been called Mexico's "safety valve," a means for venting the pressures associated with a rate of population growth that has outpaced the growth of jobs. Millions of Mexicans have made the trek to the north over the past half century. In the past, most went with the intention of staying only temporarily, just long enough to earn sufficient money to support a growing family, generate the capital to improve the family's housing back home, or invest in a small business or truck or taxi. Many who worked temporarily in agriculture, construction, or manufacturing jobs in the United States would return home. In recent years, however, Mexicans increasingly have come to consider migration as a permanent solution to their lack of economic opportunity at home. Because most Mexicans have family members or friends from their villages or neighborhoods living in the United States, the other side of the border has come to be regarded as less foreign and less forbidding. Moreover, they can use those family and neighborhood connections to secure employment, which makes it easier for them to consider bringing their families along. The ratio of young women to young men in the migrant pool has increased in recent years, too.

For Mexico, the earnings of migrants to the United States have served as an important source of foreign exchange. It is not surprising that the Mexican government would prefer to see the border remain relatively open. Yet, efforts by President Fox to convince the United States to ease border restrictions on labor migration ran into a wall after the September 11 attacks. Fox was the first Mexican president to openly admit that his nation depends heavily on remittances from Mexicans working in the United States, seeking to make a virtue of migrant labor rather than trying to deny the importance of that labor flow.

The Mexican experience with ISI thus brought mixed results, just as it did for most nations that chose to follow an industrialization strategy largely focused on producing manufactured products for the domestic market. The state, as the "rector" of the economy, promoted industrial development that certainly benefited millions of Mexicans, but there were many unexpected consequences of that industrialization. The cities exploded, the rural poor could not be adequately absorbed into the labor force, income remained maldistributed, and eventually, the state developed a large presence in the economy that threatened the private sector.

ISI had its last stand in Mexico in the 1970s. Activist President Luis Echeverría (1970–76) sought to reintroduce the populist policies of Cárdenas, including new land reforms, greater government spending on social programs, and more state ownership of industry. He thereby provoked a conflict with the private sector, which ended with massive capital flight and the first devaluation of the peso since the 1950s. His handpicked successor and boyhood friend, José López Portillo (1976–82), initially mended relations with the private sector, a move aided by discoveries of large petroleum reserves off Mexico's gulf coast. However, his government also spent billions of dollars (borrowed from Western banks with future oil revenues as collateral) to please nearly all constituencies: businesspeople, the poor, oil and construction workers, and the middle class. When the high oil prices of the late 1970s plummeted in 1981, however, Mexico was faced with a cash flow problem of global proportions. The threat that Mexico would default on its foreign loans in 1982 set off a global debt crisis. Capital flight and another devaluation accompanied the economic calamity, to which López Portillo responded by nationalizing privately owned banks in the last great act of Mexican populism.

Eventually, with the help of the U.S. government, Mexico's foreign debt was restructured. López Portillo's successors, Miguel de la Madrid (1982–88) and Carlos Salinas (1988–94), finally abandoned the ISI strategy of development, opting instead for incorporation into the rapidly globalizing world economy in an attempt to position Mexico as an exporter of manufactured goods, especially to the United States. Mexico's decisions to join the General Agreement on Tariffs and Trade (GATT) and to become a part of NAFTA cemented the redirection of the nation's economic strategy. (In 1995 the GATT was succeeded by the World Trade Organization.) That new strategy, called **neoliberalism**, involved the lowering of the nation's barriers to imports, a reduction in state subsidies for staples (like cooking oil and tortillas) and in expenditures on social welfare, and the privatization of most of the state-owned enterprises accumulated since the 1930s. Foreign investment in Mexico, once discouraged by laws that limited foreign ownership of enterprises to 49 percent of a company's stocks, became welcomed into the country with fewer encumbrances.

Neoliberalism led to a dramatic restructuring of Mexican industry. Much new investment improved the competitiveness of Mexican exporters. Many entrepreneurs made billions of pesos as new opportunities came their way, not least by being able to acquire equity stakes (stock) in newly privatized firms. After nearly a decade of economic depression in the 1980s, Mexico's economy began to grow again under Salinas. However, the adjustments associated with the "lost decade" of the 1980s and the economic restructuring of the 1990s were borne disproportionately by the poor. The end of subsidies for consumer staples hurt the poor much more than it did the middle classes. Bankruptcies by (mostly smaller) firms unable to compete with foreign imports led to worker layoffs. State employees saw their salary increases lag inflation, making their real incomes decline. Overall, real wages may have dropped as much as 41.5 percent between 1983 and 1988.[28] To make up for lost income, families had to send a second or third wage earner into the workforce, or the principal breadwinner had to take on additional income-earning tasks. The size of the informal sector of the economy—jobs where income is not reported, such as itinerant sales (street vendors), housekeeping, and repair work—grew in the 1980s. The financial crisis at the beginning of Ernesto Zedillo's presidency in 1994–95, described in Chapter 11, demonstrated that the restructured Mexican economy remained vulnerable to sudden international capital flows associated with the loss of investor confidence, perhaps even more so than in the 1970s and early 1980s. In the year following that downturn, Mexicans suffered yet one more sustained period of unemployment and job changes. The accumulated economic crises of the last quarter of the twentieth century, coming after the apparent successes of the Mexican miracle, played an enormous role in undermining the legitimacy of the PRI's rule.

Mexico's Protracted Democratization

Although many scholars were impressed with the stability imposed on Mexico by the postrevolutionary PRI elite, the party's monopoly of power ended in 2000. Twenty-first century Mexico differs substantially from the country of the third quarter of the twentieth century. A president from a party other than the PRI sat in the president's chair for a dozen years, and no party commands a majority in either house of congress. Politicians from the PAN and the Democratic Revolutionary Party (PRD) have sat in many governors' chairs. Almost all of Mexico's largest cities and many of its state capitals, including Mexico City, Guadalajara, Monterrey, and Ciudad Juárez, have been headed by PAN or PRD mayors and city councils in recent years. These opposition governments, including PRI state governors when the PAN held the presidency, have challenged centralism.[29] Mexicans of all social backgrounds have joined popular organizations and social movements in the past 30 years, attempting to circumvent the clientelist linkages preferred by the PRI and created by organizations associated with it. The top electoral agency in the country, the Federal Electoral Institute (IFE), gained autonomy from the PRI and the government. Maybe the most spectacular development of all was that a rebellion of indigenous (Indian) people in Chiapas was able to stand up to the regime in the 1990s. The *Zapatistas* in Chiapas were not able to get the PRI government to concede to their demands for local autonomy and a new development strategy, but neither was the PRI government willing to destroy them militarily in the way that it would likely have done a generation ago.

What factors account for these changes in the political system? The main sources of change can be summarized in two categories: the modernization of Mexican society and major political failures by the ruling elite and its party, the PRI.

Modernization Mexico's economic modernization, a process at work since the 1940s, altered the social structure upon which the PRI's hegemony was based. The Mexico of the 1980s, when political change began to accelerate, had become more urban, more educated, and more influenced by the outside world than was the Mexico of the 1930s when Lázaro Cárdenas built the PRI-dominated regime. Consequently, Mexicans in the 1980s were less subject to the control of the PRI's corporatist organizations, more informed about alternatives to the PRI, and more attracted to the democratic practices observed outside Mexico, especially in the United States. A more complex social structure meant that public policy could not please all Mexicans all the time. As economic development proceeded, support for the opposition grew. In more modern parts of the country, especially in the cities, the opposition performed much better than in the past. However, economic modernization cannot by itself explain the sudden fall in the PRI's electoral fortunes in 1988 and thereafter.

Policy and Political Failures Equally important in the erosion of the PRI's dominance was a series of policy and political failures that delegitimated the PRI's rule. The first came in 1968 when a large student movement that began as an objection to government interference in the National Autonomous University (UNAM) developed into a protest against the regime's development strategy. Students and others questioned the government's priorities when it spent millions of dollars hosting the 1968 Summer Olympics in Mexico City while poverty remained widespread throughout the country. A political standoff between students and the government ended tragically when troops fired on a large assembly, killing a still unknown number of protesters. In that event the regime lost the support of the intelligentsia and found its democratic façade torn away.

A second blow to the regime's image came with the debt crisis of the 1980s. The debt crisis revealed that the government had squandered the opportunities presented by the oil boom of the late 1970s. When López Portillo nationalized the banks to halt capital flight, he angered much of the private sector and the middle class, leading them into more vigorous electoral activity in support of the PAN. Miguel de la Madrid's administration chose to respond to the debt crisis with an austerity program that became a liberalization project that promoted the business sector. Salinas accelerated the liberalization program. The pain resulting from austerity and liberalization severely afflicted peasants and workers, the very sectors whose support played such a key role in PRI electoral victories. The sudden change in the development strategy also produced severe divisions within the PRI. In 1987, Cuauhtémoc Cárdenas, the son of the man who had shaped the PRI, defected from the party and declared his candidacy at the head of a union of left-wing parties and groups known as the *National Democratic Front (FDN)*. Mexico's "lost decade of the 1980s," during which economic growth stagnated, contributed significantly to the growing dissatisfaction of many sectors of the society with the government.

Cárdenas's presidential candidacy, the first by a PRI maverick since 1952, ruptured the stability of the hegemonic party system. His success at drawing millions to his campaign rallies and then to vote for him indicated significant disaffection from the ruling elite. To defeat Cárdenas, the PRI and the government had to take extraordinary measures, even by their own standards. The electoral authorities' computer allegedly crashed on the night of the election, the vote tallies of nearly half of the polling places were never reported, and those ballots were subsequently destroyed. Even then, Carlos Salinas received only half the votes. Consequently, he entered office with the legitimacy of his presidency questioned by substantial portions of the Mexican population, the effective leader of a party whose capacity to carry elections had come under question.

Salinas's presidency became a defining era in Mexico's development. Demonstrating his political acumen, Salinas went right to work to restore the legitimacy he had lost in his contested election. He jailed corrupt union bosses who had unofficially supported Cárdenas's candidacy, including leaders of the powerful petroleum workers union. And he accelerated the privatization of state-owned firms and the reduction of Mexico's high barriers to trade. Quickly Salinas became admired at home and abroad for his forceful leadership.

His two most controversial acts were to agree to NAFTA and to reform Article 27 of the constitution. The reform of Article 27 essentially put an end to land reform in Mexico. Land reform had been moribund for many years, the spectacular actions of populist president Echeverría notwithstanding. With this reform, Salinas made it possible for the *ejido* land, which was owned in common by local communities, to pass to private investors. Salinas put an end to ISI and Mexican populism, forcing his country into the new century with a new development model.

Manifestations of Political Change

Aspects of Mexico's transition to democracy include the rise of two parties (PAN and PRD) that have defeated the former ruling party in important elections, the development of a freer press, and the emergence of many popular organizations and social movements. These forces together propelled Mexico into a democratic era in which the PRI's string of victories and its control of governments at all levels came to an end.

Opposition Parties and Electoral Reform The first significant electoral reform came in 1977. It relaxed the rules that had previously restricted the registration of opposition parties. It also reserved one-quarter of the seats (100 of 400) in the Chamber of Deputies for opposition parties, selected on the basis of proportional representation, and instituted a mixed system for elections to the legislature roughly similar to those used in Germany and Japan. The remaining 300 seats are chosen on the basis of single-member districts. Opposition parties were stimulated by this reform and by new rules that lowered the requirements for registration as parties. However, because the barriers to entry for new parties were set quite low, the opposition parties of the left remained divided and small. In 1986, the de la Madrid government doubled the number of deputies chosen by proportional representation to 200 (increasing the Chamber of Deputies to 500 seats at the same time).

Other electoral reforms in the 1990s leveled the playing field for the parties, reducing the advantages held by the PRI as an incumbent party. These included making the agency that oversees elections (the IFE) autonomous from the government and reforming campaign financing so that the opposition parties were not at a severe disadvantage compared to the PRI. Electoral reform contributed to the effective emergence of challengers to the PRI, especially the PRD and the PAN (see Table 18.3).

Democratic Revolutionary Party (PRD) Cuauhtémoc Cárdenas's presidential campaign in 1988 enjoyed the support of a wide range of left-wing parties, some independent

Table 18.3 Recent Elections to the Chamber of Deputies

	PAN		PRI		PRD		OTHERS	
Year	% of Vote	No. of Seats	% of Vote	No. of Seats	% of Vote	No. of Seats	% of Votes	No. of Seats
1991	18%	89	61%	320	8%	41	13%	50
1994	27	119	50	301	17	70	6	10
1997	27	121	39	239	26	125	9	15
2000	41	223	39	209	20	68	0	0
2003	33	153	37	224	19	95	12	28
2006	34	206	29	123	30	158	7	13
2009	30	143	40	237	13	71	17	49
2012	26	114	32	207	18	100	24	79

Notes: In 2000, PAN ran with the Mexican Green Party (PVEM) in the Alliance for Change, with PAN receiving 208 seats and the PVEM 15. The PRD joined with four smaller parties in the Alliance for Mexico, from which the PRD received 40 seats and the other parties 28. In 2003 the PRI and the PVEM ran in coalition in several states. In 2006 the PRI and PVEM formed the Alliance for Mexico coalition; the PRD, the Labor Party (PT), and the Convergence Party ran in coalition as the Coalition for the Good of All.

The percentages of the vote reported in Table 18.3 are the percentages of the total votes received by parties eligible for seats (that is, those receiving more than 2.0 percent of the vote in 1997 and 2000, or 1.5 percent in earlier elections).

Source: Instituto Federal Electoral.

and some that had collaborated with the PRI. These parties initially banded together under the umbrella of the National Democratic Front (FDN). The core of the FDN subsequently changed its name to the **Democratic Revolutionary Party (PRD)**. Although former socialists composed an important contingent of the original PRD at the leadership level, they were gradually overwhelmed by ex-PRI members who defected to the PRD. The PRD has had to deal with a number of internal struggles over ideological and strategic issues as well as personal differences among leaders.

Revolutionary nationalism has motivated most followers of the PRD, but most also recognize that the former policies of economic nationalism and ISI will not lead Mexico to economic prosperity. PRD militants continue to hold very bad feelings toward the PRI because of the 1988 elections and the repression of many party militants in the years that followed, especially in southern states such as Michoacán and Guerrero.

As a party that came together out of other organizations of the left and from the defection of a substantial portion of the left wing of the PRI, the PRD remains faction-ridden. PRD leaders have had to trade off the need to reward those PRD members who have supported them for many years with the desire to attract new PRD members who come from other organizations—both popular organizations and the PRI itself. Squabbles among leaders have been widely reported in the press, contributing little to the party's public image. These internal weaknesses have made the consolidation of the PRD as the party of the left somewhat disappointing to those who saw a bright opportunity in the 1988 *cardenista* campaign.

The PRD's control of the Mexico City government since 1997 has meant the party and its popular mayors have been able to reward supporters and lure potential voters with public spending projects. Spending in the capital has not convinced voters throughout Mexico that the PRD is a credible alternative to either the PAN or the PRI, however. Like the PAN (see below), the PRD is tending in the direction of a catchall party that is anchored on the left, but in catching many former PRI

activists as well as people from many other progressive currents, it has built into its organization much of the historical fractiousness of the Mexican left.

The PRD's most popular politician since Cárdenas faded from the scene has been Andrés Manuel López Obrador, former mayor of Mexico City and twice the PRD's presidential candidate. In 2006 the PAN's Calderón defeated López Obrador by a margin of only 233,831 votes out of almost 41 million cast—a less than 0.6 percent margin (see Table 18.1). López Obrador's legal challenges to the outcome failed when the ruling of Mexico's electoral court produced only very minor changes to the result announced the day after the election. The loser, however, refused to yield, continuing to rally his supporters and proposing to form an alternative government.[30] After a heated standoff, including the occupation of public spaces in Mexico City that lasted until Calderón's inauguration in December 2006, the López Obrador challenge faded from public attention. In 2012 he finished second behind Peña Nieto. He later announced he would leave the PRD.

The National Action Party (PAN) The PAN since its founding has been the main party of legal and gradual reform. The influx of middle-class and business militants such as Vicente Fox into the party in the early 1980s (in reaction to López Portillo's nationalization of the banks) may have made the party seem more stridently opposed to state intervention in the economy than ever before, but the PAN has always stood for constraints on state power. Because of its pro-market orientation and its middle-class base, the PAN's opponents often depict the party as being on the right. Although Fox's voting base crossed the whole ideological spectrum, since the 1980s the PAN's following has become concentrated among two often incompatible segments of Mexican society, social conservatives and supporters of free-market policies.

When the PAN won the gubernatorial races in Baja California and Chihuahua in 1989 and 1992, respectively, Salinas allowed those victories because they allowed him to point to PAN wins as evidence of a political opening to the opposition. Thereafter the party focused on winning local and state races as a way to build party strength, taking several governorships and city halls from 1995 onward.

Indeed, as the PAN advanced electorally, the experience of governing large states and municipalities produced leaders capable of presenting themselves as realistic presidential candidates in the future, perhaps no one more so than Vicente Fox, former governor of Guanajuato and Mexico's president from 2001 to 2006.

PROFILES   Vicente Fox

Vicente Fox was elected president of Mexico in 2000.

Millions of Mexicans will remember July 2, 2000, as the day they brought democracy to their country. On that election day, more Mexicans voted for Vicente Fox of the PAN than voted for Francisco Labastida of the ruling PRI, an outcome that forced the PRI to relinquish power at last. After the polls closed and the television networks broadcast the results of exit polls indicating that—unexpectedly—Fox had won, Mexicans streamed into the streets to celebrate what they regarded as a vote for change. They agreed with Fox's campaign slogan: *¡Ya!* (Enough Already!).

If one had to choose the profile of the ideal candidate to end the PRI's long lock on the presidency, Vicente Fox would come very close to matching it. Tall, handsome, brash, and successful in business, Fox was a perfect candidate for the first Mexican presidential campaign largely waged by television. While hardly a perfect embodiment of the PAN, a party he had been active in only since 1988, Fox represented perhaps the best of the former businessmen who chose to enter politics in the 1980s to oust what they saw as the increasingly corrupt PRI.

Fox was born in 1942, the grandson of an American immigrant of Irish descent and the son of a Spanish-born mother. He was educated at Jesuit schools in Mexico and Wisconsin and attended college at Ibero-American University in Mexico City. He later took an executive education course at Harvard.

Before entering politics, Fox rose through the ranks of Coca-Cola's Mexican and Central American division, eventually becoming its president. However, he declined an offer to take charge of the company's entire Latin American operation, choosing instead to go into a family business in Guanajuato—he and his brother raised vegetables for export and produced shoes. Manuel Clouthier, the party's rabble-rousing 1988

presidential candidate, drew Fox into the PAN along with many other mostly northern businessmen who shared the view that the PAN had to challenge the PRI head-on, with no holds barred. For their more audacious approach to opposition politics, these PAN members became known as the barbarians of the north. They were distrusted by PAN leaders in Mexico City who were more comfortable with an elitist approach to opposition politics, seeing their role as a loyal opposition more than as true contenders for power.

Fox won a seat in the Chamber of Deputies in 1988. In 1994, Fox won the Guanajuato gubernatorial election. As governor, he put his efforts into promoting Guanajuato's agricultural and manufacturing industry in international markets, traveling far and wide to open markets and attract investment capital.

Knowing that the national leadership of his party distrusted him, Fox created an organization called *Amigos de Fox* outside the structure of the PAN. Amigos de Fox represented a major effort to transcend the financial and human limitations of Mexico's opposition parties by building a mass, nonpartisan association dedicated to electing a single politician. Fox sought to court friends among the political elite, too. His campaign team included several Mexican intellectuals, most notably Jorge Castañeda and Adolfo Aguilar Zinser, leftist public intellectuals who saw in Fox an opportunity to defeat the PRI.

Fox led a rollicking campaign. He dressed in boots, jeans, an open-collared shirt, a cowboy hat, and a giant "Fox" belt buckle to emphasize his popular roots and to argue that he had been a working man all his life. Political commentators and his opponents dwelt on what they regarded as the vulgar language Fox used on the stump. Negative campaigning had never been a major element of Mexican electoral politics, but it entered in a massive way in 1999–2000.

More than anything, Fox's message of change—throwing the rascals out—won him the presidency. Governing Mexico proved more difficult for Fox than campaigning, however. During his term of office, Mexico was saddled with a constitutional structure in which a presidential system coexisted with a congress in which no party held a majority. Fox suffered from comparisons with past Mexican presidents who had enjoyed large majorities in that congress. A pattern of policy making in which PRI presidents dictated to congress had become the norm by which presidential performance was measured. Fox's inability to push through major policy initiatives may have looked like presidential failure when it was little more than a reflection of the existing political constraints. Fox's term will not be remembered for policy breakthroughs. Mexicans, however, will remember Fox as the man who ended the PRI's 71-year hold on the presidency.

Although primarily a party of the middle class, the PAN could not have won the gubernatorial races it has won without attracting working-class voters. Hence, since 1988 the PAN has converted itself into a catchall party with a somewhat right-of-center ideology. But this conversion is less the result of changes in ideology than changes in circumstance, principally the rise of the rival PRD.

When he assumed the presidency, Fox appointed many PAN leaders to his cabinet and other key administrative posts. However, because his cabinet selections also included businessmen and leftist intellectuals, Fox's relationship with the party was troubled at times. At the same time, the PAN was regarded as the party in power by most Mexicans; so when they voted in midterm elections in 2003, Mexicans punished the PAN for Fox's inability to achieve the many reforms he had promised when elected three years earlier. The PAN's congressional delegation plunged from 206 members in 2000–03 to 153 for the 2003–06 term, rebounded to 206 for 2006–09, but then declined again to 143 for 2009–12 and 114 for 2012–15, just barely ahead of the PRD's 104.

Other Parties In the past 25 years there have been a number of other opposition parties. Some have contested elections either as members of political alliances with one of the major parties or separately. Mexican electoral rules since 1977 have generally favored the development of small parties. A cynical way to look at this phenomenon (but probably the correct way) is to say that the PRI encouraged the fragmentation of the independent parties of opposition by keeping the barriers to creation of new parties low.[31] Those low barriers tended to encourage the fragmentation of the left in the late 1970s and 1980s, until the emergence of the PRD. The Mexican Green Party (PVEM), a party whose commitment to the environment is questioned by knowledgeable Mexicans, has proven capable of attracting a significant vote share (over 6 percent in 2012) and acting independently in the congress. Other parties have arisen in recent years, most notably Citizens' Movement (*Movimiento Ciudadano*), which began as the Convergence for Democracy in 1999; the New Alliance Party (PANAL), which grew out of the National Union of Education Workers, Latin America's largest trade union, led by Elba Esther Gordillo, a former PRI secretary general; and the Labor Party (*Partido del Trabajo*, PT), which has contested elections since 1991. Together the latter parties take greater than 12 percent of the popular vote in congressional elections.

The Media and Civil Society

The Mexican media traditionally exhibited a prejudice in favor of the PRI and maintained an uncritical attitude toward the close U.S.–Mexican relations. This bias has weakened in some areas within the media in recent years.

The Media and Politics The major private television network, Televisa, which owns major radio stations as well, started with close ties to Miguel Alemán, president from 1946 to 1952). The state owns one of the other major television stations. The uncritical attitude of television news toward the government inhibited public debate about major issues essential to democracy, especially because the majority of Mexicans rely on television and radio for their news. However, campaign finance reforms and new laws mandating that broadcasters provide equal time to all major parties, which took effect before the 1997 midterm elections, weakened some of the excessively pro-government, pro-PRI orientation of the broadcast media. In the 2000 elections the broadcast media finally broke its longstanding practice of favoring the PRI in news coverage. The decision of Televisa and its rival, TV Azteca, to be neutral in their coverage contributed significantly to Fox's successful campaign in 2000.

In contrast to the relatively pro-regime attitudes of broadcasters, the print media have become much more critical of the political system and of specific public policies over the past 30 years. Mexico City and the cities of the north have been especially well served by newspapers that have shown a willingness to criticize the government and in which opposition politicians and intellectuals could add their perspectives to the debate about public policy. Newspapers such as *Unomásuno* and *La Jornada* and magazines such as *Proceso* and *Nexos* gave a voice to the left and permitted investigative journalists to publish articles that revealed government corruption and described the way some critical public decisions were made. The Mexico City daily *Reforma*, launched by a media enterprise that published Monterrey's *El Norte*, has set a new standard for investigative reporting in Mexico. Several critical intellectuals have written regular columns for *Reforma*, *La Jornada*, and *Proceso*, meaning that anti-PRI perspectives got circulated before 2000. However, these newspapers are not the most widely read periodicals in Mexico. Mexico now has a free and critical press, essential to democracy.[32]

Popular Organizations and Civil Society Mexico, like several other Latin American countries, has experienced a surge in popular organizations and social movements, especially in the aftermath of the 1968 student movement. These organizations have varied widely in their size, the issues they address, and the extent to which they try to maintain a distance from the government. In the 1980s, popular movements, most of which had sprung up at the grass roots in poor urban neighborhoods as well as among peasant communities, began to make connections among themselves, thus forming networks of similar groups that started sharing ideas and seeking collective responses to the government. Many of those who have studied such social movements argued that they held more promise for a democratization of Mexican life than the political parties and that the flowering of popular organizations witnessed in the past two decades indicates that many Mexicans increasingly wish to create a more participatory society.[33]

Popular organizations typically begin with very local objectives that are closely related to the material needs of their members, such as clean water or other city services, the regularization of land titles, or the government's response to the 1985 Mexican earthquake. Veterans of the 1968 student movement organized many such organizations, but others have sprung up as the result of local leaders' initiatives. Popular movements often have an explicit commitment to internal democracy. Moreover, in both membership and leadership, popular movements tend to redress the gender imbalance otherwise evident in Mexican public life.

In the 1970s and 1980s, popular movements more heavily emphasized socioeconomic issues, and they sought to avoid being captured by the PRI's corporatist structures. Until the 1988 presidential candidacy of Cárdenas, most of these organizations were explicitly abstentionist in electoral politics, seeing electoral politics as an arena of corruption and a distraction from more important local concerns that would never be affected by electoral politics anyway. In addition to the growth of popular movements concerned primarily with the socioeconomic needs of localities, Mexico has witnessed the emergence of movements more focused on human rights and dedicated to fairer elections and a more democratic regime. These organizations have broader membership and a more national scope than the popular movements just described. Middle-class professionals constitute a far larger share of their membership than in urban popular movements.

Human rights associations began to form in the late 1970s and early 1980s and proliferated in number. A relatively freer print media that was willing to report instances of political corruption, police abuse, and political violence; support from international human rights organizations; and a record of assassinations of Mexican journalists all helped to motivate this movement. The Catholic church and church-based groups have also contributed to the development of human rights associations.

In the 1990s, civic associations came into prominence because of their role (largely self-appointed) in watching over the electoral process. The best known of these was the *Civic Alliance*, a self-described nonpartisan network of organizations dedicated to protecting the right of Mexicans to have a free and fair electoral process. The development of such associations dedicated to promoting more democratic practices in Mexican politics contributed to a less authoritarian political system. In addition, the open sympathy of many such organizations and human rights groups toward the rebels in Chiapas served to constrain government abuses in putting down that rebellion and kept the pressure on the government to find a political solution to the armed resistance there.

Women and Politics The democratization of Mexican politics has been accompanied by a greater inclusion of women in electoral politics and in the organizations of civil society. When the PRI had a near total monopoly on legislative seats and executive appointments, women's issues received relatively little attention in national politics. The personalism of presidential power in the 1970s and 1980s often meant that the women who managed to be appointed to high office were the family members or mistresses of the president, as under José López Portillo.

The opposition's success at gaining congressional seats helped to move onto the national political agenda public policy issues that women's groups valued more highly—such as greater care for victims of sex crimes and more severe penalties for their assailants.

Greater political competition has spurred the parties to present more women candidates for office and to promote more women to important national-level positions. Women rank among the most influential leaders of the PRI and the PRD, and women have served as president or secretary general of those two parties. Amalia García served as PRD president and Rosario Robles as PRD mayor of Mexico City; both have led important factions of their party. Within the PAN, first lady Marta Sahagún de Fox was a powerful figure. The PAN's 2012 presidential candidate was Josefina Vázquez Mota, the first female candidate of a major party.

Having a critical mass of women in the congress and other positions of power seems essential to raising women's issues onto the national agenda. To that end, Mexico passed an electoral reform in 2002 that required all parties to present women in 30 percent of their congressional candidacies. In the 2003 midterm elections, this resulted in an increase of women elected from 16 percent to 23 percent, a figure that rose to 25 percent after the 2009 elections and 37 percent in 2012. Moreover, it appears that the parties, which all complied with the law, did not discriminate against these women candidates by placing them in hard-to-win seats. Thus, women are making progress in gaining access to political office.[34]

Issues in Mexican Politics

Among the many issues salient in contemporary Mexican politics, let's give a close look at economic integration and human rights.

Economic Integration On January 1, 1994, the North American Free Trade Agreement (NAFTA) came into effect, marking the culmination of President Salinas's efforts to shift the Mexican economy away from ISI toward a more outward orientation. With NAFTA, Mexico is bound by a treaty with the United States and Canada to retain its outward orientation. By joining NAFTA, Mexico's political elite made any attempt to reverse the neoliberal economic model much more difficult.

What does NAFTA mean for the Mexican economy? Trade volumes have increased dramatically among the NAFTA countries, more rapidly than their trade with the rest of the world. Direct investment by U.S. firms in Mexico has contributed to trade growth because those firms have located in Mexico specifically to produce goods for export to the United States. However, businesses from Europe and Asia have also sought to get into the Mexican and the NAFTA market by investing there.

Because of the asymmetry in the sizes of the Mexican and the U.S. economies, we should not be surprised that the impact of NAFTA on Mexico has been considerably greater than on the United States. Some U.S. firms have relocated to

Mexico, but they would likely have relocated somewhere else in the world to find lower labor costs, with or without NAFTA. Many Mexicans have suffered job dislocations since NAFTA came into effect; those working in small and medium-size firms have been especially vulnerable to bankruptcies, as have employees of privatized former state-owned firms. Many of these job losses or changes came about in the 1995 economic crisis associated with the peso devaluation of December 1994 (see Chapter 11). Those involved in agriculture, especially peasant producers of corn (maize) and beans, have found it difficult to compete against cheap grain imports from the Midwestern states. Again, to what extent NAFTA has been responsible for causing Mexicans to need to change jobs, as opposed to the overall changes in the economy brought about by Salinas and Zedillo, is not clear. But some scholars have argued that, during its first 10 years, NAFTA failed to create a significant number of jobs in Mexico and had an insignificant effect on job creation in the United States. By contrast, NAFTA's supporters have stressed its achievements.[35]

Also, it is important to recognize that the impact on Mexico of economic downturns in the United States has increased as the result of the greater integration of the two economies. The impact on Mexico of the global financial meltdown that originated in the United States in 2008 was significantly greater than it was on Brazil, for example. In Brazil the economy declined by 0.3 percent in 2009; in Mexico the corresponding figure was 6.0 percent. Mexico has rebounded since then, but the reality is that with fewer important trade partners than Brazil, Mexico is far more vulnerable to the economic policy decisions of the U.S. government and what happens on Wall Street.

Human Rights in Mexico Vicente Fox's government published thousands of pages of government documents that describe how the PRI-led governments of the 1960s and 1970s prosecuted a dirty war against dissidents and guerrillas. Government prosecutors even sought to indict former President Luis Echeverría on charges related to a massacre of students in 1971 and other charges pertaining to the suppression of the 1968 student movement. Fox also signed a transparency law that makes all government information publicly available. Mexicans can now seek to hold former government officials and members of the military accountable for their violations of human rights.

Despite these gains, however, Mexico continues to have an imperfect human rights record. Most notably, years of political corruption have created an attitude of impunity and disregard of the law by the police and local officials. Drug trafficking only exacerbates a situation in which those who seek to investigate the police, local officials, and the lawbreakers they protect must fear for their lives. The Committee to Protect Journalists reports 70 journalists and media workers killed between 1994 and 2012,[36] and attorneys and human rights activists have also been subject to political intimidation and violence. The inability or unwillingness of local police to solve violent crimes, especially against women, raises issues of fundamental human rights as well. In a notorious example, in Ciudad Juárez, the huge border city across from El Paso, Texas, hundreds of women have

been murdered over the past several years without a satisfactory resolution of their cases. Family members and human rights advocates have decried this situation, which puts so many innocent young women's lives at risk.

The widespread violence described at the start of this chapter has enormous consequences for Mexican citizens. While some parts of the country are not affected in major ways by the violence originating in the criminal gangs, thousands of Mexicans have been killed and others feel their freedom of movement has been seriously constrained by the need to avoid armed gangsters. Unfortunately, the police and the army have been accused of arbitrary acts and abuse of prisoners as they have sought to crack down on the narco-traffickers. At the same time, organized crime has been able to censor or force into self-censorship significant parts of the media and has killed or maimed individuals who have turned to the authorities with accusations against them. As a consequence, Freedom House has downgraded Mexico from the free to partly free category in the past two years.[37]

Hypotheses on Democratic Consolidation

Does Mexico have a democratic future? With Vicente Fox's election, most Mexicans had good reasons to think that democracy would be their future. With Enrique Peña Nieto's election, some wonder whether that will remain true. Rather than gaze into a crystal ball, let's review the conditions for democratization from Chapter 7, summarizing the evidence just covered.

Elites President Zedillo demonstrated a commitment to democracy unparalleled among postrevolutionary presidents. He forced the PRI to accept the opposition victory in the 1997 midterm legislative elections, and he made the party introduce primaries for the selection of gubernatorial candidates, giving away some of the meta-constitutional powers of the presidency. He also recognized Vicente Fox's presidential victory in 2000. Very few high-level members of the PRI would prefer to return to the practices of the 1960s. Since its loss in 2000, the PRI has come to behave much more like an ordinary political party, although the loss of government slush funds has made party financing a significant challenge. Zedillo's disinclination to impose his will on the PRI and his PRI successors' inability to do so has meant that in many states and localities, hard-liners in the party have engaged in the old-time practices of intimidation and repression.[38] In general, a weaker central government continues to allow regional and local elites to violate the norms of democracy in their quest to expand their power.

State Institutions The PRI's loss of the Chamber of Deputies majority in the 1997 elections helped to considerably reduce presidential domination of the congress. The PRI's loss of the presidency in 2000, along with the failure of Fox's and Calderón's PAN to gain congressional majorities from 2000 and 2009 has meant that old-fashioned presidentialism is essentially dead. The parties have attempted to build democratic processes within the congress, but they need more time to accomplish that task. So long as reelection is constitutionally proscribed, and a Calderón proposal to allow reelection was defeated in 2012, legislators cannot build legislative careers and serve as powerful committee chairs who can block presidential initiatives in the way that senators can in the United States. However, Mexican federalism has been bolstered by efforts at administrative decentralization and an increase in the revenue sharing that the federal government grants to the states. Similarly, with each of the three major parties governing many states and municipalities, a majority of Mexicans can now imagine alternation in power: They can throw the rascals out if they are angry about public services.

National Unity If anything, Mexico's indigenous people have become more demanding of their rights. They have found more and more members of the intelligentsia and the political elite willing to espouse their causes too. The Chiapas rebellion has played a critical role in bringing these issues to the attention of the wider world, so that indigenous people have international allies to help support their efforts to gain greater autonomy from the state and the PRI.

National Wealth Problems of maldistribution of income continue to cast a shadow over Mexico's path toward democratization. The violent uprisings in Chiapas, Guerrero, and other southern states have their origins in the poverty suffered by millions of Mexicans and in their perception that the neoliberal policies advocated by Salinas, Zedillo, and Fox were intended to make them bear the burden of Mexico's adjustment to globalization, a process they would just as soon not embark upon. Narcotics-trafficking organizations are peopled by poor, striving young men and women who see organized crime as a more effective way to achieve social mobility than working hard in the formal sector of the economy.

Private Enterprise In the past three decades many entrepreneurs moved over to the PAN. The presidential campaign of Vicente Fox, for instance, was funded in part by the organization called Amigos de Fox, in which businesspeople played a key role. These business connections with the PAN contributed to Mexican political pluralism. At the same time, the very wealthy members of the private sector who gained most under Salinas's privatization of the economy demonstrated little concern for political pluralism; rather, when asked by Salinas to make large contributions to the PRI's campaign war chest for the 1994 race, they willingly offered to ante up the funds.[39] Those entrepreneurs who benefited from the privatization of the economy in the 1990s include many PRI supporters.

The Middle Class More than any other group, the Mexican middle class has supported political pluralism with its votes. The PAN is a thoroughly middle-class party, and the left-wing PRD draws many of its supporters from the middle class too. To the extent that the middle class continues to grow, democracy in Mexico should benefit.

Support of the Disadvantaged for Democracy

Although the disadvantaged—the urban poor, the working class, and the peasantry—were controlled by the PRI and its corporatist organizations a generation ago, the socioeconomic changes of the past 20 years have ruptured the PRI's strong control over these social groups. The poor are now able to vote for other parties and to join popular organizations, and they do. But if the clientelism associated with the PRI has declined at the national level, it remains important at the local level and in the relationships that the poor develop with some state agencies. Thus the disadvantaged might favor democracy overall, but their weakness vis-à-vis the government in their everyday lives may mean that their votes can continue to be bought.

Citizen Participation, Civil Society, and Political Culture Mexico now has a much more vibrant civil society, with neighborhood associations, women's groups, and organizations devoted to the promotion of human rights. Mexicans by and large prefer democracy, although politically alienated Mexicans, who have withdrawn from politics or who have never taken an interest in politics, may support an authoritarian regime as quickly as a democratic polity. Overall, however, in the past three decades the forces for democracy at the grass roots have been bolstered.

Education and Freedom of Information Fewer and fewer Mexicans cannot read, so the capacity of democracy's foes to dupe the people is declining from year to year. Information is so much more available and of such high quality today that anyone in Mexico seeking political information would have no difficulty in obtaining it. Of course, Mexicans remain television watchers instead of quality newspaper readers. Even here, however, the past 15 years have brought major improvements in the degree of journalistic integrity and the extent to which critical questions are being posed.

Favorable International Environment Again, the Chiapas rebellion brought much world attention to the progress of democracy in Mexico. The globalization of communications now constrains the Mexican government in its actions toward dissident groups. At election time, the world's television cameras have been pointed on ballot boxes throughout Mexico, which limited the PRI's ability to undertake electoral shenanigans from 1994 onward. The U.S. government is more involved than ever in providing advice to its Mexican counterpart about how to treat its own citizens. However, many human rights activists have suggested that the U.S. government remains too uncritical of the political elite ruling Mexico.

Conclusions Although Mexico faces many significant political and social problems, emerging forces in the past quarter century have enabled it to confront problems directly. Most important, the forces favoring democracy have grown greatly, having seized on the opportunities granted them by government failures to throw the PRI out of power. In view of the factors just reviewed, we can regard Mexico's potential for consolidating a successful democracy as reasonably high. In 2000, Mexico elected a president from a party other than the long-ruling PRI. Millions of Mexicans took the most important step in consolidating democracy by voting the PRI out of the presidency; they recognized the historic character of their collective act. López Obrador's challenge to the 2006 electoral outcome put the integrity of Mexico's electoral institutions into question for a minority of the population, but that challenge faded quickly after Calderón took office. The widespread violence from which Mexico has suffered in the past six years had curtailed civil liberties, a setback for Mexican democracy. However, the return to power of the PRI in the form of President Peña Nieto can be taken as an indication that the Mexican electorate is prepared to turn to various political actors to meet its perceived needs. His assumption of power bears some risks for Mexican democracy given his party's record, but the PRI of today is different from the party of old. It is now a competitive party, not a ruling party. So long as the current government does not limit the capacity of the electorate to vote freely and opposition parties to campaign freely and fairly, voters can always turn the PRI out again. That, of course, is how we recognize a democracy—the capacity of the electorate to choose an alternative team of governors when it sees fit.

BRAZIL

In contrast to the political stability enjoyed by Mexico since its revolution, Brazil's political history in the twentieth century was marked by political instability. Brazil now is governed under the fifth (or perhaps sixth) distinctly different political regime since the Brazilian imperial monarchy fell in 1889. A nation of great promise, whose leaders have aspired to *grandeza*, or greatness, Brazil may be poised to deliver on that promise in the twenty-first century. A nation vast in population, territory, and resources, it has at times seemed nearly ungovernable. No other major country in the world has an income distribution so unequal, and its politics has been characterized by paradoxes and frustrations. However, Brazil is by far the most industrialized

MAP 18.2 Brazil

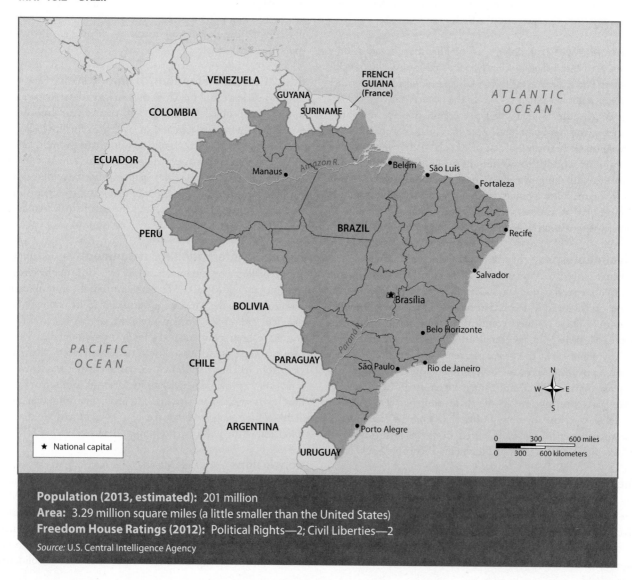

Population (2013, estimated): 201 million
Area: 3.29 million square miles (a little smaller than the United States)
Freedom House Ratings (2012): Political Rights—2; Civil Liberties—2

Source: U.S. Central Intelligence Agency

of the South American countries and has a per capita income near the top in the region. Moreover, under center-left presidents Luiz Inácio "Lula" da Silva (2003–10) and Dilma Rousseff (2011–) Brazil has enjoyed robust economic development, continuing to grow when much of the world economy suffered under the post-2008 economic crisis, leading some pundits to posit that Brazil is set for sustained development.

The Setting

Brazil occupies more than half the land mass of South America. As the largest Portuguese-speaking country in the world, Brazil has 200 million people, making it the world's fifth most populous state. As in Mexico, Brazil's struggle to industrialize led to rapid urbanization in the twentieth century. São Paulo, with almost 20 million inhabitants, rivals Mexico City's size. Its growth has been phenomenal: In 1950, São Paulo did not have 4 million people and was not even Brazil's largest city. (Rio de Janeiro was; its population currently approaches 12 million.)[40] The Amazon basin, the largest tropical rain forest in the world, remains one of the world's last frontiers. Brazilians and many foreigners have scrambled to exploit its richness—lumber, iron ore, hydroelectric power, and an extraordinary diversity of flora and fauna. In short, Brazil clearly has great potential, and it should be easily understandable that Brazilian leaders would seek to realize that potential by making the country a *grande potência*, a great power.

Regionalism Even more than Mexico, Brazil has distinct regions with different political and economic histories. One challenge of any national government is to accommodate these regional differences. Four regions can be identified: the northeast, the southeast, the south, and the Amazon and west. Let's briefly explore their distinct characters.

Sugar production made northeast Brazil the most prosperous region in its eighteenth-century heyday.[41] Sugar production also brought millions of Africans to Brazil in the Atlantic slave trade, creating the multiethnic society Brazil has become (according to the 2000 census, 54 percent of the population is white, 39 percent mulatto—mixed white and black—and 6 percent black).[42] But centuries of sugar cultivation exhausted the soil of the northeast. Combined with cycles of droughts, the decline of the sugar industry has made this Brazil's poorest region, with per capita incomes at the lowest levels in the country.[43] Yet the northeast remains home to 28 percent of Brazil's population.

In the past two centuries, the southeast has emerged as Brazil's most prosperous region. Brazil's major urban centers, including São Paulo, Rio de Janeiro, and Belo Horizonte, are located in the southeast states of São Paulo, Rio de Janeiro, and Minas Gerais,[44] respectively. The foundation for São Paulo's prosperity came from its world-renowned coffee industry, which produced much wealth in the past two centuries. Coffee profits provided the basis for industrial investments in the southeast region, where 42 percent of Brazil's population now lives on 11 percent of the nation's territory.[45] Most of Brazil's industry is located in the southeast, including its large automobile industry. The state of São Paulo is home to about half the nation's industries, where per capita income is about twice the national average.

Brazil's southern states border Uruguay and Argentina,[46] and like those Spanish-speaking nations, Brazil's south is largely agrarian. The climate here is temperate, and in the far south, the topography resembles the pampas of the two neighboring countries. The 14 percent of Brazilians who live in the south enjoy a relatively high standard of living.

The part of Brazil that the rest of the world most readily identifies as a distinct region is the Amazon (Amazonas) and the west.[47] The interest of outsiders has been drawn to the Amazon by concerns about the implications of its development for the world's environment, especially by fears that the greenhouse effect will be exacerbated by excessive clearing of the Amazon rain forest. Many Brazilians have come to share the sense that the Amazon should be saved from the clear-cutting of the forest and from development that would threaten the region's biodiversity and the lives of its indigenous inhabitants. However, in the not-too-distant past the Amazon represented opportunity to Brazilians bent upon economic development and national grandeur. It has been a magnet for northeast peasants and southeast slum dwellers heading for the frontier to break out of their poverty as well as for generals and presidents seeking the resources that could feed Brazil's growing industrial sector with abundant raw materials and cheap sources of energy. This vast region, where only 16 percent of Brazilians live, covers 64 percent of the nation's territory.

A nation of such size and regional variety can be difficult to govern from a central capital, as the experiences of other large nations (Russia, Canada, India, and even the United States) can attest. Yet, without a strong centralized government, such nations tend to fragment when regional political forces strive for autonomy. Brazil's history has reflected the tension between centralism and regional desires to avoid domination by the center. Federalism, or more precisely, the character that federalism will take (the balance between federal power and local prerogatives), thus has been a major theme in Brazilian political development.

Socioeconomic Development Brazil, like Mexico, is usually considered a middle-income country. Its economy grew rapidly in the twentieth century, with industry leading the way. Although Brazil retains a substantial agricultural sector—best known for its coffee, but also the world's leading exporter of beef, poultry, orange juice, and sugar and second in soybean exports—industrial growth has made Brazil one of the most attractive places for foreign investors to locate. Starting in the 1930s, the Brazilian state followed an import-substituting industrialization (ISI) strategy of development, like Mexico. It pursued expansionist fiscal (i.e., tax and spending) policies, protected Brazil's nascent industries against foreign competition (through tariffs and other trade barriers), and made considerable investments in the country's infrastructure (roads, bridges, and the like) and state-owned enterprises. The result was one of the most rapid spurts of economic development in the Third World. In terms of industrial development, Brazil clearly surpasses all its South American neighbors. However, as we shall learn, industrialization may have brought a relatively high per capita income to Brazil, but it has not guaranteed that the proceeds of that development have been fairly distributed.

Associated with rapid industrialization in the twentieth century has been rapid population growth and urbanization. Brazil's population was about 17 million in 1900, but it grew by 10 times in the twentieth century, now reaching nearly 200 million. Brazil includes two of the world's largest metropolises, São Paulo and Rio de Janeiro, plus several other cities whose populations exceed 1 million. At the same time, Brazil retains a large rural society: More than 25 million people live in towns and the countryside. Thus Brazil presents one of the developing world's most complex societies, a society that no political regime can easily govern.

Brazil's Political Development

As in Mexico, we can identify in Brazil a number of distinguishing features of politics that need explaining.

Prominent Features of Brazilian Politics
In the twentieth century, Brazil was subjected to several instances of military intervention in politics. Usually they were of short duration, intended to force the resignation or ouster of an unacceptable president with a view to scheduling new elections. However, the nation was governed for over two decades (1964–85) by the military as an institution, a period that saw the repression of the regime's opponents and an effort to realize Brazil's great power potential.

Brazil, like Mexico, has a history of state intervention in the economy. State ownership of industry, state financing of huge infrastructure and development projects, state-subsidized financing of private industry, and state attempts to regulate the market economy characterized the Brazilian political economy in the last half of the twentieth century. Much of the attention of recent presidents, especially Fernando Henrique Cardoso (1995–2002), was given to reducing this large state role. State corporatism characterized the government's relationship with economic actors, especially labor and business, reflecting the desire of the Brazilian state to control its economy, especially its labor force.

The centrality of the state in politics is manifested in two other political features that Brazil shares with Mexico: clientelism and corruption. Brazil's state bureaucracy has been the preserve of clientelism. Political patrons place their clients in positions in the bureaucracy not because of their merits but to reward them for their political loyalty. These patrons also use their connections in the bureaucracy to reward private-sector supporters with state contracts. The many huge construction projects undertaken by the government have provided especially lucrative bonanzas for well-connected "clients" of the political leadership. Clientelism almost naturally leads to corruption scandals when it becomes known how individuals who have benefited from these patron–client relationships have distorted the public interest, using the public purse to finance their private projects. In the most celebrated recent corruption case, President Fernando Collor de Mello (1990–92) was impeached in 1992 for the embezzlement of public funds—after running for president on a campaign to clean up corruption.

In contrast to the centralism evident in much of Brazil's political life, other forces in the society are antithetical to centralism. For our purposes, the two most important are federalism and the fragmentation of the party system.

Many of Brazil's states have sought autonomy from a federal government that they worry will govern with the interests of other regions in mind. But central government officials concerned about national security worry that granting too much power to the states may threaten national unity and invite a fragmentation of the federal union. Brazil's more authoritarian regimes have strived to promote unity by establishing central controls over the states. Brazil's more democratic regimes, in contrast, have allowed the states to gather more power to themselves at the expense of the central government.

Related to the dispersion of power associated with federalism is the weakness of the party system, even its fragmentation. Brazilian parties, reflecting the personal aspirations of politicians and regional interests, have proven unusually weak. Politicians have demonstrated little party discipline, displaying instead a marked unwillingness to sacrifice their personal interests for their party's national purposes. Quite a few have proven highly fickle, defecting from the parties that supported them for election and switching to other parties after taking their congressional seats. In this regard, the Workers Party of Lula and Rousseff has been an exception, demonstrating party unity and discipline.

In this section we'll explore the historical antecedents of these prominent features of Brazilian politics, highlighting how they emerged and how political reformers have sought to address them. (See Table 18.4 for a list of Brazil's regimes.)

Table 18.4 Brazilian Political Regimes

Date	Regime	Regime Type
1822–89	Empire	Constitutional monarchy
1889–1930	Old Republic	Oligarchical democratic republic
1930–37	Provisional government (Vargas)	Dictatorship
1937–45	Estado Nôvo	Corporatist state
1946–64	Second Republic	Democratic republic
1964–85	Military regime	Military dictatorship
1985–present	New Republic	Democratic republic

Independence and the Empire In contrast to the wars of independence that rocked Spanish America and contributed to nearly a half century of political instability in Mexico, Central America, and most of South America in the first half of the nineteenth century, Brazil's independence from Portugal came peacefully and paved the way for a century of political stability and order. Portugal's royal family fled Lisbon before Napoleon's invasion in 1808, moving to Brazil for the duration of the French occupation. When the king, Dom João VI, returned home after Napoleon's defeat, his son, Dom Pedro I, remained in Brazil. In 1822, Dom Pedro I declared Brazil to be an independent empire. He and his son, Dom Pedro II, ruled the *Brazilian Empire* for 67 years (1822–89).[48]

The monarchy came to an end in 1889 in a military coup backed by coffee planters from São Paulo. Although several issues precipitated the military's actions, the most significant was a conflict between the government and the planters over the abolition of slavery in 1888. With the end of the empire, Brazil became a republic with a presidentialist constitution.

The Old Republic, 1889–1930 The **Old Republic**, as it is now known, was given its birth with the constitution of 1891. Formally democratic, the constitution became subverted by the oligarchy, the small clique of people who actually wielded real power. Thus at best the Old Republic can be considered a limited democracy. Power was divided between the coffee-rich state of São Paulo and the cattle-raising state of Minas Gerais, which included an agreement to rotate the office of the presidency.

That procedure allowed the incumbent president to choose his successor and then enforce his decision on the electorate through a vertically downward chain of pressure. The president's choice was imposed on the state governors and *coroneis*, or local political bosses (the Brazilian equivalents of the Mexican *caciques*). The local bosses' task was to turn out the votes on election day, making sure the president's designated candidate won. *Coronelismo* is a Brazilian variant of clientelism, with local notables (usually landlords) serving as patrons to the less advantaged people in patron–client relationships.[49] Through this process, the southeast region controlled national politics, excluding the south and the northeast from political power. The Old Republic thereby introduced a strong element of federalism into Brazilian politics.

As the success of *coronelismo* implies, the rural underclass could not act independently in politics. Moreover, neither a strong business class nor a large industrial proletariat existed in Brazil at this time. Brazilian politics in the Old Republic was controlled by landowners, the country's economic development driven by the coffee growers' link to the international economy. These rural oligarchs preferred a weak central state. Federalism flourished, with regional governors rather than the central government holding the greater power.

In 1930, the Old Republic faced a crisis. Opposition to the hegemony of the São Paulo–Minas Gerais alliance had been mounting in the states of the northeast and south, particularly in Rio Grande do Sul. A group of young army officers also opposed the southeast's hegemony. These two groups were supported by the small but growing urban business class and by the coffee growers, who were hurt by President Washington Luis's policies. When the president violated the established system of rotation in office by choosing someone from his home state as his successor, the main opposition party led a revolt that threatened to overthrow both the president and his designated successor. Alarmed at the increasing polarization of the political elites, the military stepped in and imposed Getulio Vargas, the leader of the opposition party, the Liberal Alliance, as president.

Vargas and the Estado Nôvo, 1930–1945 The Liberal Alliance favored an early return to constitutional rule, though segments of the military opposed it on the grounds that elections would only return the old elite to power. In 1934, Vargas promulgated a new constitution that included elements of both political liberalism and social reformism. But as the global depression jolted Brazil, sending coffee prices tumbling and derailing the first stages of the country's industrialization, the ruling elites had to face a new constellation of opposing forces.[50]

Vargas's Liberal Alliance and the radical junior officers were quickly superseded by two mass-oriented movements, the neofascist *integralista* movement and the communist-supported National Liberation Alliance (ANL). Vargas manipulated these two oppositions to make the situation appear to be even more polarized. Since the Brazilian military feared communism every bit as much as it disliked "irresponsible" politicians, the officers intervened once again, vesting exclusive civilian authority in Vargas. Armed with military backing, Vargas established a dictatorship and began constructing his corporatist **Estado Nôvo** (**new state**). The period of the *Estado Nôvo* is important for the subsequent development of Brazilian politics because it concentrated power in the central government. In doing so it created three long-lasting effects. First, the corporatist labor legislation of the *Estado Nôvo* gave control of the labor movement to the state, particularly to the minister of labor.[51] This approach provided the government with a means of mobilizing the working class and keeping its demands under control. It deprived

Armed with military backing, Getulio Vargas established a dictatorship and began constructing his corporatist *Estado Nôvo*.

Brazilian workers of the right to organize their own unions, and cut off the outlawed communists from their natural working-class base. Second, the state began to take a strong, relatively interventionist role in the direction of the economy and economic development.[52] And third, the new state's centralization of power marked a major political dividing line for many years to come. From here on, Brazilians would be divided between those who favored an interventionist state with a strong executive and those who wished a return to the politics of the Old Republic, with its weaker executive and its diffusion of power to the states and *coroneis*.

Brazil's involvement in the Second World War on the side of the Western Allies undermined any legitimacy that the dictatorial *Estado Nôvo* might have created for itself by stabilizing social conflict. As the military fought alongside the United States and Britain to preserve the world for democracy, the lack of democracy at home became a source of incongruity. Vargas himself recognized the dilemma and therefore planned for the return of democracy by developing a strong following among the corporatized labor movement. Under his leadership, liberal democracy returned to Brazil with the end of the war. But the real key to the return of democracy lay in the perspectives of the military, who held the ultimate source of coercive power.

The Second Republic, 1946–1964 Brazilian populism emerged with the return of democratic rule.[53] In 1951 Vargas was swept back into power by a populist coalition of urban workers in the Brazilian Workers' Party (PTB) and old-time clientelistic politicians in the misnamed Social Democratic Party (PSD). His opposition was primarily composed of conservatives who favored laissez-faire policies and a weak central state. Vargas initially steered a delicate path between market-oriented orthodoxy and state-centered economic nationalism, but by 1953 had chosen the latter path, a choice revealed in his creation of the state-owned oil company, Petrobras. Vargas also came to depend more and more on his working-class following. However, when Vargas made João Goulart his minister of labor in 1953 to strengthen his support on the left, opposition to his government grew. His chief adversaries were the middle class, which was threatened by inflation, and the thoroughly anti-leftist military, for whom Goulart's pro-worker orientation was an internal security threat.

When the military moved to overthrow Vargas in 1954, he committed suicide. The 1955 elections returned the Workers Party–Social Democratic choice of Juscelino Kubitschek, with Goulart as vice president. Kubitschek continued the populist developmental policies of Vargas, perhaps with even more support from national industrialists than Vargas had received. Brazil's economic development proceeded apace, with economic growth rates reaching 8 to 9 percent annually as foreign investment and foreign loans streamed into Brazil. However, this development exacerbated both inflation and trade balance problems, leading the International Monetary Fund (IMF) to propose a stabilization plan in 1958. This stabilization plan threatened Kubitschek's ability to reach his economic development targets and to preserve his reputation

and political future. Kubitschek rejected the IMF plan in 1959, to the acclaim of Brazilian nationalists.

The 1961 presidential election was a victory for democratic constitutionalism as the left-wing alliance was defeated by Jânio Quadros, the popular governor of São Paulo. Goulart was again elected vice president. However, the apparent gain for democratic legitimacy quickly became a loss when Quadros resigned less than a year after being inaugurated. Goulart was forced to wait 14 months before taking full presidential power, ruling as a president accountable to parliament in the interim.

By the time Goulart assumed the full powers of the presidency, he was faced with a full-blown economic crisis. Inflation was mounting, mobilizing opposition from the working class on the left to the capitalists and upper classes on the right. Balance of payments pressures, reflecting an excess of imports over exports, were inhibiting Brazil's ability to import badly needed industrial goods, thus threatening future economic growth. Furthermore, the working class had gained more autonomy from political control since it was not incorporated into any of the parties.[54] The right favored stabilizing the business climate while the left favored the nationalization of privately owned companies. In this polarized climate, the presence in the presidency of a man who was suspected by the right of leftist sympathies created an unworkable situation. The right would not cooperate with Goulart, so he turned to the left for support.

In fact, Goulart turned so far to the left as to become a serious advocate of land reform. His left turn, however, only confirmed the right's view of him and gave the military a justification to move against him, ostensibly to protect Brazil from communism. In April 1964 the military removed Goulart from power. But rather than arranging new elections as it had after coups in the past, the military settled in to rule as an institution.[55]

Military Rule, 1964–1985 The two decades of military rule in Brazil proved less politically disruptive than did other Latin American military dictatorships, especially when compared with the events that followed Argentina's 1976 coup or the 1973 overthrow of Salvador Allende's socialist regime in Chile by a junta led by General Augusto Pinochet. In those nations the military clamped down severely on the left, "disappearing" thousands of progressive activists or suspected activists, effectively banning civilian politics and the public activities of politicians altogether. In contrast, Brazil's military allowed some democratic institutions to survive the fall of Goulart, although the activities of the congress were greatly restricted and the former political parties were disbanded. Elections continued to be held. Indeed, the military regime made electoral performance an indicator of its legitimacy. However, the military manipulated the electoral rules so as to ensure a government majority in the congress, thereby undermining the legislature's legitimacy.

Although government candidates won congressional majorities in 1966 and 1968, high percentages of blank ballots cast doubt on the popularity of the generals in power. After pro-Kubitschek figures won governorships in Minas Gerais and

Guanabara in 1966, the military issued Institutional Act No. 2, a government decree that abolished the existing parties. Urban guerrilla violence and agitation in the legislature followed the military's failure to carry out a promised liberalization in 1968. These events strengthened the hand of hard-liners in the military and helped to touch off the most repressive stage of the regime (1968–74), marked by the issuance of Institutional Act No. 5, which gave unlimited powers to the president to protect national security.[56] Generally, the military regime strengthened the executive and the central government to the detriment of legislative bodies and the states.

The repression unleashed by Institutional Act No. 5 proved mild by comparison to what the Chilean military did after the 1973 coup and the crimes that the Argentine military perpetrated in its "Dirty War" against "subversion" in the late 1970s. Still, the Brazilian military regime inflicted arbitrary detentions, exile, and torture on its victims. Hundreds disappeared or were killed for their politics. The Brazilian military entrusted its anticommunist crusade to an intelligence agency, the National Intelligence Service (SNI). However, in the campaign against subversion, the SNI and other intelligence agencies proved too autonomous for the comfort of many military leaders who worried that they could no longer control them.[57]

Throughout the military's rule, factional infighting between hard-liners and those military leaders more disposed to an early return to democracy gave the regime's opponents opportunities to push for a liberalization of the political system. By 1974, a major division had appeared between those who wanted to loosen the grips of the state's repression and those who wanted to maintain complete control over society. The more moderate faction prevailed, buoyed in part by fears that the repressive apparatus (the SNI and other internal security agencies) was developing an independence that could eventually allow it to be used against other elements within the military. A decompression process began.

One of the military regime's greatest challenges was legitimating its rule. Because it was not born of a true revolution (though the military called its seizure of power in 1964 by that term) and because it was not disposed to the populist, redistributive politics of social welfare for the poor, the Brazilian military could not generate the popular support that Mexico's postrevolutionary rulers enjoyed. In an effort to simulate legitimacy, the military tried to create a two-party electoral competition that would in some ways mirror Mexico's one-party-dominant regime. A pro-regime party was founded called the National Renovating Alliance, or ARENA. A smaller, weaker opposition party, the Brazilian Democratic Movement (MDB), was also encouraged to form. The idea was that, like Mexico's PRI, ARENA would always win. And like the weak opposition parties in Mexico, the MDB would contest elections but lose.

However, when the regime held very strictly controlled elections in 1974 that severely constrained the opposition, the oppositionist Brazilian Democratic Movement still won. Various efforts to stack the electoral deck in the military's favor after 1974 kept ARENA and its successors in control of congress, but no one was fooled by the blatant rigging of the contest

between regime and opposition. For example, in 1978 the military banned the existing parties (both ARENA and the MDB) in an effort to destroy the MDB before it became too popular. ARENA re-formed as the Democratic Social Party (PDS) while many members of the MDB created the Party of the Brazilian Democratic Movement (PMDB) and returned to their struggle to oust the pro-military party.

In the end, the military's rule created a larger central state presence in Brazilian society, especially in its economy. However, after the spectacular rise in oil prices in the mid-1970s, the pro-growth policies pursued by the military government led it to take on large volumes of foreign debt, which came due in the early 1980s at a time when Brazil could not repay its obligations (just like Mexico). Brazil put off a severe restructuring of its economy for longer than any other major Latin American country, waiting until the mid-1990s, a decade after the military left power, to adopt neoliberal restructuring policies. In the meantime, Brazilian society suffered a decade of hyperinflation.

The military's quest for Brazilian greatness also encouraged it to undertake massive development projects in the Amazon and other parts of Brazil, projects that have proven environmentally disastrous. These projects generally benefited society's "haves" to the detriment of its "have-nots." While the nation's gross domestic product grew immensely during the military's two decades (an average of about 7.5 percent annually),[58] the poor gained little. The military saddled its civilian successors with a development model that had exhausted its potential, enormous foreign debts, a bloated central bureaucracy, environmental crises, and the most unequal income distribution of any large country in the world. One had to ask, as civilians returned to power in the mid-1980s without the coercive force of the military behind them, "Would this society be governable?"

Brazilian Economic Development

One of the central tenets of the military's national security doctrine was the notion that subversion prospered in circumstances in which economic stagnation prevented people from achieving their goals in life. The military thus made the promotion of economic development a high priority in the struggle against communism. Once the military regime had eliminated any evidence of insurrectionary violence in the early 1970s, maintaining healthy economic growth rates became its most important source of legitimacy.

To promote economic development, the Brazilian military embarked on a state-led growth strategy. The state took on large roles both in the overall direction of the economy and in investing public money in specific industries. The military's ambitions for Brazilian grandeur led it to lean toward large projects and those that emphasized high technology. As Peter Evans has argued, this approach meant that Brazilian businesspeople often were unable to make the new investments sought by the military government because they lacked sufficient money— the projects were too big for them—or they lacked access to technology. Hence the Brazilian state encouraged foreign investors to enter some of the higher technology industries such as

10 CONDITIONS FOR DEMOCRACY

Explaining Brazilian Authoritarianism

Why did democracy fail in Brazil? How could the military manage to rule for two decades? These questions have haunted Brazilians and the social scientists who have studied their society. Let's look at the conditions for democracy laid out in Chapter 7 and see if they help us understand Brazil's experience with authoritarianism.

1 **Elites Committed to Democracy**

Various groups with elite status held at best a lukewarm commitment to democracy from the time of the fall of the Old Republic until late into the military regime. Traditional political elites—local elites (the *coroneis*), governors, and political bosses—were willing to work through formally democratic institutions, but they engaged in practices inimical to democracy. Even when operating through political parties and contesting elections, these traditional elites practiced clientelism, regionalism, and personal power.[59] Traditional elites might figure out how to manipulate democratic institutions to promote their interests, but democracy was not their primary goal. In 1964, traditional elites conspired to help bring off the military coup that ousted Goulart.[60]

Military elites also showed at best conditional support for democracy, at worst outright hostility to it. On the one hand, liberals within the military managed to retain constitutional forms during the military dictatorship, including elections and political parties. (Of course, they permitted only the parties they created rather than the preexisting parties.) These *blandos*, as they were called (the soft-liners), also pushed to liberalize the regime after 1974. However, the *blandos* were offset by the *duros* (or hard-liners), those opposed to democracy. In addition, from the late 1950s onward, the Brazilian military adopted a doctrine of national security and development alleging that threats to the nation's security came from insurgencies and other revolutionary challenges to the state. The military regarded civilian politicians as incapable of confronting these internal security threats.[61] Military elites could be indifferent to democracy or hostile to it.

One final elite group whose commitment to democracy has been in question were the technocrats who came to staff the large state bureaucracy, especially in those ministries, agencies, and state-owned enterprises charged with promoting national economic development. Many of these technocrats were trained in engineering programs or in neoclassical economics, disciplines that have emphasized the efficacy of rational planning processes. Guillermo O'Donnell has argued that technocrats tended to consider the messy politics of populism, in which politicians like Goulart or Vargas mobilized the urban masses by promising inflationary spending programs (subsidies for staple goods, cheap public transportation, higher minimum wages, and so on), to be threatening to their capacity to plan and administer the economy. Hence, civilian technocrats—many of whose services were indeed retained by the military after they came to power—and military technocrats preferred to see the masses demobilized so that they could more "rationally" operate the economy.[62]

The foregoing suggests that elites in Brazil were historically lukewarm toward democracy, if not hostile to it. Although many found themselves able to prosper under democratic institutions, they were also able to get along well under authoritarianism. Moreover, some elites considered democracy to be inimical to their interests.

2 **State Institutions**

Brazil's two previous democratic regimes came to their ends in 1930 and 1964 as the result of impasses that emerged among the civilian politicians running those regimes. In the Second Republic, state institutions—the constitutional order—contributed to the political crisis that ended with the military's seizure of power. The Second Republic had a presidential system. Popular candidates could win the presidency even without strong party backing. Unfortunately, Brazil's party system failed to produce reliable majority coalitions for any president. With three major national parties and other regional parties, no single party gained a majority in either house of the bicameral congress. Federalism encouraged politicians to pay close attention to the needs of local constituencies, often leading them to vote against their national parties on important bills. Without majorities to back their reform measures, presidents were tempted to bypass congress by issuing decrees or to engage in popular mobilization to gather support. Goulart's use of popular mobilization to push an intransigent congress into accepting agrarian reform and other populist policies provoked the military to stage its coup in 1964.[63]

3 **National Unity**

Brazil's society is far from ethnically homogeneous. Almost 45 percent of Brazilians can claim some descent from African slaves, and others are descended from native Americans (Indians). On the other hand, in contrast to societies in Eastern Europe and even to some extent the United States, these ethnic or racial differences have had little salience in Brazilian political conflict. Certainly those Brazilians of African heritage are more likely to be among the poor and thus subject to clientelistic control. Myths about "racial democracy" in Brazil have hidden the reality of prejudice, discrimination, and violence against African-Brazilians. However, ethnic differences have not been at the heart of political conflict in Brazil and have not therefore promoted dictatorship.

4 National Wealth

If the hypothesis that higher levels of national wealth tend to promote democracy were to hold true in its simplest form, we would expect Brazil to be democratic before many of its South American neighbors because its national wealth is the greatest on the continent. However, in addition to a high per capita income, Brazil has a highly unequal distribution of income and wealth, the worst among the world's largest nations. Income inequality is manifested in several ways that have implications for democracy.

In the countryside, where as many as a quarter of Brazilians still live, rural poverty and landlessness permits the local bosses, the *coroneis*, to use their economic power and their connections with the state to dominate the lives of peasants and rural workers. Their domination has kept the rural masses from effectively articulating a preference for democracy, perhaps even from realizing that democracy could be an alternative to authoritarian rule. Nor can the rural poor, often in debt to the *coroneis* and fearful of their willingness to use violence against their opponents, create a real alternative to the control of local government by the political machines of the rural bosses.

The millions of urban poor in the seemingly endless *favelas* (slums) surrounding Brazil's cities serve to remind the rich, who live as well as or better than people do in the world's richest nations, of what could become of their privileged status and their material well-being. Associated with inequality are high levels of crime in Brazil's major cities. Consequently, there has been considerable support from the prosperous for hard-line policies that would clamp down on antisocial behaviors resulting from inequality, even if at the expense of civil liberties.

5 Private Enterprise

Brazil has had a sizable private sector even while the state has owned many large firms in important industries. The private sector worried both about the growth of inflation in the years leading up to 1964 and about the populist mobilization of workers and peasants in which Goulart was engaged at the time of the coup.[64] However, Brazilian entrepreneurs came to join the opponents of the military regime in the 1970s after the economic successes of the early years of the military's rule began to wane. Furthermore, the private sector became frustrated with the growth of the state-owned sector of the economy, as businesspeople thought they were being denied opportunities to make investments in profitable industries because of the state's presence.[65] Thus Brazil's business sector has alternately opposed and supported democracy.

6 The Middle Class

Brazil's large middle class consists mainly of the many white-collar employees, self-employed professionals, and small-business owners necessary in an industrial economy. While the middle class might desire the political and personal freedoms associated with democracy, its members seek other political goals as well. Among them are price stability and prosperity. The inflation that

The seemingly endless *favelas* (slums) surrounding Brazil's cities are home to millions of urban poor.

(Continued on next page)

(Continued from previous page)

came to characterize Brazil in the early 1960s brought the middle class into the coalition supporting the coup. During the later 1960s, especially during the years of the economic miracle (1968–74), support for the military regime by the middle class was high because of the prosperity it enjoyed in those years.[66] However, middle-class support for authoritarianism has been as conditional as its support for democracy. When their interests have been adversely affected by authoritarian rule, as for example when the military's crackdowns on dissidents put their children in prison, members of the middle class have advocated democracy. Brazil's economic difficulties in the later 1970s and 1980s also led the middle class to oppose the continuation of military rule.

7 Support of the Disadvantaged for Democracy

The most important point about the support or nonsupport of the disadvantaged for democracy is that, until recently, neither the rural poor nor the urban poor were in a position to act upon a preference for democracy even if they had one. In the later 1950s and early 1960s, the working class had become increasingly politically active under the Brazilian Workers Party (PTB) and President Goulart. But the political mobilization of labor became one of the reasons other groups in society supported the 1964 coup. During much of the military regime, the government sought to use the corporatist labor laws originally written during the *Estado Nôvo* to keep organized labor under control. From 1977 onward, however, a "new unionism" within Brazilian labor played an essential role in opposing the military's continued rule, using strikes to pressure the military to leave power.[67] President Lula da Silva was a leader of the new unionism.

Others among Brazil's poor, especially those organized in grassroots social movements, also opposed military rule. Like the unions, however, these grassroots movements were weak or nonexistent in the early years of the military's rule. When in the later 1970s they were able to act, they came to promote democratization of the regime and an expansion of the definition of who ought to be allowed to participate politically. The non-existence of such organizations in the 1960s, however, made it difficult for the poor to articulate their needs to the state.[68]

8 Citizen Participation, Civil Society, and a Democratic Political Culture

As the previous comments should suggest, during the years of the Second Republic, many elements of Brazilian society were what could be described as semi-loyal to the society's democratic institutions.[69] They found themselves willing to desert the nation's democratic institutions when their interests were not served by democracy. Moreover, a major aspect of Brazilian political culture until recently could be labeled *patrimonialism:* the sense that much of society needs political patrons—local bosses, people with connections to state agencies that can provide material resources, even a state that can dole out projects that benefit specific groups or localities. Patrimonialism is necessary, in this view, because people are themselves unable to participate independently in the political system or are unable to accomplish collective projects on their own. Of course, this patrimonial political culture was much cultivated by the *coroneis*, the state governors, and other traditional political elites who came to power with its backing.

The military, in contrast, simply sought a nonpoliticized society in which people did not turn to politics to address their needs. They preferred that people focus their attention on the exploits of the Brazilian national soccer team—the world's best in the early 1970s—rather than on national political affairs. Given these attitudes held by elite groups and the pervasiveness of low levels of education among the masses, it should come as no surprise that Brazil had little in the way of an active civil society until well into the 1970s, after the military had been in power for over a decade.

9 Education and Freedom of Information

In contrast to the mass media in some of its South American neighbors—for example, Argentina and Chile—but like Mexico, Brazil's mass media have been dominated by television. Television has reached even the many illiterates or semi-literates who populate Brazil's slums, the *favelas*. Brazil's inequalities have historically extended to severe inequalities in education, and the lack of education has led many Brazilians to become trapped in the system of *coronelismo* described earlier in this chapter. Even as late as 1997, 16 percent of Brazilian adults were illiterate and 29 percent of students did not reach the fifth grade. (Mexico had 10 percent illiterate and 14 percent not reaching the fifth grade; Chile had 5 percent illiterate and less than 1 percent failing to reach the fifth grade.)[70] These low levels of educational attainment created a society vulnerable to control by political bosses and easily manipulated by the mass media. Those not subject to the control of political bosses may nevertheless have been constrained in their political choices because the media, especially television, were controlled under military rule and thus disinclined to broadcast the opposition's messages. In short, continuing low levels of education among the poor and the dominance of television among the mass media limited the capacity of Brazilians to formulate and advocate democratic alternatives during the military dictatorship.

---

10 **A Favorable International Environment**

The United States has had much less influence on South American nations than on Mexico or the small countries of the Caribbean and Central America. However, the United States can influence politics even in more distant nations like Brazil through its diplomacy and its foreign economic assistance programs. During Goulart's presidency, the U.S. embassy conspired with anti-Goulart politicians and provided some intelligence assistance to those conspirators as they aided the military in bringing off its coup. The United States then quickly recognized the new military government. U.S. assistance may not have been critical in bringing authoritarianism to Brazil, but the United States did nothing to stop it.

---

automobiles and petrochemicals. Today several of the world's largest automobile firms have sizable operations in Brazil, including Volkswagen, Ford, and General Motors. At the same time, the state's national development bank channeled investment capital to private firms to encourage them to develop other sectors of the economy. Domestic entrepreneurs came to be involved in important joint ventures with foreign firms so as to facilitate the transfer of technology in pharmaceuticals and computers in the 1970s and 1980s.[71] As Evans argues, in some state agencies very able administrators learned the skills necessary to encourage development in specific sectors of the economy.[72]

In other areas of the economy, especially where the state considered investment to be of strategic importance, the state itself became the investor, creating state-owned companies (public enterprises) designed to operate under capitalist logic. Though they were owned by the state, they had to observe the market forces of supply and demand in setting prices, and they were expected to earn profits. The state became a large investor in the steel, petroleum, aluminum, mining, and shipbuilding industries, among others. In essence, the Brazilian military propelled the economy further in the direction of import substitution as opposed to free international trade. It sought to produce not only finished light consumer goods in Brazil but also consumer durables (autos, refrigerators, televisions) as well as intermediate goods (steel, petrochemicals) and capital goods (factory equipment). The essence of this strategy was to make Brazil as economically self-sufficient as possible, reducing its dependence on imports to the lowest feasible levels.

However, the large state investments had their costs. The military's economic strategy encouraged the intensive use of energy, especially oil. But until the advent of recent discoveries, Brazil had few deposits of petroleum, making imports mandatory. The oil crises of the 1970s, which provided a great opportunity for oil-rich Mexico, threatened to wreck the Brazilian economic miracle. When world oil prices shot up in 1974, so did Brazil's oil bill. Rather than discourage consumption and slow the economy, the generals borrowed from international banks. Large infrastructure projects and borrowing to provide finance capital for the national development bank also contributed to the nation's foreign debt, which reached about $85 billion at the beginning of the 1980s.

Thus the Brazilian miracle emphasized an import substitution model that was capital intensive, technology intensive, and energy intensive. Although this model produced high economic growth rates, the nation's dependence on international sources of capital grew. This pattern of development did not begin to meet Brazilian society's needs in terms of jobs, however, a flaw in the development strategy that had unfortunate consequences for income distribution. While Brazilian incomes may have grown significantly *on average* during the military regime, income distribution became so unequal that Brazil now has one of the worst structures of income distribution in the world, with a Gini index of 51.8 (compare that number to the Ginis in Table 1.2). In the nearly 20 years since the end of military rule, elected presidents have pledged to liberalize Brazil's economy. Economic liberalization has come slowly to Brazil, however, even while it remains highly dependent on foreign capital for investment and to finance its government debts. Cutting deficit spending has proven very difficult, especially in a democratic regime in which many politicians and interest groups can effectively veto unpopular spending cuts.

Brazil's New Republic

In January 1985, Tancredo Neves, a leader of the opposition to the military regime, was elected Brazil's first civilian president in over two decades. His election came as a surprise to the military leadership, which had stacked the electoral college with its own supporters. Neves's vice presidential running mate was José Sarney, the leader of the pro-government party, the PDS. On the eve of his inauguration, Neves, a 74-year-old survivor of the Second Republic (1946–64), was hospitalized with an intestinal ailment from which he did not recover. On March 15, 1985, José Sarney assumed the presidency. Although Neves and Sarney had been elected indirectly, their successors would be directly elected by the Brazilian people. Brazil's new constitution, approved in 1988, inaugurated the **New Republic**, a presidentialist, federal republic. (For a list of Brazil's presidents, see Table 18.5.)

Although a democratic regime, the New Republic has not spared Brazil from political strife. Sarney and the new congress were immediately deadlocked over economic stabilization plans during his four-year presidential term. Unable to count on any party to support him in the congress, Sarney engaged in the widespread use of patronage in exchange for support for his economic policies. But patronage politics undermined the policy coherence of his economic stabilization efforts; distributing patronage required federal expenditures at a time when

Table 18.5 Brazilian Presidents Since 1930

Name	Term of Office	Mode of Succession
Getulio Vargas	1930–45	Populist dictator
Eurico Dutra	1946–50	Elected
Getulio Vargas	1951–54	Elected
João Café Filho	1954–55	Assumed office as vice president
Juscelino Kubitschek	1956–61	Elected
Jânio Quadros	1961	Elected
João Goulart	1961–64	Assumed office as vice president
Humberto Castelo Branco	1964–67	Military dictator
Artur Costa e Silva	1967–69	Military dictator
Emilio Garrastazú Médici	1969–74	Military dictator
Ernesto Geisel	1974–79	Military dictator
João Figueiredo	1979–85	Military dictator
José Sarney	1985–90	Indirectly elected while vice president
Fernando Collor de Mello	1990–92	Elected 1989
Itamar Franco	1992–94	Assumed office as vice president
Fernando Henrique Cardoso	1995–2002	Elected 1994; reelected 1998
Luiz Inácio "Lula" da Silva	2003–2010	Elected 2002; reelected 2006
Dilma Rousseff	2011 to present	Elected 2010

economic stabilization dictated that expenditures be curtailed. Hyperinflation resulted, nearing 2,000 percent before Sarney left office.[73]

When direct presidential elections were held in 1989, Fernando Collor de Mello, a former governor of the northeast state of Alagoas with unprecedented skills as a television campaigner, took office on a populist platform of cleaning up corruption in government. Within three years, Collor would be impeached on charges of corruption. A prime example of personalism in politics, Collor had created his own party to campaign for the presidency, but he brought few of his fellow party members into the congress and commanded very little loyalty there. Amid charges of misappropriating $20 million, he resigned in 1992. His successor was the vice president, Itamar Franco, an impulsive politician with little interest in the presidency. Only with the election to the presidency of Fernando Henrique Cardoso in 1994 did Brazil find solid leadership. Lula da Silva entered the presidency in 2003 with the most unified political party in Brazil behind him and a long track record as an advocate of the interests of Brazil's poor and of democracy. Although Lula da Silva found it difficult to implement his reform agenda because of his commitment to fiscal responsibility and due to opposition in congress, he remained a popular president and won reelection in October 2006, despite failing to win a majority of votes on the first ballot. Corruption scandals, which forced several members of Lula's cabinet to resign during his first term, dominated the campaign, but Lula's personal connection to the people of Brazil won him nearly 60 percent of the vote on the second ballot. Lula was able to promote the candidacy of his chief of staff, Dilma Rousseff, to succeed him. She won the presidential election in 2010 and assumed office at the beginning of 2011, Brazil's first woman head of state.

What were the forces that brought democracy's return to Brazil? Do the institutions put in place in the New Republic promote political stability and a capacity to confront the daunting social and economic problems facing the nation? What are the greatest challenges facing Brazil at the beginning of the twenty-first century?

Democratization Democracy came to Brazil only after a long process of political liberalization in which the military regime sought to use democratic institutions to place its allies in positions of power. The opposition fought for democracy on two fronts. The first was the electoral arena, in which an opposition party sought to deny victory to the government's allies. Initially, that party was the Brazilian Democracy Movement (MDB), which later changed its name to the *Party of the Brazilian Democracy Movement (PMDB)*. The second front consisted of nonelectoral arenas, where grassroots organizations and the organized labor movement fought for the democratization of local government and labor relations. Progress in all arenas came slowly, as the military managed to control the transition to civilian rule and to limit progress in the democratization of society. The government of President Ernesto Geisel (1974–79) began a process of decompression in 1974. A civilian (Sarney) became president in 1985, but the first direct elections for the presidency did not take place until 1989, 25 years after the military had seized power.

The most severe repression by the military regime coincided with the period known as the *economic miracle* (1968–74). By 1974, after a successful campaign against armed opponents of its rule, the military could not easily claim that repression was necessary to counter subversion, since the subversives had been killed or imprisoned. Moreover, the campaign against urban and rural guerrillas had already begun to have an impact on those members of the middle class whose family members were accused of subversion. As mentioned earlier, liberal members of the military also had become worried about the growing autonomy of the state intelligence agency in charge of countering subversion.[74]

Seeking to capitalize on the good feelings associated with the economic miracle and to rein in the hard-liners, moderates in the military supported the decompression policy, one element of which involved allowing more open elections for the federal congress and governorships in 1974. To the military's chagrin, the opposition Brazilian Democratic Movement defeated the pro-government ARENA. Having opened the electoral process, the moderates in the military could not easily close it, but they feared losing the congress to the opposition if ARENA did not have some guarantees that would ensure its victories. Thus began a long series of electoral "reforms" intended to forestall a genuine opposition win. Perhaps the most dramatic of these reforms came in 1979 when the ARENA-dominated congress voted to dissolve the existing political parties (ARENA included) and to create new rules for party registration designed to fragment the opposition by making the rules for registration easier than they had been in the past. Civilian supporters of the military formed a new party, the PDS, which continued to hold a majority in the congress, but it became increasingly obvious that it lacked genuine popular support.[75]

As economic problems such as the foreign debt crisis and the increasing restiveness of industrial workers mounted in the late 1970s and early 1980s, the government's efforts to stack the deck electorally proved inadequate. The truth was that the military's social support bases had begun to abandon the regime. The military could forestall the advent of a civilian regime, but it could not legitimize its own rule.

Perhaps the most notable allies to abandon the military's coalition in the mid-1970s were businesspeople in Brazil's private sector. Businesspeople had become dissatisfied by the growth of state-owned enterprises during the miracle, an expansion of the public sector that they saw as coming at the expense of investment opportunities that they would be denied. In 1974–76, entrepreneurs led a campaign against the expansion of the state-owned sector. Businesspeople also had become frustrated by what they saw as excessive bureaucratic autonomy under the military; they preferred the more regular access to decision makers promised by democratic institutions.[76] By the late 1970s, business leaders also felt that the military had mismanaged the economy, undermining one of the military's major justifications for being in power.[77]

Meanwhile, the difficulty of producing progressive change through the channels of representation available during the military's rule led many groups among Brazil's poor to create new organizations independent of the political parties or officially sanctioned labor unions. Although grassroots organizations and the "new labor" movement cannot be credited as the only source of democratization in the 1970s and 1980s, they did pose challenges to the military regime. Grassroots organizations ran the gamut of issue areas, from women's organizations to environmental movements to neighborhood associations. Many became active during the military government because no other political organizations—parties or government agencies—gave adequate attention to their members' needs.

Neighborhood associations, for instance, formed to make demands on state and local governments for the extension of public services: utilities, law and order, roads, and schools. These associations perceived that a transition to democracy would be necessary to get the representation that could bring responses to their demands.[78] The Catholic church, a progressive force in Brazil, supported grassroots groups and provided a critical voice when few others could be found.

The "new union" movement reflected a desire of some segments of the industrial labor force to escape the corporatist organizations of the state-run labor movement. In a wave of strikes begun in 1978–79 by metalworkers led by Lula and eventually extending to many other industries, the new union movement focused attention on the capacity of ordinary people to organize themselves and make demands on the government. The strikes produced only modest gains for workers, and they also demonstrated to the movement's leaders that they needed to create a political organization to focus their efforts at the national level. The *Workers' Party (PT)* was formed after the new law regulating party formation was passed in 1979.[79]

The pressure for democratization increased dramatically in the early 1980s. The most dramatic example of that pressure came in the *Diretas Já* (Direct Elections Now) campaign of 1984. Many opposition politicians, social movements, and labor unions participated in this mass movement, which swept the country. The military resisted the demand for direct

The "new union" movement in Brazil reflected a desire of some segments of the industrial labor force to escape the corporatist organizations of the state-run labor movement. Here in 1978 Luiz Inácio "Lula" da Silva (left), then head of the metalworkers, is shown meeting with Fernando Henrique Cardoso, then a candidate for the Senate. Both went on to become president of Brazil.

elections in 1984, but only after alienating many of its civilian allies, several of whom left the pro-government party to form a party of their own. That new party supported Tancredo Neves, the Brazilian Democracy Movement's candidate in the 1985 indirect elections; together they defeated the military's candidate, thereby ushering out the military regime.

The New Republic and Its Institutions

Brazil's transition to democracy included the writing of a new constitution, completed in 1988. In many of its fundamental elements, the lengthy new constitution drafted by the Constituent Assembly (245 articles) looks much like the constitution of the Second Republic. The military and President Sarney significantly defeated an effort by reformers to introduce a parliamentary regime in Brazil that would have increased the powers of the legislature by giving it an opportunity to vote no-confidence in the executive (including the cabinet officers in charge of the military branches).[80]

The Institutional Structure Roughly patterned on the U.S. Constitution's principle of separation of powers, the New Republic provides for a president who is both head of state and head of government (like the U.S. president). The president is now elected directly by the people.

The bicameral congress consists of the Chamber of Deputies, the lower house with 513 members drawn from the country's 26 states and the Federal District of Brasilia, the national capital, and the Senate, the upper house, which has three representatives from each state and the Federal District (81 total). Members of the Chamber of Deputies serve four-year terms; senators serve eight years. The powers of the two houses are evenly balanced, with both possessing the right to initiate legislation and review the federal budget. Congress may also override presidential vetoes. The Supreme Court has the power of judicial review.

Brazil's federal structure gives ample powers to the governors of the states and the Federal District. Each state and the Federal District also has a unicameral state legislature. County-level governments called *municipios* are the main institutions of local government.

The Electoral System and Its Consequences To most observers, the most notable aspect of relations between the executive and legislative branches is the difficulty that presidents have in putting together majority coalitions for their legislative initiatives. Consequently, Brazilian presidents have found it difficult to accomplish major policy objectives. Weak parties (and the large number of them) contribute to the challenge of governing Brazil.

Many of the ills of Brazil's new democracy can be traced to the electoral system put in place with the new constitution. In elections to the Chamber of Deputies, the representatives are chosen in a complex version of the party-list *proportional representation* system known as the *open list*. The 26 states plus the Federal District serve as the electoral districts. Because the

states vary in size, so do state deputations; some have as few as 6 seats and others as many as 70. Voters can either vote for a party's label or write in the names of individual candidates, whose names do not appear on the ballot itself. The votes received by the party label or by individuals belonging to a party are then totaled. Each party receives a number of seats from that state roughly equivalent to the percentage of the total votes its label and its candidates have garnered. So if the Party of the Brazilian Democracy Movement and its candidates get 35 percent of the vote in São Paulo state, they get roughly 35 percent of that state's total delegation to the Chamber of Deputies.

The actual composition of each party's congressional delegation depends on how many individual write-in votes each candidate receives. The candidates with the greatest number of write-in votes are the ones who tend to get elected. To stand a good chance of winning, therefore, candidates must have name recognition; membership in a particular party might help them, but only marginally. Furthermore, in many states there may be several candidates running under a party's name, thus crowding the field.

How does one gain name recognition? A politician seeking office for the first time would benefit from the help of political patrons who might urge their followers to vote for an individual—for example, a governor or senator might tell his followers to vote for a particular deputy candidate. Once a politician has gained a congressional seat, she must figure out how to reward those who have voted for her; she may, for example, direct public spending toward the localities where her votes have been concentrated or intervene to ask for public jobs for constituents. This system strongly encourages pork-barrel politics and clientelism. Politicians even attempt to focus the government's spending on those specific localities within their states in which they expect to get the most votes, so they can return from Brasilia (the capital) to those localities and claim credit for the spending. Because pork-barrel politics discourages politicians from developing strong ideological identities and because personal name recognition matters more than a party label does at reelection time, politicians have little incentive to be loyal to their parties and the programs they might put forward. Weak parties result from this electoral system.

Weak Parties and an Underdeveloped Party System

Given the incentive structure created by the electoral system, we would expect that political parties have a hard time retaining the loyalty of their elected representatives. As Table 18.6 shows, at the beginning of the New Republic, Brazilian politicians were notorious for switching parties after they were elected. Politicians jumped from party to party as they bargained for political benefits that they could distribute to their supporters. Parties' fortunes thus rose and fell even between elections, without the voters having rejected a party at the ballot box. If a politician was willing to abandon the party that elected him, would we expect him to vote with the party when crucial issues come before the congress? Surely not, if it threatened his reelection chances.

Weak parties cannot be counted on by party leaders or the president to support major policy initiatives. As a consequence,

Table 18.6 Composition of the Brazilian Chamber of Deputies by Party, 1987–90 Term

Party	February 1987	September 1988	January 1990	October 1990
Party of the Brazilian Democracy Movement (PMDB)	305	235	200	153
Party of the Liberal Front (PFL)	134	125	108	103
Democratic Socialist Party (PDS)	37	34	32	35
Brazilian Social Democratic Party (PSDB)	0	48	61	72
Democratic Labor Party (PDT)	26	28	35	43
Brazilian Labor Party (PTB)	19	29	26	32
Workers' Party (PT)	16	16	16	17
Liberal Party (PL)	7	7	19	13
Christian Democratic Party (PDC)	6	13	17	22
Party of National Reconstruction (PRN)	0	0	24	34
Others	9	24	32	43

Source: Adapted from Scott Mainwaring, "Brazil: Weak Parties, Feckless Democracy," in *Building Democratic Institutions: Party Systems in Latin America*, ed. Scott Mainwaring and Timothy R. Scully (Stanford, CA: Stanford University Press, 1995), p. 377.

presidents have had a daunting task before them when they seek to pass legislative bills they consider important: They must constantly cobble together a congressional majority by making deals with groups of legislators or individuals whose votes are essential. Controlling public spending in this context has proven very difficult; legislators expect favors for their votes, usually in the form of budgetary allocations for their home states. That is one reason inflation plagued Brazil for so long. Significantly, public spending was rarely directed toward major efforts to confront poverty or lessen inequality, for the weakness of the party system ensured that programs threatening the privileges of the better-off segment of Brazilian society simply would not pass the congress.[81] Even a party as committed to clean government and democratic processes as the PT was found to have bought votes of legislators from other parties to pass important pieces of legislation. Many of Lula's close advisors, including his chief of staff, resigned over a vote-buying scandal in 2005.

Despite incentives against the formation of strong parties, several parties have emerged that have some durability. Fortunately for Brazil, its politicians no longer exhibit the same degree of fickleness illustrated in Table 18.6, and the party system has become more stable. Not all of Brazil's parties have clear ideologies, but most have something akin to a policy stance on the important issues facing their society. The largest party on the conservative side of the political spectrum has been the *Party of the Liberal Front (PFL)*, now known as the Democrats (*Democratas*). The Democrats can trace their ancestry to the military-backed parties, ARENA and the PDS; the PFL was put together during the 1984–85 transition by PDS members seeking to erase their association with the former military regime. As a party of the right it generally favors reducing the size of the public sector; hence it favors pro-business neoliberal policies. Other parties on the right include the *Brazilian Labor Party (PTB)*, founded by Getulio Vargas's grandniece in the early 1980s, but much more conservative than its namesake during the Second Republic; the *Progressive Party (PP)*, formed in a merger of the Labor Renewal and Social Labor Parties; and several smaller parties. Together these parties of the right or

center-right took about 40 percent of the vote in 1998's Chamber of Deputies race, but only about 20 percent in 2010.

On the other end of the political spectrum, the founders of the *Workers' Party (PT)* conceptualized it as a socialist mass party with democratic operating procedures—a stark contrast to the elite-dominated parties that dot the Brazilian political landscape. Those norms of internal democracy have meant that Lula on two occasions lost when he ran for party president. Yet the PT has been closely identified with Lula, whose charismatic leadership of the metalworkers and then in the movement for democracy won him the following of Brazilian workers, intellectuals, and many others. The PT has successfully incorporated many of Brazil's marginalized groups—homosexuals, blacks, environmentalists, and women, among others. Its leader is now President Rousseff. As a party that strives to promote internal democracy, the PT has not suffered defections to the same extent as other Brazilian parties. It won nearly 17 percent of the congressional vote in 2010.

Other parties on the left have found breaking into the already crowded party system difficult because of the PT's successes. However, a *Green Party (PV)*, a *Brazilian Socialist Party (PSB)*, and two communist parties—the *Communist Party of Brazil (PC do B)* and the *Popular Socialist Party (PPS)*, formerly the Brazilian Communist Party—contend for votes. The *Democratic Labor Party (PDT)*, a populist party founded by Goulart's brother-in-law, Leonel Brizola, himself a former governor of Rio de Janeiro before the military regime, gained about 5 percent of the vote.

In the center and center-left of the party system sit the *Party of the Brazilian Democratic Movement (PMDB)* and Cardoso's *Brazilian Social Democratic Party (PSDB)*. These parties rival the Democrats and the PT in their quest to be the largest party in the nation. Each has drawn as much as 15 to 20 percent of the vote. While they can be placed in the middle of the ideological spectrum, the PMDB and the PSDB include members on both the right and the left. The PSDB itself was founded by dissidents from the PMDB in 1988 who desired a social democratic alternative in Brazil. However, the PSDB followed centrist policies after Cardoso assumed the presidency in 1994 and has drifted rightward. The PMDB, meanwhile, attracted conservative politicians to its ranks in the 1990s but is now part of the coalition supporting Rousseff's government. The PMDB is a catchall party.

Table 18.7 indicates the strength of the most important parties in different electoral settings in the past decade. Note that the largest four parties (PMDB, Democrats, PT, and PSDB) have done especially well in elections where only one candidate stands, namely, gubernatorial and senatorial races. Other parties that cannot swing a whole state or that can only rarely do so can nevertheless win several federal deputy races. Thereby they gain congressional representation, but with that representation they make coalition formation all the more difficult in the lower house. Note too that the number of seats going to other, smaller, usually more local parties has grown in the past couple of elections, suggesting that even if politicians are less fickle than 20 years ago, the electorate is seeking yet more parties to represent them.

The Presidency and the Congress The new constitution gives the president a formidable set of constitutional powers, making the Brazilian presidency on paper among the most powerful in Latin America,[82] with much more sweeping powers than the Mexican presidency. Presidents can veto legislative acts, wholly or partially, and they have exclusive rights to initiate legislation in several important policy areas, including most that deal with public spending. (The congress can override a presidential veto.) The president can also insist that the congress within a 45-day period take up legislation that she deems urgent. However, to rate the Brazilian presidency's powers on the basis of formal constitutional authority alone would be to ignore other key aspects of presidential power. As we learned by considering the Mexican presidency, if the president has sufficient partisan support in the congress, he can accomplish feats not envisioned by the constitution. In the Brazilian case, in contrast, insufficient partisan support in the congress can make it very difficult for the president to accomplish major policy objectives, much as divided government can frustrate U.S. presidents.

To get legislation passed, Brazilian presidents must attempt to hold coalitions together. Since the legislators don't always show party discipline and sometimes even defect from their parties, presidents cannot count on party leaders whipping their members to vote for a presidential initiative. Instead, presidents contribute to the clientelist politics described earlier. They control federal funds and federal jobs, both of which are coveted by members of congress seeking to satisfy their constituents. Old-fashioned horse trading may be essential to pass laws considered key to a president's agenda. It bears repeating that pork-barrel politics contributes to Brazil's out-of-control federal spending.

Even then, presidents have found it difficult to accomplish major objectives. Scott Mainwaring demonstrated that in nine policy areas critical to economic stabilization and state reform in the 1985 to 1994 period (including the privatization of state monopolies, cutting public-sector employment, passing new tax bills, even collecting debts owed to the federal government by private business), Presidents Sarney, Collor, and Franco ran into the opposition of members of congress who were protecting constituents or supporters and made no progress in those pressing policy areas.[83] Brazil's underdeveloped party system contributes to a legislature more inclined to protect the status quo and vested interests than to promote change or to address major social problems. Presidents are often forced to rule as much as possible by emergency measures, which allow the president to make laws for 30 days, after which the congress can either pass or reject the new legislation. Without those measures, presidents would find governing nearly impossible.

Table 18.7 Governors, Senators, and Deputies Elected in 1994, 1998, 2002, 2006, and 2010

Party	GOVERNORS					SENATE					CHAMBER OF DEPUTIES				
	1994	1998	2002	2006	2010	1994	1998	2002	2006	2010	1994	1998	2002	2006	2010
Party of the Brazilian Democratic Movement (PMDB)	9	6	5	7	5	22	26	19	15	19	107	83	74	89	79
Democrats (formerly the PFL)	2	6	4	1	1	18	20	19	18	6	89	105	85	65	43
Brazilian Social Democratic Party (PSDB)	6	7	7	6	8	11	16	11	15	11	62	99	71	65	53
Brazilian Progressive Party (PP) (PPB)	3	2	—	1	—	6	3	1	1	4	52	60	48	42	41
Workers' Party (PT)	2	3	3	5	5	5	7	14	11	15	49	58	91	83	88
Democratic Labor Party (PDT)	2	1	1	2	—	6	4	5	5	4	34	25	21	24	28
Brazilian Labor Party (PTB)	1	—	—	—	—	5	1	3	4	6	31	31	26	22	21
Republic Party (PR, formerly Liberal Party, PL)	—	—	1	—	—	1	—	3	3	4	13	12	27	23	41
Others	2	2	6	5	8	7	4	6	9	12	76	40	70	100	119
Total	27	27	27	27	27	81	81	81	81	81	513	513	513	513	513

Source: Maria D'Alva G. Kinzo and Simone Rodrigues da Silva, "Politics in Brazil: Cardoso's Government and the 1998 Re-election," *Government and Opposition* 34, no. 2 (Spring 1999), p. 259; Tribunal Superior Eleitoral.

PROFILES Dilma Rousseff

Released in 1972, Rousseff had to change universities to continue her education. She completed an economics degree in 1977 at Rio Grande do Sul Federal University. The year before she had given birth to her only child, Paula Rousseff Araújo. Her relationship with Carlos Araújo continued until their divorce in 2000. Rousseff returned to politics through the influential Institute of Social and Political Studies (IEPES), a think tank associated with the Movement for Brazilian Democracy (MDB). When the military regime forced the political parties to regroup in 1978, Rousseff helped to found the Democratic Labor Party (PDT). As a PDT politician she became Porto Alegre municipal treasurer, then the Rio Grande do Sul state energy minister, and finally minister of energy in Lula's first term. As energy minister she sought to extend electrical service to all Brazilians.

In 2005, in the wake of a corruption scandal involving high-ranking members of his administration, Lula appointed Rousseff his chief of staff. She became a Workers' Party (PT) member at that time. Lula reported being impressed with Rousseff's management of the energy ministry, a role that included serving as the chief executive of the huge state energy company, Petrobras. Term limits prevented Lula from running for a third term as president, and he prevailed on Rousseff to become the PT candidate. As Table 18.8 shows, she won the presidency easily.

Said to be somewhat more ideologically rigid than the pragmatic Lula, Rousseff has also been more comfortable leading an activist state. She has advocated an expansionist economic policy to encourage further Brazilian growth in the midst of the global economic stagnation associated with the 2008 financial meltdown and the sovereign debt crisis. In her short time in office Brazil has also extended affirmative action to university admissions and begun a significant infrastructure upgrade to roads and railroads. Having ducked the worst effects of the world economy's downturn, Dilma Rousseff is poised to lead Brazil further toward the *grandeza* long sought by national leaders.

Brazil's first female president, Dilma Vana Rousseff was born in Belo Horizonte 1947 to a Bulgarian immigrant lawyer and his Brazilian wife. Educated in a boarding school run by nuns and then a public high school, Rousseff became involved in politics in the late 1960s during the most repressive phase of the military regime. She married Cláudio Galeno Linhares, a leftist militant, in 1968. Rousseff became involved in an armed insurgent movement, split up with Galeno, and married Carlos Franklin Paixão de Araújo. Roussef and Araújo were arrested in 1970. Rousseff was imprisoned for three years, during which time she was tortured.

Table 18.8 Brazilian Presidential Elections, 2002, 2006, and 2010

2002			2006			2010		
Candidate	Party	%	Candidate	Party	%	Candidate	Party	%
First Round								
Luiz Inácio "Lula" da Silva	PT	46.4%	Luiz Inácio "Lula" da Silva	PT	48.6%	Dilma Rousseff	PT	46.9%
José Serra	PSDB	23.2	Geraldo Alckmin	PSDB	41.6	José Serra	PSDB	32.6
Anthony Garotinho	PSB	17.9	Heloísa Helena	PSOL	6.8	Marina Silva	PV	19.3
Ciro Gomes	PPS	12.0	Cristovam Buarque	PDT	2.6	Plínio de Arruda Sampaio	PSOL	0.9
Others		0.5	Others		0.4	Others		0.3
Second Round								
Luiz Inácio "Lula" da Silva	PT	61.3	Luiz Inácio "Lula" da Silva	PT	60.8	Dilma Rousseff	PT	56.1
José Serra	PSDB	38.7	Geraldo Alckmin	PSDB	39.2	José Serra	PSDB	43.9

Issues in Brazilian Politics

A Robust Federalism[84] That Brazil's congress overrepresents small states, most of which are rural states from the northeast and the Amazon, exacerbates a set of structural problems in the Brazilian political system. Those northeastern and Amazonian states depend more on distributions from the federal government than do the southeastern and southern states. Their representatives have parlayed the president's need for their votes in congress into continuing public spending in their states and localities. Such processes reinforce the sense held by other Brazilians that corruption and backwardness characterize the politics of the north and the northeast.

The 1988 constitution grants significant public funds to state and local governments, but it does not impose greater expectations on those subnational governments for spending on education, health, or infrastructure, the typical responsibilities of subnational authorities. Indeed, about half the nation's tax revenues collected by the federal government is returned to states and municipalities with no mandates about how that money should be spent. Governors and mayors thus have resources they can distribute to help their political clients, including members of the congress elected from their states. Consequently, governors (who can now be reelected) and mayors can use their influence over members of the congress to see that their states are favored by federal laws or that their states are recipients of federal spending in infrastructure projects and the like. Development projects in the northeast and infrastructure projects in the Amazon have thus been well supported in the congress.

The enormous influence of the states was vividly evident in 1998, when the governor of Minas Gerais—Brazil's former president, Itamar Franco—declared a moratorium on his state's $15.3 billion debt to the federal treasury. The unilateral announcement provoked a budgetary crisis that frightened foreign investors and threatened to derail President Cardoso's austerity policies, which were central to retaining the confidence of the IMF. It took all of Cardoso's political skills to resolve the issue.

Poverty and Inequality Given that Brazil has one of the worst distributions of income in the world, we would expect a Workers' Party government to try to address income inequality. Lula followed the fiscally conservative policies of his predecessor, Cardoso, to encourage investment. However, he also promised to alleviate the extreme poverty that afflicted an estimated 50 million Brazilians when he took office, and to implement his "zero hunger" program, which sought to eliminate widespread malnutrition. "If, by the end of my term, all Brazilians are able to eat breakfast, lunch, and dinner," Lula said at his first inauguration, "I will have fulfilled my life's mission."

One of Lula's most effective initiatives was a Family Fund (*Bolsa Familia*) program that provides government assistance to nearly a fifth of Brazil's families, which replaced the failed zero hunger plan. Bolsa Familia, which was partly based on a similar effort in Mexico, is a conditional cash transfer program—poor families must demonstrate that their children are enrolled in school and that they have been vaccinated in order to receive cash payments. About 50 million Brazilians eventually became enrolled in Bolsa Familia, the largest program of its kind in the world. Lula also succeeded in raising the minimum wage by 25 percent.[85] Bolsa Familia recognizes that to truly address income maldistribution requires, among other things, a commitment to rebuilding Brazil's primary and secondary educational systems. According to the World Bank, two-thirds of the glaring income gap between rich and poor in Brazil is caused by an education gap. Only a third of Brazilian teenagers attend high school, compared to 58 percent in Mexico and 98 percent in South Korea. President Rousseff has continued Bolsa Familia and sought to expand access to day care so that women are able to earn income for their families.

Women and Politics Women's movements emerged with the reduction of political restrictions in the late 1970s and early 1980s. Women demanded greater political representation and policy initiatives, such as day care and family planning, that would improve their lives. Of course, in many policy areas, such as abortion rights, feminists run up against opposition from the powerful Catholic church. And the New Republic creates many opportunities for powerful political actors to block policy initiatives.

Overall, Brazil has perhaps the most vibrant feminist movement in Latin America. In addition, during the New Republic the feminist movement has worked with elected officials to pass some of the most advanced measures to promote women's rights.[86] However, women's representation in politics has been marginal in Brazil. Although women have had the vote since 1933, few female candidates have been elected to important positions, President Rousseff notwithstanding. Currently out of 26 governors two are women. President Franco had three women in his cabinet, but his successor, Cardoso, appointed only one. When Rousseff appointed 10 women to her cabinet (of 38 members), it more than tripled the number from Lula's outgoing cabinet. In 1996 Congress introduced a quota of 20 percent for women candidates for municipal office and then extended the system to congressional offices in 1998.[87] As a result, the number of female legislators has grown. Yet nomination does not equate to election, and in 2002 only 6 percent of elected federal deputies and only 7 percent of senators and governors were women.[88] Women won 8.6 percent of the Chamber of Deputies seats in 2006 and 9.6 percent in 2010.

Human Rights in Brazil Democracy does not guarantee that human rights will be respected. Even though repression of dissidents by the central government went out along with Brazil's military regime, many human rights problems continue in Brazil. A weak central government, the persistence of local political bosses, and highly unequal economic relationships have resulted in forced labor, police brutality, inhumane prison conditions, and extrajudicial killings of activists. Police abuse of detainees, homeless people, and other marginalized persons is a particular shortcoming in Brazil's human rights record.

The experience of the Landless Workers Movement (MST) provides a very clear example of human rights abuse in Brazil. The MST is the largest social movement in Latin America; it has struggled for land reform for more than a decade. When its legal efforts to obtain land for the millions of landless rural workers fail, the MST sometimes seizes some of the thousands of acres that large landowners leave fallow. Because of its advocacy of land reform and because it is willing to engage in direct action to address its members' needs, the MST is much reviled by the thousands of large absentee landowners who own so much of Brazil's territory and by their political allies, powerful local *coroneis*.

Despite the size of its membership and the hundreds of lawyers and human rights workers who struggle on the MST's behalf, the MST has been subject to severe repression. More than 200 activists and peasants associated with the MST have been murdered in the past decade and a half. Rarely are the assassins—often moonlighting policemen—or their employers brought to justice in local courts, and even when they are, local *coroneis* exert such influence over members of juries that convictions are uncommon. Brazilians and international human rights organizations such as Amnesty International and Human Rights Watch continue to pressure for federal legislation that would make it easier to prosecute assassins and other human rights abusers in settings beyond these rigged local courts. In the meantime, though, being an advocate of the poor and the landless can be a very dangerous vocation in Latin America's largest democracy.

Hypotheses on Democracy and Democratization

Can Brazil's New Republic survive the challenges it faces? Does democracy have a future in South America's giant? Again, let's review our conditions for democratization to see if they suggest a bright or a bleak future for Brazil.

Elites Committed to Democracy

Most important, Brazil's military has apparently withdrawn from politics. If the New Republic has had a notable success, it has been in returning the military to the barracks.[89] Since the transition to democracy, most elite groups seem to support the New Republic, perhaps because the military's rule has been discredited in Brazil as in most of the hemisphere. But the depth of elite commitment to democracy has yet to be tested.

State Institutions

The institutions of the New Republic provide powerful groups many points of access to defeat measures that threaten their interests. This means that measures designed to reform the economy so as to address the needs of the poor and redistribute income can be difficulty to legislate. A legislature composed of weak and undisciplined parties whose members seek all the patronage they can acquire, and a federal system in which states and governors can use their power to defeat measures in the national congress or resist implementing them at the state and local levels, have made socioeconomic reform difficult to accomplish. A democratic process may be in place in Brazil, but it often fails to produce policies that reflect the interests of the majority of society.

Paradoxically, some political scientists argue that the fact that Brazil's political institutions allow conservative groups to veto many reform measures makes those same groups more prone to support democracy. Hence, Brazilian businesses, landowners, and locally powerful figures have become much less inclined to advocate nondemocratic acts, such as military coups or other threats against those in office. So Brazil's democracy may be stable even if the quality of democracy could be better.[90]

National Unity

Brazil's society is not homogeneous, but as we noted earlier, as yet the racial diversity of the nation has not promoted political conflict on racial lines. However, African-Brazilians and those of indigenous heritage are increasingly active politically, demanding that their voices be heard too. This new political activism regarding racially or ethnically based issues should be welcomed as one way in which Brazil's new democracy is responding to citizens' concerns.

National Wealth

Income distribution remains severely unequal in Brazil. While the opponents of income redistribution learned how to defeat redistributive measures through the institutions of democracy, the successes of the da Silva and Rousseff governments with the Bolsa Familia program are encouraging. Millions of Brazilians have risen from poverty in the past decade.[91]

Private Enterprise

The Brazilian state has divested itself of considerable portions of the public sector since the mid-1990s. In part because of the neoliberal policies followed by the government, business owners do not feel threatened by democratic institutions at this time. Having lived through a military regime that enhanced the public sector of the economy, perhaps at their expense, business has little desire to return to military rule.

Middle Class

Brazil's middle class seems solidly supportive of democracy.

Support of the Disadvantaged

Brazil's working class has become the voter base of one of its most important, prodemocratic parties, the Workers Party (PT). The PT has expanded its voter base to others among the urban poor. But poverty is a festering wound in Brazilian cities, where millions live in overcrowded shantytowns. Many of Brazil's poor are prey to criminal gangs, drugs, and flagrant police brutality.

Rural poverty and political marginalization are also endemic. Land remains heavily overconcentrated in the hands of wealthy farmers; the poorest 30 percent of Brazilians share just 2 percent of the country's arable land, and nearly 5 million people have no land at all. As Latin America's largest social movement, the MST has pushed for land reform and on many occasions has taken matters into its own hands, seizing properties that it regards as underused. These actions have both positive and negative implications for democracy. On the one hand, many applaud the activism of the MST as representing a clear example of the underclass taking political action to rectify perceived injustices. On the other hand, direct action of the type followed by the MST is often illegal, forcing the authorities to respond to such acts by *post facto* land redistribution laws or decrees. In addition, the direct action of the MST threatens landowners, who sometimes still respond violently, promoting a breakdown of rule of law. Though the constitution reserves 11 percent of Brazil's land for indigenous Indians, numbering about a quarter million, recent laws have facilitated encroachment on Indian territory for lumbering and mining purposes. Illegal encroachments spark periodic violence with native populations.[92] The rural poor have few allies in congress, while many remain controlled in clientelist networks run by local political bosses. Despite these enormous problems, however, a nondemocratic revolutionary movement representing the poor is not in evidence in contemporary Brazil, and the success of Bolsa Familia has won over more poor people to the side of democracy.

Civil Society and Political Culture Like Mexicans, many Brazilians remain skeptical about whether democracy can make a difference in their lives. Many doubt that it solves society's problems.[93] However, Brazilian civil society has much more vibrancy than it did a quarter century ago. Many social movements have organized the poor and the middle classes to promote the interests of women, indigenous peoples, and local communities and to save the environment. This more active civil society would not as easily succumb to military rule as Brazil did in 1964.

Education and Freedom of Information Although educational levels have improved in the last quarter century, and although there are many more sources of information in today's Brazil, in these dimensions of Brazilian society all is not strongly supportive of democracy. On the one hand, the news media have played an important role in investigating allegations of political corruption, thereby demonstrating a degree of journalistic independence critical for keeping politicians somewhat honest. On the other hand, the Brazilian reliance on television for news and the popularity of *telenovelas* (soap operas) among the viewing public does not promise to promote political sophistication in the mass public.

Favorable International Environment Since 1964, and especially with the end of the Cold War, the likelihood that the United States and other major powers would support a military coup in Brazil has declined drastically.

Conclusions Despite the institutional weaknesses in the New Republic that continue to encourage clientelism and the challenges that poverty and maldistribution of income pose to the regime's legitimacy, democracy is on a much firmer footing in today's Brazil than it ever has been. Absent colossal policy failures, we can expect Brazil to remain Latin America's largest and in many ways most vibrant democracy for the foreseeable future.

Conclusion

Significant forces are at work in Brazil and Mexico to promote democracy's consolidation. Certainly each nation continues to confront serious social problems and an increasingly challenging international economic environment. However, these societies' relatively recent experiences with less than democratic regimes—a civilian authoritarian regime in Mexico, military rule in Brazil—have led both elites and mass publics to prefer democratic politics. Popular sovereignty is evident in the large numbers of people who have voted in elections that, in recent years, have swept popular opposition figures such as Vicente Fox and Lula da Silva to the pinnacle of power in their respective countries. It is evident as well in the growth of civil society in both Mexico and Brazil. Legal guarantees of political and civil rights and liberties are also becoming stronger in the two countries, a far cry from the flagrant abuses of these rights that were defining characteristics of Mexico's former one-party regime and Brazil's military governments, although Mexico's inability to quell the violence related to narcotics trafficking threatens the rights and lives of thousands of its citizens. And elected officials in both countries have a keener sense of their obligation to improve the economic well-being of the people they govern than the authoritarian elites they replaced ever had.

Of course, democracy cannot instantly reverse decades of corruption, injustice, and economic inequality. As noted earlier in this book, democracies are works in progress. The progress Mexicans and Brazilians have made in recent years in surmounting powerful dictatorships and charting paths toward democracy has been exemplary, and it may well inspire other countries in Latin America to follow the same course. Democracy does not necessarily solve all problems, as Latin Americans have learned in the past 20 years. The important but yet-to-be-answered question is, do Latin Americans value democracy for its own sake?

Key Terms

Institutional Revolutionary Party (PRI)
National Action Party (PAN)
North American Free Trade Agreement (NAFTA)
Mestizos
Spanish conquest
Import-substituting industrialization (ISI)
Neoliberalism
Democratic Revolutionary Party (PRD)
Old Republic
Estado Nôvo (new state)
New Republic

Notes

1. Charles Bowden and Molly Molloy, "Mexicans Pay in Blood for America's War on Drugs," *Phoenix New Times*, July 16, 2012, http://www.phoenixnewtimes.com/2012-07-26/news/mexicans-pay-in-blood-for-america-s-war-on-drugs/. The figure of 12,000 deaths in 2011 was reported in William Booth, "In Mexico, 12,000 Killed in Drug Violence in 2011," *The Washington Post*, January 2, 2012.
2. United Nations Office on Drugs and Crime, "Estimating Illicit Financial Flows Resulting from Drug Trafficking and Other Transnational Organized

Crimes," October 2011, available at http://www.unodc.org/documents/data-and-analysis/Studies/Illicit_financial_flows_2011_web.pdf.

3. United Nations Population Division, Department of Economic and Social Affairs. "World Population Prospects: The 2010 Revision," atesa.un.org/unpd/wpp/Excel-Data/DB02_Stock_Indicators/WPP2010_DB2_F01_TOTAL_POPULATION_BOTH_SEXES.XLS.

4. World Bank, databank.worldbank.org/databank/download/GN1.pdf.

5. The U.S. population density was 84 persons per square mile in 2010; Mexico's was 145 persons per square mile. See www.infoplease.com/ipa/A0934666.html.

6. See www.worldatlas.com/citypops.htm.

7. United Nations, Department of Economic and Social Affairs, Population Division, "World Urbanization Prospects: The 2011 Revision," esa.un.org/unup/CD-ROM/Urban-Rural-Population.htm.

8. Carlos Antonio Gutiérrez, "Extienden su Constancia de Mayoria a Candidatos Ganadores en Aguascalientes," *Excelsior* (Mexico City), August 7, 1998.

9. José Luis Reyna and Richard S. Weinert, eds., *Authoritarianism in Mexico* (Philadelphia: Institute for the Study of Human Issues, 1977).

10. Wayne A. Cornelius, *Mexican Politics in Transition: The Breakdown of a One-Party-Dominant Regime* (La Jolla, CA: Center for U.S.-Mexican Studies, University of California at San Diego, 1996), p. 39.

11. Jonathan Fox, "The Difficult Transition from Clientelism to Citizenship: Lessons from Mexico," *World Politics* 46, no. 2 (January 1994).

12. For a comprehensive historical overview, see Michael C. Meyer and William L. Sherman, *The Course of Mexican History*, 5th ed. (New York: Oxford University Press, 1995).

13. They were called *científicos* because they adopted the positivist political philosophies then current in Europe that suggested pursuing scientific progress would lead to economic and social development, just as it had (according to the positivists) in Europe.

14. John M. Hart, *Revolutionary Mexico: The Coming and Process of the Mexican Revolution* (Berkeley, CA: University of California Press, 1987).

15. Charles C. Cumberland, *Mexican Revolution: Genesis under Madero* (Austin, TX: University of Texas Press, 1952).

16. The 1917 constitution had forbidden reelection for the presidency and other federal offices. Because "no reelection" had been such an important slogan of Madero, dispensing with the no reelection clause seemed unwise. Thus Obregón, who had held the presidency from 1920 until 1924, had the constitution amended to forbid only immediate reelection.

17. Meyer and Sherman, *Course of Mexican History*, p. 591.

18. Pablo González Casanova, *Democracy in Mexico*, trans. Danielle Salti (New York: Oxford University Press, 1970), p. 226.

19. Daniel Cosío Villegas, *El Sistema Político Mexicano* (Mexico City: Joaquín Mortiz, 1978).

20. Joseph L. Klesner, "Electoral Reform in an Authoritarian Regime: The Case of Mexico," Ph.D. dis., Massachusetts Institute of Technology, 1988, pp. 312–13.

21. Douglas C. Bennett and Kenneth E. Sharpe, "The State as Banker and Entrepreneur: The Last Resort Character of the Mexican State's Economic Interventions," *Comparative Politics* 12, no. 2 (January 1980), pp. 165–89.

22. Gabriel A. Almond and Sidney Verba, *The Civic Culture: Political Attitudes and Democracy in Five Nations* (Princeton, NJ: Princeton University Press, 1963), pp. 17–19.

23. John A. Booth and Mitchell A. Seligson, "The Political Culture of Authoritarianism in Mexico: A Reexamination," *Latin American Research Review* 19, no. 1 (1983), pp. 106–24.

24. Joseph L. Klesner, "Modernization, Economic Crisis, and Electoral Alignment in Mexico," *Mexican Studies/Estudios Mexicanos* 9, no. 2 (Summer 1993), pp. 187–224.

25. González Casanova, *Democracy in Mexico*, p. 217.

26. Victoria E. Rodríguez, *Decentralization in Mexico: From Reforma Municipal to Solidaridad to Nuevo Federalismo* (Boulder, CO: Westview, 1997).

27. Howard Handelman, *Mexican Politics: The Dynamics of Change* (New York: St. Martin's Press, 1997), p. 122.

28. Ibid, p. 135.

29. Victoria Rodríguez and Peter Ward, eds., *Opposition Government in Mexico* (Albuquerque, NM: University of New Mexico Press, 1995).

30. See the articles collected in Joseph L. Klesner, ed., "Symposium: The 2006 Mexican Election and Its Aftermath," *PS: Political Science and Politics*, 40, no. 1 (January 2007), pp. 11–48.

31. Klesner, "Electoral Reform in an Authoritarian Regime."

32. Chappell Lawson, *Building the Fourth Estate: Democratization and the Rise of a Free Press in Mexico* (Berkeley, CA: University of California Press, 2002).

33. Joe Foweraker and Ann L. Craig, eds., *Popular Movements and Political Change in Mexico* (Boulder, CO: Lynne Rienner, 1990).

34. Linda S. Stevenson, "Gender Politics in the Mexican Democratization Process: Electing Women and Legislating Sex Crimes and Affirmative Action, 1988–97," in *Toward Mexico's Democratization: Parties, Campaigns, Elections, and Public Opinion*, ed. Jorge I. Dominguez and Alejandro Poiré (New York: Routledge, 1999); Lisa Baldez, "Elected Bodies: Gender Quota Laws for Legislative Candidates in Mexico," *Legislative Studies Quarterly* 29, no. 2 (May 2004), pp. 231–58. Most recent figures are available at www.ipu.org/wmn-e/classif.htm.

35. For assessments, see Robert E. Scott, "The High Price of 'Free' Trade," Economic Policy Institute Briefing Paper, November 2003, at www.epinet.org/content.cfm/briefingpapers_bp147; Sidney Weintraub, "Scoring Free Trade: A Critique of the Critics," *Current History* 102, no. 670 (February 2004): 56–60; Jorge G. Castaneda, "NAFTA at 10: A Plus or a Minus?" *Current History* 103, no. 670 (February 2004): 51–55; and Robert A. Pastor, "North America's Second Decade," *Foreign Affairs* 83, no. 1 (2004): 124–35.

36. Committee to Protect Journalists, cpj.org/killed/americas/mexico/.

37. Freedom House, www.freedomhouse.org/report/freedom-world/2012/mexico.

38. Wayne A. Cornelius, Todd A. Eisenstadt, and Jane Hindley, eds., *Subnational Politics and Democratization in Mexico* (La Jolla, CA: University of California at San Diego, Center for U.S.-Mexican Studies, 1999).

39. See the account in Andres Oppenheimer, *Bordering on Chaos: Mexico's Roller-Coaster Journey Toward Prosperity* (Boston: Little, Brown, 1996).

40. See http://www.worldatlas.com/citypops.htm.

41. The northeast is made up of the states of Alagoas, Bahia, Ceará, Maranhão, Paraíba, Pernambuco, Piauí, Rio Grande do Norte, and Sergipe.

42. *CIA World Factbook*, https://www.cia.gov/library/publications/the-world-factbook/geos/br.html.

43. Rex A. Hudson, ed., *Brazil: A Country Study* (Washington, DC: Federal Research Division, Library of Congress, 1997), http://lcweb2.loc.gov/frd/cs/brtoc.html.

44. Espírito Santo joins São Paulo, Rio de Janeiro, and Minas Gerais as the four southeastern states.

45. Hudson, *Brazil: A Country Study*.

46. The states of Paraná, Rio Grande do Sul, and Santa Catarina form the southern region.

47. The Amazonian states are Rondônia, Acre, Amazonas, Roraima, Pará, Amapá, and Tocantins, while the western states are Goiás, Mato Grosso, and Mato Grosso do Sul.

48. A comprehensive political history of Brazil can be found in Peter Flynn, *Brazil: A Political Analysis* (Boulder, CO: Westview, 1978).

49. Eul-Soo Pang, "Coronelismo in Northeast Brazil," in *The Caciques: Oligarchical Politics and the System of Caciquismo in the Luso-Hispanic World*, ed. Robert Kern (Albuquerque, NM: University of New Mexico Press, 1973).

50. Thomas E. Skidmore, *Politics in Brazil, 1930–1964: An Experiment in Democracy* (New York: Oxford University Press, 1967).

51. Kenneth P. Erickson, *The Brazilian Corporative State and Working Class Politics* (Berkeley, CA: University of California Press, 1977).

52. Peter B. Evans, *Dependent Development: The Alliance of Multinational, State, and Local Capital in Brazil* (Princeton, NJ: Princeton University Press, 1978).

53. Skidmore, *Politics in Brazil, 1930–1964*.

54. Ruth Berins Collier, "Popular Sector Incorporation and Political Supremacy: Regime Evolution in Brazil and Mexico," in *Brazil and Mexico: Patterns in Late Development*, ed. Sylvia A. Hewlett and Richard S. Weinert (Philadelphia: Institute for the Study of Human Issues, 1982).

55. Alfred C. Stepan, "Political Leadership and Regime Breakdown: Brazil," in *The Breakdown of Democratic Regimes*, ed. Juan J. Linz and Alfred C. Stepan (Baltimore, MD: Johns Hopkins University Press, 1978); Michael Wallerstein, "The Collapse of Democracy in Brazil: Its Economic Determinants," *Latin American Research Review* 15, no. 3 (1980), pp. 3–40.

56. Maria Helena Moreira Alves, *State and Opposition in Military Brazil* (Austin, TX: University of Texas Press, 1985).

57. Alfred Stepan, *Rethinking Military Politics: Brazil and the Southern Cone* (Princeton, NJ: Princeton University Press, 1988).

58. Thomas E. Skidmore and Peter H. Smith, *Modern Latin America*, 3rd ed. (New York: Oxford University Press, 1992), p. 408.

59. Frances Hagopian describes their rule: "In thousands of municipalities across Brazil, local bosses exploit the economic dependence of their clients on resources they own or control to boost their position and power." See Frances Hagopian, *Traditional Politics and Regime Change in Brazil* (New York: Cambridge University Press, 1996), pp. 16–17.

60. Ibid, p. 69.

61. This particular doctrine of national security, taught at the military's Superior War College from the late 1950s onward, justified in their own eyes the military's seizure of power. See Alfred Stepan, *The Military in Politics: Changing Patterns in Brazil* (Princeton, NJ: Princeton University Press, 1971); Alves, *State and Opposition in Military Brazil.*

62. Guillermo A. O'Donnell, *Modernization and Bureaucratic-Authoritarianism: Studies in South American Politics* (Berkeley, CA: Institute of International Studies, University of California, 1973).

63. Scott Mainwaring, "Multipartism, Robust Federalism, and Presidentialism in Brazil," in Scott Mainwaring and Martin Soberg Shugart, *Presidentialism and Democracy in Latin America* (New York: Columbia University Press, 1997); Stepan, "Political Leadership and Regime Breakdown: Brazil."

64. Skidmore, *Politics in Brazil, 1930–1964.*

65. On business and democratization, see Leigh A. Payne, *Brazilian Industrialists and Democratic Change* (Baltimore, MD: Johns Hopkins University Press, 1994).

66. Thomas E. Skidmore, *The Politics of Military Rule in Brazil, 1964–85* (New York: Oxford University Press, 1988), pp. 142–43.

67. Margaret Keck, "The New Unionism in the Brazilian Transition," in *Democratizing Brazil: Problems of Transition and Consolidation*, ed. Alfred Stepan (New York: Oxford University Press, 1989).

68. Scott Mainwaring, "Grassroots Popular Movements and the Struggle for Democracy: Nova Iguaçu," in Stepan, *Democratizing Brazil.*

69. This concept is from Juan Linz, *Crisis, Breakdown, and Reequilibrium*, vol. 1 of *The Breakdown of Democratic Regimes*, ed. Juan J. Linz and Alfred Stepan (Baltimore, MD: Johns Hopkins University Press, 1978).

70. United Nations Development Program, *Human Development Report 1999*, pp. 176–77.

71. Evans, *Dependent Development.*

72. Peter Evans, *Embedded Autonomy: States and Industrial Transformation* (Princeton, NJ: Princeton University Press, 1995).

73. Mainwaring, "Multipartism, Robust Federalism, and Presidentialism in Brazil."

74. Stepan, *Rethinking Military Politics.*

75. David V. Fleischer, "Constitutional and Electoral Engineering in Brazil: A Double-Edged Sword, 1964–1982," *Inter-American Economic Affairs* 37, no. 1 (Spring 1984).

76. Stepan, *Rethinking Military Politics*, p. 56.

77. Leigh A. Payne, "Brazilian Business and the Democratic Transition: New Attitudes and Influence," in *Business and Democracy in Latin America*, ed. Ernest Bartell and Leigh A. Payne (Pittsburgh: University of Pittsburgh Press, 1995).

78. Mainwaring, "Grassroots Popular Movements and the Struggle for Democracy."

79. Keck, "The New Unionism in the Brazilian Transition."

80. Juan J. Linz and Alfred Stepan, *Problems of Democratic Transition and Consolidation: Southern Europe, South America, and Post-Communist Europe* (Baltimore, MD: Johns Hopkins University Press, 1996), p. 169.

81. Kurt Weyland, *Democracy Without Equity: Failures of Reform in Brazil* (Pittsburgh: University of Pittsburgh Press, 1996).

82. Mainwaring, "Multipartism, Robust Federalism, and Presidentialism in Brazil," pp. 65–66.

83. Ibid, pp. 99–100. See also Barry Ames, *The Deadlock of Democracy in Brazil: Interests, Identities, and Institutions in Comparative Politics* (Ann Arbor, MI: University of Michigan Press, 2002).

84. The term comes from Scott Mainwaring, "Multipartism, Robust Federalism, and Presidentialism in Brazil."

85. "Happy Families," *Economist*, February 7, 2008.

86. Mala Htun, "Puzzles of Women's Rights in Brazil," *Social Research* 69, no. 3 (Fall 2002), pp. 373–51.

87. *Brazil: A Country Study*, http://countrystudies.us/brazil/99.htm.

88. Ibid, p. 374.

89. Wendy Hunter, *Eroding Military Influence in Brazil: Politicians Against Soldiers* (Chapel Hill, NC: University of North Carolina Press, 1997).

90. Kurt Weyland, "Neoliberalism and Democracy in Latin America: A Mixed Record," *Latin American Politics and Society* 46, no. 1 (Winter 2004), pp. 135–47.

91. Weyland, *Democracy Without Equity.*

92. *Freedom in the World 1998–1999* (New York: Freedom House, 1999), pp. 104–07.

93. Linz and Stepan, *Problems of Democratic Transition and Consolidation.*

19

Nigeria and South Africa

TIMOTHY D. SISK

At midnight on March 6, 1957, Kwame Nkrumah, first prime minister of Ghana, announced the country's independence from Great Britain.

OVERVIEW

- The 55 countries of Africa share a heritage of European colonialism that left them with enormous challenges upon their independence: artificial boundaries that inhibit the formation of national identity and unity, economies oriented to the export of agricultural commodities and natural resources, and in many cases, tensions among ethnic groups that had been exploited and exacerbated by the colonial authorities.

- Nigeria has attempted to install a democratic regime four times since its independence in 1960. Democracy has been repeatedly destroyed by military rulers bent on using the state as the source of financial gains for themselves or their ethnic groups.

- Nigeria's Fourth Republic, governing an incredibly diverse society, remains fraught by ethnic and regional differences that its institutions have not been able to ameliorate. Deadly ethnic conflict breaks out regularly; the regime faces a prolonged fight against the Islamist *Boko Haram* insurgency. The electoral system has many flaws that undermine the legitimacy of the government and exacerbate regional and ethnic conflict.

- In the past 20 years South Africa has moved beyond its apartheid regime to be a multiracial democracy. Nelson Mandela and the African National Congress managed the transition away from apartheid deftly, allowing many of the old regime's supporters to accept black majority rule by carefully designing institutions that protected the interests of the minority.

- South Africa's three postapartheid presidents have come from the ANC, which dominates electoral politics. While the ANC has managed relations among ethnic groups—between whites and blacks and among blacks—effectively, long-term economic and social problems have not been addressed adequately.

Of the 55 countries of Africa, Nigeria and South Africa have emerged as vital to the continent's future. They are the most populated and wealthiest of African countries, respectively, and both of these regional powerhouses have aspirations for global leadership roles and a permanent seat on the United Nations Security Council. Yet these countries continue to struggle to consolidate democracy after an authoritarian past, to cohere as deeply diverse societies, and to promote socioeconomic development for their citizens, especially the chronically poor and marginalized portions of their populations.

In both Nigeria and South Africa, democracy continues to be tested. In Nigeria, elections have occurred regularly since the return of democracy from military rule in 1999, but each electoral cycle has been gripped by widespread fraud and rigging and election-related violence. The 2007 and 2011 elections (presidential and parliamentary) saw especially high levels of election-related fatalities, revealing a deeply fractious political system and continued weakness of core state institutions. Moreover, Nigeria is plagued with recurring bouts of religiously oriented inter-ethnic violence, low-level insurgency in the oil-rich south, urban violence in Lagos (Africa's largest metropolitan area), and, in recent years, the emergence of an Islamist terrorist organization, *Boko Haram*, which has shaken stability in the country; in 2011, the group attacked the UN local offices in Abuja, and it has claimed responsibility for a number of bombings at Christian churches in northern Nigeria, together with other terrorist attacks. In turn, the government's security forces have become more aggressive, with reports of random killings, arrests, and arbitrary detention as they wage the effort to constrain the terrorist insurgency.

The turn away from military rule to democracy in 1999 began as a promising transition, but today the country's political system has failed to deliver either more meaningful democracy or far-reaching economic development for the majority of its people despite being one of the world's top oil-exporting countries. Because of Nigeria's fractious political culture, its strong presidential system, and its dramatic urban and economic stresses, the prognosis for democracy's development in Nigeria remains, at best, mixed.

South Africa's democracy has developed in a more promising direction overall, bolstered by the political culture of bargaining and problem solving that emerged during its celebrated negotiated transition from **apartheid** (white minority rule and strict racial segregation) to democracy in 1990–96. The institutional design of South Africa, reflected in the "rainbow nation" constitution of 1996, underscores the country's commitment to tolerance, conciliation, consensus, and basic human rights free of the discrimination that marked the country's apartheid years (1948–89). The consolidation of South Africa's multiracial democracy has succeeded in large part because of the political stability the country has achieved under the African National Congress (ANC), the African nationalist party that led the struggle against apartheid. South Africa has had three postapartheid presidents from the ANC, Nelson Mandela, Thabo Mbeki, and Jacob Zuma; and the party looks set to rule at the national level for the foreseeable future.

Consequently, as a democratic but single-party-dominant state, South Africa's movement along the pathway to democratic consolidation remains an unfinished journey. Socioeconomic inequality tops the list of enduring challenges to the country's stability and performance as a democracy: Although South Africa has a productive industrialized economy, there remains a large underclass of people facing serious physical and health insecurities from the country's low rates of development. In the poorest areas, unemployment can top 60 percent and many educated young people have very little hope of finding a fulfilling job. Crime, HIV/AIDS, joblessness, illegal immigration, land scarcity, and a youth employment crisis are among the threats to the consolidation of South Africa's democracy. These factors have led to increasing radicalism among the youth, and within the trade unions, particularly in the country's vital mining sector. Over the horizon, South Africa will face major tests of its political system as the liberation-era antiapartheid coalition begins to weaken in the face of ongoing social inequality and economic underperformance for the majority of its people.

The idea of democracy, and arguably its practice, is remarkably resilient in Africa, even in states that see chronic poverty and that have been torn by political violence. Despite widespread destitution and diversity, democracy has emerged in many African countries, not just Nigeria and South Africa. While there are African states that continue to be managed by semi-authoritarian regimes (such as Ethiopia, Uganda, and Rwanda, each of which allows for some political pluralism but where the ruling elite maintains a firm grip on power), democracy has become increasingly and firmly rooted in contemporary African political culture. Democratic values and mechanisms have also been reflected in the continent's principal regional organization, the African Union, and in the charters of many of the subregional organizations. Observers in Africa and abroad argue that *more* democracy—not less—is needed for Africa's states to meet their human security and development challenges in the twenty-first century.[1] Today, democracy is viewed as a prerequisite to more inclusive economic growth and social harmony and as such it also is seen as the only political system that has a chance of managing Africa's diverse societies.

Like Chapter 18, this chapter provides a paired comparison of two countries within one world region. Comparative politics has a long history of contributing to area studies, and these final two chapters represent our foray into area studies. Area studies scholars typically take a broad interdisciplinary look at the countries and regions they study so as to fully understand the context and then focus on themes that most interest them (for us, the emergence of democracy and challenges to its consolidation). Area studies allows us to apply a version of most-similar systems comparison. The countries in particular regions often have several contextual factors that are relatively similar.

In this chapter, Nigeria and South Africa are similar in that they are the powerhouse countries of Africa: Nigeria is the most populous, and it is an influential hegemonic power in West Africa and a global player as a leading African state, particularly as the world's eighth largest oil exporter (40 percent of which comes to the United States). South Africa is the continent's largest economy, and it is both a political leader of southern Africa and the economic center for much of the continent's southern cone. Both countries had a troubled transition to democracy in the 1990s; and moving into the second decade of the 21st century, in neither country can it be said that democracy is fully consolidated. Nigeria has been led by a dominant ruling party, which has used electoral fraud and oil patronage to stay in power; the country suffers from enormous social, economic, and political challenges, not least of which is a growing insurgency and recurrent political violence along ethnic and religious lines. South Africa has had a better record of democracy, emerging from its transition with a sterling charter of human rights and a well-designed set of political institutions. South Africa, however, also has yet to see full democratization in that it remains under the rule of the liberation-era political party, and its resilience as a democracy has yet to be fully tested.

This chapter begins by setting the stage with a broad-brush look at the politics of Africa as informed by a look back at the period of decolonization and postcolonial politics that has led to a variety of regime types. We then systematically compare Nigeria and South Africa in terms of their political histories, the current issues in governance, and the political challenges these powerful states face in the coming decades. We cannot do justice to the full experience of politics in these two complex countries. Therefore, our focus will be on the difficulties of establishing democracy in Nigeria and South Africa, these countries' most recent attempts to install democratic regimes, and the prospects for the consolidation of those democracies in the twenty-first century.

AFRICA: FROM CRADLE OF HUMANITY TO CONQUEST AND COLONIALISM

Africa is increasingly an integrated regional political system that shares a history of colonial oppression; a new, but still evolving, state system; a marginalized place in the international political economy that is still reliant on primary commodity exports; and a widespread desire among its people for democracy, prosperity, and secure livelihoods. To understand where Africa's countries are headed today, including the big players of Nigeria and South Africa as case studies, we must understand their common past.[2]

Current anthropological theories concur that Africa is the cradle of all humankind. The "African genesis" theory holds that the earliest hominids—the primordial ancestors of the human race—lived in the Great Rift Valley of central Africa and the Ethiopian highlands. Thus the beginning of African history is the beginning of human history. Africa's history and its present are marked by extensive cross-border and internal migration, changing structures of authority and governance between traditional and modern forms, evolving boundaries of the state and society, and contested concepts of religious, ethnic, and national identity. Historically, great ancient kingdoms developed in Africa, including the Gao in present-day Senegal, the Mali dynasties of the twelfth and thirteenth centuries, and the regal traditions of the Ashanti in present-day Ghana. During these times, Africans interacted with Islamic traders such as the Berbers, and a vibrant system of exchange developed across the sands of the Sahara.

Early in the fifteenth century, Portuguese fortune-seekers and emissaries of imperialistic monarchies crossed the straits of Gibraltar, and eventually rounded the Cape of Good Hope, and began the European colonization of Africa. This system of colonial domination lasted in some areas until the early 1990s, when independence for Namibia marked an end to colonialism. Before European rule, traditional authority in the persons of African monarchs and chiefs, rooted in agrarian systems of livelihood, was the dominant mode of governance. Colonial rule changed Africa significantly, and its long-term effects to the present cannot be overstated.

Over the seventeenth to twentieth centuries, additional imperial powers invaded Africa. They carved up the continent along artificial and illogical boundaries, manipulated social systems, and created economic legacies that continue to bedevil African countries. An initial impetus for the colonial exploitation of Africa was the slave trade, in which at least 12 million Africans were enslaved and forcibly trafficked to destinations in the colonial Americas to work plantations of cocoa, coffee, tobacco, cotton, and sugar. The legacies of the slave trade informed the strength of anticolonial movements into the present in terms of the exploitative relationship that Africans have long had with foreigners who intervene primarily in their own interests. Indeed, just west of the capital of Dakar, Senegal, lies Goree Island, once a prison where slaves were auctioned to slave traders in passing ships; today it houses an institute for democracy, development, and human rights.[3] With the British decision to abolish slavery in 1833 and the emancipation of slaves in the Americas during the U.S. Civil War, the nature of European subjugation changed. Colonial powers annexed large swaths of African territory in an effort to fuel their industrial revolution with raw materials extracted from the rich natural resources found on the continent. Principally, these resources included cotton, peanuts, cocoa, palm oil, coffee, sisal, and minerals such as copper, gold, diamonds, and other precious or rare earth metals. Colonization accelerated in the final three decades of the nineteenth century. In 1870 only 10 percent of Africa was colonized; by 1900 only 10 percent was not. At the infamous Berlin Conference of 1884, the major European colonial powers—Britain, France, Belgium, Germany, Italy, Portugal, and Spain—divided up Africa's territory among themselves.

Their colonial "state" was rather arbitrary in terms of then-existing African social patterns. For the most part, the colonial administrative entities simply reflected the patterns of military control exercised by the colonial armies of the European

Goree Island, Senegal, was once a prison where slaves were auctioned to slave traders. Shown here is the "Door of No Return." Today the island houses an institute for democracy, development, and human rights.

imperialist powers: Whoever controlled an area took it as a colony. The borders of most African states today are the legacy of the ill-considered partition of Africa in the mid-nineteenth century, based on the "principle of effective occupation" of territory. These boundaries often did not correspond to a consistent geographic, national, or ethnic logic. Ultimately they set the stage for many of the problems of ethnic tension that challenge the majority of African countries today.[4] This process of change is ongoing, as evidenced by the secession of Eritrea from Ethiopia in 1993 or the independence of South Sudan from Sudan in 2011. Whether Eritrea and South Sudan's independence are still part of decolonization as a broad historical process or the beginnings of the unraveling of contemporary African states into smaller ones will only be known by future observers. For the present, though, it is safe to say the process of nation building and of state building in Africa remains incomplete, and that the African state system itself is still very much a work in progress.

Patterns of Colonialism

The discovery of rich diamond and gold deposits in South Africa in the 1860s heightened what became known as the "scramble for Africa." To fully exploit Africa's wealth, colonizers required ever more effective occupation and social control. Although different in their approaches—the British used "indirect rule" whereas the French, Belgians, and Germans preferred more direct administration—the colonial powers engaged in the widespread political manipulation of African societies.

- The British relied on agreements with traditional rulers to impose their policies, usually backed up with superior military might. Consequently, we find today that in erstwhile British colonies such as Ghana, Kenya, South Africa, or Uganda, traditional rulers remain very powerful as informal institutions with their own authority, legitimacy, and governance functions (for example, on land tenure), and de-facto territorial control by ethnic groups remains critically important.

- In French and Belgian colonies, centralized power was more important and to a certain extent it eroded more fully traditional power structures. The French sought to exert cultural influence through their language policy, and they ruled their colonies as an extension of France itself. Colonial subjects were to become *évolués*, or "people evolving" into Frenchmen. In contrast, though, Belgian colonies such as the vast Congo were ruled as the personal property of the eccentric King Leopold II.

- In Portuguese colonies, such as Angola, Mozambique, and Cape Verde, assimilation was encouraged and many interracial marriages occurred. As a result, *assimilados* (or mulattos, the products of mixed marriages) became an important social group that blurred the lines between colonial and indigenous rule.[5] Lusophone (Portuguese-speaking) countries in Africa today thus have social structures that are remarkably different from those of former British or French colonies, and *assimilados* are still influential leaders in these countries.

Thus another legacy of the colonial period was the stark division of a large part of Africa into Anglophone (English-speaking), Francophone (French-speaking), and Lusophone (Portuguese-speaking) colonies. These language differences affect the way today's African countries relate to one another and stymie the development of a common approach to contemporary problems. Former British colonies tend to have special ties with one another, as do former French colonies. For example, former English colonies are active members of the British Commonwealth,[6] while French West African countries have adopted a common currency (the Central African franc, or CFA, which is guaranteed by the French treasury).

The reliance on African land and labor to grow crops and extract mineral wealth in service to the colonial powers resulted in severe distortions in traditional African societies. The colonial authorities introduced European concepts with no indigenous roots in Africa: Christianity, monogamy, formal education, and wage labor, among others. New stratifications based on socio economic class came into being, ethnic identities were transformed, and basic economic infrastructures and modes of production were created to serve the single-commodity economies needed by the colonial powers. In southern Africa, European immigrants set up white minority "settler states" that systematically displaced Africans from the land and created a new form of what was described by African liberation leaders in these countries as *internal colonialism*. In many colonies, the imperial powers imposed a "head tax," in which an African peasant had to work for a European plantation owner or an enterprise to pay off debt to the metropolitan state (the colonial power).

After the creation of the Union of South Africa following the British defeat of the Dutch-origin colonists (then known as the Boers,[7] or today, the Afrikaners) in 1902, and after Germany's defeat in World War I, the shape of colonialism in Africa was nearly complete. European plenipotentiaries and bureaucrats ruled the vast continent, and their oppression of the indigenous population was nearly universal. Once Germany lost its colonies after 1918, most decisions affecting the masses of the continent were made in Paris or London, with little regard for their implications for the millions of people whom colonial policy affected. Only Liberia and Ethiopia, each owing to their own historical contingencies, were independent countries.

Legacies of Colonialism: Explaining Underdevelopment

Colonialism's legacies are thus pervasive throughout Africa some 60 years after the system of domination began to crumble beginning with Ghana's liberation in 1957 (see Table 19.1). These legacies are political, economic, and cultural.[8]

- Politically, as noted before, the territorial boundaries of today's countries are the result of the competition among the European powers over arable land, water, blue-water harbors, transportation arteries such as rivers, and precious mineral resources.

- Economically, the African colonies were reliant on single-commodity, resource-extraction economies. Urbanization

Table 19.1 The Decolonization of Africa

	INDEPENDENCE
Former French Colonies	
Algeria	July 3, 1962
Benin	August 1, 1960
Burkina Faso	August 5, 1960
Central African Republic	August 13, 1960
Chad	August 11, 1960
Congo (Republic)	August 15, 1960
Djibouti	June 27, 1977
Equatorial Guinea	October 12, 1968
Gabon	August 17, 1960
Guinea	March 6, 1957
Ivory Coast	August 7, 1960
Madagascar	June 26, 1960
Mali	September 22, 1960
Mauritania	November, 28 1960
Niger	August 8, 1960
Senegal	August 20, 1960
Tunisia	March 20, 1956
Former British Colonies	
Botswana	September 30, 1966
Gambia	February 18, 1965
Ghana	March 6, 1957
Kenya	December 12, 1963
Lesotho	October 4, 1966
Malawi	July 6, 1964
Nigeria	October 1, 1960
Sierra Leone	April 27, 1961
South Africa	May 31, 1961
South Sudan	July 9, 2011
Sudan	January 1, 1956
Swaziland	September 6, 1968
Uganda	October 9, 1962
Zambia	October 24, 1964
Zimbabwe	April 18, 1980
Former Portuguese Colonies	
Angola	November 11, 1975
Cape Verde	July 1, 1975
Guinea-Bissau	September 10, 1974
Mozambique	June 25, 1975
São Tomé and Príncipe	July 12, 1975
Former Belgian Colonies	
Burundi	July 1, 1962
Congo (Democratic Republic, formerly Zaire)	June 30, 1960
Rwanda	July 1, 1962
Former Italian Colonies	
Eritrea	Seceded from Ethiopia 1991
Libya	December 24, 1951
Somalia	July 1, 1960
Western Sahara	Disputed territory
Former German Colonies	
Cameroon	January 1, 1960
Namibia	March 21, 1990
Tanzania	December 9, 1961
Togo	April 12, 1960
Not Colonized (Dates of Historical Independence)	
Liberia (1847), Ethiopia (1895)	

Colonizing countries as of 1914. Modern names used for independent countries.

was inhibited, subsistence agriculture encouraged, and the development of diversified industrial production was stultified.

- The cultural units that had existed before colonialism were also affected, and in many regions ethnic and linguistic groups are now divided by artificial lines on a map. As a result, most African countries today are a mosaic of ethnic, linguistic, racial, and religious diversity. One of the consequences is a pattern of distorted social relations. Conflicts in Rwanda, for example, between the minority Tutsi (now 15 percent of the population) and the Hutu (84 percent) were fanned by the Belgian colonists' support for the Tutsi. A Hutu revolt in 1959 ended Tutsi domination. Violence erupted periodically after independence in 1962 as the Tutsi challenged Hutu power. In 1994, more than 800,000 people died in a hundred days in the worst genocide since World War II as Hutus lashed out against the Tutsi.

African Nationalism: The Pursuit of the Political Kingdom

World War II had significant material and psychological effects on the continent and its people. As a consequence of the war, the colonial powers were weakened and the legitimacy of occupation began to erode; at the same time, the message of the struggle for civil rights in countries such as the United States spread abroad. U.S. presidents such as Dwight Eisenhower pressed for decolonization to open Africa's markets to free trade. Encouraged by civil rights activism in the United States, African nationalist movements emerged to resist colonial rule and exploitation. Under the leadership of these movements, demands for independence from the colonial powers grew rapidly in the late 1940s and 1950s. Although there had been prior resistance to colonial rule—notably by the Ashanti Kingdom in the late nineteenth century, the Ndebele-Shona uprisings in current-day Zimbabwe in 1896–97, and the Maji-Maji rebellion in present-day Tanzania in 1905–07—more consequential resistance to European rule emerged in the continent after World War II. Among the most significant of these new awakenings was the Mau Mau rebellion in Kenya in 1950, in which Kikuyu tribespeople articulated the legitimacy of African aspirations to be free of the colonial yoke.

African nationalism arose from the frustrations of an educated elite that deeply resented that the highest positions in commerce, finance, government administration, and even religious organizations were controlled by foreigners, as were the rewards of economic success. African nationalists from within this educated elite sought independence from the colonial powers, a goal that would bring them complete control over the state apparatus and territory of their respective countries. Buoyed by the promise of the Charter of the United Nations to promote the "self-determination of peoples," and imbued with the postwar optimism reflected in the 1948 Universal Declaration of Human Rights, African leaders began to agitate for decolonization. Western-educated, skilled professional leaders organized independence movements and petitioned for independence.

Tanzania's Julius Nyerere, Jomo Kenyatta of Kenya, Leopold Senghor of Senegal, Kwame Nkrumah of Ghana, and Kenneth Kaunda of Zambia, to name a few, articulated philosophies of independence, self-reliance, and economic development for African colonies.

These men were the founding fathers of today's African states, much like Mohandas Gandhi and Jawaharal Nehru, who led India to independence in 1947. Senghor, for example, argued for a rekindling of traditional African values. He coined the term *négritude* to encompass "the whole complex of civilized values (cultural, economic, social, and political) which characterize the black people." Senghor and other nationalists believed that cultural nationalism could unify countries whose people had little in common other than their suffering to bind them in their postcolonial political units. To achieve this unity, African anticolonial nationalists sought the reins of state power. This drive for power, waged in revolutionary struggles of armed resistance and guerrilla warfare in many colonies, was heralded by Nkrumah's dictum, "Seek ye first the political kingdom." At the same time, the United States, in conformity with its own anticolonial past, pressured the European powers to loosen their control of markets and commerce with Africa. In turn, the Soviet Union saw African liberators, especially in the Afro-Marxist movements in countries such as Angola, Mozambique, and Namibia, as vanguards of a global revolution against imperialism, offering them ideological and tangible support.[9]

Independence came rapidly for many countries in the 1960s. Fueled by UN General Assembly Resolution 1514 (1960), which called for decolonization and the sanctity of existing borders, the claims of African nationalists could not be denied. As early as 1957, Ghana's Nkrumah had succeeded in his effort to seize the political kingdom. His Convention People's Party won a pivotal election, assumed power, and forced the British to relinquish control. In 1960 alone, 26 African colonies became independent, and by 1969 some 42 countries had emerged as sovereign states, becoming full-fledged members of the United Nations. In subsequent years, after bitter struggles for independence, Portuguese colonies such as Mozambique and Angola were finally freed in the mid-1970s. The settler societies of southern Africa, such as Rhodesia (now Zimbabwe), Namibia, and South Africa, also came over time to be ruled by African nationalist movements. Across the continent, in the short historical span of some 30 years, colonial-era flags went down and the flags of newly independent African countries were crafted and raised.

As it happened, however, African nationalism in these formative decades of decolonization was not tightly linked to democracy. Unlike leaders in Britain and the United States, where nationalism and democratic tendencies were virtually inseparable from the beginning, most African independence leaders defined their nationalism in pronouncedly anti-Western terms. Upon taking power, most of them quickly abandoned any pretense to Western liberal democratic ideas and practices, establishing authoritarian or semi-authoritarian regimes based on the military or one-party dominance. African democracy was set back for decades as a result.

Leopold Senghor, right, a Senegalese nationalist leader, coined the term *négritude* to encompass the complex of cultural, economic, social, and political values that characterize black people tyrannized by colonialist rule. Here he chats with Félix Houphouët-Boigny, long the president of Côte d'Ivoire (Ivory Coast), at a 1978 summit of African states.

From Liberation Struggle to Neo-Patrimonialism

Initially, the constitutions of the newly liberated states tended to establish the minimal framework of democracy: constitutionalism, the rule of law, and elections. In countries throughout Africa, the anticolonial nationalist movements—such as TANU in Tanzania, KANU in Kenya, and UNIP in Zambia—won elections. With charismatic leaders such as Nyerere, Kenyatta, and Kaunda, these movements inherited a highly centralized state and highly diverse populations. But contrary to the democratic tenets of political pluralism, which rest on free and open competition among political parties and freedom of expression, some of the most prominent leaders of African independence quickly turned to patronage forms of politics, what some scholars have called **neo-patrimonialism**.[10] Liberation elites then argued that African states needed one-party rule to unify their populations and "build nations." Creating new countries required emphasizing common struggles and sufferings; competitive, multiparty elections, in their view, would tear the nascent nations apart.

The hypothesis that multiparty competition is ill suited to African's multiethnic, impoverished societies because it divides rather than unifies is a common and recurrent theme in Africa's political development.[11] It reverberates throughout the region today. For example, Uganda's President Yoweri Museveni experimented with a system of "no-party" politics, in which candidates for office could stand as individuals and are not allowed to assume a party identification. The National Resistance Movement, which he leads, is the guiding force in the country despite a popular referendum on constitutional change in 2005 that abandoned the "no-party" notion. Although it espouses such democratic notions as market-oriented economics, freedom of expression, and free primary education (a rarity in Africa), it

resolutely monopolizes political power. At the same time, President Museveni maneuvered a change in the constitution that enabled him to serve a third term, circumventing the provision barring more than two terms in office. In elections in 2011, Museveni's party won handily with 68 percent of the vote, even as opposition leaders and international observers claimed the elections were marred by irregularities.

While rejecting British-style parliamentarism and other Western models of democracy, most African states in the postcolonial period turned to one form or another of authoritarian or semi-authoritarian rule. In virtually every newly independent African country, the formal institutions of democracy that may have been in place when self-rule began were systematically undermined by power-accumulating elites. Democratic practices and human rights fell victim to political and military elites who sought the reins of office for their own personal power and enrichment.[12] These elites relied on the centralized, bureaucratic structures of the states that they inherited from the colonial powers to become Africa's new dominant class.

In the worst instances, some countries such as Angola and Mozambique suffered from protracted civil wars in which independence movements fought against the Portuguese and among themselves over who would wield power in the independence era. In both instances, the hasty retreat of Portuguese colonizers in 1974–75 left a power vacuum in which the competing local factions vied for dominance. These factions obtained arms and ideological support (and sometimes troops) from their respective benefactors—especially the United States, the Soviets, the apartheid-era South African regime, and the Cubans—who were locked in their global Cold War confrontation. Despite several efforts and peace agreements and UN peacekeeping efforts in the 1990s, Angola's civil war continued nearly uninterrupted for 25 years. Tragically, as a result Angola has the highest proportion of victims of land mines of any country in the world, including some 100,000 land-mine victims. In 1999, an estimated 200 people died per day in Angola's tragic war. The war finally ended in 2001 when rebel leader Jonas Savimbi was killed on the battlefield; today Angola has yet to see meaningful democratization and the wartime ruling regime, the MPLA (Movement for the Popular Liberation of Angola), remains in power in Luanda. The Ivory Coast, Liberia, and Sierra Leone were also embroiled in civil wars in the 1990s and into the 2000s. International peacekeeping missions involving British, French, or (in Liberia's case) American troops, together with troops from many other countries under the UN flag, were sent to these countries to provide security, build peace, and support the development of more legitimate, inclusive, and capable state institutions.

Perhaps no country has seen postcolonial civil war in Africa more than Sudan. Since its independence from a British and Egyptian joint-rule arrangement (known as condominium), Sudan was embroiled in almost constant civil war between the mostly Islamic north and the mostly Christian and animist south, a division that also reflected differentiation between Arab and African identities. In the so-called Second Civil War of 1983–2005, more than 2 million people lost their lives, and more than 5 million were displaced, with many more suffering from famine and loss of livelihoods. The civil war in Sudan was ended only after years of international mediation in 2005 with a comprehensive peace agreement, one that turned out to be only a segue to the partition of the country with the independence of South Sudan following the UN-facilitated referendum that led to the creation of Africa's 55th country. Even with the creation of South Sudan, the region remains deeply conflicted with armed conflict over disputed territories, ethnic violence, and an ongoing food-security crisis.

Among the several forms of authoritarianism that emerged in Africa between the early 1960s and the late 1980s, one variant is *semi-authoritarian one-party rule*. Examples include TANU in Tanzania and Guinea's *Parti démocratique de Guinée*. In these and similar examples of this political system, political power is monopolized and guided by famous and generally popular political leaders. The government and party structures operate in parallel, with some similarities to the relationship between party and state in communist Russia and China. These parties voiced socialist rhetoric and have sought to achieve economic development by breaking the bonds of dependency that tied the prosperity of their country to uneven and disadvantageous trade relations with Europe. These parties still exist in most countries. Some of them remain in power despite the introduction of multiparty politics; for example, TANU (which was renamed *Chama Cha Mapinduzi*, or CCM) continues to dominate politics in Tanzania as it has since independence in 1962. Elsewhere, as in Zambia, one-party governments were defeated in elections when political liberalization began in the early 1990s.

Zimbabwe experienced a fundamental transformation of its one-party system in 2000 as a relatively new party—the Movement for Democratic Change—won nearly half the parliamentary seats up for election, delivering a stunning blow to the Zimbabwe African National Union-Patriotic Front (ZANU-PF), the party that had dominated the country for 20 years under liberation-leader President Robert Mugabe. In 2002, Mugabe claimed he had won a hotly contested presidential election against Morgan Tsvangirai, a popular trade union leader and democracy advocate. The election outcome was regarded as fraudulent by Mugabe's opponents, and in 2003 Tsvangirai was put on trial for treason. Mugabe's despotic leadership and the country's rapidly deteriorating economy have prompted some 3 million people to flee the country. In 2008, the main political parties (ZANU-PF and the Movement for Democratic Change, or MDC, headed by Tsvangarai) agreed to a power-sharing deal. In reality, though, ZANU-PF under Mugabe has continued to wield the levers of power, has intimidated MDC officials, and has been implicated in ongoing human rights abuses such as targeted assassinations and illegal property seizures; power sharing has more or less collapsed in Zimbabwe, as have meaningful constitutional reforms, and despite elections in 2013 few observers expect much change toward the return of democracy in Zimbabwe until the Mugabe era has passed.[13]

Other countries have had **patrimonial rule**, which is rule by a domineering and personalistic elite. In the Belgian Congo (later known as Zaire and now as the Democratic Republic of Congo, or DRC), a troubled decolonization process in the 1960s was marked by civil war, UN military intervention, superpower rivalry, and assassinations. Eventually, Mobutu Sese Seko seized power and ruled as a veritable monarch until his despotic regime was toppled by rebels in May 1997. Mobutu's assets at the time of his death were estimated at $8 billion in property and money, while his country had sunk to the bottom of the global list in virtually every conceivable development indicator. A prolonged war for control of the country involving both Congolese factions and interventions from no less than 11 other African states (which was dubbed Africa's "first world war") claimed 3.8 million lives. Following a South Africa-brokered peace agreement, which led to the deployment of a significant UN peacekeeping force in 2004, the DRC remains a country bedeviled by conflict and a weak state that does not have authority over its vast territory despite the continued deployment of UN peacekeepers. Indeed, in the eastern DRC an ongoing humanitarian emergency persists and rampant rape or gender-based violence has garnered the attention of the entire world as a continuing crime against humanity.

In other countries, the military stepped in and took over power from corrupt or incompetent elites. Military coups were rampant in Africa from the 1960s through the 1980s: In 74 instances between 1952 and 1990, military officers gained power through violence or the threat of it and ruled the country as dictators. In Ethiopia, military officers with pro-Soviet leanings and a Marxist ideology seized power in 1974, deposing the aging emperor, Haile Selassie. Under the despotic rule of the military committee, known as the Dergue and led by Mengistu Haile Mariam, the junta unleashed a reign of terror and embroiled the country in devastating civil wars and wars with its neighbors (notably the war with Somalia over the Ogaden desert in 1975). It used its radical Marxist-Leninist ideology to justify dictatorial rule at home and to establish international alliances with the Soviet Union, Cuba, and other communist states. After inflicting untold suffering on the Ethiopian people, Mengistu fled the country in 1991 as rebel forces closed in on the capital, Addis Ababa. (Mengistu fled to Zimbabwe, where he eventually became a "security advisor" to President Mugabe.)

Several countries in Africa—such as Botswana, Mauritius, Gambia, and Senegal, and more recently, Ghana—have managed to remain near- or partial democracies with constitutional systems, regular elections, and relatively good human rights records.[14] But only in a few instances have elections ever led to the ouster of the ruling party and the assumption of power by an opposition party. For example, in Botswana, Africa's oldest surviving democracy, elections held in 2009 returned to power the only party that has governed the country since independence in 1966. Alternation in power—the periodic transfer of state power from one party to another over a succession of elections—is a key indicator of the vibrancy of democracy as traditionally defined. Unfortunately, until the dawn of the twenty-first century it was largely absent from Africa. The relative success of some of these countries in avoiding the complete collapse of democracy has tended to stem from the responsiveness of the dominant party to ethnic and religious groups. This type of political system has been labeled a **hegemonic exchange regime** in which for the right to exercise its hegemony over the state and the population, the dominant party provides benefits to the country's main ethnic or religious groups.[15] It is equally fair to describe the post-genocide regime of President Paul Kagame of Rwanda in this fashion, although some wonder about whether instability could return to Rwanda over time.

In the 1980s and 1990s, global factors such as the collapse of communism in the Soviet Union and in Eastern Europe, together with a new assertiveness of multilateral financial institutions to advance "good governance," converged with domestic pressures to undermine the alternatives to democracy in Africa. International lending organizations, including the World Bank and the International Monetary Fund, along with aid providers such as the United States and Western Europe, increasingly insisted on "good governance," private enterprise, and trade liberalization as conditions for future economic assistance. They called on the states of Africa to root out official corruption, reduce state controls over economic activity, and remove tariffs and other barriers to trade with the outside world.[16] They also enjoined them to take more responsibility for their governance, economic development, and human rights records.[17] Sanctions on apartheid-era South Africa in the 1980s, including the country's expulsion from the Olympic Games, placed special external pressures on that country's white minority government to open negotiations with African nationalists with the aim of democratizing the entire country. Under these mounting outside pressures, political practices within individual African countries gave way to new continental and global realities.

In many countries, popular movements arose that demanded space for the development of an autonomous civil society outside the single-party framework. They called for multiparty competitive elections, new constitutional frameworks, an end to corruption, and a more equitable distribution of wealth. In Ghana, Kenya, Malawi, and Zambia, new coalitions of organizations in civil society came together and pressured the incumbent governments to open the political system to multiparty competition. Africa was clearly caught up in the third wave of democratization that spilled across the world in the early 1990s.

Over the course of the 1990s, nearly all of Africa's then 54 states underwent dramatic political changes. As we've seen, the pressures for democratization were both external, a condition of further loans, foreign direct investment, and foreign aid, and internal, the result of widespread public disaffection with the status quo.[18] Whether through negotiated agreements

("pacts"), the victory of rebel movements on the battlefield, or the passing of longtime liberation-era leaders, the stereotypical African one-party state became a relic of the past in the early 1990s. During the 1990s, Africa witnessed scores of governments that have come to power seeking to inaugurate a new era, such that some dubbed the period of the 1990s "Africa's second independence."[19]

More than anything, the process of democratization in Africa was characterized by the rush to multiparty elections. Between 1992 and 1994, 20 countries held national-level elections. These elections swept away one-party regimes in the Ivory Coast, Gabon, Mali, and Zambia. In some instances, as in Angola, Eritrea, Ethiopia, Liberia, Mozambique, Namibia, Sierra Leone, South Africa, and Uganda, votes were held to restore and legitimize a new political order after years of civil war or political violence. Many Francophone countries held "national conferences" to arrive at new constitutional rules of the game for democratic politics.

The track record of the remarkable attempts at democratization in much of Africa is demonstrably mixed.[20] Some experiments of the 1990s were relatively successful, in that legitimate government was reconstituted and the stage was set for a longer-term evolution to mature democracy and its consolidation (e.g., frequent or occasional alternation in power by governing coalitions). In Benin, Madagascar, Malawi, Mozambique, Namibia, South Africa, Uganda, and Zambia, elections have been more or less successful vehicles for ushering in fledgling democracies. But there have been failures, as well. Elections went awry in Angola, Burundi, Liberia, and Sierra Leone, leading to renewed civil violence, the suspension of human rights, and sharp declines in the standard of living as well as in the prospects for future prosperity. Observers have differed over whether the electoral contests of the 1990s produced greater accommodation among conflicting groups within these countries—especially along ethnic lines—or whether they exacerbated tensions and undermined national cohesiveness.[21]

Among the alternatives to elections as a route to democracy is the promotion of viable civil societies in Africa. Some have suggested that popular participation and consensus-building decision-making processes are more suited to Africa's divided societies than are the rough-and-tumble of Western-style competitive elections.[22] John Harbeson suggests that democratization efforts in Africa have relied too much on elections, arguing, "This overemphasis derives from an inaccurate reading of the most widely accepted definition of 'democracy,' upon which much of the contemporary democratic transitions theory appears to rest." He suggests as an alternative that "a broadened conception of democratization will result in a significantly improved understanding of the status and quality of democracy [in Africa] and the prospects for it." African countries should engage in more constitution-making exercises that establish a consensus on the rules of the democratic game before rushing into elections in the absence of that consensus, Harbeson maintains.[23]

The African Renaissance?

In recent years, some African leaders have called for a "renaissance." This appeal for a rebirth is a response to disillusioned pessimists who decry the persistence of war, authoritarian rule, and poverty in Africa and the continent's marginalization in the international economy. Thabo Mbeki, former president of South Africa, advocates for a renaissance that motivates African leaders to take responsibility for the continent's security and economic well-being. As Mbeki put it:

Renaissance has to be about democracy, peace and stability throughout our continent. It has to be about economic regeneration so that we pull ourselves out of the category "the underdeveloped" permanently. It has to be about vastly improving the quality of life of all our citizens.[24]

There is widespread agreement that, if the hoped-for African renaissance is to occur, the further broadening and deepening of democracy in African nations will be necessary. Positive signs include the much-heralded elections in Rwanda in 2003—the first since the 1994 genocide—and the introduction of a new democratically elected government in Kenya. At the same time, the tainted senate elections held in Zimbabwe in 2005 failed to force Robert Mugabe to step down; instead, Mugabe's forces have perpetrated human rights violations against white former settlers and the government's political opponents in a desperate effort to retain power. Food shortages and starvation have resulted, severely halting progress toward Africa's renaissance. In fact, the years 2007–11 saw movement away from democratic practice in Africa, as countries limited the activities of opposition parties and civil society, restricted mass protests, and conducted elections in which electoral processes lacked sufficient integrity to call the regime fully democratic. Thus, most regimes today in Africa—as seen in the 2012 Freedom House rankings of African states in Table 19.2—are at best partial or, perhaps more accurately, *façade democracies* in which there are significant restrictions on political rights and civil liberties.[25] For 2012, only 21 percent of Africa's countries were labeled "free," with 37 percent coded as "partly free," and 42 percent as "not free."

Democratization has also been problematic in postcolonial Africa as electoral processes have at times featured devastating election-related violence. In 2007–08, for example, elections in Kenya generated violence that cost an estimated 800 lives and displaced some 600,000 others. Only after international mediation by former UN Secretary General Kofi Annan, who invoked the principle that governments have a responsibility to protect innocent civilians from violence, did the violence subside. Annan succeeded in leveraging the parties into an agreement on power sharing that averted a broader civil war in Kenya. Similarly, elections in Ivory Coast in 2010, verified by the UN, put the country back on the brink of civil war (and produced some 2,000 fatalities) until the UN and the former colonial power, France, intervened forcefully to require the incumbent president (Laurent Gbagbo) to step down and hand over power to the presumed winner of the poll, Alassane Ouatarra.

Mali, a democracy thought to be stable, succumbed to a military coup in March 2012 following the seizure of the country's north by separatist Tuareg rebels together with Islamist groups, thus reversing democracy in what had been an African success story. The crisis in Mali shows the continued vulnerability of democratic African regimes to instability and conflict that may well be driven by underlying factors such as environmental change, migration, or food insecurity.

Democratization continues to be accompanied by crisis, turbulence, and sometimes violence in Africa's varied contexts, and our two case studies of Nigeria and South Africa reflect and further inform some of these broader patterns. Despite these significant obstacles, Africans as a whole tend to strongly favor democracy. In the fourth round of systematic sampling on attitudes toward democracy of the Afrobarometer (a survey carried out in 18 African countries), more than 70 percent of respondents preferred democracy to any other elected kind of government, and more than 79 percent disapproved or strongly disapproved of the statement that "elections and the parliament [can be] abolished so the president can decide everything."[26] Support for democracy in the Afrobarometer survey was strong in South Africa, with 67 percent in favor of democracy, and in Nigeria 72 percent favored democracy.[27]

For Nigeria, and then for South Africa, we will first look at the troubled transitions to democracy that each country encountered. We'll next look at each country's prospects for consolidating a pluralist political system that meets the aspirations of its people for governance that protects human rights, manages diversity, and fosters economic development into the twenty-first century.

NIGERIA

Military coups in Nigeria, some with popular backing and some with fierce opposition, historically ended experiments in democracy. But in May 1999, the military stepped aside and elections inaugurated a new period of civilian rule—the Fourth Republic—with former General Olusegun Obasanjo emerging as the country's first popularly elected president in 15 years. Turmoil and insurgency has been persistent in the oil-rich southern part of the country, where rebels are fighting for a greater share of Nigeria's oil revenues and for effective measures to address the environmental and social disruptions that result from local oil exploitation. Also, violence recurs between Christians and Muslims in a number of Nigeria's federated states, particularly in the divided city of Jos, a problem that has plagued Nigeria for decades. Some Muslim-dominated states in the north have adopted Islamic law, at times implicitly condoning violent penalties for sexual offenses (such as stoning for adultery) that conflict with the civil laws of Nigeria's central government. Political corruption on the part of government officials and politically well-connected private businesses

Table 19.2 Freedom House Rankings for Sub-Saharan African Countries, 2012

Country	Freedom Status	PR (Political Rights)	CL (Civil Liberties)
Angola	Not Free	6	5
Botswana*	Free	3	2
Burkina Faso	Partly Free	5	3
Burundi	Partly Free	5	5
Cameroon	Not Free	6	6
Cape Verde*	Free	1	1
Central African Republic	Partly Free	5	5
Chad	Not Free	7	6
Comoros*	Partly Free	3	4
Congo (Brazzaville)	Not Free	6	5
Congo (Kinshasa)	Not Free	6	6
Côte d'Ivoire	Partly Free	5	5
Djibouti	Not Free	6	5
Equatorial Guinea	Not Free	7	7
Eritrea	Not Free	7	7
Ethiopia	Not Free	6	6
Gabon	Not Free	6	5
The Gambia	Not Free	6	6
Ghana*	Free	1	2
Guinea	Partly Free	5	5
Guinea-Bissau	Not Free	6	5
Kenya	Partly Free	4	4
Lesotho*	Free	2	3
Liberia*	Partly Free	3	4
Madagascar	Partly Free	6	4
Malawi*	Partly Free	3	4
Mali	Not Free	7	5
Mauritania	Not Free	6	5
Mauritius*	Free	1	2
Mozambique	Partly Free	4	3
Namibia*	Free	2	2
Niger*	Partly Free	3	4
Nigeria	Partly Free	4	4
Rwanda	Not Free	6	6
São Tomé and Príncipe*	Free	2	2
Senegal*	Free	2	3
Seychelles*	Partly Free	3	3
Sierra Leone*	Free	2	3
Somalia	Not Free	7	7
South Africa*	Free	2	2
South Sudan	Not Free	6	5
Sudan	Not Free	7	7
Swaziland	Not Free	7	5
Tanzania*	Partly Free	3	3
Togo	Partly Free	5	4
Uganda	Partly Free	5	4
Zambia*	Partly Free	3	4
Zimbabwe	Not Free	6	6

* Indicates country's status as an electoral democracy.

Ratings reflect 2012 experience.

Source: Arch Puddington, *Freedom in the World 2013: Democratic Breakthroughs in the Balance* (New York: Freedom House, 2013), http://www.freedomhouse.org/report/freedom-world/freedom-world-2013.

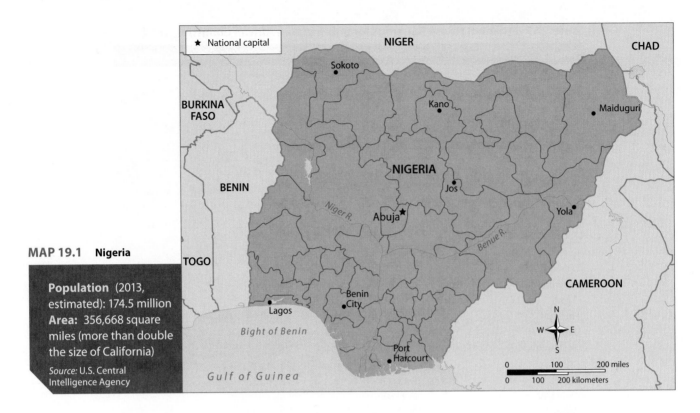

MAP 19.1   Nigeria

Population (2013, estimated): 174.5 million
Area: 356,668 square miles (more than double the size of California)

Source: U.S. Central Intelligence Agency

remains a continuing source of the abuse of power. These and other problems haunt Nigeria's troubled process of consolidating democracy. In 2012, Freedom House ranked Nigeria as partly free, which was no change over the 2011 score, noting that the People's Democratic Party (PDP) continues to dominate politics through a combination of direct intimidation of opponents and oil-based patronage politics.

Nigeria is an enigmatic case in sub-Saharan Africa. In many ways, this important country—20 percent of Africa's population—has long possessed a high potential for developing into a regional and global superpower with national wealth and a strong and vibrant democracy. Nigeria boasts abundant natural resources (especially light sweet crude oil, exports of which account for 30 percent of GDP), a vigorous civil society, highly educated elites, vibrant universities, and an enduring commitment to freedom, pluralism, and enterprise among its people. At the same time, the country has been plagued since its October 1, 1960, independence from Britain by poor leadership and a social structure that does not support national unity. Since independence, Nigeria has suffered six successful military coups d'état and many other unsuccessful ones, a brutal civil war (the attempted but failed secession attempt of the oil-rich southeast, to be the Republic of Biafra, from 1967 to 1970), costly military engagements in the region, endemic kleptocracy (rule by theft) and corruption, and deeply ingrained religious and ethnic tensions. An earlier attempt at democratization following military rule in 1979 broke down amid myriad governance failures in 1983, when the military stepped in again for another 16 years until democratization recommenced in 1999.

That Nigeria's consolidation of democracy has not been realized remains one of the most important facts of postindependence Africa, together with the realization that poor governance and the scarcity of natural resources is the principal cause of continued crisis and chronic poverty in the country. Above all, Nigeria's absence of democracy and development owes very much to poor governance.

The Mosaic of a Diverse Society

Nigeria is not only Africa's most heavily populated country; it is also one of its most diverse. There are some 250 ethnic groups in Nigeria, and nation building has been a central theme of Nigeria's political history.[28] Historical divisions centered on three major ethnic groups that account for some two-thirds of the population: the *Igbo* (or *Ibo*) in the southeast, who account for about 18 percent of the population; the *Yoruba* in the southwest (21 percent); and the *Hausa-Fulani* group in the northern third of the country (the Hausa comprise about 21 percent of the population, and the Fulani, 11 percent). Hausa, for example, is a language spoken by several distinct ethnic groups, including the Fulani, the Tiv, the Kanuri, the Nupé, and others. The Igbo, who initially lived in autonomous villages and spoke their own language and dialects, proved especially receptive to Western religious, cultural, and commercial influences. The Yoruba also had their own language.

In addition to having these ethnolinguistic divisions, Nigeria is deeply divided along religious lines. In general, the Igbo are mostly Christian and the Yoruba and Hausa-Fulani mostly Muslim. In all, Muslims comprise about half of Nigeria's population, and Christians about 40 percent. A large number of Igbo are Roman Catholics, but other Christian denominations, such as Baptist, Evangelical, and Pentecostal churches, also attract Nigerian adherents. Traditional animism remains widely practiced as well.

While the three largest ethnic groups tend to dominate Nigerian politics, it is important not to overlook Nigeria's numerous smaller minority groups, which often play an important role in regional and national politics.

The current patterns of ethnic awareness had antecedents in the precolonial period, most notably in the Yoruba kingdom, which was an identifiable entity with a shared culture and legal customs for several centuries before colonialism. But the effects of colonialism in molding today's social divisions cannot be underestimated. The British, who colonized Nigeria from the mid-eighteenth century to 1960, fostered regional devolution (indirect rule, as described earlier). They promoted the development of regional and ethnic identities in Nigerian political consciousness on the one hand and superimposed a highly centralized administrative system on the other. In many ways, this colonial system set up a tug-of-war among various regional forces in a fight over the central reins of power, creating precedents for postindependence political conflicts.

Like many phenomena in Africa, today's problems have deep roots in colonial rule. During the British colonial period, the regions of northern and southern Nigeria, fused in 1914, were only loosely integrated. Using indirect rule, the British fostered local autonomy in the more Islamic north but offered less autonomy and self-rule to those in the mostly coastal, non-Muslim south, where colonial "penetration"—the existence of civil and military administrators—was more extensive than in the hinterlands. But the British also systematically disadvantaged the northern Muslims in terms of education, access to political influence, and economic development, setting up a paradoxical problem that continues to influence Nigerian politics today. Side by side, a relatively politically powerful but economically weak Muslim north competes with a comparatively wealthy but historically less powerful south.

Regionalism fostered by the British has left a poor legacy for nation building in Nigeria. In 1939, the British divided their Nigerian territories into three regions (along with what was then the capital, Lagos, which was administratively separate): the western (predominantly Yoruba) region, the eastern (mostly Igbo), and the northern (generally Hausa-Fulani). After World War II, this regional division evolved into a federal structure. Federalism and related policies in the colonial period set up the basic dynamics that continue to threaten Nigeria's territorial integrity today. It also strongly influenced political organization, such that during the first elections in the early 1950s in the run-up to independence, ethnic parties quickly emerged and gained control of their respective territories.

As in much of Africa, rising nationalism in Nigeria in the 1950s forced the British colonizers to expand Nigerian participation in the country's administration, create elected representation, and ultimately move toward independence. The constitution of 1954 reinforced the colonial legacy by formalizing the regions and fostering the hegemony of a dominant ethnic group within each region. If it were simply a matter of constitutional structure, Nigeria might have overcome its ill-considered regional structure that reinforced social tensions. Throughout the years, through legal reforms, the number of states in Nigeria has ballooned—from 4 in the early 1960s to some 36 today—in efforts to change the regional basis of Nigerian politics. Other administrative and technical solutions to resolving ethnic tensions have been tried.

The First Republic, 1960–1966

Nigeria's first start at democracy after independence led to the creation of two broad political orientations: the Nigerian People's Congress (NPC) and the National Conference of Nigerian Citizens (NCNC). The former had its base in the northern part of the country among the largely Muslim Yoruba and Hausa, while the latter had a more southern base, rooted in the mostly Catholic Igbos. Generally, the NPC was slightly to the right of the center of the political spectrum and the NCNC slightly to the left. A high degree of unity marked the time of independence and the First Republic's initial years. The country's first president was an Igbo (Nnamdi Azikiwe), and its prime minister came from the Hausa-Fulani group (Tafawa Balewa). But corruption and ethnic tensions quickly undermined the civilian regime. In particular, a major dispute over the national census of 1964 (which was to determine the allocation of state spending) heightened antagonisms along ethnic lines. A devastating national strike also undermined the authority and capacity of the government.

Another factor that served to undermine the *First Republic*—and many Nigerian governments since then—is what Richard Joseph terms **prebendalism**, or the use of state offices as "prebends" (instruments) for creating wealth and gain for individuals and their ethnic brethren.[29] This use of the government for wealth-gathering (sometimes known as "rent-seeking") behavior has systematically undermined constitutionalism, which places an emphasis on the statutory functions of an office (that is, its legal competence as set forth in the constitution and other laws). Because prebendalism has become so prevalent, democratic competition in Nigeria has been fought with unusual vigor and often violence. Political party organization has often broken down along ethnic lines, threatening to lead the country into disintegration. These problems stalked the First Republic from its inception.

By the time the first independently administered national elections came in 1964, politics had deteriorated into a sharp struggle along north–south, Muslim–Christian, and conservative–reform lines. The election itself was hotly contested, but eventually the northern-based NPC emerged as the strongest party. Tensions mounted particularly in the western region, where the Yoruba felt repressed, and these tensions were exacerbated by regional elections. Rising violence further undermined the legitimacy of the country's first experience with democracy. Corruption, too, became endemic, and support for President Azikiwe quickly eroded.

Military Intervention and Civil War

In an abrupt move, the military intervened in early 1966, murdering the prime minister, the governors of the west and north regions, and some military officers. Most of those involved in the coup were Igbo, including the first head of the military government, Gen. Johnson Aguiyi-Ironsi. His efforts to establish an Igbo-dominated central government and his suppression of the north provoked anti-Igbo reprisals against their ethnic kin in the northern part of the country. In July 1966 Aguiyi-Ironsi was assassinated by rival northern officers, and Lt. Col. Yakuba Gowon, a Tiv, emerged as the new military head of state. Fleeing the massacres in the north, more than a million Igbos migrated eastward, and calls for secession—independence—for the eastern region grew substantially.

In July 1967, civil war broke out after a unilateral declaration of independence by the eastern region's military commander proclaimed the creation of the Republic of Biafra. In the ensuing violence, federal forces battled the mostly Igbo secessionists for three years. By January 1970 the east had been defeated. At least 600,000 people—perhaps as many as a million—perished in the bitter struggle. Most died of starvation, as government forces cut off Biafra from the outside world. Several countries recognized the breakaway republic, but many others sided with the Nigerian central government. After the Biafran secessionists were defeated, Gowon's policy of forgiveness and national reconciliation managed to keep the country together. He worked hard to foster a new national identity based on ethnic accommodation and tolerance, buttressed by a renewed commitment to federalism and equitable sharing of resources.

Gowon's military rule ushered in a long succession of military governments in Nigeria. Sometimes military takeovers have been popular, as civilian administrators squandered their opportunity to govern and lost public support. Often, civilian leaders have brought the country to ruin as a result of factionalism, personal power struggles, corruption, and ethnic favoritism. The military has thus stepped in as the guardian of order, only to rule repressively and in the interests of individual leaders. Almost always, the military in Nigeria has justified its intervention and the suspension of the constitution by promising to lead a transition to restore clean governance and democracy. But more often than not the military leaders retracted these pledges and retained their grip on power, burying hopes for democracy under a heap of broken promises.

Gowon headed the Federal Military Government from 1966 to 1975, facing continuing social and economic problems; he was then removed in a bloodless coup and succeeded by Brig. Gen. Murtala Muhammed (1975–76), a Hausa-Fulani from the north. The new military leader purged the government of thousands of corrupt officials. Soon thereafter Lt. Gen. Olusegun Obasanjo, Muhammed's chief of staff, was appointed president by the military leadership after Muhammed was assassinated in a failed coup attempt by disgruntled elements of the military who opposed his corruption-busting campaign. Obasanjo, a Yoruba from the southwest region, was genuinely interested in reestablishing democracy. Governing from early 1976 to the restoration of constitutional government in 1979, he restored order in the military and fought corruption. The Obasanjo regime led many Nigerians to believe that the military rulers were truly committed to the restoration of democracy and would respond to popular pressure for it.

Nigeria's fortunes were also buoyed by a rapid expansion of oil production, along with the bounty provided by the escalation in global oil prices during the mid-1970s. Up to 90 percent of Nigeria's foreign exchange earnings were from oil during this highly volatile period. Obasanjo's commitment to the restoration of civilian rule at a time of economic expansion set the stage for a carefully managed, protracted transition to democracy, giving birth to the Second Republic.

The Second Republic, 1979–1983

One of the most important developments in Nigeria's political history was the 1979 constitution, which established several important precedents. One such precedent was the creation of new federal states in an effort to break up the troubled regionalism. Gradually the number of states was increased to 12, and subsequently to 19. Also important to Nigeria's political evolution was the introduction of the "federal character" clause of the 1979 constitution that required equitable representation among ethnic groups in state institutions (especially the military) and an equitable allocation of Nigeria's oil bounty. This federal character principle retains its importance in today's Fourth Republic.

The constitution featured the creation of a directly elected president with substantial independent powers, a popularly elected National Assembly (lower house), and a Senate with representatives drawn from the states. Many considered the constitution to have been modeled on the U.S. system, although there is no evidence of a direct influence in the constitution-drafting process. The judiciary was fairly independent.

Nigeria's 1979 constitution also featured innovative devices designed to curb the influence of ethnic identity in political organization and leadership. To win the all-important presidential election, a candidate was required to garner an absolute majority of the electorate nationwide and at least 25 percent of the vote in each region of the country. This mechanism provided an incentive for political leaders to eschew narrow appeals to ethnicity and encouraged them to broaden the base of their political organizations to all parts of the country.[30] Political parties were to meet specific and detailed criteria to ensure they did not simply reflect regional or ethnic constituencies. The constitution also provided for compromise on the divisive issue of when Islamic law could be used to adjudicate domestic disputes. The careful compromise allowed it to be used in the Muslim northern areas but did not provide for its imposition on non-Muslims elsewhere or in instances where a party to a dispute preferred modern, constitutional legal procedures.

The Second Republic was widely seen as a reasonably good start for Nigeria's second attempt at democracy. The election results were disputed; the victor, Alhaji Shehu Shagari, won a nationwide majority, though he may not have garnered sufficient support in all the states. The election commission declared him the winner, however, and this outcome was eventually accepted by most Nigerians. But Shagari was a Hausa-Fulani, a northerner whose assumption of the leadership was resented by those who chafed under the north's domination of the central government. Thus the troubles of the Second Republic began right from its inception.

On the positive side of the ledger, political coalitions crystallized into two blocs, one predominantly right of center, or conservative on domestic social and foreign policy (now organized under the National Party of Nigeria), the other predominantly left-leaning, or more socialist in orientation (the Unity Party of Nigeria). Yet mounting ethnic violence, especially in Kaduna and Kano states where Muslim-Christian tensions flared, undermined the fragile regime. Once again, impending elections heightened tensions and popular support for democracy quickly waned. Factionalism and political infighting grew rife and increasingly violent.

The prebendal inclinations of politicians were revealed in a number of scandals, often reported by Nigeria's independent press. Ever since the advent of Nigeria's oil wealth in the mid-1970s, for example, control over the central administration had been a point of deep contention and unceasing power struggles. The central government was seen as a funnel through which the nation's oil wealth flowed. Control over the narrow end of the funnel allowed predatory politicians to siphon off the nation's wealth for their own personal enrichment. Corruption, malfeasance,

manipulation, neglect, and political thuggery undermined the legitimacy of the government and civilian politicians in general. Ultimately it eroded popular support for democracy itself.

When the next presidential elections occurred in mid-1983, they were widely perceived as fraudulent; few believed the Shagari government had been returned to power by the will of the people. Violence ensued among the major political factions, and disillusionment with democracy was pervasive.

Babangida's Dictatorship

Poor leadership and prebendal politics set the stage for the next military coup. Launched by Maj. Gen. Muhammadu Buhari in December 1983, it was led by officers who, like some of their predecessors, pledged to restore order, civility, and good governance to Nigeria. They promised a new election to overturn the theft of democracy in the failed elections earlier that year, but it was not to be. Although the military officers moved quickly to arrest hundreds of corrupt political leaders and made some headway on economic reform, they mishandled the treatment of many individuals in unfair trials, meting out especially harsh punishment to southern politicians. "Ethno-military rule"—the junta was dominated by northerners—also limited the credibility of the government's promises to restore democracy. (Buhari came from the Hausa-Fulani group.) Malfeasance and popular unrest produced a popularly supported usurpation of power by other generals.

This time the coup was led by Maj. Gen. Ibrahim Babangida, who would become one of Nigeria's most dictatorial and despised military leaders. Under Babangida, authoritarian repression intensified despite initial expectations that he would lead the country back to democracy.

Indeed, there was a brief period in which the dictator allowed party politics to resume and initiated a halting process of constitution making. From his seizure of power in 1985 to his ultimate political demise in 1993, a process of transition to democracy seemed to be under way. First, Babangida announced

Governmental control of Nigeria's enormous oil production has long occasioned corruption, malfeasance, manipulation, neglect, and political thuggery.

a drawn-out transition that was supposed to culminate in a return to democracy in 1990. In 1989 a constitution for the *Third Republic* was drafted that made modest improvements on the 1979 charter. The reforms included clarifying the electoral law while retaining the feature requiring the president to draw support from a wide variety of ethnic, regional, and religious groups. The new constitution also expanded the number of states to 30 to further encourage the development of more fluid, multiethnic coalitions. (Babangida himself was a northerner, but he came from a small ethnic group, the Gwari.) Some political prisoners from the Second Republic were released. Yet the dictatorial and kleptocratic nature of the Third Republic could not be denied.

Despite all the trappings of a transition to democracy, at the end of the day the military regime was ruling for its own immediate benefit and wealth. A bloody but failed coup attempt occurred in 1990, which nearly provoked a new civil war. During his rule, Babangida earned a reputation as the most corrupt ruler in Africa, vying for this dubious distinction with the Zairian strongman Mobutu Sese Seko. One of Babangida's most lavish projects was the creation of a new national capital in Abuja, where billions of dollars were spent on official buildings, luxury hotels, and hundreds of bridges in a city with no major river. Compared to the former capital of Lagos, Abuja was a gleaming showplace, but its amenities have been enjoyed mainly by visiting foreign dignitaries. The new capital was too expensive for ordinary Nigerians and remains virtually deserted. Under his rule, Nigeria became a pariah state subject to international sanctions. Its external reputation was in shambles, its vast oil wealth was squandered, drug trafficking flourished, and ethnic and religious tensions rose dramatically.

The 1993 Elections

Babangida's so-called transition to democracy was consistently manipulated and often deferred. Presidential elections were first slated for 1990, but they were shunted aside until June 1993. From the very beginning, the military's pledge to restore democracy lacked credibility. The ruling junta used the protracted and tightly controlled "democratization" process to enhance its power, with a view to remaining the arbiter of national politics even after its military dictatorship came to an end and a democracy governed by civilians took its place.

Among the many ways the military leaders governed Nigeria was their tight control over the registration of political parties. It was the ruling officers who required, through decrees, the creation of two centrist political parties. The military created a left-leaning Social Democratic Party and the more conservative National Republican Convention as a means to control the process of selecting candidates for office as well as the ways the parties would position themselves in the ethnically and regionally divided electorate. These parties were to be loosely based on the party structure of the First Republic, but in reality they were entirely new constructs. In 1992, the government allowed elections to the National Assembly. The voting revealed ethno-regional divisions between the northern groups backing the NRC and the southern and western groups backing the Social Democrats. The Social Democrats won a majority of seats in both the newly reconstituted Senate (earning 55 percent of the seats) and in the lower chamber, the House of Representatives (with 65 percent of the seats). The elections were flawed, however, because of the use of nonsecret voting measures and a very low turnout rate. Subsequent primary elections for presidential candidates were also troubled, with widespread vote buying and rigging. At the end of the troubled process, both presidential candidates turned out to be businessmen with close ties to the Babangida regime, although the SDP candidate, Chief M. K. O. Abiola, stood out for his cross-communal profile and broad appeal. The NRC nominated a little-known candidate, Bashir Tofa.

A genuine democratic fervor accompanied the presidential elections when they were finally held in 1993, and Babangida pledged to leave power in August. But the elections of June 12 were fraught with turmoil. At the end of the balloting, 10 days after the election, Babangida reneged on his pledge to restore civilian power. He annulled the results of the election when it became apparent that the southern traditional leader, Chief Abiola, had been elected by an estimated 58 percent of the vote. The international community was outraged, Abiola was put under house arrest, and the country was further driven into isolation and condemnation. Within a few weeks Babangida was forced to leave under pressure, but an "interim" civilian government under Ernest Shonekan fell within months to another military coup, this one led by an especially inept and corrupt military dictator, Sani Abacha.

Abacha's Dictatorship

Abacha, a northerner from the Kanuri group, ruled with an iron fist. Despite modest efforts to recruit credible civilians to his cabinet, he and his subordinates engaged in the systematic theft of the nation's wealth. Like other military leaders before him, he too announced a new draft constitution and pledged to lead the country back to civilian rule. But the military government's deeds spoke louder than its words. Corruption and arbitrary rule reached new depths. Abacha himself is thought to have embezzled billions of dollars from the national treasury, perhaps tens of billions. His cronies also profited handsomely from stolen wealth. A pivotal event in the deepening crisis in Nigeria was the execution on November 10, 1995, of Ken Saro-Wiwa and eight other activists who had sought to raise international attention to the plight of an ethnic group in the southeast, the Ogoni, whose area had been desecrated by pollution from the extraction of oil and gas. The executions led to the application of economic and political sanctions against the Abacha regime by the world community and reinforced Nigeria's status as a pariah state. In 1996, the British Commonwealth suspended Nigeria's membership and the United States imposed sanctions on the regime.

Only a bizarre twist of fate allowed Nigeria to find its way out of the abyss. Dramatically, Abacha succumbed to a heart attack June 8, 1998. Hopes rose that Abiola would now lead a transition to democracy. But exactly one month later, on July 8, Abiola died suddenly in the middle of a meeting with U.S. and Nigerian officials. Abiola's death set off riots by his supporters, many of whom suspected foul play because he was still in detention when he died. (An international investigatory team found no evidence of it.) General Abacha's demise set the stage for a new military government under General Abdulsalami Abubakar, a member of the Hausa-speaking Nupe group. Abubakar realized that the military's ability to retain power was at an end. Popular discontent was at the boiling point. He organized a rapid transition to democracy that featured local elections in December 1998 and presidential elections on February 27, 1999. Abiola's passing set aside the lingering controversy over the aborted elections of 1993. Nigeria now seemed poised for a fresh start.

From Prisoner to President: The Obasanjo Period

With the establishment of an independent election commission and heavy involvement by the international community, the 1999 elections were a major turning point for Nigeria. The presidential vote—widely seen as the most important in the transition—featured Gen. Olusegun Obasanjo, the man who had tried to restore democracy in the late 1970s, running for the People's Democratic Party. Until the transition of 1999, Obasanjo was the only Nigerian head of government who had gained power as a military leader (in 1976, when Muhammed was assassinated), only to hand over the reins of government to a civilian leader. Subsequently, in 1995, he was arrested by the military for advocating a return to civilian rule and democracy during the brutal and incompetent rule of Sani Abacha. In a secret trial, Obasanjo was convicted of plotting a coup and remained imprisoned for several years. His main opponent in the February 1999 elections, Olu Falae, was the joint candidate of the Alliance for Democracy and the All People's Party and was alleged to be a favorite candidate of the outgoing military regime.

In a vote deemed somewhat less than free and fair by independent Nigerian and international observers—including Falae, who claimed they were fraudulent—Gen. Obasanjo won a lopsided victory. With the support of a large majority (62.8 percent), mostly in the southeast and north, Obasanjo enjoyed the backing of some 18.7 million voters from all major ethnic and religious groups. Although Obasanjo is a Yoruba from the southwest (and a Christian), most Yorubas disliked him because of his past support for the Hausa-led military and his close associations with Hausa leaders during the presidential campaign. The majority of Yorubas voted for Falae, who also comes from their group, and many voiced displeasure with the election results. Nevertheless, Obasanjo's victory represented the first time someone from his region and ethnicity had been elected president with an ethnically mixed base of support. Falae garnered about 11 million votes. Despite the apparent irregularities, the victory of Obasanjo and his party was undeniable. On May 29, 1999, the military formally stepped aside and civilian rule at long last returned to Nigeria. The country's **Fourth Republic** was at last a reality.

Obasanjo was widely believed to be the one leader who could lead Nigeria out of its deep crisis. The country now had the opportunity to restore some legitimacy to its government, to begin developing anew, and to realize its long-lost potential.

The obstacles were enormous. Nigeria's tradition of democratic pluralism and constitutionalism had been undermined systematically for years by military officers and inept civilian leaders. Larry Diamond, a renowned scholar of the struggle for democracy in that country, uses the term **praetorianism** to characterize Nigeria's postindependence political system: a system in which personal power occupies the pursuits of political leaders and factions, and constitutional rules are manipulated for individual gain. Diamond perceptively argues that "the modern state was a resource, devoid of moral content or attachment, to be pursued, occupied, milked—and later plundered—for the individual politician and his support group."[31]

The Presidency of Goodluck Jonathan

Obasanjo, despite his global reputation as a devoted democrat, fell victim to the allure of power; when his two terms as president were coming to an end in 2006, he futilely attempted to modify the constitution to run for a third term. Following a political crisis and widespread condemnation, and little support from abroad, Obasanjo relented and the PDP chose a new candidate, Umaru Yar'Adua. The 2007 elections highlight a basic irony in the long-standing story of democratization in Nigeria. The electoral process was highly compromised, both through deliberate rigging and professional incompetence of the election management body, and through the systematic and deliberate use of election-related violence. The Independent National Electoral Commission (INEC) proclaimed Yar'Adua the victor against former military ruler Gen. Muhammadu Buhari of the All Nigeria-People's Party (ANPP) with a handsome presidential poll with 24.7 million votes,

President Goodluck Jonathan of Nigeria oversees a nation in which ethnic tensions and economic and resource conflict are on the rise at a time when the ruling party's grip on power seems to be slowly weakening.

10 CONDITIONS FOR DEMOCRACY

Democracy in Nigeria

The new civilian rulers of Nigeria's Fourth Republic, which finally got off the ground with the 1999 elections, must deal with a daunting array of challenges. We can critically evaluate the consolidation of democracy in Nigeria and speculate about its possible future course by measuring it against the 10 conditions for democracy discussed in Chapter 7. How has Nigeria done thus far in fulfilling these conditions, and what are its likely prospects in the future?

1 Elites Committed to Democracy

In the past, Nigerian political leaders often substituted military dictatorship for civilian democracy and used state offices to enhance their own personal wealth. The ruling elite under President Obasanjo seemed genuinely committed to democracy, though corruption remained rife in many institutions. In view of the importance of Nigeria's central government in holding the reins of power and national wealth, the commitment of its political elites to democratic rule—above all the military elites—is vital to the survivability of democracy in Nigeria. However, it seems premature to conclude that Nigerian elites are committed to democracy as opposed to self-interest.

2 State Institutions

State institutions in Nigeria have been well conceived in theory, but in practice have often proved frail and unable to withstand the pressures of ethnic and regional divisions and the temptations presented for officeholders to skim from the national coffers. The strict observance of the rule of law—and the elimination of corruption in particular—will be crucial in the coming years if democracy is to succeed in Nigeria. Similarly, a fair application of federalist principles to the country's diverse regional, ethnic, and religious groupings will also be essential. The current institutions are too new to conclude that politicians and powerful individuals will not be able to subvert them and avoid the rule of law.

3 National Unity

As we've observed, Nigeria's ethnic divisions have been a constant strain on its national unity and attempts at democracy, even though the immediate causes of the downfall of the First and Second Republics were other factors such as corruption and malfeasance. Ominous signs of religious and ethnic strife confronted the new Fourth Republic in its first year. In March 2000 and thereafter, some 800 people were killed in separate clashes between Christians and Muslims as the leaders of Muslim-dominated parts of the north sought to impose Islamic law in their localities and Christians in both the north and south vented their anger. Fortunately Nigeria's political institutions—while not fully consociational as described in Chapter 5—have been carefully crafted to help manage ethnic differences. Nigeria's diversity is thus a possible, but not inevitable, barrier to the consolidation of its democracy, depending upon how fairly the central authorities apply the constitution's federalist principles. Multiethnicity in and of itself need not undermine democracy in Nigeria.

4 National Wealth

Nigeria's national wealth is highly dependent on a single commodity, oil. Oil accounts for 95 percent of the government's revenues and the state has reaped hundreds of billions in total revenues since the 1970s. Unfortunately, about $280 billion was squandered by corrupt leaders. In the 2000s, buoyant world oil prices helped improve economic performance and increase export earnings. But the world oil market is highly volatile. Oil wealth alone will not allow Nigeria to overcome endemic poverty and structural inequality. Indeed, almost no oil-rich countries have been able to parlay oil revenues into self-sustaining economic growth and poverty alleviation. Nigeria remains one of the poorest countries in the world, with a per capita GDP in 2011 of $2,600. The country requires a structural adjustment of the economy in the form of a move away from reliance on petroleum exports, a process that is just as likely to destabilize the democratization process as lead to the consolidation of democracy.

5 Private Enterprise

The entrepreneurial spirit of many Nigerians is legendary, and the informal economy contributes significantly to the welfare of many citizens. At the same time, rampant corruption limits the ability of private enterprise to grow and prosper. (Nigeria is rated as one of the most

72 percent of the popular vote. However, the elections were mired in controversy: Nigerian author and intellectual Wole Soyinka wryly observed: "Long before the election itself took place, the election had failed. It had proceeded along unconstitutional lines, masterminded by one individual who had not yet given up his ambition of ruling that nation dictatorially, even after leaving office . . . [that attempt] is linked to the manipulation of this election, the rigging into office of a number of cronies of the departing president. . . ."[32] Indeed, some 300 people died in the electoral process. The Yar'Adua regime

corrupt countries on the globe—139th of 174 countries in Transparency International's Corruption Perceptions Index.[33]) State ownership of the country's oil reserves and nearly all its farmland has facilitated government corruption in the past. Private enterprise contributes to the consolidation of democracy only if the government can effectively root out the deep-seated corruption that limits a flourishing private sector.[34]

6 Middle Class

The development of a vibrant middle class in Nigeria has been stunted by the poor economic performance engendered by decades of misgovernment by the military. The country's oil wealth, in particular, has not trickled down to support the development of a strong and consolidated middle class. The absence of a secure middle class continues to limit the consolidation of Nigeria's democracy.

7 Support of the Disadvantaged

Endemic poverty characterizes the lives of most Nigerians today. According to World Bank estimates, nearly 85 percent of the population lived on less than $2 a day in 2010, and 68 percent survived on less than $1 a day. More than 40 percent of children under the age of five suffered from stunted growth in 2010 and 35 percent were underweight due to malnourishment. More than 14 percent died before their fifth birthday. About 36 percent of city dwellers lacked access to sanitation. (Nigeria's urban population exploded from 27 percent in 1980 to 50 percent by 2010.) Life expectancy is 51 years. In addition, Nigeria has one of the worst maldistribution of wealth patterns in the world, with a Gini index of 48.8 (compare to Table 1.2). AIDS is taking a rising toll—though not as severely as in other parts of Africa. About 3.6 percent of Nigerians were HIV-infected in 2009.[35] AIDS research and medical facilities have received scant funding in Nigeria thus far, however. Agricultural production has fallen far below the country's potential as a producer of cocoa, rubber, cotton, and other valuable commodities, thanks in large measure to inept government policies under the military. The rebellion in Nigeria's southern delta region, where oil drilling and processing are conducted by foreign-owned companies that have cut deals with the central government, raises the question of whether oil wealth is in fact a curse

rather than a blessing for oil-rich countries. The benefits of energy resources do not always reach those most affected by pollution and other negative consequences of oil extraction. Rather than promoting social cohesion in Nigeria, oil wealth inhibits it.

8 Citizen Participation, Civil Society, and a Democratic Political Culture

Nigeria boasts a vibrant civil society with a plethora of associations and trade unions. The vigor of Nigeria's civil society has been one reason military regimes have experienced strong pressures for a return to civilian rule, although at times civil society has become uncivil in that organizations have at times crossed the line into vigilante activity.[36] Nigeria's civil society will likely continue to contribute to the likelihood that democratic institutions continue to be perceived as the only truly legitimate form of government, bolstering the chances that democracy can be consolidated over time.

9 Education and Freedom of Information

Illiteracy in Nigeria is widespread. Half of adult females cannot read.[37] Without a greater emphasis on education and the extension of literacy to a great proportion of the population, Nigeria's chances for long-term consolidation of democracy are slim. Though the country boasts a vigorous free press, the newly elected government will have to take action to lift prior decrees restricting press freedoms and refrain from exercising excessive government controls over the media if democratic liberties are to be fully guaranteed.

10 Favorable International Environment

Nigeria's external environment has not been especially conducive to supporting democratic institutions; civil wars in Liberia and Sierra Leone, for example, have drawn Nigeria into costly engagements abroad. Yet the broader international community has been very supportive of democracy in Nigeria, and pressure from overseas has been one of the reasons military regimes have been compelled to return to civilian rule. Considerable international assistance—in the form of political party training, election monitoring, and development aid—continues to be critical to the long-term viability of democracy in Nigeria.

was short-lived. The president died just two years into his term after an extended illness, and he was succeeded by his deputy, current President Goodluck Jonathan, who ran for a second term and was elected in 2011. (For a list of Nigeria's leaders, see Table 19.3.)

The 2007 elections were a low point for Nigeria's Fourth Republic. In subsequent polls, principally those of April 2011, election administration improved; although there were still reports of significant and widespread irregularities, the polls were generally seen as an improvement over 2007 in terms

Table 19.3 Rulers of Postindependence Nigeria

Ruler	Dates of Rule	Ethnic Group	How Power Was Attained
First Republic, 1963–66			
Nnamdi Azikiwe	1963–66	Igbo	Appointed
Military Rule, 1966–79			
Gen. Johnson Aguiyi-Ironsi	1966	Igbo	Military coup
Lt. Col. Yakabu Gowon	1966–75	Tiv	Military coup
Brig. Gen. Murtala Muhammed	1975–76	Hausa-Fulani	Military coup
Lt. Gen. Olusegun Obasanjo	1976–79	Yoruba	Appointed by military
Second Republic, 1979–83			
Alhaji Shehu Shagari	1979–83	Hausa-Fulani	Elected
Military Rule, 1983–99; Third Republic, 1989–93			
Maj. Gen. Muhammadu Buhari	1983–85	Hausa-Fulani	Military coup
Maj. Gen. Ibrahim Babangida	1985–93	Gwari	Appointed by military
M. K. O. Abiola	1993	Yoruba	Elected; election annulled
Chief Ernest Shonekan	1993	Yoruba	Appointed by military
Gen. Sani Abacha	1993–98	Kanuri	Military coup
Gen. Abdulsalami Abubakar	1998–99	Nupe	Appointed by military
Fourth Republic (1999–present)			
Olusegun Obasanjo	1999–2007	Yoruba	Elected
Umara Musa Yar'Adua	2007–09	Fulani	Elected
Goodluck Jonathan	2009–	Ijaw	Succeeded Yar'adua 2009; elected 2011

of electoral process and the extent of fraudulence.[38] With the results favoring the PDP and leading to the re-election of Goodluck Jonathan over the erstwhile General Mohammadu Buhari (a Northerner), violence escalated in the northern part of the country, in which many victims were targeted on the basis of religious identity, leading to more than 1,000 fatalities. According to the International Crisis Group, "ethnicity and religion appear to have been intertwined with socio-economic malaise and grievances about marginalization."[39] Thus the 2011 electoral process leaves in its wake a situation in which ethnic tensions and economic and resource conflict are on the rise at a time when the ruling party's grip on power seems to be slowly weakening.

Conclusions about Nigeria

The evidence from Nigeria's checkered experience with democracy since independence and from its current situation is quite *mixed*. Positive tendencies coexist with less favorable ones. Political science predictions can by no means plot Nigeria's trajectory with any degree of certainty. Much depends on the ability of the government to manage ethnic tensions, contain political infighting, revive its flagging economy, and especially root out corruption. As a purely speculative prognosis, we can regard Nigeria's chances as doubtful, given the strains to which it will be put.

Nigeria today confronts major social, economic, and political challenges. In the social sphere, tensions are rising from the assertiveness of Muslims who insist on the implementation of Islamic law in their regions, as well as from ongoing sectarian violence between Muslims and Christians. In 2005 and 2006, Muslim sensitivities were aroused all over the world by a Danish newspaper's publication of a political cartoon that caricatured Muhammad; in Nigeria nearly a thousand people died in protest riots. The determination of traditionalists in northern Nigeria's highly conservative Muslim states to implement punishments such as stoning has created frictions with human rights advocates. These and other social conflicts were reflected in the difficult task of conducting a census in 2006, Nigeria's first attempt to count its entire population since achieving independence 35 years earlier. Previous attempts were thwarted by the exceptionally sensitive nature of ethnic and religious affiliation in the socially divided country. In 2009, an African Union peer-review assessment of Nigeria's democracy pointed to the continued threats of ethnic tensions and corruption to the consolidation of democracy in the diverse and highly mobilized society.[40] In 2010, hundreds of villagers near the central city of Jos were killed in Christian–Muslim conflicts, while in 2011 election-related violence between Christians and Muslims claimed hundreds more lives.[41]

In the economic realm, the dramatic rise in crude oil prices in recent years has certainly boosted Nigeria's GNI. Of course, volatility of world oil prices can threaten to lower GNI at any time. Incoming oil royalties have also created sharp resentments in local communities that bear the brunt of environmental degradation but do not get a fair share of the country's oil revenues. Rebels connected with the Movement for the Emancipation of the Niger Delta (MEND) in the Ogoni region are demanding greater central-government accountability. To dramatize their cause, they have kidnapped a number of foreign oil workers.

And in the political arena, Nigeria stands on the brink of crisis. In the Third Republic ethnic parties were banned. The party system today is governed by rules for party registration that require political parties to have support across the country. To be elected president, the successful candidate needs to have broad support as well: He or she must win at least 25 percent of the vote in two-thirds of the states, which essentially means that no candidate can be elected on a narrow, ethnic party platform. Provisions require that a political party name, symbol, or logo contain no ethnic or religious connotation or "give the appearance that the activities of the party are confined to a part only of the geographic area of Nigeria."[42] Moreover, there has emerged a practice in which a president from the north is succeeded by a president from the south, and vice versa, and the vice president would be from another region. This informal rule of regional alternation was put to the test in 2010–11. When Jonathan was elected president in elections in 2011, many claimed that the informal principle of regional alternation had been broken. The operation of this informal institution in the future will likely be key to overall stability in this deeply divided country.

SOUTH AFRICA

South Africa has been described as a "miracle" transition to democracy, emerging at the end of the Cold War from internal colonialism and white minority rule to become a model twenty-first-century, middle-income, globally engaged, and progressive democratic country.[43] The dramatic transition from white minority rule and apartheid—the separation of people on the basis of race and ethnicity—to democracy in 1994 reveals a remarkable story of a country that was on the brink of civil war, yet managed to avoid the abyss. In doing so, it embraced a multiracial democracy in which all citizens are entitled to vote and enjoy equal human rights regardless of race or ethnic origin. South Africa's success at democratization is a consequence of an unusual confluence of historical events, including the end of the Cold War, and the equally unique quality of its leadership, particularly Nobel Peace Prize–winning Nelson Mandela, the legendary freedom fighter who became the country's first black president. Despite its remarkable transition from apartheid to democracy, South Africa—riddled by widening inequality, continued unrest, and chronic poverty among the long disadvantaged black population—still has a long way to go before democracy can be said to be fully consolidated. The country's democracy will be put to the test in future years, as the government struggles to be responsive to the tremendous social and economic challenges it faces and the liberation-movement ruling party, the African National Congress (ANC), begins to fissure.

South Africa, with about 51 million citizens, is a very special case in Africa. Beginning in 1642, a European white minority dominated the African majority, exercising democracy for themselves while brutally exploiting and oppressing the black majority through the policies of apartheid (literally, separateness; pronounced "apart-ide"). Yet voting rights and democracy for all came in April 1994 after negotiations over a new constitution that featured enfranchisement of the country's black majority (roughly 77 percent of the population), an achievement seen as a miracle by some and by others as an inevitable

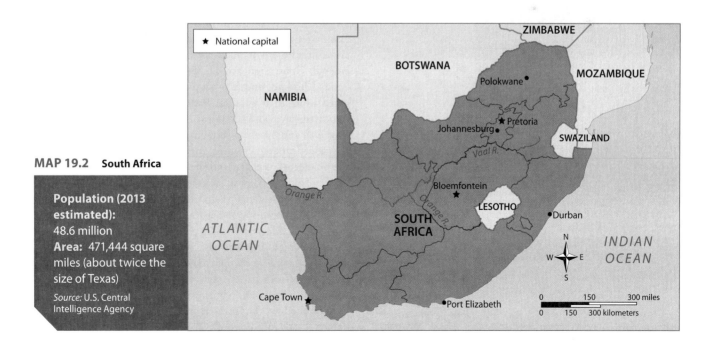

MAP 19.2   South Africa

Population (2013 estimated): 48.6 million
Area: 471,444 square miles (about twice the size of Texas)

Source: U.S. Central Intelligence Agency

consequence of the world's condemnation of apartheid-era racial discrimination.

South Africa's transition was the result of extensive negotiation and compromise among its competing political forces.[44] A white minority settler society ruled over the majority black population of South Africa for some 350 years, from the day the first settlers set foot on the Cape Peninsula in 1648. After mounting pressures in the 1980s and 1990s, the ruling regime—led by the **National Party (NP)**, which gained power in 1948 and implemented the policies of apartheid—agreed to a series of extensive negotiations on a new constitution with the leading force in the liberation movement, Mandela's **African National Congress (ANC)**. This process was turbulent: Some 14,000 people died in political violence during this widely heralded yet deeply unsettled transition. But in the end it yielded one of the most progressive democratic constitutions on the globe. Today, South Africa is a highly regarded developing country (one of the so-called BRICS, or Brazil/Russia/India/China/South Africa) and a member of the Group of 22 leading states worldwide. Although it faces tremendous challenges in confronting the legacy of apartheid, the country's prospects for the consolidation of democracy are widely considered good. How did a country ostensibly headed for a brutal war on ethnic or racial lines manage to transform itself into a model multiethnic democracy?

In 2009, South Africa successfully held a fifth postapartheid national and provincial election, and its democratic system now seems to be durable. Freedom House gives it some of the highest scores in Africa, rating it as overall "free," and assigning a 2 on both political rights and civil liberties. The organization raised concerns about restrictions on press freedoms and public-sector strikes (and in 2012 violent strikes in the critical mining sector) in which government responses have demonstrated a tendency toward a lack of accountability, together with allegations of corruption against the ruling ANC.

Apartheid, Conflict, and Liberation

Apartheid means "separateness" in Afrikaans, the language of the descendants of Dutch and French settlers of southern Africa known as *Afrikaners*. The policy of apartheid had its antecedents in the domination of the white settlers over the indigenous African peoples that began with the arrival of the first colonists in the late seventeenth century. Yet apartheid was more than just colonial domination; rather, it was a systematic division of the country's peoples based on race and ethnic origin. The policies of apartheid were intensified by the National Party, led by Afrikaners, after it took power in whites-only elections in 1948, but its roots lay deep in South African history. Indeed, some suggest that the more pernicious effects of apartheid were as much a legacy of British rule in South Africa (extending roughly from 1800 to 1910) as they were the result of the Afrikaners and the National Party. Even so, the post-1948 white-majority regime in South Africa perfected laws of racial domination—especially the exclusion of the country's majority black population from the voting franchise—and it was these measures particularly that led to a black uprising that eventually brought apartheid to an end.

South Africa's historical trajectory is rich and complicated.[45] Originally, the area was a colony of the Dutch East India Company, which needed this southern crossroads of the world as a station for ships rounding the Cape of Good Hope en route to and from the colonies of the West Indies. Soon after the founding of the Cape Colony in 1648, settlers arrived and the dynamics of a highly diverse society began to emerge. Upon their arrival, the Dutch settlers found indigenous Khoikhoi and San peoples, whom they quickly subjugated using their superior technology, firearms. The settlers imported slaves and indentured labor from Dutch colonies in East Asia and began to implement strict policies of racial segregation. Imperial contests ended Dutch rule by the turn of the nineteenth century, and the British took over the southern African colonies. British suzerainty and policies banning slave ownership led to an uprising by the Dutch-speaking settlers (known during the period as the Boers), and by 1838 all slaves in the colony had been emancipated. Consequently, the Afrikaners migrated into the vast interior of the subcontinent, in a pioneer march known as the Great Trek. At the same time, however, African tribes such as the Zulu and Xhosa had settled into the east and south, and black–white conflicts and wars erupted on the frontier. In 1838, for example, the well-known battle of Blood River occurred in which Afrikaner

Afrikaners' political identity was formed through the struggle to wrest control of the rich lands of what is now South Africa from African groups who had previously occupied it. A central monument to that struggle is the Voortrekker Monument in Pretoria. For black South Africans this monument represents the colonization of their lands and their subjugation as a people.

commandos (known as Voortrekkers) defeated the army of King Shaka of the Zulus.

By the mid-nineteenth century, the British controlled the Cape Colony as well as the eastern coastal zone of Natal. The Voortrekkers set up independent republics known as the Transvaal and the Orange Free State. In perhaps the most pivotal historical events in South African history, in 1867 diamonds and later huge gold deposits were discovered in the deep interior of the country; a rush for wealth began. Hundreds of thousands of new European settlers migrated into the Boer republics as tremendous mineral deposits were discovered. Conflict among the whites soon grew over the newfound treasure. The British governor, Sir Cecil Rhodes, sought to undermine the Boer republics and the result was the **Anglo-Boer War** of 1899–1902, in which British control of the entire territory of southern Africa was secured. The struggle embittered many Afrikaners: British troops committed untold atrocities, including the incarceration of Boer women and children in concentration camps. Although South Africa became independent in 1910, conflict among the whites and domination over blacks became the hallmarks of South African society.

Steadily throughout the early half of the twentieth century, South Africa's economy boomed from mineral wealth. Meanwhile the Afrikaners, many of whom were farmers or laborers, became increasingly nationalistic. They mobilized against black migrants to the cities who threatened their meager wages and also against English-speaking whites who controlled South Africa's capital, its mines, and the means of industrial production. Blacks were relegated to 13 percent of the land, encompassing the least agriculturally productive parcels. The Afrikaner nationalists, stirring up so-called "poor white" resentments surrounding access to jobs, unemployment, and subsistence farming, won progressively larger support among the Afrikaners, who themselves constituted a majority of the whites. They argued for stricter policies of racial segregation and discrimination against the burgeoning black population. They also claimed a Christian basis for their policies, locating its origins in a highly puritan form of Calvinism that they claimed ordained white domination over blacks in South Africa.

White Domination and Black Protest

By 1948, the Afrikaner-led National Party managed to gain power in an all-white election by employing the political and religious myths that demanded Afrikaner control of southern Africa as a matter of destiny. The policies of apartheid began to be systematically implemented. The entire population was registered by race: African (68 percent in 1960), colored (mixed ancestry, about 10 percent), Indian/Asian (3 percent), and white (19 percent). Mixed marriages and romance across the race bar were forbidden. Racially exclusive areas were demarcated, and blacks were forbidden in cities unless they had a pass that certified their employment. Blacks were assigned separate services such as water fountains, public transportation, and bathrooms, and they were denied education, health

services, and other opportunities despite the fact that it was on their backs that a prosperous, modern industrial country was being built.

In the vision of the architect of "grand apartheid," Prime Minister Hendrik Verwoerd, South Africa was to be internally partitioned. The "homelands," or reservations, were created for the 10 major black linguistic groups; gradually they became putatively independent black islands in a broader white South African sea. The South African government regarded the homelands as independent states, and their residents were not regarded as South African citizens. Hence they could be classified as migrant workers and were denied unemployment compensation and other benefits. No foreign country ever recognized the homelands' independent status, however. Apartheid was created to systematically exclude the majority black population from citizenship and economic opportunity in its own country.

At the same time that the policies of apartheid were being implemented, blacks began to develop their own competing national identity, arguing for an end to apartheid policies in their petty form (such as separate amenities) as well as in their more extensive form of "grand apartheid," which set up the system of homelands. On March 21, 1960, in the township of Sharpeville, the first black riots erupted. Blacks burned the passes that they were required to carry; 60 died as the result of police brutality. Today that date is celebrated as Human Rights Day. In a spiral of revolt and repression, black anger grew and the state responded with brutal force. The African National Congress (ANC)—the organizational arm and political party of the broader antiapartheid movement—was banned, along with other black organizations. Nelson Rolihlahla Mandela, a young ANC activist, was arrested and convicted of treason in the landmark Rivonia trial; he entered prison in 1962. As the protests grew, so did the repression and the whites' commitment to the systematic exclusion of blacks. Although some whites argued for progressive change, most supported the National Party's program of separation and domination. From 1948 to 1984, National Party governments were returned to power with enlarged electoral majorities among whites, including the support of many English-speaking whites.

Black protest grew more fervent in the 1970s. By June 1976, widespread riots erupted throughout the sprawling townships that lay astride South Africa's major cities. Beginning in Soweto near Johannesburg, youths set the country aflame, and widespread unrest drew more outside attention to the tragic oppression of the country's majority black population. In 1977 the United Nations imposed an arms embargo on South Africa and the litany of denunciations by the international community against apartheid began. Subsequent sports and cultural boycotts heightened pressure on the white government to reform. Just as the rest of the world was moving away from colonialism, racial segregation, and the denial of human rights in the 1960s and 1970s, South Africa was moving in the opposite direction.

PROFILES   Nelson Mandela

Nelson Mandela is considered the father of postapartheid South Africa.

Nelson Mandela, the father of postapartheid South Africa, led the independence struggle from his jail cell on Robben Island off Cape Town for nearly three decades, finally emerging from prison to negotiate with the white regime a new constitution that would guarantee voting rights to the majority black population. He served as the country's first president under the new political order from 1994 to 1999. Extremely popular among all segments of the population—including the white minority—he is hailed as the one individual most responsible for South Africa's dramatic transition to democracy. In 1993, he and F. W. de Klerk were awarded together the Nobel Peace Prize for their dedication to a negotiated settlement.

Born July 18, 1918, Mandela was the son of the principal councillor to the acting paramount chief of Thembuland. At an early age, he dedicated himself to the study of law. He was educated in a local mission school. Upon graduation from high school, Mandela entered the University of Fort Hare, where he was for a time suspended for protesting South Africa's discriminatory racial policies. He migrated to Johannesburg, where he studied law and began his political career by joining the African National Congress in 1942.

In Johannesburg, Mandela forged ties with other young black activists, such as Oliver Tambo and Walter Sisulu, and they founded the ANC Youth League. Mandela and his companions espoused African nationalism and began to mobilize the ANC to challenge the powerful white minority establishment.

The youth organizers eventually were elected to the ANC's National Executive Committee.

After World War II, when the National Party began to implement apartheid, Mandela and the ANC became more militant, organizing boycotts, strikes, civil disobedience campaigns, and other acts of noncooperation with the regime. Among their demands were full citizenship and direct parliamentary representation for all South Africans regardless of color. In 1955, he was instrumental in the drafting of the landmark Freedom Charter, which committed the ANC to a tolerant, multiracial South Africa with freedom and equality for all. During this time, Mandela was at times banned, arrested, and briefly imprisoned. In the early 1960s, as it became clear that the apartheid government's policies were becoming ever more cruel and discriminatory, Mandela went underground to form the armed wing of the ANC. He later wrote that only the intransigence of the apartheid government led him and his ANC colleagues to turn to violent armed struggle. Mandela became commander-in-chief of Umkhonto we Sizwe, "the spear of the nation." Although for a time he evaded the net of the white police, eventually they managed to apprehend him, and he was charged with treason. At the Rivonia trial, he conducted his own defense, uttering these words that continue to ring in the South African national psyche:

> I have fought against white domination, and I have fought against black domination. I have cherished the ideal of a democratic and free society in which all persons live together in harmony and with equal opportunities. It is an ideal which I hope to live for and to achieve. But if needs be, it is an ideal for which I am prepared to die.

Mandela was convicted at Rivonia, sentenced to life in prison, and spent the next 27 years clandestinely directing the liberation movement from prison. By the late 1980s, senior leaders of the white minority government were secretly visiting him in prison to explore a negotiated solution to the escalating conflict. Finally, in February 1990, he was released following a bold decision by de Klerk to negotiate a new constitutional dispensation. Mandela demonstrated tremendous magnanimity and called for national reconciliation, reassuring the white minority and in particular the Afrikaners of their place in a postapartheid nation. He engaged white leaders with no sign of personal bitterness and steadfastly led the ANC through the difficult negotiations that produced a new constitution. In the first full-franchise elections in April 1994, Mandela was elected president. From 1994 to 1999, he served not only as the country's chief executive, but also as its moral force, firmly launching the new democracy on a path of tolerance, moderate policies, and national reconciliation. After stepping down at the age of 81 in 1999, he traveled the world advocating international assistance to help poor children and mediating disputes in other countries such as war-torn Burundi. At age 95 (in 2013), Mandela lives near his birthplace in a quiet rural area, at times providing moral guidance to his country and the world.

Apartheid could not hold back the economic forces that led desperately poor black laborers to flock to the cities. The country's cities and their environs witnessed a growing influx of blacks—despite brutal government policies of influx control—pulled by the country's tremendous industrial development after World War II and by the diamond and gold wealth extracted from the earth. The government tried various measures to stem the tide of urbanization, such as forced removals and the deeply despised "pass" system, which required blacks to carry cards certifying their employment eligibility and thus residence rights in the teeming cities. Despite ever-increasing repressive measures, domestic discontent and international condemnation continued to ratchet up the pressure on a recalcitrant and entrenched white minority government.

By the 1980s, more comprehensive economic sanctions dried up new foreign investment, technology transfers, and trade opportunities. The once-roaring economy floundered and a recession set in during the early 1980s. About the same time, the first fissures emerged in what had been a brick wall of resistance put up by white South Africans. Under the reformist president P. W. Botha, the South African government began to ease some of the more discriminatory laws of apartheid while reinforcing its commitment to maintaining white dominance in general.

The halfhearted reforms of the 1980s eliminated some of the more overtly discriminatory laws—such as separate public amenities like drinking fountains—but not the foundation of the system, the race-based categories of citizenship. Far from defusing black anger and international disapproval, the reforms led instead to a renewed protest movement and a significant energizing of the international antiapartheid movement.[46] Widespread protests erupted again in September 1984 in a popular upsurge of demands for democracy, human rights, and full enfranchisement of the black majority. In 1986, the U.S. Congress passed the Comprehensive Anti-Apartheid Act, which included a ban on new investment and promised new sanctions if further reforms weren't enacted. Many other countries imposed stiff economic sanctions. With internal and external pressures mounting, the white minority reached a turning point by 1989, the same year that the Berlin Wall crumbled. White leaders could try to defend their policies of racial domination and face an all-out race war with the majority blacks in their country, or they could seek to reach an accommodation with black leaders such as Mandela before it was too late. Wisely, they chose the latter. Political violence was already high between 1984 and 1989, and without further reforms the black townships would once again explode in protest.

A series of unexpected events unleashed the process of transition in South Africa. In early 1989, the recalcitrant President Botha suffered a debilitating heart attack. Though he had initiated private, secret negotiations with Mandela, who was still in jail, Botha was a reluctant reformer who would not take the steps necessary to end the unrest. Later that year, the fall of communism created a situation in which the white minority—which had long claimed that the ANC was controlled by the Soviets in Moscow—could feel comfortable that black rule would not result in the widespread expropriation of property and industry. Botha was succeeded by a lesser-known figure from within the National Party ranks with a reputation as a hardliner, F. W. de Klerk, in August 1989.

The stage was now set for a dramatic change of fortune for South Africa. On February 2, 1990, de Klerk shocked white South Africans and the world. He announced the release of Mandela and scores of other political prisoners, lifted the bans on the ANC and other antiapartheid organizations, invited exiles to return home, and promised to negotiate in good faith the end of apartheid and the dawn of a fully inclusive democracy for all South Africans. Addressing the white minority government's longstanding enemies, de Klerk invited them to "walk through the open door, take your place at the negotiating table together with the government and other leaders who have important power bases inside and outside of parliament. . . . The time for negotiation has arrived." The transition had begun in earnest. Two weeks later Nelson Mandela, released unconditionally, appeared on the steps of City Hall in Cape Town before a joyous crowd after 27 years in prison.

The Turbulent Transition

The historic events of February 1990 set in motion a transition from apartheid to democracy that was full of hope for a brighter future for all South Africans but that simultaneously unleashed tremendous uncertainty. Initially, the negotiations went well, and an early accord was reached by May of that year that pledged the ANC and the government to a negotiation process that would culminate in the advent of a new, multiracial democracy in which no racial, religious, or ethnic group would dominate another. Individual human rights would prevail over structured domination by a group. All political prisoners would be released, free political activity would be allowed, and negotiations would proceed on convening a constitutional convention to draft a charter that would guide the new democracy into a more peaceful future.

Yet significant forces were opposed to the end of apartheid or were afraid that the ANC would emerge as a domineering political force despite the promises of toleration and reconciliation contained in the early agreements. In particular, the Zulu-based *Inkatha Freedom Party (IFP)*, led by Mangosuthu Buthelezi, felt excluded from the negotiations. With the help of clandestine forces in the white-led police and military, IFP cadres instigated violence, especially in the urban areas outside Johannesburg and in the already simmering province of KwaZulu-Natal, which included the traditional Zulu homelands. Although some analysts saw the emerging violence as ethnic—alleging that the ANC was primarily Xhosa in contrast to the IFP's unambiguously Zulu identity—in reality the violence reflected a political struggle over power, politics, and positioning for the postapartheid future. In the uncertainty of the transition, when apartheid was dead but the new order had not yet been created, violence among various factions soared. Thousands died in factional fighting and fingers were pointed in all directions.

Political violence soured the initial goodwill that had been generated by Mandela's release. In 1991 and 1992, mass killings, assassinations, clashes among armed militias, and continuing police brutality undermined the incipient talks on democracy. For a while in 1992 it appeared that the talks would fail and a civil war would ensue. Clashes between ANC and IFP supporters left more than 2,000 people dead in 1992 alone. Despite a major agreement in December 1991 to curb the violence—the National Peace Accord—the deaths continued to mount and several major incidents scuttled the talks. One particularly traumatic event was the June 1992 *Boipatong incident*, which left scores of innocent civilians dead after an attack by Zulu migrant laborers on a nearby township. Only after the intervention of the United Nations, which dispatched senior mediator Cyrus Vance, a former U.S. secretary of state, to investigate the violence, did the country's transition get back on track. As the killing escalated, the realization set in that the country faced a truly stark choice between anarchy and war, on the one hand, and compromise and power sharing on the other.

By late 1992, the violence had shocked the political leaders—especially Mandela and de Klerk—into reaching a series of agreements that formed the essential bargain, or democratization pact, of the negotiated transition in South Africa. Black South Africans would gain voting rights and other human rights in exchange for assurances to white South Africans that their property rights would be protected. Security force members would receive amnesty for any human rights abuses they may have committed, provided that they supplied all the details on any incidents of abuse. The African National Congress and the National Party would share power after an initial election, while a government of national unity would be installed until a final constitution could be drafted that would guarantee both

majority prerogatives and minority rights. South Africa would have a period of democratic power sharing in which decisions were to be taken by consensus among all the major political parties. This pact was sealed in multiparty talks that concluded in June 1993 with an agreement on an interim constitution and a specific plan for managing the transfer of power at the end of white-minority rule.

The IFP and some conservative Afrikaner parties, however, balked at the deal. They demanded greater autonomy for their respective ethnic groups—the Zulus and the Afrikaners—and vowed a campaign of violent resistance unless their demands were met. On the African nationalist left, opponents of the ANC, organized in the *Pan-Africanist Congress (PAC)*, also objected to the agreement, arguing that it granted too many concessions to the whites. The PAC demanded unfettered majority rule by the blacks, opposing any form of sharing power. These disaffected parties boycotted the signing of the new interim constitution and pledged to boycott—and possibly disrupt—the momentous elections slated for April 27, 1994, the elections that would end apartheid. Preparations for the culmination of the transition and the hotly contested electoral campaigns generated tremendous tension in late 1993 and early 1994. The far-right whites and the IFP as well as the PAC were poised to spoil the vote.

Mandela's renowned qualities as a conciliator, however, produced a breakthrough in early 1994 that brought the far-right *Afrikaner Volksfront* into the election. Significantly, the Inkatha Freedom Party remained outside the agreement. Preparations for the elections went ahead and a potential showdown loomed. After a bloody confrontation in downtown Johannesburg between the IFP and the African National Congress in which scores died, cooler heads once again prevailed. Deft politicking and international mediation (including an active role by U.S. Ambassador Princeton Lyman) produced a last-minute agreement among Mandela's African National Congress, the

Then South African President F. W. De Klerk, African National Congress leader Nelson Mandela, and Inkatha Freedom Party leader Mangosuthu Buthelezi represented the three largest groups that shaped the agreement out of which South African democracy emerged in 1994.

National Party government, and the Inkatha Freedom Party, leading to an end to the latter's election boycott.[47] Stickers were attached by hand on the already-printed ballots to include the IFP. South Africa's elections would proceed, and they would be broadly representative of all the country's major political forces.

Remarkably, the elections held April 26 and 27, 1994, brought South Africa some of the most peaceful days in the troubled country's history. Very little political violence was reported, the vote was relatively free and fair (despite widespread administrative irregularities), and the mood in the country was joyous. The results of the election were as expected: The ANC won a handsome majority of 63 percent of the vote, the NP garnered 20 percent, and the IFP 10.5 percent. All three parties would be in the government of national unity. Nelson Mandela, the guardian of national reconciliation, would be president. De Klerk, along with the number-two leader in the ANC, Thabo Mbeki, would be vice presidents. Buthelezi was offered a cabinet post as home affairs minister, which he eventually accepted.

The New South Africa

The new South Africa was imbued with tremendous hope for reconciliation, economic revival, and newfound legitimacy in the world. Mandela's famous acts of magnanimity toward white South Africans and his Inkatha foes—such as meeting with the widow of the former apartheid President Hendrik Verwoerd, donning the cap of the national (and historically all-white) rugby team at the 1995 Rugby World Cup (won by the mostly white South African team, the Springboks), and appointing Buthelezi acting president while he traveled abroad—did much to consolidate legitimacy for the new government. A new flag and anthem seemed to symbolically unify the nation, and many blacks and whites alike seemed relieved that the tensions generated by the enforcement of apartheid were lifted from the nation's collective shoulders.

The elections of 1994 not only produced a new power-sharing government, but they also produced a constitutional assembly that would create a new national charter to permanently guide South Africa's newfound democracy. In a process known for its thoughtful deliberations, its progressive embrace of human rights, and its delicate balance between majority demands and minority fears, the Constitutional Assembly produced a new constitution in 1996. It is in many ways the greatest achievement of the democratization process that today all the major political actors in South Africa see the constitution as a legitimate set of rules for ordering the country's political life. Among its most progressive features are the charter of human rights, which later set the stage for South Africa becoming the first country in Africa to recognize the rights of gay, bisexual, lesbian, and transgender persons. Moreover, in the election of 1994 the main political parties—under pressure from politically active women who had bravely fought apartheid—adopted voluntary quotas for the representation of women on their party lists (the electoral system is party-list proportional representation), an innovation which has since become rather widespread

in democratizing countries, including, notably, Iraq. The new constitution in South Africa and informal practices, such as the quota system for women, reflect the broader finding that transitions to democracy present windows of opportunity for expanding women's participation in politics and for progressive policies to protect the rights of vulnerable minorities, such as religious minorities or the rights of persons with disabilities.

South Africa's Government

South Africa has a *hybrid* democratic political system.

- The *Parliament* is bicameral, consisting of the *National Assembly*, its lower house, and a *National Council of Provinces*, which represents the country's nine provinces as well as local governments. The National Assembly consists of 400 deputies, elected to five-year terms on the basis of proportional representation. The National Council has 90 members selected by provincial legislatures and local governments.

- The *president* is the country's head of government and, as a member of the National Assembly, is elected by that body (not by the people). The president presides over the cabinet and appoints the *deputy president* and other cabinet ministers, and may dismiss them. The National Assembly may remove the president only for malfeasance in office or disability.

- One of the top judicial organs is the *Constitutional Court*, which hears cases on constitutional matters and has powers of judicial review. Its 11 members are appointed by the president upon the advice of the Judicial Service Commission. *The Supreme Court of Appeal* is the highest court in civil and criminal matters.

Postapartheid Politics: A Dominant-Party State

Many analysts around the world were concerned that South Africa's fledgling democracy would begin to unravel when Mandela stepped down in 2004 as president. Under Mandela's successor, Thabo Mbeki, a longtime ANC activist who was for many years its representative to the international community, the ANC was able to reassure the outside world and South Africans alike that he could successfully lead the country and carefully balance the need for change with the imperative of stability. Mbeki was for the most part a technocratic leader who took bold steps to revise the economy and work with business.[48] Mbeki also sought to assuage minority concerns and to carry on Mandela's legacy of balancing social reconciliation with the long-term transformation of South Africa's highly unequal distribution of income. In 2004 the ANC won a staggering 69.7 percent of the vote in parliamentary elections, which were widely viewed as free and fair (see Table 19.4). The party's large delegation in the National Assembly thereupon reelected Mbeki to a second term as president.

Mbeki, however, was forced by internal party dynamics to step down in 2008, after losing a power struggle to Jacob

Table 19.4 2004 and 2009 National Assembly Election: Votes and Seats

Party	2004 %	2004 Seats	2009 %	2009 Seats
African National Congress (ANC)	69.7%	279	65.9%	264
Democratic Party/Alliance (DA)	12.4	50	16.7	67
Congress of the People (COPE)	—	—	7.4	30
Inkatha Freedom Party (IFP)	7.0	28	4.6	18
United Democratic Movement (UDM)	2.3	9	0.9	4
Independent Democrats (ID)	1.7	7	0.9	4
New National Party (NNP)	1.7	7	—	—
African Christian Democrats (ACDP)	1.6	6	0.8	4
Freedom Front (FF/VF)	0.9	4	0.8	4
United Christian Democrats (UCDP)	0.8	3	0.4	2
Pan-Africanist Congress (PAC)	0.7	3	0.3	1

Jacob Zuma overcame charges of corruption and rape to become president of South Africa.

Zuma, his former vice president. Because the president in South Africa is elected indirectly—by a majority vote in the National Assembly, controlled by the ANC—the dismissal of Mbeki and the election of Jacob Zuma was entirely an internal party affair. The context for the abrupt changing of the president in South Africa in 2008, without an election, is intriguing. In 2005, while Zuma served as deputy president, he was implicated in a corruption scandal and fired by Mbeki; later that year he was charged with rape of a prominent HIV activist. Remarkably, however, Zuma was acquitted on the rape charge and later his prosecution on corruption charges was also dropped. Following this redemption, Zuma came back within the ANC by mobilizing the young populists who are disaffected over unemployment and poverty, and agitating on behalf of the restive trade unions. In the end, he outmaneuvered the sometimes aloof and less popular Mbeki to gain control of the ANC.

In the next national elections, the ANC under Zuma once again prevailed, winning nearly two-thirds of the seats in the National Assembly (down slightly from the 2004 percentage, which approached 70 percent). The opposition Democratic Alliance did a little better than in 2004, garnering 17 percent of the seats against its showing in 2004 of 12.4 percent. The voting base of the ANC, black South Africans, remained loyal to the liberation-era party, despite the arrival of new political challengers such as the Congress of the People (COPE), an ANC splinter party that was able to capture 7.6 percent of the seats in the National Assembly with a platform that criticized the ANC's record of service delivery after apartheid. In local elections in 2011, the ANC's grip on power also seems to be eroding slightly; in polls to elect new municipal councils across the country, the ANC's support slipped further to around 62 percent of the cumulative votes in the various areas while the DA rose to 24 percent. Even with these modest declines, the ANC remains a dominant party.

Under Zuma and ANC single-party control, South Africa continues to face tremendous economic, social, and political problems that have limited the aspirations and promises of the new democratic constitution. Among the critical challenges are very high levels of violent crime, economic stagnation, uneven performance in delivering key services (housing, health care, education, water, environmental quality), corruption, tensions over employment and affirmative action, and a highly unequal distribution of wealth and income.

Challenges Facing South Africa

Approaching two decades into its postapartheid era, what challenges face this consolidating democracy? The list of issues below is as daunting as any contemporary government might have to consider.

- *Reconciling justice and forgiveness for apartheid crimes.* The country created a *Truth and Reconciliation Commission* to review past crimes, hear testimonies, grant pardons for atrocities, and offer recommendations for social healing. Bishop Desmond Tutu, the Nobel Peace Prize laureate, chaired the commission. But few were satisfied with the commission's final report, issued in early 1999, because besides condemning the former white minority regime for human rights abuses it also criticized the African National Congress for abuses committed during its liberation war. It also singled out Nelson Mandela's former wife, Winnie Madzhikela Mandela, for her involvement in several killings in Soweto. A lingering question for South Africa is, how can the demands of justice be reconciled with the need for forgiveness?

- *Unemployment and poverty.* South Africa's unemployment level hovers around 25 percent of the working population, and 73 percent of the unemployed population are working-age youth; half of all youth are unemployed. About a third of the population lives on less than $2 a day, with about 14 percent subsisting on less than $1.25 a day. The maldistribution of wealth is perhaps the worst in the world; as Table 1.2 indicated, the Gini index is 63.1. Some 8 million South Africans are chronically unemployed, and nearly 45 percent of households have no income earners from pensions or the formal economy.[49] Some fear that with such widespread poverty, South African society is a cauldron that will eventually boil over.

- *HIV/AIDS and other infectious diseases.* Since 1990, South Africa has witnessed a terrible epidemic of HIV/AIDS. By 2000 it had more HIV-infected people than any other country in the world: in 2007, the UN's AIDS-prevention organization (UNAIDS) estimated that 5.7 million South Africans had HIV/AIDS, or a prevalence rate of 12 percent.[50] In many hospitals, half the emergency room patients test HIV-positive. Government efforts to combat the disease, as well as other threats to public health such as tuberculosis, have been riddled with corruption. Alcoholism is also rampant, posing additional health hazards.

- *Crime.* Johannesburg is one of the most dangerous cities in the world, with a staggering number of murders and other criminal activities. Throughout the country, carjackings, rape, violence against children, robbery, killings of farmers, extortion, and other crimes make South Africa's crime situation one of the worst in the world. The police system is crippled with the legacies of apartheid, which have left it wholly illegitimate in many communities. Many South Africans are uncertain if their country can prosper as a democracy with such high crime levels; while crime has abated in recent years, the crime wave of the 1990s and into the 2000s has led many skilled workers to leave for jobs in safer countries such as Australia, Canada, and the United Kingdom.

- *South Africa's role in Africa and the world.* Now that South Africa is a model of interracial reconciliation and a powerhouse in sub-Saharan Africa, with the largest economy and military force, it is increasingly being called upon to assume a leadership role in world affairs. Already, South African troops have intervened in neighboring states to promote stability, and the country has contributed to regional and international peacemaking and peacekeeping efforts. For example, it has played an important role in efforts to settle the war in the DRC and to mediate a power-sharing agreement in Zimbabwe. South Africa has also adopted an open international trade and finance regime, including participation as a BRICS country, though it remains vulnerable in a globalized international economy dependent on foreign oil. Foreign investment shot up after the 1994 elections, but investors remain fickle and especially wary of the country's comparatively high labor costs and labor unrest, its crime wave, labor unrest, and creeping corruption.

In some ways, South Africa is struggling with the reality that the challenges the country now faces are similar to those of many other "ordinary" developing countries. These problems are enormous, to be sure, but compared with the difficulties of the past, South Africa is well along the way toward its own renaissance.

Conclusions about South Africa

South Africa remains a society deeply divided by race, wealth, and ethnicity. While its hosting of the 2010 World Cup showed

a unified country with a strong, postapartheid national identity that transcends the divisions of race, religion, and ethnic difference, the reality is a country in which there is still significant inequality along identity lines and in which differences can still easily erupt into social struggles. Will South Africa's "miracle" transition succumb to the pressures of ethnic and racial extremism, as some competent and highly regarded analysts of politics in deeply divided societies have predicted?[51] Although there are incipient stresses in the newfound social cohesion that was the immediate outcome of the South African transition,[52] the patterns of intergroup bargaining that arose during the 1990–94 transition from apartheid to nonracial democracy are deeply embedded in many sectors of South African society, including its new governmental institutions.

Remarkably, this political culture of bargaining, steeped in the necessity of pragmatic moderation that propelled the transition, has been sustained in the postapartheid era despite the overwhelming electoral predominance of the African National Congress government. Ethnic conflict—which characterizes the vast majority of contemporary civil wars and political violence—still remains a long-term threat to this newborn democracy, if conclusions from the comparative studies of deeply divided societies are any guide.[53] Moreover, there is a growing sense that the multiracial "rainbow-nation" ethos is fading as clouds of ethnic and racial assertiveness appear on the horizon.

Moreover, South Africa's new constitution establishes rules that provide incentives for moderation on divisive ethnic and racial themes. Even though it is essentially a majoritarian constitution, conferring primary governmental responsibility on the majority party or parties, the institutions it has created contain myriad features that may check majority powers and mediate current and potential intergroup conflicts. The judiciary and an independent human rights commission, for example, have helped mediate disputes relating to own-language education and to women's rights, both in the workplace and on reproductive issues. The new political system, over time, will likely encourage the continued integration of South African society, providing institutional remedies and protections to its various minority ethnic and religious groups. For democracy to succeed, a strong civil society and a reinvigorated state (one that has earned legitimacy from its people) will be required, and South Africa appears to be well on the way to securing them.[54]

As long as South Africa's homegrown culture of bargaining, consultation, and intergroup consensus seeking is maintained—however inefficient and laborious such decision making may be—the country's transformation from being the locus of one of the most intractable ethnic conflicts on the globe to one of the world's most promising multiethnic democracies is likely to continue its present, relatively successful, course. This transformation has much to do with the high quality of its leadership, particularly the exceptional efforts of former President Nelson Mandela to keep nation building and reconciliation on the front burner of the country's political life.[55] In turn, South Africa has also taken the lead on creating a regional approach to democracy across southern Africa, and this degree of regional integration is generally seen as a model in Africa as a whole for

10 CONDITIONS FOR DEMOCRACY

Democracy in South Africa

We conclude our analysis of South Africa in the same way we concluded our exploration of Nigeria: with a brief overview of its prospects for democracy in light of the 10 conditions for democracy and democratization developed in Chapter 7. Each of these conditions constitutes an independent factor that has an impact on the emergence of democracy and its survival. Our expectation is that the more of these conditions South Africa manages to fulfill successfully, the greater its chances are of sustaining democratic institutions and practices over the long run.

How has South Africa done thus far in fulfilling these conditions, and what are its likely prospects of the future?

If present trends continue, ethnic and racial diversity will not seriously impede progress toward the consolidation of democracy in South Africa.

1 Elites Committed to Democracy

South Africa's governing elite, especially high-level leaders of the ruling ANC, fought for decades against a strong and bitter foe to gain their right to vote and exercise basic human rights. Their commitment to democracy is thus deep and strong. At the same time, civic elites such as white business leaders have dedicated themselves to working with the new black-majority government. Similarly, opposition political party leaders have learned to work very effectively within the new institutions, and they too are committed to democratic processes. It appears that elite attitudes in South Africa are conducive to long-term democratic survival.

2 State Institutions

South Africa's new democratic constitution, finalized in 1996, enjoys broad support and is widely respected within the country and abroad. It puts human rights at the forefront of state policy, strikes an admirable balance between majority prerogatives and minority protections, and shows appreciation for the principle of proportionality in representation and in the allocation of state resources. It also recognizes that South Africa must move beyond widespread economic inequality for the long-term survival of democracy. The constitution was broadly debated and is accepted by virtually all segments in South Africa's diverse social mosaic. The government's Commission on Gender Equality enforces the constitution's guarantee of equal rights for women. (About 43 percent of the National Assembly deputies are female, one of the highest such percentages in the world—see Table 1.3.) With such a widely accepted and progressive constitution, South Africa's state institutions are aptly designed and should help meet the society's needs for balancing stability and change.

At the same time, some government bodies—such as some regional governments—suffer from ineptitude and corruption. But on balance, South Africa's institutions contribute to the consolidation of democracy because of broad public support for them and for the principles on which they are based.

3 National Unity

Ethnic, racial, and religious diversity has been a challenge for South Africa since the first days of European settlement. Nevertheless, it has emerged from apartheid as one of the most progressive, multicultural countries on the globe, with a widespread commitment to unity in diversity—the "rainbow nation," as some have termed it. Blacks now comprise about 75 percent of the population, whites about 14 percent; about 9 percent are of mixed race and 2 percent are East Indian. Two out of three South Africans are Christian (including 60 percent of blacks), while about 30 percent have traditional animist beliefs. There are also small communities of Muslims (2 percent) and Hindus (1.5 percent). If present trends continue, ethnic and racial diversity will not seriously impede progress toward the consolidation of democracy in South Africa.

4 National Wealth

South Africa is the strongest regional economy in southern Africa and a significant "newly emerging market" for international investors. Its per capita GNI in 2010 was in the upper-middle-income range at $10,280 (PPP).

Much of the country's current infrastructure and economic development was built on mining as the critical sector, especially gold and diamonds. But mining revenues alone are insufficient to carry today's South Africa into the twenty-first century as a competitive country in the bustling international marketplace. Although natural endowments such as minerals still contribute to economic growth, South Africa will need to develop a more diverse economic base in high-technology industries. At present, its growth rate is only 2 percent to 3 percent per year, not enough to keep up with population pressures that add another 10 percent of job seekers into the employment market virtually every year. National wealth contributes to democracy's success in South Africa, but any decline of its growth rate could cool public attitudes toward democracy.

5 Private Enterprise

The private sector remains strong in South Africa, and the ANC's moderate economic policies have begun to woo more international investors. Although domestic and international investors are still nervous about South Africa's long-term economic prospects—especially about the power of the trade unions—the country fosters private industry and, increasingly, a burgeoning tourist economy. South Africa's strong private enterprise sectors contribute to democracy's survival.

6 The Middle Class

Class distinctions in South Africa are very pronounced, and a solid, multiethnic middle class is just beginning to form. Considerable emphasis has been placed on the development of a black middle class (to include other minority groups disadvantaged by apartheid as well), and signs that such a development is occurring are encouraging. The evidence suggests that, over the long term, South Africa will likely develop a fairly broad middle class that will contribute to democracy's survival.

7 Support of the Disadvantaged

Endemic poverty still grips many South Africans: As mentioned above, a third of South Africans live on less than $2 per day. Maldistribution of income makes South Africa one of the most unequal societies in the world (see Table 1.2). The country has alarmingly high rates of rural and urban poverty, unemployment, and health issues such as pandemics of AIDS and tuberculosis. The ANC government is committed to building a more viable social safety net even as resource scarcity limits initiatives such as building more houses for people who still live in informal settlements (shantytowns). The likely continued commitment to poverty eradication increases the probability of democratic survival in South Africa.

8 Citizen Participation, Civil Society, and Democratic Political Culture

One of the consequences of the antiapartheid struggle has been the strengthening of civic institutions, from neighborhood committees to professional associations, trade unions, women and youth groups, and numerous others. The political culture remains one that emphasizes consensus building and compromise. South Africa's diverse and sophisticated civil society and its newfound tolerant political culture are making major contributions to the survivability of democratic decision making.

9 Education and Freedom of Information

Transforming the education system in South Africa in recent years has been one of the most difficult challenges for the ANC government. Thirteen percent of the population is illiterate, according to the United Nations Development Program.[56] Years of inferior "Bantu education" for blacks, as it was known, have left a system of schools for the majority black population that are riddled with problems. Teachers and resources are extremely scarce and the administrative aspects of education have been dismal. At the same time, the country has a world-class system of higher education and a strong potential for creating new models of community college development. While education policies are improving, the travails of South Africa's education system are a serious impediment to the long-term survivability of democracy. A poor education system limits the opportunities for democratic consolidation in South Africa. Meanwhile, the country also enjoys a vigorous, capable, and independent media sector.

10 International Environment

South Africa's regional environment remains perilous. Instability in neighboring states, such as Zimbabwe and the Democratic Republic of the Congo, seriously threatens regional stability and could draw South Africa into costly military engagements—as combatants or peacekeepers. These wars and regional economic stagnation also limit South Africa's ability to be the economic engine of southern Africa, as it purports to be. At the same time, the broader support among the international community for democracy and development in South Africa remains high. International support for South Africa's nascent democracy will, on balance, bolster the likelihood that it will continue to develop as a democracy.

creating norms and standards for processes such as elections, and mechanisms for regional monitoring of elections and governance processes.[57]

In sum, we can conclude that the evidence available thus far is mostly consistent with the notion that democracy is being consolidated in South Africa, although the test will come when the ANC's power slowly fades or a split in its ranks occurs, and the moment of "alternation" in the ruling coalition arises. These grounds for optimism do not mean that South Africa won't remain deeply divided along ethnic and racial lines. The critical question for South Africa is whether its political leaders will succumb to the lure of "playing the ethnic card."[58] To what extent, for example, will they try to outbid one another in making extravagant or inflammatory promises to their constituents on sensitive ethnic and racial themes in forthcoming national, local, and provincial electoral contests? And how will the public respond to such overtures?

Conclusion

As we have seen, Nigeria and South Africa both have mixed records when it comes to the 10 conditions for democracy discussed in this book. A majority of the people in both countries seem to have embraced some of the core values of democracy, and the demand for effective governance, especially capable service delivery, is high. Above all they value freedom from colonial authoritarian rule and kleptocratic elites—whether in the form of military rule, as in Nigeria, or race-racially narrow based one-party rule, as in South Africa, or in the contemporary challenges of corruption. Most people in both countries embrace the value of inclusion in the political system on the basis of equality. But Nigeria has had significant difficulties inculcating the values of tolerance and compromise in its diverse, conflict-ridden population. The rule of law may be accepted in principle by majorities in both Nigeria and South Africa, but corruption—especially in Nigeria—undermines this principle in practice. Both countries established electoral democracies in the 1990s, providing an important element of popular sovereignty. When it comes to ensuring equal rights and liberties for all, Nigeria is still seriously deficient but South Africa has made greater strides. South Africa has also outpaced Nigeria in its attempts to improve the population's economic well-being, but both countries are plagued by a grossly uneven distribution of national wealth and reliance on primary commodities such as oil and metals, plus they have pockets of chronic poverty (particularly in large, urban slums).

Former UN Secretary General Kofi Annan, who hails from Ghana, has echoed former South African President Thabo Mbeki's call for an African renaissance. After witnessing great suffering as a result of the brutal civil war in Sierra Leone, he saw, in the midst of the atrocities of this war, a sense of optimism about Africa emanating from "the resilience and hope that form the reality of Africa today. . . . Never has Africa been more in need of political and financial help," he said. "But never, perhaps, has it been better placed to benefit from it."[59] Africa's countries are potentially on the cusp of a new era in which these societies will learn from past mistakes and embrace a course of development and prosperity. Virtually all observers agree that if such a rebirth is to occur, democratic governance will need to be fostered. As these countries evolve in the twenty-first century, a critical factor in their security and development success will be the further consolidation of their nascent democracies.

Key Terms

Apartheid
Neo-patrimonialism
Patrimonial rule
Hegemonic exchange regime
Prebendalism
Fourth Republic
Praetorianism
National Party (NP)
African National Congress (ANC)
Anglo-Boer War

Notes

1. For the rankings of African states on the United Nations Development Program's Human Development Index (a combination of a number of development indicators), see www.undp.org. For an overview of Africa's contemporary challenges, see Howard W. French, *A Continent for the Taking: The Tragedy and Hope of Africa* (New York: Alfred A. Knopf, 2004).

2. We will concentrate on the states of sub-Saharan Africa in this chapter. Although part of the African land mass and active players in African politics, the Arab states of the Maghreb region—Morocco, Algeria, Tunisia, Libya, and Egypt—are more closely associated with the Mediterranean and Middle East regions.

3. See http://www.refer.sn/sngal_ct/cop/goree/fgoree.htm. For a view of the island during the slave period, visit http://webworld.unesco.org/goree/en/wade.shtml.

4. For an analysis of the project of nation building within the colonial-era borders, see Ricardo René Laremont, ed., *Borders, Nationalism, and the African State* (Boulder, CO: Lynne Rienner, 2005).

5. See Gerald Bender, *Angola Under the Portuguese: The Myth and Reality* (Berkeley and Los Angeles: University of California Press, 1978).

6. The commonwealth consists of former British colonies or dependencies that are now independent countries. Membership is voluntary, and the organization's main function is consultation on such matters as economic cooperation, technical assistance, terrorism, and drug trafficking. At the end of 2006 there were 53 member states.

7. The term *Boer* has been abused at times as a term in the context of hate speech, particularly in recent controversies of the continued singing of a liberation-era song that includes the line "kill the farmer, kill the Boer." Thus the term in some contexts or usages is considered derogatory. At best, the term should be used in its historical contexts in South African history, and reference to the identity group should occur through the preferred contemporary term *Afrikaners*.

8. See Gus Liebenow, "The Impact of Colonialism," in *African Politics: Crises and Challenges* (Bloomington, IN: Indiana University Press, 1986).

9. See Zaki Laidi, *The Superpowers and Africa: The Constraints of Rivalry, 1960–1990* (Chicago: University of Chicago Press, 1990).

10. See René Lemarchand, "Political Clientelism and Ethnicity in Tropical Africa: Competing Solidarities in Nation-Building," *American Political Science Review* 66 (1972), pp. 68–90.

11. This argument was first articulated by Sir Arthur Lewis in his classic book, *Politics in West Africa* (London: Allen and Unwin, 1965).

12. See Robert Jackson and Carl Rosberg, *Personal Rule in Black Africa* (Los Angeles and Berkeley: University of California Press, 1982). See also

Robert H. Bates. 2006. *When Things Fell Apart: State Failure in Late-Century Africa*. Cambridge: Cambridge University Press.

13. See Robert I. Rotberg, "Winning the African Prize for Repression: Zimbabwe," in *The Worst of the Worst: Dealing with Repressive and Rogue Nations*, ed. Robert I. Rotberg (Washington, DC: Brookings Institution Press, 2007).

14. See John Wiseman, *Democracy in Black Africa: Survival and Revival* (New York: Paragon House, 1990). For an analysis of elections in Africa, see Staffan I. Lindberg, "The Democratic Qualities of Competitive Elections: Participation, Competition and Legitimacy in Africa," *Commonwealth & Comparative Politics* 41, no. 3 (2003), pp. 61–105.

15. See Donald Rothchild and Victor Oloronsula, eds., *State Versus Ethnic Claims: African Policy Dilemmas* (Boulder, CO: Westview Press, 1983).

16. See Letitia Lawson, "The Politics of Anti-Corruption Reform in Africa," *The Journal of Modern African Studies* 47 (2009), pp. 73–100.

17. See Francis Deng et al., *Sovereignty as Responsibility: Conflict Management in Africa* (Washington, DC: Brookings Institution Press, 1996).

18. See Michael Bratton and Nicolas van de Walle, "Popular Protest and Political Reform in Africa," *Comparative Politics* 24 (1992), pp. 419–42.

19. See Colin Legum, "The Coming of Africa's Second Independence," *The Washington Quarterly* 25 (Winter 1990), pp. 129–40. See also Claude Ake, "Rethinking African Democracy," *Journal of Democracy* 2, no. 1 (1991), pp. 32–44.

20. See the 2008 study commissioned by the U.S. Central Intelligence Agency, Director of National Intelligence, *Democratization in Africa: What Progress toward Institutionalization?* http://www.dni.gov/nic/PDF _GIF_confreports/african_democ_2008.pdf.

21. See Harvey Glickman, ed., *Ethnic Conflict and Democratization in Africa* (Atlanta: African Studies Association Press, 1995).

22. See Timothy Sisk and Andrew Reynolds, eds., *Elections and Conflict Management in Africa* (Washington, DC: United States Institute of Peace Press, 1998).

23. John W. Harbeson, "Rethinking Democratic Transitions: Lessons from Eastern and Southern Africa," in *State, Conflict, and Democracy in Africa*, ed. Richard Joseph (Boulder, CO: Lynne Rienner Press, 1999).

24. Statement at the African Telecom Forum, Johannesberg, May 4, 1990.

25. See Nicholas Van de Walle, "Africa's Range of Regimes," *Journal of Democracy* 13, no. 2 (2002), pp. 66–80; Afrobarometer Network, "Neither Consolidating Nor Fully Democratic: The Evolution of African Political Regimes, 1999-2008," Afrobarometer Briefing Paper No. 67 (2009), http://www.afrobarometer.org/papers/AfrobriefNo67_19may09_final .pdf.

26. See the Afrobarometer Network, "The Quality of Democracy and Governance in Africa: New Results from the Afrobarometer Round 4," Afrobarometer Working Paper No. 108, p. 7.

27. Ibid.

28. See Muhammad Sani Umar, "Weak States and Democratization: Ethnic and Religious Conflicts in Nigeria," in *Identity Conflicts: Can Violence Be Regulated?* ed. J. Craig Jenkins and Esther E. Gottlieb (Piscataway, NJ: Transaction Publishers, 2007).

29. Richard Joseph, "Autocracy, Violence, and Ethnomilitary Rule in Nigeria," in Joseph, *State, Conflict and Democracy in Africa*.

30. Donald Horowitz, *Ethnic Groups in Conflict* (Berkeley and Los Angeles: University of California Press, 1985).

31. Larry Diamond, "Nigeria: The Uncivil Society and the Descent into Praetorianism," in *Politics in the Developing Countries: Comparing Experiences with Democracy*, 2nd ed., ed. Larry Diamond, Juan J. Linz, and Seymour Martin Lipset (Boulder, CO: Lynne Rienner Press, 1995), p. 419.

32. Wole Soyinka, Testimony at the United States House of Representatives, Subcommittee on Africa and Global Health, hearing "Nigeria at the Crossroads: Elections, Legitimacy and a Way Forward," June 7, 2007, Washington, DC: Committee on Foreign Affairs, Serial 110-80, pp. 26–27.

33. www.transparency.org/cpi2012/.

34. See the special section on Nigeria in *The Economist*, January 15, 2000.

35. Data available at www.unicef.org/infobycountry/nigeria_statistics.html and data.worldbank.org.

36. See, for example, Kate Meagher, "Hijacking Civil Society: the Inside Story of the Bakassi Boys Vigilante Group of South-eastern Nigeria," *The Journal of Modern African Studies* 45 (2007), pp. 89–115.

37. 2010 data from databank.worldbank.org.

38. Dorina Bekoe, "Nigeria's 2011 Elections: Best Run, but Most Violent," Peace Brief 103, United States Institute for Peace, August 15, 2011, www .usip.org/files/resources/PB103.pdf.

39. International Crisis Group, "Lessons From Nigeria's 2011 Elections," Crisis Group Africa Briefing No. 81, September 15, 2011, www.crisisgroup .org/~/media/Files/africa/west-africa/nigeria/B81%20-%20Lessons%20 from%20Nigeras%202011%20Elections.pdf.

40. African Union, "Federal Republic of Nigeria," APRM Country Review Report No. 8, June 2009.

41. Human Rights Watch, "Country Summary: Nigeria," January 2012, www.hrw.org/sites/default/files/related_material/nigeria_2012.pdf.

42. As reported in the Report of the Commonwealth Observer Group, "Nigeria: State and Federal Elections," April 14 and 21, 2007, p. 20. Additionally, the Electoral Act of 2006 prevents campaigning on religious, tribal, or sectional basis.

43. On the miracle metaphor, see Patti Waldmeir, *Anatomy of a Miracle: The End of Apartheid and the Birth of a New South Africa* (New Brunswick, NJ: Rutgers University Press, 1998).

44. See Timothy Sisk, *Democratization in South Africa: The Elusive Social Contract* (Princeton, NJ: Princeton University Press, 1995).

45. See Leonard Thompson, *A History of South Africa* (New Haven, CT: Yale University Press, 1990).

46. See Robert Price, *The Apartheid State in Crisis: Political Transformation in South Africa, 1975–1990* (New York: Oxford University Press, 1991).

47. Donald Rothchild notes that international mediation was critical to the success of the South African transition despite the reluctance of the parties to external influence. See his *Managing Ethnic Conflict in Africa* (Washington, DC: Brookings Institution Press, 1997), pp. 191–211.

48. William Mervin Gumede, *Thabo Mbeki and the Battle for the Soul of the ANC* (Cape Town: Zebra, 2005).

49. United Nations Development Program, "South Africa: The Challenge of Sustainable Development, National Human Development Report 2003," http://hdr.undp.org/en/reports/nationalreports/africa/southafrica/ south_africa_2003_en.pdf.

50. See the 2006 "Report on the Global Aids Epidemic" produced by UNAIDS (Joint United Nations Program on HIV/AIDS), unaids.org.

51. Comparativist scholars such as Arend Lijphart, *Power Sharing in South Africa* (Berkeley, CA: Institute of International Studies, 1985) and Donald Horowitz, *A Democratic South Africa? Constitutional Engineering in a Divided Society* (Berkeley and Los Angeles: University of California Press, 1991) predicted severe ethnic strife if the cluster of political institutions they advocated for South Africa (consociational versus integrative institutions, respectively) were not adopted. Horowitz went so far as to predict "Zulu-Xhosa" polarity as the greatest threat to postapartheid South Africa. Marina Ottaway in *South Africa: The Struggle for a New Order* (Washington, DC: Brookings Institution Press, 1993) referred to the transition from apartheid as a process of conflict generation as much as conflict management and saw ethnic nationalism increasing and threatening any political settlement that might emerge.

52. Sisk, *Democratization in South Africa*.

53. See Donald Horowitz, "Democracy in Divided Societies," *Journal of Democracy* 4, no. 4, (1993), pp. 18–38.

54. See Pierre du Toit, *State Building and Democracy in Southern Africa: Botswana, Zimbabwe, and South Africa* (Washington, DC: United States Institute of Peace Press, 1995).

55. See Tom Lodge, *Politics in South Africa: From Mandela to Mbeki* (Oxford: Oxford University Press, 2003).

56. www.undp.org/content/undp/en/home/librarypage/hdr/human _developmentreport2011/.

57. See Khabele Matlosa and Kebapetse Lotshwao, "Political Integration and Democratization in Southern Africa: Progress, Problems, and Prospects," Pretoria: Electoral Institute for the Sustainability of Democracy in Africa, http://www.eisa.org.za/PDF/rr47.pdf.

58. Alvin Rabushka and Kenneth A. Shepsle, *Politics in Plural Societies* (Columbus, OH: Charles E. Merrill, 1972).

59. Kofi Annan, "Window of African Promise amid Great Suffering," *International Herald Tribune*, July 31–August 1, 1999.

Glossary

A

African National Congress (ANC) Political party that has governed South Africa since the end of apartheid in 1994. Before 1994 it served as the organizational arm and political party of the broader antiapartheid movement.

Anarchism A political philosophy that argues people are better off without an organized government. While anarchism has sparked political movements in several countries, it has not been adopted.

Anglo-Boer War A 1899–1902 war between the British colonial authorities and Afrikaans-speaking settlers in South Africa by which British control of the entire territory of southern Africa was secured.

Anticipated (snap) elections Parliamentary elections that take place before the expiration of the legislature's full term.

Apartheid A system of strict racial segregation in South Africa that permitted white minority rule. As a formal policy apartheid was in force from 1949 to 1994, but racial segregation long predated formal apartheid legislation.

Authoritarianism (dictatorship) A political regime type that places the governing authorities above the people. The people have little, if any, say in who governs them or how they are governed.

Authority The exercise of legitimate power. A ruler who exercises authority can expect the people will obey a specific command because they regard it as right.

Autonomy of the state The relative independence of state authorities from specific groups within society.

B

Basic Law The founding document of the Federal Republic of Germany that went into effect on May 23, 1949, when the Federal Republic of Germany was formally proclaimed in the western occupation zone. The Basic Law is the equivalent to the constitution of Germany.

Bicameral legislature A legislative body that consists of two houses (or chambers). Typically one of these chambers is considered the lower house (e.g., the U.S. House of Representatives) and the second is regarded as the upper house (e.g., the U.S. Senate).

Bolsheviks Lenin's party, whose name means majority, derived from their false claim to be the majority faction of the Russian Social Democratic Labor Party. The Bolsheviks evolved into the Communist Party of the Soviet Union.

Bonapartism A reference to Napoleon's populist military autocracy. This term implies a preference for a strong, centralized authority led by a popular leader such as Charles de Gaulle.

Budget deficit Circumstance arising when government expenditures exceed government revenues.

Bundesrat Upper house of the parliament of the Federal Republic of Germany that directly represents states. Bundesrat members are chosen by the state governments.

Bundestag Popularly elected lower house of the Federal Republic of Germany.

Bureaucracy Well-developed network of state organs charged with advising political decision makers about different policy options and implementing policies once they have been decided upon.

C

Catchall parties Political parties that seek to widen their base of popular support as much as possible, eschewing ideological purity in favor of electoral success.

Central bank The national government's official bank.

Centrally planned (command) economy A form of political economy that effectively fuses the state and the economy. In a centrally planned economy, investment, production, and distribution decisions are made by state authorities rather than by private investors, producers, and consumers. Centrally planned economies were implemented in the Soviet Union under Stalin and his successors and in the client states they dominated after the Second World War.

Chancellor The prime minister or head of government in Germany.

Chinese Communist Party (CCP) The Communist Party of China, which founded the People's Republic of China in 1949 and has ruled the country since then.

Chinese Nationalist Party (Kuomintang, KMT) Political party established by Sun Yat-sen, which ruled much of China in the interwar period before being expelled to Taiwan in 1949 by the Chinese Communist Party. The guiding political doctrine is the "Three Principles of the People" (nationalism, democracy, and social well-being). The KMT has ruled Taiwan for most of the post-1949 period.

Christian Democratic Union (CDU) One of the major German political parties, founded after World War II, that combined Catholics and Protestants across Germany into a single party. A right-of-center party, the CDU subscribes in a general way to Christian principles such as fellowship and reconciliation.

Christian Social Union (CSU) A more conservative sister party to the Christian Democratic Union, the CSU competes only in state elections in Bavaria while allying with the CDU in national elections.

Citizenship The relationship of a person to a state. Within a state's territory, a citizen has rights, such as those outlined in the U.S. Constitution and Bill of Rights, and reciprocally has certain duties in relation to the society and the state.

Civic culture A term coined by Gabriel Almond and Sidney Verba to refer to a combination of fairly large numbers of persons with participant and subject orientations together with a smaller number of individuals with a parochial orientation.

Civil society Those associations organized independently of the state.

Class The economic or status position of an individual or group in society. Class implies a hierarchy of status positions, with some persons having higher status and others lower status based on occupational and income differences.

Cleavages Social divisions that are meaningful enough to shape political preferences.

Clientelism A form of political organization based on authorities or political patrons dispensing benefits or favors to people in exchange for their votes or other forms of support.

Coalition government Government formed when two or more parties agree to share cabinet posts, usually to form a voting majority in the legislature.

Codetermination The relationship between workers and their employers that allows German workers to share responsibility with their employers in determining wages, working hours, work rules, and other company policies.

Cohabitation In France the situation that arises when the president is of one party and the prime minister represents an opposing party. Cohabitation is the French version of divided government.

Collective goods Material or nonmaterial goods that are shared by large segments of the community rather than being divisible among individuals.

Commonwealth of Independent States (CIS) A regional organization formed following the dissolution of the Soviet Union, the CIS was composed of the former Soviet republics, except Estonia, Latvia, Lithuania, and Georgia.

Communal activity Collective action at the neighborhood or village level whereby fellow citizens collaborate to achieve local needs, such as building a ballpark, creating and operating a neighborhood watch organization, or launching a fund drive to finance additions to a local school or clinic.

Communist Party of the Soviet Union (CPSU) The political party that ruled during the entirety of the history of the Soviet Union. The CPSU grew out of the Bolshevik Party, which rose to dominance during the Russian Revolution in 1917.

Comparative politics The subfield of political science that engages in the comparative examination of the political realities in countries all over the world. It looks at the many ways governments operate and the ways people behave in political life. It considers the actions of governments and individual political behavior comparatively, drawing inferences and conclusions by comparing and contrasting.

Confederation A loose arrangement characterized by a weak central state and a group of constituent subnational elements that enjoy significant autonomy or even independence as sovereign states. Confederations have weaker central governments than do federalist regimes.

Conservatism A political philosophy that advocates maintaining traditional political and social arrangements. In the contemporary world conservatism typically advocates minimal government interference in the economy.

Conservatives (Tories) British political party originally identified by devotion to absolutist monarchy, aristocratic rule, the House of Lords, and the established Anglican church. The contemporary Conservative Party is a catchall party with a right-of-center ideological orientation.

Consociational democracy A democratic regime that establishes political institutions that allow elite accommodation in a socially heterogeneous society, thereby limiting political conflict.

Consolidation The building of a strong and lasting democracy that withstands the tests of time.

Constitutional (limited) monarchy A political regime in which the monarch is head of state, but real decision-making power is in the hands of other institutional authorities such as legislators, the prime minister, and other officials who answer to them.

Contentious politics A form of political participation in which one or more actors engage in disruptive activities to express a political perspective, including making demands on the government in an attempt to shape public policy.

Conventional political participation Forms of political participation regarded as normal in democracies, such as voting, working through political parties to support campaigns and candidates, and lobbying through interest groups.

Corporatism A system of formal interest group participation in the state's decision-making processes.

Correlation (association) A relationship in which two or more variables change together.

Coup d'état A forceful takeover of state power by the military.

D

Decolonization The process by which colonies of imperial powers gain their independence. Decolonization took place in Asia and Africa in the decades after World War II, while Latin American decolonization occurred at the end of the Napoleonic Wars.

Deduction Reasoning process that proceeds from the general to the specific.

Democracy (1) The idea that the people should have the right to determine who governs them, and that there should be legal limits on the government's authority through guarantees that citizens will enjoy certain rights and freedoms. (2) A political regime that offers regular opportunities for peaceful competition for political power, thereby allowing the people, no segment of which is forcibly excluded from participation, to hold their political leaders accountable.

Democratic Revolutionary Party (PRD) Mexico's main left-of-center political party formed from a wide range of left-leaning parties that had banded together under the umbrella of the National Democratic Front (FDN) in the 1988 presidential election.

Democratization The transition from nondemocratic to democratic forms of government.

Dependency theory A theory of development that asserts the advanced capitalist countries of the north dominate the world economy and constitute its "core" (or "metropolis"). The poor countries are relegated to the "periphery" of the world capitalist system. They are treated as mere satellites of the rich industrialized nations and remain economically dependent on them.

Dependent variable In a cause-and-effect relationship, the variable whose change is being explained. The dependent variable is the variable whose value changes in response to changes in the value of other variables (independent variables).

Depression A prolonged period of negative economic growth, usually accompanied by a severe decline in trade, massive unemployment, and widespread bankruptcies.

Direct contacting Directly petitioning elective or appointed officials or political party leaders to ask that the government address the petitioner's specific, often very individual, needs.

Direct democracy The direct exercise of governmental power by the people themselves.

Dissidence Anti-regime behavior, usually vocal criticism, that falls short of actually toppling the government.

Divided government When the executive branch is controlled by one political party and the legislature is controlled by an opposite party or parties.

Divine right of kings The doctrine asserting that the monarch derived his or her power from God and not from the people.

Duverger's law A theory that asserts that the form of electoral system adopted in a country plays a powerful role in shaping the number of parties operating there. In particular, Duverger's law argues that single-member-district pluralist electoral systems promote two-party systems while proportional representation encourages the emergence of multiparty systems.

E

Economic democracy An approach to democracy that seeks to establish various criteria of fairness or equality as social and economic components of democracy.

e-democracy The use of advanced information and communications technologies to allow citizens a more direct involvement in political decisions. Ideally, e-democracy is direct democracy exercised via electronic communication.

Empirical analysis An approach to building knowledge by discovering, describing, and explaining facts and factual relationships, to the extent that the facts are knowable; the systematic analysis of facts.

Equality The notion that everyone should ultimately be exactly or approximately equal whether in terms of their political rights (e.g., the right to vote) or their economic and social conditions.

Equity The notion that we should accord people a reasonably fair chance to realize their ambitions and improve their well-being under the same laws that apply to everyone else.

Ethnicity A form of group identification or distinctiveness often based on a perceived common biological ancestry in the distant past.

Executive branch The part of the state that engages in the daily administration of laws and policies. The executive branch typically is led by the head of government and the cabinet and includes the ministries and agencies that answer to cabinet officers.

F

Failed state A state that loses its monopoly of coercive power and is seriously challenged by domestic groups or individuals who routinely ignore its laws.

Fascism A form of radical, aggressive nationalism that glorifies one's own people above all others. Fascist ideology emphasizes intense racism and devotion to an all-powerful, heavily militarized state. Fascist movements typically organize into parties with paramilitary organizations and adulate their maximum leaders.

Federal Constitutional Court Specialized German court endowed with the power of judicial review. The Federal Constitutional Court hears only cases related to the constitutionality of statutes; unlike the U.S. Supreme Court, it is not an appellate court.

Federal Republic of Germany Post-World War II state formed in West Germany based on the democratic Basic Law and later extended to united Germany after the fall of communism in 1989.

Federation A union of several political units known usually as states or provinces in which the central government shares real authority with the various administrative units below the national level.

Federation Council Russian legislature's upper house, which consists of two members from each of Russia's 83 constituent federal units.

Fifth Republic Presidential–parliamentary regime introduced in France at the end of 1958. The Fifth Republic's constitution remains in force today.

Fiscal policy The use by the government of taxation and government expenditures to influence macroeconomic conditions.

5 percent threshold In the German electoral system, a party must receive at least 5 percent of the national vote or win three district seats to gain its proportion of seats on the second ballot. This threshold was introduced in the 1950s to avoid the proliferation of small parties in the parliament—a problem that plagued the Weimar Republic.

Fourth Republic Nigerian democratic regime born in 1999 that remains in place.

Free Democratic Party (FDP) German liberal party formed in 1948. The FDP has been a critical coalition partner in most governments of the Federal Republic of Germany.

French Revolution Period of social and political upheaval in France beginning in 1789 that ended the absolutist Bourbon monarchy, initially ushering in a radical democratic regime. The French Revolution unleashed powerful political forces that ended feudal privileges accorded to aristocrats and the clergy and replaced them with universalist liberal principles. While supported by the urban poor, workers, and in places by peasants, middle-class elements inspired by Enlightenment principles led the French Revolution and directed it against the monarchy, the nobility, and the Roman Catholic church.

G

Gaullism Center-right political movement in France founded by Charles de Gaulle that advocates strong presidential authority at home and foreign policy activism on the world stage.

General secretary Top party official in many Communist Parties, including those of the former Soviet Union and China, who are formally in charge of the Secretariat, a small organization connected to the Politburo that handles the daily affairs of the party leadership. When Communist Parties rule, the general secretary is effectively the most powerful politician in the country.

German Democratic Republic (GDR) Post-World War II German state formed in the eastern occupation zone, controlled by the Soviet Union, ruled as a dictatorship under a single party of German communists. The GDR, or East Germany, was formally established in 1949 and collapsed in 1989–90.

Gini coefficient/index A statistical measure of the relative degree of socioeconomic inequality within a particular country.

Glasnost Refers to policies pursued by Mikhail Gorbachev in the late 1980s intended to promote transparency in the Soviet government. The term can be literally translated as "openness" and is sometimes equated with "democratization."

Globalization The growing interconnectedness of governments, nonstate actors, and populations throughout the world through a variety of political, economic, technological, cultural, environmental, and other interactions.

Government Particularly in parliamentary systems, refers to the group of individuals in the very highest levels of decision-making authority in the state, such as the prime minister and cabinet officers.

Governmental instability Situation in which governing coalitions fall apart and must be replaced fairly frequently.

Grand Coalition German government coalition between the Christian Democrats (CDU/CSU) and the Social Democrats that lasted from 1966 to 1969. Sometimes also used to refer to a similar CDU/CSU and Social Democrat coalition extending from 2005 to 2009.

Great Leap Forward A campaign promoted by the Chinese Communist Party from 1958 to 1961 intended to rapidly transform China from an agrarian society to an industrial society. The Great Leap Forward included the creation of communes, large-scale agricultural production units that eventually led to widespread famine.

Great Proletarian Cultural Revolution A sociopolitical campaign in the People's Republic of China initiated by Mao Zedong in 1966 that extended until Mao's death in 1976. In the Cultural Revolution Mao encouraged youth groups organized as Red Guards to subject party officials to harsh and relentless criticism, leading to the purge of Mao's major rivals in the party.

Greens German political party founded in the 1970s dedicated initially to advocating an ecologically sustainable society through pro-environment policies, social liberalism, and grassroots democracy. The Greens, based in West Germany, merged with Alliance '90, a prodemocracy East German group, in 1993, to form Alliance '90/The Greens.

Gross domestic product (GDP) The market value of all goods and services produced by a country's economy in a specified period of time; *per capita GDP* equals the country's GDP divided by its population.

Gross national income (GNI) The total market value of goods and services a country produces at home (the GDP), plus the net income received from foreign countries; *per capita GNI* equals a country's gross national income divided by its population.

H

Head of government Country's chief political officer responsible for presenting and conducting its principal policies. Unlike a ceremonial head of state, the head of government has real decision-making authority.

Head of state The highest ranking officer in a state who has the authority to act as the principal representative of the state. A head of state may hold a largely ceremonial position as the representative of the state that carries little or no real decision-making power. However, in some political systems (such as the United States) the head of state is simultaneously the head of government and thus is also the chief political official.

Hegemonic exchange For the right to exercise its hegemony over the state and the population, the dominant party provides benefits to the country's main ethnic or religious groups.

House of Commons In the United Kingdom, the more powerful lower house of the parliament elected by popular vote.

House of Lords In the United Kingdom, the weaker, upper house of parliament composed of hereditary peers, appointed peers, and high ecclesiastical officials of the Church of England.

Human development theory A theory that identifies causal linkages between economic development, the value of freedom, and democratic institutions. Human development theory argues that socioeconomic development sets in motion a train of processes that ultimately leads to democracy through changes in political culture.

Hundred Flowers Movement In 1957 Mao invited criticisms of the Chinese Communist Party's performance from experts and intellectuals, confident that his policy successes so far had created considerable enthusiasm and support for the regime.

Hung parliament Term used in the United Kingdom and extended to other parliamentary regimes to refer to situations in which no party succeeds in winning an absolute majority of legislative seats. Hung parliaments lead to minority or coalition governments.

Hypothesis Assumption or supposition to be tested against relevant evidence.

I

Ideology Coherent set of ideas and guidelines that defines what the nature and role of government should be and prescribes the main goals the people should pursue through political action.

Illiberal democracy Regimes that hold elections generally regarded as free and fair but that do not effectively guarantee rights and liberties.

Import-substituting industrialization (ISI) An economic development strategy that promotes development by substituting domestic manufactured consumer goods for like products that had previously been imported from more industrialized economies, thereby promoting domestic industry.

Inclusion The notion that democratic rights and freedoms must not be denied to specifically targeted elements of the population and that no one should be systematically excluded from ever acquiring any advantages through the democratic process.

Independent variable In cause-and-effect relationships, the causal or explanatory variable; the factor or characteristic that influences or causes the dependent variable.

Induction Reasoning process that goes from the specific to the general.

Inflation Steadily rising prices; a rise in the price level. The *inflation rate* is the percentage increase in the price level over a specified time period, such as a year.

Institutional Revolutionary Party (PRI) Political party formed by former revolutionaries that governed Mexico from 1929 to 2000.

Institutionalism Branch of political science that looks at how state institutions are set up and how they shape the political decision-making process.

Interest aggregation Process by which political organizations such as parties gather (aggregate) the various interests, priorities, and opinions of their leaders and constituents and shape them into common goals and policy proposals.

Interest articulation Process by which individuals and groups articulate their interests, demands, and desires. Interest articulation typically includes lobbying of political decision makers.

Interest group Organization that articulates the interests and demands of a particular group of people, often with the aim of influencing the state to do something in their behalf.

International relations Subfield of political science that examines relations between countries. Diplomacy, international law, international economic relations, war, and peacemaking are among the chief topics studied by political scientists concerned with international relations.

Intervening variables Variables in a causal relationship located between independent and dependent variables.

Islamism The view held by some Muslims that Islam should guide social and political life as well as spiritual beliefs and religious practices.

J

Judicial review The power of judicial authorities to invalidate as unconstitutional laws made by the legislature and executive bodies.

Judiciary A country's system of courts. The judiciary interprets the laws with the authority of the state.

Jus sanguinis Principle of nationality law that translates as "right of blood." States that apply *jus sanguinis* base citizenship on the basis of one's parents' citizenship.

Jus soli Principle of nationality law that translates as "right of the soil." States that apply *jus soli* base citizenship on the basis of where one was born.

K

Keynesianism The state's use of fiscal measures and public spending to promote growth in a mixed economy.

L

Labour Party Political party in the United Kingdom originally founded as the political arm of the trade union movement. In recent years the Labour Party has evolved to be a left-of-center catchall party.

Laissez-faire capitalism A system of political economy based on private ownership and market setting of prices. Laissez-faire means "let do" or "leave alone" in French. In effect, the state allows private individuals to pursue their economic activities without extensive regulation or other intervention in production and distribution of goods and services.

Law In the social sciences, a regularly occurring association (or correlation) between two or more variables.

Left Party (Die Linke) German political party formed in the 1990s as a merger of leftist mavericks from the Social Democratic Party, who were opposed to labor reforms, and the former Party of Democratic Socialism, the communist party in East Germany.

Legislature Branch of the state whose chief function, especially in democracies, is to make laws (sometimes in conjunction with the executive branch) and to represent the people in the lawmaking process.

Legitimacy The right to rule, or the popular acceptance of authority.

Leninism Political theory associated with V.I. Lenin that emphasizes the primacy of the Communist Party in leading the transition to socialism.

Liberal Democrats Political party in the United Kingdom that resulted from the merger of the Liberal Party and the Social Democratic Party, an offshoot of the Labour Party. The Liberal Democrats are the third largest party in the UK.

Liberalism A philosophy of government that emphasizes guarantees of liberty. Liberalism advocates liberal democracy as the ideal political regime and free-market capitalism as the ideal economic system.

M

Magna Carta A document signed by King John of England in 1215 that specified the rights of subjects in such matters as taxation, judicial appointments, and private property. The Magna Carta affirmed the rule of law, plainly indicating there were limits to the king's sovereign power and that the monarchy was not above the law.

Market economy An economic system in which prices are determined mainly by supply and demand. The government, in other words, does not control the price system.

Marxism A body of social and political thought associated with Karl Marx that interprets sociopolitical development on the basis of changes in technology and economic organization. Marxism emphasizes conflict among social classes as the main axis of political activity and advocates socialism.

Marxism–Leninism A reinterpretation of Marxian theory that combines Marx's revolutionary anticapitalism with Lenin's reliance on a revolutionary Communist Party and the domination of the postrevolutionary state by the Communist Party.

Mestizos In Latin America, individuals of mixed indigenous and European heritage.

Minimal winning coalition Legislative coalition that has just the bare minimum number of members to form a majority in the legislature, form a government, and win votes on the legislation it brings before parliament.

Minority government A government in a parliamentary regime that consists of one or more parties whose delegates do not constitute a majority of the legislature.

Mixed economy An economic system that combines both private enterprise and state involvement in the country's economic affairs.

Mixed member electoral system An electoral system for a legislature in which some seats are chosen in single-member-district, winner-take-all contests and the remainder are chosen by proportional representation.

Model Simplified representation of reality in descriptive or abstract form.

Modernization Refers to a model of development that emphasizes society's evolutionary progress from a traditional, largely agricultural economy to an industrial economy.

Modernization theory A body of social theorizing that contends that economic underdevelopment cannot be overcome until the society in question abandons its traditional social and institutional structures, along with their accompanying attitudes and behavioral patterns.

Monarchy A type of authoritarian regime, in which a king, queen, emperor, or prince, often flanked by blood-related aristocrats, wields effective power. In a monarchy sovereignty is embodied in a single individual, the monarch.

N

Nation Group of people whose members claim a common identity on the basis of distinguishing characteristics and a claim to a territorial homeland.

Nation building Process of developing a widely shared identity among a country's population and an effective, legitimate state.

National Action Party (PAN) Mexican political party that opposed the rule of the Institutional Revolutionary Party and advocated legal and gradual reform and constraints on state power. The PAN's pro-market orientation, its association with pro-Catholic positions, and its middle-class base led the party's rivals to depict it as being on the right.

National Assembly The lower house of France's parliament that consists of 577 deputies elected in a two-round variant of the single-member district (SMD) electoral system.

National debt The amount of money the national government owes its creditors at home and abroad.

National identity People's conscious belief that they collectively constitute a nation. It is a shared understanding that they belong together on the basis of certain characteristics that, in their own minds, transcend their differences and set them apart from other national groups.

National Party (NP) South African political party founded by Afrikaans-speaking politicians that gained power in 1948 and implemented the policies of apartheid.

National People's Congress The legislative branch of the People's Republic of China.

National Socialist Workers' Party (Nazis) The German fascist political party led by Adolf Hitler that took power in 1933 and established the Nazi dictatorship.

Nationalism Consciously formulated set of political ideas emphasizing the distinctiveness and unity of one's nation, specifying common interests, and prescribing goals for action.

Nationalization The transfer of private property, usually privately owned firms, to state ownership.

Nation-state Sovereign state consisting of one "nation" within internationally recognized boundaries.

Neocolonialism (neo-imperialism) Terms used by many leaders of the developing world to denounce what they regarded as attempts by Britain, France, the United States, or other Western states to try to dominate their economies and dictate their political orientations even after the formal termination of colonial rule.

Neo-corporatism Corporatist interest group system practiced in Germany in which the main business association and trade unions sit down with government officials on a regular basis to negotiate the country's economic and social welfare policies.

Neoliberalism Economic development strategy originally associated with Ronald Reagan and Margaret Thatcher that was implemented in many developing countries. Neoliberalism involved the lowering of barriers to imports, a reduction in state subsidies for staples and in expenditures on social welfare, and the privatization of most of the state-owned enterprises accumulated during early periods of greater state involvement in the economy.

Neo-patrimonialism Patronage form of politics in which patrons use state resources to benefit their clients.

New Republic Federalist republic established by Brazil's 1988 constitution.

New State (Estado Nôvo) A Brazilian corporatist dictatorship under President Getulio Vargas (1937–45).

Newly industrializing countries (NICs) Developing countries with relatively high economic growth rates typically due to successful implementation of development strategies that involve export of manufactured products.

Nonconventional (confrontational) political participation Forms of political participation not legally sanctioned that include mass protest, confrontational activities, and even armed rebellion.

North American Free Trade Agreement (NAFTA) A treaty between Canada, Mexico, and the United States that took effect January 1, 1994, and created a trade bloc that dramatically lowered barriers to trade among the three countries.

O

October Revolution The phase of the Russian Revolution during which the Russian state fell into Bolshevik hands as the result of a coup d'état November 7, 1917.

Old Republic Brazil's first democratic regime, a limited, elite-dominated democracy in place from 1889 to 1930.

P

Parliamentary government The form of democratic regime in which the executive power (typically the prime minister and cabinet) emerges from the legislative power (the parliament). The electorate votes for members of parliament, and then members of parliament choose the government (prime minister and cabinet).

Parliamentary supremacy Parliament is the supreme authority in the political system. The term is often used in reference to the United Kingdom, in which the parliament has ultimate authority, not the crown, the courts, or any other institution.

Particularistic parties Political parties that confine their appeal to a particular segment of the population.

Party discipline Practice by which the parliamentary deputies of a particular party vote together unanimously as a bloc.

Party system System of parties within a country, characterized by the number of parties, their ideological orientations, degree of party discipline, and various other traits.

Patrimonial rule Rule by a domineering and paternalistic elite.

Perestroika Rerestructuring of the Soviet economy and political system pursued by Mikhail Gorbachev in the late 1980s.

Plebiscitary democracy The practice of providing citizens the opportunity to vote on specific policy questions in a referendum (or plebiscite).

Pluralism Interest representation system in which many groups and interests are represented by many, mostly unregulated interest groups, leading to a dispersion of political power.

Politburo The executive committee of many communist parties, including the Communist Party of the Soviet Union and the Chinese Communist Party. The politburo makes major decisions for the party between meetings of lower level organs such as the central committee and the party congress. The politiburos of the CPSU and CCP have typically included about two-dozen party leaders.

Political culture Pattern of shared values, moral norms, beliefs, expectations, and attitudes that relate to politics and its social context.

Political economy (1) The study of how people pursue collective economic goals and deal with conflicts over resources and other economic factors in an authoritative way by means of government. (2) The relationship between the economy and the political system within a particular country or abstractly, in theory.

Political socialization Process by which individuals learn about politics and the political culture of their society.

Political sociology The study of the relationship between social identity and political behavior, and of how political power is distributed among social groups

Political subculture Political culture that deviates from the dominant culture in key respects.

Politics The process by which societies decide how to authoritatively allocate the goods, services, and nontangible items they value. Politics is about who gets what, when, and how. Politics also involves the process by which individuals and groups come to hold power in society so that they are able to authoritatively allocate those items society values.

Polyarchy Literally, "rule by the many," a term coined by Robert Dahl to refer to regimes with relatively high levels of competition for power and in which political participation is broad.

Popular sovereignty The notion that the people have the right to govern themselves.

Populism Either mass antielitism or elite efforts to cultivate the support of the disadvantaged masses.

Postmaterialism A set of political attitudes or political culture that emphasizes autonomy and self-expression, in contrast to the values of materialism, which stress economic and political security.

Postmodernization The social conditions of a postmodern society, with rising prosperity, in which the main priorities of a growing portion of the population shift from maximizing material wealth to maximizing nonmaterial forms of personal well-being and the adoption of postmaterialist values.

Praetorianism A system in which personal power occupies the pursuits of political leaders and factions, and constitutional rules are manipulated for individual gain.

Prebendalism The use of state offices as "prebends" (instruments) for creating wealth and gain for individuals and their ethnic brethren.

Presidentialism The form of democracy in which the president, usually directly elected, is both the head of state and the sole effective head of government,

constitutionally armed with real decision-making powers.

Presidential–parliamentary system A regime that features a president and a prime minister who each have significant decision-making powers. The president typically is elected by the voters. The prime minister usually must be approved by both the parliament (the lower house in bicameral legislatures) and the president.

Prime minister (premier) The senior cabinet member in a parliamentary democracy. As the senior cabinet member the prime minister is the head of the executive branch, or head of government.

Privatization The transfer of state-owned enterprises to private ownership.

Proportional representation An electoral system for legislative bodies in which a party's share (percentage) of its seats in the legislature exactly or approximately equals its share of the popular vote nationwide.

R

Recession A period of zero economic growth or negative growth, resulting in declining business activity, rising unemployment, and bankruptcies.

Regime A form of government. More precisely, the set of rules and procedures, both formal and informal, that guides the operation of state institutions.

Representative democracy Form of democracy in which the people elect state officials to represent them and make decisions on their behalf.

Revolution Overthrow of one system of the government and its replacement by a different regime, accomplished by a violent, mass uprising.

Rights and liberties Freedoms that may be guaranteed by law to the citizenry.

Rule of law Principle that the power of the state must be limited by law and that no one is above the law.

S

Science Set of rules and methods for investigating reality logically and systematically.

Self-determination The demand of a national group for self-government.

Senate In France the upper house of the parliament, composed of 348 members elected to six-year terms by a special electoral college that represents local governments throughout France.

Shadow cabinet In a parliamentary regime, the opposition party members who are assigned portfolios corresponding to cabinet post and who thereby form the implicit alternative to the government.

Shiites The second largest branch of Islam, composed of Muslims who regard only Muhammad's blood descendants as the Prophet's true successors, or imams.

Single-member-district/plurality electoral system Electoral system in which the country is divided into electoral districts each of which elect just one member to a seat in a particular legislative chamber. The electoral rules in this system dictate that the candidate who wins the most votes in the election takes the district's legislative seat.

Single-party majoritarian government Government formed when one party wins a majority of seats in the national parliament and is thereby able to form the government without coalition partners.

Social capital Resources accruing to an individual or a group due to social networks and the norms of reciprocity and trustworthiness that arise from them.

Social democracy A form of democratic regime that combines political democracy with socialist principles in economic and social relations.

Social Democratic Party of Germany (SPD) German political party that has operated in the Second Reich (pre-1919), the Weimar Republic (1919–33), and the Federal Republic of Germany. Originally an ideological party that advocated a peaceful transition to socialism, the SPD evolved into a catchall party of the left in the post-World War II period.

Social Liberalism A political philosophy advocating active government intervention in the economy and society for the purpose of promoting economic growth, community welfare, and social justice.

Social market economy Term applied to the post-World War II German economy that combines a private enterprise system, a generous welfare state for all citizens, and social protections for workers.

Social movements Segments of the population who engage in significant collective action because they believe that neither the state nor the established political parties or interest groups have adequately addressed their concerns. Social movements are characterized by the absence of extensive formal organization.

Socialism A political and economic system in which private enterprise (capitalism) is abolished and replaced by some form of common ownership of factories, farms, and other productive enterprises.

Sovereign monarchy (absolutism) Political regime in which the monarch is the supreme political authority in the land and enjoys the right to absolute power.

Sovereignty Exclusive legal authority of a government over its population and territory, independent of external authorities.

Spanish conquest Military conquest and colonization of what is now Latin America, initially led in 1519 by Hernán Cortés and his band of 550 Spaniards against the Aztec empire in what is now Mexico.

State (1) Organization that monopolizes the use of violence within a territory in order to command the obedience of those living there with the laws and policies it has issued; (2) the totality of a country's governmental institutions and officials, guided by the laws and procedures that structure their activities.

State building The effort to develop an effective government at the political decision-making level, along with supportive bureaucratic agencies that can implement government policies and programs.

State Duma Russian legislature's lower house, which consists of 450 legislators elected to a five-year term.

States (Länder) The 16 subnational political units that make up the Federal Republic of Germany, each of which has its own legislature and government.

Sunnis The largest branch of Islam, Sunnis are those Muslims who follow the words and deeds of Muhammad and acknowledge the first four caliphs as his rightful successors.

Supranationalism Efforts on the part of two or more countries to limit their sovereignty by establishing decision-making structures over and above their national governments.

T

Territorial autonomy Self-government by a distinct minority of the population over its own territory within the structure of a larger state.

Theocracy State run by religious authorities.

Theory (1) Normative political theory, that is, value-centered political philosophy (or political thought). (2) In the natural and social sciences, a generalization, or set of generalizations, that seeks to explain, and perhaps predict, relationships among variables.

Third World (or the Global South) Term coined by a French economist in the 1950s for developing countries that did not fall within the First World—economically advanced democracies associated with the Western alliance—or Second World—communist states.

Tiananmen Square Demonstrations in 1989 against the Communist Chinese government by students, workers, professionals, and others.

Totalitarianism An exceptionally intrusive form of authoritarianism in which the state monopolizes control not only over all institutions of government but also over the educational system, the media, science, and the arts, leaving little room for private liberty.

Transnationalism The concept that emphasizes the increasing movement of people and ideas across borders as the result of globalization.

U

Underdeveloped economies Term used to identify poor countries whose prospects for economic development are very low. Some social scientists use the term to imply that such economies have become poorer or less able to create self-sustaining economic growth as the result of their integration into the world economy.

Unicameral legislature Legislature consisting of only one house (or chamber) of parliament.

Union of Soviet Socialist Republics (USSR, or Soviet Union) Multinational state that ruled the lands of the former Russian Empire from 1918 through 1991. The USSR was ruled by the Communist Party of the Soviet Union, which followed a Marxist-Leninist ruling philosophy.

Unitary actor model A model of decision making in which all the elements of a state's bureaucracy work together as though they were a single actor.

Unitary state A form of state in which decision-making authority and disposition over revenues are concentrated in the institutions of a single, central government, in contrast to federalist states, where decision-making authority is shared between the central, regional, and local governments.

V

Value-added tax (VAT) A national sales tax imposed at every point in the production and marketing process of specified goods.

Values Spiritual or moral principles, ideals, or qualities of life that people favor for their own sake.

Variable Element or feature that can vary or change, that is, can take on different values.

Vote of confidence Showdown vote in parliament to determine if the government still has the support of a voting majority of legislators.

W

Welfare state A form of political economy in which the state assumes responsibility for the general welfare of its population, especially its most vulnerable elements, through spending on such items as education, housing, health care, pensions, unemployment compensation, food subsidies, family allowances, and other programs.

Credits

Image Researcher: David Tietz/Editorial Image, LLC
Interior and Cover Designer: Elise Lansdon

PHOTO CREDITS

CHAPTER 1

Opener: © James May/Alamy; **p. 2 (bottom):** © Fethi Belaid/AFP/Getty Images; **p. 2 (top):** © Joel Carillet/Lightroom Photos/The Image Works; **p. 3:** © XINHUA/Gamma-Rapho via Getty Images; **p. 13:** Courtesy of Outseve-SLDN; **p. 18:** James Foley/AFP/Getty Images; **p. 22:** © sinopictures/ullstein bild/The Image Works.

CHAPTER 2

Opener: U.S. Census Bureau, Public Information Office (PIO); **p. 26:** © KNS/AFP/Newscom; **p. 33:** © Bill Bachmann/The Image Works.

CHAPTER 3

Opener: © Erica Simone Leeds; **p. 46:** © akg-images/The Image Works; **p. 47 (left):** Library of Congress [LC-USZ62-77295]; **p. 47 (middle):** © VisionsofAmerica/Joe Sohm/Getty Images; **p. 47 (right):** Library of Congress [LC-DIG-ppmsc-03256]; **p. 48:** Library of Congress [LC-USZ62-41264]; **p. 50:** © Anu Malik/Dean Pictures/The Image Works; **p. 54:** © Press Association/The Image Works; **p. 57:** © SZ Photo/SZ Photo/The Image Works; **p. 58:** © Stefan Boness/Visum/The Image Works; **p. 62:** National Archives and Records Administration (NLK-PXDOD-CMCPHOTOS-PX66(20)(27).

CHAPTER 4

Opener: © Roberto Schmidt/AFP/Getty Images; **p. 66:** © Josep Lago/AFP/Getty Images; **p. 68:** © Sean Gallup/Getty Images; **p. 72:** © Art Chen Soon Ling-Unep/Still Pictures/The Image Works; **p. 74:** © Rogerio Barbosa/AFP/Getty Images; **p. 78:** © David Rubinger/Time Life Pictures/Getty Images; **p. 80:** © The Image Works.

CHAPTER 5

Opener: © Digital Vision/Punchstock; **p. 90:** © Pixtal/age Fotostock; **p. 92:** © Xinhua Press/Corbis; **p. 93:** © Andrejs Strokins/epa/Corbis; **p. 95:** © Onsite/Alamy; **p. 97:** © Photodisc/Getty Images; **p. 98:** © Swim Ink 2, LLC/Corbis; **p. 99:** © Wang Yahong/Xinhua Press/Corbis; **p. 107:** © Koen Suyk/ANP/Newscom.

CHAPTER 6

Opener: © Philip Coblentz/Brand X Pictures/PictureQuest; **p. 114:** © PoodlesRock/Corbis; **p. 130:** AP Photo/Odd Andersen; **p. 134:** AP Photo/Ali Haider.

CHAPTER 7

Opener: © Eric Vandeville/Gamma-Rapho via Getty Images; **p. 140:** © Walter Dhladhla/AFP/Getty Images; **p. 141:** © Ed Ou/Getty Images; **p. 143:** © Juan Mabromata/AFP/Getty Images; **p. 144:** Rex Features via AP Images; **p. 146:** AP Photo/Bullit Marquez; **p. 149:** © Bettmann/Corbis.

CHAPTER 8

Opener: The McGraw-Hill Companies, Inc./Jill Braaten, Photographer RF; **p. 159:** © Hiroko Masuike/The New York Times/Redux; **p. 163:** Kerry-Edwards 2004, Inc./Sharon Farmer, photographer RF; **p. 165:** AP Photo/Kevork Djansezian; **p. 168:** © Kent Gavin/Keystone/Getty Images; **p. 175:** © Galo Paguay/El Comercio de Ecuador/Newscom.

CHAPTER 9

Opener: © Bill Bachmann/The Image Works; **p. 188:** © FPG/Hulton Archive/Getty Images; **p. 194:** © AA/ABACA/Newscom; **p. 195:** Etienne Laurent/SIPA/dapd.

CHAPTER 10

Opener: AP Photo/Vahid Salemi; **p. 203 (left):** Library of Congress [LC-USZ62-26759]; **p. 203 (right):** Library of Congress [LC-USZ62-13040]; **p. 205:** © The Print Collector/Heritage/The Image Works; **p. 207:** Library of Congress [LC-USZ62-101877]; **p. 209:** © Bettmann/Corbis, **p. 210, p. 211, p. 212:** © Ingram Publishing RF; **p. 215:** © Bettmann/Corbis; **p. 217:** © Frederic Noy/AFP/Getty Images.

CHAPTER 11

Opener: © Philippe Wojazer/Pool/EPA/Newscom; **p. 228:** © Alexandros Michailidis/Demotix/Corbis; **p. 230:** © Ocean/Corbis RF; **p. 233:** © Hulton Archive/Getty Images; **p. 235:** © RIA Novosti/The Image Works; **p. 237:** © Bettmann/Corbis; **p. 240:** © Popperfoto/Getty Images.

CHAPTER 12

Opener: © Philippe Lissac/Godong/Corbis; **p. 250:** © Bruno Perousse/akg-images/The Image Works; **p. 251:** © John Robinson/Africa Media Online/The Image Works; **p. 252:** © Photodisc RF; **p. 256:** © Andrew Winning/AFP/Getty

Images; **p. 259:** © Sean Sprague/The Image Works; **p. 260:** © Ingram Publishing RF; **p. 265:** © Sean Gallup/Getty Images; **p. 267:** © Christine Pemberton/The Image Works.

CHAPTER 13

Page 273: © PA Photos/TopFoto/The Image Works; **p. 276:** ©The Print Collector/Heritage/The Image Works; **p. 281:** Library of Congress [LC-USW33-019093-C]; **p. 283:** © Press Association/The Image Works; **p. 284:** © AFP/Getty Images; **p. 293:** Press Association via AP Images; **p. 300:** Library of Congress [LC-U9-31687B-13A/14]; **p. 302:** © Schöning/ullstein bild/The Image Works; **p. 303:** © Actionplus/TopFoto/The Image Works.

CHAPTER 14

Page 307 (left): © Gilles Bassignac/Gamma-Rapho via Getty Images; **p. 307 (right):** © Reuters/Gerard Cerles/Corbis; **p. 308:** © Alexandre Marchi/L'est Republican/pict/Newscom; **p. 311:** © Alastair Miller/Bloomberg via Getty Images; **p. 313:** © The Bridgeman Art Library/Getty Images; **p. 318:** © Loomis Dean/Time Life Pictures/Getty Images; **p. 319:** © Jack Burlot/Apis/Sygma/Corbis; **p. 322:** © Bernard Bisson/Sygma/Corbis; **p. 335:** © Kristy Sparow/Getty Images; **p. 337:** © William Ryall 2010 RF.

CHAPTER 15

Page 344: © Snapshot-photography/SZ Photo/The Image Works; **p. 346:** © Ingram Publishing RF; **p. 349:** © Mary Evans Picture Library/The Image Works; **p. 353:** © World History Archive/TopFoto/The Image Works; **p. 356:** © ullstein bild - Roehrbein/The Image Works; **p. 365:** © Stefan Boness/Visum/The Image Works; **p. 368:** © John Macdougall/AFP/Getty Images; **p. 371:** © Axentis/ullstein bild/The Image Works; **p. 374:** © Sorge/Caro/ullstein bild/The Image Works.

CHAPTER 16

Page 378: © Peter Turnley/Corbis; **p. 379, p. 380, p. 381:** © RIA Novosti/The Image Works; **p. 386, p. 388:** © Ingram Publishing RF; **p. 390:** © Carl Mydans/Time Life Pictures/Getty Images; **p. 392:** AP Photo/Stringer/Zemlianichenko; **p. 408:** AP Photo/Misha Japaridze; **p. 412:** © RIA Novosti/The Image Works.

CHAPTER 17

Page 418: AP Photo/Jeff Widener; **p. 421:** © De Agostini Picture Library/Getty Images; **p. 422:** Library of Congress [LC-USZ62-39907]; **p. 423:** © Ingram Publishing RF; **p. 428:** © ullstein bild/sinopictures/The Image Works;

Index